shakespearean criticism

Mr. WILLIAM

SHAKESPEARES

COMEDIES,
HISTORIES, &
TRAGEDIES.

Published according to the True Originall Copies.

LONDON
Printed by Iſaac Iaggard, and Ed. Blount. 1623.

Frontispiece to the First Folio (1623). By permission of the Folger Shakespeare Library.

ISSN 0883-9123

Volume 59

shakespearean criticism

Excerpts from the Criticism of
William Shakespeare's Plays and Poetry,
from the First Published Appraisals
to Current Evaluations

Michelle Lee
Editor

GALE GROUP

Detroit
New York
San Francisco
London
Boston
Woodbridge, CT

STAFF

Lynn M. Spampinato, Janet Witalec, *Managing Editors, Literature Product*
Kathy D. Darrow, Ellen McGeagh, *Product Liaisons*
Michelle Lee, *Editor*
Mark W. Scott, *Publisher, Literature Product*

Elisabeth Gellert, *Editor*
Madeline S. Harris, Jessica Menzo, *Assistant Editors*
Mary Ruby, *Technical Training Specialist*
Deborah J. Morad, Joyce Nakamura, Kathleen Lopez Nolan, *Managing Editors, Literature Content*
Susan M. Trosky, *Director, Literature Content*

Maria L. Franklin, *Permissions Manager*
Margaret Chamberlain, Edna M. Hedblad, *Permissions Specialists*
Debra Freitas, *IC Administrator*

Victoria B. Cariappa, *Research Manager*
Sarah Genik, *Project Coordinator*
Maureen Eremic, Barbara McNeil, Gary J. Oudersluys, Cheryl L. Warnock, *Research Specialists*
Ron Morelli, Tamara C. Nott, Tracie A. Richardson, *Research Associates*
Michelle Campbell, *Research Assistant*

Dorothy Maki, *Manufacturing Manager*
Stacy L. Melson, *Buyer*

Mary Beth Trimper, *Composition and Prepress Manager*
Carolyn Roney, *Composition Specialist*

Randy Bassett, *Imaging Supervisor*
Robert Duncan, Dan Newell, Luke Rademacher, *Imaging Specialists*
Pamela A. Reed, *Imaging Coordinator*
Kelly A. Quin, *Editor, Imaging and Multimedia Content*
Michael Logusz, *Graphic Artist*

Library of Congress Catalog Card Number 86-645085
ISBN 0-7876-4697-0
ISSN 0883-9123
Printed in the United States of America

10 9 8 7 6 5 4 3 2 1

Contents

Preface vii

Acknowledgments ix

List of Plays and Poems Covered in *SC* xi

Preface

*S*hakespearean Criticism (*SC*) provides students, educators, theatergoers, and other interested readers with valuable insight into Shakespeare's drama and poetry. A multiplicity of viewpoints documenting the critical reaction of scholars and commentators from the seventeenth century to the present day derives from hundreds of periodicals and books excerpted for the series. Students and teachers at all levels of study will benefit from *SC,* whether they seek information for class discussions and written assignments, new perspectives on traditional issues, or the most noteworthy of analyses of Shakespeare's artistry.

Scope of the Series

Volumes 1 through 10 of the series present a unique historical overview of the critical response to each Shakespearean work, representing a broad range of interpretations.

Volumes 11 through 26 recount the performance history of Shakespeare's plays on the stage and screen through eyewitness reviews and retrospective evaluations of individual productions, comparisons of major interpretations, and discussions of staging issues.

Volumes 27 through 56 in the series focus on criticism published after 1960, with a view to providing the reader with the most significant modern critical approaches. Each volume is ordered around a theme that is central to the study of Shakespeare, such as politics, religion, or sexuality. The topic entry that introduces each volume is comprised of general essays that discuss this theme with reference to all of Shakespeare's works. Following the topic entry are several entries devoted to individual works.

Beginning with volume 57 in the series, *SC* provides a works-based approach; each of the four entries contained in a regular volume focuses on a specific Shakespearean play or poem. The entries will include the most recent criticism available on the works, as well as earlier criticism not previously included in *SC*. In 2001, a Topics Volume will be published; volume 60 will contain topic entries comprised of essays that analyze various topics, or themes, found in Shakespeare's works. Past topic entries have covered such subjects as Honor, Jealousy, War and Warfare, and Elizabethan Politics.

Until volume 48, published in October 1999, *SC* compiled an annual volume of the most noteworthy essays published on Shakespeare during the previous year. The essays, reprinted in their entirety, were recommended to Gale by an international panel of distinguished scholars.

Organization of the Book

An *SC* entry consists of the following elements:

- The **Introduction** contains background information that introduces the reader to the work or topic that is the subject of the entry and outlines modern interpretations of individual Shakespearean topic, plays, and poems.

- Reprinted **Criticism** for each entry consists of essays arranged chronologically under a variety of subheadings to facilitate the study of different aspects of the play, poem, or topic. This provides an overview of the major areas of concern in the analysis of Shakespeare's works, as well as a useful perspective on changes in critical evaluation over recent decades. The critic's name and the date of composition or publication of the critical work are given at the beginning of each piece of criticism. Unsigned criticism is preceded by the title of the source in which it appeared. Footnotes are reprinted at the end of each essay or excerpt. In the case of excerpted criticism, only those footnotes that pertain to the excerpted texts are included.

- A complete **Bibliographical Citation** of the original essay or book precedes each piece of criticism.

- Critical essays are prefaced by **Explanatory Notes** as an aid to students using *SC*. The explanatory notes summarize the criticism that follows.

- Each volume includes such **Illustrations** as reproductions of images from the Shakespearean period, paintings and sketches of eighteenth- and nineteenth-century performers, photographs of modern productions, and stills from film adaptations.

- An annotated bibliography of **Further Reading** appears at the end of each entry and suggests resources for additional study. In some cases, significant essays for which the editors could not obtain reprint rights are included here.

Indexes

A **Cumulative Character Index** identifies the principal characters of discussion in the criticism of each play and non-dramatic poem.

A **Cumulative Topic Index** identifies the principal topics in the criticism and stage history of each work. The topics are arranged alphabetically, by topic.

A **Cumulative Topic Index, by Play** identifies the principal topics in the criticism and stage history of each work. The topics are arranged alphabetically, by play.

Citing *Shakespearean Criticism*

When writing papers, students who quote directly from any volume in the Literary Criticism Series may use the following general format to footnote reprinted criticism. The first example pertains to material drawn from periodicals, the second to material reprinted from books.

Tetsuya Motohashi. "Body Politic and Political Body in *Coriolanus,*" in *Forum for Modern Language Studies* XXX, no. 2 (April 1994): 97-112; reprinted in *Shakespearean Criticism,* vol. 50, ed. Kathy D. Darrow (Farmington Hills, Mich.: The Gale Group, 2000), 119-128.

Mary Hamer. "Authority and Violence," in *William Shakespeare: Julius Caesar* (Northcote House, 1998), 12-20; reprinted in *Shakespearean Criticism,* vol. 50, ed. Kathy D. Darrow (Farmington Hills, Mich.: The Gale Group, 2000), 230-34.

Suggestions are Welcome

Readers who wish to suggest new features, topics, or authors to appear in future volumes, or who have other suggestions or comments are cordially invited to call, write, or fax the Managing Editor:

Managing Editor, Literary Criticism Series
The Gale Group
27500 Drake Road
Farmington Hills, MI 48331-3535
1-800-347-4253 (GALE)
Fax: 248-699-8054

Acknowledgments

The editors wish to thank the copyright holders of the excerpted criticism included in this volume and the permissions managers of many book and magazine publishing companies for assisting us in securing reproduction rights. We are also grateful to the staffs of the Detroit Public Library, the Library of Congress, the University of Detroit Mercy Library, Wayne State University Purdy/Kresge Library Complex, and the University of Michigan Libraries for making their resources available to us. Following is a list of the copyright holders who have granted us permission to reproduce material in this volume of *SC*. Every effort has been made to trace copyright, but if omissions have been made, please let us know.

COPYRIGHTED EXCERPTS IN *SC*, VOLUME 59, WERE REPRODUCED FROM THE FOLLOWING PERIODICALS:

Anglia, v. 104, 1986. Reproduced by permission.—*The Centennial Review,* v. 43, Fall, 1999. Reproduced by permission.—*Colby Quarterly,* v. 26, June, 1990. Reproduced by permission.—*College Literature,* v. 21, June, 1994. Reproduced by permission.—*Comparative Drama,* v. 27, Fall, 1993. Reproduced by permission.—*Drama in the Renaissance,* 1986. Reproduced by permission.—*English Literary Renaissance,* v. 20, Spring, 1990. Reproduced by permission.—*English Studies in Canada,* v. XI, March, 1985. Reproduced by permission.—*English Studies,* v. 65, February, 1984. © 1984, Swets & Zeitlinger. Reproduced by permission.—*The Hudson Review,* v. 51, Summer, 1998. Reproduced by permission.—*Journal of Medieval and Renaissance Studies,* v. 22, Spring, 1992. Copyright © 1992 by Duke University Press. Reproduced by permission.—*Mosaic,* v. 26, Winter, 1993. © 1993 by *Mosaic.* Reproduced by permission.—*Orbis Litterarum,* v. 43, 1988. © 1988 Munksgaard International Publishers, Ltd. Reproduced by permission.—*Renaissance Drama,* n.s. v. XXV, 1994. Copyright © 1996 by Northwestern University Press. All rights reserved. Reproduced by permission.—*The Review of English Studies,* v. 47, May, 1996; v. 50, August, 1999. Copyright © 1996, 1999 by Oxford University Press. Reproduced by permission.—*Shakespeare Jahrbuch,* v. 135, 1999. Reproduced by permission.—*Shakespeare Quarterly,* v. 43, Summer, 1992; v. 45, Fall, 1992; v. 45, Summer, 1994; v. 48, Fall, 1997. Reproduced by permission.—*Shakespeare Studies,* v. 13, 1980; v. 23, 1995. Reproduced by permission.—*Shakespeare Survey,* v. 36, 1983; v. 44, 1992; v. 9, 1973 for "The Art of Cruelty: Hamlet and Vindice" by R.A. Foakes. © R.A. Foakes 1973. Reproduced by permission.—*South Atlantic Review,* v. 51, January, 1986. Reproduced by permission.—*Texas Studies in Literature and Language,* v. 35, Spring, 1993. © 1993 by the University of Texas Press. Reproduced by permission.—*University of Toronto Quarterly,* v. 68, Summer, 1999. © University of Toronto Press Incorporated 1999. Reproduced by permission.—*Women's Studies,* v. 7, 1980. © Gordon and Breach Science Publishers, Inc., 1980. Reproduced by permission.

COPYRIGHTED EXCERPTS IN *SC*, VOLUME 59, WERE REPRODUCED FROM THE FOLLOWING BOOKS:

Bevington, David. From an introduction to *Troilus and Cressida.* By William Shakespeare, edited by David Bevington. Thomas Nelson and Sons, 1998. Editorial material © 1998 David Bevington. Reproduced by permission.—Cousins, A.D. From *Shakespeare's Sonnets and Narrative Poems.* Longman, 2000. © Pearson Education Limited 2000. Reproduced by permission.—Craik, T.W. From an introduction to *The Merry Wives of Windsor.* By William Shakespeare, edited by T.W. Craik. Clarendon Press, 1989. © Oxford University Press, 1989. All rights reserved. Reproduced by permission.—Dubrow, Heather. From "'This Blemish'd Fort': The Rape of the Hearth in Shakespeare's *Lucrece,*" in *Form and Reform in Renaissance England: Essays in Honor of Barbara Kiefer Lewalski.* Edited by Amy Boesky and Mary Thomas Crane. University of Delaware Press, 2000. © 2000 by Associated University Presses, Inc. All rights reserved. Reproduced by permission.—Edwards, Philip. From an introduction to *Hamlet, Prince of Denmark.* By William Shakespeare, edited by Philip Edwards. Cambridge University Press, 1985. © Cambridge University Press 1985. Reproduced by permission of publisher and author.—Flannery, Christopher. From *Troilus and Cressida: Poetry or Philosophy?"* in *Shakespeare as Political Thinker.* Edited by John Alvis and Thomas G. West. Carolina Academic Press, 1981. © 1981 John Alvis and Thomas G. West. All rights reserved. Reproduced by permission.—Lanham, Richard A. From *The Motives of Eloquence: Literary Rhetoric in the Renaissance.* Yale University Press, 1976. Reproduced by permission of the author.—Melchiori, Giorgio. From *Shakespeare's Garter Plays: "Edward III" to "Merry Wives of Windsor."* University of Delaware Press, 1994. © 1994 by Associated University Presses. All rights reserved. Reproduced by permission.—Muir, Kenneth. From *Shakespeare the Professional and Related Studies.* Heinemann, 1973. © Kenneth Muir 1973. Reproduced by permission.—Roe, John. From *The Poems.* Cambridge University Press, 1992. © Cambridge University Press 1992. Reproduced

PHOTOGRAPHS APPEARING IN *SC*, VOLUME 59, WERE RECEIVED FROM THE FOLLOWING SOURCES:

List of Plays and Poems Covered in *SC*

Volumes 1-10 present a critical overview of each play, including criticism from the seventeenth century to the present. Beginning with Volumes 11, the series focuses on the history of Shakespeare's plays on the stage and in important films. The Yearbooks reprint the most important critical pieces of the year as suggested by an advisory board of Shakespearean scholars. Beginning with Volume 27, each volume is organized around a theme and primarily focuses on criticism published after 1960.

Vol. 1
The Comedy of Errors
Hamlet
Henry IV, Parts 1 and 2
Timon of Athens
Twelfth Night

Vol. 2
Henry VIII
King Lear
Love's Labour's Lost
Measure for Measure
Pericles

Vol. 3
Henry VI, Parts 1, 2, and 3
Macbeth
A Midsummer Night's Dream
Troilus and Cressida

Vol. 4
Cymbeline
The Merchant of Venice
Othello
Titus Andronicus

Vol. 5
As You Like It
Henry V
The Merry Wives of Windsor
Romeo and Juliet

Vol. 6
Antony and Cleopatra
Richard II
The Two Gentlemen of Verona

Vol. 7
All's Well That Ends Well
Julius Caesar
The Winter's Tale

Vol. 8
Much Ado about Nothing
Richard III
The Tempest

Vol. 9
Coriolanus
King John
The Taming of the Shrew
The Two Noble Kinsmen

Vol. 10
The Phoenix and Turtle
The Rape of Lucrece
Sonnets
Venus and Adonis

Vol. 11
King Lear
Othello
Romeo and Juliet

Vol. 12
The Merchant of Venice
A Midsummer Night's Dream
The Taming of the Shrew
The Two Gentlemen of Verona

Vol. 13
1989 Yearbook

Vol. 14
Henry IV, Parts 1 and 2
Henry V
Richard III

Vol. 15
Cymbeline
Pericles
The Tempest
The Winter's Tale

Vol. 16
1990 Yearbook

Vol. 17
Antony and Cleopatra
Coriolanus
Julius Caesar
Titus Andronicus

Vol. 18
The Merry Wives of Windsor
Much Ado about Nothing
Troilus and Cressida

Vol. 19
1991 Yearbook

Vol. 20
Macbeth
Timon of Athens

Vol. 21
Hamlet

Vol. 22
1992 Yearbook

Vol. 23
As You Like It
Love's Labour's Lost
Measure for Measure

Vol. 24
Henry VI, Parts 1, 2, and 3
Henry VIII
King John
Richard II

Vol. 25
1993 Yearbook

Vol. 26
All's Well That Ends Well
The Comedy of Errors
Twelfth Night

Vol. 27
Shakespeare and Classical Civilization
Antony and Cleopatra
Timon of Athens
Titus Andronicus
Troilus and Cressida

Hamlet

For further information on the critical and stage history of *Hamlet,* see *SC,* Volumes 1, 21, 35, and 44.

INTRODUCTION

Hamlet is, quite simply, the best known of Shakespeare's plays and the most famous play in Western literature. It is not hard to see why it enjoys such an exalted status. The play, which dates from the middle of Shakespeare's career (around 1600-1), manages to combine a complicated plot, profound insights into the human condition, and non-stop action into one seamless whole. An extraordinary amount of criticism has been written about *Hamlet*; in fact, the journal *Hamlet Studies* is devoted solely to discussion of the play. The amount of criticism generated is matched by its variety; some critics focus on the characters or concentrate on the gender issues that the play addresses, while others examine the play's highly condensed language and imagery. Critics are also interested in how Shakespeare transformed his sources in creating *Hamlet,* as well as the play's various themes and its influence on culture.

Historically, critical attention has been concentrated on the character of Hamlet. In recent years however, critics have begun to focus on other characters as well, especially Ophelia. Gunnar Sjögren (see Further Reading), for example, looks at Ophelia from numerous different critical perspectives in order to "do justice" to her. For Sjögren, the crucial point about Ophelia's characterization is its ambiguity, and he looks to contemporary Elizabethan attitudes and important plays by Shakespeare's rivals in an attempt to judge how her character was meant to be viewed. He examines the relatively lax morals of the Elizabethan court and the characterization of Bel-imperia in Thomas Kyd's *The Spanish Tragedy* (c. 1586), and concludes that Ophelia is seduced by Hamlet. According to Sjögren, Ophelia is cast aside when she gets in the way of Hamlet's primary goal of revenge, and her madness arises from Hamlet's rejection of her. Sjögren concludes by observing that modern performances of *Hamlet* have done justice to Ophelia, for in them "Ophelia comes into her own and emerges as a very interesting part indeed." Hamlet's relationship with Ophelia has also been of interest to critics. R.A. Foakes (1973) analyzes the effect of Hamlet's cruelty on Ophelia, and Eric P. Levy (1999) examines the encounter between Hamlet and Ophelia in Ophelia's room. Jennifer Low (1999) discusses the symbolic importance of the location of the initial fight between Laertes and Hamlet, which takes place at Ophelia's grave.

It is, however, in feminist criticism and the discussion of gender roles that Ophelia has played a central part. Elaine Showalter (1985) considers how to read Ophelia's story. In an attempt to gain new perspectives on her character, she traces the "cultural history" of Ophelia's representation, both on and off the stage, and examines the connection between female sexuality and insanity. Showalter also examines the feminist revision of Ophelia's character, and contends that "there is no 'true' Ophelia for whom feminist criticism must unambiguously speak," and that Ophelia's representation depends entirely on cultural attitudes towards both women and madness. Ann Thompson and Neil Taylor (1996) review the shifting critical attitudes to the female characters in *Hamlet,* commenting that many critics have echoed Hamlet's own misogynistic attitudes towards the women in the play. Thompson and Taylor ultimately contend that the play has "relatively simplistic views of women as angels or whores."

The discussion of gender issues has always been a politically and culturally charged one. By contrast, the analysis of the language and imagery in *Hamlet* has been relatively tranquil although wide ranging. Richard A. Lanham (1976) traces the uses of rhetoric in the play. He concludes that Shakespeare's two principal preoccupations as a playwright were with style and motive. According to Lanham, the crucial insight *Hamlet* presents is that any sense of morality needs to take into account human beings' inherent theatricality—our self-conscious realization that we are always acting and are forever on stage. Imtiaz Habib (1994) emphasizes how the language of the play will always be misread due in part to Hamlet's ambiguity and in part to the very nature of language. R. Chris Hassel, Jr. (1999) examines the mouse and mousetrap imagery in *Hamlet.*

Despite the recent trend toward concentrating on gender issues and language, two older critical strategies remain well represented in contemporary criticism: source studies and thematic analyses. Cherrell Guilfoyle (1990) deepens the hunt for Shakespeare's sources by tracing Ophelia's character to the legend of Mary Magdalen as developed in medieval drama, and suggests that Shakespeare parallels Mary Magdalen in the character of Ophelia in order to stress the twin ideas of hope and atonement in a play. Frank Nicholas Clary (see Further Reading) returns, as have so many critics and scholars, to one of Shakespeare's sources for *Hamlet*—Belleforest's adaptation of the Saxo Grammaticus story—and concludes that Belleforest's work was more influential than has been previously acknowledged. Manuel Aguirre (1996) examines the literary origins of the cup from which Gertrude drinks a fatal toast to Hamlet in the play's final scene, and argues that by Shakespeare's time women's mythic role within society was being undermined. From Aguirre's perspective, Shakespeare's attention to the theme of sovereignty dramatizes the clash between older and newer ideologies. Millicent Bell (1998) also studies *Hamlet*'s concern with a particular theme: in this case, revenge. Bell shows that one of Shakespeare's intentions in *Hamlet* was to satirize the revenge-play genre by means of both the overstylized play-within-the-play and the conclusion of the play itself. The critic contends that the play-within-the-play, *The Murder of Gonzago,* is "stale bombast," and Hamlet's concern with revenge is nowhere to be seen when he is dying, noting that, rather than crying out for revenge, Hamlet asks only to be remembered.

OVERVIEWS AND GENERAL STUDIES

Philip Edwards (essay date 1985)

SOURCE: Introduction to *Hamlet, Prince of Denmark,* by William Shakespeare, edited by Philip Edwards, Cambridge University Press, 1985, pp. 40-61.

[*In the following excerpt, Edwards analyzes* Hamlet *in a linear fashion, emphasizing the complexity of the play and examining the choices open to the protagonist.*]

THE PLATFORM

Hamlet opens with soldiers on guard at night in a scene full of perturbation and anxiety. It is nervousness about the apparition which predominates, of course, 'this thing', 'this dreaded sight', looking exactly like the late king in full armour. It is an ominous thing, and the sceptic Horatio, who is quickly converted, fears that it 'bodes some strange eruption to our state'. The state is already in turmoil, being hastily put on a war footing. Fortinbras of Norway is threatening to invade Denmark to recover lands which his father lost to the late King Hamlet a generation ago. Recollection of that old combat coming on top of the apparition focuses all attention on the dead king. The practice of calling the king by the name of his country enforces an identity between king and kingdom, the health of the one reflecting the health of the other, so that the old king's death seems to mark the end of an era. 'The king that's dead' is referred to as 'the majesty of buried Denmark'. Much later, the first words of the mad Ophelia are 'Where is the beauteous majesty of Denmark?' Even a routine cry like Bernardo's 'Long live the king!' in the third line of the play takes an additional meaning as we sense the apprehension of the watch for what may be the consequences for Denmark of the loss of their hero-king.

Hamlet is about Denmark as well as its prince. How Denmark fares as a society is in our minds all the time. But of course it's not just Hamlet and Denmark. Though Hamlet is at the centre of the play, he exists in his relationships, familial, social, sexual, political, divine; and even Hamlet, the most famous 'individual' in drama, is not so

exclusively the centre that he diminishes the importance of what he is related to: family, society, God.

Since it is his threat to the kingdom which is the cause of the watch being set, young Fortinbras may be said to start the play off. In fact he encircles it, seeing that he enters at the very end to take over the kingdom without having to fight for it. Having so satisfactorily concluded his business, he will be able to give his 'landless resolutes' whatever they would like to have. Fortinbras succeeds where Hamlet fails, though Hamlet has been trying to right a great wrong and Fortinbras has been interested only in reversing the lawful outcome of his father's reckless challenge.

'I KNOW NOT SEEMS'

Prince Hamlet in black carries into the court (in 1.2) that memory of the dead king which Claudius and Gertrude are anxious to erase. His grief, he says, is real not assumed, unlike (he implies) the emotions being expressed around him. But the most determined candour could scarcely reveal in public what he pours out when he is alone: his feeling of total despair, of *taedium vitae,* of the weary meaninglessness of 'all the uses of this world'. He has no wish to continue living, but divine law forbids suicide. Why is all this? Because his father has suddenly died and his mother has speedily taken a new husband. Too slight a ground for despair? Hamlet's protestations are extreme. To call Claudius a satyr—a lecherous goat-like creature—does not make much sense to an audience who has just seen the new king efficiently managing his courtiers and the affairs of the nation. His mother's remarriage makes him call in question the constancy of all women. 'Hyperion to a satyr!' 'Frailty, thy name is woman!' Such passionate attachment to his father, such contempt for his uncle, such disgust with his mother, may seem pathological, what Eliot would call 'in excess of the facts'. Hamlet's indignation does indeed go deeper than the 'facts' but its source is not morbid.

The story of Cain and Abel is brought into the play during this scene (105) and appears again twice (3.3.38 and 5.1.65).[1] That first murder shattered the human family; it resulted from and betokened man's falling away from God. The identification of Claudius with Cain—which he himself makes—gives us the context in which we should put the 'unreasonable' bitterness of Hamlet, though as yet he knows nothing about any murder. In his book *Violence and the Sacred,* René Girard argued that cultural breakdown in early society, what he terms the 'sacrificial crisis', involves the failure to recognise acknowledged distinctions and differences. The erasure of difference shows itself in myth in the mortal rivalry of two brothers for what cannot be shared, a throne, a woman. Girard quotes the 'degree' speech in Shakespeare's *Troilus and Cressida* as an inspired perception of the chaos and violence which flow from the weakening of accepted distinctions. If, instead of the reading 'each thing meets in mere oppugnancy', he had followed the quarto text with 'each thing *melts* in mere oppugnancy', he would have shown how even more forcefully the passage conveys the rooted fear of the loss of category, of identity, of distinctiveness.

The obliteration of distinction, before Hamlet knows anything about fratricide or adultery, lies in Claudius taking his brother's place as king and husband and in Gertrude tranquilly accepting him as substitute. Their acts may offend against taste and ethics but the deeper offence is the undermining of an ideal of the person enshrined in antiquity and law. Hamlet's expressions, 'Hyperion to a satyr' and 'no more like my father / Than I to Hercules', show a mythographic ordering of the human differences. So in the closet scene Hamlet tries to force the distinction of the two men on to his mother by means of the two pictures. 'Have you eyes?' he shouts at her—

> See what a grace was seated on this brow;
> Hyperion's curls, the front of Jove himself,
> An eye like Mars, to threaten and command;
> A station like the herald Mercury . . .

> (3.4.55-8)

This matter of the blurring of distinctions in a man claiming to be his brother helps to explain Hamlet's passion against Claudius as a usurper—

> A slave that is not twentieth part the tithe
> Of your precedent lord, a vice of kings,
> A cutpurse of the empire and the rule . . .

> (3.4.97-9)

Denmark is an elective monarchy as Hamlet knows quite well (see 1.2.109, 5.2.65, 335).[2] But Shakespeare plays off this elective monarchy against his Elizabethan audience's deep emotional commitment to primogeniture and the right of a son to inherit. The Danish system condemns itself; a country which chooses its kings ends up with the rabble-cry of 'Choose we! Laertes shall be king!' (4.5.106). It has chosen for its king one who, did they but know, organised the vacancy by murder. For the audience, the system is a legalism which runs counter to their instinctive sense of rightness. There is a higher court than the court of Denmark, and in that court Hamlet is the dispossessed prince. Hamlet himself is both a Dane and an Elizabethan; whatever Danish law says, Claudius has usurped his brother, and violently appropriated a kingship he has no right to.

Gertrude's offence in confusing the two brothers is much deepened in the audience's eyes later in the first act when they learn that she committed adultery with Claudius while her husband was alive. . . . The willingness of this complaisant woman to sleep with either of two brothers is a forceful image of the failure of discrimination which is central to the tragedy of *Hamlet*.

In this second scene Hamlet is unaware of adultery or murder. But he has repudiated with contempt the appropriation of that vital distinction of fatherhood which Claudius grandly tries to add to his other appropriations. 'But now my cousin Hamlet, and my son . . .' Hamlet will not accept the relationship; it is 'more than kin'. He knows he is not Claudius's son, and the same knowledge tells him that Claudius is not Gertrude's husband, nor Denmark's king. It is this knowledge, as well as grief for a father's death and the shallowness of a mother's love, which makes the whole world an unweeded garden.

THE GHOST

Hamlet is galvanised into activity by the news of the appearance of a ghost that resembles his dead father. On the platform that night he sees it and is determined to speak to it whatever happens. It is explanation he wants; explanation and a course of action. 'Let me not burst in ignorance', he cries. 'What should we do?' Though it is specific explanation—why the Ghost has come—and a specific course of action—what the Ghost wants him to do—that he seeks, his words have a wider perspective. The Ghost may have some secret, some unimaginable truth to bring relief from those 'thoughts beyond the reaches of our souls', an explanation why things are as they are and a directive for meaningful action. To his demands in both their specific and their general senses he receives, or thinks he receives, a more than sufficient response.

The Ghost declares that he is his father's spirit, gives him the extraordinary tidings of murder and adultery, and asks him to take revenge. His injunctions are summed up in the three imperatives, 'Bear it not', 'Taint not thy mind', 'Leave her to heaven.' These interconnect. 'Bear it not' looks both backwards and forwards. The idea of retribution is implied by the Ghost's appeal to Hamlet's 'nature', that is, his filial piety. 'Bear it not' means that as a son he is not to acquiesce in and accept what has been done to his father. But it looks also to the future. The abuse of Denmark by the very continuation of this pair in sovereignty and in marriage is not to be endured: 'Bear it not.' The second imperative is very strange: 'howsomever thou pursues this act, / Taint not thy mind'. Whatever the exact meaning of 'taint'. . . , the tone of the remark is that the Ghost does not consider this matter of revenge too difficult an act, and is anxious that Hamlet should not become too disturbed about it. No doubt for the Ghost the challenge is like that which he accepted all those years ago when he agreed to face old Fortinbras in a single combat: a matter of honour, determination, courage and skill. The final injunction, 'Leave her to heaven', must temper our feeling of the Ghost's personal vindictiveness. It is more important, however, in giving a religious context to the punishment of Claudius and Gertrude. Gertrude's earthly punishment is to be her conscience: 'those thorns that in her bosom lodge / To prick and sting her'. Whatever further punishment or exoneration is hers to receive belongs to an afterlife. With Claudius it is different. By his words 'Leave *her* to heaven', the Ghost must imply that a higher justice requires the exemplary punishment of Claudius on earth, by the hand of an appointed human being. The Ghost's commands indicate not the pursuit of personal satisfaction but the existence of a world beyond the human world responsible for justice in the human world. Whether the Ghost has the authority to convey this the play never makes clear.

Awful though it is, Hamlet now has his explanation. What had seemed the degeneration of the world turns out to be a condition which is clearly and starkly the consequence of a double crime. He now also has his directive, a commission that is also a mission. His reaction to the Ghost is like a religious conversion. He wipes away all previous knowledge, all previous values, and baptises himself as a new man (1.5.95-104).

> And thy commandment all alone shall live
> Within the book and volume of my brain,
> Unmixed with baser matter.

The commandment is summed up by the Ghost as 'Remember!' 'Remember me', says the Ghost, and Hamlet repeats the word three times in his dedication. The Ghost is to be remembered 'whiles memory holds a seat / In this distracted globe', that is to say so long as this now-disordered world attributes any value to the past and its traditions, to the established standards of virtue and justice. . . . In this speech, to remember means more than to keep in mind; it means to maintain and to restore. In the section 'Of Redemption' in *Thus Spake Zarathustra,* Nietzsche deplored those who could not accept the 'It was' of time. He saw vengeance and punishment as an imprisonment of the will in concentrating on the past in an effort to undo what could not be undone. 'This, yea, this is very vengeance!—Will's abhorrence of time and its "It was".'[3] It is quite clear that Hamlet is not prepared to accept the 'It was' of time, and that he regards revenge as a task of creative remembrance, that is, the restoration of a society that has fallen to pieces. The act ends with

> The time is out of joint: O cursed spite,
> That ever I was born to set it right.

This is a terrible moment as, all exhilaration gone, he faces the burden of his responsibilities. But who has told him that it is his responsibility to put the world to rights? to restore the disjointed frame of things to its true shape? No one but himself. It is the entirely self-imposed burden of cleansing the world that he now groans under.

THE ANTIC DISPOSITION

'As a stranger give it welcome', says Hamlet to Horatio about the supernatural visitation.

> There are more things in heaven and earth, Horatio,
> Than are dreamt of in your philosophy.

He identifies himself with the world of the stranger, and shows his alienation from Denmark and its values by adopting the garb of madness. The 'antic disposition' (an essential element in the old Amleth story) puzzles and worries the man who is now his enemy and sworn victim;

it also has symbolic significance in denoting that Hamlet, like Bunyan's Christian, having received his call, considers himself a pilgrim and a stranger in his own city of Vanity Fair. Madness is conduct which does not conform to society's standards. Very well, says Hamlet, I am a madman.[4]

Shakespeare carefully marks a considerable lapse of time between Acts 1 and 2. . . . The first event in Hamlet's mission that we hear about is his silent ritual of divorce from Ophelia. Ophelia's tragedy, like Hamlet's, is the tragedy of obedience to a father. Only she really goes mad. And then—always going one step further than the prince—she doesn't stop at thinking about ending her life. At this stage in the play, she has obeyed her father and refused to see Hamlet. She now tells Polonius of the very peculiar encounter she has had with him. Hamlet, in a set piece of antic theatre, went dishevelled to her room and in total silence carried out what we might interpret as a ceremony of questioning, denunciation and separation. By this, he cuts the closest tie that binds him to the court of Denmark, and takes his school-fellow Horatio as his only confidant.

What are the values of 'Denmark' as we are shown them? The court party, Claudius, Polonius, Laertes, are much given to expressing their beliefs in resonant platitudes. Claudius knows the proper response to death, Laertes to sex, Polonius to everything. With each person, we see the insufficiency of their moralising. What Claudius is hiding we learn in 1.5 (though it is not confirmed until 3.1.50), and he is hiding it even from his new wife, who in turn tried to hide her double-life from her husband. Laertes is suspected by both his sister and his father of an inclination towards the primrose path of dalliance. Polonius advocates reticence, truth and straightdealing, but is loquacious and devious. It is the ever-ready platitudes, betrayed both by their rhetoric and by the conduct of those who utter them, that Hamlet discards as mere 'saws of books' as he enters his new life. It is interesting that the heavy moralising of the court party accompanies a low view of human nature. Polonius and Laertes both expect Hamlet to be the insouciant seducer that is their stereotype of an aristocrat. (Hamlet, on the other hand, is an 'idealist', expecting mothers to be above sexual desire.) Polonius's proclivity for spying—which leads to his own violent death—is shown in the grotesque commission to Reynaldo to keep an eye on Laertes in Paris and then in his schemes to find out what's wrong with Hamlet. Claudius has much greater need than Polonius to find out what lies behind Hamlet's strange behaviour; his elaborate plot to use Rosencrantz and Guildenstern as decoys is quickly uncovered by Hamlet.

What Hamlet is really thinking about during the long scene 2.2 is impossible to say. Everything he says to Polonius, Rosencrantz and Guildenstern has its irony, and if his hearers do not know when he is being sane and serious, nor do we. When he tells Rosencrantz and Guildenstern that he is 'most dreadfully attended' (255) he is not really talking about his servants. He may have the Ghost in mind, but chiefly he must mean his own thoughts. We are sure enough of him when he says he finds Denmark a prison. And with that extraordinary end to his joke about Polonius taking his leave—'except my life, except my life, except my life'—we must feel the warning note that the *taedium vitae* which lifted from him when the Ghost spoke is descending again and that the ultimate dilemma of 'To be or not to be' is at hand.

What we should discount as an index of Hamlet's feelings is the famous speech 'What a piece of work is a man' (286-91). So often pointed to as a brilliant perception of the anguish of Renaissance man in general and of Hamlet in particular, it is a glorious blind, a flight of rhetoric by which a divided and distressed soul conceals the true nature of his distress and substitutes a formal and conventional state of *Weltschmerz*. At the end of it he punctures the rhetoric himself.

ROGUE AND PEASANT SLAVE

We are often reminded that Pyrrhus is, with Hamlet, Laertes and Fortinbras, another son avenging the slaying of his father (Achilles). But Hamlet swings into the rant of his second soliloquy not in any desire to emulate the cruel fury of Pyrrhus but out of shame that an actor's emotion for Pyrrhus's victim, Hecuba, should outdo his own emotion for Claudius's victim, his father. He has done nothing—it is true enough. But the effect of the eloquence of the old play and the actor's moving performance is to make him confuse doing with exhibition. His outburst is violent but essentially comic. His guilt runs away with him. Feeling that if he were a proper avenger he would exhibit a huge amount of passion he lets go a mammoth display of self-accusation and rage, culminating in a great stage-cry, 'O vengeance!'

With this, he becomes ashamed of his hysterical attitudinising and rebukes himself for unpacking his heart with words. He turns from rant to action. What has to be done? The idea of using the players to test the Ghost's veracity was in his mind before he fell 'a-cursing like a very drab' (see 2.2.493-5). Hamlet had approached the Ghost knowing it might be either a demon from hell or a spirit from heaven. Perhaps he accepted it as an 'honest ghost' with too little question. That he should test the Ghost's account before he proceeds to take the king's life is the most obvious precaution. He says all that needs to be said on this subject (551-5). The Ghost could be a spirit from hell taking advantage of his distress to lure him into an act that will damn his soul.

That Hamlet in deciding to use the test of a play is guilty of procrastination is scarcely tenable. . . . Procrastination means putting off until tomorrow what you know ought to be done today. *Hamlet* is indeed a tragedy of delay, but procrastination is only one special form of delay. At least part of the reason for his delay so far must be Hamlet's fear that he is being deluded by the devil into imperilling the life of Claudius and the fate of his own soul.

'TO BE OR NOT TO BE'

Act 3 begins next day, the day that the court play is to be given. But even if we are aware of this lapse of time since Hamlet decided to use a play to test the king, it is a shock to us to find Hamlet speaking as he does, for the 'To be or not to be' soliloquy throws everything back into debate.

What *is* the question, 'to be or not to be'? All sorts of answers have been given. I can't doubt that Hamlet is asking whether one should go on living or whether one should take one's life. He is back in the depression of the first soliloquy, longing for the oblivion of death. But now the question whether life is worthwhile has much more knowledge and experience to take account of and brood over, and it assumes an entirely new significance. It is extraordinary that, at this moment in the play, the soliloquy should seem so indifferent to the immediate problem of killing the king. Implicitly the issue is there all the time, but never explicitly. The reason for that is that killing the king has become part of a much wider debate.

> To be or not to be, that is the question—
> Whether 'tis nobler in the mind to suffer
> The slings and arrows of outrageous fortune,
> Or to take arms against a sea of troubles,
> And by opposing end them. To die, to sleep—
> No more; and by a sleep to say we end
> The heart-ache and the thousand natural shocks
> That flesh is heir to—'tis a consummation
> Devoutly to be wished.

The question is which of two courses is the nobler. The first alternative is 'to be', to go on living, and this is a matter of endurance, of contriving to accept the continuous punishing hostility of life. The second alternative is 'not to be', to take one's life, and this is described as ending a sea of troubles by taking arms against it. There is only the one opposition to be made against the sea of troubles (which is the definition of our life) and that is the constructive act of suicide. Suicide is the one way in which fighting against the ungovernable tide—that mythical symbol of hopeless endeavour—can succeed.

If we accept that Hamlet's alternative in these opening lines is the course of enduring or the course of evading life's onslaught, there is an important consequence. The life that has to be suffered or evaded is described as a continuous, permanent condition of misfortune, and must therefore include the state of the world even after vengeance has been taken and Claudius killed—supposing that to happen. The whips and scorns of time, the oppressor's wrong—there is no indication that these can ever disappear from the world, except by disappearing from the world oneself. By his stark alternative in these opening lines Hamlet implicitly rejects the possibility that any act of his could improve the condition of the world or the condition of its victims. Revenge is of no avail. Whether Hamlet kills the king or not, Denmark will continue to be a prison, a place of suffering ruled by fortune. The only nobleness which is available if one goes on living is not the cleansing of the world by some great holy deed, but endurance, suffering in the mind.

But, as the soliloquy proceeds, the one positive act available to man, suicide, has to be ruled out. The sleep of death becomes a nightmare, because of the dread of damnation. What began as a question which was more noble ends as a contest in cowardliness. What is one the more afraid of, the possibility of damnation or the certainty of suffering on earth?

And so we do nothing, frightened to take the one route out of our misery. 'Thus conscience doth make cowards of us all.' 'Conscience' means what it normally means, what it means when Claudius uses it just before this (50) and when Hamlet uses it in the previous scene (2.2.558); that is to say, it has its religious meaning of an implanted sense of right and wrong. It is with this reflection that Hamlet moves away from suicide; it is with this 'regard'—this examination of the consequences of things and worrying about how they look in the eye of eternity—that *other* 'enterprises of great pitch and moment' lose the name of action. Hamlet must be thinking about killing Claudius. So, although only by inference and indirectly, Hamlet twice refers to his revenge in this soliloquy. On the first occasion we gather that he no longer has any faith that killing the king would be a cleansing act setting the world to rights; on the second, we gather that his resolution to exact revenge has been 'sicklied o'er' by respects of conscience. His conscience cannot convince him that the act is good; and, whether good or bad, it cannot change the world. We are condemned to unhappiness and to inactivity. Although this speech represents a trough of despair into which we don't see Hamlet fall again, the whole of the rest of the play is coloured by the extreme pessimism of this soliloquy.

It certainly affects his behaviour to Ophelia in the painful, cruel interview which now follows. All he says is backed by a loathing of the world, a loathing of himself, and a loathing of sex. It is hard for Ophelia that she should be in his way just at this moment, to trigger off an eruption of anger and disgust. At the same time, we realise that Hamlet sees his victim as life's victim. Her innocence cannot survive; she is unavoidably subject to the contagion of living; she will be corrupted by men as inevitably as, being a woman, she will corrupt them. When he says she should go to a nunnery, he means a nunnery. Only if she is locked up in perpetual virginity can she be saved. And there will be no more marriage. Hamlet begins to work at a new way of saving mankind—sexual abstinence.

Although I believe that *Hamlet* is primarily a religious play, and that Hamlet perpetually sees himself in a relationship with heaven and hell, yet it is noticeable that Hamlet voices very few really Christian sentiments—as contrasted with both Claudius and Ophelia. Only once, and then in his usual ironic manner, does he talk of praying (1.5.132). It is in this scene of cruelty to Ophelia, if anywhere, that behind the restless, unending teasing and taunting we might feel Hamlet's strong sense of his personal unworthiness and need of assistance. 'What should such fellows as I do crawling between earth and heaven?'

PLAY, PRAYER, MURDER

Hamlet is not content to let his 'mousetrap' play on the murder of Gonzago take its toll of Claudius's conscience without assistance. He forces its significance at Claudius as he later forces the poisoned cup at him (3.2.237-9). His insistent commentary gives Claudius the opportunity to cover his departure with righteous indignation against his nephew's impossible behaviour. At any rate, Hamlet has achieved his purpose. He is convinced of Claudius's guilt and he has made Claudius know that he knows. Hamlet does not lack courage. But what to do with this knowledge now? There is way of avoiding the fact that at this critical juncture, with the Ghost's story confirmed, he chooses to do precisely what the Ghost forbade, take action against his mother.

First there is the difficult problem of how to take his extraordinary speech about drinking hot blood.

> 'Tis now the very witching time of night,
> When churchyards yawn, and hell itself breathes out
> Contagion to this world. Now could I drink hot blood,
> And do such bitter business as the day
> Would quake to look on. Soft, now to my mother.
> O heart, lose not thy nature . . .

> (3.2.349-54)

Some say that this speech is a sign that Hamlet has committed himself to hell; some say that he is rather awkwardly trying out the traditional role of the avenger of fiction. There is a grain of truth in both these theories, but neither can of itself explain the speech. We have just seen Hamlet, who has been at a peak of emotional intensity during and immediately after the play scene, in a keen and fierce verbal attack on Rosencrantz, Guildenstern and Polonius. That he should at this point in all seriousness bellow out like some Herod of the stage 'Now could I drink hot blood' is to me incredible. The rant of the 'rogue and peasant slave' soliloquy, induced by the emotion of the Pyrrhus speech, was understandable, but this seems quite out of keeping with character and situation. But that Hamlet should *fear* his declension into hellish activity, should *fear* himself slipping into the role of the stage-avenger, I could well imagine. The contagion of hell is what he wishes to avoid, and the *last* thing he wants to do is 'drink hot blood'. He says the words with a shiver of apprehension and disgust. Then, 'Soft, now to my mother.' As so often in this play, 'soft!' is a word of warning to oneself to turn away from some undesirable train of thought and attend to an immediate problem.. . . 'O heart, lose not thy nature.' He really does fear he may do something terrible.

Action is now hedged about with all sorts of warnings and limitations concerning the good it can do to the world or the harm it can do to him, But there is one task of primary urgency, whatever the Ghost said: to shame and reclaim his mother. On the way to see her, he comes across Claudius at prayer. He goes over to kill him, then pauses as he had paused over suicide, to reflect on the consequences. Again it is the after-life that is uppermost in his mind, but the fear about damnation now is that Claudius may *not* be damned. He wants Claudius damned, and he is not prepared to take the risk that if he kills him while he is praying he will go to heaven. He will wait for an opportunity that will make revenge more complete and damnation more certain.

> Then trip him that his heels may kick at heaven,
> And that his soul may be as damned and black
> As hell whereto it goes.
>
>   (3.3.93-5)

Savagery of this order is familiar to students of Elizabethan revenge fiction.[5] Perhaps the contagion of hell *has* touched Hamlet. But, repellent though it is that Hamlet so passionately wants the eternal perdition of his victim, it is perhaps more striking that he should think that it is in his power to control the fate of Claudius's soul. It is surely a monstrously inflated conception of his authority that is governing him, distorting still further the scope of the Ghost's injunctions. In this scene the arrogance of the man who is trying to effect justice is strongly contrasted with the Christian humility of the man who has done murder.

Hamlet means what he says in the prayer scene. The procrastination theory held that once again Hamlet was finding some excuse for not acting. This cannot be right, for a minute or two later, thinking he has found Claudius in the ignominious and dishonourable position of eavesdropping behind the arras in Gertrude's chamber, he kills him—only to find that it is Polonius. The killing of Polonius is a major climax. In spite of whatever doubts and mental stress about the authority of the Ghost and the meaning of its message, about the need to do the deed or the good it would do, here deliberately and violently he keeps his word and carries out his revenge; and he kills the wrong man. This terrible irony is the direct result of his decisions since the end of the play scene, which imply his belief in his power to control the destinies in this life and in the after-life of both Gertrude and Claudius, his assumption of the role of Providence itself.

From the killing of Polonius the catastrophe of the play stems.[6] This false completion of Hamlet's revenge initiates the second cycle of revenge for a murdered father, that of Laertes for Polonius. *That* revenge is successful and ends in the death of Hamlet. By unwittingly killing Polonius, Hamlet brings about his own death.

THE CLOSET SCENE

Nothing in the play is more bizarre than that Hamlet, having committed the terrible error of killing Polonius, should be so consumed with the desire to purge and rescue his mother that he goes right on with his castigation even with the dead body of Polonius at his feet. No wonder the Ghost

enters again to whet his 'almost blunted purpose'. Hamlet well knows that in this present heat ('time and passion') he should be obedient to his vow and apply himself to a grimmer task. But he does nothing. It is remarkable that he fears the presence of the Ghost will actually weaken his resolve to kill Claudius: that his response to this shape of his dead father will be pity not retribution. The Ghost could 'convert / My stern effects' and there would be 'tears perchance for blood' (3.4.126-29). This fear for the strength of his resolution should be compared with the heavy-heartedness at the prospect of carrying out the execution as he looks at Polonius's corpse: 'Thus bad begins and worse remains behind' (180).

There seems no deep compunction for Polonius's death, however, and no lessening of the sense of his privilege to ordain for others.

> For this same lord,
> I do repent; but heaven hath pleased it so,
> To punish me with this, and this with me,
> That I must be their scourge and minister.
>
>   (3.4.173-6)

Poor Polonius! Hamlet is at his worst in these scenes. His self-righteousness expands in his violent rebukes of his mother and his eagerness to order her sex-life. 'Forgive me this my virtue', he says, going on to explain that in these upside-down times 'virtue itself of vice must pardon beg'. Yet the force of his words, and what appears to be the first intimation that her husband was murdered, instill into her that sense of difference which he has fought to re-establish. At the beginning she asks in indignation and bewilderment, 'What have I done?' But later she says, 'O Hamlet, speak no more', and 'What shall I do?'

TO ENGLAND

From this point onwards there are two plays of *Hamlet*, that of the second quarto and that of the Folio. I have argued . . . that the Folio version with its omissions and additions has much to be said for it, knowing what its hero has become by the end of the closet scene in a way that the seemingly more tentative and exploratory version in the second quarto does not. The changes in the Folio substitute for a rather contradictory talkativeness in Hamlet about being sent to England with his revenge unaccomplished a silence as mysterious and suggestive as the silence that lies between Acts 1 and 2. They also add a central passage in 5.2 in which the problem of damnation which has occupied Hamlet throughout is given an answer.

There is a real want of resolution concerning his revenge in Hamlet's going away to England, though it is concealed in the exciting scenes in which he courageously and scornfully spars with Claudius, who is now absolutely determined to destroy the man who knows his secret. It may be that he is biding his time, or is baffled and mortified by his own inability to act, as the two main passages omitted from the Folio suggest, but we feel that there are deeper things restraining him, hinted at in what he says to Horatio when he comes back.

> Sir, in my heart there was a kind of fighting
> That would not let me sleep.

(5.2.4-5)

While Hamlet is away, we see the effects of what he has so far achieved, in the madness of Ophelia and the furious return of Laertes. To avenge his father is for Laertes an inalienable duty, whatever may be its status in the eternal world.

> Conscience and grace to the profoundest pit!
> I dare damnation. To this point I stand,
> That both the worlds I give to negligence,
> Let come what comes, only I'll be revenged
> Most throughly for my father.

(4.5.132-6)

For Hamlet it is quite the contrary. Revenge in itself is uninteresting and foreign. It is only the question of its place as a creative and restorative 'remembering' deed within the values of the eternal world that is important to him.

THE RETURN

The news of Hamlet's return astounds the king, and he hastens to employ Laertes in a scheme to destroy him finally. Act 5 opens with the two clowns digging a grave for Ophelia. The joke of the senior of these, the sexton, that of all men he who builds strongest is the gravedigger, is something to ponder on at the end of the play. The sexton is the only person in the play who is a match for Hamlet in the combat of words. He manages to avoid answering Hamlet's question, 'Whose grave's this?' Not until the funeral procession arrives does Hamlet learn that the grave is for Ophelia, and it does not appear from the play that he was aware of her madness. Many people feel that in Hamlet's reflections over the empty grave on the vanity of life and the inevitability of death there is a mature and sober wisdom. But the presentation of this wisdom is entirely ironic. His truths are based on a chasm of ignorance. He speaks his words over a grave which he does not know is intended for a woman whose madness and death he is responsible for.[7] The fact of the dead girl punctures his philosophy. For us, at any rate. He never speaks of his regret for the suffering he caused her even before Polonius's death. On the contrary, when Laertes leaps into the grave and expresses, too clamantly perhaps, an affection for Ophelia which he genuinely feels, Hamlet will not accept it, and chooses this moment to advance and declare himself, with a challenge to Laertes' sincerity. He claims 'I loved Ophelia'—with a love forty thousand brothers could not match. It is hard to know what right Hamlet has to say that when we think of how we have seen him treat her. The dispute over Ophelia's grave seems very important. Laertes is more than a foil to Hamlet; he is a main antagonist, diametrically opposed to him in every way of thought and action, who is scheming to kill him by

a dreadful trick. But Shakespeare refuses to belittle him or let us despise him. And he refuses to sentimentalise his opponent or whitewash his failings. For those of us who to any extent 'believe in' Hamlet, Shakespeare makes things difficult in this scene. It is tragedy not sentimental drama that he is writing, and our division of mind about Hamlet is partly why the play is a tragedy.

In the all-important colloquy with Horatio at the beginning of the final scene, Hamlet tells him of the strong sense he has that his impulsive actions on board ship were guided by a divinity which takes over from us 'when our deep plots do pall' and redirects us. This is a critical juncture of the play, implying Hamlet's surrender of his grandiose belief in his power to ordain and control, and his release from the alternating belief in the meaningless and mindless drift of things. His recognition, vital though it is, is his own, and we do not necessarily have to share it.

The sense of heaven guiding him reinforces rather than diminishes his sense of personal responsibility for completing his mission. The discovery of the king's treachery in the commission to have him murdered in England has fortified Hamlet's determination. Yet it is with a demand for assurance that he puts the matter to Horatio.

> Does it not, think thee, stand me now upon—
> He that hath killed my king, and whored my mother,
> Popped in between th'election and my hopes,
> Thrown out his angle for my proper life,
> And with such cozenage—is't not perfect conscience
> To quit him with this arm? And is't not to be damned
> To let this canker of our nature come
> In further evil?

(5.2.63-70)

It is difficult to see how we can take this speech except as the conclusion of a long and deep perplexity. But if it is a conclusion, that question mark—conveying so much more than indignation—makes it an appeal by this loneliest of heroes for support and agreement, which he pointedly does not get from the cautious Horatio, who simply says,

> It must be shortly known to him from England
> What is the issue of the business there.

Horatio won't accept the responsibility of answering, and only gives him the exasperating response that he hasn't much time.

Once again Hamlet has raised the question of conscience and damnation. Conscience is no longer an obstacle to action, but encourages it. As for damnation, Hamlet had felt the threat of it if he contemplated suicide, felt the threat of it if he were to kill at the behest of a devil-ghost; now he feels the threat of it if he should fail to remove from the world a cancer which is spreading. This new image for Claudius, a 'canker of our nature', is important. All the vituperation which Hamlet has previously thrown at Claudius seems mere rhetoric by this. Hamlet now sees himself undertaking a surgical operation to remove a cancer from human society. Whether the slings and arrows of outrageous fortune continue or not is immaterial. To neglect, ignore or encourage the evil is to imperil one's soul.

THE SILENCE OF THE GHOST

When in reply to Hamlet's unanswerable question Horatio tells him that if he is going to act he had better move quickly, because as soon as Claudius learns the fate of Rosencrantz and Guildenstern Hamlet won't have another hour to live, Hamlet exclaims 'The interim's mine.' But of course it isn't, because the plot against his life has already been primed and is about to go off. Hamlet has no time left to act upon his new conviction that it is a religious duty to strike down Claudius. He accepts the fake challenge of the fencing match in the awareness that something may be afoot, and he faces it without any exhilaration: 'Thou wouldst not think how ill all's here about my heart.' When he says 'If it be now, 'tis not to come . . . the readiness is all', we assume he has some kind of prevision of what actually happens, the coming together of his revenge and his own death. Laertes wounds him fatally before he is able to make his second attempt to kill the king. The first time, he killed the wrong man; the second time, he kills the king indeed, but not until he is within moments of his own death.

There is no doubt of the extent of Hamlet's failure. In trying to restore 'the beauteous majesty of Denmark' he has brought the country into an even worse state, in the hands of a foreigner. He is responsible, directly or indirectly, for the deaths of Polonius, Ophelia, Rosencrantz and Guildenstern. With more justification, he has killed Laertes and Claudius. But if his uncle is dead, so is his mother.

What does the Ghost think of it all? He has disappeared. There is no word of approval, or sorrow, or anger. He neither praises his dead son nor blames him. Nor, if he was a devil, does he come back to gloat over the devastation he has caused. The rest is silence indeed.[8]

In Kyd's *Spanish Tragedy,* the ghost of the dead Andrea and his escort from the infernal world of spirits, named Revenge, were on stage during the whole of the play. It was absolutely clear that the ultimate direction of things was entirely in the hands of the gods of the underworld. At the end of the play Andrea rejoiced in the fulfilment of his revenge and happily surveyed the carnage on the stage. 'Ay, these were spectacles to please my soul!' He helped to apportion eternal sentences, whose 'justice' makes our blood run cold.

In spite of the seeming crudity of *The Spanish Tragedy,* it is a subtle and sinister view of the relation of gods and men that the play conveys. Kyd's gods are dark gods. Men and women plot and scheme to fulfil their desires and satisfy their hatreds, they appeal to heaven for guidance, help and approval, but the dark gods are in charge of everything, and they use every morsel of human striving in order to achieve their predestined purposes. Hieroni-

mo's heroic efforts to obtain justice, which drive him into madness and his wife to suicide, are nothing to the gods except as they may be used to fulfil their promise to Andrea.

Hamlet resists the grim certainties of Kyd's theology and the certainties of any other.[9] Hamlet's own belief towards the end of the play that a benign divinity works through our spontaneous impulses and even our mistakes is neither clearly endorsed by the play nor repudiated in ironic Kydean laughter. Hamlet is a tragic hero who at a time of complete despair hears a mysterious voice uttering a directive which he interprets as a mission to renovate the world by an act of purifying violence. But this voice is indeed a questionable voice. How far it is the voice of heaven, how its words are to be translated into human deeds, how far the will of man *can* change the course of the world—these are questions that torment the idealist as he continues to plague the decadent inhabitants, as he sees them, of the Danish court.[10]

His doubts, at one edge of his nature, are as extreme as his confidence at the other. His sense of his freedom to create his own priorities and decisions, and indeed his sense of being heaven's scourge and minister privileged to destroy at will, bring him to the disaster of killing Polonius, from which point all changes, and he becomes the hunted as well as the hunter. Eventually, in a new humility as his 'deep plots' pall, Hamlet becomes convinced that heaven is guiding him and that the removal of Claudius is a task that he is to perform at the peril of his immortal soul. He does indeed kill Claudius, but the cost is dreadful. What has he achieved, as he dies with Claudius?

It is very hard for us in the twentieth century to sympathise with Hamlet and his mission. Hearing voices from a higher world belongs mainly in the realm of abnormal psychology. Revenge may be common but is hardly supportable. The idea of purifying violence belongs to terrorist groups. Gertrude's sexual behaviour and remarriage do not seem out of the ordinary. Yet if we feel that twentieth-century doubt hampers our understanding of the seventeenth-century *Hamlet,* we must remember that *Hamlet* was actually written in our own age of doubt and revaluation—only a little nearer its beginning. *Hamlet* takes for granted that the ethics of revenge are questionable, that ghosts are questionable, that the distinctions of society are questionable, and that the will of heaven is terribly obscure. The higher truth which Hamlet tries to make active in a fallen world belongs to a past which he sees slipping away from him. Shakespeare movingly presents the beauty of a past in which kingship, marriage and the order of society had or was believed to have a heavenly sanction. A brutal Cain-like murder destroys the order of the past. Hamlet struggles to restore the past, and as he does so we feel that the desirability is delicately and perilously balanced against the futility. Shakespeare was by no means eager to share Nietzsche's acquiescence in time's *es war.* This matter of balance is an essential part of our answer about the ending of the play. It is a precarious balance, and perhaps impossible to maintain.

The Elizabethans too doubted ghosts. Shakespeare used the concern of his time about voices and visions to suggest the treacherousness of communication with the transcendent world. We come in the end to accept the Ghost not as a devil but as a spirit who speaks truth yet who cannot with any sufficiency or adequacy provide the answer to Hamlet's cry, 'What should we do?' Everything depends on interpretation and translation. A terrible weight of responsibility is thrown on to the human judgement and will. Kierkegaard, in *Fear and Trembling*, spoke of Abraham hearing a voice from heaven and trusting it to the extent of being willing to kill his own son; and he wrote brilliantly of the knife-edge which divides an act of faith from a demoniacal impulse. In Shakespeare's age, William Tyndale also used Abraham as an example of where faith might go outside the boundaries of ethics, but he warned against 'holy works' which had their source in what he contemptuously called 'man's imaginations'.[11] These distinctions between acts of faith and the demoniacal, between holy works and works of man's imagination, seem fundamental to *Hamlet*. We know that Hamlet made a mess of what he was trying to do. The vital question is whether what he was trying to do was a holy work or a work of man's imagination. Shakespeare refuses to tell us.

Hamlet's attempt to make a higher truth operative in the world of Denmark, which is where all of us live, is a social and political disaster, and it pushes him into inhumanity and cruelty. But the unanswerable question, 'Is't not to be damned / To let this canker of our nature come / In further evil?', if it could be answered 'Yes!' would make us see the chance-medley of the play's ending in a light so different that it would abolish our merely moral judgement. Bradley's final remark on the play was that 'the apparent failure of Hamlet's life is not the ultimate truth concerning him'.[12] But it might be. That is where the tragic balance lies. The play of *Hamlet* takes place within the possibility that there is a higher court of values than those which operate around us, within the possibility of having some imperfect communication with that court, within the possibility that an act of violence can purify, within the possibility that the words 'salvation' and 'damnation' have meaning. To say that these possibilities are certainties is to wreck the play as surely as to say they are impossibilities.

So the silence of the Ghost at the end of the play leaves the extent of Hamlet's victory or triumph an open question. To answer it needs a knowledge that Horatio didn't have, that Shakespeare didn't have, that we don't have. The mortal havoc is plain to our eyes on the stage; the rest is silence.

Notes

1. See Rosalie L. Colie, *Shakespeare's Living Art*, 1974, p. 230, and Honor Matthews, *The Primal Curse: The Myth of Cain and Abel in the Theatre*, 1967.

2. See the discussion by E.A.J. Honigmann in 'The Politics of *Hamlet*', in '*Hamlet*', ed. Brown and Harris, pp. 129-47.

3. 'Des Willens Widerwille gegen die Zeit und ihr "Es war".'

4. I am indebted here to Hiram Haydn, *The Counter-Renaissance*, 1950, p. 626.

5. See Prosser, *Hamlet and Revenge*, pp. 261-75.

6. Compare A.C. Bradley, *Shakespearean Tragedy*, 1904, p. 136.

7. See the excellent comment by Dover Wilson, *What Happens in 'Hamlet'*, 1935; 3rd edn, 1951, p. 268.

8. The absence of the Ghost at the end, in contrast with *The Spanish Tragedy*, is noted by H. Levin, *The Question of 'Hamlet'*, 1959, p. 98. A view of the reason for the Ghost's disappearance which is very different from mine is given in two adjoining articles in *Shakespeare Survey* 30 (1977), by Philip Brockbank (p. 107) and Barbara Everett (p. 118).

9. The view that Shakespeare is making a positive comment on Kyd is developed in Edwards, 'Shakespeare and Kyd', in *Shakespeare, Man of the Theatre*, ed. K. Muir, J.L. Halio and D.J. Palmer, 1983.

10. For the relation of this passage to Lucien Goldmann's *The Hidden God*, 1955, see Edwards, 'Tragic balance in *Hamlet*', pp. 45-6.

11. Edwards, 'Tragic balance in *Hamlet*', p. 51.

12. *Shakespearean Tragedy*, p. 174.

CHARACTER STUDIES

R.A. Foakes (essay date 1973)

SOURCE: "The Art of Cruelty: Hamlet and Vindice," in *Aspects of Hamlet: Articles Reprinted from Shakespeare Survey*, edited by Kenneth Muir and Stanley Wells, Cambridge University Press, 1979, pp. 28-38.

[*In the following essay, originally published in 1973, Foakes compares Hamlet to Vindice in* The Revenger's Tragedy, *contending that "it is the strength of Hamlet, not his weakness . . . that he cannot kill, that he fails to carry out his revenge."*]

Hamlet admits to cruelty only when he is about to encounter his mother in the Closet scene, and then he seeks to qualify the term

> O heart, lose not thy nature, let not ever
> The soul of Nero enter this firm bosom,
> Let me be cruel not unnatural.

(III, ii, 396-8)

The cruelty he seeks to permit himself is to be kept under a restraint, not let loose with the tyrannical savagery of which Nero served as a type. So again, at the end of the interview, Hamlet cries, 'I must be cruel only to be kind', claiming that his cruelty serves its opposite, kindness. What Hamlet seems anxious to do here is to prevent himself from inflicting cruelty for its own sake; and the fact that he alone articulates this idea in the play suggests both the measure of success he has in controlling himself, and also his awareness, so to speak, of possibilities for cruelty within himself.

If Hamlet is not at this point recalling the Ghost's speeches to him in act I, his concern about his mother, and the re-appearance of the Ghost in the Closet scene, make the link for spectator and reader. Then the Ghost had ended his account of the murder by exhorting Hamlet to revenge, but warning him too:

> Howsomever thou pursues this act,
> Taint not thy mind, nor let thy soul contrive
> Against thy mother aught . . .

> (I, v, 84-6)

It might be said that Hamlet's mind is already tainted, as the first soliloquy, 'O that this too too sullied flesh would melt', has already shown him brooding on suicide and disgusted by the speed of his mother's remarriage with a man he despises; but the Ghost himself may be seen as tainting Hamlet's mind in another way. For the Ghost, like Hamlet in his soliloquy, dwells imaginatively on what has happened in such a way as to emphasise by elaboration what is most gross and nasty. In this the Ghost and Hamlet are alike: what the Ghost speaks may be seen as articulating what is already there in Hamlet. So, like Hamlet, the Ghost dwells on remarriage in language that is itself revolting,

> So lust, though to a radiant angel linked,
> Will sate itself in a celestial bed
> And prey on garbage

> (I, v, 54-6)

There is a kind of self-indulgence in this, a relish of nastiness which does not relate to the Claudius and Gertrude we have seen in action. The Ghost continues with his account of the murder:

> Upon my secure hour thy uncle stole
> With juice of cursed hebenon in a vial,
> And in the porches of my ears did pour
> The leperous distillment, whose effect
> Holds such an enmity with blood of man
> That swift as quicksilver it courses through
> The natural gates and alleys of the body,
> And with a sudden vigor it doth posset,
> And curd, like eager droppings into milk,
> The thin and wholesome blood. So did it mine,
> And a most instant tetter barked about,
> Most lazarlike, with vile and loathsome crust,
> All my smooth body.

> (I, v, 61-73)

The Ghost seems fascinated by the details of what happened, and dwells especially on the effects of the poison, producing that 'tetter' or eruption which covers his skin with a 'loathsome crust'; it is this above all that the speech renders with the force of particularity, and which informs that great cry.[1]

> O, horrible! O, horrible! most horrible!

> (I, v, 80)

In other words, the Ghost does not just tell us *what* happened, but recreates imaginatively *how* it happened, the horrible atrocity of a murder which could, presumably, have been relatively quick and simple, a stab with a dagger, or smothering with a pillow. A passage from Dostoevsky's *The Brothers Karamazov* may be helpful at this point, for this is a novel much concerned with the nature of cruelty; at one point in it Ivan tries to explain to Alyosha why he cannot love his neighbours, and this passes into an extraordinary account of human cruelty, in which he tells Alyosha a story:

> 'By the way, not so long ago a Bulgarian in Moscow told me', Ivan went on, as though not bothering to listen to his brother, 'of the terrible atrocities committed all over Bulgaria by the Turks and Circassians who were afraid of a general uprising of the Slav population. They burn, kill, violate women and children, nail their prisoners' ears to fences and leave them like that till next morning when they hang them, and so on - it's impossible to imagine it all. And, indeed people sometimes speak of man's 'bestial' cruelty, but this is very unfair and insulting to the beasts: a beast can never be so cruel as a man, so ingeniously, so artistically cruel. A tiger merely gnaws and tears to pieces, that's all he knows. It would never occur to him to nail men's ears to a fence and leave them like that overnight, even if he were able to do it. These Turks, incidentally, seemed to derive a voluptuous pleasure from torturing children, cutting a child out of its mother's womb with a dagger and tossing babies up in the air and catching them on a bayonet before the eyes of their mothers. It was doing it before the eyes of their mothers that made it so enjoyable. But one incident I found particularly interesting. Imagine a baby in the arms of a trembling mother, surrounded by Turks who had just entered her house. They are having great fun: they fondle the baby, they laugh to make it laugh and they are successful: the baby laughs. At that moment the Turk points a pistol four inches from the baby's face. The boy laughs happily, stretches out his little hands to grab the pistol, when suddenly the artist pulls the trigger in the baby's face and blows his brains out . . . Artistic, isn't it? Incidentally, I'm told the Turks are very fond of sweets.'[2]

Ivan observes that man is distinguished from beasts by his artistry: we speak casually of 'bestial' cruelty, but no animal is as cruel as men can be, who do it for enjoyment and to display their skill as artists, while others, looking on as spectators, take pleasure in watching, and in this case, enjoy the anguish the murder of the baby causes to its mother.

Something of this artistry in cruelty seems to be shown in the murder of old King Hamlet, as the Ghost describes it; the poison chosen by his brother was one that visibly corrupts and makes horrible the body of the dying man. Even the Ghost, who speaks of it as if he had been an onlooker at his own murder, is fascinated by the details of the process of dying, horrible as they are. He says he was sleeping at the time, and so not conscious, but he narrates what happened as if Claudius, in the manner of Dostoevsky's artists in cruelty, had staged it so that old Hamlet would at once suffer and be a spectator at his own death.

The Ghost calls on Hamlet to revenge,

> Revenge his foul and most unnatural murder,
>
> (I, v, 25)

and to pursue it by any means so long as he leaves his mother to Heaven. Although the Ghost does not explicitly command him to kill Claudius, this is what, in effect, 'revenge' means, since it is the only way Hamlet can obtain satisfaction and repay the injuries received by his father. So Hamlet is required to contrive another killing, a deed ironically condemned in the very next words of the Ghost,

> Murder most foul, as in the best it is.
>
> (I, v, 27)

In her study of revenge,[3] Eleanor Prosser 'found no evidence to indicate that Elizabethans believed the law required blood revenge. The Law was absolute: murder, as such, was never justified.' The play shows Hamlet to be an artist, an actor-dramatist, ingenious contriver, and player of many parts; the Ghost, even as he condemns murder, demands that he put that artistry into the service of a cruelty Hamlet sees, at any rate in the Closet scene, as potentially there in himself.

This may seem a strange perspective when it is set against that view of Hamlet, which many hold, as a character imbued with a moral idealism or governed by a sense of moral scruple. It has been said, for example, very recently by Ivor Morris, in a careful account of Hamlet, that

> Goodness and simple humanity are Hamlet's ideal. More truly than the heroic, it is the moral that confers nobility on man . . . Human excellence for Hamlet does not imply a self-aggrandizement, but rather the forsaking of an instinctive self-will, and the disciplining of the aspiring consciousness according to values which, though humble and familiar, are yet of a power to transcend. The chief passion of Hamlet's soul, therefore, is the precise antithesis of the heroic.[4]

Well, yes—but isn't this much too simple and clear-cut? For Hamlet sees his father in an heroic image, and finds a model for himself in Horatio, more an antique Roman than a Dane. It is true that Hamlet disparages himself in saying that Claudius 'is no more like my father than I to Hercules'; yet much of his idealism is bound up with the warrior-figures of the Ghost at the beginning and Fortin-

bras at the end, so that it is important to notice how these figures are presented in the play.

Some think of the military imagery in the play as being there to 'emphasise that Claudius and Hamlet are engaged in a duel to the death',[5] or that it exists to call attention 'to the issues of public life, to the state of the nation'.[6] It may serve these purposes, but when the Ghost appears in armour from head to foot, and accompanied by indications of past triumphs, as when he smote the sledded Polacks on the ice, other connotations are at work too; for war here does not, of course, have its unpleasant modern associations, but rather a ring of chivalric heroism in the thought of personal encounters, personal courage and skill. Old Hamlet appears in a 'fair and warlike form', as 'valiant Hamlet', who, challenged to combat,

> Did slay this Fortinbras, who by a sealed compact,
> Well ratified by law and heraldry,
> Did forfeit (with his life) all those his lands
> Which he stood seized of, to the conqueror.
>
> (I, i, 86-9)

The word 'heraldry', referring vaguely to heraldic practice, suggests an almost medieval ceremony, an ancient practice, no longer meaningful in the new Denmark of Claudius, the modern politician, negotiating through ambassadors. Later on Hamlet sees another image of chivalric heroism in that 'delicate and tender prince', young Fortinbras, passing through on his way, like old Hamlet, to fight the Poles, merely for honour, and driven by a 'divine ambition'. It is enough to make him give Fortinbras his dying vote for the succession to the Danish throne.

Hamlet in this combines a nostalgia for a past that seems better than the present with the idea of a great soldier as simple, good and truthful. An audience sees also that Fortinbras is wasting his country's youth on a trivial and useless campaign; and if the Ghost really represents Old Hamlet, then he was also vindictive and morally perverse, condemning all murder, yet urging Hamlet to commit one. Hamlet's image is a partial one; Fortinbras and his father take on in his mind's eye grander proportions and finer qualities than are evidenced in the play, and Claudius appears worse to him than he does in the action:

> So excellent a King, that was to this
> Hyperion to a satyr,
>
> (I, ii, 140-1)

the sun-god compared with one who is half-beast. The heroic ideal Hamlet thinks he sees in his father merges into those classical figures that spring to his lips for a comparison, Hyperion, Mars, Mercury, Caesar, Hercules, Aeneas, and others, and all help to suggest imagined models for Hamlet himself, and to exemplify to him that possibility of the godlike in man embodied in 'What a piece of work is a man!' Hamlet tends to disclaim comparison between himself and his heroes, yet there is much of the heroic in him too,[7] complicated by other qualities, as he is more fully of the Renaissance, a man of all talents and so much less the mere warrior-hero. Trained at a university, he retains the habit of sifting evidence, even the habit of taking lecture-notes ('My tables, meet it is I set it down'). He writes more than other Shakespearian protagonists; King Lear could have been illiterate, but Hamlet is clearly an intellectual, *au fait* with classical literature, able to turn off a few lines for Ophelia, however much he is 'ill at these numbers', and to pen a speech for the players, a dozen or so lines of verse. Hamlet the writer reflects Hamlet the thinker and scholar, but he is also an accomplished swordsman, who throughout conveys a sense of absolute fearlessness, so that at the end it seems entirely appropriate when he is accorded martial honours, as four captains bear his body, 'like a soldier' to the stage.

Hamlet is a very complex character, and it won't do to say that 'goodness and simple humanity are Hamlet's ideal'. Insofar as he locates his ideal in his father and Fortinbras, it seems to be partly a longing for a simpler world, in which problems could be honourably settled in combat; and it is based on an uncritical association of these figures with a chivalric heroism. Hamlet's idealism is confused, and this confusion prevents him from seeing at once the contradiction in the Ghost's exhortations to him to do the very thing for which the Ghost condemns Claudius. Hamlet shows at times a moral delicacy and scrupulousness that mark him off from the world of Claudius, and this is brought out by the comparison with Laertes sweeping unhesitatingly to his revenge; but he is confused in his moral stances too, and fails to discipline his consciousness, or to remain, as Ivor Morris claims, 'morally consistent'.[8] He does not directly question the Ghost's command, although he avoids pursuing it, and has recourse to play-acting, to an antic disposition, and to the play within the play. Some see this as a substitute for real action, for killing Claudius, and put emphasis on Hamlet's delay, but it is as much a device to penetrate the mask of Claudius in order to discover his true nature and to expose his guilt. Beyond this it is also, more importantly, a means to accommodate himself to what he feels he has to do; the Ghost has emphasised in detail the horror of the murder of his father, and in order to accomplish his revenge, he needs to act like Claudius, and face a similar horror.

In the course of the play he makes a series of moral adjustments, notably after he stabs Polonius through the arras, and so marks himself with a blood-guilt. He assigns the responsibility for this to 'heaven', as if he has been appointed a divine agent:

> For this same lord
> I do repent; but heaven hath pleas'd it so
> To punish me with this, and this with me,
> That I must be their scourge and minister.

> (III, iv, 172-5)

The terms 'scourge' and 'minister', it seems, 'are so contradictory that they are irreconcilable', for 'God elects as his scourge only a sinner who already deserves

damnation', while a 'minister' would be a true agent and servant of God.[9] Hamlet could not be both at the same time, and the moral confusion present here is brought out further in his recognition in the same speech that, 'This bad begins, and worse remains behind.' This confusion is marked too in the way he seems to convince himself after his return from the sea-voyage in act v that it would be 'perfect conscience' to kill Claudius:

> Does it not, think thee, stand me now upon—
> He that hath kill'd my king and whor'd my mother,
> Popp'd in between th' election and my hopes,
> Thrown out his angle for my proper life,
> And with such cozenage—is't not perfect conscience
> To quit him with this arm? And is't not to be damned
> To let this canker of our nature come
> In further evil?

> (v, ii, 63-70)

Though Claudius has done these things, including the attempt to have Hamlet done to death by sending him to England bearing a commission for his own execution, Hamlet is not thereby given moral freedom to kill Claudius, to practise murder most foul, 'as in the best it is'.

In fact his claims that heaven has appointed him as its agent, and that he would be damned for not killing Claudius, do not issue in any determined action. Hamlet might be interpreted here as cheering himself up; whatever he says, he still does nothing, and rather at the end resigns himself to providence. However much he may justify murder to himself, there is no sign that he can bring himself in action to face the horror of doing it. After the encounter with the Ghost in act I, Hamlet cries out that the commandment to revenge shall alone live in his mind, but what he does is to adopt that 'antic disposition', which allows him to play any part, notably those of fool and madman. The Ghost's commandment brings out the artist in Hamlet, his concern with play-action, which is stimulated too by the entry of the players, and Shakespeare focuses our attention on these through much of acts II and III. When Hamlet first meets the players, he asks for a speech, recalling the opening of it himself: ''twas Aeneas' tale to Dido, and thereabout of it especially where he speaks of Priam's slaughter'. It is appropriate for him to have remembered this speech from a play that was 'caviare to the general', a play for the educated, based on Virgil's *Aeneid,* and so associated with that heroic world with which Hamlet likes to link himself, and which emerges especially in references to and images drawn from classical history, literature and myth. As has been skilfully shown by Nigel Alexander,[10] the player's speech also provides subtle analogies for Hamlet, as it acts out the successful vengeance of Pyrrhus upon Priam, and the destruction of a kingdom brought about by lust.

But the speech has another kind of significance which I want to emphasise; it describes Pyrrhus raging through the streets of Troy to revenge the death of his father, until eventually he finds and hacks to pieces the aged and defenceless Priam:

'Head to foot
Now is he total gules, horridly trick'd
With blood of fathers, mothers, daughters, sons,
Bak'd and impasted with the parching streets,
That lend a tyrannous and a damned light
To their lord's murder. Roasted in wrath and fire,
And thus o'er-sized with coagulate gore,
With eyes like carbuncles, the hellish Pyrrhus
Old grandsire Priam seeks.'

(II, ii, 460-8)

The language of this is inflated, but not too much so for its content and occasion, and the overall impression it makes is powerful. Of its kind, it is a good speech, vigorously presenting an image of Pyrrhus as literally covered in blood that is dried and baked on to him, so that he is 'impasted' or encrusted with it, through the heat generated by his anger ('roasted in wrath'), and slaughters fathers, mothers and sons at random. In other words, Pyrrhus images an ultimate in cruelty, beyond all control, and exemplifies the kind of pleasure in atrocity which Dostoevsky observes, as he goes on to make 'malicious sport' in mincing Priam before the eyes of Hecuba. If it is a reminder to Hamlet of what he feels he must do, it recalls also the Ghost's account of his murder, when the poison Claudius administered caused his skin to become covered with a 'vile and loathsome crust'. Like the Ghost's speech, this one dwells on the particularities of the event, recreating imaginatively the horror of it, and like that, it wins for a moment Hamlet's wholehearted involvement. In each case, however, the horror of the deed is made bearable to Hamlet through its presentation in art, in a kind of play within the play, where it is aesthetically distanced.[11] The point I would make about these scenes, is that they show how Hamlet can involve himself imaginatively in playacting or dramatising the act of cruelty, but cannot do it. Briefly now he whips himself into a heat of passion:

Is it not monstrous that this player here,
But in a fiction, in a dream of passion,
Could force his soul so to his own conceit,
That from her working all his visage wanned,
Tears in his eyes, distraction in his aspect,
A broken voice, and his whole function suiting
With forms to his conceit; and all for nothing?

(II, ii, 554-60)

In fact, it is the fiction or art that makes it possible for Hamlet to face this image of cruel murder, and it provokes him not into acting like Pyrrhus, but into arranging a performance of another play, the murder of Gonzago.

It is not 'monstrous' to 'force the soul' to display the imagined passion; it would be monstrous rather to put that passion to work in earnest. Again Hamlet's moral confusion emerges, as he forces his own soul into a rage and unpacks his heart with words in this soliloquy. For Hamlet's moral idealism emerges not in what he tries to will himself to do, which is to abandon scruple and drive to his revenge (consciously, so to speak, this is what he

thinks he is doing, as is evidenced in his confusions or rejections of morality); it is revealed rather in the energy with which he can respond to or recreate the horror imaginatively. In this the aesthetic passes into the moral; he confronts the image of what, on one level, he would like to make himself, at such a pitch of imaginative intensity, that it disables him from practising cruelty himself. His full imaginative involvement brings home to him and us the horror of what Claudius did, and of the carnage wrought by the 'hellish Pyrrhus'; so, even when he has a perfect opportunity, finding Claudius at prayer, Hamlet cannot do it, and neglects the chance to kill him. The reasons he gives have some plausibility, but behind them we sense his radical inability to become 'monstrous' or 'hellish' in deed, and carry out a willed murder.

When he does kill, it is in a fit of excitement, and an unpremeditated act, stabbing blindly through the arras, not a planned murder. The death of Polonius fastens a guilt on him, and makes it easier for him to send Rosencrantz and Guildenstern to their deaths by forging a new commission to the King of England. Even this, though ingenious, is not a direct deed of cruelty, and on his return to Denmark, it is in a condition of resignation: 'If it be now, 'tis not to come; if it be not to come, it will be now; if it be not now, yet it will come—the readiness is all.' He appears to be talking about his *own* death—but he is talking also about the death of *Claudius*—for he abandons plotting, the thought of acting as revenger, of being a Pyrrhus; and the death of Claudius happens in a muddle at the end, and only after Hamlet has his own death-wound. Horatio speaks with reason here

Of accidental judgments, casual slaughters,
Of deaths put on by cunning and forced cause,
And, in this upshot, purposes mistook,
Fallen on the inventors' heads.

(v, ii, 380-3)

It is all clumsy, casual and, on the part of Hamlet, unplanned and unprepared—he never does become a revenger, unless he might be thought one in that moment when, having given Claudius his death-wound with a venomed sword, he then forces him to drink the poisoned wine. Its effect, however, is to despatch Claudius at once, not to protract his death, or make it more horrible, and Laertes guides our response:

He is justly served;
It is a poison tempered by himself.

(v, ii, 325-6)

Hamlet shows a kind of cruelty twice in the play, once when he turns on Ophelia, recognising that she is a decoy, and later when he speaks savagely to his mother. He lashes verbally the two women he loves, and his behaviour here is not, as is sometimes argued, merely a reflection of his revulsion against sex, or of his hatred of the corruption he sees around him; it relates also, and more deeply, to his imaginative engagement with, and recoil from, the horror within himself. The cruelty expressed in words is also a substitute for action, an outlet for what he knows is in him, and might perhaps be seen too as vicariously satisfying the conscious urge to drive himself to a deed of cruelty, to revenge. His attack on Ophelia springs from an inquisition into himself, beginning in the soliloquy 'To be or not to be', in which, amongst other things, a dejected Hamlet attempts to reckon with the need for action, the task of taking arms against Claudius, in the recognition that 'the pale cast of thought' is inimical to action; the self-inspection deepens into the hyperbole of his words to Ophelia:

> I am very proud, revengeful, ambitious, with more of-
> fences at my beck than I have thoughts to put them in,
> imagination to give them shape, or time to act them in.
>
> (III, i, 125)

He has a sense of a potential in himself for unimagined, or unimaginable offences, but those we are aware of in him exist mostly in his mind or imagination. So when he confronts his mother in the Closet scene, it is to recreate in imagination, and with a nastiness belonging to his conception, to him more than to the deed itself, the activity of sexual relations between Claudius and his mother:

>   Nay, but to live
> In the rank sweat of an enseamed bed,
> Stewed in corruption, honeying, and making love
> Over the nasty sty . . .
>
> (III, iv, 91-4)

The obscenity is inside Hamlet, and bursts out in a savagery of words; if these help to bring Ophelia to suicide, and afflict Gertrude so that she cries

> These words like daggers enter in mine ears,
>
> (III, iv, 95)

nevertheless, these attacks are essentially different from the deed this line recalls, Claudius pouring poison into the ears of Old Hamlet. Ophelia cannot comprehend what Hamlet says, and both she and, initially at any rate, Gertrude, are inclined to think his outbursts are expressions of madness. I think rather that Hamlet gives rein to his tongue as an alternative to the action he cannot face; and his ability to give bitterness vent in words to them, and yet refrain from a willed or planned killing, is exactly what we might expect.

The presentation of Hamlet in this way is worth comparing to that of Vindice in *The Revenger's Tragedy,* who is also something of an artist, and likes to see himself as dramaturge, even as writer of his own play. Even in the opening speech over the skull, he already uses it as a stage-property in his own dramatisation of the court, and when he is not playing the disguised roles of Piato and a malcontent, adopted to deceive Lussurioso, he is to be found stage-managing playlets of his own, most notably in the famous scene in which the skull is again introduced, now dressed in 'tires', fitted with a head-dress as if alive. As he brings it on, Vindice uses it consciously again as a property, saying to Hippolito;

> Now to my tragic business, look you, brother,
> I have not fashioned this only for show,
> And useless property; no it shall bear a part
> E'en in its own revenge . . .
>
> (III, v, 103-6)

The skull itself is a reminder of Hamlet in the graveyard, but though Hamlet plays many parts, and fancies himself as an actor with the visiting company in Elsinore, there is a radical difference, namely that Hamlet is wholly involved in the decision whether to revenge, in those questions to do or not to do ('Now might I do it part . . .'), and to be or not to be, that reverberate in the play; but Vindice has made his decision already before his opening speech; his attention is engaged by the question, 'How can I effect my revenge in the cleverest way?' not, 'How can I do it at all?' Because his attention is on the means rather than the end, he becomes pleased with his own cleverness, designing the little play within the play in which he murders the Duke.

While Hamlet is concerned with the nature of revenge and the horror of the act of cruelty, we see in Vindice a growing detachment from the nature of what he is doing, a detachment which is made to take effect fully as part of the play's serious action. At the beginning, his moral indignation at the corruptions of the court invites our sympathy and assent. In the opening scene, his independence from the court is imaged in the visual separation of Vindice from the procession he watches and describes, but by act III, when he contrives the murder of the Duke, he has taken his place among the courtiers, and joins those he so despised at first, crying

> 'Tis state in music for a Duke to bleed.
> The dukedom wants a head, tho' yet unknown.
> As fast as they peep up, let's cut 'em down.
>
> (III, v, 224-6)

Vindice's anger at the beginning is justified insofar as he is in a position similar to that of Hamlet, unable to obtain justice for a murder in a court which seems corrupt; but when Vindice uses the skull to poison the Duke in act III, Hippolito applauds him not for a moral achievement, but more appropriately for his cleverness:

> I do applaud thy constant vengeance,
> The quaintness of thy malice.
>
> (III, v, 108-9)

It is an ingenuity ('quaintness'), an artistry, put into the service of 'malice', of cruelty, as Vindice enjoys poisoning the Duke in a kiss even while he watches his own wife and bastard son making love.

*Laurence Olivier as Hamlet in the
1948 film adaptation of* Hamlet.

It is their self-satisfaction in their skill which leads Vindice and Hippolito to boast at the end of their 'wit' in murdering the Duke, and so brings on their arrest and execution. By act v, their enjoyment in plotting has reached the point where they congratulate each other on watching an innocent nobleman carried off to execution suspected of a murder they have carried out:

> *Hippolito.*
> Brother, how happy is our vengeance!
> *Vindice.*   Why, it hits
> Past th' apprehension of indifferent wits.

(v, ii, 133-4)

In relation to this delight in cruelty, it is important to notice how much of the play is funny; its general cleverness emerges in a kind of grisly humour, as in the joking of the Duchess's youngest son as he expects release from the scaffold, a release which never comes, or in the hiring of Vindice by Lussurioso to kill his *alter ego,* Piato; or in the double masque of revengers at the end. In spite of the burning moral indignation of some of Vindice's speeches, the world of the play offers an image of human existence which excludes the possibility of the heroic and moral idealism present in *Hamlet;* it is a world in which money, power, and sex dominate, and for Vindice, intelligence and artistry replace morality. The humour is necessary to make

such a vision of human cruelty through ingenuity bearable. At the same time, the play shows in Vindice an 'artist', the stage-manager and writer of his own playlets, becoming so absorbed in his skill that he treats life merely as an exercise for his art, and so loses all moral sense. When he confronts his mother in act iv, it is not to threaten her with words like daggers (compare Hamlet's, 'I will speak daggers to her, but use none'), but to hold a real dagger to her breast, so that when she echoes Gertrude's 'Thou wilt *not* murder me', it is with a difference: Gratiana asks, 'What, *will* you murder me?' and there seems every reason to suppose Vindice and Hippolito may do so.

To return then to *Hamlet:* there is one moment in the play when Hamlet, like Vindice, yields to a sense of pleasure in the skill of plotting:

> 'tis the sport to have the engineer
> Hoist with his own petar, and't shall go hard
> But I will delve one yard below their mines,
> And blow them at the moon: O, 'tis most sweet
> When in one line two crafts directly meet.

(iii, iv, 206-10)

This occurs after the death of Polonius, and when he learns he must go to England; but in fact, Hamlet practises craft in this way only once. All his artistry in the first part of the play is aimed at understanding himself and making apparent the guilt of Claudius; he stabs Polonius in a fit of passion, and not knowing what or who is behind the arras; and at the end he declines to plot against Claudius, putting his trust in providence. Only once, in the boat to England, is he prompted to try his craft, when he alters the message Rosencrantz and Guildenstern are carrying to avoid his own death. There is no instance at all of Hamlet initiating a plot to kill anyone.

Although he is as much of an artist as Vindice, Hamlet does not confuse art and life; indeed, he has his theory of the art of playing, and his famous formulation is worth noting: 'whose end both at the first, and now, was and is, to hold as 'twere the mirror up to nature, to show virtue her own feature, scorn her own image, and the very age and body of the time his form and pressure' (iii, ii, 20). The 'end' or aim of art is to reflect what is there, and presumably by reflecting, to reveal to him what the spectator may not otherwise see; but its success in doing this depends on the apprehension of the spectator, as Vindice knew, on his sensitivity and understanding, and Hamlet's theory says nothing of his. It does not work too well for Claudius; the play within the play shows twice, first in dumb-show and then in action, something closely resembling the murder of old Hamlet, and Claudius is not much troubled by this mirror held up to nature; what does seem to stir him is Hamlet's identification of the murderer as 'one Lucianus, nephew to the King', and a few lines later, Claudius walks out, calling for lights, and 'marvellous distempered'. What he saw acted before him was not the murder of Old Hamlet so much as an image of a secret fear, the killing of himself by his nephew, Young Hamlet.

The theory works better for Hamlet himself: the play within the play seems to him to mirror Claudius's deed, and to cause him to reveal his guilt; in addition, it provides yet one more artistic expression of the nature of that murder, which is also reflected in the Ghost's speech, and in the First Player's speech on the 'hellish Pyrrhus'. Hamlet's playing dwells on the image of a murder which reflects the cruelty of the deed and the horror of revenge; and so reveals to us what is not apparent to Hamlet himself, his moral revulsion from the task he feels the Ghost has imposed on him. This fascinated loathing of the horror in its imagined recreation finds one more outlet in the Graveyard scene, when he broods on the skull of Yorick, and after drawing out the commonplaces appropriate to that *memento mori,* passes on to Alexander, another classical hero:

> *Hamlet.* Now get you to my lady's chamber, and tell her, let her paint an inch thick, to this favour she must come, make her laugh at that . . . Prithee Horatio, tell me one thing.
> *Horatio.* What's that, my lord?
> *Hamlet.* Dost thou think Alexander looked o'this fashion i'th' earth?
> *Horatio.* E'en so.
> *Hamlet.* And smelt so? pah!
> *Horatio.* E'en so, my lord.
> *Hamlet.* To what base uses we may return, Horatio! Why may not imagination trace the noble dust of Alexander till'a find it stopping a bung-hole?
> *Horatio.* 'Twere to consider too curiously, to consider so.

(v, i, 187-200)

Why may not imagination trace the dust of Alexander in this way? Horatio's answer carries weight—because it is to speculate too nicely, to go too far, to become, he might have added, self-indulgent; but there are more things in heaven and earth than Horatio sees, and his response is a limited one; Hamlet's effort to trace in imagination the full consequences of physical decay in death parallels his ability to face imaginatively the full horror of revenge; the element of indulgence in both is less significant than the power they have to work as vehicles of Hamlet's deepest moral awareness; he is right to reply here to Horatio's ''Twere to consider too curiously' with the phrase 'No, faith, not a jot!'

The greatness of *Hamlet* may be measured against the more limited, if splendid, achievement of *The Revenger's Tragedy,* in which Vindice so falls in love with his art as to commit himself entirely to it. Unable then to see its moral implications for himself, he uses it, most notably in his device with the skull, as a means to effect his revenge; so, becoming like Dostoevsky's Turks, he enjoys the display of cruelty as he makes the dying Duke watch the incestuous adultery of his own wife. By contrast, it is the strength of Hamlet, not his weakness, or only superficially his weakness, that he cannot kill, that he fails to carry out his revenge. The role of Hamlet may be seen as ironically

expanding from his opening lines, when he enters acting like a mourner in his customary suits of solemn black, and saying,

> These indeed seem,
> For they are actions that a man might play,
> But I have that within which passeth show

(i, ii, 83-5)

In the action Hamlet does, in fact, reveal what is most deep within him, not, so to speak, consciously, not even in the soliloquies, but in projecting imaginatively, into art, into shows, into plays within the play, or the rhetoric of his encounters with Ophelia and Gertrude, a sense of the potential for cruelty and viciousness in himself. Shakespeare makes this art the vehicle of the moral restraint Hamlet exercises upon what is within. The combination of his full imaginative grasp of the horror of a cruelty he recognises as potentially in himself, with a moral revulsion from it of which he is unconscious, or at best obscurely aware, perhaps helps to explain why Hamlet remains both an enigma and Shakespeare's best-loved hero.

Notes

1. This line functions too in relation to the idea immediately preceding it, of dying, 'With all my imperfections on my head', and that following in the reference to 'luxury and damned incest', but it seems to me to carry most weight as a rhetorical climax to the account of the murder as a whole.

2. The quotation is from the translation by David Magarshack (Harmondsworth, 1958), i, 278-9.

3. *Hamlet and Revenge* (Stanford, 1967), p. 18.

4. *Shakespeare's God. The Role of Religion in the Tragedies* (London, 1972), p. 371.

5. Nigel Alexander, *Poison, Play and Duel* (London, 1971), p. 25. This stimulating book in some measure provoked the present essay.

6. Maurice Charney, *Style in Hamlet* (Princeton, 1969), p. 30.

7. See G.K. Hunter's analysis of 'The Heroic in Hamlet', in *Hamlet,* edited J.R. Brown and Bernard Harris (*Stratford-upon-Avon Studies 5,* London, 1963), especially pp. 103-4.

8. *Shakespeare's God,* p. 383.

9. The quotations are from Eleanor Prosser's analysis of this passage in *Hamlet and Revenge,* pp. 199-201.

10. *Poison, Play and Duel,* p. 97.

11. In *Shakespeare the Craftsman* (London, 1969), p. 129, M.C. Bradbrook has argued that the First Player here was made up to look like Burbage playing Hamlet, so that during the Pyrrhus speech Hamlet was watching, as it were, a reflection of himself.

Eric P. Levy (essay date 1999)

SOURCE: "'Nor th' exterior nor the inward man': The Problematics of Personal Identity in *Hamlet*," in *University of Toronto Quarterly,* Vol. 68, No. 3, Summer, 1999, pp. 711-27.

[*In the following essay, Levy charts* Hamlet*'s probing of the nature of human identity and argues that the play conceptualizes an alternative to the usual inward/outward polarity.*]

Hamlet begins with an urgent questioning of identity: 'Who's there?' A similar query is soon directed at the Ghost: 'What art thou that usurp'st this time of night' (1.1.49). The interrogation is complicated by the very nature of the problem. For identity in this context is not simple but polar. That is, it comprises a totality whose two aspects are public and private or what Claudius terms 'th'exterior' and 'the inward man' (2.2.4).[1] Therefore, if the question of identity is to be answered at the most fundamental level, the proper relation of the inward and outward dimensions of identity must first be determined. As we shall find, *Hamlet* profoundly critiques prevailing assumptions regarding this relation, and dramatizes an alternate conceptualization of human identity: 'what is a man' (4.4.33).

According to the conventional schema, inward and outward are construed as reciprocal modes of the same totality. In Hegel's succinct enunciation of this traditional schema, inward pertains to 'essence' or 'identity with self'; outward pertains to 'appearance' or 'what is manifested.' In ideal configuration, '[t]he appearance shows nothing that is not the essence, and in the essence there is nothing but what is manifested' (179). A medieval example of such agreement occurs in Abbot Suger's (d. 1151) celebrated description of the clergy assembled for the consecration of the Parisian basilica of St Denis: 'their outward apparel and attire indicated the inward intention of their mind and body' (113).[2] This schema of selfhood presupposes the *primacy of inwardness,* whereby inwardness is construed as the original or exemplar of which the exterior is at best a faithful copy and at worst a deliberate dissimulation. As such, inwardness has more reality than outwardness.

Implicit in this schema is the assumption that inwardness has privileged and unerring access to its own content. That is, just as outward, as a public manifestation, is by definition perceptible by others, so inward, as a private experience, is by definition uniquely perceptible by the subject to which it pertains. Gilbert Ryle elaborates: 'Only I can take direct cognizance of the status and processes of my own mind' (11). In other words, private confirmation of inward content is deemed analogous to public confirmation of outward content. The essential differences between them concern *location* and *access.* Public objects are situated in the world or the body, and can be perceived by any appropriately placed observer; private objects are situated 'in the mind' (*Hamlet* 3.1.57), and can be perceived only

by that mind. Indeed, Hamlet invokes this assumption when distinguishing between outward display and inward feeling: 'But I have that within which passes show, / These but the trappings and the suits of woe' (1.2.85-86). Here, the private object (in this case, his own grief) is assigned a certainty of existence equivalent to that enjoyed by public objects. In fact, Katherine Eisaman Maus even claims that, in this example, the private object enjoys *superior* certainty: 'For Hamlet the internal experience of his own grief "passes show" in two senses. It is beyond scrutiny, concealed where other people cannot perceive it. And it *surpasses* the visible—its validity is unimpeachable' (4; original emphasis).[3]

THE CRITIQUE OF INWARDNESS

But Maus's claim regarding the primacy of inwardness is undermined in the world of the play, where the private object (that of which inwardness is aware) is notoriously problematic and in need of outward verification. Relevant examples include Polonius forgetting his own train of thought ('what was I about / to say?' [2.1.50-51]), and Ophelia uncertain of her own awareness, both before her madness ('I do not know, my lord, what I should think' [1.3.104]) and during it: 'Indeed would make one think there might be thought, / Though nothing sure . . .' (4.5.12-13). With respect to inwardness, Hamlet questions his own courage ('Am I a coward?' 2.2.566), and doubts whether commitment to his own purpose is really there, in the womb of interiority, when no outward action—not even verbal—to fulfil it is performed: 'Like a John-a-dreams, unpregnant of my cause' (2.2.563). Without external corroboration, there is no distinction between false and valid claims concerning inwardness. In these circumstances, the content of inwardness becomes radically problematic. An extreme example of this predicament concerns Hamlet's inventory of 'that within which passes show': 'I am very proud, revengeful, ambitious, with more offenses at my beck than I have thoughts to put them in, imagination to give them shape, or time to act them in' (3.1.124-127). Here inwardness excludes *all* outwardness—even the acts of awareness (such as thought and imagination) by which interiority is expressed. Yet, in this situation, statements about inwardness are no more than empty attributions, with no possibility of either verification or refutation.[4]

The problem of inward verification can be clarified by reference to the critique of inwardness developed by Wittgenstein and the Oxford philosophers of ordinary language. The primary conclusion of this school is that, without outward criteria, we can never *know* what another person is experiencing, because we can never *know* what we ourselves are experiencing. To pursue the implications of this extraordinary conclusion, we must first clarify the concept of knowledge on which it is based.

Explication can begin with Socrates, for whom knowledge implies infallibility (Plato, *Theaetetus* 152c). Otherwise, it would not be knowledge but error. Hence, perception of external objects cannot yield genuine knowledge, since the perceiver is always subject to fluctuation: 'Are you not sure that it [that which is perceived] does not even appear the same to yourself, because you never remain in the same condition?' (*Theaetetus* 154a). Though without acknowledging the similarity, Wittgenstein applies a variation of this argument to the notion of the private object (that which exists only in experience of the inward man). There can be no *knowledge* of the private object (e.g., pain), because in this context, there is no criterion by which truth and falsehood, accuracy and error, can be distinguished. The point here is not that there are no inward feelings, but that statements regarding them are *incorrigible;* that is, they cannot be verified by any objectively valid principle of verification, and hence are subject to no evaluation of correctness (Malcolm, 'Wittgenstein's *Philosophical Investigations,*' 101).

If the subject alone has access to his own feelings, by what criterion can the accuracy of his own perceptions or reports concerning them be verified? That is, how can the *content* of inwardness be validated? In Wittgenstein's epigram, 'An "inner process" stands in need of outward criteria' (i.e. standards of measurement and identification which are independent of their referents) (*Philosophical Investigations,* 580). Indeed, Hamlet himself refers to the need for outward criteria in order to prove that his perception of the Ghost in Gertrude's closet was *not* merely an inward process or private object: 'Bring me to the test / And I the matter will reword, which madness would gambol from' (3.4.144-46). Wittgenstein epitomizes the problem of inwardness in an example: 'Always get rid of the idea of the private object in this way: assume that it constantly changes, but that you do not notice the change because your memory constantly deceives you' (*Philosophical Investigations,* 207e). To reformulate this problem in the language of the play, what if, unknown to the subject, the same private object ('that within which passes show') changes its appearance (or magnitude, intensity, etc.) according to the mood or condition of the subject perceiving it—just as the same cloud 'seems' (1.2.76) spontaneously to change shape ('camel,' 'weasel,' and 'whale' [3.2.368, 370, 372]), according to Hamlet's shifting perceptions of it?

The consequences of this problem are profound. To begin with, the assumption that knowledge of others is derived from analogy with oneself must be abandoned. For if, *in oneself,* it is impossible to verify objectively whether a given sensation or feeling is the same as that felt at some period in the past, then *a fortiori* it is impossible to determine whether what *someone else* feels is the same as that which one feels oneself. In the realm of privacy, there is no criterion for correct use of the term 'same'—whether in reference to oneself or another. Thus, to borrow Norman Malcolm's phrasing, 'the illusion of the priority of [one's] own case' is exploded, together with 'the mistaken assumption that *one learns from one's own case* what thinking, feeling, sensation are' ('Knowledge of Other Minds,' 380, 378; original emphasis). Hence, first-person

experience is no longer valid as the paradigm in terms of which third-person experience is explained.

But without this paradigm, how is knowledge of other minds possible, or, to put the question less formally, how can the privacy of one individual be interpreted and made intelligible to another? For as Justus Hartnack indicates, '[t]he belief that states of mind or mental events are experienced by others is an inference based on analogy from one's own inner experience' (111). A pertinent version of this inference occurs in Plato's *Gorgias:* 'if mankind did not share one common emotion which was the same though varying in its different manifestations, but some of us experienced peculiar feelings unshared by the rest, it would not be easy for one of us to reveal his feelings to another' (481c).

According to this critique of inwardness, the only adequate criterion of verification regarding the private object is outward behaviour. The 'I' is *not* in a better position than others to confirm statements about his or her innermost processes, because verification requires an invariable criterion, not one that is itself an inward process whose variation might not be noticed by the subject applying it. To adopt Ryle's formulation, the subject does not enjoy 'Privileged Access to the so-called springs of his own actions' (91). Hence, as Terence Penelhum indicates, properly to attribute traits to character is 'to refer not to private episodes, but to dispositions which manifest themselves in predominantly public performances' (227). It is to posit, not properties independent of expression, but what Place terms 'capacities, tendencies . . . to behave in a certain way . . . if certain circumstances were to arise' (211).

THE CRITIQUE OF OUTWARDNESS

As we have seen, the primacy of inwardness is problematized by the need for outward confirmation of its content. But outward verification of inwardness is itself notoriously problematized in the world of the play, where the exterior man functions as an actor or 'player' (2.2.545) whose role and character are contrived by the inward man in order to manipulate the response of the 'audience' (5.2.340): ''Tis too much prov'd, that with devotion's visage / And pious action we do sugar o'er / The devil himself' (3.1.47-49); 'one may smile, and smile, and be a villain' (1.5.108); 'A face without a heart' (4.7.108). Hence, outwardness is now associated with the concealment or shamming of inwardness, while inwardness is associated with the manipulation of outwardness. Indeed, much of the action in *Hamlet* concerns the elaborate strategies by which one party attempts to hide, behind a false exterior, its own attempt to probe behind the presumedly false exterior of another. For example, Polonius and Claudius hide behind an arras in order to detect the inward cause of Hamlet's madness, which, in turn, is but an outward simulation designed to enable Hamlet to probe the inward secret of Claudius.[5]

This situation epitomizes the notorious discord between inward and outward during the Renaissance. According to

Maus, the period 'produces a distinctive way of thinking about human subjectivity that emphasizes the disparity between what a person is and what he or she seems to be to other people' (210). According to Stephen Greenblatt, 'in the sixteenth century there appears to be an increased self-consciousness about the fashioning of human identity as a manipulable, artful process' (2). The *locus classicus* of Renaissance preoccupation with self-presentation is, of course, Castiglione's *The Book of the Courtier* (completed in 1516), where the ideal of the gentleman is the *sprezzatura* or nonchalance that enables him 'to conceal all art and make whatever is done and said appear to be without effort and without almost any thought about it' (43). The obverse of this emphasis on self-presentation is suspicion concerning authenticity. For outward is now associated with the concealment of inward.

Yet the reliability of outward expression as a criterion of inward verification is problematized, not only by deliberate manipulation undertaken for personal advantage, but also by mandatory conventions governing outward presentation. Indeed, the opening dialogue foregrounds such conventions: 'Who's there?' / 'Nay, answer me. Stand and unfold yourself' (1.1.1-2). Here, knowledge of identity follows *not* from direct expression of private feeling (as when Francisco, after dismissal, refers to feeling 'sick at heart') but from outward behaviour modelled according to performative convention (1.1.9). That is, the guard confirms his identity not by outward expression of his inward state, but by a password whose utterance presupposes a shared 'custom' of usage: 'Long live the King!' (1.4.15; 1.1.3).

The Theatrical Morality

But the watchmen are not the only figures expected to adhere to performative convention. According to the dominant morality in the world of the play, when certain external circumstances are present, an appropriate state of inwardness must be prominently indicated by the appropriate outward behaviour. If a character does not display the expected emotion in response to these external circumstances, he risks disgracing his 'honour' (5.2.242, 244).[6] For, as the most coveted of possessions, honour is primarily a measure of 'performance' (4.7.150) or 'showing' (5.2.108), and hence can be gained only through appropriate public 'behaviour' (2.1.4)—to adopt a term introduced by Polonius, who uses it in the contrary sense: to indicate the actions which Laertes would *not* want his father to see, lest his own 'dishonour' (2.1.21, 27) result. But in obeying the imperative regarding appropriate emotional display, each consigns 'the inward man' to an inconsolable isolation by ensuring that 'th'exterior' man—the self presented to others—is seen, by those constituting the audience, to act according to their moral specifications, evincing only those thoughts and feelings deemed suitable to the situation.[7]

An unexpectedly apt account of the theatrical imperative appears in T.S. Eliot's celebrated—but by now anti-quated—essay 'Hamlet' (1919). There Eliot develops the notion of the 'objective correlative,' wherein the inward emotion expressed by a character must be correlated with external elements evoking it: 'in other words, a set of objects, a situation, a chain of events . . . shall be the formula of that *particular* emotion; such that when the external facts, which must terminate in sensory experience, are given, the emotion is immediately evoked' (145). Hamlet unwittingly cites the objective correlative when comparing the Player's emotional performance with his own shameful reticence: 'What would he do / Had he the motive and the cue for passion / That I have? He would drown the stage with tears, / And cleave the general ear with horrid speech . . .' (2.2.554-60).

Of course, Hamlet is unaware here of the deeper implications of his own query. But in spontaneously proposing this hypothetical case, where a professional actor exploits his skill to express emotions that for him are compellingly real, Hamlet unknowingly critiques the theatrical imperative, as brief analysis shows. His assumption that sincerity enhances the public expression of feeling presupposes another: that one is already adept at feigning what he does not feel. The primary requirement is to be an actor, '[t]h'observ'd of all observers' (3.1.156)—someone, that is, skilled at simulating the emotions deemed appropriate to the 'situation' or 'chain of events.' In a world where the suddenly sincere Player is the 'paragon' (2.2.307) of the behaviour appropriate to the situation in which Hamlet now finds himself, sincerity has no place. For it can no longer be distinguished from its contrary, false show or deception. Whether the individual actually feels the passion he displays is irrelevant because unverifiable.[8] Similarly, were the Player abruptly to intensify his acting during a performance, the audience could not tell whether the change were due to a spasm of sincerity or simply a surge of professional talent.

In a world where the suddenly sincere Player is the ideal— 'the card and calendar of gentry'—to be oneself is to be a public likeness or 'semblable' (5.2.119-20, 118) of oneself, whether the emotions expressed by speech and action are sincere or not. For to be oneself is to be construed and evaluated in terms of expectations and criteria regarding exterior self-presentation—just as we found earlier with respect to the sentries standing 'watch' on the 'platform' (1.2.197, 214). But as a result of the requirement regarding outward 'showing' (5.2.108), the inward man is denied the power of expression, just like the dead: 'That skull had a tongue in it, and could sing once' (5.1.74).

The predicament of identity uncovered thus far in the world of the play can now be recapitulated. On the one hand, inwardness requires outward expression for verification. Without external 'showing' (5.2.108), the existence of an inward trait ('that within which passes show' [1.2.85]) is no more certain than is the existence of the Ghost without corroboration by multiple witnesses. On the other hand, outward expression—the necessary criterion by which inwardness is verified—is an unreliable index of identity, for it is subservient to both inward manipulation and prevailing convention.

POSTHUMOUS EXISTENCE AS METAPHOR FOR INWARDNESS

In the course of the play, the plight of inwardness, isolated from authentic and intelligible outward expression, is powerfully symbolized by the Ghost, for whom death involves an intensity of private suffering that if disclosed to the living would occasion not comprehension but horror: 'I could a tale unfold whose lightest word / Would harrow up thy soul . . .' (1.5.15-16). For Hamlet, in his 'To be or not to be' soliloquy, death putatively involves a sleep wherein the mind is forever tormented by appalling 'dreams' (3.1.66) from which it never awakens—and of which, by implication, it can never speak. Moreover, with his four last words, 'the rest is silence' (5.2.363), Hamlet again associates death with the incommunicable privacy of that centre of interiority which he elsewhere terms 'my heart's core, . . . my heart of heart,' and 'my dear soul' (3.2.73, 63).

The linkage between the inward man and death is strengthened by a correlative association between Hamlet's inwardness and the motif of the Ghost. Hamlet's sudden visit to Ophelia's closet—his initial appearance after the dialogue with the Ghost—is the first of these occasions. To Ophelia, who receives him unexpected, Hamlet appears 'As if he had been loosed out of hell / To speak of horrors . . .' (2.1.83-84)—a condition like that of the Ghost who, loosed from Purgatory, speaks of similar things: 'O horrible! O horrible! most horrible!' (1.5.80). Later, on the second occasion when Hamlet is associated with the Ghost, Polonius and Claudius exploit Hamlet's habit of walking 'in the lobby' (2.2.161), and direct Ophelia to stand in his path while they eavesdrop behind an arras. The decision of these two characters to send out a third who will converse with an enigmatic figure regularly appearing in a part of the castle duplicates the plan of Horatio, Bernardo, and Marcellus to invite Hamlet to speak to the Ghost. Moreover, in both conversations the enigmatic figure concludes with redundant valediction: the Ghost by repeating 'Fare thee well' (1.5.88) and 'adieu' (1.5.91); Hamlet by repeating 'Farewell' (3.1.134, 139, 142).[9]

The third linking of Hamlet with the motif of the Ghost occurs at the moment of death. Hamlet's invocation of the astonished 'audience' (5.2.340) of courtiers who have witnessed the carnage at the end of the play ('You that look pale and tremble at this chance' [5.2.339]) repeats almost verbatim that spoken by Bernardo to Horatio after sighting the Ghost ('You tremble and look pale' [1.1.56]). Similarly, the Ghost's *aposiopesis* ('I could a tale unfold whose lightest word' [1.5.16]) is echoed in Hamlet's version: 'O, I could tell you . . .' (5.2.342).

This motif of the secondary ghost (that is, the ghost implied by the duplication, in one character, of attributes or utterances associated with the primary Ghost) constitutes the supreme symbol of the plight of the inward man in the world of the play. Analysis of the first example of the motif, that is, Hamlet's visit to Ophelia's closet—will position us to probe the problematics of personal identity more deeply.

What is the painful vision that absorbs Hamlet as he stares at Ophelia while thrice nodding his head and sighing in dismay?[10] The most striking element here is that, throughout their silent meeting, Hamlet seems completely unaware of Ophelia's ability to see his behaviour, but acts instead as if he were somehow still alone. He is dishevelled, but seems wholly unconcerned with his appearance. He gazes at her with prolonged and anguished attention, oblivious to her response. In fact, instead of regarding Ophelia as a separate person, Hamlet seems ultimately to see in her something which concerns only himself—almost as if he were contemplating his own reflection. And in a way, he is. To look at Ophelia is to confirm his own inescapable isolation. Perhaps this is the deepest meaning of Ophelia's comparison of Hamlet to a ghost released from hell to speak of horrors. Private pain propelled Hamlet into Ophelia's closet, but that pain only intensifies the longer he stays. Yet when he leaves, there is only one place he can go: back to his hell of silence. Hamlet's agony in Ophelia's closet is the recognition that he can never speak. More precisely, he can speak but only to hide what he can never say. As if he were already dead, Hamlet becomes the ghost of himself—a manifestation of his own absence, the living embodiment of his own dying words: 'The rest is silence.'

This encounter with Ophelia reveals Hamlet in the grip of the play's central paradox: to be *is* not to be. In a society founded on deception and the fear of disgrace, to live as a person is to live as a ghost. In public, each is encouraged to present himself as a sheer appearance which renders invisible the reality within; in private, each risks suffering pain that must remain dumb. More profoundly, each risks the pain of having to remain dumb: 'Give thy thoughts no tongue' (1.3.59); 'But break my heart, for I must hold my tongue' (1.2.158). Thus, through the need to maintain 'th'exterior' by words and actions, the secrets of 'the inward man' are as removed from communication with the living as are the dead.[11] But, as was suggested near the outset of our study, without outward expression the content of inwardness becomes problematic—even to the subject experiencing it—and is as much in need of verification as the testimony of the real Ghost.

OVERCOMING THE FIRST-PERSON PARADIGM

No character is more implicated in this predicament than Hamlet. But neither is any character more motivated to transcend it. To understand his efforts in this regard, it is useful first to review his predicament. However acutely he perceives falseness ('To be honest, as this world goes, is to be one man picked out of ten thousand' [2.2.178-9]) and however adroitly, through the ruse of madness, he exploits it, Hamlet cannot readily separate his own sense of identity from the exteriority he reviles. For his very concept of himself is grounded in concern for the exterior man and the reputation pertaining to it: 'O God, Horatio, what a wounded name, / Things standing thus unknown, shall I leave behind me' (5.2.349-50). Conversely, the more Hamlet withdraws from exteriority into inwardness, the more his view of the world is influenced by the first-person paradigm, such that everything he sees is interpreted by analogy with his own experience. This is evident in Hamlet's initial two soliloquies, where he defines both himself ('O what a rogue and peasant slave am I!' [2.2.544]) and the future ('It is not, nor it cannot come to good' [1.2.158]) in terms of his own immediate situation.

Many critics conclude that Hamlet achieves no more than an unpredictable oscillation between the poles of 'psychic opposition' (States, 127) or identity, however defined. As a result, his character is frequently labelled as incoherent.[12] But the 'yeasty collection' (5.2.188) of contraries constituting Hamlet's character undergoes leavening whose consequence is a genuine—though incomplete—integration of opposites. Or, to deploy a more active metaphor, in a labour equivalent to those of 'Hercules' (1.2.153; 5.1.286), Hamlet realigns what is 'out of joint' (1.5.196), and so achieves heroic individuation.

The process of rectification can be completed only through overcoming the first-person paradigm, for through it there is no genuine knowledge of identity, only a self-preoccupation that construes everything external by analogy to itself. In the play, of course, the first-person paradigm is often taken for granted, as when Polonius interprets Hamlet's presumed love-sickness in terms of his own experience ('And truly in my youth I suffered much extremity for love, very near this' [2.2.189-90]), Ophelia's auditors interpret, in terms of their own thinking, her mad utterances ('And botch the words up fit to their own thoughts' [4.5.10]), and Hamlet interprets Laertes' predicament in terms of his own ('For by the image of my cause I see / the portraiture of his' [5.2.77-78]).

In conjunction with this emphasis on the first-person paradigm, *Hamlet* also dramatizes the confusion created by its absence. For the advent of the Ghost obviously constitutes an instance when the first-person paradigm is temporarily suspended. By his tendency '[s]o horridly to shake our disposition / With thoughts *beyond the reaches* of our souls' (1.4.55-56; my emphasis), the Ghost literally localizes an inward experience which exceeds the relevance of the first-person paradigm and the attempt to interpret experience in terms of one's own case. Ironically, that very paradigm is invoked when Horatio compares the resemblance of the Ghost to the late King with Marcellus's resemblance to himself: 'As thou art to thyself' (1.1.63).

But a transcending in the first-person paradigm is achieved in Hamlet's third soliloquy, where 'grief' (1.2.82) over his father's death eventually deepens into awareness of the implications of mortality for 'us all' (3.1.83). Death is life-terminating but also life-enlarging, because awareness of it focuses thought on the ultimate purpose of this life which will end: 'What should we do?' (1.4.57). Though in the 'To be' soliloquy that ultimate purpose is not yet evident and the only goal of life is to endure until the end, at least the sufficiency of self-reference has been questioned. The 'sea of troubles' is far more vast than any 'single and peculiar life' can contain (3.1.59; 3.3.11), and the 'sleep of death' is far too enigmatic for any living individual to fathom.

After the performance of *The Murder of Gonzago,* movement 'beyond the reaches' (1.4.56) of the first-person paradigm is more pronounced, with the result that inward and exterior are redefined. When he unexpectedly corners his quarry at prayer, instead of killing him on the spot and finally satisfying his own immediate and painfully frustrated purpose, Hamlet defers revenge to a more opportune occasion: 'No. / Up, sword, and know thou a more horrid hent; / When he is drunk asleep, or in his rage . . . or about some act / That has no relish of salvation in't' (3.3.87-92). Were Hamlet still confined within the preoccupations of his own case, he would not defer action at this moment of intensely aroused desire whose immediate analogue is the yearning, in the 'To be' soliloquy, for the 'consummation' (3.1.63) of death. Both in that soliloquy and in the scene with the praying Claudius, Hamlet's rejection of 'action' (3.1.87) stems from speculation about posthumous experience inexplicable in terms of the first-person paradigm.

Analysis of Claudius's synchronous meditation will clarify the implications of this rejection.[13] Here the King contrasts the accuracy of divine judgment, where 'the action lies / In his true manner,' with the fallibility of human judgment, prone to be fooled by 'shuffling' (3.3.61-62, 41). In one case, the moral value of the inward man behind the action of the exterior one is revealed; in the other, dissembled. But, '[i]n the corrupted currents of this world' (3.3.57), a more insidious shuffling occurs than intentional deception—one that concerns the inadvertent confusing of two antithetical concepts of the inward man. According to the first, here represented by 'Christian' (5.1.1) eschatology, the inward man is in principle corrigible, and can therefore be evaluated in terms of 'better, and worse' (3.2.245), if an infallible criterion of judgment is applied. But according to the second, the inward man is *incorrigible*, for no criterion of verification pertains. In this context, the inward man enjoys the same unverifiability as the 'shapes' (1.2.82) of 'camel,' 'weasel,' and 'whale' indwelling in the cloud which Hamlet indicates to Polonius (3.2.368, 370, 372). Those shapes are what they are said to be, and have no status apart from the awareness formulating them. Hence, to interpolate Malcolm's account of the incorrigible private object, statements about them are neither 'in error [nor] *not* in error' ('Wittgenstein's *Philosophical Investigations,*' 103; original emphasis).

Whereas at first the problematics of personal identity in the play concerned the relation between the exterior and the inward man, they now concern the corrigibility of the inward man, regardless of his exterior manifestations. Is the inward man, like a sensation or thought, logically and existentially indistinguishable from first-person awareness of it *or* is the inward man intact and separate in its own right? The question can be deepened: is the inward man accountable or, like Hamlet in his madness, exempt from the very notion of responsibility?

These questions undergo profound examination during the scene in Gertrude's closet. Here Hamlet suggests two means by which to verify that his sighting of the Ghost pertains to a real presence, and not a mere hallucination: comparing his pulse-rate with Gertrude's and rewording the entire incident coherently. But this problem of verification becomes the analogue of another: verifying the moral condition of Gertrude's inward man (or woman): 'You go not till I set you up a glass / Where you may see *the inmost part of you*' (3.4.18-19; my emphasis). Unlike a first-person sensation or thought whose very existence is inseparable from awareness of it, the inward man or 'inmost part' is here construed to exist behind the arras of Gertrude's unawareness, just as Polonius is soon discovered behind the real arras. But by what criterion can the presence of this 'inmost part' be verified and not dismissed, like the Ghost, as 'the very coinage of [Hamlet's] brain' (3.4.139)?

Explicitly, that criterion is Gertrude's own behaviour, as described to her by Hamlet: 'Nay, but to live / In the rank sweat of an enseamed bed' (3.4.92-93). She sees her 'inmost part' in the verbal picture or mirror of her behaviour which Hamlet has constructed: 'Thou turn'st my eyes into my very soul, / And there I see such black and grained spots / As will not leave their tinct' (3.4.89-91). But once Gertrude thus witnesses her 'inmost part,' it is no longer a private object, but a public or objective one, just as on the 'platform' (1.2.214) at the beginning of the play the 'apparition' is no longer construed as a mere 'fantasy' (1.1.31, 26) after Horatio, as supplementary witness, confirms its reality.

THE ROLE OF CATHARTIC ACTION IN REALIGNING INWARD AND OUTWARD

But, according to Hamlet, behaviour does more than confirm the inmost part. It can also modify or transform it. After the influx of pity encouraged by the Ghost ('O step between her and her fighting soul' [3.4.113]), Hamlet stops castigating Gertrude, and instead exhorts her to 'reform' (3.2.38): 'Assume a virtue if you have it not' (3.4.162). Here, the *assuming* of virtue signifies, not false appearance, but a sincere imitation of virtue in order to overcome 'habits evil' (3.4.164).[14] If Gertrude acts virtuously for the sake of becoming virtuous (and not for the sake of seeming so), she will eventually succeed: 'For use can almost change the stamp of nature, / And either lodge the devil or *throw him out*' (3.4.170-71; my emphasis).[15] This kind of *cathartic* action, undertaken for moral cleansing or 'the purging of the soul' (3.3.85), is the moral contrary of the

'actions that a man might play,' prescribed by the theatrical imperative; for its end or purpose is not to simulate outwardly a given moral state but inwardly to achieve it.

Rectification of the relation between inward and exterior is consummated through Hamlet's eventual faith in end-shaping divinity—in a way clarified by analysis of the 'ends' shaped: 'There's a divinity that shapes our ends, / Rough-hew them how we will' (5.2.10-11). On the one hand, the 'ends' shaped refer to the *outcome* of individual striving. Indeed, the Player King employs the term 'ends' with this meaning: 'Our thoughts are ours, their ends none of our own' (3.2.208). On the other hand, the 'ends' shaped refer to the *purposes* of the agent intending action, not to their result.

The profundity of Hamlet's insight now emerges. In shaping ends, divinity is not simply equivalent to the influence of fate whose intervention renders consummation of individual purpose impossible or irrelevant: 'Our wills and fates do so contrary run' (3.2.206). Instead, by causing a particular purpose to fructify in a particular result, divinity shapes the meaning of that purpose.[16] For the result achieved qualifies the purpose conceived. For example, when groping '[r]ashly' (5.2.6) in the dark to extract the diplomatic 'packet' (5.2.15) purveyed by Rosencrantz and Guildenstern, Hamlet does not yet know the full implication of his purpose which is revealed to him only by its result. Here the inward man is clarified—one might accurately say constituted—by the actions of the exterior one. But conversely, this clarification by means of the exterior man depends on the initiative (what Hamlet terms 'rashness' [5.2.7]) of the inward one.

But Hamlet's anagnorisis implies more than this. Identifying through a purpose beyond himself enables him to achieve authentic self-assurance: 'This is I, / Hamlet the Dane' (5.1.250-51). His sense of identity is no longer bounded in the nutshell of the first-person paradigm. To be himself is no longer to interpret everything else by analogy with his own case, as when, in his former melancholy, he viewed the world as a 'sterile promontory' overlooking 'a sea of troubles' (2.2.299; 3.1.59). A corresponding change has also occurred with respect to his conception of the exterior man. In the course of the play, he advances from regarding the suddenly sincere player as the 'paragon' (2.2.307) to be emulated in the presentation of oneself to attacking Laertes for emulating, in 'the bravery of his grief' (5.2.78), precisely that ideal.

Yet, though Hamlet deepens his expression of both the inward and exterior man, he cannot unambiguously reconcile their reciprocal estrangement in the world of the play. The pathos of his death illumines the dilemma of his life: 'Now cracks a noble heart' (5.2.364). Unlike Gertrude, who, when confronted with her own moral identity, can simply 'throw away the worser part of it / And live purer with other half' (3.4.159-60), Hamlet must strain to reconcile incompatible halves, without the option of discarding one. Yet no matter how heroically he struggles, his task must end in failure. For the relation between inward and exterior is not under his exclusive control.

Consider the 'transformation' (2.2.5) which Hamlet's own exterior man or 'name' (5.2.349) begins to undergo as soon as Hamlet himself dies. In outlining the explanation which he intends to provide of the events leading to Hamlet's death, Horatio inadvertently sounds like an impresario drumming up interest in his repertoire: 'So shall you hear / Of carnal, bloody, and unnatural acts, / Of accidental judgments, casual slaughters, / Of deaths put on by cunning and forc'd cause . . . All this can I / Truly deliver' (5.2.385-91).[17] His diverse inventory recalls that enunciated by Polonius on introducing the Players: 'The best actors in the world, either for tragedy, comedy, history, pastoral . . . scene individable, or poem unlimited' (2.2.392-96). This emphasis on exaggerated theatrical display culminates in the last words of the play, when Fortinbras orders the exposition of Hamlet's corpse on a '*stage*' (5.2.401; my emphasis) or bier. Yet, the more Hamlet is eulogized in these 'terms of honour' (5.2.242), the less his rejection of theatrical exaggeration is understood.

Without exterior expression, the inward man undergoes an analogous 'transformation' (2.2.5). As long as inwardness passes show and remains bounded in the nutshell of interiority, there is no criterion by which to distinguish accurate predications concerning it from those that are merely 'bad dreams' (2.2.256). Ironically, with his last four words, 'the rest is silence' (5.2.363), Hamlet not only refers to interiority but seems almost to withdraw into it, as if preparing to begin the posthumous experience which has already been associated many times with precisely that pole of personal identity. But this possibility—and, of course, it is no more than a possibility—also suggests that, since now Hamlet really is dead, his interior experience entails judgment by the infallible criterion 'above' (3.3.60). For in the play divinity is the ultimate transcendence of the first-person paradigm.

We reach the double bind in the problematics of personal identity in *Hamlet*. Without exterior expression, the content of inwardness cannot be confirmed, except by divinity for whom there is no 'shuffling' (3.3.61). But with exterior expression, inwardness is equally problematized. Conventions and expectations regarding exterior manifestation distort or misconstrue the inwardness made manifest. Moreover, as we have also seen, application of the first-person paradigm leads the witnesses of outward expression to 'botch' it up 'fit to their own thoughts' (4.5.10). Hamlet cannot overcome this problem. For his task is a tragic hero's, not a 'Saviour's' (1.1.164). He can only, through his dramatic *agon,* transpose the problem to larger contexts where its conflicting terms of reference—inward and exterior—can in principle be resolved. He accomplishes this first in Gertrude's closet, where, through the notion of cathartic action, outward expression becomes the means of effecting inward reform. He further reconciles the conflicting poles of identity by his recognition of the

end-shaping divinity through whose influence, as we have seen, the inward purposes of individual agents are not only expressed but widened and transformed by outward action.

Notes

1. Cf States: 'There are two dimensions in which a character behaves and exists before us: as body, as acter, do-er and speaker of things, as entity in physical space; and as "spirit," as judgment, sensibility, thought, and imagination' (187).

2. For background, see chapter 3, 'Suger of St.-Denis,' in Von Simpson, 61-90.

3. For a recent elaboration of Maus's thesis, see Finkelstein.

4. Solipsism, of course, assumes the verifiability of the private object in the absence of outwardness. A succinct formulation of this position is provided by Windelband: 'Each individual mind has certain, intuitive knowledge only of itself and of its states, nor does it know anything of other minds except through ideas which refer primarily to bodies and by an argument from analogy are interpreted to indicate minds' (2: 471).

5. Several critics take Hamlet's madness far more literally. See, for example, Lidz, 222, and Codden. Regarding the influence of gender on madness, see Findlay.

6. As C.L. Barber has copiously demonstrated, the word 'honour' was not used univocally but acquired a wide range of meanings during the seventeenth century.

7. Cf Hobbes, *Leviathan Parts I and II,* 87: 'Desire of praise disposes to laudable actions, such as please them whose judgment they value.'

8. For an existential discussion of related notions, see the chapter 'Sincerity and the Actor' in Ilie, 78-90. For a sociological analysis, see the chapter 'Performances' in Goffman, 17-76.

9. For an earlier account of Hamlet's spectral side, see Robert F. Wilson, Jr.

10. A traditional answer is that Hamlet is confirming sadly to himself that Ophelia is too weak to help him. See Chambers, 188. Similarly, J. Dover Wilson argues that Hamlet, though wounded by Ophelia's rejection of him, urgently seeks 'some comfort or help in her company' (111-12). Kirschbaum suggests that Hamlet 'may not see Ophelia the individual as much as Ophelia the symbol of everything in life that pains him' (386). For emphasis on Ophelia's moral ambiguity, see Patrick, 139-44; and McGee, 138-53.

11. Goddard argues that Ophelia's report concerns her own hallucination of Hamlet.

12. For representative criticism on these grounds, see Bartels; Barker, 37; Eagleton, 73, and Belsey, 41-42.

13. For a discussion of Claudius's abortive repentance in the context of Church of England theology, see Frye, 239-42.

14. The belief that virtue is acquired through good moral habit derives ultimately from Aristotle, *Nichomachean Ethics,* 2.11032a14-26, as Jenkins in his edition of *Hamlet* (520) and others have noted.

15. However, according to Adelman, Hamlet's purpose here is to 'divorce' (33) Gertrude from her sexuality, in order to protect 'the boundaries of his selfhood' (31) from inundation by it.

16. Cf Cornford: 'the most important element of personality—individual purpose' (21). Contrast Herold: 'The self one performs in order better to know oneself turns out not to be one's self at all' (131).

17. On Horatio's role in confirming Hamlet's intrinsic honesty, see Halverston.

Works Cited

Adelman, Janet. *Suffocating Mothers: Fantasies of Maternal Origin in Shakespeare's Plays: 'Hamlet' to 'The Tempest.'* New York: Routledge 1992

Barber, C.L. *The Idea of Honour in the English Drama: 1591-1700.* Goteborg: Elanders 1957

Barker, Francis. *The Tremulous Private Body: Essays on Subjection.* London: Methuen 1984

Bartels, Emily C. 'Breaking the Illusion of Being: Shakespeare and the Performance of Self.' *Theatre Journal* 46 (1994), 171-85

Belsey, Catherine. *The Subject of Tragedy: Identity and Difference in Renaissance Drama.* London: Methuen 1985

Castiglione, Baldesar. *The Book of the Courtier.* Trans Charles S. Singleton. Garden City: Doubleday 1959

Chambers, E.K. *Shakespeare: A Survey.* New York: Hill and Wang 1985

Coddon, Karin S. '"Such Strange Desygns": Madness, Subjectivity and Treason in *Hamlet* and Elizabethan Culture.' *Renaissance Drama* 20 (1989), 51-75

Cornford, F.M. *From Religion to Philosophy: A Study in the Origins of Western Speculation.* New York: Harper and Row 1957

Eagleton, Terry. *William Shakespeare.* Oxford: Blackwell 1986

Eliot, T.S. '*Hamlet.' Selected Essays.* 3rd ed. London: Faber 1951

Findlay, Alison. '*Hamlet: A Document in Madness.' New Essays on 'Hamlet.'* Ed Mark Thornton and John Manning. New York: AMS Press 1994, 189-205

Finkelstein, Richard. 'Differentiating Hamlet: Ophelia and the Problem of Subjectivity.' *Renaissance and Reformation* 21:2 (1997), 15-22

Frye, Roland Mushat. *The Renaissance Hamlet: Issues and Responses in 1600.* Princeton: Princeton University Press 1984

Goddard, Harold. 'In Ophelia's Closet' *Yale Review* 35 (1946), 462-74

Goffman, Erving. *The Presentation of Self in Everyday Life.* Garden City: Doubleday 1959

Greenblatt, Stephen. *Renaissance Self-Fashioning: From More to Shakespeare.* Chicago: University of Chicago Press 1980

Halverson, John. 'The Importance of Horatio.' *Hamlet Studies* 16:1-2 (1994), 57-70

Hartnack, Justus. *Wittgenstein and Modern Philosophy.* Trans Maurice Cranston. Garden City: Doubleday 1965

Hegel, Georg Wilhelm Friedrich. *The Doctrine of Essence.* Trans William Wallace. *Hegel Selections.* Ed Jacob Loewenberg. New York: Scribner's 1957

Herold, Niels. 'Pedagogy, *Hamlet,* and the Manufacture of Wonder.' *Shakespeare Quarterly* 46:2 (1995), 125-34

Hobbes, Thomas. *Leviathan Parts I and II.* Indianapolis: Bobbs-Merrill 1958

Ilie, Paul. *Unamuno: An Existential View of Self and Society.* Madison: University of Wisconsin Press 1967

Kirschbaum, Leo. 'Hamlet and Ophelia.' *Philological Quarterly* 35 (1956), 375-85

Lidz, Theodore. *Hamlet's Enemy: Madness and Myth in 'Hamlet.'* New York: Basic Books 1975

Malcolm, Norman. 'Wittgenstein's *Philosophical Investigations.' Wittgenstein: The Philosophical Investigations.* Ed George Pitcher. Garden City: Doubleday 1966

————. 'Knowledge of Other Minds.' *Wittgenstein: The Philosophical Investigations*

Maus, Katherine Eisaman. *Inwardness and Theater in the English Renaissance.* Chicago University of Chicago Press 1995

McGee, Arthur. *The Elizabethan Hamlet.* New Haven: Yale University Press 1987

Patrick, J. Max. 'The Problem of Ophelia.' *Studies in Shakespeare.* Ed Arthur D. Matthews and Clark M. Emery. Coral Gables: University of Miami Press 1953, 139-44

Penelhum, Terence. 'The Logic of Pleasure.' *Essays in Philosophical Psychology.* Ed Donald F. Gustafson. Garden City: Doubleday 1964

Place, U.T. 'The Concept of Heed.' *Essays in Philosophical Psychology*

Plato. *Theaetetus.* Trans F.M. Cornford. *Plato: The Collected Dialogues.* Ed Edith Hamilton and Huntington Cairns. Bollingen Series 71. Princeton: Princeton University Press 1961

———. *Gorgias.* Trans W.D. Woodland. *Plato: The Collected Dialogues*

Ryle, Gilbert. *The Concept of Mind.* New York: Barnes and Noble 1949

Shakespeare, William. *Hamlet.* Ed Harold Jenkins. London and New York: Methuen 1982

States, Bert O. *Hamlet and the Concept of Character.* Baltimore and London: Johns Hopkins University Press 1992

Suger, Abbot. *Libellus Alter De Consecratione Ecclesiae Sancti Dionysii [Booklet on the Consecration of the Church of St. Denis].* Abbot Suger on the Abbey Church of St.-Denis and Its Art Treasures. Ed and trans Erwin Panofsky. 2nd ed. Princeton: Princeton University Press 1979

Von Simpson, Otto. *The Gothic Cathedral: Origins of Gothic Architecture and the Medieval Concept of Order.* 3rd ed. Bollingen Series 48. Princeton: Princeton University Press 1988

Wilson, J. Dover. *What Happens in Hamlet.* 3rd ed. Cambridge: Cambridge University Press 1956

Wilson, Robert F., Jr. 'Hamlet's Ghostly Presence.' *Hamlet Studies* 11:1-2 (1989), 80-86

Windelband, Wilhelm. *A History of Philosophy.* Rev ed. 2 vols. Trans James H. Tufts 1901; New York: Harper and Row 1958

Wittgenstein, Ludwig. *Philosophical Investigations.* 3rd ed. Trans G.E.M. Anscombe. New York: Macmillan 1958

Jennifer Low (essay date 1999)

SOURCE: "Manhood and the Duel: Enacting Masculinity in *Hamlet,*" in *The Centennial Review,* Vol. 43, No. 3, Fall, 1999, pp. 501-12.

[*In the following essay, Low examines the duel at the end of the play and contends that it is a rite of manhood that focuses Hamlet's attention on how masculinity should be shown and enables him to unite his private and public selves.*]

As many critics have remarked, *Hamlet* is framed by the deeds of Fortinbras.[1] In 1.1 Marcellus and Horatio discuss Denmark's preparations for the possibility of a Norwegian invasion; in 5.2 Fortinbras enters, flushed with his victory over the Poles, just in time to receive Hamlet's endorsement of his claim to the Danish throne. Not only does Fortinbras serve as a possible monitory double for Hamlet—a son whose father is killed and who knows how to respond—Fortinbras and his martial exploits also remind us of the public sphere that is excluded from this play. Despite the play's examination of the relation between theatricality, deceit, and public personae, much criticism has focused on psychological issues or addressed the play largely as a private and domestic tragedy.[2] But although the focus of the play is young Hamlet's dilemma, the drama's time-frame matches that of Claudius's rule over Denmark, and during that time Hamlet as a potential threat is merely one of Claudius's concerns.

Hamlet is concerned with being, not seeming, with translating genuine feeling into activity that manifests that feeling. His mourning clothes in 1.1 publicly bespeak his determination not to play a public role—to stay out of the sun. His black attire urges the community not to attempt to include him. Hamlet wishes to grieve privately, believing that the private sphere is appropriate to a good son. But he soon learns that mourning is not enough: he must also take revenge. Such an act must necessarily have a public component, as he is a prince and the son of a king. To kill Claudius is to become involved in the political arena. Action, then, is equivalent to taking a part, both in the sense of being partisan and in the sense of acting publicly, under the eyes of others. The notion of taking a part makes Hamlet uneasy, however, particularly because such a part would involve behavior that could be divorced from true feeling. But in the course of the fencing exhibition, Hamlet discovers a means of performance acceptable to him. While fencing is a courtly pastime and a way of entertaining others, it also contains the potential for decisive action; when it is not an actual duel, fencing is always (at least theoretically) practice for such an encounter. Moreover, the duellist's determination to back his challenge with his body offers Hamlet one solution to the problem of representing himself honestly. When the exhibition breaks out of its mimetic frame, Hamlet finds the opportunity apt for his revenge: this very public method of killing involves a ritual element that grants the deaths a stylized, sacrificial quality and appropriately solemnizes this drama of the royal family.[3]

Hamlet's decision to act is slowed by the need to understand all the roles that have been assigned to him. Chief among these are man and son.[4] Hamlet learns from the ghost that his role as avenger *depends* upon his identity as son:

> Hamlet: Speak, I am bound to hear.
> Ghost: So art thou to revenge, when thou shalt hear.
> Hamlet: What?
> Ghost: I am thy father's spirit.
>
> (1.5.7-9)[5]

The ghost's assertion of their relationship assumes that the moral imperative of revenge is concomitant upon their blood connection. Contrast this view to Beatrice's allusion to revenge in *Much Ado:* "It is a man's office, but not yours" (4.1.267). She implies that her newly declared lover is too distant in relation to her traduced cousin to serve as Hero's champion. In Hamlet's case, however, the task *is* his. Yet the role of avenger is incompatible with the models of manhood described throughout. The "What a piece of work is man" speech (2.2.303-08) emphasizes rationality, the infinite potential inherent in man's reason.[6] This valorization of mental faculties seems incompatible with the ghost's call to action and revenge. Insofar as the speech describes an ideal of mankind, it urges both restraint and a reverence for the godhead in man.

Later, Hamlet offers Gertrude a blazon in praise of her husband. Apparently similar to the earlier speech, it actually offers an alternative model of masculinity:

> See what a grace was seated on this brow:
> Hyperion's curls, the front of Jove himself,
> An eye like Mars, to threaten and command,
> A station like the herald Mercury
> New lighted on a [heaven-] kissing hill,
> A combination and a form indeed,
> Where every god did seem to set his seal
> To give the world assurance of a man.
>
>   (3.4.55-62)

Again the speech emphasizes man's godlike stature; it further describes King Hamlet's physical presence as manhood embodied. Young Hamlet's words create the notion of masculinity through specific signs which, taken together, offer a pictorial, almost emblematic representation of virility. Significantly, in this blazon the eye is not primarily an organ of apprehension; instead, it enacts unspoken imperatives, shaping the responses of those on whom the king glances.

In contrast, Gertrude uses eyesight as a figure for psychological perception. Her son refers to her senses to describe as an error of synesthesia her failure to recognize his father's superiority: "Eyes without feeling, feeling without sight, / Ears without hands or eyes, smelling sans all, / . . . Could not so mope" (3.4.78-81). Gertrude responds by turning inward, away from her physical senses to her inner vision: "Thou turn'st my eyes into my very soul" (89). She conceives the recognition of her error as a visual apprehension of wrong. Her words suggest that the function of her eyes is to monitor her own spiritual well being; Hamlet Senior, on the other hand, must use his eyes in a gesture of command. The old king's ability to urge the behavior of others characterizes masculine dominance as a theatrical staging (and, incidentally, recalls early modern concerns about the power of the stageplayer).[7] His mien compels, not by demonstrating force but by implying his capacity to shift to action. Action thus proves inseparable from theatricality; young Hamlet eventually learns the lesson as he finds his opportunity to act in the context of a performance.

To combine private and public is, for Hamlet, both to unite "that within" with forms and shapes, as he says (1.2.82), and to join the role of son with that of prince. While the role of prince by itself could be that of the classic protagonist of revenge tragedy, Hamlet's desire to follow his father's model of masculinity makes him perceive such an enactment as shrill and theatrical. When Hamlet blazons his father, the reference to his stance "like the herald Mercury / New lighted on a [heaven-] kissing hill (3.4.59) recalls Quintilian's assertion that action in oratory

is "a discourse, and sometimes . . . a certain eloquence of the body" (2:340). When speech and action are in harmony, their combination creates a sense of authenticity, of truth in argument. A public role for Hamlet must both derive from inward feeling and offer an acceptable presentation of himself as his father's heir.

Manhood figures largely in Hamlet's recollection of the dead king. When Horatio greets Hamlet in act 1, he comforts the grieving prince with the remembrance, "I saw him once, 'a was a goodly king" (1.2.186). Hamlet replies, "'A was a man, take him for all in all, / I shall not look upon his like again" (187-88). Unlike Fortinbras, whose eulogy upon Hamlet's corpse is, "he was likely, had he been put on, / To have prov'd most royal" (5.2.397-98), Hamlet does not see his subject's primary virtue in his royalty but in his masculinity. Though Hamlet's comment refers in part to the inevitable masculinity of all men, including kings, it also bespeaks with simplicity the nobility inherent in his conception of what it means to be a man. As Howard Felperin says in discussing the morality play as one of this tragedy's antecedents, Hamlet manifests "a troubled awareness . . . of the simultaneous resemblance and discrepancy between the play and its older models that is increasingly forced upon us as the action proceeds" (60). The player's enactment of revenge reproaches him because, unlike his father's appearance, it is an empty show. Hamlet wants to rant, yet feels he must not: he chides himself for womanly words, for his need "like a whore [to] unpack my heart with words, / And [to] fall a-cursing like a very drab" (2.2.585-86). He wants to act but cannot do so until he has discovered his own form of masculine decorum, his way of uniting private and public identities.

                    . . . . .

That the fencing match is significant should be evident from the fact that it was a departure from the original story of Hamlet. Shakespeare's depiction of Hamlet (who is, in the original version by Saxo Grammaticus, resolute and unhesitating[8]) is capped by the fencing scene. But there is a distinction between duelling and fencing, and my use of the term "duellist" differs somewhat from that of other critics who have applied the term to Hamlet. S.P. Zitner argues that Hamlet seeks to attain "a state of mind that proceeds from ethical contemplation, social awareness, a quenching of passion, and . . . the disinterestedness that abandons the private will to the will of God," assuming that Hamlet follows the precepts of the Renaissance fencing-master Vincentio Saviolo, whose writings proscribed vengeful duels (Zitner 8; Saviolo 381). But Hamlet is not a duellist in this sense. Far from attempting to kill in a moral frame of mind, he does not even definitively plan to kill his stepfather by means of the sword. He does not reject the treacherous stab in the back because it is an ignoble act but because it punishes Claudio ineffectively, permitting him (Hamlet assumes) to rise to Heaven purged of his sins. What Hamlet seeks throughout the play is a way to perform the part of a man according to his father's model.

Such a mode is that of the duellist. It corresponds to Hamlet's needs in several ways. First, the verbal challenge that precedes a proper duel pledges to prove through action what is uttered in speech; thus, it establishes a connection between word and meaning that destroys the seeming/being dichotomy. Second, the duel harks back to medieval trial ordeals, invoking both historical tradition and the attempt by civil law to involve a heavenly tribunal. The custom of the duel also bears strong overtones of courtliness and chivalry that enable young Hamlet to act publicly in a princely manner. Finally, within that courtly context, the duel embodies the notion of manhood, both through the correspondence of word and deed and through the implicit legitimization of vigilantism (and, by extension, individualism) as a means of achieving justice. Thus we should not be surprised at Hamlet's avowal of his "continual practice" of fencing since Laertes's departure for France. Later, when sport turns into violence, Hamlet's enterprise in turning Claudius's own tools against him demonstrates his ease in the role of swordsman and suggests the psychological rightness of this pastime for him.

To understand fully the significance of the contest for Hamlet, we must be aware of the history of the duel in England. In the 1580s and 1590s, Italian weaponry and customs reshaped the English combat.[9] The lightness of the Italian rapier made it popular; ease and popularity altered the nature of its use. Having passed through two distinct state-sponsored forms, the single combat evolved into an extra-legal proceeding.

The alternative term for the duel—trial by combat—derived from the duel's position in late medieval English law as a supplement to criminal trial and judgment. The practice was generally understood as a test in which God's hand would intervene on the right side.[10] Social historian Robert Bartlett clarifies its purpose: "The components, in the fifth century as in the thirteenth, are clear: the absence of other means of proof, divine judgment, single combat, a means of proof" (115). The duel was a part of due process, used to distinguish between two disputants when evidence could not determine the case.[11] The ritual was a legal trial proceeding that combined investigation, judgment, and, if a combatant was killed outright, summary execution. The presence of onlookers included the community in the ritual and reinforced the performative aspect of the custom.[12]

As English civil law developed, the judicial duel fell into disuse and another form of state-sanctioned single combat became popular: the joust.[13] What we may call the extra-judicial duel almost certainly derived, if not from the joust itself, then from the traditions of chivalry that initially structured that type of one-to-one combat (Billacois 5-6).

By the time of the Tudors, the increasing centralization of power in the monarch diminished the importance of the nobility.[14] The extra-judicial duel, or the duel of honor, helped to reaffirm the status of the aristocrat. Engaging in duels was a way for a nobleman to assert his independence from the Crown's authority, maintaining a right that had existed from the time when the nobility were essentially answerable to themselves alone (Billacois 29-30). Duels of honor fought over trivial remarks and casual insults demonstrated Italianate *sprezzatura* and enhanced one's reputation in an era when the aristocrat's role was increasingly unclear.[15]

In the late sixteenth century, the English Masters of Defence developed the fencing match as commercial entertainment for another level of society. An organization that legitimated the professional status of fencing teachers, the Masters of Defence generated publicity for their art by requiring students to engage in public matches in order to rise in the ranks of the organization. Yet because the legitimacy of the organization itself depended on the whim of the monarch (James I gave them his royal warrant, Elizabeth did not), the art of fencing remained a somewhat shady enterprise. Even before the sixteenth century, fencers tended to congregate in the suburbs of London where, later, theaters would be built. Early fencing exhibitions were staged outdoors and in taverns, but when Burbage and other entrepreneurs began to finance the playhouses, these stages were used for fencing exhibitions as they were for dramas and the other forms of secular spectacle popular at that time.[16]

When the duel is placed in the context of a theatrical production, that context interrogates the very structure of drama's mimetic framework. Because all combat is itself a performance, the performative aspect of theatre is redundant in the enactment of the duel. Staged, the duel's apparent authenticity does not depend on how successfully the actors represent a state of mind. While a staged combat is choreographed and its outcome is predetermined, it still has a reality lacking in more mimetic acts. The difference derives partly from the fact that words are extrinsic to the duel. As Cynthia Marshall says of the wrestling match in *As You Like It,*

> [T]he firmest distinction between the "game" or "spectacle" of the wrestling match and the "drama" of the surrounding action will also be the most obvious one: wrestling is an affair of bodies and not words. Le Beau's announcement of Charles's defeat—"He cannot speak" (1.2.208)—illustrates perfectly the established priority of deed over word, the capacity of pure spectacle or of violence . . . to destroy language. The ludic interval, because it presents violent physical action of a sort that is anterior to language, would seem to possess greater "reality" than the surrounding text of *As You Like It.*
>
> (276-77)

Marshall's analysis reminds us that the duel was only one instance of the plentiful spectacular violence enacted during this period. Yet the wrestling match and the duel share that element of performativity, of ludic entertainment, that separates such spectacle from its surrounding context.

From inception to conclusion, such a physical contest, staged, functions as a small drama on its own. Self-contained, a small play-within-a-play, it presents two figures whose fight resolves their conflict. The fight itself is bounded, delimited by on-stage presentation. In a way, the conventions of dramatic structure force the duel (when it is part of a drama) to revert to its earlier form as trial by combat. If the challenge to the duel is a speech-act, the staged duel is a tacit judgment of the combatants.

. . . . .

When Osric, the superfine courtier, asks Hamlet to take part in the contest in compliance with the King and Queen's wish, his account of the proposed fencing match stresses the formal nature of the exhibition. He emphasizes the courtliness of Laertes, hinting that the nature of any entertainment in which he takes part will be equally elegant:

> Osric: Sir, here is newly come to court Laertes, believe me, an absolute [gentleman], full of most excellent differences, of very soft society, and great showing; indeed, to speak sellingly of him, he is the card or calendar of gentry; for you shall find in him the continent of what part a gentleman would see.
>
> (5.2.106-11)

Osric's euphonious description of the proposed combat and his account of Claudius's and Laertes's wager both call attention to the courtly character of this ludic competition. Osric puts forth the combat as a sport of gentility, a combat in spirit and in class closer to the tilt than to the duelling exhibitions of early modern England. Hamlet and Laertes both use unusual linguistic formality when they meet for the fencing competition. Their language suggests that the fencing will be well-governed, controlled, regulated by the ceremonies of courtesy. But the ceremony, of course, has been designed by Claudius, the devious, false monarch.

Although the challenge to this combat characterizes it as an entertainment, not a duel, one participant (Laertes) and one watcher (Claudius) are aware that the combat will be lethal. Their knowledge (in which we participate) restructures the nature of the match. Yet the fencing appears sportive and friendly at first. Hamlet actually asks Laertes to judge one of his hits. In the crucial bout, in which each wounds the other with the envenomed rapier, they appear at first to be in earnest; Claudius calls out, "Part them, they are incens'd" (5.2.302). But when Hamlet refutes this, he and Laertes face one another again. It is only when Gertrude cries out at the poison and Laertes admits his treachery that disorder breaks out. The match which had seemed a lawful entertainment reveals itself as a ploy of the monarch, created by the king's design and yet unlawful, as perfidious as Claudius himself.

At this point, the device that Claudius has created for Hamlet's death grows beyond his control. As Laertes falls, he confesses his wrongdoing toward Hamlet, thereby recanting the unspoken accusation of Hamlet as his father's murderer. Moreover, his final words—"the King, the King's to blame" (5.2.320)—offer a new accusation that may be proven in blood. Hamlet attacks his uncle with the envenomed sword and, as he forces Claudius to drink the poisoned wine, makes his own accusation: "[T]hou incestious, murd'rous, damned Dane," he charges as he acts (5.2.325-26). The violence set in motion by the king becomes the swordsman's prerogative.

The first overt violence occurs earlier—in the almost comical struggle between Hamlet and Laertes in Ophelia's grave. That brawl occurs in a disjunctive setting that shows how unpromising combat is when it takes place without ceremony or due process. That combat is replayed in the fencing match set up by Claudius as a blind for murder.[17] The display of competitive sport now carries its participants beyond the bounds set by the game. Throughout, Shakespeare exploits the dynamics of violence as he has already done in *As You Like It*. As Marshall says of the ludic match in that play, one character (here, Laertes) sees violence as the sign of sincerity, authentic feeling, while another character (Claudius) sees "the formal violence of [a contest] as open to manipulation" (268). But with the denouement Hamlet recognizes both possibilities: for him the violence is public display, a chance to write his story, as well as the embodiment of feeling. Claudius's manipulations enable him to die as an avenger and a true prince.

For the court onlookers in *Hamlet,* a performance that began as a game has exploded its boundaries, breaking out of ceremony and playfulness to become brutal, sly, and real.[18] What the onlookers realize only at the bloody conclusion is that this apparent sport concealed more than one character's intention not to "act," but in fact, in deed, to do something decisive to alter his circumstances.

For us as audience, the fencing exhibition restructures the relationships within the larger play. As Jean Howard points out, the fencing places Hamlet "visually at the center, rather than the periphery of the action. Sword in hand, he is himself a public actor" (118). At that juncture, Hamlet's internal state (which has been the play's focus) and the public world of Denmark come together. Once Hamlet begins the match, he becomes an actor rather than an observer. Even though the combat is not a performance of his choosing, it offers him the opportunity to act, to *do*—in earnest as well as in the ludic context of the competition.

Notes

1. See, for example, Bevington 1071.
2. It is convenient to cite Ernest Jones's *Hamlet and Oedipus* (1949) as the beginning of the body of psychoanalytic criticism of *Hamlet*. C.S. Lewis, however, names Schlegel (1815), Hazlitt (1815), Hallam (1837-39), Coleridge (1856), Sievers (1866), Raleigh (1907), and Clutton-Brock (1922) as critics who analyze Hamlet's psychology (cited in Lewis 140-41). Maus (1995) has recently addressed the issues of theatricality and deceit in her excellent discussion of "seeming" in Hamlet (1-5).

3. James V. Holleran discusses this scene in "Maimed Funeral Rites in Hamlet." Holleran gives an interesting reading of the fencing exhibition as a distorted version of Holy Communion (87-93).

4. Masculinity in *Hamlet* is far from being a stable construct, and the assumptions about its constitution vary from one character to another. As Judith Butler says, summarizing phenomenologist theories of gender,

> gender is in no way a stable identity or locus of agency from which various acts proceed; rather, it is an identity tenuously constituted in time—an identity instituted through a *stylized repetition of acts.* Further, gender is instituted through the stylization of the body and, hence, must be understood as the mundane way in which bodily gestures, movements, and enactments of various kinds constitute the illusion of an abiding gendered self.
>
> (270)

Butler's discussion of gender forms a large part of the theoretical underpinning of my analysis of duelling and masculinity in *Hamlet*.

5. All quotations of Shakespeare's works are from William Shakespeare, *The Riverside Shakespeare,* ed. G. Blakemore Evans.

6. My discussion of rationality and revenge has been inflected by Gordon Braden's analysis of Stoicism in English Renaissance drama in *Renaissance Tragedy and the Senecan Tradition.*

7. For early modern texts that reveal anxiety about the powers of the stage-player, see J. Northbrooke, Stephen Gosson, Anthony Munday, and Philip Stubbes, among others.

8. See Saxo Grammaticus.

9. For information about the change in swordfighting brought about by the introduction of the rapier to late sixteenth-century England, see Aylward 26-75, Brian Parker 58, and Sieveking 2:389-407, among others.

10. For two conflicting views on this point, see Lea 166 and Bartlett 68.

11. But according to Bartlett, "The idea of 'letting them fight it out' is at least as strong as the sentiment 'may the best man win' (even given that 'best' means 'with the best case')" (114).

12. As Foucault says of the watchers at executions, "they must be the witnesses, the guarantors, of the punishment, and . . . they must to a certain extent take part in it. The right to be witnesses was one they possessed and claimed" (58).

13. Arguing that the judicial duel was not a thing of the past in early modern England, Francois Billacois asserts that it continued into the sixteenth and seventeenth centuries (19). For an excellent discussion of jousting and chivalry, see Maurice Keen 83-7.

14. Lawrence Stone's groundbreaking study *The Crisis of the Aristocracy, 1558-1641* was among the first to discuss this phenomenon in detail.

15. On the subject of trivial remarks as the pretext for single combats, see Parks 166-72. For the aristocrat's anxiety about his social role and the complex codes of behavior that resulted from this anxiety, see Whigham.

16. See Wickham 2.1.168 and 2.2.42 for a discussion of the various kinds of entertainment offered in Elizabethan and Jacobean London.

17. For discussion of Claudius's use of the performative fencing display as concealment for the assassination of Prince Hamlet, see Holleran 67 and Alexander 23 and 174-75.

18. I should acknowledge the debt that this point owes to Johan Huizinga.

Literature Cited

Alexander, Nigel. *Poison, Play, and Duel.* Lincoln: Nebraska UP, 1971.

Aylward, J.D. *The English Master of Arms.* London: Routledge, 1956.

Bartlett, Robert. *Trial by Fire and Water: The Medieval Judicial Ordeal.* Oxford: Clarendon, 1986.

Bevington, David. "Introduction to Hamlet, Prince of Denmark." *The Complete Works of Shakespeare.* 3rd ed. Ed. David Bevington. Glenview, IL: Scott, Foresman, 1980. 1069-73.

Billacois, Francois. *The Duel: Its Rise and Fall in Early Modern France.* Ed. and trans. Trista Selous. New Haven: Yale UP, 1990.

Braden, Gordon. *Renaissance Tragedy and the Senecan Tradition.* New Haven: Yale UP, 1985.

Butler, Judith. "Performative Acts and Gender Constitution." *Performing Feminisms.* Ed. Sue-Ellen Case. Baltimore: Hopkins UP, 1990. 270-82.

Felperin, Howard. *Shakespearean Representation: Mimesis and Modernity in Elizabethan Tragedy.* Princeton: Princeton UP, 1977.

Foucault, Michel. *Discipline and Punish: The Birth of the Prison.* Trans. Alan Sheridan. New York: Vintage, 1979.

Gosson, Stephen. *The Schoole of Abuse.* London, 1579. STC 12097.

Grammaticus, Saxo. *Saxo Grammaticus and the Life of Hamlet.* Lincoln: Nebraska UP, 1983.

Holleran, James V. "Maimed Funeral Rites in Hamlet." *ELR* 19 (1989): 65-93.

Howard, Jean E. *Shakespeare's Art of Orchestration: Stage Technique and Audience Response.* Chicago: Illinois UP, 1984.

Huizinga, Johan. *Homo Ludens: A Study of the Play Element in Culture.* Boston: Beacon, 1944, rpt. 1955.

Jones, Ernest. *Hamlet and Oedipus.* Rev. ed. New York, 1949.

Keen, Maurice. *Chivalry.* New Haven: Yale UP, 1984.

Lea, Henry Charles. *The Duel and the Oath.* 1866. Rpt. Philadelphia: Pennsylvania UP, 1974.

Lewis, C.S. "Hamlet: The Prince or the Poem?" *Proceedings of the British Academy* 28 (1942): 139-54.

Marshall, Cynthia. "Wrestling as Play and Game in As You Like It." *Studies in English Literature* 1500-1900 33 (1993): 265-87.

Maus, Katharine Eisaman. *Inwardness and Theater in the English Renaissance.* Chicago: Chicago UP, 1995.

Munday, Anthony. *A Second and Third Blast of Retrait from Plaies and Theaters.* London, 1580. STC 21677.

Northbrooke, J. *A Treatise wherein Dicing, Dauncing, Vaine Playes or Enterluds . . . are reproved.* London, 1577. STC 18670. Rpt. New York: Garland, 1974.

Parker, Brian. "*A Fair Quarrel* (1617), the Duelling Code, and Jacobean Law." *Rough Justice: Essays on Crime in Literature.* Ed. M.L. Friedland. Toronto: Toronto UP, 1991. 52-75.

Parks, Ward. *Verbal Duelling in Heroic Narrative.* Princeton: Princeton UP, 1990.

Quintilian, Marcus Fabius. *De Institutione Oratoria.* 2 vols. Trans. W. Guthrie. London: Dutton, 1805.

Saviolo, Vincentio. *Vincentio Saviolo His Practise.* London: Wolff, 1595. Rpt. in *Three Elizabethan Fencing Manuals.* Ed. James L. Jackson. Delmar, NY: Scholars' Facsimiles, 1972. 185-488.

Shakespeare, William. *The Riverside Shakespeare.* Ed. G. Blakemore Evans. Boston: Houghton Mifflin, 1974.

Sieveking, A. Forbes. "Fencing and Duelling." *Shakespeare's England.* 2 vols. Oxford: Clarendon, 1966. 2:389-407.

Stone, Lawrence. *The Crisis of the Aristocracy, 1558-1641.* Oxford: Clarendon, 1965.

Stubbes, Philip. *The Anatomie of Abuses.* London, 1583. STC 23376.

Whigham, Frank. *Ambition and Privilege: The Social Tropes of Elizabethan Courtesy Theory.* Berkeley: California UP, 1984.

Wickham, Glynne. *Early English Stages 1300 to 1600.* 3 vols. New York: Columbia UP, 1959.

Zitner, S.P. "Hamlet, Duellist." *University of Toronto Quarterly* 39 (1969): 1-18.

GENDER ISSUES

Elaine Showalter (essay date 1985)

SOURCE: "Representing Ophelia: Women, Madness, and the Responsibilities of Feminist Criticism," in *Shakespeare and the Question of Theory,* edited by Patricia Parker and Geoffrey Hartman, Methuen, 1985, pp. 77-94.

[*In the following essay, Showalter probes a number of crucial questions surrounding the character of Ophelia which involve her status in the play and bring to the forefront the relation between madness, representation, women's sexuality, and femaleness.*]

"As a sort of a come-on, I announced that I would speak today about that piece of bait named Ophelia, and I'll be as good as my word." These are the words which begin the psychoanalytic seminar on *Hamlet* presented in Paris in 1959 by Jacques Lacan. But despite his promising come-on, Lacan was *not* as good as his word. He goes on for some 41 pages to speak about Hamlet, and when he does mention Ophelia, she is merely what Lacan calls "the object Ophelia"—that is, the object of Hamlet's male desire. The etymology of Ophelia, Lacan asserts, is "O-phallus," and her role in the drama can only be to function as the exteriorized figuration of what Lacan predictably and, in view of his own early work with psychotic women, disappointingly suggests is the phallus as transcendental signifier.[1] To play such a part obviously makes Ophelia "essential," as Lacan admits; but only because, in his words, "she is linked forever, for centuries, to the figure of Hamlet."

The bait-and-switch game that Lacan plays with Ophelia is a cynical but not unusual instance of her deployment in psychiatric and critical texts. For most critics of Shakespeare, Ophelia has been an insignificant minor character in the play, touching in her weakness and madness but chiefly interesting, of course, in what she tells us about Hamlet. And while female readers of Shakespeare have often attempted to champion Ophelia, even feminist critics have done so with a certain embarrassment. As Annette Kolodny ruefully admits: "it is after all, an imposition of high order to ask the viewer to attend to Ophelia's sufferings in a scene where, before, he's always so comfortably kept his eye fixed on Hamlet."[2]

Yet when feminist criticism allows Ophelia to upstage Hamlet, it also brings to the foreground the issues in an ongoing theoretical debate about the cultural links between femininity, female sexuality, insanity, and representation. Though she is neglected in criticism, Ophelia is probably the most frequently illustrated and cited of Shakespeare's heroines. Her visibility as a subject in literature, popular culture, and painting, from Redon who paints her drowning, to Bob Dylan, who places her on Desolation Row, to Cannon Mills, which has named a flowery sheet pattern after her, is in inverse relation to her invisibility in Shake-spearean critical texts. Why has she been such a potent and obsessive figure in our cultural mythology? Insofar as Hamlet names Ophelia as "woman" and "frailty," substitut-ing an ideological view of femininity for a personal one, is she indeed representative of Woman, and does her mad-ness stand for the oppression of women in society as well as in tragedy? Furthermore, since Laertes calles Ophelia a "document in madness," does she represent the textual archetype of woman *as* madness or madness *as* woman? And finally, how should feminist criticism represent Ophelia in its own discourse? What is our responsibility towards her as character and as woman?

Feminist critics have offered a variety of responses to these questions. Some have maintained that we should represent Ophelia as a lawyer represents a client, that we should become her Horatia, in this harsh world reporting her and her cause aright to the unsatisfied. Carol Neely, for example, describes advocacy—speaking *for* Ophelia—as our proper role: "As a feminist critic," she writes, "I must 'tell' Ophelia's story."[3] But what can we mean by Ophelia's story? The story of her life? The story of her betrayal at the hands of her father, brother, lover, court, society? The story of her rejection and marginaliza-tion by male critics of Shakespeare? Shakespeare gives us very little information from which to imagine a past for Ophelia. She appears in only five of the play's twenty scenes; the pre-play course of her love story with Hamlet is known only by a few ambiguous flashbacks. Her tragedy is subordinated in the play; unlike Hamlet, she does not struggle with moral choices or alternatives. Thus another feminist critic, Lee Edwards, concludes that it is impos-sible to reconstruct Ophelia's biography from the text: "We can imagine Hamlet's story without Ophelia, but Ophelia literally has no story without Hamlet."[4]

If we turn from American to French feminist theory, Ophelia might confirm the impossibility of representing the feminine in patriarchal discourse as other than mad-ness, incoherence, fluidity, or silence. In French theoretical criticism, the feminine or "Woman" is that which escapes representation in patriarchal language and symbolism; it remains on the side of negativity, absence, and lack. In comparison to Hamlet, Ophelia is certainly a creature of lack. "I think nothing, my lord," she tells him in the Mousetrap scene, and he cruelly twists her words:

> *Hamlet:* That's a fair thought to lie between maids' legs.
> *Ophelia:* What is, my lord?
> *Hamlet:* Nothing.

> (III.ii.117-19)

In Elizabethan slang, "nothing" was a term for the female genitalia, as in *Much Ado About Nothing.* To Hamlet, then, "nothing" is what lies between maids' legs, for, in the male visual system of representation and desire, women's sexual organs, in the words of the French psychoanalyst Luce Irigaray, "represent the horror of having nothing to

see."[5] When Ophelia is mad, Gertrude says that "Her speech is nothing," mere "unshaped use." Ophelia's speech thus represents the horror of having nothing to say in the public terms defined by the court. Deprived of thought, sexuality, language, Ophelia's story becomes the Story of O—the zero, the empty circle or mystery of feminine dif-ference, the cipher of female sexuality to be deciphered by feminist interpretation.[6]

A third approach would be to read Ophelia's story as the female subtext of the tragedy, the repressed story of Hamlet. In this reading, Ophelia represents the strong emotions that the Elizabethans as well as the Freudians thought womanish and unmanly. When Laertes weeps for his dead sister he says of his tears that "When these are gone, / The woman will be out"—that is to say, that the feminine and shameful part of his nature will be purged. According to David Leverenz, in an important essay called "The Woman in *Hamlet,*" Hamlet's disgust at the feminine passivity in himself is translated into violent revulsion against women, and into his brutal behavior towards Ophelia. Ophelia's suicide, Leverenz argues, then becomes "a microcosm of the male world's banishment of the female, because 'woman' represents everything denied by reasonable men."[7]

It is perhaps because Hamlet's emotional vulnerability can so readily be conceptualized as feminine that this is the only heroic male role in Shakespeare which has been regularly acted by women, in a tradition from Sarah Bern-hardt to, most recently, Diane Venora, in a production directed by Joseph Papp. Leopold Bloom speculates on this tradition in *Ulysses,* musing on the Hamlet of the actress Mrs Bandman Palmer: "Male impersonator. Perhaps he was a woman? Why Ophelia committed sui-cide?"[8]

While all of these approaches have much to recommend them, each also presents critical problems. To liberate Ophelia from the text, or to make her its tragic center, is to re-appropriate her for our own ends; to dissolve her into a female symbolism of absence is to endorse our own marginality; to make her Hamlet's anima is to reduce her to a metaphor of male experience. I would like to propose instead that Ophelia *does* have a story of her own that feminist criticism can tell; it is neither her life story, nor her love story, nor Lacan's story, but rather the *history* of her representation. This essay tries to bring together some of the categories of French feminist thought about the "feminine" with the empirical energies of American historical and critical research: to yoke French theory and Yankee knowhow.

Tracing the iconography of Ophelia in English and French painting, photography, psychiatry, and literature, as well as in theatrical production, I will be showing first of all the representational bonds between female insanity and female sexuality. Secondly, I want to demonstrate the two-way transaction between psychiatric theory and cultural representation. As one medical historian has observed, we could provide a manual of female insanity by chronicling the illustrations of Ophelia; this is so because the illustrations of Ophelia have played a major role in the theoretical construction of female insanity.[9] Finally, I want to suggest that the feminist revision of Ophelia comes as much from the actress's freedom as from the critic's interpretation.[10] When Shakespeare's heroines began to be played by women instead of boys, the presence of the female body and female voice, quite apart from details of interpretation, created new meanings and subversive tensions in these roles, and perhaps most importantly with Ophelia. Looking at Ophelia's history on and off the stage, I will point out the contest between male and female representations of Ophelia, cycles of critical repression and feminist reclamation of which contemporary feminist criticism is only the most recent phase. By beginning with these data from cultural history, instead of moving from the grid of literary theory, I hope to conclude with a fuller sense of the responsibilities of feminist criticism, as well as a new perspective on Ophelia.

. . . . .

"Of all the characters in *Hamlet*," Bridget Lyons has pointed out, "Ophelia is most persistently presented in terms of symbolic meanings."[11] Her behavior, her appearance, her gestures, her costume, her props, are freighted with emblematic significance, and for many generations of Shakespearean critics her part in the play has seemed to be primarily iconographic. Ophelia's symbolic meanings, moreover, are specifically feminine. Whereas for Hamlet madness is metaphysical, linked with culture, for Ophelia it is a product of the female body and female nature, perhaps that nature's purest form. On the Elizabethan stage, the conventions of female insanity were sharply defined. Ophelia dresses in white, decks herself with "fantastical garlands" of wild flowers, and enters, according to the stage directions of the "Bad" Quarto, "distracted" playing on a lute with her "hair down singing." Her speeches are marked by extravagant metaphors, lyrical free associations, and "explosive sexual imagery."[12] She sings wistful and bawdy ballads, and ends her life by drowning.

All of these conventions carry specific messages about femininity and sexuality. Ophelia's virginal and vacant white is contrasted with Hamlet's scholar's garb, his "suits of solemn black." Her flowers suggest the discordant double images of female sexuality as both innocent blossoming and whorish contamination; she is the "green girl" of pastoral, the virginal "Rose of May" and the sexually explicit madwoman who, in giving away her wild flowers and herbs, is symbolically deflowering herself. The "weedy trophies" and phallic "long purples" which she wears to her death intimate an improper and discordant sexuality that Gertrude's lovely elegy cannot quite obscure.[13] In Elizabethan and Jacobean drama, the stage direction that a woman enters with dishevelled hair indicates that she might either be mad or the victim of a rape; the disordered hair, her offense against decorum, suggests sensuality in each case.[14] The mad Ophelia's bawdy songs and verbal license, while they give her access to "an entirely different

range of experience" from what she is allowed as the dutiful daughter, seem to be her one sanctioned form of self-assertion as a woman, quickly followed, as if in retribution, by her death.[15]

Drowning too was associated with the feminine, with female fluidity as opposed to masculine aridity. In his discussion of the "Ophelia complex," the phenomenologist Gaston Bachelard traces the symbolic connections between women, water, and death. Drowning, he suggests, becomes the truly feminine death in the dramas of literature and life, one which is a beautiful immersion and submersion in the female element. Water is the profound and organic symbol of the liquid woman whose eyes are so easily drowned in tears, as her body is the repository of blood, amniotic fluid, and milk. A man contemplating this feminine suicide understands it by reaching for what is feminine in himself, like Laertes, by a temporary surrender to his own fluidity—that is, his tears; and he becomes a man again in becoming once more dry—when his tears are stopped.[16]

Clinically speaking, Ophelia's behavior and appearance are characteristic of the malady the Elizabethans would have diagnosed as female love-melancholy, or erotomania. From about 1580, melancholy had become a fashionable disease among young men, especially in London, and Hamlet himself is a prototype of the melancholy hero. Yet the epidemic of melancholy associated with intellectual and imaginative genius "curiously bypassed women." Women's melancholy was seen instead as biological, and emotional in origins.[17]

On the stage, Ophelia's madness was presented as the predictable outcome of erotomania. From 1660, when women first appeared on the public stage, to the beginnings of the eighteenth century, the most celebrated of the actresses who played Ophelia were those whom rumor credited with disappointments in love. The greatest triumph was reserved for Susan Mountfort, a former actress at Lincoln's Inn Fields who had gone mad after her lover's betrayal. One night in 1720 she escaped from her keeper, rushed to the theater, and just as the Ophelia of the evening was to enter for her mad scene, "sprang forward in her place . . . with wild eyes and wavering motion."[18] As a contemporary reported, "she was in truth *Ophelia herself*, to the amazement of the performers as well as of the audience—nature having made this last effort, her vital powers failed her and she died soon after."[19] These theatrical legends reinforced the belief of the age that female madness was a part of female nature, less to be imitated by an actress than demonstrated by a deranged woman in a performance of her emotions.

The subversive or violent possibilities of the mad scene were nearly eliminated, however, on the eighteenth-century stage. Late Augustan stereotypes of female love-melancholy were sentimentalized versions which minimized the force of female sexuality, and made female insanity a pretty stimulant to male sensibility. Actresses

*Jean Simmons as Ophelia in the
1948 film adaptation of* Hamlet.

troupe in 1827, his Ophelia was a young Irish ingénue named Harriet Smithson. Smithson used "her extensive command of mime to depict in precise gesture the state of Ophelia's confused mind."[21] In the mad scene, she entered in a long black veil, suggesting the standard imagery of female sexual mystery in the gothic novel, with scattered bedlamish wisps of straw in her hair. . . . Spreading the veil on the ground as she sang, she spread flowers upon it in the shape of a cross, as if to make her father's grave, and mimed a burial, a piece of stage business which remained in vogue for the rest of the century.

The French audiences were stunned. Dumas recalled that "it was the first time I saw in the theatre real passions, giving life to men and women of flesh and blood."[22] The 23-year-old Hector Berlioz, who was in the audience on the first night, fell madly in love, and eventually married Harriet Smithson despite his family's frantic opposition. Her image as the mad Ophelia was represented in popular lithographs and exhibited in bookshop and printshop windows. Her costume was imitated by the fashionable, and a coiffure "à la folle," consisting of a "black veil with wisps of straw tastefully interwoven" in the hair, was widely copied by the Parisian beau monde, always on the lookout for something new.[23]

Although Smithson never acted Ophelia on the English stage, her intensely visual performance quickly influenced English productions as well; and indeed the romantic Ophelia—a young girl passionately and visibly driven to picturesque madness—became the dominant international acting style for the next 150 years, from Helena Modjeska in Poland in 1871, to the 18-year-old Jean Simmons in the Laurence Olivier film of 1948.

Whereas the romantic Hamlet, in Coleridge's famous dictum, thinks too much, has an "overbalance of the contemplative faculty" and an overactive intellect, the romantic Ophelia is a girl who *feels* too much, who drowns in feeling. The romantic critics seem to have felt that the less said about Ophelia the better; the point was to *look* at her. Hazlitt, for one, is speechless before her, calling her "a character almost too exquisitely touching to be dwelt upon."[24] While the Augustans represent Ophelia as music, the romantics transform her into an *objet d'art*, as if to take literally Claudius's lament, "poor Ophelia / Divided from herself and her fair judgment, / Without the which we are pictures."

Smithson's performance is best recaptured in a series of pictures done by Delacroix from 1830 to 1850, which show a strong romantic interest in the relation of female sexuality and insanity.[25] The most innovative and influential of Delacroix's lithographs is *La Mort d'Ophélie* of 1843, the first of three studies. Its sensual languor, with Ophelia half-suspended in the stream as her dress slips from her body, anticipated the fascination with the erotic trance of the hysteric as it would be studied by Jean-Martin Charcot and his students, including Janet and Freud. Delacroix's interest in the drowning Ophelia is also reproduced to the

such as Mrs Lessingham in 1772, and Mary Bolton in 1811, played Ophelia in this decorous style, relying on the familiar images of the white dress, loose hair, and wild flowers to convey a polite feminine distraction, highly suitable for pictorial reproduction, and appropriate for Samuel Johnson's description of Ophelia as young, beautiful, harmless, and pious. Even Mrs Siddons in 1785 played the mad scene with stately and classical dignity. . . . For much of the period, in fact, Augustan objections to the levity and indecency of Ophelia's language and behavior led to censorship of the part. Her lines were frequently cut, and the role was often assigned to a singer instead of an actress, making the mode of representation musical rather than visual or verbal.

But whereas the Augustan response to madness was a denial, the romantic response was an embrace.[20] The figure of the madwoman permeates romantic literature, from the gothic novelists to Wordsworth and Scott in such texts as "The Thorn" and *The Heart of Midlothian,* where she stands for sexual victimization, bereavement, and thrilling emotional extremity. Romantic artists such as Thomas Barker and George Shepheard painted pathetically abandoned Crazy Kates and Crazy Anns, while Henry Fuseli's "Mad Kate" is almost demonically possessed, an orphan of the romantic storm.

In the Shakespearean theater, Ophelia's romantic revival began in France rather than England. When Charles Kemble made his Paris debut as Hamlet with an English point of obsession in later nineteenth-century painting. The English Pre-Raphaelites painted her again and again, choosing the drowning which is only described in the play, and where no actress's image had preceded them or interfered with their imaginative supremacy.

In the Royal Academy show of 1852, Arthur Hughes's entry shows a tiny waif-like creature—a sort of Tinker Bell Ophelia—in a filmy white gown, perched on a tree trunk by the stream. The overall effect is softened, sexless, and hazy, although the straw in her hair resembles a crown of thorns. Hughes's juxtaposition of childlike femininity and Christian martyrdom was overpowered, however, by John Everett Millais's great painting of Ophelia in the same show. . . . While Millais's Ophelia is sensuous siren as well as victim, the artist rather than the subject dominates the scene. The division of space between Ophelia and the natural details Millais had so painstakingly pursued reduces her to one more visual object; and the painting has such a hard surface, strangely flattened perspective, and brilliant light that it seems cruelly indifferent to the woman's death.

. . . . .

These Pre-Raphaelite images were part of a new and intricate traffic between images of women and madness in late nineteenth-century literature, psychiatry, drama, and art. First of all, superintendents of Victorian lunatic asylums were also enthusiasts of Shakespeare, who turned to his dramas for models of mental aberration that could be applied to their clinical practice. The case study of Ophelia was one that seemed particularly useful as an account of hysteria or mental breakdown in adolescence, a period of sexual instability which the Victorians regarded as risky for women's mental health. As Dr John Charles Bucknill, president of the Medico-Psychological Association, remarked in 1859, "Ophelia is the very type of a class of cases by no means uncommon. Every mental physician of moderately extensive experience must have seen many Ophelias. It is a copy from nature, after the fashion of the Pre-Raphaelite school."[26] Dr John Conolly, the celebrated superintendent of the Hanwell Asylum, and founder of the committee to make Stratford a national trust, concurred. In his *Study of Hamlet* in 1863 he noted that even casual visitors to mental institutions could recognize an Ophelia in the wards: "the same young years, the same faded beauty, the same fantastic dress and interrupted song."[27] Medical textbooks illustrated their discussions of female patients with sketches of Ophelia-like maidens.

But Conolly also pointed out that the graceful Ophelias who dominated the Victorian stage were quite unlike the women who had become the majority of the inmate population in Victorian public asylums. "It seems to be supposed," he protested, "that it is an easy task to play the part of a crazy girl, and that it is chiefly composed of singing and prettiness. The habitual courtesy, the partial rudeness of mental disorder, are things to be witnessed. . . . An actress, ambitious of something beyond cold

imitation, might find the contemplation of such cases a not unprofitable study."[28]

Yet when Ellen Terry took up Conolly's challenge, and went to an asylum to observe real madwomen, she found them "too *theatrical*" to teach her anything.[29] This was because the iconography of the romantic Ophelia had begun to infiltrate reality, to define a style for mad young women seeking to express and communicate their distress. And where the women themselves did not willingly throw themselves into Ophelia-like postures, asylum superintendents, armed with the new technology of photography, imposed the costume, gesture, props, and expression of Ophelia upon them. In England, the camera was introduced to asylum work in the 1850s by Dr Hugh Welch Diamond, who photographed his female patients at the Surrey Asylum and at Bethlem. Diamond was heavily influenced by literary and visual models in his posing of the female subjects. His pictures of madwomen, posed in prayer, or decked with Ophelia-like garlands, were copied for Victorian consumption as touched-up lithographs in professional journals. . . .[30]

Reality, psychiatry, and representational convention were even more confused in the photographic records of hysteria produced in the 1870s by Jean-Martin Charcot. Charcot was the first clinician to install a fully-equipped photographic atelier in his Paris hospital, La Salpêtrière, to record the performances of his hysterical stars. Charcot's clinic became, as he said, a "living theatre" of female pathology; his women patients were coached in their performances for the camera, and, under hypnosis, were sometimes instructed to play heroines from Shakespeare. Among them, a 15-year-old girl named Augustine was featured in the published volumes called *Iconographies* in every posture of *la grande hystérie*. With her white hospital gown and flowing locks, Augustine frequently resembles the reproductions of Ophelia as icon and actress which had been in wide circulation. . . .[31]

But if the Victorian madwoman looks mutely out from men's pictures, and acts a part men had staged and directed, she is very differently represented in the feminist revision of Ophelia initiated by newly powerful and respectable Victorian actresses, and by women critics of Shakespeare. In their efforts to defend Ophelia, they invent a story for her drawn from their own experiences, grievances, and desires.

. . . . .

Probably the most famous of the Victorian feminist revisions of the Ophelia story was Mary Cowden Clarke's *The Girlhood of Shakespeare's Heroines,* published in 1852. Unlike other Victorian moralizing and didactic studies of the female characters of Shakespeare's plays, Clarke's was specifically addressed to the wrongs of women, and especially to the sexual double standard. In a chapter on Ophelia called "The rose of Elsinore," Clarke tells how the child Ophelia was left behind in the care of a peasant couple when Polonius was called to the court at Paris, and raised in a cottage with a foster-sister and brother, Jutha and Ulf. Jutha is seduced and betrayed by a deceitful knight, and Ophelia discovers the bodies of Jutha and her still-born child, lying "white, rigid, and still" in the deserted parlor of the cottage in the middle of the night. Ulf, a "hairy loutish boy," likes to torture flies, to eat songbirds, and to rip the petals off roses, and he is also very eager to give little Ophelia what he calls a bear-hug. Both repelled and masochistically attracted by Ulf, Ophelia is repeatedly concerned by him as she grows up; once she escapes the hug by hitting him with a branch of wild roses; another time, he sneaks into her bedroom "in his brutish pertinacity to obtain the hug he had promised himself," but just as he bends over her trembling body, Ophelia is saved by the reappearance of her real mother.

A few years later, back at the court, she discovers the hanged body of another friend, who has killed herself after being "victimized and deserted by the same evil seducer." Not surprisingly, Ophelia breaks down with brain fever—a staple mental illness of Victorian fiction—and has prophetic hallucinations of a brook beneath willow trees where something bad will happen to her. The warnings of Polonius and Laertes have little to add to this history of female sexual trauma.[32]

On the Victorian stage, it was Ellen Terry, daring and unconventional in her own life, who led the way in acting Ophelia in feminist terms as a consistent psychological study in sexual intimidation, a girl terrified of her father, of her lover, and of life itself. Terry's debut as Ophelia in Henry Irving's production in 1878 was a landmark. According to one reviewer, her Ophelia was "the terrible spectacle of a normal girl becoming hopelessly imbecile as the result of overwhelming mental agony. Hers was an insanity without wrath or rage, without exaltation or paroxysms."[33] Her "poetic and intellectual performance" also inspired other actresses to rebel against the conventions of invisibility and negation associated with the part.

Terry was the first to challenge the tradition of Ophelia's dressing in emblematic white. For the French poets, such as Rimbaud, Hugo, Musset, Mallarmé and Laforgue, whiteness was part of Ophelia's essential feminine symbolism; they call her "blanche Ophélia" and compare her to a lily, a cloud, or snow. Yet whiteness also made her a transparency, an absence that took on the colors of Hamlet's moods, and that, for the symbolists like Mallarmé, made her a blank page to be written over or on by the male imagination. Although Irving was able to prevent Terry from wearing black in the mad scene, exclaiming "My God, Madam, there must be only *one* black figure in this play, and that's Hamlet!" (Irving, of course, was playing Hamlet), nonetheless actresses such as Gertrude Eliot, Helen Maude, Nora de Silva, and in Russia Vera Komisarjevskaya, gradually won the right to intensify Ophelia's presence by clothing her in Hamlet's black.[34]

By the turn of the century, there was both a male and a female discourse on Ophelia. A.C. Bradley spoke for the Victorian male tradition when he noted in *Shakespearean Tragedy* (1906) that "a large number of readers feel a kind of personal irritation against Ophelia; they seem unable to forgive her for not having been a heroine."[35] The feminist counterview was represented by actresses in such works as Helena Faucit's study of Shakespeare's female characters, and *The True Ophelia*, written by an anonymous actress in 1914, which protested against the "insipid little creature" of criticism, and advocated a strong and intelligent woman destroyed by the heartlessness of men.[36] In women's paintings of the *fin de siècle* as well, Ophelia is depicted as an inspiring, even sanctified emblem of righteousness.[37]

While the widely read and influential essays of Mary Cowden Clarke are now mocked as the epitome of naive criticism, these Victorian studies of the girlhood of Shakespeare's heroines are of course alive and well as psychoanalytic criticism, which has imagined its own prehistories of oedipal conflict and neurotic fixation; and I say this not to mock psychoanalytic criticism, but to suggest that Clarke's musings on Ophelia are a pre-Freudian speculation on the traumatic sources of a female sexual identity. The Freudian interpretation of *Hamlet* concentrated on the hero, but also had much to do with the re-sexualization of Ophelia. As early as 1900, Freud had traced Hamlet's irresolution to an Oedipus complex, and Ernest Jones, his leading British disciple, developed this view, influencing the performances of John Gielgud and Alec Guinness in the 1930s. In his final version of the study, *Hamlet and Oedipus,* published in 1949, Jones argued that "Ophelia should be unmistakably sensual, as she seldom is on stage. She may be 'innocent' and docile, but she is very aware of her body."[38]

In the theater and in criticism, this Freudian edict has produced such extreme readings as that Shakespeare intends us to see Ophelia as a loose woman, and that she has been sleeping with Hamlet. Rebecca West has argued that Ophelia was not "a correct and timid virgin of exquisite sensibilities," a view she attributes to the popularity of the Millais painting; but rather "a disreputable young woman."[39] In his delightful autobiography, Laurence Olivier, who made a special pilgrimage to Ernest Jones when he was preparing his *Hamlet* in the 1930s, recalls that one of his predecessors as actor-manager had said in response to the earnest question, "Did Hamlet sleep with Ophelia?"—"In my company, always."[40]

The most extreme Freudian interpretation reads *Hamlet* as two parallel male and female psychodramas, the counterpointed stories of the incestuous attachments of Hamlet and Ophelia. As Theodor Lidz presents this view, while Hamlet is neurotically attached to his mother, Ophelia has an unresolved oedipal attachment to her father. She has fantasies of a lover who will abduct her from or even kill her father, and when this actually happens, her reason is destroyed by guilt as well as by lingering incestuous feelings. According to Lidz, Ophelia breaks down because she fails in the female developmental task of shifting her sexual attachment from her father "to a man who can bring her fulfillment as a woman."[41] We see the effects of this Freudian Ophelia on stage productions since the 1950s, where directors have hinted at an incestuous link between Ophelia and her father, or more recently, because this staging conflicts with the usual ironic treatment of Polonius, between Ophelia and Laertes. Trevor Nunn's production with Helen Mirren in 1970, for example, made Ophelia and Laertes flirtatious doubles, almost twins in their matching fur-trimmed doublets, playing duets on the lute with Polonius looking on, like Peter, Paul, and Mary. In other productions of the same period, Marianne Faithfull was a haggard Ophelia equally attracted to Hamlet and Laertes, and, in one of the few performances directed by a woman, Yvonne Nicholson sat on Laertes' lap in the advice scene, and played the part with "rough sexual bravado."[42]

Since the 1960s, the Freudian representation of Ophelia has been supplemented by an antipsychiatry that represents Ophelia's madness in more contemporary terms. In contrast to the psychoanalytic representation of Ophelia's sexual unconscious that connected her essential femininity to Freud's essays on female sexuality and hysteria, her madness is now seen in medical and biochemical terms, as schizophrenia. This is so in part because the schizophrenic woman has become the cultural icon of dualistic femininity in the mid-twentieth century as the erotomaniac was in the seventeenth and the hysteric in the nineteenth. It might also be traced to the work of R.D. Laing on female schizophrenia in the 1960s. Laing argued that schizophrenia was an intelligible response to the experience of invalidation within the family network, especially to the conflicting emotional messages and mystifying double binds experienced by daughters. Ophelia, he noted in *The Divided Self,* is an empty space. "In her madness there is no one there. . . . There is no integral selfhood expressed through her actions or utterances. Incomprehensible statements are said by nothing. She has already died. There is now only a vacuum where there was once a person."[43]

Despite his sympathy for Ophelia, Laing's readings silence her, equate her with "nothing," more completely than any since the Augustans; and they have been translated into performances which only make Ophelia a graphic study of mental pathology. The sickest Ophelias on the contemporary stage have been those in the productions of the pathologist-director Jonathan Miller. In 1974 at the Greenwich Theatre his Ophelia sucked her thumb; by 1981, at the Warehouse in London, she was played by an actress much taller and heavier than the Hamlet (perhaps punningly cast as the young actor Anton Lesser). She began the play with a set of nervous tics and tuggings of hair which by the mad scene had become a full set of schizophrenic routines—head banging, twitching, wincing, grimacing, and drooling.[44]

But since the 1970s too we have had a feminist discourse which has offered a new perspective on Ophelia's madness as protest and rebellion. For many feminist theorists, the madwoman is a heroine, a powerful figure who rebels against the family and the social order; and the hysteric

who refuses to speak the language of the patriarchal order, who speaks otherwise, is a sister.[45] In terms of effect on the theater, the most radical application of these ideas was probably realized in Melissa Murray's agitprop play *Ophelia,* written in 1979 for the English women's theater group "Hormone Imbalance." In this blank verse retelling of the Hamlet story, Ophelia becomes a lesbian and runs off with a woman servant to join a guerrilla commune.[46]

While I've always regretted that I missed this production, I can't proclaim that this defiant ideological gesture, however effective politically or theatrically, is all that feminist criticism desires, or all to which it should aspire. When feminist criticism chooses to deal with representation, rather than with women's writing, it must aim for a maximum interdisciplinary contextualism, in which the complexity of attitudes towards the feminine can be analyzed in their fullest cultural and historical frame. The alternation of strong and weak Ophelias on the stage, virginal and seductive Ophelias in art, inadequate or oppressed Ophelias in criticism, tells us how these representations have overflowed the text, and how they have reflected the ideological character of their times, erupting as debates between dominant and feminist views in periods of gender crisis and redefinition. The representation of Ophelia changes independently of theories of the meaning of the play or the Prince, for it depends on attitudes towards women and madness. The decorous and pious Ophelia of the Augustan age and the postmodern schizophrenic heroine who might have stepped from the pages of Laing can be derived from the same figure; they are both contradictory and complementary images of female sexuality in which madness seems to act as the "switching-point, the concept which allows the co-existence of both sides of the representation."[47] There is no "true" Ophelia for whom feminist criticism must unambiguously speak, but perhaps only a Cubist Ophelia of multiple perspectives, more than the sum of all her parts.

But in exposing the ideology of representation, feminist critics have also the responsibility to acknowledge and to examine the boundaries of our own ideological positions as products of our gender and our time. A degree of humility in an age of critical hubris can be our greatest strength, for it is by occupying this position of historical self-consciousness in both feminism and criticism that we maintain our credibility in representing Ophelia, and that, unlike Lacan, when we promise to speak about her, we make good our word.

Notes

1. Jacques Lacan, "Desire and the interpretation of desire in *Hamlet,*" in *Literature and Psychoanalysis: The Question of Reading: Otherwise,* ed. Shoshana Felman (Baltimore, 1982), 11, 20, 23. Lacan is also wrong about the etymology of Ophelia, which probably derives from the Greek for "help" or "succour." Charlotte M. Yonge suggested a derivation from "ophis," "serpent." See her *History of Christian*

Names (1884, republished Chicago, 1966), 346-7. I am indebted to Walter Jackson Bate for this reference.

2. Annette Kolodny, "Dancing through the minefield: some observations on the theory, practice, and politics of feminist literary criticism" (*Feminist Studies,* 6 (1980)), 7.

3. Carol Neely, "Feminist modes of Shakespearean criticism" (*Women's Studies,* 9 (1981)), 11.

4. Lee Edwards, "The labors of Psyche" (*Critical Inquiry,* 6 (1979)), 36.

5. Luce Irigaray: see *New French Feminisms,* ed. Elaine Marks and Isabelle de Courtivron (New York, 1982), 101. The quotation above, from III. ii, is taken from the Arden Shakespeare, *Hamlet,* ed. Harold Jenkins (London and New York, 1982), 295. All quotations from *Hamlet* are from this text.

6. On images of negation and feminine enclosure, see David Wilbern, "Shakespeare's 'nothing'," in *Representing Shakespeare: New Psychoanalytic Essays,* ed. Murray M. Schwartz and Coppélia Kahn (Baltimore, 1981).

7. David Leverenz, "The woman in *Hamlet:* an interpersonal view" (*Signs,* 4 (1978)), 303.

8. James Joyce, *Ulysses* (New York, 1961), 76.

9. Sander L. Gilman, *Seeing the Insane* (New York, 1981), 126.

10. See Michael Goldman, *The Actor's Freedom: Toward a Theory of Drama* (New York, 1975), for a stimulating discussion of the interpretative interaction between actor and audience.

11. Bridget Lyons, "The iconography of Ophelia" (*English Literary History,* 44 (1977), 61.

12. See Maurice and Hanna Charney, "The language of Shakespeare's madwomen" (*Signs,* 3 (1977)), 451, 457; and Carroll Camden, "On Ophelia's madness" (*Shakespeare Quarterly* (1964)), 254.

13. See Margery Garber, *Coming of Age in Shakespeare* (London, 1981), 155-7; and Lyons, op. cit., 65, 70-2.

14. On dishevelled hair as a signifier of madness or rape, see Charney and Charney, op. cit., 452-3, 457; and Allan Dessen, *Elizabethan Stage Conventions and Modern Interpreters* (Cambridge, 1984), 36-8. Thanks to Allan Dessen for letting me see advance proofs of his book.

15. Charney and Charney, op. cit., 456.

16. Gaston Bachelard, *L'Eau et les rêves* (Paris, 1942), 109-25. See also Brigitte Peucker, "Dröste-Hulshof's Ophelia and the recovery of voice" (*The Journal of English and Germanic Philology* (1983)), 374-91.

17. Vieda Skultans, *English Madness: Ideas on Insanity 1580-1890* (London, 1977), 79-81. On historical cases of love-melancholy, see Michael MacDonald, *Mystical Bedlam* (Cambridge, 1982).

18. C.E.L. Wingate, *Shakespeare's Heroines on the Stage* (New York, 1895), 283-4, 288-9.

19. Charles Hiatt, *Ellen Terry* (London, 1898), 11.

20. Max Byrd, *Visits to Bedlam: Madness and Literature in the Eighteenth Century* (Columbia, 1974), xiv.

21. Peter Raby, *Fair Ophelia: Harriet Smithson Berlioz* (Cambridge, 1982), 63.

22. Ibid., 68.

23. Ibid., 72, 75.

24. Quoted in Camden, op. cit., 247.

25. Raby, op. cit., 182.

26. J. C. Bucknill, *The Psychology of Shakespeare* (London, 1859, reprinted New York, 1970), 110. For more extensive discussions of Victorian psychiatry and Ophelia figures, see Elaine Showalter, *The Female Malady: Women, Madness and English Culture* (New York, forthcoming 1985).

27. John Conolly, *Study of Hamlet* (London, 1863), 177.

28. Ibid., 177-8, 180.

29. Ellen Terry, *The Story of My Life* (London, 1908), 154.

30. Diamond's photographs are reproduced in Sander L. Gilman, *The Face of Madness: Hugh W. Diamond and the Origin of Psychiatric Photography* (New York, 1976).

31. See Georges Didi-Huberman, *L'Invention de l'hystérie* (Paris, 1982), and Stephen Heath, *The Sexual Fix* (London, 1983), 36.

32. Mary Cowden Clarke, *The Girlhood of Shakespeare's Heroines* (London, 1852). See also George C. Gross, "Mary Cowden Clarke, *The Girlhood of Shakespeare's Heroines,* and the sex education of Victorian women" (*Victorian Studies,* 16 (1972)), 37-58, and Nina Auerbach, *Woman and the Demon* (Cambridge, Mass., 1983), 210-15.

33. Hiatt, op. cit., 114. See also Wingate, op. cit., 304-5.

34. Terry, op. cit., 155-6.

35. Andrew C. Bradley, *Shakespearean Tragedy* (London, 1906), 160.

36. Helena Faucit Martin, *On Some of Shakespeare's Female Characters* (Edinburgh and London, 1891), 4, 18; and *The True Ophelia* (New York, 1914), 15.

37. Among these paintings are the Ophelias of Henrietta Rae and Mrs F. Littler. Sarah Bernhardt sculpted a bas relief of Ophelia for the Women's Pavilion at the Chicago World's Fair in 1893.

38. Ernest Jones, *Hamlet and Oedipus* (New York, 1949), 139.

39. Rebecca West, *The Court and the Castle* (New Haven, 1958), 18.

40. Laurence Olivier, *Confessions of an Actor* (Harmondsworth, 1982), 102, 152.

41. Theodor Lidz, *Hamlet's Enemy: Madness and Myth in Hamlet* (New York, 1975), 88, 113.

42. Richard David, *Shakespeare in the Theatre* (Cambridge, 1978), 75. This was the production directed by Buzz Goodbody, a brilliant young feminist radical who killed herself that year. See Colin Chambers, *Other Spaces: New Theatre and the RSC* (London, 1980), especially 63-7.

43. R.D. Laing, *The Divided Self* (Harmondsworth, 1965), 195n.

44. David, op. cit., 82-3; thanks to Marianne DeKoven, Rutgers University, for the description of the 1981 Warehouse production.

45. See, for example, Hélène Cixous and Catherine Clément, *La Jeune Née* (Paris, 1975).

46. For an account of this production, see Micheline Wandor, *Understudies: Theatre and Sexual Politics* (London, 1981), 47.

47. I am indebted for this formulation to a critique of my earlier draft of this paper by Carl Friedman, at the Wesleyan Center for the Humanities, April 1984.

Ann Thompson and Neil Taylor (essay date 1996)

SOURCE: "*Hamlet* and Gender," in *William Shakespeare: Hamlet,* Northcote House, 1996, pp. 42-50.

[*In the following essay, Thompson and Taylor review the shifting critical attitudes to the female characters in* Hamlet.]

'A female Hamlet is one thing but a pregnant prince is quite another' says Dora Chance in Angela Carter's novel *Wise Children* (1991). Dora and her identical twin sister Nora are stars of vaudeville and illegitimate daughters of Sir Melchior Hazard, the great Shakespearean actor. The novel contains many references to *Hamlet,* including the moment when the hero's most celebrated soliloquy becomes the inspiration for a song and dance routine with the two sisters dressed as bellhops in a hotel corridor, debating whether a package should be delivered to '2b or not 2b' (p. 90). The pregnant prince (in this case Dora's and Nora's grandmother Estella Hazard, pregnant with their natural father Melchior and his twin brother Peregrine, who passes for their father) belongs to the level of subversive fantasy and the cheerful appropriation of Shakespeare's texts by twentieth-century low culture, but in fact the notion of Hamlet as female has a lengthy history in the critical and theatrical reception of the play.

Hamlet himself, . . . sees his inaction in general and his verbosity in particular as effeminate in his soliloquy after his first encounter with the Players:

> Why, what an ass am I! This is most brave,
> That I, the son of a dear father murthered,
> Prompted to my revenge by heaven and hell,

> Must like a whore unpack my heart with words,
> And fall a-cursing like a very drab.

> (II. ii. 582-6)

As Patricia Parker points out in *Literary Fat Ladies,*

> In the traditional opposition of genders in which 'Women are words, men deeds', Hamlet's comparison of his verbal and deedless delay to the impotent anger of a 'drab' [prostitute] sets up a link between his entire period of inactivity and delay and womanish wordiness, in contrast to such one-dimensional emblems of masculinity as Laertes and the aptly named Fort-in-bras [strong-in-arms].

> (1987, p. 23)

Much later, just before the fatal duel with Laertes, Hamlet dismisses his sense of 'how ill all's here about my heart' as 'such a kind of gaingiving [misgiving], as would perhaps trouble a woman' (V. ii. 212-16). He sees his own behaviour and his capacity for feeling as more appropriate to a woman than to a man, but is behaving and feeling like a woman the same as being a woman? Fears about Hamlet's apparent lack of essential masculinity have often been expressed by critics who focus on his weakness, his vacillation, his melancholy—all seen as feminine traits. Goethe was apparently the first to say that Hamlet was 'part woman', and an extensive critical tradition draws on what now looks like fairly crude gender stereotyping to perpetuate this point. It came to a climax in 1881 with the publication of Edward P. Vining's book *The Mystery of Hamlet,* which developed the theory that in revising his play Shakespeare dallied with the idea that Hamlet was in fact born female and was educated from infancy to impersonate a male. This book inspired the fine silent film version directed in Germany by Sven Gade and Heinz Schall in 1920 in which Asta Nielsen played the hero precisely as a princess passed off as a prince by her mother, anxious to secure the succession when it is feared just as she is giving birth that Old Hamlet has been killed by Old Fortinbras. . . .

Those who have written about this film, both when it was released and more recently, have insisted on its distance from Shakespeare, though it is in fact closer to the text than they allow, and provides some fascinating reflections on gender issues in the play. But on the stage too a large number of women have acted Hamlet (as a man, that is), from Sarah Siddons in 1776 and Elizabeth Edmead in 1792 to at least Frances de la Tour in 1979 and Diane Venora in 1983. And these were not necessarily seen as freakish or one-off performances: Siddons played Hamlet in Birmingham, Manchester, Liverpool, Bristol, and Dublin between 1776 and 1802, while Millicent Bandmann-Palmer performed the part over a thousand times from 1887 to 1902; she is referred to in James Joyce's *Ulysses* when John Eglinton tells Stephen Daedalus that 'an actress played Hamlet for the fourhundredandeighth time last night in Dublin'. There was serious acclaim for actresses such as Charlotte Cushman (from 1848), Alice Marriott (from 1861) and Sarah Bernhardt (from 1899) in the role during the nineteenth century (see Jill Edmonds, 'Princess Hamlet', in Gardner and Rutherford, eds., *The New Woman and Her Sisters,* 1992).

Many of these women were in the position of actor-managers and could choose to play Hamlet simply because it was the best part available, but they also exploited what was seen as a feminine ability to convey the interiority of the character and to do justice to Hamlet's romantic sensitivity. The dominant view of Hamlet as a poetic dreamer, played even by male actors as an aesthetic, even pre-Raphaelite figure, no doubt helped to make these interpretations acceptable. Eugène Delacroix apparently used a female model for his lithographs of Hamlet in 1834-45. . . . (see Foakes, *'Hamlet' versus 'Lear',* 1993, p. 23). By 1979 however Frances de la Tour's performance was admired for quite different qualities. As one reviewer put it: 'She is tough, abrasive, virile and impassioned. Indeed it's a good performance compact with every female virtue except femininity' (Michael Billington, *The Guardian,* 20 October 1979). Asked about the phenomenon of women playing Hamlet fifteen years later, de la Tour herself explained

> I think it is because it is universal youth, expressing all the emotions of youth and of life, and there isn't another part to match it . . . There would be no need and no desire for a woman to play Lear. It's not the same as Hamlet.

> (*The Observer Review Extra,* 9 October 1994, and BBC2 programme *Playing the Dane,* broadcast 30 October 1994)

But Hamlet's own misogyny remains an issue. 'Frailty, thy name is woman!' he says (I. ii. 146) when he is left alone on stage at the end of the second scene of the play to reflect on the speed with which his widowed mother has married his uncle. Later he exclaims 'O most pernicious woman!' (I. v. 105) on hearing the Ghost's tale of Gertrude's 'falling off' from the 'celestial bed' of her first marriage to the 'garbage' and 'damned incest' of her second (I. v. 56-7, 83). Similarly, he feels betrayed by Ophelia who in obedience to her father rejects his attentions and returns his letters and gifts. Reserving his idealization for men (his dead father and Horatio), he attacks both women vehemently, Ophelia in the 'nunnery' scene (III. i) and Gertrude in the 'closet' scene (III. iv), on both occasions evoking a somewhat baffled response in so far as the women do not seem to be absolutely clear what they are being accused of. Some editors and directors have felt it necessary to bring Hamlet onstage early in III. i so that he overhears Polonius and the King plotting to spy on him and his anger against Ophelia becomes motivated by her complicity in this. Ophelia herself clearly cannot understand his attitude but can only attribute it to madness (III. i. 151-62).

Gertrude, three scenes later, admits and regrets what she has already described as her 'o'erhasty marriage' (II. ii. 57), but seems sincerely shocked—'As kill a king!' (III. iv. 30)—by her son's suggestion that she was actually implicated in the murder of her first husband. Curiously, they neither of them pursue this more serious charge which is also implied by the Player Queen's line 'None wed the second but who killed the first' (III. ii. 180), while the Ghost's repeated admonitions to Hamlet to 'Leave her to heaven' (I. v. 86) and to 'step between her and her fighting soul' (III. iv. 113) would seem if anything to attest to Gertrude's relative innocence. The focus is instead on Hamlet's disgust at his mother's sexual activity 'In the rank sweat of an enseamed bed' (III. iv. 92) and his insistence that she begin to practise celibacy: 'Let not the bloat king tempt you again to bed' (III. iv. 182).

Hamlet's priggish attitude here—'You cannot call it love, for at your age / The heyday in the blood is tame, it's humble, / And waits upon the judgment' (III. iv. 68-70) has been endorsed by critics and editors who worry about Gertrude's age, and indeed Hamlet's since, as they see it, if he is really thirty as the Gravedigger says (V. i. 142-62), she must be too old to excite the King's interest. It seems typical of her opacity as a character, or perhaps of the play's refusal to present her other than through Hamlet's eyes, that we do not know what impact this conversation has on her. While she seems to accept Hamlet's harsh judgement in this scene, and to be prepared to obey his commands and keep his secrets, her relationship with the King through the remainder of the play seems unchanged—or at least there is no clear indication in the text that they have become estranged, though some productions do play it in this way. Nor is it clear why in the last scene she becomes what Janet Adelman calls

> a wonderfully homey presence for her son, newly available to him as the loving and protective mother of his childhood, worrying about his condition, wiping his face as he fights, even perhaps intentionally drinking the poison intended for him.

> (*Suffocating Mothers,* 1992, p. 34)

The fact that this last suggestion has been made quite often, again without any clear warrant from the text, seems an indication of how baffled critics are by Gertrude. It is also an option in the stage tradition, though it is quite a challenge for the performer to convey this intention to the audience by meaningful looks at a point when attention is more likely to be focused on Hamlet. Nineteenth-century Gertrudes sometimes said 'I have [drunk]' rather than 'I will', apparently to soften the act of deliberate disobedience to the King, and even then might be sent offstage to die. The entire role was severely and quite consistently cut from 1755 to 1900 (and frequently after that) in such a way as to eliminate any possibility of Gertrude being affected by the closet scene encounter with Hamlet (see O'Brien, 'Revision by Excision', in *Shakespeare Survey 45,* 1992). The 1920 film goes to the other extreme from the self-sacrificing mother in having Gertrude deliberately prepare the poison for her daughter Hamlet who has by this time already been responsible for the death of the King.

The extent and nature of the guilt projected on to Gertrude and by association on to Ophelia and indeed all women has much exercised the play's psychoanalytic critics. Freud saw Hamlet as a hysteric and many Freudians have offered interpretations which tease out parricidal or matricidal motives. Ernest Jones provided the classic Oedipal reading of the play in 1949, arguing that Hamlet is unable to kill the King because he represents the fulfilment of Hamlet's own repressed erotic desire for his mother. In her essay on 'Sexuality in the Reading of Shakespeare' (in Drakakis, ed., *Alternative Shakespeares*) Jacqueline Rose traces how influential male readers of the play—T.S. Eliot as well as Ernest Jones and the Freudians—have echoed Hamlet's misogyny and blamed Gertrude for what they saw as the aesthetic and moral failings of the play overall. Picking up on Eliot's analogy for *Hamlet* as 'the Mona Lisa of literature', she argues that in his reading

> the question of the woman and the question of meaning go together. The problem with *Hamlet* is not just that the emotion it triggers is unmanageable and cannot be contained by the woman who is its cause, but that this excess of affect produces a problem of interpretation: how to read, or control by reading, a play whose inscrutability (like that of the *Mona Lisa*) has baffled—and seduced—so many critics.

(pp. 97-8)

Femininity itself becomes the problem within the play, and within attempts to interpret it, but paradoxically femininity is also seen as the source of creativity and the very principle of the aesthetic process in other psychoanalytic readings in which the focus shifts from character to author: Shakespeare, unlike his hero, can be claimed to have effected a productive reconciliation with the feminine in his own nature.

Modern male editors of the play are not necessarily more enlightened when it comes to talking about the women. Harold Jenkins remarks condescendingly of Ophelia that, rejected by Hamlet, she has 'little left to do . . . but to bewail her virginity . . . Her tragedy of course is that Hamlet has left her treasure with her' (Arden 2, pp. 151-2). G.R. Hibbard quotes this approvingly, adding that, as a virgin, she dies 'unfulfilled'. Moreover, he says, 'It is Ophelia's tragic fate to pay the price in pain and suffering for Gertrude's sins' (this despite the fact that he is very confident she was not privy to the murder), and goes on, 'Woman's sexuality has evidently become an obsession with [Hamlet]; and to this extent at least he is genuinely mad' (Oxford edition, p. 51). Surely such a definition of madness would include a sizeable proportion of the men in any given audience of the play?

The fate of Ophelia, specifically the scene of her drowning ('There is a willow grows askaunt the brook') is paradoxically one of the most vivid, iconic moments in the play. . . . Paradoxically, because it is not of course staged but rather described by Gertrude in elaborate detail (IV. vii. 166-83), shocking perhaps to the naturalistically trained 'modern reader [who] cannot suppress his astonishment that Gertrude should have watched Ophelia die without lifting a finger to help her' (Edwards, New Cambridge edi-

tion, 1985, p. 212). It has become familiar through decorative, dreamy paintings such as the one by John Everett Millais in the Tate Gallery in London, and it does tend to be represented in film and video versions of the play; Eleuterio Rodolfi was clearly inspired by Millais for the depiction of the death of Ophelia in his 1917 film (which has Pre-Raphaelite decor throughout), as was Olivier in 1948. Unfortunately, suicide by drowning has also become a typically feminine death, both in real life, from Mary Wollstonecraft's failed attempt in 1795 to Virginia Woolf's successful one in 1941, and in fiction, from the Jailer's Daughter (another failed attempt) in Fletcher's and Shakespeare's *The Two Noble Kinsmen* in 1614 to Edna Pontellier in Kate Chopin's *The Awakening* (1899) and beyond.

In his identification of the 'Ophelia complex' Gaston Bachelard discussed the symbolic connections between women, water, and death, seeing drowning as an appropriate merging into the female element for women who are always associated with liquids: blood, milk, tears, and amniotic fluid. Moreover, as Elaine Showalter has demonstrated, the particular circumstances of Ophelia's madness have made her 'a potent and obsessive figure in our cultural mythology': she represents a powerful archetype in which female insanity and female sexuality are inextricably intertwined. Men may go mad for a number of reasons, including mental and spiritual stress, but women's madness is relentlessly associated with their bodies and their erotic desires. As Showalter notes, melancholy was a fashionable disease (or attitude) among young men in London from about 1580, but it was associated with intellectual and imaginative genius in them, whereas 'women's melancholy was seen instead as biological and emotional in its origins' ('Representing Ophelia' in Parker and Hartman, eds., *Shakespeare and the Question of Theory,* 1985, p. 81). The very word 'hysteria' implies a female, physiological condition, originating as it does from Greek 'hystera' meaning womb. King Lear, fighting off his own impending madness, equates '*Hysterica passio*' with the medical condition involving feelings of suffocation and giddiness known as 'the mother' (II. iv. 56-7). (See also Juliana Schiesari, *The Gendering of Melancholia,* 1992.)

On stage and in critical reception, Showalter argues that 'the representation of Ophelia changes independently of theories of the meaning of the play or the Prince, for it depends on attitudes towards women and madness' (pp. 91-2). She traces how stereotypes of female insanity affected the staging of the mad scene (IV. v), from sentimentalized Augustan versions through intense Romanticism to Pre-Raphaelite wistfulness. Post-Freudian Ophelias have signalled an incestuous interest in Polonius or Laertes, while the most recent performers have indicated schizophrenia, either as a serious mental illness or (in a feminist appropriation of the work of R.D. Laing) as an intelligible response to the experience of invalidation or the double bind within the family network.

When the well-known American feminist Carolyn Heilbrun reprinted her essay on 'Hamlet's Mother' in 1990 and used it as the lead piece in her book *Hamlet's Mother and Other Women,* she noted that when she first published it in 1957 she was 'a feminist critic waiting for a cause to join'. Her basic line in the essay was that critics and readers of the play have been too ready to accept Hamlet's view of Gertrude without questioning whether the overall view taken by the play (or its author) might be different. Many have joined the cause since 1975, the publication date of Juliet Dusinberre's *Shakespeare and the Nature of Women,* the first full-length feminist study of Shakespeare, and the date selected by Philip C. Kolin as the starting point for his annotated bibliography of *Shakespeare and Feminist Criticism* which lists forty-four items relating to *Hamlet* published between 1975 and his cut-off point in 1988. (More have of course appeared since.) This total is lower than those for *The Merchant of Venice* (forty-eight), *As You Like It* (fifty), *The Winter's Tale* (fifty-eight) and *Othello* (sixty-nine), and only just ahead of *The Taming of the Shrew* (forty-three), testifying to the prominence given to comedy in this period of feminist criticism, and the dominance of *Othello* amongst the tragedies. (*King Lear* gets thirty-eight items, *Antony and Cleopatra* thirty-four, and *Macbeth* thirty-three.)

Most of the items on *Hamlet* in these first thirteen years of feminist criticism are studies of the female characters—of Gertrude as a rare and problematic example of a Shakespearian mother, and of Ophelia as a victim, weak and silenced. This last adjective is perhaps surprising, given the extent to which her discovery of a voice in her madness causes the other characters considerable stress and embarrassment, but the obscenity and sexual innuendo in Ophelia's songs has still not been properly addressed by feminist critics although they are surely not as worried by it as nineteenth-century readers who felt the need to invent rustic wet-nurses for Ophelia's childhood (like the Nurse in *Romeo and Juliet*) to account for her knowledge of such things.

Some more general essays discuss the larger issues of femininity and masculinity in the play, covering such areas as the supposed effeminacy of Hamlet himself and the desire for male bonding, especially in Hamlet's relationship with Horatio. Many of the authors (especially those from North America) could be described as psychoanalytic critics as well as feminist critics and they are concerned to investigate the overlapping territories of language, fantasy, and sexuality. This emphasis has continued in post-1988 writing, though, . . . recent feminist critics have also been concerned with questions of history and staging.

Given that the majority of students of literature today are female as well as an increasing number of their teachers, it is probably the case that feminist critics have been responsible for the reordering of the canon, whereby a play like *Hamlet* with its relatively simplistic views of women as angels or whores becomes less interesting as a text to teach and/or write about. We are perhaps more critical of crude gender stereotypes, and while this can make for more interesting performances by actors who can

allow Hamlet to be sensitive as well as virile without making the two mutually exclusive, students today (male as well as female) find it more difficult to empathize with a hero who seems so casual in his cruelty to the women in his life.

On a more positive note, the present critical climate may offer more scope for investigation of the phenomenon whereby Hamlet has been seen as effeminate in the past partly because he was seen as an intellectual: for a man to be intellectual was to be womanish, while at the same time it certainly did not follow that actual women were seen as intellectual, or that intellectual women were seen as anything other than unnatural. It should be possible for modern feminist critics to reassess at least this aspect of gender stereotyping in a more positive way as they both analyse and contribute to the extraordinarily rich afterlife of the play.

LANGUAGE AND IMAGERY

Richard A. Lanham (essay date 1976)

SOURCE: "Superposed Plays: *Hamlet,*" in *Shakespeare's Middle Tragedies: A Collection of Critical Essays,* edited by David Young, Prentice Hall, 1993, pp. 18-28.

[*In the following essay, originally published in 1976, Lanham traces the use of rhetoric in* Hamlet *and investigates the relation between elaborate and theatrical rhetoric in the play.*]

Shakespeare uses a variation on the sonnets strategy in *Hamlet.* He writes two plays in one. Laertes plays the revenge-tragedy hero straight. He does, true enough, veer toward self-parody, as when he complains that crying for Ophelia has interfered with his rants: "I have a speech o' fire, that fain would blaze / But that this folly drowns it" (4.7.189-90). But he knows his generic duty and does it. No sooner has his "good old man" (Polonius's role in the straight, "serious" play) been polished off than he comes screaming with a rabble army. He delivers predictably and suitably stupid lines like "O thou vile king, / Give me my father" (4.5.115-16). And the Queen can scarcely manage a "Calmly, good Laertes" before he begins again: "That drop of blood that's calm proclaims me bastard, / Cries cuckold to my father, brands the harlot / Even here between the chaste unsmirchèd brows / Of my true mother" (4.5.117-20). And just before the King begins to calm him, to the villainous contentation of both: "How came he dead? I'll not be juggled with. / To hell allegiance, vows to the blackest devil, / Conscience and grace to the profoundest pit!" (4.5.130-32). He plays a straight, hard-charging revenge-hero.

Against him, Ophelia reenacts a delightfully tear-jerking madwoman stage prop. The King mouths kingly platitudes well enough ("There's such divinity doth hedge a king . . ." [4.5.123]), comes up with a suitably stagey, two-phase fail-safe plot, and urges the hero on ("Revenge should have no bounds"). And the whole comes suitably laced with moralizing guff. So the King plays a Polonius-of-the-leading-questions: "Laertes, was your father dear to you?" Laertes, with unusual common sense, returns, "Why ask you this?" And then the King is off for a dozen Polonian lines on love's alteration by time: "Not that I think you did not love your father, / But that I know love is begun by time . . ." 4.7.109-10. Only then can he get back to, as he phrases it, "the quick o' th' ulcer." And the Queen plays out a careful scene on the brookside where Ophelia drowned. And wrestling in Ophelia's grave, Hamlet, annoyed at being upstaged by Laertes, protests, "I'll rant as well as thou." And, as superb finale, Laertes, at the fencing match, stands there prating about honor with the poisoned rapier in his hand. The poisoner-poisoned motif releases the Christian forgiveness that forgives us, too, for enjoying all that blood. *Hamlet* offers, then, a story frankly calculated to make the audience as well as the compositor run out of exclamation points.

Hamlet obligingly confesses himself Laertes' foil. "In mine ignorance / Your skill shall, like a star i'th'darkest night, / Stick fiery off indeed" (5.2.244-46). It is the other way about, of course. Laertes foils for Hamlet. Shakespeare is up to his old chiasmatic business, writing a play about the kind of play he is writing. The main play overlaps as well as glossing the play criticized—again, a strategy of superposition. Polonius plays a muddling old proverb-monger, and a connoisseur of language, in the Hamlet play, as well as good old man in the Laertes play. Ophelia, though sentimental from the start, is both more naive and more duplicitous in the Hamlet play; and so with the King and Queen, too, both are more complex figures. Shakespeare endeavors especially to wire the two plots in parallel: two avenging sons and two dead fathers; brother's murder and "this brother's wager"; both Hamlet and Laertes in love with Ophelia; both dishonest before the duel (Hamlet pretending more madness than he displays when he kills Polonius), and so on.

Now there is no doubt about how to read the Laertes play: straight revenge tragedy, to be taken—as I've tried to imply in my summary—without solemnity. We are to enjoy the rants as rants. When we get tears instead of a rant, as with the Laertes instance cited earlier, an apology for our disappointment does not come amiss. We are not to be caught up in Laertes' vigorous feeling any more than in Ophelia's bawdy punning. We savor it. We don't believe the fake King when he maunders on about Divine Right, the divinity that doth hedge a king. We don't "believe" anybody. It is not that kind of play. For explanation, neither the ketchup nor the verbal violence need go further than enjoyment. The more outrageous the stage effects, the more ghastly the brutality, the more grotesque the physical mutilation, the better such a play becomes. Shakespeare

had done this kind of thing already and knew what he was about. Such a vehicle packed them in. Just so, when part-sales were falling, would Dickens kill a baby.

The real doubt comes when we ask, "What poetic do we bring to the Hamlet play?" As several of its students have pointed out, it is a wordy play. Eloquence haunts it. Horatio starts the wordiness by supplying a footnote from ancient Rome in the first scene, by improving the occasion with informative reflection. Everybody laughs at Polonius for his moralizing glosses but Hamlet is just as bad. Worse. Gertrude asks him, in the second scene, why he grieves to excess and he gives us a disquisition on seeming and reality in grief. The King follows with *his* bravura piece on grief. Everybody moralizes the pageant. The Hamlet play abounds with triggers for straight revenge-tragedy response. The whole "mystery" of Hamlet's hesitant revenge boils down to wondering why he doesn't go ahead and play his traditional part, complete with the elegant rants we know he can deliver.

The rhetorical attitude is triggered not only by obvious stylistic excess, as we have seen, or by *de trop* moralizing, but by talking about language, by surface reference to surface. This surface reference occurs at every level of the Hamlet play in *Hamlet,* as well as, of course, throughout the Laertes play. Polonius plays a main part here. His tedious prolixity ensures that we notice everyone else's tedious prolixity. And his relish of language, his speech for its own sake, makes us suspect the same appetite in others and in ourselves. The Queen's rejoinder to the marvelous "brevity is the soul of wit" speech in 2.2 could be addressed to almost anybody in the play, including the gravedigger: "More matter, with less art."

Everyone is manipulating everyone else with speechifying and then admitting he has done so. Every grand rhetorical occasion seems no sooner blown than blasted. Polonius offers the famous Gielgud encore about being true to oneself and then sends off Reynaldo to spy and tell fetching lies. The King plays king to angry Laertes then confesses to Gertrude that he has been doing just this. Ophelia is staked out to play innocent maiden so Hamlet can be drawn out and observed. *Hic et ubique.* Is she a stage contrivance or a character? What kind of audience are we to be? Everyone is an actor, Hamlet and his madness most of all. The play is full of minor invitations to attend the surface, the theme of speaking. Even the ghost has to remind himself to be brief—before continuing for thirty-odd lines (1.5). Theatrical gestures are not simply used all the time but described, as in Hamlet's inky cloak and windy suspiration for grief, or the costuming and gesture of the distracted lover, as the innocent Ophelia describes Hamlet's visit:

> My lord, as I was sewing in my closet,
> Lord Hamlet, with his doublet all unbraced,
> No hat upon his head, his stockings fouled,
> Ungartered, and down-gyvèd to his ankle,
> Pale as his shirt, his knees knocking each other,
> And with a look so piteous in purport
> As if he had been loosèd out of hell

To speak of horrors—he comes before me.

. . . . .

He took me by the wrist and held me hard.
Then goes he to the length of all his arm,
And with his other hand thus o'er his brow
He falls to such perusal of my face
As 'a would draw it. Long stayed he so.
At last, a little shaking of mine arm
And thrice his head thus waving up and down,
He raised a sigh so piteous and profound
As it did seem to shatter all his bulk
And end his being. That done, he lets me go,
And with his head over his shoulder turned
He seemed to find his way without his eyes,
For out o'doors he went without their helps
And to the last bended their light on me.

(2.1.77-84, 87-100)

This might have come from an actor's manual. Do we take it as such, respond as professional actors?

The Hamlet play turns in on itself most obviously when the players visit. Dramatic self-consciousness retrogresses a step further as the tragedians of the city talk about themselves doing what they are just now doing in a play depicting them doing just what. . . . The debate is about rightful succession, of course, like both the Laertes and the Hamlet plays. "What, are they children? Who maintains 'em? How are they escoted? Will they pursue the quality no longer than they can sing? Will they not say afterwards, if they should grow themselves to common players (as it is most like, if their means are no better), their writers do them wrong to make them exclaim against their own succession?" (2.2.338-44). Who are the children in the "real" plays? Hamlet had invoked a typical cast a few lines earlier (314 ff.) such as *Hamlet* itself uses and stressed that "he that plays the king shall be welcome." Hamlet will use the play, that is, *as a weapon,* the propaganda side of rhetorical poetic, to complement the Polonius-pleasure side. But before that, there is a rehearsal, for effect, to see whether the players are good enough to play the play within the play. Here, even more clearly than in the Laertes play, we confront the connoisseur's attitude toward language. Polonius supplies a chorus that for once fits: "Fore God, my lord, well spoken, with good accent and good discretion" (2.2.454-55). This to Hamlet, a good actor, as Polonius was in his youth. They proceed in this vein, nibbling the words; "That's good. 'Mobled queen' is good."

The main question pressing is not, How does the feedback work? What relation is there, for example, between rugged Pyrrhus and Hamlet, or Laertes? Or what relation with the King, who also topples a kingdom? And why is Hamlet so keen to reach Hecuba? The main question is, How does all this connoisseurship affect the "serious" part of *Hamlet*? *Hamlet* is one of the great tragedies. It has generated more comment than any other written document in English literature, one would guess, reverent, serious comment on it as a serious play. Yet finally can we take *any* of its rhetoric seriously? If so, how much and when? The play is full of the usual release mechanisms for the rhetorical

poetic. And, at the end, the Laertes play is there as stylistic control, to mock us if we have made the naive response. But what is the sophisticated response?

Hamlet focuses the issue, and the play, the plays, when he finally gets to Hecuba. He who has been so eager for a passionate speech is yet surprised when it comes and when it seizes the player:

O, what a rogue and peasant slave am I!
Is it not monstrous that this player here,
But in a fiction, in a dream of passion,
Could force his soul so to his own conceit
That from her working all his visage wanned,
Tears in his eyes, distraction in his aspect,
A broken voice, and his whole function suiting
With forms to his conceit? And all for nothing,
For Hecuba!
What's Hecuba to him, or he to Hecuba,
That he should weep for her? What would he do
Had he the motive and the cue for passion
That I have?

(2.2.534-46)

Hamlet makes the point that dances before us in every scene. Dramatic, rhetorical motive is stronger than "real," serious motive. Situation prompts feeling in this play, rather than the other way round. Feelings are not real until played. Drama, ceremony, is always needed to authenticate experience. On the battlements Hamlet—with ghostly reinforcement—makes his friends not simply swear but make a big scene of it. Laertes keeps asking for *more ceremonies* for Ophelia's burial and is upset by his father's hugger-mugger interment. Hamlet plays and then breaks off ("Something too much of this") a stoic friendship scene with Horatio in 3.2. The stronger, the more genuine the feeling, the greater the need to display it.

The answer, then, to "What would he do . . . ?" is, presumably, "Kill the King!"? Not at all. "He would drown the stage with tears / And cleave the general ear with horrid speech" (2.2.546-47). He would rant even better. And this Hamlet himself, by way of illustration, goes on to do:

Yet I,
A dull and muddy-mettled rascal, peak
Like John-a-dreams, unpregnant of my cause,
And can say nothing. No, not for a king,
Upon whose property and most dear life
A damned defeat was made. Am I a coward?
Who calls me villain? breaks my pate across?
Plucks off my beard and blows it in my face?
Tweaks me by the nose? gives me the lie i'th'throat
As deep as to the lungs? Who does me this?
Ha, 'swounds, I should take it, for it cannot be
But I am pigeon-livered and lack gall
To make oppression bitter, or ere this
I should ha' fatted all the region kites
With this slave's offal. Bloody, bawdy villain!
Remorseless, treacherous, lecherous, kindless villain!
O, vengeance!

(2.2.551-67)

Hamlet is here having a fine time dining off his own fury, relishing his sublime passion. He gets a bit confused, to be sure: saying nothing is not his problem. If somebody did call him villain or pluck his beard it would be better, for his grievance would then find some dramatic equivalent, would become real enough to act upon. But he enjoys himself thoroughly. He also sees himself clearly, or at least clearly enough to voice our opinion of his behavior: "Why, what an ass am I! This is most brave, / That I, the son of a dear father murdered, / Prompted to my revenge by heaven and hell, / Must like a whore unpack my heart with words" (2.2.568-71).

Hamlet is one of the most appealing characters the mind of man has ever created but he really is a bit of an ass, and not only here but all through the play. He remains incorrigibly dramatic. Do we like him because he speaks to our love of dramatic imposture? Because his solution, once he has seen his own posturing as such, is not immediate action but more playing? "I'll have these players / Play something like the murder of my father / Before mine uncle" (2.2.580-82). Playing is where we will find reality, find the truth. The play works, of course, tells Hamlet again what he already knows, has had a spirit come specially from purgatory to tell him. But that is not the point. Or rather, that is the point insofar as this is a serious play. The rhetorical purpose is to sustain reality until yet another dramatic contrivance—ship, grave scene, duel—can sustain it yet further.

We saw in the sonnets how a passage can invoke opaque attitudes by logical incongruity. Something of the sort happens in the scene after this speech, the "To be or not to be" centerpiece. Plays flourish within plays here, too, of course. The King and Polonius dangle Ophelia as bait and watch. Hamlet sees this. He may even be, as W.A. Bebbington suggested,[1] reading the "To be or not to be" speech from a book, using it, literally, as a stage prop to bemuse the spyers-on, convince them of his now-become-suicidal madness. No one in his right mind will fault the poetry. But it is irrelevant to anything that precedes. It fools Ophelia—no difficult matter—but it should not fool us. The question is whether Hamlet will act directly or through drama? Not at all. Instead, is he going to end it in the river? I put it thus familiarly to penetrate the serious numinosity surrounding this passage. Hamlet anatomizes grievance for all time. But does *he* suffer these grievances? He has a complaint indeed against the King and one against Ophelia. Why not do something about them instead of meditating on suicide? If the book is a stage prop, or the speech a trap for the hidden listeners, of course, the question of relevancy doesn't arise. The speech works beautifully. But we do not usually consider it a rhetorical trick. It is the most serious speech in the canon. But is it? It tells us nothing about Hamlet except what we already know—he is a good actor. Its relevance, in fact, may lurk just here. The real question by this point in the play is exactly this one: *Is* Hamlet or not? Or does he just act? What kind of self does he possess?

The whole play, we know, seeks authenticity, reality behind the arras, things as they are. Hamlet, we are to assume, embodies the only true self, the central self amidst a cast of wicked phonies. The play, seen this way, provided a natural delight for both the Victorians and the existentialists; their sentimentalism about the central self ran the same way. Yet the question really is whether Hamlet is *to be,* to act rather than reenact. Much has been written on the Melancholy-Man-in-the-Renaissance and how his problems apply to Hamlet. Much more has been written on Hamlet's paralysis. Yet, how irrelevant all this commentary is to the real problem, not *what* Hamlet's motive is but *what kind of* motive. Why can't he act? Angels and ministers of grace, he does nothing else. Polonius, Rosencrantz and Guildenstern, Laertes, Claudius, all go to it. But Hamlet never breaks through to "reality." His motives and his behavior remain dramatic from first to last. So, in spite of all those bodies at the end, commentators wonder if *Hamlet* amounts to a tragedy and, if so, what kind. Hamlet lacks the serious, central self tragedy requires. We are compelled to stand back, hold off our identification, and hence to locate the play within rhetorical coordinates, a tragicomedy about the two kinds of self and the two kinds of motive.

We see this theme in that Q^2 scene (4.4) where Fortinbras and his army parade, with seeming irrelevance—at least to many directors, who cut it—across the stage. They parade so that Hamlet can reflect upon them. The theme is motive. The scene begins as a straightforward lesson in the vanity of human wishes. They go, the Captain tells Hamlet, "to gain a little patch of ground / That hath in it no profit but the name" (4.4.18-19). Hamlet seems to get the point, "the question of this straw," the absurd artificiality of human motive, and especially of aristocratic war, war for pleasure, for the pure glory of it. But then out jumps another non sequitur soliloquy:

> How all occasions do inform against me
> And spur my dull revenge! What is a man,
> If his chief good and market of his time
> Be but to sleep and feed? A beast, no more.
> Sure he that made us with such large discourse,
> Looking before and after, gave us not
> That capability and godlike reason
> To fust in us unused. Now, whether it be
> Bestial oblivion, or some craven scruple
> Of thinking too precisely on th' event—
> A thought which, quartered, hath but one part wisdom
> And ever three parts coward—I do not know
> Why yet I live to say, "This thing's to do,"
> Sith I have cause, and will, and strength, and means
> To do't.
>
> (4.4.32-46)

What has reason to do with revenge? His question—why, with all his compelling reasons, doesn't he go on—is again well taken. Shakespeare has carefully given him the realest reasons a revenge hero ever had—father murdered, mother whored, kingdom usurped, his innocent maiden corrupted in her imagination. The answer to Hamlet's question marches about on the stage before him. As usual, he does not fully understand the problem. It is the Player King's tears all over again. Fortinbras's motivation is sublimely artificial, entirely dramatic. Honor. It has no profit in it but the name. Hamlet cannot act because he cannot find a way to dramatize his revenge. Chances he has, but, as when he surprises Claudius praying, they are not dramatic. Claudius is alone. To fall upon him and kill him would not be revenge, as he says, not because Claudius will die shriven but because he will not see it coming, because nobody is watching.

So, when Hamlet continues his soliloquy, he draws a moral precisely opposite to the expected one. Again, logical discontinuity triggers stylistic attitude:

> Examples gross as earth exhort me.
> Witness this army of such mass and charge,
> Led by a delicate and tender prince,
> Whose spirit, with divine ambition puffed,
> Makes mouths at the invisible event,
> Exposing what is mortal and unsure
> To all that fortune, death, and danger dare,
> Even for an eggshell. Rightly to be great
> Is not to stir without great argument,
> But greatly to find quarrel in a straw
> When honor's at the stake. How stand I then,
> That have a father killed, a mother stained,
> Excitements of my reason and my blood,
> And let all sleep, while to my shame I see
> The imminent death of twenty thousand men
> That for a fantasy and trick of fame
> Go to their graves like beds, fight for a plot
> Whereon the numbers cannot try the cause,
> Which is not tomb enough and continent
> To hide the slain? O, from this time forth,
> My thoughts be bloody, or be nothing worth!
>
> (4.4.46-66)

He sees but does not see. In some way, Fortinbras represents where he wants to go, what he wants to be, how he wants to behave. But he doesn't see how, nor altogether do we. If ever an allegorical puppet was dragged across a stage it is Fortinbras. Yet he haunts the play. His divine ambition begins the action of the play; he gets that offstage introduction Shakespeare is so fond of; he marches to Norway to make a point about motive; and he marches back at the end, inherits Denmark. Yet he stays cardboard. It is not real motive he represents but martial honor much rather.

Shakespeare sought to give *Hamlet* a pronounced military coloration from first to last. The play begins on guard; the ghost wears armor; Denmark is a most warlike state. Military honor is the accepted motive in a Denmark Fortinbras rightly inherits. Honor will cure what is rotten in Denmark, restore its proper values. Hamlet cannot set the times right because he cannot find in martial honor a full and sufficient motive for human life. Hamlet, says Fortinbras, would have done well had he been king, but we may be permitted to doubt it. He thinks too much. Yet honor and the soldier's life provide the model motive for *Hamlet.*

All his working life, Shakespeare was fascinated and perplexed by how deeply the military motive satisfied man. It constituted a sublime secular commitment which, like the religious commitment, gave all away to get all back. Hamlet's selfconsciousness keeps him from it, yes, but even more his search for real purpose. Chivalric war—all war, perhaps—is manufactured purpose. Hamlet can talk about clutching it to his bosom but he cannot do it, for there is nothing *inevitable* about it.

Military honor is finally a role, much like Laertes' role as revenge hero. Both roles are satisfying, both integrate and direct the personality. But once you realize that you are playing the role for just these reasons, using it as a self-serving device, its attraction fades. As its inevitability diminishes, so does its reality. War and revenge both prove finally so rewarding because they provide, by all the killing, the irrefutable reality needed to bolster the role, restore its inevitability. Thus Shakespeare chose them, a revenge plot superposed on a Fortinbras-honor plot, for his play about motive. They provided a model for the kind of motive men find most satisfying; they combine maximum dramatic satisfaction with the irrefutable reality only bloody death can supply. In the Elizabethan absurdity as in our own, men kill others and themselves because that is the only real thing left to do. It is a rare paradox and Shakespeare builds his play upon it.

But even death is not dependable. We can learn to make sport of it, enjoy it. So the gravedigger puns on his craft. So, too, I suppose, Fortinbras laconically remarks at the end of the play: "Such a sight as this / Becomes the field, but here shows much amiss." Death's reality can vanish too. All our purposes end up, like the skull Hamlet meditates on, a stage prop. It is not accidental that the language which closes the play is theatrical. Hamlet even in death does not escape the dramatic self. When the bodies are "high on a stage . . . placèd to the view" Horatio will "speak to th' yet unknowing world," will authenticate the proceeding with a rhetorical occasion. Hamlet's body, Fortinbras commands, is to be borne "like a soldier to the stage, / For he was likely, had he been put on, / To have proved most royal."

Nor is it accidental that Hamlet kills Polonius. The act is his real attempt at revenge, Polonius his real enemy. Polonius embodies the dramatic self-consciousness which stands between Hamlet and the roles—Avenger and King—he was born to play. But Polonius pervades the whole of Hamlet's world and lurks within Hamlet himself. Only death can free Hamlet. Perhaps this is why he faces it with nonchalance. Much has been said about Hamlet's stoicism, but how unstoical the play really is! Honest feeling demands a dramatic equivalent to make it real just as artifice does. Stoicism demands a preexistent reality, a central self beyond drama, which the play denies. Stoicism is death and indeed, in *Hamlet,* the second follows hard upon the avowal of the first. We have no choice but to play.

And so Hamlet chooses his foil and plays. I have been arguing that the play invokes rhetorical coordinates as well as serious ones. It makes sense, if this is so, that it should end with a sublime game and the triumph of chance. Hamlet never solves his problem, nor does chance solve it for him, nor does the play solve it for us. No satisfactory model for motive, no movement from game to sublime, is suggested. Hamlet can finally kill the King because the King thoughtfully supplies a dramatic occasion appropriate to the deed. And Hamlet can kill Laertes because dramatic motive has destroyed naive purpose. And vice versa. But Hamlet cannot get rid of his dramatic self, his dramatic motives. The duel allegorizes the quarrel between kinds of motive which the play has just dramatized. And the duel, like the play, is a zero-sum game. Interest for both adds up to zero. The play leaves us, finally, where it leaves Hamlet. We have savored the violence and the gorgeous poetry and been made aware that we do. We have been made to reflect on play as well as purpose. We have not been shown how to move from one to the other. Nor that it *cannot* be done. We are left, like those in the play, dependent on death and chance to show us how to put our two motives, our two selves, together.

Shakespeare as a mature playwright is not supposed to be an opaque stylist. The great unity of his mature tragedies is a style we look through, not at. The gamesman with words fades out with the nondramatic poems and early infatuations like *Love's Labor's Lost. Hamlet* shows, by itself, how wrong this view of Shakespeare's development is. The play depends upon an alternation of opaque and transparent styles for its meaning. The alternation almost *is* the meaning. *Hamlet* is a play about motive, about style, and thus perhaps, of the mature plays, an exception? I don't think so. Where Shakespeare is most sublime he is also most rhetorical and both poetics are likely to be present in force. To illustrate such a thesis would constitute an agreeable task. The lines it would follow are clear enough. They would yield explanation of the double plot more basic than the comic/serious one. They would render the comic/tragic division altogether less important than it now seems.

In play after play the same stylistic strategy illustrates the same juxtaposition of motive, of play and purpose. Richard cannot learn the difference. Hal must. Lear can play the king but he has never *been* a king. *Antony and Cleopatra* juxtaposes not only public and private life but two poetics and two selves. The double plot becomes, over and over, a serious plot-poetic and a play plot-poetic. The fatal innocence of Shakespeare's characters turns out, over and over, to be innocence about the real nature of their motivation. All through the *Henriad* political rhetoric can be *seen* as rhetoric. Egypt is meant to be *seen* as more wordy and more metaphorical than Rome. *Romeo and Juliet* depends on our seeing the Petrarchan rhetoric as such, else we will mistake the kind of play it is, a play where death authenticates game. Lear on the heath, that centerpiece of Shakespearean sublimity, alters his outlines considerably within rhetorical coordinates. Shakespearean tragedy may come to seem, as in *Hamlet,* a juxtaposition of the two motives with a hole in the middle, with no way to connect

them. The comedies collapse them. And the problem plays and romances try to make a path between the two, see them in dynamic interchange. The two things that obsessed Shakespeare were style and motive, and his career can be charted coherently from beginning to end in terms of their interrelation. In this he typifies the stylistic strategy of the Renaissance as a whole. The real question of motive lay beyond good and evil. It was the principal task of the self-conscious rhetorical style to point this moral. Human flesh is sullied with self-consciousness, with theatricality, and these will be the ground for whatever authentic morality any of us can muster.

Note

1. "Soliloquy?," *Times Literary Supplement,* 20 March 1969, p. 289.

Imtiaz Habib (essay date 1994)

SOURCE: "'Never Doubt I Love': Misreading *Hamlet,*" in *College Literature,* Vol. 21, No. 2, June, 1994, pp. 19-32.

[*In the following essay, Habib offers a close reading of Hamlet's love poem to Ophelia and argues that Hamlet deliberately intends his poetry to be misread. The critic further contends that misreading of all kinds is central to the action and meaning of* Hamlet.]

> Doubt thou the stars are fire,
> Doubt that the sun doth move,
> Doubt truth to be a liar,
> But never doubt I love.
> O dear Ophelia, I am ill at these numbers. I have not
> art to reckon my groans, but that I love thee best, O
> most best, believe it. Adieu.
> Thine evermore, most dear lady, whilst this machine
> is to him, Hamlet.[1]

Hamlet's love poem to Ophelia, which Polonius reads out to Claudius and Gertrude in 2.2.116-24 of *Hamlet,* is an awkward, doubtful business. The love relationship between Hamlet and Ophelia is, admittedly, a minor strand in this complex tragedy. But readers trained in resolving the balanced antinomies of sixteenth- and seventeenth-century English love poetry often reach for a generalized meaning in Hamlet's poem too quickly to notice the conflicts of its particular oppositions. The conventional response to the poem would be to regard it as a hyperbolic assertion of Hamlet's love for Ophelia in the tradition of Elizabethan and Jacobean syllogistic love poetry (as in Donne's "Go and Catch a Falling Star"). "Doubt the most believable things," Hamlet's poem seems to say, "but never doubt that I love you." To construct this sense from a close reading of the poem, however, involves one in considerable difficulties.

The problem centers on the variable relationship between the sense of "doubt" and the statements that are made to be the subject of that doubt in each of the poem's first three lines, and on the consequent uncertainty of the sense of "doubt" and of Hamlet's "love" in the poem's last line. There is an inversion of the meaning of "doubt" either in the second line or in the third or in both, depending on our taste in paradox. If "doubt" in the last line means what it seems to mean in lines 2 and 3, i. e., suspect, fearfully surmise, tentatively believe *(O.E.D.* 1: 616-17),[2] then the line amounts to a disavowal of love. Is Hamlet asking to be believed as a lover or disbelieved? Is the poem an avowal of love or a denial of it? No wonder that many modern European poets and writers in over a hundred attempts have had a hard time translating Hamlet's poem, as Alexander and Barbara Gerschenkron have shown.[3]

Among the critics who have noticed Hamlet's problematic poem and responded to it, Robert Bozanich in 1980 made the interesting suggestion that Hamlet's poem, with its semantic inversions, could be seen as a psychic mirror or "Rorschach blot" that is intended to mockingly reflect the assumptions of the poem's readers rather than those of its author. Thus, Claudius sees in Hamlet's lines ambition, Gertrude shame, Polonius frustrated sexuality, and Ophelia Hamlet's impending madness, which in turn reflects her own future madness (90-93). The Gentleman's comment in 4.5.7-13 that hearers interpret Ophelia's mad words to suit "their own thoughts" could apply to Hamlet's poem as well.

What is interesting about Bozanich's idea of seeing Hamlet's poem as a psychic mirror is that it seems to explain not just responses to the poem within the play but also those outside it, among its critical readers. Those comfortable in their assumptions about the poem's Petrarchan pedigree and about Hamlet's strained courtship of Ophelia have insulated themselves from the lurking discomfiture of Hamlet's lines by simply glossing over them (Meader 149-50; Doran 37-38; King 52; Blanke 22).[4] Others, wanting to contain the poem and its disturbances, have attempted to domesticate the problem by minimizing the ambiguity of the lines and giving such ambiguity an incidental miscellaneous value: the poem is unquestionably an avowal of love although there is enough room for ambiguity in the lines (Jenkins 462-63; Hibbard 209). Still others have tried to defuse the problem by either apologizing for Hamlet (Levin 54), or for us (Skulsky 485).

Extending what Geoffrey Hartman has pointed out about the play's opening lines—"Who's there?"—we can say that Hamlet's cryptic poem seems to challenge all those who read it to declare themselves, i. e, to be *read* themselves (3-19; qtd. in Patterson 49).[5] In its interrogative designs and subversive disturbances, the poem seems to lend itself naturally to phenomenological and deconstructive analyses, neither inappropriate perhaps for a play as concerned as *Hamlet* is with the reflexions of textuality and the dysfunctions of meaning. To grapple with the significance of Hamlet's cryptic love poem is to go beyond an exploration of any local Shakespearean improprieties and be caught in a network of subversive relations between Hamlet and the world. Hamlet's four-line poem is the text for a pervasive system of misreading that dominates the play, or, as Stephen Booth put it in an important discussion of the poem, it is "a model for the experience of the play as a whole" (173).[6]

The text, in Wolfgang Iser's terms, is "a structured prefiguration . . . that has to be received, and the *way* in which it is received depends as much on the reader as on the text" (107). Furthermore, "the work interrogates and transforms the implicit beliefs we bring to it, disconfirms our routine habits of perception," and rather than merely reinforcing our given perceptions, it "violates or transgresses these normative ways of seeing." Thus, "The whole point of reading . . . is that it brings us into a deeper self-consciousness, catalyzes a more critical view of our own identities."[7] Transferred to the realm of interpersonal behavior, these functions of reading acquire strategic implications. To the extent that we can read others we can control others and vice-versa. We would, obviously, like to read others without ourselves being read. As Carol Cook has put it in the related context of her reading of gender differences in *Much Ado About Nothing,* "To read others is an act of aggression; to be read is to be emasculated. Masculine privilege is contingent on the legibility of women." Reading as a subversive strategy of manipulation shades off into misreading: we would like to read others and want them to misread us. We would like to transmit false readings and receive none, and thus misreading shades off into misleading: we would like to mislead others but not ourselves be misled. In Cook's terms, "Beatrice alternately challenges others' misreadings of her humorist's masks and encourages them to take her as she appears" (186-91). Hamlet's poem is difficult to read because Hamlet, like Beatrice, does not wish to be understood satisfactorily, wishes to be misread.

Love, of course, is the primary location of the secret self and its primary point of vulnerability, and therefore of critical importance in the struggle for self-possession that defines human experience. It is going to be the first subject of concealment, for Hamlet as well as for Ophelia, Gertrude, and Claudius (as evidenced for the latter, for instance, in the densely equivocal announcement of his marriage to Gertrude in the third scene of the play). Patricia Fumerton has suggested that in Elizabethan cultural taste the little, privately circulated love poem with its curious mix of artifice and sentiment—like both the aristocratic Elizabethan country house with its stately rooms that also connect to private ones, and the miniature portrait that is at once displayed and hidden—is a representation of an impulse of self-revelation that is also implicitly an instinct of self-concealment, an invitation to a reading of the self that only yields a misreading of it (104-11). Paralleling Hamlet's love poem is Queen Elizabeth's own love poem, "On Monsieur's Departure":

> I grieve and dare not show my discontent
> I love and yet am forced to seem to hate
> I do and dare not say I ever meant,
> I seem stark mute but inwardly do prate.

I am and not, I freeze and yet am burned,
Since from myself another self I turned. . . .

(1-6)

Hamlet's self-rescinding love poem is, then, at once a literary analog to a cultural attitude and a semantic code for the dramatized community in which it appears. It is a key to the historical world of Elizabeth as well as to the dramatic world of Elsinore. It is also an index to the (mis)representations of Hamlet's self in speech and behavior in the play.

The text of misreading that Hamlet's poem contains, it is worth noting, is of a particularly impenetrable quality. The poem's meaning is lost in the *aporia* between an assertion and its implicit opposite, which threatens to cancel it. The declaration that he loves Ophelia is infected by the possibility that he does not love her, the affirmation of the one merely passing into a validation of the other and an impersonation of it, and vice-versa. The deconstructive reflexivity of the unstable signifier "doubt" that creates this aporia is a perfect barrier against the intrusion of legibility into the poem. In a world of hidden intentionality the poem is a declaration of love that reverses and thereby conceals itself—a sign that announces itself by its disappearance. The self-canceling design of Hamlet's poem is replicated by the evasive movement of the last line of the letter that encloses it—"But that I love thee best, O most best, believe it"—a compulsive rhetorical gesture that directs attention away from the *fact* of his love to an assumption of it, and in doing so obscuring the fact and implicitly erasing it (Bozanich 91). The self-negation of Hamlet's statement happens on the verbal and cognitive level, on the level of speech and understanding. Hamlet is unmaking the word and with it, as we shall see later, the world.[8] Irrespective of their precise circumstance (whether they were written before or after Polonius's injunction to Ophelia to rebuff Hamlet), the poem and the letter neither seek nor find any readership with Ophelia or with anyone else because, like the other human gestures in the play, love has become one more cipher in a text that refuses to, because it cannot, be deciphered. In being unable to exist except through and in its own annulment, Hamlet's declaration of love affirms subversion as the chief ideology of Elsinore and misreading as its principal text, and announces his mastery over both.

Predictably, the esoteric method of Hamlet's poem is not unlike the dubious style of the other letters that he writes in the play. On the way to England he re-writes Claudius's order for his execution in such a way that the meaning of the order is clear but not its manner: the justification he offers for the order is deliberately obscure and sarcastic ("As peace should still her wheaten garland wear / And stand a comma 'tween their amities, / And many such like as's of great charge" [5.2.41-43]). As Jonathan Goldberg has put it, "Hamlet's skilled hand insures the force of the document, but it does not reveal the writer" (323). Likewise, in the strange letter he sends Claudius announcing his return to England, it is unclear whether his mes-

sage is contrition or defiance: the letter's reference to seeking "pardon" (4.7.46) is mocked by its stilted, artificial language of royalty. In both of these writings, as in his poem to Ophelia, content is distorted by the variability of intention. Hamlet's own remark to Horatio that, even though he used royal handwriting to re-write the execution order, he normally holds it "A baseness to write fair" (5.2.34), aptly describes his penchant not just for illegibility in handwriting but also for incommunicability in substance. The puzzling love poem, in other words, sets the pattern for Hamlet's enigmatic compositions elsewhere in the action.

The origin of this ideology of subversion and its text of misreading cannot be wholly situated, by Hamlet or by us, in a specific causal event—the murder of a King by his brother. For, even as the Ghost's radical tale of treachery rewrites, revises, and blocks other readings of Elsinore, it is itself a misreading. Its opaque ghostly authority, its manipulative implication of Hamlet in filial duty and an agenda of revenge, and the impenetrability of its ambiguities about Gertrude (who wavers in the Ghost's account between being a reluctant lover, an adulteress, and a murderess [1.5.42-57]) are all dubieties that undermine the validity of its text. The very strength of the Ghost's reading of Elsinore makes it a misreading since excessive magnification will always blur the total picture. As Harold Bloom has put it, a strong "[r]eading is always a misreading" (3). Hamlet's difficulties with the Ghost's account are implicit here in the lament with which he ends the scene, "The time is out of joint—O cursed spite! / That ever I was born to set it right!" (1.5.88-89), and later in his momentary revaluation of the Ghost's words in his decision to put on the play-within-the play (2.2.594-605).

That is, all readings are tainted with the suspicion of misreading, become misreadings. True readings remain inaccessible, uncertain and unknown. One of Roland Barthes' comments is pertinent here:

> To read, in fact, is a labor of language. To read is to find meanings and to find meanings is to name them; but these named meanings are swept towards other names; names call to each other, reassemble, and their grouping calls for further naming; I name, I unname, I rename; so the text passes; it is a nomination in the course of becoming, a tireless approximation, a metonymic labor.

(11)

To this we may perhaps add the observation that causality is the last human illusion. To be able to ascribe reasons to phenomena is to be able to know them, and if knowledge is power a belief in the causality of phenomena is implicitly a desire for one's ability to control phenomena. These are goals as human as they are philosophically elusive. In the endless chain of cause and effect we may discern *local* connections and even learn to contribute to them, but to uncover the *first* cause—the original reason why the world is the way it is—that is surely beyond human fathoming. This is to say that in the short range the world is decipherable but in the long range, in terms of origins, it is unknowable. Thus, the misreadings of Elsinore are both intentional and inexplicable: as Hamlet cannot read the world so he will not let the world read him.

To Hamlet, the death of his father, by natural or unnatural causes, is the inexplicable cue for the extinction of a rational civilization. It is the occasion for the rise of a King whose namelessness in the play (Claudius is the only Shakespearean King never addressed either by his official title [Calderwood xv] or by his name [Goldberg 326]), matches the equivocal blankness of his speech (as for instance, in 1.3). That death is the setting for the rise of a world in which a celestially angelic Gertrude, a "Niobe" in her "tears," can be with the "satyr," Claudius, as readily as she was with the "Hyperion" that was her husband (1.2.140-49). This is a world in which, from behind the pomp and glitter of a coronation ceremony, the riddle of incest decouples things from their names, thoughts from their expression, and ideas from their representation.[9] But this event—the death of his father—cannot be given any status save that of a desultory event. It cannot be afforded any attribute of causality because causality has the legibility of logic that is denied by the world that Hamlet confronts. The subversion and misreadings of Elsinore are, in other words, causeless, a random phenomenon in the dynamics of chaos. For reasons unknown, Elsinore and the world have become unreadable to Hamlet, and with that Hamlet has become unreadable to others and to himself. In this sense, the text of misreading that Hamlet affirms in his poem is his horrible practical joke, his real gruesome revenge upon the world for the incomprehensibility of its text. This, we note, is a revenge that Hamlet's audience would relish, for, as Stephen Orgel has recently pointed out, "the Renaissance often found in incomprehensibility a positive virtue" (436). Indeed, in his poem Hamlet exemplifies Montaigne's words from "On the Inconsistency of Our Actions": "I have nothing to say about myself absolutely, simply and solidly, without confusion and without mixture, or in one word" (242).

That misreading is *the* principal Elsinorean activity, and a phenomenon that *precedes* the Ghost's disturbing revelations, is in fact evident from the play's very beginning. The characters of Elsinore are all trying to impose their reading of events and phenomena on others while blocking those of others (Payne 100-11). Hartman has suggested (in the reference given above), that the whole plot of the opening scene with its play of murky happenings and confused identities enacts the phenomenology of readings that challenge the reader. The principal element in that phenomenology is the riddling apparition that resists the semantic probings of the skeptic philosopher, Horatio. The nocturnal visitor affords neither him, nor Barnardo, Francisco, or Marcellus, any more sense than the vague discomfort that "it bodes some strange eruption" to the state (1.1.69), or, as Marcellus articulates it later, that "Something is rotten in the state of Denmark" (1.4.89). The blocked reading merely renews the desire to read, with the hope that the "dumbness" of illegibility may give

way to the legibility of "speech" with a changed reader—"young Hamlet" (1.1.170-71).[10] But the request for a reading privileges a legibility in that reader himself that cannot pass unchallenged by him. The aim of Hamlet's canny cross-examination of Horatio and the guards is to flush out any hidden agendas they may have in inviting him to read the specter as his father:

> Ham: Arm'd say you?
> Hor: Arm'd, my lord.
> Ham: From top to toe?
> Hor: My lord, from head to foot.
> Ham: Then saw you not his face? . . .
> Ham: His beard was grisl'd, no?
> Hor: It was, as I have seen it in his life, a sable silver'd.
>
> (1.2.226-40)

Of course, Hamlet's attempt to read Horatio and the guards' failure to read the spectral phenomenon have both been preceded by Claudius's and Gertrude's attempt to read *him* earlier in the same scene. There, Claudius's Kingly reading tries to situate him as "a cousin" and "son" and thereby demands, by executive and filial privilege, to know the source of "the clouds" of melancholic despair that plague him. Hamlet counters this with a defensive misreading of himself as someone who is neither "kin" nor "kind," and who is not at all under the weather but in fact "too much in the sun," the punning between "son" and "sun" obscuring both the content and the intent of his reply. The attempted precision of Claudius's reading of Hamlet is neatly dissipated by the brazen ambiguity of Hamlet's misreading of himself, with the particular diagnosis of behavior of the one being silently replaced by that of the other. In this tense verbal thrust and parry, readability, i. e., knowability, is established as the besieged site of a fierce Elsinorean tactical struggle for dominance.

Unsurprisingly, as is the state so is the family. The most developed family depicted in the play, Polonius's, merely replicates within itself the pattern of interaction within the court. The cute scenario in the third scene of the play, of a cocky elder brother and an officious father fussing over the danger of a young commoner girl's liaison with royalty, is also an attempt to govern a young girl's mind. Laertes' prognosis of "the chariest maid['s] . . . prodigal[ity] . . . If she unmask her beauty to the moon"—otherwise "the shot and danger of desire" (1.3.35-38)—is a notion of Ophelia's sexuality that he is implicitly seeking to validate. Likewise, Polonius's inquisitorial suggestion, a few lines later, of a busy affair between her and Hamlet is a reading of her behavior that Polonius intends to confirm: "What is between you? Give me up the truth" (1.3.98). The teasing maidenly reticence with which Ophelia instinctively sidesteps such testing preserves her sovereignty over her own decipherability and with that, her options of personal freedom. The same struggle to regulate behavior permeates the relationship between father and son, as for instance when Polonius facetiously advises Laertes about the necessity of behaving duplicitously with the world while remaining true ("above all") to himself (1.3.58-80). Later, he instructs Reynaldo to spy on his son by using "indirections [to] find directions out" (2.1.38-63). Both speeches exemplify a technique of understanding others while withholding understanding from them—a technique, in short, of reading others while remaining unread or misread oneself. It is in this context of the pervasive misreadings of Elsinore that Hamlet's quizzical love poem is inscribed.

Given the dense inexplicability of Elsinore, Hamlet's feelings for Ophelia can only be the occasion for his riddling equivocation and paradoxical behavior, with her and with others. His visit to her in her closet, which Ophelia describes in 2.1.73-97 is an act that is simultaneously an affirmation and a denial. He goes to her but does not speak to her. He goes to her in an instinctive gesture of communication but ends up in a silent scrutiny of her face. He stares at her, reads her, without letting her read him, or, making sure that she misreads him and encouraging her misreading of him (as transmitted through Polonius) as mad. The uncertainty of what he reads in her is matched and cloaked by the uncertainty of what Ophelia and Polonius, and we with them, can read in him. Each reading—that he is mad, that he is love-sick, that he is testing her through an "antic disposition"—is instantly challenged by the others and thus ends up as no more than a misreading of him.

Again, he flaunts this same riddling behavior before her in the "nunnery" scene in Act 3. He did and did not love Ophelia, he says (3.1.114-18)—playing again on the compulsive verb "believe," but this time in a direction opposite that of the letter. If she "believed" he loved her, he asserts bluntly that he loved her not—imposing his belief on hers and blocking it. The instability of the signifier "nunn'ry" with which he ends his tirade (3.1.129)—poised as it is between its formal sober connotation as a retreat of sanctity and its bawdy popular Elizabethan denotation as a brothel (*O.E.D.* 1: 264; Jenkins 282)—masks perfectly the sense of his feelings for her, now or in the past. His insistence later, in the grim verbal and physical scuffle with Laertes in Ophelia's grave, that he "lov'd Ophelia" (5.1.269), declares his rights over the politics of intentionality. If Laertes' love for his sister allows him to rant against Hamlet for causing her death, then Hamlet's love for Ophelia allows *him* to vent his fury at Laertes for blackening his name. Hamlet will not let his feelings for Ophelia become Elsinore's vehicle of legibility into him, a foreground of its mastery over him. What he will give up, to Ophelia, Polonius, Laertes, Gertrude, Claudius, and to us, is only the misreading of incoherence. The more anyone tries to read Hamlet the more he will be misread.

The desire to be misread is the desire to be mysterious, and to be mysterious to the world is to confuse it. Hamlet traps Rosencrantz and Guildenstern when they come to him in 2.2 as robotic extensions of Claudius's probing of his mind, to demonstrate his ability to deflect Elsinore's attempt to plumb him back upon itself. Somewhat Iago-like, Hamlet offers Rosencrantz and Guildenstern not a paucity of motives for his melancholic behavior but a

plethora of them—thwarted ambition, love sickness, depression. In this bag of motives the dilemma of choice transforms visibility into inscrutability and sense to confusion, as Guildenstern later reports to Claudius:

> Nor do we find him forward to be sounded
> But with a crafty madness keeps aloof
> When we would bring him on to some confession
> Of his true state.
>
> (3.1.7-9)

To preserve the sovereignty of the self, it must not be allowed to have a text because a text invites reading. The "angelic action" and "God[-like] apprehension," and the "quintessen[tial]" dust of man, in Hamlet's speech to Rosencrantz and Guildenstern on the nature of man (2.2.303-10), are free signifiers in Hamlet's unmaking of the text of the self of man. Hamlet's unmaking of the text of the self has affinities with what Michael F. McCanles has described as Shakespeare's deconstructive character analysis,

> the notion of . . . textuality put forth by Jacques Derrida and Julia Kristeva: a text without a centered self or substantive origins, a fluid melting of multiple texts thrown up momentarily, coalescing, then disappearing, to be replaced by still other texts.
>
> (201)

The unmade text of the self is what Hamlet describes, both to Guildenstern at the end of the play scene when he forces him to play the recorder, and immediately after to Polonius when he forces him to decipher the shape of a cloud that looks like a weasel and like a whale. The chaotic self of man in Hamlet's unmaking of it, cannot be "play[ed]" and "sound[ed]," and the "heart" of its "mystery" cannot be "pluck[ed] out" (3.2.364-71). And the text of the self of man must be unmade if the world is to be unmade. If sense—the logical connected arrangement of units of meaning, i. e., a readable text, or what Terence Hawkes in a related context has described as "the unity, progression, coherence" that are "part of the [world's] ruthless and rigorous process of domestication [and control]" (324)—if this is what holds the world together, then confusion is what will unmake it. If the world has already become an unreadable text, then, Hamlet's text of misreading will accelerate that unreadability. Behind the text of misreading that Hamlet affirms lies a grim malevolence towards a malevolent world.

In trying to destroy the text of the self and of the world, Hamlet's text of misreading is also intended to disallow the very idea of a text itself. The textlessness of his soliloquies matches the textlessness of the play he puts on to rewrite both the play he has inherited from the Ghost and the play he himself is set in. His soliloquies seem to show transparently the processes of thought and decision-making but actually give us only their opaque results. For instance, in the "Rogue and peasant slave" soliloquy (2.2.550-605) and in the "To be or not to be" one (3.1.55-88), the tortuous self-analyses that Hamlet conducts have little connection to the conclusions he quickly reaches for—deciding to put on a play in the former and choosing inaction in the latter.[11] This is identical to the way that the signifiers of an anti-text have ineffectual links with the signifieds they couple with, the result in both cases being a refusal to communicate with a reader.

So too, "The Murder of Gonzago" rewrites the text of the *Hamlet* play and the Ghost's in a manner that pretends to speak with the audience, but in fact, in its deliberate conflation of the roles of brother and nephew, killer and revenger, in the figure of Lucianus, and in its incompleteness (it stops midway and we do not know how much of it, if any, was left to be performed), declines to do so. If Claudius's angry exit is provoked by his uncertainty and suspicion of the staged play's intentions, this fuels *our* uncertainty about precisely what Claudius finds suspicious (the spectacle of regicide, the murder of a brother, the manner of the killing, or the murderer's quick wooing of the victim's widow), and about what he understands of the staged play (does he see the dumb show, and, if he does, why does he ask what its "argument" is?). Both uncertainties, Claudius's and ours, combine to make the entire episode resist the cohering control of textuality. In denying textuality Hamlet is not so much destroying a textuality that the world still has as he is participating in, and deliberately contributing to, its rampant anti-textuality.

In making the staged play episode resist a textuality, its author is himself resisting the textual authority of the larger play of which he is a part. Just as the staged play refuses to make full sense Hamlet himself refuses to make full sense, his exuberance at the performance's end being but a deceptive signifier of his authorial conclusions about the success of his staged text. (If Claudius *has* seen the dumb show and failed to respond to it, then the Ghost's words cannot be taken "for a thousand pound" [3.2.286]).[12] Hamlet's deliberate collapsing of selfhood and textuality begins the disintegration of Elsinore and the *Hamlet* play, both of which become sites of defiance of form and meaning.

To be unable to read is to die, misreading is dying. The disappearance of a text of self and of textuality itself can only be a prelude to the world's slide into the random incoherence of death. With no textuality to hold them, lives crumple, characters fall and are expunged. Polonius's "sudden, rash, intruding" death at the hands of Hamlet, the first of the play's many deaths, is without explanation or apology because it belongs to no script. Unsupported by any role in family or state because of his inability to read and domesticate either his wayward daughter, her dangerous lover, or the "transformed" Prince, Polonius falls—a miscellaneous end to a life suddenly become miscellaneous. Cast adrift by the illegibility of her lover and the dubiety of her father, Ophelia's slide into madness perfectly replicates her textual redundancy. Her disjointed songs in 4.5, with their conflation of the texts of sexual betrayal and elegiac lament for the loss of a loved one in death, are as contextless as her own death, in Gertrude's

evocative description (4.7.166-83), by a drowning closely observed but not prevented.

As royal order breaks in Elsinore, first signalled by Claudius's disruptive exit from the dramatic performance, the King's assassins are themselves assassinated. Rosencrantz and Guildenstern die quietly off-stage as the game of cheap espionage in which Claudius had cast them is terminated, literally in Hamlet's re-writing of his assassination orders on board ship to England. Baffled by the wild behavior and hallucinatory antics of her son in her bed chamber and caught by his "wild, whirling words," some of which strike home in the direction of her wedded Queenly bliss, Gertrude's notions of maternality, wifedom, and Queenliness are at once confused. She floats in a tide of seeping self-sickness, dreading to face the mad Ophelia and seeing her death in the accents in which perhaps she would like to see her own (in the passage cited above). Her intervention on Hamlet's side in his graveyard scuffle with Laertes prefigures her fatal, albeit unwitting, intervention in Claudius's design of the poisoned wine cup intended for her son and she dies a blundering death marginally lamented by husband and son. Displaced by Ophelia's death from the scenario of strutting protective brotherhood, and impelled by his father's murder into a desperate revenge plot, Laertes falls in the play's last scene, caught in the cross-pull of Hamlet's sincere sportsmanship and Claudius's manipulative stratagem of hidden retribution, unable to read fully or relate to either.

As Elsinore's texts disintegrate and characters collapse, its center, and its chief reader and author, Claudius, begins to deconstruct, losing his authority over both language and action. Within the arranged self of majesty in Claudius the memory of criminal instinct stubbornly intrudes, stirred by Polonius's chance remark about the perfidy of necessary deceptions when they are rehearsing Ophelia's entrapment of Hamlet before the "nunnery" scene:

> O 'tis too true!
> How smart a lash that speech doth give my conscience!
> The harlot's cheek, beautied with plast'ring art
> Is not more ugly to the thing that helps it
> Than is my deed to my most painted word.
>
> (3.1.48-52)

Reinforced by the experience of Hamlet's subversive play, such insistent memories erode self-authority in Claudius, dividing thought from action, speech from intent, and driving them up against each other, so that as he prays his "words fly up" but his "thoughts remain below" (3.3.97-98). The loss of self-authority releases hardened and hidden desires in Claudius—for the "crown," the "ambition," the "Queen"—that he cannot forsake (3.3.55), and for the violence by which he acquired them. Claudius's Kingship begins to die in the "pestilent" public speeches of an uncontrollable Laertes demanding redress for a father's murder that "Like . . . a murd'ring piece" gives Claudius "superfluous death" (4.5.91-96), and this death signals the release of the cold-blooded killer in him. In fact, by this time the practiced killer in Claudius has already emerged, in his compulsion for the purging of the "hectic in [his] blood" by the killing of Hamlet (4.3.65-68).

The loss of authority in the Kingly self can only reflect the loss of authority in the state, the textual subversion of the one merely compounding that of the other. As the secret assassination of Hamlet goes awry and the assassins are themselves assassinated, so the killing of Hamlet in the duel fails to hold true and instead also kills the killers. The physical death of Claudius in the play's last scene recalls the textual death of King Claudius earlier in the scene of Laertes' riotous entry into the castle and replicates in its savagery the ferocity of the killer Claudius's own compulsive violence.

Claudius's death is both textual and textless. It is textual in that it completes the object of the revenge text—the retributive killing of the killer. It is textless in the sense that the manner in which it is accomplished destroys that textuality. Hamlet kills Claudius in a frenzy of spontaneous action that has little to do with premeditated vengeance, particularly of the sort stipulated by the Ghost's text. If it is vengeful at all, that vengeance is an immediate response to the local plan of Claudius to poison him, and has little to do with his father's murder. Claudius falls in a welter of confused violence that the court can only misread as "Treason!" (5.2.323). Somewhat as Hamlet's declaration of love in his riddling poem had announced itself by its own disappearance, the revenge text of *Hamlet* completes itself by its own erasure. The litter of bodies that fills the play's last scene is not just conventional. It is uniquely a function of this play's compulsion to consume itself.

For Hamlet the greatest problem in his dramatized life is the desirability and danger of communication in an indecipherable world. To have a text of living is to be read and destroyed. Yet not having a text is to die. One can live, then, only by subverting life. By extension one can speak only by not speaking. Through one's silences one can understand by not understanding. One can live—triumph over death—by having a text that cannot be read. One can meet the indecipherability of the world by destroying the world as one is destroyed by it. This compound apocalyptic ethic can only be grounded in a celebration of silence as the sole good in a meaningless "unknowing" universe where "readiness" is but "all" (5.2.222). Horatio doesn't fail Hamlet's dying request "to tell [his] story." As Hamlet himself erases meaning from his instructions to Horatio about what his text should contain—by his dying gesture of deferral, "the rest is silence" (5.2.358)—so, Horatio's bare account of "unnatural acts," "accidental judgments" and "purposes mistook / Fall'n on the inventors' head" (5.2.380-86), is the prologue to an unfulfilled text—one that the play's physical end elides from our view.[13]

Thus Hamlet's play, like his poem, is built on a system of misreading that subverts meaning in the very process of its communication, that conceals as it reveals, and that exists only in its self-cancellation. As the poem subverts its own Petrarchan tradition by asserting love through the process of denying it, the play hides its literary lineage by accomplishing revenge through the process of destroying its textual framework (Waller 27; Hawkes 330). Just as Hamlet's struggle in his poem to find an original voice against the burden of a literary tradition leads him to his discovery of silence as a form of speech, Shakespeare's struggle to achieve a unique play amidst the pressure of a burgeoning copycat literary culture produces a text that de-textualizes itself to preserve its own integrity.[14] Just as the origins of Hamlet's love letter are mysterious and hidden (exactly when was it written, is it authentic or a forgery? [Goddard 40; Ferguson 308 n. 21]), so the dramatic origins and models of Shakespeare's play are uncertain and unknown (who wrote the *Ur-Hamlet* and when?). As the subject of Hamlet's letter and poem—his love for Ophelia—is lost in its own doubts, the subject of Hamlet's play—the tragedy of his life—is buried in its own deletions, trapped in our endless misreadings of it. If *Hamlet* is a deconstructive play (Patterson 47; Calderwood xv), the enigmatic love letter to Ophelia, tucked away in one small corner of the play, contains much of the energies of such a modality and helps in executing it.

Notes

1. All citations from Shakespeare use the Riverside edition unless otherwise noted.

2. Examples of this usage from the *O.E.D.* include: "I havying doute of harmes of my body . . . dyd assemble these persones," 1411, *Rolls of Parliament,* III, 650/2, and "The pinne or web is likewise to be doubted to happen in that year," 1574, Hyll, *Conject. Weather,* ii. Also see Shakespeare's own use of this word earlier in the same scene, in Gertrude's words in line 56, as Stephen Booth has pointed out (174). For instances of this use of the word elsewhere in Shakespeare see *King Lear* 5.1.6 and *Timon of Athens* 1.2.155. Jonson in *Volpone* 3.7 has Bonario say of Mosca: "I do doubt / this fellow."

3. The article is cited by the editors of Harold C. Goddard's posthumously published book *Alphabet of the Imagination* (57 n. 9).

4. Also see John J. Murray's "mathematical" resolution of the problem. For examples of nineteenth-century dismissals of Hamlet's letter see Furness 2: 209.

5. That the poem "reads" its readers is also the substance of Goddard's trenchant comment (43). Goddard also argues that the poem is a partial forgery by Polonius (48-52; qtd. in Taylor 51 n. 9).

6. Booth's analysis, which is dependent on the concept of complementarity popularized by Norman Rabkin in his book *Shakespeare and the Common Understanding,* has affinities with the phenomenological and deconstructive argument I am using. My essay explores some of the implications of Booth's discussion. In a general sense, I have also profited from the

Ethan Hawke as Hamlet and Julia Stiles as Ophelia in the 1999 film adaptation of Hamlet.

critical methods and ideas of James Calderwood in *To Be and Not To Be.*

7. Paraphrased by Eagleton in his summary of Iser's theories (79).

8. On the use of negation in *Hamlet* see Calderwood's incisive discussion: "If poetic negation is positive then Not this exists on an equal footing with This. The absent is present, the denied affirmed, the forbidden consummated in the verbal act of negation itself" (61). On the breakdown of language generally in Shakespeare's tragedies, see also Danson, and Hawkes (*Shakespeare's Talking Animals*).

9. On the connection between incest and riddles see Levi-Strauss (34-39; qtd. in McAlinden 59 and Calderwood 205 n. 14).

10. On the greater importance of speech than of sight for producing meaning in phenomena, particularly here in the scenes of the Ghost's appearance before the guards and before Hamlet, see Don Parry Norford's essay. Norford says "Only when [the Ghost] speaks to Hamlet does the meaning of its appearance become known" (567).

11. That the conclusions of the soliloquies *seem* to arise from the context of the soliloquies but actually do not, may be less readily evident in the latter of these two soliloquies than in the first. That inaction is going to be Hamlet's choice in the "To be or not to be" soliloquy is indicated from the very beginning by the way it is associated with, and thereby valorized by, "being," despite conventional expectations that "being" will mean living well and acting heroically, i. e., being active. Partly perhaps to hide this inversion in values, Hamlet, after setting out "being" and "non-being" in the first four lines as items in a particular series, switches their order and proceeds to discuss the *latter* item—non-being—first. He returns to "being" only afterwards, as a preferable alternative (3.1.59-68). In other words, what appears to be a debate really isn't one—Hamlet has already made up his mind about inaction before the speech begins and in the soliloquy he is only looking for ways to justify that decision. This is like his having suddenly decided, in the earlier soliloquy, to put on a play and *then* merely looking for reasons to do so (2.2.598-605). Harold Jenkins provides a good discussion of

the hidden inversions in Hamlet's "To be or not to be" soliloquy in his edition of the play (484-91).

12. For an effective discussion of the dubieties of what the play-within-the-play "proves" about Claudius, see Brent Cohen (235-37). Stanley Cavell has offered a sophisticated Freudian rejection of what Hamlet's play actually proves about Claudius's guilt (179-91).

13. Calderwood, of course, says that this is a moment of termination as well as a beginning. Horatio's story is the text for the play's next performance before another audience (182-84).

14. I am referring, of course, to the busy, competitive production of sonnets, history plays, and romances, as well as revenge plays, in England in the late sixteenth and early seventeenth centuries. In Stanley Cavell's words, in *Hamlet* Shakespeare "is writing the revenge play to end revenge plays" (181).

Works Cited

Atkins, G. Douglas, and David M. Bergeron, eds. *Shakespeare and Deconstruction*. New York: Peter Lang, 1988.

Barthes, Roland. *S/Z*. Trans. Richard Miller. New York: Hill and Wang, 1974.

Blanke, N. F. *Shakespeare's Language: An Introduction*. New York: St. Martin's, 1983.

Bloom, Harold, *A Map of Misreading*. New York: Oxford UP, 1973.

Booth, Stephen. "On the Value of *Hamlet*." *Reinterpretations of Elizabethan Drama*. Selected Papers of the English Institute. Ed. Norman Rabkin. New York: Columbia UP, 1969. 136-76.

Bozanich, Robert. "The Eye of the Beholder: Hamlet to Ophelia 2.2.109-24." *Shakespeare Quarterly* 31 (1980): 90-93.

Calderwood, James L. *To Be and Not To Be: Negation and Metadrama in Hamlet*. New York: Columbia UP, 1983.

Cavell, Stanley. "Hamlet's Burden of Proof." *Disowning Knowledge in Six Plays of Shakespeare*. New York: Cambridge UP, 1987.

Cohen, Brent. "'What Is It You Would See?': *Hamlet* and the Conscience of the Theater." *ELH* 44 (1977): 222-47.

Cook, Carol. "The Sign and Semblance of Her Honor: Reading Gender Difference in *Much Ado About Nothing*." *PMLA* 101 (1986): 186-202.

Danson, Laurence. *Tragic Alphabet: Shakespeare's Drama of Language*. New Haven: Yale UP, 1974.

Doran, Madeleine. *Shakespeare's Dramatic Language*. Madison: U of Wisconsin P, 1976.

Eagleton, Terry. *Literary Theory: An Introduction*. 1983. Minneapolis: U of Minnesota P, 1989.

Elizabeth I, Queen. "On Monsieur's Departure." *The Norton Anthology of English Literature*. 6th ed. Vol. 1. Gen. Ed. M.H. Abrams. New York: Norton, 1986. 998.

Ferguson, Margaret. "*Hamlet*: Letters and Spirits." Parker and Hartman 292-309.

Fumerton, Patricia. "Secret Arts: Elizabethan Miniatures and Sonnets." *Representing the English Renaissance*. Ed. Stephen Greenblatt. Berkeley: U of California P, 1988.

Furness, H.H., ed. *Hamlet: A New Variorum Edition*. 2 vols. Philadelphia: Lippincott, 1877.

Gerschenkron, Erica, and Alexander Gerschenkron. "The Illogical Hamlet: A Note on Translatability." *Texas Studies in Literature and Language* 8 (1966): 301-36.

Goddard, Harold C. *Alphabet of the Imagination: Literary Essays of Harold C. Goddard*. Ed. Eleanor G. Worthen and Margaret Goddard Holt. Atlantic Highlands: Humanities, 1974.

Goldberg, Jonathan. "Hamlet's Hand." *Shakespeare Quarterly* 39 (1988): 307-27.

Hartman, Geoffrey. *The Fate of Reading*. Chicago: U of Chicago P, 1975.

Hawkes, Terence. *Shakespeare's Talking Animals: Language and Drama in Society*. Tottowa: Rowman and Littlefield, 1973.

———. "Telmah." Parker and Hartman 310-31.

Hibbard, G.R., ed. *Hamlet*. The Oxford Shakespeare. Oxford: Clarendon, 1987.

Iser, Wolfgang. *The Act of Reading*. Baltimore: John Hopkins UP, 1978.

Jenkins, Harold, ed. *Hamlet*. The Arden Shakespeare. London: Methuen, 1983.

King, Walter. *Hamlet's Search for Meaning*. Athens: U of Georgia P, 1982.

Levi-Strauss, Claude. *The Scope of Anthropology*. Trans. S. O. Paul and R. A. Paul. London: Cape, 1967.

Levin, Harry. *The Question of Hamlet*. New York: Oxford UP, 1959.

McAlinden, T. *Shakespeare and Decorum*. London: Barnes and Noble, 1973.

McCanles, Michael F. "Shakespeare, Intertextuality and the Decentered Self." Atkins and Bergeron 193-211.

Meader, William G. *Courtship in Shakespeare*. New York: Octagon, 1971.

Montaigne, Michel de. *The Complete Essays of Montaigne*. Trans. Donald M. Frame. Stanford: Stanford UP, 1958.

Murray, John J. "Hamlet and Logic." *PMLA* 90 (1975): 120-21.

Norford, Don Parry. "'Very Like a Whale': The Problem of Knowledge in *Hamlet*." *ELH* 46 (1979): 559-76.

Orgel, Stephen. "The Poetics of Incomprehensibility." *Shakespeare Quarterly* 42 (1991): 431-37.

Oxford English Dictionary. 1971. Compact ed. 2 vols. Oxford: Oxford UP, 1980.

Parker, Patricia, and Geoffrey Hartman, eds. *Shakespeare and the Question of Theory*. New York: Methuen, 1985.

Patterson, Annabel. "The Very Age and Body of the Time His Form and Pressure." Atkins and Bergeron 47-67.

Payne, Michael. "What's Wrong with Hamlet?" *Perspectives on* Hamlet. *Collected Papers of the Bucknell-Susquehanna Colloquium on* Hamlet. *April 27-28, 1973*. Ed. William G. Holzberger and Peter B. Waldeck. Lewisburg: Bucknell UP, 1975. 100-11.

Rabkin, Norman. *Shakespeare and the Common Understanding*. New York: Free, 1967.

Shakespeare, William. *Hamlet. The Riverside Shakespeare*. Ed. G. Blakemore Evans. Boston: Houghton Mifflin, 1974.

Skulsky, Harold. "I Know My Course: Hamlet's Confidence." *PMLA* 89 (1974): 477-86.

Taylor, Mark. "Letters and Readers in *Macbeth, King Lear* and *Twelfth Night*." *Philological Quarterly* 69 (1990): 31-53.

Waller, Gary. "Decentering the Bard: The Dissemination." Atkins and Bergeron 21-45.

David Farley-Hills (essay date 1999)

SOURCE: "Hamlet's Account of the Pirates," in *Review of English Studies*, Vol. 50, No. 199, August, 1999, pp. 320-31.

[*In the following essay, Farley-Hills defends George Miles's linguistic argument (from 1870) that Hamlet planned his meeting with the pirates before he left for England. His defense involves some comparison of the Q2 and F versions of the play.*]

The view that Hamlet had been planning, before he leaves Denmark, to be rescued by pirates on the journey to England has received short shrift from most Shakespeare commentators and editors since it was first given lengthy and forceful promulgation by the American scholar and author George Miles in his monograph of 1870, *A Review of Hamlet*. Miles made his suggestion provisional on the possibility of a pun on the word 'craft' at Q2 III. iv. 199: 'If the word *crafts* had its present maritime significance in Shakespeare's time, the pun alone is conclusive of a pre-arranged capture.'[1]

W.W. Lawrence regarded the whole of Miles's argument as 'an absurd idea',[2] and most of those few critics who have noticed Miles at all have substantially concurred. Later attempts to support Miles's view, such as Martin

Stevens's article in *Shakespeare Quarterly*,[3] have fared no better. The main objection, however, has often been that the use of 'craft' to mean 'ship' was unknown in Shakespeare's day or too rare to be a meaningful reference. The German scholar Robert Petsch, for instance, in his article refuting Miles's argument, argues that even if the word could have meant 'ship' in Elizabethan English, the usage would have been too rare and technical for a general audience to understand.[4] Modern editors have been more forthright: G.R. Hibbard's note on Q2 III. iv. 190, for instance, comments (with rather strange logic): 'The earliest instance of *craft*, signifying "boat", cited by the *OED* belongs to 1671-2, so there is little likelihood that Hamlet is quibbling.'[5] In providing evidence that Hibbard and those many commentators and annotators who share a similar view are mistaken in this assumption, I think it worth again raising the ghost of Hamlet's planned meeting with the pirates.

In the 'closet' scene of the Q2 version of *Hamlet* Shakespeare gives Hamlet nine lines in his last speech that do not occur in either Q1 or the Folio version. The last of these lines may or may not contain a pun on the word 'crafts':

> O, 'tis most sweet
> When in one line two crafts directly meet.
>
> (III. iv. 198-9)[6]

'Crafts' here certainly means (as most annotators agree) something like 'cunning plots' (Harold Jenkins). G.R. Hibbard rather ingeniously suggests in explanation of the last line: 'when two exponents of the same skill or cunning device—in this case mining and counter-mining—meet one another head-on'. A problem with this, however, is that Hamlet promises to dig 'one yard below their mines'. Jenkins too thinks that it is unlikely that the word also means 'ships' here: 'A pun on *crafts*, ships, is (at this date) unlikely',[7] and elsewhere, in notes to III. iv. 207-11 and IV. vi. 19, finds 'no justification' for inferring that the pirates were in league with Hamlet in a plot to get him back to Denmark. At first sight the *OED* seems to give support to this scepticism; but as well as giving the date of the first known use of 'craft' meaning 'ship' as 1671 the compilers also add to the entry the note: 'These uses were probably colloquial with watermen, fishers and seamen some time before they appeared in print, so that the history is not evidenced.' Some support is given to the suggestion that this usage of the word is to be found earlier by the entry in Coles's *English Dictionary* (1676), where one definition of 'craft' is 'small vessels as ketches etc.', which may imply it was a well-established usage by this date. But the *OED* compilers need not have resorted to conjecture. Kurath and Kuhn give two relevant entries in their *Medieval English Dictionary* where 'Craft 9a' is partly defined as 'something built or made . . . a building, ornament, painting, ship etc.', and for their example of the meaning 'ship' they quote Beryn *c.*1460:

> Wel was hym þat coude bynd or ondo
> Any rope with-in shippe, þat longit to þe crafft.

Under 'ship-craft (c)' (meaning 'ship'), they give as an example Scrope 1450: 'The King sent . . . to get þingis that myght abide with thayme that their ship-crafte brake not in the see.' An example can be cited from the late fourteenth century in *Richard the Redeless,* iv. 74-7, where we read:

> Than lay the lordis a-lee, with laste and with charge,
> And bare aboute the barge, and blamed the maister,
> That knewe not the kynde cours, that to the crafte longid,
> And warned him wisely, of the wedir-side.[8]

We can even go further back than this, for the Bosworth and Toller *Anglo-Saxon Dictionary* enters under 'Cræft IV' 'a craft, any kind of ship'. In view of these examples it can be regarded as certain that the usage was current in Shakespeare's day; indeed Shakespeare himself may be using it elsewhere in a pun in *Troilus and Cressida* (IV. v. 103-4) where Troilus runs riot with piscatorial metaphors:

> Whilst others fish with craft for great opinion,
> I with great truth catch mere simplicity.[9]

Jenkins's objection clearly has no force against the weight of this evidence. Trusting to etymological evidence, then, to refute Miles's argument turns out to be relying on 'false fire'.

A more fundamental objection, however, becomes clear in Jenkins's comment on Hamlet's earlier lines (III. iv. 207-11), 'Let it work . . . at the moon': 'Hamlet's confidence in the outcome will prepare the audience for it, but affords no justification for supposing that he has any precise plan for bringing it about (which he ultimately does by sudden inspiration, V. ii. 6-53), still less that he "has planned in advance for the intervention of the pirates" (*SQ,* xxvi, 279)'. Jenkins rejects the possibility of a pun on 'crafts' because he refuses to contemplate the reading of these lines it would imply.

The possibility of a pun on 'crafts' does not, of course, prove that Shakespeare intended one, but it does open up the possibility of a different understanding of Hamlet's reaction to being sent to England. The phrase 'two crafts directly meet' suggests accommodation to a pun because literally it would be against Hamlet's interest for the plots or stratagems to meet directly, and his aim is obviously to keep his plans secret. It would be very much in character for Hamlet to express through a pun what he does not wish to reveal openly (as he shows in the first words he speaks in the play). It is true that the reference to 'crafts' in the 'closet' scene would be puzzling to an audience, because it is the first we hear of Hamlet's intention of initiating the counterplot (though the meaning 'ships' is the first, not the second, meaning that springs to mind to a modern audience, and this might well have been the case with a popular audience in Shakespeare's time if the *OED* is right that the meaning, far from being 'technical', was a popular one). In any case Hamlet constantly likes to keep friend, foe, and even audience guessing at his precise inten-

tions. Shakespeare is constantly engaged in mystification in *Hamlet* (as befits a play which questions the adequacy of 'your philosophy'), especially in the later versions, as, for instance, when he substitutes in Q2 and F a far more ambiguous response of the Queen to Hamlet's revelation that he knows of his father's murder, compared to her unambiguous response in Q1: 'I never knew of this most horride murder'. The difference between Q2 and F in their account of the meeting with the pirates might well be explained by a later decision in F to make the nature of the encounter more ambiguous. We can also accept Jenkins's explanation that the purpose of the Q2 passage in III. iv. 207-12 is to 'prepare the audience' for what is to come.

Miles points out that Hamlet is surprisingly acquiescent when Claudius tells him he must board the boat for England (IV. iii. 44). He simply repeats Claudius's command 'For England' (F turns it into a question) and then says 'Good', followed by the somewhat mysterious remark: 'I see a cherub that sees them' (referring to Claudius's 'purposes'). Jenkins finds in this 'a hint that Hamlet perceives more than the King supposes', but it is the cherub that sees Claudius's intention; Hamlet merely sees the cherub. He only finds out Claudius's true intentions when he opens the letter addressed to the King of England on board ship. Hamlet may be intimating that he sees a glimmer of providential help in the journey to England and that it might provide him with an opportunity if properly understood and prepared for, or it might simply be, as Petsch suggests, that Hamlet is here appealing to the conscience of the King to remember that God sees all.[10]

Miles interprets the nine additional lines of Q2 (III. iv. 204-12) as Hamlet's first revelation of an attempt to take advantage of such an opportunity:

> Ther's letters sealed, and my two Schoolfellowes,
> Whom I will trust as I will Adders fang'd,
> They beare the mandat, they must sweep my way
> And marshall me to knavery: let it work,
> For tis the sport to have the enginer
> Hoist with his own petar, an't shall goe hard
> But I will delve one yard belowe their mines,
> And blowe them at the Moone: o tis most sweete
> When in one line two crafts directly meete.[11]

Jenkins's note on 'knavery' here is interesting, because it indicates a refusal to contemplate Hamlet's taking the initiative (the a priori assumption is the Romantic one found in Goethe and Coleridge that he is too inward-looking and too kind to act ruthlessly): 'knavery' therefore is interpreted as 'to be suffered, of course, not committed by the speaker, cf. V. ii. 19' (the reference to 'royal knavery' in V. ii. 19 is not relevant to the point). For similar reasons 'marshall me to knavery' is glossed by Hibbard as 'ceremoniously conduct me into a trap'.[12] It is clear from the next lines, however, that Hamlet is talking about taking a lead from his erstwhile schoolfellows; he will 'blowe them at the Moone' by 'undermining' them at their own game. In any case he has no idea at this point that they are leading him into a trap; he has simply lost all trust in them. 'Marshall' means 'lead me to knavery', as it does for Macbeth when he addresses the phantom dagger: 'Thou marshall'st me the way that I was going' (*Macbeth*, II. i. 42). Hamlet's position is clear: he has lost trust in the friendship of Rosencrantz and Guildenstern and suspects they are being used in some way by the principal plotter ('engineer') Claudius, although he does not know exactly how until he opens the letter to the King of England on board ship. He will therefore take counter-measures and destroy their plans by the kind of underhand means ('knavery') they are using against him. Given this reading, it is not unreasonable to interpret the reference to 'two crafts' as a pun by which Hamlet is suggesting covertly (as is his wont) that the preparations for this counterplot are already under way in arranging a meeting of the two craft at sea. It is perhaps indiscreet of Hamlet even to hint obscurely at such intentions, but one of the most intriguing features of Hamlet's complex character is the all too human mixture of discretion and indiscretion in his conduct. At this stage it seems unlikely that his plan involves having Rosencrantz and Guildenstern killed, in spite of the violence of the metaphors; but a plan to engineer a quick and unexpected return to Denmark might well enable him to 'hoist' Claudius 'with his own petar'. Whether Hamlet has had time to arrange such a meeting is immaterial, so long as we feel there has been sufficient stage time. Claudius first mentions the intention of sending Hamlet to England in open conversation with Polonius, and in the presence of Ophelia, before the play scene (III. i. 171). Much happens between this and Hamlet's first mention of the journey, which Gertrude says she has 'forgot' (III. iv. 203)—a subtle intimation that she had the information some time before.

At this point it might be well to quote Miles's commentary on these lines:

> One would think it required a miraculous allowance of critical obtuseness to ignore a counterplot so strikingly pre-arranged. Yet, opening Coleridge, you find 'Hamlet's capture by the pirates: how judiciously in keeping with the character of the over-meditative Hamlet, ever at last determined by accident or by a fit of passion!' And opening Ulrici . . . God save the mark! 'Accident frustrates his plans. Captured by pirates he is set on shore in Denmark against his will' etc. And opening *Wilhelm Meister* you find Hamlet's 'capture by pirates, and the death of the two courtiers by the letter which they carried', regarded as 'injuring exceedingly the unity of the piece, particularly as the hero has no plan'. After such obvious, amazing misconception, one may be pardoned for believing he sees
>
>   Two points in Hamlet's soul
> Unseized by the Germans yet.[13]

To make assurance doubly sure, comes the letter to Horatio, 'In the grapple, I boarded them; on the instant they got clear of our ship: so I alone became their prisoner. They have dealt with me like thieves of mercy; but they knew what they did'. Can circumstantial proof go further? Could any twelve men of sense

on such a record, acquit Hamlet of being an accessory before, as well as after, the fact?[14]

The letter from Hamlet to Horatio (IV. vi. 17-20) is interpreted very differently by Jenkins (who quotes Miles at this point):

> There is no justification for inferring (as Miles *A Review of Hamlet*, 1870, pp. 70-1 and recently in *SQ*, xxvi, 276-84) that they were therefore in league with Hamlet and the whole pirate encounter a plot to get him back to Denmark. In that case Hamlet could hardly have spoken of their 'mercy'. The implication is that they showed mercy in calculated exchange for services to be rendered.[15]

Jenkins's interpretation of the letter is not implausible if taken alone from what has preceded it and what is to come. Hamlet certainly seems to be giving the impression here to Horatio that the meeting with the pirates was fortuitous:

> Ere we were two days old at sea, a pirate of very warlike appointment gave us chase. Finding ourselves too slow of sail, we put on a compelled valour, and in the grapple I boarded them. On the instant they got clear of our ship, so I alone became their prisoner. They have dealt with me like thieves of mercy. But they knew what they did: I am to do a turn for them . . . I have words to speak in thine ear will make thee dumb; yet are they much too light for the bore of the matter . . . Rosencrantz and Guildenstern hold their course for England; of them I have much to tell thee.
>
>   (IV. vi. 14-28)

Miles has not helped his case by omitting the words at the end of his quotation: 'I am to do a turn for them', because it looks as if Hamlet is suggesting he did some sort of deal with the pirates on the spot, though it does not necessarily mean this. On the other hand, Hamlet's remark, 'But they knew what they did', sounds suspiciously like an acknowledgement that the whole episode was under control in a way not usually associated with fights at sea, and his description of their behaviour as like 'thieves of mercy' is not incompatible with Miles's view that the meeting had been prearranged, especially if he is not being totally frank with Horatio. 'Thieves of mercy' would be a good phrase to describe pirates who have agreed to his rescue plan, whether or not they have received good payment. Robert Petsch argues against Miles's view that Hamlet is sparing with the information he imparts to Horatio, arguing that Hamlet always treats Horatio 'with boundless trust',[16] but the text of the play hardly bears out the contention. Hamlet has all along been economical in what he tells his friend: he refuses to explain what the Ghost has said to him, for instance (I. v. 123 f.), and he does not reveal that earlier plot to catch the conscience of the King until just before the players enter (III. ii. 75-87), although he has been hard at work for some time arranging it. Even in this letter he is too cautious to reveal how he has behaved towards his old school-fellows, and the information that they 'hold their course for England', while perfectly true, is full of the irony of disingenuousness. Miles's comment would appear to be justified: 'Horatio's ignorance of the capture is no argument against its being premeditated. It would have been very unlike Hamlet, either to compromise his friend, who remained at Court in service of the King, or to extend his secret needlessly.'[17]

The implausibility of the story as Hamlet tells it also gives Hamlet's letter the impression of disingenuousness. It is difficult to believe that by chance Hamlet is the only person who boarded the pirate ship and that by chance the pirates immediately sailed away with Hamlet still on board without their attempting any further assault. Pirate ships would presumably usually attack in order to seize more than the first man who came on board, even if they immediately (by chance) happened to recognize who he was and his potential for ransom. Shakespeare need not have given all these circumstantial details or made them so prominent unless he wanted to draw special attention to Hamlet's conduct on the occasion. Indeed Q1 makes no mention of pirates and is none the worse in its plotting for that. Many earlier commentators have found Hamlet's account of the encounter with the pirates implausible, including those who for one reason or another come to accept that the meeting was accidental. Lawrence, for instance, remarks that it 'strains probability',[18] while the nineteenth-century commentator D.J. Snider remarks: 'The whole proceeding is so suspicious that were such an event to occur in real life, everybody would think at once of collusion.'[19] Petsch argues in general that the events of the story, as Hamlet tells it, are thoroughly in character, and in particular that the impulsiveness of Hamlet's nature would make his rash attempt to fight single-handed thoroughly typical.[20] Our impression of Hamlet's character, however, must derive from the particularities of the text, not govern the text's interpretation, and it is these particularities that are in question here.

Jenkins follows earlier commentators in arguing that Hamlet's final account of the meeting with the pirates in Act V, scene ii is the key to understanding what happened. The dialogue at V. ii. 6-53, in which Hamlet gives Horatio an account of the forging of Claudius's letter to the King of England and the ultimate fate of Rosencrantz and Guildenstern, clearly indicates, says Jenkins, that Hamlet's behaviour on board ship was the result of 'sudden inspiration', and so the author of the *Shakespeare Quarterly* article (Martin Stevens) is wrong. The same view had been taken some hundred years earlier by D.J. Snider, who finds Hamlet's description of what happened in this scene decisive in rejecting what he otherwise regards as the persuasive view that the meeting with the pirates was planned: 'Yet this view, apparently so well founded, we must abandon when we read Hamlet's account of the affair (V. ii). In that he ascribes his action wholly to instinct; there was no premeditation, no planning at all.'[21] Lawrence endorses this view in quoting Snider.[22]

Miles's interpretation of Hamlet's narrative at this point is very different: the opening of Claudius's letter to the King of England is

a sudden inspiration . . . It is the only second hope on which he can count; for if the chances of the sea prevent the contemplated rescue, he is infallibly lost without that earnest conjuration. The whole 'rash' undertaking is a supplemented plot; a reserved escape, an 'indiscretion' only meant to serve in case his pirate plot should fail.[23]

By opening the letter Hamlet providentially obtains the public proof of Claudius's guilt that he would otherwise lack, and he can thereby justify his actions before the Danish people when he finally takes his revenge.

In contrast to Jenkins's view that Hamlet links the finding of the letter and the meeting with the pirate ship as examples of providence coming to his aid, Miles contrasts the planning of the encounter with the pirates with the unplanned opening of the letter. Hamlet's second account of the episode (V. ii) says very little about the meeting with the pirates on the grounds that he has informed Horatio of that already (V. ii. 55). Instead he concentrates almost exclusively on the discovery of Claudius's letter and the substitution of his own version of it. His comments on the intervention of providence arise entirely in the context of the narrative concerning the letter, and it is therefore not unreasonable to conclude that that is what it is referring to. Miles's view seems to me much more closely in accordance with Hamlet's words than that of either Jenkins or Snider:

> Rashly—
> And prais'd be rashness for it: let us know
> Our indiscretion sometimes serves us well
> When our deep plots do pall; and that should learn us
> There's a divinity that shapes our ends,
> Rough-hew them how we will.
>
> (V. ii. 6-11)

Neither a chance meeting nor a planned meeting with the pirates could be regarded as an 'indiscretion', although Hamlet's action in boarding the ship might be. But at this point Hamlet is describing the moments before he steals the letter, not the later event. The rashness clearly refers to the sudden decision to steal the letter just before he leaves his cabin to seek out in the dark the sleeping Rosencrantz and Guildenstern (V. ii. 12-18). Hamlet only cursorily mentions the sea-fight next day nearly forty lines later (V. ii. 53-5). He must, therefore, be *contrasting* the unpremeditated opening of the letter with those 'deep plots' that he fears may have gone wrong—if he is thinking of a particular 'deep plot' it could only be the one Miles mentions, for he is hardly likely to be looking at the matter from Claudius's point of view. It is worth noting that Shakespeare does not use the word Pope thought appropriate here—'fail'—but 'pall/paule',[24] a word meaning 'falter', suggesting doubt over whether it ('they') will succeed or not. At the moment he is referring to he would not have known whether the agreement with the pirates was going to succeed. Miles's interpretation is further strengthened by the imagery of lines 10-11, for if he had arranged the meeting with the pirates he would have 'rough-hewn' a plan that providence then refined by inspiring the impromptu opening of the letter. 'Rough-hew' would seem to be a perfect expression to describe the formulation of the plan, for there seems to have been no specific plan for dealing with Claudius when Hamlet arrives back. Imagery could hardly have a greater preciseness. The main argument, then, that Jenkins produces to defend his position turns out to be flawed. The orthodoxy that Lawrence, Jenkins, and Hibbard espouse is seen to be based on the a priori assumption that Hamlet lacks the initiative to finish the task of revenge, not on a plausible reading of the text (especially the Q2 text).

It is strange, however, that the best evidence to justify Miles's viewpoint comes from the text that also includes that long soliloquy 'How all occasions do inform against me' (IV. iv. 32-66) that the Folio suppresses. Strange because while the plot to meet up with the pirates suggests verve and initiative, the soliloquy is the most insistent example of that other theme in the play, Hamlet's own doubt and uncertainty whether he is able to carry out the revenge entrusted to him. It is apparent, however, that throughout *Hamlet* Shakespeare has tried to steer a difficult course between a sufficiently heroic tragic protagonist and the profound psychological interest in the character that results from Hamlet's constant introspection, which is the play's greatest achievement. That even some of his contemporaries had doubts whether he had achieved the right balance is evident (if somewhat obscurely) from two very different contemporary reactions to the play. For instance, in the account given of Burbage's interpretation of the part in the anonymous funeral elegy of 1618 (although scanty it gives his role as Hamlet the fullest treatment), we seem to be hearing of a vigorous, heroic figure:

> He's gone and with him what a world are dead,
> Which he revived, to be revived so.
> No more young Hamlet, old Hieronimo,
> Kind Lear, the grieved Moor, and more beside,
> That lived in him, have now for ever died.
> Oft have I seen him leap into the grave,
> Suiting the person, which he seemed to have,
> Of a sad lover, with so true an eye
> That there I would have sworn he meant to die;
> Oft have I seen him play this part in jest,
> So lively that Spectators and the rest
> Of his sad crew, whilst he but seemed to bleed,
> Amazed, thought even then he died indeed.[25]

On the other hand the parody of *Hamlet* by Shakespeare's fellow playwrights Marston, Chapman, and Jonson in the Blackfriars' play *Eastward Ho!* mocks the lady Gertrude's footman called Hamlet for his unheroic incompetence in love ('he gives no . . . milke, as I have an other servant does', III. ii. 44-5), as well as his incompetence in his other duties. The very fact that he is given the role of a servant emphasizes the playwrights' view that he is unsuitable to be a tragic hero.

This is, no doubt, slight evidence to go on, but it might give us an indication of why Q2 and F differ as they do.

In Q2 the attempt to strike a balance involves the inclusion both of the lines in which Hamlet expresses his wish to blow his enemies to the moon and his determination to outplay Claudius in knavery, shortly followed by a long soliloquy accusing himself of unnecessary delay, of cowardice, and of 'thinking too precisely on the event' (IV. iv. 41). The two passages are not absolutely contradictory since the soliloquy ends with a resolution to affect bloody thoughts from henceforth, a sentiment which, it could be argued, inspires the earlier passage. On the other hand there is a considerable contradiction in the tone of self-confidence with which he punningly announces his plan of action and the despondency and self-recrimination of the soliloquy. This contradiction becomes more disruptive if (as I have argued) the plan that Hamlet is announcing in his pun on 'crafts' turns out to have been put into effect later. The objection, of course, is not that people may not realistically be self-contradictory in this way, but that the suggestion of inadequacy in the soliloquy and the retrospective futility it accords the earlier vaunting (which in the light of the soliloquy is made to look like braggadocio) undermine Hamlet's tragic status. By taking out both these passages in the Folio text Shakespeare (assuming the modification is Shakespeare's) avoids both the element of contradiction and making so large an issue of Hamlet's inadequacy, though of course the issue is raised elsewhere in the play. A further consequence is to make the plan to meet the pirates more obscure and indeed, as the history of *Hamlet* commentary suggests, invisible to most subsequent readers. The same process of wanting to make Hamlet's initiative less prominent may also account for the substitution in F of 'deare plots' for Q2's 'deep plots' (V. ii. 9), for while 'deep' might well hark back to the mining metaphor of III. iv. 196-8, its change to 'deare' seems to suggest the more general theme of the vanity of human wishes. Even the question mark in F in place of the full stop in Q2, after Hamlet's repetition of Claudius's order that he must embark for England: 'For England?' (IV. iii. 47), is a curious addition seeing that Hamlet has informed his mother earlier that the order has already been given (III. iv. 202). It would be wrong, however, to insist here on a more precise interpretation of punctuation than Elizabethan practice required.

The influence of the F reading seems to have prevailed in spite of its greater obscurity, but there may have been another influence at work in masking Shakespeare's intention here. There is some evidence that there has been a shift in stage presentation of Shakespeare over the years away from emphasis on speech performance and towards a greater emphasis on action and stage business. Bertram Joseph, in his excellent account of the importance of elocution in the Elizabethan educational system and its influence on Shakespeare's style, suggests a level of aural sophistication in Shakespeare's contemporary audiences that no modern audience could hope to match.[26] The importance given to recitation not only accounts for the delight in the set speech in Elizabethan drama, but also for the propensity towards elaborate 'undramatic' narrative accounts of offstage events. There is some evidence too, I think, that Elizabethan stage presentation was considerably more static than our modern approach allows. We know, for instance, that it was the custom before Garrick for actors to stand around, inattentive to the speaker, until it was their turn to speak—which suggests that long speeches were treated more like operatic arias than as parts of realistic dialogue. Indeed we are informed by Francis Gentleman in his *Dramatic Censor* (1770) that it was common practice before Garrick to 'sing' Shakespeare's lines: '[Garrick] certainly, as a lover of nature, despised the titum-ti, monotonous sing-song then fashionable, and indeed equally admired, till within these last thirty years'.[27] Some hint that these 'operatic' techniques applied in Shakespeare's day is provided by that same anonymous elegy to Burbage I have already quoted, for there we are told that the other actors on stage, like the audience, were 'amazed' by Burbage's lifelike performance, suggesting that they were less concerned with responding in character than as ordinary onlookers. The new Globe in London, with its obscuring onstage pillars, also suggests, I think, that Elizabethan audiences were willing to accept a more static presentation of the acting that perhaps allowed the speaker to come forward, as in the older style of opera production on the modern stage. The fact that now even modern opera production, with its highly artificial conventions, attempts—sometimes ludicrously—a degree of realistic movement, shows how absurdly far we have gone along the road of misunderstanding the conventional nature of all drama. However, this is not the place to discuss acting techniques, but merely to point out that such tendencies towards stage realism add to the obscurity of Shakespeare's intentions.

Hamlet's meeting with the pirates is presented entirely in narrative in the play; we see nothing of the action on stage, while the prominence of the meditative Hamlet on stage with his soul-searching soliloquies has become all the more highlighted by the contrast with the activity that surrounds him. This might be at least part of the explanation why Miles's plausible reading of the text of *Hamlet* has been either ignored or condemned out of hand. The same fate has attended the more recent attempt to revive the argument by Martin Stevens in the *Shakespeare Quarterly*. The difference in the two texts of the play may indicate that the process of undermining Hamlet's heroic status may have been begun by Shakespeare himself, or at least by the players' interpretation of the play during Shakespeare's lifetime. If this softening of the Prince occurred so early, it might also account for why, even in the early responses to the play, we find a discrepancy between those, like Burbage's elegist in 1618 and the caricature of Hamlet in *Eastward Ho!*

Notes

1. As quoted in *Variorum Hamlet*, ed. H.H. Furness (London and Philadelphia, Pa., 1877), i. 354. Furness may be quoting from the version of Miles's commentary in the *Southern Review* (Apr./July 1870), which I have not seen. The version of this sentence in the Boston publication, G. Miles, *A Review of Hamlet* (Boston, Mass., 1870, reprinted 1907), from which I generally quote, is somewhat toned down.

2. W.W. Lawrence, 'Hamlet's Sea Voyage', *PMLA* 59 (1944), 53 n. 23.

3. M. Stevens, 'Hamlet and the Pirates: A Critical Reconsideration', *Shakespeare Quarterly*, 26 (1975), 276-84.

4. R. Petsch, 'Hamlet unter den Seeräuben', *Englische Studien*, 36 (1905), 235.

5. *Hamlet*, ed. G.R. Hibbard (Oxford and New York, 1994), appendix A, p. 361.

6. Quotations are from the Arden Shakespeare edition of *Hamlet*, ed. H. Jenkins (London and New York, 1982), unless otherwise stated.

7. Ibid., note to III. iv. 212.

8. William Langland, *Richard the Redeless*, ed. W.W. Skeat (London, 1954), i. 628.

9. References to Shakespeare's plays other than *Hamlet* are to *The Complete Works*, ed. S. Wells and G. Taylor (Oxford, 1988).

10. Petsch, 'Hamlet unter den Seeräuben', 234: 'hier wie sonst handelt es sich um einen heftigen appell an das gewissen des verbrechers'.

11. I quote the text of the facsimile *Hamlet* (second quarto), 1605 (Menston, Ill., 1972), sig. I4^v.

12. *Hamlet*, ed. Hibbard, appendix A, x. 4.

13. Robert Browning, *Bishop Blougram's Apology*, ll. 946-7.

14. Miles, *A Review of Hamlet* (Boston, Mass., 1870, reprinted 1907), 162-4.

15. *Hamlet*, ed. Jenkins, note to IV. vi. 19.

16. Petsch, 'Hamlet unter den Seeräuben', 233: 'aber, fragen wir, hat Hamlet solche geheimnistuerei gegenüber Horatio nötig, dem er doch grenzenloses vertrauen schenkt und den er als rechten confident in seine geheimsten pläne einweiht?'

17. Miles, *A Review of Hamlet*, 179-80.

18. Lawrence, 'Hamlet's Sea Voyage', 52.

19. Quoted in *Variorum Hamlet*, ed. Furness, ii. 184.

20. 'Dass Hamlet sofort den kampf persönlich aufnimmt und als erster an das feindliche schiff springt, finden wir ja in seinem Naturell hoffentlich genügend begründet': Petsch, 'Hamlet unter den Seeräuben', 236.

21. Quoted in *Variorum Hamlet*, ed. Furness, ii. 184.

22. Lawrence, 'Hamlet's Sea Voyage', 53 n. 23.

23. Miles, *A Review of Hamlet*, 176, 178.

24. There seems little doubt that this is what Shakespeare wrote even though 'corrected' versions of Q2 change the word to 'fall'.

25. *Critical Responses to Hamlet,* ed. D.L. Farley-Hills (New York, 1997), i. 8. This elegy might be by Middleton, I think; cf. Middleton's poem in praise of *The Duchess of Malfi,* ed. F.L. Lucas (London, 1966), ii. 34.

26. B. Joseph, *Acting Shakespeare* (London, 1960).

27. See *Critical Responses to Hamlet,* ed. Farley-Hills, i. 216.

R. Chris Hassel, Jr. (essay date 1999)

SOURCE: "Mouse and Mousetrap in *Hamlet,*" in *Shakespeare Jahrbuch,* Vol. 135, 1999, pp. 77-92.

[In the following essay, Hassel examines the mouse and mousetrap imagery in Hamlet.*]*

When Hamlet names "The Murder of Gonzago" for Claudius, he calls it "The Mousetrap", adding, "Marry how? Tropically".[1] Since Hamlet has already told us that he hopes to use the play to "catch the conscience of the king" (2.2.591), we quickly hear several teasing puns and figures. Hamlet the mouser may be playfully connecting the "trap" of "trapically" with the "marry" of Claudius' marriage to "his mouse" Gertrude. He is also probably punning on "tropically" as "in the way of a trope; metaphorically, figuratively", using the common Renaissance figure of the mousetrap as "A device for enticing a person to his destruction or defeat".[2] But though we quickly get Hamlet's "tropical" gist, his general meaning, we have not done so well with its ingenious particularity. John Doebler has made a good start by suggesting that the well-known Augustinian trope of the *muscipula diaboli,* the mousetrap of the devil, highlights and informs the mouse and mousetrap imagery in *Hamlet.* Doebler also shows that popular Renaissance beast-lore combines with this theological context to present in a mouse-like Claudius "all that was gluttonous, lascivious, corrupt, and defiling":

> "What better image for the corrupter of Denmark, the polluter of the royal wedding bed, the one who banqueted in a time proper to mourning? Claudius is consistently presented by Shakespeare as being both diabolic and erotic."[3]

However, by focusing his interpretation almost exclusively on Claudius and by assuming a basically redemptive Hamlet, Doebler misses some of the most interesting possibilities of this material. What are we to make, for example, of Hamlet's perplexing portrayal as mouse and mouser, the tragic destroyer paired ambiguously with the heroic redeemer? How are we to understand Hamlet's problematic fury over what he considers Gertrude's excessive lasciviousness, and the resultant associations of his mother with the mouse and the mousetrap? Doebler has also left relatively unexplored the traditional associations of the mouse with secretive destructiveness and the play's persistent pairing of the destructive and the lascivious

Claudius. Undetected mouse-predators, mouse-banes, and mouse-medicines are also lurking in the darker corners of *Hamlet.* Legendary mouse-quellers like St. Gertrude and Apollo may share some of these hiding places. Finally, theological and iconographic traditions may connect Hamlet with Joseph the archetypal maker of mousetraps in ways that Doebler has not suggested. Neither Shakespeare, his characters, nor his audience could be expected to have kept all of these associations suspended in one rich and contradictory mixture, but each would have known some of them. The quality of their theatrical experience, and ours, is enhanced by their recovery. Let us start our own unique and imperfect concoction with Gertrude.

GERTRUDE AS MOUSE AND MOUSETRAP

Hamlet embarrasses Ophelia with his quips about "country matters", lying in "laps" and "between maids' legs" just before the "mousetrap" play begins, and he jokes easily with his schoolmates about Fortune's "secret parts" (3.2.109, 113; 2.2.232). However, from the start of the play he is also obsessed by what he perceives as his mother's lasciviousness. He calls her sexual "frailty" worse than "a beast", who would with "wicked speed" "post / With such dexterity to incestuous sheets" (1.2.146, 150-51, 156-57). He insults her more publicly with the Player-Queen's outrageous promise of a fidelity that will survive her first husband's death: "Such love must needs be treason in my breast", she says, and "A second time I kill my husband dead / When second husband kisses me in bed" (3.2.170, 176-77). In her closet after the play, Hamlet is even more voluble on the subject of what he considers Gertrude's inappropriate lust. It is at the end of this scene that Hamlet spits out Claudius's sobriquet "mouse", the name he imagines his stepfather using when he is about to make love to Gertrude (3.4.184). "What have I done", she asks him, "Ay me, what act"? (3.4.40, 52). His answer roars and thunders her salaciousness at her:

> [It] blurs the grace and blush of modesty,
> Calls virtue hypocrite, takes off the rose
> From the fair forehead of an innocent love,
> And sets a blister there, makes marriage vows
> As false as dicers' oaths.
>
> (3.4.42-46)

"[S]uch a deed / [. . .] from the body of contraction plucks / The very soul, and sweet religion makes / A rhapsody of words!" Her lust and the resultant times are to Hamlet "ulcerous", "corrupt", "infecting unseen", "pursy" or corpulent, like a "compulsive ardor" to "charge" in battle. She has let reason pander to will, virtue's wax melt in the flaming fires of youth. She lies in "the rank sweat of an enseamed bed, / Stewed in corruption, honeying and making love / Over the nasty sty."[4] At Hamlet's urging Gertrude finally sees in her own soul "such black and grained spots / As will not leave their tinct" (3.4.46-49, 148-50, 154, 83-89, 91-95). Of course, this general remorse does not concede all of Hamlet's outrageous charges against her. Gertrude certainly comes off better than her son in this scene, who seems if not mad drunk with a moral outrage and an accompanying misogyny that would seem to indict his own imbalance as much as his mother's lust.[5]

This "mouse" Hamlet refers to could of course be merely a term of endearment in Shakespeare and the proverbs and poems of his near-contemporaries. In *Love's Labour's Lost* (5.2.19), for example, Rosaline calls Katherine "mouse" innocently enough. We see the potential misogyny more clearly in *Romeo and Juliet*. When Lady Capulet wants to call her husband "a nocturnal prowler after women" (Pelican gloss), she says "You have been a mouse-hunt in your time" (4.4.11). The joke or the insult can be gender-neutral, as in the poem "Our Sir John" a century or so before Shakespeare, where neither the woman nor the friar can resist their lust:

> Ser Iohn ys taken in my mouse-trappe:
> ffayne wold I haue hym bothe nyght and day.
> he gropith so nyselye a-bought my lape,
> I haue no pore to sa[y hym nay.][6]

But while Andreas Alciatus and Edward Topsell concede that "white mouse" or "bad mouse" can be applied as Doebler does "to a man who is lascivious or of immoderate lust", this pejorative is more commonly applied to a woman. Topsell reflects the misogynistic early modern commonplace that among mice (and men of course) "the female is much more venerious than the male", and Meyer Schapiro mentions from popular tradition that the mouse is often "the womb, the unchaste female, the prostitute". Topsell illustrates this same prejudice when he credits Alciatus with the saying, "she was a mouse's hole, signifying that her virginity was lost, and that she suffered any lovers as a mouse-hole doth any mouse". This tradition of the salacious female mouse is so strong that the story reappears in many sources of a dead pregnant female mouse cut open to reveal "all the young females within her belly [. . .] also found pregnant".[7] English proverbs are also fond of connecting the devil's entrapment of human lust with the mousetrap. One of Whiting's proverbs reads "Women are the devil's mousetraps", and a similar one in the Oxford *Proverbs* "Women are the devil's nets".[8] The mouse is also in the popular tradition an animal in which witches and the devil sometimes manifest themselves, and a form taken by the graven images of vicious, malignant, and evil gods. As Schapiro says, "the mousetrap is, at the same time, a rich condensation of symbols of the diabolical and the erotic and their repression; the trap is both a female object and the means of destroying sexual temptation".[9]

Though it wears a fur coat, the misogyny woven into the lining of this tradition is as clear as the female lasciviousness it purports to describe. However unfair it is to Gertrude, she is to her son this "unchaste female", virtually Alciatus's emblem of female lasciviousness. As Hamlet urges his mother Gertrude to amend what he considers her lack of chastity and sanctity, "Repent what's past, avoid what is to come," (3.4.151), he often uses terms that suggest the diabolic as well as the erotic associations of the

mouse. Her lust is like "Rebellious hell", mutinying "in a matron's bones". This "Devil" "of habits" is lust as well as custom, and Claudius seems to be, and to bear, the "devil" lust that "cozened" Gertrude "at hoodman-blind". If she can just "[r]efrain to-night", Hamlet says, "that shall lend a kind of easiness / To the next abstinence; the next more easy". Not to repress her sexuality, yielding to Claudius's "damned fingers", is yielding to the devil himself. With practice she will be able to "either . . . the devil, or throw him out / With wondrous potency" (3.4.77-84, 162-171). I would conjecture "trip" or "trap" against the more traditional "curb" or "quell" for the missing verb here, especially since Hamlet names her "mouse" and asks her to help him trap Claudius at the end of this conversation: "Let the bloat king tempt you again to bed, / Pinch wanton on your cheek, call you his mouse" (3.4.183-84). But Hamlet's fear that she will not be able to abstain from Claudius' bed even after all of his chastising words also confirms the lyric's picture of a woman with "no power to say him nay".

The tension between Hamlet's perception and his mother's reality is emphasized by one of the most curious pieces of mouse-lore in *Hamlet*. St. Gertrude of Nivelle, a woman of great sanctity and absolute chastity, was well-known in England and throughout northern Europe because she stopped a plague of mice. She was for this reason invoked as often as the more material vermifuge wormwood against rats and mice, and is pictured iconographically with mice running around her or on her crozier. One wonders if Shakespeare changed her name from Geruthe in Belleforest to emphasize Hamlet's confusion?[10] Hamlet's "That's Wormwood" just as the Player-Queen is about to "protest too much" her eternal fidelity to her first husband could inject more mouse-lore into his relationship with Gertrude (3.2.173; 221-22). Wormwood is of course both rotten timber and the bitter Biblical taste of contrition or mortification. It is also according to Topsell a common herbal remedy against mice: "Wormwood laid among clothes, and skins, defend them from mice; and also the water of wormwood sod, sprinkled upon clothes, hath the same operation" (p. 512). Hamlet seems to hope that once the "mouse" of Gertrude's lasciviousness is out, once his own "wormwood" has begun to have its shriving way with his mother, he will be able to persuade her to be wormwood as well as taste and use it, to repel the mouse of her own lust and Claudius in whom it resides.[11]

Oedipal impulses compete with self-righteous ones as Hamlet perceives his mother as the paradoxical combination of subject and object of temptation, attraction and repulsion of lust. He seems to see her at once as the snare that catches the devil Claudius (and the son Hamlet?) in lust, and snared herself in the same devil's mousetrap. She is a potentially repellent wormwood who tastes in her own mouth its corrective gall even while inspiring Hamlet's galling words. In most productions, Hamlet's repulsion and attraction are blazoned across the stage or screen in the looming bed on which they often perform some enigmatic rite. Only in some productions, most notably the

Olivier *Hamlet*, does Gertrude cool towards Claudius after the bedroom scene, apparently as a direct result of Hamlet's shriving. The 1982 Time-Life BBC videotape is I think more characteristic, where Gertrude remains Patrick Stewart's mouse. In almost every case Hamlet's perception of his mother's demonic sexuality competes interestingly with her more modest representation on the stage. Commonly her own allegiance remains as painfully divided as Hamlet's relationship to her.

THE LASCIVIOUS AND DESTRUCTIVE CLAUDIUS

In Shakespeare's *Henry V* the destructiveness of the mouse is thought of as underhanded, secretive work, sometimes connected to human thievery; the "weasel Scot" "[c]omes sneaking, and so sucks her princely eggs, / Playing the mouse in absence of the cat" (1.2.170-72). "Mouse" can also be a verb meaning "to ransack, rummage, pillage": "They have rifled and mowsed the cofer by a false key thei made" (1589) (*OED* 2 *Mouse* 4). Whiting cites an English proverb about destructiveness from 1546, "A mouse in time may bite a cable in two" (M738). In *Troilus and Cressida* Nestor is similarly called "that stale old mouse-eaten dry cheese" (5.4.9-10). Sometimes the mouse's destructiveness takes on especially sacrilegious, even diabolical overtones. Noah, according to Riegler, had to throw his glove at a mouse that was gnawing away at the hull of the Ark, and Rowland illustrates it "nibbling the sacred host", the communion wafer.[12]

In describing Claudius, Hamlet characteristically connects the lascivious and the destructive, the main characteristics that Alciatus, Shakespeare and the English proverbs all associate with the mouse. In fact, their pairing becomes something of a formula for understanding his mouse-uncle. Just before Hamlet decides to use the play as "the thing / Wherein I'll catch the conscience of the king", he calls Claudius a "Bloody, bawdy villain", and then a "treacherous, lecherous" one for killing his father and marrying his mother. His act is both "remorseless" in its destructiveness and "kindless", unnatural, in its heedless, incestuous lechery. We hear another reference to this pair of sins in the line "Upon whose property and most dear life / A damned defeat was made" (2.2.590-91, 565-66, 555-56). In Hamlet's eyes Gertrude as well as the kingdom is the erotic property, his father's the diabolically destroyed life. Finally, in Act 5, Claudius is called "incestuous, murd'rous damned Dane" by Hamlet and "carnal, bloody, and unnatural" (5.2.314, 370) by Horatio. Earlier in the same scene Hamlet describes Claudius as "He that hath killed my king, and whored my mother" (5.2.64). Claudius is "Bloody, bawdy villain", and "treacherous, lecherous, kindless villain"; he has "killed" and "whored"; he is "incestuous, murderous", "carnal, bloody". Such concise and formulaic statements of the destructive and lascivious impulses in this Claudius reinforce Hamlet's obsession with his uncle as the perfect quarry for a mousetrap.

The ghost of Hamlet's father is similarly fixated on Claudius's combination of lechery and treachery. He calls him "that incestuous, that adulterate beast", who "won to his shameful lust / The will of my most seeming-virtuous queen". Claudius is "lewdness", "lust", "garbage" in the same sequence. Denmark's bed is called "A couch for luxury and damned incest" (1.5.42, 45-46, 54-57, 83). At the same time that Hamlet is hearing what his father's ghost describes as Gertrude's "lust" and "luxury" with Claudius, he learns of his destruction of his father's body and the imperilment of his soul. "The leperous distilment [. . .] / [. . .] a most instant tetter barked about / Most lazar-like with vile and loathsome crust / All my smooth body", and left me "Unhouseled, disappointed, unaneled, / No reck'ning made, but sent to my account / With all my imperfections on my head" (1.5.64, 71-73, 77-79). Hamlet hears of this lechery and destructiveness, and he believes. As late as 4.4.56-57 the formula still holds: "How stand I then, / That have a father killed, a mother stained?" Treacherous, lecherous Claudius is a memory that never leaves "the book and volume of [Hamlet's] brain" or his father's (1.5.103).

Claudius shares this dual perception. To Polonius's "'Tis too much proved, that with devotion's visage / And pious action we do sugar o'er / The devil himself" (3.1.47-49), Claudius replies:

> How smart a lash that speech doth give my conscience!
> The harlot's cheek, beautied with plast'ring art,
> Is not more ugly to the thing that helps it
> Than is my deed to my most painted word.

> (3.1.50-53)

In this self-indictment Claudius admits killing his own brother and covering it up, sugaring it o'er, with the "plast'ring art" of the harlot. But though experiencing "The Mousetrap" may remind Claudius of his sexual as well as his political guilt, the king is more concerned about his treachery than his lechery as a result of seeing the play. He mentions the queen as one of the "effects for which I did the murder", but the "rank" offense, the crime that "smells to heaven", the "primal eldest curse" is Cain's sin, "A brother's murder" (3.3.54, 36-38). Catching Claudius's conscience in that treachery is also the primary purpose of Hamlet's strategy. It is "murder, though it have no tongue, [which] will speak", and "the murder of my father" (2.2.579, 581) that he will play before his uncle. Claudius feels deep remorse after "The Mousetrap", but "Though inclination be as sharp as will" he says that he cannot give up "th'effects" of his sin, the sexual and political property he has gained by killing his brother. Thus in the midst of his apparent moment of honest contrition, honest self-appraisal, a moment of "purging" close to "heaven" in Hamlet's mistaking eyes, Claudius is still ironically self-deceived. By confusing "can" and "will" he implies that he is unable to repent, rather than unwilling. But he will not repent. Therefore his prayer, beyond Hamlet's wildest hopes, "Has no relish of salvation in't". Though Claudius's "heels may kick at heaven", "his soul may be as damned and black / As hell, whereto it goes" (3.3.39, 54, 85, 74, 65-66, 92-95). Even without Hamlet's help, Claudius is hell-bound.

Of the dumb-show to "The Mousetrap", Hamlet tells Ophelia "This is miching mallecho; it means mischief" (3.2.131-32). Is Hamlet referring here not only to his own mischief but also to the mouse-thief of his father's life, crown and wife, and of his own hopes? Hanmer thought it meant "secret, covered, hidden iniquity", from the Spanish *malhecho*. So did Malone (misdeed). Warburton preferred lying in wait for the poisoner, from the eponym Malhechor (who is probably a criminal rather than a poisoner). Capell suggests an ill-looking, munching animal, compared to the mean figure of the poisoner in the dumb-show, and paralleling the Iniquity figure from the moralities.[13] In *Henry IV, Part 1* a similar micher munches blackberries (2.4.389-390). Combining these readings could yield "munching mischief", with Claudius as the muncher. Interestingly, Robert Herrick once called such a stealing, sneaking creature a "miching mouse", a phrase reminiscent of Hamlet's description of the "miching mallecho" of the murderer in the dumb-show. Whatever "mallecho" refers to, nonsense, mischief, poisoning, or something yet undiscovered, "miching" can definitely refer to the secretive destroying or theft of a mouse. But Hamlet could also be referring to himself and the play as the truant means to reverse the wrongs of the sneaking pilferer Claudius. This would support the image pattern of undermining the underminer, hoisting the engineer with his own petar (3.4.207-8), a secretive destruction that may be the mole's work as well as the mouse's. The "vicious mole of nature" (1.4.24) may then be the imperfection all must carry, even Hamlet, imaged as the underground destructiveness of these rodents that were associated with mice in the symbolic contours of the Renaissance mind.[14] Once again, Hamlet seems both mouse and mouser in this ingenious imagery.

HAMLET AS MOUSE AND MOUSER

One of Hamlet's first insults of Claudius is the cryptic "I am too much in the sun" (1.2.67). We usually assume he means that he is closer than he wants to be, in kin if not in kind, to this new father-king, the sun of Denmark, and this is surely one of Hamlet's meanings. But in the same scene Hamlet also calls his father "Hyperion" to Claudius's "satyr" (1.2.140). Hyperion is the father of Helios, the sun-god who is identified with Apollo by the fifth century B.C. Is Hamlet playing Apollo to his father's Hyperion? One of the names by which Apollo (*Iliad* 1.39) is known, "Sminthius", means "mouse-killer". Like the St. Gertrude we mentioned earlier, Apollo eliminated a plague of mice to earn this epithet. Hamlet shares Apollo's idealized nature, his love of philosophy, his inculcation of virtue.[15] Does he also share with him this role of exterminator? He certainly hopes to rid Denmark of its rodent-king. The connections are as provocative as they are unexpected.

There are grounds more relative than this. Predators of mice like the cat and the hawk and the owl occur in *Hamlet* in obscure but potentially threatening places. Hamlet's "The cat will mew" (5.1.279) during Ophelia's funeral promises the reassertion of the proper order of things,

good triumphing over evil, morality and hierarchy restored. In *Henry V* the absent cat is understood as this sort of mice-warden (1.2.170-72). But pictures of gleeful mice (or rats) dancing around caged cats embody the same reversal of natural order that now seems to reign in Denmark. In the epigram in Geffrey Whitney's emblem book, for example, these mice are called "the wicked sort", the trapped cats "worthy men". Even Dürer's little mouse in "The Fall of Man" is still held by the tail under Adam's foot, though he looks ready to spring loose as soon as Eve takes the serpent's proffered apple. The cat there looks languid; perhaps before the fall he knew nothing of mice, or of the need to catch them.[16] Hamlet's "I know a hawk from a handsaw" is similarly elusive and threatening, possibly connecting competent predation and pruning with a carpenter's competence to tear down and rebuild. Hamlet's manipulative playfulness with Polonius about the weasel-shaped cloud (2.2.370; 3.2.364) adds another mouse-predator to the cat and the hawk. Topsell tells us that the weasel was the mouse's worst enemy, "not only more inclined to hunt after them, than the cat, but [. . .] more terrible also unto them" (p. 508).

The cat-like, teasing method in Hamlet's madness is nowhere more clearly revealed than when he also refers to a mouse-bane just before "The Mousetrap". begins. The king asks "How fares our cousin Hamlet?" Hamlet replies, "Excellent, i'faith, of the chameleon's dish" (3.2.89-90). Now the chameleon was thought, as Maplet and Topsell both reveal, to eat air,[17] and so Hamlet is certainly referring to all of the false promises in the air of Denmark as well as Claudius's deceptive coloration. But Topsell tells us that chameleon (*OED Chameleon* 3) is also a potent mouse-poison: "The juice of the root of the herb Camelion, mixed with water and oil, draweth mice unto it, and killeth them by tasting thereof, if they drink not presently" (p. 512). Hamlet would indeed "fare" well if this mouse who is soon to be caught in "The Mousetrap" were drawn to eat of the chameleon's dish; unfortunately, their eating of death is almost simultaneous.

Oddly, mouse could also have had medicinal uses for Hamlet and his father. Topsell tells us, for example, that "the flesh of a mouse is hot and soft, [. . .] and doth expel black and melancholy choler". As Hamlet says of "my melancholy", the devil "is very potent with such spirits" (2.2.588). But if young Hamlet could use some of this medicine, Topsell gives us three good reasons why Old Hamlet could also. First, "Mice being cut and placed into wounds which have been bitten by Serpents, [. . .] do [. . .] cure and perfectly heal them". Old Hamlet calls his poisoner "The serpent that did sting thy father's life". Second, as a result of Old Hamlet's poisoning, "a most instant tetter barked about / Most lazar-like with vile and loathsome crust / All my smooth body". According to Topsell, "The dust of a mouse pounded and beaten to powder, and mixed with a certain oil, is very good and wholesome, for those which are grieved with a tettor or scab which may overrun their whole body". Finally, mouse is also considered good for "pain in his ears" (pp. 514-16).

Claudius, of course, "did pour / The lep'rous distilment" "into the porches" of Old Hamlet's ears (1.5.38, 71-73, 63-64).

Art historian James Snyder connects Joseph's mousetraps in the Merode Altarpiece to Joseph's apparent unimportance to Satan: "The marriage of Mary and Joseph was staged to make the miraculous birth of Christ less conspicuous to Satan by hiding the fact of his divine parentage. According to Saint Augustine, the marriage took place to fool the devil just as mice are fooled by the bait of the trap.[18] Hamlet, playing the fool or madman with Polonius, Claudius, Ophelia and Gertrude just before the performance of his own "Mousetrap", hopes similarly to disarm his adversaries by exaggerating his own weakness and asserting therefore his implausibility as an avenger. The second of Hamlet's two carpenter images, "There's a divinity that shapes our ends, / Rough—hew them how we will—", also connects Hamlet with Joseph as two carpenters humbly acquiescing in the superior craftsmanship of providence.[19] Hamlet's "I must be idle" underlines this strategy of disarming humbleness. But the many negatives of Claudius's "Nor what he spake [. . .] / Was not like madness." suggest that he is alerted, not disarmed, by the feigning conversation with Ophelia: "I do doubt the hatch and the disclose / Will be some danger;" (5.2.10-11; 3.2.87; 3.1.163-64, 66-67). He will not be an easy prey for Hamlet's mousetrap.

Punctuated as it is with the poisoned rapier and the poisoned cup, the final scene illustrates one last time how often the play's imagery of ironic reversal is associated with iconography of mouse and mousetrap. The rapier, which can symbolize honor but also sexuality and murder, is here the rodent king's means to pervert honor in a last underhanded plot of destructive treachery. The cup, emblem of fellowship and forgiveness but also of gluttony, serves Claudius's mouse-like drunkenness until the end, and then joins the rapier in more secretive and destructive mischief.[20] Even Claudius's mouse Gertrude dies by coming between the incensed points of these fearful adversaries. "Not a mouse stirring" is the tenth line of the play. In *Hamlet* the trap eventually silences all of them. Doebler finds clarity and closure as he finishes his exploration of the imagery of mouse and mousetrap in *Hamlet*. Hamlet is the redeemer; Claudius is the villain; Gertrude is discreetly omitted from the picture. But to me the transparent paradox that the trapper must himself die to purify a diseased kingdom, "set it right", (1.5.189) is not the play's last word.

The mousetrap trope becomes instead part of a pattern of images in *Hamlet* that poises the clarity of poetic justice against a universe of dark unknowing. On the one hand Laertes proclaims himself caught "as a woodcock to mine own springe", "justly killed with mine own treachery." Rosencrantz and Guildenstern, who would "sweep [Hamlet's] way / And marshall [him] to knavery.", will instead serve as "sport to have the enginer / Hoist with his own petar". Hamlet "will delve one yard below their mines / And blow them at the moon." Polonius "find'st to be too busy is some danger." Finally, Claudius is "hurt" with his own "envenomed" point. But as Horatio summarizes the play we are challenged to question Laertes' naive and dying notion that Claudius is "justly served", even if "It is a poison tempered by himself" that kills him, and forced to look again at Hamlet's reassuring if momentary sense of "a divinity that shapes our ends, / Rough—hew them how we will—". To Horatio the "judgments" seem "accidental" and the "slaughters" "casual". What "purposes" there are, in the human universe, at least, are "mistook". Horatio may hope of Hamlet that "flights of angels sing thee to thy rest"; but neither angels nor providence are asserted to govern similarly these "carnal, bloody, and unnatural acts" on earth. Hamlet is part of Horatio's bloody summary. Mouse and mouser are all carried off in the end by "this fell sergeant, Death," Augustine's "Bailiff",[21] and we are left deeply moved but also darkling.

One last proverbial tradition concerning the mouse would seem apposite to this troublesome denouement. In 1629 T. Adams says in a sermon: "The empiric to cure the fever, destroys the patient; so the wise man, to burn the mice, set on fire his barn." In 1816 Wolcot (P. Pindar) echoes this commonplace in his 2nd Epistle to Mrs. Clarke (WKS. 4:446), when he says, "Who, but a Bedlamite, would fire his house / To wreak his vengeance on a pilfering mouse".[22] One answer, apparently, is Hamlet. His reluctant doctoring loses a lot of patients, breaks a lot of bones, to reset time's dislocated joint. Is he then a Bedlamite? Hamlet the obsessed son and spiritual physician may think that only contribution, the wormwood of mortification, can cool those "fires that mutine in a matron's bones". Hamlet the moral and political exterminator may hope that his complex arsenal might at once expel the mouse-like lust in his too-lascivious mother and deter the object of her lust, the devilish, mouse-king Claudius, thus killing two mice with one application. Hamlet says he "must be cruel only to be kind." and he and Laertes also apparently "exchange forgiveness" (3.4.179; 5.2.318, 321), but neither the prince nor his audience can know how his wholesale destructiveness will weigh against the cure in the balance. The inner mystery in this play is almost as dark as the outer. On earth at least, here if not hereafter, Hamlet is punished along with his victims in his double role. And though he promises his mother earlier to "answer well / The death I gave" (3.4.177-78), such answers are not much in evidence in Denmark's dark world of mice and mousers.

Far from "plucking out the heart of his mystery", this learning impresses us with the unfathomable complexity of Hamlet's mind and his heart, as he plays, and is, Gertrude's loving but imperfect son and Denmark's scourge and minister. His lowest note would be the mischievous schoolboy, the sadistic spoilsport, the frustrated prince and the obsessive reformer, revelling in the public and private embarrassment and bitterness he is causing the mice Gertrude and Claudius to suffer. The "top of [his] compass" would be Hamlet's enactment of the deepest caring and the profoundest ministry to the "black and grained spots" of his mother's immortal soul. But even in that ministry there is something rank, choleric and diseased. We may play upon Hamlet even as we tease so "much music", such "excellent voice" (3.2.353-54) out of Shakespeare's uses of mouse and mousetrap lore. We cannot thereby know Hamlet, any more than Hamlet can know himself. In Denmark's unweeded garden it is as hard to distinguish mouse from mouser as it is to know which plants are poisonous, and which medicinal.

Notes

1. *The Complete Pelican Shakespeare,* (ed. by) Alfred Harbage (New York: Viking, 1984), 3.2.229; subsequently cited in text.

2. *Mousetrap* 1b and *Tropically* 1 in J.A. Simpson and E.S.C. Weiner, *The Oxford English Dictionary,* (2nd ed.) (Oxford: Clarendon, 1989); subsequently cited as *OED*. On the "trap" "trope" pun, see *A New Variorum Edition of Shakespeare, Hamlet,* (ed. by) H.H. Furness (Philadelphia: J.B. Lippencott, 1905), 1: 255.

3. John Doebler, "The Play Within the Play: the *Muscipula Diaboli* in *Hamlet*", *SQ* 23 (1972), 162-69; see also Meyer Schapiro's classic, "'*Muscipula Diaboli*', The Symbolism of the Merode Altarpiece", *Art Bulletin* 27 (1945), 182-83, 186.

4. "Swine" is also one of Luther's favorite metaphors for our uncontrolled desires; see *Index,* (ed. by) Joel W. Lunder in *Luther's Works* (Philadelphia: Fortress, 1986), for over thirty references. See "Hamlet's 'Too, Too Solid Flesh'" in *The Sixteenth Century Journal* 25 (1994), 609-22, for my argument that Luther's idea of the prudence or wisdom of the flesh might gloss Hamlet's problems with doing and knowing perfectly in a fallen world.

5. As Cherrell Guilfoyle says, *Shakespeare's Play Within Play* (Kalamazoo: Medieval Institute Pubs., 1990), p. 9, Hamlet often suffers from the "delusion of female wantonness". John King, *Tudor Royal Iconography* (Princeton: Princeton University Press, 1989), p. 183, and Arthur McGee, *The Elizabethan Hamlet* (New Haven: Yale University Press, 1987), pp. 152-53, remind us of its biblical heritage.

6. *Secular Lyrics of the Fourteenth and Fifteenth Centuries,* (ed. by) Russell Hope Robbins (Oxford: Clarendon, 1955), p. 20.

7. Andreas Alciatus, *Emblemata cum commentariis* (Padua, 1621; first published 1531) (New York: Garland, 1976), pp. 348-49; and Edward Topsell, *The History of Four-Footed Beasts* (London: William Jaggard, 1607), pp. 505-6. See also Pliny, *Natural History,* trans. Philemon Holland (London: A. Aslip, 1601), pp. 304-5.

8. Bartlett Jere Whiting, *Proverbs, Sentences, and Proverbial Sayings* (Cambridge: Harvard University Press, 1968), W530; *The Oxford Dictionary of English Proverbs* (3rd. rev. ed.) F.P. Wilson (Oxford: Clarendon, 1970), p. 910.

9. R. Riegler, "Maus", in *Handwörterbuch des deutschen Aberglaubens,* (ed. by) Bächtold-Stäubli (Berlin & Leipzig: W. de Gruyter, 1934-35) 6: 31-59; Schapiro, p. 186.

10. Riegler, 6: 39; S. Baring-Gould *The Lives of the Saints,* (rev. ed.) (Edinburgh: J. Grant, 1914), 1:viii, says, "People forget the age and parentage of St. Gertrude, but they remember the mice running up her staff." For another illustration see Baring-Gould 3: 306.

11. See my article "'Wormwood, Wormwood'," *ShJb* (1993), 150-62.

12. Riegler 6: 50; Beryl Rowland, *Animals With Human Faces* (Knoxville: University of Tennessee Press), 1973, p. 129.

13. See *Hamlet Variorum,* 1: 243-4, and *OED* 1 *Mitching.*

14. Topsell affirms this belief by disagreement (p. 498).

15. See *Oxford Classical Dictionary,* (ed. by) M. Cary and others (Oxford: Clarendon, 1949), pp. 68, 375, 445.

16. Geffrey Whitney, *A Choice of Emblems* (Leyden: Christopher Plantyn, 1586), p. 222; *Emblemata: Handbuch zur Sinnbildkunst des XVI. und XVII. Jahrhunderts,* (ed. by) Arthur Henkel und Albrecht Schöne (Stuttgart: J.B. Metzler, 1967), pp. 590-99. Erwin Panofsky, *Albrecht Dürer* (Princeton: Princeton University Press, 1948), 2: fig. 117.

17. See Pelican gloss; see also John Maplet, *A Green Forest, or a Natural History* (London: Henry Denham, 1567), p. 76, and Topsell, p. 114; Topsell is, however, skeptical.

18. James Snyder, *Northern Renaissance Art* (New York: Harry N. Abrams, 1985), p. 121. On this metaphor in Augustine's writing and its history see J. Rivière, *Le dogme de la rédemption chez saint Augustin* (Paris, 1933), pp. 117 ff., 320-38, cited in Schapiro, "A Note on the Merode Altarpiece", *Art Bulletin* 41 (1959), 327-28.

19. On Joseph's humble acquiescence to God's will, see Luther, *Sermons on the Gospel of St. John* (1957), 22: 76. On the association of carpentry tools with humility, see Luther, *Selected Psalms II* (1956), 13: 378; and *Lectures on Genesis* (1970), 6: 133, 157 (all ed. by) Jaroslav Pelikan, in *Works* (St. Louis: Concordia).

20. "Drunk as a mouse" is a common simile from the 14th to the 16th century. Whiting gives examples from Chaucer, Lydgate, Greene, Skelton, and three others.

21. 5.2.295-96; 3.4.205-10, 34; 5.2.310-17, 10-11, 369-74, 349, 325. So Schapiro, *"Muscipula"*, p. 182, translates Augustine's *"quasi praepositus mortis"*, when, speaking of the devil's mousetrap, he says "He has rejoiced in Christ's death, like a bailiff of death."

22. *The Oxford Dictionary of English Proverbs,* (ed. by) William George Smith, rev. Sir Paul Harvey (Oxford: Clarendon, 1948), p. 69.

SOURCES

Cherrell Guilfoyle (essay date 1986)

SOURCE: "'Ower Swete Sokor': The Role of Ophelia in *Hamlet,*" in *Shakespeare's Play within Play: Medieval Imagery and Scenic Form in Hamlet, Othello, and King Lear,* Western Michigan University, Medieval Institute Publications, 1990, pp. 7-19.

[*In the following essay, originally published in 1986, Guilfoyle traces Ophelia's character to the legend of Mary Magdalen as developed in medieval drama.*]

The virtuous disguise of evil in woman is described most bitterly by Shakespeare in *King Lear* (IV.vi.120-29): "Behold yond simpering dame / Whose face between her forks presages snow . . . / But to the girdle do the gods inherit, / Beneath is all the fiends'." If she can be separated from sexual considerations, for example in royalty or in comedy, woman can appear on a level with, if not equal to, man; but where his feelings are most deeply aroused, in love and veneration, or in lust and frustration, the writer finds her angel or devil, separately or interchangeably. In the opening cantos of *The Faerie Queene,*[1] Spenser presents the two pictures of woman which combine in a potent myth in the literature of all ages: the pure, young, innocent Una, characterized by her name, and her exact physical duplicate, who is, behind the façade, a filthy fiend. This sinister figure is later presented as Fidessa/Duessa, but in her first appearance she usurps the fair form of Una, the one truth. In one of the fragments of Euripidean tragedy, there is the saying "Woman brings to man the greatest possible succour, and the greatest possible harm."[2] The words for "greatest possible succour" are *ophelian . . . megistan.*

Ophelia's name links her to the idea of succor; "ower swete sokor" was a phrase used of Mary Magdalen in the Digby Magdalen play. In different ways, Ophelia and Magdalen embody the "angel/devil" dichotomy of woman, and the figure of Magdalen appears in the imagery of Ophelia's scenes throughout *Hamlet.* Conventions in Shakespeare are often hidden, because in his hands they do not appear conventional, but if the strands of the Magdalen legends are examined, it can be seen that many of them are woven into Ophelia's words and actions. These images reflect Shakespeare's preoccupation, not with the horrific figure described by Lear, but with innocence or good faith mistaken—for example, Desdemona mistaken by Othello, Hermione by Leontes, Imogen by Posthumus,

Cordelia by Lear—and Ophelia by Hamlet. The young woman in the Saxo and Belleforest versions of the *Hamlet* story was not virtuous (and not, of course, called Ophelia); Shakespeare changes this into the figure which seems to have haunted him. The tragic mistake is explicit in *The Tragedy of Hoffman,* a crude revenge play which borrows much from *Hamlet* and may have been commissioned on the heels of *Hamlet's* success. Mathias describes the innocent Lucibella thus: "Shee is as harlots, faire, like guilded tombs / Goodly without; within all rottenness . . . Angel in show, / Divell in heart."[3]

In *The Faerie Queene,* angel and devil are presented in simple allegorical form, as two different figures that look the same. The Red Cross Knight abandons Una, because he assumes that the girl he finds *in flagrante dilectu* is his virgin fallen. In *Hamlet,* the duality is used differently, but basically the same thing happens. Hamlet abandons Ophelia, maligning her in the most brutal terms, because he assumes her to be corrupt or, at the least, on the first step downwards. Archimago creates the false Una; Hamlet, on this occasion as on others, combines the roles of hero and villain in creating for himself his false Ophelia. He, like the Red Cross Knight, is mistaken; but his mistake is not retrieved.

The presentation of the relationship between Hamlet and Ophelia at first seems contradictory. In Act I.iii Polonius and Laertes warn Ophelia that Hamlet's wooing may not be honorable, and she is instructed to avoid his importunities. It should be noted that his wooing is of recent date: "He hath my Lord of late made many tenders / Of his affection to me." But in Act III.i, she appears as the neglected mistress and reproaches Hamlet for his coldness. This may be an inconsistency, but it may alternatively reflect a major change in Hamlet. Between the picture of the ardent young lover given by Ophelia to her father, and Hamlet's bitter comments to her father (II.ii.181ff) and to herself (III.i.103ff), there is the key encounter of Hamlet and Ophelia in her closet.

Images from the various Magdalen stories appear in all Ophelia's scenes except the "fatal mistake" scene in the closet, recounted in Act II.i. It is therefore entirely appropriate that this scene should be offstage, as an unseen key to the tragic role of Ophelia. For she is not the prostitute, the early Magdalen taunted by Hamlet in the nunnery scene; she is pure, as her name suggests and as her brother repeatedly describes her, "Whose worth . . . / Stood challenger on mount of all the age / For her perfections." She is the figure not of the repentant sinner, but of the purity which can atone for the sins of others. She is to intercede, in her "orisons," in the nunnery, as a ministering angel. Her prayers are all for others—"O help him, you sweet heavens!" "O heavenly powers, restore him!" "God dild you!" "God be at your table!" "God ha' mercy on his soul! And of all Christian souls I pray God," "God bye you." Her final utterance (reported) is "snatches of old lauds."[4] She opposes truth to Hamlet's feigning and feinting; he pretends to be mad, she is really mad; he meditates on death, she dies. Critics have noted that Ophelia never mentions her love for Hamlet. Her function goes far beyond that of a girl caught up in an unhappy love affair.

The Magdalen imagery serves to illumine on the one hand the succor which the pure Ophelia can offer through atonement; and on the other, the delusion of female wantonness from which Hamlet suffers and which is part of his tragedy.

"O my lord, my lord, I have been so affrighted!" introduces the description of Hamlet face to face with female depravity—depravity that exists only in his imagination, as the scene itself exists only in the imagination of the audience. Hamlet has seen something of the rottenness within in his mother's summary grief and incestuous marriage; he subsequently hears from the ghost the story of the murder, the stain of which, together with the stain of adultery, is added to the defaced image of his mother. Distracted, he runs to Ophelia, to gaze on the pure young face which between her forks presages snow. What he sees is presumably what Fradubio saw when he came upon Duessa bathing herself in origen and thyme, and saw her "in her proper hew." Hamlet leaves Ophelia with his head over his shoulder in the gesture of the damned, that of the runner in Dante's seventh Circle of Hell, and of Trevisan fleeing Despair.[5]

Hamlet makes no reference to Ophelia in the play until after this encounter. We hear of Hamlet as an ardent young lover and as the author of the exaggerated and very youthful jingle beginning "Doubt thou the stars are fire." But once he has rejected womankind, including Ophelia, he never (until the funeral scene) speaks or refers to her except with the imagery of sexual corruption. He calls Polonius a fishmonger (or brothel keeper) and after what seems to be a passing reference to the sun breeding maggots in a dead dog, he says of the "fishmonger's" daughter: "Let her not walk i' the sun; conception is a blessing, but as your daughter may conceive—friend look to't." Traditionally, the serpent's egg was hatched by the sun; Brutus, resolving on the death of Caesar, decides to "think him as a serpent's egg / Which hatched, would as his kind grow mischievous" (*Julius Caesar* II.i.32-33). Ophelia's "kind" is now, in Hamlet's thoughts, the progeny of the serpent; and possibly, if we go back to the maggots, the swarming brood of Error, "soon conceiv'd," which will devour its mother.[6] With Ophelia in the nunnery scene, Hamlet is still haunted by this image: "Why wouldst thou be a breeder of sinners?"

From the time of his fatal mistake, Hamlet is without the support, the *ophelia,* that he needs. His mother is sunk in adultery, incest, and complicity in murder;[7] he is forced to reject her, and with her he rejects all women, and Ophelia suffers the same fate as Una.

By Act IV, Ophelia's rejection is total, her brother gone, her father dead, her lover brutally estranged from her having killed her father and treated her as a prostitute. In her rejected state, she rejects reason. In this she is like Lear,

and like Lear, she will die, the will to live being annihilated. In her mad scene she can only "play" the tragedy in which she is caught up, like Cassandra helplessly enacting what she can truly see but cannot intervene to prevent.

The mad scene is, at first glance, a jumble of songs, dialogue, and lament. However, characters who go mad in renaissance drama frequently speak more truth, and deeper truth than when sane, and this can be said of Ophelia (who is sadly confused when her wits are about her) as of Lear. It is the order of what she says that is disturbed. "Oh when degree is shak'd . . . the enterprise is sick";[8] conversely, in the Elizabethan world picture, when the mind is sick, the divine order by which man can live in harmony is shaken and in chaos. What happens to Ophelia is what she has described as having happened to Hamlet— the sweet bells are jangled, out of tune and harsh, as bells will be if rung out of order. The images of her mad scene show derangement in its literal sense, but they are nonetheless images of the truth—the truth in chaos because of the havoc in her mind. Laertes, who provides a commentary on her madness, sums this up when he says, "This nothing's more than matter." It is "nothing" because evil derangement has taken over the order of a rational mind; but the disordered fragments are of something good and precious, which has been under attack ever since Hamlet's irruption "as if he had been loosed out of hell."

The Magdalen legends bear strongly on the detail of Ophelia's mad scene, and it is therefore appropriate now to consider the outline of the legends. In these, the images of virtue and depravity in woman, as symbolic of the problem of good and evil, provide the emotive power. Little of this power can be gleaned from the New Testament. The legends grew firstly by the identification of various women mentioned in the Gospels as the one Magdalen—including the woman taken in adultery, the "Mary" who was the sister of Lazarus, and the woman of Samaria—and secondly by a process of polarization of her states of sin and repentance. She is made not merely a sinner, but a prostitute, not just a repentant disciple, but a saint. From a practitioner of the oldest profession, she rises to be no less than the "beata dilectrix" of Christ.[9] In medieval literature she and Christ address each other as "love," "true love," and "lover."[10] She is the most important figure at the tomb of Christ (in the Coventry Resurrection play costumes were provided for Magdalen and for "two side Maries"),[11] and was the first witness of the Resurrection. Her tears were symbolic of the purifying waters of baptism. Her hold on dramatists, ballad writers, and artists can be well understood.

One other aspect of her legend bears on the parallel imagery of Ophelia, and that is the threefold interpretation of her relationship with God. God for Magdalen is father, lover, and brother—all as manifestations of the same divine love. In the ballad "The Maid and the Palmer" an old man—the figure of the Father—appears to the woman at the well, identified in medieval tradition as Magdalen. She hopes he is "the good old man / That all the world beleeves vpon." In a Scandinavian version of the ballad, it is Jesus who appears in the pilgrim's robe.[12] Magdalen's Christ/brother is Lazarus, whose raising from the dead prefigured the Resurrection, and Ophelia's brother at one stage briefly enacts this. In the deeply symbolic graveyard scene in *Hamlet,* with a setting redolent of the Last Judgment plays in the mystery cycles, Laertes leaps into his sister's open grave and then emerges from it.

The young woman in the known sources of the *Hamlet* story has neither father nor brother; the provision of both in Shakespeare's play opens the way for the multiple imagery of the threefold relationship in Ophelia's mad scene.

Three religious plays—the Digby *Mary Magdalene,* Wager's morality play *The Life and Repentaunce of Marie Magdalene,* and the Benediktbeuern Passion play—are convenient texts from which to trace parallels with Shakespeare's heroine.[13] Shakespeare may not have known the plays, but the legends were common knowledge, and the plays contain many of them. In the main, the following parallels are traced through the Digby play, which has been dated late fifteenth or early sixteenth century. The play begins with an affectionate family scene between Magdalen, her sister Martha, her father Cyrus, and her brother Lazarus. The family is about to be scattered, as Cyrus divides his estates between his children. It can be seen that although the topic of conversation is different from *Hamlet* I.iii, there is some similarity in the characters present and in the occasion. After leaving her home, Magdalen is led to an inn by Luxuria, and is seduced by Curiosity, who gets the better of her, so to speak. Curiosity's conversation with her, in a tone of mock gallantry mixed with indecency, is reminiscent of the cruel banter with which Hamlet assails Ophelia in the play scene. In Wager's play there is a similar conversation between Magdalen and Infidelitie, the Vice. It is interesting to see Hamlet so nearly assuming the role of vice, or villain, in this instance.

The seduction in *Hamlet* is described in Ophelia's "valentine" song. In the Digby play, Magdalen becomes a prostitute and is seen in her "erbyr" waiting for her "valentynys"—"A, God be wyth my valentynys, / My byrd swetyng, my lovys so dere!" (ll. 564-65). In the Wager play she decks herself in elaborate costumes and jewels, and is persuaded to buy cosmetics to paint her face. In the Benediktbeuern play, she visits a shop with her fellow prostitutes to buy cosmetics. Hamlet in the nunnery scene adopts the tone of a contemporary preacher rebuking the painted ladies of the town: "I have heard of your paintings too, well enough; God hath given you one face, and you make yourselves another; you jig, you amble, and you lisp, and you nickname God's creatures . . ." (III.i.145-48). The "sweet ladies" to whom Ophelia later bids good-night, the coach for which she calls, are part of this life *in gaudio.*[14]

In the mad scene Ophelia is acting out, among other facets of the tragedy, the role of harlot which Hamlet has foisted on her. To the king she suddenly says, "They say the owl was a baker's daughter." This is perhaps the only direct reference to a legend almost certainly linked with Magdalen. According to a country legend cited by Douce, Jesus asked for bread at a baker's shop; the girl in the shop cheated him, and he punished her by changing her into an owl.[15] This is typical of many New Testament apocryphal stories, in which the character of Jesus is made stern and retributive to sinners. The outline of the story is similar to that of the ballad "The Maid and the Palmer." There an old man asked for water at a well. The girl at the well refused him, and he punished her by changing her first to a stepping stone and then to a bell-clapper, and lastly by sending her to hell for seven years. The ballad tells one of the stories of Magdalen and Jesus which grew up after identification of Magdalen with the woman of Samaria. The owl and the baker's daughter may have derived from stories of St. Mary of Egypt, who was always depicted with loaves of bread, and was often confused with Magdalen.[16]

The Digby Magdalen described herself when a prostitute as "drynchyn" (drowned) "in synne" (l. 754). In her death Ophelia re-enacts this drowning in sin; the "long purples," which some critics have found so incongruous in the Queen's speech describing the drowning, can be seen as the key to this re-enactment.[17]

The waters that meet over Magdalen's head are those of baptism, and she emerges repentant. In token of her changed condition, she sheds her jewels and dresses in black.[18] Later she will assume the appearance of the Donatello Magdalen, her hair dishevelled, her face drawn, her clothing in rags. Early in the nunnery scene, Ophelia returns to Hamlet the "rich gifts," "remembrances of yours," which he had given her.[19] There is no reference to her appearance in the mad scene, except for the Q.1 stage direction ("Enter Ofelia playing on a Lute, and her haire downe singing"), but traditionally she assumes the disorder of the penitent's hair and dress, which is equally indicative of mental derangement. It is worth noting, because other similar instances will emerge, that the "nighted colour" of mourning which Hamlet wears is also the outward show of repentance; Hamlet is, in a sense, wearing Magdalen's color when he confronts Ophelia.

The central scene of the Magdalen story is the Resurrection. She first visits the sepulchre with the two "side" Maries, bearing herbs and spices to anoint the dead body of Jesus. They find the tomb empty and are told by an angel that Christ is risen. Left alone, Magdalen is the first person to see the risen Christ. This scene, described in the gospels with some variations, is also the subject of the first recognizably dramatic ceremony in the liturgy— *"Quem quaeritis in sepulchro,"* "whom seek ye in the sepulchre?" to which the angel adds, "He is risen, he is not here" (*"non est hic, surrexit"*).[20] This scene is linked in Magdalen legend with a passage from *The Song of Solomon,* for Magdalen, the *beata dilectrix* of Christ and sister of Lazarus the Christ-figure, was identified with the sister/spouse of the Old Testament: "I will . . . seke him that my soule loueth; I soght him, but I founde him not. / The watchemen that went about the citie founde me; to whome I said, Haue you sene him whome my soule loueth?"[21]

It takes little imagination to see that from this line one could continue directly with the first line of Ophelia's song—"How should I your true love know?"—which like Raleigh's "As you came from the Holy Land," seems to start from an old ballad about a pilgrimage to Walsingham, but finishes in the poet's own idiom.[22] Since Magdalen traditionally calls Jesus her love, the song which (with interruptions) runs through the mad scene can be seen as the negative *Quem quaeritis* of an evil, disordered world. Parts of the song, including the opening lines, are missing; it is jumbled and broken up, and spoken by various persons who are not identified. But the answer to the seeker's question is clear: the true love, or Father, or brother, is dead, not risen; "he will not come again." The lines beginning "And will a not come again?" are full of negative-resounding doom—*not, not, no, no, never*—and give the counsel of despair, "Go to thy death-bed."

The true love is to be recognized "by his cockle hat and staff / And his sandal shoon"—the pilgrim's dress worn by the risen Christ on the road to Emmaus, and by the man at the well in "The Maid and the Palmer." The pilgrim is buried, "At his heels a stone"—an indication that he is not in a grave, where the stone would be at the head, but in a sepulchre sealed by a stone. The "O, ho!" which follows this line is the mourner's cry of grief, as Magdalen wept over her brother Lazarus and at the sepulchre of Christ. The white shroud of the martyr is "Larded all with sweet flowers," the equivalent of the herbs and spices that Magdalen brought to the tomb. The faulty rhythm of "Which bewept to the grave did not go" points the intrusive *not;* this body was not destined for the grave. The "true love showers" are the tears of the mourner (cf. *Richard II,* V.i.20: "And wash him fresh again with true-love tears"); Magdalen's tears are among the most famous ever shed. But Shakespeare is always alive to a double meaning, and "showers" are also pangs, the bitter pains felt by the "true love." In the Digby play Lazarus exclaims, "A! A, now brystyt myn hartt! þis is a sharp showyr!" (l. 822), and the word was in use in this meaning as late as 1637. The first part of the song ends, and Ophelia, after greeting the king, says, "they say the owl was a baker's daughter."

The lament over the dead love begins again with "They bore him barefaced on the bier." The "hey non nonny" line which follows is not in Q.2 and looks like an interpolation.[23] The many tears again recall the copious water which flowed from Magdalen's eyes. The figure in the last verse is that of the father—indeed, of the Ancient of Days: "His beard was as white as snow, / All flaxen was his poll" (cf. *Daniel* 7.9: "the Ancient of daies did sit, whose garment was white as snowe, and the heere of his head like the pure woll"). The earthly father dead, and the earthly brother who has gone away, are mourned by Ophelia in her visionary state as Magdalen mourned Jesus, who was at once the heavenly Father and her "true love," and also Lazarus, her brother who was a type of Christ. Thus it is not, in this strangely haunting scene, a particular death and absence which is lamented; it is the death of Ophelia's whole world, and she symbolizes this also with the flowers which she scatters among the assembled company. They are funeral flowers, handed to those who will shortly die— the King, the Queen, Laertes, and herself.

The legends of Magdalen's later life describe her as a preacher, converting the heathen, and as a hermit in the wilderness, where is fed by angels until her death and ascent to heaven. In a long poem published at Lyon in 1668,[24] Magdalen is described as preaching to her former fellow-prostitutes and exhorting them to enter nunneries. With no earlier reference, this cannot be directly related to Hamlet's repeated exhortations to Ophelia to "get thee to a nunnery," but it is at least likely that the Magdalen of legend would do this, as the patron saint of reformed prostitutes and as a preacher.[25] If so, Hamlet in the nunnery scene is opposing the repentant Magdalen to the figure of her former self which he sees in Ophelia. He not only wears Magdalen's "nighted colour" but also speaks her words.

In the death of Ophelia, borne down the weeping brook, the main image is of another suffering innocent, the Fair Maid of Astolat, who floated down the Thames. This story from Malory may also have influenced the funeral scene, for it is the King (Arthur) who commands arrangements for the funeral, and the ceremony is attended by the Fair Maid's "true love" (Lancelot) and brother (Lavaine).[26] These images may testify to the "embryology" (to use T.S. Eliot's word[27]) of the episodes of the drowning and of the funeral rather than to their meaning; but it may be worth noting that Claudius's "arrangements" for Ophelia's funeral are the reverse of what they seem. According to the Clowns, Ophelia killed herself, and only by "great command" was she allowed Christian burial; even so, only "maimed rites" were permitted. Yet it is clear from the Queen's description that Ophelia did not deliberately throw herself into the water; it appears that although the Queen knew well enough what happened, different information was given to the "crowner," which deprived her of the benefit of the full funeral service. It is Claudius who has "maimed" the rites, not for the first time, as Polonius her father was interred "hugger-mugger"; and his action aligns Ophelia's funeral with the hasty burial of Christ, leading in turn to Magdalen's visit to the tomb with herbs and spices.

The stage properties which accompany Ophelia are, significantly, specified in the text. The traditional symbol of Magdalen's contempt of the world, the skull, is thrown from Ophelia's grave early in the funeral scene, and lies nearby as her body is prepared for burial. Earlier, in the nunnery scene, she carried a book, the symbol of Magdalen the contemplative. The flowers in the mad scene may be taken to stand for the funeral herbs and spices which Magdalen carries in her traditional ointment jar. The rue, which she probably hands to the King since it must be worn "with a difference" (that is, with a sign that he is not in the main line of succession),[28] is also the "herb of grace," a phrase as relevant in this context as the "long purples" are to the drowning.

In tracing religious imagery in *Hamlet,* it is instructive to compare it with *Der Bestrafte Brudermord,* a corrupt German version of Shakespeare's play in which all religious reference is omitted. Thus in Ophelia's part, there is no scene with her father and brother; no account of her confrontation by Hamlet in her closet; no book or skull; no drowning (she commits suicide by throwing herself from the top of a hill); her mad scenes are utterly secular nonsense, and there is no graveyard scene.[29] The Magdalen imagery changes all this. As has been noted above, the drowning is parallel to the "drowning in sin" of the early Magdalen, and the water to which Ophelia is as "native and indued" is reminiscent both of the tears shed over the feet of Christ and of the redemptive waters of baptism; water is as much part of Ophelia's story as it is of Magdalen's. Laertes, Ophelia's commentator in this as in the mad scene, evokes the saint-like figure that she is to be, the fair and unpolluted flesh in earth, the "minist'ring angel" in heaven. The idea of *ophelia,* succor, is implicit in "minist'ring."[30]

Like Cassandra, like Iphigenia, Ophelia suffers for the sins of the house. Johnson's famous comment can therefore be seen in an unusual light: "the gratification which would arise from the destruction of an usurper and a murderer is abated by the untimely death of Ophelia, the young, the beautiful, the harmless, and the pious." The devout Johnson would undoubtedly have been shocked at the suggestion that the untimely death of Christ robs us of any gratification arising from the defeat of Satan; but without the idea of atonement, the power of Ophelia's tragedy cannot be fully grasped. In her mad scene she mourns the loss and absence which has doomed the court of Denmark, polluted by lust and murder. "Where," she asks, "is the beauteous majesty of Denmark?" Where, indeed? Her words echo the transferred epithet of Horatio's lines in the first scene of the play, "What art thou, that usurp'st this time of night, / Together with that fair and warlike form / In which the majesty of buried Denmark / Did sometimes march?" Ophelia's death is the signal for the retributive action which at last is taken when her beloved brother unwittingly provides the poisoned weapon for Hamlet's hand.

As Ophelia is not the double character of the legendary Magdalen, but only the purer half, the other half being painted in by false accusation, why should Shakespeare choose the image of Magdalen to illumine the role of Ophelia? The popular appeal of Magdalen is that she epitomizes hope. She sins, she repents; she is forgiven, and by grace she is made pure. She is therefore the hope of every sinner. For Hamlet, "all is not well," "how ill all's here about my heart"; but Ophelia says "I hope all will be well." The Magdalen raised from prostitution to sainthood provides a resolution of the Una/Fidessa riddle. The sin in Magdalen could be atoned for, sinner and penitent made one and purified. Ophelia acts this atonement through the scenes of Magdalen's life. Hamlet speaks of the ghost as a hellish resurrection, out of the "ponderous and marble jaws" of his father's sepulchre, "making night hideous"; Ophelia evokes the heavenly resurrection in the search for her "true love."

The idea of atonement (*adunamentum*) brings us back to Spenser's Una, who like Ophelia is the face of true purity. With his "Una," Hamlet might have reached the Castle of Holiness; he rejects the woman who could have been his "swete sokor"—the phrase used of Magdalen by her grateful disciples in the Digby play (l. 1963). Laertes gives the key lines on his sister: "O Rose of May, / Dear maid, kind sister, sweet Ophelia." The rose of May is probably the white rose, the symbol of both the Virgin and Magdalen, whose tears were supposed to have washed it white. The "dear maid" is a virgin, pure in spite of all Hamlet's suspicions; the "kind sister" is in contrast to the incestuous and therefore unnatural (unkind) sister-in-law of Claudius; and "sweet Ophelia" is a version of "swete sokor."

To go back to woman's nature as described by Euripides, Ophelia could have given to Hamlet the means of salvation, *ophelian megistan;*[31] but he is fatally convinced that she brings him only the greatest harm. Nothing could be more decisive than his rejection; he first abuses her, and then forgets her. Her living image is only fleetingly recalled in the funeral scene, and the last reference to her in the play is Hamlet's half-mocking challenge which brings his rejection of her to its conclusion: "Be buried quick with her, and so will I."[32]

Notes

Quotations from *Hamlet* . . . are from the New Shakespeare Edition, ed. John Dover Wilson, 2nd ed. (Cambridge: Cambridge Univ. Press, 1936). Quotations from the Bible are taken from *The Geneva Bible: A Facsimile of the 1560 Edition,* ed. Lloyd E. Berry (Madison: Univ. of Wisconsin Press, 1969).

1. Book I.vii.1; note also Book IV.i.17 (the theme runs through much of *The Faerie Queene*). Citations are to *The Works of Edmund Spenser: Variorum Edition.*

2. August Nauck, ed., *Tragicorum Graecorum Fragmenta* (Hildesheim: Georg Olms, 1964), p. 384 (Stob. Flor. LXIX.7). This Stobaic fragment is taken from a lost play by Euripides on Alcmaeon. Editions of the fragments of ancient Greek collected by Stobaeus were published, in Greek and in Latin, at various times through the sixteenth century, and it is possible that Shakespeare had some knowledge of them, as F.P. Wilson suggested (in *Shakespeare's Reading,* quoted by Emrys Jones, *The Origins of Shakespeare* [Oxford: Clarendon Press, 1977], p. 91). For discussion of the possible link between *Hamlet* and the

story of Alcmaeon, see my chap. IV, in *Shakespeare's Play within Play: Medieval Imagery and Scenic Form in Hamlet, Othello, and King Lear,* Western Michigan University, Medieval Institute Publications, 1990. J. P. Collier lists a play on Alcmaeon (now lost) given in the court revels before Elizabeth (*The History of English Dramatic Poetry to the Time of Shakespeare* [London, 1831], III, 24). See also ibid., I, 207. Either at second hand from this play or directly from Stobaeus, Shakespeare might have come across the word which named his heroine.

3. Henry Chettle, *The Tragedy of Hoffman, or A Revenge for a Father,* Malone Soc. Reprints (Oxford, 1950), II.823ff.

4. Q2. The emphasis is changed in F1—"snatches of old tunes."

5. *Faerie Queene* I.ii.40, I.ix.21.

6. *Julius Caesar* V.iii.69; cf. *Faerie Queene* I.i.25.

7. In his own eyes, at least; *vide* "As kill a king and marry with his brother" (III.iv.29).

8. *Troilus and Cressida* I.iii.101-03.

9. Louis Réau, *Iconographie de l'art chrétien,* III, Pt. 2 (Paris: Presses Universitaires de France, 1958), 848.

10. See the Digby Mary Magdalen play, in *The Late Medieval Religious Plays of Bodleian MSS Digby 133 and e Museo 160,* ed. Donald Baker, John L. Murphy, and Louis B. Hall, Jr., EETS, 283 (1982): l. 1068 ("I his lover"), l. 1588 ("mary my lover"); and the version of *Noli me tangere* in the York Winedrawers' play: "negh me not, my loue, latte be" (l. 82). For the York plays, see the edition of Richard Beadle (London: Edward Arnold, 1982).

11. Thomas Sharp, *A Dissertation on the Mysteries or Dramatic Pageants Anciently Performed at Coventry* (Coventry, 1825), p. 47; *Coventry,* ed. R.W. Ingram, Records of Early English Drama (Toronto: Univ. of Toronto Press, 1981), pp. 240-41.

12. Francis James Child, ed., *The English and Scottish Popular Ballads* (1882; rpt. New York, 1957), I, 228.

13. *Late Medieval Religious Plays,* ed. Baker *et al.,* pp. 24-95; Lewis Wager, *The Life and Repentaunce of Marie Magdalene,* ed. F.I. Carpenter (Chicago, 1902); *Ludus de Passione,* in Karl Young, *The Drama of the Medieval Church* (Oxford: Clarendon Press, 1933), I, 518-33.

14. See E.K. Chambers, *The Mediaeval Stage* (London: Oxford Univ. Press, 1903), II, 90.

15. Horace Howard Furness, ed., *Hamlet,* New Variorum Edition (Philadelphia: Lippincott, 1877), I, 332.

16. See Edith C. Batho, "The Life of Christ in the Ballads," *Essays and Studies,* 9 (1924), 81; Réau, *Iconographie,* III, Pt. 2, 847.

17. The connotation of "long purples" is most explicit in Q2 (IV.vii.170), for which most editors substitute the F1 version: "But our cull-cold maydes doe dead mens fingers call them."

18. See Robert Potter, *The English Morality Play* (London: Routledge and Kegan Paul, 1975), p. 48; Chambers, *Mediaeval Stage,* II, 75-76.

19. Cf. Dover Wilson's stage direction: "*she takes jewels from her bosom and places them on the table before him*" (p. 61).

20. Chambers, *Mediaeval Stage,* II, 9-10.

21. *The Song of Solomon* 4.9, 3.2-4; cf. the sub-title *Soror mea sponsa* of Raymond Léopold Bruckberger's *Marie Madeleine* (Paris: La Jeune Parque, 1952).

22. Cf. Sir Walter Ralegh, *The Poems,* ed. Agnes M.C. Latham (London: Constable, 1929), pp. 100, 184.

23. "Hey nonny nonny" and, later, "down-a-down," both common phrases in ballad refrains, may indicate the disorder and parody of her song. Cf. Wager's opening lines, spoken by Infidelitie: "With heigh down down and downe a downe a, / Saluator mundi Domine, Kyrieleyson, / Ite, Missa est, With pipe vp Alleluya."

24. Pierre de S. Louys, *La Madeleine au désert de la Sainte Baume en Provence,* Book IV; cited by Françoise Bardon, "Le thème de la Madeleine Pénitent au XVIIème siècle en France," *Journal of the Warburg and Courtauld Institutes,* 31 (1968), 293.

25. The Order for reformed prostitutes (Pénitent de Sainte Marie-Madeleine), known as *Dames blanches* or *Weissfrauen* because they were dressed in white, was first set up in the early thirteenth century; see Victor Saxer, *Le Culte de Marie Madeleine en Occident* (Auxerre: Société des fouilles archéologiques et des monuments historiques d'Yonne, 1959), pp. 222-23.

26. *Caxton's Malory,* ed. James W. Spisak (Berkeley and Los Angeles: Univ. of California Press, 1983), I, 531.

27. In "The Music of Poetry," in *Selected Prose of T.S. Eliot,* ed. Frank Kermode (New York: Harcourt, Brace, and Jovanovich, 1975), p. 111.

28. Cf. *Much Ado about Nothing* I.i.69: "If he have wit enough to keep himself warm, let him bear it for a difference between himself and his horse." Of course, the real "difference" between Ophelia and the King is between the pure and impure.

29. Geoffrey Bullough, *Narrative and Dramatic Sources of Shakespeare* (London: Routledge and Kegan Paul, 1973), VII, 146-56.

30. Cf. John Ruskin, *Munera Pulveris,* quoted in Furness, ed., *Hamlet,* II, 241; see also *Matthew* 27.55-56.

31. Cf. Richard Helgerson, "What Hamlet Remembers," *Shakespeare Studies,* 10 (1977), 91: "his [Hamlet's] misogynism keeps him from discovering the grace that might redeem both him and the natural world."

32. Cf. Harley Granville-Barker, *Prefaces to Shakespeare* (1930; rpt. London: Sidgwick and Jackson, 1958), I, 244: "he, at heart, is as dead as she. This is, indeed, the last pang he is to suffer."

THEMATIC ROLES

Manuel Aguirre (essay date 1996)

SOURCE: "Life, Crown, and Queen: Gertrude and the Theme of Sovereignty," in *The Review of English Studies,* Vol. 47, No. 186, May, 1996, pp. 163-74.

[*In the following essay, Aguirre examines the symbol of the cup from which Gertrude drinks in the play's final scene, and attempts to "delve further into the mythological status of Gertrude and, beyond this, to explore the role, and the fate, of myth in Hamlet."*]

In a short preliminary paper[1] I sought to establish the presence in Hamlet of the traditional symbol of the Cup of Sovereignty. Briefly the argument was this: when Hamlet speaks of the 'dram of evil' that obscures a man's virtues (I. iv. 36-8), he is constructing a metaphor for the cup Claudius drinks out of to celebrate his marriage, and giving this vessel connotations which, on the moral plane, resemble those found in the several poisons used in the play: moral corruption is as inherent in that cup as physical infection is in Lucianus', Laertes', or Claudius' poisons. The significance placed on this cup seems out of all proportion to its apparent function in the play, until we stop looking for a realistic explanation and recall that the cup was a symbol for the transmission of Sovereignty in Celtic tales: when the queen handed a vessel or otherwise offered drink to the hero she was granting him her sexual favours and/or sovereignty over her territory. No reader of Hamlet can fail to notice the analogy with Claudius' cup in I. iv which symbolizes both his sexual union with Gertrude and his accession to the Danish throne. The argument, then, claims a traditional, non-realistic reading for this aspect of the play. The present article seeks to delve further into the mythological status of Gertrude and, beyond this, to explore the role, and the fate, of myth in Hamlet. To forestall misunderstandings it will be expedient to state here that this article does not make any pronouncements on woman, her social status, her 'archetypal' nature, or her numinous qualities. The point is worth some emphasis, if only because the border between fact and fiction is often made to look so elusive nowadays. That 'Goddess' which has caught many a receptive imagination since the 1980s is none of my concern here; my goal is to explore Renaissance changes in the application of a traditional literary metaphor. Nothing is said about 'woman', much is claimed about a literary device.

1. MYTH

Though more research has been done into the Celtic—especially Irish—manifestations of the theme of Sovereignty,[2] this theme is equally widespread in Greek and Germanic myth; according to the twelfth century scholar Snorri Sturluson, the function of the Valkyries was to serve the sacred mead in Val-hall;[3] Brynhild's acceptance of Sigurd was signalled by the rune-cup she handed him after he woke her up on her flame-encircled mountain;[4] in canto x of *The Odyssey* Circe offered Odysseus' men a bowl containing food and wine mixed with a drug that enslaved their minds and bodies to her will. In all three cases the vessel is a token of acceptance or rejection, of love or death. A variation on this symbol appears in the tale of Hamlet's precursor, the hero Amleth whose exploits Saxo Grammaticus relates in his *Historia*.[5] He was sent to England with two devious friends bearing orders for his execution; once in England, all three were invited by the king to a feast at which Amleth abstained from eating and drinking; when asked why he had refrained from it all 'as if it were poison', he replied that the bread, meat, and drink were tainted with human blood, human flesh, and iron rust. As a result of these revelations (which turned out to be true, thus proclaiming his more-than-human wisdom), Amleth obtained the hand of the king's daughter and the execution of his treacherous friends. Symbolically, the feast was a test which his companions (like Odysseus' men before Circe's drink) failed, but which Amleth (like Odysseus) passed. Loss of life or loss of humanity is the penalty; the lady's favour, and Sovereignty, the reward.

The cup is not the only symbol relevant to an understanding of Hamlet; there is also the symbolism of water, which traditional myth again significantly relates to the figure of an Otherworld woman. The Irish Cuchulainn crosses the sea in search of the sorceress Scathach, who will either kill him or teach him the craft of arms; eventually she gives him her own daughter.[6] The Welsh Macsen journeys from Rome to Anglesey to meet the lady of his dream, Elen of the Hosts; she will eventually help him to reconquer Rome.[7] The Irish Conle, Bran, and Mael Duin all put to sea to reach the Island of Women, where love and immortality await them.[8] Like the Celtic fairy women, Circe, Calypso, Nausicaa, and Penelope all live on islands towards which Odysseus must sail. On reaching the Rubicon, Caesar sees a vision of Rome personified as a mighty woman who mourns the coming civil war and begs him not to cross the river.[9] When Thomas Rymer was led to Elfland by a fairy queen,

> He wade thro red blude to the knee,
> And he saw neither sun nor moon,
> But heard the roaring of the sea.[10]

Having sailed to England, Saxo's Amleth will marry the English king's daughter; when Shakespeare's Hamlet is sent to England he undergoes a change (similar to that mysterious 'seachange' which is the essence of The Tempest) and returns a new man to Denmark—to witness (and here lies a fundamental difference) the burial of his lady and, shortly after, the death of the Queen. Time and again, in Celtic, Germanic, and classical myth, the hero's encounter with Woman, whether Queen, Goddess, Fairy, or Sorceress, is made dependent on his crossing a sea or river[11] - a voyage at the end of which she awaits in majesty to bestow or withhold Sovereignty, or else to subjugate or destroy him.

Woman is also the Spinner, the Great Weaver, the Embroiderer. As the Greek Moirai and the Roman Parcae, she spins, measures, and cuts the threads of human destinies; as the Queen of the Island of Women, she retains Mael Duin with a magic ball of yarn which cleaves to his palm; as Ariadne, she gives Theseus the thread that will allow him to extricate himself from the Labyrinth; as Clytemnestra, she casts a net over her husband Agamemnon so that he will be helpless before the sword of her lover Aegistus; as Bertilak's wife, she gives Gawain a magic girdle to protect himself from the Green Knight's blow; as the giantess Grid she lends Thor a girdle of might to fight Geirrod the giant.[12] As Queen Gerutha in Saxo's tale, she spends a year knitting a vast hanging to cover the walls of her palace; at the end of the year, as a banquet is held in honour of dead Amleth, the hero returns from England to everyone's confusion. He puts on a wild disposition, takes up the office of drink-bearer and plies everyone with drink; but when they are all drunk asleep he cuts down his mother's hanging to immobilize the sleepers on the floor, and burns the hall down on them. As both Gerutha and Gertrude, she hides a spying courtier behind an arras (under a quilt in Saxo's and Belleforest's versions), which will result in his death at the hands of her son; 'I took thee for thy better', says Hamlet; and 'It had been so with us, had we been there', confirms Claudius.

And indeed, Polonius is a surrogate-king, a stand-in for his better, King Claudius, and dies a king's death—Agamemnon's. Time and again myths metaphorize fate as the operations of a Woman who spins, knits, weaves, or embroiders men's destinies; for whom yarns, webs, nets, and hangings are instruments to entangle, protect, or extricate the seeker.[13] Hamlet displays the same metaphors in a conspicuous manner.

So cup, sea-voyage, and yarn or web or cloth are all symbols central to the tale of the meeting between the hero and Sovereignty. Their presence is amply evident in Saxo's story; I think I have shown that all three are present in Shakespeare's, if under certain important modifications. Let me now formulate the idea as it applies to Shakespeare's text: the cup is Gertrude's, not Claudius'; the Danish crown was not his to take, it was hers to give; she it was who yielded Sovereignty to him; and Claudius' own explanation of the event is hollow: he could not have wedded Gertrude to save the unsettled orphan country because that decision was not for him to make.

2. GERTRUDE

Several questions arise directly from the foregoing: (a) what is Gertrude's status? (b) why did Gertrude give Sovereignty to Claudius? And (c) that most vexed question: has the Queen committed adultery?

To answer the first: Claudius refers to Gertrude in 1. ii. 9 as 'Th' imperial jointress to this warlike state'; Jenkins has pointed out that

> From the reference to the Queen as 'jointress' Dover Wilson infers that Gertrude had a life-interest in the crown, and it may be that Shakespeare had in mind how in earlier versions of the story Hamlet's father acquired the throne by marriage; but the rights he accords Gertrude as dowager he is content not to define. What is clear is that Claudius became king before taking her 'to wife' but consolidated his position by a prudent marriage.[14]

Actually it is not that simple. First, as to earlier versions of the story: Saxo tells us that King Rorik of Denmark had appointed Amleth's father, Horwendil, ruler of Jutland jointly with his brother Feng. Horwendil 'held the monarchy for three years, and then, to win the height of glory, devoted himself to roving'.[15] We may presume that, meanwhile, Feng stayed on as king, though Saxo does not tell us. Then Horwendil slew King Koll, married Rorik's daughter Gerutha, and was slain by Feng, who then wedded his brother's widow. Belleforest adds that Fengon killed his brother 'craignant d'estre depossede de sa part du gouvernement, ou plustost desirant destre seul en la principaute';[16] clearly, his Fengon had remained king all along while Horwendil lived as a rover, and feared eviction once Horwendil returned.[17] Both brothers, therefore, were rulers before they married Gerutha. Jenkins's statement that Hamlet's father obtained the throne through marriage in earlier versions does not agree with the story as told by Saxo and Belleforest.

And yet: it is not easy to dispel the impression that their wedding does have something to do with their status as rulers. It is a matter of immediacy: sexual union or sexual harassment of women are mentioned immediately before or after the death of a ruler, or in explicit juxtaposition to kingship. Both Saxo and Belleforest make the point that Feng/Fengon's first concern after killing his brother was to marry his widow; Belleforest furthermore states that Fengon wedded 'celle qu'il entretenoit execrablement, durant la vie du bon Horvvendille':[18] he had already had sexual relations with her before her husband's death. Saxo then tells us that when Wiglek succeeded Rorik his first move was to harass Amleth's mother, why, we are not told; further we learn that as soon as Amleth had been slain by Wiglek his widow Hermutrude, again for no reason one can discern, 'yielded herself up unasked to be the conqueror's spoil and bride'.[19] All of this goes beyond mere coincidence: while there is nowhere an indication to the effect that marriage is a precondition for kingship, time after time we encounter an inevitable link between sexual union and sovereignty.[20] The terse grammar of myth employs a paratactic structure giving us little more than concomitancy; any connectives between the three events (death, enthronement, sexual union) we have to make up, but significance is of the essence.

Ethan Hawke as Hamlet, Diane Venora as Gertrude, and Kyle MacLachlan as Claudius in the 1999 film adaptation of Hamlet.

If we read Gertrude's marriage as a sequel to Claudius' coronation, we assign a very poor role to her: she becomes a helpless victim of circumstances; she loses a husband, then a new king is elected with little regard for her possible interest in the state as 'jointress', then she is seduced by the new king, who finally weds her for political reasons. It is doubtlessly part of the playwright's intention to present her in this light . . . , yet there is more to Gertrude in the text. Something of the paratactic grammar of myth has rubbed off on Shakespeare. Laertes tells Claudius that he is there 'to show my duty in your coronation'; Horatio tells Hamlet he came 'to see your father's funeral'; Hamlet replies sarcastically it must have been 'to see my mother's wedding'. All three statements are found in the same scene (I. ii). We are not told which of the three events came first, which last, though we infer from Claudius' speech in I. ii. 1 ff. that the wedding has just taken place. On this same critical day Hamlet mourns his father's death 'But two months dead—nay, not so much, not two'; seven lines later: 'within a month'; his pain makes his reckoning of time unreliable, but if it is Gertrude's wedding that, as Claudius seems to imply, has taken place on this day, when did the coronation take place? If some time before the wedding, why is Laertes still in Elsinore, seeing that

he only came for the coronation? If Horatio came to see the funeral, and 'has been a month and more in Denmark, Hamlet would have been likely to know of his presence';[21] yet the latter greets him as if they had not seen each other all this time—in fact, as if the funeral had only taken place yesterday (which is what a grief-stricken Hamlet feels, anyway). Judging from each of the three statements by Laertes, Horatio, and Hamlet, we feel they all bear the same immediacy to the present. My argument is that reading the three events in temporal succession yields serious inconsistencies, and that this is not simply the result of carelessness on Shakespeare's part but arises from a conflict between a modern perspective and a traditional theme. The modern view seeks linearity, temporal order, causality; the traditional theme involves concomitancy, simultaneity, significance. This is most clearly brought home by Old Hamlet in I. v. 74ff.: 'Thus was I, sleeping, by a brother's hand,[O]f life, of crown, of queen at once dispatch'd'. At once, indeed: for the queen is the life is the crown. Again, consider the following exchange (I. v. 39ff.):

> Ghost. The serpent that did sting thy father's life
> Now wears his crown.
> Hamlet. O my prophetic soul! My uncle!
> Ghost. Ay, that incestuous, that adulterate beast,

With witchcraft of his wit, with traitorous gifts—
O wicked wit, and gifts that have the power
So to seduce!—won to his shameful lust
The will of my most seeming-virtuous queen.

The main statement in this five-line outburst is 'Ay, that beast won the will of my queen'. Now this statement has nothing to do with the ostensive meaning of the Ghost's previous lines: he was trying to reveal his murderer to Hamlet, suddenly he raves off extempore about how this murderer has seduced Gertrude. 'Ay' is meant to confirm Hamlet's exclamation 'My uncle!', and thus to identify the killer; since this 'Ay' is followed by a comma, it introduces what should by rights contribute to the identification; a string of epithets would do; but when they emerge they become the subject of a new sentence, one which does not confirm anything said before but moves on to a different track, yielding a logically incongruous sequence which could be summarized as follows:

> Ghost. My murderer is the present king
> Hamlet. My uncle!
> Ghost. Yes, he seduced my wife.
> Incongruous, indeed: unless the Queen's will does
> have a relevance to life and crown.

3. THE QUEEN'S WILL

For us it would be a simple matter to read here that the Queen is guilty, or at least hopelessly weak; that she has conspired or connived in the King's murder; that, being of a fickle will, she has let herself be seduced, and proven frail and inconstant, if not treacherous. For the more traditional, mythical mind, on the other hand, the Queen simply exercises a prerogative, and it is her deliberate choice that results in a king's death and another man's enthronement: the Queen is indeed the life is the crown. Now, Shakespeare's text stands half-way between these two readings; it contains a persistent if subdued association of the Queen with 'life and crown' as well as several important ingredients of the traditional theme of Sovereignty, but for Hamlet they are no longer intelligible, even though he, like Claudius, dimly recognizes their import. And so he is outraged by his mother's deed, a deed which he, like ourselves, must interpret in a 'realistic' way and therefore without the framework of myth to justify it.

Nor is this such a far-fetched notion. Our contemporary, 'post-modernist' literature is currently dealing with its exact opposite: for it exploits our absolute faith in realism and startles or thrills us with the sight of a character caught out of his reality: we feel puzzled or amused when an author intrudes into the story to tell his creation what's what, when the immutable frame of reality-in-the-novel breaks down and characters become suddenly conscious of their fictional status.[22] But what happens when a creature of myth comes, quite possibly in spite of himself, to believe in a reality divested of symbolic qualities? What should we say of a character who gets trapped into a pitilessly real space and becomes unable to explain his world because he no longer has the wider reference framework

of myth to validate it? Elsewhere I have used the expression 'the closure of the world' to identify the process whereby an increasing realism shuts the Renaissance culture against the world of the non-rational, the world of Numens, archetypes, and myths, with the resulting loss of meaning for the inhabitants of the human world.[23] Hamlet, one such victim of this closure, vainly tries to understand by means of reason what is in effect a mythical deed; he rejects much that goes on in Elsinore; but most he rages at his mother's choice. With 'a scholar's tongue' he runs through all the human faculties, senses, and emotions which might have been responsible for Gertrude's inexplicable act; he concludes that the operations of memory, love, judgement, sense, and shame must have been suspended at the time; even reason must have been perverted, for 'reason panders will'. This, an incomprehensible will which he can only see as perverse, is all that remains after such an analysis.

And the will is the key to the problem. In the context, the word will may signify sexual desire, or passion generally, but it cannot be reduced to either; the word is contrasted with 'conscience', 'thought' (III. i), 'reflection', 'reason' (III. iv): a contrast central not only to Hamlet but also to a proper understanding of the Renaissance. Medieval Christianity had always emphasized the will, whether in a literature of action or in its religious concern with free will. On the other hand, ever since the Renaissance our culture has stressed consciousness, while placing a lavish emphasis upon the evils of the will. The myths of Faustus and Don Juan, of Macbeth and Satan, Don Quixote's rashness and Hamlet's indecision, all point to a new understanding of the will as an evil or ineffective faculty whose operations are to be mistrusted. The rise of Elizabethan drama and the birth of the picaresque novel signal a new type of writing which stresses the ubiquitousness of deception, the importance of mistrust, the need to reflect before acting. The modernity breeds a literature of reflection in which the world is no longer the known arena where the central question was whether to follow one or the other of two well-understood courses of action; but a bewildering realm where the question is rather whether to act at all, given our uncertainty about the motives, means, and outcome of action.[24]

As the Queen carries out her one mythical deed, on which the whole play depends, the new hero ponders its import, agonizes over his own response, and endlessly reflects about motives and consequences; in his eyes her will becomes an evil faculty unchecked by reflection. Her choice of consort should be understood in symbolic terms—but a 'realist' son finds it meaningless and outrageous; it should be seen as a manifestation of the theme of Sovereignty—but without the dignity of myth, it becomes a mere case of adultery.

4. ADULTERY

Do not weep, kind cuckold, take comfort, man, thy betters have been beccos: Agamemnon Emperor of all the merry Greeks, that tickled all the true Troyans, was a cornuto; Prince Arthur, that cut off twelve kings' beards, was a cornuto; Hercules, whose back bore up heaven, and got forty wenches with child in one night . . . yet was a cornuto.

(Marston, *The Malcontent,* IV. v. 54ff.)[25]

This is the 'realist', cynical view; unwittingly, however, it once again looks back to myths. All three heroes mentioned by Marston perished as a result of their wives' infidelity or involvement with another man. Both Agamemnon and Hercules died much like Polonius when covered with a fateful piece of clothing (net, shirt) woven by their wives. As for Arthur, we learn from Geoffrey of Monmouth's *History* that, 'at the beginning of August', he left for Rome, delegating 'the task of defending Britain to his nephew Mordred and to his Queen, Guinevere'. A year later, 'when summer came', he learned 'that his nephew Mordred, in whose care he had left Britain, had placed the crown upon his own head. What is more, this treacherous tyrant was living adulterously and out of wedlock with Queen Guinevere, who had broken the vows of her earlier marriage'.[26] The resemblance to Hamlet is noteworthy; but here the presence of myth is much more obvious. The summer king leaves, a new summer comes; usurpation of kingship is simultaneous with usurpation of the king's marital rights. Geoffrey, of course, lays part of the blame on Guinevere, like his contemporary Saxo does on Queen Hermutrude: woman is inconstant. But both authors preserve glimpses of an older tradition, and other myths allow us to uncover its pattern. King Cormac dreamt that his wife Ethne slept with Eochu Gunnat, after which she went back to her husband; when asking his druid for an interpretation, he was told: 'thy kingship will sleep with him, and he will be but one year in the kingship of Tara'.[27] Blodeuwedd and her lover planned to slay her husband, the Welsh hero Lleu Llaw Gyffes; but he could only be killed by a spear forged 'in a year of Sundays'; and so Lleu was struck down exactly one year after the plan was conceived.[28] The death of the year equates the death of the husband; either event signals (or is signalled by) the Queen's or Lady's attachment to another man.

The drift of my argument is that we have to do with ritual. I do not mean this in any anthropological sense, the sort of ritual at which, as Robert Graves[29] tells us, the Queen rid herself of a Yearly or Half-Yearly King in a bloody sacrifice. Rather I mean mythic, ultimately literary ritual. From the point of view of literary analysis, the entire concept of Sovereignty and its transmission must be seen as a stupendous metaphor devised to convey the basic rhythm of earth and seasons. The metaphor is presented in a variety of images centred around Woman which include the Voyage, the Test, the Cup, the Yarn or Net or woven garment; abduction, hierogamy, and adultery; deliverance and bondage; betrayal, death, and renewal. It is because these are all metaphors for a sacred round—it is because they are transcendent images—that they are used by traditional cultures. The general principle, of which adultery constitutes a special case, is renewal, and in the mythic heart of medieval Europe this principle is still

strong enough to assert itself from behind the growing realism of its literature.

And so when we come to the Renaissance we find the theme of Sovereignty still very much a literary issue; but instead of asserting the theme, the literature of the new age questions it, literalizes and plays down its mythic import. In the metaphor of earth and seasons, woman was nature and her behaviour was therefore predictable in a mythic, cyclic—as opposed to linear—view of time. Take this myth away, and woman's behaviour will appear incomprehensible and therefore perverse; it is then but inevitable that this perversion should attach to the metaphor itself, to all female symbols of nature. At this point, Laertes' speech on learning of Ophelia's death sums up the whole issue:

> Too much of water hast thou, poor Ophelia,
> And therefore I forbid my tears; but yet
> It is our trick; nature her custom holds,
> Let shame say what it will. When these are gone,
> The woman will be out. Adieu, my lord,
> I have a speech o' fire that fain would blaze
> But that this folly drownes it.

(Hamlet, IV. vii. 184 ff.)

The concepts Laertes is contrasting can be summarized thus:

Man shame (honour) fire blazing speech

Woman nature tears, water drowning folly

'The woman will be out.' This is the unconscious goal towards which the new culture strives: the eradication of the significant presence of the feminine principle from the Western definition of the universe. She is water that has to be opposed with fire; she is folly that has to be mastered with that most rational faculty, speech; she is shameless nature that has to be restrained by a manly sense of honour; she stands for myth that must be replaced with a realistic view of things. But she is also strong: too strong for the patriarchal culture to destroy her; she may be outrageously unintelligible, but her folly can yet drown a speech of fire. The only way to defeat her age-old power is to get the imagery to shortcircuit itself, as it were: the metaphor implodes, and Woman drowns in the very water she symbolized; it implodes again, and she dies of the very drink that was her most sacred prerogative. With the deaths of Ophelia and, especially, Gertrude, the traditional concept of Sovereignty passes from woman's hands, and a decisive step is taken towards the Modernity.

To conclude, then, Hamlet does not just express the new point of view concerning woman's Sovereignty, but presents the conflict itself between the old and the new as embodied in a modern hero's confrontation with an ancient myth. Shakespeare does not limit himself to the use of traditional material to convey a present-day concern; he seems rather to have realized that this is precisely the root of the problem—that the spirit of the modernity is ill at ease with traditional modes of expression, that the new man must come to terms with the loss of the old frameworks; ultimately, that there is no place in the new ideology for the traditional metaphors, though these cannot be lightly abandoned.

Notes

1. M. Aguirre, 'The Dram of Evil: Medieval Symbolism in *Hamlet*', *Proceedings of the 2nd International SEDERI Conference* (Oviedo, Spain, 1992), 23-7.

2. See e.g. G. Goetinck, *Peredur: A Study of Welsh Tradition in the Grail Legends* (Cardiff, 1975), and sources there given.

3. *The Edda,* tr. A. Faulkes (London, 1987), 31.

4. *The Saga of the Volsungs,* tr. J.L. Byock (Berkeley, 1990), ch. 21.

5. See I. Gollancz (ed.), *The Sources of* Hamlet: *With an Essay On the Legend* (Oxford, 1926).

6. *The Tain Bo Cuailnge,* tr. T. Kinsella (Oxford, 1982).

7. 'The Dream of Macsen Wledig', in *The Mabinogion,* tr. G. and T. Jones (London, 1978).

8. 'Echtra Condla', ed. and tr. H.P.A. Oskamp, *Etudes Celtiques,* 14 (1974), 207-28; *The Voyage of Bran Son of Febal to the Land of the Living,* ed. and tr. K. Meyer (London, 1895); 'Immram Curaig Mailduin', ed. and tr. W. Stokes, *Revue Celtique,* 9 (1888), 452-95; 10 (1889), 50-95.

9. Lucan, *The Civil War,* tr. J.D. Duff (London, 1877), 185 ff.

10. 'Thomas Rymer', in G. Grigson (ed.), *The Penguin Book of Ballads* (Harmondsworth, 1975).

11. Crossing a boundary, whether fence, threshold, mountain, river, or sea, traditionally signals a journey into the Otherworld. See A. and B. Rees, *Celtic Heritage: Ancient Tradition in Ireland and Wales* (London, 1978); Aguirre, 'The Hero's Voyage in Immram Curaig Mailduin', *Etudes Celtiques,* 27 (1990), 203-20.

12. See Aguirre, 'Weaving-Related Symbolism in Early European Literature', in N. Thomas (ed.), *Celtic and Germanic Themes in European Literature* (Lampeter, 1994), 1-11.

13. The function of these is not dissimilar from that of the labyrinth: as the Theseus story illustrates, yarn and labyrinth are merely two versions of one same symbol; like net and web, the labyrinth—whether cave or catacomb, castle or ocean, forest, darkness, or riddle—is the great symbol of the testing, wherein the seeker loses or finds the wielder of Sovereignty—and loses, or finds, himself. See Aguirre, 'The Riddle of Sovereignty', *MLR* 88 (1993), 273-82.

14. William Shakespeare, *Hamlet,* ed. H. Jenkins (London, 1990), 434.

15. See Gollancz, *Sources of* Hamlet, 95.

16. Ibid. 184.

17. These two conform to a motif often found in Saxo, as in Snorri's Edda and other Scandinavian texts, which involves the eternal alternation between a land-king and a sea-king. It must be clear that Horwendil and Feng are alternate kings, much as Atreus and Thyestes are in Seneca's tragedy—much as, in a more obscure way, Old Hamlet and Claudius are. This quality reinforces the mythological status of Shakespeare's 'characters'.

18. Gollancz, *Sources of* Hamlet, 188.

19. Ibid. 161.

20. A debased German redaction of Shakespeare's play, the 18th-century *Der Bestrafte Brudermord* ('Fratricide Punished'; in G. Bullough (ed.), *Narrative and Dramatic Sources of Shakespeare* (London, 1975), vii. 128-58) explicitly adopts the traditional view: 'Alas, my only son has entirely lost his reason! And I am much to blame for it! Had I not taken in marriage my brother-in-law, I should not have robbed my son of the crown of Denmark' (*Der Bestrafte Brudermord,* IV. vi). There it is, in all its coarse simplification: the crown depends on the queen's marriage, and it is her choice of husband that has led to the present state of affairs.

21. *Hamlet,* ed. Jenkins, 191.

22. Metalepsis, the violation of narrative levels, is rife in post-modernism; for discussion see B. McHale, *Post-modernist Fiction* (New York, 1987).

23. See Aguirre, *The Closed Space: Horror Literature and Western Symbolism* (Manchester, 1990), esp. ch. 3.

24. See Aguirre, 'A Literature of Reflection', *Forum For Modern Language Studies,* 29 (1993), 193-202.

25. *Jacobean Tragedies,* ed. A. H. Gomme (Oxford, 1982).

26. *The History of the Kings of Britain,* tr. L. Thorpe (Harmondsworth, 1982), VII. x.

27. 'Cormac's Dream', retold in P. MacCana, 'Aspects of the Theme of King and Goddess in Irish Literature', *Etudes Celtiques,* 7 (1955-6), 76ff., 356 ff.; 8 (1958-9), 59 ff.

28. 'Math Son of Mathonwy', in *The Mabinogion.*

29. Graves, *The Greek Myths* (Harmondsworth, 1960).

Millicent Bell (essay date 1998)

SOURCE: "Hamlet, Revenge!," in *The Hudson Review,* Vol. 51, No. 2, Summer, 1998, pp. 310-28.

[*In the following essay, Bell contends that Hamlet does not fulfill his expected role as a revenger because Shakespeare's intent was to satirize the revenge-play genre that was popular at the end of the sixteenth century.*]

When, at the end of the second act, Hamlet bawls, "Bloody, bawdy villain! / Remorseless, treacherous, lecherous, kindless Villain! / Oh vengeance!", the audience laughed, I guess, the way modern audiences laugh when viewing Mel Brooks's *Young Frankenstein*. They recognized a horror-thriller style old-fashioned enough to be funny; this was the way the Revenger hero of Thomas Kyd's *Spanish Tragedy* had ranted on the stage fifteen years before. Shakespeare's modern editors disagree about the "Oh vengeance," which appears only in the 1623 Folio version of the play. The editor of the Arden edition, who commits himself to an earlier Quarto text, where it is missing, thinks it must have been put in later by someone else, probably an actor. It jars, he feels, with the brooding self-reproach Hamlet has just expressed after hearing the player orate about the avenging of Achilles by his son Pyrrhus and about the grief of Hecuba over slaughtered Priam. The editor of the New Cambridge *Hamlet* thinks Shakespeare wrote it himself: "This cry, the great climax of the rant with which Hamlet emulates the Player, exhausts his futile self-recrimination, and turns, in proper disgust, from a display of verbal histrionics to more practical things." I, too, think it was Shakespeare's, but I disagree about its tone and intent. It is really a nudge to the funny bone of the sophisticated theatergoer of 1602. It resulted from the irrepressible leaking out of the playwright's satiric impulse in the midst of high seriousness.

If so, it is a small sign of what happens elsewhere. The elocutionary set piece that has moved Hamlet is itself an imitation of the style of a creaky older play about Queen Dido of Carthage. Hamlet is not put off by its stiff rhetoric; the mercilessness of the blood-smeared Pyrrhus and Hecuba's lamentation stir him profoundly by their application to his case. But the theater buffs in the audience must have been amused. Perhaps also by "The Murder of Gonzago," which the company of strolling players puts on according to Hamlet's instruction. This is to be another "Revenge Tragedy"—as the type is called—one, like Kyd's, with a Spanish setting, but it will represent his own father's murder and so cause his uncle to acknowledge his crime. Its parodic character is indicated by Hamlet's impatient exclamation to the actor who comes on as the murderer: "leave thy damnable faces and begin. Come, the croaking raven doth bellow for revenge."

"The Murder of Gonzago" is, I would say, a fictitious play invented by Shakespeare as an example of the kind of play he makes fun of at various points in *Hamlet*. Though Hamlet is supposed to have added some lines there is no evidence of the voice we know him by in the fragment we hear before a terrified Claudius rises from his seat. It is stale bombast cast into out-of-style couplets, unlike the naturalistic dialogue enclosing it. Shakespeare seems to have wanted to exaggerate its theatricality. He sets it in contrast with the reality of a modern—though medieval—Denmark. At the same time, Shakespeare is letting the audience know it is going to see the unfolding in *his* play, despite its realism, of just another such tale of teeth-grinding and bloody setting-to-rights as those it used to

find so thrilling. The *Hamlet* world is a contemporary realm, and the thought behind it, as I shall be suggesting, belongs to that latest Renaissance moment which Shakespeare shares with Montaigne. Yet it deliberately frames its modernity within an archaic kind of story (ultimately finding its model in Seneca), that of its probable source, a lost Revenge Tragedy, also by Kyd. This "ur-Hamlet," as the scholars call it, was undoubtedly the play remembered by a contemporary as including a "ghost which cried so miserably at the Theatre, like an oyster-wife, *Hamlet revenge*." Shakespeare's *Hamlet* has all the prescribed features of the once popular genre (and its surprising retro success helped bring the genre back into popularity). It has a ghost who demands revenge for a murder and a hero who promises to achieve it, pretends to be mad, indulges in philosophic soliloquies, and does not succeed in his purpose till the end of five acts. Even the play-within-a-play is a favorite of older plays of this kind. Like *The Spanish Tragedy,* which has all the features just mentioned, *Hamlet* also has a secondary revenge plot which brings about the completion of the main plot; it is Laertes' drive to avenge the death of *his* father, Polonius, which takes the action to its finish. The audience would recognize these reprises and wait for the turn Shakespeare would put on them. What he did was employ them all with a difference—make a teasing mystery of the delay of the execution of revenge which once had served just to extend suspense, make his hero's detached soliloquies exceed in profundity and poetry anything the theater had ever heard, make the madness the Revenger is supposed to feign to conceal his purposes an occasion for paradoxical wit and cynical philosophy as well as a symptom of the hero's mental anguish, introduce in Laertes the model of the effective Revenger yet use Hamlet's relation to the Polonius family as an opportunity to contrast him with "normal," or ordinary, persons. But, as though reminding the audience of his effort to reincarnate the old Revenger persona, Hamlet will still shout at the end, when Laertes threatens to outdo him in melodramatic grief for Ophelia, "I'll rant as well as thou!"

Hamlet's postmodern status as "metatheater"—theater about theater—is obvious enough. We might suspect a personal self-reflexiveness in it. Was not Shakespeare himself an actor? Shakespeare was a theater man, fascinated by the problems of his craft—and his Hamlet not only knows the history of Elizabethan drama but gives judicious advice to actors and can act creditably himself, can write a dramatic script or part of one, and he loves to see a play put on, quite aside from its possible use as a conscience-catcher. As a result, there are, from the earliest moment to the last, occasions when the curtain between the theatrical and the supposedly real is rent—beginning with Hamlet's remark when the ghost can be heard groaning as it retreats to its purgatorial exile: "You hear this fellow in the cellarage"—"cellarage" being a term that reminds the audience that an actor is making noises down in the space beneath the stage.

"Metatheatricality," as it may be too modish to call it, is detectable elsewhere in the literature of the Elizabethan stage, and Shakespeare's earlier plays give an emphasis to common terms that suggest the theater, words like tragedy, play, perform, show, act, scene or part, are frequent. *Hamlet* is particularly rich in such language. What has not been noted is that Hamlet's theater interest—and all the hints and references to the theatrical in the play—constitute a metaphoric motif and the tracking sign of a dominating theme. *Hamlet* abounds in situations in which the actors are audiences. When Hamlet observes Claudius at prayer, he is the unseen watcher who does not detect the deception in the performance; the King's repentance is momentary only and will not gain him salvation. Hamlet himself is watched by Polonius from behind an arras both in the "nunnery" scene with Ophelia and parallel scene with his mother in her closet. With Ophelia, Hamlet is, perhaps, consciously "playing a scene" for her benefit but unaware of hidden witnesses. Most productions of the play want to make it somehow possible for Hamlet to demonstrate that he knows about Polonius' proximity—and improvise a rustle behind the arras at which Hamlet starts before he asks Ophelia where her father is. But the theatricality of the situation lies precisely in Hamlet's oblivion—as an actor must be oblivious of the audience in the darkened theater. Meanwhile, the "nunnery" scene itself is more than an occasion for the abuse of poor Ophelia; it is a commentary on the unreliability of appearances, for Hamlet will tell her not to trust the seeming in men, not even his own pose as a lover ("We are arrant knaves all, believe none of us"). He abuses her as though she were herself a deceiving person—or an actress ("God hath given you one face and you make yourselves another").

In the play-within-the-play, the player king is a representation not only of the dead King Hamlet but of Claudius, an usurper who plays at being the true king ("a king of shreds and patches"), and brings to mind the way Richard II is represented continually as one who can say, "thus play I in one person many people." "The Murder of Gonzago" is a representation of the main play's actuality. But this actuality is itself the matter of the play, Shakespeare's *Hamlet*. And this flow of theatricality expands outward from the edge of the stage. Those ranks of interested spectators in the Danish court who watch the performance by the visiting players are mirrored by the theater filled with the spectators of *Hamlet*. Each spectator in either audience is, besides, not only a viewer of the action but an actor, too. "All the world's a stage," as Jacques says in *As You Like It*. We who watch *Hamlet* are not only spectators but actors in parts prescribed—some larger cosmic theater enclosing us.

That Shakespeare did not take the Revenge plot altogether seriously is signified by the way he let its coherence lapse. Much has been made of Hamlet's reasons for delay. He himself gives no reasons. What is clear is that his slowness to execute revenge against Claudius is not due to the explanation available in his sources—that it is difficult to get at a monarch surrounded by his guards; Shakespeare omits the guards present in these earlier versions of the story. Hamlet never complains of lack of opportunity.

Though he pretends to be mad it is not evident what purpose this really serves; in the revenge plays it diverts suspicion while in *Hamlet* it actually arouses it, and it is not always clear if or when Hamlet is pretending to be crazy or when indulging in a bizarre humor or when expressing his desperate but sane anguish. The soliloquies seem even more disconnected from the action surrounding them than is true in other plays of the type. The first announces Hamlet's desire for suicide—that this "too too solid flesh would melt"—without justifying cause beyond his mother's remarriage, since he still has not learned about his father's murder. In "O what a rogue and peasant slave am I," having just heard the player's Pyrrhus-Hecuba speech, Hamlet reproaches himself because he can "say nothing" to match such passion, then shifts, illogically, to accuse himself of having been like "a whore" who can only "unpack [his] heart with words" instead of acting. "To be or not to be," following shortly upon his resolution to confirm Claudius' guilt by means of his expectable reaction to "The Murder of Gonzago," reverts to the theme of suicide so inappropriately that some scholars feel that it must have been misplaced in the texts we have. "How all occasions do inform against me," which follows the appearance of Fortinbras and his troops in the fourth act, renews his resolution ("from this time forth, / My thoughts be bloody") when the moment for action may well be passed, even though it is at this time that Hamlet most clearly reproaches himself ("I do not know / Why yet I live to say this thing's to do, / Sith I have cause, and will, and strength, and means / To do't"). The fact of the matter is that he is about to board ship in forced exile to England. But precisely these "weaknesses," these denials of the dramatic coherence the standard Revenge plot provides, open up larger questions of human identity and destiny. In his indifference to causality even when available in his models, Shakespeare reveals the nature of his struggle to evade tradition and audience expectations.

There is a discrepancy between the hero and the play, but this results from what I take to be a general skepticism to be felt in the tragic plays Shakespeare would write from *Hamlet* on—a skepticism threatening our confidence in the consistency of character and in the linking of character to either its origin in outer circumstance or its effect in action. The cavalier way in which Shakespeare ignores the logic that his sources often provide, inferior as they are, has not been sufficiently observed—so great is our admiration for his wonderful art. But as he does in the case of *Hamlet,* Shakespeare will actually reduce the motivation available in his source for *Macbeth*. In Macbeth he seems to want to show us the *inexplicable* spectacle of a good man doing an evil deed. *Othello,* also, ignores the suggestion of comprehensible causes for Iago's malignity which Shakespeare's source provides. And it is not only Iago who is "motiveless," as Coleridge said, having no real reason for his fiendish malice. Othello's jealousy arises from provocation so inadequate that it is difficult to understand how anyone so reasonable could have been inflamed by it—and so, Iago's persuasive powers must be made nearly demonic. In acting out his preposterous rage Othello's character must be temporarily transformed from what it was.

Hamlet is a mystery play, and concealment and secrecy are essential to its style, but they serve, also, to reinforce the idea that appearances, like the actor's role, are deceptive. The ghost itself is forbidden, it tells Hamlet, to tell the secrets of its prison house; otherwise, it could a tale unfold of horrors to make the hearer's hair stand on end like porcupine quills! The murder is known only to the perpetrator; Claudius' guilt is "occulted." As the ghost relates, Hamlet's father was killed, significantly, by poison in the ear, "by which the whole ear of Denmark is by a forged process of my death rankly abused." Hamlet himself continues to keep it secret, swearing Horatio and Marcellus to silence not only about the ghost but about his plans to assume a mask himself, to put on an "antic disposition" to hide his purposes. Of course the usurping murderer is the supreme example of dissembling; and Hamlet cannot get over the way "one may smile, and smile, and be a villain." The play is full of spying—another way of seeing those spectatorial moments when a hidden witness watches a performance as though shown in a theater. Polonious, who sends a spy to look into the life abroad of his own son, is ludicrous and inefficient in his secret-service surveillance of Hamlet, and dies for his spying upon the Prince. Only when he is dead is he said by Hamlet to be, at last, "most still, most secret, and most grave." But deception and disguise do not break down, finally, to reveal the unchangeable truth—as in detective fiction; the character of Hamlet remains identified only with a succession of appearances.

As the play, in the first act, shifts from Hamlet to the Polonius family, Laertes' counsel to his sister to resist the sweet speeches of the Prince suggests that human nature, especially a prince's, is determined by social position—and has no other meaning. "He may not, as unvalued persons do, / Carve for himself, for on his choice depends / The sanctity and health of this whole state." Hamlet's love is definable only by his limited power to "give his saying deed." Polonius' advice to his son, which seems a string of stale truisms—because so often repeated as counsel to the young—boils down to the idea that self-expression should not be attempted. "Give thy thoughts no tongue, / Nor any unproportioned thought his act." But if the self should not be expressed, what is the meaning of the famous conclusion, "This above all, to thine own self be true"? Is there a self to which one can be "true" without letting it be heard or seen in speech and action? To Ophelia he gives advice that echoes her brother's resort to the familiar metaphor of theatrical costume. Hamlet's vows, he tells her, wear false vesture (he uses the unusual word "investments"). They plead "unholy suits" while pretending holy intent. The idea that personal reality is something shaped or "carved," not inherent in character, may be implied even when Hamlet facetiously ponders with Polonius over the shapes of clouds. He seems to have in mind the arbitrariness of all our interpretations which impose form and meaning on the meaningless, but it has been noted that the passage resembles one in *Antony and Cleopatra* when Antony says to Eros, after describing cloud shapes that resemble now this, now that,

> My good knave Eros, now thy captain is
> Even such a body. Here I am Antony
> Yet cannot hold this visible shape, my knave

I suspect that in *Hamlet* the talk about clouds also implies something about the way our characters seem fixed in one form or another but are really capable of infinite change. Hamlet tells Ophelia that he has "more offences at my beck than I have thoughts to put them in, imagination to give them shape, or time to act them in." He is all potentiality. There is no limit to the unenacted, unthought, unimagined "offences" of which he might be capable.

Hamlet's first utterance in the play is a reference to the problematic relation of essence and appearance and, at the same time, to the representation of this problem by the theatrical. He comes on stage clothed in the black of mourning, and the Queen, already speaking metaphorically, asks him for a change of mood, saying, "cast thy nighted colour off." She asks him why death "seems so particular" to him, and he answers,

> Seems, madam? nay it is. I know not seems.
> 'Tis not alone my inky cloak, good mother,
> Nor customary suits of solemn black,
> Nor windy suspiration of forced breath,
> No, nor the fruitful river in the eye,
> Nor the dejected haviour of the visage,
> Together with all forms, moods, shapes of grief,
> That can denote me truly. These indeed seem,
> For they are actions that a man might play,
> But I have that within which passes show—
> These but the trappings and the suits of woe.

This is more complex than appears at first glance. Hamlet is not saying that he has put on a false appearance to cover a true self. He does not deny the message of his appearance, for it declares his grief. Yet the way he looks and behaves constitutes *only* signs, after all, "actions that a man might play" as on the stage, a collection of gestures established by tradition for a role and easily enacted by the accomplished actor. If there is an inner mystery of some sort it is one that escapes all arts of action or expression and can hardly be spoken of, for no terms of description or manifestation exist for it. Shakespeare, the creator of theatrical character, expresses his own recognition of the conventionality of all the ways in which drama represents the self, and also the conventionality and insufficiency of all self-conceptions by means of which men and women carry on.

Hamlet resists all typological confinement. Is he bold or hesitating, passionate or sluggish, loving or cold, refined or coarse? The evidence for the first term in these pairs is what attracts us to him, yet the evidence for the second set of terms is plentiful—and those many attempts to summarize his character and explain his behavior in a unitary way must founder. Some of his negative aspects are off-putting enough to threaten his position as the hero. His reluctance to kill Claudius when he was kneeling in prayer—because then he might not send him straight to hell—shocked Dr. Johnson. His contrived killing of his sleazy false friends, Rosencrantz and Guildenstern, has seemed to many to be something that should have been beneath him. He is too brutal and vulgar with his mother and Ophelia. Yet we endure these spectacles for the glimpses given of that noble nature that Ophelia remembers, his tender filial memory and his appreciation of Horatio's friendship, and his generosity to the rash Laertes, who deals him his death blow. And the elevation of his mind, his play of wit and philosophy, his keen understanding of others and of society. Horatio's loyalty is a warrant we accept, for Horatio is our representative in the play—the sensible, decent, ordinary man who gives his complete loyalty to someone worthy of it. But the contradictions remain. Shakespeare's hero may be seen as someone who wants to be undetermined, unclassifiable, though, ultimately, he can find no selfhood outside of prescribed forms, no history but in established plots. He cannot be anything other than the Revenger the play sets out to make him.

Some say too quickly that Hamlet is a humour type—a melancholic, or a victim of an excess of black bile; he himself wonders if the devil has not been able to delude him with a false ghost "out of my weakness and my melancholy, / As he is very potent with such spirits." Then there is his madness to which one might refer his inconsistency; sometimes put on but perhaps not always. At the very end he apologizes to Laertes for his intemperate wrath.

> I am punished
> With a sore distraction. What I have done,
> That might your nature, honour and exception
> Roughly awake, I here proclaim was madness.

But neither melancholy nor madness is really the right explanation for the overmastering philosophic doubt—and the mood that leads to Hamlet's desire for death. In *Hamlet* the incoherence of what men do is profoundly and continuously explored. The famous "To be, or not to be" soliloquy at the beginning of the third act, spoken on the day the court play is to be presented, says not a word about this imminent test of Hamlet's suspicions and does not mention revenge. The question it opens is, most critics have supposed, again the issue of suicide. "To be" may be read as, simply, "to live," and "not to be" as, simply, "to die." If this is the choice that poses "the question" and if it is meant to be paralleled (A:B as C:D) in the alternatives then offered—whether it is "nobler in the mind to suffer / The slings and arrows of outrageous fortune, / Or to take arms against a sea of troubles, / And by opposing, end them"—one must assume, somewhat implausibly, that the ending of his troubles by the taking of arms against them is deliberate and certain suicide. But the choice is phrased so abstractly that one can also say that these terms are syntactically in opposition ("chiasmatically," their order

reversed to make the comparison A:B as D:C) with the ideas of passive suffering and active battle. In this way, to act is "to be." Merely to feel is "not to be." Hamlet may be reflecting that there is no being aside from our deeds. Still, are we only our acts? If Hamlet seems to be appealing to an "inmost part" of Gertrude when, in the closet scene, he proposes to set a glass before her in which she may view her true self, he also pleads with her to be an actress, "to assume a virtue if you have it not," with the hope that the appearance of virtue will, somehow, create an essence.

That Hamlet is inconsistent, variable, even uncertain himself as to who he is—this corresponds to his skepticism about human conceptions in general. The play, we must remember, is contemporaneous with Montaigne's *Essays*. Florio's English translation was published in London only months, perhaps, after the staging of Shakespeare's play. Perhaps Shakespeare saw the Florio Montaigne even before it was published; the very phraseology of the English version as well as Montaigne's balancing of contrary arguments is echoed, some think, in the soliloquies. Hamlet brings Montaigne to mind when he says about Denmark being a prison, "There's nothing good or bad but thinking makes it so"—a reflection expressed in Montaigne's essay, "That the taste of goods or evils doth greatly depend on the opinion we have of them." But Montaigne particularly denied the stability—or even reality—of personal essence, saying, "there is no constant existence, neither of our being, nor of the objects. We have no communication with being, for every human nature is ever in the middle between being born and dying, giving nothing of itself but an obscure appearance and shadow." Montaigne also wrote, in the essay, "Of the Inconstancie of our Actions," "We are all framed of flaps and patches and of so shapeless and diverse a contexture, that every peece and every moment playeth his part. And there is as much difference found betweene us and our selves, as there is betweene our selves and other." What being we have, then, is only what we assume in that phantasmic play in which we struggle to escape and to fulfill an idea of ourselves which owes its shape to cultural formulations.

"All the world's a stage" has so long been a platitude that one is apt to forget how revolutionary it might have sounded when first uttered, and how the idea is likely to shock us still when expressed by a modern thinker like Clifford Geertz in his well-known statement, "There is no such thing as human nature independent of culture." In Shakespeare's time the tension felt by those who adventured out of the bounds of inherited status—new classes, new professions—was intense, and what one was, as an individual, became more problematic. The process that Stephen Greenblatt calls "Renaissance self-fashioning" was strenuous and fraught with anxiety. For Shakespeare, a "new man" who was making a name and a fortune for himself in a once-despised trade, the problem of selfhood was fundamental. But the literature of the theater, changing with such rapidity in the few years of his participation, directly dramatized the contest between prescribed form and innovation. The standardized types into which mankind might be classified were no longer fixed in society nor were they for more than a moment useful literary conventions. What Shakespeare thinks of such types is represented in his portrait of Laertes—the perfect avenger, but stupid and not really so honorable when he consents to have his rapier poisoned in order to make sure he will win the duel with Hamlet. Osric, the courtier fop, a comic type himself, is the spokesman for fading categories when he describes Laertes in typecasting terms as the "absolute gentleman . . . the card or calendar of gentry; for you shall find in him the continent of what part a gentleman would see."

Hamlet's personal speeches, even aside from the soliloquies, often express an excessive despair that has baffled the critics. He tells Rosencrantz and Gildenstern,

> I have of late, but wherefore I know not, lost all my mirth, foregone all custom of exercises, and indeed it goes so heavily with my disposition that this goodly frame, the earth, seems to me a sterile promontory; this most excellent canopy, the air, look you, this brave o'erhanging firmament, this majestical roof fretted with golden fire—why, it appeareth no other thing to me but a foul and pestilent congregation of vapours. What a piece of work is a man! How noble in reason, how infinite in faculties, in form and moving how express and admirable, in action how like an angel, in apprehension how like a god! The beauty of the world, the paragon of animals—and yet to me, what is this quintessence of dust? Man delights not me—no, nor woman neither, though by your smiling you seem to say so.

It is complained that Hamlet's expression of such thoughts to such auditors, who can only respond with stupid snickers, is preposterous. Besides, he does know why he has lost all his mirth. The explanation generally offered is that he is trying to throw these spies off the scent. The Cambridge editor of the play says, "So often pointed to as a brilliant perception of the anguish of Renaissance man in general and of Hamlet in particular, it is a glorious blind, a flight of rhetoric by which a divided and distressed soul conceals the true nature of his distress and substitutes a formal and conventional state of *Weltschmerz*." But I would say that the instinctive response of reader or hearer to the power of the famous speech is sounder than this critical insistence upon its plot-logic. Hamlet has ceased to be, as he so often ceases to be, simply the character whose motives advance the plot. What he expresses is the root of his gloom, his sense of the paradox in the contradictions of human nature. Hamlet's desire for suicide, which continually erupts in the midst of the action and seems to have no sufficient explanation in the plot, derives from the discrepancy between what is felt and what is done that the play will go on to reinforce after the first soliloquy. To lose all one's mirth without apparent cause is to be someone whose altered response to life is all-inclusive and goes beyond specific occasions. In contrast with his ghostly, impalpable sense of self, the outer man and his roles are "too too solid."

Hamlet's "lunacy," as Polonius calls it, may have been apparent before Hamlet heard the ghost's tale. His melancholy, as the first soliloquy showed, has already aroused that loathing for sexuality which even causes him to wish that his own flesh would melt. But he can put on the madman act, as he shows in his exuberant teasing of Polonius or of Rosencrantz and Guildenstern—and yet baffle them by the famous "method" in his madness. Ophelia's report to her father about Hamlet's strange behavior makes it appear that he has been driven out of his mind by the repulse she has administered at her father's command. Polonius is conversant enough with conventional typology to recognize in Ophelia's description the standard symptoms of what was called "love ecstasy." But the audience may legitimately suspect it was all "an act"—an exhibition of that pretended madness Hamlet has resolved upon. Beyond this uncertainty, however, I want to point out another which is generally overlooked. Simulated or no, Hamlet's appearance of madness is a representation of the fragility of that notion of identity in which he has ceased to believe. It is this uncertainty that is even expressed in Ophelia's authentic mad talk. "Lord, we know what we are, but we know not what we may be," she says. Is not madness what we call "not being oneself"—an alienation from the essential consistency one prefers to believe in? But what if one has ceased to believe in it? By keeping us in continual doubt about Hamlet's madness, Shakespeare raises this suspicion of essences and of any truth beyond appearance.

Hamlet's transformation into an avenger requires him to surrender, as much as he can, his character as lover. He has sworn to the ghost that he will wipe away from the table of his memory "all trivial fond records" and let only the ghost's command remain. In this process his previous character has been constricted. The nature of man as a sexual being, and of woman as one, also, is reduced. From the outset of the play Hamlet is oppressed by the idea of sex as a perversion; his mother has caused him to look at the consummation of marriage with loathing, as an incestuous horror. In retrospect, he regards even her feeling for his father as a kind of gluttony: "she would hang on him / As if increase of appetite had grown / By what it fed on." No one is chaste in the Danish court—not even Ophelia, in his view. It is unnecessary, I think, to psychologize this, as has so often been done—to see Hamlet as suffering from oedipal fixation on his mother, hatred for the usurper father now represented by Claudius. Hamlet's rejection of the "normal" sexual and familial set of attitudes is still another mark of the shrinking of identity with which he is afflicted.

Does Hamlet ever come close to accepting entirely—or rejecting without question—the Revenger model? There is one moment when, I believe, he invokes it consciously—and puts it aside. As he goes to meet his mother in the third act he revs himself up with an old-style invocation of dark powers—then dismisses their prompting,

> 'Tis now the very witching time of night,
> When churchyards yawn, and hell itself breathes out
> Contagion to this world. Now could I drink hot blood,

And do such bitter business as the day
Would quake to look on. Soft, now to my mother.
O heart, lose not thy nature; let not ever
The soul of Nero enter this firm bosom.
Let me be cruel, not unnatural:
I will speak daggers to her but use none.

"When churchyards yawn" is a reminder to himself of the ghost who returned from the realm of death to lay its demand upon him. Now it is the "witching hour," as we still say, when he "could drink hot blood," as murdering witches were believed to drink the blood of their victims. Now he could do the unnamable horror that "the day would quake to look on." But he draws back. He will "speak daggers" to his mother but he will not commit the crime of Nero, the matricide. He calls upon something almost never acknowledged in this drama of borrowed, fabricated selfhood—upon the promptings of the heart, "of nature." But it is not "nature" that keeps him from killing the King when he comes upon him in prayer—on the way to the Queen.

"Nature" as a term for an original human nature that persists despite the impositions of borrowed form appears rarely in *Hamlet*. The principal reference that comes to mind is that curious comment on Danish drunkenness which Hamlet makes as he listens in the first act to the "heavy-headed revel" of the royal wedding feast. Hamlet speaks here of "nature" as a source of human defect: "So oft it chances in particular men, / That for some vicious mole of nature in them, / As in their birth, wherein they are not guilty, / Since nature cannot choose his origin." The passage, deleted from the Folio, seems out of place as a reflection Hamlet might make as he waits for his father's ghost to appear—except, perhaps, for the fact that the ghost refers to his own "days of nature" when he committed the crimes for which he suffers now.

But "histrionics" is never discarded altogether by Hamlet. He had wondered, after hearing the player's recital, that he himself was so inferior in expression, having "the motive and the cue for passion" that he had. He found himself in competition with an actor who lacked his own great "cue": "What's Hecuba to him?" He is in a similar competition later on, in the fourth act, with the Norwegian Prince, Fortinbras. Fortinbras, who has put aside his original desire to revenge his own father's death and recover his property, now marches to Poland with an army of twenty thousand to gain a worthless scrap of land, finding "quarrel in a straw"—while Hamlet, "a father killed, a mother stained," still has not acted. And Hamlet is stirred and humbled by such an exhibition of pure performance without motive— which is really like the actor's. "How all occasions do inform against me / And stir my dull revenge," he begins his last soliloquy.

Witness this army of such mass and charge,
Led by a delicate and tender prince,
Whose spirit with divine ambition puff'd
Makes mouths at the invisible event,
Exposing what is mortal and unsure

To all that fortune, death, and danger dare,
Even for an eggshell.

The difficulty with Fortinbras' presence in the play has not been addressed properly by the critics. Most commentators think of him in comparison or contrast with Hamlet because he is heard of at the very beginning as a son aroused to reprisal by a father's cruel death; one is tempted to see a parallel between him and Laertes and even ancient Pyrrhus as instances of unhesitating filial action. Laertes really is a misguided hothead and Pyrrhus a butcher who makes Hecuba, with her copious tears, a foil to Gertrude who has dried her own too quickly. But they fulfill their avenger roles. Fortinbras, however, disappears as an avenger promptly. Claudius averts his threat to Denmark by sending envoys to Fortinbras' uncle, the King of Norway—and by return mail, one might say, news arrives that this rash young man has promised to give up his personal project and embrace instead an assignment to lead his soldiers elsewhere. Has he any persisting role in the play? Well, someone has to be there at the end to pick up the pieces and assume the throne—Horatio would hardly do as Denmark's new king; he is not a royal person. The great Harvard Shakespearean, George Lyman Kittredge, made the matter even simpler. The dramatic character of highest rank customarily spoke the speech which brings an Elizabethan play to a close, and so "this accounts for the presence of Fortinbras in *Hamlet*. But for him there would be no one left of sufficient rank to fulfill this office." But there may be a special meaning in the resemblance of Hamlet's late envy of Fortinbras and his early envy of the stage actor who performs his part with such noble fervor. In both cases it does not seem to matter that the brilliant performances of the theatrical actor and the soldier are without personal motive. Their merely spectacular action for action's sake seems superior to Hamlet's inadequate expression of what he calls "excitements of my reason and my blood." Hamlet's envy even expresses that existential lack of confidence in essences and in the connection of character and deed which is at the heart of the play, for only acts, in this skeptical view, count, not intention. Pragmatically, Man is no more than "a beast" if "capability and godlike reason . . . fust in us unus'd." Inner selfhood has no real existence compared to the show of those who "find quarrel in a straw / When honour's at the stake." Earlier, in the "To be or not to be" soliloquy, as I have noted, "to be," may be interpretable as action, mere "in the mind to suffer" as "not to be." But such a challenge to the importance of essential being and the necessary relation it bears to doing may have been too radical and disturbing a skepticism for Shakespeare's audience. Because Hamlet seems finally ready to acknowledge his laggardliness as an avenger, modern directors often retain the fourth act Fortinbras passages even though self-reproach seems out of place at a moment when Hamlet has been rendered powerless and is a virtual prisoner. Shakespeare might have had second thoughts about this dramatic illogic. But, besides, the skeptical paradox posed by the Fortinbras model was bound to puzzle many. This final soliloquy of Hamlet and the preceding scene which provokes it are found in the quarto, probably Shakespeare's own earlier script, but they are absent from the later Folio text of *Hamlet,* the longest of such cuts in a revision which may have been made with the playwright's consent. Perhaps the acting company's director or even Shakespeare himself cried "Cut!" at this point when the play was first run through.

Death, of course, is the ultimate loss of selfhood, and the jesting of the gravediggers and of Hamlet in the last act is not merely comedy but reflects that mystery. Where are those selfhoods of the politician, the courtier, the lawyer, "with his quiddities now, his quillets, his cases, his tenures, and his tricks," of the lady painting herself an inch thick, and of Alexander the Great and Caesar, and of Yorick? Yet it is precisely at this moment when the awfulness of the loss of identity by death is brought to mind that Hamlet is also made to recall his own childhood, when, as a little boy, he was carried on Yorick's shoulders. When he leaps into Ophelia's grave to contest with Laertes, it is not only with the declaration of the love he has denied, but with a momentary sense of recovered selfhood. "This is I, Hamlet the Dane," he shouts in thrilling tones as though setting himself into history along with his father, who bore the same name. Yet this renewed identity is, after all, the rage of the old action-man that his father was and expected him to be. To Laertes, he says in a desire not to be exceeded, "Woo't weep, woo't fight, woo't fast, woo't tear thyself? / Woo't drink up eisel [vinegar], eat a crocodile? / I'll do it."

Finally, Hamlet is ready to acknowledge how impossible it is to avoid role-playing. He will accept the end shaped for him in the role he has been unable to elude. Describing to Horatio how he had—accidentally—discovered and foiled the plot against him on the ship taking him to England, and sent Rosencrantz and Guildenstern to their deaths, he says,

> Our indiscretion sometimes serves us well
> When our deep plots do pall, and that should learn us
> There's a divinity that shapes our ends,
> Rough-hew them how we will—

A good many critics have found Hamlet's easy disposal of this paltry pair, "no shriving-time allowed," as somehow too brutal for the "sweet prince" we love, and wince at the fact that when he kills Claudius at last it is not only with the "envenom'd" rapier but, gratuitously, by a forced swallow from the cup of poisoned wine as well. But Hamlet has accepted the Revenger role, and the crude ruthlessness which goes with it, by this time. The divinity that shapes our ends is commonly thought to be a reference to God's determination, to which, it is said, Hamlet at last acquiesces. But the religious note is so scantily sounded in this play that one may as properly think of the shaping force Hamlet calls "a divinity" as simply Destiny—something assigned to us as much by custom and circumstance as by Divine intention. Hamlet may be alluding to Matthew 10:19 when he tells Horatio, as he prepares for his duel with Laertes, "There is a special providence in the fall of a sparrow. If it be now, 'tis not to come; if it be not to come, it will be now; if it be not now, yet it will come—the readiness is all." But his sense of ineluctable necessity is a part of the acceptance of the role into which he has been "shaped" by determinants that are not necessarily heavenly. I think of them, in relation to my idea of Shakespeare and his times, as the determinants Geertz refers to when he speaks of "culture" as the definer of character.

The ghost (very uncertainly a divine messenger; there is strong Protestant theological argument behind Hamlet's idea that it could be an impersonating fiend) appears as an agent whose task it is to haunt Hamlet literally and figuratively with reminder of his Revenger role. In the closet scene with Gertrude it appears to "whet [Hamlet's] almost blunted purpose." Hamlet has passionately inveighed against her "act / That roars so loud and thunders in the index"—her marriage to his uncle, "in the rank sweat of an enseamèd bed, / Stewed in corruption, honeying and making love / Over the nasty sty"—but has said not a word about the murder. There is a tradition that Shakespeare himself took the part of the ghost in performance. In a sense it is Shakespeare who is both haunted and haunting. It is he himself who tries to escape the expectations of his audience—yet, ultimately, cannot really do so. As the play wears on, the ghost quite disappears. At the last, when its appeal for revenge is about to be answered, Hamlet hardly speaks at all about his father except to mention that he used his signet to seal the death warrant of Rosencrantz and Guildenstern, and to refer to the murder of his father (whom he now calls, more impersonally, "my king") as one item only in his charges against his uncle:

> He that hath killed my king, and whored my mother
> Popped in between th'election and my hopes,
> Thrown out his angle for my proper life,
> And with such cozenage—is't not perfect conscience
> To quit him with this arm? And is't not to be damned
> To let the canker of our nature come
> To further evil?

—a speech in which, among other reasons for killing Claudius, one hears of frustrate ambition, which Rosencrantz and Guildenstern had scented in Hamlet (much to one's annoyance, when one heard them say so). The word "revenge," which one would expect to hear at the end, is never sounded. Hamlet, in a last reminder of theatricality, turns to the audience in the theater as well as to witnesses on the stage when, dying, he says,

> You that look pale, and tremble at this chance,
> That are but mutes or audience to this act
> Had I but time, as this fell sergeant death
> Is strict in his arrest, oh I could tell you—
> But let it be. Horatio, I am dead,
> Thou livest; report me and my cause aright
> To the unsatisfied.

But what account of Hamlet Horatio will give is no longer clear. "Story," in a received sense, the story of Hamlet and his "cause"—has collapsed, and Horatio now speaks only of the "accidental" and "casual" and mistaken chances that produced the carnage on the stage. He does not speak of revenge, that chain of calculated steps leading inexorably to conclusion.

> How these things came about. So shall you hear
> Of carnal, bloody, and unnatural acts,
> Of accidental judgments, casual slaughters,
> Of deaths put on by cunning and forced cause,
> And in this upshot, purposes mistook
> Fallen on th'inventors' heads.

If there is another story to tell, only the play itself tells it.

FURTHER READING

Criticism

Aggeler, Geoffrey. "Nobler in the Mind: The Dialectic in *Hamlet*." In *Nobler in the Mind: The Stoic-Skeptic Dialectic in English Renaissance Tragedy,* pp. 145-61. Newark: University of Delaware Press, 1998.

Distinguishes between the degrees of Stoicism in the characters of Hamlet and Claudius and follows the development of the Stoic philosophy in the play as a whole.

Belsey, Catherine. "Sibling Rivalry: *Hamlet* and the First Murder." In *Shakespeare and the Loss of Eden: The Construction of Family Values in Early Modern Culture,* pp. 129-74. New Brunswick, N.J.: Rutgers University Press, 1999.

Describes the biblical story of the murder of Abel by his brother, Cain, and then connects it to the story of familial loss, rage, and bloodshed in *Hamlet.*

Charney, Maurice. "*Hamlet* as Comedy." In *Hamlet's Fictions,* pp. 131-51. New York: Routledge, 1988.

Asserts that while *Hamlet* is not a tragicomedy, it is a play that depends upon substantive comedic elements to make its tragic conclusion more powerful and convincing.

Clary, Frank Nicholas. "'The Very Cunning of the Scene': Hamlet's Divination and the King's Occulted Guilt." *Hamlet Studies,* 18, Nos. 1-2 (Summer 1996): 7-28.

Studies the play-within-the play, *The Murder of Gonzago,* in order to point out that Francois de Belleforest's adaptation of the Saxo Grammaticus story influenced Hamlet more than previously believed.

Dickson, Lisa. "The Hermeneutics of Error: Reading and the First Witness in *Hamlet.*" *Hamlet Studies* 19, Nos. 1-2 (Summer 1997): 64-77.

Describes *Hamlet* as a play about boundaries, citing the conflict between public and private worlds as well as the conflict between the self and its sense of identity.

Floyd-Wilson, Mary. "Ophelia and Femininity in the Eighteenth Century: 'Dangerous conjectures in ill-breeding minds.'" *Women's Studies* 21, No. 4 (September 1992): 397-409.

Contends that eighteenth-century censorship of the character Ophelia transformed her into a more sexualized and subversive character than Shakespeare had intended her to be.

Knights, L.C. "An Approach to *Hamlet.*" In *Hamlet and Other Shakespearean Essays,* pp. 1-20. Cambridge: Cambridge University Press, 1979.

Assesses *Hamlet* in relationship to Shakespeare's other plays, focusing, for example, on the recurrent theme of deception.

Leverenz, David. "The Woman in Hamlet: An Interpersonal View." In *Representing Shakespeare: New Psychoanalytic Essays,* edited by Murray M. Schwartz and Coppélia Kahn, pp. 110-28. Baltimore: The Johns Hopkins University Press, 1980.

Suggests that the tragedy in *Hamlet* results from the conflict between masculine power, feminine feeling, and the ultimate defeat of feeling.

Levy, Eric P. "'Things standing thus unknown': The Epistemology of Ignorance in *Hamlet.*" *Studies in Philology* 97, No. 2 (Spring 2000): 192-209.

Observes that *Hamlet* is a play about the relentless search for knowledge warring with a desperate need for denial.

McGee, Arthur. "The Last Act." In *The Elizabethan Hamlet,* pp. 162-76. New Haven, Conn.: Yale University Press, 1987.

Reevaluates *Hamlet*'s character as representative of madness and of the medieval morality figure, Vice, rather than of noble aims.

Russell, John. "The Failure of the Son: Hamlet's Delay." In *Hamlet and Narcissus,* pp. 114-45. Newark: University of Delaware Press, 1995.

Gives a psychoanalytical reading of the play, locating *Hamlet*'s slowness to avenge his father's murder in his own ambivalent preoccupation with death.

Sheidley, William E. "Hamlets and Hierarchy." *Peace Review* 11, No. 2 (1999): 243-49.

Focuses on *Hamlet*'s sources and on several productions of the play in order to demonstrate that the fundamental plot deals with social hierarchies and the need either to reform or destroy them.

Sjögren, Gunnar. "Doing Justice to Ophelia." In *Hamlet the Dane: Ten Essays by Gunnar Sjögren,* pp. 66-91. Lund: CWK Gleerup, 1983.

Examines the character of Ophelia from multiple perspectives: historical, critical, and textual.

Stanton, Kay. "*Hamlet*'s Whores." In *New Essays on Hamlet,* edited by Mark Thornton Burnett and John Manning, pp. 167-88. New York: AMS Press, 1994.

Examines the dual reading of the line "Get thee to a nunnery," and its implications for the female characters in *Hamlet.*

Waters, D. Douglas. "*Mimesis* and Catharsis as Clarification in *Hamlet.*" In *Christian Settings in Shakespeare's Tragedies,* pp. 208-46. Rutherford, N.J.: Fairleigh Dickinson University Press, 1994.

Asserts that Shakespeare drew heavily upon Aristotelian theory in constructing his play, and that in Prince Hamlet he created a character he genuinely admired.

The Merry Wives of Windsor

For further information on the critical and stage history of *The Merry Wives of Windsor,* see *SC,* Volumes 5, 18, 38, and 47.

INTRODUCTION

While *The Merry Wives of Windsor* has generally remained popular in performance, this comedy of the ne'er-do-well knight Falstaff and his disastrous efforts to romance two clever city housewives has not always been well received by literary critics. According to T.W. Craik (1989), the play fell into disregard early in the nineteenth century when critics dismissed it in favor of thematically complicated Shakespearean comedies such as *Twelfth Night.* Critics have since charged that the Falstaff in *The Merry Wives of Windsor* is a pathetic caricature of the crafty Falstaff in the *Henry IV* plays. This objection was reinforced by those who believed that the play was written not out of inspiration but in answer to Queen Elizabeth's command that Shakespeare write a play showing the fat knight in love. More recently, however, literary critics have begun to reexamine the play's sources and overall structure and now place a higher value on its comic variety and its portrayal of Elizabethan society.

Both Giorgio Melchiori (1994) and Barbara Freedman (1994) cast doubt on the argument that *The Merry Wives of Windsor* is a so-called "occasional" play that had been ordered by the Queen for a courtly celebration. Indeed, Freedman suggests that the comedy is too rich in topical references to have been written for any single occasion, and that what is in fact more interesting about the play is the manner in which it reveals Shakespeare's virtuosity in applying the current events of his time in an engaging way to traditional comedic forms. The precise nature of these comedic forms is examined by G. Beiner (1988) and Robert S. Miola (1993). Beiner describes Falstaff as a "pharmakos" or potential threat to the community of the play—one that has to be united against and routed so that the final act can resolve itself into a "festive celebration" of marriage between Fenton and Anne Page. Further, Beiner asserts that Falstaff's role as pharmakos is important to Shakespeare's works overall because it firmly connects *The Merry Wives of Windsor* with other plays such as *Twelfth Night,* where the "malcontent" Malvolio likewise serves to draw the play to a festive close. While literary critic Miola remains unimpressed with the comedic resolution to *The Merry Wives of Windsor,* describing it as "flawed" and at times "badly garbled," he nevertheless credits Shakespeare for incorporating a variety of European comedic forms into the play which are then used to greater advantage in his comedy *All's Well That Ends Well.*

Finally, several critics have focused on *The Merry Wives of Windsor* as representative of Elizabethan urban life. For example, while R.S. White (1991) acknowledges that the characters make very conscious references to themselves as participants in the artificial world of a play, he adds that the setting of this play is a very realistic portrayal of sixteenth-century London life and examines how it differed from the rural life beyond the town. Camille Wells Slights (1985) also looks at the play's juxtaposition of urban and rural, arguing that in the cynical London setting of the play, idealized "pastoral values" are achieved when Fenton and Anne Page ultimately ask her parents to bless their marriage. Alternatively, Charles Stanley Ross (1994) sees the play's setting in a more ambiguous light. He argues that fraud is the focus of *The Merry Wives of Windsor,* and the fraudulent practices reflect the ambiguous morals of Renaissance society. The critic also notes that in his attempt to cheat the wives, Falstaff is the most flagrant practitioner of fraud in the play.

OVERVIEWS AND GENERAL STUDIES

T.W. Craik (essay date 1989)

SOURCE: Introduction to *The Merry Wives of Windsor,* by William Shakespeare, edited by T.W. Craik, Clarendon Press, 1989, pp. 13-25.

[*In the following excerpt, Craik provides an overview of* The Merry Wives of Windsor, *focusing in particular on the plot structure and comparing it to several other works of the Renaissance.*]

SHAKESPEARE'S ENGLISH COMEDY: THE
SUBSTANCE AND THE DRAMATIC STRUCTURE OF
THE PLAY

The Merry Wives of Windsor is unique among Shakespeare's comedies in being set in England, rather than in Ephesus, Athens, France, Italy, Illyria, or ancient Britain. This English setting—a very local one, with its allusions to Windsor, Eton, Frogmore, and Datchet—goes to confirm the play's connection both with the Garter Feast and with the English history plays. Its social world is that of the Gloucestershire scenes of *2 Henry IV,* where there are no kings or dukes, and none of the characters is above the rank of a knight. The incidents in which its central character, Falstaff, is discomfited recall the spirit of the Gadshill robbery episode in *1 Henry IV.* Everything points to Shakespeare's having intended to write a comedy of which the material should be his English histories with the history left out. Falstaff, already a more important figure in the histories than his subsidiary role required him to be, was now to have a whole play to himself.

For this new Falstaff play Shakespeare needed a plot, a plot involving a succession of comic discomfitures from which Falstaff would emerge defeated but irrepressible, as he had done from the Gadshill robbery. On the face of it, it is not likely that any ready-made plot would serve his purpose, and so it is not surprising that no source for the play as a whole has been found. (That a lost play called *The Jealous Comedy*, performed by the Lord Chamberlain's Men in 1593, was the source is the merest conjecture.)[1] Shakespeare, then, may be assumed to have invented his own plot, drawing upon his memory for suitable incidental material, as he remembered Chaucer's *Knight's Tale* when inventing the plot of *A Midsummer Night's Dream*. The most substantial piece of material of this sort is a story from a collection of *novelle*, Ser Giovanni Fiorentino's *Il pecorone*.[2] In this story a student asks a professor to teach him the art of love (that is, of seduction), and duly applies the teaching and reports his progress to the professor; suspecting that the woman is his own wife (as she is), the professor follows the student to the house, but does not find him because the wife has hidden him under a heap of damp washing; next day the student reports his adventure to the professor, who consequently stabs the heap of washing the next time he follows the student to the house; the student, of course, has escaped in a different way, and the professor is treated as a madman by his wife's brothers, whom he has caused to witness his search. Though there are major differences (chiefly that in the *novella* adultery takes place), there are striking resemblances. The lover's confiding in the husband, the concealment under the washing, and the husband's assault on the washing upon the second occasion, all suggest that Shakespeare knew this story, particularly because another story in *Il pecorone* is agreed to be the source of the main plot (the bond, the wife disguised as a lawyer, and the business of the ring) of *The Merchant of Venice*, which he probably wrote in 1596 or 1597. No other proposed source for elements of the play comes anywhere near so close as this, which may be taken to be the point from which Shakespeare's plot grew.[3]

Ser Giovanni's *novella* is a simple comedy of ironic situation, satisfying enough within its conventional limits but strictly limited in characters and in incidents.[4] It would not in itself make a play. Shakespeare seizes on its situational irony and develops round this a humorous comedy of character. He also substitutes for the amoral sexual opportunism of the original a quite different moral spirit, in which 'wives may be merry and yet honest too', and in which not only is Falstaff's lechery frustrated but also Ford's jealousy is cured—yet all this without sententious moralizing or undue seriousness. One method by which the mood of the whole play is kept light and cheerful is the multiplying of the dramatic interest. Though Falstaff's first two discomfitures take place at Ford's house and turn upon his attempts to seduce Mistress Ford, the facts that

he has also written a love-letter to Mistress Page, that the two women have compared their letters, that Ford and Page have both been told of his intentions by his discarded hangers-on, that Falstaff has been (as he thinks) independently engaged by the supposed Brook to seduce Mistress Ford, and that Ford has Page and two or three eccentrics in tow when he searches his house for Falstaff, all go to confirm that there are to be no unpleasantly lifelike treatments of sexual misconduct or of marital jealousy.

Along with this filling-out of his main plot Shakespeare introduces two subsidiary actions. In the first of these, Page's daughter is courted by three suitors, two of them ridiculous, and is won by Fenton, the young gentleman whom she favours, while her two unwelcome suitors (the respective choices of her father and mother) are ludicrously disappointed, in the final scene. The second subsidiary action centres upon one of Anne Page's two ridiculous suitors, Dr Caius the French physician, and the Welsh parson of the town, Sir Hugh Evans; the former challenges the latter to a duel for intervening to forward Slender's courtship of Anne, the Host of the Garter Inn frustrates the duel by appointing them contrary places, and they combine to revenge themselves on him by arranging for some pretended Germans to run away with his horses. Their revengeful trick is so lightly sketched in that several critics have supposed one or more scenes to have been lost, but there is no necessity for more than a sketch of this very minor element in the plot. Its usefulness, apart from further filling out the play with the humours of Caius, Evans, and the Host, is that it adds the Host to the number of those who suffer reverses in the latter part of it—Page and Slender, Mistress Page and Caius. It is important that Falstaff should not be the only loser.

Shakespeare gives most of the principal characters more than one function in the play's multiple action. Mistress Page, for instance, is both Mistress Ford's confidante and an intriguer on behalf of Caius in his suit to her daughter Anne; Page intrigues on behalf of Slender and is also a foil to the jealous Ford; Mistress Quickly, besides being Caius's housekeeper, acts as go-between in Mistress Ford's dealings with Falstaff; Caius and Evans, besides being absurd would-be duellists, are reasonable spectators of Ford's searches of his house, and Caius is also a suitor and Evans a pedant who conducts a Latin lesson; the Host, in addition to his involvement in the duel and in the duellists' revenge, is an assistant in Fenton's elopement with Anne Page.

It is typical of Shakespeare's method, which the following discussion will explore, to have more than one action afoot in a comedy. The opening scene proclaims the breadth of interest, in event and character, that we are to be offered. The first three persons on stage—Justice Shallow, his nephew Slender, and Sir Hugh Evans—are a trio of notable eccentrics, and presently they are confronted with an equally eccentric quartet in Falstaff and his hangers-on, Bardolph, Pistol, and Nim. The only normal people—Page and his wife, their daughter, and Mistress Ford—are outnumbered, and provide a scale by which the abnormality of the others can be measured. Shallow's complaint against Falstaff, which gives the scene and the play their kick-start, is never heard of again, and the chief business set going is the wooing of Anne Page by (or rather, on behalf of) Slender, which is carried on in the second scene when Sir Hugh sends Slender's servant Simple with a letter to Mistress Quickly asking her to use her influence with Anne. Only then, in Scene 3, do we reach the beginning of the main action, with Falstaff proposing to make Mistress Ford and Mistress Page his East and West Indies, cashiering Pistol and Nim for refusing to deliver his love-letters, and thereby motivating their betrayal of his scheme to Ford and Page. Among Shakespeare's artful touches in these first three scenes Falstaff's one speech to Mistress Ford is to be noted:

> Mistress Ford, by my troth, you are very well met. By your leave, good mistress.

Even if general kissing breaks out after the next line, when Page says, 'Wife, bid these gentlemen welcome', Falstaff's speech and kiss have made their dramatic point, with their conscious gallantry; consequently his announcement of his scheme in Scene 3, though it has all the impact of novelty, has continuity too. We may also notice that Falstaff has already parted with his third follower, Bardolph, to the Host—in whose employment he will be dramatically useful later—before he breaks with the other two and gives both letters to his page Robin (another minor character who will have his uses: 'And Falstaff's boy with her!').[5]

Ford, who grinds out the line just quoted, does not appear until well into the first scene of Act 2. In the mean time, true to Shakespeare's usual method of alternating action, Sir Hugh's letter is delivered to Mistress Quickly, and her employer Dr Caius discovers the messenger, becomes incensed at Sir Hugh's meddling on behalf of a rival suitor, and sends him a challenge. The French doctor is obviously the Welsh parson's equivalent in the play's gallery of eccentrics, though not so obviously as if they were themselves rival suitors, which would be too obvious a device for Shakespeare. Before the scene is over, Fenton—Anne's third suitor, and so evidently the successful one that there is no need, here or later, to spend more than the minimal time in establishing the fact—also appears. Then, in the first scene of Act 2, the main plot is greatly developed: Mistress Page and Mistress Ford compare their letters, Ford and Page are informed of Falstaff's scheme by Pistol and Nim, Mistress Quickly is engaged by the wives as a messenger to Falstaff, and Ford arranges with the Host that he shall be introduced to Falstaff under the assumed name of Brook.

Shakespeare's skill in dramatic construction is so easy that it is the easiest thing in the world to ignore it. In this scene the arrival of the Host, whom Caius has appointed umpire in his duel with Sir Hugh, with Shallow at his heels, allows Ford to come to his arrangement with the former while the latter talks to Page about the duel. And

this dialogue with Page allows Shallow to vent his opinions on modern swordsmen and to reflect with satisfaction on his own feats of former days:

> 'Tis the heart, Master Page; 'tis here, 'tis here. I have seen the time, with my long sword, I would have made you four tall fellows skip like rats.

This is a good instance of how, in this play as in others, Shakespeare gives his scenes room to breathe. Then, with the exits of the Host, Shallow, and Page, Ford is left on stage to reinforce our knowledge of his intention to visit Falstaff in disguise in a very short soliloquy.

Of course, we are eager to see him put his plan in practice, and the sight of Falstaff browbeating a crestfallen Pistol is our assurance that Ford is even now on his way. But first Mistress Quickly must arrive and appoint Falstaff's assignation for next morning. The result is that Ford's arrival finds Falstaff in a hubristic mood of self-gratulation:

> Sayst thou so, old Jack? Go thy ways. I'll make more of thy old body than I have done. Will they yet look after thee? Wilt thou, after the expense of so much money, be now a gainer? Good body, I thank thee. Let them say 'tis grossly done, so it be fairly done, no matter.[6]

Master Brook offers Falstaff money for seducing Ford's wife. The oddity of this proposal from one who declares himself in love with her is not lost on Falstaff, so Master Brook has to justify it. The dialogue is conducted, at some length, with great politeness on both sides, which throws into strong relief the contrast in style when Falstaff begins to talk of Ford, 'the jealous rascally knave her husband'. Every change is rung on the abusive terms—'poor cuckoldly knave', 'jealous wittolly knave', 'cuckoldly rogue'— and Falstaff's exuberant invention supplies new ones like 'mechanical salt-butter rogue'. This serves to work Ford up to the explosive fury of his soliloquy—a long one this time—with which he ends the scene.

The next two scenes show Caius and Evans respectively waiting for their opponents, the Host having appointed them contrary places. These are leisurely scenes—plenty of breathing-room here—and are almost wholly displays of humorous character. Their only consequence, at a long interval, is the stealing of the Host's horses by the pretended Germans.

By the middle of Act 3 we return to the main action with the buck-basket scene, out of which Shakespeare gets full comic value. Especially worth noting, in this scene of so much activity, is the point of rest, when the buck-basket has left by one of the doors (of Shakespeare's stage) on its way to Datchet Mead and the Thames, and Ford and his neighbours have left by the other door to search the upstairs rooms of the house. Mistress Ford and Mistress Page have the whole stage to themselves, and their remarks make sure that the audience has got the comedy in the right moral focus:

*Maurice Good as Sir Hugh Evans, Alan Scarfe as Frank Ford, Lewis Gordon as George Page, and Robert Selkirk
as townsperson in the 1978 Stratford Festival production of* The Merry Wives of Windsor.

MISTRESS PAGE Is there not a double excellency in this?
MISTRESS FORD I know not which pleases me better—
that my husband is deceived, or Sir John.

What is doubly excellent about this exchange is its
combination of moral rightness and artistic rightness: its
neat summing-up of the moral situation springs naturally
from the symmetry of the stage action. On the occasion of
Falstaff's second assignation (4.2) the different stage situation allows a different form of moral comment, when Falstaff has fled upstairs to disguise himself, Mistress Ford
has gone to summon the servants to carry the buck-basket,
and Mistress Page remains on stage to speak the moral
couplets that refer to the play's title:

> We'll leave a proof, by that which we will do,
> Wives may be merry and yet honest too.
> We do not act that often jest and laugh;
> 'Tis old but true: 'Still swine eats all the draff.'

Falstaff's three unsuccessful assignations are the chief
structural feature of the play, and perhaps no other of
Shakespeare's comedies so thoroughly exploits the

pleasures of variety-within-repetition. Johnson has a
somewhat discontented editorial comment on 'I spied a
great peard under her muffler' (4.2.179-80):

> As the second stratagem, by which *Falstaff* escapes, is
> much the grosser of the two, I wish it had been
> practised first. It is very unlikely that *Ford* having been
> so deceived before, and knowing that he had been
> deceived, would suffer him to escape in so slight a
> disguise.

But he overlooks the fact that by being practised second
this stratagem permits the reappearance of the buck-basket,
for the sake of which we willingly turn a blind eye to the
alleged improbability.

In the Herne's Oak scene (5.5), the third of Falstaff's assignations, every reader and every spectator must be struck
by the way in which this domestic comedy turns fantastical. There is a much greater shift here than at the end of
As You Like It when Rosalind, as Ganymede, undertakes to
bring Orlando his true Rosalind by magic, and is then led

in, in her own person, by one representing Hymen the marriage-god. *As You Like It* has already developed a lyrical romantic mood bordering on the fantastic: it needs only a touch to steer it to this mythological tableau. Many critics have felt that the last scene of *The Merry Wives of Windsor* is produced not by a touch in the right direction but by a wrench in the wrong one. Falstaff frightened of fairies is more than they can endure.

It must be admitted that Falstaff is the last person one would expect to believe in fairies, and that he would not easily be persuaded to come to Herne's Oak at midnight wearing a pair of antlers. Still, Shakespeare himself cannot have been unaware of the implausibility of these things, so it is worth trying to understand his purpose in ending *The Merry Wives of Windsor* in this way.

In the last movement of the play he evidently has two objects in view. The first is to finish off the main plot with the third assignation and Falstaff's final and public discomfiture. The second is to finish off the minor plot with Anne Page's marriage to Master Fenton. This minor plot has hitherto been kept alive rather than developed; it is less a plot than an existing situation. But it has provided one strategically placed scene (3.4) that has brought together Fenton and Anne, Slender and Shallow, Page and Mistress Page, and Mistress Quickly, and has emphasized that Fenton is Anne's own choice, Slender is her father's choice, and Caius is her mother's choice. Much of that scene is in blank verse—not, of course, anything said by Slender, Shallow, or Mistress Quickly—and blank verse, in Shakespearian comedy, is often a gesture towards romance. No more than a gesture here: a touch of *Romeo and Juliet* would be quite out of keeping. Nevertheless, the blank verse in this scene (the first scene in which it appears in any quantity and with other than burlesque intention) points forward to the next blank verse scene (4.4), between Page, Ford, Mistress Page, Mistress Ford, and Evans. Of these only Sir Hugh is confined to prose throughout the scene. Ford, who opens it, uses blank verse to express his wholehearted conversion from jealousy:

> Pardon me, wife. Henceforth do what thou wilt.
> I rather will suspect the sun with cold
> Than thee with wantonness. Now doth thy honour stand,
> In him that was of late an heretic,
> As firm as faith.

Page, here as always the reasonable man, approves of Ford's sentiments but cuts short his expression of them and gets down to business:

> But let our plot go forward. Let our wives
> Yet once again, to make us public sport,
> Appoint a meeting with this old fat fellow,
> Where we may take him and disgrace him for it.
> FORD
> There is no better way than that they spoke of.
> PAGE How, to send him word they'll meet him in the Park at midnight?
> Fie, fie, he'll never come.

> EVANS You say he has been thrown in the rivers, and has been grievously peaten as an old 'oman. Methinks there should be terrors in him, that he should not come. Methinks his flesh is punished; he shall have no desires.
> PAGE So think I too.
> MISTRESS FORD
> Devise but how you'll use him when he comes,
> And let us two devise to bring him thither.
> MISTRESS PAGE
> There is an old tale goes that Herne the Hunter,
> Sometime a keeper here in Windsor Forest,
> Doth all the winter-time, at still midnight,
> Walk round about an oak, with great ragg'd horns
> . . .

The dialogue has been quoted at some length to show how Shakespeare anticipates the charge of implausibility by letting Page and Evans voice it in prose, and then meets it with Mistress Ford's confident verse reply, which he follows with Mistress Page's speech reminding them of the legend of Herne the Hunter. As this speech runs on, we yield ourselves to the stream:

> Nan Page my daughter, and my little son,
> And three or four more of their growth we'll dress
> Like urchins, oafs, and fairies, green and white,
> With rounds of waxen tapers on their heads . . .

This is not a matter of convincing us that what will happen is true to life but of persuading us to suspend our disbelief for the sake of enjoying what will happen.

Shakespeare might still have some difficulty in persuading us to do this if the whole scene were devoted to the planning of Falstaff's discomfiture. But the fairy disguise has started a train of thought in Page's mind: hearing that Anne is to be the queen of the fairies, 'Finely attirèd in a robe of white', he says

> That silk will I go buy. (*Aside*) And in that time
> Shall Master Slender steal my Nan away
> And marry her at Eton.

A few lines later, left alone on the stage, his wife determines that Dr Caius shall have her daughter. The minor plot thus comes right to the foreground, and it is kept there in the next scene, where Fenton (again in verse) confides to the Host that he and Anne mean to elope while Slender and Caius are diversely obeying her parents' different instructions. The effect of this sudden concentration on the marriage of Anne Page is to deflect our attention from the improbability of the device against Falstaff, who, when we next see him, is already persuaded to the assignation, not in process of being persuaded to it.

Shakespeare has a further object besides finishing off his two plots and combining them; he uses the denouement as a vehicle for his compliments to the Queen, to Windsor Castle, and to the Order of the Garter. By setting the last scene in a wood—whether in the Little Park or in the Great Park (Windsor Forest) is left vague[7]—he removes the action further from the commonplace houses, inns, streets, and fields in which it has been taking place. *The Merry Wives of Windsor* and *A Midsummer Night's Dream* are as different from each other as any two of his comedies, but there can be no doubt that his earlier fairy play was in his mind when he was planning the end of this one. Perhaps the original connection was his remembering the compliment to the Queen as the 'fair vestal thronèd by the west' which he had worked into Oberon's speech about the magic flower (*Dream*, 2.1.158). In neither play has the Fairy Queen an allegorical, or even allusive, reference to Elizabeth, the Faerie Queene of Spenser's poem, but it would have been impossible to compliment the Queen in the 1590s without having Spenser's immense tribute in mind. Shakespeare's fairies are nothing like the inhabitants of Spenser's Faerie Land, but belong to the popular tradition of playful, mischievous, and punitive immortals who live in the country and sometimes enter mortals' houses. In making them pinch Falstaff he may have remembered Lyly's complimentary court comedy of 1588, *Endymion* (where Elizabeth is allegorically portrayed as Cynthia), in which they pinch Corsites.[8] Of course it can never have crossed his mind to bring real fairies into *The Merry Wives of Windsor* as he had done in *A Midsummer Night's Dream;* these fairies are William Page and other children of Windsor. Yet in the Fairy Queen's speech the lines in which she invokes an everlasting blessing on Windsor Castle are in the elevated tone in which Theseus's palace is blessed at the end of *A Midsummer Night's Dream.* There is undeniable incongruity here, but anyone who regards the incongruity as a fault is out of tune with the spirit of this final scene. For Shakespeare's original court audience the unexpected complimentary flourish would be a delightful surprise, and even now that the play's occasion is far in the past his ingenuity can still delight us.

There is incongruity of a different kind in Falstaff's interjection, after Sir Hugh's line 'But stay! I smell a man of middle earth',

> Heavens defend me from that Welsh fairy, lest he transform me to a piece of cheese!

The incongruity lies in Falstaff's joke—for a joke it undeniably is—at the expense of one of the fairies while he is in awe of them collectively:

> They are fairies; he that speaks to them shall die.
> I'll wink and couch; no man their works must eye.

In that speech he is subdued to the couplets of the surrounding verse, but his prose interjection (like 'Rebellion lay in his way, and he found it', interjected into the serious blank-verse altercation between the King and Worcester before the battle of Shrewsbury)[9] shows him in his usual irreverent and irrepressible mood. It is one of Shakespeare's surest artistic touches. It provides us with an escape from the conclusion that Falstaff is filled with craven terror, while at the same time it does not go so far in the other direction as to suggest that he is only pretending to be afraid.[10]

The success of the final scene depends on the maintaining of a delicate balance. The sudden development of the Anne Page plot, as has been said, predisposes us to accept Falstaff's comic tormenting by the fairies. In this final scene the elopement of Anne with Fenton, and the carrying-off by Slender and Caius of boys whom they mistake for Anne, acts as a distraction from his plight, which might seem too moralistically presented if it demanded our whole attention. It also provides excellent theatre, especially when, as we anticipate, Slender and Caius return to complain—each in his characteristic style—of how they have been deceived. And it distributes the discomfiture, which is not allowed all to fall on Falstaff's head; Page and his wife, as well as Slender and Caius, whom they respectively favoured, have missed their aim. The return of Fenton and Anne, whom Page and his wife finally congratulate upon their marriage, makes the play end as a comedy of forgiveness and reconciliation and not as one of retribution and satirical exposure. Ford, of course, must have his speech of triumph at Falstaff's expense, and reclaim the money that he paid over as Master Brook. This speech occurs when everyone is uniting to denounce Falstaff, before the reappearance of Slender, Caius, Fenton, and Anne. But at the very end, it is Ford who presses Mistress Page's invitation on Falstaff ('Let it be so, Sir John'),[11] and his final couplet,

> To Master Brook you yet shall hold your word,
> For he tonight shall lie with Mistress Ford,

is best taken as his happy afterthought, and as a joke which Falstaff can share.

Notes

1. Oliver, H.J., *The Merry Wives of Windsor*, Arden Shakespeare, p. lx, reviews the arguments that have been brought forward to support this theory.

2. Bullough, Geoffrey, *Narrative and Dramatic Sources of Shakespeare,* ii. 19-26, gives a translation of this story (*Il pecorone* (1558), Giornata I, Novella II).

3. Leo Salingar, *Shakespeare and the Traditions of Comedy* (Cambridge, 1974), pp. 231-2, suggests that the play originated in Plautus' *Braggart Soldier* (*Miles Gloriosus*), in which 'the boaster, inordinately vain about his sexual charm, . . . is lured into an intrigue with a married woman (a pretended married woman in Plautus), steals into his neighbour's house, is soundly thrashed and is terrified into avowing his fault'.

4. Its denouement is that the student, going to the university as usual next day, learns that the professor is mad and confined to his house. When he pays a sympathetic call, with other students, he recognizes with astonishment that his visits were to the professor's wife, but conceals his surprise and in his turn addresses the professor with commiseration. The professor bids him go away, for he has learned only too well at his teacher's expense. The wife hastily declares that the professor's words are just part of

his madness, and the student leaves Bologna and returns home.

5. The order in which Shakespeare worked out his plot cannot, of course, be known; but it seems probable, assuming that the play precedes *Henry V* and that Nim makes his first appearance here, that he was created because Shakespeare needed two characters, each with a distinctive mannerism of speech, to warn Ford and Page simultaneously—a much better situation than if Pistol warned them both, either simultaneously or consecutively.

6. This is the fat Falstaff's equivalent of the deformed Richard's soliloquy after successfully wooing Lady Anne:

> Upon my life, she finds, although I cannot,
> Myself to be a marv'lous proper man.
> I'll be at charges for a looking-glass,
> And entertain a score or two of tailors
> To study fashions to adorn my body.
>
> *(Richard III,* 1.3.240-4)

Both speakers adopt an ironical tone, but whereas Richard is under no illusion about his looks, Falstaff really does feel complacency.

7. The wives propose to send Falstaff word that 'they'll meet him in the Park at midnight' (4.4.16-17). Herne the Hunter is said to have been 'Sometime a keeper here in Windsor Forest' (4.4.26). After making a fool of Falstaff the conspirators will 'mock him home to Windsor' (4.4.62). Falstaff says to Ford (as Brook), 'Be you in the Park about midnight, at Herne's Oak, and you shall see wonders' (5.1.9-10). Page, Shallow, and Slender go to 'couch i'th' Castle ditch' till they see the lights carried by the fairies (5.2.1-2), which suggests that the assignation will be in the Little Park adjoining the Castle. Mistress Page bids Caius 'Go before into the Park. We two must go together' (5.3.3-4: implying that she and Mistress Page will also go there). Falstaff calls himself 'a Windsor stag, and the fattest, I think, i'th' forest' (5.5.12-13). Mistress Page says that Falstaff's horns 'Become the forest better than the town' (5.5.107). The tradition that identified an oak in the Little Park as Herne's Oak (Green, p. 18) probably arose from the play's popularity and is unreliable as evidence either of the location of 5.5 or of the antiquity of the Herne story. More than one tree has been so identified (Roberts, p. 149 n. 59).

8. Bullough, ii. 55-8. In *Endymion,* as in Shakespeare's play, the pinching is accompanied by a song in trochaic metre.

9. *1 Henry IV,* 5.1.28.

10. In a review of the Royal Shakespeare Company's 1955 production (*Bolton Evening News,* 15 July 1955) it was noted that it received not only the usual laughter but 'even some applause, as if it were extempore'.

11. On the punctuation of Ford's final speech see Commentary, 5.5.236.

COMIC STRUCTURES

G. Beiner (essay date 1988)

SOURCE: "The Libido as Pharmakos, or The Triumph of Love: *The Merry Wives of Windsor* in the Context of Comedy," in *Orbis Litterarum,* Vol. 43, 1988, pp. 195-216.

[*In the following essay, Beiner takes a close look at the comedic structure of* The Merry Wives of Windsor *in order to show that this play is not an anomaly but is instead related in style and theme to the rest of Shakespeare's comedies as well as to other comedies of the era.*]

I

The history of the criticism of *The Merry Wives of Windsor* shows a radical evaluative disparity between a high critical regard and popularity on the stage until the eighteenth century and, on the other hand, romantic hostility and modern neglect.[1] The modern neglect, at least until recently,[2] is particularly noticeable in the context of the increasing critical interest in Shakespeare's comedies, manifested especially in a number of book-length studies which have greatly contributed to our understanding of the plays, and have rescued some (for instance, *Love's Labour's Lost*) from previous neglect. From these studies *The Merry Wives* is usually excluded for varying reasons, and sometimes without a stated reason.[3] Since conceptual tools for dealing with the genre of comedy and the corpus of Shakespeare's comedies (tools of which there used to be a great dearth) have been developed, especially since the seminal work of Northrop Frye and C.L. Barber, it is also glaringly obvious that this play has not received proper analytical and conceptual attention. It has simply suffered from neglect, partly because of a persisting prejudice in character evaluation (Falstaff is supposed to show a great falling off in comparison to the aplomb and incisiveness in *Henry IV,* especially Part One), and partly because generic issues have been obscured by driving a wedge between the other comedies and this one.

Neglecting *The Merry Wives* is detrimental not only to our understanding of the play. It harms our perception of the development of Shakespearean comedy from *Errors* to *Twelfth Night,* of the coordinates of values asserted in the corpus, and of Shakespeare's choice of comic strategies. Much can be learned, for instance, about the comic strategy in *Twelfth Night* (with its juxtaposition of a main level of errors and resolutions of love with a subplot of exposure and comic punishment) by observing the relationship between the punitive manipulation of Falstaff and the level of Fenton—Anne Page. More generally, in analyzing *The Merry Wives* closely, we can perceive a great deal about the values which inform Shakespeare's comedies—about what is asserted and what is rejected, what leads to a festive resolution, what is tolerated even when comically exposed, and what is cast out.

One should not place evaluation before elucidation and interpretation, as such an order becomes prejudicial, but rather engage in evaluation only after a meticulous analysis. This is the procedure in the present essay. The analytical work is carried out with the help of generic tools, and an awareness of the relevant traditions of comedy—for the sake of contrast (which reveals Shakespeare's creative originality) as much as for comparison (which shows that he did not create in a void and out of nothing). For the purpose of dealing with exposure/punishment/casting out in comedy, two related terms are particularly useful, and are often invoked in the following analysis of the play. The social/anthropological term 'pharmakos' helps to elucidate the dimension of communal solidarity against a threat and an aberration, and the aspect of physical punishment, with its comic echoes of punitive rituals. The specifically comic term 'alazon' is directly related to the coordinates of comic values (in this case, the blocking force in the comedy), as is its counterpart 'eiron' (the character who exposes the alazon).[4] The comic dialectic of eiron versus alazon is a central pattern in the traditions of European comedy, and it is used by Shakespeare not only in relation to characters (whom he does not always define strictly as belonging to the negative or to the positive group) but more generally in relation to attitudes (which are positive or negative, ironic or earnest) and to stances. The appropriate definition of the terms for Shakespeare's comedy is given here in the process of analyzing the dynamics of *The Merry Wives,* and relevant parallels or contrasts from European comedy are adduced.

II

> "Comedy is a game played to throw reflections upon social life"
>
> Meredith, *The Egoist.*

The Merry Wives creates an overall pattern through a number of levels, and through their interactions and juxtapositions. Any analysis of the play, whatever the focus of its interest, has to take into account the existence of the various interconnected levels, and the dependence of the overall meaning of the play upon juxtapositions.[5] Without the overall pattern, concentrating on one level (the exposure of Falstaff, for instance) is bound to distort.

On one level Falstaff, the would-be seducer who aims at pecuniary gain, devises a campaign designed to combine business with pleasure; he plans to assault the social fortress of marriage. Or, to change the military metaphor for a theatrical one, he devises a play, in which he casts himself in the role of manipulator, successful seducer, and the cuckolder who fleeces the husbands. Falstaff's way, as the opening scene emphasizes in connection with Shallow' complaint, is not to hide his offences against social order. He is no hypocritical Tartuffe, who disguises practical, immoral designs under a cloak of pretended piety and respectability. He is avowedly immoral. Nor does he excuse himself when he is accused. Whether "a fault confessed is half redressed," as the proverb says, or "if it be confessed,

it is not redressed" as Shallow says, is not a relevant issue for him.[6] He does not aim to redress, and an open admission is only part of his method. When he attempts seduction, he also employs the attack direct: no "courtly love," and no beating about the bush, but a brazen boarding (II.i.4ff.). "I cannot cog, I cannot prate," he says (III.iii.42).

Against the foolish Shallow, the "miles gloriosus" of reminiscences, this method is successful: Falstaff is not punished, intimidated, or thrown out of the homes of the citizens of Windsor. But Mrs. Ford and Mrs. Page are not Shallow, either in determination or in the ability to punish an offender. All they need in order to be effective against Falstaff is knowledge, and this is conveniently supplied as a result of Falstaff's characteristic thrasonical behaviour. His hyperbolical self-confidence (which is, of course, characteristic of the "miles gloriosus" and is normally either a cause of defeat or a main object of ridicule in connection with this comic type) in duplicating the letters of seduction leads to the wives' knowledge of his double scheme. At the same time, Falstaff's confident and bragging disclosure of his plans to his disgruntled followers, at the moment of antagonizing them, also makes the knowledge of the scheme available to the husbands. The attitudes and behaviour of husbands and wives are juxtaposed from then on, with the wives being clearly superior in awareness and control; but, from the outset, Falstaff is consistently at the bottom of the scale of awareness, at least on the level on which he functions.[7]

With knowledge available to the merry wives, and Falstaff ignorant of their decisions, his campaign, or prospective play, is turned upside-down. The saturnalian figure, who would make fun of moral values and social institutions, is taught a comic lesson which asserts moral norms. The would-be Lord of Misrule pushes himself willingly yet unwittingly (no less than the kill-joy Malvolio does vis-à-vis the festive revellers in *Twelfth Night*) into the role of pharmakos, in the comedy which the merry and chaste wives engineer. He is not only the resistible force applied to immovable objects—though he thinks he is an irresistible lover. He is manipulated, fooled, punished, and ultimately exposed in a sequence which culminates in a masque—a play in which make-believe is intertwined with the reality of the participants—where the Windsor society unites against the threat represented by the "Prince of Libido."[8] Falstaff is punished, like Acteon, for prohibited desires: he assumes the part of a beast (thinking himself a virile stag and another Joye, only to discover that he is made an ass), and he wears the horns of ridicule he thought he would place on the foreheads of Ford and Page (as Ford reminds him, in Act V, scene v, 110ff.).

Falstaff's fantasy of prowess and success fails before it begins, not just at the end; and his self-confidence and gullibility lead him repeatedly to try once more after each unpleasant lesson. Even as he speaks eloquently of his suffering after each punishment, and decides not to go to the wives any more, he commits the same mistake again in swallowing the old bait thrown to him via Mistress

Quickly. Though his intentions are antisocial, Falstaff is not effective even in selfish terms. We find the most delightful verbal exuberance in Falstaff when he complains about his treatment in the course of his most uncourtly love—that is, when he functions as a comic victim. Since he does not learn a lesson from painful experience though he says he does, there is a clear indication that his wit bears no relation to awareness or cleverness. Such dubious verbal triumphs as he has—e.g., over Simple, IV.v.31ff.—do not take him out of the role of comic butt and victim.

Falstaff's aims represent a threat which is directed at a fundamental social value, embodied in marriage. To this we have to add a Shakespearean characteristic, which is found in all the comedies from *Errors* to *Twelfth Night,* and which distinguishes them from many a comedy either in the classical or the medieval tradition. Generally, comic values (what is desired, and what constitutes a resolution) need not always be identical with moral/social values. A comedy may relate to such values by saturnalian inversion, and may even challenge and subvert them. Successful seductions by young men of old men's wives, and the willing adulteries of young wives are cases in point— whether we find them in medieval fabliaux (like the Miller's Tale in *The Canterbury Tales,* and many a tale in the *Decameron*), or in the erudite plays in the "new comedy" tradition (like Machiavelli's *Mandragola*). In either tradition, the underlying pattern of the triumph of virile youth over impotent, jealous, obstructive old age emphasizes the saturnalian relationship between comic triumph and conventional comic values. Given such patterns, and their prominence in the traditions of comedy, we need to emphasize that in Shakespeare's comedies the social institution of marriage is used in a way which also embodies comic values—not an opposition between the two. The final resolutions, with the accompanying celebrations, are assertions which indicate a correspondence between social and comic values. Furthermore, in Shakespeare's comedies, the middle phase (of complications, release, and comic exploration) is not a "period of sexual license,"[9] if that phrase is understood in terms of sexual relations. There are revealing errors, and departures from everyday norms of behaviour (whether in the form of a temporary freedom from conventional restrictions, as with Rosalind in *As You Like It,* or a "midsummer madness" of emotion, as in *A Dream* and *Twelfth Night*); but there is no freedom in sexual relations, which would be in opposition to marriage.

The assertion represented by marriage in Shakespearean comedy is not, of course, absolute and uniform. As there are different levels of perception within Shakespearean comedies, so are there different levels in the comic resolutions. Given what is revealed about Proteus and Claudio, or given the level of sentiment on which Touchstone functions, the respective marriages are considerably less-than-ideal, though they are integral to the resolutions of *The Two Gentlemen, Much Ado,* and *As You Like It.* Similarly, the comic exposure directed at the conventional love-game

of Lucentio and Bianca comes to a climax (rather than being removed) after the young lovers outwit the parent and the undesirable suitors and get married; but there is no suggestion that an illicit relationship, or no relationship would have been preferable. The ironic point at the end of *The Shrew* (on the Bianca-Lucentio level) is that marriage based on conventional love-at-first-sight and achieved through conventional comic intrigue is not what the young man supposes it is, or what it should ideally be. To take a further example, the marital problems of Adriana and the Ephesian Antipholus in *Errors* are not resolved at the end in a way which fully answers all complaints raised by the wife, or which promises perfect stability. But, just as nothing untoward really happens when the wife locks the wrong man with her in the house (no adultery is committed, unlike what happens when Amphytrio's loving wife unwittingly welcomes her husband's divine look-alike in Plautus's play), so the marital reconciliation is, for all its limitations, an integral part of the various reunions (and the one new union) which constitute the resolution in *Errors.*

Many unions in Shakespearean comedy are less-than-profound (e.g., the young Athenian lovers in *A Dream,* or Oliver and Celia in *As You Like It*). We have to emphasize the point in the present context, so as not to convey the misleading impression that Shakespeare is a stuffy moralist whose aim in comedy is to give us moral *exempla,* to preach, and to show virtue rewarded. His comic resolutions are not emblems of perfection, profundity of sentiment, and total stability. There is a wide range. At the higher end we may put the genuine mutual relationship established after obstructive attitudes are altered (Benedick and Beatrice, and, more one-sidedly, Petruchio and Katherina). These are contrasted with relationships and attitudes which are comically exposed as deficient (Claudio-Hero, Lucentio-Bianca). Also at the highest end of the range are the cases where the woman's loyalty triumphs in spite of the man (Julia, Viola); or where there is a combination of commitment with a vivacious playacting, which produces comic exposure but also comic remedy and resolution (Rosalind). To put the point in a somewhat different way, comic exposure and clarification bring out problems and deficiencies, but Shakespearean comedy also establishes positive norms of values, which are asserted in the resolution—itself the "telos" of the comic movement. Whether the focus of comic exposure is on conventions of declarations and behaviour in love (a recurrent comic motif in Shakespeare's comedies), or on the question of reliability of sentiment, or on misunderstandings and friction—resolutions in Shakespearean comedy are connected with marriage, both as a formal device for creating a "sense of an ending" (in Frank Kermode's phrase) and in terms of an assertion of values. This is one reason why much can be learnt about Shakespearean comedy in general by examining the comic values and comic obstacles in *The Merry Wives;* and, conversely, much light is cast on this play by placing it in its proper context among Shakespeare's comedies, rather than putting it in quarantine as "- farce," "citizen comedy," or "Shakespeare's English comedy." In this play, there is a multiple assertion, and a final celebration, of values represented by marriage. The comic action (which moves from an initial threat to well-being, via complications, to resolution) and the comic clarification (which exposes values and deficiencies) have to do here with the external threat to marriage (which is punished and cast out), an internal problem within marriage in the form of jealousy (which is eventually remedied), and the obstacle of parental opposition to the young lovers' choice (which is overcome through the initiative of the lovers).

In a simplified distinction, one kind of assertion in *The Merry Wives* is manifested in the comic "via negativa"; the exposure, punishment, and removal of the opposition to basic values. The other kind may be called positive, in that it shows the triumph, fulfilment, and celebration of the values which the comedy upholds. As we shall see, the distinction is by no means absolute: the process of comic exposure is based on an assertive, normative stand taken by characters in the play; and the usual "new comedy" pattern of the triumph of young love includes, as it often does in Shakespearean comedy (though very briefly here), a querying of the motives and intentions of the young man. However, the basic distinction does exist. It is expressed in the two principal levels in the play, and in their relationship of juxtaposition.

One level involves exposure, a thwarting of designs, and comic punishment which reaches the proportions of a casting out of the pharmakos. Falstaff is at its centre, on the receiving side, and he must have felt—as Northrop Frye puts it—that "after being thrown into the water, dressed up as a witch and beaten out of the house with curses, and finally supplied with a beast's head and singed with candles, he had done all that could reasonably be asked of any fertility spirit."[10]

In fact, Falstaff is not really a fertility spirit. He is an antagonist/alazon, who is basically on the same side of the comic scale as obstructing old men, or old lechers, and other characters in whom libidinal desires are seen as negative and ridiculous. As we can see in two well-known non-Shakespearean comedies, which are typical of a major European tradition—Beaumarchais's *Barber of Seville* and Molière's *L'Avare*—such negative traits can be combined in one character, who can be a grouch, a miser, and a lecher, and who is the comic loser. A Bartholo (guardian of the young Rosine, whose rejection of her suitors has to do with his plan to marry her himself), or Harpagon (the old miser, who wants to marry the young woman his son loves, and to match the son with an old widow) are alazones, and occupy the most negative and most obstructive positions in the comic scheme. These examples (which could be multiplied from Menander's *Dyskolos* and Plautus's *Aulalaria* almost "ad infinitum") are typical of a major pattern in the "new comedy" tradition: a conflict between the young and the old on sexual relations—where the old competitors are negative, and are exposed to ridicule and comic punishment. Although Shakespeare

shows the triumph of young love in his comedies, he does not usually employ the pattern of young vs. old—and he avoids the father/son competition altogether; though when the superannuated lover (Gremio, the "pantaloon" in *The Shrew,* Shallow in our play) does appear, he occupies the conventionally ridiculous position. Falstaff is not a competitor against young lovers; Mrs. Ford and Mrs. Page are past the holiday time of their beauty (II.i.1), as well as being married. But he is on the same side of the comic scale as old lovers and lechers, and his defeat is juxtaposed with Fenton's triumph. Falstaff's scheme is negative, that of the young lovers positive.

The usual "new comedy" structure, which unfolds from an initial combination of a goal of well-being (what is desired) and obstructions, via complications, to a resolution in which the goal is achieved, may create a contradiction between the comic value defined by the goal and social requirements; often, this is combined with the conflict between generations (with the old people holding the purse strings, as well as having social authority). The parental/social position may be in line with normal social preoccupation with money and status (e.g., when the father objects to his child's choice in love because the prospective mate is poor or socially inferior); or, it may involve a comically perverse competition between the old father and the young son for a young woman; or, and equally negative obstruction from an old man but without the Oedipal dimension of the previous pattern.[11] All these major versions place the old man in a comically negative position. As examples we may take Terence's *Andria* (a young man in love with a girl who does not seem to meet the parental requirements for social rank and money), Plautus's *Casina* (the father wanting an affair with the girl his son desires), and Plautus's *Rudens* (where the obstruction and seeming misfortune have to do, not with a father but with an old pimp). "New comedy" resolutions may completely remove the opposition between desires and social norms by making the former acceptable, as a result of fortunate discoveries, in terms of the latter (*Andria*); or, as a roughly equivalent case, the resolution may provide a fortunate removal of all obstructions (whether connected with status and money, or not) in a way which is both desirable and socially acceptable, as well as moral (*Rudens*); or, it may defeat the ridiculous and perverse parental competition (*Casina*), and celebrate a saturnalian triumph of the young over the old (Plautus's *Pseudolus,* where this is combined with the victory of the slave over the old master). As an even more extreme comic inversion of ordinary social norms, a comedy may push the last-mentioned version to the point where the young man defeats not only the old man but also the institution of marriage (Machiavelli's *Mandragola*). In short, the comic victory, which is "right" in comic terms, may finally correspond or be opposed to what is right in moral/social terms. If we bear in mind these options, we can see which one Shakespeare chose consistently.

In Shakespearean comedy, the emphases are different from those of ancient, or of Italian Renaissance, "new comedy"—even though he uses the same basic structure. There is no concentration on a conflict of generations (though Egeus in *A Dream,* Proteus's father and the Duke in *The Two Gentlemen,* and Baptista in *The Shrew* are recognizable "senex" figures), and the focus is not simply on the young lovers finally achieving their goal.[12] Shakespeare's comedies explore sentiments, declarations of commitment, the degree of perception of various characters, and the process of finding comic remedies through comic release and testing (in addition, that is, to resolving comic fortune).

The sentiment of love is not a donnee (as it usually is in Roman comedy, where the young woman hardly appears on the stage), a goal which the young man wants to achieve in spite of external obstacles, but an emotion, a commitment, and a relationship which are themselves explored. The goal of achieving a proper and reliable relationship faces inner obstacles (connected with the lovers' attitudes) no less than external/social obstructions. Even when the external obstacles are formidable (as at the beginning of *A Dream,* with the father's arbitrary opposition and the backing he has from social authority), a Shakespearean comedy proceeds to examine love itself—i.e., the inner, rather than the external, problem—before it brings the resolution.

We have to add, in order to avoid misleading implications, that neither the comic clarification (what is exposed) nor the comic resolution (which confirms what is asserted) in Shakespearean comedies rely on a Petrarchan or a neo-Platonic idealization of love. Here we find one of the distinctive contributions of Shakespearean comedy, both in relation to the dramatic traditions he uses (as we have remarked above) and vis-à-vis the cultural issues he deals with in his comedies. If the focus on love, which is a dominant feature in Renaissance literature, distinguishes these plays from Plautine/Terentian comedy, as well as from medieval farce, the comic perspective on love distinguishes them from Renaissance lyrics, epic poetry dealing with love, philosophical "dialoghi d'amore," and even romance narrative—in short, from literary works which treat love with a solemn intensity. The conventional and idealizing formulae are themselves explored. But Shakespearean comedy does assert a positive norm, based on a mutual choice free from parental/social tyranny; a norm of constancy of sentiment and of a genuine relationship. It is in relation to this norm that the comedies expose aberrations—such as changing allegiance (e.g., in *A Dream*), superficiality of sentiment (Claudio in *Much Ado*), saturnalian errors of emotion (*Twelfth Night*), a merely conventional love-game (Lucentio in *The Shrew*), and other problems or comic obstacles. Marital relations are also examined in relation to similar norms (in *Errors,* in *A Dream* with the fairy monarchs, in *The Shrew* when the newlyweds are juxtaposed, and in *The Merry Wives*): there are obstacles to a proper relationship, which may be removed after, indeed as a result of, being comically exposed. The norm which Shakespeare's comedies assert does not subvert moral/social values (like some of the "new comedy" patterns we have mentioned), though they

expose deficiencies—including inadequacies in conventions. There is no difference in principle between those comedies which concentrate on young love and those in which marital relations are an object of comic exploration; in fact, the two topoi are often combined, as is the case in our play.

In *The Merry Wives,* the exposure and punishment of Falstaff by the chaste wives is juxtaposed with the triumph of Fenton and Anne Page. The young lovers are not so much at the centre as at the climax of the positive comic assertion, which is timed to coincide with the festive ending of the comedy. The casting out of the pharmakos—who threatens marriage, or would if he were effective—is combined with the achievement, acceptance, and celebration of the young lovers' marriage in accordance with their mutual choice. The explicit indication of the appropriateness of the triumph of love is given by the young man, after the marriage is secured. "You," he says to Anne's parents, "would have married her most shamefully / Where there was no proportion held in love." "Th' offence is holy that she has committed, / And this deceit loses the name . . . / Of disobedience, or unduteous title, / Since therein she doth evitate and shun / A thousand irreligious cursed hours / Which forced marriage would have brought upon her" (V.v.221ff.). These words have an almost Blakean force in regarding conventional compulsion as a sacrilegious destruction of human dignity. They certainly convey the comic norm of the triumph of love and mutual choice.

The distinction between levels in the play is not absolutely defined as exposure vs. assertion. In punishing Falstaff, the wives assert values; and there is comic exposure on the level which deals with the competition for the "pretty virginity," Anne Page. Furthermore, each level has ramifications. The thwarted designs of the "miles gloriosus" of seductions (the external threat) bring out an internal threat in marriage: the husband's jealousy.

Ford's jealousy does not come into existence in the dramatic present, it has been a chronic tendency (II.i.99-103), but it is brought out, comically explored by being pushed "ad absurdum," and integrated in the overall comic movement—which progresses through release to resolution.[13] Ford's jealousy, which is juxtaposed with Page's confidence in his wife (while the wives have similar, not contrasted attitudes), is treated in a way which reveals a great deal about the Shakespearean comic perspective.

The jealous husband, like the superannuated lover, the grouch, or the young woman's guardian, is generally an "alazon" figure; and comedy delights in holding him up for ridicule, punishing and defeating him. In the comic scale of values from comic "minus" to comic "plus" (whether moral or not),[14] such figures are emphatically given as a comic "minus"—whatever social claims (as husbands, parents, or guardians) they may have. Even a moralistic poet without a bent for comedy like Spenser could write a rather powerful fabliau piece (or partly fabliau) on the punishment of the jealous husband. The story of Hellenore, Malbecco, and Paridell (*The Faerie Queene,* III.ix,x)[15] may be said to show a sordid picture of unchastity. The lecherous young wife is in the end no better than a whore, and the lover she runs away with "having filcht her bels, her up he cast / To the wide world" (III.x.35). Nonetheless, the most unequivocally negative figure is the miserly, impotent, and jealous old husband: "all his mind is set on mucky pelf," and he is "unfit fair ladies service to supply" (III.ix.4,5). He is humiliated and cheated even by the ridiculous Braggadochio, and witnesses how the jolly satyr has fun with his wife ("nine times he heard him come aloft ere day" (III.x.48)). The force of comedy and medieval fabliau comes to the fore even in the moralistic scheme of Spenser's allegory. "Not for nought his wife [the satyrs] loved so well" (III.x.48): there are reasons why a May is faithless to a January, and the old man bears the brunt of the blame. Even when the moral perspective is applied to adultery, the old husband is both negative and ridiculous, in spite of his official claim, which is sanctioned by laws. No wonder that in comedy the January or Malbecco figure (e.g., Harpagon in *L'Avare*) is negative, as ordinary morality is not the guideline (e.g., in the *Mandragola*); at least, youthful desires are usually regarded in comedy as normal and seasonable (to use a notion which is mentioned explicitly in *Love's Labour's Lost*). A lenient treatment of the jealous husband is rare in comedy. An interesting example is *The Jealous Old Husband,* one of the "entremeses" by Shakespeare's contemporary Cervantes, where the comic pattern of a young wife, a jealous husband, and a young man unfolds in the usual trajectory without reaching the expected point of defeat for the husband. Cervantes parts company with the conventions he uses by being tolerant. Another case in which the well-known comic convention concerning the young wife and the old husband is used with an unconventional focus and conclusion is Garcia Lorca's *The Love of Don Perlimplin* and *Belisa in the Garden.* The marriage of the January character (Don Perlimplin) to the young, erotic May figure (Belisa) leads to sexual infidelity. But, in the event, this is not quite the triumph of potent youth over impotent old age—which in traditional comic terms would be a "plus." At the cost of his life, the husband asserts a depth of emotion which shows that the young wife is as immature as she is sexually vital. Such plays are striking in their departure from comic conventions; or, we may say, they use well-known norms in order to create and express through contrast. If this is one of the general manifestations of the relationship between norm and form in literature—where new forms emerge through the use of old norms—the use, rather than the contravention of existing norms is no less common. In our play, the norm which regards a husband's jealousy as negative is indeed employed, though in a distinctive Shakespearean pattern, and in a Shakespearean spirit.

In *The Merry Wives* the husband's jealousy is ridiculous, and unquestionably negative (it is an obstacle to well-being), but it exists only temporarily for comic exposure. It is not accompanied by ultimate punishment and defeat:

there is comic remedy (connected with the realization of error), and there is a resolution. In part, this is due to the fact that here the opposition between would-be seducer and jealous husband is not the comic pattern of virile youth vs. old age—in which, by comic standards, the former triumphs even when it opposes itself to conventional morality. To a large extent, Shakespeare's remedial pattern is also due to the fact that the wives, who are in control of the comic situation in relation to Falstaff and to Mr. Ford, do not permit the seducer's triumph, and do not keep the husband in the dark for very long. Ford's specific suspicions are an error, which is removable by the disclosure of truth; in other words, as in other comedies of errors, there is a built-in possibility for a resolution, in addition to the possibility given by the existence of controlling figures within the comedy. But, most of all, the logic of the comic pattern which Shakespeare creates here and in his other comedies (a pattern which is quite distinct from satire, even if it employs ridicule, and from farce) is that of *temporary* release, which exposes underlying problems while complicating the initial situation, terminated eventually so as to produce a constructive and assertive (which is not to say unqualified) resolution. A Shakespearean comedy in its totality (not just one phase in it) is not a saturnalia, though it incorporates a phase which may be termed saturnalian. Within the unfolding comic progression from initial problems via revealing complications to a resolution, the phase of release is eventually superseded by the removal of the obstacles to well-being. The resolution represents and celebrates a norm (which is implicit from the outset in the comic goal of well-being, in what we perceive to be right—or a comic "plus"), though the tolerant Shakespearean comic perspective does not require perfection as a condition for including characters in the resolution. There are comic remedies to problems, errors and deficiencies, but they vary in scope and profundity; and the plays do not include in the final resolutions only the superior, the profound, or the perfect. The norm asserted in Shakespearean comic resolutions is not moralistic, though it is a value relevant for everyday, and not just for saturnalian holiday (to use Barber's terms).

In *The Merry Wives,* the norm embodied in marriage is asserted both by the punishment of Falstaff (the external threat) and by the eventual removal of the husband's jealousy (the internal threat in marriage). In unfolding the jealousy, comic release brings out a latent tendency in Ford, and pushes it to ridiculous extremes. Extremism is one of comedy's means for exploration, as well as for remedy. With Ford we also have yet another character who pushes himself unwittingly into a comic role through a fantasy which he projects without justification onto reality (as we see with Falstaff). His visions of cuckoldry (II.ii.276ff., III.ii.26ff., III.v.129ff.), and his determination to make a public spectacle of his supposed shame—an attitude condemned even by such imperfect characters as Shallow, Evans, and Caius—push Ford into the ridiculous comic role of jealous husband, though he has no real cause. Initially he aims at a test (which should, in principle, admit a positive or a negative result, II.i.227), but his conviction soon displaces the positive alternative, and loses contact with reality. He is determined to confirm his obsession with cuckoldry, not to investigate the truth. As the audience is well aware, Ford is no more justified in his fears than Falstaff is in the anticipation of triumph.

Ford's imaginary script is inherently self-destructive as well as wrong; he would be the loser if he were right, whereas Falstaff at least imagines success. And yet, Ford is not ultimately the loser, while Falstaff is. The difference is prescribed by the scheme of values in the play. Ford (le malade imaginaire) has to be cured, so that the marital relationship is also remedied; the libidinal Falstaff has to be punished and defeated, in order to secure the same norm of marital relations.

Ford's determination to push Falstaff into assaulting Mrs. Ford's chastity, and his masochistic insistence on making a public spectacle of his search for proof that he is a cuckold, move on a trajectory to destruction; or, rather, they would do so if the play were not a comedy. As usual in Shakespearean comedy, the "contrary valuation" of tragedy[16] (anchored in this case on the sentiment of jealousy, which can be destructive—as *Much Ado* points out in a comic perspective, and *Othello* in a fully tragic one) is evident within the comic movement, but serves as a measure of the actual comedy—by contrast to the possible but excluded alternative.[17] Our attention is directed at the exposure of the malady of jealousy, without fear that disaster would ensue; and at the game of lack of awareness played between Falstaff and Brook/Ford, in which the former unwittingly torments the husband, and the latter does not perceive that the would-be seducer can offer only hopes of success and accounts of actual failure.

One of the clearest signs of the would-be trickster's ineffectiveness (in addition to his repeated punishment, and the guaranteed failure) is that he does not benefit from the husband's offer to subsidize the adultery. Such a situation is usually a great comic advantage to the seducer (as we see, for instance, in the *Mandragola,* or in The Shipman's Tale in *The Canterbury Tales*), and an added level in ridiculing the husband. Falstaff does not even realize that Brook is Ford, and his actual tormenting of the husband (II.ii.25ff., III.v.64ff.) is unwitting. Since in this play jealousy can be cured in the end (as error is removed, and no irreparable harm is done in the meantime), while attempted seduction remains unacceptable, Falstaff is the loser in the game with Ford—but not because Ford is more perceptive, or better able to get out of the situation his fantasy has created. The decisive point is that what Ford's jealousy represents in the scale of comic values in the play is a removable obstacle, while Falstaff's aims are an intolerable one. We are aware of this scheme of values from an early point, so that we can observe with detachment both Falstaff's schemes, which are doomed to be ineffective, and the spectacle of Ford's jealousy, which does not turn into a real threat.

Given the comic control in the play (which excludes destructive alternatives, and secures solutions) and the comic perspective (which ensures our detachment), we can also delight in the way in which the jealous husband unwittingly steps into the comedy arranged by the wives at Falstaff's expense. He provides the actual justification for treating the would-be seducer as scapegoat, where only an imaginary excuse was to be used; and he does so while insisting on giving a comic exhibition of his obsession. As Mrs. Page says, there is a "double excellency in this" (III.iii.162). Indeed, there is a triple one: Falstaff is punished as he would have been in accordance with the initial script, Ford is allowed to punish himself, and he unwittingly cooperates in punishing the supposed cuckolder. That the alazon Ford is eventually enlightened and cured is not the result of awareness he acquires, or a lesson he learns by himself. On his own, he would be dominated by the "humour" of jealousy. He is an extremist, in being reconciled no less than in jealousy (IV.iv.10ff.), but the comedy accommodates him nonetheless. Indeed, it has to if the marital problems are to be resolved. The only figure who cannot be accommodated—who is the consistent loser, comic butt, and recipient of punishment—is Falstaff. What he represents cannot be corrected, tolerated, or included in the resolution (except in the form of the willingness to let him partake of a meal).

The process of revealing and curing Ford's malady is juxtaposed to Page's confidence in his wife. Page is in a similar situation, but behaves very differently. He even reproaches Ford for his irrational behaviour (III.iii.198). Ford refers to Page as a "secure and wilful Acteon" (III.ii.38), but he is the one who is determined to uncover his supposed horns (though, in the end, the horns are placed on Falstaff). These and other juxtapositions point to the system of values in the comedy, which does not necessarily rely on fixed functions for the characters. The most obvious case in point is that of Page and his wife. In relation to Falstaff's negative designs, they both have a positive function. Unlike Ford, Page has full confidence in his wife's chastity (II.i.173ff.); and Mrs. Page, like Mrs. Ford, proves that she is a chaste wife. However, in relation to Anne Page, both parents have the traditional role of alazon, in conflict with the wishes of the young lovers. They are obstructive, as they scheme separately, but in symmetrical ways, to marry her to one of her ridiculous suitors for the sake of a financial or a social position. As Anne shrewdly observes, "a world of ill-favour'd faults / Looks handsome in three hundred pounds a year" (III.iv.31ff.). However, if it looks so to the parents, the comic perspective clearly gives a different valuation; and comic control sees to it that the positive valuation is achieved at the end.

In keeping with the same comic values which justify the punitive exposure of Falstaff and the ridiculous effect of Ford's jealousy, the parental schemes for their daughter are defeated—by the mutual agreement of Anne and Fenton. The young lovers' manoeuvre, which outwits the obstructive parental schemes and the ridiculous competitors, is more than merely successful. Upon being publicly discovered, the triumph of love is socially accepted; ultimately, there is no conflict between love and the parental/social level, and no radical conflict of generations. The communal festive celebration at the end of the play goes well beyond a merely formal resolution resulting from the removal of obstacles as a way of ending the comic game. It is a manifold assertion of principles represented by marriage: the would-be seducer is punished and removed, jealousy is cured, and the young people's marriage is secured on the basis of mutual choice—with subsequent social approval.

On the level of young love, which is more a framework than a major element in the middle phases of the comedy (but becomes prominent towards the end), the young man's aim is momentarily queried about possible mercenary thoughts. When Fenton refers to Page's objections to his rank (which is too high for a bourgeois family), his character, and his motive in wooing (seemingly to gain a fortune)—Anne, who is an alert and spirited young woman, responds by saying "maybe he tells you true" (III.iv.4ff.). There is scope at that point for comic exposure and interplay, as well as for expanding the dramatic role of the young woman. But Fenton is not subjected to the extensive comic exploration we find in other Shakespearean comedies concerning the young men's sentiments, the reliability of their declarations, or the stability of their commitments; nor is Anne's role developed to the proportions of a Rosalind, who can mock and playact while in love. This play focuses on other matters, and does not need to expand the Anne-Fenton level. Fenton's frank admission that his first move was a venture (if we may borrow a suggestive word from *The Merchant of Venice*), and his declaration that love has superseded the initial pecuniary aim (II.iv. 13ff.) are sufficient. Anne will have him, if possible with the father's permission, if not otherwise. The decisive comic action on this level of the play is not anchored on an exploration of love (which would have to do with errors and remedies), rather, in line with the time-honoured "new comedy" tradition, it shows the triumph of the young lovers' choice over parental authority, and over inappropriate suitors who have parental backing. The irredeemable silliness of Slender and his ridiculous wooing (III.iv.38ff.), and the preposterous irascibility of Dr. Caius—one of the offenders against the King's English in the play—are comically exposed before their aims are thwarted (assuming we can say Slender has aims). The comedy leaves no room for doubt that the parental selections are wrong.

III

"Nor is the moving of laughter always the end of comedy"

Ben Jonson, *Timber.*

Slender (the worthy heir to Shallow, and suitably attended by Simple) and Caius are part of a comic gallery, in which we also find Evans, Quickly, and more minor characters like Pistol (whose mind is full of garbled literary bombast and melodramatic clichés). Their various forms of linguistic incompetence are all ridiculous. Some of the hu-

mour created by such abuses, and by the duping of those who are ignorant of the English language (e.g., Caius in II.iii.55ff.) is, in my view, of an inferior kind. Like some comedians' gags which rely on nothing more than an accent to create humour without a joke, this type of humour relies on the sheer prejudice against the "foreigner": the automatic solidarity and sense of superiority which even the illiterate members of a community feel over the incompetence of a foreigner in their language. That is repeatedly the case with Evans and Caius, and this element is not among the achievements in the play. Without defending this kind of humour, I can point to its place in the general pattern in the comedy—which is of a higher order. The play exposes anti-social behaviour or deviations from social norms; linguistic abuses are among them. These range from the lower end of the foreigner's incompetence (Caius) and the exaggerated version of a dialect (Evans), through the mad mixture of supposedly elevated and literary language (Pistol), the bare articulateness and sometimes non-articulateness of the simpleton (Slender), malapropisms with a bawdy slant (Quickly), and jocular superfluity and hyperbole (less an offence against normal usage than a saturnalian departure from it, and found especially in the merry Host). To this list we may add the pseudo-learned school Latin which Evans pumps into his pupil, while the ignorant Quickly finds bawdy meanings in the unknown words, and the equally ignorant mother (the otherwise sharp Mrs. Page) is proud of the boy's education (IV.i). All such deviations centered on the use of language are ridiculed in the play—though without making the use, referentiality, and intelligibility of language the central issue it is in *Love's Labour's Lost*. None of these characters is a Bottom (whose "reason and love keep little company together" is highly relevant, even if he cannot know the full relevance) or a Dogberry (the shallow fool who brings to light the crucial truths which the wisdom of his social betters does not see)—let alone a Feste or a Touchstone. They exhibit aberrations, not folly as a vehicle for dramatic clarification.

In so far as some of the abusers of the King's English are also involved in negative action, they fail in their schemes. However, unlike Falstaff, whose schemes are a threat which cannot be tolerated or accommodated, these characters are integrated in the final festivities. From the opening scene, and repeatedly in the course of the play, it is evident that there is a community—whatever the points of friction within it—and that Falstaff is an outsider. The climax of this distinction is at the end of the play, where the various characters leave their quarrels and differences and participate in the communal solidarity against the *pharmakos*. Mistress Quickly, the panderess and mistress of malapropism, can even play the Fairy Queen in the masque of scapegoating; and other characters who have been exposed as foolish, ridiculous, or deceived take part in that masque on the positive side—in opposition to Falstaff. We are not meant to ask at that point how the speech deficiencies of Quickly, Caius, and Evans are cured, and Pistol's style is improved. The comic exposure of their aberrations is simply suspended—without the explanation of a miraculous transformation we get in *As You Like it* when threatening evil is removed. When the time for a resolution comes, all deficiencies which are not an intolerable threat are remedied, suspended, or bypassed—and the characters concerned can participate in the resolution. Only Falstaff remains unassimilable.

As we see in other Shakespearean comedies, a profound transformation is not a precondition for resolution. A removal of obstacles to well-being, and the achievement of goals which embody comic values, are the fundamental requirements. If, exceptionally, a play insists on a strict test of profound change (as happens at the end of *Love's Labour's Lost*), the resolution does not take place—and there is a rupture in the comic form. Otherwise there is a comic resolution, and from it are absent (as a result of exclusion or, more commonly, self-exclusion) characters who are incompatible with it and with festive celebration: a melancholy Jacques, a Malvolio whose "amour propre" is hurt, a Don John who flees.[18]

The exposing, punitive manipulation of the pharmakos, and the positive and successful manoeuvre arranged by the young lovers are not the only manipulatory actions in the play. From the opening scene to the last there is, on every level and in the links between levels, a multiplicity of schemes and manipulations—some of them doubled-edged. The overall comic clarification relies heavily on a juxtaposition of levels, but, unlike the complex system of reflectors in *As You Like It*, it is inseparable from a multiple action of intrigue. In addition to the intrigues we have mentioned, which create the central pattern of punishing the pharmakos and securing the triumph of love, the play contains a number of manipulations. Apart from the vindictive scheme carried out by Falstaff's followers against him (which is instrumental to the wider action of exposing and defeating the bulky impostor), we have Mistress Quickly and the merry Host. Quickly is active in a triple game of match-making, while she herself is unaware of the situation. "I know Anne's mind as well as another does" (I.iv.158), she says, but she is wrong; the triumph of Fenton and Anne Page comes about without her services and without her knowledge. She is also the go-between in the double game of the wives with Falstaff—again without being in the known (except in the end, when all Windsor knows), and certainly without controlling the game.

The merry Host, whose verbal ebullience is on occasion more striking than Falstaff's, successfully manipulates Evans and Caius. He extracts as much fun as can be had from the belligerent physician (who gives him potions and motions) and the incensed parson (who gives proverbs and no verbs, III.i.94), while making sure that no physical harm comes from their verbal violence. "Let them keep their limbs whole, and hack our English" (III.i.71), he says. But when he praises himself jocularly for being a subtle Machiavel, who uses policy to prevent combat, the would-be duellists are reconciled only to join forces in a plan of revenge against him. The Host, in his turn, becomes the victim of manipulation, though he does not lose in the

end. His losses are made good by Fenton as a reward for helping him with the scheme to marry Anne (IV.vi.3ff.).

If the various comic aberrations, and the schemes and manipulations may be regarded as farcical (or comic stuffing)—the fundamental comic pattern relies on a dual progression. The pharmakos is punished and exposed by an entire community, and in the process there is a catharsis of the anxiety of jealousy; while young love triumphs and is accepted by the community. Like other Shakespearean comedies, *The Merry Wives* moves through comic release both in order to provide clarification and in order to culminate in a constructive comic resolution, which is accompanied by festive celebration. Without being moralistic, the resolution and cumulative clarification are based on moral values. And moral values require punishment and exclusion, as well as assertion, tolerance, and celebration.

Notes

1. A good critical survey of the history of criticism of *The Merry Wives* is given by Jeanne Addison Roberts in *Shakespeare's English Comedy* (Lincoln and London, Univ. of Nebraska Press, 1979).

2. Apart from Professor Roberts's book-length study of the play, there is at least one other deliberate attempt to analyze the comedy without negative prejudices, and to place it in relation to Shakespeare's other comedies: Ruth Nevo's *Comic Transformations in Shakespeare* (London, Methuen, 1980). Both books are recent. Two somewhat earlier books on Shakespearean comedy have chapters on *The Merry Wives*: Bertrand Evans's *Shakespeare's Comedies* (Oxford, Clarendon Press, 1960), and Ralph Berry's *Shakespeare's Comedies* (Princeton, Princeton Univ. Press, 1972). Evans's systematic, if somewhat mechanical, application of the concept of discrepant awareness contributes something to our understanding of how the play works, but casts little light on what it says. Ralph Berry dismisses, in effect, the play as a farce which brings out the worst tendencies in an audience, and was supposedly a burden to its creator; he does not tell us how he can support these views. "The revenge motif unleashes much sadism in the audience . . . the quality of *The Merry Wives of Windsor* is perfectly expressed in its jokes . . . the piece is a Public Record Office of graffiti . . . one imagines that Shakespeare laid down his pen with some relief" (p. 148, p. 149, p. 153). This is a rather extreme example of the prejudice against the play, as well as of the critical impediments, and even patronizing attitude, which this prejudice can create.

3. So, for instance, C.L. Barber does not analyze the play in his important book *Shakespeare's Festive Comedy* (Princeton, Princeton Univ. Press, 1959), though he deals with the Falstaff of the history plays. Alexander Leggatt omits *The Merry Wives* from his good study of the comedies up to *Twelfth Night, Shakespeare's Comedy of Love* (London, Methuen,

1974) on the grounds that it is comparable to citizen comedy (and is not a comedy of love).

4. The term 'alazon' is, of course, Aristotelian. Aristotle gives it a general ethical value, which need not be related only to comedy, though it happens to be most suggestive when employed both in relation to Old Comedy (with its dialectical structure and agon, as well as the frequent punishment of negative characters) and to New Comedy (with its teleological structure directed at resolution, which involves the need to overcome obstructions). Both comic strategies appear in *The Merry Wives* (and also in *Twelfth Night*), as an impostor is exposed and punished on one level, and fulfilment is achieved and celebrated on another level; and both levels are integrated into the overall multiple plot of the comedy.

For Aristotle's definition of the impostor/boaster (alazon) and of his opposite extreme, the ironical man (eiron), see *The Nicomachean Ethics*, IV,7. An easily available English translation is that of J.A.K. Thompson (Harmondsworth, Penguin, 1974; first published 1953), where the directly relevant passage is on page 133.

The Aristotelian ethical terms are specifically given as types constituting the ethos of comedy in *The Tractatus Coislinianus*. See Lane Cooper, *An Aristotelian Theory of Comedy . . . And a Translation of the 'Tractatus Coislinianus'* (Oxford, Basil Blackwell, 1924), p. 226. The widest critical application and currency to these terms have been given by Northrop Frye in a number of essays on comedy. See, for instance, *The Anatomy of Criticism* (Princeton, Princeton University Press, 1971; first published 1957), p. 171ff. Frye is particularly illuminating in dealing with dramatic *function,* and the dynamism in which the characters are involved.

As far as the term 'pharmakos' is concerned, I should emphasize that I do not use it in a directly anthropological sense (to refer to an actual ritual of casting out the scapegoat). We are concerned with the comic transposition and echoes of such rituals, the comic structuring of the dialectic of exposure, and the comic values on which this process relies. However, just as the ethical term alazon is useful for dealing with characters and their function in action, so the ritual term pharmakos can throw light on the pattern of punishment, and its significance. As my title suggests, what is cast out in the end is an attitude (the libidinal) more than a character; and, at the same time, there is an assertion of sexuality in the form of young love. Punishment and assertion are given in tandem.

5. For an illuminating study of the interrelationship of plot levels in Elizabethan and Jacobean Drama generally, see Richard Levin, *The Multiple Plot in English Renaissance Drama* (Chicago and London, Univ. of Chicago Press, 1971). Levin does not deal with *The Merry Wives* in his book, but his general points are most useful for a critical analysis of the play.

In this connection, see also Leo Salingar's *Shakespeare and the Traditions of Comedy* (Cambridge, Cambridge Univ. Press, 1974), especially p. 228 ff.

6. See I.i.96, and the note on this line, in the Arden Shakespeare edition of *The Merry Wives of Windsor,* ed. H.J. Oliver (London, Methuen, 1971). All textual quotations are from this edition.

7. In this connection, see Evans, *op. cit.,* p. 98ff.

8. See Nevo, *op. cit.,* p. 15.

9. Frye, *A Natural Perspective* (New York, Harcourt, Brace and World, 1965), p. 76.

10. Frye, *Anatomy,* p. 183.

11. A delightful indication of the traditional comic motif of an Oedipal conflict is Synge's *Playboy of the Western World,* which also puts it to a good comic use. Like Oscar Wilde's *The Importance of Being Earnest,* which has fun with the convention of "cognition," Synge's play both uses a comic tradition and gives a comic perspective on it. One of its effects, which is particularly illuminating for critical purposes, is to remind us that in the "vis comica" the Oedipal conflict, a prominent element in the tradition, is funny—whatever its effect in tragedy.

12. There is, of course, a great difference between classical comedy, where the woman is a desirable object, but hardly a dramatic character, and Renaissance comedy—especially Shakespearean comedy—where the women are at the very least equal to the men, and often markedly superior to them.

13. I am changing here Barber's well-known formula "through release to clarification." The plot progresses to resolution, and its effect is clarification.

14. The morally neutral terms "plus" and "minus" are defined in terms of what is desirable vs. what is obstructive. They are particularly useful in accommodating an entire relevant range. As I have already indicated, we need terms which do not have an automatically moral connotation, but which can correspond to moral values, when these appear.

15. The edition I use is *Spenser, Poetical Works,* ed. J. C. Smith and E. de Selincourt (Oxford, Oxford Univ. Press, 1970 [1912]).

16. I borrow this useful phrase from Philip Edwards, *Shakespeare and the Confines of Art* (London, Methuen, 1968), ch. 1.

17. In the complex forms of the "problem plays" and "romances," Shakespeare expanded considerably the stresses which can lead to tragedy, while maintaining the overall comic framework. This combination is not absent in the comedies proper. The point emerges not only when we juxtapose *A Dream* and *Romeo and Juliet, Much Ado* and *Othello, As You Like It* and *Lear,* but also in the way in which the comedies, from *Errors* onward, indicate internally the road not taken.

18. For reasons which I cannot pursue here, I would argue that *The Merchant of Venice* is best understood in the context of the "problem plays," hence the exclusion of Shylock is not listed here.

Robert S. Miola (essay date 1993)

SOURCE: "*The Merry Wives of Windsor:* Classical and Italian Intertexts," in *Comparative Drama,* Vol. 27, No. 3, Fall, 1993, pp. 364-76.

[*In the following essay, Miola asserts that despite its weaknesses in plot,* The Merry Wives of Windsor *reveals Shakespeare's skill at adapting comedic forms outside of English dramaturgy.*]

Current theory has distinguished between two opposite intertextual perspectives, synchronic and diachronic. Dismissing all notion of temporality and hence of sources, the synchronic perspective views all texts as existing simultaneously with each other. "An endless *ars combinatoria* takes place in what has been variously termed 'musée imaginaire' (Malraux), 'chambre d'échos' (Barthes), or 'Bibliothèque générale' (Grivel)." Contrarily, the diachronic perspective recognizes temporality and thus constructs well-ordered "archives" (Foucault) of intertextuality that meticulously chronicle "every code and register its continuities and discontinuities."[1] The latter perspective opposes the former's endless Derridean deferral and dispersion, that kind of detheologized hermeticism in which all signifiers ultimately signify nothing. It enables criticism by affording more spacious perspectives—perspectives which stretch beyond the familiar landscapes and delusory comforts of verbal echo and the parallel passage to newer vistas composed of ancient and evolving *topoi,* conventions, and traditions.[2]

Mapping these vistas in Shakespeare's *The Merry Wives of Windsor* begins with recognition of its New Comedic substrata. *Wives* draws on the braggart soldiers of *Miles Gloriosus* and *Eunuchus* and on enormously popular descendant traditions. Moreover, the play, fluently recombining other New Comedic themes, motifs, and characters, draws on configurations and conventions originating in Plautus' *Casina.*[3] Though R.S. Forsythe overstated the case, he set forth persuasive evidence for this influence, well observing that both *Casina* and *Wives* feature a husband and wife who support different suitors to a young girl, that this girl loves a third person and eventually marries him, that both sets of wives similarly conspire against a foolish husband, that both dramas work to the climax of a mock-wedding in which the bride is discovered to be a male. Here we need not succumb to the fallacy of misplaced specification to recognize important affinities.

In *Wives,* as elsewhere, Shakespeare arranges the New Comedic elements in Italian style.[4] Oscar James Campbell notes the Italianate triple wooing of Anne Page and observes the *pedante* in Falstaff and Sir Hugh Evans, the *zanni* in the Host, the *medico* in Dr. Caius, and the *fantesca* in Mistress Quickly. Leo Salingar remarks Shakespeare's use of the Italianate double plot "with its confusions of identity and crossed complications," his preference for multiple marriages and subordinate deceptions (like *beffe*), and concludes: "paradoxically, the play in which he comes nearest to a wholesale adoption of Italian methods and an Italian manner is *The Merry Wives of Windsor,* his only comedy set in England."[5]

These observations suggest an approach that can justly evaluate Shakespeare's wide-ranging eclecticism in this play and assess its complex topography. The central alazon, Falstaff, descendant of Pyrgopolynices and Thraso, resides in a world created by Italian dramatists. *The Merry Wives of Windsor* belongs specifically to that family of plays that adapt *Casina,* mixing in other contemporary and classical elements, often a braggart soldier. Beatrice M. Corrigan first noted the common elements and variations in this group of plays—Machiavelli's *Clizia* (1525), Berrardo's *La Cassina* (1530), which is a translation of Plautus, Dolce's *Il Ragazzo* (c.1541), Della Porta's *La Fantesca,* Lanci's *La Ruchetta* (1584), Cecchi's *I Rivali,* and the anonymous and unpublished Sienese *Il Capriccio* (1566-68).[6] To this list we may also add a descendant of *Clizia,* Gelli's *Lo Errore* (1556). Offering a wide range of dramatic and interpretive possibilities, these plays represent a related series of ingenious adaptations rather than a coherent group; together they gather contemporary responses to a seminal classical play and present a lexicon of theatrical possibilities. Shakespeare need not have studied this lexicon directly to have picked up the language; in this regard traditions speak much louder and longer than individual texts. Shakespeare's reworking of *Casina, The Merry Wives of Windsor,* freely recombines all the important constituent elements of the Italian versions: the emphasis on jealousy, sometimes embodied in a scheming wife; a ridiculous *senex amans;* a boasting soldier; romantic young lovers; and, the signature motif, a male disguised as a bride. (There are also echoes in *Wives* of other Italian innovations—an impudent boy and a Latin-speaking *pedante.*) *Wives* arranges the standard elements into new configurations: the jealousy appears in the husband Ford, not the wife, and motivates a parallel action; the wife becomes the merry wives who control the major intrigues of the play, a transformation that recovers the original dynamic of *Casina.* The *senex amans* and *miles gloriosus,* along with various other medieval and classical figures, conjoin in the stuffed figure of Falstaff. Eros turns into romance Italian style: the lusty *adulescens* becomes the loving Fenton, the silent and absent Casina, the winsome Anne Page. The boy disguised as a bride, doubled, provides a climax to a subordinate plot and accompanies the other humiliating exposures in the play. Shakespeare brilliantly redefines and rearranges traditional elements to create an English comedy that is, paradoxically, both classical and Italianate as well.

Annotating Plautus' *Casina,* Lodovico Castelvetro suggested that the son's love affair was "*senza niun valore, che bastava che la moglie si fosse aveduta, che il marito fosse inamorato della serva*" ("without value; it was sufficient that the wife be jealous and the husband be in love with the servant").[7] Castelvetro's identification of jealousy as an essential plot element echoes in the Italian adaptations, which often portray this passion. Della Porta's *La Fantesca,* for example, features Jealousy as the prologue, and this passion motivates the major actions of the play. Transferring the jealousy from the wife to Ford, Shakespeare depicts it as another form of the *alazoneia* that overestimates the self and underestimates a woman. The wives' battle against the tendency to reduce them to sexual objects, possessions carefully guarded but easily stolen, has actually two fronts, one without and one within Windsor; Falstaff's noisy narcissism finds reflection in Ford's obsessive jealousy. Like a braggart soldier, Ford congratulates himself on his own percipience and vigilance: "God be prais'd for my jealousy!" (II.ii.309). He mocks the trusting Page as "an ass, a secure ass" (ll. 300-01), and delights in his own invention, his plot to expose his wife, whom he misprizes as "a false woman" (l. 292).

Ford's jealousy motivates a subordinate action that mirrors the main action of *Casina*—namely, the exposure of a foolish husband by a smart wife. To portray Ford's folly, Shakespeare reverts to his earliest experiment with Plautus, *The Comedy of Errors.* Like Antipholus of Syracuse who wonders whether he is "Sleeping or waking, mad or well-advis'd" (II.ii.213), Ford ponders his state, "Hum! ha? Is this a vision? Is this a dream? Do I sleep? Master Ford, awake!" (III.v.139-40). Here Plautine bewilderment results not from the simple error of mistaken identity but from more complex misjudgment of his wife and self. Moreover, like the other twin, Antipholus of Ephesus (III.i), Ford angrily storms his house in the company of restraining friends (III.ii-iii, IV.ii). And both times he, like the town twin, leaves dissatisfied, convinced that his wife has been unfaithful. This scenario, deriving ultimately from *Amphitruo,* occurs also in *Ado,* when Claudio and Don Pedro spy on Hero's supposed rendezvous. Here Shakespeare works a new variation on the dramatic situation, this time portraying the jealous husband as a complementary fool to the braggart soldier-lover. (Jonson uses essentially the same strategy with Kitely and Bobadill in *Every Man In His Humor,* a play in which Shakespeare acted.) In contradistinction to Falstaff, however, Ford moves from ostentatious self-love to the humble trust of another in marriage, a progress that recalls similar developments in *Errors, Shrew,* and *Ado.* Ford repents in verse, in lines dignified and convincing:

> Pardon me, wife, henceforth do what thou wilt.
> I rather will suspect the sun with cold
> Than thee with wantonness. Now doth thy honor stand,
> In him that was of late an heretic,
> As firm as faith.
>
> (IV.iv.6-10)

Together husband and wife plan the final exposure of the other *alazon,* Falstaff, appropriately bedecked in horns.

Shakespeare's striking transformation of the classical *matrona* into Mrs. Page and Mrs. Ford has rarely been noted or appreciated. Though these wives differ markedly from their unchaste counterparts in the novella tales frequently adduced as sources, critics have been reluctant to consider classical precedents. Most, subscribing too closely to the notion of stock characters, have in fact seen the wives as anti-classical; witness, for example, Ruth Nevo: "Shakespeare's New Comedy inverts traditional feminine roles, thus transforming a male-oriented, male-dominated perspective into its antithetical opposite."[8] Such a generalization, though commonly held, ignores the demonstrable diversity of women and their roles in New Comedy, not to mention the dominating females of Aristophanes' *Lysistrata, Ecclesiazusae,* and *Thesmophoriazusae.* Plautus and Terence depict the chaste and virtuous *matrona* Alcumena (*Amphitruo*) as well as the virago Artemona (*Asinaria*). Sostrata, instead of scolding her husband, gets scolded by him and is wrongly held responsible for her son's problems throughout *Hecyra.* And, of course, we need look no further than *Casina* itself to find precedent for Shakespeare's merry wives. As Walter E. Forehand has shown, Plautus presents here Cleustrata, a highly individualized matrona who outmaneuvers her husband through clever tricks.[9]

It is a long way from Cleustrata to Mistress Ford, but some of the distance had already been traveled by Italians. The two playwrights who follow *Casina* most closely, Lanci and Machiavelli, expand the roles and characters of the matrona. In the conclusion of *La Ruchetta* Cassandra pardons her erring husband at the request of her friend Gostanza ("*Horsu Cassandra perdonategli per amor mio*"); the husband gratefully responds, "*Non credo che sia al mondo huomo, che habbia la piu piaceuol moglie della mia*" ("I don't think there is a man in all the world who has a more pleasing wife than mine"). Recognizing her long-lost daughter, Ruchetta, Gostanza exclaims: "*Oh Cassandra quanto giubilo, quanta allegrezza ho io?*"[10] Discussing *Clizia,* Radcliff-Umstead notes the major changes in Machiavelli's portraiture:

> Whereas Plautus' Cleostrata is always finding fault with husband, insulting him at every occasion, Sofronia attacks Nicomaco only because of his failure to preserve the dignity of his age and because of the bad example he has set for his son. Sofronia is never jealous; Cleostrata is jealous even when there is no cause. . . . Cleostrata forgives her husband only because of the technical necessity of ending the comedy, but Sofronia pardons her husband because of her affection for him. All the efforts of the wife in Machiavelli's play are made to shock Nicomaco out of his amorous madness; Sofronia has to use brutal means to wake him from his dream of sensual delight. When he surrenders, she is ready to forget everything. Machiavelli has depicted this woman as a thoughtful and loving wife.[11]

In Gelli's reworking of this play, *Lo Errore,* Mona Francesca likewise humiliates her husband, then grants him forgiveness but not before she forces him to agree to their son's marriage. Mrs. Ford makes one with this good company of women: all defend themselves and their marriages from the crazed passion of the husband; all use for a principal weapon a remarkable *astuzia;* and in the end, all are loving and forgiving wives in reconstituted partnerships.

Falstaff too embodies and transforms New Comedic and Italian characters, expanding them well beyond the boundaries, however spacious, of any single type.[12] Primarily, he is a *miles gloriosus,* that boasting soldier/lover who descends from Euripides' Herakles, Aristophanes' Lamakhos and Dionysos, down through Menander's soldiers and those of Plautus and Terence, through Italian and English ancestors as well.[13] Here too he resembles the familiar *senex amans,* the old man who presumes to be a lover but is found to be "Old, cold, wither'd, and of intolerable entrails" (V.v.153-54). These two classical types were traditional targets of much Italian comedy, including those plays descending from *Casina* (Della Porta's *La Fantesca* features two braggarts, Capitano Dante and Capitano Pantaleone). Freely adding other types and traditions, Shakespeare combines them into one enormous figure, drawing all into coherence by the fat rogue's "admirable dexterity of wit" (IV.v.117-18).[14] In his mixed ancestry Falstaff resembles Molière's great comic creation Harpagon of *L'Avare,* direct descendant of Plautus' miserly Euclio, simultaneously the *senex amans* in rivalry with his son and the blocking father who opposes his daughter's marital plans.

Falstaff's military braggadocio appears throughout the play. He woos like a "soldier" in "soldier-like phrase" (II.i.11-13); he promises to stare Ford "out of his wits" (II.ii.279), thus boasting of the basilisk eye that was stock weaponry in the braggart's arsenal; he threatens to awe Ford with the cudgel: "it shall hang like a meteor o'er the cuckold's horns" (ll. 280-81). Moreover, both *Miles Gloriosus* and *Wives* use the conventional dialogue with the parasite to reveal the vanity of the boasting soldier. The importance and flexibility of this pairing, first appearing in Greek Middle comedy, is amply attested by Francesco Andreini's collection of *commedia dell'arte* dialogues between Capitano Spavento and Trappola.[15] In Plautus' *Miles Gloriosus* Pyrgopolynices converses with his parasite Artotrogus; Falstaff converses with the equivalents—Pistol, Nym, and Bardolph. There are, however, important dissimilarities in presentation. The classical boaster usually has his illusions fed by a wily parasite who encourages him for selfish purposes, ridicules him in asides, and gleefully plots the final puncturing of the balloon. In I.iii Falstaff himself fantasizes about Mrs. Ford's "leer of invitation" and Mrs. Page's "judicious iliads" (ll. 45-46, 60-61), expounding the dream of his own sexual attractiveness that motivates the entire action. He is as vain as Pyrgopolynices but needs no flatterer to puff him up. Falstaff feeds his own illusions as well as his own belly. His attendants, far from inflating the foolish fantasy, seek to deflate it:

Falstaff:
. . . sometimes the beam of her view gilded my foot, sometimes my portly belly.
Pistol:
Then did the sun on dunghill shine.
Nym:
I thank thee for that humor.

(ll. 61-64)

Pistol and Nym indignantly refuse to bear Falstaff's letters to the ladies. Whereas Pyrgopolynices sees himself by reflection, by the false images that others are only too happy to provide, Falstaff creates his own self-image and acts accordingly. This invention, of course, argues a kind of wit in Falstaff, a poetic fancy that sets him apart from the merely gullible and stupid prototypes. But this difference also isolates the fat knight in his illusions and makes him solely responsible for his folly as well as its consequences.

In classical and neoclassical plays the comeuppance begins with the boaster's entrance into the lady's house. Plautus' Milphidippa assures Pyrgopolynices that the husband will be absent (l. 1277). Mistress Quickly twice tells Falstaff that the husband will be out and that Mrs. Ford awaits him (II.ii.83-84, III.v.44-46). We recall the humorous stage play and resonant symbolism of the locked door in *Amphitruo* and *Menaechmi,* and in *Errors, Twelfth Night,* and *Ado,* as Shakespeare stages two variations of the device here. Twice entering the woman's house, twice unlocking the locked door, Falstaff reenacts the other entrances, real and feigned, in full expectation of the sexual reward. Like Plautus' courtesans, the merry wives, however, have wittily revised the New Comedic script. He who fancied himself a sexual imperialist, an extravagant voyager in love, trading with the East and West Indies of Windsor wives (I.iii.71-72), gets locked in a laundry basket and, the second time, beaten in women's clothes. The ignominious adventure in the suffocating and odorous laundry basket has some precedent in *Il Pecorone* and other novella tales, but similar enclosures regularly extinguish the ardors of foolish lovers in neoclassical comedy: the *senex amans* in Piccolomini's *Alessandro* gets locked in a bathroom ("*in quella camera del necessario*") where he suffers from the horrendous stench ("*il puzzo horrendo*");[16] the scene changes to a coal-house in Chapman's *May Day,* his adaptation of *Alessandro;* in *La Calandria* the amorous old fool gets stuffed into a large trunk that is about to be dumped in a river; and in *Les Fourberies de Scapin* the wily servant tricks Géronte into a sack and then beats him.

The conflation of martial and amorous ardors evident in Falstaff clearly shows the twin delusions rampant in Windsor—the overestimation of the self as a soldier for all seasons, and the underestimation of the woman, here reduced to the status of a military objective, a thing to be lost or won. Dr. Caius, another "Hector" (II.iii.33), presents an extreme and illuminating case of both delusions. He woos Anne arrogantly and ineffectually with his sword, mistaking his competition (he seems to be unaware of

*Act II, scene i. Mrs. Ford and Mrs.
Page. By J. Perker Norris.*

(III.ii.67-69). Unlike the others in the play, Fenton actually woos the lady in person and, though rejected by her father, shows faith in her, "Why, thou must be thyself" (III.iv.3). He does not see Anne as a military objective or as merchandise to be fought for or bargained over—the prevalent attitude typified, for example, by Evans: "Seven hundred pounds, and possibilities, is goot gifts" (I.i.65). He pointedly disavows materialistic motives in the wooing, stung by Mr. Page's accusation that he views Anne "but as a property":

> No, heaven so speed me in my time to come!
> Albeit I will confess thy father's wealth
> Was the first motive that I woo'd thee, Anne;
> Yet wooing thee, I found thee of more value
> Than stamps in gold, or sums in sealed bags;
> And 'tis the very riches of thyself
> That now I aim at.
>
> (III.iv.12-18)

Fenton's use of a military metaphor later in this scene—his promise to "advance the colors" of his love "against all checks, rebukes, and manners" (III.iv.80-81)—measures the difference between him and the other suitors. War is a mere metaphor for the hostile circumstances and for his own steadfast persistence. He doesn't actually boast of soldierly prowess, woo with the sword, or consider Anne a military prize. Instead, he takes the trouble to win her heart and sends a ring (III.iv.100). The letter he receives from her later, a direct contrast to the presumptuous epistles of Falstaff, "mutually" answers affection (IV.vi.10); together Fenton and Anne plot to outwit parents and foolish suitors. Those who come to wive by swaggering, in Windsor as in Illyria, never thrive.

Fenton), misdirected to the duel, that Italian innovation which here, as in *Twelfth Night,* exposes the folly, usually cowardice, of the braggart. Dr. Caius works through agents like Mrs. Page and Mistress Quickly, and does not once speak directly to Anne in the play. Consequently he is perpetually in the wrong place at the wrong time. His fortunes, running through swaggering folly to public humiliation, clearly mirror Falstaff's progress from Windsor boaster to country gull.

Opposed to these military lovers in the play is the young Fenton. Shakespeare's transformation of the absent youths of *Casina* into young lovers perfectly accords with Italian theory and practice. Castelvetro, as we have seen, thought the classical lovers extraneous. Italian playwrights expanded their roles and integrated them into the action, as did later adaptors, including John Dennis, who made "*everything Instrumental to* Fenton's *Marriage,*" as well as Boito and Verdi in their opera.[17] With regard to the Italian plays Beatrice Corrigan has observed: "the characters who assume paramount importance in the Renaissance versions are precisely those of the young lovers, particularly of the men."[18] Similarly adapted is Shakespeare's *adulescens,* Fenton, who also resembles a Chaucerian "clerk": "He capers, he dances, he has eyes of youth; he writes verses, he speaks holiday, he smells April and May"

Similarly, the silent and absent virgo becomes Anne Page, a transformation well prepared by the Italians. Corrigan observes similar changes in Machiavelli's Clizia, still absent but good and beautiful, Dolce's Livia, a "*gentildonna fanciulla*" who reciprocates love, in Cecchi's Persilia, who appears briefly on stage, and in Lanci's Ruchetta, who asks for time to find her parents (with the help of *il cielo*) before beginning an undesired marriage. Berrardo's translation of *Casina* expanded the *virgo*'s role and, according to Jean Braybrook, encouraged the fuller portrayal of Antoinette in yet another adaptation, Belleau's *La Reconnue.*[19] Shakespeare continues the trend with Anne Page, who, like his other *virgines* Bianca and Hero, has more stage presence than her small part suggests and than many commentators allow. Anne tolerates the idiotic Slender with kindliness and grace; she protests vigorously against her mother's choice, Dr. Caius: "Alas, I had rather be set quick i' th' earth, / And bowl'd to death with turnips!" (III.iv.86-87); going Ruchetta one better, she chooses and plays her role in the final marital pageant.

This pageant features the substitution of boys for brides, a multiplied replay of Chalinus' imposture in *Casina.* Plautus plays this substitution for bawdy slapstick as the chagrined lover gets his comeuppance.[20] Machiavelli,

Dolce, and Lanci follow suit, reprising the raucous tone and genital humor. There were other interesting variations: in *La Fantesca* there is no girl at all but a boy, Essandro, in disguise throughout the play; and in Aretino's *Il Marescalco* the duped suitor, preferring men to women, is delighted with the trick. Jonson's adaptation, *Epicoene,* derived partly from *Il Marescalco,* makes the switch a surprising stage trick that culminates a scene of legal satire and comic confusion. Shakespeare, more simply, focuses on the deceivers deceived, on Slender who says in shock and surprise, "she's a great lubberly boy" (V.v.184), and on Caius, who exits for the last time, as we might expect, huffing and puffing, "Ay, be-gar, and 'tis a boy. Be-gar, I'll raise all Windsor" (V.v.209-10).

The Merry Wives of Windsor presents an Italianate appropriation of New Comedic characters, conventions, and plays. Like the errors plays—*The Comedy of Errors* and *Twelfth Night*—it multiplies incident and character into complicated design, romanticizes classical eros, dramatizes mistaken identity. Like the intrigue plays—*The Taming of the Shrew* and *Much Ado About Nothing*—*Wives* focuses on marriage, featuring many tricks and deceits—in Bertrand Evans' judgment, "the greatest accumulation of practices in any play of Shakespeare's except *Cymbeline.*"[21] And, like *Shrew* and *Ado,* the play exhibits in one of its plots (the wooing of Anne Page) a Plautine romantic configuration that plays off another more eclectic story line. This line, the duping of Falstaff, reprises significant New Comedic elements as well, liberally combining them with other traditions. And yet as always Falstaff finally transcends the classical types he subsumes. Speaking a lively prose much different from the usual Thrasonical huffe-snuffe,[22] he narrates the adventure of the buck-basket in hilariously vivid detail and is capable of occasional *eironeia*—as in, for example, the witty sally he directs at himself:

> *Quickly:*
> Alas the day! good heart, that was not her fault. She does so take on with her men; they mistook their erection.
> *Falstaff:*
> So did I mine, to build upon a foolish woman's promise.
>
> (III.v.38-41)

Shakespeare's *Wives* explores the moral and psychological complexities behind classical comic action. The *miles gloriosus* here, seen variously in Falstaff, Pistol, and Caius, continually overestimates himself and underestimates others, particularly women. To such delusions the wives apply stringent corrective. Falstaff's *cognitio,* consequently, differs from the standard classical recognition of identity by token or the neoclassical variant brilliantly exploited in Italian comedy and in Shakespeare himself: the throwing off of disguise or unmasking. Instead, he discovers the folly of his misconceptions, of his evil thinking. The fairies berate him for "sinful fantasy" (V.v.93), the onlookers mock him as "A puff'd man" (l. 152). The *processus turbarum* illustrates in a comic way the truth of the Garter motto, *Honi soit qui mal y pense* (V.v.69), "Evil be to him who evil *thinks*" (italics mine).

Few today would argue that *Wives* is a seamless success for all of its rambunctious fun. Earlier critics, however, focusing on plot and on the comic unities, thought the play one of Shakespeare's purest comedies. The line of praise includes John Dryden, Nicholas Rowe, and Charles Gildon, and culminates in Samuel Johnson's comment, "perhaps it never yet had reader or spectator who did not think it too soon at an end."[23] But to our eyes even the plot seems flawed. The revenge on the host, the business with the horses, is badly garbled and, in the present state of the text, entirely extraneous. Nor are Falstaff's subordinates, Bardolph, Pistol, and Nym, well integrated into the action. To be sure they amplify exploration of *alazoneia* and provide some comic color, but the revenge plot against Falstaff, like Pistol's suit to Mistress Quickly, simply evaporates as the wives take over the play. In fact, Pistol and Nym themselves disappear as the play moves on; they do not reflect on the main action and characters as consistently and tellingly as they do in *2 Henry IV* and *Henry V.* Here Shakespeare works with comic relations and traditions which he will use with greater skill and subtlety in *All's Well.* There Pistol will reappear as Parolles, and the subordinate *miles gloriosus* figure will bear a relationship to the action and main characters that is important and purposeful.

Notes

1. Heinrich Plett, ed., *Intertextuality* (Berlin: Walter de Gruyter, 1991), pp. 25-26. References to Shakespeare are cited to *The Riverside Shakespeare,* ed. G. Blakemore Evans *et al.* (Boston: Houghton Mifflin, 1974); to Plautus, *Comoediae,* ed. W.M. Lindsay, Oxford Classical Texts (1904-05; rpt. Oxford: Clarendon Press, 1989), 2 vols. All translations are mine.

2. The diachronic perspective is discussed and deployed variously by Thomas M. Greene, *The Light in Troy* (New Haven: Yale Univ. Press, 1982) and *The Vulnerable Text* (New York: Columbia Univ. Press, 1986); R.J. Schoeck, *Intertextuality and Renaissance Texts* (Bamberg: H. Kaiser Verlag, 1984); the essayists in *Literary Theory/Renaissance Texts,* ed. Patricia Parker and David Quint (Baltimore: Johns Hopkins Univ. Press, 1986).

3. See Northrop Frye, *The Anatomy of Criticism* (Princeton: Princeton Univ. Press, 1957), p. 167; Leo Salingar, *Shakespeare and the Traditions of Comedy* (Cambridge: Cambridge Univ. Press, 1974), p. 173; Geoffrey Bullough, ed., *Narrative and Dramatic Sources of Shakespeare* (London: Routledge and Kegan Paul, 1957-75), II, 9; R.S. Forsythe, "A Plautine Source of *The Merry Wives of Windsor,*" *Modern Philology,* 18 (1920), 401-21. Forsythe, however, did not take into account the possibility of intermediation. The feature of three rival suitors, for example, is an Italian innovation already put to good use in *TGV* and *Shrew.*

4. That Italian adaptations of New Comedy created the principal family lines for European Renaissance comedy is a proposition long verified and long ignored. Stephen Gosson (*Plays Confuted in Five Actions* [1582], ed. Arthur Freeman [New York: Garland, 1972], sig. D5v) complained of Italian plays "ransackt, to furnish the Playe houses in London"; Chapman casually mentioned four Italian plays in the dedication to *The Widow's Tears.* Summarizing past work and reformulating the proposition with erudition and cogency is Louise George Clubb, *Italian Drama in Shakespeare's Time* (New Haven: Yale Univ. Press, 1989).

5. Oscar James Campbell, "The Italianate Background of *The Merry Wives of Windsor*," *University of Michigan Publications, Language and Literature,* 8 (1932), 81-117; Salingar, *Shakespeare and the Traditions of Comedy,* p. 190; see also Clubb, *Italian Drama,* pp. 24-25.

6. Beatrice M. Corrigan, "*Il Capriccio:* An Unpublished Italian Renaissance Comedy and its Analogues," *Studies in the Renaissance,* 5 (1958), 74-86. These plays engendered others, thus extending the family lines; Dolce's *Il Ragazzo,* e.g., found new life in Pierre de Larivey's *Le Laquais.*

7. Lodovico Castelvetro, "Parere di Ludovico Castelvetro sopra ciascuna comedia di Plauto," ed. Giuseppe Spezi, *Il Propugnatore,* 1 (1868), 68.

8. Ruth Nevo, *Comic Transformations in Shakespeare* (London: Methuen, 1980), p. 160. The play resists the schematic gender readings now in fashion. Backing the suit of Dr. Caius, Mrs. Page, no less than Mr. Page, plays a comic blocking figure whom the young lovers outwit. David O. Frantz (*Festum Voluptatis* [Columbus: Ohio State Univ. Press, 1989], pp. 230-45) discusses the play in the context of Renaissance erotica.

9. Walter E. Forehand, "Plautus' *Casina:* An Explication," *Arethusa,* 6 (1973), 233-56.

10. *La Ruchetta* (1584), pp. 92, 93, 98.

11. Douglas Radcliff-Umstead, *The Birth of Modern Comedy in Renaissance Italy* (Chicago: Univ. of Chicago Press, 1969), p. 137.

12. See George E. Duckworth, *The Nature of Roman Comedy* (Princeton: Princeton Univ. Press, 1952), p. 416; John W. Draper, "Falstaff and the Plautine Parasite," *Classical Journal,* 33 (1938), 390-401; Madeleine Doran, *Endeavors of Art* (Madison: Univ. of Wisconsin Press, 1954), p. 159: "the discomfited Falstaff of the *Merry Wives* is far nearer the type of amorous old man of Plautine and Italian comedy than is the more complex Falstaff of the history plays." Anne Barton ("Falstaff and the Comic Community," *Shakespeare's "Rough Magic,"* ed. Peter Erickson and Coppélia Kahn [Newark: Univ. of Delaware Press, 1985], pp. 131-48) finds precedents in Aristophanes.

13. Aside from his earlier incarnation in the history plays, the Windsor Falstaff's most important ancestor is the Italianate Spaniard Armado (see Oscar James Campbell, "*Love's Labour's Lost* Re-studied," *Univ. of Michigan Publications, Language and Literature,* 1 [1925], 3-45). Both soldiers engage in a senex-puer dialogue with a page; both are compared to ancient heroes and mythological figures (*LLL* I.ii.63ff, 173ff, the show of the Worthies; *Wiv.* I.iii.6ff). Both pursue unreceptive women by a letter which is derisively read aloud (*LLL* IV.i; *Wiv.* II.i). The pursuits culminate in a pageant or "sport," wherein each suffers exposure and mockery. After the pageant there are some motions of reintegration: Armado vows to "hold the plough" (V.ii.883-84) for Jaquenetta for three years; the abashed Falstaff gets invited to dinner at Page's house (V.v.170-73).

14. Mrs. Page calls him "a Herod of Jewry" (II.i.20), thus evoking the boastful tyrant from the miracle plays. As always, Falstaff exuberantly displays some characteristics of the Vice, the Prodigal Son, and the Lord of Misrule. In addition, several have argued that Falstaff enacts the role of the scapegoat or the central character in folk rituals: Jeanne Addison Roberts, *Shakespeare's English Comedy* (Lincoln: Univ. of Nebraska Press, 1979), pp. 77-83; J.A. Bryant, Jr., "Falstaff and the Renewal of Windsor," *PMLA,* 89 (1974), 296-301; Anne Parten, "Falstaff's Horns: Masculine Inadequacy and Feminine Mirth in *The Merry Wives of Windsor*," *Studies in Philology,* 82 (1985), 184-99.

15. See T.B.L. Webster, *Studies in Later Greek Comedy,* 2nd ed. (1970; rpt. Westport, Conn.: Greenwood Press, 1981), p. 64; Andreini, *Le bravure* (Venice, 1607).

16. Piccolomini, *Alessandro* (Venice, 1562), p. 36.

17. John Dennis, *The Comical Gallant* (London, 1702), sig. A2ᵛ. On Boito and Verdi's work, see Gary Schmidgall, *Shakespeare and Opera* (New York: Oxford Univ. Press, 1990), pp. 329-30.

18. Corrigan, "*Il Capriccio:* An Unpublished Italian Renaissance Comedy," p. 82.

19. Ibid., pp. 82-83; Remy Belleau, *La Reconnue,* ed. Jean Braybrook (Geneva: Droz, 1989), pp. 10, 15. Corrigan describes another variation, the bawdy Giglietta of *Il Capriccio.*

20. W.T. MacCary and M.M. Willcock (eds., *Casina* [Cambridge: Cambridge Univ. Press, 1976], p. 37) note that the false bride scene may have been popular in Atellan farce and has a prototype in comic treatments of the marriage of Herakles and Omphale; see also Webster, *Studies,* p. 161.

21. Bertrand Evans, *Shakespeare's Comedies* (Oxford: Clarendon Press, 1960), p. 99.

22. Compare for example the outrageous bluster of Huanebango in Peele's *The Old Wives Tale* (1595): "Phy-

lyda phylerydos, Pamphylyda floryda flortos, / Dub dub a dub, bounce quoth the guns, with a sulpherous huffe snuffe: / Wakte with a wench, pretty peat, pretty love, and my sweet prettie pigsnie; / Just by thy side shall sit surnamed great Huanebango" (ll. 646-49).

23. See for convenience Brian Vickers, ed., *Shakespeare: The Critical Heritage,* (London: Routledge and Kegan Paul, 1974-81), I, 137, 255 (Dryden); II, 195 (Rowe); II, 221 (Gildon); V, 521 (Johnson).

DATE, TEXT, AND SOURCES

Barbara Freedman (essay date 1994)

SOURCE: "Shakespearean Chronology, Ideological Complicity, and Floating Texts: Something Is Rotten in Windsor," in *Shakespeare Quarterly,* Vol. 45, No. 2, Summer, 1994, pp. 190-210.

[*In the following essay, Freedman suggests that* The Merry Wives of Windsor's *confusing mixture of dramatic genres, topical references, and historical allusions cast doubt on the argument that the play was written for a single occasion.*]

> I warrant he hath a thousand of these letters, writ with blank space for different names (sure, more!); and these are of the second edition.
>
> (*The Merry Wives of Windsor,* 2.1.74-77)

I

If at one time the literary scholar's double bind could be summed up by the conflicting imperatives "always deconstruct" and "always historicize," at present a third command triangulates the critic's desire—always localize.[1] In the context of theory's latest turn of the screw to local history and thick description, a return to Shakespeare's last remaining so-called occasionalist play should prove both timely and unsettling. Widely accepted as Shakespeare's most topical play, *The Merry Wives of Windsor* boasts the stunning fact of being the only play in the corpus still generally believed to have been composed for a specific court occasion and, even more specifically, as a compliment to Elizabeth. Yet the sheer range and variety of the play's topical references belie the occasionalist argument, since we are no closer to resolving such long-standing intertextual conundrums as the relation of this play to other two-wives comedies, to the dating and characters of the Henriad, or to the elder/younger Cobham's complaints resulting in the Oldcastle/Falstaff, if not Brooke/Broome, censorship. More simply, the play's generous topicality seems to have complicated rather than clarified accounts of its textual and theatrical history, since the more evidence

that is brought forward to ballast the occasionalist argument for dating the play, the less convincing that argument appears.

That *Merry Wives* offers an embarrassment of riches for the topically minded scholar is a problem that has never been squarely faced or followed to its logical conclusions. Part royal compliment and part bedroom farce, best known as a Falstaff play and widely recognized as Shakespeare's only topical satire, part citizen comedy, part city comedy, part humors comedy, and part court comedy, *Merry Wives* offers so many conflicting leads that to choose one as its source of composition is to err on the side of willful simplicity. How do we account for references to the fairy queen and to Elizabethan diplomatic affairs, as well as to the king and to Cotswald games, to rural and urban life, to April court ceremonies and to country harvest homes? How do we account for the reception in the late 1590s of topical jokes known only in limited circles in the early 1590s? How do we explain references so private and yet so public, so early and then so late? How could a play with so many topical references to Elizabethan diplomatic and Garter court affairs be Shakespeare's only bedroom farce mocking foreigners? Who was or who could be the audience for such a play?

Equally confusing is the play's heavy-handed yet half-hearted efforts to connect itself up to the Henriad. How can this play be considered a commissioned sequel to *1* or even *2 Henry IV* when so many of its characters, such as Falstaff and Quickly, not only speak and act differently than their counterparts in the Henriad but actually fail to recognize one another? Why should *Merry Wives* appear later than *1* and *2 Henry IV* and yet seem earlier, promise us a return to Falstaff only to show how easily Falstaff's characteristic trait—the ease with which he avoids pocketing up shame—is so readily and repeatedly abandoned? And, should this caveat be answered, how do we integrate references to him as a "scholar" (2.2.180), a "metamorphised youth" (Allen and Muir, 576), and an "Old, cold, wither'd" fat man (5.5.153)?[2] Further, why would anyone composing a personal compliment to Elizabeth represent her in the person of Mistress Quickly? Finally, how could this most topical of comedies have led our most reliable scholars to date the play as early as 1592 and as late as 1602 and have led current editors of the play to bicker between dates of composition as early as 1597 and as late as 1601?

Symptomatic of this free-floating topicality is the unabashed presence of two competing conclusions to the play, neither of which has been proven anterior to the other. Despite the obvious superiority of the Folio text, no editor of the play treats either its Folio or Quarto versions as autonomous.[3] Yet editors seeking to safely anchor the date of the play's composition often obscure this fragile state of codependency. The occasionalist court-dating of this play, for example, depends on references to a Windsor Garter occasion which appear only in the Folio version; the Quarto lines diverge markedly at this point in ways that suggest to many scholars a link with some as yet undiscovered London comedy:

> Where is *Pead*? go you & see where Brokers sleep,
> And Foxe-eyed Seriants with their mase,
> Goe laie the Proctors in the street,
> And pinch the lowsie Seriants face.
>
> (Allen and Muir, 576)

Whether or not these lines and other Quarto references to Dr. Caius's "counting house" and "stall" are indeed "pure" London, or whether the writing here is even "pure" Shakespeare is much disputed, and for good reason. But surely the absence of the term *proctor* from the *Harvard Concordance to Shakespeare* reminds us once again of the need for more work on the Quarto, for a Quarto concordance, and for discussion of bad quartos appended to the editions of plays we study and teach.

That we are no closer to mapping the play's territorial confines, despite this plethora of topical pointers, suggests that we may inadvertently be confusing revision with source and interpolation with text and pursuing clues that are indeed nothing more than signs of extensive revision. Rather than ignore such leads, we might use them in another context, since they lend substantial weight to recent arguments for a revisionist Shakespeare whose topicality was more inclusive than exclusive.

II

Not surprisingly, the more we overcome the confusion provoked by topical references, the more ideologically inflected appear arguments for dating a play based on them. For example, although there is no dearth of studies exploring the ideological assumptions behind choices of textual variants in *Merry Wives,* no one has examined how these same assumptions govern the logic used to date the play.[4] Despite the welcome recent focus on *Merry Wives'* popular aspects and on its Quarto/Folio variants by scholars such as Steven Urkowitz, Peter Erickson, and Leah Marcus, none challenges the 1597 occasionalist court-dating of the play urged by Leslie Hotson, William Green, H.J. Oliver, and Jeanne Addison Roberts.[5] Thus the received belief on *Merry Wives*—that the play was commissioned by Lord Hunsdon to be performed at his 1597 Garter election—still prevails. Loyalty to this argument is surprising given the widespread discrediting of the occasionalist theory of Shakespeare's plays.[6] But such loyalty is baffling when exhibited by revisionists who are committed to using quarto evidence to rethink our concepts of audience, textual history, topicality, and theatrical history. When the same critics who contest editorial preference for the conclusion in the 1623 Folio *Merry Wives* over the more popular conclusion in the 1602 Quarto remain undisturbed by the occasionalist court argument and dating, one is left to conclude that something is rotten in Windsor scholarship.[7]

For centuries the question dominating *Merry Wives* scholarship has been not *how* to evaluate the evidence of the topical references to Garter ceremonies but *which* court Garter ceremony offered the most likely conditions for its performance. This questionable line of reasoning alone led Leslie Hotson, in the early 1930s, to redate the play; the same logic governed the scholarly revival and acceptance of Hotson's dating in the 1970s. In his 1971 Arden edition of *Merry Wives,* Oliver claimed that "easily the most persuasive explanation of the occasion and date of the play is that advanced by Leslie Hotson in his *Shakespeare versus Shallow,* although unfortunately it falls short of final proof."[8] Oliver's endorsement and elaboration of Hotson's thesis, though qualified, was forceful enough to lead a host of scholars, including the general editor of the Riverside Shakespeare, to abandon the standard date of 1600 in favor of 1597.[9] In a 1976 review of the Arden edition of *Merry Wives,* Charles Forker both reflected and spread the growing mood of overconfidence: "If Oliver cannot precisely be said to have settled the dating problem beyond dispute, he has at least shifted the burden of proof—a heavy burden—to the shoulders of the opposition."[10] Most enthusiastic was Jeanne Addison Roberts, whose comprehensive 1979 book on the play set forth the following challenge: "since nothing that is known about the history of *The Merry Wives* rules out a specifically commissioned performance in April 1596-97, since the main arguments against this date have been answered, since the arguments for it are powerful, and since everyone now seems to agree that the Garter allusions in the final masque support the idea of special commission, we are approaching a consensus on the date of the play."[11]

In the twenty years since the Hoston revivalists appeared on the scene, no such consensus has been reached. In fact convincing arguments against the 1597 dating have been lodged by G.R. Hibbard, Gary Taylor, Giorgio Melchiori, and Anne Barton, though their complaints are not being sufficiently heard or integrated into mainstream criticism.[12] The burden of proof shifts back to the Hotson camp when we add to these complaints the arguments that Oliver fails to counter, the conflicts within the occasionalist camp itself, and a number of overlooked sources—including Garter-related diplomatic and trade affairs.[13] Rather than enshrine *Merry Wives* as a court play written in 1597 to compliment Elizabeth and the Order of the Garter, I want here to use Garter evidence to undermine that claim, to lend weight to dissenting arguments for other dates of composition, and to liberate a more unsettling textual history from the aristocratic stronghold that for too long has fascinated Shakespeareans.

III

There are any number of ways to call a fixed chronology into question. The easiest way is to emphasize the fact that no decisive proof exists for such a date; the more difficult task is to prove that the assertions on which the argument rests are improbable. One can easily demonstrate the absence of decisive proof in the occasionalist argument. First, no scholar has provided evidence of any topical satire—indeed of any full-length play—performed at any

Garter ceremony at any time. Nor has any scholar offered proof that Hunsdon or anyone else ever commissioned a play for either Elizabeth or the Garter. In contrast, there is more than ample evidence that Shakespeare's plays were performed on the public stage before they were considered for court performances. Thus, not only is there no proof that *Merry Wives* is a commissioned Garter play; the weight of probability actually resists the occasionalist thesis.

The question is not whether Garter references exist in *Merry Wives* but how to read them. Such references (in Act 5 of the Folio version) have been noted since the eighteenth century.[14] In addition to the Garter motto, "*Honi soit qui mal y pense*" (5.5.69), the play includes commands to the Windsor fairies to scour "The several chairs of order" with balm (l. 61); to bless "Each fair installment, coat, and sev'ral crest, / With loyal blazon" (ll. 63-64); and to "nightly . . . sing / Like to the Garter's compass, in a ring" (ll. 65-66). These references indeed suggest a nod to the 23 April English Feast of Saint George, when knights of the Order were elected after a feast at Whitehall and, a few weeks later, were invested at Windsor Castle.[15] But in what context that nod was made—when, for whom, and why—remains a mystery.

That Shakespeare's company attended the 1597 Windsor Garter ceremonies is quite probable,[16] though this probability cannot be adduced as evidence for the argument that *Merry Wives* was composed to be performed during those ceremonies. Not only do we have ample evidence that Shakespeare's patron, Lord Hunsdon, would have needed special permission to avoid the Windsor ceremonies, but records indicate that his servants and retainers would be expected to travel with him. And we possess solid evidence of Garter-related theatrical activities at Windsor, although no 1597 occasionalist has ever referred to it. Charting the moves of the Lord Admiral's Men in the spring of 1600, E. K. Chambers observes: "Apparently the summer season was diversified by a visit to Windsor for the Garter installation of Henry IV of France on 27 April."[17] Henslowe's diary reads: "Lent vnto the company to goo to winswarth to the installinge the 27 of aprell 1600."[18]

The question is not which Garter ceremony provided the right conditions for the performance of *Merry Wives* but what proof exists for Garter-related theatrical activities, as opposed to Garter-commissioned compliments, and how the two may be distinguished from one another. Given the choice between a theatrical season diversified by a visit to Windsor and a play commissioned and composed for a Garter feast, all the evidence points toward the former. There is no dearth of information regarding Garter entertainments, including a painstakingly detailed account of the 1595 Garter feast and similar material contained in the Ashmole manuscripts. Yet all describe a type of entertainment similar to Accession Day tilts and royal progresses, which directly fulfilled the diplomatic and ideological aims of these occasions. Garter ceremonial

feasts, installations, and investitures would be inappropriate occasions for full-length bedroom farces with jokes about urinals, codpieces, and turds; or for topical satires on those to be inducted; or for mocking treatment of foreign ambassadors' accents and mishaps. In the absence of any record of any play performed at these ceremonies, the occasionalist argument for *Merry Wives*' dating remains conjectural at best.

Hotson's argument that Hunsdon commissioned this play as a compliment to Elizabeth is equally improbable. Those familiar with the sorts of public compliments that Elizabeth regularly required and elicited at Accession Day tilts, pageant plays, and royal progresses will concede that *Merry Wives* hardly fits the category of encomium. To cite Dekker's *Old Fortunatus:* "Some cal her *Pandora:* some *Gloriana;* some *Cynthia:* some *Belphoebe,* some *Astroea:* all by seuerall names to expresse seuerall loues"[19]—but who to the same end would address her as Mistress Quickly? The late 1590s reveal an Elizabeth especially sensitive to remarks about her age and fading attractiveness. It is doubtful that she would have been flattered by the middle-aged Mistress Page's wise response to a foolish love letter: "What, have [I] scap'd love-letters in the holiday-time of my beauty, and am I now a subject for them?" (2.1.1-3). Nor would the references to Mistress Ford as the "doe with the black scut" (5.5.18) have proven any more welcome an identification, particularly at a diplomatic occasion. Nor would Falstaff's "Ask me no reason why I love you" have been viewed as flattery, given that the most flattering reason he devises is that "You are not young, no more am I; go to then, there's sympathy" (2.1.4, 6-7). Nor would young or old consider it a high honor to be represented in the final scene by that bawd and notorious queen of malapropisms, Mistress Quickly. Granted, her role is sanitized here in comparison to her role in *1 Henry IV* but not enough to render her appearance as Fairy Queen at *Merry Wives*' conclusion a fitting court compliment. The ease with which Shakespeare could have avoided this embarrassment, and his failure to do so, further subverts the compliment thesis. Nor do the play's two lines on the Fairy Queen imply the commendation that Green and others claim; they simply observe that, in the context of a concern with good housewifery and cleanliness, "Our radiant Queen hates sluts and sluttery" (5.5.46).

The Elizabeth-Garter connection is equally suspect. The 1602 Quarto title page advertises the performance of the play "Both before her Maiestie, and else-where." Combining that information with the Folio Garter references, Green concludes that the play's first performance could have occurred only during a year such as 1597 when Elizabeth attended the Garter ceremony, since it is "hard to believe that the Quarto reference to presentation 'before her Maiestie' can apply to aught but the first performance."[20] But there is simply no reason to conclude that the performance for the queen and the Garter ceremony occurred at the same time, especially since presentations before the queen were often received by her representative. For example, at the 1595 Garter Feast, William Brooke represented Elizabeth: "At this table sat Mylord Cobham all alone, who at this festival had to represent the Queen. He was also served and waited upon exactly as if Her Majesty had been present in person."[21]

The reliance of the occasionalist argument on hearsay further undermines its credibility. John Dennis informed us in 1702 that Elizabeth commanded Shakespeare to write *Merry Wives* in a fortnight.[22] Yet Dennis later revised "fortnight" to "ten days" without explanation, and he had a personal and financial stake in circulating this story; he promulgated the rumor only after the resounding failure of *The Comical Gallant,* his stage revision of *Merry Wives.* In a dedication to his play, Dennis writes that his ill-wishers had believed the original "to be so admirable, that nothing ought to be added to it; the others fancied it to be so despicable, that any ones time would be lost on it."[23] Only in this context does he circulate the news that the play had found favor with Queen Elizabeth. In 1709 Nicholas Rowe embellished the rumor begun by Dennis: according to Rowe, the queen was so pleased with Falstaff in the *Henry IV* plays that she personally asked Shakespeare to write a play about Falstaff in love.[24] Like so many rumors, this one doesn't square with the facts as we know them. No evidence for such personal requests exists, and if it did, one would need to explain why Shakespeare refused to fulfill Elizabeth's demand, since *Merry Wives* never portrays Falstaff in love. And if Elizabeth so enjoyed the Falstaff of *1* and *2 Henry IV,* why would Shakespeare write her a sequel in which both Falstaff and Mistress Quickly have new and different backgrounds and ways of speaking and fail to recognize one another? If Shakespeare wrote *Merry Wives* before completing *2 Henry IV*—as Oliver and Roberts contend—then Rowe's account, which places Elizabeth's request after *2 Henry IV,* must be discredited.[25]

Acceptance of the 1597 argument also requires that we discount a much-respected vehicle for dating Shakespeare's plays, since Francis Meres's 1598 *Palladis Tamia: Wit's Treasury* never mentions *Merry Wives.*[26] While a single play might have slipped Meres's attention, court entertainment was news rather than gossip, and thus hard to avoid. If the play had been performed at the 1597 Garter Feast, knowledge of it could only with exceeding difficulty have escaped the attention of someone who resided in London in 1597 and who was composing a list of Shakespearean plays in 1598. Green attributes *Merry Wives'* absence from this list to Meres's preference for symmetry over accuracy; but surely this argument is strained.[27] It is unlikely that a play written and performed for the queen at a public occasion the year before Mere's list was composed would have been omitted from it.

The use of a single topical reference to fix a date of composition is itself suspect, but Green's contention that the Garter lines are extraneous to the action of the play undermines his own argument.[28] Further, since most editors believe that both the Quarto and Folio offer later, revised versions of the play, neither can provide decisive evidence for its original date and place of composition. Yet Green treats the occasionalist theory as a matter of fact and continually refers to *Merry Wives* as "presented as a salute to the Order of the Garter."[29] And scholars continue to treat this fictional event as historical fact, although it is just as fantastic as David Scott's 1840 "portrait" of Elizabeth viewing *The Merry Wives of Windsor.. . .*[30]

IV

Ironically, Green, in his effort to strengthen Hotson's argument, brings forth a considerable body of evidence that actually undermines it. When Green refurbishes Hotson's argument, he deletes those aspects of it that were dependent on the much-disparaged Justice Shallow-satire theory and unearths additional Garter information to situate the play in the context of British politics and trade relations. The diplomatic material he points to offers new evidence against the occasionalists.

Hotson's genius was to connect the play's Garter references with its allusions to a German duke. Three such allusions occur in the play: Bardolph tells the Host that "the [Germans desire] to have three of your horses. The Duke himself will be to-morrow at court"; the Host replies: "What duke should that be comes so secretly? I hear not of him in the court" (4.3.1-5); and Dr. Caius later mockingly informs the Host: "it is tell-a me dat you make grand preparation for a duke de Jamany. By my trot, dere is no duke that the court is know to come" (4.5.86-89). The German duke had already been identified by Charles Knight as Frederick, Count Mompelgard, later duke of Wurtemberg, based on the Quarto's variant "three sorts of cosen garmombles" (TLN 1364) for the Folio's "three cozen-germans" (4.5.79).[31] Hotson reasoned that since both Count Mompelgard and Lord Hunsdon were elected to the Garter in the spring of 1597, the play must have been written for that occasion.

While the evidence for a connection between Shakespeare's text and Hunsdon's election is unpersuasive,[32] the Mompelgard allusions cannot be ignored. Notorious for his efforts to be elected an English Garter Knight, Count Mompelgard was addressed by Elizabeth as "cozen," and so was at once a "duke de Jamany," a cousin germane or German relative, and a cozening German with a well-known and particularly outrageous connection to the Garter ceremonies. In 1592, after a visit with Elizabeth, Frederick somehow misconstrued her language as a promise of election to the English Order of the Garter. On his return home he actually had coins struck anticipating his election as a Garter Knight. In vain he yearly sent letters, bribes, and embassies to achieve his goal. The stream of requests ended in October 1597, when the count was informed he had been named a Knight-Elect, but started up again the following year as he sought the official investiture that Elizabeth continued to withhold. James was left to foot the costly bill for Frederick's investiture in 1603 and for his final installation in 1604. Oliver claims: "The theory that

The Merry Wives of Windsor was written for the Garter Feast in 1597 . . . alone makes sense of allusions in the play [to Mompelgard] that were first discussed by Charles Knight."[33] But since Frederick was annoying the crown over Garter matters from as early as 1592 to as late as 1603, a better argument for a 1597 date needs to be advanced, and the conflicting evidence more closely explored.

The economic and diplomatic basis of Garter elections, and especially of Mompelgard's election in 1597, strongly undermines the hypothesis of a Garter-related satire in 1597. We know that Elizabeth wisely reserved Garter elections for economic purposes and therefore held out as long as possible before each election, investiture, and installation. Less important than the difficulty that Frederick, like others, experienced in waiting for formal Garter ceremonies are the economic conditions that resulted in his election in 1597.[34] Green correctly observes that for over a decade Frederick spent considerable sums of money in order to be elected to the Garter. But in February 1597, a letter to Cecil from Dr. Christopher Parkins, Elizabeth's advisor on German relations, requesting that either Frederick or some other German prince be favored for diplomatic reasons achieved the coveted election within two months.[35] In 1596 one Garter member had nominated Frederick; in 1597 Frederick was unanimously nominated and elected. The letter seems to have done the trick. Green draws the logical conclusion that "Frederick was elected to the Order out of sheer political expediency," and he marshals ample evidence to prove this point.[36] But if the diplomatic nature of the 1597 Garter election be granted, the real question is why Elizabeth would commission a play that insults Frederick at the very ceremony where she sought to honor him.

Frederick's absence from the 1597 ceremonies is often pointed to by occasionalists to answer this complaint. But since Garter affairs were diplomatic in nature and since news about what happened at these feasts was common knowledge, Frederick's absence by no means licenses the theory that a satire about him was performed at the Garter Feast. Nor does the repeated misreading of "What duke should that be comes so secretly" bolster this argument. Oliver and others contend that this line is an insiders' joke which refers to the fact that Frederick did not arrive—secretly or otherwise—because he was not informed of his election in time to attend the Garter ceremony.[37] But a funnier and more convincing reading is offered by his envoy's journal, which reminds us that, on separate occasions more than three years apart, both Frederick and later his envoy Hans Jacob Breuning von Buchenbach did in fact arrive secretly at Elizabeth's court and wreaked much havoc as a result. In 1592, Frederick arrived unannounced at London for lengthy court visits and caused numerous problems, as well as unintended comic entertainment for the court. Three years later Breuning arrived in London not only unannounced but in disguise. Breuning's journal, which neither Oliver nor Roberts uses,[38] also clarifies another line misinterpreted by the occasionalists. Quickly's refrain,

"Out upon it! what have I forgot?" (1.4.165), need not refer, as is claimed, to Elizabeth's 1597 omission of Frederick's invitation; a more convincing reading connects it to Elizabeth's 1595 statement—reported by an overwrought Breuning—that she had no memory of any promise to Frederick: "It amazes me that you so often, both now and on the last occasion, make mention of my promise. . . . But to speak truth, I have not the least recollection of ever having made any such promise."[39]

Green claims that a "study of each of the Feasts from 1593 to 1601 reveals that not one of them—except that of 1597—offered the proper circumstances for the special composition and presentation of the *Merry Wives*."[40] But the evidence Green finds should have led him to conclude that 1597 was just as unlikely an occasion. In fact the strained state of English-German trade relations that Green uncovers explains precisely why 1597 is an especially unlikely date for a play satirizing the Germans in general and Frederick in particular. On 22 July/1 August 1597, Emperor Rudolph II banned all English merchants from Germany.[41] The ever-politic Elizabeth withheld retaliation until January 1598, at which time she formally banished all German merchants from England.[42] This further confirms spring 1597 as a time of much-needed foreign diplomacy. During the mid- to late 1590s, a satire on cozening Germans would have been welcome on the public stage; any time after January 1598 would have been ideal; at the spring 1597 Garter ceremonies alone, however, such a performance would have been problematic.

In sum, the Mompelgard argument is indeed convincing, and ample evidence exists to suggest a parallel between Frederick and Falstaff in the public imagination. Both ludicrous, pompous fools are baited by women whose scorn and delay in turn reduce them to objects of public ridicule. But 1597 would have been the only year when this parallel would not have been tenable, since it is the only year when Elizabeth was not fooling Frederick but rewarding him. Between 1592 and 1596 Frederick was baited with election; between 1598 and 1602 he was baited with investiture; and between 1602 and 1603 he was baited with installation. Only in 1597 was he not being baited at all. Given the satirical mode of *Merry Wives*, then, the weight of probability is against a spring 1597 Garter-commissioned performance.

V

The possibility that *Merry Wives* was originally composed for a public audience familiar with Garter events has never been entertained, even though it is far more plausible than the court occasionalist argument. Peter Erickson has studied "the double appeal of the Garter ceremony to both elite and public" as "particularly pertinent to the theme of class reconciliation in *The Merry Wives of Windsor*, for it counters the notion that a popular audience could have no interest in Garter lore pertaining exclusively to aristocratic need and suggests instead a convergence of classes around an all-purpose symbol." But Erickson does not question the court occasionalist argument, nor does he consider the Garter material to be interpolated.[43]

Breuning's journal proves that popular knowledge of *Merry Wives'* topical references extended well beyond Garter affairs. Not only does Breuning describe the popular audience outside the 1595 Garter Feast he attended,[44] but he describes in detail how his disastrous adventures in London were received by "high and low." No sooner did Bruening arrive in London to win Frederick's election to the Garter than he discovered, while dining at a local pub, that a fellow German named Stamler had been passing himself off as Frederick's envoy in an attempt to export cloth duty free. Breuning decides to take on the case before negotiating for Frederick's election and writes to Frederick: "I was of the opinion that this unpleasant affair must first of all be settled and removed from our path; the more so because both high and low spoke so contemptuously and derisively of it, and he [Stamler] by his demands had alienated from us the prominent men." Disguised "in very homely garb and unrecognized," Breuning met with Stamler at the White Swan tavern. Breuning's efforts to resolve the Stamler affair on his own were notorious; his attempts to resolve the affair with Essex's help further problematized his efforts to bribe courtiers into electing Frederick to the Garter. Breuning complains that the Stamler case "was the daily topic at table, on 'Change, and . . . talked of at Court with so much contempt, reproach and opprobrium that I was hurt to the quick and could not sleep of nights."

In the late 1590s Breuning was a more logical choice and a much easier target for a topical satire than was Frederick, who had not visited England since 1592. This stranger to court with the terribly funny name—Buchenbach—daily wrote an unending stream of letters (in triplicate, as did Falstaff) to further his aims. He also outraged many Londoners with his attempts to make purchases and to borrow money and was forced to admit that they perceived him as "a very suspicious character."[45] Not only did he travel widely over the English countryside, but he apparently offended the town of Windsor by his unexpected decision not to stay overnight at the local inn where he had dined.[46] This explains the frustrated response of *Merry Wives'* Windsor Inn Host, who had made such great preparation in honor of a "duke de Jamany." Breuning also acted badly at table over precedence. At the 1595 Garter Feast he created havoc by refusing to sit down to dinner unless seated above Count Philip of Solms, envoy to the Landgrave Maurice of Hesse. Yet in his report to Frederick, he proudly recounted each gaffe as a diplomatic triumph: "Before we had risen from table this scene, as I was afterwards reliably informed, was reported to Her Majesty and to all the Knights and bruited about at Court. The English nobles who waited upon us put their heads together and did not know what to make of the whole business. . . . And so henceforth I was held in higher esteem by the English than ever before, as *not only the Court but all London* busied itself with the affair" (my emphasis).[47]

Whether or not Breuning's peculiar behavior is later caricatured in *Merry Wives'* Cousin Slender, who also refuses to sit down to dinner, or in his Uncle Shallow's behavior over precedence and courtesy, need not be answered decisively. Annabel Patterson persuasively argues that it was both more common and certainly a wiser practice for Renaissance dramatists to avoid the one-to-one correspondence of personal satire in favor of a more complex functional ambiguity.[48] Arguments that *Merry Wives* cannot be "about" Frederick because it is "about" some other noteworthy figure—whether Breuning, Essex, Brooke, or Monsieur de Chastes—ignore the way in which Elizabethan authors protected themselves from censorship by conflating a variety of sources and incidents. It is far more likely that the "garmombles" who fool a Windsor host conflate caricatures of Frederick, who sought revenge on the Garter; of the French representative de Chastes, who stole post-horses to attend a 1596 Garter celebration; of Breuning, who cozened a Windsor innkeeper; and of Germans in general, who were widely perceived as having duped the British in trade relations. Since "both high and low" knew of these affairs, there is every reason to suppose that *Merry Wives* was written to be performed on the public stage.

Curiously, Green argues against an April 1600 Garter performance of *Merry Wives* precisely because Monsieur de Chastes stood in for the French king, Henri IV, at the Windsor installation: "On the surface it may appear that the *Merry Wives* conceivably could have been part of that great and magnificent entertainment. But Monsieur de Chastes is the same French envoy who became involved in a major post-horse scandal on September 4, 1596. . . . The circumstances surrounding this incident are so startlingly similar to those described in the fourth act horse-stealing subplot of the *Merry Wives* that . . . I believe the affair served as the prototype for the subplot."[49] Here Green repeats J. Crofts's argument, peremptorily dismissed by Oliver and Roberts, that *Merry Wives'* post-horse scene, widely thought to be abridged or censored in both Q and F, played on a well-known post-horse crisis.[50] In 1596 de Chastes was rushing back to France for a reception for the English, who had just honored his king with a Garter election. Unable to procure a horse, he stole horses belonging to private travelers and took them beyond the appointed posts. News of the affair, which wrought havoc with the English transportation system, spread quickly and was well publicized. Green argues: "that Shakespeare would knowingly mirror an unpleasant incident in the life of an individual of the stature of de Chastes is beyond the wildest imagination." Yet it is precisely de Chastes's stature, the inappropriateness of this episode, and the texts' confused state, that invites the hypothesis that the scene was censored.[51] That Edmond Tyllney would censor a hit at de Chastes is particularly likely given his own diplomatic and Garter-related work. In *Edmond Tyllney, Master of the Revels and Censor of Plays: A Descriptive Index to His Diplomatic Manual on Europe,* W.R. Streitberger provides ample proof that Tyllney would be especially sensitive to ambassadors' perceptions of plays and all too aware of who was being mocked and when. Tyllney's *Topographical Descriptions,* primarily designed as an overview of foreign policy, included much information essential to diplomatic relations. Streitberger points out that the lord chamberlain and his aides entertained foreign ambassadors due to the lack of a master of ceremonies and adds: "No doubt Tyllney was called upon to help in this matter."[52] Crofts's argument for the importance of the de Chastes affair thus deserves a new hearing.[53]

Further indications of a popular audience for *Merry Wives* emerge from the study of such textual variants as the Quarto's repeated identification of the Folio's wise woman of Brainford as Gillian of Brainford. Robert Copland's *Gyl of Brainfords Testament* offers a less likely source for this character's popularity and name recognition in the late 1590s than does the title of a play purchased by Henslowe in 1599.[54] Henslowe's diary entry reads: "Lent vnto Thomas dowton & samwell Redly [Rowley] the 10 of febreary 1598 to bye A boocke called fryer fox & gyllen of branforde."[55] The interaction between a citizen wife and one Sir John (a term for a friar) may provide a basis for future study. References to Gyllen of Branford in plays of the early 1600s, such as Dekker and Webster's 1604 *Westward Ho!,* further underline the probability that this character's currency with popular audiences would have been more likely after 1597.

VI

The most likely direction for further research is provided by the work of Melchiori, Taylor, and Hibbard—all of whom contend, based on the dating of the Henriad, that *Merry Wives* recycled rather than anticipated the 1597 Garter events.[56] The most convincing argument to date is Gary Taylor's theory for a February 1598 date of composition and performance:

> Hotson's dating of *Merry Wives,* though plausible, remains conjectural, and by pushing the composition of *1 Henry IV* back into 1596 it further cramps the chronology for 1595-6, and leaves 1597-8 by comparison relatively empty. If we abandon the 1597 Garter Feast as the play's origin and occasion, then *1 Henry IV* could have been written in 1597 (after the death of William Brooke, Lord Cobham, briefly Lord Chamberlain, whose title descended from Oldcastle), and performed at court early in the Christmas season of 1597-8 (where the Chamberlain's Men played on 26 December, 1 and 6 January). The censorship could have occurred at that time, and Queen Elizabeth's request for a play on Falstaff in love could have been made in anticipation of a later court performance that Whitehall season (on 26 February). The officially instigated publication of *1 Henry IV,* in order to advertise the change of Sir John's name, would then have followed very soon after the censorship itself.[57]

A February 1598 date would capitalize on English hostility toward German merchants, who had been expelled from London the month before. It also suggests an intriguing connection with the January 1598 performance of an unidentified comedy performed by Shakespeare's company and reported by the French ambassador, Monsieur de Maisse.[58] This date confirms Eliot Slater's rare-vocabulary test, which places *Merry Wives* in close proximity to *2 Henry IV.*[59] Finally, an early 1598 date for Shakespeare's play would provide a more reasonable connection to Henslowe's 10 February 1599 purchase of the book called "fryer fox & gyllen of branforde"; to his 31 January 1599 purchase of "tafetie for ij womones gownes for the ij angrey wemen of abengton";[60] and to other dramatists' references to Gyllen of Branford in early 1600.

The consequences of undermining the 1597 occasionalist argument in favor of a 1598 date of composition are more far-reaching than might at first appear. Not only should it demolish the myth of Shakespeare's occasionalist plays, of which *Merry Wives* is the last remaining example, but it should help to resolve arguments concerning which Brooke family member complained about the use of Oldcastle; could influence current debates on the dating of the Henriad and of Jonson's *Every Man in His Humour;* and may suggest new areas of research into the tradition of two-wives and humors comedies.[61] For example, the later date undermines the reasoning behind theories that the Brooke/Broome change was made at the same time as the Oldcastle/Falstaff change and that *Merry Wives* is an attack on the elder Brooke.[62] "The play would still have been written with a court performance in mind," Taylor explains, "honouring by allusion the company's patron, and satirizing by contrast Henry Brooke, the new Lord Cobham, who would have been instrumental in the censorship of *1 Henry IV.*"[63] Since the elder Cobham died on 6 March 1597, it is unlikely that Shakespeare would spoof Brooke for Elizabeth in April, a month after Brooke's death.

A 1598 date for *Merry Wives* places the conflict between Essex and the younger Brooke, and this context receives further backing given the notorious hostility between the two men.[64] And Essex's references to the younger Brooke as Falstaff make sense only in this context. Essex adds an amusing postscript in a 1598 letter to Sir Robert Cecil: "I pray you commend me allso to Alex. Ratcliff and tell him for newes his sister is maryed to S[r] Jo. Falstaff"; a 1599 letter written by Elizabeth Wriothsley, Countess of Southampton, reads: "Al the nues I can send you that I thinke wil make you mery is that I reade in a letter from London that Sir John Falstaf is by his M[rs] Dame Pintpot made father of a godly milers thum, a boye thats all heade and veri litel body; but this is a secirt."[65] Hotson has convincingly supported the thesis that these references are to Henry Brooke, the younger Cobham; that it was he who was referred to as Falstaff by Essex; he who was interested in Margaret Ratcliff (much to her brother's concern); and he who, in the spring of 1599, was rumored to have fathered a little cob (since cob, like miller's thumb, also refers to a small fish with a large head). That he was also rumored to have been interested in marrying Sir John Spencer's daughter may be relevant; Hotson considers his interest in the countess of Kildare, daughter to the lord admiral, in terms of the Admiral's Men's *Oldcastle* play.[66] That Breuning sought to bribe Brooke and that Essex was the chief officer involved in resolving many of the problems Breuning raised point to a further connection. Finally, if *1 Henry IV* were speedily published to advertise the name change from Oldcastle to Falstaff, this might explain *Merry Wives'* unsuccessful efforts to relate its characters to the Henriad.

What is at least indisputable is that too much of this mess was known to the public, that the Brooke family's sensitivity was itself cause for public gossip and humor, and that *Merry Wives* inevitably played on popular knowledge of this fiasco. Instead of treating topicality as merely reflecting contemporary incidents, we may consider its power to influence them. Just as the Oldcastle saga continued to plague the Brooke family, confusing and interrelating life and art, so the difficulty we experience in pinning down *Merry Wives'* date of composition may reflect how the Mompelgard saga served as local humor. With Frederick pestering the court for over a decade, the affair probably became increasingly humorous and outlandish, encouraging further improvisation and revision of the play itself. *Merry Wives* depended on and contributed to the local knowledge of this affair, and so not only reflected but helped to shape popular Elizabethan culture. Pierre Bourdieu's strategy of "making use of indeterminacy" provides a useful model for making use of topical indeterminacy in this play; it reminds us that the conditions under which a play is performed in turn may become a condition of its performance, as in much ritual action.[67]

For their epigraph to *Shakespeare's Plays in Quarto,* Michael Allen and Kenneth Muir lift a line from the Folio *Merry Wives:* "I warrant he hath a thousand of these letters, writ with blank space for different names (sure, more!); and these are of the second edition" (2.1.74-77). The tell-tale line accurately glosses what we must surmise of the history of the always already divided text that is *Merry Wives.* Blank spaces can express both anonymity and particularity, both an emptiness and a determined inclusiveness. Such anticipatory receptivity alone ensures that the local and the specific will survive and flourish. The ability of *Merry Wives* to withstand alteration and censorship, to append itself to the vogue of humors comedy and to the Henriad alike, to capitalize on local events and to rewrite them suggests that its topicality functions less as a liability than as a survival strategy. By emphasizing the particular, the daily, and the unexpected, this comedy inscribes an improvisational power and topicality not only open but attentive to the restraints and revisions of performance realities. In the face of such evidence, Shakespearean scholars may want to rethink how consensus can drive "the grossness of the foppery into a receiv'd belief, in despite of the teeth of all rhyme and reason" and "how wit may be made a Jack-a-Lent, when 'tis upon ill employment!" (5.5.124-29).

Notes

1. Most influential in the return to local readings has been the work of David Bevington, *Tudor Drama*

and Politics: A Critical Approach to Topical Meaning (Cambridge, MA, 1968); and, more recently, Leah S. Marcus, *Puzzling Shakespeare: Local Reading and Its Discontents* (Berkeley, 1988). All recent studies of Shakespeare's multiple-text plays are deeply indebted to Steven Urkowitz's *Shakespeare's Revision of* King Lear (Princeton, 1980); and to *The Division of the Kingdoms: Shakespeare's Two Versions of "King Lear,"* Gary Taylor and Michael Warren, eds. (Oxford, 1983). See also Warren, "Textual Problems, Editorial Assertions in Editions of Shakespeare" in *Textual Criticism and Literary Interpretation,* Jerome J. McGann, ed. (Chicago, 1985), 23-37; Urkowitz, "Reconsidering the Relationship of Quarto and Folio Texts of *Richard III,"* *English Literary Renaissance* 16 (1986): 442-66; and Annabel Patterson, "Back by Popular Demand: The Two Versions of *Henry V,"* *Renaissance Drama* 19 (1988): 29-62. For a critique of work in this area, see Richard Knowles's review of Urkowitz in *Modern Philology* 79 (1981): 197-200, and his review of Warren and Taylor, titled "The Case for two *Lears,"* in *Shakespeare Quarterly* 36 (1985): 115-20; see also Marion Trousdale, "A Trip Through the Divided Kingdoms," *SQ* 37 (1986): 218-23.

2. Quotations of quarto texts are from *Shakespeare's Plays in Quarto: A Facsimile Edition of Copies Primarily from the Henry E. Huntington Library,* ed. Michael J. B. Allen and Kenneth Muir (Berkeley, 1981); quotations of through-line numbers are from the 1910 edition of the 1602 Quarto *Merry Wives,* ed. W.W. Greg (Oxford, 1910); other quotations follow the *Riverside Shakespeare,* ed. G. Blakemore Evans (Boston, 1974).

3. In *Shakespeare and the Post-Horses: A new study of The Merry Wives of Windsor* (University of Bristol Studies 5 [Bristol, 1937]), J. Crofts surveys the history of critical opinion on this matter: "All authorities are therefore agreed that the two texts are derived in some way from a common original" (51). In their introduction to the Cambridge edition of *Merry Wives* (Cambridge, 1921), Arthur Quiller-Couch and J. Dover Wilson explain that Q is "so eminently a Bad Quarto that every editor finds himself inflexibly driven back upon the Folio version. . . . And yet he must be constantly collating: since, bad though it so obviously is, at any moment out of the Quarto's chaos some chance line, phrase or word may emerge to fill a gap or correct a misprint in the better text" (xi). In his 1910 edition of the 1602 Quarto *Merry Wives,* W.W. Greg contends, in regard to a Folio/Quarto line variant in *Merry Wives,* that "both readings are unquestionably genuine Shakespeare. I think there can be little doubt that we have to do with a case of revision" (67, n. 467). Yet oddly, William Green maintains in *Shakespeare's* The Merry Wives of Windsor (Princeton, 1962) that "there is no basis for the supposition that both the Q and F texts stem from a common original. The F text is, with minor

modifications, the authoritative version of the *Merry Wives,* and basically represents the script played at the 1597 Feast of the Garter" (102). In "Another Masque for *The Merry Wives of Windsor*" (*SQ* 3 [1952]: 39-43), John H. Long argues that Shakespeare wrote both the Q (for Elizabeth) and F (for James) conclusions. For a sustained argument that Q is an abridgment of F, see William Bracy, The Merry Wives of Windsor: *The History and Transmission of Shakespeare's Text* (Columbia, MO, 1952). The theory that Folio/Quarto variants are the result of authorial revision, possibly in the interests of two separate audiences, goes back at least as far as Alexander Pope.

4. Elizabeth Schafer does, however, touch on this point in "The Date of *The Merry Wives of Windsor,*" *Notes & Queries* 38 (1991): 57-60. In this succinct but cogent argument, Schafer contends: "The 1597 dating argument generally depends on speculation rather than proof; it seems to have become orthodoxy mainly because it has been repeated so many times— and certainly the Garter connection and the links with *2 Henry IV* offer no solid support for dating *Merry Wives* 1597" (60).

5. The so-called "consensus" on Leslie Hotson's occasionalist reading of *Merry Wives* in *Shakespeare versus Shallow* (London, 1931) has received backing from two separate camps: first, Green's development of Hotson's thesis, in *Shakespeare's* The Merry Wives of Windsor, and Jeanne Addison Roberts's reception of Green's argument, in *Shakespeare's English Comedy:* The Merry Wives of Windsor *in Context* (Lincoln NE, and London, 1979); and, second, H.J. Oliver's quite different reception of Hotson in his introduction to the Arden edition of *Merry Wives* (London, 1971). Peter Erickson's "The Order of the Garter, the Cult of Elizabeth, and class-gender tension in *The Merry Wives of Windsor*" (in *Shakespeare Reproduced: The text in history and ideology,* Jean E. Howard and Marion F. O'Connor, eds. [New York and London, 1987], 116-40) is the first essay to argue persuasively for "the double appeal of the Garter ceremony to both elite and public" (127). Erickson, however, never questions the ideological implications of the 1597 occasionalist dating. Valuable treatments of the Quarto which also fail to challenge the 1597 date include Steven Urkowitz's "Good News about 'Bad' Quartos" (in *"Bad" Shakespeare: Revaluations of the Shakespeare Canon,* Maurice Charney, ed. [London and Toronto, 1988], 189-206, esp. 193-96), and, more recently, Leah S. Marcus's "Levelling Shakespeare: Local Customs and Local Texts" (*SQ* 42 [1991]: 168-78), where she adopts the 1597 dating for the court version without addressing the question of the dating of the popular version and observes: "I have no quarrel with this account of the Folio's [1597 Garter] occasion" (173).

6. In *Tudor Drama and Politics,* Bevington explains: "Regular plays . . . were financed by a theatrical audience. The patron offered nominal protection in return for sporadic services; he did not commission the work. For these reasons it is unsafe to assume that plays like . . . *The Merry Wives of Windsor* fostered individual campaigns of flattery and begging on behalf of certain courtiers, as did the courtly entertainment. And in fact no Tudor document exists to demonstrate such a condition of performance" (10). And yet, as Annabel Patterson notes in *Shakespeare and the Popular Voice* (London, 1989), the occasionalist myth persists in scholarly responses to plays such as *A Midsummer Night's Dream:* "Despite the difficulty that critics experience in finding an appropriate marital occasion during 1595-6, and an uneasy recognition that the play seems rather to *problematize* than celebrate marriage, it is somewhat alarming to see how readily this hypothesis has been absorbed as fact into texts designed for students" (58). Although Patterson points to Wolfgang Clemen's introduction to the Signet edition of *A Midsummer Night's Dream* (New York, 1963), we might note here that Green's introduction to the Signet edition of *The Merry Wives of Windsor* (New York, 1965) exemplifies the same pattern.

7. In their introduction Quiller-Couch and Wilson correctly describe the Bad Quarto as "one of the most tantalising in the whole canon"; when they later casually refer to its "naughtiness," they demonstrate how textuality recapitulates morality (vii and xi). In *Shakespeare and the Popular Voice,* Patterson argues that preference for the courtly folio readings of Shakespearean texts over more popular quarto readings constitutes as much as it reflects an ideologically based class preference. Her thesis appears to be borne out by such comments as Oliver's: "Behind the Quarto text, then, there would seem to be *The Merry Wives* that was designed for an audience not aristocratic and not primarily intellectual, whereas the full Folio text has much that would appeal only to the more sophisticated. Here perhaps lies also the explanation of the main differences between the two forms of the final scene" (xxx). Since the Quarto offers a much funnier, more dramatic, and more drawnout discovery and punishment of Falstaff, and since the Folio ending is not really intellectual but actually includes more elaborate song and dance, scholarly preference for this "sophisticated," "aristocratic," and "intellectual" ending exemplifies the class ideology of textual studies.

8. Oliver, ed., xlv.

9. See, for example, Ralph Berry, *Shakespeare's Comedies: Explorations in Form* (Princeton, 1972), 146; Alexander Leggatt, *Citizen Comedy in the Age of Shakespeare* (Toronto, 1973), 7; and Leo Salingar, *Shakespeare and the Traditions of Comedy* (Cambridge, 1974), 228. In the section on "Chronology and Sources" in the Riverside edition of *Merry Wives,* Evans describes *Merry Wives* as composed in 1597 and revised c. 1600-1601 and attributes the re-

dating to Hotson and the support of that redating to Oliver: "Until relatively recently *Merry Wives* was regularly dated 1601-2, but Hotson's suggestion . . . [regarding dating] is being more and more strongly supported (see New Arden ed.)" (52). More recently, Yoshiko Kawachi, in *A Calendar of English Renaissance Drama 1558-1642* (New York and London, 1986), has also credited Hotson.

10. Review of the Arden *The Merry Wives of Windsor, Shakespeare Studies* 8 (1975): 419-25, esp. 423.

11. Roberts, 50.

12. See G.R. Hibbard's introduction to the New Penguin edition of *The Merry Wives of Windsor* (Middlesex, UK, 1973), 47-50; Gary Taylor, "The Canon and Chronology of Shakespeare's Plays" in Stanley Wells and Gary Taylor, with John Jowett and William Montgomery, *William Shakespeare: A Textual Companion* (Oxford, 1987), 120; Giorgio Melchiori, "Which Falstaff in Windsor" in *KM80: A Birthday Album for Kenneth Muir,* comp. Philip Edwards (Liverpool, UK, 1987), 98-100; and Melchiori's introduction to the New Cambridge edition of *The Second Part of King Henry IV* (Cambridge, 1989), 5. The fact that these arguments have not been integrated is especially disturbing when contradictions occur within the same text. Evans confirms a 1597 date in his section on chronology in the Riverside Shakespeare (52), and yet Anne Barton's introduction to the play in the same volume is noncommittal at best; she summarizes the controversy, raises questions that seem designed to catch the 1597 camp off guard, and concludes: "For some commentators, the idea is palpably absurd; for others, it represents an entirely plausible account of what happened" (287). In the section on chronology in *A Textual Companion,* Gary Taylor argues for a date of 1598 (120); in the section on the play (approved by Taylor) in the same volume, John Jowett refers to "the recorded court performance of 1597 for which the play was probably commissioned" (341). And the Oxford Shakespeare, also edited by Gary Taylor and Stanley Wells, confirms the 1597 dating (see *William Shakespeare: The Complete Works* [Oxford, 1986]). In the introduction to his Oxford Shakespeare edition of *The Merry Wives of Windsor* (Oxford, 1993), T.W. Craik strongly supports the 1597 occasionalist argument. Indeed the paperback edition's back cover enticingly claims: "*The Merry Wives of Windsor* was almost certainly required at short notice for a court occasion in 1597." Craik approvingly refers to "the consensus of the majority of scholars that *The Merry Wives of Windsor* was written for the Garter Feast of 23 April 1597" (27) and states, despite evidence to the contrary (see note 57), that Gary Taylor "accepts the generally agreed date of 23 April 1597 for the first performance" (10).

13. The divided reception of Green's 1962 book is typical of divisions within the occasionalist camp; Oliver

concludes that "Green's *Shakespeare's 'Merry Wives of Windsor'* tries to build on Hotson's argument but adds little to it" (xlv, n. 3); in contrast Roberts finds "Green's thesis . . . convincingly defended" (36). For other significant disagreements between Oliver and Roberts, see notes 25 and 61. Other problems with the occasionalist argument are noted by scholars who endorsed 1600 after Hotson and before the 1970s revival of his argument; see W.W. Greg's review of Leslie Hotson's *Shakespeare versus Shallow* in *Modern Language Review* 27 (1932): 218-21, esp. 220; Greg, *The Shakespeare First Folio: Its Bibliographical and Textual History* (Oxford, 1955), 337; *The Complete Works of Shakespeare,* ed. George Lyman Kittredge (Boston, 1936), 63; James G. McManaway, "Recent Studies in Shakespeare's Chronology," *Shakespeare Survey* 3 (1950): 22-33, esp. 29; E. K. Chambers, *William Shakespeare: A Study of Facts and Problems,* 2 vols. (Oxford, 1951), 1:434; Fredson Bowers's introduction to the Penguin *Merry Wives of Windsor* (Baltimore, 1963), 17; J. M. Nosworthy, *Shakespeare's Occasional Plays: Their Origin and Transmission* (London, 1965), 88. Since the 1970s revival, the New Penguin dating remains committed to 1600. See also Schafer's compelling arguments against 1597.

14. Edmond Malone, *The Plays and Poems of William Shakspeare . . . ,* 10 vols. (London, 1790), 1:329.

15. For additional Garter information, see Elias Ashmole, *The Institution, Lawes & Ceremonies* Of the most Noble *Order of the Garter* (London, 1672); and *Memorials of the Most Noble Order of the Garter,* ed. George Frederick Beltz (London, 1841; rpt. New York, 1973), which contains Elizabeth's 1567 decree effectively reserving Windsor for installations rather than for feast days (ciii-civ). For recent work on the Garter, see Roy Strong, "Saint George For England: The Order of the Garter," *The Cult of Elizabeth: Elizabethan Portraiture and Pageantry* (Wallop, UK, 1977), 164-86; and Arthur B. Ferguson, *The Chivalric Tradition in Renaissance England* (Washington, DC, 1986).

16. In *Shakespeare versus Shallow,* Hotson refers to a description of Hunsdon entering the Garter Feast accompanied by three hundred followers (118-19) which was first recorded in *Historical Manuscripts Commission, Report on the Manuscripts of Lord de L'Isle & Dudley Preserved at Penshurst Place,* ed. C.L. Kingsford, 20 vols. (London, 1925-42), 2:265, hereafter cited as *HMC Penshurst.*

17. *The Elizabethan Stage,* 4 vols. (Oxford, 1923), 2:160.

18. *Henslowe's Diary,* ed. R.A. Foakes and R.T. Rickert (Cambridge, 1961), 133.

19. *The Dramatic Works of Thomas Dekker,* ed. Fredson Bowers, 4 vols. (Cambridge, 1953-61), 1:105-206, esp. 113. For representative works written as compliments to Elizabeth, see *The Queen's Garland: Verses Made by her Subjects for Elizabeth I, Queen of*

England Now Collected in Honour of Her Majesty Queen Elizabeth II, ed. M.C. Bradbrook (London, 1953).

20. Green, *Shakespeare's* Merry Wives, 42-43.

21. Quoted in *Queen Elizabeth and Some Foreigners* . . . , ed. Victor von Klarwill, trans. T.H. Nash (London, 1928), 379.

22. In his dedicatory epistle to *The Comical Gallant* (London, 1702), Dennis writes: "That this Comedy was not despicable, I guess'd for several Reasons: First, I knew very well, that it had pleas'd one of the greatest Queens that ever was in the World. . . . This Comedy was written at her Command, and by her direction, and she was so eager to see it Acted, that she commanded it to be finished in fourteen days; and was afterwards, as Tradition tells us, very well pleas'd at the Representation" (i). Dennis reduces the time to ten days in his *Original Letters, Familiar, Moral and Critical,* 2 vols. (London, 1721), 2:232.

23. Dennis, *Comical Gallant,* i.

24. In his "Some Account of the Life of Mr. William Shakespeare" (prefixed to his edition of *The Works of Mr. William Shakespeare,* 6 vols. [London, 1709]), Rowe reports that Elizabeth "was so well pleas'd with that admirable character of *Falstaff,* in the two Parts of *Henry* the Fourth, that she commanded him to continue it for one Play more, and to shew him in Love. This is said to be the Occasion of his Writing *The Merry Wives of* Windsor" (1:viii-ix).

25. In *A New Variorum Edition of the First Part of Henry the Fourth* (Philadelphia, 1936), Samuel Hemingway credits H. N. Paul with having first suggested the precise point at which Shakespeare interrupted his work on *2 Henry IV* in order to compose *Merry Wives* (355). Roberts concurs with Paul; Oliver is noncommittal but finds the theory persuasive; and Green disagrees.

26. For Meres's list, see Chambers, *Elizabethan Stage,* App. C, 4:246.

27. Green, *Shakespeare's* Merry Wives, 209-13.

28. Green finds the Garter lines "completely extraneous to the plot of the play" (10) and maintains that "not one of the Court-Garter passages is essential to the action of the *Merry Wives*" (96). For an opposing view, see Erickson, 126, and note 43 below.

29. Green, *Shakespeare's* Merry Wives, 118.

30. See James Fowler, "David Scott's *Queen Elizabeth Viewing the Performance of the 'Merry Wives of Windsor' in the Globe Theatre (1840)*" in *Shakespeare and the Victorian Stage,* Richard Foulkes, ed. (Cambridge, 1986), 23-38. Oliver hypothesizes that "there was an alternative ending to the play for use— probably on the public stage—when, perhaps, the special occasion for which the original text was prepared was simply not relevant" (xxxii).

31. *The Standard Edition of the Pictorial Shakespeare,* ed. Charles Knight, 7 vols. (London, 1846), 2:143. The Quarto "garmombles" can be read not only as Mompelgard but also as *geremombles,* a term that signified confusion. Thomas Nashe uses *geremumble* as a term of abuse in his *Strange Newes* and his *Lenten Stuff;* see *The Works of Thomas Nashe,* ed. Ronald B. McKerrow, 5 vols. (1904-10; rpt. Oxford, 1958), 1:321 and 3:207. See also J. Douglas Bruce, "Two Notes on 'The Merry Wives of Windsor,'" *MLR* 7 (1912): 239-41.

32. If Hunsdon had commissioned the play, we would expect to find the customary dedication or, at the very least, some reference to him in the play. And the mere fact that Hunsdon borrowed money for the occasion of his election is hardly reason to argue that he also commissioned *Merry Wives;* in fact it raises the question of why he would use those funds to satirize the Garter activities he was so busy promoting.

33. Oliver, ed., xlvi.

34. No less royal a fellow Knight-Elect than France's Henri IV awaited the Garter insignia and investiture a good deal longer; elected in 1590, the king of France was not invested until 1596 and not formally installed at Windsor until 1600. As Green correctly points out, Elizabeth failed to send Henri the insignia until she was negotiating a treaty with France (139).

35. Dr. Christopher Parkins informed Cecil: "advice hath been given that Spain moveth in Denmark and in the Empire to hinder the quiet trade of her Majesty's subjects, wherefore some means is to be thought of for everting this endeavor. . . . As for the Empire, the Hanses use commonly to be the means for the hindering the trade there. . . . Yet if her Majesty send a man to Denmark, he may, as it were by the way, give any of the cities *occasion to become suitors to her for some their good, giving them hope of good success in reasonable requests.* . . . it seemeth convenient that her Majesty deal with some of the Princes of the Empire to that effect, either by letters, either by the man sent to Denmark, as it were by the way saluting them from her Majesty, which may seem the fitter *if there were any other matter wherein they were now especially to be confirmed.* The fittest Princes for like occasions are Breame, Magdiburg, Saxon, Rhene, Hassia and Wirtenberg" (*Historical Manuscripts Commission: Calendar of the Manuscripts of the Most Honorable the Marquis of Salisbury,* 18 vols. [London, 1899], 7:77-78 [my emphasis], hereafter cited as *HMC Salisbury*).

36. Green, *Shakespeare's* Merry Wives, 136. Ample additional material can be found in *HMC Salisbury;* the entire eighteenth volume concerns English foreign policy with France and the Low Countries in the context of the war against Spain. During the spring of 1597, the Spanish were trying to convince the German princes to join with them against the English,

and Hanse trade with England was in great danger. Although Parkins is scheming as early as February, by 15 March he urges particular speed since "The merchants of the East country had yesterday intelligence from Denmark that there is a constant purpose to arrest their ships that shall pass by the Sound" (18:114). The clearest statement of a problem appears in the negotiations between Spain and Lubeck on 1 and 25 June 1597: "First. That the King of Spain is willing the Hances shall, without breach or hindrance, enjoy their privileges, for which purposes his ambassador with the Emperor is very instant that the privileges taken from them by the Queen of England by his means may be restored" (18:271).

37. Oliver, ed., xlvii.

38. Although Geoffrey Bullough quotes extensively from Breuning's journal, he offers only an excerpt from the section on Mompelgard's travels, which may be one reason why scholars have neglected its importance as a source for *Merry Wives;* see *Narrative and Dramatic Sources of Shakespeare,* 8 vols. (New York, 1957-75), 2:13-16 and 44-49.

39. Quoted in von Klarwill, ed., 388, n. 41.

40. Green, *Shakespeare's* Merry Wives, 38.

41. *HMC Salisbury,* 7:307-8.

42. See *Calendar of State Papers, Domestic Series, of the Reign of Elizabeth, 1598-1601,* ed. Mary Anne Everett Green, 13 vols. (London, 1869), 5:5-6.

43. Erickson, 127. He states further: "I contend that the Garter reference is not incidental and anomalous but directly relevant and integral to the play as a whole since the play's concern with courtly forms is part of its overall ambience" (126).

44. Quoted in von Klarwill, ed., 378-79. Roy Strong, citing the official records of the Garter Feast, reports that "by 1592 the crush of people was so great that the ceremonies were held up awaiting the arrival of Knights who had failed to penetrate the throng" (172). In *Letters of Philip Gawdy . . .* (ed. Isaac Herbert Jeayes [London, 1906]), Gawdy records a "great press of people" at the 1594 feast (81-82). Of the 1595 feast, Breuning observes: "There was a great crush in the chapel, as many of the common people had thronged thither"; he writes that the queen, followed by her noblemen and ladies, "marched round the yard three times so that everyone could have a good view of them" and notes that the queen "spoke most graciously to everyone, even to those of the vulgar who fell upon their knees in homage" (81-82).

45. For the preceding quotes from Breuning's journal, see von Klarwill, ed., 400-403.

46. For a description of this event, see Bullough, 2:14.

47. Quoted in von Klarwill, ed., 382-83.

48. *Censorship and Interpretation: The Conditions of Writing and Reading in Early Modern England* (Madison, WI, 1984).

49. Green, *Shakespeare's* Merry Wives, 37.

50. Oliver maintains that Crofts's post-horse theories "have little to recommend them" (xlviii); Roberts terms Crofts's reasoning "inadmissible" (30), and after examining all the theories advanced, she concludes: "One is left with the feeling that the horse-stealing plot is as far as ever from a really satisfactory explanation" (37).

51. Green, *Shakespeare's* Merry Wives, 37. The vast majority of critics, including Green, believe that the status of the scene is fragmentary and unsatisfactory. In Wells and Taylor's *Textual Companion,* Jowett observes of the horse-stealing plot that both Q and F have "an almost unintelligible subplot whose deficiencies cannot be attributed to incomplete foul papers" (341). In both *The Editorial Problem in Shakespeare: A Survey of the Foundations of the Text* (2d ed., [Oxford, 1951]) and in *The Shakespeare First Folio,* Greg regards censorship as a viable explanation (72 and 336-37, respectively). For an unconvincing effort to explain why the post-horse scene is not censored, as well as for a survey of scholarly argument to the contrary, see Green, *Shakespeare's* Merry Wives, 151-76.

52. (New York, 1986), 14. Although Tyllney was never knighted, "the College of Heralds confirmed his official position with knights on 18 March 1600" (11). Streitberger points out that Tyllney's name was suggested by the ambassador from Spain as a possible envoy to Spain, which further indicates his status in diplomatic circles (10).

53. Contemporary documents support Crofts's position. For example, on 29 February 1600, John Chamberlain writes to Dudley Carleton: "We heare there is some great man comming out of France, in shew about the Kinges installation at Windsore, whatsoever other errand he may have in secret" (*Letters Written by John Chamberlain during the Reign of Queen Elizabeth,* ed. Sarah Williams [Westminster, 1861], 68). The French king, Henri IV, is listed in *Memorials of the Most Noble Order of the Garter* as follows: "El. 24 April 1590; inv. 10 Oct. 1596; inst. by proxy 28 April 1600" (clxxxii). In a letter to Sir Robert Sidney dated 26 April 1600, Rowland Whyte observes: "The Feast of St. *George* was solemnised with more then wonted Care, in Regard of Monsieur *Le Chates* being here. . . . This morning, Monsieur *Le Chatre* is gone to *Winsor* to be for the *French* King installed" (*Letters and Memorials of State . . . Faithfully Transcribed from the Originals at Penshurst Place . . . ,* ed. Arthur Collins, 2 vols. [London, 1746], 2:190); on 4 May, de Chastes returned to London to attend an evening feast given by the lord of Shrewsbury at which the tumbler Peter Bromville performed; on 5 May he left for France (2:193). See also *HMC Penshurst,* 2:457.

54. Old-style dating marks the new year at 1 March; I refer to new style whenever possible. See Nashe's references to *Gyl of Brainfords Testament, Newly Compiled* (c. 1560) in McKerrow, ed., 3:235, 314; 4:421; 5:195; and see [Sir John Harrington] *Vlysses upon Aiax* (London, 1596), sig. B4. In his notes to the Yale Shakespeare edition of *The Merry Wives* (New Haven, 1922), George van Santvoord claims that the woman of Brainford refers to the "witch of Brentford," "a well-known personage of Shakespeare's day [who] kept a tavern at Brentford, a town on the Thames about twelve miles directly east of Windsor" (116-17), yet offers no source for this information.

55. Foakes and Rickert, eds., 104.

56. Of the three, only Hibbard argues for the possibility that the play refers to the 1599 Compton-Spencer marriage. According to Hibbard, "the Fenton-Anne Page story reflects the affair between Lord Compton and Elizabeth Spencer" and so "must have been completed after 18 April 1599" (48).

57. "The Canon and Chronology of Shakespeare's Plays" in Wells and Taylor, *A Textual Companion,* 120.

58. *A journal of all that was accomplished by Monsieur de Maisse Ambassador in England from King Henri IV to Queen Elizabeth Anno Domini 1597,* trans. and ed. G. B. Harrison and R.A. Jones (London, 1931). De Maisse saw a number of comedies performed before the queen in January 1597/98 (91-92); the editors remind us that "both the Lord Chamberlain's company of players (to which Shakespeare belonged) and the Lord Admiral's acted at Court this Christmas" (145). De Maisse also provides significant information regarding the troubles between England and the German princes at the time, as well as significant Garter-related information.

59. "Word Links with 'The Merry Wives of Windsor,'" *N&Q* 22 (1975): 169-71; reviewed in M.W.A. Smith, "Word-Links and Shakespearian Authorship and Chronology," *N&Q* 35 (1988): 57-59.

60. Foakes and Rickert, eds., 104.

61. For arguments on the relation of *Merry Wives* to other two-wives comedies, see Andrew Gurr, "Intertextuality at Windsor," *SQ* 38 (1987): 189-200; see also Roslyn L. Knutson, "Intertextuality at Windsor: A Rejoinder," and Andrew Gurr, "Intertextuality in Henslowe: A Reply," both in *SQ* 39 (1988): 391-93 and 394-98, respectively. The continuing controversy over the play's relation to the Henriad is glossed in Oliver, in Melchiori, and in A.R. Humphrey's introduction to the Arden editions of *The First Part of King Henry IV* and *The Second Part of King Henry IV* (London, 1960 and 1965). Gary Taylor has contributed to the Oldcastle/Falstaff controversy in "The Fortunes of Oldcastle," *SS* 38 (1985): 85-100; see also "William Shakespeare, Richard James and the House of Cobham," *Review of English Studies* 38

(1987): 334-54. For the Brooke/Broome censorship, see Oliver, who adopts the same position taken by Alfred Hart in *Stolne and Surreptitious Copies: A Comparative Study of Shakespeare's Bad Quartos* (London, 1942) in contending that this change was made as late as 1604 (lvi-lviii); Oliver terms Green's theory of the Brooke/Broome change "desperate" (lvi, n. 2). Jeanne Addison Roberts, on the other hand, agrees with Green's argument that the change was made in 1597 and disagrees with Oliver's claim (38-40).

62. See, for example, Robert J. Fehrenbach, "When Lord Cobham and Edmund Tilney 'were att odds': Oldcastle, Falstaff, and the Date of *1 Henry IV,*" *ShStud* 18 (1986): 87-101.

63. Wells and Taylor, *Textual Companion,* 120.

64. For ample proof of the bad blood between Essex and Henry Brooke, the younger Cobham, see Leslie Hotson, *Shakespeare's Sonnets Dated and Other Essays* (London, 1949), 147-52. Hotson compiles a good deal of evidence to back up his claim, including a letter from Essex to Sir Robert Sidney which refers to Henry's "base villainies . . . towards me (which to the world is too well known)" and a letter from Essex which makes clear that he advertised their disputes to other privy councilors: "I made it known unto them that I had just cause to hate the Lord Cobham for his villainous dealing and abusing of me; that he hath been my chief persecutor most unjustly; that in him there is no worth" (151).

65. Hotson, *Shakespeare's Sonnets Dated,* 147; Chambers, *William Shakespeare,* 2:198.

66. Hotson, *Shakespeare's Sonnets Dated,* 147-57.

67. Pierre Bourdieu uses the phrase "making use of indeterminacy" in chapter 3 of his *Outline of a Theory of Practice,* trans. Richard A. Nice (Cambridge, 1977). In *Drama of a Nation: Public Theater in Renaissance England and Spain* (Ithaca, NY, 1985), Walter Cohen argues that the material conditions of dramatic production are subject to a peculiar form of ideological reversal: "However aristocratic the explicit message of a play, the conditions of its production introduced alternative effects. The total theatrical process meant more than, and something different from, what the dramatic text itself meant" (183).

Giorgio Melchiori (essay date 1994)

SOURCE: "Reconstructing the Garter Entertainment at Westminster on St. George's Day 23 April 1597," in *Shakespeare's Garter Plays: Edward III to Merry Wives of Windsor,* University of Delaware Press, 1994, pp. 92-112.

[*In the following essay, Melchiori examines the textual and historical clues in and surrounding* The Merry Wives of Windsor *in his attempt to discover the exact date, location, and occasion on which the play was first performed.*]

Most recent editions of *The Merry Wives of Windsor* (with the notable exception of George Hibbard's New Penguin of 1973) accept the date of 23 April 1597 for the first performance of the play, as part of the Garter feast celebrated at Westminster, when George Carey, second Baron Hunsdon, the patron of the company of which Shakespeare was a sharer, was one of the five newly elected knights solemnly invested by Queen Elizabeth with the Order of the Garter. This view was first put forward by Leslie Hotson in his *Shakespeare versus Shallow* (1931), but the most cogent arguments in favor of it were those advanced in 1962 by William Green, in a painstaking study[1] minutely reconstructing on the basis of contemporary historical documents the ceremonies held on that occasion, to show that the performance of a play containing a celebration of the Order of the Garter would have been most appropriate after the supper held at Westminster in honor of the new knights on the evening of 23 April. In fact, though some kind of entertainment would be in order at such a time, no extant document mentions it or specifies its nature; and, at all events, entertainments offered on such occasions were generally in the form of masques rather than two-hour plays. Was, then, the Garter entertainment a much shorter dramatic piece that only some time later was partly incorporated in a full play for the public theatre?

Garter Play and/or Garter Entertainment

The main stumbling block met by the supporters of 1597 as the date of composition of the whole play of *The Merry Wives*—at a time when Shakespeare might have just completed *Henry IV, Part One,* and changed the names of Sir John Oldcastle, Rossill, and Harvey into those of Falstaff, Bardolph, and Peto respectively—is the presence in it, in very marginal roles, of characters who had become popular only after their appearance in Histories performed not before but after 1597: Shallow and Pistol in *2 Henry IV* (1598), Nym in *Henry V* (1599). Besides, the role of Sir Hugh Evans is a typical vehicle for an actor specializing in the comic Welshman, and this fits the bill of Robert Armin, who had joined the company only in 1599, "creating" the character of Fluellen;[2] and the introduction of Doctor Caius can best be explained in terms of exploitation of the comic French linguistic *pastiche* successfully used in *Henry V*. There are other incongruities: for instance, how comes it that Shallow, described as a justice of the peace in Gloucestershire in *Merry Wives* 1.1.5. (but not in the Quarto version of 1602), as well as in *2 Henry IV,* has now a deer park in Windsor? And why is so little trace left in the play of the episode of the "Germans" who steal the Host's horses, which has been rightly taken as an allusion (appropriate to the Garter entertainment) to the Mömpelgard affair?[3] The only reasonable explanation of these anachronisms and inconsistencies is that *Merry Wives* was a new play hurriedly put together around 1600, incorporating parts of an earlier Garter entertainment, dating back to 1597.

The main reason for considering *Wives* a "Garter play" is, of course, the speech of Mistress Quickly impersonating the Fairy Queen at 5.5.58-79—a speech that does not figure in the 1602 Quarto, suggesting that at least on occasion it was not used in public performances, though the rest of the scene was. The speech is a formal celebration of the Order of the Garter, but it does not place the stress on military virtue and valor as attributes of the Garter knights; by quoting the French motto, *Honi soit qui mal y pense,* it emphasises a different aspect of the virtue expected from the members of the Order. George Hibbard[4] remarks that this speech, and the part of the scene in which it is included

> is singularly masque-like. The Fairy Queen, the fairies, the Satyr, Hobgoblin—all these are exactly the kind of figures that are to be found in several of the royal 'Entertainments' that have survived. These entertainments are masque-like shows which were put on for the Queen's amusement when she visited the homes of her more important subjects . . . [In 1591], at Elvetham in Hampshire, the fourth day's proceedings began with a speech from the Fairy Queen, after which she and her fairy maids danced about Elizabeth, and then sang a song in praise of her.

Hibbard concludes:

> It therefore seems a reasonable hypothesis that either Hunsdon or the Queen may well have asked Shakespeare and his company to put together such an entertainment for the Garter celebrations of 1597. It would certainly be something that they could do in a fortnight, and it would fit the occasion. Then later, when it was all long over, Shakespeare, with the economy so characteristic of him, salvaged the entertainment, made the necessary changes to fit Falstaff into it, did not bother to insert indications of Welshness into the Satyr's speeches when they were handed over to Evans, and used it for the denouement of his new comedy. It is not a theory capable of outright proof, but it is more consistent with the play . . . than is Dennis's story.[5]

Falstaff and the 1597 Garter Entertainment

My only disagreement with Hibbard's theory concerns the "fitting" of Falstaff into the new play, which implies that the figure of the fat philandering knight was not present in the earlier Garter entertainment. In the following pages I look for new circumstantial evidence in support of the general view expressed by Hibbard (with the proviso just mentioned), and outline the Garter entertainment presented on 23 April 1597 as distinct from the comedy of *The Merry Wives of Windsor.*

The basic issue, I feel, has been obscured by the fact that, whereas a very great deal of attention has been rightly paid to the relationship between the Shakespearean comedy and the other Falstaff plays, to establish, among other things, their chronological sequence, too little account has been taken of the emergence and development of the character of Falstaff and his companions. In the first place, as Hibbard noted, royal entertainments for particular occasions were generally much shorter than regular plays, and all or mostly in verse. *Merry Wives* instead has, by far, the lowest percentage of verse (12 percent, including Pistol's doggerel) of any Shakespeare play. The only partially versified scenes in it—apart from the masquelike Garter celebration and the exposure of Falstaff at 5.5.40-105—are those connected with the Fenton-Anne Page love story and parental interference (3.4.1-21 and 67-94), the Pages's and Fords's preparations for the Herne the Hunter's masquerade in Windsor Forest at Falstaff's expense (4.4.6-16, 26-79 and 82-90; Evans's prose interventions in the scene look like later interpolations), Fenton's arrangements with the Host of the Garter for the elopement with Anne Page during the fairies masque (4.6.1-55), and Fenton's and Anne's reappearance after the masque, celebrating their happy union against the miseries of enforced marriage, as part of the final rejoicing and merry making (5.5.216-45).

Hibbard's suggestion that *Merry Wives* was hastily written (either at the Queen's command or just as a money-making proposition) in 1599-1600 accounts for the presence of these verse passages: together with the "Garter speech," I take them to be the only parts of the play borrowed and adapted (with changes and insertions of new lines) from the entertainment presented by the Hunsdon Men before the Queen at Westminster Palace on 23 April 1597 for the Feast of the Garter—an appropriate occasion for the company in that one of the five new Knights of the Garter elected that day was their patron, George Carey Lord Hunsdon.

A most suitable central feature of an entertainment devised for such an occasion would be a masque in which the Fairy Queen (an obvious allegorical projection of Queen Elizabeth) ordered her court to make the necessary preparations for the installation ceremony that was to take place a month later in Windsor Castle (see 5.5.56-74). And it was for such a queen to stress, among the duties of the Garter knights, the virtue of chastity.[6] The latter would suggest the subject matter for the antimasque[7] that was to complete the day's entertainment. This view is supported by the verse sections from the Garter show incorporated in *Merry Wives*. The Fenton-Anne story underlines the dangers to married chastity represented by parentally enforced marriage (see 5.5. 218-27), whereas Falstaff is the knight unworthy of the Order of the Garter because he is "corrupt, and tainted in desire." The general outlines of the Garter entertainment of 1597, then, were based on the honorable deception of the parents practiced by a pair of lovers and the punishment of a corrupt knight unworthy of the Order, culminating in the celebration of the Garter virtues and of the "radiant Queen" who "hates sluts and sluttery" (5.5.46). There was no room in this simple scheme for the "irregular humourists" of the Henry plays: in the original Westminster masque (corresponding to *Merry Wives*, 5.5.37-102), the speakers were the Fairy Queen and her followers, awkwardly replaced in the later comedy version by Mistress Quickly, Evans, and Pistol utterly deprived of their individual speech mannerisms, whereas Falstaff's prose speech at ll.81-82, detecting the

Welsh accent of a "fairy," is an obvious later interpolation, intruding in a perfect rhymed couplet spoken by the original fairies.[8] But before attempting an ampler reconstruction of the 1597 entertainment, let us take a closer look at its hero, or rather anti-hero. The question to be asked at this point is: Which Falstaff in Windsor?

There is reason to suspect that not only the unworthy knight, contrary to Hibbard's conclusions, figured already in the 1597 entertainment, but also that his name was from the beginning Sir John Falstaff. The very idea of presenting a knight unworthy of the Order would have suggested that name. The only other occasion in the whole of Shakespeare's work when the Order of the Garter and the duties of its members are mentioned at some length is in *1 Henry VI*, 4.1.9-47, the scene in which the English national hero Talbot tears the Garter from Sir John "Falstaffe"'s leg for "Prophaning this most Honourable Order."[9]

FASTOLF AND FALSTAFF VERSUS OLDCASTLE—AND A GRANT OF ARMS

A difficulty arises at this point. In Shakespeare's *1 Henry VI*, the name of the historical character who deserted the battle of Patay "without any stroke stricken," as Hall and Holinshed put it, though he had been "the same year for his valiantness elected to the order of the garter," is consistently spelled "Falstaffe"; but in the chronicles from which Shakespeare drew his information it is given as "Fastolf," "Fastolfe," or "Fastollfe." He was actually "disgartered" not by Talbot but by Bedford, the Regent of France, and Shakespeare, though taking a hint from it, decided to ignore the further report by the chroniclers that "Sir John Fastolffe" was able to justify his behavior at Patay, and "was restored to the Order against the mind of the Lord Talbot." A fact not unknown to the librarian Richard James when, in his epistle to Sir Henry Bourchier,[10] he tried to disentangle both the Oldcastle/Falstaff muddle and the question of how Falstaff could be alive under Henry VI if he had died under Henry V:

> In Shakespeare's first shewe of Harrie ye fift, ye person with which he vndertook to playe a buffone was not Falstaffe, but Sr Ihon Oldcastle, and . . . offence beinge worthily taken by personages descended from his [title . . .], the poet was putt to make an ignorant shifte of abusing Sr Ihon Fastolphe, a man not inferior [of] Vertue though not so famous in pietie as the other.[11]

The learned librarian simply imputes to Shakespeare's ignorance the confusion of the names and of the characters. Editors of the plays defend him from the accusation by maintaining that he had actually made a clear distinction between the two, later obliterated by a scribe or a compositor of the First Folio. True it is that, though *1 Henry VI* was already very successful on the stage in 1592, it appeared in print only posthumously in the 1623 Folio, so that the latest editor of the play, Michael Hattaway, is justified in stating:

> Throughout the Folio text and in all editions of the play before that of Theobald he is called 'Falstaffe',

because, no doubt, of scribal or compositorial confusion with the famous character in *1* and *2 Henry IV*.[12]

Perhaps "no doubt" is supererogatory. The question of the name has been amply debated,[13] and I find far from improbable the suggestion that the altered spelling may be authorial. Because in any case Sir John was meant to be the type of the knight unworthy of the Garter, Shakespeare may well have seen from the beginning, when he first introduced him as such in *1 Henry VI*, the allusive possibility offered by a slight variant in the name, from Fastolf to Fall-staff or False-staff, branding him as a false bearer of the emblem of military valor, staff or shaft being synonymous of spear—a notion familiar to the playwright whose grandfather Richard's family name is set down in the Snitterfield court rolls as both Shakeschafte and Shakstaff.[14] The significance of Shakespeare's own surname in connection with the name of Falstaff has been remarked upon by T.W. Herbert and Harry Levin,[15] who detect a suggestion of cowardice both in "Shake-spear" and in "Fall-staff," to which Roberts,[16] in the second instance, adds that of impotence, appropriate to the final scene of *Merry Wives*. This is perhaps going too far. Shakespeare was certainly aware of the martial quality of his family name, the very opposite of "Fall-" or "False-staff," and at all events its full significance was brought home to him by the grant to his father John and to "his children yssue and posterite" of

> This shield or cote of Arms, viz. Gould, on a Bend Sables, a Speare of the first steeled argent. And for his creast or cognizaunce a falcon his winges displayed Argent standing on a wrethe of his coullers: supporting a Speare Gould steeled as aforesaid sett vppon a helmett with mantelles & tasselles.[17]

The grant by the Garter principal king of Arms is dated 20 October 1596, and it must have amused Shakespeare to include, in an entertainment for a Garter celebration that he was called to devise shortly afterward, the type of the unworthy knight: the derogatory implications of the name borrowed from that of the dishonorable historical character who had put in a brief appearance in *1 Henry VI*, suggested for him a coat of arms with a falling spear—in ironical contrast with Shakespeare's own.

It is likely, therefore, that the royal entertainment on 23 April 1597 presented a knight actually called Falstaff, as yet a different person from what we know as the Sir John Falstaff triumphantly appearing in the two parts of *Henry IV* in 1597-98. But we should recall once again that, when a play on Henry IV was written and possibly performed in 1596, the "villainous abominable misleader of youth" was not called Falstaff but sir John Oldcastle, and that the use of his name was objected to by the powerful Brooke family, connected with that Oldcastle whom John Foxe had celebrated as a protomartyr of the Protestant religion. William Brooker Lord Cobham, Lord Chamberlain from August 1596 till his death in March 1597, was in a particularly strong position to exact the suppression of a play containing a slanderous presentation of his ancestor. I

have already illustrated[18] my view that the replacement of the "Oldcastle" version of *Henry IV* (originally, I believe, a single play) was a fairly laborious task undertaken in late 1596 or early 1597. The Garter entertainment presenting the Sir John Falstaff revived from *1 Henry VI* was produced at a time when Shakespeare was busy rewriting with considerable changes and amplifications the role of Oldcastle in the new version of *Henry IV*, and looking for a new name for the knight. Why not adopt the name used on the occasion of the Garter Feast, which added to Sir John Falstaff's earlier taint of cowardice the further imputation of lechery and corruption?

In other words:

1. The Sir John Falstaff exposed at Windsor in the Garter entertainment of 23 April 1597 was the same as the one even more dishonorably exposed in some brief scenes of *1 Henry VI*.

2. The Garter entertainment gave Shakespeare the idea of replacing with "Falstaff" the name of "Oldcastle" that had given offense to his descendants, in the rewriting of *Henry IV* as a new play or plays in 1597-98.

3. When, for whatever reason, Shakespeare was asked in 1599-1600 to write a comedy about the *new* Falstaff who had been successful in the two parts of *Henry IV*, he remembered the earlier Garter entertainment located in Windsor and, fusing together old and new, transferred to Windsor—improbable as it may appear—the irregular humourists that in the Histories had haunted Eastcheap, Gadshill, Gloucestershire, and even the fields of France.

A Chronology of Shakespeare's Work on the Histories

Here is a detailed prospect of the chronological sequence of the plays and entertainments in which Shakespeare had a hand between 1596 and the end of the century, apart from the romantic comedies and *Julius Caesar*:

1596

Early in the year Shakespeare writes for the Chamberlain's Men a remake of the first part of *The Famous Victories of Henry V*, under the title of *Henry IV*, covering events from the first rebellion in the North to the king's death, stressing the wildness of Prince Hal and his reformation, and developing the characters of his companions, Rossill (Sir John Russell), Harvey, Pointz, and particularly Sir John Oldcastle. The play is successfully staged.

23 July: The Lord Chamberlain, Henry Carey, first Baron Hunsdon, dies. The company passes under the patronage of his son, George Carey, second Baron Hunsdon, and is renamed the Lord Hunsdon's Men.

August: William Brooke, seventh Baron Cobham, is appointed Lord Chamberlain. He objects to the presentation on the public stage of Sir John Oldcastle. The play is withdrawn. Shakespeare undertakes to rewrite it for the next season, developing the role of Oldcastle under a less offensive name.

At about this time Queen Elizabeth decides to fill the next year the vacancies in the Order of the Garter by electing new knights, among whom George Carey, Lord Hunsdon. The latter commissions from his company an entertainment in view of the festivities for the investiture, on Saint George's day 23 April 1597.

1597

5/6 March: William Brooke Lord Cobham dies.

17 April: George Carey Lord Hunsdon is appointed Lord Chamberlain.

23 April: In a solemn ceremony at Westminster Queen Elizabeth invests five new Knights of the Garter: Frederick Duke of Württemberg (formerly Count Mömpelgard) in absentia, Thomas Lord Howard de Walden, George Carey Lord Hunsdon, Charles Blount Lord Mountjoy, Sir Henry Lee. Though there is no record of it, it is likely that, after the supper that followed evensong, the Chamberlain's Men presented an entertainment celebrating the Order and Queen Elizabeth in the person of the Fairy Queen, while the comic antimasque would center on the figure of a knight unworthy of the Order because of his sexual uncleanness (a homage to the cult of chastity promoted by the virgin queen). The knight was named after the infamous Sir John Fastolf (False-staff) disgraced for his cowardice in *1 Henry VI*.

At the same time, Shakespeare was busy rewriting the play on Henry IV and looking for new names to replace those used the year before. He gave the main character the name and title that had been revived on the occasion of the Garter entertainment: Sir John Falstaff. The new play—published the next year simply as *The History of King Henry IV*—was presented successfully on the stage.

1598

In view of this success, the Chamberlain's Men commissioned and presented a sequel to it. . . , ending with the promise of a third Falstaff play, *Henry V*, where "Falstaff shall die of a sweat," and with an apology for calling him Oldcastle in an earlier version.

1599

When it was presented at the newly built Globe, the rewriting of the second part of *Famous Victories* as *Henry V* did not keep the promise of showing Falstaff, possibly because Shakespeare had become aware of the historical Fastolf's gallant behavior at Agincourt, but introduced new comic roles: Fluellen the Welshman, suited to Robert Armin, the new Clown of the company; corporal Nym, with his recurring tag "That's the humour of it";[19] and the French Dauphin.

1599-1600

Presumably for commercial reasons, rather than obeying a Royal command, Shakespeare devised a new comedy centering on the figure of Falstaff, partly incorporating the Garter entertainment of 1597, exploiting some typical situations in Italian and English novels, and reintroducing the most successful comic figures in the recent Histories: Bardolph (1H4), Pistol (2H4), Nym (H5), Shallow (2H4), a new Mistress

Quickly that shared only her linguistic oddities with her previous namesake, the well-meaning Welshman (Fluellen = Evans), the pompous Frenchman (Dauphin = Caius).

THE BROOK/BROOME AFFAIR AND THE POOR KNIGHT OF WINDSOR

The result of the process I have summarized was *The Merry Wives of Windsor,* a dual-purpose comedy, for both court presentation (even if we do not credit the story of the royal command) and the public stage. The Garter masque (albeit the Fairy Queen of the original Garter entertainment was redimensioned as Mistress Quickly, the Satyr as Evans, and Hobgoblin as Pistol) would please both audiences, whereas the "Latin lesson" (4.1) is obviously meant only for the sophisticated court audience rather than for the more general one of the Globe—and on occasion also the Garter speech by the Queen of Fairies might have sounded out of place. This accounts for the two major omissions (the whole of 4.1 and the speech at 5.5.58-76) in the 1602 Quarto of the play, which appears to be a "reconstructed" text based on a public performance. The Folio text reflects instead the full version of the 1599-1600 play, including the substitution of Ford's assumed name "Broome" for the original "Brooke" to avoid any further possible offence to the Cobham family.

The Brooke-Broome change has caused serious difficulties to the supporters of 1597 as the date of composition of the entire comedy, including editors of the play like H.J. Oliver[20] and the most recent, T.W. Craik,[21] as well as Jeanne Addison Roberts.[22] If we acknowledge instead that Shakespeare wrote the play, as distinct from the Garter entertainment, in 1599-1600, the use of the assumed name Brooke for the suspicious Ford can be seen as the author's little revenge for having been forced by the earlier Lord Cobham, William Brooke, to substitute the name of Oldcastle, whereas the further change to Broome may well have been caused by the resentment of the surviving Brookes. But the change itself from Brooke to Broome could be a further insult to the Brookes: Ernst Honigmann[23] has shown that in 1595 the wife of a Mr. Broome was, with her husband's consent, under the "protection" of William Brooke. Honigmann comments: "having been ordered to remove the name Brooke from *Merry Wives,* Shakespeare or his colleagues added insult to injury by dragging in the Broomes. This would have been a clever counterthrust; the Cobham-Mr Broome-Mrs Broome triangle is repeated in the play, with Cobham (i.e. Oldcastle, i.e. Falstaff) offering to cuckold 'Mr Broome.'"

It is now time to leave the Falstaff of *The Merry Wives*—a pale reflection of the one appearing in the two Parts of *Henry IV*—and to go back to the other Falstaff, modeled in the 1597 entertainment not on the Sir John Oldcastle who had been Prince Hal's companion in *The Famous Victories of Henry V,* but on the cowardly Garter knight who had deserted Talbot at Patay in *1 Henry VI*. The lost entertainment can only be reconstructed in its general outlines from hints offered by the later comedy. The first

valuable clue is represented by the presence in a secondary role of a new character, the Host of the Garter, and by
the choice of the Garter Inn as Falstaff's permanent lodg-
ing in Windsor. The satirical intention is obvious. The
poor knights of Windsor were a well-known institution:
they were commoners who had acquired their title through
services rendered as soldiers, but, having no hereditary
property, were kept as Crown Pensioners. Falstaff is one
of them—not a nobleman but a retired captain. His lodg-
ing at the Garter Inn is a sign of both his frustrated ambition of ranking with the top nobility of the Kingdom (the
twenty-six Knights of the Order of the Garter), and his gift
for equivocation: being a knight and living at the Garter
Inn he could be referred to as "the knight of the Garter."

THE GARTER ENTERTAINMENT OF 1597—A
RECONSTRUCTION

From the evidence of the versified parts of the comedy,
which were the most likely to have been borrowed and
adapted from the earlier Garter Entertainment of 1597, it
appears that the latter required a much smaller cast, apart
from the fairies in the masque. Granting that the Garter
entertainment was built round three main interwoven
strands, here are the basic requirements of each of them:

1. Love plot. A young gentleman (= Fenton); a young
girl (= Anne Page); the parents of the girl, either one or
both of whom wanted her to marry a person of their
own choice; the person or persons chosen for her by
her parent(s). It is difficult to determine if each of the
parents favored a different pretender for the girl (as in
Merry Wives) or if only one did so. At all events, the
love plot did not need more than six actors.

2. The unworthy knight plot. Only two actors were essential: the knight himself, a poor pensioner of Windsor who aspired to a higher rank and saw himself as an
irresistible lady-killer; the Host of the Garter Inn, where
the knight lodged. The knight wanted to restore his
fortunes by seducing the girl's mother and/or other
wives of well-to-do Windsor commoners.

3. The "German Duke" plot, intended as a satire on the
behavior of the Duke of Württemberg, formerly Count
Mömpelgard (see *Wiv.*, 4.3 and 4.5). In fact, there was
hardly any need to present on the stage the three other
lodgers in the Garter Inn who, under pretense of attending on a German Duke, cheated the Host of his
horses; the episode could as well be reported by the
Host's servant or tavern drawer. This would explain
why, when some years later Shakespeare wrote his
comedy, dragging into it Falstaff's companions, Bardolph is very soon transferred from the knight's service
to that of the Host of the Garter (1.3.4-19; Folio, sig.
D3):

Fal. Truely mine *Host*; I must turne away some of my
followers. . . .

Ho[st]. Discard, (bully *Hercules*) casheere; let them
wag; trot, trot. . . . I will entertaine *Bardolfe*: he shall
draw; he shall tap; said I well (bully *Hector*?)

. . . . .

Fal. Bardolfe, follow him: a *Tapster* is a good trade: an

old Cloake, makes a new Ierkin: a wither'd Seruing-
man, a fresh Tapster: goe, adew.

Ba[rdolph]. It is a life that I haue desir'd: I will thriue.[24]

Bardolph had to replace the presumably anonymous drawer
bringing the news of the confidence trick played on the
Host.

The entertainment may well have begun by introducing
the overbearing knight in conversation with the Host of
the Garter Inn, laying his plans for the seduction of rich
Windsor wives. Mention might have been made on this
occasion of his fellow lodgers, the "three Gentlemen"
(Quarto version), or "Germans" (Folio) waiting for the arrival of a Duke, along the lines of the short exchange
between the Host and Bardolph at 4.3 (Folio, sig.E4):

Bar. Sir, the Germane desires [Germans desire] to haue
three of your horses:[25] The Duke himselfe will be to
morrow at Court, and they are going to meet him.

Host. What Duke should that be comes so secretly? I
heare not of him in the Court: let me speake with the
Gentlemen, they speake English?

Bar. I sir? Ile call him to you.[26]

Host. They shall haue my horses, but Ile make them
pay: Ile sauce them, they haue had my houses[27] a week
at commaund: I haue turn'd away my other guests,
they must come off, Ile sawce them, come.

Exeunt

Such a short scene, sandwiched between two much longer
ones, the second of which (4.4) begins with exactly the
same characters on the stage who were present at the end
of the earlier one (4.2), looks like an intrusion inherited
and adapted from a version in which the dialogue was part
of a different longer scene.

The rest of the Garter entertainment must have interwoven
this slender satirical (and topical) strand with the story of
the unworthy lodger in the inn attempting to seduce the
mother of the heroine of what can be considered the main
plot line: the love story of a young girl whose father has
different plans for her marriage. The versified parts of 3.4,
reproducing the original love scene between Anne and
Fenton, suggest that Mistress Page is not so averse to let
her daughter have her way: it is Master Page who has
other plans for her. Again, the verse sections of 4.4 and
4.6 indicate the further development of this plot: on the
one hand, the father plans the punishment of the knight
who has designs on his wife (though in the later comedy
there is a duplication of the situation, through the introduction of the "Italianate" story of the deception of the jealous husband); on the other hand, the young lover enrolls
the help of the Host of the Garter to deceive the father of
the heroine. Adding to this the deception of the Host
himself by the followers of the "German Duke," we have
the simple comedy of errors that constitutes the antimasque of the Garter entertainment. It should be noted that it
dispenses with the Ford/Brooke play of disguises, the hid-

ing of Falstaff and the other episodes that Shakespeare devised later, when he engaged in the writing of a full-fledged comedy, having recourse to new Italian sources and to some of the characters that had become popular by appearing in the Histories he had written in the meantime.

The Garter masque proper, led by the Fairy Queen, with the celebration of the Order, the punishment of the unworthy knight and the triumph of true love against enforced marriage, was the conclusion of the courtly entertainment offered to the Queen and to the old and new Knights of the Order on Saint George's day 23 April 1597.

POSTSCRIPT: THE DUAL CHRONOLOGY OF THE FALSTAFF PLAYS

An imperfect consensus. In spite of the assurance by Jeanne Addison Roberts[28] that "we are approaching a consensus on the date" of composition of *Merry Wives,* i.e., 1596-97, even the supporters of a close connection between the comedy as it stands now and the Garter celebrations of 1597, though dismissing as irrelevant the fact that the play was not mentioned by Francis Meres in his *Palladis Tamia* (1598), find it difficult to place it within the sequence of the other Falstaff plays. They are forced to push back to 1596, against all known evidence, the date of completion and stage presentation of both Parts of *Henry IV.* An ingenious compromise is suggested by the editors of the Oxford *Complete Works.*[29] Though accepting Roberts's surmise[30] that to write the new Garter comedy, "Shakespeare interrupted his work on *2 Henry IV* at 4.3" when he "had already invented Shallow and Pistol," they doubt that by April 1597 he could have reached this point in the writing of the history, so they advance the opinion that

> Queen Elizabeth's request for a play on Falstaff in love could have been made in anticipation of a later court performance that Whitehall season (on 26 February 1598). . . . *Merry Wives* could . . . have recollected, rather than anticipated, the Garter ceremonies of spring 1597; the play would still have been written with a court performance in mind, honouring by allusion the company's patron, and satirizing by contrast Henry Brooke, the new Lord Cobham, who would have been instrumental in the censorship of *1 Henry IV.* Shakespeare's composition of *2 Henry IV* would have been interrupted by the request for *Merry Wives,* and *2 Henry IV* as a consequence would not have been completed until spring or early summer of 1598.[31]

The forest of conditionals and subjunctives is a clear indication of strain in devising a solution that, on the one hand, connects the play with a court occasion, and on the other, suggests acceptable dates for the two Parts of *Henry IV.* But why recall a Garter celebration and announce an installation ceremony some ten months after the event? And why borrow from the as yet incomplete and unperformed *2 Henry IV* the characters of Shallow and Pistol, which the audience would not recognize because they had never appeared before on the stage? Why devise for the occasion of a court play to be performed on 26 February 1598 the new character of Corporal Nym, so obviously

intended to satirize the theatrical fashion set by Jonson's comedy of humors—he uses the word *humor* twenty times in eleven of the twelve speeches allotted him—when the earliest possible date of performance of *Every Man in His Humour* is July of that year? Roberts[32] argues that "Shakespeare invented Nym specifically to fill a plot need in *The Merry Wives,*" namely, "to balance Pistol"; but that is true of *Henry V* rather than *Merry Wives.*

The Humor of It. In his turn, William Green[33] notices that Nym's well-known tag line or "verbal tic," "that's the humor of it," appearing six times in the Folio text of *Henry V* (and eight in the bad quarto), is instead constantly varied in *Merry Wives,* but in the 1602 bad Quarto of the comedy turns up five times in the form "and there's the humor of it." This is explained by the fact that the reporter of the bad Quarto text of *Merry Wives* replaced the imperfectly remembered varied mentions of humors with a constant formula modeled with a slight variant on the one consistently used in the history play. But it is no proof that the comedy had been written two years before the history; it is more likely that Shakespeare, writing *Merry Wives* shortly after *Henry V,* would deliberately play variations on the tag line already familiar to the audience from Nym's previous appearance in the history play. Corporal Nym, Bardolph, Pistol, and even Mistress Quickly, are no longer full-blown human characters; they are, one and all, in contrast with their appearances in the histories, presented merely as "humours," counting exclusively on their linguistic peculiarities. In fact, *Merry Wives* is Shakespeare's ironical tribute paid to the new theatrical genre of the comedy of humors, and the title page of the 1602 bad Quarto is fully justified in describing it as "Entermixed with sundrie variable and pleasing humours." Shakespeare could neither adopt nor satirize the genre before 1599, when, thanks to Jonson's comedies, it triumphed on the London stage.

Recurring Characters. Green supports his theory on the sequence of composition of the plays (*1 Henry IV,* late 1596; *2 Henry IV,* January-April 1597, completed if not performed; *Merry Wives,* April 1597; *Henry V,* Summer 1599), by producing a "Chart of Military Titles in the Falstaff Plays," including the characters of Falstaff, Bardolph, Peto, Gadshill, Pistol, Nym.[34] Such a chart, which has to acknowledge the disappearance of any military title in the comedy, except in the case of Nym, is further evidence of the wrongness of the sequence suggested. The omission of indications of rank means simply that they were presented no longer as functionally linked to the action of the play, but as stage figures already well known to the audience from their previous appearances, whereas Nym retained his title because he was a recent addition to the group of "irregular humourists," not yet as familiar as the others. Let us now complete the chart with the designations of the other characters without military rank who figure in more than one Falstaff play, leaving out Gadshill (not a military but merely a "setter," the robbers' decoy, appearing in only one play) and including instead Mistress Quickly, Poins, Doll, Falstaff's page, and Shallow, and place them in what I consider the correct sequence.

Designations of Recurring Characters in the Falstaff Plays

	1H4	*2H4*	*H5*	*Wiv*
FALSTAFF	knight	knight captain	(mentioned)	knight
QUICKLY	hostess married	hostess widow	hostess remarried	house-keeper spinster
BAR-DOLPH	no mention of rank	corporal	corporal lieutenant	no mention of rank
POINS	gentleman	gentleman	(absent)	(mentioned)
PETO	lieutenant	no mention of rank	(absent)	(absent)
PISTOL	(absent)	ancient lieutenant	ancient lieutenant	no mention of rank
SHALLOW	(absent)	justice	(absent)	justice
DOLL	(absent)	?gentle-woman	(mentioned)	(absent)
FALST'S PAGE	(absent)	boy, page	boy	Robin, boy page
NYM	(absent)	(absent)	corporal	corporal

Quickly Metamorphosed. The transformation of Mistress Quickly is the most striking. If we accept any of the theories maintaining that the whole play of *Merry Wives* was completed by 23 April 1597 (or, according to the Oxford editors, by 26 February 1598) we must accept as well that:

1. Shakespeare created, in the first place, the conventional type of the Hostess, a "most sweet wench" and "an honest man's wife," who has not much to say for herself in *1 Henry IV* (1596-97).

2. When writing the unplanned sequence to that play in 1597-98, he transmuted her into a superannuated widow, a bawd whose delusions of respectability are reflected in her magnificent use of linguistic equivocation.

3. *At the same time,* in *Merry Wives,* she figures as the spinsterish housekeeper of a French doctor in Windsor, using the same language for her side-trade of go-between.

4. Finally in *Henry V,* once again as a hostess, as well as Pistol's wife, "her genius for unintended and unperceived obscenity," in Gary Taylor's words,[35] "helps make her report of Falstaff's death perhaps the most moving . . . messenger speech in the canon."

But if *Merry Wives* postdates *Henry V* the transition from full-blown character to mere stage type or humor, in her case as in that of the other characters borrowed from the histories, is justified.

The Two Chronologies. The attempts at dating the comedy have confused two distinct sorts of chronology: on the one

hand, the actual chronology of composition of the Falstaff plays, and on the other, the fictional chronology of the events represented in those plays.. . . . Shakespeare had decided not to keep the promise of showing Falstaff in the French campaign, as the Epilogue of *2 Henry IV* had stated. Mindful of the ten-mile banishment from Westminster of Falstaff and his crew at the end of that play, Shakespeare was careful, in *Henry V,* not to specify the location of the inn where Mistress Quickly, now married to ancient Pistol, is plying her trade as a hostess, from whence Falstaff is gathered "to Arthur's bosom," and his followers are summoned to join the French expedition. The mention of Staines at 2.3.2 suggests a place up the Thames to the west of London, at the opposite end from Eastcheap, down the river in the heart of the City. To fit into the play a character meant to mock the growing fashion for "humours" on the stage, Shakespeare created Corporal Nym as the unsuccessful rival of Pistol for the hand of the hostess. Later, though, Nym becomes associated with Bardolph rather than Pistol, because "Nim and Bardolph are sworn Brothers in filching" (3.2.44), which leads to their death, in contrast with Pistol who, as the Boy comments (4.4.69-74), is not a thief simply for lack of courage:

> The empty vessel makes the greatest sound, Bardolfe and Nym had tenne times more valour, then this roaring diuell i'th olde play . . . and they are both hang'd, and so would this be, if hee durst steale any thing aduenturously.

The Boy himself was soon to come to a sad end, cruelly massacred by the French.

Reviving Falstaff. It was Falstaff's absence from *Henry V* that caused the demand—by public theater audiences rather than by the Queen—for a comedy where he would appear again, to dispel the gloomy impression left not only by the announcement of his death, but also by the fate of his followers, including Corporal Nym, a posthumous addition to them. In improvising, at short notice, the new play, Shakespeare was faced with the same sort of problem that confronted many authors of serials and sequels for the press, the stage, or the large or small screen in the following centuries. To justify the revival of his hero, he could not present, as did Conan Doyle at the end of last century, the death of Falstaff, like that of Sherlock Holmes, as mere pretense, nor could he pretend, as did, in more recent times, the harassed scriptwriters of *Dallas,* that Henry the Fifth's famous victories in France, like the death of Bobby Ewing, had never taken place, being merely a hallucination. History left Shakespeare no other choice except that of presenting the comedy, hastily put together from Italianate sources and the recollection of the 1597 royal entertainment where a different Sir John Falstaff had appeared, as a marginal episode in the life of the fat knight, at the time of his banishment from London. The clue was given by Henry's rejection speech (*2 Henry IV,* 5.5.66-70; 1600 Quarto, sig. K4v):

> For competence of life, I will allow you,
> That lacke of meanes enforce you not to euills,
> And as we heare you do reforme your selues,

We will according to your strengths and qualities,
Giue you aduauncement.

What other "competence of life" could be offered a discredited and impecunious knight except a pension and a place among the poor knights of Windsor? His companions (the king is addressing Bardolph, Pistol, and the page, as well as Falstaff) would of course follow him there. To them Shakespeare added his latest creation, Corporal Nym (also to keep up the joke about humors); not Poins: already in *2 Henry IV* he is Prince Hal's rather than Falstaff's companion, he is not present at the rejection and does not figure at all in *Henry V.* In *Merry Wives* we are slyly reminded of his different role and status in the passing mention (3.2.73) of the fact that the young gentleman Fenton (not the commoners Pistol and Bardolph) "kept companie with the wilde Prince and *Pointz*."

Reviving Mistress Quickly. The revival of Mistress Quickly presented a different problem. She had been a hostess in Eastcheap, and in *Henry V* we had seen her in the same capacity, remarried to Pistol, in an unspecified locality necessarily òutside London. It could not be Windsor, because the inn there was emblematically called the Garter Inn, and the personality of its Host had already been firmly established in the Garter entertainment of 1597. Shakespeare had no choice but to imagine that, in the interval between the rejection of Falstaff and the preparations for the French campaign, Mistress Quickly had temporarily changed her trade in order to figure plausibly in Windsor. Hence her role as housekeeper and general busybody, a merry former and future wife. Astutely, Shakespeare drops a hint about her future when Pistol, following her off-stage, exclaims (2.2.137-39):

This Puncke is one of *Cupids* Carriers,
Clap on more sailes, pursue: vp with your fights:
Giue fire: she is my prize, or Ocean whelme them all.

The hint is hardly developed in the rest of the play, though Pistol as Hobgoblin partners Quickly as Queen of Fairies in the Folio version of the Windsor forest revels.

In the chronology of "history" Shakespeare has endeavored to insert *The Merry Wives of Windsor* between the action of the Second Part of *Henry IV* and that of *Henry V.* But he could not have done so if, in the chronology of composition, he had actually written the comedy before the last of his "histories" of the Lancastrian cycle.

Notes

1. William Green, *Shakespeare's Merry Wives of Windsor* (Princeton: Princeton University Press, 1962). Roberts, *English Comedy,* already mentioned, is a more recent study along the same lines.

2. This appears from Armin's own play, *The Two Maids of More-Clacke,* see A.S. Liddie's introduction to his critical edition of the play (New York: Garland, 1979). Armin reserved for himself in it the part of a comic Welshman as well as that of the clown. The

language of Owen Glendower in *1 Henry IV,* written before Armin's advent, counts for comic effect on its grandiloquence, but it shows no trace of the equivocations caused by the Welsh accent, which characterize instead Fluellen and Sir Hugh Evans.

3. The curious intervention of Bardolph in the extremely brief scene 4.3, and the inconsequential scene (4.5.60-86) when the Host of the Garter is informed that three Germans have stolen his horses under pretense of needing them to meet a duke, has been taken to allude to a German nobleman who, when visiting England in 1592 as Frederick Count Mömpelgard, had maneuvred to be elected to the Order of the Garter, but when, having become Duke of Württemberg, the honor was conferred upon him in 1597, did not attend the installation ceremony. William Green (121-76) devotes a whole chapter to "The Duke of Jarmany."

4. G. Hibbard, ed. *The Merry Wives of Windsor* (New Penguin Shakespeare, Harmondsworth: Penguin Books, 1973), introduction 49-50.

5. A reference to Dennis's statement that the comedy was written in a fortnight at the Queen's command, quoted in "The Garter Comedy" section of chapter 4 in *Shakespeare's Garter Plays: Edward III to Merry Wives of Windsor,* University of Delaware Press, 1994.

6. On the Elizabethan cult of chastity see Philippa Berry, *Of Chastity and Power* (London: Routledge, 1989).

7. Anne Barton, introducing *The Merry Wives of Windsor* in The Riverside Shakespeare, ed. G. Blakemore Evans (Boston: Houghton Mifflin, 1974), 286, remarks that "a comedy concerned, as this one is, with the punishment of a knight whose principles and behaviour contravene all the ideals of his rank would be appropriate, almost as a kind of antimasque, at a Garter feast."

8. The two lines of the couplet (80 and 83) were spoken alternately by Satyr and Hobgoblin (Folio, p.51, sig. E6):

[*Evan.*] But stay, I smell a man of middle earth.

Pist. Vilde worme, thou wast ore-look'd euen in thy birth.

9. Quotations of *1 Henry VI, . . .* are from the First Folio of 1623, Histories, 110, sig. 13v.

10. See chapter 3, note 24 in *Shakespeare's Garter Plays: Edward III to Merry Wives of Windsor,* University of Delaware Press, 1994. Taylor ("Fortunes") believes that the epistle was written in 1634 rather than about 1625, the date commonly accepted.

11. Quoted by Taylor, "Fortunes," 86.

12. *The First Part of King Henry VI,* ed. Michael Hattaway (New Cambridge Shakespeare. Cambridge: Cambridge University Press, 1991), 64.

13. George Walton Williams, "Fastolf or Falstaff," *ELR,* 5 (1975), 308-12; Robert F. Willson, Jr, "Falstaff in *Henry IV:* What's in a Name?" *SQ* 27 (1976), 199-200; Norman Davis, "Falstaff's Name," *SQ* 28 (1977), 513-15; G. W. Williams, "Second Thoughts on Falstaff's Name," *SQ* 30 (1979), 82-84.

14. E. K. Chambers, *William Shakespeare: A Study of Facts and Problems* (Oxford: Clarendon Press, 1930), 2.27, and 2.371-75 ("Spelling and Significance of the Name").

15. T. Walter Herbert, "The Naming of Falstaff," *Emory University Quarterly,* 10 (March 1954), 1-11; Harry Levin, "Shakespeare's Nomenclature." *Essays on Shakespeare,* ed. G. W. Chapman (Princeton: Princeton University Press, 1965), 87.

16. Roberts, *English Comedy,* 48.

17. Chambers, *Shakespeare,* 2.18-32.

18. See chapter 1, "The Corridors of History: Shakespeare the Remaker." and chapter 2, "Reconstructing the Ur-*Henry IV,*" in *Shakespeare's Garter Plays: Edward III to Merry Wives of Windsor,* University of Delaware Press, 1994.

19. A likely jocular reference to the new genre of the comedy of humors, established by Ben Jonson's *Every Man in His Humour,* a play presented on the stage between July and September 1598, with Shakespeare as one in the cast.. . .

20. *The Merry Wives of Windsor,* ed. J.H. Oliver (New Arden Shakespeare, London: Methuen, 1971).

21. *The Merry Wives of Windsor,* ed. T.W. Craik (Oxford: Oxford University Press, 1990).

22. Roberts, *English Comedy,* 38-40.

23. E.J.A. Honigmann, "Sir John Oldcastle: Shakespeare's Martyr," in J.W. Mahon and T.A. Pendleton, eds., *"Fanned and Winnowed Opinions" Shakespearean Essays Presented to Harold Jenkins* (London: Methuen, 1987), 118-32.

24. The exchange is practically identical in the earlier version of the play, the 1602 Quarto (sig. B1v), except for Bardolph's last speech that reads: "I will sir, Ile warrant you Ile make a good shift to liue."

25. In 1602 Quarto, sig.F3: "Syr heere be three Gentlemen come from the Duke the St[r]anger sir, would haue your horse."

26. 1602 Quarto: "Ile call them to you sir."

27. 1602 Quarto: "House."

28. Roberts, *English Comedy,* 41-50.

29. 1986, text of the play edited by John Jowett, checked by Gary Taylor.

30. Roberts, *English Comedy,* 45.

31. *Textual Companion,* 1987, 120.

32. Roberts, *English Comedy,* 46.

33. Green, *Merry Wives,* 88-92.

34. Green, *Merry Wives,* 190-92.

35. *Henry V,* ed. Gary Taylor (Oxford: Oxford University Press, 1982), 63-64.

SOCIETY

Camille Wells Slights (essay date 1985)

SOURCE: "Pastoral and Parody in *The Merry Wives of Windsor,*" in *English Studies in Canada,* Vol. XI, No. 1, March, 1985, pp. 12-25.

[*In the following essay, Slights examines the community of* The Merry Wives of Windsor *and contends that the humiliation of Falstaff "forces him to bow to social pressures and prepares him to understand and accept his place within the society."*]

Sir Hugh Evans, the Welsh parson in *The Merry Wives of Windsor,* tries to arrange Master Slender's marriage to Anne Page and in the process offends another of Anne's suitors, Doctor Caius, who challenges him to a duel. Act three finds Parson Evans waiting, with considerable trepidation, to answer the challenge:

> Pless my soul, how full of chollors I am, and trempling of mind: I shall be glad if he have deceived me. How melancholies I am! I will knog his urinals about his knave's costard when I have good opportunities for the 'ork. Pless my soul!
>
> (III.i.11-15)[1]

Suddenly, in the course of expressing his malevolence and apprehension, he breaks into song:

> To shallow rivers, to whose falls
> Melodious birds sings madrigals;
> There will we make our peds of roses,
> And a thousand fragrant posies.
> To shallow—
>
> (ll. 16-20)

The delivery of a familiar text in Evans's comic Welsh accent compounds the incongruities inherent in the situation of a clergyman preparing to fight a duel of honour over his role as go-between in a romantic intrigue. Moreover, as Ronald Huebert has pointed out, the Marlowe quotation not only reminds us of Evans's incongruous position but also parodies the conventions of the pastoral love song that were becoming literary clichés by the late 1590s.[2] In the robustly middle-class world of Shakespeare's Windsor, the delicate beauty of Marlowe's poem seems absurdly out of place.

Nevertheless, while the singer and his song may appear ridiculous, Evans's choice of musical texts is less incongruous than critics have allowed. Indeed, the lines he quotes are apt and illuminating both for his immediate situation and for the comic world he inhabits. In a time of anxiety and anticipated danger Evans recalls Marlowe's pastoral lyric not because his thoughts have turned to love but because he longs for the world of peace and safety Marlowe evokes. To Evans, this pastoral ideal of human and natural harmony seems poignantly inaccessible, and he breaks off, exclaiming that he feels as much like crying as singing. When he resumes his song, he interpolates a more melancholy line of pastoral poetry:

> Mercy on me! I have a great dispositions to cry.—
> Melodious birds sing madrigals—
> Whenas I sat in Pabylon—
> And a thousand vagram posies.
> To shallow, etc.

> (ll. 21-25)

He interjects into Marlowe's love poem a line from Psalm 137, which in a similar metrical version begins:

> When as we sate in Babilon,
> the riuers round about,
> and in remembraunce of Sion,
> the teares for griefe burst out:
> We hangd our harpes and instruments,
> the willow trees vpon:
> for in that place men for their vse,
> had planted many one.[3]

Clearly, Psalm 137 intrudes into Evans's memory because it combines the pastoral imagery of river, trees, and music with the direct expression of grief and with elegiac longing for an idealized harmonious community.[4] Like most people, Parson Evans turns to pastoralism when the stress and complexity of the world are too much with him and he yearns for the peace and innocence of a better world.

The most delightful irony implicit in Evans's evocation of the pastoral tradition is the fact that he is in the midst of that harmonious world without knowing it. Specifically, he is in no danger from Doctor Caius's sword. The genial host of the Garter, who has no intention of losing either his doctor or his priest, has misdirected the would-be adversaries to opposite sides of town in order to avoid bloodshed. More generally, the Windsor of Shakespeare's comedy is a community of human and natural harmony where rural virtue triumphs over courtly sophistication. Sir Hugh's quotations signal that the pastoral, along with Plautine comedy, medieval farce, and Italian novelle, is among the generic antecedents of the play's comic form.

The Windsor of *The Merry Wives* is admittedly an unlikely *locus amoenus*. Sir John Falstaff attempts to seduce Mistress Page and Mistress Ford in a busy village, not the fields of Arcady or the forest of Arden. The fat knight and those respectable matrons and their families, not lovesick shepherds and innocent nymphs, are at the centre of the dramatic action. Still, while Windsor does not provide a wholly natural contrast to urban artificiality, the green world is all around and easily accessible. The basic staples of pastoral landscape are ready to hand: fields with birds, woods with deer, a flowing river, and even an ancient oak all play notable parts in the action and serve the traditional function of bringing sophistication, ambition, and greed to terms with natural simplicity.

For all of Falstaff's natural exuberance, his designs on the deer and the women of Windsor constitute an attack by the civilized vices of greed and pride on bucolic contentment. In scene one, when he is accused by Shallow of beating his men and killing his deer, Falstaff arrogantly admits the charges, brags that he has also kissed the keeper's daughter and broken Slender's head, and taunts Shallow that he would make a laughingstock of himself by his threatened complaint to the Council. Falstaff's attempt to seduce Mistress Page and Mistress Ford originates in greed and is nurtured by vanity. He plans to solve his financial problems by making love to the women, whom he believes to control their husbands' ample purses. His social rank and his personal vanity make him confident of success. Mistress Page, he brags, "examined my parts with most judicious oeillades: sometimes the beam of her view gilded my foot, sometimes my portly belly" (I.iii.56-58), and she understands his proposal as a temptation to ambition, confiding to her friend that "if it were not for one trifling respect, I could come to such honour! . . . If I would but go to hell for an eternal moment or so, I could be knighted" (II.i.43-48). Falstaff woos Ford's wife by flattering her that nature intended her for a more exalted social sphere: "thou wouldst make an absolute courtier, and the firm fixture of thy foot would give an excellent motion to thy gait in a semi-circled farthingale" (III.iii.55-58), and he has no doubts that he can "predominate over the peasant" her husband (II.ii.270-71).

While Sir John and his followers clearly exhibit the vices of civilization, the denizens of Windsor may seem too concerned with economic advantage and social status and too busy with schemes of matchmaking and revenge to illustrate the contrasting pastoral virtues of humility and contentment. For example, the play opens with Shallow's indignant assertions of the dignity of his social rank and family lineage. Economic considerations, moreover, determine both Master and Mistress Page's choice of husband for their daughter, Mistress Page supporting Doctor Caius, who has money and powerful friends at court, and Master Page favouring Slender, who has land and 300 pounds a year. Even Fenton, Anne's own choice, admits that he was first attracted to her by her father's wealth. In addition, Falstaff's aggression against the gamekeeper is echoed in Shallow's repeated boasting of the combative prowess of his youth, in Doctor Caius's challenge to Evans, and in the beating Ford administers to the supposed old woman of Brainford. The citizens of Windsor have even been accused of sharing Falstaff's gluttony, exhibiting inordinate appetites for food and drink.

In short, acquisitiveness, pride, and pugnacity are as natural to the inhabitants of Windsor as to Falstaff and his followers. And that similarity, I think, is just the point. Desires for food, drink, sex, money and prestige are as basic to life in Windsor as to life in the most worldly and self-indulgent urban or courtly society, but in the simple rural community they are held in check. The citizens of Windsor are conscious of distinctions of social rank but are fundamentally unimpressed by them. The merry wives are immune to the temptation of a knightly lover. Justice Shallow is asserting his right to respect in spite of Falstaff's superior rank when he blusters, "If he were twenty Sir John Falstaffs, he shall not abuse Robert Shallow, Esquire" (I.i.2-4). Although Anne's parents prudently want to secure their daughter's social and economic position through her marriage, they are not socially ambitious and do not want an aristocratic son-in-law who would marry her "but as a property" (III.iv.10) to repair his own depleted fortune. Essentially, economic and social status function in Windsor as means of establishing membership within the community, not as means of asserting individual superiority.

The sense of community, moreover, controls the appetitive and aggressive impulses of the citizens. It is true, as Barbara Freedman comments, that "eating seems to be the major preoccupation of Windsor society; everyone is always coming from or going to a dinner,"[5] but it is equally notable that no one eats alone: the references to dining are almost always in the form of invitations offered and accepted. While Falstaff poaches another man's deer, Shallow gives deer to Page, who invites everyone to share his venison pasty and wine. By the same token, the men of Windsor are naturally combative, as Shallow boasts:

> Bodykins, Master Page, though I now be old, and of the Peace, if I see a sword out, my finger itches to make one. Though we are justices, and doctors, and churchmen, Master Page, we have some salt of our youth in us; we are the sons of women, Master Page.

(II.iii.41-45)

But for all their irascibility and nostalgia for youthful exploits, they accept transformation into pillars of the community. Shallow remembers that he is a sworn Justice of the Peace come to pacify Caius not to "make one" in his quarrel. Reminded of their responsible roles in the community as "a curer of souls" and "a curer of bodies" (II.iii.35-36, cf. III.i.90) and learning how they have been tricked by the Host, Evans and Caius drop their quarrel rather than be "laughingstocks to other men's humours" (III.i.78-79).

Life in Windsor is not uneventful, but on the whole people live together there peacefully, controlling potentially explosive situations through various forms of social pressure. Act one, scene one, sometimes criticized as superfluous, demonstrates the social group functioning smoothly, reconciling differences through good will and hospitality. Settling the quarrel between Evans and Caius requires more complicated manoeuvres and recourse to the harsher weapons of trickery and ridicule. In both cases the peacemakers act as a group: Evans, Page, and the Host are the self-appointed umpires for the deer-stealing controversy, and Shallow, Slender, Page, and the Host co-operate to reconcile Caius and Evans. While they are effective as representatives of the community, not as individuals, they transmit the group judgment personally and informally rather than through impersonal institutions, and their power is accepted rather than imposed. With the notable exceptions of Falstaff and his followers, the residents of Windsor have a sense of themselves as part of a group and are willing to bend to social pressure in order to retain the reassurances of community.

Although critics have made much of Falstaff's status as an outsider, the fact that he is a visitor is less crucial than his imperviousness to public opinion and his refusal to identify with the group. After all, for an English village, Windsor has a remarkably heterogeneous population, including a Welsh parson and a French doctor as well as the Fords, Pages, and Justice Shallow with his three-hundred-year-old coat of arms. Even Shallow and Slender, like Falstaff, are visitors, guests at the inn (II.iii.53, 69).

Being a visitor or an alien is no bar to participation in Windsor society. Although there are jokes about Evans and Caius, they are mocked affectionately as members of the group. Their accents are ridiculed as Mistress Quickly's malapropisms are, as personal idiosyncracies, and cause no real problems in communication. In contrast, Nym's affected language earns Master Page's distrust and defeats his attempt to make Page jealous. And Falstaff, whose command of the King's English surpasses all other characters', utterly misunderstands Mistress Quickly and Mistress Ford. He boasts that Mistress Ford "gives the leer of invitation; I can construe the action of her familiar style, and the hardest voice of her behaviour, to be Englished rightly, is, 'I am Sir John Falstaff's'" (I.iii.42-45). As Pistol says, he has "translated her will—out of honesty into English" (ll. 46-47), and he suffers for his mistranslation. Society is held together, then, not so much by a shared language as by shared values, in this play especially by agreement about permissible sexual activity. The scene where Mistress Quickly hears indecencies in young William's recital of his Latin lesson comically demonstrates that, as society transmits its culture to the young, it passes on not merely grammar and vocabulary but attitudes and assumptions and that the two are distinguishable: proficiency in one does not necessarily imply understanding of the other.

While the heterogeneity of Windsor's population suggests that enjoying the bucolic peace and innocence traditionally symbolized by a pastoral setting depends not on place of nativity or social rank but on values and attitudes, the physical presence of the court itself at Windsor suggests that the courtly vices of ambition and sexual intrigue are temptations for country men and women as well as for courtiers. Mistress Quickly assures Falstaff that he is not the first courtly suitor to address Mistress Ford:

there has been knights, and lords, and gentlemen, with
their coaches—I warrant you, coach after coach, letter
after letter, gift after gift . . . that would have won any
woman's heart . . . and yet there has been earls, nay,
which is more, pensioners, but, I warrant you, all is
one with her.

(II.ii.60-74)

Although this flight of fancy is not to be believed literally,
it reminds us of the immanence of the court and establishes
that it is a matter of conscious choice that the court has no
effective reality in the lives of the characters. Just as a
harmonious social life is possible for a French doctor, a
Welsh clergyman, and a down-at-heels aristocrat as well as
for the Fords and Pages, so the civilized decadence and
individual ambition associated with the courtly ambience
are possibilities within ordinary life. Caius, who boasts of
his practice among earls, knights, lords, and gentlemen,
and Fenton, who is reputed to have "kept company with
the wild Prince and Poins (III.ii.66-67), as well as Falstaff,
have connections with the court, but their preference for
integration with the humbler Windsor community is
expressed by their desire to marry Anne Page.

The Windsor community that accepts considerable
diversity and tolerates a good deal of aggressive, anti-
social behaviour severely punishes Falstaff for his
proposed adultery. By attacking marriage, the basis of
social structure, Falstaff has repudiated the friendliness
and hospitality that are the means both of creating and of
expressing communal solidarity. Also, his smug assumption of the acceptability of his proposal threatens the
women's sense of their own identity, which depends
largely on their public status as virtuous wives. Mistress
Ford's reaction on receiving Falstaff's letter is to reflect
uneasily on her own behaviour:

> What an unweighed behaviour hath this Flemish
> drunkard picked . . . out of my conversation, that he
> dares in this manner assay me? . . . I was then frugal
> of my mirth. Heaven forgive me!

(II.i.22-28)

Mistress Page expresses even more explicitly the disorien-
tation they both feel at this threat to their sense of
themselves:

> *Mrs. Ford.* What doth he think of us?
>
> *Mrs. Page.* Nay, I know not: it makes me almost ready
> to wrangle with mine own honesty. I'll entertain myself
> like one that I am not acquainted withal; for, sure, un-
> less he know some strain in me that I know not myself,
> he would never have boarded me in this fury.

(ll. 80-86)

Because their sense of themselves depends on their public
image, they cannot simply refuse Falstaff's proposal but
must prove to him and to the community at large how
totally wrong he is. Thus their revenge is as much educa-
tive as retributive. They do not denounce Falstaff and send
him packing; instead they teach him a lesson by humbling

his aggressive individualism to the values and authority of
their rural community. They put him through a series of
experiences that forces him to bow to social pressures and
prepares him to understand and accept his place within the
society.

Appropriately, the staging of Falstaff's humiliation utilizes
burlesque versions of pastoral motifs. In the first episode,
the ubiquitous flowing brook of the pastoral landscape has
been transformed to the muddy banks of the Thames into
which Falstaff is thrown. The traditional symbolism of
purity is rendered comically in the domestic details of
laundering, and Falstaff's urgent need for purification is
reified in the dirty, smelly linen that he shares the buck
basket with. The man who woos with talk of jewels and
courtly finery is unceremoniously "rammed . . . in with
foul shirts and smocks, socks, foul stockings, greasy
napkins, that . . . there was the rankest compound of villainous smell that ever offended nostril" (III.v.80-84).

As the merry wives anticipate, this first treatment does not
cure Falstaff's "dissolute disease" (III.iii.177). Like Duke
Senior, who finds that natural adversities "'feelingly
persuade me what I am'" (*AYL* II.i.11), Falstaff is reminded
by his rude immersion in the Thames of what kind of man
he is—a man with "a kind of alacrity in sinking," "a man
. . . that am as subject to heat as butter; a man of continual
dissolution and thaw" (III.v.12, 105-08). But while he is
made conscious of his physical grossness and vulnerability,
he remains unrepentant and unashamed. He recounts the
experience with indignation at the discomfort he has suffered and with undiminished arrogance and contempt for
Master Ford, whom he again plans to cuckold, and for
Mistress Ford, whom he plans to pass on afterwards to
Master Brook.

In his next encounter with the Windsor wives, Falstaff is
disguised as a woman. Although a shepherd's costume is a
more usual pastoral disguise, Falstaff's female clothing is
not unprecedented. Pyrocles in Sidney's *Arcadia* also puts
on women's clothing to disguise his pursuit of a forbidden
love. But while Pyrocles disguises himself as a splendidly
beautiful and war-like amazon, Falstaff appears as an
outcast old woman. Again, the details of the punishment
appropriately travesty the fat knight's pretensions. His
favourite persona as suitor has been that of a blunt, virile
soldier. For example, his initial love letters concluded:

> "Let it suffice thee . . . if the love of soldier can suf-
> fice—that I love thee. I will not say pity me—'tis not
> a soldier-like phrase—but I say, love me. By me,
>
> Thine own true knight,
> By day or night,
> Or any kind of light,
> With all his might
> For thee to fight,
>   John Falstaff."

(II.i.9-19)

And at his first assignation with Mistress Ford he disdain-
fully contrasts his own manly courting with that of those

effeminate "lisping hawthorn-buds that come like women in men's apparel" (III.iii.65-66). At their next meeting when he hears that her husband is coming, this mighty knight begs the women to devise a disguise for him—"any extremity rather than a mischief" (IV.ii.65-66). Pyrocles, disguised as the amazon Zelmane, feels only momentary shame at being discovered in his female disguise and justifies his adopted motto, *Never more Valiant,* by fighting bravely and victoriously. But the merry wives have mischievously dressed Falstaff as "the fat woman of Brainford" (IV.ii.67), whom Master Ford believes to be a witch and has threatened to beat, so that, in addition to betraying his cowardice, Falstaff receives a thorough drubbing from the "peasant" Ford.

This experience shakes Falstaff's self-confidence even if it does not damage his self-esteem. He rather defensively boasts to "Master Brook" that, although he has been beaten "in the shape of a woman[,] . . . in the shape of man . . . I fear not Goliath with a weaver's beam" (V.i.20-22). In soliloquy he admits that he has been "cozened and beaten too" (IV.v.89), but he boasts to Mistress Quickly of the "admirable dexterity of wit" (IV.v.112) with which he avoided the further humiliation of being exhibited as a witch in the common stocks. He fears public humiliation, but the authority and judgment he respects are the court's:

> If it should come to the ear of the court how I have been transformed, and how my transformation hath been washed and cudgelled, they would melt me out of my fat drop by drop, and liquor fishermen's boots with me; I warrant they would whip me with their fine wits till I were as crest-fallen as a dried pear.
>
> (IV.v.89-95)

Abashed but unrepentant, he wants revenge rather than forgiveness from Windsor society.

His desire to be revenged on Ford incites him to meet Mistress Ford once more and so to fall into the last trap set for him. Mistress Ford and Mistress Page understand that Falstaff has been sufficiently frightened by the last fiasco not to renew his solicitations but that his punishment will not be complete until his shame is made public. Falstaff suffered his dunking in the Thames privately and his beating anonymously; his final humiliation takes place before the entire community. It also penetrates most deeply to the core of his pride. When Ford, disguised as Master Brook, flatters Falstaff that he is renowned for his "many war-like, court-like, and learned" (II.ii.220-21) endowments, he shrewdly articulates Falstaff's image of himself. Although his soldierly swaggering and his courtly wooing are perhaps largely tongue-in-cheek, pride in his "admirable dexterity of wit" is wholly genuine. For example, it provides his enjoyment in mocking country obtuseness and superstition when Slender sends Simple to consult the fortune-telling woman of Brainford (IV.v.28-53). And, of course, a sense of intellectual superiority underlies his whole cony-catching scheme. Just as being treated as a piece of dirty laundry has tarnished his pretensions to

courtly grandeur and receiving a beating as a weak old woman has undermined his war-like boasting, the last plot is designed to attack his intellectual pride.

For the last, much elaborated punishment, Mistress Ford arranges a midnight rendezvous in Windsor forest by an old oak tree reputed to be haunted by the spirit of Herne the hunter. Falstaff, wearing stag antlers in disguise as Herne the hunter, is caught up in the fabulous, numinous atmosphere:

> The Windsor bell hath struck twelve; the minute draws on. Now, the hot-blooded gods assist me! Remember, Jove, thou wast a bull for thy Europa; love set on thy horns.
>
> (V.v.1-4)

Although he had planned to manipulate the women sexually for his own financial purposes, they now arouse him to an erotic frenzy:

> My doe with the black scut? Let the sky rain potatoes; let it thunder to the tune of 'Greensleeves', hail kissing-comfits, and snow eringoes; let there come a tempest of provocation, I will shelter me here.
>
> (ll. 18-22)

Suddenly, his sexual fantasy-come-true is interrupted by Evans, Quickly, and the Windsor children disguised as fairies, and the women flee. Falstaff, who had mocked Simple's credulity so wittily, is totally duped and hides his eyes in terror: "They are fairies; he that speaks to them shall die" (l. 48). The "fairies" discover and torment him until the Pages and Fords arrive to complete his disgrace by mocking him.

The scene at Herne's oak is a burlesque version of the supernatural centre at the heart of the pastoral landscape. Speaking of the multiple setting of Renaissance pastoral romances, Walter R. Davis suggests thinking of "a center with two concentric circles surrounding it." The pattern, he says, implies

> a kind of purification of life proceeding inward: from the . . . naturalistic outer circle, to the refined pastoral inner circle, and then to the pure center of the world.
>
> The center is always supernatural, usually either a shrine . . . or the dwelling of a magician. It may be the actual dwelling place of the god, who may reveal himself . . . there.[6]

The spectacle of a fat old man with deer antlers tied to his head being pinched by a motley assortment of villagers got up as fairies obviously is a long way from Calidore's vision of the Graces dancing on Mount Alcidale in Spenser's Legend of Courtesy, yet, for all its absurdity, the scene at Herne's oak functions much as the visit to a supernatural centre does in more orthodox pastorals. Calidore, who withdraws from his heroic quest into a pastoral world and then happens upon the Graces dancing to Colin Clout's

William Hutt as Falstaff, Alan Scarfe as Frank Ford, Lewis Gordon as George Page, Jennifer Phipps as Mistress Page, and Domini Blythe as Mistress Ford in the 1978 Stratford Festival production of The Merry Wives of Windsor.

piping, gains momentary access to the poet's vision of perfect order that embraces the natural and human worlds while transcending them. Falstaff witnesses a humbler artistic production, but even Mistress Quickly is unexpectedly dignified in her role as fairy queen and evokes quite eloquently an image of natural and social order:

> And nightly, meadow-fairies, look you sing,
> Like to the Garter's compass, in a ring:
> Th'expressure that it bears, green let it be,
> More fertile-fresh than all the field to see;
> And *Honi soit qui mal y pense* write
> In em'rald tufts, flowers purple, blue, and white,
> Like sapphire, pearl, and rich embroidery
> Buckled below fair knighthood's bending knee:
> Fairies use flowers for their charactery.
>
> (V.v.66-74)

The basic action of the pastoral romance, according to Davis, consists of the hero's journey from the heroic world of the outer circle to the peaceful pastoral world, and then to the supernatural centre, where the hero resolves his internal conflicts and is prepared for his return to the outer world.[7] Sometimes the resolution is simply the supernatural gift of a god, but sometimes the illumination is gained more painfully. In Sidney's *Arcadia,* for example, the centre is not a shrine but a cave, which serves as a focus for events that are "degrading and even shameful as well as instructive and humiliating."[8] For Falstaff the process is painful and increasingly humiliating. First, the "fairies" taunt and torture him for the sinful fantasies of his corrupted heart. After the fairy vision vanishes, the mockery of the assembled company forces him to realize that the only metamorphosis to occur at Hearne's oak is, as he ruefully admits, that "I am made an ass" (l. 120). What most astonishes him is his own gullibility—that he, witty Jack Falstaff, "in despite of the teeth of all rhyme and reason" took the villagers for fairies: "See now how wit may be made a Jack-a-Lent, when 'tis upon ill employment!" (ll. 126-29). The Fords and the Pages taunt and insult him, but it is Parson Evans's voice that Falstaff reacts to most strongly:

Have I lived to stand at the taunt of one that makes
fritters of English? This is enough to be the decay of
lust and late-walking through the realm.

                                                    (ll. 143-46)

The chorus of ridicule culminates with Evans's denunciation, which elicits Falstaff's surrender:

> Well, I am your theme: you have the start of me. I am
> dejected; I am not able to answer the Welsh flannel;
> ignorance itself is a plummet o'er me; use me as you
> will.
>
>   (ll. 162-65)

When Falstaff's wit is humbled to Evans's ignorance, the
pastoral values of simplicity and humility have triumphed
over wit and worldliness, communality has triumphed over
selfish individualism, and Falstaff's punishment is over.
He has been exposed, humiliated, and hence controlled.
The goal has not been ostracism or even conversion but
rather integration, and the Pages begin the process by
extending yet one more hospitable invitation, including
"Sir John and all" (l. 240). Once the threat of adultery has
been defeated, the group turns its attention to celebrating
marriage—sexuality in its socially controlled form. Anne
Page's elopement is discovered and forgiven, and the play
ends with a joking reference to middle-aged, married
sexuality:

> *Ford.*   Sir John,
> To Master Brook you yet shall hold your word,
> For he to-night shall lie with Mistress Ford.
>
>   (ll. 240-42)

In this way, Windsor combines two traditions: the pastoral
world as a place of innocence and chastity and the pastoral
world as a place of full sensual gratification.

While *The Merry Wives* ends happily with plans for
everyone to return to town and "laugh this sport o'er by a
country fire" (l. 239), mockery, the weapon that brings
Falstaff's greed and lust under social control, also can be
socially divisive. Suffering scorn and ridicule creates the
desire to mock others in revenge. Thus when the Host
ridicules Caius and Evans, they abandon their duel rather
than be laughingstocks only to ally themselves in a plot to
have revenge on him. Poor Master Ford's double fear, of
being revealed to public scorn as a cuckold and of being
ridiculed by Page as a "jealous fool" (IV.ii.120) for unwarranted suspicion, drives him to the absurd position of wanting to prove his wife guilty of adultery so that he can "be
revenged on Falstaff, and laugh at Page" (II.ii.299-300).
This potentially destructive process of mockery begetting
mockery does not develop into an uncontrolled cycle of
revenge largely because of its communal nature. No one
pursues a goal of private vengeance; instead, each person
who feels aggrieved enlists friends and neighbours in his
scheme, whose end is always public ridicule. No one
rejects the group judgment or perpetuates his grudge
beyond the public acknowledgement of guilt. For example,

Ford explicitly submits himself to the judgment of the
group each time he sets out to prove Falstaff's adultery
(III.iii.138-40; IV.ii.147-51) and admits his fault and asks
for forgiveness when his suspicions prove wrong
(III.iii.210; IV.iv.6-9). Although Parson Evans occasionally
reminds him of his weakness, Mistress Ford asks no additional penance, and Master Page, rather than gloating,
exemplifies characteristic Windsor moderation by warning
Ford against being "as extreme in submission / As in offence" (IV.iv.11-12).

The pattern works out most clearly, indeed almost
schematically, in the three plots against Falstaff. The first
involves only the women—Mistress Ford, Mistress Page,
and Mistress Quickly. In the second, the men cooperate
unwittingly: Ford beats Falstaff without knowing it.
Significantly, as the group opposing Falstaff widens, Falstaff's sub-group disintegrates, and the men's involvement
results directly from his followers' revenge against him for
turning them away. Finally, the men, women, and children
of Windsor all participate in the last plot. In the first
episode, the women Falstaff has most directly misjudged
and insulted punish him. In the second, the agent of
persecution is Master Ford, the man he has consciously
tried to injure. In the third, that role is taken by Parson
Evans, a disinterested representative of the community.
Once Falstaff has submitted, he is invited to participate in
the favourite communal activities of feasting and shared
laughter.

On the whole, then, social solidarity and co-operation
operate beneficently in the Windsor of Shakespeare's
imagination, defeating anti-social aggression and controlling the use of the powerfully coercive weapons of social
pressure. But the play also acknowledges the danger to
individuality inherent in the power of social coercion.
Abraham Slender, who is perfectly willing to marry anyone
Justice Shallow tells him to but cannot comprehend the
idea that his own feelings could be at all relevant to the
matter, is a potent warning of how the individual mind and
will can be stunted in a tightly knit society. Still, Slender
is the only happy and hopeless victim of this power we
see. If the threat of divisive individualism is defeated by
social cohesion, the possible tyranny of this cohesion is
prevented by its fluidity and informality. Anne Page can
disobey her parents and marry the man she wants because
her mother and father disagree. They close ranks to defeat
a common enemy but pursue their goals for Anne singly
and secretly. This division enables Anne to act independently and justifies her doing so. Mistress Page's attempt
to outwit her husband and Anne's success in outwitting
both her parents do not constitute a direct assault on ideas
of patriarchal, hierarchical authority, but they suggest,
perhaps even more subversively, that such orthodoxies are
irrelevant abstractions with little relation to the actual
functioning of a harmonious society. When Anne and Fenton return and defer obediently to Anne's parents, the
group rallies to reconcile the Pages to the marriage, and
the rebellious marriage becomes part of the "sport" that
"Sir John and all" will laugh over by their country fire.

The narrative patterns of *The Merry Wives* draw heavily on the conventions of the pastoral tradition and dramatize its assumption that outside the pressures and rigidities of sophisticated society people can achieve natural freedom and harmony with their environment. In one line of action, a man embroiled in conflict retires to a natural setting where, after a period of contemplation, he puts away his sword, makes peace with his enemy, and re-enters society as a peacemaker and moral instructor. In another plot line, a young aristocrat, who is good at heart but corrupted by worldly society (indicated by his mercenary motives and reputation for profligacy), falls in love with a village lass. Purified by the experience, he overcomes obstacles and wins her hand in marriage. In the main plot, a knightly exile from court enters a rural society where, although evil exists, moral issues are simplified and clarified and where his pride is humbled. Impelled by disappointment in love, he moves further from man-made institutions into the natural world until he reaches a sacred place where the human and divine meet. Here he experiences humiliation and a revelation about the natural sources of social harmony and then re-enters society a sadder but wiser man.

While the play's plot structure and symbolic motifs derive from the highly artificial, conventionalized traditions of pastoral literature, the tone and texture of the dramatic action are realistic, farcical, and unromanticized. The action on stage is often rowdy and boisterously physical. The setting is rural England, not a remote and glamorous Arcadia. The cast of characters includes popular comic fictional characters and ordinary bourgeois English men and women rather than lovelorn shepherds. The prose dialogue contains a good deal of "hack[ing] our English" (III.i.72) and very little of the rhetorical elegance of Sidnean or Spenserian pastoral. This incongruous combination is doubly satirical, pointing at once to the pastoral conventions' distance from reality and to ordinary life's banality and pettiness in comparison with the idylls of the poetic imagination. But the parodic tension between pastoral framework and low-comedy rendering does not destroy the connection between them. After all, poetry typically works by disjunctions, disrupting familiar associations and established connections and forging new ones. In *The Merry Wives* the disparity offers an interpretation of the pastoral ideal of human harmony compatible with recognizing the imperfections of human nature. The harmony in this imaginative model may derive from nothing more exalted than natural human sociability (the desire to belong that is the other side of the fear of mockery and isolation), but, for all that, the amity and unity of its attainment should not be despised. In Shakespeare's Windsor the pastoral values of simplicity, humility, and fidelity are elusive and transitory but always accessible; dramatic action grows out of the struggle by the inhabitants to maintain this equilibrium.

Notes

1. I quote throughout from the New Arden edition, ed. H.J. Oliver (London: Methuen, 1971).

2. Ronald Huebert, "Levels of Parody in *The Merry Wives of Windsor*," *English Studies in Canada*, 3, 2 (Summer 1977), 136-52. For useful discussions of the evidence for dating the play 1597, see Oliver's New Arden introduction, pp. lii-lvi, and Jeanne Addison Roberts, *Shakespeare's English Comedy: 'The Merry Wives of Windsor' in Context* (Lincoln, Neb.: University of Nebraska Press, 1979), pp. 41-50.

3. Thomas Sternhold and John Hopkins, *The Whole Booke of Davids Psalmes* (London: John Daye, 1582), pp. 343-44.

4. Huebert argues that since Psalm 137 concludes by calling for God's vengeance on the enemies of Israel, Evans implicitly is invoking divine wrath on Doctor Caius, and "the threatening rumble of the Babylon Psalm is the bugle-call of the knight-at-arms." Because Evans as knight is more notable for discretion than valour, the effect is mock heroic (Huebert, p. 141). I think that the original audience, like the modern, would have associated Psalm 137 with waters, willows, harps, and tears more readily than with bugles, that is, with elegaic pastoral rather than with heroic poetry or epic.

5. Barbara Freedman, "Falstaff's Punishment: Buffoonery as Defensive Posture in *The Merry Wives of Windsor*," *Shakespeare Studies*, 14 (1981), 167.

6. Walter R. Davis and R.A. Lanham, *Sidney's 'Arcadia'* (New Haven: Yale University Press, 1965), p. 35.

7. Davis, pp. 38-39.

8. Davis, p. 175.

R.S. White (essay date 1991)

SOURCE: "The Town of Windsor," in *Twayne's New Critical Introductions to Shakespeare: The Merry Wives of Windsor,* Twayne Publishers, 1991, pp. 1-16.

[*In the following essay, White asserts that* The Merry Wives of Windsor *provides a realistic portrayal of sixteenth-century life due to its contemporary English setting.*]

It is dangerous, and perhaps impossible, to claim that any work of literature or art is 'realistic'. All that art can give us is a model of a possible world, and we as spectators locate ourselves either close to or distant from that world. The work of Ernst Gombrich and John Berger in the field of pictorial art, and the developing ideas of semioticians, prove that art works through conventions and codes which we as viewers and readers feel either comfortable with or uneasy in decoding. Moreover, as 'metatheatrical' critics (J.L. Calderwood is the main exponent) have insistently shown, Shakespeare in particular rarely allows us to forget that we are watching (or reading) a stage play rather than observing what pretends to be unmediated 'reality'. Such theatrical consciousness is at work in this play. On several occasions characters use theatrical terms when speaking of their own activities:

Mistress Ford. Mistress Page, remember you your cue.
Mistress Page. I warrant thee; if I do not act it, hiss me.

(III. iii. 34-5)

Falstaff. . . . after we had embraced, kissed, protested, and, as it were, spoken the prologue of our comedy . . .

(III. v. 68-9)

The scene in the Forest at the end is presented as a masque by characters who are very conscious of the fictive roles they play. The effects of such 'metatheatrical' aspects of presentation can be very problematical (as in *Hamlet*) and it may even be an open question as to whether the effect is to distance us from the action or, paradoxically, to make us feel it is more naturalistic. Comments such as Mistress Page's can simultaneously make us aware that we are in a theatre watching actors and contribute to the overall sense that the play itself has its distinctive, internally consistent 'possible world' with its own norms of what is real and what is not.

In terms of the 'possible worlds' given to us by Shakespeare in his plays, some are either more or less remote from what we recognise as a specific 'locality' with its own ethos within which we can assume a proximity to a 'realistic' setting. His comedies generally give us never-never lands like the dreamy Illyria, the literary Forest of Arden (or Ardennes, as the New Oxford Shakespeare insists), the romantic Belmont or the commercially-minded and vindictive Venice, the madcap forest outside Athens. Such settings take us away from any recognisable day-by-day existence. There is a stratum of such 'romantic' conventions in *The Merry Wives* found in the wooing of Anne Page, the comic disguises of Falstaff as the fat lady of Brainford, of Mistress Quickly as the Fairy Queen, of Slender and Doctor Caius, Anne and Fenton, and indeed all characters except Falstaff in the last scene. In this scene we even have a forest which has its transformative magic, able to bring couples together (and back together, like the Fords).

However, compared with full-blooded romantic comedy, Windsor in our play seems solidly rooted in its specified town planning, its diurnal activities, its local customs. It is, after all, English (the only comedy Shakespeare set in England), and it is a geographically precise location whose central landmark, the pub called the Garter Inn, still exists. The play is also the one and only example by Shakespeare of Citizen Comedy, a genre which was popular in the early seventeenth century, showing the middle class involved to a large extent in believable commercial transactions as well as love, rather than the aristocratic, fantasy milieu of romantic comedy. There may even be a little joke by Shakespeare in all this, since by mentioning Windsor he may have raised audience expectations about seeing the private life of the court, since the town is where the Royal Palace was (and still is), only to disappoint them by scrupulously not showing court life. This is not,

however, to say that what Shakespeare does with the town of Windsor is necessarily 'realistic', and still less is it to say that the characters are 'real', for a more eccentric lot could hardly be imagined. The play is certainly not in the mould of 'social realism' as the term is understood today, and the plot is too elaborately crafted in multi-layered fashion to be a 'slice of life'.

No matter how we need to qualify the statement, it is possible to talk about the Windsor of the play as a small, self-sufficient society which is 'characterised' by local references. Early on we get chatter about town life which is inconsequential to the plot but is important in building up a social setting. Mr Page thanks Justice Shallow for a gift of venison, Shallow regrets it is not of the top quality (it was badly killed, perhaps by Falstaff), and he enquires after Mistress Page's health. Slender indulges in gentle banter about Shallow's greyhound which is rumoured to have lost a race at a meeting in the Cotswolds. And then the dialogue returns to the matter in hand, the troubles caused by Falstaff. There are neighbourly meals, one to be held before a sea-coal fire (sea-coal was gathered at Newcastle upon Tyne and Sunderland and shipped down to the south, thus acquiring something of a status symbol for its price and superior quality). One meal concludes with pippin apples and cheese. When dogs bark, Slender surmises that there are bears in town and he recalls seeing the famous London bear Sackerson 'loose twenty times' (I. i. 274). This detail partly fixes Slender as one who enjoys male, violent pursuits (he has bruised his shin at fencing with a sword and dagger, revels in bear-baiting, and will later collude in a duel), and it also helps to characterise the township's men in general.

Geographical references are often particularised. John and Robert, Ford's servants, must take the laundry-basket 'among the whitsters in Datchet Mead, and there empty it in the muddy ditch close by the Thames side' (III. iii. 14-15). The fat woman impersonated by Falstaff is from Brainford (now Brentwood in Essex), and she is well known in Windsor. While the plot moves between the Garter Inn, Mistress Ford's house, the fields and Herne's oak in the Park, there is awareness of the close proximity of Windsor Castle and of the 'big city' of London from where some of the characters have come. The events in the forest may be just as fictive as those in the Forest of Arden or the Forest outside Athens, but the name itself would have had a real reference point for a contemporary audience as a semi-provincial, largely agricultural but regally significant town. All these details may simply be the consequence of the play having been commissioned and adapted to be played in Windsor, but since the play does not have to be played there (and usually is not), we can make the point that topical detail builds up a little world with its own rough town-plan, sports, occupations, friendships and rivalries, a rooted locality in which characters 'live', some permanently and some temporarily.

Much the same can be said, incidentally, of the settings of most of Shakespeare's comedies, even the most fantastical, for they are all essentially about people interacting in social groups. For example, through the accumulation of apparent and conspicuous irrelevancies of detail, Illyria, in *Twelfth Night,* is given a strong presence as a social setting which contains and is distinct from its citizens. The same could be said of Messina in *Much Ado About Nothing,* or the contrasted cities of Belmont and Venice in *The Merchant of Venice.* This is not just to make a point about atmosphere or background. The 'characterisation' of the town of Windsor extends to an underlying value-system, a set of tacit assumptions about the way life is, and should be, led. These attitudes may be espoused and practised by its citizens, but there is a feeling that they have been inherited from generations of Windsor-dwellers. They have the status of customary, unquestioned, and settled routines and beliefs. It is the solidity of these values which are tested and threatened by those who enter from the outside, in the clash which motivates the plot.

CIVILITY AND INCIVILITY

A brief exchange between Slender and Parson Evans reveals something of the underlying attitudes that bind Windsor society together. Slender regrets having become drunk in the company of Falstaff's men, since he has had his pocket picked as a consequence:

> *Slender.* . . . I'll ne'er be drunk whilst I live again, but in honest, civil, godly company, for this trick. If I be drunk, I'll be drunk with those that have the fear of God, and not with drunken knaves.
> *Evans.* So Got 'udge me, that is a virtuous mind.
>
> (I. i. 166-71)

Drunkenness is no vice in itself, but takes its colour from the company, as the local vicar confirms. In 'honest, civil, godly company' drunkenness may be the activity of a 'virtuous mind'. Honesty is almost next to godliness, separated only by 'civility'. The three qualities make one a good citizen, and it is this word that best sums up the ethos of Windsor. Mistress Quickly pays the highest compliment to Mistress Page:

> . . . and, let me tell you in your ear, she's as fartuous a civil modest wife, and one, I tell you, that will not miss your morning nor evening prayer, as any is in Windsor, who'er be the other.
>
> (II. ii. 93-6)

Windsorites do not seem to have an exact definition of civility, and they apply the concept mainly to keeping good company and attending church regularly. Basically, it is the kind of conduct that keeps the cogs of this society turning harmoniously. Making money may certainly be done 'in the way of honesty' as Mistress Quickly says (II. ii. 70-1), so long as any potential dishonesty is not visible. She herself is receiving money from two suitors to Anne Page, and she claims to be working for both of them, but she does it with 'discretion' (another Windsor word, used by Evans five times). Similarly, the Host of the Garter Inn makes money out of his tenants, and although he shows

signs of deviousness and even roguish hypocrisy, he is trusted by all as honest and civil. The families that make up Windsor life (Pages, Fords and Shallows in particular) all show signs of being moderately prosperous, landowning and involved in trade or agriculture. Having money is, if anything, a sign of solid virtue. To historicise this aspect of the play, we could interpret the linkage between money-making, relative honesty, churchgoing and civility with the rise at the end of the sixteenth century of protestantism which eventually led to the clash between court and upper bourgeoisie that lay behind the English Revolution in the 1640s. Of course, such tensions are comically contained in this play, but they are latent as part of its 'world'.

Incivility is that which disrupts town life and significantly it is equated with ungodliness. 'There is no fear of Got in a riot' (I. i. 34) warns Parson Evans, commenting upon the nuisances committed by Falstaff and his men in their open 'coney-catching' (theft by deception), beating Shallow's men, killing his deer, and breaking open his lodge. Falstaff's men, in one sense or another, are identified with the London court and the aristocracy (as is Fenton) but ironically the real sin is their impecunity, their inability to pay their way. Non-payment of the rent at the Inn is as bad as the more open crimes. Whether Falstaff is down from London for a holiday or for the express purpose of making money, he is forced into deception by the very necessities of having to pay not only his own way but also those of his men, Pistol, Bardolph and Nym and his page Robin. First he lays off Bardolph from his retinue by allowing him to work for the Host as a tapster (barman). Then he gets rid of Nym and Pistol in order to save money and to disassociate himself from their manifest crimes, thus entering into a state of 'French thrift' (I. iii. 79) by retaining only his 'skirted page', the boy Robin. His plans backfire since they give his former cronies the motive for betrayal and revenge.

It is 'thrift' (I. iii. 39), the need to pay one's way and to avoid at all costs 'waste' (ibid.) in money-conscious Windsor, that next prompts Falstaff to woo the wives, in a desperate attempt to gain access to their husbands' wealth. Mistress Page is, in his eyes, 'a region in Guiana, all gold and bounty' (I. iii. 64). He calls both 'exchequers' to him (ibid.) and sends his letters off to 'golden shores' (I. iii. 75). The imagery gives away his acquisitive motive. We shall see more evidence of commercial motivation in other characters, but the general point is that every single male character is driven by the need to make or maintain wealth. It is the central fact of (male) Windsor life, and the one that can either cause greatest havoc in society and in marriage, or conversely can keep everything in orderly, civil harmony.

Another quality which arouses the suspicions of people living in Windsor is, again in Parson Evans' word, 'affectations' (I. i. 140). He uses the word in reproof of Pistol's language, which is indeed grandiose, mannered ('He hears with ears' (I. i. 138)) and hyperbolical. Page, aroused to contempt by Falstaff's letter to his wife, says that he is 'a fellow frights English out of his wits', 'a drawling, *affecting* rogue' (II. i. 129-32, my italics). Suspicion of 'affectation' hangs over everybody who is in some way different or new: Fenton's courtly suavity (he speaks in iambic pentameters while Windsorites for the most part speak sober prose), Doctor Caius' Gallic English, as well as Falstaff's raffish and ostentatious crew are examples. Again, there is some irony in this, since some Windsorites speak in very individual ways and there are few examples of 'the King's English'. Parson Evans unconsciously draws humour from the audience, and from Falstaff who openly ridicules him, for his Welsh accent. Mistress Quickly commits malapropisms and amusing mishearings, the Host speaks with a bluff heartiness that does not carry the ring of sincerity, Shallow is easily sidetracked into irrelevancies and the speech of Simple and Slender is defined by their names. They are, in short, all to some extent at least linguistically eccentric and each could be described as 'affected'. The difference lies between acceptance and non-acceptance into Windsor. The ethos is fundamentally one that runs on conservativeness and conformity, where the familiar and habitual are considered safe, while the new is intrusively dangerous. So long as the basic rules of civility (godliness, paying one's way, modesty, discretion and thrift) are observed, then all other divergences from a norm of behaviour will be tolerated and even overlooked. Mistress Page, for example, is sympathetic to Caius as a potential 'naturalised' Windsorite because he has money. But if these rules are not obeyed, or if outsiders are suspected on these grounds (as is Fenton), then all deviation of conduct will be regarded as 'affectation' and, generally speaking, as foreign to Windsor.

Class

Windsor is conservative also in its insistence on a stable hierarchy based on status and rank. So much is revealed in the exchange that opens the play:

[Enter Justice Shallow, Slender, and Sir Hugh Evans]

> *Shallow.* Sir Hugh, persuade me not. I will make a Star-Chamber matter of it. If he were twenty Sir John Falstaffs, he shall not abuse Robert Shallow, Esquire.
> *Slender.* In the county of Gloucester, justice of peace and Coram.
> *Shallow.* Ay, cousin Slender, and Custalorum.
> *Slender.* Ay, and Ratolorum too. And a gentleman born, master parson, who writes himself Armigero—in any bill, warrant, quittance, or obligation, Armigero.
> *Shallow.* Ay, that I do, and have done any time these three hundred years.
> *Slender.* All his successors gone before him hath done't; and all his ancestors that come after him may. They may give the dozen white luces in their coat.
> *Shallow.* It is an old coat.

(I. i. 1-18)

What rankles with Shallow is that Falstaff is theoretically above him on the social scale, for Sir John is a knight

while Shallow is an 'Esquire' and merely a provincial Justice of the Peace, however time-honoured the position. This inescapable fact is unaffected by the differences in wealth. Falstaff mercilessly uses his rank to defy the jurisdiction of Shallow's over him. The digression about Shallow's 'old coat' is fuelled by his impotent rage that although 'a gentleman born' and one that stands in a hereditary line, he can be upstaged and flouted by a penniless knight slumming from London.

Below Shallow in social standing are Ford and Page. They are landowners, moneyed citizens who are clearly accustomed to getting their own way in Windsor by working closely with Justice Shallow and dining with him frequently. They respect his authority as he respects their wealth and it is they (or more specifically Page) who set the standards of behaviour in the town. Page warns his daughter about the dangers of being wooed by Fenton because he is a courtly gentleman (although, like Falstaff, he needs money), nobly born and above her status. Page's class-suspiciousness is useful for the plot since he is motivated to act like the comic *senex,* the patriarchal figure who tries to prevent his daughter from marrying according to her desires. There may even be a parallel history to this situation, for if we may believe Mistress Quickly, Mistress Ford was unsuccessfully wooed by powdered gentlemen from court (II. iii. 60ff.) in an earlier siege of Windsor, before choosing the other local, landed yeoman, Ford. Page's choice for Anne's husband (and more pertinently the future recipient of his own money and status) is Shallow's nephew, Abraham Slender. Such a marriage would satisfy the men in Windsor, for it joins wealth and status, and keeps everything 'in the town'. Meanwhile, Mistress Page's choice is Doctor Caius, presumably because he is wealthy (he can pay his way at the Inn and can afford to pay Mistress Quickly and keep his man John Rugby), and also because a physician would have been respectably placed in status close to the parson-schoolmaster, Evans. Caius could also be expected to settle in Windsor, whereas Fenton would undoubtedly take Anne back to court. Both Mistress Page and her husband are able to overlook glaring personality defects in Doctor Caius and Slender respectively, because they place financial and class circumstances above the personal. In a sense Mrs Page is right in one thing at least. She wishes Anne to marry somebody who is in love with her and has no ulterior, fortune-hunting motive, and Caius seems to be sincere in his courtship. Equally, Anne is right in a deeper sense because, as well as not loving Caius, she also avoids the fate of Mistress Ford since the Doctor reveals himself to be as violently jealous as Ford.

Hugh Evans is deftly but unforgettably sketched as the local parson and schoolteacher. So convincing is he as a provincial schoolmaster that biographers scurry to the records to find a Welshman who may have taught Shakespeare in Stratford. His Welsh English is treated with contemptuous amusement by the aloofly metropolitan Falstaff, but he has clearly been fully accepted by Windsor for his professional contributions. Paradoxically for somebody who must once have been an 'outsider', Evans has established himself as a very central figure to the town's ethos, and it is he who expresses most overtly the high priority placed upon the god-fearing virtues and upon the sanctity of 'thrift'.

Some other characters, while definitely lower on the social scale than these, are socially indeterminate. The Host of the Garter Inn and Mistress Quickly need to make money where they can, and the economic imperative leads them to disguise or suppress their own opinions. They are go-betweens, useful to the dramatist for their accessibility to all classes high and low, which makes them ideal 'plotters'. While seeming trustworthy and even sycophantic to their social superiors, they prove themselves to the audience to be devious and hypocritical. The only judgments they make concern who can pay most. This mercenary quality may superficially appear to be a moral weakness, but before we condemn them we should acknowledge that their stations in life, respectively landlord of an ailing tavern with impecunious tenants and housekeeper to an erratic foreigner with a violent temper, are the least secure of any characters in the play. They must shift as they can to maintain a precarious living. Morals, in a town like Windsor, may be a luxury available only to those privileged with wealth. In a sense the modern equivalents of the Host and Mistress Quickly are the army of people in Britain today who depend on tourists, and who have an ambivalent attitude towards their employers, poised between obsequious flattery and disguised contempt.

> *Caius.* Rugby, come to the court with me.
> [To Mistress Quickly] By gar, if I have not Anne Page, I shall turn your head out of my door. Follow my heels, Rugby.
>
> [Exeunt Caius and Rugby]
> *Mistress Quickly.* You shall have—An fool's-head of your own. No, I know Anne's mind for that. Never a woman in Windsor knows more of Anne's mind than I do, nor can do more than I do with her, I thank heaven.
>
> (I. iv. 120-6)

Beneath even these characters on the social scale are a bevy of servants, more or less silent like John and Robert who are Ford's servants and carry out the linen-basket containing Falstaff, Jack Rugby who is Doctor Caius' servant, Robin, Falstaff's page and Peter Simple, Slender's servant. In the social hierarchy they are regarded more as embellishments to their respective masters than as characters in their own right. A condition of their service is that they keep quiet about their employers' foibles and vices. If we look at the dramatis personae with an eye to class, we discover that characterisation is not so much a function of individualism and inner identity (as is often assumed with Shakespearian characters), but of economic station. Certainly, this is how people in Windsor view and judge their neighbours.

INSIDERS AND OUTSIDERS

The structure of *The Merry Wives of Windsor* is built upon the coherence of the society which we have just analysed.

The values held by Windsorites are tacitly agreed upon and zealously defended. The society has a hierarchy, but there is definitely a sense in which all those who are accepted share the values of thrift, sobriety and social ranking. Justice Shallow and Mr Page between them stand for what they see as sensible qualities that bind them all together in a form of trust. Oddities, eccentrics and even simpletons can be accepted into the circle so long as they prove their tacit agreement with an ethical and economic system. They are the 'insiders'.

'Outsiders' are regarded with mistrust. Fenton is eventually accepted into the society, as, in a more provisional way, is Doctor Caius. Falstaff is the most dangerous of all, because he threatens the stable structure of Windsor values. He is eventually purged in ritualistic fashion, as some sort of germ that must be ejected for the sake of the health of the society. And yet, as germs can be most threatening because their genetic make-up mirrors something in the organism they attack, so Falstaff (and in their different ways the more penitent and corrigible Fenton and Caius) simply clarifies, parodies and exaggerates tendencies already existent in Windsor. Ford is just as culpable as Falstaff in equating love with possession. His jealousy is simply the other side of Falstaff's desire to possess women in both sexual and commercial senses. It is Ford who pays Falstaff to test his wife's fidelity, saying 'if money go before, all ways do lie open' (II. ii. 164), words that are echoed by Falstaff in his own military idiom with 'Money is a good soldier, sir, and will on' (II. ii. 165). The Host of the Garter and Mistress Quickly are just as hypocritical and crafty as Falstaff in their readiness to take money for dubious causes. Anne Page and the 'merry wives' are just as devious in their plotting, though they can be seen as more effectively artful and also as more morally justifiable. Even Shallow, Page, Evans and Slender are as commercially-minded and acquisitive as Falstaff, although they, of course, would see their attitudes as prudent. The real danger of Falstaff is that he represents traits that already lie within the society of Windsor and must be kept under close control. His worst crime is to display in a kind of distorting mirror what all are like beneath the carefully maintained façade. This, more than his 'outsider' status, leads to his firm ejection from the society, and his final accommodation only at the cost of penitence and humiliation.

Christian values, modest but secure wealth, middling social status, prudent behaviour—these are the qualities which gain social acceptance and even respectability in Windsor. Difference of any kind is regarded as 'affectation' until the person is accepted by the community. The agreed values are defined as 'civil' and 'civic'. Gambling is not acceptable, and in a real sense both Falstaff and Fenton are gambling for women and wealth. High status is suspect, for why, the logic runs, would courtiers be in Windsor except to make money out of the town? 'Riotous' behaviour is frowned on and any form of excess, even excess in pleasure, is considered disruptive. Falstaff is excessive in body as in behaviour and he arouses most vilification. In such a society change will be resisted, the status quo preserved against all threats. Outsiders of any ilk are considered a risk to the stability of tradition and to the secure, generational rhythms of provincial English town life.

HISTORICAL CONTEXT

The historically-minded reader will want to draw a different set of conclusions from this analysis of Windsor. Just as the town is seen as a backwater under siege from the London court and Europe, so also can it be seen, in Elizabethan terms, as a bulwark of 'traditional' values which were being threatened in the late sixteenth century by the increasing dominance of London, and even by the threat posed by Queen Elizabeth marrying a foreigner in a diplomatically arranged marriage. Windsor is a town representative of a nostalgic concept of the 'organic community' based largely on agriculture and ancient status claimed now by a local, family-based hierarchy. It had its glorious past, as Mistress Quickly says, 'when the court lay at Windsor' (II. ii. 60-1), but its significance fell dramatically when the court was transferred to London and Windsor Palace had become something of a holiday-home for the monarchy rather than a political force. (As I have said, the play makes nothing of the Royal Palace except for this one, almost elegiac phrase.) It is a place which time has left behind but, in terms of the play, is considered by the outside world as a catchment area for finance. Shallow, in his first appearance in *2 Henry IV*, is seen as inveterately nostalgic for his lost youth, his wild times at the Inns of Court where he studied Law with Falstaff. 'We have heard the chimes at midnight, Justice Shallow' (*2 Henry IV*, III. ii. 228) is Falstaff's weary contribution to the backward-looking mellowness of dimming memory. Even in *The Merry Wives* (where Falstaff has very clearly outstayed his welcome), Shallow itches to be young again to teach troublemakers a lesson with the sword. At the same time, Falstaff and Fenton are buccaneers, entrepreneurial risk-takers with their assets (Falstaff's rhetoric, Fenton's good looks and status) come to rob the town of its wealth. They are, at least in this respect, prototypes of the new capitalists, men in the sixteenth century forced by inflation into economic insecurity and destined to search for new worlds, to pirate foreign ships (Falstaff's imagery in this respect is telling), or marry into rural families in order to acquire a stronger economic basis. What is happening in Windsor provides a microcosm of what was happening in England in the 1590s in social and economic terms. The play gives a reflection of a tension between 'old', 'civil' and even feudal virtues and 'new', more dangerous but potentially profitable tendencies, the tension between an 'investment' and a 'risk-taking' mentality.

Shakespeare's insights into such social tensions are acute throughout his works, and in this he must have been helped by his own, socially mobile experience. He grew up in Stratford-upon-Avon, which cannot have been totally unlike Windsor as depicted in the play. He went to London to 'make his fortune' as an actor and playwright, and was so successful that he could play before the Queen in the acting company commissioned as The Queen's Men and, if legend is correct, he could even be commissioned to write a play at the request of Elizabeth. He was later to retire to Stratford to buy land and become one of the town's wealthiest men. If there is a 'moral' to the tale in the play, it may strike us as a provisional and perhaps suspect one. The older virtues of Windsor are glowingly presented at the end of the play as generous and forgiving ones, for both Fenton and even Falstaff are invited to the feast. If the older community on a cusp with threatening pressures may absorb the voguish—allow a little of the new into the settled verities of the old—it may survive unscathed and need not make major changes. The sardonic mind may see this as a moral which is deeply comforting to those who inherit the wealth of England, deeply unjust and pessimistic to those who do not have a place in the ordered hierarchy created by wealth. It was a complacency to be challenged in succeeding centuries but which might still have its legacy in England today.

Charles Stanley Ross (essay date 1992)

SOURCE: "Shakespeare's *Merry Wives* and the Law of Fraudulent Conveyance," in *Renaissance Drama*, n.s., XXV, 1994, pp. 145-69.

[*In the following essay, originally presented in 1992, Ross examines the fraudulent practices that occur in* The Merry Wives of Windsor, *which center principally but not exclusively around Falstaff, and argues that the ambivalent outcomes of these practices reflect the ambiguous morals of Renaissance society.*]

Several forms of fraudulent conveyance characterize Shakespeare's *Merry Wives of Windsor:*[1] Fraudulent conveyance may be defined as putting realizable assets beyond [a] creditor's process, whatever form that process might take" (Glenn 2). Laws against such transfers of assets occur in every society that recognizes the obligation to pay debts. The flip side is that civil societies have a certain tolerance for people who devise means to avoid the clutches of creditors.

The concept of fraudulent conveyance was found in Roman law;[2] it arose in canon law, where the pauper status of clerics complicated the collection of debts;[3] and it had a noble history in England, where complex legal mechanisms were constantly devised to frustrate judicial processes that sought to take property for the benefit of creditors. From the time of the Magna Carta, the Parliament of England regularly protected royal interests against fraudulent conveyances. A series of statutes provided remedies against mortmain, subinfeudation,[4] conveyances to defeat a lord of his wardship,[5] the seeking of sanctuary to escape financial liabilities,[6] fraudulent deeds used by those accused of treason to protect family property, as well as other devices, some still being invented in Shakespeare's day.[7] For legal historians the most significant of these statutes is 13 Eliz. 5 (1571), because Sir Edward Coke, the queen's attorney general, gave the statute two readings, in Twyne's case (3 Co. Rep. 80b [1601]) and Packman's case (6 Co. Rep. 18b [1585]).[8] The language of the statute—still present in the law of many states—forbids

> fraudulent feoffements, Giftes, Grantes, Alienationes, Conveyances, Bondes, Suites, Judgements and Executions as well of Landes and Tenements, as of goods and Cattells [sic] . . . devised and contrived of malice, fraud, covin, collusion or guile, to the end, purpose and intent, to delay, hinder or defraud, creditors and others of their iust and lawfull Actions, Suites, Debts.
>
> (13 Eliz. 5)

Garrard Glenn characterizes the statute as purely political and punitive, designed to protect the interest of the Crown in land.[9] That it was not aimed at creditors can be deduced from the fact that a bankruptcy statute passed the same year did not mention fraudulent conveyance. The political purpose of similar statues explains why Spenser frequently mentions fraudulent conveyance in his *View of the Present State of Ireland* (1596), written but not published within a few years of Shakespeare's composition of *The Merry Wives*.[10] Just beginning a tenure as sheriff of Cork, the Protestant poet complains, through the medium of the *View,* that the Irish practice fraudulent conveyance when they deed their property to a relative before going into rebellion. According to English law, a dead rebel had to forfeit his property to the queen. If the man no longer had title to his land, the queen was deprived of her "escheat" (the reversion of land to the Crown). Spenser warns the authorities in London that much land has been conveyed secretly for this purpose.

A few modern instances should suggest the range and moral ambiguity of fraudulent transfers that make them a perennial concern. First, a man or woman facing bankruptcy may seek to put assets in the name of a spouse or child. The law will generally void such transfers as an attempt to defraud creditors. (Most states provide certain exemptions as a matter of policy to preserve the family unit.) Second, some forms of Medicaid provide free care for the indigent. Is it fraudulent to give your lifetime savings to your children to prevent their depletion by nursing-home expenses that Medicaid will cover? One view regards the practice as mere "asset planning"; another regards those who transfer for less than full value as lacking a "modicum of decency."[11] The classic American standoff between farmers and bankers provides a third example.[12] Midwest farmers routinely ship grain to distant elevators to keep their product out of the hands of bankers in case they default on crop loans.[13] This example suggests that the form of the conveyance is of marginal importance. (Narrowly defined, a conveyance is a means for transferring estates in land.) Although it might make all the difference whether one must only send a truck for hidden grain rather than tracing property that may have been sold several times to a series of *bona fide* purchasers, morally

the issue is simply whether society will allow certain practices to defeat creditors.

Shakespeare's composition and revision of a play that echoes such practices coincided with the first important appearance of the concept of fraudulent conveyance in the debtor law of England. Twyne's case (1601) also records the first instance in which Justice Coke spelled out the "badges of fraud" that determined whether a conveyance was fraudulent or not. A creditor sought to attach the sheep of a man named Pierce in payment for debt, but Pierce "conveyed" them to a man named Twyne by deed. Because Pierce conveyed the sheep to Twyne to avoid his debt, the English court declared the deed void and allowed the creditor to obtain possession of the animals. Coke defended his belief that the conveyance was meant to defraud by pointing to several indicators: the gift was made in secret, the sheep retained the original owner's mark, Pierce had no other assets, and the deed unnecessarily proclaimed itself *bona fide*. The prominence of the case suggests that the courts were moving to protect creditors' rights in new ways. Coke believed he could guess Pierce's intentions.[14] Understanding Falstaff's conveyancings in *The Merry Wives* proves more difficult.

I

A law and literature analysis typically considers what a legal perspective can tell us about a work of art, or what a literary understanding reveals about the law, or the regulation of literature by law. Although Shakespeare's play may open our eyes to the acceptance of fraud (or near fraud) in the law of conveyancing, this essay concentrates on the first approach for the most part.

The plot of *The Merry Wives* involves many legal themes: Justice Shallow's suit against Falstaff for a deer poached by the fat knight, Falstaff's attempts to avoid debt, the several marriage negotiations concerning Anne Page, the clever ways the wives avoid adultery by fending off Falstaff's advances, the rules of the duel, and the theft of horses. There is even a hint of the issue of same-sex marriage at the end of the play when two suitors find they have carried away boys instead of Anne Page. The element of fraud these adversarial situations share raises what Richard Posner calls the "fundamental problems of law, which is how to control human behavior effectively by means of rules" (105). Fraud becomes socially acceptable when laws no longer reflect the mores of a society. The colonial context in which Spenser operated, as an English agent in Ireland, reminds us that what looks fraudulent from the creditor's perspective often seems, from the debtor's angle, to be a legitimate way to protect a family inheritance from an antagonistic political power or impersonal creditor

The link between law and literature is rarely literal. Law as a subject matter is usually "just a metaphor for something else" (Posner 15). Anthony Trollope is a rare exception, as is a certain passage in Vladimir Nabokov's

Lolita, in which Humbert Humbert brilliantly parodies a legal memo on the issue of interstate travel with an under-age companion for immoral purposes.[15] The literary use of the law is usually much less exact: Portia's trial of Shylock in *The Merchant of Venice* is a legal farce and—to take another well-known example from the law and literature field—Melville probably did not have his eye on naval law when he wrote *Billy Budd* (Posner 162). In the same way, the law of fraudulent conveyance forms an interesting and necessary background to *The Merry Wives of Windsor,* but the play is not about legal technicalities.

Yet Shakespeare's play has long been recognized for the legal language that distinguishes the Folio from the Quarto text: characters use words and phrases such as quorum, Star Chamber, Justice of the Peace, *custalorum,* "bill, warrant, quittance, or obligation,"[16] "the register" (of follies), "fee'd every slight occasion," "exhibit a bill in the parliament,"[17] building on another man's ground, fee simple, fine and recovery,[18] waste, cheaters,[19] exchequers, egress and regress, suits and oyers.[20] An earlier generation of critics used this language to argue that Shakespeare was a trained lawyer; more sober reflection has shown that these words and phrases were readily available and rarely employed with technical exactness.[21] Nowhere do we find a "conveyance" in the narrow sense of a transfer of title by deed, but the recent work of Patricia Parker has revealed a "discursive network" that "links the transporting or translating of words with the transfer, conveying, or stealing of property" in the play.[22]

It is the possibility and practice, not the legal technicality, of the law of fraudulent conveyance that enters the comedy. As Parker has shown, conveying plays a large metaphoric role in *The Merry Wives,* introducing not merely signs of the law (the legalisms pursued by earlier scholars) but subversive practices that inspired the law, such as fraud. For this reason, conveyance operates as a paradigm for actions that illustrate a relationship between law and literature: a parody or parallel more productive than the illusion of legal substance, the representation of the adversarial process, or the use of legal terminology.

A true theory of law and literature requires a conception of the jurisprudence that underpins the ways an author employs legal materials, by which I mean the author's assessment of the source and function of law in society. A creative writer need not be bound by a single jurisprudence, but if sensitive to the operation of law, he or she may create a dramatic interaction between different ways of understanding society's formal rules. As analysts of law and literature, our task begins with the identification of traditional categories of jurisprudence, such as natural, customary, and positive law, as well as the fields where law functions: property, family, commerce, administration, torts, procedure, contracts. The story told will either be one of conflict or transition: a clash between fundamental values, or changing conceptions of law based on our historical assessment of a given society. A competition between legal and literary modes of dispute resolution will naturally recur from work to work, providing the possibility of a sustained approach to literary history.

If, as Richard Weisberg claims, "literature provides unique insights into the underpinnings of law" (*Poethics* 3), and if Shakespeare's *Merry Wives* provides such insight into the practice of fraudulent conveyance, nonetheless Posner rightly warns us about a fundamental incompatibility of the outward structures of the law and a play. This incompatibility requires us to make three critical assumptions that separate *The Merry Wives* from the law. First, we presume organic unity in a work of art—that the various actions that comprise the plot express a single theme—in contrast to a series of separable issues that compose legal thinking. Second, we regard *The Merry Wives* not as a brief about fraudulent conveyance but as a dramatic presentation of what lawyers today call the "public policy" to which laws eventually conform. Third, we recognize that the bourgeois characters of *The Merry Wives* use mercantile and legal language even when the matter is not mercantile and legal, so sometimes they talk literally and other times metaphorically. These characters serve as foils to Falstaff, who sometimes seems out of touch with, but sometimes is perceptive about, certain matters of fraud.

II

Shakespeare's *Merry Wives* finds Falstaff financially embarrassed and involved in a number of carryings on to obtain money. Early in the play he plans to seduce two wives of Windsor, Mistress Page and Mistress Ford, not for love but to gain access to the moneybags of their rich husbands. Much of the drama's humor derives from Falstaff's failure to dissimulate his intentions effectively.

The wives learn of Falstaff's plot when he sends them each an identical love letter. Falstaff's men, Pistol and Nym, then reveal his game to the wives' husbands. The result is a series of humiliations: most famously, Mistress Ford's servants secretly "convey" Falstaff in a buck-basket of dirty laundry from Mistress Ford's house to the Thames for a dunking. The conveyance saves Falstaff from the wrath of a jealous husband while punishing him at the same time. But Falstaff's conveyance in a buck-basket is only the most spectacular of several imitations of legal deception in the play.

In *2 Henry IV* Falstaff recalls his time as a law student at Clement's Inn (3.2.308). Although Mistress Page, as a woman, would not have attended the Inns of Court, she often sounds more like a lawyer than Falstaff. Traditionally the first act of fraud was Jacob's deception of Isaac to win Esau's birthright (Parker, *Literary* 74). Mistress Page cites it when she compares her letter from Falstaff to Mistress Ford's: "heere's the twynbrother of thy Letter: but let thine inherit first, for I protest mine never shall" (Folio 2.1). Later, after Falstaff is beaten as a woman, Mistress Page produces the densest legalism in the play: "if the divell have him not in fee-simple, with fine and recovery, he will never (I thinke) in the way of waste, attempt us againe" (4.2). Mistress Page compares Falstaff's beating to an exorcism of the devil, who has surely been driven out unless he has undisputed possession of Falstaff ("fee simple"), a fee often obtained, in the late sixteenth century, by the legal maneuver of "fine and recovery."[23] Mistress Page not only uses legal language; she is also alert to fraud and deception.

For the second part of Mistress Page's sentence compares Falstaff's attempts on the ladies' virtue to a dispute over rights to exploit real estate. Paul S. Clarkson and Clyde T. Warren correctly gloss "waste" as "the unauthorized use of land," "the spoil or destruction done, or permitted, to houses, lands, trees, or other corporeal hereditaments by the tenant in possession to the prejudice of the reversioner or remainderman in fee simple or fee tail," noting the objection that "Falstaff was certainly no tenant (metaphorically, of course)" (166-67). But this account misses the point that such waste was a recognized form of fraudulent conveyance.[24] In 1601 Elizabeth's Parliament passed a statue that reflects the wider association of fraud and waste: 43 Eliz. 8, "an act against fraudulent administration of Intestates goods," targeted estate administrators who managed to give away goods before creditors could be paid because the creditors, "for lack of knowledge of the place of habitation of the Administrator, cannot arrest him," or if they find him and sue him, learn he is unable to pay "the value of that he hath conveyed away of the intestates goods, or released of his debts, *by way of wasting*" (*Anno xliii;* emphasis added). Mistress Page identifies *herself* as one with the potential to *waste* and understands that waste is a form of fraudulent conveyance.

Besides making a legal pun on *waste* and *waist,* Mistress Page also plots. She vows revenge when she receives Falstaff's letter; she enlists Mistress Quickly; she suggests disguising Falstaff as a woman when he will not enter the basket a second time; and she invents Falstaff's third humiliation, the Herne the Hunter scenario.[25] Most spectacularly, she instigates Mistress Ford to convey Falstaff in a buck-basket when Ford, like a judgment creditor, demands that his wife hand over Falstaff.

Finally, Mistress Page associates legal language with the plans she conceives. For example, the Folio assigns Mistress Page a significant use of the word "convey" in the play, one of several legalisms by which Shakespeare's revisions find legal language to catch up with and recognize the nature and complexity of the plot.[26] In the Quarto Falstaff first uses the word "convey" in reference to his concealed transport in Mistress Ford's buck-basket ("convey me hence" [3.3]), but his usage seems to be accounted for by the presence of the word in *Tarlton's News out of Purgatorie,* a probable source (Bullough 31). By contrast, when Mistress Page says "convey" in the Folio, one first feels that the word signals a character's awareness of its legal and ethical associations: "If you have a friend here, convey, convey him out," she tells Mistress Ford. "Bethinke you of some conveyance. . . . Looke,

heere is a basket" (3.3). Something similar happens when Richard II shouts "Conveyers are you all!" at Bullingbroke after he orders his men to "convey" Richard to the Tower (*Richard II* 4.1).

The exquisite humor of the buck-basket parody lies in the double sense of conveyance as both the means of transferring title and the property itself. Where real property is at issue, a "conveyance" is always metaphorical (even when livery of seisin is confirmed by dropping a clod of earth). A deed may be "conveyed," but it or another document has value only through what it represents. A marriage debt is similarly metaphorical, even though it may entail physical activity. Falstaff expects the wives to betray their husbands, to whom they owe their loyalty, by loving him instead. Mistress Ford and Mistress Page, however, protect their reputations and chastity by secretly conveying Falstaff out of Ford's house. The buck-basket parody works because it inverts the literal and metaphorical aspects of a fraudulent conveyance. The "conveyancing" of Falstaff actually takes place, and Falstaff becomes, literally, the conveyance.

III

An overlooked element of fraud also lies concealed in another well-known legalism, Ford's reference to building on another man's land. Having learned Falstaff intends to seduce his wife, Ford disguises himself as a stranger named Brooke (Broome in the Folio). He meets Falstaff at the Garter Inn, claiming he loves Mistress Ford and offering to pay Falstaff to seduce her on the theory that, having once fallen, she will then favorably receive his entreaties. Amazed at Brooke's profession of love and confession of failure that drives him to this extreme, Falstaff asks him, "Of what quality was your love then?" Ford responds with a legal metaphor, comparing his love of Mistress Ford "to a fair house, built on another mans ground, so that I have lost my edifice, by mistaking the place, where I erected it" (2.2.215). Clarkson and Warren echo earlier legal scrutinists, that "at common law if a man by mistake erected a house upon another man's land it became a part of the land and the property of the landowner" (164). The rule is that whatever is affixed to the soil belongs to the soil (*"quicquid plantatur solo solo cedit"; "aedificium solo cedit"*).[27] The idea occurs in Shakespeare's sonnet 146: "Why so large cost, having so short a lease, / Dost thou upon thy fading mansion spend?" (Dunbar Barton 114). The rule was a commonplace of the law.

Criticism of *The Merry Wives* has not noticed, however, the opportunity the rule provided for mischief. Consider a tenant who seeks a twenty-year lease knowing that he wants to construct a building. The tenant will naturally bargain for a lease price discounted to reflect the future value of the building that will belong to the landlord once the lease expires. Yet if the landlord can manage to accelerate the lease—perhaps by demanding payment when the tenant blunders into insolvency, or even by driving the tenant into financial trouble—the landlord will effect a

Act V, scene v. Falstaff, Mrs. Ford, Mrs. Page, Sir Hugh Evans, Pistol, Mistress Quickly, Ann Page, and others.

conveyance to himself. Modern lawyers describe a similar situation as a *constructive* fraudulent conveyance (meaning the effect against other creditors is the same, although strictly speaking there is no *conveyance*) (Kennedy). Such a situation occurs when a landlord terminates a lease, leaving the lessee/debtor with no income to pay his creditors, thereby causing the tenant to forfeit his building or premises.

Exactly this process occurred in Shakespeare's circle in the 1597, when the twenty-year lease that James Burbage had taken from Gyles Allen for land on which to build the Theatre expired. Allen had the law on his side. He owned the land, and when the lease was up he owned the building.[28] And yet, to the Burbages and their resident theater company, including Shakespeare, it doubtless seemed that Allen was morally or contractually obligated to renew the lease. When Allen refused, and Burbage's plans to cover himself by moving into Blackfriars ran into trouble, Shakespeare's company reacted as if Allen had effected a constructive fraudulent conveyance, and they took measures to void it. They literally disassembled the Theatre from Allen's property on 28 December 1598, and then floated the timbers across the Thames to construct the new Globe Theatre.

Like the conveyance of an entire theater—a gesture initiated by actors alert to maintaining their assets—the buckbasket that carries Falstaff humorously suggests a theatrical representation of statutes on fraudulent conveyance. As Posner writes, law functions best in literature not as "a complex of rules and institutions" but as a "practice" that can be "imitated" in the Aristotelian sense (79). The practice at which the statutes aimed was amazingly widespread. A. W. B. Simpson has called the late sixteenth and early seventeenth centuries "the age of fantastic conveyances," as lawyers manipulated legal estates to outwit the Statute of Uses and the Statute of Enrollments passed under Henry VIII: "The chaotic state of the land law on points such as these was all the more lamentable during a period of social upheaval marked by an increase in the prosperity and social status of the lesser landowners, which, in its turn, brought an accompanying desire to 'found families' and ensure that the family estate should not be alienated out of the family in the future" (Simpson 186). This common topic was readily available to Shakespeare and his circle in popular and indexed epitomes, such as those of Robert Brook, William Rastell, Fernando Pulton, William West, and Edmund Plowden, many published by Richard Tottel.[29]

We do not know if Shakespeare read these works, but we do know his friends (if not he himself) practiced the deceptions these books describe. For not only did Shakespeare's acquaintances take a dim view of the termination of Burbage's lease, but, in a related gesture, they themselves readily conveyed property to avoid creditors. For example, before he died, John Brayne had been James Burbage's partner in constructing the Theatre. In 1591 an attorney named Henry Bett mentioned in a deposition that Brayne habitually prepared deeds of gift whenever he anticipated being imprisoned for debt. Bett implied that Brayne acted to defraud creditors, commenting, "That yt was a Common thinge, wth the said John Braine, to make deedes of gifte of his goodes and Chattelles, the reason was . . . to prevent his Credito^rs aswell before buildinge of the Theatre, as since, for he beinge redie to be imprisoned for debt he would prepare sutch safetie for his goodes, as he could / by those deedes" (Wallace 86). At the time he wrote, Bett was an ally of the Burbages in defending their interests against Brayne's widow, who acted at the instigation of a man named Robert Miles. Later he witnessed the assignment of the lease of the Theatre to Cuthbert Burbage.

Another legally ambiguous conveyance occurred in 1596, when James Burbage protected his estate "by making a deed of gift to Cuthbert of all his personal property, and another deed of gift of the Blackfriars to his second son, Richard" (Shakespeare's acting partner) (Wallace 23-24). As a result of this gift, Robert Miles filed suit in 1597 against Cuthbert, Richard, and Ellen Burbage. Miles charged that James Burbage fraudulently conveyed his estate to defeat Miles and other creditors of their due. Perhaps because the law was still unsettled, Miles lost his legal action, as did Gyles Allen, who raised the same issue in 1599 when he sued the Burbages for the value of his lost building.

The prevalence and uncertainty of the practice of fraudulent conveyancing gives layers of meaning to Ford's speech to Falstaff. We have seen, for example, that an unscrupulous landlord might let someone who was ignorant of his title build on his land. Ford, disguised as Brooke, similarly encourages Falstaff to "build" on his "ground" (his wife). The metaphor works at least two ways: first, "Brooke" builds false hope upon another man's ground; second, Ford suspects someone has made "shrewd construction" on his wife's "enlarged mirth." In the latter case the "building" is not vain desire but a sexual erection: Mistress Quickly unknowingly blunders onto the truth a few lines later. Falstaff catches her meaning, but he is remarkably unaware of the risk he takes of being defrauded by Brooke, since he himself will be "building" on another man's (Ford's) "ground." Instead, Falstaff's mind conjures a law that arises from the works of nature (nature to which his

mind compares woman), when he says that he has mistakenly built upon a "woman's promise" (3.5.41). Ford's "building" image refers to a form of fraudulent conveyance under a lease, but Falstaff (fresh from a dunking in the Thames) thinks, rather quaintly, in terms of riparian rights. Land is stable, but a riverbank can shift in flood, and the changing course of a stream may eliminate one's property interest.[30] A "woman's promise," Falstaff suggests, shifts like a shoreline, and one's possessions may be washed away.

IV

Like Mistress Page and Ford—and in contrast to Falstaff's somewhat retrograde activity—the Host also thinks like a contemporary lawyer. He is eager to use the legal terminology of "egress and regress" ("said I well?"),[31] and he worries that "Brooke" has a "shute [suit] against my knight." He somewhat suspiciously keeps a room for Falstaff even when the Garter has been taken over by Germans ("They have had my [house] a week at command. I have turn'd away my other guests" [4.3.8]).[32] He also seems to have a precocious sense of what in later contract law will be called "mutual mistake" when he assigns Caius and Evans to different locations for their duel, effectively preventing their encounter. (A contract is void when a broker makes a sale by describing a different article to each party; cf. Tiffany 3.) The result is good comedy.

The Host also connives with Falstaff with regard to the employment of Bardolphe. The dismissal of a servant to evade debt is a very old legal trick. Justinian mentions fraudulent manumission and gives an example: "A grant of freedom amounts to fraud on creditors when the grantor is already insolvent at the time of the manumission or will become so by freeing the slaves" (Justinian, *Institutes* 41 [1.6.3]). Bardolphe is not a Roman slave, of course, but in *2 Henry IV*, Falstaff says he "bought" him at St. Paul's. When Falstaff follows his announcement that he needs to "turn away" some of his followers by saying "I sit at ten pounds a weeke" (1.3), the Host of the Garter is not slow to realize that he receives most of that expense. (The tavern bill found on Falstaff in *1 Henry IV* suggests that Falstaff spends thirteen shillings a day for food and drink, which with half a crown or so for rent, comes to about ten pounds a week.) Mine Host picks up Bardolphe's hire because he values a good customer. He is the beneficiary of Falstaff's transfer of Bardolphe, and the transfer verges on fraud because of a trust relationship between Falstaff and the Host to the detriment of other creditors (although it was legitimate to *prefer* one creditor over another). As a tapster, Bardolphe will spend much of his time doing what he would do anyway, fetching sack for Falstaff.

Falstaff's show of concern for finding new employment for Bardolphe conceals the fact that a transfer of assets is taking place. Openly, Falstaff defends letting Bardolphe go by claiming he has lost his skill in filching. Pistol—who has just heard Falstaff rationalize his dismissal of Bardolphe by claiming that he stole not in time—perhaps puts a right name to what has happened. Shakespeare's characters usually base their puns and wordplay on something someone else has just said or done. Pistol has heard Nym use the word "steal" a moment before, but he may have come up with the word "convey" in response to the way Falstaff engineers Bardolphe's new occupation when he offers a synonym for theft: "Convay, the wise it call. Steal? foh: a fico for the phrase!"

Falstaff has told his followers he needs to practice deceit— "to shuffle, to hedge, and to lurch"—thus coloring even his inadvertent actions with a degree of intentionality. Pistol's suspicion of Falstaff's secret dealings helps account for his and then Nym's refusal to carry Falstaff's love letters. The distaste for pimping that they express seems like a sudden attack of virtue, but their possible suspicion is borne out when Falstaff seizes his chance to cashier his two remaining followers. Whatever his true motive, and whether or not the Host connives with him (as Twyne did with Pierce), Falstaff gets a kind of fresh start by releasing Bardolphe. He reduces his expenses, and he may also make money if Bardolphe, Pistol, and Nym are receiving a military salary that Falstaff can pocket. We remain uncertain as to whether Falstaff makes a sly reference to the deceptive practice of fraudulent conveyance when he refers to Bardolphe's new occupation as a "good trade," but others, including the perspicacious Host, seem well aware of what is happening.

Ford, Mistress Page, and the Host constitute a pattern of legal thinking that reflects the increasingly mercantile world of turn-of-the-century England. Their values contrast with those of the knightly class to which Falstaff belongs. England's gentry and aristocracy embraced a romantic ideology of exploration and commercial adventure that also colors Falstaff's language.[33] As an apologist for empire, or like an old aristocrat, the knight believes that fortunes are made by wooing women for their wealth.[34] Falstaff is certain the wives of Windsor will yield riches: he declares that Mistress Ford and Mistress Page are lands of "gold, and bountie: I will be Cheaters to them both, and they shall be Exchequers to mee: they shall be my East and West Indies, and I will trade to them both" (1.3.29ff.). He means, "I will deceive them; they will be my source of wealth. I will take money first from one, then the other." But Falstaff's language undercuts him by echoing a commercial world to which he seems a stranger. In real life, "cheaters" were tax collectors, and they were capable of fraud. The situation at Cadiz in 1596 shows such a corrupt representative of the Exchequer at work, as J. E. Neale tells the story:

> Both Howard and Essex were under promise and orders to save the plunder of the voyage for the Queen: they gave it with a bountiful hand to their men. An official had been attached to them to see the order carried out: he plundered with the rest.
>
> (346)

Whether or not Shakespeare knew about Cadiz, the problem of repossessing property that such embezzlers bought with the king or queen's money is typical of a series of cases in James Dyer's *Reports* on fraudulent conveyance.[35] This close connection between "escheators" for the Crown and fraud suggests the limited range of Falstaff's ideas on trading and cheating: he maintains an epic attitude of bravado and lying in a world where economic activity was increasingly seen as a technically sophisticated adventure.

The problem of Falstaff's legal knowledge surfaces most acutely in the final act, when Ford announces that Falstaff owes "Brooke" (the name that Ford assumes in disguise) the sum of twenty pounds, money that Falstaff has accepted in exchange for his promise to Brooke to seduce Mistress Ford. In the Quarto version of the play Ford mentions "a further matter" to Falstaff: "There's 20 pound you borrowed of M. Brooke Sir John, /And it must be paid to M. Ford Sir John" (5.5.117). Mistress Ford tells her husband to forgive his debtor, thereby effecting a reconciliation appropriate to the comedy's conclusion: "Nay husband let that go to make amends, / Forgive that sum, and so weele all be friends."

In the Folio, however, Mistress Ford says nothing about forgiving Falstaff, while Ford announces that Falstaff's "horses are arrested" to ensure repayment of the debt. Lewis Theobald retained the Quarto reading, noting, in a quasi-judicial manner, that "Sir John Falstaff is sufficiently punished, in being disappointed and exposed. The expectation of his being prosecuted for the twenty pounds, gives the conclusion too tragical a turn. Besides it is *poetical justice* that Ford should sustain his loss, as a fine for his unreasonable jealously" (216). I believe Theobald overreacts. For one thing, Ford's legal move may have been merely practical: in *1 Henry IV*, when Prince Hal hides Falstaff's horse before the Gadshill robbery, he knows that the fat knight is not likely to move far unmounted.

If Ford has not taken Falstaff's horses as a joke, then the term "arrest" may be a legalism. Falstaff may have been compelled to give horses to the sheriff as pledges that he will appear in court. His horses would have been "arrested" because the writ that forced Falstaff to pledge the horses was the *capias ad respondendum*, a common writ used to start a case.[36] But nothing indicates Falstaff knows what has happened. John Cowell's *Interpreter* (1601) offers another possible gloss in the writ of *arrestandis bonis ne dissipentur*, "which lyeth for him, whose catell or goods are taken by another, that, during the controversie, doth, or is like to make them away, and will be hardly able to make satisfaction for them afterward."[37] Yet this writ fits the facts of the case imperfectly, since Falstaff did not take horses from Ford.[38]

It is tempting to suggest that perhaps old Falstaff knows a thing or two about fraudulent conveyances and that Ford is merely blustering when he claims to have arrested Falstaff's horses. Falstaff seems unperturbed by the news, and it may be that Ford sent the bailiff too late. I am not the first to think that those horses of the Host stolen by the

"Germans" may well have been Falstaff's, doubtless on their way to a place beyond the reach of creditors.[39]

Falstaff's conveyance of his horses would be fraudulent if he had no other assets with which to repay his debt. He has clothes, and his room at the Garter counts as an asset if he has paid for it in advance. He may have an income either from an inheritance or as a military captain. Falstaff also has an uncertain number of horses—say four, one each for himself and his men—whose value we may estimate at about five pounds apiece, suggesting that "Brooke" knew his man if he purposely limited his lending to twenty pounds.[40]

Falstaff's notable failure to convey his horses beyond the reach of his creditor—which Ford's action presumes—illustrates how conveyancing suits comic drama. In Plautus and Terence, the creditor often takes the form of a distant father or husband or brothel owner to whom a girl owes a duty that she seeks to convey to a young man, whom she will marry.[41] Indeed, so suited is conveyancing, like revenge, to literary treatment that Erich Segal observes how young men typically court bankruptcy in the Roman comedies.[42] The lovers' insolvency—like Falstaff's (who therefore symbolically stands in for Anne Page's suitor Fenton, who has money enough but lacks the goodwill of Anne's parents)—allows comedy to represent the "breaking of restrictions" that is the "'heart' of the genre" (Segal 17-18). Like fraudulent conveyance, comedy can take many forms. In Moliere's *Le Festin de pierre,* for example, Don Juan gets rid of his creditor Monsieur Dimanche by professing such warm friendship and sharing such solicitude for him that the creditor never gets to demand his money (Olson 59). Shakespeare's comedies typically turn on sudden shifts in affection, as when a young man like Proteus in *The Two Gentlemen of Verona* claims to give one woman his heart (the title) but conveys his affection (the use) elsewhere. As Elder Olson observes, comedy contrasts to the narrow genre of tragedy, because comedy has an enormous range of plots.

The comic form of *The Merry Wives of Windsor* remains intact, despite what Theobald thought, if we follow the text and assume Ford did manage to arrest Falstaff's horses. Falstaff has traditionally been regarded as a *miles gloriosus* figure, the alazon or braggart of Roman comedy, or as a derivative of vice in the old morality plays. Recent critics, seeking to interpret the final pageant of *The Merry Wives,* see him as a carnival figure, a victim of folk ritual, or a scapegoat who bears the vices of misplaced sexuality and deception "shared by the very citizens who taunt him" (Hinely; Foley; Parten). I believe he is an effigy of fraud as well. The original Twelve Tables of Rome allowed creditors to divide the body of a debtor among them.[43] Falstaff therefore echoes the old Roman law when, reveling with the wives at Herne the Hunter's oak tree, he offers to divide himself up for their benefit, a haunch to each. Falstaff's symbolic role as a figure of fraud helps explain why Falstaff invites Brooke to Herne's oak to watch him give himself to Mistress Ford and also why Falstaff is ultimately forgiven his trespasses by the townspeople who mock him.

The reconciliation of Falstaff with the citizens of Windsor mirrors the general acceptance of this form of fraud by Shakespeare's society. Mistress Page's legal language suggests that she is an astute woman who recognizes the delightful way Falstaff's carriage in a buck-basket parodies the practice of fraudulent conveyance. Mr. Ford conjures a form of "constructive" fraudulent conveyance when he compares making love to someone else's wife with building on another man's land. The Host of the Garter also thinks like a lawyer. He takes over Bardolphe's employment to help Falstaff manage his affairs. Compared to these characters, Falstaff appears curiously retrograde in his awareness of legal matters: the end of the Folio version holds up the possibility that Falstaff, said to owe Ford twenty pounds, has missed an opportunity to fraudulently convey his horses. In each case the play draws on a common issue in the legal thinking of sixteenth-century England.

The moral ambivalence of fraudulent conveyance unifies the play and explains its legal metaphors. Although there have been recent defenses of Falstaff's role in the comedy, he has generally been taken to be a lesser wit than the knight of the history plays. A. C. Bradley called Falstaff's degradation "horrible."[44] Samuel Johnson said that the danger of Falstaff's vice is its attractiveness to others.[45] I believe Bradley's view is misguided and that Johnson's observation applies to *The Merry Wives* as well the history plays. Falstaff reflects a society in which fraud is endemic and social rules, including legal forms of conveyance, are in flux.

As a figure of the shifting ethics of conveyancing, Falstaff operates both openly and secretly, intentionally and perhaps instinctually. Jill Levenson observes that the narrative movement of comedy is often accompanied, in the Renaissance, by "a series of debates" or *dianoia:* "that ongoing process of reasoning and problem-solving which the commentators suggest is the action of comedy" (268, citing Altman 139, 157-61). In Shakespeare's history plays, Falstaff's illegal behavior threatens to mislead Prince Hal and derange society (Kornstein 134-42). Shakespeare's comedy, however, absorbs Falstaff's deceptive stratagems because the mores of the society represented in the play show the same ambiguity that characterizes Falstaff.

Falstaff's simultaneous punishment and escape reflects the moral ambiguity of fraudulent conveyancing. The terms debtor and creditor are like the image of a vase that becomes the profile of two women as we stare at it. Depending on our situation, we will sympathize with one or the other. Fraudulent conveyance operates in this shifting moral sphere, where power blurs the line between right and wrong. Anyone, including Falstaff, who appears unfairly oppressed by circumstances or misfortune will arouse sympathy.

Notes

This essay was first presented at the Indiana College English Association, 30 October 1992, and at the Shakespeare and Law section, organized by Constance Jordan, of the 1994 meeting of the Shakespeare Association of America. I would like to thank David Bevington, Michael Murrin, the anonymous reader for *Renaissance Drama,* and Frances Dolan for providing written comments on previous versions. Thanks also to Patricia Parker, Seth Weiner, and Slaney Ross, who made several editorial suggestions.

1. Quotations are taken from the facsimile editions listed in the Works Cited. The editors of the Quarto facsimile give line numbers that correspond roughly to those of the Globe edition based on the Folio. Leah S. Marcus ("Levelling") comments on the different versions: *The Merry Wives of Windsor* "exists in a Quarto of 1602 with an urban setting strongly suggesting London or some provincial city, and the standard copytext, the 1623 Folio version, which sets the play in and around the town of Windsor and includes numerous topographical references to the area, its palace, park, and surrounding villages" (173). "Both versions of *Merry Wives* are teeming with folk rituals, but the way we interpret them will depend on which version we choose" (175). This essay suggests that what Marcus says extends to legal rituals as well.

2. Radin; Glenn 82.

3. Helmholz 8, 12; Martines 176; Simpson 174 (comparing the medieval use to modern tax evasion, as when the Franciscans, to maintain poverty, "found it convenient that property should be held by others to their use").

4. 9 Hen. III 35 was a statute against mortmain and subinfeudation (conveyance of lands to a religious house in order "to take the same land again to hold of the same house"). "A tenant might convey land to a church with the understanding that the church would subinfeudate him for lesser services. The result was that the superior lord now had the church for a tenant, with the resulting loss of feudal dues, but the erstwhile tenant still had the benefit of the land with his obligations considerably reduced" (Kempin 146).

5. 52 Hen. III 6.

6. 50 Edw. III 6 was aimed at those who, to avoid creditors, give their tenements and chattels to friends, who agree to pass on the profits, and then seek sanctuary in "the Franchise of Westminster, of S. Martin le graund of London, or other such priviledged places." The Parliament of Henry VII repeated the injunction of 50 Edw. III 6 against deeds of gift made to defraud creditors by those who seek "Sanctuary, or other places privileged" (3 Hen. VII c. 4).

7. A series of statutes under Richard II (11 Ricc. II 1-6) was aimed at five specific peers of the realm, accused of high treason, to void the "fraudulent conveyances of their goods to deceive the King." One bill under Henry VIII forced a single man, Sir John Shel-

ton, to repeal fraudulent deeds and conveyances made to defeat the king and others of wardship, primer seisin, and relief, and to make clear that he, condemned to die, did so while seised of those lands, which the king could then reach (33 Hen. VIII 26). Later laws were aimed at recusants who sought by "convenous conveyance" "to defraud any interest, right, or title, that may or ought to grow to the Queen" or anyone else (23 Eliz. 2 and 29 Eliz. 6). Another statute (27 Eliz. 4, passed in 1585 and made perpetual in 1597 by 39 Eliz. 18) prohibited fraudulent conveyances to defeat purchasers (in other words, it gave statutory form to the obvious notion that you should not sell the same thing to two people at the same time). In 1603, between the Quarto and Folio versions of *Merry Wives,* King James's first Parliament made fraudulent conveyance an act of bankruptcy (the law applied only to merchants). The issue in Elizabethan times was the *trade rule* in bankruptcy, which was added to the 1543 statute in 1571. After 1571, courts gradually clarified what manufacturers of tangible goods could be covered by bankruptcy law: shoemakers in 1592, drapers in 1610, dyers in 1621, bakers in 1623, carpenters in 1688 (Weisberg, "Commercial" 22-24). (Much later the issue would become discharge or the modern "fresh start.") The next act of this legal history occurred in 1623 when James's new bankruptcy bill (21 Jac. 19) incorporated the specific language of 13 Eliz. 5 and Twyne's case, which survives to this day in many states ("to delay, defraud, or hinder" creditors and others). The bill also uncannily echoes Falstaff's debt, since the fraudulent conveyancing provision only applies to amounts of twenty pounds or more. Another threshold in the bill is that the debtor's obligations must be one hundred pounds, the amount Fenton offers the Host to help him convey away Anne Page.

8. "Our notion of the fraudulent conveyance traces to a statute of Elizabeth . . . due to the restatement of the law which was made by Sir Edward Coke. . . . Later, no one cared to go back further; and so our law of fraudulent conveyances may be ascribed to Coke" (Glenn 79).

9. Glenn observes that the first Elizabethan statute against fraudulent conveyance had less to do with creditor's rights than with providing the queen with a legal means to enrich the royal treasury. The statute of 13 Eliz. 5 provided that, in Glenn's summary, "'all and every the parties' to a fraudulent conveyance, 'being privy and knowing of the same,' shall forfeit one year's value of the land, if land was the subject, and 'the whole value of the goods and chattels,' one half to the Queen and the other half to any party who may be aggrieved" (92).

10. In addition, *A Briefe Note of Ireland,* if Spenser's, refers to fraudulent conveyancing in the last words the poet wrote: "Whereas manie of the lords of the Countrie not longe before the confederating of his rebellion procured there freeholders to take there

lands of them selues by lease manie of which are since now gone into rebellion / That provision may be made for the avoyding of such fraudulent conveyances made onelie to defeat hir Maiestie of the benefitt of theire attainder" (245).

11. See Carlson. See also (for convenience I cite in law-review style): Dobris, *Medicaid Asset Planning by the Elderly*, 24 REAL PPTJ 1 (cloud of fraudulent conveyance law creates no safe haven for divestment planning); *cf.* Randall v. Lukhard, 729 F.2d 966, at 969 (4ᵗʰ Cir. 1984) (dissent said anyone who transfers for less than full value and then applies for Medicaid lacks even a "modicum of decency" and has sunk to "immoral depths"); State v. Goggins, 546 A. 2d 250 (Conn. 1988) (allegation that transfer of Medicaid patient's property was fraudulent conveyance).

12. David Ray Papke reveals how American agrarian law valorized debtors ("Rhetoric").

13. This suspicion reflects the opinion of rural bankers I spoke with during a visit to the federal Bankruptcy Court in Lafayette, Indiana.

14. Coke, the queen's attorney general, paid no attention to the Crown's rights or interests "but he put life into the Statute by applying it to the rights of the citizen who has been cozened" (Glenn 99).

If Shakespeare knew the case, he would have read legal French, of which I give a sample: "[I]n camera Stellata, pur contriver et publication dun fraudulent done des byens; Le case sur lestatute de 13 Eliz. cap. 5, fuit tiel: Pierce fuit endebt al Twyne en 400.li." Pierce had "byens et chateux al value de 300.li. en secret fait general done per fait, de touts ses byens et chateux reals & personals quecunque al Twyne." Twyne resisted "ad *Fieri facias* direct al Vicont de South." When he came to execute the brief, it was found that "cest done fuit fraudulent" under the statute because the gift had "les ensignes et markes de fraude": the gift was general without exception for clothing ("son apparel ou ascun chose de necessitie"). Also, the gift said it was done "honestly, truely, & bona fide," a phrase that aroused suspicion because "secrecie est un marke de fraude." Coke objects to the abundance and the growth of fraud "pluis que en former temps"; therefore the court must read the statute broadly and presume fraud: "tout Statutes faits encounter fraud serra liberalment & beneficialment expounde a suppresser fraud" (Coke, *Le Tierce Part* 80-82).

15. Anthony Trollope provides a brilliant legal analysis of intent in a charge of murder in *The McDermots of Ballycloran* (1847). The passage I have in mind in *Lolita* begins "Query: is the stepfather . . ." (Nabokov 174).

16. These first terms occur in the opening conversation of Justice Shallow and Slender, whose legal knowledge finds its image, a little later, in his apparent preference for Richard Tottel's *Songs and Sonnets* instead of that publisher's legal tomes.

17. The last three examples are cited by H.J. Oliver, who declares the significance of the legalisms hard to detect (lxxviii). When Mrs. Page says she will "exhibit a bill in the parliament for the putting down of men" (2.1.27), she sounds like Beatrice.

18. For an explanation of a simple fine, see note 23.

19. "Shakespeare used the word 'cheater', either in its original sense of escheator or officer who enforced escheats or forfeitures to the Crown, or in its derivative sense of a 'swindler' or 'cheat'" (Dunbar Barton 154-55).

20. "[T]he commencement of the mock trial of Falstaff at Herne the Hunter's Oak in Windsor Park at midnight . . . is shortly followed by a parody of ordeal by fire" (Phillips 89). Shakespeare "compares the starting of a fairy revel to the opening of a Court of Assize. The fairy Hobgoblin figures as Crier of the Courts; and is ordered to open the revels as if it were an Assize: 'Crier Hobgoblin make the fairy o-yes'" (Dunbar Barton 84).

21. Dunbar Barton 7, 159; Underhill 381; Keeton 301.

22. See Parker's *"The Merry Wives"* 236. I am indebted to her *Literary Fat Ladies* for the original inspiration of the first draft of this essay, which I rewrote after she kindly referred me to her article. Neither she nor Sandra K. Fischer (*Econolingua* 59), however, catches the legal sense of "conveyance," nor does William Carroll, who also comes near my topic, list it among the forms of transgression in the play (206). Otherwise my thesis finds a parallel but not overlapping path in Fischer's contrast between King Henry's use of new terms of contract and exchange in contrast to Richard's obtuseness in *Richard II* and her remarks on how Hal learns "which debts to keep and when and how to pay" from Falstaff and his father ("He means" 159).

23. "The conveyancers quickly developed ways of breaking entails, for the benefit of tenants-in-tail who wanted to alienate the land that came to them. The conveyancers' cleverest invention was the *common recovery*. It was known that a tenant for life or a term of years sometimes fraudulently conveyed away the fee simple of the land he occupied by means of a collusive action: the purchaser claimed the land in court, and the tenant made only a gesture of defense, so that the purchaser 'recovered' the land by a legal judgment" (Harding 91). For the more complex "fine and recovery," see Clarkson and Warren 127; Underhill 405; Kempin 157.

24. William Rastell lists the rule that one who sustains damage can have a "writ of waste out of the Chancery against the escheator for his act" (522).

25. The moral ambiguity of fraudulent conveyance colors Mistress Page's behavior in the play. It can be argued that adultery has some attraction for her, just as fraudulent conveyance appeals to debtors. She is clever enough to put Mistress Ford at risk by arrang-

ing for Falstaff to come to her friend's house, although once there she plays a separate game by accusing Falstaff (who has sent two love letters) of two-timing her. Also, Anne's seven hundred-pound income (Folio 1.1.50) may have been assured by Mrs. Page's father as easily as by Mr. Page's side of the family (there is no textual way to choose), skipping a generation, perhaps creating some bitterness and giving Mistress Page reason to think hard about the transfer of property.

26. The Folio seems to me to be a later version of the play: Grace Ioppolo argues it was probably revised several times for "several Garter feasts" (120).

27. Dunbar Barton 122. William Rushton traces the maxim to Justinian and gives a variation in George Chapman's *May Day* (23-25). Clarkson and Warren (166) cite Dekker's *Shoemaker's Holiday* for a similar sexual metaphor: "hee / that sowes in another mans ground forfeits / his harvest."

28. Burbage knew his lease would expire and spent six hundred pounds on the Blackfriars, but a neighborhood petition drove him out. Shakespeare's company played at the Rose and the Swan for an interim year, then made plans to build the Globe: it was to finance this project that the Burbages allowed Shakespeare and five or so others to invest and thereby become part owners. "[B]y 1597 [the Theatre] was empty because of trouble with the lease of the land on which it stood" (Gurr, *Stage* 130).

In a private communication, Andrew Gurr expressed certainty that the law was not on the side of Shakespeare's confederates. He restated his position on the date of the play: if *The Merry Wives* was composed in 1597, then the reference "Brooke" makes would have been innocent; if composed in 1599, then it becomes a topical reference to Shakespeare's own situation. I believe this answers Elizabeth Schafer's objections to Gurr, "Intertextuality," that a 1597 date for the Folio, based on the lease reference, is only "speculation" (58).

29. W. F. Bolton counts over 225 editions of such law books and reports between 1553 and 1591, including works by Thomas Fortescue, Thomas de Littleton's *Tenures,* and James Dyer's *Reports* (54).

30. Spenser draws on a similar law of the sea in the tale of the two sons of Milesio, owners of eroding islands, when Artegall convinces them that they must be content with what the sea delivers them and what it takes away (*Faerie Queene* 5.4.4-20).

31. 2.1. Clarkson and Warren gloss "egress and regress" as derivative of words of leases that signify departure and return to some part of land (69-70).

32. English bankruptcy laws, like those of Rome, generally created some form of sanctuary, a place where a debtor could be free from arrest while he reorganized. See Thornley 183-86; Marcus, *Puzzling* 165-66; 32 Hen. VIII c. 12 ("places of priviledge and tuition for

terme" included Welles in Somerset, Westminster, Manchester, Northampton, Norwich, York, and Darby). Usually a church or abbey lands served as a sanctuary, but as Bacon recognized in his *Learned Reading upon the Statute of Uses,* debtors desired to find a retreat to live in after conveying their assets to a friend (412). They could then negotiate with their creditors, who would be willing to settle their claims at a discount because they would otherwise be unable to reach property held in trust for the debtors (Glenn 84). The Garter Inn operates symbolically in this way—rather like a "homestead" in modern law—for Falstaff lives there uninterruptedly, giving him time to effect the transfer of Bardolphe's employment to the Host of the Garter and to send love letters to Mistress Ford and Mistress Page, wooing them for their money.

33. David Quint notes that although plunder is "the normal means for an epic hero to acquire portable property," there was a tradition of debased heroes who ventured among the merchants (ancient critics called Ulysses a hording merchant, and Juvenal referred to Jason as "mercator Jason") (259). The old categories were breaking down by 1600 when Elizabeth gave a charter to the East India Company to trade wool cloth in the Indian Sea: "Commerce was the motive of exploration as well as warfare, and all three were combined in some of the greatest deeds of that generation. Romance and money-making, desperate daring and dividends, were closely associated in the minds and hearts of men" (Trevelyan 346-47).

34. Falstaff represents what Immanuel Wallerstein calls the old view of the world of trade as a trade in luxuries (food and handicraft production), not "bulk" goods (18).

35. Dyer's *Reports* cites a cluster of cases based on debt, sanctuary, and fraudulent conveyance, including the case of a man who purchased land with the money of the king: "Walter de Chyrton Customer al Roy esteant graunde dettour a luy, purchase terre ove le money le Roy, et prist lestate del terre a ses amyes a defrauder le Roy, mes il mesme prist les profits, ceux terres fuerot extende al Roy in *Scaccario*" (295). The court of Exchequer voided the conveyances and gave the land to the king.

36. Normally the creditor would enlist a bailiff to execute the debt "against the body" of the debtor: this is the language used in 1582, for example, when the bailiff of the Manor and Liberties of Stebneth executed a debt of one hundred pounds against John Brayne (Wallace 91).

37. Dr. Cowell was Reader in Civil Law at the University of Cambridge; he published *The Interpreter* in 1601 (Keeton 342).

38. Notice that Ford arrests Falstaff's horses, not Falstaff. George W. Keeton observes that Antipholus threatens Angelo with a suit for wrong arrest in *The*

Comedy of Errors (114). Other methods of distraint would be available *after* a judgment in court, which we may presume Ford has not yet sought. At that point a judgment creditor in the king's court could send a sheriff to levy on the debtor's animals by a writ of *fieri faciat,* employing a legal process that went back at least to 3 Edward I 18; *elegit* (a transfer of the debtor's personal property to his creditor at an appraised price); and *capias ad satisfaciendum* (where a local sheriff arrests the judgment debtor, who stayed in prison until he paid his fine) (Epstein 66; Dunbar Barton 85 and 92).

39. Geoffrey Bullough condemns the horse-stealing episode: "As it stands in both Q and F this is surely the worst-handled episode in all Shakespeare's plays" (11). W.W. Greg calls it "curiously fragmentary" (336); Robert S. Miola "badly garbled" (374).

40. Indictments involving the theft of horses often included the value of the animal. J.S. Cockburn lists prices in 1600: six pounds each for a black and a sorrel gelding (#2973); fifty shillings for a gray mare (#2975); three pounds for a gray gelding; five pounds for bright-bay horse; three pounds for a sorrel horse (#3011): five pounds for a gray gelding, but twenty-six shillings for a white gelding (#3011). I owe this information on prices to Shawn Smith, my former student at Purdue who is currently completing a Ph.D. at Yale University.

41. In *The Ghost,* for example, Philematium is in debt to Philolaches for buying her freedom with his own money, so she pays back her debt by loving him exclusively, despite the advice of Scapha, who argues that Philematium overpays her debt, since Philolaches will certainly leave her. In other dramas of Plautus, slave girls are typically conveyed from house to house or given sanctuary to protect them from brothel keepers.

42. The theme also occurs in *Astrophil and Stella* 18, where Sidney wants only to lose "more" of what heaven "hath lent":

> With what sharpe checkes I in my self am shent,
> When into Reason's audite I do go:
> And by just counts my selfe a banckrout know
> Of all those goods, which heav'n to me hath lent:
> . . . . .
> I see and yet no greater sorrow take,
> Then that I lose no more for *Stella's* sake.

43. See Sandars xv; Posner 93.

44. Other have defended Falstaff's role in the comedy. Brian Vickers complains that the plot requires that Falstaff by "easily duped" (141). But Oliver denies that there is a "gap" between the Falstaff who "loses the battle of wits over the Gadshill robbery and is not allowed to forget it" and "the one who can so easily be made to look foolish by the kind of honest women of whom he has little experience, or between the Falstaff who is frightened of being found by a jealous husband and the one who ran away at Gadshill." Like others, he observes that Falstaff's defeat is necessary to the comic drama (lxvii). Anne Barton concludes that Falstaff is a "lesser creature" because his character is "not . . . an end in itself" but an expression of the play's comic plot (287), a point made also by E. K. Chambers, cited by G.R. Hibbard (55).

45. "The moral to be drawn from this representation is, that no man is more dangerous than he that with a will to corrupt, hath the power to please; and that neither wit nor honesty ought to think themselves safe with such a companion when they see *Henry* seduced by Falstaff" (Johnson 356 [the last note to *2 Henry IV*]). Falstaff's double nature seems similar to Justinian's observation that fraud may be admirable: "[T]he old lawyers described even malice or fraud as good and held this expression to stand for ingenuity, especially where something was devised against an enemy or robber," and so they "added the world 'evil'" (Non fuit autem contentus praetor dolum dicere, sec adiecit malum, quoniam veteres dolum etiam bonum dicebant) (Justinian, *Digest* 119).

Works Cited

Altman, Joel B. *The Tudor Play of Mind: Rhetorical Inquiry and the Development of Elizabethan Drama.* Berkeley: U of California P, 1978.

Bacon, Francis. *Learned Reading upon the Statute of Uses. The Works of Francis Bacon.* Ed. James Spedding, Robert Leslie Ellis, and Douglas Denon Heath. 14 vols. London: Longman, 1861. New York: Garrett, 1968. 7: 389-450.

Barton, Anne. Introduction. *The Merry Wives of Windsor. The Riverside Shakespeare.* Ed. G. Blakemore Evans. Boston: Houghton, 1974. 286-89.

Barton, Dunbar Plunket. *Shakespeare and the Law.* 1929. New York: Blom, 1971.

Bolton, W. F. "Ricardian Law Reports and *Richard II.*" *Shakespeare Studies* 20 (1988): 53-65.

Bradley, A. C. "The Rejection of Falstaff." *Oxford Lectures on Poetry.* London: Macmillan, 1909. 247-75.

Brook, Robert. *Auscun novel cases de les anz et tempz le roy H. 8 Edw. 6. & la roigne Mary le I.* London (?), 1576.

Bullough, Geoffrey. "Tarltons Newes out of Purgatorie." *Narrative and Dramatic Sources of Shakespeare.* 8 vols. 1957-75. Vol. 2: *The Comedies, 1597-1603.* London: Routledge, 1958. 26-34.

Carlson, David Gray. "Is Fraudulent Conveyance Law Efficient?" *Cardozo Law Review* 9 (1987): 643-83.

Carroll, William. "'A Received Belief': Imagination in *The Merry Wives of Windsor.*" *Studies in Philology* 74 (1977): 186-215.

Clarkson, Paul S., and Clyde T. Warren. *The Law of Property in Shakespeare and the Elizabethan Drama.* Baltimore: Johns Hopkins UP, 1942.

Cockburn, J.S. *Calendar of Assize Records. Essex Indictments: Elizabeth I.* London: HMSO, 1978.

Coke, Edward. *Exact Abridgement.* London, 1651. Newberry Library Case SA 1877.

———. *Le Tierce Part des Reportes del Edward Coke Lattorney generall le Roigne.* London, 1602.

Cowell, John. *The Interpreter.* 1601. London, 1607.

Dyer, James. [*Reports.*] *Cy ensuant ascuns novel cases.* London, 1601.

[England-Statutes.] *Anno xliii. Reginae Elizabethae. At the Parliament . . . 1601.* STC 9495.

———. *A Collection in English, of the Statutes now in force, continue from the beginning of the Magna Charta.* London, 1598. STC 9321.

Epstein, David G. *Debtor-Creditor Law.* Nutshell Series. 4th ed. St. Paul: West, 1991.

Fischer, Sandra K. *Econolingua: A Glossary of Coins and Economic Language in Renaissance Drama.* Newark: U of Delaware P, 1985.

———. "'He means to pay': Value and Metaphor in the Lancastrian Tetralogy." *Shakespeare Quarterly* 40 (1989): 149-64.

Foley, Stephen. "Falstaff in Love and Other Stories from Tudor England." *Exemplaria* 1 (1989): 227-46.

Glenn, Garrard. *Fraudulent Conveyances and Preferences.* 2 vols. Rev. ed. New York: Baker, Vorrhis, 1940. Vol. 1.

Greg, W.W. *The Shakespeare First Folio.* Oxford: Clarendon, 1955.

Gurr, Andrew. "Intertextuality at Windsor." *Shakespeare Quarterly* 38 (1987): 189-200.

———. *The Shakespearean Stage, 1574-1642.* 2nd ed. Cambridge: Cambridge UP, 1980.

Harding, Alan. *A Social History of English Law.* 1966. Gloucester, MA: Smith, 1973.

Helmholz, R.H. *Canon Law and English Common Law: Selden Society Lecture Delivered in the Old Hall of Lincoln's Inn, July 5th, 1982.* London: Selden Soc., 1983.

Hibbard, G.R. Introduction. *The Merry Wives of Windsor.* 1973. Harmondsworth: Penguin, 1981.

Hinely, Jan Lawson. "Comic Scapegoats and the Falstaff of *The Merry Wives of Windsor.*" *Shakespeare Studies* 15 (1982): 37-54.

Ioppolo, Grace. *Revising Shakespeare.* Cambridge: Harvard UP, 1991.

Johnson, Samuel, ed. *The Plays of William Shakespeare.* 7 vols. 1765. New York: AMS, 1968. Vol. 4.

Justinian. *The Digest of Justinian.* Ed. Theodor Mommsen, Paul Kreuger, and Alan Watson. 4 vols. Philadelphia: U of Pennsylvania P, 1985. Vol. 1.

———. *Justinian's Institutes.* Trans. Peter Burks and Grant McLeod. Ithaca: Cornell UP, 1987.

Keeton, George W. *Shakespeare's Legal and Political Background.* New York: Barnes & Noble, 1968.

Kempin, Frederick G., Jr. *Historical Introduction to Anglo-American Law.* Nutshell Series. 3rd ed. St. Paul: West, 1990.

Kennedy, Frank R. "Involuntary Fraudulent Transfers." *Cardozo Law Review* 9 (1987): 531-80.

Kornstein, Daniel J. *Kill All the Lawyers?: Shakespeare's Legal Appeal.* Princeton: Princeton UP, 1994.

Levenson, Jill. "Comedy." *The Cambridge Companion to English Renaissance Drama.* Ed. A.R. Braunmuller and Michael Hattaway. Cambridge: Cambridge UP, 1990. 263-300.

Marcus, Leah S. "Levelling Shakespeare: Local Customs and Local Texts." *Shakespeare Quarterly* 42 (1991): 168-78.

———. *Puzzling Shakespeare: Local Reading and Its Discontents.* Berkeley: U of California P, 1988.

Martines, Lauro. *Lawyers and Statecraft in Renaissance Florence.* Princeton: Princeton UP, 1968.

Miola, Robert S. "*The Merry Wives of Windsor:* Classical and Italian Intertexts." *Comparative Drama* 27 (1993): 364-76.

Nabokov, Vladimir. *Lolita.* New York: Putnam's, 1955.

Neale, J.E. *Queen Elizabeth I.* 1934. Harmondsworth: Penguin, 1973.

Oliver, H.J., ed. *The Merry Wives of Windsor:* The Arden Shakespeare. 1971. London: Routledge, 1993.

Olson, Elder. *The Theory of Comedy.* Bloomington: Indiana UP, 1968.

Papke, David Ray. "Discharge as Denouement: Appreciating the Storytelling of Appellate Opinions." *Journal of Legal Education* 40 (1990): 145-59.

———. "Rhetoric and Retrenchment: Agrarian Ideology and American Bankruptcy Law." *Missouri Law Review* 54 (1989): 871-98.

Parker, Patricia. *Literary Fat Ladies: Rhetoric, Gender, Property.* London: Methuen, 1987.

———. "*The Merry Wives of Windsor* and Shakespearean Translation." *Modern Language Quarterly* 52 (1991): 225-62.

Parten, Anne. "Falstaff's Horns: Masculine Inadequacy and Feminine Mirth in *The Merry Wives of Windsor.*" *Studies in Philology* 82 (1985): 184-99.

Phillips, O. Hood. *Shakespeare and the Lawyers.* London: Methuen, 1972.

Plowden, Edmund. *Les Comentaries, ou les Reportes.* London, 1571 (pt. 1), 1578 (pt. 2).

Posner, Richard. *Law and Literature: A Misunderstood Relation.* Cambridge: Harvard UP, 1988.

Pulton, Fernando. *De Pace regis et regni, viz. A Treatise declaring which be the great and generall offenses of the Realme.* London, 1608. STC 9548.

Quint, David. *Epic and Empire: Politics and Generic Form from Virgil to Milton.* Princeton: Princeton UP, 1993.

Radin, Max. "Fraudulent Conveyances at Roman Law." *Virginia Law Review* 18 (1931): 109-30.

Rastell, William. "To the Gentle Reader." *A Collection in English, of the Statutes now in force, continue from the beginning of Magna Charta.* London, 1598. STC 9321.

Rushton, William Lowes. *Shakespeare's Legal Maxims.* 1907. New York: AMS, 1973.

Sandars, Thomas Collett, ed. *The Institutes of Justinian.* 7th ed. London: Longman, 1952.

Schafer, Elizabeth. "The Date of *The Merry Wives of Windsor.*" *Notes and Queries* ns 38 (1991): 57-60.

Segal, Erich. *Roman Laughter: The Comedy of Plautus.* 2nd ed. New York: Oxford UP, 1987.

Shakespeare, William. *The Merry Wives of Windsor* (1602). Shakespeare Quarto Facsimiles, No. 3. Oxford: Clarendon, 1963.

———. *Mr. William Shakespeares Comedies, Histories, & Tragedies.* A facsimile edition of the First Folio prepared by Helge Kökeritz. Intro. Charles Tyler Prouty. New Haven: Yale UP, 1954.

Simpson. A. W. B. *A History of the Land Law.* 1961. 2nd ed. Oxford: Clarendon, 1986.

Spenser, Edmund. *A Briefe Note of Ireland. The Prose Works.* 233-45.

———. *A View of the Present State of Ireland. The Prose Works.* 39-232.

———. *The Works of Edmund Spenser: A Variorum Edition.* 11 vols. 1932-49. Ed. Edwin Greenlaw et al. Vol 9: *The Prose Works.* Ed. Rudolf Gottfried. Baltimore: Johns Hopkins UP, 1949.

Theobald, Lewis L. Cited in *The Plays of William Shakespeare.* 21 vols. Ed. George Steevens. London, 1803. Vol. 5.

Thornley, Isobel D. "The Destruction of Sanctuary." *Tudor Studies Presented.* Ed. R. W. Seton-Watson. London: Longmans, 1924. 182-207.

Tiffany, Francis B. *Handbook of the Law of Sales.* 2nd ed. St. Paul: West, 1908.

Trevelyan, G. M. *Illustrated History of England.* 1926. London: Longmans, 1956.

Underhill, Arthur. "Law." *Shakespeare's England.* 2 vols. 1916. Oxford: Clarendon, 1950. 1: 381-412.

Vickers, Brian. *The Artistry of Shakespeare's Prose.* London: Methuen, 1968.

Wallace, Charles William. *The First London Theatre.* 1913. New York: Blom, 1969.

Wallerstein, Immanuel. *The Modern World-System: Capitalist Agriculture and the Origins of the European World-Economy in the Sixteenth Century.* New York: Academic, 1976.

Weisberg, Richard. *Poethics, and Other Strategies of Law and Literature.* New York: Columbia UP, 1992.

Weisberg, Robert. "Commercial Morality, the Merchant Character, and the History of the Voidable Preference." *Stanford Law Review* 39 (1986): 3-138.

West, William. *Symbolaeographia.* London (?): Tottel, 1590.

FURTHER READING

Criticism

Battenhouse, Roy. "Falstaff as Parodist and Perhaps Holy Fool." *PMLA* 90, No. 1 (January 1975): 32-52.

> Explores Falstaff's role as a jester in *The Merry Wives of Windsor* and the *Henry IV* plays.

Clark, Sandra. "'Wives may be merry and yet honest too': Women and Wit in *The Merry Wives of Windsor* and Some Other Plays." In *"Fanned and Winnowed Opinions": Shakespearean Essays Presented to Harold Jenkins,* edited by John W. Mahon and Thomas A. Pendleton, pp. 249-67. London: Methuen, 1987.

> Uses *The Merry Wives of Windsor* to demonstrate that women's wit in the Renaissance was based on action, in contrast to men's wit which was based on speech.

Foley, Stephen. "Falstaff in Love and Other Stories from Tudor England." *Exemplaria* 1, No. 2 (Fall 1989): 227-46.

> Looks at *The Merry Wives of Windsor* in relation to contemporary stories of courtship, deceit, and marriage.

Marcus, Leah S. "Purity and Danger in the Modern Edition: *The Merry Wives of Windsor.*" In *Unediting the Renaissance: Shakespeare, Marlowe, Milton,* pp. 68-100. London: Routledge, 1996.

Examines the folio and quarto versions of *The Merry Wives of Windsor* and argues that rather than trying to find a definitive version of the play, scholars should treat each one as a separate entity worthy of study.

Scolnicov, Hanna. "The Zoomorphic Mask in Shakespeare." *Assaph: Studies in the Theatre* 9 (1993): 63-74.
  Remarks on Shakespeare's very limited use of masks in his plays, and suggests that Falstaff's Herne the Hunter mask is meant first to reinforce and then subvert the playgoers' assumptions about male virility and female infidelity.

Wall, Wendy. "'Household Stuff': The Sexual Politics of Domesticity and the Advent of English Comedy." *ELH* 65, No. 1 (Spring 1998): 1-45
  Defines *The Merry Wives of Windsor* as a typical English comedy by focusing principally on an earlier Renaissance play, *Gammer Gurton's Needle.*

The Rape of Lucrece

For further information on the critical history of *The Rape of Lucrece,* see *SC,* Volumes 10, 33, and 43.

INTRODUCTION

The Rape of Lucrece—Shakespeare's narrative poem and companion piece to the lighter *Venus and Adonis*—tells the story of Lucrece, the chaste wife of Collatine, whose rape by the Roman prince, Tarquin, leads to suicide, revenge, and the founding of the Roman Republic. Although not generally as well known as Shakespeare's plays, *The Rape of Lucrece* has inspired significant discussion among scholars. Critical interest surrounds the poem's structure, its Roman and medieval sources, and its rich imagery, as well as its relationship to Shakespeare's plays. Also of interest are the poem's characters, specifically Lucrece and her role in and reaction to her patriarchal society.

After comparing *The Rape of Lucrece*'s more formal structure with that of *Venus and Adonis,* Kenneth Muir (1973) comments that a preoccupation with rape and female virtue recurs in several of Shakespeare's plays, such as *Measure for Measure* and *Troilus and Cressida.* Muir notes a parallel between Angelo's lust for the virgin Isabella in *Measure for Measure* and Tarquin's arousal by Lucrece's purity. He concludes that Shakespeare wisely chose not to turn the story of Lucrece into a play because "the long period between the rape and the suicide . . . is pathetic rather than tragic, and static rather than dramatic."

Closely connected to the focus on structure and theme is scholarly assessment of the vivid imagery that pervades the poem. Sarah Plant (see Further Reading), for example, observes that there are references to bees and their behavior sprinkled throughout the *The Rape of Lucrece.* Plant remarks that bees had been regarded as symbols of chastity since classical times, and that Shakespeare's use of this image to organize his poem reflected a growing interest during the Renaissance period regarding the virtues of "modesty and temperance" and their link to the nation's governance by a female monarch. The invasion of dwellings forms another insistent image in the poem, according to Heather Dubrow (2000). Dubrow focuses on an ironic twist embedded within this image: as a Roman homemaker, Lucrece is also keeper of the family hearth, but when Tarquin rapes her in a fiery passion, he subverts the warmth and safety of the home fire into the horror of a family-destroying blaze.

Lucrece and her interactions with the two other principal characters in the poem have received scrutiny from feminist critics. Catharine R. Stimpson (1980) avers that

in *The Rape of Lucrece* as well as in several of his plays, Shakespeare revealed genuine sympathy rather than "titillation" concerning rape. Nevertheless, Stimpson concludes that for all his sympathy, Shakespeare insisted that the patriarchal status quo must be maintained, and that therefore women who are raped must bear it stoically, or, as in the case of Lucrece, end their lives with dignity. In fact, Lucrece's resort to suicide has been much debated. While several scholars have blamed Lucrece for her passivity and her decision that death is preferable to living with what she and her society regard as the stigma of rape, several recent critics have by contrast emphasized her strength and independence. Philippa Berry (1992), for instance, acknowledges Lucrece's victimization by the Roman patriarchy but notes that, whether inadvertent or not, Lucrece has the final word when her suicide destroys the monarchy in which her husband, Collatine, wields influence. Jane O. Newman (1994) goes farther; she refers to the fact that the myth of Philomela is mentioned twice in Shakespeare's poem. Newman points out that when Philomela is raped and mutilated by her brother-in-law, she chooses not to commit suicide but to conspire with her sister for revenge. While Newman admits that the image of Philomela occurs only briefly in the poem, she contends that it continues to "haunt" the reader as an example of the will and ability of women to rely upon themselves rather than men for justice. Finally, A.D. Cousins (2000) takes a completely different approach with regard to the characters in *The Rape of Lucrece.* He sees the chaste Lucrece, her adoring husband, Collatine, and the lustful Tarquin as parodic types. In this scenario, Cousins describes Lucrece as the Petrarchan mistress pursued by the ardent Petrarchan lover, Tarquin, whose desire is accidentally manufactured by the "hubris" of Collatine when he boasts about his wife's virtues.

OVERVIEWS AND GENERAL STUDIES

Kenneth Muir (essay date 1973)

SOURCE: "*The Rape of Lucrece,*" in *Shakespeare the Professional and Related Studies,* Heinemann, 1973, pp. 187-203.

[*In the following essay, Muir briefly describes the structure of* The Rape of Lucrece, *connects the poem to such later Shakespearean plays as* Measure for Measure, *and reviews the scholarly responses to the poem's themes and imagery.*]

Lucrece was the 'graver labour' promised by Shakespeare in the Dedication to *Venus and Adonis.* It is written in rhyme royal, the stanza form employed by Chaucer in *Troilus and Criseyde* and by Sackville in his Induction to the *Mirror for Magistrates,* and it has a slower, graver movement than the six-line stanza of *Venus and Adonis.* There may have been a draft in the six-line stanza of *Venus and Adonis,* since Suckling quoted several stanzas in this form.

In *Venus and Adonis* Shakespeare had written of a chaste youth repelling the assaults of an amorous goddess. In the companion poem he writes of a chaste wife violated by a lustful guest. Adonis is successful in preserving his chastity, but he is slain by a boar, and bewailed by Venus; Lucrece, unable to endure the shame, commits suicide.

By providing a prose 'argument'—concerned partly with previous events—Shakespeare was able to plunge into the middle of the story, and to concentrate on the struggle in Tarquin's mind before the rape, on Lucrece's appeal to him to spare her, and on her lament afterwards.

Lucrece is interesting as a forerunner and there are many links between it and later plays. One of the most significant is with *Macbeth.* Just before the murder of Duncan, Macbeth has a soliloquy describing an imaginary dagger which seems to lead him to Duncan's chamber, inciting him to the deed. The speech continues:

> Now o'er the one half world,
> Nature seems dead and wicked dreams abuse
> The curtained sleep. Witchcraft celebrates
> Pale Hecate's offerings; and withered murder,
> Alarumed by his sentinel the wolf
> Whose howl's his watch, thus with his stealthy pace
> With Tarquin's ravishing strides, towards his design
> Moves like a ghost.

Shakespeare's mind went back some twelve years to the earlier scene in *Lucrece,* to that other deed of darkness—a rape being a symbolic murder. Many editors have observed that a large number of details of the two scenes are identical, whether because Shakespeare was consciously drawing on his narrative poem, or because the various scenic properties are natural concomitants of the violent deeds—the starless night, the noise of owls and wolves:

> Now stole upon the time the dead of night,
> When heavy sleep had clos'd up mortal eyes;
> No comfortable star did lend his light,
> No noise but owls' and wolves' death-boding cries;
> Now serves the season that they may surprise
>   The silly lambs. Pure thoughts are dead and still,
>   While lust and murder wake to stain and kill.

Baldwin points out[1] that this is partly derived from Ovid's description of the rape beginning *Nox erat,* and this would send Shakespeare's mind to a similar passage in Virgil, Book IV, describing Dido's sleeplessness in the toils of love.[2]

More significant than the background of the two scenes is the fact that Tarquin is, in a sense, the first of Shake-speare's tragic heroes. Richard III is a tragic villain, conscious of the evil he commits, but not seeking to repent until the last act of the play. Tarquin is fully conscious of the sin he contemplates and the first 51 stanzas are devoted to the conflict in his mind before he definitely succumbs to evil. In this respect he is much closer to Macbeth than he is to Richard.

Like Angelo, whose passions are aroused by the sight of the novice, Isabella, Tarquin is sexually stirred by the reputed chastity of the heroine:

> Haply that name of 'chaste' unhaply set
> This bateless edge on his keen appetite . . .
>
> Perchance his boast of Lucrece' sovereignty
> Suggested this proud issue of a king;
> For by our ears our hearts oft tainted be.
> Perchance that envy of so rich a thing,
> Braving compare, disdainfully did sting
> His high-pitched thoughts that meaner men should vaunt
> That golden hap which their superiors want.

When Tarquin goes to his bedroom, he weighs 'the sundry dangers of his will's obtaining'. He realizes, as Macbeth was later to realize, that he is liable to forfeit the things that should accompany old age, 'As honour, love, obedience, troops of friends', but his desire brushes these unpleasant facts on one side.

> And when great treasure is the meed proposed,
> Though death be adjunct, there's no death supposed.
>
> Those that much covet are with gain so fond
> That what they have not, that which they possess
> They scatter and unloose it from their bond,
> And so, by hoping more, they have but less;
> Or, gaining more, the profit of excess
>   Is but to surfeit, and such grief sustain
>   That they prove bankrupt in this poor-rich gain.
>
> So that in vent'ring ill, we leave to be
> The things we are for that which we expect;
> And this ambitious foul infirmity,
> In having much, torments us with defect
> Of that we have; so then we do neglect
>   The thing we have and, all for want of wit,
>   Make something nothing by augmenting it.

(It will be noted that considered as poetry such passages of argumentation are inferior to the passages of description in the poem.)

Even when Tarquin leaps from his bed to go to Lucrece's chamber, he is still 'madly tossed between desire and dread', but 'honest fear' is 'bewitched with lust's foul charm'. He upbraids his own lust. He knows perfectly well that he should 'offer pure incense to so pure a shrine', and that 'fair humanity' abhors the deed he contemplates. He knows that it is a shame to knighthood, a slur on his own ancestry, a disgrace to bravery, and a scandal to his descendants.

What win I if I gain the thing I seek?
A dream, a breath, a froth of fleeting joy.
Who buys a minute's mirth to wail a week?
Or sells eternity to get a toy?
For one sweet grape who will the vine destroy?
Or what fond beggar, but to touch the crown,
Would with the sceptre straight be strucken down?

Moreover, Collatinus, Lucrece's husband, is not his enemy, but his dear friend and kinsmen. So Macbeth reminds himself that he is Duncan's kinsman. Then, like Lady Macbeth, telling her husband that it is the eye of childhood that fears a painted devil, Tarquin answers his own scruples:

Who fears a sentence or an old man's saw
Shall by a painted cloth be kept in awe.

St Thomas Aquinas says somewhere that no man can deliberately choose evil; he has first to delude himself that the choice is good for him. So, in the disputation between frozen conscience and hot-burning will, Tarquin persuades himself that the temporary possession of Lucrece is a 'good' which outweighs all other considerations. 'What is vile shows like a virtuous deed'.

I have stressed the importance of Tarquin as a forerunner of later dramatization of sin, although the demands of the narrative form, while allowing for more direct commentary by the poet, are different from those of the drama; and Shakespeare never forgets that he is writing a narrative poem.

The next section of the poem (stanzas 52-98) deals with the debate between Tarquin and Lucrece and the actual violation by means of blackmail. He tells her that if he kills her under the pretence that he had caught her committing adultery with a servant, her reputation will be blasted, her children will be bastardized, and her husband will suffer more than if she submits to Tarquin's will:

But if thou yield, I rest thy secret friend:
The fault unknown is as a thought unacted;
A little harm done to a great good end
For lawful policy remains enacted.

The choice for Lucrece is not a simple one between death and dishonour, but between death and apparent dishonour on the one hand, and life and secret dishonour on the other. The arguments Lucrece uses to plead with Tarquin are those he had himself used. She appeals to religion, knighthood, friendship, pity, laws human and divine, hospitality, his own royal birth since the man who rules a country should be able to govern his passions.

After the rape and Tarquin's departure, Shakespeare switches attention from criminal to victim, and from victim to criminal, in alternate lines, and it has the effect of alternating shots in a film.

She bears the load of lust he left behind,
And he the burthen of a guilty mind.

He like a thievish dog creeps sadly hence,
She like a wearied lamb lies panting there;
He scowls and hates himself for his offence,
She, desperate, with her nails her flesh doth tear.
He faintly flies, sweating with guilty fear;
    She stays, exclaiming on the direful night;
    He runs, and chides his vanish'd loath'd delight.

He thence departs a heavy convertite,
She there remains a hopeless castaway;
He in his speed looks for the morning light;
She prays she never may behold the day.

Coleridge said that in *Lucrece* Shakespeare 'gave ample proof of his possession of a most profound, energetic, and philosophical mind'. The evidence for this is mostly contained in the long soliloquy in which the heroine rails at Night and Time and Opportunity (stanzas 113-147). It is a foretaste of the tirades of the early Histories, and it looks forward to the soliloquies of the mature plays. It exemplifies Shakespeare's amazing facility of expression, and his daring virtuosity in utilizing and displaying all the resources of rhetoric, and contains passages as great as anything in Elizabethan non-dramatic poetry.

Lucrece begins with an invocation of Night, in which there is an accumulation of epithets and images. Night is associated with hell, with tragedies performed on the Elizabethan stage, with chaos, prostitution, death, conspiracy, fog, poison, sickness and impurity, because Night was an accomplice of Tarquin in his crime. This leads Lucrece to a reflection on his hypocrisy, the contrast between the virtue he talked of and the deed he committed. This is followed by a whole catalogue of examples of similar contrasts, all convential, but obtaining their effect by accumulation: worm in the bud, cuckoo in the nest, toads fouling fountains, misers who suffer from gout, unruly blasts in the spring, weeds growing side by side with flowers, the adder hissing while birds are singing. This again leads on to a diatribe against Opportunity, probably suggested by these remarks of Erasmus:[2]

So much force has opportunity as to turn honesty into dishonesty, debt into wealth, pleasure into heaviness, a benefit into a curse, and vice versa; and, in short, it changes the nature of everything.

But Shakespeare is concerned only with the evil effects of Opportunity, not with their opposite. Opportunity is the cause of treachery, fornication, murder, incest, nay

all sins past, and all that are to come
From the creation to the general doom.

Opportunity is Time's servant, as Time is copesmate of Night; so Lucrece proceeds to address Time, 'Thou ceaseless lackey to Eternity', in lines partly inspired by the last book of Ovid's *Metamorphoses*. Time, though he is the destroyer and overturner of the works of man and nature, is also the power which brings truth to light; and Lucrece appeals to him to overthrow Tarquin and bring him to despair.

T.W. Baldwin, in his account of what he calls the literary genetics of *Lucrece,* has a number of examples of Shakespeare's method of composition in the stanzas we have been discussing. Perhaps the neatest example is the stanza about the miser.[3]

> The aged man that coffers up his gold
> Is plagu'd with cramps and gouts and painful fits,
> And scarce hath eyes his treasure to behold,
> But like still-pining Tantalus he sits,
> And useless barns the harvest of his wits,
>   Having no other pleasure of his gain,
>   But torment that it cannot cure his pain.

Ovid refers briefly to the story of Tantalus in the *Metamorphoses* (IV), and in a note on the passage (probably in the edition used by Shakespeare) Regius suggests that Tantalus is a type of avarice. The connection between the story of Tantalus and avarice is also brought out in Horace's first satire, a passage quoted by Erasmus in his *Adagia.* The same point is made in one of Sidney's sonnets, but that Erasmus was the source is supported by another quotation from one of Horace's odes:

> magnas inter opes inops.

If Shakespeare knew the ode, or looked it up, he would know that the stanza which this line concludes runs:

> contemptae dominus splendidior rei,
> quam si quicquid arat impiger Apulus
> occultare meis dicerer horreis . . .

Baldwin does not point out that these granaries are the link between avarice and the parable of the covetous rich man in the Bible, Luke XII. The rich man proposed building greater barns only to be told 'O fool, this night will they fetch thy soul from thee'. On this parable, the Genevan version has the marginal note:

> Christ condemneth the arrogancy of the rich worldlings, who as though they had God locked up in their coffers and barns, set their whole felicity in their goods, not considering that God gave them life and also can take it away when he will.

The coffers and barns, used as nouns in this note, are taken over by Shakespeare and used as verbs:

> The aged man that coffers up his gold . . .
> And useless barns the harvest of his wits.

The 31 stanzas describing the painting of the destruction of Troy are partly based on Virgil's account in the first two books of the *Aeneid;* but, as Professor Root has shown,[4] the Virgilian account is amplified by details derived from the 13th book of the *Metamorphoses* in which Ovid describes the contest between Ajax and Ulysses, and gives an account of Hestor and Hecuba. The order of the scene—Ajax, Ulysses, Nestor, Hecuba—is the same as Ovid's. The idea of introducing the painting was perhaps suggested by the similar device in Samuel Daniel's *Complaint of Rosamund,* in which the heroine, just before her seduction, contemplates a casket decorated with mythological pictures, given her by her royal lover.

Nine of the stanzas describe the crafty Sinon, who is compared by Lucrece to Tarquin. Both men united 'outward truth and inward guile . . . saintly seeming and diabolical purpose':

> For even as subtle Sinon here is painted,
> So sober-sad, so weary, and so mild,
> As if with grief or travail he had fainted,
> To me came Tarquin armed; so beguil'd
> With outward honesty, but yet defil'd
>   With inward vice. As Priam him did cherish,
>   So did I Tarquin; so my Troy did perish.

Shakespeare knew from his reading of Livy, although curiously enough he did not mention it, that Tarquin had engaged in a stratagem which makes the comparison with Sinon more relevant. Like Sinon, he had gone to the besieged inhabitants of Gabii

> as a suppliant outcast, with a forged tale of woe, and displaying in his person the marks of cruel usage, Tarquin had roused their sympathy, and secured a welcome he turned to account by conspiring against his friends and benefactors, and compassing their speedy destruction.

Lucrece also inveighs against Helen and Paris, whose lust was the cause of the war. She asks:

> Why should the private pleasure of some one
> Become the public plague of many moe?
> Let sin, alone committed, light alone
> Upon his head that hath transgressed so;
> Let guiltless souls be freed from guilty woe.
>   For one's offence why should so many fall,
>   To plague a private sin in general.

These stanzas are also interesting on two other grounds. They throw light on Shakespeare's views on painting which he shared with most of his contemporaries. In *Venus and Adonis,* there is a stanza describing Adonis's horse:

> Look when a painter would surpass the life
> In limning out a well-proportioned steed,
> His art with nature's workmanship at strife,
> As if the dead the living should exceed;
>   So did this horse excel a common one
>   In shape, in courage, colour, pace, and bone.

So in the painting of Troy Lucrece admires the way

> In scorn of nature, art gave lifeless life.

The panoramic view of the siege is filled with hundreds of vivid details which seem to be painted from life; but Lucrece (or Shakespeare) admires the psychological truth even more than outward verisimilitude—the ashy lights in dying eyes, other eyes seen through loopholes, and eyes in the distance looking sad, pale cowards with trembling paces, the triumphant faces of great commanders, the art of physiognomy in the portraits of Ajax and Ulysses, Nestor's beard wagging up and down, and Hecuba gazing on Priam's wounds:

> In her the painter had anatomiz'd
> Time's ruin, beauty's wrack, and grim care's reign;
> Her cheeks with chaps and wrinkles were disguis'd;
> Of what she was no semblance did remain:
> Her blue blood chang'd to black in every vein,
> Wanting the spring that those shrunk pipes had fed,
> Show'd life imprison'd in a body dead.

These stanzas also show that Shakespeare's attitude to the Trojan war did not change substantially during the next ten years. His treatment of the subject in the Dido play in *Hamlet* and *Troilus and Cressida* is essentially the same. It may well be that the time-theme, which is so prominent in *Troilus and Cressida,* was suggested by Lucrece's tirade against time which comes just before the description of the painting.

It is true that in the *Sonnets* we have a forerunner of the Troilus situation—an obsessive concern with the power of Time and a realization of the vulnerability of constancy. But in *Lucrece,* written before many of the Sonnets, the heroine's tirade against Time precedes, as we have seen, the description of the painting of Troy. Time is described as 'carrier of grisly care', 'eater of youth', 'virtue's snare' and 'the ceaseless lackey to eternity'. Some of the imagery used in the poem links up with four famous speeches in *Troilus and Cressida:*

> Thou grant'st no time for charitable deeds . . .
>
> (l. 908)
>
> Time's glory is to calm contending kings . . .
>
> (l. 939)
>
> To ruinate proud buildings with thy hours,
> And smear with dust their glitt'ring golden towers
> . . .
>
> (ll. 944-5)
>
> To feed oblivion with decay of things . . .
>
> (l. 947)
>
> Let him have time a beggar's orts to crave,
> And time to see one that by alms doth live
> Disdain to him disdained scraps to give.
>
> (ll. 985-7)

Ulysses's speech on Time is spoken in answer to Achilles's question: 'What, are my deeds forgot?' And in the course of his reply Ulysses mentions 'good deeds past', the scraps which are 'alms for oblivion', the charity which is subject to 'envious and calumniating time', and the 'gilt o'er-dusted' which is no longer praised. In the next act, when Troilus parts from Cressida, he makes use of Lucrece's epithet:

> Injurious time now with a robber's haste
> Crams his rich thievery up, be knows not how:
> As many farewells as be stars in heaven,
> With distinct breath and consign'd kisses to them,

> He fumbles up into a loose adieu,
> And scants us with a single famish'd kiss,
> Distasted with the salt of broken tears.
>
> (IV. iv. 44-50)

Here we have the same image of Time with a wallet, and also the cooking imagery first pointed out by Walter Whiter,[5] to the significance of which we shall have occasion to return. When Ulysses prophesies the destruction of Troy, Hector replies:[6]

> the end crowns all,
> And that old common arbitrator, Time,
> Will one day end it.

The fourth speech having links with the lines quoted from *Lucrece* is spoken by Troilus after he has witnessed Cressida's unfaithfulness:

> The fractions of her faith, orts of her love,
> The fragments, scraps, the bits and greasy relics
> Of her o'er-eaten faith, are bound to Diomed.
>
> (V. ii. 158-60)

Some of the food images in *Lucrece* and the *Sonnets* are connected with the Ovidian idea of devouring Time; the remainder associate sexual desire with feeding, and its satisfaction with surfeiting. The association is a natural extension of the various meanings of the word *appetite.* Tarquin considers that

> the profit of excess
> Is but to surfeit;

his lust is compared to the 'sharp hunger' of a lion; and he is described after his crime as 'surfeit-taking':

> His taste delicious, in digestion souring,
> Devours his will, that liv'd by foul devouring.

A few lines later, we have another image of surfeiting:[7]

> Drunken Desire must vomit his recept,
> Ere he can see his own abomination.

There are some twenty-five food images in *Lucrece* and more than three times that number in *Troilus and Cressida.* In the poem there is a link between the Time imagery and the Food imagery: Time is not merely a devourer, but also a bloody tyrant; and the ravisher is not merely a devourer of innocence, but a tyrant as well.

The analogy between love and war is to be found in the work of numerous poets between Ovid and Shakespeare. In one of Ovid's *Elegies,* there is a detailed comparison between the lover and the soldier:[8]

> Lovers are always at war, with Cupid watching the ramparts:
> Atticus, take it from me: lovers are always at war.
> What's the right age for love?—the same as that for a soldier.

What the captains demand, agressiveness, ardor of
spirit,
That's what a pretty girl wants when a man's on the
hunt.
The soldier's service is long; but send a girl on before
him,
And the unfaltering lover plods the road without end.

In the middle ages, the siege of Love's castle was common enough; and it is natural that Tarquin should be
compared to a soldier entering a breach in the walls, that
Shakespeare should speak of honour and beauty being
'weakly fortressed'; that in the account of the actual rape,
Tarquin's hand should be compared to a 'Rude ram, to
batter such an ivory wall'; that Lucrece's breasts should
be called 'round turrets'; that her white face should look
like a flag of surrender; and that Tarquin should say he
comes to scale her 'never-conquer'd fort'. As Professor
Allen points out,[9] the image is turned against Tarquin
when, after the crime, his soul complains that her walls
have been demolished by his deed:

> She says her subjects with foul insurrection
> Have battered down her consecrated wall,
> And by their mortal fault brought in subjection
> Her immortality, and made her thrall
> To living death and pain perpetual.

Whereas the walls of Tarquin's soul are battered down—we
are reminded of the sonnet 'Poor soul the centre of my
sinful earth, Hemmed by these rebel powers that thee
array'—the house of Lucrece's soul is sacked,

> Her mansion batter'd by the enemy,
> Her sacred temple spotted, spoil'd, corrupted,
> Grossly engirt with daring infamy.

She wishes therefore to leave her body—'this blemish'd
fort'—by killing herself.

Brutus, at the end of the poem, comments on Lucrece's
suicide:

> Thy wretched wife mistook the matter so,
> To slay herself that should have slain her foe.

Is Brutus right? Professor Don Cameron Allen in the article
to which I have referred (*Shakespeare Survey* 15), shows
how there was a long controversy about Lucrece's suicide
which dates back to the Fathers of the Church. Tertullian
praised her as a 'splendid example of domestic virtue'.
But St Augustine argued that 'if suicide is extenuated,
adultery is proved . . . If she was adulterous, why is she
praised? If she was chaste, why was she killed?'

Camerarius expressed the same idea in verse (as translated
by an Elizabethan poet)

> Were that unchaste mate welcome to thy bed,
> *Lucrece,* thy lust was justly punished.
> But if foul force defil'd thine honest bed,
> His only rage should have been punished.

A really chaste woman would have died rather than surrender.

Professor Allen thinks that Shakespeare read the story of
Lucrece in its Christian context. 'Lucrece should have
defended herself to the death, or, having been forced, lived
free of blame with a guiltless conscience'.

Professor Roy Battenhouse in his *Shakespearean Tragedy*
(1969) likewise argues that the poet was writing from St
Augustine's standpoint. The 'pearly sweat' on Lucrece's
'hand that is lying the outside the coverlet' is a sign of her
unchaste nature. When Tarquin warns her that if she
refuses to yield, he will use force, 'deny she does—as if
subconsciously she wished force to work his way'. Surely,
Battenhouse continues,

> if Lucrece really wishes rescue, she has plenty of time
> to cry out for it; for Shakespeare, in contrast to Ovid,
> makes much of Tarquin's long dallying. And surely
> there are servants in the house to answer calls for help
> . . . Shakespeare is but giving his reader time to real-
> ize that actually Lucrece's resort to complaints is her
> way of escaping from calling for help.

Her grief is put down to her fear 'for loss of social status'.
Her suicide is 'paganism's dark substitute for the Christian
Passion story'.

Such an interpretation seems to conflict with the obvious
meaning of the text, and is not really supported by the fact
that Middleton in his feeble imitation of Shakespeare
makes the ghost of Lucrece come from hell.

Both Allen and Battenhouse seem to leave out of account,
or at least to gloss over, the reason for Lucrece's capitulation, and also the reasons she gives for her suicide. It was
not fear of death that made her give up the struggle, but
fear for her reputation after death. For Tarquin blackmailed
her with the threat that he would kill her and a servant and
say he had caught her in the act of adultery. When one
considers the high value set by the Elizabethans on reputation, and also that this story would be more damaging to
her husband than her actual rape, one can see that in the
circumstances Lucrece's duty was not clear, even if she
had been in a position to think clearly. Just before she kills
herself, Lucrece asks the bystanders:

> What is the quality of my offence,
> Being constrain'd with dreadful circumstance?
> May my pure mind with the foul act dispense,
> My low-declined honour to advance?
> May any terms acquit me from this chance?
>   The poisoned fountain clears itself again;
>   And why not I from this compelled stain?

She is assured by Brutus and Collatine that

> Her body's stain her mind untained clears.

But she cannot accept this assurance:

> "No, no," quoth she, "no dame hereafter living
> By my excuse shall claim excuse's giving".

She felt, rightly or wrongly, that she could only prove that she had not consented to rape—that the rape was not half-desired—if she refused to go on living. She wished to set an example to women who came after, who might pretend that they had been forced when they had welcomed the opportunity of committing adultery with a clear conscience. I am reminded of two modern French plays. In Giraudoux's *La Guerre de Troie N'Aura Pas Lieu,* Hector asks Paris if Helen consented to the rape. Paris replies that all women in such circumstances resist, but they afterwards consent with enthusiasm. The other play is André Roussin's farce, *La petite hutte,* in which the heroine allows herself to be seduced by a supposed native of the isle on which she is shipwrecked, ostensibly to save the life of her husband, who has been tied up by the native. Roussin makes clear that her real motive, or at least her unconscious motive, is different from her avowed one.

On the whole, it must be admitted, *Lucrece* has been less popular among the critics as well as with the general reader than *Venus and Adonis*. It lacks something of the freshness of the earlier poem. It is as though Shakespeare felt hampered by the necessity of producing a graver labour for his patron. It is obvious that he took immense pains with it. He showed that he could surpass all his contemporaries in the tragic lament. It is better than Daniel, better even than Spenser. It is a beautifully composed poem. It could be used to illustrate a text-book on rhetorical devices. Every stanza exhibits a rhetorical figure. Shakespeare ransacked the work of his predecessors and amplified the various themes and topics in accordance with the best critical opinion. The verse is for the most part melodious and varied, the rhymes unforced except some of the feminine ones. There are some lines as magnificent as any he ever wrote, and even when they are not magnificent, they frequently exhibit considerable art. For example, if one takes the commonest of all rhetorical figures—alliteration—one finds that Shakespeare never overdoes it.

> To blot old books and alter their contents . . .
> Thy violent vanities can never last . . .
> Muster thy mists to meet the eastern light . . .
> Cave-keeping evils that obscurely sleep . . .
> For men have marble, women waxen minds . . .

The two halves of the line are frequently bound together by this subtle, and not obtrusive, alliteration.

It could be argued that although the poem is less attractive than *Venus and Adonis,* it shows greater dramatic power. It remains a narrative poem, a 'complaint' (one of the most popular forms in the 1590s); but Shakespeare would never have made a play on the subject, as Heywood was afterwards to do. How sound his instinct was can be seen from Obey's *Viol de Lucrèce* which is very closely based on Shakespeare's poem. Obey, indeed, translates many of Shakespeare's stanzas and puts them into the mouth of his chorus. The play is impressive in its way; but the long period between the rape and the suicide in which we see a voluble and suffering innocence is pathetic rather than tragic, and static rather than dramatic.

Notes

1. T.W. Baldwin, *The Literary Genetics of Shakespeare's Poems and Sonnets* (1950) p. 118.

2. Baldwin, *op. cit.,* p. 136.

3. Baldwin, *op. cit.,* p. 133.

4. R.K. Root, *Classical Mythology in Shakespeare* (1903), p. 35.

5. *A Specimen of a Commentary* (1794), p. 136.

6. IV. v. 224-6.

7. *Lucrece,* ll. 138-9, 421-2, 699-700, 703-4.

8. Tr. Rolfe Humphries.

9. *Shakespeare Survey 15,* p. 94.

John Roe (essay date 1992)

SOURCE: Introduction to *The Poems: Venus and Adonis, The Rape of Lucrece, The Phoenix and the Turtle, The Passionate Pilgrim, A Lover's Complaint,* by William Shakespeare, edited by John Roe, Cambridge University Press, 1992, pp. 22-41.

[*In the following excerpt, Roe looks at the range of interpretations—from Christian to feminist—of* The Rape of Lucrece, *cites several sources for the poem, and assesses Shakespeare's relationship to his patron, Southampton, for whom he wrote the poem.*]

The Poem and Interpretation

The Rape of Lucrece is the antithesis of *Venus and Adonis*. Sexual desire, which aggressively yet also touchingly and humorously characterised Venus, returns to its familiar role as the preoccupation of the male; chastity, so ill-suited to the improbably coy Adonis, recovers its conviction in the person of Lucrece. *Venus and Adonis* is a poem of the fresh outdoors, which salutes procreative energy even as it recognises its inevitable shortcomings. *Lucrece* is a poem of interiors, of physical and spiritual darkness. The corridors down which Tarquin stalks, illuminated by his own 'lightless fire', lead into a circle of complexity, at the centre of which he meets the innocent but no less confused Lucrece.[1]

The poem starts with Tarquin, ruminates on his quickly conceived lust, and, like *Macbeth,* contemplates his inexorable pursuit of an aim that can only destroy him. But unlike *Macbeth* it ceases to concentrate on the perpetrator, once he has done the deed, and switches attention to the victim. As soon as the rape has been accomplished it is clear that the poet intends to devote the rest of his story to vindicating the heroine. The comparison with *Macbeth* (a play which contains echoes of the poem, including references to Tarquin) illuminates the different sort of progress *Lucrece* follows after the offence. Whereas Macbeth purges his guilt within and through his own fate, the discarded Tarquin cannot fulfil this function himself. The purgation comes instead through Lucrece, who sheds her own blood. Does this make her Tarquin's counterpart in guilt, or does it merely mean that fate is unfairly forced on her as a sacrificial victim? The very change of direction in the poem, so different from the inexorably logical sequence of *Macbeth,* helps explain both the quandary experienced by Lucrece as victim and the uncertainty and confusion into which interpretation tends to fall.

This brings up first of all the question of the poem's moral perspective, in particular the nature of Lucrece's 'self-slaughter' and her motive in performing it.

St Augustine attacked the Lucrece of classical legend by reminding her supporters that a truly clear conscience had nothing to fear. He was concerned to dispute the morality of suicide, and argued that if Lucrece were truly an innocent victim she should not have killed herself: killing an innocent is also a crime.[2] If on the other hand Lucrece secretly consented to being raped, she was no heroine. The paradox as Augustine presents it is indeed a thorny one since it involves the notoriously difficult and contentious issue of victim complicity in sexual aggression. Shakespeare however avoids this spectre by inviting his readers to think further along the lines of the rape victim's own attitude to her experience. Unlike Augustine, Shakespeare does not ignore the cultural imperatives and taboos of an ancient society, in which pollution, even of an utterly innocent family member, brings shame on the family, shame which the victim's death is believed to cleanse. At the same time, Shakespeare is writing in a Christian culture, in which the law forbade suicide. The resulting moral debate arises from the Christian emphasis on the supreme importance of the individual soul, whereas classical Roman culture gave greater importance to the family and, under certain circumstances, allowed suicide.

A significant passage occurs at what might be described as the moment of 'transference', that is, following the rape when Tarquin slinks away and leaves Lucrece musing on the event:

> Ev'n in this thought through the dark night he stealeth,
> A captive victor that hath lost in gain;
> Bearing away the wound that nothing healeth,
> The scar that will despite of cure remain;
> Leaving his spoil perplexed in greater pain.
>   She bears the load of lust he left behind,
>   And he the burden of a guilty mind.
>
> He like a thievish dog creeps sadly thence;
> She like a wearied lamb lies panting there.
> He scowls, and hates himself for his offence;
> She, desperate, with her nails her flesh doth tear.
> He faintly flies, sweating with guilty fear;
>   She stays, exclaiming on the direful night;
>   He runs, and chides his vanished loathed delight.
>
> He thence departs a heavy convertite;
> She there remains a hopeless castaway.
> He in his speed looks for the morning light;

> She prays she never may behold the day:
> 'For day', quoth she, 'night's scapes doth open lay,
>   And my true eyes have never practised how
>   To cloak offences with a cunning brow.
>
>   (729-49)

Like any rape victim Lucrece feels that she has been contaminated and finds it hard, in fact impossible, to distinguish between Tarquin's culpability and her own personal shame. Even though pollution has been foisted on her ('the load of lust'), she cannot help regarding it as her own. As the poem proceeds towards its dénouement a chorus of voices urges her to believe in her innocence; but Lucrece has resolved on suicide as the only solution long before her husband and countrymen arrive on the scene, and there is no wavering on her part. Medical science, at least in Shakespeare's application of it, seems to bear out her sense of contamination, for her spilt blood divides into pure and corrupt elements:

> Some of her blood still pure and red remained,
> And some looked black, and that false Tarquin stained
> . . .
>
> And ever since, as pitying Lucrece' woes,
> Corrupted blood some watery token shows,
>   And blood untainted still doth red abide,
>   Blushing at that which is so putrified.
>
>   (1742-3, 1747-50)

However inviolate her mind, the blood is evidence of those 'accessary yieldings' (1658) to which the body, despite its owner's will, succumbs (Chaucer—see below, p. 38—maintains that she was unconscious throughout, which clears her of even involuntary physical participation.) Augustine would say that none of this matters; but it is plain that Shakespeare took the body—soul dualism seriously, as *Venus and Adonis* shows. In the earlier poem the two are kept separate by careful contrivance (the man's inclination to chastity being decisive), but in *Lucrece* the act of sex brings them together: a chaste mind finds itself occupying a defiled body, and the resultant confusion will not be dispelled except by drastic action. The poem accordingly salutes her suicide as a triumphant release of her soul from its circumstances of defilement:

> Even here she sheathèd in her harmless breast
> A harmful knife, that thence her soul unsheathèd:
> That blow did bail it from the deep unrest
> Of that polluted prison where it breathèd.
>
>   (1723-6)

There is no evidence that Shakespeare wishes to think the matter out more subtly than this. Indeed, he probably sensed that he did not need to. While culpable in the view of the Church, suicide performed with such a fine and conscientious regard to personal honour would undoubtedly strike a chord of sympathy with the laity (hence Tyndale's worries over Lucrece's popularity).[3] Shakespeare has thoroughly integrated this Roman lady (who in line 1694 appeals to her kinsmen as 'knights') in a familiar chivalric context, one which is characteristically adept at blurring theological principle and, with whatever effect on logic, regarding the actions of sympathetic characters in a morally favourable light.

From this perspective, the distinction between stoical Rome and contemporary England is not very marked. Of responses on the page, we have only those of Lucretius, Collatine, and Brutus to judge by, the rest standing 'stone-still, astonished with this deadly deed' (1730). Lucretius deplores her action as an inversion of the natural order, as a result of which children now predecease the parents, depriving fathers like himself of the consolation of survival through progeny. This cannot be enlisted as a Christian objection to what she has done, and indeed it too closely resembles one of Lucrece's own laments on the disorder of things to do much more than supplement her own plaintive rhetoric. Collatine feels uxorious rage at Tarquin's violation of his spouse, but soon falls to a futile competition with his father-in-law over who has greatest claim to grief—a further stylistic means of emphasising the pathos of her loss. Brutus criticises her for having plunged the knife into the wrong culprit, less a measured judgement of Lucrece and more a clever rhetorical means of establishing a case against the Tarquins. In each spokesman, style and performance hold sway over the finer points of moral inquiry, the effect taken as a whole contributing to the depiction of a Lucrece who has behaved in a sombre but laudable manner in conformity with Sidney's commendation of 'the constant though lamenting look of Lucretia, when she punished in herself another's fault' (*Apology*, p. 102).

In his overall handling of the theme, then, Shakespeare shows greater interest in the requirements of style—and in particular genre—than ethics, further supporting evidence for this being that the formal character of *Lucrece* can be traced to his activities in the theatre. He had lately completed the dynastic first Tudor tetralogy (echoes of which can be heard in some of the lines of *Lucrece*), which concerns itself with the transmission of guilt from one generation to the next by inherent curse or pollution; as well as this, his tragic instinct was shaped by the code of revenge drama, with its insistence on the extirpation or purgation of guilt through blood, to which his own recent Roman tragedy *Titus Andronicus*—again echoed sporadically by the language of the poem—belongs. (All of this is connected with the contemporary practice of putting Senecan ideas on to the Elizabethan stage.) The solution Shakespeare finds for the dilemmas confronting and expressed via Lucrece is the formalist one of subduing the abstract puzzles of conscience to the emotive force of the complaint genre, on the reasonable assumption that the pathos it produces will take care of any lingering ethical doubts.

To a large extent he succeeds. Readers generally object less to contradictions in the handling of the morality of the subject and more to the extended apostrophes of such bleak personifications as Night, Time, and Opportunity

(what William Empson has described as 'the Bard doing five-finger exercises in rhetoric at the piano', *Signet*, p. 1670b). Despite the Augustinian school's suspicion that here is a lady protesting too much, the more obvious danger of such speeches is their inordinate length unsupported by a viable dramatic context. Shakespeare does all he can to elicit sympathy for the heroine as victim, but the lengths to which he goes risk an over-exposure of technique, sometimes culminating in stridency.

As Lever (p. 28) points out, we need to remember the circumstances of the time. Similar rhetorical extravagance had already worked on the stage in Kyd's *Spanish Tragedy,* which was to enjoy a later revival. Compared to this, Lucrece's speeches are not at all excessive. Also, the poem enjoys the advantages of being read in solitude, which makes for a different experience altogether from the reception of dramatic utterance. The demands of naturalism constantly forced the theatre to renew its style, and Shakespeare himself contributed decisively to the modification in rhetorical habit which was taking place on the stage. By contrast, the spaciousness of the narrative mode allows the mind to absorb the immediate drama and to contemplate at length the metaphysical condition which it expresses. Nowhere is this more powerfully done in such poetry than in the stanza just prior to the rape, where we witness the helplessness of the victim and the terrible (again Ovidian) transformation that has taken place in her attacker:

> Here with a cockatrice' dead-killing eye
> He rouseth up himself, and makes a pause;
> While she, the picture of pure piety,
> Like a white hind under the gripe's sharp claws,
> Pleads, in a wilderness where are no laws,
>   To the rough beast that knows no gentle right,
>   Nor aught obeys but his foul appetite.
>
>   (540-6)

Such descriptions never lost their appeal for Shakespeare's contemporaries, for the poem went into at least six editions in his lifetime, including one in the year he died. But a modern readership needs, to some degree, to recover the technique of appreciating the principles by which such a passage functions.

It is accordingly from the perspective of rhetorical practice that we must judge how theme and action are presented, and in particular how the heroine is perceived. In the early part of the narrative Shakespeare impresses upon the reader Lucrece's artlessness and simple good faith. Such unsuspecting honesty of disposition is hard to render without running the risk of making its possessor appear naive or unintelligent. Anyone else would suspect Tarquin was up to no good arriving unannounced and without a prior word from Collatine. But in order that she should epitomise uncomplicated virtue, Shakespeare has her accept the visit as quite natural; suspiciousness in her at this stage would cloud our impression. The antithetical structure of the poetic argument enables Shakespeare to present matters in extremes, ideal chastity opposed to base lust:

This earthly saint, adorèd by this devil,
Little suspecteth the false worshipper;
For unstained thoughts do seldom dream on evil;
Birds never limed no secret bushes fear.
So guiltless she securely gives good cheer
  And reverend welcome to her princely guest,
  Whose inward ill no outward harm expressed.

                                                    (85-91)

As the last line shows, antithesis works internally in the case of Tarquin, indicating his inner turmoil and self-division, whereas Lucrece shows no such innate contradiction.[4] Tarquin has the devil's view of the sleeping, innocent Lucrece as he enters the sanctity of her bedchamber at a narrative moment in which the playful effects of the description trouble some readers as inappropriately precious:[5]

Her lily hand her rosy cheek lies under,
Coz'ning the pillow of a lawful kiss;
Who, therefore angry, seems to part in sunder,
Swelling on either side to want his bliss;
Between whose hills her head entombèd is,
  Where like a virtuous monument she lies,
  To be admired of lewd unhallowed eyes . . .

Her hair like golden threads played with her breath,
O modest wantons, wanton modesty!
Showing life's triumph in the map of death,
And death's dim look in life's mortality.
Each in her sleep themselves so beautify,
  As if between them twain there were no strife,
  But that life lived in death, and death in life.

Her breasts like ivory globes circled with blue,
A pair of maiden worlds unconquerèd,
Save of their lord no bearing yoke they knew,
And him by oath they truly honourèd.
These worlds in Tarquin new ambition bred,
  Who like a foul usurper went about
  From this fair throne to heave the owner out.

                                                    (386-92, 400-13)

Doubtless for the modern reader, more accustomed to expect moments of unbroken dramatic plausibility, such narrative pauses seem an artificial and stilted slowing of the action. But their function is to state and recall to us the poem's governing themes. Lucrece, in this image of her, has the power to resolve contradictions which in Tarquin, as in ordinary sinners, are only exacerbated. Differences of life and death are annulled, as they were in paradise, which knew no mortality. The outcome of anger is sweetness, and so on.

In addition, the picture does contain a significant element of erotic psychology, whereby an unconscious, innocent posture calls forth a voluptuous response. Shakespeare takes his cue for this from Ovid, whose original description of Lucrece as the dutiful housewife at her loom he has carefully adapted to the dramatically charged bedroom setting. (By contrast, Ovid spends few preliminaries on the rape.) A comparison shows how Shakespeare incorporates something of Ovid's delicacy of physical description and suspenseful erotic anticipation in his description of Tarquin's stealthy advance on his sleeping victim. John Gower's awkward verse translation of 1640 (the first in English) renders the Roman passage as follows:

Her lilie-skin, her gold-deluding tresses,
Her native splendour slighting art him pleases.
Her voice, her stainless modesty, h'admires:
And hope's decay still strengthens his desires.
Day's horn-mouth'd harbinger proclaim'd the morn;
The frollick gallants to their tents return.
His mazing fansie on her picture roves;
The more he muses still the more he loves:
Thus did she sit, thus drest, thus did she spin,
Thus plai'd her hair upon her necks white skin;
These looks she had, these rosie words still'd from
her;
This eye, this cheek, these blushes did become her
As billows fall down after some great blast,
Yet make some swelling when the wind is past:
So though her person from his sight was tane,
Yet did that love her person bred remain.
He burns; and prick'd with spurs of basest lust,
Against her chast bed plots attempts unjust.

                                                 (Bullough, 1, 194)

Whereas Ovid's Tarquin turns these images of Lucrece over in his mind while still in the camp, Shakespeare, as the above passage shows, weaves them into the scene in which he beholds her in bed without her knowledge. The conceits are entirely appropriate to the complexity and contradictoriness of the situation whereby chastity kindles lust and the mutually inimical instincts of modesty and lasciviousness find themselves drawn indivisibly together.

There is a rhetorical purpose to Shakespeare's rearrangement of source material, and that is to concentrate all the particulars of the tragedy in these few strategically placed stanzas. The artistic conceit of life alternating with death in the image of the sleeping woman announces the eventual fate of Lucrece, which is, again paradoxically, made beautiful by its quality of heroic sacrifice. Like the Troy ecphrasis (see below, p. 31), though on a smaller scale, the picture given here summarises in concentrated form the thematic concerns to be demonstrated in the course of the action. Far from merely contributing an elusive and momentary lyric voice to the sombre epic tale, the stanzas signal the dimension of tenderness and pathos which unify the whole experience. An Elizabethan audience, looking less for naturalism of mood and more alert to the demands of thematic contemplation, would enjoy the manner in which these conceits maintain their fragile, delicate play while encompassing a wider significance.

While the device or strategy is more characteristic of narrative poetic art, Shakespeare none the less sometimes makes use of it in his mature tragic dramas, an interesting example occurring in *King Lear* (Quarto version) where the description of Cordelia given by the Gentleman to Kent fulfils, even to the evocation of her sympathetic tears, all the requirements of the ecphrasis mode of concentrated pity:

KENT. Did your letters pierce the Queen to any
demonstration of grief?
GENT. Ay, [sir], she took them, read them in my pres-
ence,
And now and then an ample tear trill'd down
Her delicate cheek. It seem'd, she was a queen
Over her passion, who, most rebel-like,
Sought to be king o'er her.
KENT. O then it mov'd her.
GENT. Not to a rage, patience and sorrow [strove]
Who should express her goodliest. You have seen
Sunshine and rain at once; her smiles and tears
That play'd on her ripe lip [seem'd] not to know
What guests were in her eyes, which parted thence,
As pearls for diamonds dropp'd. In brief,
Sorrow would be a rarity most beloved,
If all could so become it.

(*Lear* 4.3.9-24)

Another relevant example occurs in Macbeth's description
of the murdered Duncan immediately upon rousing his
household (lines which have often puzzled later generations of critics and readers):

Here lay Duncan,
His silver skin lac'd with his golden blood,
And his gash'd stabs look'd like a breach in nature
For ruin's wasteful entrance.

(2.3.111-14)

The use of non-naturalistic epithets to describe the King's
face and blood enable the play (even allowing for the
duplicity of the speaker) to raise in a single image one of
the central themes, the sacredness of kingship, for which
gold and silver are appropriate epithets. Johnson's observation that Macbeth's seemingly odd choice of diction
plausibly depicts a hypocritical mind trying to feign innocence is attractive but incorrect. The audience would
have recognised that even in the mouth of a perjurer and
murderer (indeed, especially in such a mouth) these words
capture precisely the reverence and awe of majesty. The
appearance in plays of such vigorous temper as *King Lear*
and *Macbeth* of images so firmly rooted in narrative poetic
art bears testimony to the easiness, for Elizabethan readers
and playgoers alike, of the artificial mode.

After the rape, Lucrece for the first time experiences
antithesis as self-division—which Tarquin has known all
along. The poem is ready now to dispense with him and
concentrate fully on her. Lucrece registers her new-found
sense of topsyturviness by railing on Time, Night, and Opportunity, all of whom appear to her to behave perversely.
A psychologically effective moment occurs when Lucrece,
gazing with suspicion on the blushing groom (1338-44),
discovers that she can no longer distinguish innocence
from evil. The play on faces uneasily reddening contrasts
with the earlier artless blushing of Lucrece that so appeals
to Tarquin when he pays his furtive visit (50-77).

Aware of self-division, another expression for her fallen
condition, Lucrece chooses not to live. This is the tragic
hero's decision, and it comes as no surprise; anything less

would be unheroic. At this point Shakespeare introduces
the much-debated Troy *excursus* (or *ecphrasis*—see
Supplementary Notes). Despite arguments favouring political allegory, the Troy passage functions most obviously
and effectively as a means of providing Lucrece with an
appropriate heroic dimension: she sees her own fate, as we
are meant to see it, depicted in the 'skilful painting':

At last she calls to mind where hangs a piece
Of skilful painting, made for Priam's Troy,
Before the which is drawn the power of Greece,
For Helen's rape the city to destroy,
Threat'ning cloud-kissing Ilion with annoy;
    Which the conceited painter drew so proud
    As heaven, it seemed, to kiss the turrets bowed.

(1366-72)

The last line in particular indicates the tragedy's attempt at
assuming cosmic proportions which its bedroom and
palace-chamber setting have so far inhibited. The allegory
explored by the painting is explicable entirely in personal
rather than political terms: Lucrece finds herself in Hecuba
and her husband and father variously in both Priam and
Hector, while Tarquin is clearly represented by Sinon but
also by Pyrrhus. The armies on either side, as well as the
city and its fortifications, recall and expand those many
images of 'servile powers' (295), 'ranks of blue veins'
(440), 'round turrets' (441), 'sweet city' (469), and 'troops
of cares' (720) which have previously represented the bodies, feelings, attitudes of mind, and souls of rapist and
victim.

But some recent criticism, as well as abandoning the old
Augustinian dilemma, would dissent from the reading just
proposed. Among the more interesting of these are the attempts at a political interpretation (i.e. closer to the spirit
of Livy than Ovid) put forward first by E.P. Kuhl in a
seminal article and revived again by Michael Platt.[6] Kuhl
argues that the main purpose of the poem is exemplary: it
intends to demonstrate to Southampton the dangers of
abusing power and status. Tarquin's initial scruples, as he
nerves himself up, over unlawful possession and betrayal
of trust (not unlike Macbeth's prior reflections on the duties of kinship) are repeated to him by Lucrece as she tries
to reason him out of his determined course. Quite apart
from the patent embarrassment that would be likely to issue from so close an alignment of Tarquin with Shakespeare's patron, the limitation of this idea is that it largely
ignores the sufferings and reactions of Lucrece herself,
which take up about two thirds of the narrative.

Platt, on the other hand, attempts to demonstrate the political meaning of the poem in terms of its overall structure,
and shows great ingenuity in doing so. Despite his title he
does not in fact see Shakespeare as advocating republicanism, even indirectly, but rather as pleading for responsible
government. (Like Kuhl he belongs to the advice-to-a-
prince school.) Platt bases his argument on the device of
synecdoche: a partial statement or observation stands for
something larger, as in the stanza in which Achilles' spear

represents the warrior (1422-28). Correspondingly, the indulgence of individual passion symbolises the abuse of political power and consequent instability. Platt's interpretation of the Troy ecphrasis is more or less the opposite of the one given above. Gazing on the picture (1366-1568), Lucrece sees her own rape in the rape of Troy, and vice versa (Platt, pp. 65-66). But in the picture she also sees Hecuba, with whose sufferings she empathises, and she looks in vain for Helen—whose beauty she would destroy if by so doing she could prevent the awful fate incessantly visited on womankind as punishment for its power to attract men. While it is possible to read political meanings into individual actions, as Platt does, the poem insists on confronting us with the sufferings and predicament of the heroine as a woman, and only incidentally as a political symbol.

As might be expected, by her very sex Lucrece has attracted to the poem an increasing number of feminist studies. These take a different political line from Kuhl or Platt in examining the role of Lucrece within a patriarchy (where, it is argued, her body is perceived as an emblem of territorial possession rather than as a thing of her own). In such a perspective there is little that distinguishes the rapist from the other men in the poem: Collatine's original foolishness in boasting about his wife has kindled Tarquin's lust even more than her beauty; Lucrece is regarded by both men as an extension of male identity; the dispute between husband and father as to whose grief is the greater (1793-1806) is a selfish one with little genuine concern for the victim; the rape itself demonstrates Lucrece's essential passiveness, which is her condition in marriage, with the result that she is compelled to see her violation primarily as an offence against her husband; Brutus, like the others, indulges in suspect oratory and makes opportunistic use of Lucrece's death.[7]

Curiously enough, such studies resist implicating the author himself in the patriarchal conspiracy and prefer, like old-fashioned criticism, to keep him aloof from the vice of artifice practised by his characters, even though his poetic manner seems prey to it. As one interpreter puts it, not altogether plausibly, 'Shakespeare moves in two directions at once: he dramatically calls into question descriptive fashion while amply demonstrating that he controls it.'[8]

One need not be a feminist reader to concur with some of the positions described above. Collatine's behaviour at the beginning of the poem is ill-advised (though not as foolish as that of Posthumus Leonatus, in *Cymbeline,* who wagers on his wife's fidelity), and one wonders what Lucrece's reaction might have been had she learned that her husband was partly responsible for her predicament. But as with other politically angled interpretations, most feminist readings ignore the fact that the poem concentrates so much of its imagination on Lucrece herself, on her inner woe, and only a relatively small amount on her context. Context, indeed, where it is registered, acts mainly as a foil for the heroine's personal drama. Collatine and Lucretius are

inadequate not because they selfishly cultivate their own grief, even if this is what they do, but because helplessness is expected of them: theirs is the role of the traditional grieving chorus, powerless to assist the main tragic figure.

Like *Venus and Adonis,* from which in so many other respects it differs, *The Rape of Lucrece* ends on a death and strikes a note of pathos. The determination expressed by the Romans to oust tyranny is merely chorus to this effect. This at least appears to have been Shakespeare's artistic solution; but as we have seen, the poem has not been received in so unexceptional a fashion. The pathos he succeeds in wringing from the theme does not wholly dispel the ethical disquiet caused by Lucrece's dilemma and the answer she finds to it. And though readers sympathetic to the poem's rhetorical principles will respond to its carefully orchestrated moods of sorrow and reflection, a majority will doubtless always prefer the brio and dispatch of *Venus and Adonis.* Donaldson concludes his excellent chapter on Lucrece as follows:

> Behind the lengthy rhetorical laments of the poem, one senses some uncertainty in Shakespeare's handling in particular of the principal issue of the poem, that of the proper course of action for a 'dishonoured' woman to take; an issue to which he was to return with greater thoughtfulness in the work of his maturity.
>
> (Donaldson, p. 56)

In fact, no woman of Shakespeare's mature period confronts dishonour on so immense a scale: Desdemona and Hermione, two paragons of domestic loyalty, are beset with smears and suspicions but never literally violated. To treat of rape was always going to be difficult. In *Titus Andronicus* Shakespeare attempts to communicate the pathos ensuing from its violence by emphasising the visually horrific. In *The Rape of Lucrece* he adopts a more bearable introspective formula, without entirely succeeding, as he had superbly with *Venus and Adonis,* in subduing the poem's troubling ethical questions to the requirements of form. In this matter, indeed, he may not be so far adrift of his practice in certain of the great tragedies. Eliot accused him of resorting to stoicism for the ending of *Othello,* and in *Hamlet* Shakespeare brings a *feeling* of satisfaction to the close while perhaps leaving some of the questions posed by the theme of revenge still unanswered.[9] But the historical fame of the Lucrece story and the fact that it has received such careful theological scrutiny more than usually expose the poet's customary habit of making his resolutions only partially answerable to the requirements of rationally conceived ethics. Be that as it may, henceforward the greatest outrages his heroines had to suffer were the insecurities and perversities of men's minds—complex enough matters in themselves, but artistically easier to solve.

The Southampton Connection

In offering *The Rape of Lucrece* to Southampton in 1594, Shakespeare seems to have fulfilled his promise to present him with a work which would qualify as that 'graver labour' foreseen at the time of the publication of *Venus and Adonis*. The dedication to *Lucrece* is even more fulsome and self-confident in its artificial self-abasement, and it has often been taken as a sign of the growth of intimacy between poet and patron. Yet we know nothing of Southampton's response. We may imagine that he liked its erotic predecessor, or Shakespeare would not have risked a second venture. But whether the poet thought it his own moral duty to try to educate the earl in more serious matters of conscience and statecraft, as some scholars have imagined,[10] is a more dubious proposition. For one thing, Shakespeare would hardly have dared tell Southampton how to behave in so public a poem; for another, the implicit identification of the earl with Tarquin would be rashness of a quite un-Shakespearean kind. It would hardly come under the humanist heading, 'education of a prince', since such treatises, fairly popular in the sixteenth century, assume a certain artlessness, and even innocence, in the pupil and limit themselves to general political matters while particularly warning against ill advisers.[11] Echoes of such things can be heard here and there in the poem, but not in a sustained, programmatic way. By contrast, artful tacticians of moral flattery such as Ben Jonson adopted the foolproof ploy of applauding their superiors for already possessing virtues they hoped they would acquire. Giving one's patron a stark lesson in self-damnation is hardly the way to keep open preferment's door; we may suppose rather that Shakespeare intended the poem as a compliment to the sage and serious part of Southampton's character. Whereas *Venus and Adonis* may well have accommodated in-jokes and personal references without losing its poise, the nature of *The Rape of Lucrece,* with its strong mixture of traditional morality, makes for a stiffness and solemnity which are quite the reverse of the more malleable myth of Eros. Besides all this, the main emphasis falls not on Tarquin, who effectively disappears about a third of the way through the poem, but on the feelings and fate of the heroine. In expressing such interest Shakespeare is not alone.

A woman whose story has exercised fascination from its occurrence at an early formative point in western history, Lucrece has been subjected to fearsome scrutiny: examined as a political figure, extolled as a suffering heroine, and alternately revered and denigrated for her chastity and actions of conscience. The treatments preceding Shakespeare's which have bearing on his version need to be considered.

Sources

The two main Roman sources are Livy's history of Rome, *Ab Urbe Condita,* and Ovid's *Fasti* (or 'Festivals'). Livy's account takes up the relatively short space of three chapters in the first book of his historical narrative, and forms part of a series of significant events in the story of the city. In particular it serves Livy's political sympathies, since in his interpretation it plays an important role in the transition from monarchy (or tyranny as Livy describes it) under the Tarquins to republicanism. Lucrece (a heroine of the sixth

century BC) receives nothing in the way of psychological depiction but assumes the person of a martyr to the cause; an almost equal emphasis is placed on Lucius Junius Brutus, who leads the successful revolt against the Tarquin family. Painter made a fairly close translation of Livy in his *Pallace of Pleasure* (1566),[12] which the author of 'The Argument' (see commentary), whether Shakespeare or another, drew upon in some detail. The rape is described in military terms (though not in the elaborate poetic metaphor of Eros as siege and invasion), and Tarquin regards his victim as a 'conquest'. Livy gets in a crack about his easily satisfied heroic instinct which glories in overcoming a woman's honour ('profectusque inde Tarquinius ferox expugnato decore muliebre');[13] Lucretia in turn grieves as if over a larger-than-life calamity or public disaster ('maesta tanto malo'). However, Livy does make a point of distinguishing between the evil that has befallen her body and her inviolate mind.[14] As she claims purity of conscience, which none of her listeners dreams of denying her, she forestalls the possibility of subsequent female backsliding by identifying her suicide as a defence of the name of (Roman) women:

> though I cleare my selfe of the offence, my body shall feele the punishment; for no unchast or ill woman shall hereafter impute no dishonest act to Lucrece.[15]

This appears in Shakespeare's poem as,

> 'No, no', quoth she, 'no dame hereafter living
> By my excuse shall claim excuse's giving.'
>
> (1714-15)

Her resolve matches the tenor of public responsibility which Livy is eager to cultivate, and emphasises that personal conscience accords with devotion to the good of the patria. Similarly, Tarquin's selfish pursuit of pleasure destroys confidence in his virtue (or, to be exact, his father's virtue) as a ruler. The importance of rape as a personal action is second to its meaning in the political sphere, and this is the line Livy follows.[16] Although, as we have seen, some critics have tried to interpret *The Rape of Lucrece* also primarily in political terms, Shakespeare is on balance more interested in depicting personal conscience and its part in individual fate; and to that extent he draws more fully on Ovid than on Livy.

Ovid throughout creates a characteristic atmosphere of beauty and horror, even down to the detail of macabre pathos as the deceased Lucrece apparently signals her support of Brutus's resolute vow:

> She at his words her sightless eyes doth move,
> And shook her head as seeming to approve.
>
> (Bullough, I, 196)

Like the *Metamorphoses,* the *Fasti* has for its ultimate purpose the glorification of Roman destiny. Following the lead of Livy, who never misses an opportunity to enlist supernatural endorsement of the events he considers favourable to the cause of Rome, Ovid accords the death of Lucrece the status of a portent which Brutus interprets correctly by calling for the end of Tarquinian tyranny (the spirit of Lucrece giving its blessing). Livy chooses the less extraordinary miracle of the astonishing transformation in Brutus's character from a seeming dolt and party-liner to a man of decision and initiative ('stupentibus miraculo rei, unde novum in Bruti pectore ingenium': Livy, 1.59). Despite clear differences in emphasis, such as his customary fascination with the mentality of the sexually obsessive, Ovid shares, then, his compatriot's intention to justify the progress of Roman history.

The fame of Lucrece was to outlive such temporal concerns, however, and later treatments such as Chaucer's (in *The Legende of Good Women*), though based closely on Ovid's text, concentrate more on chastity as a virtue in itself. What survives in Chaucer's estimate is not so much Roman triumph as Lucrece's own good name as a type of wifely devotion:

> But for that cause [ie. the Roman] telle I nat this story,
> But for to preyse, and drawen to memory
> The verray wife, the verray trewe Lucresse,
> That for hir wifehood, and hir stedfastnesse,
> Not only that these payens hir commende,
> But he that y-cleped is in oure legende
> The grete Austyne hath grete compassyoun
> Of this Lucresse that starf at Rome toun.

> (Bullough, I, 184)

Chaucer overstates St Augustine's compassion, but in concentrating on Lucrece as an emblem of universal female virtue, he breaks the domination of historical and political perspective. Brutus's role as an inspired republican matters little to Chaucer, who ends the account by a pointed comparison between the dispositions of men and women, drawing together the poem's twin themes of male treachery and female integrity:

> For wel I wot that Christe himselfe telleth,
> That in Israel, as wyde as is the londe,
> Nat so grete feythe in al that londe he fonde,
> As in a woman; and this is no lye.
> And as for men, loketh which tirannye
> They doon al day,—assay hem whoso lyste,
> The trewest is ful brotil [brittle] for to triste.

> (Bullough, I, 189)

As he acknowledges at the beginning of his account, Chaucer merely touches on the 'grete' (outline) of the political and historical dimension. Similarly, it may be that 'The Argument' of Shakespeare's *Lucrece* functions as a framework from which the poem selects certain details. Being a prose account, 'The Argument' naturally follows Livy—or more probably Painter (see Supplementary Notes). The proportion of narrative it gives to the historical question certainly exceeds that afforded by the poem; and in this Shakespeare may be re-employing Chaucer's tactic of using Roman history as a source of something which survives it. The fate of Tarquinius Superbus poses a

special problem for any poet living under a monarchy, but Chaucer solves this by suggesting that the Tarquins have brought a curse upon themselves in offending against divinity (the one authority earthly kings must kneel to):

> Ne never was ther kynge in Rome toun
> Syn thilke day; and she was holden there
> A seynt, and ever hir day y-halwed dere.

> (Bullough, I, 188)

There is a touch of fairy-tale to this, not unlike the Pied Piper's punishment of the townspeople of Hamelin by depriving them of their children. If kings misbehave, they may be lost to their subjects. Lucrece's saintliness, however, might not be acceptable to those who think that the very nature of Tarquin's offence to some degree involves her complicity, however unwilling.[17] Chaucer, as well as disingenuously (and disarmingly) enlisting the authority of a chief member of the opposition—Augustine—deals forthrightly with sceptics by insisting on her complete and utter senselessness at the moment of violation:

> That, what for fere of sklaundre, and drede of dethe,
> She lost attones both wytte and brethe;
> And in a swowgh she lay, and woxe so ded,
> *Men myghten smyten of hir arme or hed,*
> She feleth nothinge, neither foule *nor feyre.*

> (Bullough, I, 187; my italics)

Chaucer, then, produces a particularly sympathetic defence of Lucrece, and the forceful nature of his assertions on her behalf suggests that he knew that his choice of her as a typical 'good woman' would not go unquestioned—hence the conciliatory gesture towards the Augustinian viewpoint. Something of this problem is to appear later in Shakespeare.

Politics and conscience were to be brought together in a new formula at the end of Mary Tudor's reign, and more pertinently at the start of Elizabeth's, in a series of stern, lugubrious poems collectively known as *The Mirror for Magistrates,* which continued to be published until the early seventeenth century. The theme connecting these poems is that of implacable fortune enacting the will of God in bringing individuals down from whatever brief height of happiness or triumph they may enjoy. The idea is a familiar medieval one and derives from the teachings of 'tragical morality'.[18] The poems in the *Mirror* collection confront the reader with a figure who unfolds an exemplary tale of personal woe. The speaker is invariably a ghost or spirit who complains of the particular event, action, or circumstances that have caused his doom. While often a king or potentate, he may equally be a rebel or political misfit (along with the confessions of Richard II we hear those of Owen Glendower and Jack Cade); and sometimes the figure is a woman, as most notably in the case of Jane Shore whose story Thomas Churchyard contributed to the collection, with a shaping effect on later poems in the 'complaint' genre, including of course *Lucrece.*

As with all Elizabethan narratives, *The Mirror for Magistrates* keeps an eye on past performances, a noteworthy sign of this appearing in the introductory poem (or 'Induction') to the sequence, in which Sorrow takes the poet on a journey to Pluto's hell and there presents to him, along with other scenes of human malady and folly, a view of the destruction of Troy:

> But Troy, alas! methought above them all,
>   It made mine eyes in very tears consume,
> When I beheld the woeful weird befall,
>   That by the wrathfull will of gods was come;
> And Jove's unmoved sentence and foredoom
>   On Priam king and on his town so bent,
>   I could not lin [cease], but I must there lament.

> (E.K. Chambers, ed., *The Oxford Book of Sixteenth Century Verse*, 1932, p. 125)

Scenes like this no doubt acted as a prompt to Shakespeare when he in turn led Lucrece to the painting which depicted the fall of Troy and the sorrows of Hecuba (1366-1568). A source for all such depictions is the second book of Virgil's *Aeneid*, in which Aeneas explains to Dido how his city fell to the Greeks. More specifically, Marlowe's description in *Dido Queen of Carthage* exercised an undoubted influence on Shakespeare in his choice of images or words describing the sack and carnage.[19] Influence builds on influence, and *The Rape of Lucrece* is accordingly a poem in which many previous voices can be heard mingling with and modifying one another, making it difficult to decide where to attribute a particular effect or to determine how much conscious selection has been at work. However, as in Chaucer, though at much greater length, the main emphasis falls on Lucrece and our judgement of her.[20]

Responsibility for this may lie particularly with Samuel Daniel's *The Complaint of Rosamond*, published only a short while before in 1592. Daniel's poem derives quite clearly from the *Mirror* narratives in that it confronts the reader with the ghost of a woman who has fallen prey to misfortune. The nature of her transgression is her untimely love (for a king no less), the punishment for which has been undertaken by the jealous wife and queen. In developing his story, Daniel transforms the homiletic sternness of the *Mirror* tradition into the romantic genre of the complaint; other examples quickly followed, dealing in the main with sorrowful heroines whose tearful confessions begged pity rather than censure.[21] Daniel establishes sympathy for Rosamond by depicting her as an unwilling victim of her own fate. She too is an object of lust, though this is the rather melancholic, hesitant lust of an older man who asks a matron of the court to intercede for him. This woman explains the king's interest to Rosamond, who accepts him as her lover. Henry's eventual grief on discovering the poisoned corpse of his mistress is genuine and meant to be redemptive. All this of course we have only from the mouth of Rosamond herself, but there is nothing in the poem to suggest that we should distrust her. Daniel gives his heroine a voice in which to keen at length, and

LONDON.
Printed by Richard Field, for Iohn Harrifon; and are to be fold at the figne of the white Greyhound in Paules Churh-yard. 1594.

Title page of The Rape of Lucrece *(1594).*

in adapting the tactic for his poem Shakespeare for the first time presents a version of Lucrece in which the victim expresses her own motives and misery. Until then she had been a silent witness to the statements made about her by poets and historians.

Shakespeare's poem resembles Daniel's in a good many respects: each uses rhyme royal, and a similar rhetorical play of argument occurs in both, so much so that certain stanzas could be transferred from one to the other without detection. The moral argument or conscience-wrestling undertaken by Rosamond interestingly makes her combine in one person elements of both of Shakespeare's protagonists, as if a more sympathetic version of Tarquin were to meet with a less resolute Lucrece:

> But what? he is my King and may constraine me,
> Whether I yeelde or not I live defamed:
> The world will thinke authority did gaine me,
> I shal be iudg'd hys love, and so be shamed:
> We see the fayre condemn'd, that never gamed.
>   And if I yeeld, tis honorable shame,
>   If not, I live disgrac'd, yet thought the same.[22]

One further detail linking Daniel to Shakespeare is the casket, a present to Rosamond from Henry, who hopes that its richly inwrought erotic motifs will nudge her thoughts in the direction of desire. But Rosamond notes rather the pathos of those women who represent seductive beauty:

> The day before the night of my defeature,
> He greets me with a Casket richly wrought:
> So rare, that arte did seeme to strive with nature,
> T'expresse the cunning work-man's curious thought;
> The mistery whereof I prying sought.
>   And found engraven on the lidde above,
>   *Amymone* how she with Neptune strove.
>
> *Amymone* old Danaus fayrest daughter,
> As she was fetching water all alone
> At *Lerna:* whereas Neptune came and caught her,
> From whom she striv'd and strugled to be gone,
> Beating the ayre with cryes and pittious mone.
>   But all in vaine, with him sh'is forced to goe:
>   Tis shame that men should use poore maydens so.
>
> There might I see described how she lay,
> At those proude feete, not satisfied with prayer:
> Wailing her heavie hap, cursing the day,
> In act so pittious to express despaire:
> And by how much more greev'd, so much more fayre;
>   Her teares upon her cheekes poore carefull gerle,
>   Did seeme against the sunne cristall and perle.
>
>   (372-92)

As well as the overall similarity, a number of verbal parallels connect this passage with Lucrece's larger survey of the Trojan scene. While civil strife and the horror of war and bloodshed make for a different emphasis from this small-scale story of seduction, rape underlies Lucrece's need for solace in the first place. Both accounts draw on a classical and mythological source. The interest in 'curious' workmanship is common to each; and each of them dwells on the relationship of art to life and on the power of representation to affect the spectator. Verbal details, as in phrases like 'There might I see' (386), recur in *Lucrece* (e.g. 1380, 1388, etc.), and a phrase like, 'how she lay / At those proud feet' (386-87) seems echoed in the line, 'Which bleeding under Pyrrhus' proud foot lies' (*Lucrece* 1449). The sheer bloodiness of the Troy scene limits its similarity with the casket depiction, but elsewhere the picture of the grieving Lucrece strikes a common chord with Daniel's poem. Compare lines 391-92 (quoted above) of *Rosamond* with the following description of Lucrece and her maid:

> A pretty while these pretty creatures stand,
> Like ivory conduits coral cisterns filling.
> One justly weeps, the other takes in hand
> No cause but company of her drops spilling:
> Their gentle sex to weep are often willing,
>   Grieving themselves to guess at others' smarts,
>   And then they drown their eyes or break their hearts.
>
>   (1233-9)

Rosamond is moved at the sight of another woman's tears (albeit artificial ones), just as Lucrece's maid responds to her mistress's sorrow. What both descriptions have in common is that they effect a moment of contemplative pathos centred on a female figure (or figures) or conveyed through a female sensibility. This brings us back once more to the question of the conflicting demands of rhetorical practice and dramatic or psychological plausibility. Another Shakespearean instance, already touched on, is the delicate tableau of the sleeping Lucrece, a picture of purity in her (literal) unconsciousness of Tarquin's gaze (386-420). Such moments, asking from the reader a tender awareness of the beauty of pathos, function ecphrastically (though in a briefer space than the Troy scene) as a statement of the overall pitifulness expressed by the main theme. The extent to which they detach themselves from their immediate context enables them to encompass the feelings and ideas of the poem as a whole. Such distillations of pity summarise the concern the poem wishes to establish over the eventual fate of the heroine, its registration at an earlier narrative point bearing on the mood intended to be dominant at the end.

Notes

1. One critic has recently argued that the antithesis which opposes the two antagonists to each other also works by producing an unexpected resemblance between them. See Dubrow's account of the poem's syneciosis ('strange harmony', as the Elizabethan stylist John Hoskyns called it), in *Captive Victors,* esp. pp. 80-142.

2. *Augustine concerning the City of God against the Pagans,* tr. H. Bettenson, 1972, 1.19.19-20.

3. St Jerome had extolled the courage and resolve of Lucrece and saw her as a worthy example for Christians to follow—even though she was a pagan. Tertullian further commented that concern for personal glory was acceptable to God if it accorded with his design. The Augustinian position, however, was alive and well in Shakespeare's day thanks to the efforts of Tyndale. See Donaldson, pp. 34 and 174-5.

4. Pursuing the notion of syneciosis (see above, p. 23, n), Dubrow argues that the contradictoriness involves Lucrece in terms of motive as it does Tarquin, and appears to see this as part of Shakespeare's design. But if this is what happens, it is more likely to be an incidental and unplanned development, since the poet bases his account of Lucrece's triumph on her resistance to compromise. See Dubrow's conclusion, p. 168.

5. Consider Lewis's objection: 'The conceit which makes Lucrece's pillow 'angrie' at 388 would have been tolerable in *Hero and Leander* but is here repellent' (*English Literature,* p. 499).

6. See Kuhl, 'Shakespeare's *Rape of Lucrece*', *Philological Quarterly* 20 (1941), 352-60, and Platt, 'The

Rape of Lucrece and the Republic for which it stands', *Centennial Review* 19 (1975), 59-79.

7. See variously articles by Coppélia Kahn, 'The rape in Shakespeare's *Lucrece*', *Shakespeare Studies* 9 (1976) 45-72; Nancy Vickers, '"The blazon of sweet beauty's best": Shakespeare's *Lucrece*', in *Shakespeare and the Question of Theory,* ed. Parker and Hartman, 1985, pp. 95-115; and Catherine R. Stimpson, 'Shakespeare and the soil of rape', in *The Woman's Part: Feminist Criticism of Shakespeare,* ed. Lenz, Greene, and Neely, 1980, pp. 56-64.

8. Vickers, '"The blazon"', p. 109.

9. See T.S. Eliot, 'Shakespeare and the Stoicism of Seneca', in *Selected Essays,* 3rd edn, 1951, pp. 126-40; and Philip Edwards, *Hamlet,* New Cambridge Shakespeare: 1985, pp. 60-1.

10. See Akrigg, p. 200, and E.P. Kuhl, 'Shakespeare's *Rape of Lucrece*', pp. 352-60.

11. See below on *Mirror for Magistrates,* p. 38.

12. See Geoffrey Bullough, ed., *Narrative and Dramatic Sources of Shakespeare,* 1957, I, 196-9.

13. The detail is not in Painter.

14. See Donaldson's careful analysis of the various treatments of the rape both before and following Shakespeare (chs. 1-2, 4-5).

15. Painter (Bullough, I, 198).

16. It is worth remarking, as the question of justifiable suicide arises, that taking one's life was not a matter of indifference to the Romans. Cicero argues that only if God has summoned one is it permissible, or if one is sure God has given a valid reason (as in the case of high-minded men such as Socrates or Cato). (See *Tusculan Disputations* 1.30.73-4.)

17. Lucrece herself seems to subscribe to this view—see above, p. 24.

18. See J.W. Lever, ed., *The Rape of Lucrece,* 1971, p. 123.

19. See Douglas Bush, *Mythology and the Renaissance Tradition in English Poetry,* 1932, p. 152n. and *Luc.* 1554n.

20. Furnivall suggests that Shakespeare combines the theme of *The Legende of Good Women* with the style of extended lament characteristic of *Troilus and Criseyde* (H.E. Rollins, ed., *Shakespeare: The Poems* (New Variorum), 1938, p. 419).

21. See the section on *A Lover's Complaint,* pp. 62-5, below.

22. *The Complaint of Rosamond,* lines 337-43 (Samuel Daniel, *Poems and a Defense of Rhyme,* ed. A Colby Sprague, 1930, p. 50).

CHARACTER STUDIES

Philippa Berry (essay date 1992)

SOURCE: "Woman, Language, and History in *The Rape of Lucrece,*" in *Shakespeare Survey,* Vol. 44, 1992, pp. 33-39.

[*In the following essay, Berry asserts that Lucrece is not simply a victim of patriarchal power, but that she more importantly functions as a strong voice for action and political change.*]

Recent feminist criticism of Shakespeare's *The Rape of Lucrece* (or *Lucrece,* as it was titled in its first five quartos) has stressed the extent to which the idea of woman which it represents is one overdetermined by patriarchal ideology, and has typically interpreted Lucrece herself as a sign used to mediate and define men's relationships to men.[1] While I am partially in agreement with such interpretations of the poem, I want here to question the view that at no point in the poem is Lucrece represented as posing any contradiction, any *aporia,* within patriarchal discourse. Nancy Vickers, in her celebrated essay, '"The blazon of sweet beauty's best": Shakespeare's *Lucrece*', argues that:

> In *Lucrece* occasion, rhetoric, and result are all informed by, and thus inscribe, a battle between men that is first figuratively and then literally fought on the fields of woman's 'celebrated' body. Here, metaphors commonly read as signs of a battle between the sexes emerge rather from a homosocial struggle, in this case a male rivalry, which positions a third (female) term in a median space from which it is initially used and finally eliminated.[2]

Of course Vickers is right in her assertion that Lucrece, as a third and female term, occupies 'a median space' in the poem. She identifies this inbetween space with Lucrece's body (as Georgianna Ziegler has recently pointed out, this space is also the private domestic space associated with female identity by patriarchal culture).[3] Lucrece's body does indeed begin and end the poem as the object of masculine rhetoric. None the less, it is strange that Vickers, in focusing her influential feminist analysis upon men's use and abuse of language in Shakespeare's poem, failed to discuss Lucrece's own language—her speech at her death, and her more private but much longer rhetorical performance, in the privacy of her chamber, immediately before and after her rape. For Lucrece's 'inbetweenness' can also be related to the importance which her voice assumes at the dead centre of the poem, in a textually constituted space which corresponds to the very depths of night according to Shakespeare's narrative. It is in this median and very dark space, under the threat of rape and death, that Lucrece utters her first words in the poem, thereby beginning a long rhetorical performance (albeit one that is occasionally interrupted) which runs from line 575 until her death at line 1722, and in which the number of lines actually spoken by Lucrece is 645—in other words, just over a third of the total number of lines in the entire poem.

The greater part of this long speech is an extended lament or complaint by Lucrece for her lost virtue, and here Shakespeare departs most strikingly from his sources in that throughout most of this lament Lucrece is alone. In the classical sources of the poem, notably Ovid's *Fasti* and Livy's *History,* Lucrece's lament is much shorter, and always addressed to an audience—her husband Collatine, her father, and their two friends, Junius Brutus and Publius Valerius. The same masculine audience for this utterance is posited in the rather longer speech found in the extremely popular *Declamatio Lucretiae,* written by the Florentine humanist Coluccio Salutati in the fourteenth century. Not only does Shakespeare's Lucrece speak most of her lament while she is alone; Shakespeare also added a number of details to the quite simple form of the lament found in his sources: in particular, Lucrece's three impassioned apostrophes to Night, Time, and Opportunity, and her meditation upon a painting of the fall of Troy. Yet while these changes have been noted by critics, they do not appear to have provoked much interest. Even a fairly extensive consideration of this part of the poem, by Don Cameron Allen, concentrates only upon the second stage of the lament, in which Lucrece meditates upon a painting of violated Troy.[4]

In this essay, therefore, I will consider the complex implications of the often forgotten centerpiece of the poem, which is one of the most extended tragic utterances attributed to a woman in English Renaissance literature, and will assess its possible importance for a feminist—and a political—reading of this poem. My contention is that Lucrece is represented in the poem as an important but unorthodox example of Renaissance *virtù,* for this quality is given most powerful expression in the poem, not through her actions, but through her private use of language—a use which implicitly stresses its performative, even magical powers. It is in fact in this secret and powerful feminine eloquence that we can find the clearest indication of republican political ideals in the poem. The Earl of Southampton, to whom the poem is dedicated, is known to have been interested in republican thought, and Shakespeare's choice of subject matter for his poem naturally suggests such an interest, since it was of course Lucrece's death which caused the end of Roman kingship with the downfall of the Tarquins, and the establishment of the Roman republic by Junius Brutus.[5] Significantly, the connection of Shakespeare's narrative with republican politics is never directly stated in the poem (presumably for reasons of political expediency). It is in Lucrece's lament, however, that the question of political justice is raised most directly.

Of course Lucrece's utterances in Shakespeare's poem are always to some extent implicated within a masculine poetic discourse: a discourse which is framed by the two male poetic exemplars of Orpheus and Virgil, as well as by the voice of the implicitly male narrator. Yet in contrast to the poem's emphasis upon the vulnerability of the female body, the female voice is here represented, not only as much less susceptible to manipulation by men, but even as the catalyst of an extraordinary political force: Lucrece's complaint enables her to replace Tarquin as the controlling figure in the narrative until the moment of her death. She only speaks, of course, when she is forced into the position of social outcast and scapegoat through the loss of her chastity—as in many other examples of English Renaissance literature, it is not until a female figure assumes a position of obvious marginality to conventional society (as opposed to the unacknowledged marginality to which all women are condemned in a patriarchal society) that she finds a voice. But through her discovery of a voice at the moment of personal disaster, Lucrece also develops a plan of action.

Without disputing the oft-stated feminist view that Lucrece's suicide is closely related to her acceptance of a patriarchal ideology of female chastity, I would suggest that this central section of Shakespeare's narrative challenges any interpretation of his Lucrece as being simply history's victim. Instead, it positions her as a partially independent, if somewhat unorthodox (and confused) historical agent, who uses an Orphic private utterance to initiate historical change. Close analysis of her lament reveals Lucrece as the deliberate rather than accidental cause of that historical change which follows her death, and which leads to the expulsion and death of the Tarquins and the establishment of the Roman republic (although as I shall show later on, Lucrece never fully grasps the implications of the historical change which she initiates). It also shows her to be a figure who is learning, along with vocal self-expression, a political art of dissembling or concealment—a skill which will be most apparent in her planning of her suicide. Seemingly, Lucrece acquires and exercises a certain degree of political skill specifically through her use of language; in the first instance, she does this by appealing to a series of ideas which figured prominently in Renaissance mythographies: Night, Time and Opportunity (Opportunity being usually referred to as Occasio or Fortuna).[6] In this part of her lament, she expresses a powerful desire to reshape history and, specifically, to make it just. This struggle with history is seen primarily as a struggle with supernatural forces.

The effort of the man of *virtù* to shape fortune to his will was of course an important theme of Renaissance humanism, a theme especially prominent in the political thought of Machiavelli.[7] In his *Discourses,* which extolled the virtues of republican government, Machiavelli praised Junius Brutus as the Roman whose exemplary *virtù* led to the establishment of the Roman republic. But he also referred to the frequently important rôle played by women in the downfall of tyrannical rulers:

> we see how women have been the cause of many troubles, have done great harm to those who govern cities, and have caused in them many divisions. In like manner we read in Livy's history that the outrage done to Lucretia deprived the Tarquins of their rule . . .

Among the primary causes of the downfall of tyrants, Aristotle puts the injuries they do on account of women, whether by rape, violation or the breaking up of marriages.[8]

Shakespeare's Lucrece is represented through her lament as a woman attempting to replace a loss of a specifically feminine 'virtue' with a *virtù* which can enable her to take control of her tragic fate. Yet her feminine discovery of this quality is importantly different from the typically public manifestation of *virtù* usually associated with men. Her attempt to master the forces which have led to her tragedy—Night, Time and Opportunity (or Fortune)—is conducted privately, and through a highly poetic use of language which simultaneously stresses language's magical, incantatory properties. This lament begins with Lucrece according supernatural priority to a primordial female divinity, Night. Only as a result of this private struggle to assert her *virtù* is Lucrece able to express it in more public terms at the end of the poem, with her speech and suicide before the four men whom she has summoned.

In its appeal to Night, Lucrece's speech seems on one level to represent an early attempt by Shakespeare to use a figurative association of woman with darkness or blackness to challenge Petrarchan emphasis upon appearances in the poetic representation of women—it is her red and white perfection whose praise by Collatine at the beginning of the poem has contributed to Lucrece's tragedy. As in his use of images of darkness in connection with women in works which include the *Sonnets, Love's Labour's Lost,* and *Romeo and Juliet,* Shakespeare seems in *The Rape of Lucrece* to be trying to define an unorthodox, dynamic version of female identity in terms of hiddenness or concealment. Lucrece appeals to Night to protect her reputation by concealing her under shadow of darkness:

> O night, thou furnace of foul reeking smoke,
> Let not the jealous day behold that face
> Which underneath thy black all-hiding cloak
> Immodestly lies martyred with disgrace!
> Keep still possession of thy gloomy place,
>   That all the faults which in thy reign are made
>   May likewise be sepulchred in thy shade.
>
> Make me not object to the tell-tale day:
> The light will show charactered in my brow
> The story of sweet chastity's decay,
>
> (799-808)

Yet at the same time, Lucrece's speech makes clear the moral ambiguity of Night: an ambiguity which is also suggested in its invocation by two such different tragic heroines as Juliet and Lady Macbeth.[9] Indeed, when considered in relation to the political themes of this poem, the associations of Night with concealment also imply a connection with the sixteenth-century humanist motif of politic dissembling, set out most explicitly in Machiavelli's *The Prince.* Breaking with earlier humanist emphasis upon the morality of *virtù,* Machiavelli had stressed that its practitioner must often dissimulate, and certainly a

concealment and dissimulation associated with Night is central to Lucrece's practice of *virtù.* Not only does she conceal the fact of the rape until her husband and father are in her presence; the theme of hiddenness also characterizes Lucrece's lament or complaint, most of which is uttered secretly, under cover of darkness.

But the aesthetic and political implications of Lucrece's emphasis upon Night become clearer when these are related to the metaphysical significance of this concept. Night figured prominently in Orphic theology, a web of ideas which was granted considerable importance in the syncretic Christian Platonism of the Renaissance. For Renaissance Platonists, because Orpheus was described in myth as imposing order upon chaos through his extraordinary eloquence, he was seen not only as the inspired poet par excellence, but also as a magician, one of the *prisci theologi*—the ancient theologians whose thought was held to have prefigured Platonism as well as Christianity.[10] Pico della Mirandola asserted that: 'In natural magic nothing is more efficacious than the Hymns of Orpheus', and identified the Orphic principle of Night with the supreme deity of the Jewish Kabbalists, the En Soph.[11] Within the Orphic cosmogony, Night was represented as a force which could overturn the authority even of the king of the gods.

The Orphic hymns, first published in the Renaissance at Florence in 1500, were an important literary influence upon the French Pléiade poets in the mid sixteenth century, but in England interest in this material is not apparent until 1594, when, in the same year as *The Rape of Lucrece,* George Chapman's *The Shadow of Night* was published.[12] This poem was explicitly indebted to the Orphic hymns. The first of its two parts was a long hymn or incantation to Night as a primordial goddess. Night is represented by Chapman as inspiring her poet with a *virtù* which is expressed through eloquence rather than strength, but which is none the less capable of ending human injustice and vice. For Chapman, Orpheus' attempt to rescue Eurydice from hell is an allegory of his fervent desire to restore justice on earth.[13] As the new Orphic poet, he appeals to Night to stage an apocalyptic overthrow of all present 'tyrannies':

> O then most tender fortress of our woes,
> That bleeding lye in vertues overthroes.
> Hating the whoredome of this painted light:
> Raise thy chaste daughters, ministers of right,
> The dreadful and the just Eumenides,
> And let them wreake the wrongs of our disease,
> Drowning the world in bloud, and staine the skies
> With their spilt soules, made drunke with tyrannies.[14]

The relationship between the works of Shakespeare and Chapman has of course been a subject of controversy since Arthur Acheson, Frances Yates and Muriel Bradbrook asserted that a reference to the 'school of night' in *Love's Labour's Lost* represented a satiric attack on the intellectual views of Chapman's circle (whose members included Raleigh and the Earl of Northumberland).[15] In my view, however, the rhetorical importance accorded to Night in *The Rape of Lucrece* (together with the use of similar imagery in several other works by Shakespeare) should prompt a reconsideration of this question; especially since the poem's date of composition seems likely to have been quite close to that of *Love's Labour's Lost.*

That Shakespeare's version of Night is indebted to the Orphic tradition is further suggested when Lucrece is herself directly compared to Orpheus, just before the first time that her words to Tarquin are reported by the narrator:

> Here with a cockatrice' dead-killing eye
> He rouseth up himself, and makes a pause,
> While she, the picture of pure piety,
> Like a white hind under the gripe's sharp claws,
> Pleads in a wilderness where are no laws
>   To the rough beast that knows no gentle right,
>   Nor aught obeys but his foul appetite.
>
> But when a black-faced cloud the world doth threat,
> In his dim mist th'aspiring mountains hiding,
> From earth's dark womb some gentle gust doth get
> Which blows these pitchy vapours from their biding,
> Hind'ring their present fall by this dividing;
>   So his unhallowed haste her words delays,
>   And moody Pluto winks while Orpheus plays.
>
>   (540-53)

The reference suggests that while Lucrece's powers of language are comparable to those of Orpheus, at this stage they are unable to help her. It is not until after the rape, when Tarquin has fled, that her eloquence finds unconstricted expression. It is now that she appeals to 'comfort-killing' Night—a force which, as the poem emphasizes, has indirectly served as Tarquin's accomplice—to desert to her side, and stage a reordering of time:

> O hateful, vaporous, and foggy night,
> Since thou art guilty of my cureless crime,
> Muster thy mists to meet the eastern light,
> Make war against proportioned course of time.
>
>   (771-4)

She appeals to Night:

> Let my good name, that senseless reputation,
> For Collatine's dear love be kept unspotted;
> If that be made a theme for disputation,
> The branches of another root are rotted.
>
>   (820-3)

A few lines later, Lucrece makes explicit this metaphoric connection between natural mutability and the sphere of politics, in what seems a restatement of the Machiavellian theme that all states are subject to decay, because of the natural depravity of man. Her words hint at a covert criticism of all models of kingship:

> Why should the worm intrude the maiden bud,
> Or hateful cuckoos hatch in sparrows' nests,
> Or toads infect fair founts with venom mud,
> Or tyrant folly lurk in gentle breasts,

> Or kings be breakers of their own behests?
>   But no perfection is so absolute
>   That some impurity doth not pollute.
>
>   (848-54)

Lucrece follows her invocation of Night with an attack on Time and 'thy servant opportunity' (or Fortune) for behaving unjustly in betraying her to this misfortune. She demands of Opportunity:

> When wilt thou be the humble suppliant's friend,
> And bring him where his suit may be obtained?
> When wilt thou sort an hour great strifes to end,
> Or free that soul which wretchedness hath chained,
> Give physic to the sick, ease to the pained?
>   The poor, lame, blind, halt, creep, cry out for thee,
>   But they ne'er meet with opportunity.
>
>   (897-903)

Finally, she asks Time:

> Why work'st thou mischief in thy pilgrimage,
> Unless thou couldst return to make amends?
>
>   (960-1)

And she urges Time to punish Tarquin:

> Thou ceaseless lackey to eternity,
> With some mischance cross Tarquin in his light.
> Devise extremes beyond extremity
> To make him curse this cursèd crimeful night.
>
>   (967-70)

Lucrece's lament is therefore also both invocation and imprecation. Through its language, she figuratively seizes control of history, rather than remaining its passive victim. Thereby, from the magical perspective of Orphic poetics, she actually begins to change it. Thus the poem seems to be associating a new, feminine model of *virtù*, expressed through the language of grief and mourning, with the capacity to disorder time and its processes.

But it would be a mistake to overestimate Lucrece's understanding of her own relationship to language or to history. Her desire for a universal justice is confusedly interwoven in this part of her lament with concern for Collatine's honour; moreover, she seems to underestimate the power of her own language, seeing her apostrophes to Night, Time, and Opportunity as having been made in vain. This lack of self-knowledge is even more apparent in the second phase of her solitary lament, which reveals her as extraordinarily anxious about the association of certain kinds of language with historical change, and as unable to face the implications of her desire to be revenged. While it was a Greek poet, Orpheus, who had influenced her invocations of Night, Time, and Opportunity, Lucrece's contemplation here of a painting of the fall of Troy is indebted to the writings of a Roman poet: to Books I and II of Virgil's *Aeneid*. And in this episode, the Greeks are identified with the treacherous power of language for deceit and destruction, through references to the 'golden words' of Nestor and the 'enchanting story' of Sinon. This emphasis upon the Greeks' powers of language suggests that the narrator may regard them with some sympathy and admiration; but Lucrece certainly views them with loathing, and grieves for ruined Troy. The episode indicates that at the same time as desiring justice, she is extremely fearful concerning the possible outcome of such a demand. Lucrece asks of Paris' cause of the fall of Troy through his abduction of Helen:

> Why should the private pleasure of someone
> Become the public plague of many moe?
> Let sin alone committed light alone
> Upon his head that hath transgressèd so;
> Let guiltless souls be freed from guilty woe.
> For one's offence why should so many fall,
> To plague a private sin in general?
>
> (1478-84)

As her identification with Troy shows, Lucrece is profoundly implicated in the hierarchical system of values and government which her appeal for revenge will eradicate. We are told of the fall of Troy:

> the skies were sorry,
> And the little stars shot from their fixèd places
> When their glass fell wherein they viewed their faces.
>
> (1524-6)

Thus in spite of her concern about Collatine's honour, Lucrece does not grasp the extent to which she is now a traitor to that system. Shakespeare would have known from his sources that the expulsion of the Tarquins would ultimately mean a loss of political power for the family of her husband Collatine, who was cousin to Tarquin. It is striking that in her meditation upon the Troy painting, Lucrece directs especial hostility, firstly, towards Helen, a woman whose rape, like her own, causes the fall of a dynasty of kings; and secondly, towards 'perjured Sinon':

> whose enchanting story
> The credulous old Priam after slew;
> Whose words like wildfire burnt the shining glory
> Of rich-built Ilion,
>
> (1521-4)

We are told, moreover, that Sinon had:

> Cheeks neither red nor pale, but mingled so
> That blushing red no guilty instance gave,
> Nor ashy pale the fear that false hearts have.
>
> (1510-12)

and that 'For every tear he falls a Trojan bleeds' (1551).

In other words, although Lucrece compares this traitor to the Trojans to Tarquin, he seems more closely to resemble herself. While her face is first described in the poem as a picture of red and white beauty, when she appears before the four men at the end of the poem the misfortune she has experienced is 'carved in it with tears' (1713), and this

clearly adds to her rhetorical impact. Hence in her intense hostility to Helen and Sinon, Lucrece may imply a buried anxiety about her own ambiguous status as both member of and traitor to her society. At the same time, her criticism of Sinon also articulates a profound uncertainty about the ethics of a use of language to produce political change. Yet in spite of such reservations, Lucrece never fully acknowledges either her own contradictory historical position, or her personal recourse to the manipulative and performative resources of language. She goes on to stage the last act of her own tragedy, unaware of the full political and historical implications of the private as well as the public phases in this compelling performance.

Notes

1. See in particular Coppélia Kahn, 'The Rape in Shakespeare's *Lucrece*', *Shakespeare Studies*, 9 (1976), 45-72; and Nancy Vickers, '"The Blazon of Sweet Beauty's Best": Shakespeare's *Lucrece*', in *Shakespeare and the Question of Theory*, ed. P. Parker and G. Hartman (London, 1985), pp. 95-115.

2. Vickers, 'The Blazon of Sweet Beauty's Best', p. 96.

3. Georgianna Ziegler, 'My Lady's Chamber: Female Space, Female Chastity in Shakespeare', *Textual Practice*, 4, 1 (Spring 1990), 73-90.

4. Don Cameron Allen, *Image and Meaning,* 2nd edn (Baltimore, 1968), ch. 4.

5. See Margot Heinemann, 'Rebel Lords, Popular Playwrights, and Political Culture: Notes on the Jacobean Patronage of the Earl of Southampton', *Yearbook of English Studies: Politics, Patronage and Literature in England 1558-1658,* 21 (1991), 63-86.

6. For the frequent identification of Fortune with Opportunity or Occasio, see Howard R. Patch, *The Goddess Fortuna in Medieval Literature* (London, 1927), pp. 115-16.

7. The view of several Florentine humanists was that *virtù vince fortuna:* fortune need not overwhelm a man who does not fear to swim with her fierce current. Niccolò Machiavelli explored the problematic relationship between man and fortune (a personification whose feminine gender he stressed) in chapter 25 of *The Prince.* This book, together with Machiavelli's *Discourses,* was printed in England (in Italian) in 1584, under a false Italian imprint.

8. Machiavelli, *The Discourses,* ed. Bernard Crick, trans. Leslie J. Walker SJ (London, 1983), 3, p. 26. I am indebted to Patricia Klindienst Joplin for the discovery of this quotation, which she cites in '"Ritual Work on Human Flesh": Livy's Lucretia and the Rape of the Body Politic', *Helios* 17, 1 (Spring 1990), 51-70.

9. *Romeo and Juliet* 2.2.10-16; *Macbeth* 1.5.50-4.

10. See D.P. Walker, *The Ancient Theology: Studies in Christian Platonism from the Fifteenth to the Eighteenth Century* (London, 1972).

11. Pico della Mirandola, 'Conclusiones secundam propriam opinionem . . . hymnos Orphei', ii and xv, in *Conclusiones* (Rome, 1486).

12. See Françoise Joukovsky, *Orphée et ses disciples dans la poésie française et néo-latine du XVIe siècle* (Geneva, 1970).

13. *The Poems of George Chapman,* ed. Phyllis Brooks Bartlett (New York, 1941), 'The Shadow of Night: Hymnus in Noctem', lines 151-2.

14. Ibid., lines 247-54.

15. See Arthur Acheson, *Shakespeare and the Rival Poet* (London, 1903); M.C. Bradbrook, *The School of Night: A Study in the Literary Relationships of Sir Walter Ralegh* (Cambridge, 1936); F. A. Yates, *A Study of 'Love's Labour's Lost'* (Cambridge, 1936).

A.D. Cousins (essay date 2000)

SOURCE: "Lucrece," in *Shakespeare's Sonnets and Narrative Poems,* Longman, 2000, pp. 63-81.

[*In the following excerpt, Cousins argues that Tarquin and Lucrece can be seen as parodies of Petrarchan lovers and that Lucrece's husband, Collatine, is a braggart who unwittingly turns Tarquin's violent attention towards Lucrece.*]

(III) Tarquin, Lucrece, and Collatine

As might be expected, much of the more recent commentary on *Lucrece* has focused on the interrelated matters of politics, gender and subjectivity. The poem's representation of the Roman world and its politics, especially its sexual/gender politics, has been studied; how *Lucrece* emerges from the variously political discourses of later Elizabethan society, and its negotiations with them, have been considered; the poem's representations of subjectivity in relation to patriarchy and to rape—and their connections—have been widely discussed.[1] In focusing on those matters, most commentary has inevitably centred on the characterization of Lucrece herself. But as a result the mutually defining nature of characterization in the poem has received insufficient attention.[2] Here I want to propose that by examining the reciprocal formation of consciousness and of role among Shakespeare's Tarquin, Collatine and Lucrece as far as the beginnings of his poem's rape scene (that is, approximately from lines 1 to 441) one sees that the characterizations established early in *Lucrece* are more complex in their discursive relations than has been acknowledged. Recognition of their being so helps to illuminate not merely subsequent happenings in the poem, such as Lucrece's insistent denial of her own innocence and her decision to commit suicide, but also crucial concerns of the poem, such as the sceptical interrogation of exemplarity, the interaction between exemplarity and historical process.

In particular, I shall argue here that while Tarquin is a tyrant figure, and distinctly a Platonic type of the tyrant, he is as well a demonic parody of the Petrarchan lover insofar as he pursues a lady, Lucrece, who is portrayed as at once an exemplar of the chaste Roman matron and an incarnation of the Petrarchan mistress. Violating her, Shakespeare's Tarquin sexually heightens and violates the Petrarchan discourse of love. Yet it is not Lucrece's primary misfortune that, in her guise as Petrarchan mistress, she attracts a tyrant figure (in fact, a proto-tyrant) who defines himself specifically, as a tyrant, in relation to her via the role of grimly parodic Petrarchan lover. Rather, as is argued here, it seems that Lucrece's primary misfortune lies in the hubris of her husband, Collatine. When part of the Roman army besieging Ardea, Collatine tries to gain a personal victory over the king's son, his superior and kinsman: Collatine's boastful vying with the proto-tyrant redirects Tarquin's violence and desire from the enemy/foreign/public to the kindred/Roman/private. The poem registers that redirection of Tarquin's violence and desire not only in terms of Petrarchan discourse but also in terms of the myths of the Golden Age and of Eden. Tarquin becomes an analogue to Satan; Lucrece, indicated as embodying both Tarquin's and Collatine's notions of the absolute good on earth, becomes an analogue to the earthly paradise and (an incorruptible) Eve; Collatine thus figures as a self-betraying Adam, who brings the serpent to Eden and tempts the serpent into violating his (unwilling) Eve.

When the intricate interactions among Tarquin, Collatine and Lucrece in the early part of Shakespeare's poem are seen especially as expressed through those Platonic, Petrarchan and Golden Age/Edenic discourses, then the immediately relevant consequences are as follows. Tarquin's mutually intensifying, interconnected roles, read in conjunction with the also mutually intensifying and interconnected roles of Lucrece, which are antithetic to his, clarify her comprehensive sense of violation and contamination. Thus clarified, too, is her deep sense of defacement, of her innermost self's having been stolen; both clarifications, in turn, help to illuminate her decision to commit suicide. Light is shed, moreover, on the sceptical questioning of exemplarity and on other of the poem's concerns. The final consequence, then, appears to be that a new perspective is offered on the poem as a whole: important happenings can be viewed from a revealingly unfamiliar angle; things not previously observed, such as the sceptical questioning of exemplarity, come sharply into view.

The easiest way to start specifying what has been outlined above is probably by looking at the characterization of Tarquin, for with him the poem itself begins. Tarquin's historical role as proto-tyrant seems to be his basic one in the poem. Shakespeare's narrator may also picture Tarquin in the roles of parodic Petrarchan lover and of Satan, but it is indicated that they are Tarquin's expressions of his tyrannic role in relation to Lucrece. At the beginning of the 'Argument', the narrator signals that Tarquin's immediate role model is his father, whose pride, treachery, violence and violations—of family bonds, of laws and of custom—manifest his will to power, his will to tyranny (ll. 1-6). The poem reveals, of course more thoroughly than does the 'Argument', that Tarquin is certainly his father's son.[3]

The opening of *Lucrece* predominantly characterizes Tarquin in terms of desire. The 'Argument' emphasizes his underlying role to be that of proto-tyrant, the opening stanzas do so as well; but as proto-tyrant he is initially and chiefly characterized in the poem by the 'desire' (l. 2) which informs the expressions of his tyrannic role in relation to Lucrece.[4] The narrator implies several things about the nature of that desire: its treachery ('trustless' and 'false', in l. 2, suggest that it betrays Tarquin while impelling him to betray Collatine and Lucrece); its possession of Tarquin (he becomes '[l]ust-breathed', the narrator says in l. 3); its sinister, even demonic, energy (ll. 4-7); its violence which displaces the military violence directed by Tarquin against Ardea. Desire, treachery and violence are, according to Plato's *Republic,* marks of the tyrannic character.[5] In fact, desire and the need to gratify it tyrannize over the tyrant. He becomes driven by a 'master passion' in whose service he will violate even domestic sanctities (9, 572-5). The characterization of Tarquin as proto-tyrant accords in those respects, then, with Plato's type of the tyrant in his *Republic.*[6] And it does so in others as well. According to Plato's text, desire possesses the tyrant but he is vulnerable also to fears: 'He is naturally a prey to fears and passions of every sort' (9, 579b). Tarquin's soliloquy in his chamber dramatizes the compelling force of his desire in conflict with the constraining power of his fears (ll. 190-280).[7] Further, Plato describes the tyrant as bestial and, more specifically, as a wolf to his fellow citizens (8, 569b and 565d-566a). Shakespeare's narrator compares Tarquin, just before the rape of Lucrece, to a 'cockatrice' (l. 540), a 'gripe' (l. 543; that is, to a vulture or an eagle) and to a 'foul night-waking cat' (l. 554). Tarquin is thereafter compared to a 'wolf' when he rapes Lucrece (ll. 676-7). Subsequently he is figured as a 'full-fed hound or gorged hawk' (l. 694) and 'thievish dog' (l. 736). In his primary role as proto-tyrant, Tarquin seems deliberately represented in accord with Plato's account of the tyrannic character. He may be, as Ovid had indicated and Shakespeare apparently accepted from Ovid, truly his father's son but he is also more than a reincarnation of his tyrannic father.

How much more than that he is can be seen from his relations to Lucrece. The ways in which Tarquin perceives Lucrece and defines himself in response to his understanding of her express, of course, his desire for her and thus his role as Platonic tyrant figure in relation to her. As has been foreshadowed above, one such expression of his role as tyrant in relation to her is his role as parodic Petrarchan lover. When first the narrator describes Tarquin, characterizing him predominantly in terms of desire, it seems that '[l]ust-breathed' Tarquin (l. 3) is as a man possessed. What tyrannizes over the proto-tyrant is desire for a woman pictured to him, by her husband, in a way that anachronis-

tically celebrates her as a type of the Petrarchan lady: 'Collatine unwisely did not let / To praise the clear unmatched red and white / Which triumph'd in that sky of his delight' (ll. 10-12). The narrator confirms that image of Lucrece by adding to his report of Collatine's imprudent eulogy. He praises Lucrece's eyes, identifying them with the stars. They are, he says, '[M]ortal stars as bright as heaven's beauties' (l. 13). Reworking the Petrarchan motif of the lady's eyes being, or resembling, stars, Shakespeare's narrator confirms what his report of Lucrece's public celebration by Collatine has previously, and likewise metonymically, indicated through Petrarchan allusion ('red and white', l. 11): Lucrece's role as Petrarchan object of desire. So Tarquin, the Platonic tyrant figure tyrannized by desire for a woman imaged to him as virtually prefiguring Laura, becomes in relation to her a counterpart to the Petrarchan lover.[8] But the differences between Tarquin and, say, Petrarch's speaker in '*Passa la nave . . .*' are more important than the similarities. In particular, the latter's desire for his lady seems ambivalent. Tarquin's desire for Lucrece is, however, solely unspiritual, a 'lightless fire' (l. 4) concerned only with the body and with violation: 'lurk-[ing] to aspire, / And girdle with embracing flames the waist / Of Collatine's fair love, Lucrece the chaste' (ll. 5-7). Expressing his will to tyranny, his proto-tyrannic role, Tarquin's desire makes him a brutal parody of the Petrarchan lover as a species; it makes his pursuit of Lucrece a sexual heightening and violation of the Petrarchan discourse of love. As might be expected, Shakespeare's narrator implies that very distinctly and emphatically in his account of Lucrece's rape.

The interaction between that parodic role and Tarquin's other main roles in relation to Lucrece is intriguing; nonetheless, before it can be looked at those roles through which her subjectivity is chiefly fashioned in the poem must be considered. Lucrece's initial and main role in the poem is, almost inevitably, that of chaste Roman matron: the narrator first identifies her as 'Collatine's fair love, Lucrece the chaste' (l. 7). Her subsequently established guise of Petrarchan lady complements her initial one by heightening the reader's sense of both her chastity and her beauty (see especially ll. 12-14). The two roles also have a less obvious harmony, for they can be seen—though in different ways—as imposed. Lucrece's initial role gives her selfhood in terms of a conventional category of the female in her society. In that sense the basic role given to her in the poem, which concurs with her own notion of who she basically is, appears to be culturally imposed. And not only does Lucrece acknowledge the role of chaste Roman matron to be in fact essential to her idea of who she is; she acknowledges, too, her feeling or consciousness of its being imposed from without (by implication, socially). Her most explicit acknowledgement occurs, I think, just after her three long complaints, when she is pondering suicide: 'I was a loyal wife: / So am I now,—O no, that cannot be! / Of that true type hath Tarquin rifled me' (ll. 1048-50).[9] The reader may not agree with Lucrece's refusal to accept her own innocence but, that aside, it would seem clear that she thinks of herself as being primarily a chaste Roman matron and as having received that role from without—of her basic selfhood as therefore ultimately able to be erased from without.

Lucrece's externalized sense of her ultimate self thus appears to be inseparable from, and to clarify, at once her profound consciousness of herself as an exemplar of chastity and her profound fear of becoming an exemplar of unchastity. She recognizes that others have established her as the former and that they can turn her into the latter: she recognizes her vulnerability as an exemplar, how indifferent to her inner life and beyond her control that aspect of her selfhood is (see ll. 519-39 and 806-40). Her consciousness of herself as exemplar seems to clarify, in turn, her sense of being immersed in historical process. Rape impels Lucrece to look anxiously to the future and also anxiously to the past, as well it might.[10] But for her, as exemplar, there is a special reason for its doing so. Exemplarity, in her world as of course in Shakespeare's, is a means of illuminating and stabilizing historical process, of defining subjectivity within it. Anticipating misrepresentation of her role as exemplar, its unjustly parodic inversion, Lucrece simultaneously anticipates the falsification of history (see, for example, ll. 813-26). To preserve her existence as an exemplar of chastity is likewise, for her, significantly if partly to save the present from future misinterpretation, to protect history from false tradition. The case is alike yet interestingly different when she turns to the past. Looking to a picture of the Trojan past for comfort, she seeks consolation in discovering an exemplar of misery (ll. 1443-56), not merely in order that she may find a companion in her distress but, as well, that she may find another self—one whom she may vindicate and so, through whom, amend history (ll. 1457-98).

Lucrece's preoccupation with her exemplarity and with control of meaning and of subjectivity in interpretation of the past will be examined again below. For the moment, discussion must focus on what seem to be her other main roles in the poem. Those other roles are, much like the ones previously considered, imposed from without. That is to say, although they are revealed by the narrator as consonant with personal appearance and impulse in Lucrece, they are also revealed by him as in effect deriving from Collatine's devotion to her and from Tarquin's perception of her via the celebratory picture drawn by her husband. They connect with, as well as complement, her roles as chaste Roman matron and Petrarchan lady, just as they evoke from Tarquin roles linked to his guises of Platonic tyrant figure and parodic Petrarchan lover. They are, moreover, syncretic and in part anachronistic: as was indicated earlier, they figure Lucrece as a type of the earthly paradise and (an incorruptible) Eve; Tarquin therefore comes to figure as a type of Satan (later, of course, he becomes an analogue to Sinon); Collatine thence comes to figure as a self-betraying Adam, who unwittingly tempts the serpent to violate, to steal. It is a powerful mingling of discourses—Platonic, Petrarchan, Golden Age/ Edenic—that combines with what is chiefly an Ovidian

historical discourse to characterize the three main actors in Shakespeare's narrative and thereby re-present the rape of Lucrece.

The representation of Lucrece in terms of Golden Age/ Edenic discourse begins with the initial picturing of her as an ideal Petrarchan lady. When Shakespeare's narrator first mentions Collatine's unwary celebration of Lucrece, he affirms her husband's reported and summarized speech by describing her face as the 'sky of [Collatine's] delight; / Where mortal stars as bright as heaven's beauties, / With pure aspects did him peculiar duties' (ll. 12-14). The Petrarchan allusions in those lines have already been discussed; what I wish to emphasize here is that the Petrarchan imagery suggests Lucrece to be Collatine's heaven on earth ('lent' to him by 'the heavens', as the narrator subsequently remarks in another context).[11] With the initial use of Petrarchan discourse in the poem, then, another discourse also emerges, the Golden Age/Edenic: from that signifying of Lucrece to be Collatine's heaven on earth follows imaging of her as the earthly paradise and as Eve. In fact Lucrece's face, 'that sky of [Collatine's] delight' (l. 12), is soon after described twice by the narrator as a 'fair field' (l. 58; 'her fair face's field', l. 72).[12] The elaborate, conventional trope seems important for several reasons. First, it suggests that Lucrece's face is an ideal landscape and so it complements the preceding image of her face as Collatine's 'sky of . . . delight' (l. 12). Further, the trope forms part of a compressed allegory that, in emphasizing the fusion of beauty and virtue in Lucrece, indicates her to be a Golden Age innocent living in a world far removed from the 'world's minority' (l. 67; see ll. 52-73). Then, too, it pictures Lucrece so attractively (and as so vulnerable) at the moment when she is welcoming Tarquin into her home. Finally, the trope derives from Petrarchan tradition, as ll. 71-2 signal, and thus hints at the extent to which Golden Age/Edenic discourse in the poem is generated by Petrarchan discourse.[13] The latter also initiates the former, as it happens, in what is the last identification of Lucrece as an earthly paradise before she is raped.

That moment of identification, which deserves closer attention than it is often given, occurs in the report of Tarquin's long, intense gazing on the sleeping Lucrece (see ll. 365-71, 386-420), the visual assault that precedes his more directly physical one. The narrator starts his account as follows:

> Her lily hand her rosy cheek lies under,
> Coz'ning the pillow of a lawful kiss;
> Who therefore angry, seems to part in sunder,
> Swelling on either side to want his bliss:
> Between whose hills her head entombed is,
>   Where like a virtuous monument she lies,
>   To be admir'd of lewd unhallowed eyes.
>
> Without the bed her other fair hand was,
> On the green coverlet; whose perfect white
> Show'd like an April daisy on the grass,
> With pearly sweat resembling dew of night.
> Her eyes like marigolds had sheath'd their light,

And canopied in darkness sweetly lay,
Till they might open to adorn the day.

(ll. 386-99)

Petrarchan images of 'lily' and of 'ros[e]' (l. 386), used
recurrently to describe Lucrece, introduce the passage.
They serve immediately to eroticise the picture of the
sleeping woman in terms of propriety and of impropriety
('Coz'ning', 'lawful' in l. 387). The '[c]oz'ning'/'lawful'
conceits, in themselves, obliquely contrast the playfully
imagined, innocent, frustrated desire of the 'pillow', which
may rightfully 'kiss' Lucrece, to Tarquin's unlawful,
violent and as yet unfulfilled desire to possess her physically. However, insofar as those conceits are at once suggestive of conflict (the mock conflict between 'hand' and
'pillow') and linked to Petrarchan imagery, they serve also
to remind the reader that it is especially the Petrarchan images used to describe Lucrece throughout the poem that
tend to identify her as a site of conflict. The first instance
of Petrarchan imagery, for example, identifies her as the
embodiment of perfect beauty through whom Collatine
can vaunt his superiority over Tarquin, but through whom,
likewise, Tarquin will assert his tyrannic will and role over
Collatine (see ll. 7-14). According to the narrator,
moreover, a struggle between 'beauty and virtue' (l. 52) as
to which 'should underprop [Lucrece's] fame' (l. 53) can
be seen in the 'silent war of lilies and of roses' (l. 71) occurring 'in her fair face's field' (l. 72). It is interesting and
significant, too, that the Petrarchan images beginning the
passage lead subsequently to the notion of Lucrece as
monument, a notion connecting with her sense of herself
as an exemplar of chastity (see ll. 390-2). But it seems
most interesting and most significant that then, only after
associating her with conflict and emphasizing her role as
exemplar (an emphasis with overtones of death), the Petrarchan images introduce the picture of her as an earthly
paradise.

There is a striking contrast between the playful, ominous,
reverential prelude to that picture and the picture itself. An
unspoiled, tranquil, natural richness is suggested by the
picture's vivid detail: the 'perfect[ly] white' hand (l. 394)
lying on 'the green coverlet' (l. 394), which is likened to
an 'April daisy on the grass' (l. 395); the 'pearly sweat
resembling dew of night' (l. 396); the 'eyes like marigolds'
that have 'sheath'd their light' (l. 397). Metonymically that
detail associates the inviolate, perfectly beautiful Lucrece
with an inviolate, perfectly beautiful nature. And one sees
Petrarchan images both introducing that picture of Lucrece
and helping to create it. Lucrece's 'other fair hand', like
the one beneath her head, is of 'perfect' whiteness; further,
the narrator celebrates the splendour of her eyes in terms
that form a counterpart to those used by him near the
poem's beginning.[14] Lucrece thus appears as both an
earthly paradise and a Golden Age innocent; but those
representations of her do not alone imply her role as a
type of Eve. Her husband and Tarquin chiefly impose that
on her.

Like Chaucer's narrator in *The Legend of Good Women*,
Shakespeare's narrator emphasizes Collatine's responsibil-

ity for exciting the interest of Tarquin in Lucrece. Although
he speculates on a number of specific possibilities—that
Lucrece's very chastity aroused Tarquin (ll. 8-9), that Collatine's vaunting her 'sov'reignty' provoked the king's son
(ll. 36-7) or that Tarquin's own 'envy' and pride did so (ll.
39-42)—the narrator emphatically blames Collatine's
imprudence for causing Lucrece's misery. 'Collatine
unwisely did not let / To praise' his wife in Tarquin's hearing, the narrator says (ll. 10-11).[15] '[I]n Tarquin's tent,' he
adds by way of elaboration, Collatine '[u]nlock'd the
treasure of his happy state: / What priceless wealth the
heavens had him lent, / In the possession of his beauteous
mate' (ll. 15-18). '[W]hy is Collatine the publisher / Of
that rich jewel he should keep unknown / From thievish
ears, because it is his own?' he asks (ll. 33-5). Yet it is not
merely Collatine's imprudence that the narrator stresses.
He emphasizes, too, the hubris that makes Collatine fatally
incautious. In his account of Collatine's 'boast of Lucrece'
sov'reignty' (l. 36), the narrator tells of him '[r]eck'ning
his fortune at such high proud rate / That kings might be
espoused to more fame, / But king nor peer to such a peer-
less dame' (ll. 19-21). In a moment when military conflict
with a foreign enemy is deferred, Collatine uses his wife
as a means of seeking personal victory over his superior
and kinsman; the result of his hubris is that he redirects
Tarquin's violence and desire from the enemy/foreign/
public to the kindred/Roman/private.[16] His overreaching
pride—an aggressive, patriarchal vanity that firmly links
him with the otherwise dissimilar Tarquin—leads him to
flaunt the wife who is his heaven on earth, his earthly
paradise and, in effect, an innocent from the Golden Age,
before the proto-tyrant. The latter, then perceiving her as
'the heaven of his [own] thought' (l. 338), quickly resolves
to dispossess him. So, as has been suggested earlier, Collatine unknowingly tempts Tarquin to violate and thus to
steal the woman represented by the narrator as an embodiment of Golden Age/Edenic discourses. In doing that, he
also unwittingly refigures both himself as a self-betraying
Adam (an Adam who falls through pride) and Lucrece as
an innocent, unfallen Eve. Simultaneously and appropriately, of course, he thereby helps to refigure Tarquin
as a type of Satan, Tarquin's subsequent actions reinforcing his own role and that imposed on Lucrece.

The process of characterization outlined above results,
then, not merely from some trivial, male rivalry. It derives
from Collatine's attempt to impose over Tarquin's will to
illegitimate power—as proto-tyrant and son of a tyrant—
his own will to illicit power, functioning within and
expressed through the notionally unthreatening and not to
be threatened sphere of the domestic.[17] In that attempt, of
course, Lucrece is objectified and so Tarquin perceives
her; on the other hand, the end of the poem suggests that
Lucrece has always been objectified by her husband and
by her father.[18] Tarquin, moreover, could arguably never
have perceived her except as 'an *object* of consciousness',
although he may not have seen or particularly considered
her at all had not Collatine set her image compellingly
before him.[19] The end of that struggle between wills to illicit power, between domestic and public regimes

(respectively Collatine's and Tarquin's), seems immediately to be the mutual defining of subjectivity for its participants, including Lucrece as an unknowing participant. The struggle of wills generates, in short, refigured subjectivities for each participant and thence a comprehensively refigured myth of the Fall.

One can now consider, I suggest, Tarquin's role as a type of Satan. That role seems implicit from virtually the moment he enters Lucrece's home. The narrator says, referring initially to Lucrece and subsequently to Tarquin:

> This earthly saint adored by this devil,
> Little suspecteth the false worshipper;
> For unstain'd thoughts do seldom dream on evil,
> Birds never lim'd no secret bushes fear:
> So guiltless she securely gives good cheer
>   And reverend welcome to her princely guest,
>   Whose inward ill no outward harm express'd.
>
> For that he colour'd with his high estate,
> Hiding base sin in pleats of majesty,
> That nothing in him seem'd inordinate,
> Save sometime too much wonder of his eye. . . .
>
>   (ll. 85-95)

The allusion to Lucrece as '[t]his earthly saint' (l. 85) evokes her connected roles as chastity's exemplar and Petrarchan lady; it harmonizes, too, with the notion that she is Collatine's heaven on earth. More to the point, however, the trope allows the narrator to characterize Tarquin antithetically to her as a 'devil' (l. 85), a 'false worshipper' (l. 86) and agent of 'evil' (l. 87), who conceals from her his 'inward ill' (l. 91), his 'base sin' (l. 93). That insistently demonic representation of Tarquin is elaborated on by the narrator's subsequent references to his 'parling looks' (l. 100), which are likened to 'baits' and 'hooks' (l. 103). But it is specifically an emphasis on innocence in the characterization of Lucrece, and allusion to her as an embodiment of the earthly paradise, that indicate Tarquin to be Satanic rather than merely demonic, here and subsequently in the narrative.

As has been argued above, the opening description of Lucrece as '[t]his earthly saint' develops into a representation of her as someone naturally innocent. '[U]nstain'd thoughts do seldom dream on evil, / Birds never lim'd no secret bushes fear . . . ,' the narrator says (ll. 87-8), explaining her 'guiltless' (l. 89) and unsuspecting reception of her visitor.[20] The images initiating perception of Lucrece as naturally innocent point back to the image of 'her fair face's field' (l. 72), with its connotations of an ideal landscape and of Golden Age virtue, and forward to the description of her, just prior to Tarquin's assault, as a type of the earthly paradise, of uncontaminated nature (ll. 386-99). And it is precisely her natural innocence which the narrator proceeds to emphasize in describing how she responds to the intense, erotic gaze of Tarquin—the 'inordinate' stare (l. 94) that she necessarily notices but cannot decipher. According to the narrator:

> . . . [S]he that never cop'd with stranger eyes,
>   Could pick no meaning from their parling looks,

> Nor read the subtle shining secrecies
> Writ in the glassy margents of such books;
> She touch'd no unknown baits, nor fear'd no hooks:
>   Nor could she moralize his wanton sight,
>   More than his eyes were open'd to the light.
>
>   (ll. 99-105)

Unable to read, much less to interpret, the language of seduction in Tarquin's eyes, Lucrece perceives no harm in his gaze. In being unaware of the artifice of seduction, she is like a fish that neither recognizes enticement nor fears to be snared (l. 103): an allusion to a familiar Petrarchan motif. Thus Lucrece, represented predominantly in terms that both suggest her natural innocence and evoke her recurrent presentation as a type of the earthly paradise (which thereby refigures her as Eve), is unwittingly betrayed by her husband (in effect, an overreaching Adam) to temptation by the demonized (Satanized) Tarquin. He, moreover, disguised as his apparent self, knowingly falls from high estate in pursuing her.[21] The poem's narrator puts before the reader a Romanized, Petrarchized, revisioned story of the Fall—and in doing so arguably generates much of the intellectual intricacy, as well as emotive power, in Shakespeare's version of the Lucretia story.

Lucrece seems to be no simple Eve figure; certainly, she becomes a quite complex one as the poem progresses. Lucrece/Eve fights back, so to speak, and makes Tarquin/Satan experience not just a fall from the dignity of high estate, from the honour code of the Roman aristocracy, but a fall from high estate itself in Rome. Tarquin, likewise, appears not to be simply refigured as, and refiguring, Satan. For a start, his nocturnal soliloquy on whether or not to rape Lucrece shows him pondering in effect whether to abandon or to deepen his Satanic role.[22] What seems particularly relevant at this point, however, is that the Petrarchan discourse used recurrently throughout the earlier part of the poem to fashion Tarquin's subjectivity appears strikingly at the end of his speech, to signal his consciously imperfect resolution of his inner conflict. Near the very end of his soliloquy, he declares:

> Affection is my captain, and he leadeth;
>   And when his gaudy banner is display'd,
>   The coward fights, and will not be dismay'd.
>
>   (ll. 271-3)

And the final words of his speech are:

> Desire my pilot is, beauty my prize;
> Then who fears sinking where such treasure lies?
>
>   (ll. 279-80)

The lines first quoted evoke Petrarch's sonnet '*Amor, che nel penser mio vivo e regna*', translated by Wyatt and by Surrey; Tarquin's words offer a desperately pugnacious reworking of the love-as-warfare allegory in Petrarch's poem. Tarquin's concluding words perhaps likewise evoke a sonnet by Petrarch, '*Passa la nave mia colma d'oblio*'; if so, they offer an aggressive reworking of the love-as-a-perilous-sea-voyage allegory in that poem.[23] There is a Petrarchan finale, as it were, to Tarquin's soliloquy—and appropriately so. Tarquin's acute self-consciousness in his soliloquy can be seen in his sensitivity to history: paradoxically enough, like Lucrece he is all too aware of how he may be officially represented, of how his existence may be constructed (but not in his case misconstrued), in years to come (see ll. 202-10, 223-4). Exemplarity is a concern for him as it is for Lucrece. His acute self-consciousness can also be seen in his sensitivity to his own speechmaking, in his politician's sense of the rhetorical nature, the theatricality, of his moment of decision (see ll. 225-7, 267-8). A Petrarchan finale certainly befits such a speech but it seems especially suitable because Petrarchan discourse acknowledges, notionally with regret, reason's incapacity to govern desire.[24] Petrarchan discourse can be used, therefore, to legitimize one's denial of constraint by reason. So, in effect, it is used here by Tarquin. The proto-tyrant making up his mind to commit rape is shown *de facto* to misappropriate and, likewise, desperately to rework Petrarchan discourse.[25] He is thus represented in order for the reader to perceive the dishonesty of his characterizing himself as the warrior compelled now to fight in the service of passion, the lover overwhelmed by desire.[26] The Petrarchan ending to the soliloquy signals his consciously specious resolution of his dilemma.

That ending signals, of course, other things as well. It confirms how thoroughly parodic a Petrarchan lover Tarquin is. Yet arguably, too, it confirms something about Tarquin as a Platonic tyrant figure and type of Satan: he can possess, and then momentarily, 'the heaven of his thought' (l. 338) only by violation, which he knows to be also self-violation because violation of the aristocratic Roman code of conduct by which he, at any rate, thinks his existence primarily defined.[27] Moreover Tarquin's final, mock-Petrarchan characterization of himself as love's warrior leads to what can be perceived, after his piously inaccurate remark about the gods' abhorrence of rape (ll. 349-50), as his committing a rape which distantly parodies the myth of Mars' rape of Rhea Silvia. Certainly, the rape of Lucrece does seem an ironic counterpart to that myth. The ancient myth tells of a rape which is an originary event for Rome: the chaste Rhea Silvia, raped by the god of war, conceives Romulus and Remus. The rape of Lucrece is, likewise, an originary event for Rome, but in a significantly different way: the Roman Republic is unwittingly and indirectly engendered by a warrior/parodic 'warrior of love', a self-confessed enemy to the gods (ll. 344-57), who in doing so initiates the overthrow of the monarchy and hence his own downfall.

What might now, and finally, be considered here is the means through which Tarquin primarily expresses himself as a Platonic tyrant figure, a parodic Petrarchan lover, and a type of Satan in relation to Lucrece before he expresses those roles through directly physical sexual violence. It seems that he does so through the male gaze. The pervasiveness of the male gaze in his relating to her can be readily shown. When Tarquin first sees Lucrece, the

narrator refers to his 'traitor eye' (l. 73): traitorous to the 'beauty and virtue' displayed in her face (l. 52), and ultimately to himself as well. That 'traitor eye' initially succumbs to the purity of what it perceives (l. 73); it is initially intimidated, and Tarquin looks at Lucrece with the 'silent wonder of still-gazing eyes' (l. 84). The innocent Lucrece, of course not recognizing Tarquin for what he is (at that moment, a Satan figure), nonetheless remarks the 'sometime too much wonder of his eye' (l. 95). She stands vulnerable to 'his wanton sight' (l. 104).

But Tarquin himself falls victim to the gaze in imposing it on Lucrece. At the end of his soliloquy he announces: 'My heart shall never countermand mine eye' (l. 276). The gaze imposed on Lucrece subdues the man imposing it, a phenomenon interestingly linked with Tarquin's role as parodic Petrarchan lover at that moment of the narrative. Not much later, Tarquin notes with approval that, because it is night, he is free from the divine gaze: 'The eye of heaven is out, and misty night / Covers the shame that follows sweet delight' (ll. 356-7). Imposing the gaze, and victim of his imposing it, he is also subject to a cosmic and sacred form of it. Lucrece would escape his infliction of it if she could (ll. 540-6); he seems relieved to have escaped the divine, transcendent gaze antithetic to his own.

Feeling liberated from the divine gaze, he then tyrannically indulges his: the male gaze thence expressing, in particular, his roles of Platonic tyrant figure, and type of Satan, in relation to Lucrece. When, according to the narrator, '[i]nto [Lucrece's] chamber wickedly he stalks' (l. 365), Tarquin 'gazeth on her yet unstained bed[;] / The curtains being close, about he walks, / Rolling his greedy eyeballs in his head' (ll. 366-8). 'By their [his eyes'] high treason is his heart misled', adds the narrator (l. 369).[28] The proto-tyrant's compulsion and betrayal by desire are metonymically indicated by means of the gaze, which thereby signals his role as a Platonic tyrant figure. Thereafter, at the moment of symbolic violation when Tarquin opens the curtain to Lucrece's bed (ll. 372-8), the narrator describes Tarquin's gaze in cautiously Petrarchan terms which lead to representation of him as Satan. Viewing Lucrece, Tarquin is dazzled: '[T]he curtain drawn, his eyes begun / To wink, being blinded with a greater light' (ll. 374-5). The narrator suggests that the brightness blinding Tarquin—and so negating the gaze—may be the light reflected from Lucrece herself (ll. 376-7), a plausible suggestion given his previous and subsequent praise of her skin's whiteness. That being the case, then *by itself* the innocent beauty of the Petrarchan lady repels the gaze: a Petrarchan convention. Even if it is not the case (l. 377), then, nonetheless, in imposing the gaze Tarquin is blinded like any less transgressive Petrarchan lover looking too rashly or too long at a chaste and resplendent lady. If only the power of the gaze had at that moment been broken, the narrator laments (ll. 379-85). But of course it is not; on the contrary, having been temporarily blinded as if some merely rash or insistent Petrarchan lover, Tarquin again imposes the gaze (ll. 414-17) and in doing so figures as a type of Satan (ll. 386-99, discussed above). His unchecked gaze, the narrator remarks, both 'slak[es]' his lust and stimulates it to more directly physical sexual violence (ll. 425 and 427).

To trace Tarquin's imposition of the gaze on Lucrece is to demonstrate its pervasiveness, and necessarily to suggest its prime importance, as a means through which he in his various guises relates to her. A more precise account of that importance requires, however, some further discussion of Tarquin and the gaze. I should like briefly to consider three things: the aesthetics of the gaze; the power of Tarquin's male gaze; the reader's implication in and distancing from Tarquin's imposition of the gaze on Lucrece. When Tarquin first imposes his 'traitor eye' (l. 73) on Lucrece and his gaze is overpowered, the narrator says: 'Therefore that praise which Collatine doth owe [to Lucrece's beauty] / Enchanted Tarquin answers with surmise, / In silent wonder of still-gazing eyes' (ll. 82-4). The words 'Enchanted', 'wonder' and 'still-gazing' seem allusions to, but certainly evoke, the then current, and linked, aesthetic categories of *meraviglia* (wonder) and *stupore* (astonishment or amazement).[29] That Lucrece should be perceived by Tarquin as marvellous and so fill him with wonder, stupefy him with amazement, is not itself wonderful given her role as ideal Petrarchan lady. Yet that is not the immediately relevant point. Venus, in Shakespeare's earlier narrative poem, would perfect Adonis as an aesthetic and erotic object (see l. 21 of that poem, for example); here, Tarquin's initial response to Lucrece objectifies her in aesthetic and erotic terms. At the same time, however, Lucrece's unique combination of beauty and virtue both overcomes and elevates his male gaze: rendered relatively passive, raised from the solely carnal to an aestheticized eroticism, Tarquin's male gaze ascends for an instant beyond unrefined *curiositas* (lust of the eyes) and simple concupiscence. At the moment when Tarquin is about to be assigned his Satanic role, he views Lucrece much as Milton's Satan momentarily views Eve: '[T]he evil one abstracted stood / From his own evil, and for the time remained / Stupidly good . . .' (9, 463-5).[30] Subsequently, of course, his gaze resumes its power.

As the narrator recounts what Tarquin could see of the sleeping Lucrece (ll. 386-420), he says:

> Her breasts like ivory globes circled with blue,
> A pair of maiden worlds unconquered;
> Save of their lord, no bearing yoke they knew,
> And him by oath they truly honoured.
> These worlds in Tarquin new ambition bred;
>   Who like a foul usurper went about,
>   From this fair throne to heave the owner out.
>
> (ll. 407-13)

To Tarquin's male gaze, the narrator suggests, Lucrece's breasts are so much new, sexual geography: 'maiden worlds' (l. 408) for him to conquer as if he were an Alexander the Great of sex (l. 411). The implicit emphasis on the colonizing impulse in Tarquin's gaze thus emphasizes,

too, Tarquin's characterization as proto-tyrant and as Platonic tyrant figure. Further, it contributes to his identification as a type of Satan, one who ejects a self-betraying Adam (Collatine) from possession of his earthly paradise/Eve.[31] Demonized though Tarquin's male and colonizing gaze affirms him to be, however, it does not in itself distinguish him from other personae fashioned in verse by Shakespeare's contemporaries or successors. For example, the persona in Donne's Elegy 19 says to the lady supposedly subordinated to his male gaze: 'O my America, my new found land, / My kingdom, safeliest when with one man manned' (ll. 27-8). A more complex example is the persona in 'The Sun Rising'. Using the languages and categories of the world beyond the walls of his and his lady's bedroom, he constructs the fiction that he and his lady inhabit a private utopia of love, one which variously refigures, subsumes and displaces the outer world—transcending time and space, class and riches. Yet in his alternative world, the 'good place' that is also 'no place' but in his fiction, he reinscribes patriarchal, Jacobean rule. With reference to his lady, he orders the sun: 'Look, and tomorrow late, tell me, / Whether both th'Indias of spice and mine / Be where thou left'st them, or lie here with me' (ll. 16-18). Again with reference to his lady, he announces: 'She'is all states, and all princes, I' (l. 21). The beloved on whom the persona focuses his gaze (ll. 13-14) is not merely objectified. She is colonized: in his eyes she becomes a body of claimed territory that, as he tells it, lies subject to his autocratic rule. Shakespeare's Tarquin and the Donne personae discussed above may be different in ways that are many and clear; nonetheless, they are not insignificantly alike.[32]

To have explored the power of the gaze is necessarily to have raised questions about resistance and implication. For example, how and where in the narrative is the gaze resisted? Is the reader never implicated in Tarquin's imposition of it on Lucrece? Perhaps those questions, and some others, can be usefully if partly answered by one's returning to the episode in which the narrator describes Lucrece as she lies asleep (ll. 385-420). His description of her is at once stylized, vivid and intimate. Its being so seems to make it curiously ambiguous. Allowing the reader to see what Tarquin sees when he gazes on Lucrece, the description offers a celebration of and commentary on her beauty; it ends with emphasis on the vehemence of Tarquin's response to that beauty. Thus it offers shared visions, mingled gazes. At once praising Lucrece's body in fairly intimate detail and commenting on the innocence and vulnerability of her beauty, the description implicitly sets the narrator's moralized male gaze in opposition to the male and colonizing gaze of Tarquin. For all that, the self-indulgent intimacy and ludic elaboration of the description (as in ll. 386-9 and 401) indicate the narrator's gaze to be indeed a moralized *male* gaze which, though certainly resisting and condemning Tarquin's, does not merely allow the reader to see what, and something of how, Tarquin saw, but also implicates the narrator and the implied male reader in Tarquin's violating gaze. There is an irony, then, in the narrator's questions, 'What could he

[Tarquin] see but mightily he noted? / What did he note but strongly he desired?' (ll. 414-15). Tarquin's is not the only 'wilful eye' (l. 417).[33]

From that concluding discussion of Tarquin and the gaze, one might now turn to consider what studying the reciprocal formation of consciousness and of role among Tarquin, Lucrece and Collatine can be said to reveal about the establishing of characterization in Shakespeare's second narrative poem. For a start, doing so strongly suggests that the characterizations established early in *Lucrece* are more complex in their discursive relations than has been acknowledged. The three main figures in the poem are not merely translated from the pages of Ovid: they are at once Ovidian and comprehensively transformed. In particular, they become actors in a Romanized, Petrarchized, revisioned myth of the Fall—a version in which the type of Eve is innocent and betrayed, not betraying (a version, too, in which she ultimately gains her revenge on the counterpart to Satan).

Moreover, thus perceiving the characterizations of Tarquin, Lucrece and Collatine early in the poem seems to illuminate both subsequent happenings in it and some of its main concerns. When one recognizes that Tarquin's sexual assault involves his forcing on Lucrece his mutually intensifying, connected roles, which are antithetic to hers, then the scope of his violence can be seen more clearly: his assault appears to involve unusually comprehensive psychic violence in conjunction with extreme physical violence. Lucrece's profound sense of contamination seems, therefore, even more understandable. So too does her decision to commit suicide. Yet if those later occurrences in the poem are illuminated, what are arguably among its main concerns appear as well to have new light shed on them. The mutually defining nature of characterization early in the poem indicates that Lucrece's interactive roles are variously imposed on her from without and, further, that she well knows her basic role as chaste Roman matron to have been externally imposed and to be removable. Recognizing the externality of Lucrece's selfhood, and her partial awareness of its being so, perhaps first clarifies yet more distinctly her feeling of contamination and her decision to commit suicide: one comes to see that she thinks of Tarquin's assault as having stolen her main role in her world. And Lucrece's sense that her role as chaste Roman matron derives from without seems at the same time to shed light, too, on her insistent denial of her innocence. To her mind, apparently, Tarquin's assault has erased her basic self and thus she is no longer chaste and hence not completely innocent. Those matters aside, however, the externality and imposition of Lucrece's selfhood arguably have more important implications.

Lucrece's awareness of her basic role's imposition from without is firmly linked to her consciousness of herself as an exemplar of chastity. That link raises questions about exemplarity in, and beyond, the poem. Well aware that her role of exemplar, like her one as chaste Roman matron, derives from without, Lucrece believes that her rape immediately deletes the latter but also that it will subsequently make ambiguous or delete the former. To regain the one, to preserve the other, she resolves upon suicide. Her perception of who she ultimately is, and the self-negating decision that results from it (to lose herself in order to save herself), seem to raise several major questions about exemplarity. First, if one's role as exemplar is imposed from without, in light of external circumstance and with no, or little, precise knowledge of one's inner life, then how reliable can exemplarity be as a means of defining subjectivity, of identifying an incarnation of an ideal? Further, how can exemplarity therefore be regarded as a reliable means of interpreting history, of clarifying and stabilizing it? That question has a special relevance, I think, because the intertextual relations of Shakespeare's narrative suggest how often and how variously Lucrece's role as exemplar has been reconstructed: continuity, variation and contradiction all mark its descent. Moreover, what does it indicate about exemplarity if Lucrece has to kill herself to preserve its/her integrity and hence the integrity of historical tradition? Lucrece successfully preserves her exemplarity, preserves historical tradition, and seemingly reveals the hermeneutic limitations or incapacity of exemplarity. There are of course other questions implicitly raised; nonetheless, my main point here is as follows. Exemplarity appears not merely to be subverted in the poem, though aspects of it certainly are; rather, it is subjected to close and sceptical examination.[34] Shakespeare's narrative suggests that exemplarity is reliable and unreliable as a means of defining subjectivity and interpreting history: it is more or less simply accurate in Tarquin's case, for instance; however, because of its dependence upon externals and contamination by opinion, it has to be made accurate in the case of Lucrece. It works and it does not. Perhaps in some of Montaigne's essays, rather than in contemporary English writings, one finds the counterpart to Shakespeare's sceptical treatment of exemplarity in *Lucrece*.[35]

Just as exemplarity is sceptically examined in the poem, so too is neoplatonism. Although an account of the poems' sceptical inquiry into neoplatonism cannot be offered without *Lucrece* having been considered as a whole, some things can nonetheless be suggested now in connection with the poem's establishing of characterization. Lucrece tends, unknowingly, to read human subjectivity in neoplatonic terms. In so reading Tarquin she makes a tragic mistake, as she soon discovers and in effect acknowledges (ll. 1527-61): his soul is not to be read in his appearance. Yet hers is, as Tarquin sees at once when he meets her. That contradiction, for all its bluntness, has more subtlety than might at first be thought. It seems primarily to indicate that a neoplatonic reading of human subjectivity, like a reading of subjectivity and of history by means of exemplarity, can be seen as unreliable and as reliable: sometimes not working, sometimes working well. Yet the contradiction seems also to imply that Lucrece, chaste matron of early Rome and *mulier economica* (woman in the role of household manager), necessarily lacks the education and experience required for her to understand the problems inherent in the neoplatonic scheme of reading—outlined for Shakespeare's contemporaries by Castiglione, among others. His outline of those problems, however, arguably heightens rather than resolves the contradiction, for the words he has Bembo speak on the matter do not help one to recognize when, or not, appearance can be read as truly indicative of the soul.[36]

Finally, here, a few remarks need to be made about the gaze and the counter-gaze in the earlier episodes of *Lucrece*. It might be mentioned again that more than one gaze is alluded to in those episodes. There, to be sure, the narrator indicates that Tarquin most vigorously imposes it but Tarquin himself draws the reader's attention to the divine gaze: that of '[t]he eye of heaven' (l. 356). His allusion to the divine gaze, particularly to its being 'out' (l. 356), evokes and queries the notion of divine providence, which Lucrece in effect considers when lamenting her misfortune (ll. 764-1015, for example). It might be mentioned again, likewise, that if the divine gaze is suggested by Tarquin to be in contradiction to his own, a counter-gaze is also implicitly exercised by the narrator (especially in ll. 386-420). As has been argued above, however, gaze and counter-gaze elide—if not always, then nonetheless often enough and significantly, as at the crucial moment when Tarquin surveys the sleeping Lucrece (ll. 386-420). The counter-gaze seems either to be absent or treacherously to merge with the thing it should oppose. To study the establishing of characterization in *Lucrece* leads one to encounter a use of the gaze, a transformation of myth, a scepticism, more complex than can be seen in *Venus and Adonis*.

Notes

1. For examples of the critical approaches and concerns mentioned above, see: M. Platt, *Rome and Romans According to Shakespeare* (Salzburg: English Institute, 1976), pp. 1-40; C. Kahn, 'The Rape in Shakespeare's *Lucrece*', *Shakespeare Studies,* 9 (1977), 45-72; R.S. Miola, *Shakespeare's Rome* (Cambridge: Cambridge University Press, 1983), pp. 18-41; T. French, 'A "badge of fame": Shakespeare's Rhetorical Lucrece', *Explorations in Renaissance Culture,* 10 (1984), 97-106; N.J. Vickers, '"This Heraldry in Lucrece' Face"', *Poetics Today,* 6 (1985), 171-84; K.E. Maus, 'Taking Tropes Seriously: Language and Violence in Shakespeare's *Rape of Lucrece*', *Shakespeare Quarterly,* 37 (1986), 66-82; J. Fineman, 'Shakespeare's *Will:* The Temporality of Rape', *Representations,* 20 (1987), 25-76; G. Ziegler, 'My Lady's Chamber: Female Space, Female Chastity in Shakespeare', *Textual Practice,* 4 (1990), 73-100; D. Willbern, 'Hyberbolic Desire: Shakespeare's *Lucrece*', in *Contending Kingdoms,* eds M.-R. Logan and P.L. Rudnytsky (Detroit: Wayne State University Press, 1991), pp. 202-24; P. Berry, 'Woman, Language and History in *The Rape of Lucrece*', *Shakespeare Survey,* 44 (1991), 33-9; L. Woodbridge, 'Palisading the Elizabethan Body Politic', *Texas Studies in Literature and Language,* 33 (1991), 327-

54; H. James, 'Milton's Eve, the Romance Genre, and Ovid', *Contemporary Literature,* 45 (1993), 121-45; J. Bate, *Shakespeare and Ovid* (1993; rpt. Oxford: Clarendon Press, 1994), pp. 65-82; J.O. Newman, '"And Let Mild Women to Him Lose Their Mildness": Female Violence, and Shakespeare's *The Rape of Lucrece*', *Shakespeare Quarterly,* 45 (1994), 304-26.

2. In fact, none as far as I am aware.

3. That is likewise implicit in Ovid's narrative.

4. See ll. 1-8, 30-4 of the 'Argument', ll. 20-1 and 36-42, of the poem itself, and ll. 3-7 of the poem on desire as informing his expressions of his tyrannic role in relation to Lucrece.

5. Reference is to Plato, *The Republic,* trans. D. Lee, 2nd edn (rev.) (1974; rpt. Harmondsworth: Penguin, 1979). R. Bushnell discusses Plato's characterization of the tyrant in her *Tragedies of Tyrants,* pp. 9-18.

6. See also ll. 652-65 of Shakespeare's poem, spoken by Lucrece.

7. Cf. ll. 120-89.

8. Reference to Petrarch will be to the edition and translation by R.M. Durling: *Petrarch's Lyric Poems,* trans. and ed. R.M. Durling (Cambridge, Mass. and London: Harvard University Press, 1976).

9. Cf. ll. 519-39, 806-40, 1184-211, and so on.

10. Her doing so is, as well, one of the elements of her characterization that connect her with the personae of the *Heroides*.

11. See l. 17.

12. The 'field' trope is of course derived from heraldry.

13. In general connection with the argument being pursued here, the reader might care to consult two other volumes in this series: R. Kirkpatrick, *English and Italian Literature from Dante to Shakespeare* (1995); R. Sowerby, *The Classical Legacy in Renaissance Poetry* (1994).

14. Compare ll. 397-9, especially 399, with ll. 13-14.

15. Cf. ll. 36-8.

16. In connection with Collatine's hubris, see especially l. 19.

17. Functioning and expressed safely, as he is apparently to be taken as thinking, if he is to be taken as thinking at all.

18. See especially ll. 1751-1806.

19. The phrase is Bakhtin's, from his *Problems of Dostoevsky's Poetics,* trans. C. Emerson (Manchester: Manchester University Press, 1984), p. 293.

20. In conjnction with ll. 87-8, see ll. 386-99.

21. See ll. 90-4, 190-301, 491-504. In ll. 362-4 he is compared to a 'serpent'.

22. See ll. 127-301, especially 181-2, 190-245, 253-80.

23. See ll. 9-14 of the former poem, ll. 13-14 of the latter.

24. See '*Passa la nave . . .*' l. 13, with its reference to passion's defeat of reason.

25. Compare ll. 248-52 with ll. 271-3 and 279-80.

26. Compare ll. 197-201 with 271-3.

27. See l. 348. See also ll. 197-224.

28. Cf. l. 73.

29. See, again, D. Summers's *Michelangelo and the Language of Art* (Princeton, N.J.: Princeton University Press, 1981), here at pp. 171-6.

30. Reference to Milton is from *The Poems,* ed. J. Carey and A. Fowler (London: Longmans, 1968).

31. See ll. 412-13; cf. ll. 386-99.

32. Cf. the discussion of Elegy 19 in the preceding chapter.

33. Cf. ll. 419-20.

34. One aspect of exemplarity subverted in the poem is that of its unquestionable interpretative authority, as asserted by some sixteenth-century writers.

35. For an illuminating account of Montaigne and exemplarity, see T. Hampton's *Writing From History,* pp. 134-97.

36. Castiglione, *The Book of the Courtier,* trans. C. S. Singleton (New York: Doubleday, 1959), pp. 342-5.

GENDER ISSUES

Catharine R. Stimpson (essay date 1980)

SOURCE: "Shakespeare and the Soil of Rape," in *The Woman's Part: Feminist Criticism of Shakespeare,* edited by Carolyn Ruth Swift Lenz, Gayle Greene, and Carol Thomas Neely, University of Illinois Press, 1980, pp. 56-64.

[*In the following essay, Stimpson demonstrates that Shakespeare's portrayals of rape in works such as* The Rape of Lucrece *indicate his sympathy towards women; nevertheless, Stimpson concludes that Shakespeare uses rape as a plot device to emphasize the primacy of patriarchy and the loss that men endure when rape occurs within their own family.*]

Shakespeare's sympathy toward women helps to create an attitude toward rape that is more generous and less foolish than that of many of our contemporaries. He never sniggers and assumes that women, consciously or unconsciously, seek the rapist out and then enjoy the deed: brutal, enforced sex; the ghastly tmesis of the flesh. He never

gives "proud lórds" the right to "Make weak-made women tenants to their shame."[1] Nor does the act dominate his imagination, as it might that of a lesser writer as concerned with violence, war, and sexuality as Shakespeare is. In the complete works, the word "rape" occurs only seventeen times; "rapes" three; and various forms of "ravish" thirty-eight.[2] "Ravish" is perhaps like a poetic gloss that both hints at and denies rape's brutal force.

When rape occurs, it is terrible in itself. Like murder, it displays an aggressor in action. Shakespeare and his rapists use stridently masculine metaphors of war and of the hunt to capture that flagrant energy. Tarquin

> . . . shakes aloft his Roman blade,
> Which, like a falcon tow'ring in the skies,
> Coucheth the fowl below with his wings' shade, . . .
>
>   (*Lucrece,* lines 505-7)

Like murder, rape also pictures a helpless victim, powerless vulnerability. Because rape's violence is sexual, an audience watching it can live out voyeuristic fantasies. Moreover, Shakespearean rape signifies vast conflicts: between unnatural disorder and natural order; raw, polluting lust and its purification through chastity or celibacy; the dishonorable and the honorable exercise of power; "hot-burning will" and "frozen conscience" (*Lucrece,* line 247); and the sinful and righteous begetting of children. A chaste wife, a "clean" marriage bed, guarantee that property rights will pass to a man's blood heirs. For a man to rape a woman, then, is to take sides; to make a series of choices. Rape tempts and tests him, physically and morally.

The structure of Shakespearean rape scenes itself embodies a conflict. The language in which rapes are imagined and then enacted is vivid, immediate, extended, garish, sometimes hallucinatory: "Night-wand'ring weasels shriek" (*Lucrece,* line 307); Lucrece's breasts are "like ivory globes circled with blue" (line 407). The breast, at once erotic and maternal, swells to symbolize the body that will be overcome. However, the setting of the rape scenes in the plays is remote in time or place or both, usually near Italy, if not actually within it. The result is a dramatic sexuality that has the simultaneous detail and distance of a dream/nightmare. The dream/nightmare also contains frequent references to past rapes, to the Trojan War, to the legend of Philomel. Shakespeare compares Lucrece to "lamenting Philomele" (line 1079), a bitterly poignant allusion she herself will make. In *Titus Andronicus,* both Aaron and Marcus will join Philomel and Lavinia in a female community of suffering (II.iii.43; II.iv.26). Aaron judges Lavinia as pure as Lucrece. (II.ii.108.) Such reminders give the dream/nightmare the repetitive weight of myth and history, of experiences that have occurred before and will occur again.

When a man pursues, besieges, and batters a woman's body, he assaults a total world. The female flesh is a passive microcosm. Lucrece is a world, a "sweet city" (line 469). In *Coriolanus,* Cominius says to Menenius:

You have help to ravish your own daughters and
To melt the city leads upon your pates,
To see your wives dishonour'd to your noses—
     . . . . .
Your temples burned in their cement, and
Your franchises, whereon you stood, confin'd
Into an auger's bore.

(IV.vi.81-83, 85-87)

In *Titus Andronicus,* "Lavinia and Tamora may be seen as symbolic personifications of female Rome."[3] The question then becomes, "To whom does the world belong?" The order of Cominius's clauses, as well as his pronouns, provides an answer. The world belongs to men: fathers, husbands, lovers, brothers. Because in Shakespeare only well-born women are raped, their violation becomes one of property, status, and symbolic worth as well. The greater those values, the greater the sense of power their conquest confers upon the rapist.

Because men rape what other men possess, rape becomes in part a disastrous element of male rivalry. The woman's body is a prize in a zero-sum game that men play. Collatine's boasting about Lucrece, an act of excess that is a rhetorical analogue to Tarquin's sexual will, helps to provoke the ruler's desire to conquer the pride of his subordinate. In *Titus Andronicus,* the vicious competition of Demetrius and Chiron parallels the sibling hostilities between Saturninus and Bassianus. However, Demetrius and Chiron stop fighting over Lavinia when it comes time to rape, mutilate, and humiliate her. The joys of controlling a woman together subsume the difficulties of deciding which one will control her independently. Their horrible, giggling plan—to use Bassianus's "dead trunk" as "pillow to our lust" (II.iii.130)—deflects and satisfies their need to defeat other men, to deprive them of their rights and gratifications. When their mother gives birth to Aaron's child, their half-brother, Demetrius and Chiron also unite in their disgust, an emotion that yokes Oedipal jealousy, racist revulsion at miscegenation, and fear of the Roman political consequences of their mother's adultery.

Such rivalry can occur within a man as well as between men. Tarquin, in his long internal debates, struggles between the good self, who argues against rape, and the bad self, who demands sexual triumph. Tarquin is unable to use the common justifications for rape: political or familial revenge. He is equally unable to forget that Collatine is a principal man in his army, a kinsman, and a friend; these are male bonds that invert and undermine male rivalries. Tarquin mourns:

Had Collatinus kill'd my son or sire,
Or lain in ambush to betray my life,
Or were he not my dear friend, this desire
Might have excuse to work upon his wife,
As in revenge or quittal of such strife;
But as he is my kinsman, my dear friend,
The shame and fault finds no excuse nor end.

(lines 232-38)

In psychoanalytical terms, Tarquin's ego is torn between the demands of a libido and a superego whose appeals Lucrece vainly tries to reinforce. After the rape, the superego takes its belated revenge. Guilt immediately deprives Tarquin of any sense of sexual pleasure. In *Measure for Measure,* Angelo will later act out Tarquin's struggle. He will put Isabella in the position of a potential rape victim, for the "choice" he offers her—submit to me sexually or commit your brother to death—is a version of the "choice" Tarquin presents to Lucrece—submit to me sexually or commit yourself to death.[4]

For women, rape means both submission, death, and more. Shakespeare never falters, never hedges, as he shows how defenseless women are before sexual violence and the large destructiveness it entails. Forced sexual submission enforces female death. For the loss of chastity, "a dearer thing than life" (*Lucrece,* line 687) stains women irrevocably. Lavinia knows that being murdered is better than being subjected to a "worse than killing lust" (*Titus,* II.iii.175) that will deprive her of her reason for living. Women are unwillingly responsible for a "cureless crime" (*Lucrece,* line 772). Lucrece, her act at once sacrificial, redemptive, and flamboyant enough to make her husband's friends wish to revenge her, must kill herself. Because "the girl should not survive her shame" (v.iii.41), Titus stabs Lavinia. Their deaths purge the lives and honor of the men whom they have ornamented: Lucrece's husband and father, whose mournings mingle over her corpse; Lavinia's father alone, her husband being dead.[5]

Few of Shakespeare's dramas about traumatic injustice are as clear, or as severe, as those about the raped woman who must be punished because she endured an aggression she never sought and against which she fought. Shakespeare deploys the voice of moderate men to comment on such unfair expiations. In *The Rape of Lucrece,* Brutus thinks Lucrece's suicide a final act of excess in a Rome Tarquin and his family have ruled. Discarding the mask of silliness he has expediently worn to now reveal an authentic self, he tells Collatine not to "steep thy heart / In such relenting dew of lamentations . . ." (lines 1828-29). He urges Collatine to abandon private grief for political action and rid Rome of Tarquin. In a sense, Brutus uses Lucrece's anguish as a weapon in a struggle between men for power. In *Titus Andronicus,* Marcus asks for compassion for his niece and shows her how to publicize her plight. The reasonableness of a Brutus or Marcus contrasts to the despicable excesses of will of the rapist and the dangerous excesses of rhetoric of husbands who brag about their wives' chaste fidelity. Oddly, moderate women (like Paulina) who play prominent, articulate roles defending the victimized woman in Shakespeare's explorations of sexual jealousy, are missing from the examinations of rape.[6] Their absence starkly points to women's inability to control and to influence in benign ways the public structures that judge rape and the psychosexual needs that generate it.

Indeed, women assist in the rapes that attack other women. In *Lucrece,* night is allegorically female, a sable "mother of dread and fear" (line 117). In *Titus Andronicus,* Tamora wants to destroy Lavinia. Like Clytemnestra, she seeks revenge for the sacrifice of her children. She is also annoyed and threatened because Bassianus and Lavinia have discovered her sporting with Aaron in the woods. However, Tamora's encouragement of her sons to rape not simply Lavinia but any Roman woman has a lascivious quality that flows beyond these motives. Letting her boys "satisfy their lust" (II.iii.180) expresses her enjoyment of her sons' potency, which veers toward and approaches a sublimated incest.

Tempting such taboos, Tamora deliberately turns away from Lavinia. She ignores the plaintive cry, "O Tamora! thou bearest a woman's face—" (II.iii.136) and denies, as Lady Macbeth will do, her own femaleness. This is but one act in a series that will end when she eats her dead children; when she incorporates them back into her body it is an inversion of the release of a living child that marks natural maternity. The forest setting of Lavinia's rape increases the play's sense of distorted, squalid sexuality. The soil is soiled in a perversion of nature comparable to the perversion of domesticity Tarquin creates in Collatine's and Lucrece's marriage bed. The pit that becomes Bassianus's grave, "unhallowed and blood-stained" (II.iii.210), symbolizes the violated female genitalia and womb as well.

Self-reflexive Shakespeare, ever rewriting his materials, also offers a darkly comic study of imagined rape. In *Cymbeline*, Posthumus flaunts Imogen's virtue before Iachimo and dares him to assail it. Iachimo does not physically rape Imogen, but his theft of her good reputation, like his penetration of her bedchamber, is a psychic equivalent. He admits this when he compares himself to Tarquin. Learning that Posthumus thinks her a strumpet and her sex a regiment of strumpets, Imogen begins to imitate Lucrece by stabbing herself in the heart. In addition, clod Cloten sees Posthumus as his rival. Cloten's fantasies parody a conflict between men in which victory means the right to assume the identity of the vanquished, to wear his clothes, to have his wife. Cloten also desires to revenge himself upon the woman who, defending herself against his advances, has offended him. With the encouragement of his mother, he imagines his sexuality as a vehicle of punishment. So he mutters:

> . . . With that suit [Posthumus's] upon my back will I ravish her; first kill him, and in her eyes. There shall she see my valour, which will then be a torment to her contempt. He on the ground, my speech of insultment ended on his dead body, and when my lust hath dined (which, as I say, to vex her I will execute in the clothes that she so prais'd), to the court I'll knock her back, foot her home again. She hath despis'd me rejoicingly, and I'll be merry in my revenge.
>
> (III.v.140-50)

However, crude Cloten cannot transform fantasy into act. Such inadequacies become a grossly comic figure. In *Cymbeline,* comedy blunts the force of Shakespeare's analysis of male enmity and the reunion of Posthumus and Imogen

"Death of Lucretia" by Marc Antoine Raimondi, engraving.

mitigates the force of his brief against the wagers, literal and figurative, that men place on women's virtue.

The fact of having been raped obliterates all of a woman's previous claims to virtue. One *sexual* experience hereafter will define her. Such a strict interpretation of rape may be an index to a shift in the position of women during Shakespeare's time. One historian has suggested: "What the Reformation era witnessed was the changing delineation of women's roles. As this period drew to a close, women's roles became defined increasingly by sex—to the detriment of all women—rather than by class."[7] Other historians have postulated that the more controlled female sexuality is in particular societies, the less power women have. Shakespeare warns his audience about breakdowns in the boundaries on male sexuality, showing rapists as vicious and out of control. However, he also reminds his audience about the boundaries that marriage places on female sexuality. His protest is not against such confinements, but against assaults upon them. If Shakespearean rape does indeed signify such a double retraction—of female identity to sexual identity, of female sexual expressiveness to marital fidelity—it might illustrate the intricate development, between 1580 and 1640, of what Lawrence Stone has named the Restricted Patriarchal Nuclear Family. Stone writes: ". . . both state and Church, for their own reasons, actively reinforced the pre-existent patriarchy within the family, and there are signs that the power of the husband and father over the wife and the children was positively strengthened, making him a legalized petty tyrant within the home."⁸ Coppélia Kahn then correctly reads *The Rape of Lucrece* as the poetic version of an ideology that justifies this male power through imputing "a sort of natural inevitability to the relationship between men and women as the relationship between the strong and the weak. . . ."⁹ In brief, the rape victim may be painfully emblematic of the plight of women during a period of constriction. Her sexual terror stands for the difficulty of her sex. Men, who have more power than women, abuse it. Women, who have less power than men, must absorb that abuse. In Shakespeare, women also have language and the dignity of stoicism as well as the choral commentary of decent men to provide a sympathetic response to their condition.

Psychologically, Shakespeare's rape sequences shrewdly unravel some of the reasons why men rape and the justifications they offer for such exploitation of their strength. Morally, the sequences compel sympathy for women, though they offer, as an inducement to the audience, some recoiling titillation. Shakespeare acutely shows—through Lucrece's speeches, through Lavinia's amputations—the agony a woman experiences after rape. Yet breeding that agony is the belief that the unwilling betrayal of a man's patriarchal position and pride matters more than the destruction of a woman's body and sense of being. Shakespeare deplores warped patterns of patriarchal authority but not the patterns themselves. I cannot prove that the Judith Shakespeare Virginia Woolf imagined in *A Room of One's Own* would have more skeptically asserted that patriarchy itself, not simply malicious and overweening representatives of it, helps to nurture rape. No fabulist, I cannot manufacture texts for history, a "Lucrece" by Judith Shakespeare. We must attend to what we have: Shakespearean victims to mourn, victimizers to despise, and a hierarchical order to frame them both.

Notes

1. *The Rape of Lucrece,* lines 1259-60. All quotations are from *The Complete Works of Shakespeare,* ed. by George Lyman Kittredge (Boston: Ginn, 1936).

2. Marvin Spevack, *A Complete and Systematic Concordance to the Works of Shakespeare,* V (Hildesheim: Georg Olms, 1970), 2713-14, 2718.

3. David Wilbern, "Rape and Revenge in *Titus Andronicus,*" *English Literary Renaissance,* 8 (1978), 164.

4. In contrast, the deceiving of Angelo in the matter of the bed-trick, though underhanded, is not comparable

to rape. Angelo is neither forced into something against his will nor conscious of pain and humiliation during the sexual act.

5. Leo C. Curran, "Rape and Rape Victims in the Metamorphoses," *Arethusa,* 11, Nos. 1/2 (1978), 223, also points out that rape is "perceived primarily as an offense against the property or honor of men." In brief, rape in a shame culture makes women guilty.

6. Because husbands perceive rape as a form of infidelity, their psychic response to the raped wife has similarities to the attitude toward a possibly unfaithful wife: a disruptive suspicion, confusion, anger, and sense of loss, conveyed metaphorically through references to the sheets of the marriage bed that no longer seem white.

7. Sherrin Marshall Wyntjes, "Women in the Reformation Era," *Becoming Visible: Women in European History,* ed. Renate Bridenthal and Claudia Koonz (Boston: Houghton Mifflin, 1977), p. 187. See, too, in the same volume, Joan Kelly-Gadol, "Did Women Have a Renaissance?" pp. 137-64, and Richard T. Vann, "Toward a New Lifestyle: Women in Preindustrial Capitalism," pp. 192-216.

8. Lawrence Stone, *The Family, Sex and Marriage in England, 1500-1800* (New York: Harper & Row, 1977), p. 7. Others have likewise claimed that the junction of the sixteenth and seventeenth centuries was "an important crisis in the historic development of Englishwomen." I quote from Alice Clark, *Working Life of Women in the Seventeenth Century* (New York: Harcourt, Brace and Howe, 1920), p. 2. Stone, though he realizes that women were important economic assets, denies the view "that the economic contribution of the wife to the family budget necessarily gave her higher status and greater power, and that her progressive removal from the labour force as capitalism spread prosperity slowly downward was the cause of her social degradation" (p. 200). Clark supports such a theory.

9. Coppélia Kahn, "The Rape in Shakespeare's *Lucrece,*" *Shakespeare Studies,* 9 (1976), 68. After giving the first version of this paper, I read in manuscript Kahn's essay which explores several of the same issues with admirable depth, subtlety, and persuasiveness.

Works Cited

Allen, P.C. "Some Observations on *The Rape of Lucrece.*" *Shakespeare Survey,* 15 (1962), 89-98.

Hulse, S. Clark. "'A Piece of Skilful Painting' in Shakespeare's 'Lucrece.'" *Shakespeare Survey,* 31 (1978), 13-22.

Kahn, Coppélia. "The Rape of Shakespeare's *Lucrece.*" *Shakespeare Studies,* 9 (1976), 45-72.

Jane O. Newman (essay date 1994)

SOURCE: "'And Let Mild Women to Him Lose Their Mildness': Philomela, Female Violence, and Shakespeare's *The Rape of Lucrece*," in *Shakespeare Quarterly*, Vol. 45, No. 3, Fall, 1994, pp. 304-26.

[*In the following essay, Newman remarks that on first examination,* The Rape of Lucrece *appears to be a poem about the patriarchal victimization of women. However, Newman proposes that a closer look reveals the poem's subtext of Philomela's violent revenge against her rapist—a story which presents an independent response from women to the male society that dominates them.*]

In Shakespeare's *The Rape of Lucrece,* as all readers of the poem know, the progress of the narrative is frequently interrupted by interior monologues and rhetorical set pieces that dilate Livy's and Ovid's essentially political story of Lucrece's rape and suicide into a lengthy, almost psychological investigation of the motivation for and implications of both Lucrece's and Tarquin's actions.[1] Among these rhetorical interludes, Lucrece's address to Night, Opportunity, and Time (ll. 764-1022) and her ekphrastic self-identification with the fall of Troy (ll. 1366-568) have in particular been the subject of no little scholarly debate, perhaps in some measure because they seem both to figure and to result from supposedly Shakespearean innovations that distinguish *The Rape of Lucrece* from its sources and from other early modern versions of the same material.[2] Yet the surrounding matter and circumstances of one of these "Shakespearean" sections—namely, the lengthy apostrophes to Night, Opportunity, and Time, where the figure of the bird-woman, Philomela, twice appears— demand that we look again at the question of *Lucrece*'s source texts. They do so not because they reveal something "new" or "modern" about Lucrece's "psychology" but because they reveal a great deal about Shakespeare's representation of rape and of women's political agency. Obscured in both the Shakespearean representation of Lucrece's story and in its critical reception is an image of woman's reaction to rape that differs radically from Lucrece's. This image, which is uncovered when one examines contemporary editions of Ovid's *Fasti* (one of *Lucrece*'s source texts), is well represented by the Philomela legend mentioned by Lucrece, and it offers an alternative to the ideological script played out by the Lucretia story, a script that blames the victim, allows her to internalize guilt, and defines her as an agent of political change solely in terms of a male's ability to avenge her.

Philomela belongs to and represents the countertradition of vengeful and violent women associated with Bacchic legend. This tradition is replete with images of different, more direct forms of political agency for women, images that in fact challenge the fundamental organization and distribution of power in the Western, patriarchal state. I will argue that this tradition, which materializes onstage in copies of Ovid's *Metamorphoses* in both *Titus Andronicus* and *Cymbeline,* is also pointedly invoked—but then just as

pointedly excised—in and by Shakespeare's *Lucrece.*[3] It nevertheless haunts the margins (both literally and figuratively) of the sources of *Lucrece,* of the poem itself, and of its critical reception. Investigating these margins and the sources represented in and by them allows us to read *Lucrece* as figuring the ways in which criticism can permit one set of images and political options to recede when those options jostle the foundations of conventional ideological assumptions about gender, power, and the state. Claire McEachern has suggested that "traditionally the relationship between Shakespeare and his literary sources . . . has been imagined as linear and determinative, an empirical matter of subtractions and additions." She argues for a new kind of source criticism in which questions of the "transference of formal ingredients" are replaced by questions of how Shakespeare read his sources and how he intervened in the ideology inscribed in them.[4] Like McEachern, I am interested in how ideology both produces and is produced by literary and critical texts. At the same time, however, I will argue that we can discern ideology formation precisely at the level of such "empirical matters" as early modern annotational practice. Philology, source study, and ideology criticism are thus not at odds with one another but rather collaborate to reveal specific instances of ideology formation. In the case of Shakespeare's references to Philomela in *Lucrece,* "excavating" the text's margins uncovers the traces of ideologically less-familiar images of women's responses to rape; these traces can, in turn, reveal how the need to create a monolithic image of mediated political agency for women often shapes the way "textual choices" are made.[5]

The motif of excavation in relation to the identity of Rome is one favored by Freud, and I rely on Freud's understanding of Rome as a diffuse, multilayered archaeological site in my exemplification of a method of reading the textual artifact of *Lucrece,* the complex dramatic poem that arguably initiated Shakespeare's concern with the Eternal City and that takes the question of how to read (textual) foundations as its central topic.[6] When Lucrece cries "How Tarquin must be us'd, *read* it in me: / Myself thy friend will kill myself thy foe, / And for my sake serve thou false Tarquin so" (ll. 1195-97 [my emphasis]), she invokes Brutus's ability to give an activist political reading to the text of the rape and her suicide, a reading that clearly distinguishes itself from her father's and her husband's passive reactions. Given the political power invested in the raped female body, it is not by chance that Freud uses an archaeological metaphor in discussing the roots of women's identity. As he suggests in "Female Sexuality" (1931) and as Luce Irigaray has pursued in "This Sex Which is Not One" (1977), the sociopolitical and ideological self-image as well as the survival of patriarchal culture depend on the repression and exclusion of all but vague traces of an archaic and alternative female civilization.[7] Coppélia Kahn has shown that much of *Lucrece* is concerned with the definition and perpetuation of patriarchal political values and forms, including honor and fidelity, as well as with women's role as sexualized object in the reproduction of patriarchal norms.[8] Small wonder, then, that in the reception of *Lucrece* alternate forms of women's political agency not complicit in the reproduction of patriarchy have been as repressed, as silenced, as Philomela herself, since what was at stake was the construction of the ideological text of a gender hierarchy in which the virtue and moral integrity of a Lucretia must be transplanted to the biological *vir* (here Brutus) in order to produce political change.

Following Freud's, Irigaray's, and Kahn's lead, I propose to expand the notion of what it means to read early modern texts and their sources both "historically" and "politically" by addressing the complexity of the multilayered textual foundations of *Lucrece*. My goal is to problematize the concept of source study and philology as disinterested methods, as well as to expand on their capacity to explain textual details that collude with but also point to ideology formation. Like Brutus, authors and critics often find and interpret a text according to local ideological and political needs; they nevertheless seek to mask, elide, and silence these needs by claiming, in discussions of Shakespeare's poem, for example, to have located or established in "objective" fashion the "historical" texts that Shakespeare "could have known and used."[9] "It is in the significant *silences* of a text, in its gaps and absences," however, as Terry Eagleton has written, "that the presence of ideology can be most positively felt."[10] My own essay is of course just as politically motivated as past source studies have been, but I will not be silent about that motivation; I seek to demonstrate that beneath the surface of Shakespeare's "hybrid" poem lies an ideology of gender that represses traditions of female political agency more threatening to patriarchy than Lucrece's.[11] "Excavating" the "lost" historical "scenario" of female violence present in the margins of *Lucrece* allows that scenario to become visible.[12]

I

The text of Shakespeare's *Lucrece* twice calls attention to the tale of Philomela, the chaste woman raped by a tyrannical relative. Both references are brief and appear almost parenthetical, even ornamental. The first reference to Philomela occurs at the close of Lucrece's apostrophes to Night, Opportunity, and Time and seems designed to create syntactical parallels between the two violated women. The text reads:

> By this, lamenting Philomele had ended
> The well-tun'd warble of her nightly sorrow,
> And solemn night with slow gait descended
> To ugly hell, when lo the blushing morrow
> Lends light to all fair eyes that light will borrow;
>   But cloudy Lucrece shames herself to see,
>   And therefore still in night would cloist'red be.
>
> (ll. 1079-85)

The juxtaposition of the bird with Lucrece, who has, like Philomela, just completed a "well-tun'd warble of . . . sorrow," seems to suggest similarities between the two. Yet the lines just preceding these strain to point out the ironic dissonance of the reference. Lucrece has just

claimed that she will not "hide the truth of this false night's abuses. / My tongue shall utter all, mine eyes like sluices, / As from a mountain spring that feeds a dale, / Shall gush pure streams to purge my impure tale" (ll. 1075-78). Most of Shakespeare's readers would have heard echoes here of the Ovidian Philomela in Book VI of *Metamorphoses,* who threatens to take revenge for the "unspeakable act" ("*nefas*" [l. 524])[13] of rape committed by Tereus the king by publicly speaking it:

> If I should have the chance, I would go where people throng and tell it; if I am kept shut up in these woods, I will fill the woods with my story and move the very rocks to pity. The air of heaven shall hear it, and, if there is any god in heaven, she shall hear it too.
>
> (ll. 545-49)

But the horrific difference in Ovid's tale is that Philomela's "tongue" cannot "utter all," because Tereus cuts out the tongue that she means to use against him and then violates her mutilated, speechless body again and again. In contrast, Lucrece's continuing ability to speak the story of her shame and to name Tarquin as the rapist thus appears to give her access to a form of rhetorical political agency that the legendary Philomela is initially and horribly denied. And indeed, in telling her tale, the legendary Lucretia's rhetoric (re)produces rhetoric and political action in turn. Seneca writes: "to Brutus we owe liberty, to Lucretia . . . we owe Brutus." Lucretia's "first imitator," Brutus, realizes the promise of her "heroic" self-sacrifice, "tak[ing] over from Lucretia the function of preserving chastity" in and restoring honor to a Roman world.[14] The apparent contrast of a silent Philomela, robbed of the potential for such an impact on the political moment to which she belongs, effectively casts Lucretia's suicide as the only form of political intervention available to women.

A similarly complex interaction between the two stories and figures characterizes the second reference to Philomela in *Lucrece,* where Lucrece claims that it is "Philomele" whom she seeks to "imitate":

> Come, Philomele, that sing'st of ravishment,
> Make thy sad grove in my dishevell'd hair;
> As the dank earth weeps at thy languishment,
> So I at each sad strain will strain a tear,
> And with deep groans the diapason bear;
>   For burthen-wise I'll hum on Tarquin still,
>   While thou on Tereus descants better skill.
>
> And whiles against a thorn thou bear'st thy part
> To keep thy sharp woes waking, wretched I,
> To imitate thee well, against my heart
> Will fix a sharp knife to affright mine eye,
> Who if it wink shall thereon fall and die.
>   These means, as frets upon an instrument,
>   Shall tune our heart-strings to true languishment.
>
> (ll. 1128-41)

Here again what strikes one initially is the similarity between the women. Lucrece can be read as imitating the bird-woman in her own songs "of ravishment" that follow, in her meditation on suicide (ll. 1156-211), and in the Troy ekphrasis (ll. 1366 ff.). But the musical harmony suggested by Lucrece's "diapason" and the bird's "descant" instead signals difference, in that the songs are in different registers and in dramatically different musical forms. The reference to Philomela ultimately makes visible precisely what distinguishes Philomela's "sad strain[s]" from Lucrece's "deep groans," makes us aware, that is, that the two women represent the story of rape in different keys, so to speak, keys that have been diversely handled in their reception.[15]

Two recent feminist readings of the poem by Katharine Eisaman Maus and Laura G. Bromley, for example, in their disagreement about whether Lucrece is in the end like Philomela or not, reveal the submerged dissonance between the two legends that the poem seeks to harmonize by recalling only their formal complementarity in the reference to the "humming" and "descanting" of the victimized women.[16] But it is at the level of plot that the story of Philomela most clearly diverges from that of Lucrece. Critics have long assumed that Shakespeare knew Ovid's version of the Philomela story (in Golding's translation). And yet, while it is true that the invocation of a self-wounding Philomela explains how Lucrece could be made to serve as a model for all women subjected to the needs of male culture, the scenario of a self-wounding Philomela does not appear in Ovid's text. Considering the Ovidian intertext in its entirety allows us to understand why references to "the nightingale leaning on a thorn," whose paradoxical "muteness" represents her "mutilation," do not fully account for the significance of the Philomela story in Shakespeare's poem, especially in its contrapuntal role.[17]

Insofar as Ovid's *Metamorphoses* tells the story of an honorable woman raped by a loathsome tyrant, it would of course initially seem to offer the parallel to the story of Lucretia that Shakespeare's text attempts to make. Philomela is, like Lucrece, the lamb ("*agna*") to Tereus's wolf (*Metamorphoses* VI, ll. 527-28; cf. *Lucrece,* l. 677); like Lucrece, she tears her hair and laments after the rape. But Ovid's rape victim differs radically from her Renaissance sister in that she recognizes more rapidly and with greater clarity where to place the blame for the crime. Lucrece delays, first accusing Time, Opportunity, and Night; Ovid's Philomela rails against Tereus immediately and calls down his sword upon her when she threatens to declaim the deed in public. His dismemberment of her is a kind of second rape (he draws his phallic sword from its sheath, the "*vagina*" [*Metamorphoses* VI, l. 551]); then follow a third, fourth, and still more rapes ("*repetisse*" [l. 562]), as Tereus's violence seeks to break the spirit of a rebellious woman. He then abandons her to a sequestered existence in the "hut deep hidden in the ancient woods" (l. 521).

Joplin has made clear that, although maimed and isolated, Philomela nevertheless remains true to her word. She is thus as "vocal" about Tereus's crime as Lucrece is about Tarquin's. Yet not only the parallels but also the divergences are remarkable. Philomela communicates by means of a nonverbal rhetoric that represents woman's language of gesture (as opposed to Lucrece's almost obsessive compliance with the phallogocentric logic of reading and writing[18]), weaving in nimble silence the tapestry (l. 576) on which the story of her violation is told. This is the alternative "text" (from *texere,* to weave) that she sends to her sister, Procne, Tereus's wife. The effect of Philomela's ingenious form of rhetoric is profound (and pointedly unlike Lucrece's seemingly analogous description of the tapestry or painting of Troy, which rewrites and thus silences the act of weaving, a rebellious act as undertaken by Philomela, by repeating a story of violation to no direct political end).[19] First, Philomela inspires another woman, her sister, Procne (rather than a man, Brutus), to threaten the tyrant's hold on phallocratic power by mimicking his abuse of it. Indeed, Procne usurps the (male) position as the avenger of the rape victim. Just as unsentimental as Brutus in Livy's, Ovid's, and Shakespeare's texts, who proclaims an end to weeping over Lucretia's/Lucrece's body, Ovid's Procne has "no room for tears" (l. 585; cf. also l. 611) and, like Brutus, calls for an avenging sword (l. 612). Siding with her sister against her husband, Procne promises to imitate him by cutting out *his* tongue and castrating him (ll. 616-17), thus taking aim at the symbolic source of patriarchal power and the literal offending member in the crime of rape. In contrast to Lucrece, then, Procne threatens to turn the sword against the victimizer rather than against the victim; the rape of a chaste woman will, she makes clear, cause the dissolution rather than the perpetuation of phallocratic rule.[20]

What follows in *Metamorphoses* is precisely the reverse of Lucrece's act of self-sacrifice for the sake of the state, although in both cases the tyrant is ultimately eliminated. Not by chance, it is "the time when the Thracian matrons were wont to celebrate the biennial festival of Bacchus" (*Metamorphoses* VI, ll. 587-88). Joining a female community of Bacchic celebrants, Procne attires herself as a devotee of the god:

> The queen . . . equips herself for the rites of the god and dons the array of frenzy; her head was wreathed with trailing vines, a deer-skin hung from her left side, a light spear rested on her shoulder. Swift she goes through the woods with an attendant throng of her companions, and driven on by the madness of grief, Procne, terrific in her rage, mimics thy madness, O Bacchus!
>
> (ll. 591-97)

With her women, she finds the maimed Philomela and dresses her, too, in the "trappings of a Bacchante" (ll. 598-99). Distorted elements of familiar Greek rites associated with Dionysianism—particularly the emphasis on the dismemberment of a living being, the women's access to the tools of ritual slaughter, and the confusion of distinct forms of ceremonial practice—appear in the subsequent substitution of Procne and Tereus's son, Itys, for his father and thus of a male body for Lucrece's female body in the act of bloody sacrifice:[21]

> While Procne was thus speaking Itys came into his mother's presence. His coming suggested what she

could do, and regarding him with pitiless eyes, she said: "Ah, how like your father you are!" . . . And when they reached a remote part of the great house, while the boy stretched out pleading hands as he saw his fate, and screamed, "Mother! mother!" and sought to throw his arms around her neck, Procne smote him with a knife between breast and side—and with no change of face. This one stroke sufficed to slay the lad; but Philomela cut his throat also, and they cut up the body still warm and quivering with life. Part bubbles in brazen kettles, part sputters on spits; while the whole room drips with gore.

(ll. 619-22, 638-46)

The murder of Itys by the women dislodges men from the position of political agency and responsibility heretofore reserved for them in a way that the Lucrece story does not. Philomela and Procne, pretending that they have prepared a "sacred feast after their ancestral fashion" ("*patrii moris sacrum mentita*" [l. 648]), feed pieces of the boy to Tereus, who goes mad when he realizes that his body has become the tomb of the heir to patriarchal rule (l. 655). Rather than reviolating herself (as Lucrece does in committing suicide and as the truncated story of Philomela as a self-wounding nightingale would have us think is Lucrece's only option), Philomela becomes jubilantly violent, "hurl[ing] the gory head of Itys straight into his father's face; nor was there ever any time when she longed more to be able to speak, and to express her joy in fitting words" (ll. 658-60). To escape the raging Tereus's sword, both she and her sister are then transformed into birds; but the image Ovid leaves us with is that of a triumphant rather than a lamenting Philomela, who, engaging in an act of ritualized violence, acts as a jubilant witness to the end of Thracian tyranny.[22]

Scholars of *Lucrece*'s source texts have attended to the Ovidian intertext and to Shakespeare's use of the story but have not investigated the nature of the relationship between the violent Philomela and the self-sacrificing Lucrece. In neglecting to do so, they have enacted a selective process not unlike Shakespeare's own, though they have been perhaps less aware than he of the act of elision in which they have engaged. As Baldwin writes, Shakespeare's Lucrece does not "go into the story" of Philomela in any detail.[23] This brevity can now be seen to have been well motivated, for to have done so would have intervened in her (and Baldwin's) ability to reinscribe the inevitability of the role assigned to Lucrece since Livy, namely the conversion of rape into suicide, of abuse into self-sacrifice for the sake of the state. The manifest absence, even deletion, of the revenge alternative from Lucrece's options is figured in the truncation of the full Philomela story. Women's response to rape and their participation in political renewal are thereby limited, ideologically speaking, to actions that require their self-destruction.

It could be argued that Shakespeare's elision of significant details from the Philomela story (an elision reproduced by source criticism to date) was an oversight if there were not a moment in the text of *Lucrece* that invokes but then im-

mediately dismisses the alternative of violent female reprisal. In her address to Time, Lucrece explicitly calls up the specter of a response to her violation that echoes the actions of Procne and Philomela. She begs Time to

> Devise extremes beyond extremity,
> To make [Tarquin] curse this cursed crimeful night.
> . . . . .
> Let there bechance him pitiful mischances
> To make him moan, but pity not his moans;
> Stone him with hard'ned hearts harder than stones,
>   And let mild women to him lose their mildness,
>   Wilder to him than tigers in their wildness.

(ll. 969-70 and 976-80)

Lucrece's Bacchic visions, which read as if she would have Tarquin become a character in a neo-Senecan tragedy of revenge, are almost immediately displaced by self-contempt at her own use of "idle words" in a "case" that is "past the help of law." "The remedy indeed," she decides, "Is to let forth my foul-defiled blood" (ll. 1016, 1022, and 1028-29). But the invocation of "wild women's" work of the very sort done by Procne and Philomela is uncanny in the technical sense, since it signals the return of a repressed scenario (or, perhaps, a scenario that will be displaced onto Brutus, the only man in the family whose heart is "hard'ned" enough in the end to avenge Lucrece's violation and death[24]). *Lucrece* thus both participates in and reveals the mechanism behind the closing off of the option of female violence against the rapist.

It might be objected that, unlike *Titus Andronicus*, Shakespeare's *Lucrece* contains no reference to the violent Philomela of *Metamorphoses* VI explicit enough to provide evidence for an act of repression at *Lucrece*'s textual foundations. Here the other Ovidian source pointed out by Baldwin is helpful.[25] As Baldwin notes, the Lucretia story is also told in *Fasti;* there it recalls precisely the Bacchic alternative. Ovid's story of Lucretia (*Fasti* II, ll. 685-856) concludes with a four-line allusion to the story of Philomela. The text reads:

> Do I err? or has the swallow come, the harbinger of spring, and does she not fear lest winter should turn and come again? Yet often, Procne, wilt thou complain that thou hast made too much haste, and thy husband Tereus will be glad at the cold thou feelest.[26]

The relationships among these lines, *Metamorphoses* VI, and *Lucrece* initially seem subtle. First, the reference to the sadistic pleasure that Tereus will feel when Procne, as swallow, arrives too early in the spring and feels the cruel cold of winter is dependent on the violence that marks the end of the intertext of *Metamorphoses* VI. Procne's harrowing by Tereus may thus be understood as the "reward" she receives in the four-line coda to the Lucretia story in *Fasti* for her actions in the lengthier *Metamorphoses* VI. Second, the description of Tereus's sadism in *Fasti* II can be seen as an intertext for Tarquin's masochistic musings just before his rape of Lucrece, when Tarquin "reads" the delays that the "locks," "unwilling portal," "wind," and "glove" (*Lucrece*, ll. 302-29) afford him:

"So, so," quoth he, "these lets attend the time,
Like little frosts that sometime threat the spring,
To add a more rejoicing to the prime,
And give the sneaped birds more cause to sing.
Pain pays the income of each precious thing. . . .

                                        (ll. 330-34)

The reference in these lines to the "frosts" of an impending "spring" works as a submerged citation of Tereus's delighted invocation of Procne's pain, caused in *Fasti* by the "cold" of a returning winter.

When we turn to marginal glosses by Paulus Marsus on the four lines that conclude Ovid's tale of Lucretia, the relationships among the texts are no longer hidden or subtle. That Marsus's commentary was important and available to Shakespeare has long been known. Baldwin goes to great lengths to demonstrate the impact of a contemporary edition of Ovid's *Fasti* with its lengthy marginal commentary by Marsus. Citing an edition printed in 1550, Baldwin states that Marsus's notes on Ovid were considered "the standard commentary of that day."[27] Baldwin further maintains that Shakespeare had "used a copy of Ovid with the notes of Marsus, who had correlated most of the other Latin sources, especially Livy," when composing *Lucrece*. I find it significant that Baldwin, in discussing the "variorum Ovid" that he identifies as Shakespeare's source for *Lucrece*, does not include Marsus's commentary on *Fasti*'s four lines about Procne.[28] Ovid's lines, quoted above in English, read as follows in the 1510 Latin edition:

> *Fallimur an veris praenuncia venit hirundo*
> *An metuit neque* [!] *versa recurrat hyems:*
> *Saepe tamenn progne nimium properasse quaereris*
> *virque tuo thereus frigore laetus erit.*[29]

Marsus begins his commentary on these lines (853-56) just to the right of the last line. The gloss spills over onto the following page, where we read in his annotation to the reference to "*thereus*": "*Thereus: de quo supius diximus in caristiis*" ("Tereus: about whom I said [more] above in the section on the Caristia [the family love feast held at Rome in February]").[30] When we look *supius*—above—for the prior point in the narrative where a reference to Tereus is made, we find it at line 629 in the explanations of the February feastdays. When Ovid explains who is specifically *not* invited to partake in the Caristia, he names, among others: "*et soror et Procne Tereusque duabus iniquus*" ("Procne and her sister and Tereus, who wronged them both").[31] The exclusion of Philomela, Procne, and Tereus from the feast is not surprising, since it would hardly be appropriate to include those involved in rape, incest, and infanticide in a "family love feast."

It is significant that Marsus draws our attention at line 856 to Ovid's mention at line 629 of Tereus, Procne, and Philomela's exclusion from the feast, thus reminding us of the reasons for this exclusion, namely their violent and bloody story; more significant are his additional marginal glosses at line 629. In the margin to the right of that line of *Fasti*

II, Marsus writes: "*Therei Prognes & philomenes fabula latius in metamorphoses libri vi*" ("The story of Tereus, Procne, and Philomela is told at greater length in Book VI of the *Metamorphoses*"). Marsus then proceeds to relate the entire story in a lengthy marginal note, with special emphasis on the Bacchic aspect of Procne's reaction to the tapestry that Philomela wove—"*orgia simulans in silvas venit*" ("imitating the wild festivals of Bacchus, she entered the woods"). His commentary underscores the horror of Itys's murder by stressing the role played by Philomela in the deed; although the boy's fate has already been described in Marsus's summary ("*Itim filium interemit pr*[?]*ique epulandum apposvit*" ["She killed the boy, Itys, and served him up at the banquet"]), Marsus elaborates: "*Absit et progne et soror: hoc e*[?] *Philom*[?]*ea: qua ambae in necem Itys conspiravere*" ("Let both Procne and her sister, Philomela, stay away [from the festival of Caristia], the Philomela who conspired with her in the death of Itys"). The marginal note in fact gives the rape victim herself a considerably greater role in the act of vengeance than does Ovid's original text.[32]

Among the several sources for *Lucrece* cited by Baldwin is Thomas Cooper's *Dictionarium Historicum & Poeticum*, published with his *Thesaurus Linguae Romanae et Britannicae* in 1565. Cooper's version of the Philomela story is just as long as his tale of Lucretia and similar to it in its indebtedness to the classical sources. Yet, interestingly, Cooper alters the Philomela story that Ovid tells to emphasize the Bacchic elements in particular:

> Philomela, . . . beinge very cunnynge in woorkyng and imbrodering, did in such sorte set out the whole matter in a garme[n]t, . . . and sent the same by a servaunt to hir sister Progne, Tereus his wyfe. Who, although she weare greatly moved with the matter, yet she did deferre the reve[n]gement, untill the sole[m]ne sacrifices of Bachhus. At which tyme, beyng accompanied, as the manner was, with a great number of other women, she taketh hir sister out of pryson, and bringeth hir into the palaice. Wheare by hir counsayle she killed hyr yonge sonne Itys, and served hir husbande with it at supper. . . .[33]

Had Cooper consulted any contemporary edition of Ovid, he would have found ample support for his emendations of the tale. Had Shakespeare used either Cooper's *Dictionarium* or an edition of the *Fasti* similar to the one edited by Marsus, as Baldwin suggests he did, he would have found information about a maenadic Philomela which calls into significant question his (and any other) Lucrece's claim to "imitate" her "well" while internalizing the blame for and consequences of the rape.[34]

Both Cooper and, for that matter, Paulus Marsus were, like Shakespeare, men of their time, and they used the available editions in composing their glosses and commentaries on classical figures and texts. Cooper's and Marsus's common desire to emphasize the infanticidal element of the Philomela story and to associate the sisters' behavior with orgiastic Bacchic rites resulted not from an idiosyncratic reading of the sources, I would maintain, but from careful consideration of a still earlier tradition of Ovid commentary. The source for Marsus's knowledge of *Metamorphoses,* for example, was probably an edition of the work with annotations by the sixth-century Christian grammarian Luctatius Placidus (called Lactantius), whose *Argumenta in Ovidii Metamorphosin* some scholars attribute to the famous Donatus. Most sixteenth-century editions of the *Metamorphoses* also contained notes by Raffaele Regio of Bergamo (called Raphael Regius), who published his commentary on the *Metamorphoses* in 1492. Although Marsus's first version of his commentary on *Fasti,* published in 1482, clearly could not have relied on Regius (since it predated the publication of Regius's notes), it may have been via Lactantius that both scholars were led to emphasize the Bacchic elements of the legend.[35] In any case, an examination of these commentaries suggests that the mention of Philomela would have conjured up the image of women reacting with violence against those who violated them rather than against themselves, with violence sanctioned, moreover, by its inscription in a ritualistic (Bacchic) frame.

The narrative of a violent Philomela seems to have been the object of some fascination in Shakespeare's time. In a 1543 edition of the *Metamorphoses* printed in Basel, for example, an edition that contains both Lactantius's and Regius's notes, the opening lines of the Philomela story in the center of the page are dwarfed by the massive annotations that surround it. Lactantius's notes, printed first, summarize the entire story at the outset in an "Argumentum." For him the relationship of Procne's and Philomela's actions to Bacchic rites appears obvious: *"et more bacchantis ad stabula venit, sororem raptam in regiam duxit, filium Ityn interemit, et dapibus immiscuit"* ("and as was the Bacchic custom, she [Procne] came to the hut, led her violated sister to the palace, killed her son, Itys, and mixed his body in with the sacrificial meal").[36] In this edition, printed in the margins after Lactantius's notes and following them in locating the murder of the boy in the context of ritual violence, Regius's notes elaborate on the Bacchic aspect in particular:[37]

> *Progne vero furijs accensa Bacchi sacra se celebrare simulans, una cum Bacchis ad sororem venit. eamque secum pampinis tectam in urbem adduxit, in cubiculoque suo occultavit. Perfectis vero Bacchi sacrificijs Progne Ityn communem filium interemit, cujus carnes coctas patri apposuit comedendas.*

> (But Procne, driven by the furies [and] imitating the sacred rites of Bacchus, came with the Bacchantae to her sister and, with them, draped in vines, led her to the city, hiding her there in her bedchamber. Procne, having accomplished the Bacchic sacrifices, [then] killed Itys, the son [whom she had borne to Tereus], and served his cooked flesh up for his father to eat.)[38]

In Regius's view, Itys's death and the act of cannibalism that follows it are accomplished in the context of traditional Bacchic behavior. Several pages later, in glosses on the lines that narrate the murder, he offers additional

material on the intricacies of such practices, making it impossible to think of the consequences of the initial rape in anything other than the context of the cult.[39]

The historical source texts and traditions that Marsus and, in turn, Cooper and Shakespeare could have known and used in their research on both Lucretia and Philomela thus display a clear fascination with maenadic behavior. Even if Shakespeare had been a man of such "small Latine" as Anthony Brian Taylor has recently asserted, the emphasis on the Bacchic elements of the story and on Philomela's collusion with Procne in the butchering of her son would have been difficult to overlook.[40] Shakespeare's reference to Philomela represents a (perhaps deliberate) deviation from this textually widespread tradition, a turn away from the tradition of wild women not unlike the one Lucrece herself performs. And yet his very reference to women's wildness calls attention to this tradition, one explicitly not represented by his text. The failure to report the historicity of this tradition as it was associated with Philomela has made it possible for critics to tell a story about the sources of Shakespeare's *Lucrece* that bypasses the opportunity to evaluate fragmentary evidence as a clue to the text's historical origins in favor of a narrative about the inevitability of women's ongoing (self-)victimization.[41]

II

The extent to which the tradition of a vengeful Philomela involved in infanticidal blood sacrifice has been repressed in both Shakespeare's text and scholarship about the text makes visible precisely what is at stake in the early modern version of Lucrece's story: namely, the guarantee that political renewal be conceived of in very narrow terms as a transfer of power within an essentially closed phallocratic political economy in which monarchy (the transfer of power from father to son) is replaced by a republic (the transfer of power from one group of men to another group of men not necessarily related to them other than under the auspices of the state). Women clearly play a limited if crucial role in this transfer and form of renewal, which can justifiably be understood as a "traffic in women," particularly insofar as it is over their violated and dead bodies that men (again, in Lucrece's case Brutus) rise to seize power and thus effect change.[42] The countertradition of women who intervene directly in this transfer of power by killing the heir, thereby providing the conditions for more thoroughgoing political change, is represented in the story of Philomela and particularly in the distorted version of Dionysian ritual it contains. In this ritual, acts of infanticide and cannibalism were not only permissible but fundamental to the symbolic structure of the expiatory myth.

Elements of what later became sacrificial tradition in Bacchic circles are visible on the surface of the Greek myth as recounted by Marcel Detienne:

> The plot is simple. A god in the form of a child is jointly slaughtered by all the Titans, the kings of ancient times. Covered with gypsum and wearing masks of

white earth, the murderers surround their victim. With careful gestures they show the child fascinating toys: a top, a rhombus, dolls with jointed limbs, knucklebones, and a mirror. And while the child Dionysus contemplates his own image captured in the circle of polished metal, the Titans strike, dismember him, and throw the pieces in a kettle. Then they roast them over a fire. Once the victim's flesh has been prepared, they undertake to devour it all. They just have time to gobble it down, all except the heart, which had been divided into equal parts, before Zeus' lightning comes to punish their crime and reduce the Titan party to smoke and ashes, out of which will be born the human species.[43]

The tradition of the Dionysia was sanctioned, indeed institutionalized by the state apparatus in Athens as part of the annual ceremonies of renewal, and only later, in its Roman form as Bacchanalia, did it become subversive. It was eventually made illegal in 186 B.C. But even in its early Greek form, Dionysianism was identified with the immorality, licentiousness, and frenzy of its female devotees.[44] The most threatening of the acts associated with its initiates, namely, the occupation by women of the place of ruling-class Titans in the myth and the subsequent unleashing upon men of latent female "wildness," quickly became those acts most readily identified as crucial to the cult. They are familiar to us from such texts as Euripides's *Bacchae,* in which another son, Pentheus, is torn limb from limb by his own mother under the influence of the god. This image is invoked by Shakespeare's Lucrece in the call for women's wildness but is immediately dismissed in favor of "heroic" self-victimization.[45]

Detienne has argued with great eloquence that the theory and practice of ritual sacrifice lay at the center of the organization of political power in classical Greece and has used as a primary example Dionysianism and its relationship to dominant politico-religious sacrificial practices, which involved ritual slaughtering, cooking, and consumption of the victim. The Greeks performed these rites as a way of guaranteeing the "harmonious functioning of society" in all areas of civic activity, relying heavily in the process on the moment of (re)generation central to the original Dionysus myth. According to Detienne, those who refused to participate in the ceremonies or who performed them in unconventional ways (as in the cults of Orphism or Dionysianism) demonstrated their refusal to subscribe to the "rules of conduct" and to the political organization represented by the dominant sacrificial code, a code designed to secure the health of the state.[46]

The terms of acceptable and successful sacrificial ceremony, for example, clearly legislated the identity of the *mageiros*—the butcher, sacrificer, and cook—and his professional duties. Significant for our discussion here, the *mageiros* was always male; "just as women [were] without the political rights reserved for male citizens, they [were] kept apart from the altars, meat, and blood." This "male monopoly in matters of blood sacrifice" kept women away from and characterized them as unqualified to handle the kettle, spit, and knife, thus pushing both them and other politically marginal groups, such as cult members, into forms of vegetarianism as a sign of their exclusion from political affairs. Stories of women wielding these instruments of blood sacrifice are rare. But when they occur, they have great significance, since they reveal the fraught nature of the relationship between the sexes and the instability of a political hierarchy based on gender distinction, particularly in terms of who was admitted to positions of privilege in the sacrificing economy and who was excluded.[47]

In this context the Greek story of Procne and Philomela and their slaughtering of Itys offers a perverse challenge to traditional politico-sacrificial behavior and resonates with the threat that the Bacchanalia must have represented to Rome. In Ovid's account Procne acts as priestess-butcher, slaying the victim in a carefully aimed blow ("with a knife between breast and side"). Philomela seems to "conspire" in the ceremony (Marsus's word) by cutting Itys's throat with a sword ("*ferro*" [*Metamorphoses* VI, l. 643]). In a shocking deformation of traditional sacrificial practice, the women then cut up the body and prepare it for consumption, simultaneously roasting part of it and boiling the rest ("*pars inde cavis exsultat aenis, / pars veribus stridunt*" [ll. 645-46]), confusing and collapsing the steps of boiling and roasting, which were strictly separated by sacrificial decorum.[48] The challenge to traditional gender roles as well as to the distribution of power within the state is thus intensified by their willful mockery of the expiatory sacrificial ceremony itself. The murder of Itys in the Procne/Philomela story can thus be located within the realm of traditional if contested sacrificial behavior. Itys's death and the cooking and eating of his body are represented as outlandish but also as ritually necessary to expiate Tereus's crime. The son is the substitute victim, ironically offered to and consumed by the offending father, whose crime (incest/rape) is all the worse because he is king.

The two legends being considered here, of course, come out of a Greek context, in the case of Philomela explicitly so, since her father was Pandion of Athens and the rapist was Tereus of Thrace. In the case of Lucretia, the Greek tradition is present at a latent level. The story originally belonged not to Rome but to Ardea and thus to "the most ancient religious legends of the Latin stock," legends whose origins rested in "imported Greek myths" and cults "transplanted to Rome in the second half of the fourth century," as Ettore Pais has pointed out.[49] Recalling the less well-known but nevertheless traditional method of state purification associated with Bacchic women's usurpation of the expiatory apparatus is not as strange as it might initially seem, given the Hellenized context of both stories. Ovid's close association of a vengeful and violent Philomela with the story of a self-sacrificing Lucretia in *Fasti* can in part be explained by the common Greek provenance of both legends. Both legends also address a similar need for displacing the tyrant, and both find ways to do so that involve cleansing rituals of blood sacrifice.

The association that underlies Ovid's juxtaposition of the Lucretia and Philomela stories in *Fasti* is also present in Shakespeare's text. *Lucrece* depicts a politically explosive moment not unlike the one presented to us in the Philomela story, a moment that is nevertheless resolved in an act of blood sacrifice pointedly unlike the one chosen by the sisters. Against the background of the similarity of the two situations, a similarity that the text strains to reinforce, the magnitude of the gap between the two solutions becomes legible as a distension of the connection between two permissible poles of political behavior by women. The reader is meant to consider but then to dismiss the Philomela option in her/his reading of *Lucrece*.

III

Reading the (margins of the) story of Lucrece through the lens of the traditions that shaped Shakespeare's fragmentary references to the Philomela myth in the late sixteenth century allows us to read other parts of the text historically, that is, as historically produced (and ideologically driven) in response to the potentially dangerous message of legitimate female violence as part of a mechanism of political renewal. Repressed in both Lucrece's response to her rape and in criticism of *Lucrece* but reappearing, as I noted above, with emphasis in the poem itself are, in turn, precisely those elements that would seem to make expiatory blood sacrifice necessary, elements that derive from the "origin" of Shakespeare's text in contemporary editions of Ovid. In *Fasti* the story of Lucretia appears in the entry for 24 February, the day on which the *Regifugium,* a celebration of the ejection of a polluted king from the city, was traditionally reenacted.[50] Ovid's reference, at the end of the Lucretia narrative, to the tale of a violent Philomela, with its representation of an incestuous rape committed by a tyrant and of the rituals of banishment and political cleansing by blood sacrifice in expiation of the king's sin, is, then, structurally related to the *Regifugium*. When seen in the context of *Lucrece*'s historical textual origins, Shakespeare's Lucrece's/*Lucrece*'s rejection of the tale of Philomela and its Bacchic afterlife in the Renaissance begins to seem even more clearly motivated by the need to remove the possibility of female revenge. That the repressed story of the rituals associated with the *Regifugium* does reemerge elsewhere in the poem helps to explain, in a way that scholarship has so far been unable to do, the text's "innovative" emphasis on the rape as a political crime (rather than as an opportunity for sentimentalized images of female purity and devotion), as well as on the need for expelling the king who is the source of pollution. Politicizing rather than sentimentalizing rape allows us to read *Lucrece* anew.

The special emphasis that Shakespeare places on Tarquin's rape as a crime of incest, and thus an instance of sexual pollution that violates the bonds of familial trust, may be understood as the most obvious indication of Shakespeare's awareness of the tale's original political context in Ovid.[51] That Sextus Tarquinius has raped the wife of his cousin, Lucius Tarquinius Collatinus, is obvious, although

not emphasized, in Livy's narrative of the Lucretia story; Collatine's full name appears twice, first in the initial scene of boasting and again at the end of the story, where Collatine is made consul.[52] That the rape is also a sexual act between relatives by marriage is only slightly more visible in Ovid's rendering of the tale in *Fasti*. He alludes briefly to the fact that Lucretia and Sextus Tarquinius are related when he explains that she received him "courteously" ("*comiter*") because he was a relative by blood ("*sanguine iunctus erat*" [*Fasti* II, 1. 788]), but he does not explore the implications of the fact that rapist and victim are related.

Annotations of Ovid's *Fasti* do, however, stress the family connections. In the 1510 edition of the *Fasti,* for example, line 788 is glossed by Antonius Constantius, whose commentary on the *Fasti* was first published in Venice in 1502.[53] They are relatives by blood, Constantius notes, "*quia Tarquinius collatinus vir lucretiae sorore tarquinii superbi genitus fuerat: ut diximus supra*" ("because Collatinus Tarquinius, the husband of Lucretia, was the son of Tarquinius Superbus's sister, as we say above").[54] Paulus Marsus's glosses repeat the same information in briefer form. When we look *supra* to the commentary on lines 725-26, where the two men are mentioned together in the context of the initial dinner conversation, we find a lengthier note by Constantius that addresses the obscure reference to "*Tarquinius juvenis.*" (Various commentators up through the twentieth century have debated whether this term refers to Tarquin or Collatine.) The gloss includes information about the Tarquin family tree which reappears later in an abbreviated form. Marsus's notes also underscore the Tarquin lineage, again in a somewhat more concise note. William Painter probably knew these notes, as well as the references to Livy that they contain, since his Lucretia novella in *The Palace of Pleasure* (1575) also gives Collatinus's full name at the outset, thus drawing attention to the family tie. Cooper's *Dictionarium* also underlines themes of kinship: his Lucretia is a "noble woman of Rome, wyfe to Tarquinius Collatinus," who "enterteyned" Sextus Tarquinius "for kinreds sake in hir house."[55]

In light of the marginalia, then, it is not surprising that Shakespeare should have paid extra attention to the incestuous aspect of the rape. He has Tarquin himself mention the kinship:

> "Had Collatinus kill'd my son or sire,
> Or lain in ambush to betray my life,
> Or were he not my dear friend, this desire
> Might have excuse to work upon his wife,
> As in revenge or quittal of such strife;
>   But as he is my kinsman, my dear friend,
>   The shame and fault finds no excuse nor end."
>
> (ll. 232-38)

Lucrece herself describes incest as "that abomination; / An accessary . . . / To all sins past and all that are to come, / From the creation to the general doom" (ll. 921-24). The pollution of the state represented by the incestuous, immoral behavior of the king's son is intensified by association with a crime against the family, "'gainst law" and "duty" (l. 497). The crime is all the worse in Rome, moreover, where the family was the model of a patriarchal political structure.

Shakespeare's poem also raises the specter of illegitimacy. There is no mention of Lucrece's childbearing capacities, of other children, or of a possible pregnancy in either Livy or Ovid. In *Lucrece,* Tarquin first mentions Lucrece's children, threatening, if she refuses him, to kill her and to put her in bed with a dead slave, thus bringing shame on her issue:

> "So thy surviving husband shall remain
> The scornful mark of every open eye;
> Thy kinsmen hang their heads at this disdain,
> Thy issue blurr'd with nameless bastardy."

> (ll. 519-22)

The horror of pregnancy as a result of the rape is very real for Lucrece, for whom the solution of suicide seems all the more promising because it will eliminate such visible testimony to her violation and, as Kahn points out, will avoid confusing the patrilineal line as well.[56] Through her suicide, Lucrece says, "This bastard graff shall never come to growth. / He shall not boast who did thy [i.e., Collatine's] stock pollute, / That thou art doting father of his fruit" (ll. 1062-64). Tarquin's claim that it is for her "children's sake" (l. 533) that she should yield to him nuances Kahn's reading, which emphasizes Lucrece's complicity in patriarchal structures but overlooks Tarquin's exploitation of her concern. Lucrece's reference to the possibility of impregnation works to suggest that she ultimately kills herself for the sake of her progeny—unlike Procne, who rejects maternal instinct and kills her offspring for her sister's sake (l. 633). Yet Lucrece's is a mother love more concerned with the reputation of the "princely name" (l. 599) of the house of Collatine and thus more with its status within the Roman sociopolitical hierarchy than with the intimacy of the nursery.

The "innovative" emphasis in Shakespeare's *Lucrece* on the rape as a crime against the family and the state, one exacerbated by the possibility of illegitimate offspring, testifies to the political crisis just below the text's surface. It is an emphasis that explains the peculiar and yet consistent characterization of Tarquin as a "Roman lord" and as a potentially legitimate authority figure whose primary sin is compromising his political reputation by raping his cousin's wife. The granting to Tarquin of a Roman identity and thus the exaggeration of the impact of his crime on the state can again be understood as the displaced emergence of the latent Philomela option, with its ultimate emphasis on another traditional, albeit oppositional form of political cleansing. The dimensions of the crime become visible, in turn, only against the background of the elided alternative. On the one hand, the sources and the historical record make clear that the Tar-

quins came to Rome from Etruria, were thus "alien[s] by blood," and could thus be considered illegitimate usurpers of power in the Latin political landscape.[57] Shakespeare's Tarquin, although "fault-full," is nevertheless clearly and consistently identified as a "lord of Rome." It is all the worse, then, that he perverts Roman values by committing the rape. Nowhere in the sources is there evidence of anything other than a morally corrupt Sextus Tarquinius ("*vir iniustis,*" Ovid calls him [*Fasti* II, l. 688]). In Shakespeare's version, however, even Lucrece posits an originally and essentially moral Tarquin, to whom she openly appeals in her self-defense:

> In Tarquin's likeness I did entertain thee;
> Hast thou put on his shape to do him shame?
> To all the host of heaven I complain me:
> Thou wrong'st his honor, wound'st his princely name.
> Thou art not what thou seem'st, and if the same,
>   Thou seem'st not what thou art, a god, a king;
>   Kings like gods should govern every thing.

> (ll. 596-602)

While there is an earlier suggestion that Tarquin may have feigned this godlike, kingly identity (he is a "false lord" [l. 50], who hides "base sin in pleats of majesty" [l. 93]), there emerges repeatedly a sense of loss or privation, a sense that Tarquin was noble, a good leader and worthy scion of his (Roman) family, who loses this identity in the act of rape: "His honor, his affairs, his friends, his state, / Neglected all, with swift intent he goes / To quench the coal which in his liver glows" (ll. 45-47). Shakespeare's deliberate (mis)identification of Tarquin as a Roman thus exaggerates the impact of his actions on the state; the rape threatens the very definition of Roman civic identity and leadership. The "foul dishonor" to his "household's grave" (l. 198) that the violation represents clearly signifies the collapse of the integrity of a Roman political system organized by familial metaphors. To restore order, Tarquin must be made to "flee the city" (as in the ceremony of the *Regifugium*) in "everlasting banishment" (l. 1855).

It is because Tarquin's personal actions are construed within this political framework that it is "high treason," even "mutiny," for his eyes to betray the sense of values located in his "Roman" heart (ll. 369 and 426). The politico-military organization of the rapist's faculties, in which the "veins" are "[o]bdurate vassals" and his own "beating heart, alarum striking, / Gives the hot charge, and bids them do their liking" (ll. 427-34), emphasizes the fact that Tarquin's very body is inscribed in a public discourse. His crime appears all the worse, then, because it was directed against the political unit of the family and committed by the individual whom Shakespeare identifies with the profile of a king. Ovid suggests the connection in a terse comment: "[*Haec*] *te victoria perdet. / heu quanto regnis nox stetit una tuis*" ("This victory will ruin thee. Alack, how dear a single night did cost thy kingdom!" [*Fasti* II, ll. 811-12]). But Shakespeare's text makes this insight central to the message of Tarquin's *psychomachia* (ll. 127-280), where the choice to remain regal is clearly offered but just as clearly rejected. As a result Shakespeare's Tarquin falls further than his classical predecessors:

> The baser is he, coming from a king,
> To shame his hope with deeds degenerate;
> The mightier man, the mightier is the thing
> That makes him honor'd, or begets him hate;
> For greatest scandal waits on greatest state.
>   The moon being clouded presently is miss'd,
>   But little stars may hide them when they list.

(ll. 1002-8)

In a context in which, as Kahn writes, "the rape of Lucrece . . . parallels the abuse of kingship in Rome."[58] the sin against the state must be promptly and thoroughly expunged.

Shakespeare's Brutus articulates the solution to the king's pollution of the body politic by gendering the city of Rome as female:

> But kneel with me and help to bear thy part,
> To rouse our Roman gods with invocations,
> That they will suffer these abominations
> (Since Rome herself in them doth stand disgraced)
> By our strong arms from forth her fair streets chased.

(ll. 1830-34)

He then interprets the text of Lucrece's suicide as a blood sacrifice, invoking its power to cleanse a feminized city of the offending member:

> Now by the Capitol that we adore,
> And by this chaste blood so unjustly stained,
> By heaven's fair sun that breeds the fat earth's store,
> By all our country rights in Rome maintained,
> And by chaste Lucrece' soul that late complained
>   Her wrongs to us, and by this bloody knife,
>   We will revenge the death of this true wife.

(ll. 1835-41)[59]

Since Rome cannot "bleed," it is the "bleeding body" of another female that seals the covenant.

The ritualized nature of Brutus's vow, complete with choreographed gestures and imitation of the priest's actions by the representative citizenry surrounding him (ll. 1842-48), reminds us quite clearly, as does the emphasis on the rape as a crime with devastating implications for the stability of the state, of the original context for one of Shakespeare's sources, namely, the calendar of feastdays represented by Ovid's *Fasti* and specifically of the *Regifugium* rites of late February. The Lucretia legend appears in direct connection with the ceremony in *Fasti,* the Philomela story indirectly but still closely associated with it, and for good reason, since both fulfill the formal requirements for atoning for the sin of the king and thus cleansing the city. The choice that Shakespeare's text about female self-sacrifice stages—with its invocation and then rejection of a Renaissance commentary tradition fascinated

by the particulars of Bacchic-Dionysian expiatory rituals that depend on and permit women's violence—becomes glaringly obvious behind the heightening of the princely crime in *Lucrece.*

IV

Other legends survive of women who use well-motivated and politically recognizable forms of violence against corrupt rulers, as in Hecuba's blinding of Polymnestor and her slaughter of his sons. Such tales suggest that a complex tradition of women participating in sacrificial rites of revenge and expiation existed in antiquity and continued to be transmitted in the Renaissance.[60] In this tradition the corruption of the (phallocratic) state could be expunged at its origin through the murder of the unjust king or his sons, rather than indirectly via the symbolic sacrifice of a woman. The rejection of the Philomela/Procne option in Shakespeare's text and by its critics demonstrates how a text can become implicated in the crafting of an ideological script that excludes women from the work of political renewal if that work is identified with the actions of women like the violent sisters, actions derived from and representative of a tradition of state ritual that empowered the underclass.

The repression of the full story of Philomela can be explained as the result of the ideological pressure of a postclassical gender code organized around preserving political agency for the male. The manifest absence, indeed even dismissal, of this story and of the Bacchic-Dionysian alternative for Lucrece has been reproduced in the invisibility of any alternative to the doubled act of violence against the female body (rape and suicide) in the critical reception of *Lucrece.* This invisibility makes possible feminist readings of the poem that, while quite correctly pointing out that both Roman and early modern women were trapped in positions of victimization by historical and cultural circumstance, at the same time fail to locate an alternative to that position either for earlier women or for modern readers. It also underlies interpretations of the text such as those by Sam Hynes or Richard Levin. Hynes's 1959 article "The Rape of Tarquin" sees the rape of Lucrece as symbolic of "the spiritual quality in Tarquin which his deed violates"; the scene of violence to women is read as a metaphor of the importance for men of preserving their "own moral sense."[61] Levin's reading of *Lucrece* in his 1981 essay similarly elides (perhaps unwittingly) the brutality of rape by excluding any readings of the poem that do not understand the heroine and others like her as "models of [and for] their sex."[62]

Caught in the scholarly crossfire between readings that see no escape from the position of victim and readings that represent victimization as noble, both beginning and advanced readers of *Lucrece* may be forced into a position of critical identification with and reproduction of the Roman matron's suicidal politics as long as the fragments of the Philomela scenario in the poem are left unexamined. The tradition of violent women, present in *Lucrece*'s sources but only partially visible in the text, deserves to be unearthed. Historical readings of these sources such as the present one make it possible to excavate their foundations in order to uncover an image of woman that is "not one"—that is, neither exclusively, naturally, or necessarily victimized nor the unwilling accomplice in the reproduction of patriarchy's political forms.

Notes

1. The sources for Shakespeare's *Lucrece* have been discussed by T.W. Baldwin in *On the Literary Genetics of Shakspere's Poems & Sonnets* (Urbana, IL, 1950), 97-153; and by Geoffrey Bullough in *Narrative and Dramatic Sources of Shakespeare,* 8 vols. (London and New York, 1957-75), 1:179-99. Hans Galinsky investigates the Lucretia tradition in *Der Lucretia-Stoff in der Weltliteratur* (Breslau, 1932), as does Ian Donaldson in *The Rapes of Lucretia: A Myth and its Transformations* (Oxford, 1982). The story is conventionally recognized as political in the versions by Livy and Dionysius of Halicarnassus and as sentimental in the version by Ovid. Critics rarely note the political context in Ovid, even though this context, conveyed in the description of the origins of the *Regifugium* feast, is central. See below, p. 321.

2. On Machiavelli's use of the Lucretia story in Book 3 of the *Discourses* and in *Mandragola,* see Hanna Fenichel Pitkin, *Fortune is a Woman: Gender and Politics in the Thought of Niccolò Machiavelli* (Berkeley, Los Angeles, and London, 1984), 111-12. On Coluccio Salutati's political reading of the Lucretia story in *Declamatio Lucretiae* (c. 1496), see Stephanie H Jed, *Chaste Thinking: The Rape of Lucretia and the Birth of Humanism* (Bloomington and Indianapolis, IN, 1989). Unless otherwise noted, all quotations of Shakespeare follow the *Riverside Shakespeare,* ed. G. Blakemore Evans (Boston, 1974).

3. The same mechanism of inclusion followed by refusal shapes the text of *Titus* as well. There the example of Lucrece is invoked multiple times (4.1.63-64, 90-91, for example) only to be rejected in favor of the Philomela option in 5.2. Although it is not how I proceed in the present essay, a comparative study of the two texts, *Lucrece* and *Titus,* and of their interdependence specifically in producing images of women's "legitimate" reaction to rape is a desideratum. Additionally, a historical investigation of their varying receptions might reveal which scenarios of female behavior are considered "proper" and for whom. J.C. Maxwell, editor of the Arden *Titus* (London and New York, 1987), would discourage such comparisons. He takes pains to try to separate the play from the poem in matters of dating (xxiv) and speaks of a scholar's "natural reluctance" to attribute the play to Shakespeare (xx).

4. McEachern, "Fathering Herself: A Source Study of Shakespeare's Feminism," *Shakespeare Quarterly* 39 (1988): 269-90, esp. 269 and 272. McEachern's argu-

ment that Shakespeare challenges the patriarchal attitudes present in the sources of *Much Ado About Nothing* and *King Lear* and is thus not as complicit in the reproduction of patriarchy as some feminist critics have claimed is convincing, but it can be challenged by examining his interaction with and transformation of the sources for *Lucrece.* Of course Shakespeare is not monolithic and can himself be read, in McEachern's words, as a "document" of the "contradictions, inconsistencies, and incongruities" of Renaissance gender ideology (270-71).

5. Gillian Murray Kendall writes of the "textual choice" that Titus makes to "remember" or invoke one specific source for and version of the story of the Roman woman, Virginia, rather than any of the many others available at the time; see "'Lend me thy hand': Metaphor and Mayhem in *Titus Andronicus,*" *SQ* 40 (1989): 299-316, esp. 313.

6. See Sigmund Freud, "Civilization and its Discontents" in *The Standard Edition of the Complete Psychological Works of Sigmund Freud,* ed. and trans. James Strachey and Anna Freud, 24 vols. (London, 1953-74), 21:57-243. On Freud's use of the image of Rome as an archaeological site, see Marjorie Garber, *Shakespeare's Ghost Writers: Literature as uncanny causality* (New York and London, 1987), 52-54; and David Damrosch, "The Politics of Ethics: Freud and Rome" in *Pragmatism's Freud: The Moral Disposition of Psychoanalysis,* Joseph H. Smith and William Kerrigan, eds. (Baltimore and London, 1986), 102-25. I am grateful to Kelley Delaney of the University of California, Irvine, for the Damrosch reference.

7. See Freud, "Female Sexuality," 21:225-43; and Luce Irigaray, *Ce Sexe Qui n'en Est Pas Un* (Paris, 1977), 21-32.

8. See Kahn, "The Rape in Shakespeare's *Lucrece,*" *Shakespeare Studies* 9 (1976): 45-72.

9. See Baldwin, *Literary Genetics,* 99. See also Richard Levin's essay "The Ironic Reading of *The Rape of Lucrece* and the Problem of External Evidence" (*Shakespeare Survey* 34 [1981]: 85-92) for an attack on critics who claim to be interested in "reconstructing the historical meaning of the poem" (85). Levin's own definition of a historical approach to the text is as limited as Baldwin's, although in a different way.

10. See Eagleton, *Marxism and Literary Criticism* (Berkeley and Los Angeles, 1976), 34-35.

11. The notion of the hybrid text is based on my understanding of the implications of Donna Haraway's classic essay "A Manifesto for Cyborgs: Science, Technology, and Socialist Feminism in the 1980s" in *Coming to Terms: Feminism, Theory, Politics,* Elizabeth Weed, ed. (New York and London, 1989), 173-204; Haraway offers a theory of intertextuality appropriate to the insights provided by postmodern theory.

12. On reading texts for such lost scenarios, see Julia Reinhard Lupton, "Afterlives of the Saints: Hagiography in *Measure for Measure*," *Exemplaria: A Journal of Theory in Medieval and Renaissance Studies* 2 (1990): 375-401, esp. 380.

13. *Metamorphoses,* trans. Frank Justus Miller, vols. 3 and 4 of *Ovid in Six Volumes,* ed. G.P. Goold, The Loeb Classical Library (Cambridge, MA, and London, 1984-89). Unless otherwise noted, all quotations of the *Metamorphoses* will follow this edition and will be cited parenthetically in the text by book and line number.

14. "*Bruto libertatem debemus, Lucretiae Brutum*"; see Seneca, "To Marcia: On Consolation" ("*Ad Marciam De Consolatione*"), *Moral Essays,* ed. and trans. John W. Basore, 3 vols. (Cambridge, MA, 1951), 2:1-97, esp. 48-49. For Brutus as Lucretia's "first imitator," see Judith Still, "Lucretia's Silent Rhetoric," *Oxford Literary Review* 6, 2 (1984): 70-86, esp. 84. On Brutus's visibility in the political tradition, see Jed, 11.

15. I am grateful to J. Hillis Miller for calling my attention to how the musical imagery ironizes the relationship between Lucrece and Philomela at this point in the text. The two distinct ways in which they sing of rape nevertheless also point to how the two tales ultimately depend on one another, as do the two parts of the song.

16. In apparent response to the critical tradition that interprets Shakespearean texts as the site of women's silencing, Maus and Bromley both take the reference to Philomela in *Lucrece* as the occasion to point to places in the text where a female protagonist does gain a voice. They disagree, however, on Lucrece's relationship to Ovid's character. For Maus, Lucrece is like Philomela, while for Bromley they are more different than alike; see Maus, "Taking Tropes Seriously: Language and Violence in Shakespeare's *Rape of Lucrece,*" *SQ* 37 (1986): 66-82, esp. 73; and Bromley, "Lucrece's Re-Creation," *SQ* 34 (1983): 200-211. Nancy Vickers discusses the legend of the bird-woman briefly in her analysis of some of the sonnets but does not comment on its presence in *Lucrece;* see "'The blazon of sweet beauty's best': Shakespeare's *Lucrece*" in *Shakespeare and the Question of Theory,* Patricia Parker and Geoffrey Hartman, eds. (New York and London, 1985), 95-115. Parker builds on Vickers's interpretation of *Lucrece* by explicating the sociopolitical and rhetorical structures of gendered "commodification" that drive the rhetorical "displays" Vickers analyzes; see Parker's "Rhetorics of Property: Exploration, Inventory, Blazon," *Literary Fat Ladies: Rhetoric, Gender, Property* (London and New York, 1987), 126-54, esp. 126-31.

17. While Patricia Klindienst Joplin considers the truncation of the Philomela legend in Shakespeare's version to be revealing, she does not pursue this critical lacuna in her essay. Joplin's article is not really about Shakespeare's *Lucrece,* which is mentioned only in a note; see "The Voice of the Shuttle is Ours," *Stanford Literature Review* 1 (1984): 25-53, esp. 30 and 31, n. 11.

18. Lucrece identifies herself as a text several times, as in "The light will show, character'd in my brow, / The story of sweet chastity's decay . . ." (ll. 807-8), and in her challenge that the text of her suicide be "read" by others (l. 1195).

19. For another reading of the Troy ekphrasis as politically effective, see S. Clark Hulse, "'A Piece of Skilful Painting' in Shakespeare's *Lucrece,*" *SS* 31 (1978): 13-22. For Hulse, Lucrece is invested with agency only through her "power . . . in the realm of art" (21), an art that ultimately remains no more than art for art's sake. For a discussion of texts and images that represent women's weaving as subversive in a different way, see Georgianna Ziegler, "Penelope and the Politics of Woman's Place in the Renaissance" in *Gloriana's Face: Women, Public and Private, in the English Renaissance,* S.P. Cerasano and Marion Wynne-Davies, eds. (Detroit, 1992), 25-46.

20. Lucrece's suicide means the continuation of phallocratic forms of government despite the fact that it causes the shift from tyranny to a republic, since the two forms of political organization differ only externally and do not challenge the transfer of power from male to male (see pp. 317-18, below). In *Titus Andronicus* (5.2. 166-205), of course, the power to avenge is once again wrested out of a woman's hand in intertextual fashion, so to speak, as Titus himself declares that he will usurp "Progne's" role (l. 195) in the act of dismemberment and cooking.

21. On the significance of the details of these echoes of sacrificial practice, see pp. 318-20, below.

22. It is probably not by chance that the lines that follow the Philomela story tell of the subsequent early death of her and Procne's father, Pandion of Athens (*Metamorphoses* VI, ll. 675-76). Here, too, the male leader who has held his power only by engaging in the "traffic in women" meets an early end. For an analysis of Pandion's actions in marrying Procne to Tereus in the first place, see Joplin, 31-38.

23. See Baldwin, *Literary Genetics:* "there is only a bare mention of the Tereus story in *Lucrece.* Lucrece simply calls on Philomel to sing of Tereus while she sings of Tarquin (1128-48), but does not go into the story" (132). Bullough fails to even mention the bird-woman by name: "The end of the night takes Lucrece's mind back to the nightingale (which had ended 'The well-tun'd warble of her nightly sorrow' [1080]) and the likeness between Tarquin and Tereus (1133-34)" (1:181).

24. On the "chastening" of Brutus, who rebukes the "effeminate" tears of Lucretius and Collatine in Livy and Shakespeare, see Jed, 10-11.

25. Baldwin, *Literary Genetics,* 132.

26. "[F]allimur, an veris praenuntia venit hirundo / nec metuit, ne qua versa recurrat hiems? / saepe tamen, Procne, nimium properasse quereris, / virque tuo Tereus frigore laetus erit" (Fasti, trans. James George Frazer, vol. 5 of Ovid in Six Volumes [cited in n. 13 above]). Unless otherwise noted, all quotations of Fasti will follow this edition and will be cited parenthetically in the text by book and line number.

27. Baldwin, *Literary Genetics,* 99.

28. Baldwin, *Literary Genetics,* 153. For Baldwin's discussion of the "variorum Ovid," see 106. According to Marsus himself, his glosses on the Fasti first appeared in 1482. Here I quote the edition printed in Milan in 1510. On the history of editions of Ovid's *Fasti,* see P. Ovidius Naso, *Die Fasten, Herausgegeben, übersetzt, und kommentiert von Franz Bömer,* 2 vols. (Heidelberg, 1957), 1:56-57. In the 1482 edition of the *Fasti* printed in Venice, Marsus comments: *"Anni. Mcccclxxxii annotamus quo quidem anno haec excripsimus & imprimenda dedimus."* I consulted the Bodleian copy of the 1482 edition (Shelfmark Auct. O 2, 23) and the Tübingen copies of the 1510 (Shelfmark Ce 425 R) and the 1550 (Shelfmark Ce 417 R) editions.

29. fol. 74ʳ. Abbreviations in the Latin original have been silently expanded.

30. fol. 74ᵛ; my translation.

31. *Fasti* II, l. 629; my translation.

32. For Marsus's commentary on *Fasti* II, l. 629, see the 1510 Milan edition, fol. 67ʳ. English translations of his commentary are my own.

33. See Cooper, *Dictionarium Historicum & Poeticum,* "Philomela." All Cooper citations refer to individual entries in the *Dictionarium,* reprinted as part of the *Thesaurus Linguae Romanae et Britannicae* (Menston, UK, 1969), No. 200 in *English Linguistics 1500-1800: A Collection of Facsimile Reprints,* comp. and ed. R.C. Alston. The manuscript abbreviation *!!emacr!* has been expanded to either *en* or *em* throughout. According to Alston's prefatory note to the 1969 edition, Cooper's 1565 *Thesaurus* was reprinted in 1573, 1578, 1584 (twice), and 1587.

34. The important exception to this standard version of the story is, of course, the Philomela-Lucrece connection in John Quarles's *Tarquin Banished,* printed along with *Lucrece* in the 1655 edition, in which an angry band of nightingales swarms around Tarquin and "pickt out his eyes." Quarles's text is available in *A New Variorum Edition of Shakespeare: The Poems,* ed. Hyder Edward Rollins (Philadelphia and London, 1938), 439-46, esp. 445.

35. On Lactantius, see Christian Gottlieb Jöcher, *Allgemeines Gelehrten-Lexicon,* 2 vols. (Leipzig, 1750-51; rpt. 1960), 2:2570; and on Regius, see *Contemporaries of Erasmus: A Biographical Register of the Renaissance and Reformation,* Peter G. Bietenholz

and Thomas B. Deutscher, eds., 3 vols. (Toronto, 1986-87), 3:134.

36. fol. 139; my translation. I consulted the Tübingen copy of the 1543 Basel edition of the *Metamorphoses* (Shelfmark Ce 410 fol. R). Abbreviations in the Latin original have been silently expanded.

37. Baldwin maintains that Shakespeare was familiar with Regius's commentary; see *William Shakspere's Small Latine and Lesse Greeke,* 2 vols. (Urbana, IL, 1944), 2:439.

38. fol. 140; my translation. Abbreviations in the Latin original have been silently expanded.

39. Cf. fol. 145.

40. See Taylor, "Golding's Ovid, Shakespeare's 'Small Latin', and the Real Object of Mockery in 'Pyramus and Thisbe,'" *SS* 42 (1989): 53-64. Even Taylor indirectly acknowledges that Shakespeare would have resorted to some versions of the *Metamorphoses* in Latin; "for *Metamorphoses* . . . he used the original or Golding. . . . In his case, however, a comparative lack of facility in reading Latin probably accentuated the use of a favoured translation like Golding" (54, n. 12).

41. Carlo Ginzburg has suggested comparing philology (and with it the question of sources) with the other so-called "conjectural sciences" of archaeology and psychoanalysis, all of which are based on the study of fragments, traces, as symptomatic evidence of historical occurrences. Such traces can be read as "revealing clues" (11) about the nature of origins that are manifestly absent from the present of the text; see "Morelli, Freud and Sherlock Holmes: Clues and Scientific Method," *History Workshop* 9 (1980): 5-36.

42. Gayle Rubin, "The Traffic in Women: Notes on the 'Political Economy' of Sex" in *Towards An Anthropology of Women,* Rayna R. Reiter, ed. (New York, 1975), 157-210.

43. Detienne, "Culinary Practices and the Spirit of Sacrifice" in *The Cuisine of Sacrifice among the Greeks,* Marcel Detienne and Jean-Pierre Vernant, eds., trans. Paula Wissing (Chicago and London, 1989), 1-20, esp. 1. Below I also cite Detienne's essay in the same volume, "The Violence of Wellborn Ladies: Women in the Thesmophoria," 129-47.

44. For the distinction between the Greek and Roman festivals, see the excellent entry on the Dionysia in *Harper's Dictionary of Classical Literature and Antiquities,* Harry Thurston Peck, ed. (New York, Cincinnati, and Chicago, 1963), 520-22.

45. The buried presence of the Bacchic tradition in Renaissance texts is worth further consideration. Richard Halpern's investigation of the "Dionysian mythology" that Milton's *A Mask* "half-invokes in order to suppress" offers a fine example of how to structure such an investigation; see "Puritanism and Maenadism in *A Mask*" in *Rewriting the Renais-*

sance: The Discourses of Sexual Difference in Early Modern Europe, Margaret W. Ferguson, Maureen Quilligan, and Nancy J. Vickers, eds. (Chicago and London, 1986), 88-105, esp. 89.

46. Detienne, "Culinary Practices," 3 and 8.

47. For above quotations, see Detienne, "Wellborn Ladies," 131 and 133, respectively.

48. Detienne, "Culinary Practices," 2.

49. See Pais, *Ancient Legends of Roman History* (1905), trans. Mario E. Cosenza (Freeport, NY, 1971), 189-97: "In the earliest history of the Roman Republic we frequently meet with legends whose origins were due to imported Greek myths. From such legends there are later developed events that are historical in appearance. . . . The stories of Lucretia and of Virginia are thus but later elaborations of legends related to the cults of Ardea which were transplanted to Rome in the second half of the fourth century. The cults of all the neighboring Latin cities were, at different times, similarly transferred to the capital of Latium. Therefore, it is fully intelligible how, in adapting itself to new soil, the myth should have been enriched with new elements of local color, and how various touches, historical in character, were added by the annalists of the second and first centuries B.C." (193 and 197).

50. See Frazer's illuminating notes on the *Regifugium* in his appendix to *Fasti,* 2:394-97.

51. See the entries on *incesto* and *incestum* in the *Oxford Latin Dictionary,* where the scope of incest is represented as having been understood widely as any form of "improper sexual relations." Kahn devotes considerable attention to the infringement on Collatine's and Tarquin's "friendship" (52-55) but does not note that they are related, both in Ovid and in *Lucrece.*

52. Livy, I, 57, and I, 60.

53. On Constantius, see Jöcher, 1:2070. Antonius Constantius's commentary on the *Fasti* was first published in Venice in 1502; his notes appear alongside Marsus's in most sixteenth-century editions. Abbreviations in the Latin original have been silently expanded.

54. fol. 72[r].

55. Cooper, *Dictionarium,* "Lucretia."

56. Kahn, 60-61.

57. Livy I, 33.

58. Kahn, 55.

59. Brutus's oath is similar to the one sworn over Caesar's corpse in *Julius Caesar,* 3.2.105-10.

60. The absence of Hecuba's story from the Troy ekphrasis and from critical treatments of that portion of the poem seems to parallel the pattern of elision of the full Philomela tale in *Lucrece* and in *Lucrece* criticism. A similar story could be told of the "historical" presence of an angry and vengeful Hecuba in the margins of *Lucrece.* Cooper wrote of Hecuba in his entry on Polydorus: "queene Hecuba scratched out the eies of Polymnestor." Euripides's *Hekabe,* in which the vengeance scene is described at length, had been available in multiple editions since 1503, among them Erasmus's Latin translation, published by Froben in 1524. See Kjeld Matthiessen, *Studien zur Textüberlieferung der Hekabe des Euripides* (Heidelberg, 1974), 19-22. Ovid also retells Hecuba's tale in *Metamorphoses* XIII, the text Baldwin explicitly refers to as the "source" for the Troy scene. But Baldwin neglects to address the differences between the silent, victimized Hecuba of Shakespeare's text and the violent Hecuba who appears in the source (*Literary Genetics,* 142-46).

61. See Hynes, "The Rape of Tarquin," *SQ* 10 (1959): 451-53, esp. 453.

62. Levin, 89.

Stephen J. Carter (essay date 1995)

SOURCE: "Lucrece's Gaze," in *Shakespeare Studies,* Vol. 23, 1995, pp. 210-21.

[*In the following essay, Carter argues that once Tarquin has defined Lucrece in traditional, patriarchal terms by raping her, she redefines herself by placing her consciousness within the painting of Troy on a wall in her home, identifying with the painting's subjects and thereby preparing herself for her suicide at the close of the poem.*]

I

In Shakespeare's *The Rape of Lucrece* Tarquin's and Lucrece's acts of seeing precede their speaking. I shall argue that a specific, constructed experience of social space *produces* their ability to speak through a sequence of narratable actions. This spatial figuration projects along gender lines. How vision is socially put together reveals the linguistic means by which Lucrece, Tarquin, 'their' narrator, and the narrative's audience come to be screens for the imaginal projection of gender.

A useful beginning may be to investigate the phenomenological acquisition of sight as documented in clinical situations. When patients who had been blind from birth first started receiving cataract operations, records of the doctors' reports on the patients' progress were collected in a study by Marius von Senden.[1] As it turned out, such "newly sighted" patients were not merely confronting a surfeit of new, different data. Their task was to learn a thoroughly new intellectual skill: how to put together the vast sensory experience contained in even the simplest, smallest movement of one's body through space. Their experience constitutes persuasive evidence that we are "taught" to posit not only an objective world outside ourselves, but also, and perhaps more importantly, a curiously objective gender inside, inseparable from our experience of being subjects. "I showed her my hand," wrote one of the doctors of a patient,

> and asked her what it was; she looked long at it, without saying a word; I then took her own hand and held it before her eyes, she said with a deep sigh: 'That's my hand.' A blind person has no exact idea even of the shape of his own body; so that I first had to hold her own hand before her in order for her to recognize mine as a hand also.[2]

The patient could be described as passing through Lacan's mirroring ego-ideal stage; she *emerges* on this side of what she sees, as a subject—opposite to and abstracted from a constructed tableau. To see, in a sense, is to be the author of oneself. Another patient described seeing

> an extensive field of light, in which everything appeared dull, confused, and in motion. He could not distinguish objects.[3]

In the course of time, however, by trial and error s/he learns to pick out such static patterns of nonmovement from the swirling of forms and colors: objects. This, as noted above, can be interpreted as the initiating, establishing event in subjectivity, setting in motion all of a life's subsequent events. Like vision, then, *being* a subject is an acquired mental process, a process of mirroring. A subject/object grid is deployed between observer and observed, such that vision does not merely interpret, but organizes, in effect produces, our social, gendered reality.

This process of linking with one's reality effects a cognitive "lack of being," the recognition that one's "realization lies in another actual or imaginary space."[4] Such a patient, like Lacan's infant,

> only sees [his] form as more or less total and unified in an external image, in a virtual, alienated ideal unity [. . .][5]

—in a mirror. The "gendered Other" gazes at his/her untouchable virtuality. Male/female as Other only knows itself by the mediating image(s) it has of the mirror-subject. It knows what it is by what it is not. This "lack of being" is initiated by, produced, and grows *with* one's capacity for sight. A patient's lack—this "rushing in" of gender—occurs in the act of making himself real in an imaginary space.

In *The Rape of Lucrece* this spatial metaphorizing of gender is apparent in the linguistically partitioned actions, and therefore the identities, of the two primary characters, Lucrece and Tarquin. I shall focus primarily, though not exclusively, on the scene of Lucrece "reading" the wall painting in which Troy's defeat is depicted. I shall argue that in her surveying of the painting—in her return from a journey into sightedness—she constructs herself as a rhetorical, gendered Other, whom she then projects back into herself as subject. As a subject she becomes a "newly

sighted" space that frames what might be termed her former feminine unseen-ness. By examining the tension between the rhetorical and painterly registers in this passage (spoken by Lucrece and the narrator), in the context of its ordering of narrative voices, I shall reconstruct the means of her transformation.

II

The story of Lucrece would have been well-known to Elizabethan audiences. Its passive/active linking of her rape/suicide was left largely unquestioned. The presumed choice presented in the poem between death or shame was a foregone conclusion. The theological position counseled choosing shame, of which one could be shriven, over suicide, a mortal sin. Preferring death implied that rape was necessarily, regardless of the purity of mind, a pollution of the *body's* chastity, an effect which could not be undone. The Elizabethan audience could imagine, and perhaps praise, a woman's choosing a public transformation of unchastity through death, over the private shame of bodily pollution, however technically virtuous of mind she remains. A gap opens up here socially between an audience's deploying of a secular discourse within the larger theological context. The former produces a reading of female space as that which needed to be kept enclosed, unseen, pure—within a larger, allegedly protective male space. The latter, however, produces a reading that condemns Lucrece's actions as, in St. Augustine's view, a failure to see

> that while the sanctity of the soul remains even when the body is violated, the sanctity of the body is not lost; and that in like manner, the sanctity of the body is lost when the sanctity of the soul is violated, though the body itself remains intact.[6]

Shakespeare's text intriguingly anticipates and conflates these two readings. Lucrece's choice of suicide is *not* presented as the automatic secular choice it was assumed to be. The process of her reaching her decision is represented as a discursively critical task in which she challenges the casting of her rape as bodily pollution. The Elizabethan audience was potentially being made aware of its emphatically split reading: that she courageously chose and acted on a theologically incorrect reading, for which she could not be held responsible given the Roman setting of the story.

III

The activity of her "looking at" the wall painting occurs within a larger terrain of envisioning modes. These take many forms in the poem: the mutable register of Tarquin's gaze at Lucrece and Collatium's interior, and similarly of Lucrece's "regard" (for Tarquin, the Apostrophic objects, and the painting); the mind's eye of lust and shame, which as signifieds, look inward at their objects; the varied surfeit(s) of what is seen (focalized); and the presence of "painted" eyes within, and looking back from, the painting.

Jennie Tourel as Female Chorus, Regina Resnick as Lucretia, Harry Mossfield as Tarquinius, and John Vickers as Male Chorus in the Stratford Festival's 1956 production of The Rape of Lucretia.

The narrator gradually escalates the activity of Tarquin's 'seeing' of Lucrece: from his "wanton sight,"[7] to "lustful eye" (179), to "greedy eyeballs" (368), to "willful eye" (417), to "a cockatrice' dead-killing eye" (540). Such rhetorical anaphora proliferate in tandem with the violent expansion of Tarquin's envisioning space; his license to "look," to penetrate with ever greater intensity, inscribes his movement across and into the female space of corridors, doorways, and the bedchamber of Collatium, which enclose the chaste, untrespassed inner female space of Lucrece's body. The nature of his seeing—surveying and violently reaching out—is being employed here to construct a version of incursive male space.

Female space is possessed within the envisioning male, whether Collatine or Tarquin. As the signified within Tarquin's mind's eye, she contracts.

> Within his thought her heavenly image sits,
> And in the self-same seat sits Collatine.
> That eye which looks on her confounds his wits:

> That eye which him beholds, as more divine,
> Unto a view so false will not incline [,]
>
> (288-92)

Her eye (as his signified) "which him beholds" proceeds *to, but not beyond* the boundary of his inner gaze.

> But she that never cop'd with stranger eyes,
> Could pick no meaning from their parling looks,
> Nor read the subtle shining secrecies
> Writ in the glassy margents of such books.
> She touch'd no unknown baits, nor fear'd no hooks,
>   Nor could she moralize his wanton sight,
>   More than [that] his eyes were opened to the light.
>
> (99-105)

Her enclosed passivity here seems to preclude any worldly understanding of what waits there to be read (or not) in his eyes and looks. Imposed chastity works to contain vision; it reverses the seeing/speaking progression for the female such that Lucrece literally does not see Tarquin's lust until he speaks it. Tarquin however is allowed to cross the boundary of his gaze, to pierce his own inner outrushing "look."

> Then looking scornfully, he doth despise
> His naked armor of still-slaughtered lust [,]
>
> (187-88)

An ineffectual armor against fear, his lust self-reflexively slaughters even as he inwardly gazes on its self-replenishing object.

Who does Tarquin rape? He rapes Collatium, the home and room, as female space. His vision precedes his movement through its corridors and doorways, pushing him steadily deeper into "her." He proceeds "As each unwilling portal yields him way" (309); he forces "The locks between her chamber and his will" (302); he ignores that "The threshold grates the door to have him heard" (306). He rapes as he sees.

> Now is he come unto the chamber door
> That shuts him from the heaven of his thought,
> Which with a yielding latch, and with no more,
> Hath barr'd him from the blessed thing he sought.
>
> (337-40)

What he sees/rapes is nothing less than the patriarchically programmed, enclosed, inrushing space of the constructed feminine. Georgianna Ziegler[8] draws on Peter Stallybrass's useful analogy between Bakhtin's notion of the grotesque, and the Renaissance reading of female vision—the grotesque as transgressive, anti-hierarchical, unfinished, obscene.[9] Such potentiality within female space is normatively constrained by patriarchy—"her signs are the enclosed body, the closed mouth, the locked house."[10] Rape becomes a rending of gendered space; what undergoes pollution is not a body, but a patriarchal construction of female space her "body" occupies.

IV

What is our response upon viewing an effectively conceived and executed visual representation? Writing on narrative painting, Leonardo da Vinci states that if the work

> represents terror, fear, flight, sorrow, weeping, and lamentation; or pleasure, joy, laughter and similar conditions, the minds of those who *view* it ought to make their limbs *move* so that they seem to find themselves in the same situation which the figures in the narrative painting represent.[11]
>
> (italics mine)

As an *audience* before the Troy painting Lucrece herself does this, and more. We need to observe, however tritely, that she must have walked by this artwork, glanced at it, and doubtless viewed it at length on countless occasions during the years she lived at Collatium. Yet on this occasion she deliberately seeks it out. Faced by a representation-as-event, one that exerts a gradually

intensifying, cathecting hold on her, she experiences herself mimicing and voicing the physiological and emotional states of its varied characters. In doing so she temporarily *steps into* the representation. Not surprisingly, the meaning she makes of herself in the painting is to a considerable degree determined by the remembered image of the violence of her rape—an image, some critics argue, unduly "stimulated" by her own language.

"Narratives," as R. Rawdon Wilson claims, can "catch, hold, illude, and frequently delude their narratees."[12] The painting-as-narrator tells Lucrece her own story. Moreover, being "caught" by an ostensible illusion can work no less genuine a transformation on a viewer/listener than that worked by a real sight. The Trojan figures she moves among open up and frame Lucrece's own narrative, that is the internal struggle between the two poles of violence she endures, rape and suicide. The gaze of the text-as-narrator at the painting (over Lucrece's shoulder) directs, constructs, and contains her (and our) gaze.

Let us take a brief, initial "wide-angle" look at the sweep of narration, Apostrophic address and prosopopoeic voice that speak in this scene of the "skillful painting." First the narrator throws his peripatetic, focalizing eye here and there over the painting in a cinematic manner—panning, cutting, tracking in and back, tilting—that gradually escalates. The linguistic effect of installing vision in this way intensifies the very reality (not the realism) of the representation, opening up a space in her own enclosed image of self.

It is during *her* first narration of (and address to) the painting that Lucrece, in effect, crosses over into what she sees, and also into herself as representation (Other). Indeed, the rhetorical features of her speech in this passage emphasize an emerging detachment from female space.

In the narrator's second passage, half the length of the first, Lucrece's impassioned response from within the painting is narrated. The text implements Simonides's aphorism mentioned earlier when Lucrece prosopopoeically gives language to the silent, painted figures, who in turn give to her her own movements and expressions. The narrator's language rearranges Lucrece's reality within her reading of the painting and herself. However, in her second passage, in which Lucrece responds emphatically to the artist's perjury of Sinon's face (linking Sinon to Tarquin), she takes control of her own seeing by the linguistic rearranging of what she sees.

In the narrator's third passage Lucrece is represented as having pulled back from her former rage, directed not only at Sinon/Tarquin, but also at the circumstances of her own (now oblique) "story."

The possibility of conferring worldhood on her own story, a place to which she returns from the embedded narrative of the painting, undergoes an anachronic shift. The space Lucrece's newly sighted eyes now project has little in common with her former world. At the moment of her death her language, actions, and seeing have a curious unity that allows us in, while holding back the males present in the scene.

V

Let us now "track in" for a closer look at the rhetorical, visual, and narrative components of each of these passages in the wall painting scene. In the narrator's first passage (1366-1463) we are gradually introduced to the "skillful painting." The narrator's initial, tentative address to the reader, "These *might* you see [. . .] / " (1380), "That one *might* see [. . .] / " (1386), and "You *might* behold [. . .] / " (italics mine) acknowledge the painting as "mere" representation, of which we are rightly to be skeptical. By the midpoint of this passage, however, by a grammatical shifting from the conditional to the simple past, the language inserts us into that representation.

This process is emphasized in the cinematic movement of narrative focus. Whom and what do we see? The most visual sequence within this passage directs our eye as follows: a "medium shot" on

> Ajax and Ulysses, O what art
> Of physiognomy might one behold!
>
> (1394);

CUT to a "close shot" on

> The face of either cipher'd either's heart
>
> (1396);

CUT to an 'extreme close' on

> Ajax' eyes blunt rage and rigor roll'd
>
> (1398);

PAN to

> the mild glance that smiling Ulysses lent.
>
> (1399);

CUT to a "medium" on Nestor; PULL BACK to a "long" to bring into frame the silent, listening faces of the soldiers; and follow with a slow "pan" among

> The scalps of many, almost hid behind,
> To jump up higher seem'd to mock the mind.
>
> (1413-14)

With this there is a shift back, in language, from what occurs in the painting-as-narrative to a look at the painter's technique itself. A subsequent description of the painterly device of *overlap* intensifies this:

> That for Achilles' image stood his spear,
> Grip'd in an armed hand, himself behind
> Was left unseen, save to the eye of the mind[:]
>
> (1424-26)

Space, in effect, is being constructed through an acknowledgement of what perception contributes—our learning to view the real in fragments. Fragments imply gaps; the text signals that what is "left unseen" is where the reader's role enters, to fill in such space. A whole is merely a consensus among the senses of a thing "they" willfully put together. From the poem's above-noted technical description of painterly special effects there is a further shift to the description of the Trojan mothers' contradictory spectatorship:

> And from the walls of strong-besieged Troy,
> When their brave hope, bold Hector, march'd to field,
> Stood many Troyan mothers, sharing joy
> To see their youthful sons bright weapons wield,
> And to their hope they such odd action yield
>   That through their light joy seemed to appear
>   (Like bright things stain'd) a kind of heavy fear.
>
> (1429-35)

We are compelled to read in both directions here. Our line of sight travels to the walls, and from there to the field, simultaneously reflected back from the "light" of the "bright weapons" to the mothers' eyes. Is vision an inter-subjective agency, or an activity by which space invents itself between two sites of seeing? It would seem that we learn not to see how we have learned to see.

This progress of the first passage—a pull back from the painted representation as deep cinematic reality, to a framing of technique, and back again to a framing of the problematics of vision itself—leaves the reader at a considerable distance from Lucrece. We hear and see her identification with Hecuba, yet cannot follow her as she crosses over.

Escalating rhetorical density has a stroboscopic effect on the space this passage produces, as demonstrated in: the piling on of anaphora (1467-8) in her first stanza, the chiasmus (1475-6) in the second, an epanalepsis (1480) in the third, and the combined anaphora and assonance (1487-8) in the fourth, each involving variations on the strategic repetition of key words. Critical opinion has often tended to resist the reflexivity of rhetorical forms, arguing that rhetoric closes down the possibilities for the development of narrative and character otherwise present in a scene. All language, however, has a rhetorical dimension, of which audiences choose to be aware. Lucrece's rhetoricity can perhaps best be read as her awareness of her own transformation. She *knows* she can step outside her ideologically grounded female space, yet she also knows she cannot escape the similarly grounded expectations her social frame places on her.

The chiasmus of her second stanza warrants more specific attention.

> Thy eye kindled the fire that burneth here,
>   And here in Troy, for trespass of thine eye[,]
>
> (1475-76)

It is Paris's inescapable, space-making eye that activates lust and destruction (of Helen and Troy), piercing, penetrating, fixing on its object: spatial absence as allotted the female. She sees that it is male envisioning that frames a woman's seeing and speech.

In the narrator's second passage Lucrece's intense sorrow over Troy's destruction is initially foregrounded. The literal sympathetic exchange between the silent painted figures and her rhetoricizing voice, "She lends them words, and she their looks doth borrow" (1498-9), removes her even further from our view. Her identification with the painting as embodying the Real, as being more than representation, reaches the stage where "Such signs of truth in his [Sinon's] plain face she spied" (1532) are such "That she concludes the picture was belied." (1533) She is seeing, in effect, two paintings—one she assembles in her mind (of which she is a part), and another she can designate as merely "the picture." The emphasis here on separating the painting (as embedded narrative) from Lucrece's viewing of it incites her to momentarily rescript Sinon's role in Troy's defeat. In the last stanza of this passage language rearranges both itself and Lucrece within what is (and is not) spoken.

> "It cannot be," quoth she, "that so much guile"—
> She would have said, "can lurk in such a look";
> But Tarquin's shape came in her mind the while,
> And from her tongue "can lurk" from "cannot" took:
> "It cannot be" she in that sense forsook,
> And turn'd it thus, "It cannot be, I find,
> But such a face should bear a wicked mind.
>
> (1534-40)

The active past tense is parried by the conditional past, what was spoken by what nearly was, the unspoken "can lurk" by the sense of the spoken "cannot." By the last two lines she recursively participates in the rearrangement of her own speech. With these spoken/unspoken phrases she gasps out her incredulity, her struggle with herself as narratee (after the spatial stroboscopy of the painting).

In her second narrative passage she responds directly to Sinon's treason, and commands herself to

> Look, look how list'ning Priam wets his eyes,
> To see those borrowed tears that Sinon sheeds!
>
> (1548-49)

By the end of this passage she is no longer having her speech rearranged *for* her, she actively rearranges what she says and sees in a complex series of inversions:

> Such devils steal effects from lightless hell,
> For Sinon in his fire doth quake with cold,
> And in that cold, hot burning fire doth dwell;
> These contraries such unity do hold
> Only to flatter fools, and make them bold:
> So Priam's trust false Sinon's tears doth flatter,
> That he finds means to burn his Troy with water.
>
> (1555-61)

She takes a certain distracted enjoyment in her ability to manipulate the painting's reality.

In the narrator's third passage her language and sight collide, as

> She tears she senseless Sinon with her nails,
> Comparing him to that unhappy guest
> Whose deed hath made herself herself detest.
>
> (1564-66)

The violence of her action returns her to 'herself'; she collapses back into the world of *her* narrative. Space contracts as, with the arrival of Collatine, Lucretius, and Brutus, the narrator pulls back slightly. A period of time is elided, "But now the mindful messenger, come back" (1583), until Collatine "[. . .] finds his Lucrece clad in mourning black." (1585) When she speaks next, it is to address her husband and his guests.

She has stepped back into her former space, but with a difference. She looks ahead to her suicide from a vantage in which the text conflates the pagan Roman and Augustinian readings of her story.

> Though my gross blood be stain'd with this abuse,
> Immaculate and spotless is my mind;
> That was not forc'd, that never was inclin'd
> To accessary yieldings, but still pure
> Doth in her poison'd closet yet endure.
>
> (1655-59)

She has come to see her pollution in Augustinian terms, that her virtue is untouched, yet the text acknowledges that this is still governed, framed by, her society.

She does not escape through death; nor does she become a symbol of Chastity for others to follow; nor indeed does she become an ironized subject in the text. Her suicide is a reassertion of the differently constructed space she sighted within the painting, and from which she returns, transformed.

Notes

1. Marius von Senden, *Space and Sight* (London: Methuen & Co. Ltd., 1960).

2. Ibid., 109.

3. Ibid., 130.

4. Bice Benvenuto and Roger Kennedy, *The Works of Jacques Lacan: An Introduction* (New York: St. Martin's Press, 1986), 55.

5. Senden, *Space and Sight,* 130.

6. *A Select Library of the Nicene and Post-Nicene Fathers of The Christian Church,* Vol. II, "St. Augustin's [*sic*] City of God and Christian Doctrine" Philip Schaff, ed. (Grand Rapids, Mich.: Wm. B. Eerdmans Publishing Co., 1956), 13.

7. William Shakespeare, *The Riverside Shakespeare,* ed. G. Blakemore Evans (Boston: Houghton Mifflin, 1974), 1. 104. All subsequent references to the poem will appear in the text of the paper.

8. Georgianna Ziegler, "My lady's chamber: female space, female chastity in Shakespeare" *Textual Practice* 4.1 (1990): 73-90.

9. I partially concur with the position Ziegler argues with reference to Stallybrass, however in her conclusion regarding "these two female poles" she seems to essentialize the female grotesque as the authentic pole opposite female enclosure as a constructed normative. Rather, both "poles" are equally such constructions.

10. Peter Stallybrass, "Patriarchal territories: The body enclosed", in *Rewriting the Renaissance,* ed. Margaret W. Ferguson (Chicago: University of Chicago Press, 1986), 124.

11. Leonardo da Vinci, *Treatise on Painting,* trans. by A. Philip McMahon (Princeton, N.J.: Princeton University Press, 1956), 110.

12. R. Rawdon Wilson, "Shakespearean Narrative: *The Rape of Lucrece* Reconsidered," *Studies in English Literature* 28 (1988): 55.

LANGUAGE AND IMAGERY

Heather Dubrow (essay date 2000)

SOURCE: "'This blemish'd fort': The Rape of the Hearth in Shakespeare's *Lucrece*," in *Form and Reform in Renaissance England: Essays in Honor of Barbara Kiefer Lewalski,* edited by Amy Boesky and Mary Thomas Crane, University of Delaware Press, 2000, pp. 104-26.

[*In the following essay, Dubrow observes that the invasion or destruction of public and private dwellings occurs repeatedly as an image in* The Rape of Lucrece; *she notes that this imagery is particularly poignant when it directly represents the fire of Tarquin's passion destroying the home that Lucrece has created and that her husband, Collatine, is meant to protect.*]

[The soul's] house is sack'd, her quite interrupted,
Her mansion batter'd by the enemy,
Her sacred temple spotted, spoil'd, corrupted,
Grossly engirt with daring infamy:
Then let it not be call'd impiety,
    If in this blemish'd fort I make some hole
    Through which I may convey this troubled soul.

(1170-1176)

I

Loss haunts *The Rape of Lucrece* as insistently and menacingly as it haunts the recently bereaved. And its sometime companion, recovery, plays as volatile and complex a role in the poem as in the trajectory of actual mourning. Staged repeatedly and overtly on the level of plot, the losses in the poem focus on the title character's deprivation of chastity as she conceives it and of life itself, but include as well that "thievish dog" (736) Tarquin's forfeiture of his integrity, Collatine's and Lucretius's privation of wife and daughter, and the multiple versions of absence associated with the depiction of Troy, itself a trace in sixteenth-century English culture.

The language of the poem also both inscribes and enacts other versions of loss. The movement from originary purity, noted by many critics,[1] is echoed in the decline from the stability and clarity implied by epithets and appository constructions like "Collatine's fair love, Lucrece the chaste" (7) to ironically ambiguous adjectives such as the reference to Sinon's "plain" (1532) countenance or Lucrece's "bright" (1213) weeping eyes. Previously analyzed by Joel Fineman in terms of erotic movements of crossing and folding and by myself in relation to tensions, rivalries, and border states, the rhetorical figure syneciosis also stages loss.[2] This trope links together opposites, with the oxymoron one of its most familiar incarnations and the tellingly entitled privative form "x-less x" its most characteristic manifestation in *The Rape of Lucrece*. For phrases like "helpless help" (1056) or "liveless life" (1374) themselves rob linguistically, taking away the word they seem to offer.

Of all the losses in the poem, however, those involving dwelling places are among the most significant.[3] The plot of the narrative pivots on Tarquin's threats to the home of Lucrece and Collatine. And on the rhetorical level tropes repeatedly evoke imperilled, corrupted, or destroyed dwellings: for example, Tarquin acknowledges that "his soul's fair temple is defaced" (719); his victim describes her body as a "polluted prison" (1726); and a number of images refer to fortresses (see, for example, ll. 28, 482), thus linking the public and private, as is so often the case in this text.

My aim in emphasizing such allusions is not to diminish the primacy or the poignancy of Lucrece's rape and suicide. Indeed, the attack on her home is often conflated with the assault on her body and being; the poem emphasizes that connection in the many references to Tarquin's forcing locks and more subtly conveys it in Lucrece's letter to her husband, where the second prepositional phrase in "So I commend me from our house *in grief*" (1308; italics inserted) could refer either to the mourning writer of the letter or the grieving house and thus links the two. The issue of threatened dwellings is important not least because it generates reinterpretations of the threatened human victim. In so doing, however, this topic also offers new and sometimes surprising perspectives on a number of other questions about the text, ranging from the workings of characteristic tropes and generic norms to the workings of male subjectivity.

To be sure, the role of houses and homes in the poem has not gone unnoticed. Important earlier analyses of *The Rape* of *Lucrece* have, as it were, opened the door to further discussions of that issue, with Coppélia Kahn identifying connections between Lucrece and the goddess Vesta, Katharine Maus observing the parallel between Lucrece's body and a house or fortress, Linda Woodbridge adducing anthropological theories of purity and contagion to connect the violation of the borders of the body and of a house, and Georgianna Zeigler encompassing this text when she discusses Shakespeare's conception of a private space.[4] Suggestive though all of these observations are, however, they touch only briefly on the issue of home in the course of other arguments, and hence they necessarily neglect certain perspectives that would variously expand, nuance, and challenge their assumptions. In particular, as I will demonstrate, archival documents on marriage crystallize complex relationships between home and protection, redefining the identification between a dwelling and the maternal body and insisting on cognate connections between lodgings and male subjectivity as well.

New historicism and feminism, the capacious homes that have nurtured so much important recent work in early modern studies, deserve credit for intensifying interest in such texts. Fully to understand the significance of dwelling places in *The Rape of Lucrece,* however, one also needs to return to intellectual homes from which many younger members of the profession have eagerly migrated, visiting the older-generation scholars still ensconced there either not at all or only for brief and tense holiday encounters—that is, source studies and close readings of literature. A *festschrift* is an appropriate occasion and *The Rape of Lucrece* an apt text for redefining the protocols of such visits. New historicism and feminism direct our attention to issues in the poem and its antecedents that might otherwise have been overlooked, while the putatively old-fashioned methods I have cited variously buttress and challenge certain presuppositions of new historicism and feminism. Above all, it is at the crossroads where all these approaches meet that we find questions about and answers to the twinned subjects on which this essay pivots: the gendered destruction of a house and the gendered construction of subjectivities.

II

Three intimately related tropes among the many figures crammed into this text particularly call for that sort of close analysis—and reward it by demonstrating why *The Rape of Lucrece* is so concerned with the loss of home and how that preoccupation relates to the representation of Lucrece:

> "If, Collatine, thine honor lay in me,
> From me by strong assault it is bereft:
> My honey lost, and I, a drone-like bee,
> Have no perfection of my summer left,
> But robb'd and ransack'd by injurious theft.
>   In thy weak hive a wand'ring wasp hath crept,
>   And suck'd the honey which thy chaste bee kept."
>
>   . . . . .

> Why should the worm intrude the maiden bud?
> Or hateful cuckoos hatch in sparrows' nests?
>
>   (834-40, 848-49)

Both the wasp and the cuckoo imperil a home (and one might more tentatively add that the innocence represented by the bud is frequently a characteristic associated with home). These lines indicate as well how and why dwellings are threatened throughout the poem. Each of these figures presents the nexus of intrusion, robbery, and contamination that recurs in the actual rape. The second and third suggest as well sexual violations—the destruction of purity and a threat to maternity—and in so doing demonstrate a propensity for seeing such transgressions in terms of that nexus. In the first case, that of the bee and the wasp, violation also involves an outsider threatening a rightful occupant, an analogue to military invasion, while in the instance of the cuckoo, the lawful owner is actually displaced. Homes no less than homelands are threatened by aliens, these figures suggest, and the desire for a dwelling, like other versions of desire, is triangulated in these tropes, as in many other Shakespearean passages.

A closer analysis demonstrates that lines 834-40 insistently establish Lucrece's vulnerability through not only overt statements but also grammatical patterns. After a conditional where the context encourages us to gloss "if" as "since," the trope proceeds to assume her guardianship of her husband's honor. She has internalized that patriarchal truism, an ironic assumption given that, as I will argue, the poem implies that his behavior has in fact threatened her honor in ways that render him a careless watchman at best. And his home has need of the most attentive sentinels. For the hive itself is "weak" (839), an allusion that may or may not refer to Lucrece herself. In any event, her own weakness is established in many other ways; here, as so often in the poem, threats to dwellings are associated not only with invaders but also with protectors who variously do not or cannot discharge their responsibility. At the beginning of the quotation she is not the subject of the main phrase but rather appears in short prepositional phrases ("in me, / From me" [834-35]), and, similarly, at the end she is the subject only of a relative clause ("which thy chaste bee kept" [840]). In the course of the passage, Lucrece is associated with a verb of possession, not action, "Have" (837). In the next line rather than writing "I am robb'd and ransack'd by injurious theft," Shakespeare leaves the first two of those words out: appropriately enough, both the noun and verb referring to her remain implicit, much as her subjectivity and agency have themselves been threatened by the rape. The character who will speak laments punctuated by exclamatory phrases, the character who will feel constrained to terminate her own self and her own future by suicide, here precisely mirrors those actions through her position in a world of adjectives rather than nouns and verbs. All this serves to emphasize the power of the wasp and the vulnerability of the bee.

In the succeeding image of the womb, the verb "intrude" (848) signals the many resonances of intrusion throughout the poem. In the late sixteenth century one meaning of *intrude* was "To thrust oneself into any benefice, possession, office, or dignity to which one has no title or claim; to usurp *on* or *upon*."[5] Hence the word itself links the political and domestic intrusions, two levels of the poem between which critics have sometimes felt obliged to choose.[6] "Maiden" (848) is apparently deployed here in two senses common in Shakespeare's period, "a young (unmarried) woman" or "a virgin";[7] thus this overtly sexual image, like the later reference to Lucrece's breasts as "maiden worlds" (408), associates this matron with not marital chastity but asexual or presexual purity.[8]

More to our purposes now, the line in question is succeeded immediately by the question, "Or hateful cuckoos hatch in sparrows' nests?" (849). "Hatch" plays the customary innocence of the newborn against the deceit aptly characterized by the adjective with which it alliterates. Aliens invade the nests as the wasp did the unfortunate hive, dispossessing the children who rightfully belong there. This figure anticipates the later allusion to the weasel, which was itself sometimes associated with usurping a nest.[9] And the figure looks forward as well to Lucrece's fears that her own children could be threatened by an illegitimate offspring if she has been impregnated. But the line surely also invokes the political undertones of "intrude," the threat of usurpation, again demonstrating the dovetailing of the political and domestic at many key moments in the poem.

Shakespeare's emphasis on a wife's obligation to protect her husband's honor and his home is hardly surprising. But juxtaposing his tropes with a particularly intriguing, though neglected, passage from the discourses of marriage nuances and complicates common critical generalizations about that responsibility. Preaching shortly after the marriage of Princess Elizabeth, John King, Bishop of London from 1611 to 1621, extends Psalm 128's brief characterization of the wife as a fruitful vine into a series of conceits suggesting that both the spouses are vines on the couple's house. Not surprisingly, in the instance of the wife he deploys the notion literally to naturalize her obligation to stay close to the house. More unexpectedly, he develops the psalm's procreative image into a trope of protectiveness. The female vine, King emphasizes, guards the house—transforming the dependency in a trope common to the epithalamium tradition, the woman as a vine clinging to her tree-like husband, into an image of strength and power: "We have found already that the *vine* is *sustentaculum* some kinde of stay and assistance to the house; 2. *umbraculum* an arbour or shade unto it; now 3. it is *propugnaculum*, being spred upon the sides of the house, a fense against the violence of the weather."[10] Rather than simply being protected from her own evil or threats from without by her house, as common generalizations about the early modern imperative to keep women inside would lead one to expect, the bride herself protects and even strengthens the house. Perhaps writing about a princess marrying a foreigner encouraged King to emphasize female power, and certainly the paradox of describing vines as powerful

shelters may suggest some ambivalences about female potency even when its exemplar is the daughter of the king of England. But the presence of passages emphasizing female power in many other marriage treatises discourages the reader from entirely explaining away King's image in those terms.[11]

Playing Shakespeare's rhetoric of female guardianship against King's, then, supports familiar commonplaces: the wife is responsible for preserving her spouse's honor, and this is figured in terms of safeguarding the home that safeguards her. At the same time, the passages demonstrate that on the issue of the female weakness that might interfere with the wife's role as sentinel and shelter the discourses in question are quite as complex and ambivalent as the expositions of male guardianship to which I will turn shortly. First of all, they do not necessarily stress such frailty to the extent facile generalizations about the early modern period might lead one to believe, as the citation from King and many other passages demonstrate. In evoking the potency of his vine by means of an image that risks compromising it, however, he gestures towards another type of complexity, more marked in texts other than his own: marriage manuals and sermons typically juxtapose celebrations of female moral and ethical agency with laments about women's incapacities.

Moreover, the discourses of marriage and related literary texts challenge some common interpretations of patriarchy in a second way that is equally germane to Shakespeare's figure of the bee: they differ significantly among and within themselves on how they deploy the limitations they do gender female. Accusations of moral weakness could be and often were used to blame the woman and justify suppression of her, another point to which I will shortly turn. Here, however, Shakespeare does not identify a culpable frailty whose name is woman but rather implies that the incapacity in question is more an inevitable physical limitation than a moral flaw. In fact, in a later passage he explicitly asserts,

> Then call them not the authors of their ill,
> No more than wax shall be accounted evil,
> Wherein is stamp'd the semblance of a devil.
>
> (1244-46)

The reference to the devil creates an unsettling conclusion despite its ostensible reassurance, again demonstrating ambivalence. But Shakespeare's overt and primary aim is to deny female culpability, presumably including women's guilt in situations where they fail in their role as guardians. Though the text elsewhere hints that Lucrece's naïveté makes her susceptible to the force and fraud of Tarquin, certainly its predominant and recurrent theme is her innocence of the guilt she attributes to herself.[12] This bee cannot be faulted in any major way for the intrusion of the wasp, as Lucrece herself acknowledges in lines 842-47.

In short, then, the tropes of the invasive wasp, worm, and cuckoo figure woman as guardian of a home subject to invasion. Shakespeare's text, unlike King's, emphasizes not only the wife's duty to protect that threatened dwelling but also her incapacity to do so. Men, too, are responsible for protecting nests and hives, the poem elsewhere suggests, and it proceeds to emphasize that they, unlike Lucrece, are deeply culpable for their failure in that role.

III

Five of the principal episodes in the poem—Collatine's initial exposure of his wife, Tarquin's rape, the descriptions of Troy, the conflict between Brutus and the familial mourners, and the political change at the conclusion of the narrative—involve to various degrees and on various levels the issue of home, exploring the responsibilities of male characters to guard it and in so doing further explicating the trope of the beleaguered bee. If, as Coppélia Kahn persuasively suggests, the story of Lucrece is "one of the founding myths of patriarchy,"[13] Shakespeare's rendition of that narrative emphasizes not only how that myth may attempt to justify rape, the point that Kahn stresses, but also how it may engender a responsibility to safeguard that, though potentially far more positive than the attitudes of a would-be rapist, is not wholly unproblematical even when it is successfully performed.[14]

In the Argument, which closely follows the version of the story in Livy's *Historia* and Ovid's *Fasti,* we learn that Collatine participates in—but apparently does not originate—a boasting contest that culminates in an apparently mutually agreed on trip back to Rome:

> In that pleasant humor they all posted to Rome, and intending by their secret and sudden arrival to make trial of that which every one had before avouched, only Collatinus finds his wife (though it were late in the night) spinning amongst her maids; the other ladies were all found dancing and revelling, or in several disports; whereupon the noblemen yielded Collatinus the victory, and his wife the fame. At that time Sextus Tarquinius being inflamed with Lucrece' beauty . . .

Focusing on Tarquin's response to the boast, the poem itself omits the trip to Rome; some critics believe it is implied, while others ground interpretations in the assumption that it never occurred.[15] Whichever of these positions one adopts, however, Shakespeare presents Collatine's behavior as imperiling not only Lucrece but also the home that encases and in some though not all senses represents her.

Extensive and often acute, previous commentary on his culpability has focused on the dangers of the boast, one of the most common and pernicious weapons in the deadly sport of male rivalry, and on the gaze that Collatine's vaulting language invites.[16] Though this perspective is valuable, it has directed attention away from a closely related but distinct consequence of the proud husband's behavior: that is, he invites not only gazing but also entry into a previously closed space, literally and metaphorically opening his home to those he should not have admitted. In

the Argument, he initially does so figuratively by boasting and hence inviting his listeners not only to look at Lucrece but also to look into the house that encases and in some senses represents her. He then literalizes these actions when he and his companions return to Rome. If, as readers have rightly noted, Tarquin's villainous passage through the house and into Lucrece's bedroom mimetically anticipates his sexual penetration of her, those actions are in turn proleptically mirrored by Collatine's opening of his home: a dubious version of hospitality anticipates a despicable perversion of it. Shakespeare's language in the Argument flags the connection between the two series of events: the military leaders are "secret and sudden" in their arrival back in Rome, and only a few lines later we learn that Tarquin "privily" withdrew from the camp. In the poem itself, if the visit is implicit, Collatine again first unlocks his home linguistically and then does so more literally; alternatively, if we are to assume that the visit does not take place, in any event the telling phrase "unlock'd the treasure of his happy state" (16) at once participates in the obvious commodification of Lucrece while also reminding us that Lucrece, too, is a treasure whose container can readily be unlocked. Similarly, in describing her husband as the "publisher" (33) of this jewel, Shakespeare draws attention not only to the role of language in his ill-conceived boast but also to the act of making a private space public.[17]

Comparing the text with its sources clarifies the threats to which Collatine subjects his wife and their imbrication with questions about houses and homes. Both Livy and Ovid emphasize the idleness and heavy drinking at the camp, implying that these are possible motivations for the ensuing contest; given that *The Rape of Lucrece* is, as Ian Donaldson observes, concerned with government in the sense of self-control, one might expect Shakespeare to include or even highlight such explanations.[18] In omitting them, however, he makes the competitiveness behind the boast appear a more common and widespread characteristic, not merely the product of the peculiar conditions at the camp. Many irresponsible young men, not only bored and inebriated soldiers, he implies, participate in mimetic desire. Shakespeare's version also diffuses guilt by omitting the statement, clear in both Livy and Ovid, that Collatine himself suggests the trip back to Rome.

The guilt of not only Collatine but also his comrades is, however, emphasized by Shakespeare's most significant, and most neglected, change in his sources. In the classical versions, in Painter, and in Chaucer, the test of the wives culminates in a joyous reunion. "Adveniens vir Tarquinii-ique excepti benigne; victor maritus comiter invitat regios iuvenes" ("As Collatinus and the Tarquinii approached, they were graciously received, and the victorious husband courteously invited the young princes to his table"), according to Livy (*Historia*, I.lvii.10).[19] Painter's version of Livy goes so far as to suggest the visitors welcomed the chance to spend the night with their wives. The author of the *Metamorphoses* characteristically renders the scene more emotional and more personal. Having come upon a weeping Lucrece, Ovid's Collatine comforts her with his presence: "'pone metum, veni!' coniunx ait. illa revixit / deque viri collo dulce pependit onus" ("'Fear not, I've come,' her husband said. She revived and on her spouse's neck she hung, a burden sweet" (II.759-760).[20] Even in the abbreviated Argument, Shakespeare could have readily referred to such a homecoming by adding after "whereupon the noblemen yielded Collatinus the victory, and his wife the fame" a phrase like "and the happy victor warmly greeted his lady and invited his companions to dine with her."

Notice what a big change that small addition effects. By not using this or a similar locution, Shakespeare omits a moment of domestic happiness, thus further distancing that possibility, elsewhere described as ephemeral as dew. And he plays up the disturbing implications of the visit home: rather than its culminating on the traditional comedic ending of the feast or a loving reunion, nothing mediates the original intrusion into the home, so the parallel with Tarquin's subsequent intrusion deepens. In short, Collatine, whose resemblances to the rapist many critics have noted, literally brings the military world within his house. Or, as Joel Fineman wittily put it in a Lacanian phrase that implicitly emphasizes the invasion of the house, the king's son is the letter that Collatine sends to his own address.[21]

Shakespeare's original readers, however, would have blamed Collatine for the violent depredations of Tarquin (that letter turned letter bomb) even more than contemporary readers have done. Studies of marriage in early-modern England have often focused on the marital ideologies that direct the husband to contain the wife's body and suppress her speech. Though sermons and marriage manuals indubitably proffer such directives, they figure within complex and often contradictory admonitions about wifely subjection and autonomy, as I suggested above. And more to the point now, imperatives about restraining and controlling a wife coexist with frequent admonitions about protecting her.

As we saw, a series of crucial tropes draws attention to Lucrece's responsibility to safeguard the house and her husband's honor. Similarly, marriage manuals do not gender the responsibility to protect exclusively male; witness the passage from King cited above. William Gouge's *Of Domesticall Duties* likewise emphasizes that both members of a couple have the obligation to protect each other's good name.[22] But these tracts more often associate the role of defender with the male. In prayers appended to his *Of Domesticall Duties,* Gouge advises the husband to pray "to protect her against such as may seduce her in her soule, hurt her in her body, or impaire her credit" (sig. Kk2ᵛ-Kk3). Similarly, Robert Cleaver and John Dod's *[G]odly Forme of Householde Government,* a highly influential sixteenth-century marriage manual, declares, "the best rule that a man may holde and practise with his wife, to *guard* and governe her, is to admonish her often" (italics inserted); a few pages later, the authors declare that

the husband "must lovingly defend . . . her."[23] Several other manuals trope protection in terms of concealment, again hinting at guilt that is gendered female even while expressing solicitude and respect. William Perkins advises "a wise and patient bearing or covering of her infirmities . . . in respect of the weakenesse of her sex," a passage whose language hints at the male's implication in those infirmities and also coalesces covering in the sense of protection and concealment, with the latter sense also perhaps hinting at the role of accessory.[24] Similarly, explicating the Biblical description of Abraham as a veil of Sarah, Henry Smith explains he is called that "because he should shield her; for a vaile is made to save."[25]

How do these repeated commands to shelter the wife relate to generalizations about gendered suppression and intimidation? The two strains are far from mutually exclusive: as the lines quoted from Cleaver and Dod suggest, the need to protect may function ideologically as a rationale for dominance and a pretext for criticism, a point on which contemporary teenagers are prone to instruct their parents. The ideology of protection demands more attention from students of this poem and early-modern culture not least because it may itself protect its male readers by concealing an ideology of domination. This again reminds the contemporary reader, if one needed any reminding, that the vulnerability that this poem sympathetically and respectfully attributes to Lucrece can be deployed very differently.

Yet, as the discourses of marriage demonstrate, suppression and criticism are but two of the valences of a tellingly frequent preoccupation with protection. The abuses justified by solicitude do not render it a mere code or screen; it serves more admirable functions as well in the discourses in question. For example, imperatives about protecting a wife are often explicitly invoked to forbid physical abuse, *pace* less informed generalizations about widespread toleration for wife beating. As that instance reminds us, the frequently cited analogy between the relationship of husband and wife and that of Christ to his church surely should not merely be dismissed as mystification of power.

Assessing the material implications of the imperative to protect one's home demands equal caution. There is no doubt that on one level that duty rephrases the desire to safeguard possessions and hence buttresses recent scholars' emphasis on the rise of the bourgeois household. Shakespeare, after all, refers to "the possession of [Collatine's] beauteous mate" (18), a phrase in which the first noun primarily represents a gerund, "the possessing of," but also inevitably signals the senses in which Collatine no less than Gilbert Osmond numbers his wife among his other belongings. Indeed, the passage proceeds immediately to deploy another expression that tellingly conflates the material and abstract, "his fortune" (19) and to refer to Lucrece as a "rich jewel" (34), a jewel, one might add, that makes its owner rich. Yet once again this interpretation, though valid, tells a partial story. The text repeatedly suggests a tenderness between Lucrece and Collatine that extends beyond a miser's delight in his treasure. Might one perhaps even argue that material possessions in the early-modern home (and perhaps other homes as well) were valued in part because they represented a wife and family treasured for emotional and ethical reasons, not just vice versa? Nuanced and shifting in its ideologies, patriarchy demands from its critics analyses as qualified and subtle as the institution itself.

It is also telling that certain passages in marriage manuals and sermons associate not only the wife but also the husband with the house itself. He is, we are repeatedly told, a sanctuary for his wife, and that sanctuary is often figured as a building. "Shee is come to thee as to a sanctuary," Cleaver and Dod declare (p. 210); Smith virtually copies their language about havens, exemplifying the plagiarism that is not uncommon in marriage manuals (p. 56). In his sermon on the Palatine wedding King explicates the phrase *"uxor tua"* ("your wife") by declaring, "The one, the margarite or pearle, *wife;* the other, the cabbinet or arke to keepe this Jewell" (p. 6). Metaphors of purity and value are immediately followed by metaphors indicating the need to enclose such a treasure, a responsibility again assigned to the husband. If "arke" elevates and justifies that role by rendering it implicitly spiritual, it is also noteworthy that the tropes for the husband transform him into versions of a house. And King proceeds to reinforce the point by returning to the same language: "We have found the treasure, we must adde the cabbinet to keepe the treasure" (p. 8). Such passages suggestively raise the intriguing possibility that domestic edifices were associated with the male body as well as the female, just as domestic space figured male as well as female subjectivity. It is telling that in this poem Collatine's compound is called "Collatium," and in early modern England the connections between a man's castle and himself may be quite as intimate if less overt.

I am not, however, making the tempting but deceptive claim that early modern England witnessed a unique and radically new conception of male subjectivity based on protection. Surely that type of husbandry has been associated with husbands in many cultures; surely well documented medieval land disputes offer immediate proof of one situation in which the predecessors to early modern husbands engaged in protecting their households. But granted that domestic safeguarding has been a value in other cultures and probably enjoyed a varied and volatile status in Tudor and Stuart England, some hypotheses are worth exploring. Many cultures preceding early modern England are likely to have emphasized and valorized other types of protection over the domestic—whether represented as the mutual commitments of the comitatus, or feudal obligations to a lord, or the responsibilities of the romance journey to save the imperilled lady. Arguably early modern England, in contrast, attached increased significance to the home as the place where men were protected and, more importantly, were obliged to protect. To put it another way, that activity, so often associated with public arenas in

other cultures, became intimately, though by no means exclusively, attached to the private spaces of the home. The Protestant emphasis on the home as source of religious instruction drew attention to the spiritual protection it could afford even as the Protestant development of the ideal of companionate marriage focused concern on the guardianship that a close relationship could facilitate.

How, then, do the discourses of marriage explicate Shakespeare's narrative of a marriage that, *pace The Ladies Home Journal*'s columns on the subject, cannot be saved? Collatine, according to these early modern conceptions of wedlock, had a deep obligation to protect his wife by creating a home that was a sanctuary and becoming a haven himself. In opening his home to an invader, he is tragically derelict, at once neglecting his obligations in relation to that literal edifice and his own responsibility to serve as a kind of sanctuary. In one sense he is himself the "weak hive" (839). Thus the changes Shakespeare made in his sources become all the more telling.

Certain recent studies have constructed early modern dwelling places from an apparently opposite perspective, emphasizing home as the a locus of danger and the wife as its source more than its victim.[26] These arguments are not in fact wholly incompatible with mine; but my emphases on the inconsistency of representations of the wife and on the responsibilities of the husband reinterpret some of these widely accepted paradigms. The treatises I have cited link the vulnerability and culpability of what a later generation would refer to as the angel in the house, and arguably, aggression towards a female source of danger could, by the processes of reaction formation, encourage tender safeguarding of the woman herself. Perhaps, too, in Shakespeare's culture guilt or anxiety about male failures in this role were not infrequently deflected onto accusations of women who had not fulfilled it. One might even speculate, though cautiously and tentatively in the absence of clear-cut evidence within the poem, that *The Rape of Lucrece* stages a telling inversion of that process: if the male obligation to protect was widely established and accepted, might not Lucrece's unexpressed and unacknowledged anger at her husband for failing to protect her, opening his nest to an invader, perhaps emerge via deflection in her intense self-blame and again via reaction formation in her intense praise of her spouse? Less speculatively, however, it is clear that the emphasis on domestic danger intensified the male responsibilities traced in this essay.

Of course, Tarquin himself is the primary target for the poem's opprobrium, and the rape is the second episode in which the text explores the valences of home, especially its connections with gender and subjectivity. Again the cultural history of the period reveals historically specific resonances to the blame the narrator and Lucrece have assigned to Tarquin. The narrative is, as readers often note, loaded with references to Tarquin's role as thief and the staining that ensues: he is a "creeping thief" (305), "a thievish dog" (736) who tries to turn the tables by claiming that his victim's beauty "purloin'd" (1651) his eyes. As I have argued elsewhere, thievery in its many incarnations was at once the source of many fears in Tudor and Stuart England and a trope for a whole range of other perils involving displacement and category crises.[27] Burglary, the version that typically involves intrusion into a house was feared particularly (indeed, some definitions of the crime associate it specifically with the fear it excites in its victims), as the harsher penalties attached to it indicate. This is partly because of its association with sexual penetration, though, as I have also asserted, robbery was feared so much in its own right that it would be misguided to assume it merely coded sexual behavior.[28] In any event, when he penetrates Lucrece's home Tarquin is associated with a felony arguably even more heinous to Shakespeare's original readers than to twentieth-century ones.

At a pivotal moment in the poem, the lines in its first stanza that introduce Tarquin, Shakespeare associates him with fire:

> Lust-breathed Tarquin leaves the Roman host,
> And to Collatium bears the lightless fire,
> Which in pale embers hid, lurks to aspire,
>   And girdle with embracing flames the waist
>   Of Collatine's fair love, Lucrece the chaste.
>
>   (2-7)

The reference recurs only six stanzas later: "with swift intent he goes / to quench the coal which in his liver glows" (46-47). Not surprisingly, twentieth-century readers are likely to interpret these lines as conventional references to passion, and certainly that level of meaning is present, as subsequent allusions to incendiary desire (see, for instance, 1475) demonstrate. Also present is a proleptic allusion to the burning towers of Troy, and in fact Shakespeare repeatedly described Sinon as an arsonist. But other meanings of fire were also significant for Shakespeare's early modern readers. For Arthur Dimmesdale, the warning "Only you can prevent forest fires" would have had sexual resonances the clean-living Smokey did not anticipate, and, conversely, for Shakespeare's early modern readers conflagrations represented a clear and present physical danger to their dwellings, not just the perils of desire.

In assessing the threat of literal flames, we confront the methodological problems attending on the social history of the period. Research by a few practitioners of that discipline has culminated in a series of articles and a useful gazetteer of fires between 1500 and 1900.[29] But the authors of that survey are the first to acknowledge the limitations of their statistics. For example, in this instance, as in the records of early modern crime, the northern counties receive inordinately little attention. The documentation of damage from fires includes reports from victims attempting to obtain financial relief, hardly the circumstances under which one would underestimate one's losses.[30]

It is clear, however, that fires were a clear and present danger in early modern England. Wood remained the predominant building material in many areas during the sixteenth century and well into the seventeenth, though this phenomenon, like so many others in social history, needs the nuancing of regional variations (for example, wood construction was especially popular in southeastern England because of its supply in the large forest known as the Weald, an availability that encouraged a distinctive and delightful style of architecture known as the Wealden house but may well have encouraged conflagrations as well). Thatched roofs of course intensified the dangers of timber framing, as did the continuing presence of open hearths in older buildings even after the chimney had become popular in new ones. Animal fat could all too easily ignite such a roof.

Such dangers were especially intense in towns, where fire could readily spread from one dwelling to the next. If the Great Fire of London (1666) apparently destroyed some 13,200 houses, apparently the sixteenth century witnessed some twenty-five fires in provincial towns in which at least ten houses were destroyed, and that figure is likely to be underreported.[31] Moreover, Stratford-upon-Avon endured at least three such fires in the 1590s, as well as one in 1614, leading one to speculate how much Shakespeare heard about them and whether he witnessed one or more of them.[32] Thus the domestic resonances of fire rendered the tropes connecting that element with Tarquin more disturbing, with the material threat fire posed to a house literalizing and thus intensifying the perils associated with the flames of passion.

Lucrece's role as prey of the fire in Shakespeare's trope is as telling as Tarquin's position as its purveyor. As I noted above, Coppélia Kahn has persuasively demonstrated the association between Lucrece and the Roman goddess Vesta, guardian of the household fires. Tarquin violates home and its mistress by turning fire from servant and symbol of the home to its dread antagonist—and by turning Lucrece from protector of a sacred fire to victim of a pernicious one. And this is the very point. Having reversed the role of honored guest into dreaded predator, he transforms as well the semiotics of fire and the position of its domestic guardian.

The violation of Vesta is, however, but part of the workings of this trope. Fires were, of course, also associated with martyrs in sixteenth-century England, a connection that glosses from a new perspective the reference to the flames encircling Lucrece. Described as a martyr in the Latin "incipit" heading in Chaucer's *Legend of Good Women*,[33] she is implicitly turned into one by this reading of Tarquin's fire. And thus the reference again links Lucrece and the physical edifice in which she dwells: both suffer Tarquin's incendiary plot.

A threat to Lucrece's home, fire is of course also the agent that destroyed Troy, the originary homeland of English national myth. Not surprisingly, the poem repeatedly alludes to its tall towers, and it evokes the blaze that destroyed them not only through repeated direct references to it but also through a metaphor that again evokes fire ("Like dying coals burnt out in tedious nights" [1379]). Such passages are the third principal locus for examinations of destroyed homes and related questions about subjectivity. If even the proud towers of Troy can burn, a method of destruction that, as we have seen, was particularly unsettling for many members of Shakespeare's original readership, then lesser cultures and residences must be vulnerable as well. At the same time, if Troy is a homeland lost through the destruction of war, it is recovered in part through the visual representation Lucrece views and her own identification with the characters she scrutinizes; thus, like Lucrece's suicide, the poem's episode involving Troy erodes the distinctions between loss and recovery.

Finally, the reactions to Lucrece's death once more involve home in the senses of literal dwelling place, protected private locale, and country. Lucretius and Collatine respond to Lucrece's tragic fate by returning home at her request and mourning over her body. Tellingly evoked by a reference to "publish[ing] Tarquin's foul offense" (1852), Brutus's alternative solution pivots on leaving the home by carrying her body to the marketplace. The verb in question signals the movement from the private sphere of home to the public arena of the marketplace, from complaint to epic action, and from grief to anger. The dovetailing of private and political elsewhere in the poem culminates in a revenge that necessitates leaving the domestic sphere for a communal one.[34] Fittingly, the result of that act is exile: having destroyed Lucrece's home, Tarquin, like the rest of his family, loses both home and homeland himself. A poem that has stressed transitoriness and mutability achieves closure on the words "everlasting banishment" (1855).

IV

Examining the significance of dwellings in *The Rape of Lucrece* can illuminate generic and narrative patterns elsewhere in Shakespeare's canon, as well as broad questions about the relationship between homes and subjectivities both in his culture and in our own. First, then, tracing the relationship of the poem to pastoral provides an appropriate culmination to an essay honoring Barbara Kiefer Lewalski, student and teacher of genre throughout her career. A prototype for its author's later and more overt versions of pastoral even though it does not conform to the literary type in question in some ways, *The Rape of Lucrece* shows Shakespeare beginning to test his sometimes uneasy preliminary response to that genre in general and its relationship to loss in particular. In the poem we encounter *genre en procès*.

The loss of home on which so many figures and episodes in the poem pivot is implicitly but closely connected with both the loss of that originary home Eden and to the deprivations of literal dwellings and metaphoric homes that recur so frequently in pastoral, notably in Virgil's first and ninth eclogues. To begin with, the pure, asexual world associated with Lucrece has analogues to the Edenic in-

nocence sometimes, though not invariably, associated with pastoral,[35] and the vision of the women spinning their wool is related in more ways than one to fantasies of shepherds minding their sheep. The intrusion of Tarquin into that world anticipates the entry of the court into Hal's pastoral tavern or Polixenes's duplicitous entry into the realm of celebrating shepherds. Not the least parallel is that in all these instances the intruder crystallizes or draws attention to something analogous to his own presence that was already there, thus eroding the boundaries between two worlds and at the same time calling the very existence of such demarcations into question. The absolute virginal purity that is the fantasy behind *The Rape of Lucrece* is, of course, just that, a fantasy—which is not to say, of course, that Lucrece is impure in senses that the poem endorses. Needless to say, each of the texts deals with these issues about the erasure of boundaries and the adulteration of an apparently ideal world differently, which makes their early appearance in *The Rape of Lucrece* all the more interesting. Furthermore, at the end of Shakespeare's narrative poem those characters who survive leave the pastoral home for the marketplace, anticipating as well one of the most fundamental structural patterns in Shakespeare's pastoral plays, the return to court.

Or, to put it another way, all of these texts, like many of Shakespeare's other contributions to the form in question, are metapastorals, a not-surprising classification for works in this typically self-conscious genre. The trope of the intruder enacts on the narrative level what happens to pastoral itself, a genre in which ostensibly antithetical values and even competing genres often intrude—much as the suffix "-less" intrudes into an otherwise positive word in phrases like "helpless help" and much as the wasp and cuckoo intrude in Lucrece's revealing tropes.

The threats to dwellings in *The Rape of Lucrece* suggest connections not only with plays that are more overtly and directly pastoral but also with the many Shakespearean dramas that pivot on some version of the loss of a home or other dwelling. The deprivation or abandonment of a dwelling place is a recurrent anxiety in Shakespeare's culture that is variously reinterpreted, resolved, and intensified in his dramas and poems. Thus comedic characters, as critics have long recognized, temporarily abandon their customary dwellings, sometimes for a sojourn in an *unheimlich* world, which helps to explain the sexuality of the woods in *A Midsummer Night's Dream*. The fates of the characters in *A Comedy of Errors* often involve lost dwellings or, more specifically, the inability to return home. In some of the comedies, the loss of a dwelling is a repeated process, as occurs in *As You Like It* when Rosalind, previously denied her home with her father, is cast out from another edifice by Duke Ferdinand. Or the plays may refer briefly to additional, related losses. Oliver, Adam warns Orlando, plots to burn his younger brother's dwelling. (This threat does not appear in Lodge's *Rosalynde*, but it might well have been suggested by repeated tropes there of the older brother's resentment as a hidden fire; if so, the literalization of those figures into arson neatly demonstrates how cultural conditions like the fear of fire I traced can ignite the tinder of literary sources.) In the histories and tragedies, physical exile often represents other types of estrangement, a fate resonant in a culture where courtiers who had displeased the queen risked banishment from court. Coriolanus must seek "a world elsewhere" (III.iii.135). Claudius sends Hamlet to England; Richard II banishes Bolingbroke and Mowbray. Similarly, romance heroes in Shakespearean plays, like other texts in that genre, are wanderers: the peregrinations of Pericles, who literally distances himself from his dwelling and country and loses as well the family that represents home, are extreme but not atypical. The shipwrecks of romance, like other comedic patterns, enact versions of reduplicated loss: their victims, having lost or abandoned a dwelling on land when they climbed aboard the ship, suffer the shattering of that vessel as well.

The losses in question at first seem too varied to permit any generalizations, but my examination of *The Rape of Lucrece* gestures towards some recurrent patterns that can help to explicate imperilled dwellings in Shakespeare's texts and his culture. We have seen that the loss of home was both a danger in its own right and the locus for many other fears. Generalizing about those fears is complicated by the realization that terms like "dominant culture" risk implying more consistency on issues about gender than a careful reading of early modern texts justifies. But nonetheless it is clear that in early modern England not only female subjectivity but male as well were profoundly associated with the house and the often neglected or compromised obligation to protect it and what it represented. Repeatedly threatened by literal intruders like burglars and forces such as fire that figured invasion, domestic spaces at once signalled security and continuing threats to it; the signification of *home* was as unstable and permeable as the material dwelling place. And thus arguably the male bodies that trope and are troped by such dwellings were encoded as complexly as female bodies, being associated both with the strength needed to protect homes and the vulnerability and instability of those edifices.

Hence studying the contamination and destruction of dwellings in *The Rape of Lucrece* also gestures toward a wide range of questions about Shakespeare's worlds and ours. For example, how does the male obligation to protect gloss domestic tragedies, notably *Arden of Feversham?*[36] And how do the issues raised in Shakespeare's poem explicate the decision by early modern Catholics to harbor a priest, an action that at once protects him and endangers one's own family? Turning to perils in late-twentieth-century America, comparing and contrasting the early modern constructions of the male responsibility to protect might clarify some debates about the possession of guns. This perspective may illuminate the workings of our own domestic tragedies as well. My father, a distinguished gynecologist, once observed to me that although losing a

child is always a traumatic event for a couple, he had repeatedly noticed that the parents suffered much more intensely from their loss if they had brought the infant home from the hospital, even if only for the briefest period. Although one obvious explanation is that the mother and father are likely to become more involved with the care of a baby at home, it is also probable that once the infant crosses the threshold of the house, the obligation to protect assumes new dimensions and a new intensity. As this extreme instance suggests, *The Rape of Lucrece* invites its current readers to rethink the connections among the loss of a dwelling and many other losses in early modern England and modern America—and in so doing to rethink as well the multiple and complex links between gender and home.

Notes

1. See especially Joel Fineman, "Shakespeare's *Will:* The Temporality of Rape," particularly 177-78, in his collection of essays, *The Subjectivity Effect in Western Literary Tradition: Essays Toward the Release of Shakespeare's Will* (Cambridge: MIT Press, 1991). I part company with Fineman, however, on some of his analyses of the originary purity: for example, it is not associated with vision to the extent he suggests throughout his essay.

2. See Fineman, "Shakespeare's *Will,*" esp. 175, 191-97; Dubrow, *Captive Victors: Shakespeare's Narrative Poems and Sonnets* (Ithaca: Cornell University Press, 1987), especially 80-84.

3. Conceptions of home were complex and volatile in the early modern period, as in many others. It is clear, however, that Lucrece inhabits a home in several senses; it is a family abode clearly associated with domestic responsibilities and hospitality. A lengthy discussion of the issue of home is outside the scope of the present article; useful recent scholarship includes Mary Thomas Crane's forthcoming study, *Shakespeare's Brain: Language, Cognition, and Culture* (working title); Frances E. Dolan, *Dangerous Familiars: Representations of Domestic Crime in England 1550-1700* (Ithaca: Cornell University Press, 1994); Lena Cowen Orlin, *Private Matters and Public Culture in Post-Reformation England* (Ithaca: Cornell University Press, 1994).

4. See two essays by Coppélia Kahn, "The Rape in Shakespeare's *Lucrece,*" *Shakespeare Studies* 9 (1976): 50-51; "*Lucrece:* The Sexual Politics of Subjectivity," in *Rape and Representation,* ed. Lynn A. Higgins and Brenda R. Silver (New York: Columbia University Press, 1991), 146-47; Katharine Eisaman Maus, "Taking Tropes Seriously: Language and Violence in Shakespeare's *Rape of Lucrece,*" SQ 37, no. 1 (1986), 70-71; Linda Woodbridge, *The Scythe of Saturn: Shakespeare and Magical Thinking* (Urbana: University of Illinois Press, 1994), 45-85; Georgianna Ziegler, "My Lady's Chamber: Female

Space, Female Chastity in Shakespeare," *Textual Practice* 4, no. 1 (1990): 73-90. (The chapter in Woodbridge's book appeared in earlier form: "Palisading the Elizabethan Body Politic," *TSLL* 33, no. 3 [1991], 327-54.)

5. *OED,* s.v. "intrude."

6. See, e.g., Annabel Patterson's insistence that other critics have emphasized Lucrece's experience at the expense of the political ramifications of the poem (*Reading Between the Lines* (Madison: University of Wisconsin Press, 1993), 297-309.

7. *OED,* s.v. "maiden."

8. Also see Kahn's persuasive suggestion that her maidenhood is connected to the association between Lucrece and Vesta ("Sexual Politics," 146-47).

9. See D.C. Allen, "Some Observations on *The Rape of Lucrece,*" *Shakespeare Survey* 15 (1962): 92.

10. King, *Vitis Palatina: A Sermon Appointed to be Preached . . . after the Mariage of the Ladie Elizabeth her Grace* (London, 1614), 23-24. Subsequent references to this sermon will appear in my text. Throughout this essay I have retained Renaissance spellings but regularized ampersands, capitalization in titles, and the usage of i/j and u/v.

11. See my discussion of such passages in *A Happier Eden: The Politics of Marriage in the Stuart Epithalamium* (Ithaca: Cornell University Press, 1990), especially, 1-27. Also cf. Orlin, *Private Matters,* 85-104.

12. For an analysis of the problems of her innocence and naïveté, see one of my earlier studies of the poem in *Captive Victors: Shakespeare's Narrative Poems and Sonnets* (Ithaca: Cornell University Press, 1987), 97-117. Some readers asserted that I was blaming the victim, which I believe is too bald a summary of my stated aim of asking "what type of person is prone to be victimized by evil?" (97). (Also see the distinctions on the issue of blame propounded on 97.) I still maintain that, despite the sympathy for her that the poem evokes, it draws attention to the dangers of her naïveté. I would add, however, that those dangers complicate the question of culpability in a way I did not initially acknowledge: the patriarchal values that enclose her within her house can be charged with those dangers, a possibility that the poem itself may hint at but does not pursue. On the one hand, then, here, as so often in his plays, Shakespeare demonstrates that innocence not only represents but also creates circumscriptions; but on the other hand, neither I nor the poem is suggesting that Lucrece bears a major responsibility for its events or that she could have prevented the rape.

13. Kahn, "Sexual Politics," 141.

14. Male subjectivity in early modern England has been extensively examined, though from perspectives dif-

ferent from mine, in Coppélia Kahn, *Man's Estate: Masculine Identity in Shakespeare* (Berkeley: University of California Press, 1981).

15. For examples of these positions, see, respectively, Bruce E. Brandt, "Shakespeare's *The Rape of Lucrece:* Argument, Text, and Interpretation," in *Proceedings of the First Dakotas Conference on Earlier British Literature,* ed. Jay Ruud (Aberdeen, SD: Northern State University Press, 1993); René Girard, *A Theater of Envy: William Shakespeare* (New York: Oxford University Press, 1991), 21-28. Assuming that Tarquin never sees his victim, Girard cites the rapist's motivation as a textbook example of mimetic desire; that process might remain a primary though not exclusive etiology even if he has seen her, however.

16. On the dangers of boasting see Nancy Vickers, "'The blazon of sweet beauty's best': Shakespeare's *Lucrece,*" in *Shakespeare and the Question of Theory,* ed. Patricia Parker and Geoffrey Hartman (New York: Methuen, 1985); Patricia Parker, *Literary Fat Ladies: Rhetoric, Gender, Property* (Methuen: London, 1987), chapter 7. On the "scopic economy" of the poem, see especially Kahn, "Lucrece: The Sexual Politics of Subjectivity," 143-46.

17. Although he does not focus on the issue of home, Arthur Little notes the significance of exposure in this text, like the other works about sacrificed women that he analyzes. See Arthur Little, "Picturing Rape in *Titus Andronicus*" in his forthcoming book *Sacrificial Altar: Virginity, Race, and Pornography in Shakespeare and Early Modern Culture,* forthcoming, Stanford: Stanford University Press.

18. Ian Donaldson, *The Rapes of Lucretia: A Myth and its Transformations* (Oxford: Clarendon, 1982), 116-17.

19. I cite *Livy,* trans. B.O. Foster, vol. 1 (Cambridge and London: Harvard University Press and Heinemann, 1961).

20. The citation is to *Ovid's Fasti,* trans. James George Frazer (Cambridge and London: Harvard University Press and Heinemann, 1959).

21. Fineman, "Shakespeare's *Will,*" 198.

22. Gouge, *The Workes of William Gouge,* 2d ed. (London, 1627), 145-46. In the case of this and later citations, page references after the first one appear within my text. In all quotations from Renaissance texts, I have retained the original spelling but regularized the capitalization of titles and the use of i/j and u/v.

23. Robert Cleaver and John Dod, *A Codly [sic] Forme of Householde Government* (London, 1598), 168, 172. In attributing the tract to both writers, I am following common practice, but its authorship has been disputed; see A. W. Pollard et al., *A Short-Title*

Catalogue of Books Printed in England, Scotland, and Ireland, 2d ed., 2 vols. (London: Bibliographical Society, 1976-1986), I, 242.

24. Perkins, *Christian Oeconomie* (London, 1618), 691.

25. Smith, *A Preparative to Mariage* (London, 1591), 56.

26. See especially Dolan, *Dangerous Familiars.*

27. See my essay, "'In thievish ways': Tropes and Robbers in Shakespeare's Sonnetes and Renaissance/ Early Modern Studies," *JEGP* 96, no. 4 (1997): 513-44. This argument is also pursued in my book *Shakespeare and Domestic Loss: Forms of Deprivation, Mourning, and Recuperation* (Cambridge: Cambridge University Press, 1999).

28. Dubrow, "'In thievish ways,'" 534-35.

29. See especially E.L. Jones, S. Porter, and M. Turner, *A Gazetteer of English Urban Fire Disasters, 1500-1900,* Historical Geography Research Series, 13 (Norwich: Geo Books, 1984); C.J. Kitching, "Fire Disasters and Fire Relief in Sixteenth-century England: The Nantwich Fire of 1583," *Bulletin of the Institute of Historical Research* 54, no. 129 (1981): 171-87; Stephen Porter, "The Oxford Fire Regulations of 1671," *Bulletin of the Institute of Historical Research* 58, no. 138 (1985): 251-55.

30. On these and other methodological challenges, see Jones, *Gazetteer,* 7-13.

31. Jones, *Gazetteer,* 42, 46.

32. Jones, *Gazetteer,* 39, 43.

33. These headings may, however, be scribal rather than authorial.

34. Critics have disagreed on the putative culpability of Brutus's actions. For an attack on them, see Dubrow, *Captive Victors,* 125-28; for a defense, Patterson, *Reading Between the Lines,* 297-12. I now believe that Brutus's behavior is less blameworthy than I originally claimed though still ethically problematical.

35. A.D. Cousins argues that Lucrece is described in terms of the discourses of the Golden Age and Eden, though he does not develop the point in relations to the pastoral genre; I am not persuaded that references to Eden do invariably occur where he finds them, but the argument is an intriguing one to which I am indebted here ("Subjectivity, Exemplarity, and the Establishing of Characterization in *Lucrece,*" *SEL,* forthcoming).

36. Orlin's treatment of the play stresses connections between Arden's limitations as a householder and a landowner, though her focus is on governing rather than the closely related but separate issue of protecting (*Private Matters,* chapter 1).

FURTHER READING

Criticism

Camino, Mercedes Maroto. "'Smoke of Words': Lucrece and The Voicing of Rape." In *"The Stage Am I": Raping Lucrece in Early Modern England,* pp. 50-64. Lewiston, N.Y.: The Edwin Mellen Press, 1995.

> Describes Lucrece as a representative of the silenced female that functioned merely as an object of economic exchange in Renaissance society.

Freund, Elizabeth. "'I See a Voice': The Desire for Representation and the Rape of Voice." In *Strands Afar Remote: Israeli Perspectives on Shakespeare,* edited by Avraham Oz, pp. 62-85. Newark: University of Delaware Press, 1998.

> Compares the use of the aural versus the visual as a means of domination in *The Rape of Lucrece, Troilus and Cressida,* and a music video by the singer Madonna.

Hart, Jonathan. "Narratorial Strategies in *The Rape of Lucrece.*" *Studies in English Literature 1500-1900* 32, No. 1 (Winter 1992): 59-77.

> Examines Shakespeare's use of a variety of voices— Tarquin's, Lucrece's, and an anonymous narrator's—to entangle the reader in this story of "love, lust, and violence."

Kietzman, Mary Jo. "'What Is Hecuba to Him or [S]he to Hecuba?' Lucrece's Complaint and Shakespearean Poetic Agency." *Modern Philology* 97, No. 1 (August 1999): 21-45.

> Compares *The Rape of Lucrece* with *Hamlet* principally through the generic device of the "complaint"—a monologue usually delivered in solitude.

Montgomery, Robert L., Jr. "Shakespeare's Gaudy: The Method of *The Rape of Lucrece.*" In *Studies in Honor of DeWitt T. Starnes,* edited by Thomas P. Harrison, Archibald A. Hill, Ernest C. Mossner, and James Sledd, pp. 25-36. Austin: The University of Texas, 1967.

> Asserts that *The Rape of Lucrece* is intentionally non-dramatic and that its heavily rhetorical language is instead meant to reveal the emotions of the characters.

Plant, Sarah. "Shakespeare's Lucrece as Chaste Bee." *Cahiers Élisabéthains,* 49 (April 1996): 51-57.

> Contends that Shakespeare connects Lucrece with the popular Elizabethan image of a bee as a symbol not only of chastity but of temperance and rational governance; further, Plant suggests that once Lucrece is raped, she sees herself as diminished into an expendable drone.

Platt, Michael. "*The Rape of Lucrece* and the Republic for Which It Stands." *Centennial Review* 19, No. 2 (1975): 59-79.

Argues that through Lucrece's rape and the resulting founding of the Republic of Rome, Shakespeare tried to reinterpret the history of Rome and, more specifically, to characterize the Roman sense of self and of virtue.

Quay, Sara E. "'Lucrece the Chaste': The Construction of Rape in Shakespeare's *The Rape of Lucrece.*" *Modern Language Studies* 25, No. 2 (Spring 1995): 3-17.

Questions feminist readings of *The Rape of Lucrece* which focus on the repercussions of the rape and instead looks at the ways in which Shakespeare's Lucrece is defined and made vulnerable, or "rapable," by her society.

Scholz, Susanne. "Textualizing the Body Politic: National Identity and the Female Body in *The Rape of Lucrece.*" *Shakespeare-Jahrbuch* 132 (1996): 103-13.

Presents Shakespeare's Lucrece as a model of the Renaissance notion that a woman's economic and political worth was dependent upon her chastity.

Troilus and Cressida

For further information on the critical and stage history of *Troilus and Cressida,* see *SC,* Volumes 3, 18, 27, and 43.

INTRODUCTION

The story of the Trojan War and of the unfortunate lovers Troilus and Cressida is one that had been told and retold numerous times before Shakespeare adapted it into a play. Significantly, Shakespeare's own particular treatment of this classical myth is controversial to the extent that over the centuries, critics have argued about its standing as one of the playwright's "problem" plays. Central to this debate are the ambivalent actions of the characters, the play's early placement as a comedy in Shakespeare's canon, the play's possible relevance to Renaissance England, and what many scholars have described as an unsatisfactory conclusion to the play's final act. Kristina Faber (1990) deals with the issues of genre and conclusion simultaneously when she argues that *Troilus and Cressida* is in fact not a comedy but a tragedy that is problematic since its catastrophes—the betrayal of Troilus and the death of Hector—offer no catharsis at the end because neither character is sympathetic. David Bevington (1998) traces the play's problematical nature back to its creation in the closing years of the sixteenth century, when playwrights were quarreling over the guidelines for proper literary form and politicians were jockeying for influence over the aging Queen Elizabeth; the critic speculates whether the actions in the play might be a reflection of both of these occurrences.

Perhaps most compelling to critics have been the ambiguities of the characters themselves. Cressida, for example, was maligned by early scholars not only for betraying Troilus but also for being manipulative of and promiscuous with men in general. Later, this view was reversed so that Cressida became a victim of the war and of male dominance. M.M. Burns (1980) and Grace Tiffany (1993) take issue with each of these interpretations. Tiffany sees Cressida as a character with a will of her own who surrenders on her own to male authority when she fails to make her voice heard. Alternatively, Burns proposes that the actual character in the play is the war itself, which does irreparable violence to the relationships between men, such as Troilus and Ulysses, and women, such as Cressida. Stephen J. Lynch (1986) switches the perspective to Troilus, arguing that his innocence and idealism are actually selfishness and that his supposed betrayal by Cressida results from his lack of "self-knowledge." Elaine Eldridge (1986), on the other hand, asserts that the dynamics of the play revolve around the Trojan "headstrong trio" of Hector, Troilus, and Cressida, each of whom is contending

with one or the other over the questions of love and honor. Peter Hyland (1993) focuses on another character entirely—Thersites—who is set apart from the rest by his bitter remarks as well as by his illegitimate birth. The "voice" of Thersites, Hyland observes, is of special interest today "because it represents . . . the real and painful impotence of the great mass of the dispossessed whose voices we now never hear at all."

Another source of interest to scholars is the powerful imagery of *Troilus and Cressida.* Juliet Dusinberre (1983) traces the references to beauty in the play, most of which reside in Helen and the fairness or foulness of women and of people's actions. Dusinberre concludes that authentic beauty exists not in the mythical Helen and her tenuous existence within the corrupt world of warring nations, but in the linguistic creation of "the play itself." Stephen X. Mead (1992) comments on the prevalence of monetary imagery in the play. He contends that Shakespeare's use of "terms of coinage, currency, exchange rates, counterfeiting, and minting practices" emphasizes the theme of morals as a commodity in *Troilus and Cressida,* even while it underscores the Renaissance obsession with its unstable economy. David Hillman (1997) also sees Shakespeare's imagery as a link between Renaissance life and the world of the play. After acknowledging the mythical, abstract status of Helen and of the oft-told story of the Trojan War, Hillman suggests that the playwright drew upon the preoccupations of his own time concerning digestive disorders as a means of grounding the play in reality. In a discussion of Renaissance politics and power, Christopher Flannery (1981) illustrates the political significance of the play's language when he asserts that Shakespeare crafted *Troilus and Cressida* knowing full well that its language, as well as that of all his drama and poetry, could be used by his own generation and those that followed it as an instrument of political change.

The theme of sexuality resonates for those who have made a close study of *Troilus and Cressida.* Barbara Hodgdon (1990), for instance, is interested in the ways in which twentieth-century directors have dealt with the male characters in the play, who debase Cressida by treating her as an object worth only being stared at or dominated. Several directors, Hodgdon notes, have made skillful use of costume and staging to emphasize the sexual tension that pervades the play. James O'Rourke (1992) refers to *Troilus and Cressida*'s "systematic critique of sexuality in a patriarchal culture" and observes that within the play, the words "whore" and "woman" become synonyms for one another. At the same time, O'Rourke is unwilling to blame either Troilus or Cressida for the disintegration of their romantic love. Finally, Michael Yogev (1998) draws upon the psychoanalytical texts of Sigmund Freud to demonstrate the falseness of the codes of chivalry and heroism in the play—codes which ultimately allow the fearful male characters to separate themselves from and dominate the female characters, whom they see as threats to their sexual identity.

OVERVIEWS AND GENERAL STUDIES

David Bevington (essay date 1998)

SOURCE: Introduction to *Troilus and Cressida,* by William Shakespeare, edited by David Bevington, Thomas Nelson and Sons, 1998, pp. 1-29.

[*In the following excerpt, Bevington presents the debates surrounding the historical context of* Troilus and Cressida *and discusses whether or not Shakespeare was using the play to mock some of his fellow playwrights; Bevington also takes a close look at the classical subject matter of the play itself and how it has been interpreted in twentieth-century productions.*]

'A NEW PLAY, NEVER STALED WITH THE STAGE':
GENRE AND THE QUESTION OF ORIGINAL
PERFORMANCE

An enigmatic publicity blurb inserted in a revised Quarto edition of *Troilus and Cressida* in 1609, addressed to 'an ever reader' from 'a never writer', offers to the 'eternal reader' a 'new play, never staled with the stage, never clapper-clawed with the palms of the vulgar, and yet passing full of the palm comical'. In praising the dramatist as a writer of such 'dexterity and power of wit' that even those who are 'most displeased with plays' are sure to be 'pleased with his comedies', this publisher's preface goes out of its way to flatter a discriminating readership that prefers literature to stage performance. The appeal is neoclassical, learned, even academic in its insistence that the play deserves to be ranked 'as well as the best comedy in Terence or Plautus'. The potential buyer is urged to acquire a copy before the dramatist's comedies are 'out of sale'. The publisher represents himself as having made such a collectors' item available to his select reading public against considerable odds, 'since by the grand possessors' wills I believe you should have prayed for them rather than been prayed'. He does not say who these 'grand possessors' were who wished to keep back *Troilus and Cressida* from the *cognoscenti,* but his animus appears to be directed at the acting company. The dramatist is not named, although his name does appear on both versions or 'states' of the 1609 Quarto title-page: 'Written by William Shakespeare'.

Seldom has the publication of a book been surrounded with so many mysteries. We learn from this preface that Shakespeare was a name with which to sell books by 1609, and that some readers at least associated him with high

culture. We do not learn, however, why publication was delayed some years after it was registered on 7 February 1603, or why a Quarto edition was finally published in 1609 in two states with two different title-pages and front matter, one advertising the play as having been acted by the King's Majesty's servants (Shakespeare's acting company) at their public theatre, the Globe, the other insisting that the play was never acted. Folio publication presents a puzzle as well. Why was the compositorial work on *Troilus and Cressida* evidently held up in the printing of the First Folio in 1622-3, leaving the play unlisted in the 'Catalogue' or table of contents, unpaginated for the most part and oddly placed between the histories and the tragedies?

Some details of textual history and bibliographical anomalies can be examined later on, but the puzzles themselves are essential to our understanding of the play's ambivalent status and genre. As many readers have observed,[1] the prefatory note 'to an ever reader' presents the play as a comedy, 'passing full of the palm comical', worthy of comparison with the best of Terence and Plautus. The two Quarto title-pages (see Figs 13 and 14, pp. 124-5) offer the play as 'The Historie of Troylus and Cresseida' and 'The Famous Historie of Troylus and Cresseid'. The first page in the Folio text calls it 'The Tragedie of Troylus and Cressida', and places it first among that volume's tragedies—or else last among the histories; the 'Catalogue' or table of contents for the Folio does not make clear to which category it belongs. The evidently last-minute decision to insert the play in an anomalous location between the histories and the tragedies appears to underscore the play's generic indeterminacy. Even the original publishers of Quarto and Folio seem not to have known what to call it.

Troilus and Cressida has struck many critics as in a genre, or *mélange* of genres, all to itself. To S.T. Coleridge, 'there is no one of Shakspere's plays harder to characterize'; one scarcely knows 'what to say of it'. Hazlitt finds *Troilus* 'the most loose and desultory of our author's plays'; Swinburne declares it to be a hybrid that 'at once defies and derides all definitive comment'.[2] Yeats and Jan Kott refer to it as a tragicomedy. Northrop Frye argues that the play is hard to fit into the usual Shakespearean categories—comedy, history, tragedy and romance—'because it has so many elements of all four'. L.C. Knights argues a kinship to the morality play.[3]

Those who see the play as a tragedy of 'defeated potential' and 'tragic waste' readily concede that it lacks catharsis and does not invite deep sympathy for its characters.[4] Defenders of the play as a 'history' of the Trojan war emphasize its episodic structure and mixture of comedy with high seriousness, and point out that a number of history plays like *King John* and *Richard II* contain elements of tragedy,[5] but must also confront the fact that the so-called tragedies (such as *Julius Caesar* and *Coriolanus*) are often historical. 'Satirical comedy' or 'problem play' are useful terms in analysing the play's insistent mocking and raillery,[6] but are too easy or too nebulous for some observers; general agreement as to what constitutes a 'problem play' is hard to find.[7] If any consensus is to be found, it is that *Troilus and Cressida* is an experimental play, characterized throughout by an intermingling of mode, tone, genre and style. Such an open-ended play needs to be read inclusively, rather than being racked on some Procrustean bed of generic classification.[8]

The experimentalism of *Troilus* can be seen in context when we compare it with other works written during the pivotal years of Shakespeare's development, from about 1599 to 1603. *Hamlet* (c. 1599-1601), like *Troilus,* expresses disillusionment about human frailty and sexual inconstancy; so do the *Sonnets,* hard to date with any precision but at times close to *Troilus* in their exploration of the disabling consequences of female desertion. *Henry V,* in 1599, is an astonishing prelude to *Troilus,* as though seeming to measure the vast distance between the real if complex heroism of a charismatic English monarch and the fallen idols of the ancient classical world. *Julius Caesar,* also produced in 1599, gives a more sardonic anticipation of disillusionment with its ironic perception that republican efforts to forestall a dictatorship, however idealistically intended, lead ultimately to a collapse of the very senatorial freedoms that Brutus has conspired and fought for. *Measure for Measure* (1603-4) and *All's Well That Ends Well* (some time around 1601-5) are well matched with *Troilus* as 'problem' plays in their depiction of male inabilities to come to terms with sexual desire and, especially in *Measure for Measure,* a sense of social moral decline. In its experimentation and bleakness, *Troilus* anticipates *Timon of Athens.*[9] Whether performed (if it was performed) in public or possibly at one of the Inns of Court, or both, *Troilus* would presumably have found a receptive audience for its experimental dramaturgy and disillusioning ambiance; we should not assume that public audiences would not have been fascinated by its mordant dramatization of hotly contemporary issues. At the same time, the play is manifestly difficult, controversial, even avant-garde.

'AN ENVIOUS FEVER OF PALE AND BLOODLESS EMULATION': HISTORICAL CONTEXT IN THE LAST YEARS OF ELIZABETH'S REIGN

Another aspect of *Troilus*'s generic instability and obscure early stage history can be seen when we look at the play in its immediate historical environment: the last years of the reign of Queen Elizabeth. *Troilus* takes on the dimensions of a *fin-de-siècle* work, exploring the disillusionment of troubled times. Two issues may be of particular relevance. The first is the play's putative role in the so-called 'War of the Theatres', to the extent that such a 'war' in fact existed among Ben Jonson, John Marston, Thomas Dekker and others about the competitive merits of 'public' and 'private' acting companies, popular morality versus the avant-garde and the like—the 'Rival Traditions' characterized by Alfred Harbage.[10] The second concerns the career of Robert Devereux, second Earl of Essex, and his catastrophic attempt at a coup d'état in 1601. Is *Troi-*

lus's depiction of insolent and divided leadership in time of war a reflection of contemporary disillusionment with some of England's governing elite? These questions depend upon, and can perhaps help determine, the dates of the play's composition and (if it was in fact performed) its performance(s).

The 'War of the Theatres', a major fascination in the 'old' historicism of the late nineteenth and earlier twentieth centuries, has been cut down to size more recently. At its height, the supposed 'stage quarrel' was imagined to have dominated the London scene in the years 1597-1603 or thereabouts and to have brought into the fray virtually every practising playwright.[11] The matter has been blown out of proportion. Still, the remark of an actor playing Will Kempe (in Part 2 of the anonymous *The Return from Parnassus,* acted at Cambridge University during the Christmas season of 1601-2), that 'our fellow Shakespeare puts them all down, ay, and Ben Jonson, too', has potential implications for *Troilus.* Did Shakespeare in fact 'put down' Jonson and others? 'O, that Ben Jonson is a pestilent fellow!' continues Kempe in his imagined conversation with Richard Burbage. 'And he brought up Horace giving the poets a pill, but our fellow Shakespeare hath given him a purge that made him beray his credit' (1809-13). The offensive 'Horace' who attacks other poets and playwrights is patently Jonson himself, whom Dekker and perhaps Marston had pilloried in *Satiromastix* (1601) by way of satirical riposte to Jonson's *Cynthia's Revels* (1600). In Act 5 of Jonson's *The Poetaster* (1601, written quickly by Jonson to anticipate *Satiromastix*), the poets Crispinus and Demetrius (thinly disguised lampoonings of Marston and Dekker) are arraigned for slandering Horace, whereupon Crispinus is administered emetic 'pills' by Horace and proceeds to vomit up scraps of Marston's recognizably eccentric dramatic language.[12] The 'pill' mentioned by Kempe is thus clearly identified, with its resulting purgative effect; but did Shakespeare then carry the attack further with his own 'purge'?

Jonson did take a swipe or two at Shakespeare in *Every Man Out of His Humour,* 1599. He parodied 'O judgement! Thou art fled to brutish beasts, / And men have lost their reason' (*JC* 3.2.106-7; compare 'Reason long since is fled to animals, you know', *Every Man Out* 3.4.33), and mockingly quoted '*Et tu, Brutè*' in an absurd context (*JC* 3.1.78; *Every Man Out* 5.6.79), evidently in wry dismay at Shakespeare's amateurism as a neoclassicist. His chorus figures sardonically question how it comes about 'that in some one play we see so many seas, countries, and kingdoms passed over with such admirable dexterity?' (Induction, 281-6). The motto of the clown Sogliardo in *Every Man Out,* 'Not without mustard' (3.4.86), may glance at the motto *Non sans droict* on the coat of arms that Shakespeare had obtained for his father and himself in 1599.[13] Might this have elicited some response from Shakespeare? Jonson did at any rate append an 'apologetical dialogue' to *The Poetaster* in 1601, regretfully commenting that 'Some better natures' among the players had 'run in that vile line' of attack on him (ll. 141-52). Jonson, who elsewhere consistently views Shakespeare as of a gentle nature, seems to suggest that the latter was never the main target of his anger, and that Shakespeare's brief succumbing to the vituperative tactics of Marston and Dekker was much to be regretted.[14]

Could Jonson have taken the view, in 1601, that the portrait of Ajax in *Troilus* was modelled on him? The pun on Ajax and 'a jakes' or privy (see, for example, 3.3.247 and note), made notorious at this time by John Harington's scatological *The Metamorphosis of Ajax* (1596), might seem to be implicitly critical of 'the very basis of the cathartic theory of comedy that Jonson was currently proposing'.[15] Alexander's description of Ajax to Cressida as a man into whom Nature has discordantly 'crowded humours' of lion, bear, elephant, folly, discretion, and melancholy (1.2.19-30) might suggest a parody of the Jonsonian character sketch. The likening of Ajax to a bear could point to Jonson's shambling bulk, while 'slow as the elephant' might suggest Jonson's well-known laboriousness of style and slow pace of production. (Jonson berated Shakespeare for never blotting a line in his writing.) The virulent revilings of Ajax and Thersites against each other might conjure up the notorious quarrelling of Jonson and Marston. Thersites' 'gleeful morbidity' and his colourful ravings at the depraved sexuality he finds so fascinating have reminded several critics of Marston.[16]

Particular *roman-à-clef* identifications seem far-fetched and too reliant on analogies that can instead be explained by the play's internal dynamics.[17] Still, Jonson's apparent sensitivity and Kempe's allegation that Shakespeare had administered Jonson and others some kind of 'purge' could point to the way in which *Troilus* deliberately employs a consciously different kind of social critique from that of Jonsonian humours comedy. Beginning with a clear reference to the 'armed Prologue' of Jonson's *The Poetaster* (l. 2), the Prologue of *Troilus* insists that he comes as 'A Prologue armed, but not in confidence / Of author's pen or actor's voice' (23-4). He thus introduces a play that will not choose the Jonsonian path of authorial self-assertion and certitude. Shakespeare's play chooses instead to explore disillusionment and multiple perspectives in an experimental way that implicitly criticizes Jonson's more dogmatic approach. As James Bednarz argues, Shakespeare in effect negates 'the first principles on which Jonson had grounded his perspective—the self-confident conviction that he was capable of obtaining a knowledge of truth'.[18] Shakespeare may be addressing other satirists as well, like Marston, George Chapman and Joseph Hall, whose work had enjoyed so much notoriety in the late 1590s in non-dramatic publishing as well as on stage; venomed spleens like theirs had been subjected by Shakespeare to a quizzical crossfire of debate about the merits and social dangers of formal satire by Jaques and Duke Senior in *As You Like It* (2.7.42-87).[19] If *Troilus* seems to lack the 'purge' that Kempe crows about in Part 2 of *The Return from Parnassus,* the forbearance is thoroughly in line with all that we know about Shakespeare, and might well have encouraged Shakespeare's company to take the view that Shakespeare had had the last word in this now ended Poets' War.

The circumstances of the debate tend, at any rate, to confirm a date for *Troilus. The Poetaster* and *Satiromastix* were performed in 1601; *Satiromastix* was registered for publication on 11 November 1601. The second part of *The Return from Parnassus,* announcing Shakespeare's 'purge' of Jonson, was acted at Cambridge in the Christmas season of 1601-2. 'The booke of Troilus and Cresseda as yt is acted by my lo: Chamberlens Men' was entered in the Stationers' Register on 7 February 1603. The Prologue's reference in *Troilus* to a 'Prologue armed' (Folio text only) seemingly alludes to *The Poetaster.* This evidence points to a date of composition of some version of the play, including the Folio Prologue, in late 1601.[20]

Troilus and Cressida's seeming comment on the Earl of Essex and his ill-fated rebellion of 1601 may also illuminate the play's experimental nature and the topical pertinence of its date of performance. Essex was often compared with Achilles in the last years of Elizabeth's reign. Both were controversial and notorious figures, at once mistrusted and admired. Achilles was suspect in Troy-sympathizing Elizabethan England simply because he was Greek; he was, moreover, truculent in refusing to fight alongside his fellow generals and treacherous in his slaying of Hector. On the other hand, he is, in the *Iliad,* an almost godlike figure whose mighty wrath is Homer's announced theme. George Chapman, whose translation of *Seven Books of the Iliads* in 1598 Shakespeare must have known, found in Achilles an admirable hero worthy of comparison with Essex, as though Homer, by 'sacred prophecy', did but 'prefigure' in Achilles the Earl of Essex as the 'now living instance of the Achillean virtues'. Nor was Chapman the first to laud Essex thus; Hugh Platt had done so in 1594, and Vincentio Saviolo had called him 'the English Achilles' in 1595.[21]

Chapman's comparison of Essex and Achilles, both known for arrogant dissension, was bound to be controversial. Even though Essex's star might still appear to be rising in 1598, his career as a politician had been turbulent. He had turned the Accession Day festivities of 1595, nominally intended to laud Queen Elizabeth on the anniversary of her coming to the English throne, into unabashed propaganda for himself in his candidacy to become leading adviser to the crown. Avidly anti-Spanish and interventionist in military affairs, he had led the successful attack on Cádiz in 1596 and the failed attack on the Azores in 1597, only to be passed over for supreme command in the aftermath of those raids. His surly withdrawal from court in 1597 for an extended period drew notices of disapproval. 'I have lately heard the different censures of many about thy absence in this high Court of Parliament', wrote a concerned follower to Essex; 'some, earnestly expecting the worthy advancement of thy most noble house and posterity, wish their service might ransom thy contentment; others, who make daily use of thy absence, confess thy worthiness, and in words only wish with the rest'. Essex's open impatience and 'discontentment' ended temporarily when the Queen relented in late 1597 by appointing him Earl Marshal.[22] He quarrelled with Elizabeth over his personal right to ransom the prisoners he had taken, like Hotspur in *1 Henry IV.* Much as Achilles does with Queen Hecuba in *Troilus,* Essex secretly corresponded with Spain and Scotland over the question of the English succession.

Elizabeth's uncertainties and vacillations in dealing with Essex did not end with his appointment as Lord Marshal. Claiming to be an heir of Edward III, Essex offered himself as the saviour of English interests in Ireland against the rebel Tyrone in 1598, to the enthusiastic cheering of many hawkish Englishmen, including Edmund Spenser. Shakespeare seems to have joined in the praise. The chorus to Act 5 of *Henry V,* acted probably in 1599, applauds 'the General of our gracious Empress' who may in good time, 'from Ireland coming', bring 'rebellion broached on his sword'. The allusion is, for Shakespeare, unusually explicit in its topicality, and seemingly dates from the interval of time between March of 1599, when Essex hopefully set forth to Ireland, and late September of that same year, when he returned in utter failure to stand trial before a specially constituted court for abandoning his station and for contracting a dishonourable treaty with Tyrone.[23]

By the time Shakespeare had completed *Troilus and Cressida,* probably in late 1601, Essex had been arrested and executed for treason. Having persuaded Lord Mountjoy (who was to become Essex's more victorious successor as Lord Deputy of Ireland later in 1601), the Earl of Southampton and others to join him in a conspiracy to rid the Queen of her pusillanimous advisers, Essex tried to raise the city of London on his behalf, failed to do so, was proclaimed traitor, and went to his death on 25 February 1601. The disillusionment was complete. All the emotional and military build-up of 1599-1600, as the English braced themselves for another possible Spanish invasion and pored over campaign bulletins from Ireland, collapsed into the dismal reality of a tarnished hero.

The case for Shakespeare's having written *Troilus and Cressida* with this unhappy saga at least partly in mind is circumstantial. It depends in part on Chapman's explicit linking of Achilles and Essex, on Shakespeare's likely acquaintance with Chapman's translation, and on Shakespeare's unusual tribute to Essex in *Henry V.* The case is strengthened by the thematizing of chivalry in *Troilus.* By 1599-1600, Essex was not only the 'now living instance of the Achillean virtues'; he was also the embodiment of a charismatic chivalry that posed a threat to the late Elizabethan regime. In its nostalgia for a rapidly disappearing social order in which aristocrats defended their nation and their ladies' honour, the idealizing of neofeudal chivalry naturally chose as its great image Sir Philip Sidney and the Protestant war party he had espoused, prominently including Essex in 1595 and the years following. The struggles between the Essex faction and the more cautious group gathered around Burghley and then (after Burghley's death in 1598) his son Robert Cecil became the central political story of *fin-de-siècle* England.[24] Essex was immensely popular with Londoners and theatre-goers,

as *Henry V* attests. His campaign to brighten England's honour worked its appeal and then collapsed. Shakespeare's one-time patron, the Earl of Southampton, was caught up in the Essex débâcle and was condemned to death though reprieved and imprisoned 'during the Queen's pleasure'. Shakespeare's acting company was severely interrogated for its performance of *Richard II,* seemingly at the instigation of Essex's supporters, on 7 February 1601, the eve of the fateful rebellion. After the events of early 1601, the ideals of neofeudal heroism seemed no longer workable.

As Eric Mallin writes, 'the chivalric premise lay behind virtually every late Tudor court formality': its masques and pageants, its Accession Day celebrations, its ceremonial diplomatic missions. Yet this 'fashion of chivalry' was barely able to contain the contradictions of which it was composed. In its medieval form, 'chivalry masked savage and unregenerate self-interest'. Knighthood 'glorified bravery and martial prowess, but in so doing legitimated and rewarded rapacity'. These tensions were, moreover, exacerbated by conflicts of gender, in which the ideals of service on behalf of womanly honour ran into conflict with male anxieties at court about a woman ruler. Essex's notorious quarrels with Elizabeth—his insolent challenges and disrespectful references to her ageing person, her *volte-face* of bestowing special favours on him and then taking them away—gave visible definition to the paradoxes of chivalry as a 'forum for the visibility of masculine courtier power'.[25]

Whether or not we are meant to see a personal portrait of Essex in Shakespeare's Achilles (Mallin in fact argues that the play gives us a bifurcated image of Essex in the opposed characters of Achilles and Hector) is less to the point than the similarities between the play and important social changes at work in late Elizabethan England. The nation was fascinated during these years with the story of the Trojan war, as though out of fear that if the great commercial city of Troy fell, so must London or 'Troynovant'.[26] The decline of feudal aristocracy in the late sixteenth century was synchronous with an increase in bourgeois mercantilism. Clinging to an outmoded feudal ideology and to the orthodoxies of an unchanging social order based on order and degree, those who had ruled medieval England found themselves displaced to an ever-increasing extent by new wealth. Their protest took rebellious forms of sexual licence and the practice of duelling, forbidden by the Tudor state.[27] Essex was the personification of this beleaguered chivalry. The insistent commercial metaphors of *Troilus,* as we will see, reflect unease in late Tudor England over social change. This is not to argue that Shakespeare takes sides in the conflict, but rather to suggest that he gives expression to many voices of anxiety and discontent in the England for which he wrote this play.

If Shakespeare wrote *Troilus and Cressida* in the wake of the Essex disaster, that event could explain a number of puzzling circumstances: the lapse of time between the

Stationers' Register entry of February 1603 and eventual Quarto publication in 1609 after a change of ownership, the substitution of a second title-page and addition of a preface to the reader, and then still more delays to printing the play in the Folio of 1623. According to the hypothesis of Ernst Honigmann, Shakespeare's company may have found itself in a delicate position in the wake of Essex's abortive coup attempt. Whether Shakespeare and his acting associates had intended to make a political statement or not, their production of *Troilus* precipitated them into controversy. The connection between Essex and Achilles was a familiar one in England from 1594 onwards; so too were analogies of Burghley and then Cecil to Nestor and Ulysses. If the play Shakespeare had written proved too hot to handle in the upshot of a failed rebellion (and the company had been in trouble over their revival of *Richard II* in early 1601 on the eve of that attempted coup), the actors may have found it prudent to hold *Troilus* back. The players are to be identified, then, with the 'grand possessors' whom the publisher's preface in 1609 describes as having been reluctant to see the play in print. Other critics too have identified the 'grand possessors' as Shakespeare's company; and in any case the preface clearly refers to someone who tried to prevent 'the scape it hath made amongst you'. The proviso in the Stationers' Register entry of 1603 conferring rights of publication on James Roberts 'when he hath gotten sufficient aucthority for yt' should not be regarded as a 'blocking entry', since that romantic notion of a stratagem to forestall piracy has now been exploded as a fiction, but it does bespeak the need for authorization that may not have been granted.[28]

Might this scenario explain the substitute title-page and added preface in 1609 (see Figs 1, 13 and 14, pp. 2, 124-5), done in haste and at some expense and difficulty, removing all mention of performance from the first title-page, 'As it was acted by the King's Majesty's servants at the Globe', and speaking as though the play had never even been performed? The phrasing sounds more like an attempt at finding safe refuge than a reporting of the truth, in view of the conflicting evidence that the play was in fact acted. Cecil, now the Earl of Salisbury and more powerful than ever after the fall of Essex, was not a person to take lightly any lampoons that might seem slanderously aimed at him.[29]

Shakespeare and his colleagues seem to have found themselves with what was essentially a banned play on their hands. *Troilus and Cressida* is, moreover, a sophisticated play, highly satirical at times, experimental in genre and attuned to an avant-garde idiom not unlike that of private-theatre plays performed with scandalous success by the boy actors. *Troilus* is rather like the play that Hamlet describes to the First Player as 'caviar to the general'; it 'pleased not the million' (*Ham* 2.2.436-7). *Hamlet* is such a play as well; both seem aimed at discriminating audiences whose judgements matter. In both *Hamlet* and *Troilus*, we seem to hear Shakespeare answering his critics with a defence of art that is experimentally difficult.

'Wars and Lechery': Demystification of the Heroes of Ancient Greece

The experimentalism of *Troilus and Cressida* may well have contributed to a lack of stage success and belated publication in the 1600s, but that same quality has served the play well in the twentieth century. As the record of performance on stage can testify (see 'Performance history', pp. 87-117), *Troilus and Cressida* has come into its own in recent years. Critically, as well, the play has come to be appreciated for its major originality in achieving a balance between the war story and the love story in a way that no previous extant version does (see the essay on 'Shakespeare's sources', pp. 375-97 below). In good part, this is because the play is now perceived as speaking to our modern condition with vivid if dismaying relevance. Nowhere in Shakespeare can our present generation hope to find a more striking dramatization of the grim interconnectedness of war and the pursuit of eros.

We are constantly aware that Shakespeare, in metatheatrical fashion, is playing tricks with time.[30] He represents the action as taking place at the time of the great Trojan war, far back in the mythical past, and yet he also expects us to listen and interpret with a modern awareness. The result, again and again, is that the characters in the play seem to anticipate their own destinies. Troilus, Cressida and Pandarus, in particular, appear to understand that history will hold them up as exemplars, even as stereotypes. 'Let all constant men be Troiluses, all false women Cressids, and all brokers-between panders', proposes Cressida's uncle, to which they all cry 'Amen' (3.2.197-9). Our knowledge that Pandarus' very name has passed into the language as a term for a pimp enriches the irony. Caught up in their hopes and excitement of the moment, these characters do not know what we know all too well, that nothing can save them from playing out the roles that history and legend have determined for them.

The war itself suffers perhaps the greatest demystification in this play about love and war. Shakespeare knew Homer's *Iliad* in George Chapman's translation (1598), at least in part, certainly enough to have savoured its tragic grandeur and its insistence on the war's great significance to the gods and to the human race. The *Iliad* has its share of disillusionment, to be sure, but finds greatness in its noble characters and denounces insubordination in Thersites. Shakespeare's depiction of war, contrastingly, focuses on the absurd.

Both sides in the conflict are aware of the ironies that link them to one another even as they long for slaughter. The rhetorical figure of oxymoron well expresses the paradox of friendly enemies who 'know each other well' and 'long to know each other worse'. Their exchanges of vaunts and loving invitations constitute 'the most despiteful'st gentle greeting, / The noblest hateful love, that e'er I heard of', concludes Paris (4.1.32-5). The two sides come increasingly to resemble each other as they compete for the same woman, and speak in metaphors that elide the difference between martial and erotic conflict. 'Better would it fit Achilles much / To throw down Hector than Polyxena' (3.3.209-10), Ulysses warns Achilles, using 'throw down' in a way that signifies both fighting and a sexual encounter laden with homo-erotic suggestion.[31] (Terry Hands's 1981 Royal Shakespeare Company production is only one of many in recent years that have made an erotic spectacle of the male body; see p. 104.) The bonds that link enemies are also heterosexual and familial, for men in this play 'traffic' in women and exploit family ties as a function of their homosocial interactions. Well-informed persons on both sides know that Achilles is secretly pledged to Priam's daughter Polyxena (194-204). All are aware that Ajax is half-Trojan, being the son of Priam's sister Hesione, which means that he is a 'cousin-german' to the very Hector whom he is chosen to battle in the lists.[32] As Hector acknowledges his dilemma, an 'obligation of our blood forbids / A gory emulation 'twixt us twain' (4.5.123-4), and yet they fight.

Diomedes, plain soldier and artful seducer that he is, perceives with sardonic clarity the meaninglessness of a war fought over Helen. When asked by Paris who is more deserving of Helen, Paris himself as her current lover or Menelaus as the estranged Greek husband, Diomedes has his ready assessment of the rivals: they are 'Both alike'. Menelaus, 'like a puling cuckold, would drink up / The lees and dregs of a flat 'tamed piece', that is, would settle for the stale sediment of a broached wine keg, while Paris must be content to breed his heirs out of 'whorish loins'. Diomedes is bitter because 'She's bitter to her country', indeed to both sides. 'For every false drop in her bawdy veins / A Grecian's life hath sunk.' The toll is no less appalling on the Trojan side (4.1.55-76). Diomedes' critique is all the more devastating because it is inspired by no moral idealism like that appealed to by Troilus and Hector. Diomedes is a soldier who sees this war as absurd in its cost. Women are to be enjoyed and used, but not at such a fantastic price.

As Linda Charnes has observed, a 'notorious identity' hovers over most of the characters in the play,[33] not simply Troilus, Cressida and Pandarus in their prospective roles as archetypal constant man, faithless woman and go-between, but also the major contenders on both sides. Shakespeare's dramaturgical techniques are those of disillusionment. Agamemnon, 'great commander, nerve and bone of Greece' (1.3.55), is also presented as a figure of ridicule.[34] His noble insistence that the Greeks' hardships are 'But the protractive trials of great Jove', designed to test and thereby sort out those who are resolute from those who, like chaff, deserve to be blown away by the 'wind and tempest' of Fortune's frown (20-6), must do battle with Thersites' reminder to us that Agamemnon 'loves quails' (5.1.50-51)—i.e. prostitutes—as do most men. Agamemnon does quarrel with Achilles over a woman in the *Iliad*, to be sure, but is not subjected in that poem to the satirical comedy of contradiction. In *Troilus and Cressida*, on the other hand, even his authoritarian bearing and 'topless deputation' or supreme power are the subject of mirthful parody when, as Ulysses reports to his fellow generals, Patroclus and Achilles amuse themselves in their tent with slanderous pageants (1.3.151-8). Recent stage productions have tended to see Agamemnon as dim-witted and obtuse (see pp. 105, 110). We do not necessarily assent to Patroclus' send-ups, but we find them diverting and informative because they represent a demystifying point of view.

Nestor is a figure of contradiction merely because he is old. Although Ulysses acknowledges a fit reverence for Nestor's 'stretched-out life', Ulysses is also unkind enough to relate to his fellow generals how the lampoons of Patroclus and Achilles use Nestor's 'faint defects of age' for their 'scene of mirth'. Ulysses obligingly imitates the way in which Nestor is perceived 'to cough and spit, / And with a palsy fumbling on his gorget / Shake in and out the rivet' as he prepares for military action (1.3.61, 172-5). Nestor's honourable career as a warrior reaches back further than anyone's, to the expedition against Troy headed by no less a hero than Hercules in reprisal for Laomedon's having defrauded Hercules over the building of the walls of Troy. Hector's grandfather Laomedon thus set in motion a war and lost his daughter Hesione to Telamon as a prize of war, prompting the Trojans to seize Helen in reprisal and thereby precipitate the present and most famous war of Greeks against Trojans. Nestor is a 'good old chronicle' that has 'walked hand in hand with time', known repeatedly as 'Most reverend Nestor' (4.5.203-5). Yet he is no less a tedious and senile old man, ready at a moment's notice to recall when 'I have seen the time' (210) and to ramble on through sententious truisms about shallow boats giving way before 'ruffian Boreas' and the like (1.3.31-54) as though he were actually adding something to what his fellow generals have already said.[35] Their polite condescension suits his role as one who never has an idea of his own and is all too willingly led by the nose by someone as clever as Ulysses. Recent stage productions have generally seen him as a wordy bore, slobbering over an orange (in Hands's 1981 production; see p. 105), ineffectual and weak.

Ajax is perhaps the figure whom the capricious memories of history and legend have treated most unmercifully.[36] He is no longer the mighty warrior of the *Iliad* but instead a fatuous, self-important gull, easily exploited as the tool of Ulysses' machinations aimed at goading Achilles into action. His dull-witted swapping of insults with Thersites, and his inevitable recourse to threats of physical violence when he is bested at the game of wits, make him a pathetic figure even in comparison with the play's most contemptible railer. To a modern producer like Hands (1981), he is a vacuous, gullible athlete, a 'roaring head-banger' out of Monty Python, practising karate chops on empty ammunition boxes (see p. 105).[37]

Broad parody thus offsets the play's more subtle demystifications of Homeric heroism. Ulysses is an interesting figure in this regard, because his character is in some ways close to the Odysseus of Homer. He is 'the sly Ulysses' celebrated in Homer's poem. Yet slyness or cunning is an asset in the Greek lexicon, an admired cultural trait, a way of dealing with dangerous enemies.[38] Shakespeare's Ulysses turns his cleverness and devious manipulations mainly against his own fellow officers like Achilles and Ajax, employing strategies of flattery, emulation and tantalizing.[39] Even his alliances are manipulative, as for example in his conspiratorial talk with Nestor. The wisdom of his speech in praise of order and degree (1.3.75-137), so often quoted out of context, takes on a more complex dimension when we hear Ulysses using his masterful rhetoric to encourage the very emulation he inveighs against.[40] On stage, the speech can be made to seem the vacuous locution of a pseudo-intellectual, as in Davies's 1985 production, when Ulysses' fellow officers rolled their eyes heavenwards in response to his pontificating (see p. 110). Ulysses is an old hand at gathering of intelligence and at deploying that information in a kind of elegant blackmail (3.3.198-210).

About women Ulysses is contemptuously wary. Cressida is for him only one more confirming instance of 'these encounterers, so glib of tongue, / That give accosting welcome ere it comes, / And wide unclasp the tables of their thoughts / To every tickling reader' (4.5.59-62). Alone among the Greek generals who greet Cressida with sex-hungry leers and kisses, Ulysses refuses to beg a kiss. Never will be soon enough for him (53). He is appalled by the spectacle of grown men demeaning themselves before a woman; it puts him in mind of the root cause of the Trojan war. There they are, on Dardan plains, risking their very lives 'to gild his [Menelaus'] horns', that is, to put a specious appearance of decency on Menelaus' cuckoldry. This is the 'deadly gall and theme of all our scorns' (31-2). Perhaps it is not surprising that this most self-possessed and rational of all the Greek leaders, this apostle of self-control and control of others, should wish to rid himself of any indebtedness to 'the woman's part'.[41]

Achilles' decline in historical reputation, as dramatized in this play, is all the more dismaying in that it pertains to the tragic hero of the *Iliad.* Arrogant, sullen, envious, the Achilles of Homer's epic is notwithstanding a man whose choice not to fight and then to fight is of great consequence. The intensity of loyalties in conflict is for Homer a major theme. Shakespeare is not without sympathy, as theatrical performance can make clear, but he does allow his Achilles to luxuriate 'Upon a lazy bed, the livelong day' in indolent resentment, breaking 'scurril jests' and abetting insubordination (1.3.147-8). We seldom see him without Patroclus or Thersites, or both.[42]

Prurient whisperings about Achilles' relationship with Patroclus refuse to go away. Thersites may be partly mocking when he calls Patroclus 'boy' and reports saucily to him that 'Thou art thought to be Achilles' male varlet', or, in plainer terms, 'his masculine whore' (5.1.14-17), and Patroclus bridles at the charge as though denying its validity, but the assumption is inevitable and widespread. Achilles and Patroclus are virtually inseparable tent-mates. Achilles' refusal to fight is generally understood to be the consequence of his 'great love' for Patroclus, and Patroclus' 'little stomach to the war' (3.3.222-3). Achilles' love for Patroclus is of course central to the *Iliad,* but the unwillingness to fight is occasioned in the first instance by Achilles' quarrel with Agamemnon over a woman. By deleting this factor, Shakespeare focuses with special intensity on the friendship of Achilles and Patroclus. Achilles' being secretly in love with Priam's daughter Polyxena evinces a heterosexual desire that evidently accommodates bisexuality as well; such a desire, as Eve Kosofsky Sedgwick argues, often misogynistically eclipses women.[43] Male relations generally in this play 'work to the detriment of the females'.[44] Yet despite the subversively anti-authoritarian nature of his relationship to Achilles, Patroclus is treated as a hero in his death: the event is reported by Agamemnon in an epic catalogue of Greek casualties, and Patroclus' body is to be taken by soldiers to Achilles (5.5.13-17). As in Homer, he takes his place among the heroes of the war.[45]

The issue of bisexuality thus hovers ambiguously over this relationship, as it does also in Homer. Various voices give us contrasting surmises and interpretations. Theatre directors of late, ever since the pace-setting production of John Barton in 1968, have opted almost unanimously to flaunt a highly visible homosexuality of bared torsoes, shaved legs and drag costume (see pp. 102-3 and Fig. 5). We may take the view that Achilles' and Patroclus' sexual preferences are their own business into which we should not pry, but the play will not let us forget the question, perhaps because it bears so meaningfully on the issue of love and war. Troilus and Cressida struggle to find mutual comfort in a time of dislocation; so, in their various ways, do Paris and Helen, Hector and Andromache. The deep and eroticized friendship of Achilles and Patroclus is still another response to the need for human closeness in an anarchic world, all the more timely in that war brings men into such close and dependent relationship with one another. The friendship of Achilles and Patroclus is a counterpart to Ulysses' response to the sexual urge, which is to repress it and owe nothing to women—or men—in this sexual sense.

Achilles' brutal slaughter of Hector is the last definitive undoing of his reputation. Goaded by Ulysses into bestirring himself lest he fall victim to ungrateful Time, and then by thoughts of revenge for the death of Patroclus, Achilles takes the surest means possible of offending reputation by premeditated savagery that savours, in Bruce Smith's view, of a 'homosexual gang rape'.[46] Modern directors have transformed the scene into that of a firing squad (in Davies's 1985 production) or trench warfare (BBC, 1981; see pp. 108, 110-1). Homer of course provides a precedent for the killing and the desecration of Hector's corpse, but Shakespeare has chosen to play up the worst aspects of post-Homeric legend (see p. 390). We see Achilles instruct his Myrmidons to fall upon Hector 'In fellest manner' and 'Empale him with your weapons round about' (5.7.5-6). To Hector's protest that 'I am unarmed. Forgo this vantage, Greek' (5.9.9), Achilles has no answer other than the fulfilment of what he has planned to do. Without remorse, he announces his intent to tie Hector's body to his horse's tail and drag him 'Along the field' (21-2). Achilles' exit line is his own epitaph as a man of any pretensions to honour in battle.

History has also dealt unkindly with Menelaus. He is a minor figure in Shakespeare's play, reduced to caricature. Virtually every mention of him refers to the inglorious fact of his being a cuckold, and he himself acknowledges the subject, albeit unwillingly (4.5.182). In a macho world of wars and lechery, where the men routinely challenge one another in the name of their mistresses, Menelaus is the emblem of what every man fears to be: an inadequate male. Modern directors like Davies (1985) generally find him a blockhead and despised nonentity (see pp. 110-1).[47] Reputation becomes the reality: to be known as a cuckold is to become subsumed by that identity.

Notes

1. For example, Alexander, 'TC', 286; Morris, 481; Fiedler, 50-1; Snyder, 89; Muir, 'TC', 28. Elton, 'Textual Transmission', proposes that the preface was written by John Marston, a friend of Henry Walley, who, with Richard Bonian, entered the play in the Stationers' Register in 1609; see also Finkelpearl.

2. Coleridge, 306; Hazlitt, *Characters of Shakespeare's Plays*, in *Works*, 1.221; Swinburne, 196-202, esp. 200. See also Heine, 3n. below.

3. Yeats, *Essays*, 240, and *Autobiography*, 286, cited by Mowat, 80 n. 1; Kott, 82; Frye, *Myth*, 62; Knights, 'TC', cited by Tillyard, 49.

4. See A. Stein, 163-6; Chambers, 'Epilogue', 400; Bayley, *Tragedy*, 97; Coghill, 78, 125; Hargreaves, 58; Frye, *Fools*, 16, 59, 66, 69; Morris; Heine, 'Shakespeares Mädchen und Frauen' (1839), trans. C. G. Leland (1891), also in *Heine on Shakespeare*, trans. Ida Benecke (1895), 42-5, reprinted in Var, 523, and in Martin, 44-5; Dollimore, 49; Rossiter, 147; Kott, 83; Danson, 75, 93; Oates, 142; Kaufmann, 'Ceremonies', 140; Stockholder, 539; Alexander, *Life*, 197, quoted in Coleman, 117; J. O. Smith, 167.

5. Dodd. Tatlock's contention (769n.) that 'There is absolutely no essential difference between *Troilus* and *Henry IV*' runs into a similar reductive difficulty. Cited and argued against by Lawrence, *Problem*, 169-70.

6. Michael Long, 104-5; Schlegel, 419, quoted in Martin, 34-5; Symons, quoted in Martin, 61-3; Brooks, 21, 24; Evans, esp. 169-70; Campbell, 185ff.; Jagendorf, 199; Everett, 125; Sacharoff; Kernan; Lawrence, *Problem*, 170-2; Lawrence, 'Troilus', 429-31; Boas, 375-8; Tillyard, 46; Bentley, 43-4. On Thersites as a satirist, see Bredbeck, 37-8; on Thersites as a railing fool, see Elliott, 137-9.

7. Lawrence, *Problem;* Tillyard; Toole; Rossiter; Ure; Schanzer. For a review of ideas about what constitutes the 'problem play', see Jamieson, 1-2.

8. Colie, 342-5; Helton, 120; Kernan, 192-8; Langman, 57, 67; Schwartz, 304-7; Foakes, 'TC', 142-3; Marsh, 182; Seltzer, xxvi-xxxiv; Mowat, 88.

9. See Goddard, 2.21-8; Wheeler, *passim;* Kaufmann, 'Ceremonies', 141-2; Lawrence, *Problem*, 128ff.; Coghill, 78-127; Meyer, 51-2; Campbell, 191-3.

10. Harbage, *Rival Traditions, passim*.

11. Among the main proponents of a full-fledged War of the Theatres, see Fleay, 1.359-70, 2.68-72, Small, Penniman and Sharpe. On reducing the often extravagant claims of these earlier researchers, see Enck.

12. For a review of the literary exchanges among Jonson, Marston and Dekker, see Bednarz, 176-7, and Bevington, *Politics,* 279-88.

13. See Bednarz, and Elton, 'Ajax'.

14. Chambers, *Shakespeare*, 1.71 and 2.202-11, is generally sceptical of personal identifications in the Poets' War and in *Every Man Out* in particular, but he does allow that 'Shakespeare may be one of the "better natures"' (2.204).

15. The pun, first proposed by Elton, 'Ajax', with citations from contemporary literature (745), is developed by Bednarz, 188-9. The linkage of Ajax to Jonson was first proposed by Fleay in an overstated case. In a similarly reductive vein, see Small, and Jonson, esp. 1.406-10, 418-27.

16. Bednarz, 203, citing Harbage, *Rival Traditions*, 116 and 118. See also Potts, Kimbrough, 9, 20 and Ramsey, 238-9.

17. Those who reject or criticize topical portraiture, of Jonson particularly, in *Troilus* include Tatlock, 726-34; Chambers, *Shakespeare,* 1.71-2 and 2.202-11; Ard[2], 19; Kimbrough, 21.

18. Bednarz, 206.

19. Bevington, 'Satire', 120.

20. Earlier attempts to date the play in 1598 tend to be based on allegorical readings of the Essex affair, assuming that Shakespeare was urging him in 1598 to emerge from retirement and take action. See especially Harrison, 'Essex'. J.D. Wilson, 101-2, opts for late 1600. See also Honigmann, 'Shakespeare Suppressed', 112-14, opting for 1601. A date in late 1601 need not presuppose that it was written after the passage in 2.2.337-62 of *Hamlet* with seeming reference to the stage quarrel; that Folio-only passage may have been written later, and could refer, as Knutson argues, to more serious matters of offence to members of the Privy Council and other noblemen.

21. Chapman, Dedication to *Seven Books of the Iliads* (1598), title and lines 60-1; see Briggs, 59. On Platt and *Vincentio Saviolo His Practice* (1595), see

Honigmann, 'Shakespeare Suppressed', 115. See also J.A.K. Thomson, 211.

22. *State Papers Domestic,* 265.10 (series 1, vol. 4, 532-4), loosely paraphrased by Harrison, *Elizabethan,* 2.235; see also 245 and 294. See Briggs, 60-2; Harrison, *Essex,* 183-210; Poel, 108ff., for a relevant document also quoted in Var, 377-8. On Essex and Accession Day, see McCoy; Strong, 141; Mallin, 166 and n. 68; Hammer. On Essex's communications with Spain and Scotland, see Honigmann, 'Shakespeare Suppressed', 116.

23. *DNB,* sv. Devereux, Robert. For a minority view arguing that the Prologue to Act 5 of *Henry V* may refer to Mountjoy rather than Essex, see W. Smith. Muir, Oxf[1], 7, is also sceptical that Essex is intended, but T.W. Craik, in his edition of *Henry V* (Ard[3]), offers a powerful argument for Essex (1-3). On Hotspur and Essex, see Harrison, 'Essex', and *Elizabethan,* 2.135.

24. For the suggestion that Nestor and Ulysses can be taken as glancing at the Cecil faction, see Norbrook, 155; Honigmann, 'Date and Revision', and 'Shakespeare Suppressed', 115; Brooke, 76. Similarly, Campbell, 219-23, argues that any well-informed spectator in 1601 would have recognized in the comradeship of Achilles, Patroclus and Thersites an echo of the Essex group and especially of Essex's relationship with Southampton and with Essex's secretary, Henry Cuffe, a one-time professor of Greek at Oxford and reckless adviser of Essex who was executed for treason in 1601. J.D. Wilson argues that Shakespeare's intent in *Troilus* was to 'goad the earl into action', though not advocating rebellion (101).

25. Mallin, esp. 154 and 157; Montrose; McCoy, 313-20; Harrison, *Essex,* 42. J. Speed's *History* (1611) relates how the Earl of Essex, about to depart from Lisbon in May of 1589, 'in the courage of his martial blood, ran his spear and brake it against the gates of that city, demanding aloud if any Spaniard mewed therein durst adventure forth in favour of his mistress to break a staff with him' (Q. Eliz. Monarch 61, chap. 24, p. 865, cited by Palmer, Ard[2], 142 n. 274). In 1591, Essex wrote to the Marquis of Villars, Governor of Rouen, proclaiming 'that I am better than you, and that my Mistress is fairer than yours' (Harrison, *Essex,* 62, cited by Savage, 50, and by Mallin, 166). See Potter, 27-8. See also below, pp. 68-71.

26. Bruster. On the bifurcated image of Essex as both Achilles and Hector, see Mallin, 168. Savage, citing Merritt Clare Batchelder, 'The Elizabethan Elements in Shakespeare's *Troilus and Cressida*', unpublished University of Iowa dissertation, 1935, pursues overzealously the identification of Hector with Essex.

27. Clarke; Mead.

28. Honigmann, 'Shakespeare Suppressed'. The 'blocking entry' scenario proposed by Pollard has been refuted by, among others, Blayney, 'Publication'.

29. Honigmann, 'Shakespeare Suppressed'.

30. See Bayley, 'Time'; Berger, 135-6; and Charnes, 75-6, on the 'here and now' time sense of theatre, with everything taking place in and ending with the theatrical present. For an analysis of 5.2 in these terms, see Clifford Lyons, and Levine.

31. See Charnes, 83, 92-3; Sedgwick, 38; Lévi-Strauss, 29ff., esp. 42-51; and Rubin, on men's 'exogamous' trafficking in women. See also Bowen, *Gender,* 3-22; Cook, 42-3; French, 103; Jardine, 8; Patke, 16; B. Smith, *Desire* 59ff.; B. Smith, 'Rape'; and Spear, 409-12, on the homo-eroticizing aspects of warfare.

32. Nass, 7.

33. Charnes, *passim.*

34. See Daniels, 286-7, Danson, 71, and Adamson, 36-9. For a more sympathetic reading of Agamemnon's rhetoric as 'close-woven' and 'virile', see Ellis-Fermor, 61, and Ard[2], 42-3.

35. See Danson, 71-2, on Nestor's garrulity. Again, Ellis-Fermor (61) is more generous.

36. On the conflation of legends of two Ajaxes, Ajax Telamon and Ajax Oileus, see Edelman, 126-7; Cam[1], xxxiv; Oxf[1], 18; Dodd, 43; Bullough, *Sources,* 6.101; J.A.K. Thomson, 213.

37. See Girard, 201, and Hyland, *TC,* 73. On the use of music to underscore the ludicrousness of Ajax' situation, see Sternfeld, 203.

38. Those who support Ulysses as a valid commentator include Brower, 243, 253, Bethell, 99-101, and Tillyard, 75. More disillusioned appraisers include Burns, 124, A. Stein, 160, Adams, 91 n. 7, and Leech, 12. See 25 n. 2 and 54 n. 3 below.

39. Girard, 205-6.

40. Those who view this speech as enacting its own loss of order and control through excessive use of accumulation, climax, neologisms and the like include Norbrook, 154-6; Grudin; Potter, 33; Elton, 'Ulysses', 98-100; Knights, 'Theme', 68-9; Roberts, 4-5 and 84; Goddard, 2.12-15. For more orthodox defences of the speech as an embodiment of noble ideas of order and degree, see, e.g., T. Spencer, 21-5, and Rossiter, 139-40; and see 24 n. 4 above.

41. The phrase, from *Cym* 2.5.20-2, also serves as the title of an influential collection of essays subtitled *Feminist Criticism of Shakespeare* (ed. Lenz *et al.*).

42. For a low estimate of Achilles as lazy, arrogant, etc., see, e.g., Chambers, *Survey,* 197-8, and Lawrence, 'Troilus', 435. On the other side, see Powell.

43. Sedgwick, 20-1, 33, 36.

44. Mallin, 159-65, esp. 163. See also G. Williams, *Sex,* 103.

45. Bredbeck, 27, 33-48, esp. 39; Mallin, 160-1; Skura, 23.

46. B. Smith, *Desire,* 61. See also Charles Lyons, 239-41. Shakespeare's account of the death of Hector is drawn in good part from Caxton's telling of the death of Troilus (638-9) and perhaps that of Lydgate (4.2647-779); see 'Sources', p. 390.

47. In Jacques Offenbach, *La Belle Hélène, morceau* 7B, Menelaus is derisively referred to as the ridiculous husband of Helen. Kott, 76, briefly pursues the comparison.

CHARACTER STUDIES

M. M. Burns (essay date 1980)

SOURCE: *"Troilus and Cressida:* The Worst of Both Worlds," in *Shakespeare Studies,* Vol. 13, 1980, pp. 105-30.

[*In the following essay, Burns suggests that the play's negative portrayal of Cressida is in fact meant to reflect critically on those characters who condemn her and, more generally, to demonstrate the corrosive effects of war upon humanity.*]

One of the better-known scenes in *Troilus and Cressida* is IV,v, in which Cressida enters the Greek camp and is kissed in "particular" and "in general" (IV.v.20-21)[1] by the leaders of the Greek army. Given Aristotle's dictum that all knowledge comes through either generals or particulars, these parameters of knowledge which Ulysses tries punningly to manipulate may be greatly significant in the play: certainly, readers often think that they "know" Cressida through this scene. More than Cressida's character alone enters into question here, however; when Ulysses obfuscates the difference between the "general" and the "particular" in human interaction, he undermines the very possibility of that interaction. To discriminate particular individuals and identify with them among the faceless mass of humanity, on one hand, and to abstract—to learn—from individuals about general human nature, on the other, are the dual process through which people relate to each other. I believe that *Troilus and Cressida* dramatizes the destruction of this dual process of interaction by the forces of aggression set loose in a world at war. Human relations having become savage and distorted, the very image of man—and especially the image of woman—is shattered; neither individually nor collectively can the characters in this play sustain a viable concept of personhood. Thus the image of humanity presented by *Troilus and Cressida* finally disintegrates, like the action of the play, but I would argue that this disintegration is evidence of the play's thesis and not of artistic disunity.[2] The play does contain recognizable patterns, parallels, and principles of organization, some of which I wish to discuss.

Set in "the matter of Troy," which evoked for the Jacobean period the same image of spiritual wreckage evoked for us today by the name of Vietnam,[3] *Troilus and Cressida* dramatizes the fundamental misdirectedness of aggression. For example, we first hear of Hector, the play's very emblem of warrior nobility, "whose patience / Is, as a virtue fixed," that "he chid Andromache, and struck his armorer" (I.ii.4-6)—out of anger at Ajax. When a society falls into a general state of aggression, even people like Hector cease to deal fairly with others as individuals; as Ulysses advocates (for ulterior reasons), they cease to distinguish "particular" people. At least one character in this play, however, does try to distinguish among other individuals and to distinguish as an individual, in the faceless flux of aggression around her.

In so doing, Cressida surely contravenes the usual critical assessment of her character. This standard assessment probably needs little review here; resting mainly on pejorative assumptions about Cressida's sexual awareness, it amounts to little more than name-calling.[4] I do wish to observe, however, that literary criticism of *Troilus and Cressida* has in some ways become a metadramatic extension of the play:[5] the voice which pronounces the word "whore" in real-world criticism of the play testifies to the contagion of that aggression which the play portrays. To examine Cressida's character without preconception, by means of her own language and situation, changes one's view both of her character and of the whole play.

Troilus and Cressida begins by juxtaposing two parallel scenes: the first presents Pandarus in a dialogue with Troilus; the second presents Pandarus in a dialogue with Cressida. In impressive consensus, readers usually judge that the latter scene undercuts the former and that it also undercuts the character of Cressida.

> In the first scene we meet the lovesick Troilus and hear him extol Cressida's charms to Pandarus in good Petrarchan fashion. In the next scene we meet the "pearl" of Troilus' eulogy capably exchanging bawdy jokes with her servant and Pandarus. . . . The portrayal of a Cressida who would lie on her back to defend her belly mocks Troilus' description of her as "too stubborn-chaste" to be won.[6]

> The appearance of the real Cressida whom Troilus has idealized into a courtly lady, is anti-climactic in the extreme. She engages in bantering remarks, first with her page and then with Pandarus; with the latter her conversation becomes increasingly suggestive.[7]

Interestingly, while readers often remark on the "bawdy" or "suggestive" quality of Cressida's conversation with Pandarus, they seldom remark that Troilus' efforts to get Cressida into bed with him (the substance of his scene with Pandarus) might also be considered "bawdy." Such a perspective in literary criticism seems to me swallowing a camel and straining at a gnat.

Looking at Cressida's language, furthermore, one must demur that her conversation with the serving man, at least, simply cannot be considered "bawdy." The lines which follow constitute all but one of her speeches in the entire exchange:

> Who were those that went by?
> And whither go they?
> What was his [Hector's] cause of anger?
> Good; and what of him [Ajax]?
> But how should this man, that makes me smile, make Hector angry?
> Who comes here?
>
> (I.ii.1-39)

As must be noticed, Cressida's conversation here consists of questions—about Hecuba and Helen, Hector and Ajax—questions which show that Cressida notices the people and events around her. In spite of the dehumanizing impact of her world, she still takes an interest in people as people. Indeed, in this conversation with the servant, Cressida has only one line which is not a question. When the serving man says of Ajax that "They say he is a very man per se, / And stands alone," Cressida replies, with some apparent scorn, "So do all men, unless they are drunk, sick, or have no legs" (15-18). This reply, while perhaps "bantering," can hardly be called "bawdy." Chiefly, it expresses a rather reasonable skepticism about what makes "a very man per se," in this world whose course is predetermined by the Trojan War. When Cressida points out that all men stand alone (or should do so), she is arguing against the unfair use of the word "man" as an honorific term applied only to a few men: she recognizes the human denominator in all men.[8]

Even in her first scene, Cressida shows herself able both to individualize and to abstract in the observation of people. This capacity, briefly established in her conversation with the servant, is further established in her conversation with Pandarus, chiefly by the contrast between her and Pandarus. The difference between the two characters shows immediately in the different ways they talk about Hector. On Pandarus' entrance, Cressida is saying that "Hector's a gallant man," and throughout the scene she continues to show that she values him (as does Helen, incidentally, a few scenes later). Pandarus, in contrast, only uses Hector as a conversational means to his own objective, which is to get Cressida into bed with Troilus:

> he'll lay about him to-day, I can tell them that: and there's Troilus will not come far behind him; let them take heed of Troilus, I can tell them that too.
>
> (58-61)

When Cressida reacts to this head-and-shoulders introduction of Troilus with her ironical, "What, is he angry too?" Pandarus replies, "Who, Troilus? Troilus is the better man of the two" (62-63). As this foolish assertion shows, Pandarus is little concerned with truth, and throughout the scene his clumsy efforts at manipulation contrast unfavorably to Cressida's clearer sight and straighter language.

> Cres. O Jupiter! There's no comparison.
> Pan. What, not between Troilus and Hector? Do you

know a man if you see him?
> Cres. Ay, if I ever saw him before and knew him.
>
> (65-69)

Again, exactly as in her dialogue with the servant, Cressida resists the use of the word "man" as an honorific term; she again applies the word to all men. This repetition of the same play on words (which can hardly be mere accident) underscores the serious weight of Cressida and Pandarus' conversation; beneath the bantering surface, their topic is the very concept of personal identity.

> Pan. Well, I say Troilus is Troilus.
> Cres. Then you say as I say; for, I am sure, he is not Hector.
> Pan. No, nor Hector is not Troilus in some degrees.
> Cres. 'Tis just to each of them; he is himself.
>
> (70-75)

Pandarus, whose role anyway is to obliterate the differences between one man (or woman) and another—so that he can obliterate the barriers separating men and women—always comes out worse in the exchange:

> Pan. You have no judgment, niece: Helen herself swore th' other day, that Troilus, for a brown favour—for so 'tis, I must confess,—not brown neither,—
> Cres. No, but brown.
> Pan. 'Faith, to say truth, brown and not brown.
> Cres. To say the truth, true and not true.
>
> (101-06)

The difference between Pandarus and Cressida, regarding their valuation of people, becomes further apparent as they stand on the walls of Troy, watching the soldiers passing by. While Pandarus is concerned only with Troilus, Cressida asks the same kind of questions she asked the serving man, earlier:

> Who's that?
> Will he give you the nod?
> Be those (marks on Hector's helmet) with swords?
> Can Helenus fight, uncle?
>
> (205-41)

Cressida is almost the only character in the play who notices the efforts of other soldiers besides the legendary heroes of Troy; Pandarus, in scurrilous contrast, dismisses from consideration everyone who does not come within the limited purview of his own advantage:

> Cres. Here come more.
> Pan. Asses, fools, dolts! chaff and bran, chaff and bran! porridge after meat! I could live and die i' the eyes of Troilus.
>
> (261-65)

Consistently, Cressida places more value on people than does Pandarus. It is her language which gives the scene its substance:

Pan. But there was such laughing. Queen Hecuba
laughed that her eyes ran over.
Cres. With millstones.
Pan. And Cassandra laughed.
Cres. But there was more temperate fire under the pot
of her eyes. Did her eyes run over too?

(156-61)

Appropriate to the tragic figures in the discussion—the
"Trojan women"—Cressida's images of millstones and
boiling cauldrons are tragic props. Troy, we are reminded,
is doomed, and in the general destruction the helpless
women will be caught up. Hecuba, Andromache, and Cassandra all contribute to the paradigm for destruction which
also encompasses Cressida's situation.

"You are such a woman a man knows not at what ward
you lie," says Pandarus, Cressida's uncle and nominal
protector, reminding Cressida that he is indeed attacking
her and that she must defend herself against him as against
others.

> Upon my back, to defend my belly; upon my wit, to
> defend my wiles; upon my secrecy, to defend mine
> honesty; my mask, to defend my beauty; and you, to
> defend all these: and at all these wards I lie, at a
> thousand watches.
>
> . . . if I cannot ward what I would not have hit, I can
> watch you for telling how I took the blow; unless it
> swell past hiding, and then it's past watching.

(282-96)

Undoubtedly, this is the speech which has caused typical
assumptions about Cressida's bawdiness—rather oddly, in
my view, given the context of Shakespearean drama
overall, in which the lightest utterances often comprise
scabrous jokes that most English professors today would
hesitate to use. Leaving aside obvious examples like those
in *The Taming of the Shrew,* or Touchstone's parody of
Orlando's poetry, or the innumerable references to cuckoldry or to syphilis in the plays, we often find briefer
touches of the same quality: even a character like the
"honest old Councellor," Gonzalo, in *The Tempest,*
describes the ship as "as leaky as an unstanched wench"
(I.i.46, New Arden ed.). In any case, the chief impact of
Cressida's speech surely lies not in some carelessly assumed salaciousness but in its disclosure of extreme
vulnerability. Obviously, a woman cannot defend her belly
by lying on her back, nor can Cressida depend on Pandarus to defend her; this entire speech relates solely that,
in fact, Cressida has no defenses. In order to deal with the
world in which she lives, she must needs be "at a thousand
watches."

This vulnerability partly shapes her actions: although she
loves Troilus, her awareness of her situation has caused
her to resist him. The speech in which Cressida expresses
her sense of her vulnerability, however, has aroused further
negative assessments of her character.

> Yet hold I off. Women are angels, wooing:
> Things won are done; joy's soul lies in the doing.
> That she beloved knows nought that knows not this:

> Men prize the thing ungain'd more than it is:
> That she was never yet that ever knew
> Love got so sweet as when desire did sue.
> Therefore this maxim out of love I teach:
> Achievement is command; ungain'd, beseech:
> Then though my heart's content firm love doth bear,
> Nothing of that shall from mine eyes appear.

(312-21)

While these lines can surely be read as evidence of
insecurity, many readers see them as evidence of cold-
blooded calculation,[9] a view which would be more
plausible if Cressida could be said to gain some material
or emotional benefit from holding out against Troilus. But
she does not. Unlike Richardson's Pamela, Cressida is not
upping the ante; she neither aspires to nor attains to material reward. It might be noted here, incidentally, that Troilus never mentions the idea of marriage to Cressida (a
lapse which seems not to dismay Shakespearean critics,
since they never—as far as I know—mention it either).

The negative treatment accorded to Cressida by literary
criticism can be explained only partly by reference to the
play, and even less by reference to her own character. One
contributing factor in this negative view, however, must be
that *Troilus and Cressida* is the ugliest of all Shakespeare's
plays in its language about women overall.[10] Negative images of women, purveyed by self-interested or biased or
neurotic characters, abound in the play; Thersites, the
obvious example, is only the most extreme; his view is
shared by—among others—Diomedes, Ulysses, Troilus,
and Hector. Not one character in the play, not even Hector,
is capable of speaking in women's defense. Perhaps, then,
it is not surprising that the critical traditions surrounding
the play have been infected by this climate of opinion
within the play. The same point will arise again in this
paper; for now, I wish to focus briefly on the character of
Troilus.

Troilus' rather dubious view of women becomes manifest
in his (and the play's) first scene; ironically, his view
manifests itself in the guise of his love-longing for
Cressida. Troilus, like the very young man he is, blames
his "weakness," meaning his unfitness for fighting, on his
love.

> I am weaker than a woman's tear,
> Tamer than sleep, fonder than ignorance,
> Less valiant than the virgin in the night,
> And skilless as unpracticed infancy.

(I.i.9-12)

His very choice of images projects Troilus' own weakness
onto the object of his desire: the speech linguistically conflates sleep, ignorance, weakness, and womanliness.
Similarly, he replies to Aeneas:

> *Aene.* How now, Prince Troilus! wherefore not afield?
> *Tro.* Because not there. This woman's answer sorts,
> For womanish it is to be from thence.

(108-10)

Even in his love scene with Cressida, even when Cressida has just confessed that she loves him, Troilus falls into the same vein:

> O that I thought it could be in a woman—
> As, if it can, I will presume in you—
> To feed for aye her lamp and flames of love;
> To keep her constancy in plight and youth,
> Outliving beauty's outward, with a mind
> That doth renew swifter than blood decays!
> Or that persuasion could but thus convince me,
> That my integrity and truth to you
> Might be affronted with the match and weight
> Of such a winnow'd purity in love;
> How were I then uplifted! but, alas!
> I am as true as truth's simplicity
> And simpler than the infancy of truth.
>
> *(165-77)*

This speech does not make much sense; moreover, what sense it has seems rather unloverlike. Not only does Troilus assert his "integrity and truth" at the expense of Cressida's, he goes so far as to say that he *cannot* be persuaded of Cressida's constancy (because he is too simple and "true" to be imposed on by "persuasion"—a peculiar argument). Indeed, the speech virtually forbids Cressida's constancy: first, because Troilus says he cannot believe in it, and second, because he says he will "presume" it anyway. Neither the willful distrust nor the equally willful presumption calls for—or allows for—any response from the woman herself.

The condition of women in *Troilus and Cressida* is an index to the condition of humanity as represented in the play; all these characters are being subjected to the pressures of a war, and such a situation does not produce fairmindedness. Troilus, for example, viewing women with distrust, almost inevitably displaces his frustrations with the war onto a woman:

> Peace, you ungracious clamours! peace, rude sounds!
> Fools on both sides! Helen must needs be fair,
> When with your blood you daily paint her thus.
> I cannot fight upon this argument;
> It is too starved a subject for my sword.
>
> *(I.i.92-96)*

Like others among the soldiers who fight with him, Troilus displaces his anger at the war onto the ostensible object of that war. In spite of the fact that he himself refers to Helen as an image—an "argument," a "subject"—he still cannot see that, being an image, Helen is devoid of responsibility for the fighting. If Helen is an image, then Troilus and the other warriors act according to their perception of her, not according to her real nature.

Thus it is not surprising that when his perception of Helen changes (partly), Troilus becomes as willing to fight "for Helen" as he was unwilling in I.i. His change manifests itself in II.ii, which contains the famous debate with Hector about continuing the war. Troilus' persuasion scenes,

by the way, form one of the unhappiest patterns in this play: when he persuades Cressida to go to bed with him and when, in two scenes, he persuades Hector to fight, he imposes his wishes on another person in spite of the manifest danger to that other.

The debate between Troilus and Hector calls for some attention. When Hector says of Helen, "Brother, she is not worth what she doth cost / The holding," Troilus replies—as most readers tend to remember—"What is aught, but as 'tis valued?" (51-53). Herein lies the debate about real and ideal values in the play which has generated many a similar debate in criticism about the play. Troilus' argument, indeed, has persuaded others besides Hector:

> A value is sufficiently objective or real if it makes demands on the prizer, imposes restraints, requires consistency of behavior, elicits noble action, and—most important—converts a world of indifferent objects into a significant field worthy of one's trouble and attention. Helen is a case in point: if women are whores, are they not accorded generous treatment in being considered pearls? If Thersites is right, do not Hector and Troilus improve Helen by making her a symbol of their own noble urges?[11]

Among these "noble urges," presumably, is the urge to kill Greeks. In any case, passing over the orotund tautology of the word "sufficiently," I would respectfully say that the answers to these questions are no, and no. Helen remains Helen, whatever she is, by virtue of her own actions, not the actions of others. Individual responsibility—that crucial concept which is skirted by both Troilus and Hector in this scene—greatly disposes individual identity. Professor Berger, however, even outstrips his initial argument, just quoted:

> Helen's shortcomings offer a challenge to the heroic imagination, . . . proof of its force lies in its ability to shape such recalcitrant material to its own higher uses.

Again, these "higher causes" presumably include the "causes" of killing Trojans and Greeks, espoused respectively by Greeks and Trojans. Professor Berger's point, of course, is that the "heroic imagination" is its own reward:

> For if life is such that trial necessarily frustrates the "unbodied figure of thought," Trojan idealism could—in the right hands—become a practical as well as a noble posture: By expecting no reward from the "universe of event . . ."

In other words, an imagination which is too heroic to need to believe in anything could hardly be disappointed at anything (a practicality which, in Berger's own terms, should surely diminish its heroism). For the metaphysics of true belief, we can substitute the heroic imagination of nonbelief.

To return to Troilus' language, the pungent array of images which Troilus marshals in support of his argument reveals his evaluation of Helen:

We turn not back the silks upon the merchant,
When we have soil'd them, nor the remainder viands
We do not throw in unrespective sieve,
Because we now are full.

(69-72)

Such a prize is not easily distinguishable from garbage. But in any case, as Troilus reveals when he continues, he is not really talking about Helen—the person Helen—at all:

Is she worth keeping? why, she is a pearl,
Whose price hath launch'd above a thousand ships,
And turn'd crowned kings to merchants.

(81-83)

"Was this the face that launched a thousand ships / And burnt the topless towers of Ilium?": having taken these lines from a man who did not greatly like women, Shakespeare gives them appropriately to Troilus. Whatever their opinion of Helen, however, Marlowe and Troilus at least refer to her as a "face"; their synecdoche is polite compared to that of Diomedes:

You, like a lecher, out of whorish loins
Are pleased to breed out your inheritors.

(I.i.63-64)

"Face" from one perspective, "whorish loins" from the obverse, Helen's image is a Duessa-like compound of concealed ugliness and menace which, I would argue, comes from her explicit association with the seductions of war.[12] But Helen herself is as much a victim of this war as anyone else. The image of the "face" is the image imposed on the ugly deeds of war by misdirection and self-interest; it remains merely an image. Therefore, Marlowe's question requires a negative answer: those ships were not in fact launched by a "face," nor were the towers burnt by it; only fighting soldiers perform such deeds. Shakespeare's alteration of the original line suggests this distinction: in changing "face" to "price," Shakespeare places the responsibility for the war not on Helen but on the men who "desire to buy" her (IV.i.76). But while Troilus voices this distinction, he himself does not recognize it; when he describes Helen, he continually objectifies her:

She is a theme of honor and renown,
A spur to valiant and magnanimous deeds,
Whose present courage may beat down our foes,
And fame in time to come canonize us.

(199-202)

A "pearl" of "price" (in neat parody of the biblical image), a "theme," and a "spur," Helen metamorphoses into everything but a person; she becomes by turns a series of objects whose particular form seems hardly to matter but whose function is always to allow people to shuffle the responsibility for their actions. Troilus may call her "a theme of honor and renown," as long as he is in the mood to do so, but she more weightily embodies a question about moral responsibility.

The fundamental point about the "matter of Troy," the red herring known as "Helen of Troy," is this: the decision to fight the war, and therefore the responsibility for the war, rests not with the object of the war but with the fighters; Hector's question of whether to continue fighting cannot be determined, one way or the other, by reference to Helen. That the very interposition of Helen's "worth" is specious, in this context, becomes readily apparent when we try to deal with it logically. Thus, what personal attributes would make Helen "worth" fighting for? more beauty? chastity? good cooking? And how long would she continue to be "worth" fighting for? until the first ten thousand men had died? the second ten thousand? No, the real question in this scene, and in this play, is why these men are fighting for something they so clearly do not want, and the dramatist shows us that they are blind to their own responsibility.

In this blindness, Troilus and Hector both address their arguments about the war to the moot question of Helen's merits. Following the general pattern of the play, Hector displaces his frustration with his situation onto Helen (just as he displaced his earlier anger at Ajax onto Andromache and his armorer). When Hector makes his shocking about-face at the end of the debate, therefore, his essential collapse is merely becoming belatedly apparent: like Cressida in another scene, he was only "hard to *seem* won" (III.ii.125). Because he has been contending for a non-strategic position, his battle was actually lost from the start.

Indeed, the play establishes several points of resemblance between Hector and Cressida, and the first of these is that both Hector and Cressida must contend with Troilus. In their self-divided conflict with Troilus, moreover, both Hector and Cressida must also contend against the fixed codes of conduct—the fixed roles—which Troilus marshals against them; Troilus exhorts Hector to be a fiercer warrior and Cressida to be his mistress in analogous applications of a sexist tradition.[13] When Hector and Cressida give in to Troilus, then, their resemblance becomes even closer; they both give in partly because they love Troilus and partly because they cannot argue against the traditions which he musters against them. One of the tragic ironies of the play is that Troilus contributes so largely to his own dual bereavement of Hector and Cressida.

Troilus' arguments thus reflect the overall action of *Troilus and Cressida,* for the whole play portrays the analogous manipulation of women and soldiers, always for ulterior reasons and always with disappointing results. Generally speaking, both the women and the soldiers become commodities to exploit, in an overall debasement of human values indicated by the play's ubiquitous images of commerce and merchandising.[14] Troilus' language fits him into this context, too; as other readers have pointed out, Troilus uses the same terms to describe Cressida that he uses for Helen:

Her bed is India; there she lies, a pearl:
Between our Ilium and where she resides,
Let it be call'd the wild and wandering flood,

Ourself the merchant, and this sailing Pandar
Our doubtful hope, our convoy and our bark.

                                          (I.i.103-07)

Himself a "merchant" and "sailing Pandar" his "bark,"
Troilus cannot see that the mercantile theme of his world
does indeed reduce kings to merchants, just as it reduces
an uncle to a procurer and leaders of men into manipulators of their soldiers' courage.[15]

If Cressida and Hector play parallel roles, so do Pandarus
and Ulysses; when people like Cressida and Hector (and
Ajax and Achilles) become commodities to exploit, Pandarus and Ulysses—another pair of characters who partly
reflect each other—become merchants. In the convocation
of the Greek generals in I.iii, Ulysses explicitly identifies
himself so:

Therefore 'tis meet Achilles meet not Hector.
Let us, like merchants, show our foulest wares,
And think, perchance, they'll sell; if not,
The lustre of the better yet to show,
Shall show the better.

                                          (358-62)

Playing a kind of pander, Ulysses tries to procure Achilles
for the battle. And with Ulysses acting as go-between, it is
only appropriate that Achilles should play a kind of coy
mistress:

Having his ear full of his airy fame, [he]
Grows dainty of his worth.

                                          (I.iii.144-45)

Or so Ulysses describes Achilles. Such a stance of passive
resistance on Achilles' part, of course, inconveniences
those about him greatly; indeed, as Patroclus warns Achilles, resistance can become intolerable in either a woman
or a soldier:

A woman impudent and mannish grown
Is not more loathed than an effeminate man
In time of action.

                                          (III.iii.217-19)

The play contains no more succinct statement of its
dualistic code of conduct for men and women, the
encroachment against individual identity which becomes a
weapon against both women and soldiers. One of the
subsidiary ironies of the tragic action in this play is that
poor Patroclus goes to his doom much as the great Hector
does, having belatedly subscribed to a "heroic" code of
self-destruction; having decided to play the part of a man,
Patroclus plays the tragic part of dying on the battlefield.

Not to put too fine a point upon it, the author of this play
reveals that the deck is stacked: for Cressida, Patroclus,
Hector, Ajax, and all the myriad characters, greater and
lesser, who might be either useful or inconvenient to
someone else, there is virtually no protection. The point is
brought home when, in order to draw Ajax and Achilles

into battle, Ulysses fixes a lottery. Here, undoubtedly, is
Ulysses' sincere comment on the axiom that "In the
reproof of chance / Lies the true proof of men" (I.ii.33-
34). Consider briefly this scheme evolved by Ulysses and
Nestor. The two chieftains agree, at the end of I.iii, to use
Ajax and Achilles to egg each other on by emulation:

Two curs shall tame each other: pride alone
Must tarre the mastiffs on, as 'twere their bone.

                                          (391-92)

Ulysses and Nestor's sordid travesty of leadership
discloses the dynamics of aggression; much of the play's
action is explicated by aggression's unworthy aims, its
unworthy means, and its subsequent failure. Like the other
manipulation throughout the play, it transforms persons
into objects—commodities, animals, images—to be used.
To render the lesson explicit, Thersites enters as the next
speaker, railing at Ajax:

thou scurvy-valiant ass! thou art here but to thrash
Trojans: and thou art bought and sold among those of
any wit like a barbarian slave.

                                          (II.i.49-52)

With the appropriate dramatic irony, furthermore, the
scheme does not succeed in any case; while Ajax is bought
and sold readily enough (within a hundred lines), the
scheme goes awry in that he now, like Achilles, "grows
dainty of his worth": "now is the cur Ajax prouder than
the cur Achilles, and will not arm today" (V.iv.14-15).
Consequently II.ii, in which the Greek leaders bait Ajax
like a pack of "curs" themselves around a bear, resembles
the bungling interferences of Pandarus rather than the epic
shrewdness traditionally associated with Ulysses and
Nestor.

To return to Cressida: although she is in love with Troilus,
Cressida has resisted the importunities of Troilus and Pandarus "for many weary months" (III.ii.124). Incidentally,
in case this question of Cressida's resistance does bear
greatly on her character, the play provides three indications of its length. One, the line just quoted from III.ii,
receives corroboration from Troilus' reply: "Why was my
Cressida then so hard to win?" (125). In I.i, furthermore,
Troilus refers to Cressida as "too stubborn-chaste to be
won," in that speech which readers generally choose to
discount; and a speech of Troilus' in IV.iv seems to suggest the same:

We two, that with so many thousand sighs
Did buy each other. . . .

                                          (41-42)

These signals have been ignored, as a rule, by readers who
wish to assume that Cressida's giving in to Troilus implies
previous great experience on her part.

In any case, Cressida does give in to Troilus, in a scene
whose tone is set by her many misgivings:

. . . if my fears have eyes . . .

Blind fear, that seeing reason leads, finds safer
Footing than blind reason stumbling without fear.
To fear the worst oft cures the worse.

                                        (III.ii.72-77)

                      See, we fools!
Why have I blabb'd? who shall be true to us,
When we are so unsecret to ourselves?

                                        (131-33)

          in this rapture I shall surely speak
The thing I shall repent.

                                        (138-39)

I am ashamed. O heavens! what have I done?

                                        (146)

          I have a kind of self resides with you;
But an unkind self, that itself will leave,
To be another's fool.

                                        (153-55)

This entire scene, with its ominous emphasis on Cressida's sense of herself as divided, underscores the tremendous fear which shadows Cressida's actions; and it should be borne in mind here that Shakespeare does not employ the literary tradition which makes Cressida a widow. While others may choose to see Cressida's reiterated misgivings as mere coyness, therefore, I think that she sincerely fears the outcome of her involvement with Troilus. Indeed, considering the vulnerability of her situation and the intensity of her fears, her involvement with Troilus may be a braver action than many performed in the war; even at the worst, Cressida at least is baited with love rather than with "pride."

The action of *Troilus and Cressida* through Act III develops the pressures brought to bear on characters like Cressida and Hector, Ajax and Achilles; the rest of the play shows the disintegration of humane values and human affection under such pressures. Cressida having lost her battle, Patroclus enters the fray; he having been destroyed, Achilles at last joins battle—finally to kill Hector, the one warrior of either camp who possesses enough humanity to spare an enemy's life. Greek and Trojan soldiers alike, incited one after another to throw themselves into the bloody mill of battle, are destroyed, and the very possibility of nobility in war is also destroyed: "Hector is dead."

For Cressida, the first consequence of her union with Troilus is that he hands her over to the Greeks: his desire for her has been fulfilled. The series of scenes (IV.ii, iii, and iv) which develops this action deserves careful attention. The first of these, the leavetaking between Troilus and Cressida the morning after they have slept together, presents an antiphony between Cressida's desire for reassurance and Troilus' desire to be gone:

Tro. Dear, trouble not yourself: the morn is cold.
Cres. Then, sweet my lord, I'll call mine uncle down;
He shall unbolt the gates.

Tro. Trouble him not;
To bed, to bed: sleep kill those pretty eyes. . . .
Cres. Good morrow, then.
Tro. I prithee now, to bed.
Cres. Are you a-weary of me?
Tro. O Cressida! but that the busy day. . . .
Cres. Prithee, tarry:
You men will never tarry.
O foolish Cressid! I might have still held off,
And then you would have tarried.

                                        (1-18)

When Pandarus enters, at this point, his voyeuristic humor at Cressida's expense evidently alienates Troilus even further from Cressida. Cressida, with an understandable wish for privacy from the unknown men who are knocking roughly at her door, begs Troilus to come back into her room—and Troilus laughs at her as though she meant to seduce him (37-43).

The men at the door are the Trojan policy makers, who have just made a deal to send Cressida to the Greeks and who have arrived to tell her about it. First, however, they inform Troilus of the news: after one night together, the lovers are to be parted—to which blow Troilus responds, "Is it so concluded?" (68). While Troilus' remarkable terseness at this point could be played as the silence of deep feeling, the rest of the scene does not necessarily warrant such an interpretation. Although Cressida has only one hour to remain in Troy, for example, Troilus does not remain with her; he does not even acquaint her with the news about her fate. Instead, he goes away to join the men who have made the bargain: "How my achievements mock me! / I will go meet them" (71-72). By "achievements," presumably, Troilus means his conquest of Cressida; in any case, he leaves her to hear the news from Pandarus or from whoever will bother to tell her, assuaging his conscience meanwhile by chivalrously protecting her reputation (or his own): "and, my Lord Aeneas, / We met by chance; you did not find me here" (72-73). Similarly, Troilus expressed his manifest desire to leave, after getting out of bed, in his ostensible concern that prolonged farewells might cause Cressida to catch cold.

In this scene, however, Troilus expresses not one word of concern for Cressida's safety or welfare in the enemy camp. More strangely yet, Troilus never expresses any direct regret over the fact that Cressida must leave. Even in his long farewell speech (IV.iv.35-50), he laments not the leavetaking itself but the haste of the leavetaking—creating the effect, once again, of his own haste:

We two, that with so many thousand sighs
Did buy each other, must poorly sell ourselves
With the rude brevity and discharge of one.

Remarkably, the play never acquaints us with any reason for all this hurry. Why must Cressida be delivered up "ere the first sacrifice" (IV.ii.66)? And why have readers not asked this question before? And why does Troilus not ask it? We cannot even ascertain that Cressida is permitted to pack her belongings. As in the famous "double time" of *Othello,* man's inhumanity to man (or to woman) creates in *Troilus and Cressida* an independent impetus, a spurious urgency which sweeps up human action to the detriment of human values. This hasty action in the play does, of course, contribute to the delineation of character, especially of Troilus' character. Troilus has two scenes of leavetaking with Cressida, scenes parallel in more than one respect but chiefly in that both of them present Troilus as a young man in a hurry. His youthful insensitivity in this regard may attest to more than his own character, incidentally; if, as readers contend, Troilus' faith in Cressida betrays his inexperience, then surely his actions betray *her* inexperience in hoping to rely on him.

> I'll bring her to the Grecian presently;
> And to his hand when I deliver her,
> Think it an altar, and thy brother Troilus
> A priest there offering to it his own heart.
>
> *(IV.iii.6-9)*

A feeling of sacrifice does indeed underly these scenes, but whether Troilus understands what (or, rather, who) is actually being sacrificed remains dubious. Pandarus says, "The young prince will go mad" (IV.ii.78), and Paris says, "I know what 'tis to love" (IV.iii.10), but Troilus performs an action surely unique in a romantic lead: on the very "morning after," he himself delivers Cressida to their common enemy.

Following this action comes that exemplary scene mentioned at the beginning of this essay, of Cressida's entrance into the Greek camp. E.M.W. Tillyard's comments instruct us as to the critical tradition regarding this scene:

> . . . two characters are exempt from the inflation, the comedy, and the antique quaintness alike. The first is Troilus, whose dejected look causes Agamemnon to ask who he is and Ulysses to testify so splendidly to his surpassing merit and courage. . . .
>
> The second is Ulysses, who towers right above the other Greeks in good sense and acute perception and he speaks in full Shakespearean idiom [sic]. He sees through Cressida instantly, while the other Greek leaders make fools of themselves.[16]

One would never guess, reading Tillyard's appraisal, that Ulysses suggests the "general" kissing in the first place:

> *Aga.* Most dearly welcome to the Greeks, sweet lady.
> *Nes.* Our general doth salute you with a kiss.
> *Uly.* Yet is the kindness but particular;
> 'Twere better she were kissed in general.
>
> *(IV.v.18-21)*

More like Pandarus than ever, Ulysses suggests the general kissing so that—of course—Cressida will kiss him in particular. As with his scheme for Achilles and Ajax, however, the readily adopted plan quickly fails.

Throughout the first half of her scene, Cressida is silent, for reasons which can only be conjectured. She breaks her silence with Menelaus, whose situation is almost as tenuous as her own and who is the first of these Greeks to ask for a kiss: "I'll have my kiss, sir. Lady, by your leave" (35). Cressida's responses are all negative:

> *Men.* I'll give you boot, I'll give you three for one.
> *Cres.* You're an odd man; give even, or give none.
> *Men.* An odd man, lady! every man is odd.
> *Cres.* No, Paris is not; for you know 'tis true,
> That you are odd, and he is even with you.
>
> *(IV.v.40-44)*

This exchange between the two picks up the theme of "every man" and some men from Cressida's first scene: Cressida seems to have become aware of the melancholy distinctions which set some men apart from others. Here, Ulysses breaks in, evidently frustrated by the ongoing action in which he has not taken part:

> *Men.* You fillip me o' the head.
> *Cres.*   No, I'll be sworn.
> *Uly.* It were no match, your nail against his horn.
> May I, sweet lady, beg a kiss of you?
>
> *(45-47)*

While Tillyard seems to imply that Ulysses refuses to kiss Cressida, the language in their exchange indicates the reverse.

> *Cres.* You may.
> *Uly.*   I do desire it.
> *Cres.*   Why, beg then.
>
> *(48)*

Like a Vaudeville exchange, the old joke goes, "May I ask . . . ?"—"You may *ask*. . . ." Whereupon Ulysses, rebuffed, tries to turn the joke away from himself: "Why then for Venus' sake, give me a kiss, / When Helen is a maid again, and his." In the final stichomythic exchange, Cressida promises never to kiss Ulysses: "I am your debtor, claim it when 'tis due." And Ulysses takes the point: "Never's my day, and then a kiss of you" (49-52). Hence, Ulysses bursts out with his famous verdict on Cressida (after her exit), in all the vigor of sour grapes:

> Fie, fie upon her!
> There's language in her eye, her cheek, her lip,
> Nay, her foot speaks; her wanton spirits look out
> At every joint and motive of her body.
> O, these encounterers, so glib of tongue,
> That give accosting welcome ere it comes,
> And wide unclasp the tables of their thoughts
> To every ticklish reader! set them down
> For sluttish spoils of opportunity
> And daughters of the game.
>
> *(54-63)*

Ulysses' speech reveals more about himself than about Cressida. Far from showing herself "glib of tongue,"

Cressida does not speak a word until the scene is half through; far from unclasping the tables of her thoughts, she must be making some considerable effort to conceal her thoughts. Nor, of course, would the Greek officers listen to her thoughts if she did "unclasp" them. Ulysses' speech here is realistic only insofar as it displays the way a Greek captain would probably deal with a Trojan woman: aside from the motive of frustrated desire, is it likely that Ulysses would laud Cressida, thereby reflecting adversely on his own efforts to destroy her homeland? Guy de Maupassant would understand these Greek officers perfectly. Cressida is indeed the "spoils of opportunity," her situation determined by the forces set loose in her world; naturally, her captors must seek to justify her being "spoils" by asserting her to be "sluttish" as well.

Considered realistically, however, Cressida's situation is pathetic, and in IV.v the pathos underscores a very obvious double standard: Cressida is despised for being kissed by the men who are kissing her. Surely, therefore, to stage or to teach this scene as though it vindicated Ulysses' idea of "daughters of the game" violates the play; we are not being shown images of aggression so that we can league ourselves with the aggressors. Simple theatrical concerns, furthermore, enforce the same conclusion; to take Ulysses' speeches at face value results in underplaying the part, turning Ulysses into a pasteboard "statesman" instead of a real character, less noble but more interesting. Consider Ulysses' pattern of action: he bears tales to Nestor and Agamemnon about Patroclus' ridicule, which he could not have heard without eaves-dropping (I.iii); he breaks in on Menelaus' exchange with Cressida to divert Cressida's attention to himself (IV.v), and then tries to create an image of wantonness about Cressida; he interrupts Nestor's courtesies with Hector, to predict—to Hector—the fall of Troy (IV.v.217-21). He makes a point of telling Troilus about Diomedes' interest in Cressida, while asking insinuatingly,

> As gentle tell me, of what honour was
> This Cressida in Troy?
>
> (IV.v.288-89)

And finally, Ulysses escorts Troilus to spy on Cressida and prevents his doing anything but spying on her, by referring to a danger which must be exaggerated, given Ulysses' own status (V.ii). In short, Ulysses is a meddler. An attention-seeker, a flatterer, a talebearer, an eavesdropper, a contriver of plans which sound plausible but consistently fail, a man caught up in a war over someone else's wife, Ulysses exemplifies that aggressive behavior in which one surmounts one's own frustrations by making trouble for other people. Not surprisingly, therefore, Ulysses seems also to admire aggression in others: while he objects to Cressida's kissing Greeks, he highly praises Troilus' prowess in killing Greeks (IV.v.96-112)—notwithstanding that he himself is a Greek. "Masculine" aggression, even in an enemy, wins his approval, where an element of self-defensive behavior in the woman who is virtually a captive arouses his disdain.

Cressida's entrance into the Greek camp is paralleled weightily, in the same scene, by Hector's entrance into the Greek camp; Cressida's situation is reflected by Hector's. For in spite of the Greeks' sexual jollification with Cressida and their elaborate courtesies with Hector, Cressida and Hector still remain "spoils of opportunity," alike; they are similarly handed over to the Greeks and similarly, in effect, carved up. The two characters resemble each other not only in situation but also in language. Thus Hector, like Cressida, initially tries to divide "particulars" from the "general":

> Were thy commixtion Greek and Trojan so
> That thou couldst say 'This hand is Grecian all,
> And this is Trojan; the sinews of this leg
> All Greek, and this all Troy; my mother's blood
> Runs on the dexter cheek and this sinister
> Bounds in my father's'. . . .
> Thou shouldst not bear from me a Greekish member
> Wherein my sword had not impressure made
> Of our rank feud.
>
> (IV.v.124-32)

Unable to partition Ajax up as he wishes, however, Hector himself ends in being carved apart; refusing to kill Ajax (since his conscience prohibits killing the whole man), he falls prey to Achilles, even in anticipation:

> Tell me, you heavens, in which part of his body
> Shall I destroy him? whether there, or there, or there?
> That I may give the local wound a name
> And make distinct the very breach whereout
> Great Hector's spirit flew:
>
> (242-46)

In simpler terms, these great warriors have become so many illustrious butchers, who wish to carve each other up like cuts of meat:

> Now, Hector, I have fed mine eyes on thee;
> I have with exact view perused thee, Hector,
> And quoted joint by joint. . . .
> I will the second time,
> As I would buy thee, view thee limb by limb.
>
> (231-38)

Here is the culmination of the play's mercantile imagery as it applies to Hector and to Cressida (whose "every joint and motive" has already been "with exact view perused" by Ulysses).

This macabre emphasis on human "joints" in the later part of *Troilus and Cressida* parodies the earlier thematic distinction of "particular" from "general." Unable to distinguish people, as people, from the fact of their enmity, these Greeks and Trojans have degenerated to the hideous travesty of distinguishing particular "joints" of people from the whole person. Inevitably, therefore, the characters become what they have been denominated; they become fragmented instead of whole. Cressida too undergoes this transformation, but rather than dividing up other people on

Len Birman as Diomedes, Martha Henry as Cressida, and Peter Donat as Troilus in the 1963 Stratford Festival production of Troilus and Cressida.

the battlefield, she turns the process inward; in a traditional self-punishing fashion, she divides herself up:

> Troilus, farewell! one eye yet looks on thee;
> But with my heart the other eye doth see.
> Ah, poor our sex! this fault in us I find,
> The error of our eye directs our mind;
> What error leads must err; O, then conclude
> Minds sway'd by eyes are full of turpitude.

> *(V.ii.107-12)*

Having been divided into "joints," into "particular" parts, Cressida no longer acts as a whole person; V.ii fulfills the hints of self-division in III.ii. There is a tragic irony in the echoes of the earlier scene:

> *Tro.* What offends you, lady?
> *Cres.* Sir, mine own company.
> *Tro.* You cannot shun yourself.

> *(III.ii.151-52)*

Having been punished—as she evidently feels—for giving in to Troilus, Cressida sustains the self-defeating pattern by punishing herself; she turns to Diomedes, the very caricature of a "guardian" (V.ii.146). At the beginning of the play, Cressida knew the difference between "true and not true" in the world around her. When she turns to Troilus, however, she relinquishes that perception about others; when she turns to Diomedes, she relinquishes the distinction even within herself; she herself becomes "true and not true": "This is, and is not, Cressid" (146). Where Cressida is so divided, Troilus is in some sense right in saying, "rather think this not Cressid" (133).

In the patterns of aggression which schematize this play, men are turned into objects of fear, to be cut apart physically, and women are turned into objects of scorn, to be cut apart figuratively. The spuriously heroic chivalric ideal of man as warrior and woman as mistress dissolves in a parody of itself, in which men die and women go to the proverbial fate worse than death. Thus it would be a mistake to apply only half the play's lesson: *Troilus and Cressida* is not the story of a valiant hero's betrayal by an unfaithful woman. The play is more balanced (so to speak) than that; people of both sexes are subjected to pressures which destroy their essential humanity. I would like to end this discussion by pointing briefly to a speech of Hector's which illustrates the position of men and women in the wartime world of *Troilus and Cressida*. This passage comes from Hector's chivalric challenge to the Greeks:

> Hector, in view of Trojans and of Greeks,
> Shall make it good, or do his best to do it,
> He hath a lady, wiser, fairer, truer,
> Than ever Greek did compass in his arms,
> And will to-morrow with his trumpet call
> Midway between your tents and walls of Troy,
> To rouse a Grecian that is true in love:
> If any come, Hector shall honour *him;*
> If none, he'll say when he retires,
> The Grecian *dames* are sunburnt and not worth
> The splinter of a lance. Even so much.
>
> (I.iii.273-83)

It is no accidental figure of speech that the projected outcome of this "chivalric" encounter is honor for the man and disgrace for the women; nor is it accidental that the disgrace will be living and the "honour" connected only with death.

Notes

1. All quotations from the text refer to the *Troilus and Cressida* in Hardin Craig, ed., *The Complete Works of Shakespeare* (Chicago: Scott, Foresman, 1961).

2. See Richard Fly, "'Suited in Like Conditions as Our Argument': Imitative Form in Shakespeare's *Troilus and Cressida*," *Studies in English Literature*, 15 (1975), 273-92, for a discussion of the play's apparent disunity as the manifestation of its "devastating and form-denying vision."

3. Jarold W. Ramsey, "The Provenance of *Troilus and Cressida*," *Shakespeare Quarterly*, 21 (1970), 223-40.

4. For a good brief overview of this history of name-calling, see Grant L. Voth and Oliver H. Evans, "Cressida and the World of the Play," *Shakespeare Studies*, 8 (1975), 231-39, especially the notes. This excellent article itself is one of the few exceptions to the general censorious rule, as is R.A. Yoder's "'Sons and Daughters of the Game': An Essay on Shakespeare's *Troilus and Cressida*," *Shakespeare Survey*, 25 (1972), 11-25. To exhaust the list of critics who hold the pejorative view would be impossible here, but it includes readers otherwise so disparate as E.M.W. Tillyard, *Shakespeare's Problem Plays* (London: Chatto and Windus, 1950), on one hand, and Jan Kott, *Shakespeare Our Contemporary* (Garden City, N.Y.: Doubleday, 1964), on the other. Not even an otherwise enlightened view of the Trojan War saves Cressida from a fate worse than death: see Kott; Harold C. Goddard, *The Meaning of Shakespeare* (Chicago: Univ. of Chicago Press, 1951); and Emil Roy, "War and Manliness in Shakespeare's *Troilus and Cressida*," *Comparative Drama*, 7 (1973), 107-20.

5. I am using the term "metadramatic" in the sense in which I understand it from James L. Calderwood, *Shakespearean Metadrama* (Minneapolis: Univ. of Minnesota Press, 1971). See especially the first chapter. *Troilus and Cressida* is a play which seems to lend itself to this approach; see Fly, n. 2 above.

6. Camille Slights, "The Parallel Structure of *Troilus and Cressida*," *Shakespeare Quarterly*, 25 (1974), 42-51.

7. Carolyn Asp, "Th' Expense of Spirit in a Waste of Shame," *Shakespeare Quarterly*, 22 (1971), 345-57. This same view is also found in Tillyard's book, cited above, and in an otherwise very helpful article by Elias Schwartz, "Tonal Equivocation and the Meaning of *Troilus and Cressida*," *Studies in Philogy*, 69 (1972), 304-19.

8. Shakespeare uses the same pun and calls attention to it elsewhere; see *1 Henry IV* II.i.100-05.

9. See, for example, Asp, Schwartz, and even Voth and Evans.

10. The *Concordance* is instructive in this context. The word "whore" is used more in *Troilus and Cressida* than in any other Shakespearean play besides *Othello* (a fact which itself comments on the play); when women are mentioned in any context, it is almost always negatively. Not only women suffer thus, however; such language degrades the general image of humanity as well. Thus, the word "cur" is used more—applied to men—in this play than in any other play of Shakespeare's (including *The Two Gentlemen from Verona*, which contains a real dog). Not even "babies" are exempt: Troilus, for example, more than once uses the image of infancy, as he uses the image of womanhood, to express his own frailty. It is as though home and family are doomed to suffer in this play, even in image.

11. Harry Berger, Jr., "*Troilus and Cressida:* The Observer as Basilisk," *Comparative Drama*, 2 (1968), 122-36.

12. This composite image, of course, is an abiding tradition. Aldous Huxley, for example, employs it in *Time Must Have a Stop:* "Is this the face . . . ?" his character asks, looking at a rear-view painting of a woman bathing. The image is one variant of the "loathly lady" motif in literature.

13. This analogy was pointed out to me by a most helpful reader of my essay, Connie M. Ericson.

14. Other readers have discussed this imagery of commerce; see, for example, Yoder.

15. I have borrowed here, almost verbatim, from an unpublished essay by a colleague, Dr. Judy Matthews Craig. Throughout this discussion, I am indebted to Dr. Craig's reading both of the play and of my writing.

16. Tillyard, p. 75. Also, consider Tillyard's remarks on the previous scenes:

The next three scenes, IV.2, 3, and 4, are part comic, part pathetic: not tragic, because Troilus thinks he can trust Cressida and that he can visit her among the Greeks. They are scenes splendidly suited to the stage, very varied in passions, full of living characterisation. For instance when Cressida in her grief at parting calls herself "a woful Cressid 'mongst the merry Greeks," we feel that even then the thought flashes through her that the merry Greeks may compensate for what she is losing. Troilus behaves with dignity, already an older man than the youth of the play's opening scene: a clear analogy with Hamlet.

(p. 74)

Arlene N. Okerlund (essay date 1980)

SOURCE: "In Defense of Cressida: Character As Metaphor," in *Women's Studies*, Vol. 7, No. 3, 1980, pp. 1-17.

[*In the following essay, Okerlund analyzes the reassessments of Troilus, Cressida, Ulysses, and Pandarus that have occurred continuously since* Troilus and Cressida *was first produced, and concludes that our final judgment of these characters should be that none is evil or good in his or her own right, but that all are embodiments of human nature.*]

Fashions in literary criticism change. Not only do the theoretical stances shift from the new criticism to contextualism to Freudianism to historicism to formalism to Marxism to the newly-heralded reader-response criticism (to restrict examples to only a few decades of the twentieth century). but the sense of the meaning, or achievement, of an individual literary work can change just as dramatically. Perhaps no work better illustrates this critical reality than Shakespeare's *Troilus and Cressida*. Until well into the twentieth century, something of a consensus of interpretation existed—particularly regarding characterizations in this drama: Cressida was a prostitute deserving only scorn for the evils she perpetrated (a character assessment corroborated by citations of her Renaissance reputation),[1] Troilus was a naive, but honorable young knight abused by that disreputable, fickle woman (corroborated by theories of courtly love),[2] and Ulysses was a wise and respected philosopher expounding ideals of order and degree necessary for society's survival and prosperity (corroborated by quotations from E.M.W. Tillyard).[3] That is not to say there were no problems. The critical spirit was kept sprightly by confusion about *genre* (the title page calls it a history, the Quarto's preface a comedy, and Heminges and Condell a tragedy). And there were problems of authorship: not so much who wrote it, but how could he? The bitter, unmitigated, diseased images of *Troilus and Cressida* do not complement the idealized vision we would like to fantasize about Shakespeare.

Nevertheless, in discussing these puzzlements and despite sometimes dissenting voices, a consensus of the play's conceptual achievement gradually emerged: Shakespeare was opposed to both war and lechery. And the play reflected "a world of value and vision ruled by murderous and senseless time, who, ignorant and inexorable, pursues his endless course of destruction and slavery, cramming up his rich thievery, 'he knows not how'. The less noble and beautiful seem to win. Time slays the love of Cressid. Hector, symbol of knighthood and generosity, is slain by Achilles, lumbering giant of egotism, lasciviousness, and pride: but all the fires of human nobility and romance yet light Troilus to the last."[4]

With O.J. Campbell's *Comicall Satyre and Shakespeare's "Troilus and Cressida,"* however, critics were forced to reassess their understanding of this drama.[5] In pointing out that Troilus did, after all, share the same sensual bed with Cressida, Campbell raised questions about the integrity of the young knight's character and compelled a reevaluation of the play's achievement. And ever since, the journals have been filled with elaborations of the controversey. J.C. Oates agrees with Campbell that Troilus and Cressida constitute a well-matched couple in which "the woman is not inferior."[6] Katherine Stockholder further claims that Cressida is a "sex object" cynically used by Troilus to gratify his lust.[7] In a psycho-sexual analysis typical of much twentieth century criticism, Jan Kott notes that Cressida was "eight, ten or twelve years old when the war started," that she and Troilus were "wartime lovers . . . given just one night," and that the events of Cressida's life *require* her "to destroy everything, so that not even memory remains."[8] R.A. Yoder reminds us that Cressida's "playful bawdry and sharp passion are commonly found in the speeches of Shakespeare's virginal heroines, Rosalind or Juliet, for example" and her witty quips should not indict her alone of Shakespeare's heroines.[9] Such sentiments contrast sharply with the earlier condemnations of Cressida which began with John Dryden, the first critic to sniff that not only is this woman left alive, but she is "false, and is not punished."[10]

Troilus has enjoyed a similar reversal of reputation—except that his has moved in the opposite direction. For more than three centuries. Troilus basked in his accolades: G. Wilson Knight praised him for fidelity[11] and Frederick Boas for heroism.[12] W.W. Lawrence commended the "ardent, high-spirited boy who gives all the fervour of his idealistic young love to a false and shallow woman, and tastes the bitterest dregs in the cup of disillusion."[13] But as the above remarks about Cressida indicate, recent critics have permitted Troilus to share the ignominy, as well as the action, with Cressida.

So, too, critics have composed all possible variations on the Ulysses theme. From Tillyard's canonization to H.C. Goddard's disapprobation,[14] Ulysses has shifted back and forth from saint to villain. Karl F. Thompson sensibly analyzed Ulysses' character as representative of Shakespeare's "insights into the true nature of men engaged in statecraft,"[15] but subsequent articles have reverted to generally one-sided visions—with the majority viewing Ulysses as the philosophical hero representing order and restraint in a world berserk with ego and sex and death.[16]

Where do such contradictory interpretations lead us in our understanding of this play? Do they reflect only the relative historical-cultural milieu or the moralistic idiosyncrasies of the individual critic who is interpreting a text? Is the recent defense of Cressida, for instance, related to the changing sexual standards of the twentieth-century—exacerbated, perhaps, by the increasing participation of women in the activities of the world and in the practice of literary criticism (from Dryden on, after all, most critics who have praised Troilus and condemned Cressida have been fairly exclusively male).

Or perhaps Shakespeare's achievement is more complex than we have hitherto perceived. As the preceding summaries have indicated, critics frequently assign Shakespeare's characters to stereotypical categories: Cressida is either a deceitful prostitute *or* sex object, Troilus an ideal lover *or* passionate playboy, Ulysses a wise philosopher *or* pragmatic politician. But such assessments overlook the complexity of the play's structure in which the characters interact with each other within the dynamic, shifting social setting created by the war. In following Cressida through the play's action, for instance, we discover that she undergoes a significant change in character—evolving from an innocent young woman with all the intelligence and energy of Shakespeare's comic heroines into a faithless, capricious dissembler. Initially, Cressida possesses the wit, charm, vitality and passion of Rosalind or Portia. But the society in which Cressida lives is immoral and corrupt, and as the action develops, Cressida becomes caught up by the evil that surrounds her. To survive, she not only adopts the evil ways of the world, but ultimately perpetuates corruption herself.

Cressida, in fact, is the central metaphor of the play—reflecting what happens to people who live in this universe of Greeks and Trojans. Beginning with her quite sincere love for Troilus, Cressida is victimized by misfortunes over which she has no control: the war and its attendant malignancies make her its hostage. But once involved in its politics, she no longer suffers as innocent victim but turns into the feminine analogue of Ulysses and Troilus and their compatriots: "What error leads must err" (V, ii, 111).[17] Cressida's role thus incarnates the process of evil in the world, reflecting the method through which perversion extends itself throughout human experience. It is a process that reaches out in ever-widening circles to engulf the formerly innocent. And its progress is continuous with no perceptible beginning and no apparent ending.

The play's structure simulates this process with its beginning *in medias res,* in the midst of the war caused by Cressida's predecessor Helen, another innocent victim in an on-going quarrel among goddesses. That quarrel, too, produced its ever-widening circles of evil, first engulfing Helen and Paris, then extending to the larger societies of Greece and Troy. Thus, the setting in which Troilus and Cressida find themselves creates irresolvable problems for them. Shakespeare emphasizes that setting with the Prologue, who appears in armor to tell us that the play is beginning in the middle of the war being fought over the "ravished Helen" and the "wanton Paris." Indeed, the Prologue's unpleasant, negative adjectives establish the atmosphere that will prevail to the end of the play: "orgulous," "chafed," "cruel," "ravished," "wanton," "warlike." His verbs are equally ugly and threatening: "ransack," "disgorge."

Another part of the problem is Pandarus, the older uncle who urges his protégés on to sensuality and license. Pandarus ought to protect and preserve his abandoned niece from the dangers of the surrounding war. The kinship is emphasized—pronounced three times by Pandarus himself (I, i, 44; 76; 77) and three times by Cressida and Alexander, who address him as "uncle" (I, ii, 39; 43; 47). But as we all know, Pandarus uses his position to subvert Cressida's honor, and that irony forever underscores Cressida's vulnerability. Both Troilus and Cressida know Pandarus for what he is and denounce his manipulative talents with a directness that contributes to the uneasy tenor of the opening scenes. Troilus complains:

> . . . instead of oil and balm,
> Thou lay'st in every gash that love hath given me
> The knife that made it.
>
> (I, i, 61-63)

Cressida, too, recognizes her Uncle's vulgarity, but rather than suffer his outrageous and lewd insinuations with traditional feminine submission, she gives as good as she takes. It is Pandarus, however, who always initiates the badinage: when Cressida speaks of Hector, Pandarus interjects, "And there's Troilus will not come far behind him. Let them take heed of Troilus, I can tell them that too . . . Troilus is the better man of the two" (I, ii, 59-64). Cressida will have none of such nonsense and scoffingly rejects Pandarus' claims, prefacing her remarks, it must be admitted, with an unladylike oath: "Oh Jupiter! There's no comparison" (I, ii, 65). William Hazlitt is quite right about the woman: unlike Chaucer's earlier heroine, Shakespeare's Cressida is not "grave, sober, and considerate."[18] And the absence of those qualities has caused innumerable critics to ignore her good attributes—her wit, her spiritedness, and her common sense. Her soliloquy at the end of this scene, for instance, reveals a knowledge of human nature that is keen and discerning:

> . . . Women are angels, wooing.
> Things won are done, joy's soul lies in the doing.
> That she beloved knows naught that knows not this—
> Men prize the thing ungained more than it is.
> That she was never yet that ever knew
> Love got so sweet as when desire did sue.
> Therefore this maxim out of love I teach:
> Achievement is command; ungained, beseech.
>
> (I, ii, 312-19)

Even fairly limited experience with life informs us that Cressida is not far wrong about man's nature. But her insistence on viewing the world as it is, rather than as it ought to be, has ruined her reputation with some critics. Boas, for instance, quotes the above lines as proof that Cressida is a "scheming, cold-blooded profligate."[19] Yet, her analysis of human relationships hardly differs from the Friar's in *Much Ado,* who remarks as he plots to reunite Hero and Claudio: "That what we have we prize not to the worth / Whiles we enjoy it; but being lacked and lost, / Why, then we rack the value, then we find / The virtue that possession would not show us / Whiles it was ours" (IV, i, 220-24). Why such insights as the Friar's represent "wisdom" and Cressida's "profligacy" constitutes one of the unexplained mysteries of literary criticism. Perhaps we should evaluate the accuracy of Cressida's analysis in terms of the actions which follow.

Central to those actions, of course, are the deeds of Troilus, who next appears in the Trojan Council arguing for the war. Enough has already been written about honor and reason, as represented by Troilus and Hector, but little has been written about the developing character of Troilus in this scene. Perhaps that is because he is hardly admirable here. His arguments in the Council must be viewed in the context of his earlier actions in the war—actions that were few, indeed. Troilus, we must remember from Act I, Scene i, stayed home while his brothers fought and lamented his frustrations while they shed blood (behavior he shall repeat in Act III, Scene i). During the Council discussion, however, Troilus suddenly becomes the vigorous advocate of pursuing the fight. He turns on Helenus with sarcasm: "You are for dreams and slumbers, brother priest" (II, ii, 37). Yet, *we* know who has been dreaming. He rejects his brother's deference to reason with contempt:

> . . . Nay, if we talk of reason,
> Let's shut our gates, and sleep. Manhood and honor
> Should have hare hearts, would they but fat their thoughts
> With this crammed reason. Reason and respect
> Make livers pale and lustihood deject.

> (II, ii, 46-50)

Troilus' contempt of reason in a philosophical system that believed the intellect controlled man's physical nature (and reflected man's correspondence with God) should certainly raise questions about the young knight's character. Troilus relies on passion to effect Hector's concession, a passion that fast becomes his identifying characteristic.

When he next appears in the orchard, for instance, his diction reveals a passionate nature that borders on the bestial: "I *stalk* about her door . . . give me swift transportation to those fields / Where I may *wallow* in the lily beds" (III, ii, 9-13, italics mine). Or as his oft-quoted description of love reveals: "This is the monstrosity in love, lady, that the will is infinite and the execution confined, that the desire is boundless and the act a slave to limit" (III, ii, 88-90). Troilus apparently finds the "expense of spirit" to constitute the totality of possible relationships between men and women. Never does he indicate any perception of a soul or spirit within Cressida's lovely body; indeed, as soon as Cressida admits her love for him, he belittles and distrusts her with doubts about her integrity:

> Oh, that I thought it *could be* in a woman—
> As, *if* it can, I will presume in you—
> To feed for aye her lamp and flames of love,
> To keep her constancy in plight and youth,
> Outliving beauty's outward, with a mind
> That doth renew swifter than blood decays!
> Or that persuasion *could* but thus convince me
> That my integrity and truth to you
> *Might* be affronted with the match and weight
> Of such a winnowed purity in love.
> How *were* I then uplifted!

> (III, ii, 165-75, italics mine)

The subjunctive neatly undercuts the possibility of such "uplifting." Yet at this point in the action, Troilus has no basis for such suspicions, no reasons for his cynicism about Cressida's ability to love. Perhaps his doubts about her sincerity originate in the debauched atmosphere that defines Troy: the leering carnality of Pandarus, the lewd jokes of Helen and Paris. Whatever the source, Troilus' distrust of women certainly causes him to act dishonorably in the succeeding actions. Immediately following his assignation with Cressida, for instance, Troilus reveals embarrassment—or more accurately, shame—at being discovered at her home:

> . . . And, my Lord Aeneas,
> We met by chance, you did not find me here.

> (IV, ii, 72-73)

Paraphrase is always redundant, but past reverences of Troilus as a courtly lover require that we emphasize the meaning of this line: "Hey, fellows, don't tell Daddy where I spent last night." If he is concerned with propriety, such concern would be unique in this society, a society that accepts Paris and Helen and Margarelon rather uncritically. Troilus does not need to skulk around at night, to hide behind bedroom doors, among these men who proclaim their loves to the world. His conduct toward Cressida, in fact, pointedly contrasts with Hector's love for Andromache, which is boldly announced to the Greek camp in a challenge to combat:

> He hath a lady, wiser, fairer, truer,
> Than ever Greek did compass in his arms,
> And will tomorrow with his trumpet call
> Midway between your tents and walls of Troy,
> To rouse a Grecian that is true in love.

> (I, iii, 275-79)

Never does Troilus indicate such pride in the woman he loves. Instead, when Cressida is ordered to the enemy camp, Troilus effectively abandons her. The persuasive Troilus, who earlier had single-handedly argued the entire Trojan Council into submission about retaining Helen, utters *not one word* in defense of Cressida, but sacrifices her to the expediency of the war effort without protest. Further, at this moment when Cressida surely needs comfort and sympathy, he again insults her integrity with a series of imperatives: "Hear me, my love. Be thou but true of heart" (IV, iv, 60). Eight lines later: "Be thou true, / And I will see thee." Seven lines later: "But yet, be true." And later: "But be not tempted." Cressida is offended, for Troilus' passion is conditional—hinging on "if's" and "but's." Its imperatives surely recall Cressida's soliloquy: "Achievement is command . . . ." Its sentiments are rather far removed from a love that alters not when it alteration finds.

After such experiences, we can hardly blame Cressida for her subsequent acts in the Greek camp. Abandoned by her father, pimped by her uncle, delivered to the enemy by her lover, dare we censure her for developing strategies to survive in the hostile world? With father, uncle, and lover *proven* untrustworthy, only the self is left; thus, Cressida turns to her only assets—her wit and personality and sex—to survive among the enemy commanders. Her kissing of the Greek lords provokes Ulysses' contempt (and the subsequent disdain of many latter day critics), but such action simply does not merit Ulysses' conclusion that Cressida is a "daughter of the game." Desdemona's kissing of Cassio, for instance, never receives comparable criticism. In fact, when Iago objects to such conviviality, we brand *him* as the malcontent well on the way to villainy. And if we admit some extrinsic evidence from Desiderius Erasmus—not exactly a wanton profligate, himself—Cressida's manner of greeting the commanders would have been viewed by Shakespeare's contemporaries as the usual social custom. In Epistle 98, Erasmus writes to Faustus Andrelinus about his experiences in England:

> There is a fashion which cannot be commended enough. Wherever you go, you are received on all hands with kisses; when you take leave, you are dismissed with kisses. If you go back, your salutes are returned to you. When a visit is paid, the first act of hospitality is a kiss, and when guests depart, the same entertainment is repeated; wherever a meeting takes place there is kissing in abundance; in fact whatever way you turn, you are never without it. Oh Faustus, if you had once tasted how sweet and fragrant those kisses are, you would indeed wish to be a traveller, not for ten years, like Solon, but for your whole life, in England.[20]

Yet Ulysses' claims have been widely accepted as an accurate assessment of Cressida's character. No one notices that Ulysses is the one who urged the kissing in the first place: "Yet is the kindness but particular, / 'Twere better she were kissed in general" (IV, v, 20-21). No one observes that Ulysses asks to participate himself. No one notes that his words as opposed to his actions merely prove that the Greeks subscribed to the double standard, too.

Ulysses' interpretation ought to be questioned—especially since he is not exactly a disinterested observer of this scene. As a Greek commander, he must surely resent the exchange of Antenor for this woman, since the warrior's return to Troy can only strengthen the enemy cause. And considering the trouble Polyxena has been causing, the introduction of Cressida into his camp must seem a terribly poor bargain to the wily commander. Or perhaps Ulysses is merely angered by Cressida's denial of a kiss to him alone of the Greek leaders. Such speculation extends beyond the facts of the text, which never adequately explain the motivation behind Ulysses' hostility toward Cressida, but whatever the motivation, the casual social greeting Cressida bestows on Agamemnon, Nestor, and the others does not warrant the conclusion that

>   . . . her wanton spirits look out
> At every joint and motive of her body.
> Oh, these encounters, so glib of tongue,
> That give accosting welcome ere it comes,
> And wide unclasp the tables of their thoughts
> To every ticklish reader! Set them down
> For sluttish spoils of opportunity,
> And daughters of the game.
>
>   (IV, v, 56-63)

Too often, I fear, past critics have permitted Ulysses' sharp mind and eloquent rhetoric to seduce them into accepting his words at face value without evaluating their larger context—in this case, the discrepancy between Cressida's actions and Ulysses' interpretation of them.

Swayed by the rhetoric, we have failed to perceive the inconsistencies in Ulysses' logic and the blatant political opportunism that motivates his every action. If his oft-quoted speech on order and degree expresses a philosophical ideal, it also includes exactly the right details to goad Nester and Agamemnon into action:

> The large Achilles, on his pressed bed lolling,
> From his deep chest laughs out a loud applause,
> Cries "Excellent! 'Tis Agamemnon just.
> Now play me Nestor, hem, and stroke thy beard,
> As he being dressed to some oration.'
>
>   (I, iii, 162-66)

A master psychologist, Ulysses manipulates all his victims to achieve his desired ends. He flatters Ajax until the warrior turns into a swaggering, prideful fool, then joins the other Greeks in making fun of the "blockish" dolt—duplicitous behavior that characterizes Ulysses' every deed. His rigging of the lottery whereby Ajax is chosen to meet Hector is another instance demonstrating that honesty does not necessarily pertain to Ulysses' policy.

Such dishonesty characterizes Ulysses' philosophical positions also. When he shifts his attention to Achilles, he taunts the sulking hero with details of Ajax's new-found fame and expounds a facile philosophy about honor:

>   . . . Good deeds past . . . are devoured
> As fast as they are made, forgot as soon
> As done.
>
>   (III, iii, 148-50)

This individual who earlier had preached to Agamemnon and Nestor about the immutable certainties that govern man's society on earth now insists that no absolute values exist in this shifting, changing world. Man's worth, Ulysses claims, depends upon "reflection, / As when his virtues shining upon others / Heat them, and they retort that heat again / To the first giver" (III, iii, 99-102).[21] He convinces the prideful Achilles of this "truth," but one wonders how readers and critics who are familiar with such antithetical propositions as "Woe unto you, when all men shall speak well of you! for so did their fathers to the false prophets" (Luke 6:26), can agree with Ulysses so readily. For the wily commander, philosophy is an expediency, a bludgeon to force others into compliance with his will. Philosophical verities—always self-serving—shift with the listener.

Equally self-serving is the over-blown flattery of Ulysses' address to the Greek leaders. He prefaces the order and degree speech with a greeting to Agamemnon as the "great commander, nerve and bone of Greece . . . most mighty for thy place and sway" (I, iii, 55-60). Those titles should surprise us a bit, since they follow immediately upon Agamemnon's own admission of ineptitude in leading the troops. When Aeneas later enters, Ulysses' flattery creates one of the few genuinely comic moments in this drama, for Aeneas looks directly at the nerve and bone of Greece, asks for the "great Agamemnon" five times, and participates in forty lines of dialogue before he discovers he has been speaking to him all along. The delayed recognition should caution us to be somewhat wary of Ulysses' introductions, at least.

These several examples of linguistic and philosophic agility should raise our suspicions about everything Ulysses says and does. He offers to escort Troilus to Calchas' tent only after he has appraised Troilus as

> . . . A true knight,
> Not yet mature, yet matchless, firm of word,
> Speaking in deeds and deedless in his tongue,
> Not soon provoked nor being provoked soon calmed.
>
> (IV, v, 96-99)

"Provocation" is exactly what will result if Troilus observes the meeting between Cressida and Diomedes. Ulysses already knows about Cressida's lover in Troy (IV, v, 289-92), and Troilus' insistence on visiting her tent certainly makes him a likely candidate for that role. But Ulysses is intent on instigating action between the two armies. Thus, he leads Troilus to an ideal vantage point and guides the young man's responses with judicious prompting: first a contemptuous taunt, "She will sing any man at first sight" (V, ii, 10); then some condescending solicitude, "This place is dangerous, / The time right deadly. I beseech you, go."—advice not likely to be followed by a "true knight / Not yet mature." When Troilus questions whether this woman was really his Cressida, Ulysses' response is quick, "Most sure she was" (V, ii, 126). The immature knight is no match for the wily commander,

and as the ensuing slaughter indicates, Ulysses succeeds in his goal. But success does not necessarily constitute a moral and philosophical ideal. Ulysses, the pragmatic psychologist, should never be mistaken for the philosopher who seeks truth and preaches virtue. In his efforts for the Greek cause, Ulysses panders for war as surely as Pandarus conspires for lechery, and the policy of the crafty swearing rascal, ". . . that same dog fox Ulysses, is not proved worth a blackberry" (V, iv, 11-12).

Yet it is Ulysses' commentary that has largely created Cressida's reputation. He *tells* us she is a whore and we believe him. Thus, Cressida reaps all the blame for the Diomedes scene, even though Diomedes is the calculating master of the game the two play. Like a child who threatens to run home if he cannot have his way, Diomedes turns to leave every time Cressida hesitates in fulfilling his demands. Yes, Cressida *should* reject his advances, but her vulnerable position among enemies makes that expectation rather unrealistic. Throughout this scene, she is obviously torn between Diomedes' ultimata and her memories of Troilus, and even as she hands over the sleeve, she regrets her action (a point usually overlooked in charges against her). Her obvious distress deserves pity more than blame, for she recognizes her iniquity and chastizes herself even before Thersites begins calling her names:

> Ah, poor our sex! This fault in us I find,
> The error of our eye directs our mind.
> What error leads must err. Oh, then conclude
> Minds swayed by eyes are full of turpitude.
>
> (V, ii, 109-12)

Self-knowledge never excuses misdeeds, of course, but it does avoid the hypocrisy of Troilus' egoistic perfidy. Moreover, when Cressida finally acquiesces, she agrees only to meet Diomedes—and that after much vacillation and embarrassing servility: "I prithee do not hold me to mine oath. / Bid me do anything but that, sweet Greek" (V, ii, 26-27). The play ends before the situation resolves itself, but the absence of a conclusion has not prevented Thersites, that most lubricious of voyeurs, and Cressida's other critics from believing the worst. Absolutely, Cressida is fickle and weak in allowing Diomedes to manipulate her, but the action of the text does not justify the collective denunciation she has reaped.

In short, Cressida is no worse (although she is certainly no better) than the other characters of this play. Among the "heroes," as we well know, are the prideful Achilles, the envious Ajax, the slothful Patroclus, the scurrilous Thersites, the impotent Menelaus, the playboy Paris, the egoistic Troilus, and the wily Ulysses. Everyone in this universe except Hector is corrupt. And Hector is murdered for his virtue. Further, everyone shares in Hector's murder—Troilus who argues him into submission, Ulysses who sets up the combat, Achilles who gives the order, and the Myrmidons who slay him. As Troilus forewarns us, men like Hector must necessarily die in such a society:

> When many times the captive Grecian falls,
> Even in the fan and wind of your fair sword,

You bid them rise and live.
Hect. Oh, 'tis fair play.
Tro.   Fool's play, by Heaven, Hector.

(V, iii, 40-43)

Fair play produces ugly corpses. That is the fact Cressida faces as she strides into the Greek camp to play the social game according to the rules she has learned from friend and foe. Like Shakespeare's comic heroines, she looks fortune in the eye and faces it down, refusing to give in to the exigencies of a world that is hostile. The problem is that the Greek and Trojan universe contains no green world where man's debilitated life can renew itself. Cressida leaves Troy not to enter the forest of Arden, but a forest of Greek tents filled with debauched, demoralized, manipulative inhabitants. To survive, she resorts to their self-serving, duplicitous, expedient actions.

Thus, the cycle of evil perpetuates itself: "What error leads must err." And thus, this play which begins *in medias res* never ends, for Pandarus' final action extends the cycle to the audience, accusing it of the self-same deeds just enacted on the stage. Contemporary Winchester geese merge the fictional world of Helen and Cressida with the real world of seventeenth-century London, reiterating the cyclic history of man wherein each era replicates within its brief moment the recorded tragedies of past human experiences. Nor is there any promise that the cycles will end. Unlike Shakespeare's tragedies, no rational force restores order to the chaotic world. No Fortinbras strides on stage to assume command, no Cassio survives to govern the state. Nor is there an Albany, a Malcolm, or even an Octavius Caesar. Only the self-serving, the self-indulgent, the murderers of Hector remain. And if the audience hisses that fact, its members find Pandarus' rude finger pointing at them.

And that, of course, is Shakespeare's point. For even now—thirty centuries after Troy—self-indulgent men still assert their power by waging wars and annihilating other men. Politicians still manipulate the destiny of their societies—mindless of the deaths of the individuals who comprise those societies. "Honor" still remains synonymous with military victory and worldly fame and narcissistic pride. "Love" still masks sexual gormandizing. In *Troilus and Cressida,* Shakespeare points out the perversion of such traditional and unexamined attitudes by turning art into a literal mirror of life—a mirror reflecting images of the vices that pass for virtue in society. And if we miss that point, the epilogue explicitly tells us that all the time we have been watching Troilus and Ulysses and Cressida and Pandarus, we have been looking at ourselves:

    . . . If you cannot weep, yet give some groans,
Though not for me, yet for your aching bones.
Brethren and sisters of the hold-door trade,
Some two months hence my will shall here be made.
It shold be now, but that my fear is this—
Some galled goose of Winchester would hiss.
Till then I'll sweat and seek about for eases,
And at that time bequeath you my diseases.

(V, x, 50-57)

Small wonder this play has seldom been staged and is read only in college classrooms, for it compels a reassessment of social and personal morality that most of us prefer to avoid. As victims of the satire, we want to escape its accusations or, at least, ignore them in hopes that they will go away. Certainly, literary criticism has reflected exactly this impulse. In villainizing Cressida, it has offered a scapegoat to excuse the continuing evils of society—without bothering to search out the causes of such evils. In adopting Ulysses as philosophical spokesman, it has embraced his techniques without challenging the duplicities of his rhetoric and logic. My own neglect of Thersites in this discussion, in fact, may derive not so much from the necessity to keep the manuscript to a reasonable length as from the greater necessity to avoid admitting that he is one of us—perhaps *is* us. But perhaps we have also reached a point in history where we can look at the characters and actions of *Troilus and Cressida* head-on. Perhaps we have caught up to Shakespeare's vision in 1600 and can examine the evils of society as they actually exist. If we can face those truths honestly, we may begin to correct our human imperfections. Some day, we might even be able to contemplate the play's ending without hissing.

Notes

1. Hyder Rollins in "The Troilus-Cressida Story from Chaucer to Shakespeare," *PMLA* 32 (1917), 382-429, summarizes the few positive and many negative references to Cressida in Renaissance literature.

2. See, for instance, Mary Ellen Rickey, "'Twixt the Dangerous Shores: *Troilus and Cressida* Again," *SQ* 15 (1964), 4, an article which commends Troilus as "traditionally the near-perfect lover, [who] chooses an object unworthy of his affections and so loses reason and happiness."

3. *The Elizabethan World Picture* (New York: Random House, n.d.) uses the order and degree speech of Ulysses as the quintessential summary of Renaissance philosophy.

4. G. Wilson Knight, *The Wheel of Fire: Interpretations of Shakespearian Tragedy with Three New Essays* (1930; rpt. London: Methuen, 1956), p. 71.

5. *Comicall Satyre and Shakespeare's Troilus and Cressida* (San Marino, CA.: Huntington Library, 1938).

6. "The Ambiguity of *Troilus and Cressida*," *SQ* 17 (1966), 149.

7. "Power and Pleasure in *Troilus and Cressida,* or Rhetoric and Structure of the Anti-Tragic," *CE* 30 (1969), 541.

8. *Shakespeare Our Contemporary,* Boleslaw Taborski, trans. (Garden City, N.Y.: Doubleday, 1964), pp. 71-73.

9. "'Sons and Daughters of the Game': An Essay on Shakespeare's *Troilus and Cressida*," *Sh S* 25 (1972), 22.

10. *"Troilus and Cressida,* 'Preface: Containing the Grounds of Criticism in Tragedy'," quoted from *Essays of John Dryden,* W. P. Ker, ed. (Oxford: Clarendon Press, 1900), I, p. 203.

11. *The Wheel of Fire,* p. 62.

12. *Shakspere and His Predecessors* (New York: Charles Scribner's Sons, 1896), p. 373.

13. *Shakespeare's Problem Comedies* (Baltimore: Penguin, 1960), pp. 130-31.

14. *The Meaning of Shakespeare* (Chicago: Univ of Chicago Press, 1951), pp. 397-408.

15. "The Unknown Ulysses," *SQ* 19 (1968), 128.

16. In a recent article, Hawley C. Taylor elevated Ulysses into a Stoic "model of ideal behavior, the complete *homo viator.*" "The Stoic Philosophy and Shakespeare's *Troilus and Cressida,*" *San Jose Studies* 4 (February 1978), 90.

17. All quotations are from *Shakespeare: The Complete Works,* G. B. Harrison, ed. (New York: Harcourt, Brace & World, 1968).

18. *The Complete Works of William Hazlitt,* P.P. Howe, ed. (London: J.M. Dent and Sons, 1930), IV, 224.

19. *Shakspere and His Predecessors,* p. 375.

20. *The Epistles of Erasmus from His Earliest Letters to His Fifty-first Year Arranged in Order of Time,* Francis Morgan Nichols, trans. (1901; rpt. New York: Russell & Russell, 1962), I, 203.

21. G. B. Harrison cites this speech (III, iii, 95-215) as "the best possible advice to Achilles, reminding him of the universal truth—the touch of nature that makes the whole world kin—that men always follow the newest fashion and soon forget the old," *Shakespeare: The Complete Works,* p. 976.

Barry Nass (essay date 1984)

SOURCE: "'Yet in the Trial Much Opinion Dwells': The Combat Between Hector and Ajax in *Troilus and Cressida,*" in *English Studies,* Vol. 65, No. 1, February, 1984, pp. 1-10.

[*In the following essay, Nass describes* Troilus and Cressida *as a play which focuses on the search for authentic, individual identity as well as for loyalty and love within the chaos of war.*]

Critics of *Troilus and Cressida* often regard the combat between Hector and Ajax (IV.v.) as a dramatic failure or as yet one more jarring episode in Shakespeare's satiric and unsettling portrayal of the Trojan War. Reuben A. Brower speaks for the majority when he observes, with disappointment, that 'the effect of the scene is lamely anti-climactic'. Daniel Seltzer confirms this judgment from a theatrical perspective, describing the duel as 'a red-herring for the director, . . . dramatically uninteresting compared to other portions of the scene . . . [and] especially pale compared to the byplay between Achilles and Hector'. T. McAlindon, on the contrary, declares the aborted combat to be an artful ploy and asserts that 'the anticlimax was part of Shakespeare's whole conception of the play'. The neologisms, Latinate diction, and elaborate conceits so prominent in Hector's speeches are, McAlindon states, deliberate stylistic effects 'debasing Hector's inherently respectable motive for withdrawal'.[1]

On its surface this long-anticipated confrontation indeed seems to come to nothing: Hector's 'roisting challenge'[2] and Ulysses' elaborate scheme to lure Achilles back into battle collapse ingloriously in a halfhearted exchange of blows followed by a lusty embrace between the two champions. The combat immediately gains stature, however, if we consider the reasons why Hector refuses to fight Ajax and the implications of his refusal with respect to a problem that afflicts all the characters in this play—the task of satisfactorily establishing identities and loyalties in the confused and confusing world of Troy.[3] From beginning to end the combat consistently emphasizes this dilemma by raising it within the framework of the military plot. Then only moments after the duel is over, the love plot depicts perhaps the drama's most striking example of the difficulty characters face in trying to determine identities and loyalties. Led through the Greek camp by Ulysses, Troilus discovers Cressida's liaison with Diomedes and struggles to absolve his beloved of infidelity by postulating, against all logic, the existence of two Cressidas (V.ii. 137-60). The significance of Troilus' metaphysical labors cannot be fully understood, however, without taking the conclusion of the combat into account. There Hector's refusal to divide Ajax into Greek and Trojan parts so that he might kill the Greek half (IV.v. 119-38) provides an ironic—and subversive—contrast to Troilus' futile attempt at dividing Cressida into two different women. Moreover, just before Troilus' speech Cressida resorts to the same device, explaining her own penchant for faithlessness in terms of a divided self that contains two Cressidas (V.ii. 107-12). In many ways, then, the combat is not a dramatic flaw, nor does its only virtue lie in once again defeating audience expectations, although much more needs to be said about precisely what desires are frustrated in this scene. Carefully integrated with the whole of the play, the combat in fact occupies a most unusual status in *Troilus and Cressida:* it begins by reiterating the impulses and attitudes at the heart of the Trojan conflict, and it ends by challenging them.

The irreverent depiction of the Trojan War in *Troilus and Cressida* owes much, as is well known, to the medieval and Renaissance texts which denounced its folly and condemned its participants for sacrificing their lives on behalf of a cuckold and his queen.[4] Rosalie L. Colie has shown that Shakespeare translates this loss of nobility and moral direction into dramatic action by portraying characters who are continually straining to identify friends, enemies, or even lovers. Their persistent questioning of the names and identities of people they ought to know well contributes markedly to the satiric atmosphere of the play by draining actions, people, and epic conventions associated with naming of their once-heroic value and meaning. It is extraordinarily difficult for Greeks and Trojans alike to get their bearings in this war, to act purposefully, or to preserve their sense of who and what they are. Chaos, not glory, reigns in Shakespeare's Troy.[5]

From its first mention in I.iii., the combat involves these problems in ascertaining identities and loyalties. Aeneas delivers Hector's challenge that the Greeks choose—or identify—a champion. But Aeneas does not recognize Agamemnon on seeing him and asks, much to majesty's chagrin: 'How may / A stranger to those most imperial looks / Know them from eyes of other mortals?' (I.iii. 223-25). Surprising and comic after seven years of fighting, Aeneas' query is a parody of the highly formal salutation an emissary may be expected to render.[6] It undermines as well the ancient supposition, both literary and social, that men can readily identify a king or hero by his superior visage. Finally, this inability to discern 'those most imperial looks' also undercuts the series of speeches Ulysses and Nestor have just given on the dire consequences of failing to identify and obey one's rightful king and leader. Indeed, when Aeneas cannot single out the king, he strengthens Achilles' contention that Agamemnon has no unique or godlike privilege to command. And the threat Ulysses so vividly describes in his oration on degree—the disorder that erupts when 'The specialty of rule hath been neglected' (I.iii. 78) appears one step closer as a result of Aeneas' neglect in identifying Agamemnon.

The basis for Hector's challenge suggests still more about the world of *Troilus and Cressida* and its values. Focusing on individuals rather than armies, the invitation to single combat reiterates on a personal scale the origins of the Trojan conflict.[7] Hector presses the enemy to select a champion who will fight for the reputation of his mistress and, by extension, the glory of the Greek camp. Trojan and Greek are therefore to do battle for the same reasons they have been doing battle over Helen: to preserve a lady's honor and that of a nation. In fact, the duel is particularly symbolic of the war because its antagonists are especially representative of both armies. In reprisal for the rape of Hesione, Hector's aunt and Ajax's mother, the Trojans stole away Helen. As Troilus puts the matter when addressing the issue of the war itself: 'Why keep we her [Helen]? The Grecians keep our aunt' (II.ii. 80).[8]

During the Trojan debate, from which Troilus' statement comes, the connection between the war and the combat is made explicit. At the outset of the scene Hector proposes that Helen be returned to the Greeks, condemning Paris and Troilus as men led by passion not reason in their desire to continue the bloodshed. But after invoking Aristotle and 'these moral laws / Of nature and of nations' (II.ii. 184-85) in support of his position, Hector suddenly withdraws his objections and joins his brothers

> In resolution to keep Helen still,
> For 'tis a cause that hath no mean dependance
> Upon our joint and several dignities.

(II.ii. 191-93)

When Troilus celebrates this decision, calling Helen 'a theme of honor and renown' (II.ii. 199), Hector again pledges his loyalty to the Trojans. For several reasons he then alludes to the combat. It is 'a theme of honor and renown'. It allows him to associate the public cause with the private, the nation's defense of Helen's honor with his own defense of Andromache's. And it provides an opportunity for contrasting the renewed solidarity of the Trojans with the reputed disunity of the Greeks:[9]

> I am yours,
> You valiant offspring of great Priamus.
> I have a roisting challenge sent amongst
> The dull and factious nobles of the Greeks
> Will [strike] amazement to their drowsy spirits.
> I was advertis'd their great general slept,
> Whilst emulation in the army crept:
> This I presume will wake him.

(II.ii. 206-13)

'Video meliora proboque, deteriora sequor'. Indefensible by any rational standard, this surprising turnabout necessarily colors responses to Hector, the war, and the combat. As Alice Walker observes: 'Hector is, indeed, more culpable than Troilus, for he abandons what he knows to be prudent and right to satisfy his own obsession—love of honour'.[10] In repudiating his own appeal to the precepts of natural and civil law, Hector openly deserts the reasonable and just course of action in favor of communal and individual honor, 'our joint and several dignities'. But his approval of further carnage on behalf of Helen—or the idea of a Helen—cannot blot out his earlier contention that 'she is not worth what she doth cost / The keeping' (II.ii. 51-52). As a consequence of the debate, the prestige of the war and its participants is dulled still more. Tarnished as well is the combat, which Hector holds up while committing himself anew to a conflict whose validity he has so severely challenged. As Hector's final pronouncement and the last issue mentioned in the debate, the duel therefore becomes a conspicuous emblem of Troy's morally suspect allegiance to chivalry and honor.

One can, of course, understand Hector's love of fame. One can also sympathize with his change of heart by recognizing, as does R.J. Kaufmann, that 'people are self-destructive, people are flawed *and* noble'.[11] Indeed, the endorsement of Hector's volte-face by so many readers indicates that in scenes like this *Troilus and Cressida* is tapping an audience's potential for condoning actions that cannot be justified rationally but nonetheless appeal to powerful emotions such as honor, pride, or nationalism. With Hector again at the center, these ambiguous responses to the war will come directly into play during the combat because its outcome also raises a series of questions about the audience's distance from the passions lying behind the Trojan War.

Up to this point the combat has reflected the preoccupations with love and honor that sustain the war. The duel also brings the problems of ascertaining identities and loyalties into high relief, but it does so by eliminating the confusion these difficulties effect elsewhere in the play. Consequently, the supposed 'anticlimax' of this scene, the reconciliation between Hector and Ajax, is in fact a victory over the chaos that efforts at naming and identification usually wreak in Troy. It is a victory as well over the hostility that separates two weary armies in their seven years' conflict over Helen.

This shift in perspective becomes apparent before the two opponents meet. In a distinct departure from the muddle over identities and origins that prevails among Greek and Trojan, all those present at the duel know Hector and Ajax are cousins (IV.v. 83ff.). Given this knowledge, the combatants themselves must weigh family loyalty against national loyalty, and honor gained in a duel against honor lost by failing to respect a blood-relationship. For the moment the ties of kinship prove stronger than the temptation to cross swords. When Hector declares his relationship with Ajax to be of greater consequence than the contest that is a microcosm of the war, he reveals that men may find other principles more compelling than the desire to perpetuate bloodshed. He also shows that by affirming bonds rather than differences, men may discover significant alternatives to battle and slaughter.[12]

Since Diomedes and Aeneas halt the combat before either man is injured, it seems proper to ask just how admirable Hector's decision to cease fighting really is. An emphasis on the degree of violence the duel entails should not detract, however, from its symbolic importance or from Hector's role in stopping it. After hearing Aeneas deliver Hector's challenge, Nestor remarks: 'Though't be a sportful combat, / Yet in the trial much opinion dwells' (I.iii. 335-36). In war, he is well aware, any test of prowess speaks loudly. Concern that the reputation of the Greeks would be badly damaged should Achilles lose even this 'sportful' contest therefore prompts Nestor and Ulysses to rig the lottery in Ajax's favor. At the duel itself Achilles learns the antagonists are cousins and predicts 'a maiden battle' (IV.v. 87); that is, one in which the opponents are not expected to draw blood. Matters threaten to turn out differently, however. The spectators' shouts, from which we must infer what happens, indicate that Hector does fight sluggishly. Not surprisingly, Troilus is more concerned with honor than harmony, and for appearance's sake urges his brother on: 'Hector, thou sleep'st, / Awake thee!' (IV.v. 114-15). Missing, as it were, the cues for a milder confrontation is Ajax. His 'well-disposed' blows, praised by Agamemnon (IV.v. 116), suggest that he battles vigorously. Perhaps seeing the danger this zeal poses, Diomedes and Aeneas interrupt the duel and call for its end. The responsibility for terminating the combat nevertheless rests fully with Hector, particularly since Ajax protests, 'I am not warm yet, let us fight again' (IV.v. 118). Hector rejects this proposal, however, and therefore rejects the symbolic implications of the duel he himself initiated.

When Achilles, Aeneas, and Agamemnon anticipate a peaceful conclusion to the combat, the word 'half' appears eight times in the space of just eleven lines:

> Aeneas. This Ajax is *half* made of Hector's blood,
> In love whereof, *half* Hector stays at home;
> *Half* heart, *half* hand, *half* Hector comes to seek
> This blended knight, *half* Troyan and *half* Greek . . .
>
> Agamemnon.   The combatants being kin
> *Half* stints their strife before their strokes begin.
>
>   (IV.v. 83-93. Italics mine)

With respect to Troilus' speech on the two Cressidas, which very shortly follows in V.ii., this repeated emphasis on division into two parts holds the utmost importance. Hector strikes no blows in earnest because he is unable, through any 'madness of discourse' (V.ii. 142) such as Troilus later practises, to invent two separate Ajaxes, one his enemy and the other his cousin. Hector cannot say, 'This is, and is not, Ajax,' and then cut down the supposedly Grecian half of his antagonist. 'This blended knight, half Troyan and half Greek' thwarts efforts to divide him because Hector recognizes that one cannot distinguish the Greek from the Trojan in a man's flesh or blood. To divide the indivisible violates the laws of logic and, in the case of the duel, a familial obligation sacred to the gods:

> Were thy commixtion Greek and Troyan so
> That thou couldst say, 'This hand is Grecian all,
> And this is Troyan; the sinews of this leg
> All Greek, and this all Troy; my mother's blood
> Runs on the dexter cheek, and this sinister
> Bounds in my father's,': by Jove multipotent,
> Thou shouldst not bear from me a Greekish member
> Wherein my sword had not impressure made
> [Of our rank feud]; but the just gods gainsay
> That any [drop] thou borrow'dst from thy mother,
> My sacred aunt, should by my mortal sword
> Be drained! Let me embrace thee, Ajax.
>
>   (IV.v. 124-35)

The effect of prematurely concluding the combat is disconcerting: we expect a fierce duel to take place and are disappointed when it does not. But this sense of dissatisfaction, which the critical views cited earlier indicate is widespread, invites further scrutiny. Rather than assume Shakespeare has let a scene fall flat or has introduced merely another anticlimax into a play riddled with anticlimaxes, we might more productively inquire why the audience has been induced to feel such discontent. That is, we might ask whether an audience expressing its displeasure at the duel's peaceful outcome should instead be surprised by its own sins in feeling cheated of a bloody encounter? Far from being bathetic or a dramatic failure, the combat is in fact a remarkable theatrical device that draws the audience into a desire for violence which it would immediately condemn outside the playhouse. In the Trojan debate, as we have seen, Hector's sudden and suspect resolution to support the fighting garners approval. In the same way the long-awaited combat lures the audience far enough into the universe of the war that it accepts the premise of doing battle over a lady and finds the refusal to maim another person on behalf of such a cause not admirable but anticlimactic.[13]

Although Hector proposes creating two Ajaxes, he quickly dismisses that notion, leaving his antagonist a whole man and pledging his loyalty to a cousin whose blood is incontestably a mixture of Greek and Trojan. In the scenes that follow, Hector's decision contrasts markedly with Troilus' extensive attempt at making two Cressidas from one and also with Cressida's use of the same ploy in justifying her own infidelity. By focusing in several different ways on the desire to generate two persons from one, Act IV, Scene v and Act V, Scene ii therefore become dramatic pendants that gain deeper significance and irony through their interaction with each other.

When Troilus sees Cressida give herself to Diomedes, the idealized world he has built around her constancy and love collapses. To escape the consequences of her betrayal, he creates two Cressidas, an idea which takes shape with another of the play's ubiquitous questions about identity: 'Was Cressid here?' (V.ii. 124). This query is followed by a series of assertions to a bewildered Ulysses that, despite appearances, she was not. For the distraught Troilus it is imperative to 'think this not Cressid' (V.ii. 133). By insisting on the existence of two Cressidas, Troilus allows his beloved to remain true to him, while the other Cressida, a woman he has never known, can yield to Diomedes:[14]

> This she? no, this is Diomed's Cressida . . .
>
> If there be rule in unity itself,
> This was not she. O madness of discourse
> That cause sets up with and against itself!
> Bi-fold authority, where reason can revolt
> Without perdition, and loss assume all reason
> Without revolt. This is, and is not, Cressid!
>
> (V.ii. 137-46)

In effect, Hector and Troilus are united by the same dilemma. Each must reevaluate his loyalty to a person associated with the enemy; and each at first tries to resolve this quandary by generating two persons from one. The martial vocabulary prominent in Troilus' speech underscores the fact that, in literal and metaphorical ways, he too is engaged in a combat. While Hector's battle is public, Troilus' is private and internal. It is a psychomachia whose adversaries are reason and the senses, and whose battleground is the soul, where 'there doth conduce a fight / Of this strange nature, that a thing inseparate / Divides more wider than the sky and earth' (V.ii. 147-49). Moreover, Troilus is in the enemy camp to observe the result of a challenge that asserts Hector 'hath a lady wiser, fairer, truer, / Than ever Greek did couple in his arms' (I.iii. 275-76). In seeking out Cressida, Troilus wants to assure himself that his lady also is true. But he learns to his dismay that she is not. The tightly knit sequence of the duel and Troilus' unhappy discovery therefore evokes a number of ironic parallels between the war plot and the love plot, parallels deriving special force from long-established literary conventions which interchange the language of warfare and love.

Given Hector's speech on the impossibility of dividing Ajax into two persons, Troilus' agonized attempt to invent two Cressidas stands out sharply as an exercise in the denial of truth and logic. Indeed, since he surely hears Hector's words of reconciliation with Ajax during the duel, his efforts to resurrect the same ploy in defense of Cressida appear all the more desperate and pitiable. The strain in reviving this flawed argument becomes clearer still because Troilus is unable so to 'invert th' attest of eyes and ears' (V.ii. 122) that he can bring himself to believe fully in the fiction Hector has just discounted. Much more slowly than in Hector's case, the desire to create two persons from one yields to the reality of accepting the many—and even contradictory—attributes embodied in an individual. But Troilus' emotional responses are always extreme. Cressida is either faithful forever (III.ii. 158ff.) or so much a traitor to his affections that she can never be redeemed:[15]

> O Cressid! O false Cressid! false, false, false!
> Let all untruths stand by thy stained name,
> And they'll seem glorious.
>
> (V.ii. 178-80)

In the light of the combat and Troilus' speech, it is noteworthy that Cressida also uses the image of the divided self when she must confront demands on her loyalties. Conscious of her own failings, she regretfully identifies in herself two selves; and in this way she warns Troilus that she cannot be the ideal of constancy and womanhood for which he longs. She describes these two selves by playing on the word *kind* as the noun meaning 'type' and as the adjective meaning 'in accordance with nature or the usual course of things', 'sympathetic', 'loving', or 'grateful'.[16] Since she claims to exercise no control over this cruel and unnatural self, both she and Troilus are susceptible to its whims:

> I have a kind of self resides with you;
> But an unkind self, that itself will leave
> To be another's fool.
>
> (III.ii. 148-50)

Her prophecy becomes fact in the Greek camp. Thinking she is alone after her rendezvous with Diomedes, Cressida again admits to having two selves which assure her lapses from fidelity. In her confession the puns on 'eye/I' point once more to the play's focus on the problem of establishing identities and loyalties:[17]

> Troilus, farewell! one eye yet looks on thee,
> But with my heart the other eye doth see.
> Ah, poor our sex! this fault in us I find,
> The error of our eye directs our mind.
> What error leads must err; O then conclude,
> Minds swayed by eyes are full of turpitude.
>
> (V.ii. 107-12)

As in the preceding statement Cressida here projects a sense of passivity, picturing her better self at the mercy of a tyrannical second self. But the speeches of Hector and Troilus both emphasize how much this second self can be an evasion, a refuge from the obligation to make troubling choices or resolve conflicting allegiances. Recourse to this second self can also be a means of avoiding the fact that vice and virtue coexist in the same person. 'The web of our life is of a mingled yarn, good and ill together', comments a lord in *All's Well That Ends Well* (IV.iii. 71-72), and touches the heart of the matter. There is only one Ajax and only one Cressida. Hector accepts the good and ill bound together in Ajax by acknowledging that he is simultaneously Trojan and Greek. Troilus, by contrast, sees only good or ill in his beloved; for him Cressida is either true or false. And while Cressida isolates virtuous and base characteristics in herself, she gives these separate existences so that she need never take responsibility for her own actions and desires.

In each of these instances the act of dividing one person into antithetical selves highlights in different ways the problem of ascertaining identities and loyalties which besets all the characters in *Troilus and Cressida*. With respect to this dilemma, Troilus' speech on the two Cressidas most vividly illuminates the epistemological and moral confusion of this process and of the war itself. As Rosalie L. Colie has remarked, Troilus' assertion 'This is, and is not, Cressid!' (V.ii. 146) exemplifies a rhetorical formula present throughout the play, a formula cast in 'the language of is-and-is-not, the terms of the familiar Liar-paradox'.[18] Simultaneously affirming and denying the same proposition, the equivocal language of the Liar-paradox reflects a world of instability and uncertainty. Nothing is fixed. Names, identities, and the choices people make shift constantly between the poles of what-is-and-is-not. In the case of Troilus' speech the Liar-paradox also promotes instability: by stating 'This is, and is not, Cressid!', Troilus attempts to avoid the need, which living in any society imposes, of dealing with people as they are, not as he might wish them to be. And by inventing two selves over which she claims to have no control, Cressida evades the responsibility, which being part of any society also demands, of acting with some degree of consistency and constancy.

At first glance the combat between Hector and Ajax appears to be another example of this disorder. But the 'anticlimactic' outcome of this duel in fact renounces the chaos and destructiveness of the Trojan War. The reconciliation of Hector and Ajax emphasizes, in familial and symbolic terms, the bonds that unite rather than divide members of the human community. Declaring that their blood-relationship forbids them to fight, Hector also resists the impulse to condone through the duel the sacrifice of yet more lives in the pursuit of honor and renown. Moreover, in halting the combat because they are cousins, Hector and Ajax successfully define their identities and loyalties in a universe where the sense of self is always elusive, ever-changing, and subject to the opinion of oth-ers rather than one's own perceptions and actions. As we have seen in the speeches of Troilus and Cressida, the problem of establishing identities and loyalties is epitomized by the process of generating two persons from one. When Hector raises and then quickly rejects the possibility of creating two Ajaxes during a duel that mirrors the issues at stake in the war itself, he shrugs off for a moment the confusion so pervasive in Troy. And that is no small thing.

Notes

1. Brower, *Hero and Saint* (New York and Oxford, 1971), p. 267; Seltzer, Introd., *Troilus and Cressida*, in *The Complete Signet Classic Shakespeare*, ed. Sylvan Barnet et al. (New York, 1972), p. 1001; and McAlindon, 'Language, Style, and Meaning in *Troilus and Cressida*', *PMLA*, 84 (1969), 29. For a study of Shakespeare's debts to and departures from previous literary accounts of Hector's challenge and the combat, see Robert K. Presson, *Shakespeare's* Troilus and Cressida *and the Legends of Troy* (Madison, 1953), pp. 28-35 and pp. 43-57. Further commentary on the combat includes E.M.W. Tillyard, *Shakespeare's Problem Plays* (Toronto, 1949), pp. 78-9; Brian Morris, 'The Tragic Structure of *Troilus and Cressida*', *SQ*, 10 (1959), 484; Robert Kimbrough, *Shakespeare's* Troilus and Cressida *and Its Setting* (Cambridge, Mass., 1964), pp. 58-9 and pp. 134-5; Alice Shalvi, 'Honor in *Troilus and Cressida*', *SEL*, 5 (1965), 288-91; Patricia Thomson, 'Rant and Cant in *Troilus and Cressida*', *Essays and Studies*, 22 (1969), 37; Richard Levin, *The Multiple Plot in English Renaissance Drama* (Chicago and London, 1971), pp. 160-8; Lawrence Danson, *Tragic Alphabet* (New Haven and London, 1974), pp. 84-6; and Susan Snyder, 'Ourselves Alone: The Challenge to Single Combat in Shakespeare', *SEL*, 20 (1980), 208-13.

2. II.ii. 208. All citations of Shakespeare's plays are from *The Riverside Shakespeare*, ed. G. Blakemore Evans (Boston, 1974).

3. See especially, Rosalie L. Colie, *Shakespeare's Living Art* (Princeton, 1974), pp. 333-49. Other studies on the problem of identity in *Troilus* are R.J. Smith, 'Personal Identity in *Troylus and Cressida*', *English Studies in Africa*, 6 (1963), 7-26; Charles Lyons, 'Cressida, Achilles and the Finite Deed', *Etudes Anglaises*, 20 (1967), 233-42; and Norman Rabkin, *Shakespeare and the Common Understanding* (New York, 1967), pp. 31-48 and p. 130.

4. See J.S.P. Tatlock, 'The Siege of Troy in Elizabethan Literature, Especially in Shakespeare and Heywood', *PMLA*, 30 (1915), 673-770; Hyder E. Rollins, 'The Troilus-Cressida Story from Chaucer to Shakespeare', *PMLA*, 32 (1917), 383-429; Presson, passim; Alice Walker, ed. *Troilus and Cressida*, The New Cambridge Shakespeare (Cambridge, England, 1957), x-xlvi; and Kimbrough, pp. 25-46.

5. Colie, pp. 333-6. The problems of disorder and value in *Troilus* are also analyzed by Una Ellis-Fermor,

'Discord in the Spheres', in *The Frontiers of Drama,* 2nd ed. (London, 1946), pp. 56-76; Winifred M.T. Nowottny, '"Opinion" and "Value" in *Troilus and Cressida*', *EIC,* 4 (1954), 282-96; Frank Kermode, 'Opinion, Truth and Value', *EIC,* 5 (1955), 181-7; W.R. Elton, 'Shakespeare's Ulysses and the Problem of Value', *Shakespeare Studies,* 2 (1966), pp. 95-111; Harry Berger, Jr., '*Troilus and Cressida:* The Observer as Basilisk', *Comparative Drama,* 2 (Summer 1968), 122-36; Arnold Stein, '*Troilus and Cressida:* The Disjunctive Imagination', *ELH,* 36 (1969), 145-67; Danson, pp. 68-96; Richard D. Fly, '"Suited in Like Conditions as our Argument": Imitative Form in Shakespeare's *Troilus and Cressida*', *SEL,* 15 (1975), 273-92; and Gayle Greene, 'Language and Value in Shakespeare's *Troilus and Cressida*', *SEL,* 21 (1981), 271-84.

6. See R.A. Foakes, '*Troilus and Cressida* Reconsidered', *Univ. of Toronto Quarterly,* 32 (1963), 145; McAlindon, pp. 36-7; Elias Schwartz, 'Tonal Equivocation and the Meaning of *Troilus and Cressida*', *SP,* 69 (1972), 309; and Colie, pp. 334-5.

7. Observing that no precedent exists in the accounts of the Troy legend for the chivalric motive behind Hector's challenge, Presson (pp. 33-4) remarks that the motive is 'an example of that continual association of war and women, which, though traditional, is so conspicuous in *Troilus and Cressida*'. See also Levin, pp. 161-5. Snyder discusses the single combat in Shakespeare 'as a personal response to a public situation' (p. 201).

8. William Empson (*Some Versions of Pastoral* [London, 1935], pp. 34-5) remarks that the political concerns in *Troilus* are 'chiefly about loyalty whether to a mistress or the state . . . The breaking of Cressida's vow is symbolical of, the breaking of Helen's vow is cause of, what the play shows (chiefly by the combat between Hector and his first cousin Ajax) to be a civil war'.

9. Mark Sacharoff, 'Tragic vs. Satiric: Hector's Conduct in II.ii of Shakespeare's *Troilus and Cressida*', *SP,* 67 (1970), 523-5.

10. Walker, xiii. See also Oscar James Campbell, *Comicall Satyre and Shakespeare's* Troilus and Cressida (1938; rpt. San Marino, Calif., 1965), pp. 205-7; Theodore Spencer, *Shakespeare and the Nature of Man,* 2nd ed. (New York, 1949), pp. 112-3; Virgil K. Whitaker, *Shakespeare's Use of Learning* (San Marino, Calif., 1953), pp. 199-211; Robert Ornstein, *The Moral Vision of Jacobean Tragedy* (Madison, 1960), pp. 242-5; Kimbrough, pp. 113-9; and Rolf Soellner, 'Prudence and the Price of Helen: The Debate of the Trojans in *Troilus and Cressida*', *SQ,* 20 (1969), 255-63.

11. Kaufmann, 'Ceremonies for Chaos: The Status of *Troilus and Cressida*', *ELH,* 32 (1965), 141. Kaufmann also notes that Hector 'defers civilly to the ceremonial sense of identity he shares with his brothers in Helen's captivity' (p. 148). As we shall see, Hector locates his identity elsewhere during the combat.

Approving and even laudatory views of Hector's decision are to be found in William R. Bowden, 'The Human Shakespeare and *Troilus and Cressida*', *SQ,* 8 (1957), 174; Willard Farnham, 'Troilus in Shapes of Infinite Desire', *SQ,* 15 (Spring, 1964), 262-3; and Jean Gagen, 'Hector's Honor', *SQ,* 19 (1968), 129-37.

12. The confusion regarding names and identities continues outside the confines of the combat proper: Agamemnon does not know Troilus (IV.v. 94), nor Hector Achilles (233). Their lack of knowledge sets off the unique status of the duel all the more sharply.

13. Obvious here is my debt to the methodology of Stanley E. Fish in *Surprised by Sin: The Reader in Paradise Lost* (1967; rpt. Berkeley, 1971). In his essay 'On the Value of Hamlet' (in *Reinterpretations of Elizabethan Drama,* ed. Norman Rabkin [New York, 1969], pp. 137-76), Stephen Booth uses a similar critical approach to examine 'the problems of *Hamlet* [which] arise at points where an audience's contrary responses come to consciousness' (p. 156).

14. The literature on this speech is vast, but to my knowledge no critic has linked its emphasis on identity and division to the combat. An early survey of critical responses to the speech appears in L.L. Schucking, *Character Problems in Shakespeare's Plays* (1922; rep. Gloucester, Mass., 1959), pp. 52-9. See also O.J. Campbell, *Shakespeare's Satire* (New York, 1943), p. 116; Spencer, pp. 119-21; G. Wilson Knight, *The Wheel of Fire,* 4th rev. and enl. ed. (London, 1949), p. 69; Tillyard, pp. 81-5; Kenneth Muir, '*Troilus and Cressida*', *Shakespeare Survey,* 8 (1955), pp. 36-7; Richard C. Harrier, 'Troilus Divided' in *Studies in the English Renaissance Drama,* ed. Josephine W. Bennett et al. (New York, 1959), pp. 151-3; and Colie, pp. 341-3.

15. A penchant for hyperbole is common to Shakespeare's tragic heroes, as Maynard Mack observes in 'The Jacobean Shakespeare', in *Jacobean Theatre,* Stratford-Upon-Avon Studies 1, ed. John Russell Brown and Bernard Harris (New York, 1960), pp. 13-15. But Troilus' praise of Cressida or Helen is so much in excess of the devotion these women merit that tragedy drifts into satire.

16. *OED: kind,* sb., 14; and adj., 1, 5, 6, 8. For a more kindly view of Cressida's being 'fearful of this new identity Troilus creates for her', see Carolyn Asp, 'In Defense of Cressida', *SP,* 74 (1977), pp. 410-1.

17. The motif of division in these scenes is noted by John Bayley in *The Uses of Division: Unity and Disharmony in Literature* (New York, 1976), pp. 207-8. It is discussed in greater detail, but with conclusions different from those reached here, by

M.M. Burns, '*Troilus and Cressida:* The Worst of Both Worlds', *Shakespeare Studies,* 13 (1980), pp. 126-7.

18. Colie, pp. 336-7.

Elaine Eldridge (essay date 1986)

SOURCE: "Moral Order in Shakespeare's *Troilus and Cressida:* The Case of the Trojans," in *Anglia,* Vol. 104, Nos. 1-2, 1986, pp. 33-44.

[*In the following essay, Eldridge examines the characters of Hector, Cressida, and Troilus, asserting that their common heritage as Trojans has more to do with their behavior than do the play's themes of love and war.*]

An established critical doctrine claims there is no discernible moral order within Shakespeare's *Troilus and Cressida*[1]. To say that is to say that the characters do wrong without punishment or suffer without cause. I would like to suggest a way of looking at the play that will show it less morally chaotic than so many readers have found it. The first step in this process—observing Cressida is a Trojan—is small but crucial. Critics have traditionally divided *Troilus and Cressida* into the Greeks and the Trojans or the love story and the war story, either ignoring Cressida or dismissing her as a slut[2]. While it is true that Cressida is tangential to the war story, that fact by no means relegates her to an inconsequential role in the love story. As Empson points out, "her case has to be taken as seriously as the whole war because it involves the same sanctions and occupies an equal position in the play"[3]. Yet too often Cressida is described as "a chatty, vulgar little piece", "a wanton", a character "without intrinsic merit"[4]. And as often as she is described this way, her case—her significance to the play—is not taken seriously. The argument seems to be that sluts and prostitutes are not worthy of dignified notice, and therefore Cressida isn't, either.

But it is axiomatic to say that social acceptability does not prescribe dramatic significance for Shakespeare—in this play, for example, consider how seriously Thersites has been read. By taking Cressida "seriously"—by accepting her as a Trojan—we can recombine the traditional divisions of the double plot (love story/war story and Greeks/Trojans) and place Cressida where she belongs, alongside the other major Trojans, Hector and Troilus. Such a recombination lets us look at Shakespeare's complex arrangement from a new angle. A shaping moral force will never strike us straight off as a significant characteristic of this play, but seeing how each of these three Trojans commits a wrongdoing and suffers for that wrongdoing should dispel, if not obliterate, the sense that there is no moral force or vision in *Troilus and Cressida*. Hector's and Cressida's cases are parallel with respect to Troilus: both characters clearly state their positions, know what actions are in their best interests, and willfully go against those actions in agreeing to agree with Troilus. Each violates a

major virtue (for Hector, honor; for Cressida, love) and each suffers an appropriate punishment. Troilus, the central figure in this headstrong trio, has the unhappy distinction of violating both virtues and hence suffering doubly.

I. HECTOR ON HONOR

In Act II.2, the Trojans, most notably Hector, gather deliberately to follow a destructive course of action. Like Ulysses in the Greek council (Act I.3), the Trojans want to continue business as usual, but they are far more emphatic than the Greeks in their resistance to change. The Trojans contemplate a change of policy that could save Troy, then decisively reject it, while the Greeks, having already experienced an undermining change in hierarchy, peevishly want their chain of command restored. Hector is smugly amused, in fact, that Agamemnon and the "dull and factious nobles of the Greeks" (II.2.209) have allowed their power to be corrupted. But he cannot afford a similar corruption. It is essential that by the end of the meeting the brothers agree, willingly or not, whether to keep Helen. Hector is quietly reasonable: indisputably, too many Trojans have died "To guard a thing not ours nor worth to us" (II.2.22). He concludes his opening argument by asking:

> What merit's in that reason which denies
> The yielding of her up?
>
> (II.2.24-25)[5]

A second time he insists that Helen "is not worth what she doth cost / The keeping" (II.2.51), and argues against Troilus' claim that value is not inherent, but attributed only by the observer. Finally, Hector argues, Helen is undeniably "wife to Sparta's king" (II.2.183), and the

> moral laws
> Of nature and of nations speak aloud
> To have her back returned. Thus to persist
> In doing wrong extenuates not wrong,
> But makes it much more heavy. Hector's opinion
> Is this in way of truth. Yet ne'ertheless,
> My spritely brethren, I propend to you
> In resolution to keep Helen still;
> For 'tis a cause that hath no mean dependence
> Upon our joint and several dignities.
>
> (II.2.184-93)

Hector uses reason to argue for moral action: the pragmatic putting of one's house in order assumes moral force. If "the specialty of rule hath been neglected" (I.3.78) in the Greek camp, then neither is Troy a "well-order'd nation" (II.2.180) as Hector describes one. The voices of reason, pragmatism, and morality call out for the Trojans to reconsider their "bad cause". Yet in the concluding lines of this famous speech Hector might as well stand up and announce, "I am going to make the false, foolish, and immoral choice". Hector does not merely "change his mind" as part of a bungled characterization. By having him so abruptly abandon his argument, Shakespeare unmistakably directs our attention to his wrongdoing. By giving in to family and personal pride, Hector ignores his "opinion [. . .] in way of truth" (II.2.188-89). For it is pride, rather than genuine honor, that is at stake here[6]. Hector has not for a moment stopped believing that Helen is not of them nor worth to them. But because he is powerful, he can defy his own belief, as well as his sister Cassandra's divinely inspired warning, that Helen should be returned. In agreeing to agree with Troilus, then, Hector deliberately, knowingly abandons the moral and pragmatic course of action, and so irreparably damages his own honor, which he claims to hold so dear, and the welfare of Troy, which he is bound in honor to defend.

A brief exchange in Act IV between Hector and Ulysses shows that Hector willfully continues to ignore the moral imperative of ending the war. Like Cassandra, Ulysses has prophesied the fall of Troy:

> Ulysses: My prophecy is but half his journey yet;
> For yonder walls, that pertly front your town,
> Yon towers, whose wanton tops do buss the clouds,
> Must kiss their own feet.
> Hector: I must not believe you.
>
> (IV.5.218-21)

"I must not believe you" is a willed declaration of belief in the face of contrary knowledge, the same sort of declaration Hector makes in the Trojan council when he rejects Cassandra's warning and turns his back on his "opinion [. . .] in way of truth". Having deserted that truthful "opinion" for his honor—that is, having vowed to keep the stolen Helen rather than yield her to the Greeks' legitimate claim—in Act V.3 Hector again rejects a moral argument in the name of honor. He has sworn to fight, and will not listen to the objections of his wife and sister. Cassandra argues that "the gods are deaf to hot and peevish vows" (V.3.16); Andromache tries to persuade her husband that it is not "holy / To hurt by being just" (V.3.19-20). But he is insistent:

> Hold you still, I say.
> Mine honor keeps the weather of my fate.
> Life every man holds dear; but the dear man
> Holds honor far more precious-dear than life.
>
> (V.3.25-28)

In the remainder of this scene he ignores further pleas from Andromache and his parents to stay home. Having sworn to fight, he goes out to face Achilles protected only by his prideful honor.

In short, in almost all his appearances Hector rejects a moral or logical argument in favor of honor. His murder by Achilles' Myrmidons is fitting: he dies asking for the "fair play" which he has, in his refusal to return Helen, already denied the Greeks.

II. Cressida on Love

Cressida's actions in love parallel Hector's on honor: she states her position, reverses herself, violates the love she embraces, and is subsequently punished. The soliloquy which ends her first appearance bears close attention because it explains her later behavior: her toying with Troilus' affections, her attempt to recall her declaration of love for him, her betrayal. From the outset Shakespeare shows Cressida as deeply mistrustful of love:

> Women are angels, wooing;
> Things won are done, joy's soul lies in the doing.
> That she beloved knows nought that knows not this:
> Men prize the thing ungained more than it is;
> That she was never yet, that ever knew
> Love got so sweet as when desire did sue.
> Therefore this maxim out of love I teach:
> Achievement is command; ungained, beseech.
> Then, though my heart's content firm love doth bear,
> Nothing of that shall from mine eyes appear.
>
> (I.2.286-95)

These lines reveal Cressida's fixed hopelessness and devaluation of love. The repetition of the "maxim out of love" emphasizes her belief in love as an organized sport in which love and lovers are won as prizes. Women are things to be gained and done. After a woman is "won" the arbitrary value placed on her will fall.

Yet in practice the maxim proves false. Troilus values her until she deprives him of his good opinion; Diomedes commands before he "wins" her. But because Cressida believes she can maintain her slight edge only as long as she keeps her relationship with Troilus static, she tries to protect herself by teasing him. Confusing power and stability, she cannot imagine a love more stable than when desire sues; she cannot imagine that Troilus might love her; she cannot imagine herself but as something to be won or lost in the game: she is only, as yet, "the thing ungained". Unable to see herself as possessing any inherent worth and lacking any goodness around her, Cressida fails to discover anything better than holding off a little longer. Her position is clear: she loves Troilus, but lovers are not to be trusted with power. From the beginning, then, Cressida undervalues both love and Troilus' potential fidelity.

Act III.2, in which Cressida reverses her position to say she loves Troilus, is parallel in action and function to the Trojan council (Act II.2), in which Hector reverses himself to agree with Troilus. A comparison of these scenes shows how the two stories of the double plot are related. The comparison is worth making because it draws our attention away from the sometimes jarring surface differences between the love story and the war story and directs it to their underlying similarities. In fact, Act III.2 is as much a companion scene to the Trojan council as is the Greek council (Act I.3).

The lovers' meeting reflects Cressida's assumption that Troilus will quickly tire of her and be false. She is genuinely surprised that he has been constant in his desire:

> Troilus: O Cressid, how often have I wished me thus!
> Cressida: Wished, my lord? The gods grant—O my lord!
>
> (III.2.61-62)

What should the gods grant? That Cressida be wrong. But she can imagine she may be wrong only fleetingly. Next moment her pessimistic, fearful thoughts are again "more dregs than water" (III.2.67).

But for a moment the seesawing between love and mistrust is quelled:

> Boldness comes to me now and brings me heart.
> Prince Troilus, I have loved you night and day
> For many weary months.
>
> (III.2.113-15)

Cressida's announcement of her love exactly parallels Hector's announcement "in resolution to keep Helen still". Both characters willfully sacrifice their safety for something they want, running headlong against their stated beliefs. But Cressida's resolution, unlike Hector's, is brief. Immediately following her statement of love she repents her weakness and tries to regain her former position:

> I was won, my lord
> With the first glance that ever—pardon me;
> If I confess much you will play the tyrant.
>
> (III.2.117-19)

"If I confess much you will play the tyrant" is a variation of the earlier "Achievement is command". Yet speaking modifies the true statement of fear and mistrust to a flattering appeal to Troilus' power, as the "pardon me" appeals to his curiosity. Her entire speech follows this halting pattern, offering a series of lover's confessions that she then tries to retract. Cressida wants to say and unsay simultaneously, to express private thoughts with no fear of the consequences of being unsecret. In the same way, in the Trojan council Hector wants to enhance his honor by both returning and defending Helen. In both cases the characters will their situations to be as they wish and turn away from the dangers of doing so.

Cressida's capitulation to Diomedes in Act V.2 follows unavoidably from her arguments about the untrustworthiness of lovers. She assumes, incorrectly, that Troilus will desert her. And she assumes, correctly, that she is without protection in the enemy camp. Readers who describe Cressida as the smoothly practiced "wanton" expected by Elizabethan audiences overlook her abject and unsteady wooing of Diomedes. She was able to tease and manipulate the young, infatuated Troilus, but is no match for the older, more experienced man. Diomedes is in charge; he keeps straight to business until he gains his bargain, at his price.

Shakespeare's treatment of Cressida is awful in its precise balance. She has reasons—sound ones—for her fearfulness. She must do what she can to defend herself in a world that has left her less than defenseless: in Troy, her uncle panders for her; in the Greek camp, her father assumes the duty. Neither the Greeks nor the Trojans value her. But her betrayal of Troilus' trust is unmitigated and ultimately unjustified; the surrender of his sleeve to Di-

omedes, unnecessarily cruel. Dryden objected that Cressida was "false, and [. . .] not punish'd"[7]. But Shakespeare devised the exactly appropriate punishment for Cressida's transgression against love. In betraying Troilus, she simultaneously punishes herself, for what could be worse than falling into the hands of the "Greekish whoremasterly villain" (V.4.7), "a false-hearted rogue, a most injust knave" (V.1.88-89)?

Shakespeare satisfies not only our expectations from the Troy legends (Cressida will be false, Achilles will kill Hector), but does so by making the characters accomplices in their downfalls—they help set up the conditions for their own punishments. Cressida could not forestall her trade for Antenor; but her deliberate pessimism leads her to believe that Troilus will forget her, and that leads her straight to Diomedes. Similarly, Hector is partially responsible for his death. He receives repeated warnings to turn back, and does not. Even Troilus warns him that it is dangerous and foolish to be merciful to fallen enemy soldiers. Still Hector insists that the demands of his honor must be met. Within minutes (of stage time) he allows Achilles to live when he is winded, and then is naively surprised that Achilles will, indeed, kill him at a disadvantage. Achilles has more than the help of the Myrmidons to murder Hector.

III. TROILUS ON HONOR AND LOVE

Troilus also sets up the conditions for his downfall in love and war, both by acting against his stated beliefs and by not fulfilling the demands of the virtues he claims to value. He is brave and faithful, but neither honorable nor loving.

In the first instance, his treatment of honor is like Hector's: Troilus abandons reason and substitutes pride and glory for honor:

> Nay, if we talk of reason,
> Let's shut our gates and sleep! Manhood and honor
> Should have hare-hearts, would they but fat their thoughts
> With this crammed reason.
>
> (II.2.46-49)

Troilus' argument for keeping Helen is bulletproof. If something—a woman, for example, as the war supposedly concerns possession of a woman—is chosen by a man, he cannot honorably change his mind about her. "I take to-day a wife" (II.2.61), he proposes:

> How may I avoid,
> Although my will distaste what it elected,
> The wife I chose? There can be no evasion
> To blench from this and to stand firm by honor.
>
> (II.2.65-68)

Further, he argues, Helen's theft was just retaliation for an earlier injury. Although he briefly argues that Helen is herself valuable ("Is she worth keeping? Why, she is a pearl / Whose price hath launched above a thousand ships

/ And turned crowned kings to merchants" (II.2.81-83)), Troilus' main argument insists that fighting to keep Helen is honorable because the Trojan brothers say it is honorable. To Cassandra's warning that "Troy must not be" (II.2.109), Troilus responds:

> Her brainsick raptures
> Cannot distaste the goodness of a quarrel
> Which hath our several honors all engaged
> To make it gracious.
>
> (II.2.122-25)

Later, he refers to Helen as "a theme of honor and renown / A spur to valiant and magnanimous deeds" (II.2.199-200). The point ignored in all his argument, of course, is that Helen is a false symbol of honor. Her own virtues are not worth defending. Earlier Troilus himself recognizes that she is "too starved a subject for my sword" (I.1.96), and Shakespeare pointedly shows her as mindless, careless of the death and suffering perpetrated in her name. She honorably and rightfully should be returned to the Greeks, as Hector first argues. Finally, she is a theme not of honor but of a military pride and glory that kills Greek and Trojan soldiers alike.

Troilus' actions in the council and his meeting with Cressida are the same: in both cases he decides what he wants and aggressively pursues it, heedless of the cost to others or the warnings against his desires. As he substitutes pride and glory for honor, Troilus substitutes sex and self-regard for love. Readers have long noted that Troilus is more in love with sex than with Cressida[8]. He longs to wallow in Cressida's lily beds:

> I am giddy; expectation whirls me round.
> Th' imaginary relish is so sweet
> That it enchants my sense.
>
> (III.2.18-20)

I hope I'm never so old as to find anything wrong with such expectation, but calling fervid anticipation love stretches that term beyond endurance. It is not the act in which Troilus errs, but—as with honor—the misnaming.

Nor is there anything wrong or unusual about interest in one's own happiness. But Troilus' singleminded pursuit of his own interests in the name of "love" shows that he reserves his true love for himself. As he ignores Cassandra's warning of Troy's fall to argue for honor, he ignores Cressida's warning of her potential fall to argue for his own virtue:

> O that I thought it could be in a woman—
> As, if it can, I will presume in you—
> To feed for aye her lamp and flames of love;
> [. . .]
> Or that persuasion could but thus convince me
> That my integrity and truth to you
> Might be affronted with the match and weight
> Of such a winnowed purity in love:
> How were I then uplifted!
>
> (III.2.158-60; 164-68)

That such a marvel of truth and integrity could be uplifted is hard to imagine. What we hear in Troilus' speech is not, as Cressida fears, someone in love with power or the abuse of the lover, but a man wholeheartedly in love with himself.

Troilus continues to show himself more concerned with Troilus than with Cressida when Aeneas brings the news of her exchange for Antenor. He thinks first of his own happiness ("How my achievements mock me!" IV.2.69) and second of his reputation ("and, my Lord Aeneas, / We met by chance; you did not find me here", IV.2.70-71). The last instance of Troilus' self-regard occurs as he watches Cressida's betrayal. One night with her hardly justifies the claim that the "bonds of heaven are slipped, dissolved, and loosed" (V.3.152), yet Troilus shakes in piercing disbelief as he watches her surrender to Diomedes. Given that he began the play describing himself as a "merchant" longing to possess Cressida ("Her bed is India, there she lies, a pearl", I.1.100), his jealous pain is apt reward for his lust and unwarranted possessiveness. This does not deny his pain or his fidelity: the point is that the betrayal is the only fitting punishment for a love which was based on sex and preoccupation with self.

I began by suggesting that *Troilus and Cressida* is more morally coherent than many readers have found it, and I have tried to show how that coherence can be observed by tracing the actions of the three—not two—major Trojans. My suggestion rests not on rejecting the traditional divisions of the double plot (war story/love story and Greeks/Trojans), but by realigning the characters within them. Shifting Cressida's emphasis from the love story to the Trojans helps us refocus our attention on Shakespeare's deliberate repetition of wrongdoing and punishment among Cressida, Hector, and Troilus, a pattern quite different from the moral jumble readers have often seen.

And the Greeks? Unappealing as they are, they cannot be said to have done anything undeniably wrong. They do nothing right, certainly, and not one among them represents or affirms any virtue. But they can always claim to have suffered the first wrong.

Notes

1. Dryden was the first critic to complain that *Troilus and Cressida* lacked an obvious moral. See John Dryden, *Preface to 'Troilus and Cressida'. Containing the Grounds of Criticism in Tragedy* (1679), rpt. *Literary Criticism of John Dryden,* ed. A.C. Kirsch (Lincoln, 1966), p. 125.

   Later critics who find the play morally unsatisfying include F.B. Dyer, Jr., "The Destruction of Pandare", *Shakespeare Enconium*, ed. A. Paolucci (New York, 1964), p. 125, p. 129. P.M. Kendall, "Inaction and Ambivalence in *Troilus and Cressida*", *English Studies in Honor of James Southall Wilson,* ed. F. Bowers (Charlottesville, 1951), p. 135, pp. 143-144. D.R.C. Marsh, "Interpretation and Misinterpretation: the Problem of *Troilus and Cressida*", *Shakespeare*

Studies, 1, ed. J. Leeds Barroll (Cincinnati, 1965), 184, 196-197. R. Ornstein, *"Troilus and Cressida", Modern Shakespearean Criticism: Essays on Style, Dramaturgy, and the Major Plays,* ed. A.B. Kernan (New York, 1970), p. 311. F. Turner, *Shakespeare and the Nature of Time: Moral and Philosophical Themes in Some Plays and Poems of William Shakespeare* (Oxford, 1971), p. 108, p. 113.

2. Critics who emphasize the Greek/Trojan aspect of the double plot include N. Coghill, "Morte Hector: A Map of Honour", *Shakespeare's Professional Skills* (Cambridge, 1964), pp. 108-109. N. Council, *When Honour's At the Stake: Ideas of Honour in Shakespeare's Plays* (London, 1973), p. 75. L.C. Sears, *Shakespeare's Philosophy of Evil* (North Quincy, Mass., 1974), p. 107.

   Critics who have placed greater importance on the love story/war story include W. Empson, *Some Versions of Pastoral* (1935; rpt. New York, 1974), p. 34. Kendall (see note 1), p. 136. N. Rabkin, "The Uses of the Double Plot", *Shakespeare Studies,* 1, ed. J. Leeds Barroll (Cincinnati, 1965), 272. W.B. Toole, *Shakespeare's Problem Plays* (The Hague, 1966), p. 209.

3. Empson (see note 2), p. 36.

4. In order, these quotations are from A.P. Rossiter, *Angel With Horns and Other Shakespeare Lectures,* ed. G. Storey (New York, 1961), p. 132. Kendall (see note 1), p. 136. W.B. Drayton Henderson, "Shakespeare's *Troilus and Cressida,* Yet Deeper in Its Tradition", *Essays in Dramatic Literature: The Parrot Presentation Volume,* ed. H. Craig (Princeton, 1935), p. 138.

5. All references are to *The Riverside Shakespeare,* ed. G.B. Evans (Boston, 1974).

6. For a general discussion of honor in the Renaissance, see C.B. Watson, *Shakespeare and the Renaissance Concept of Honor* (Princeton, 1960). For a discussion specific to *Troilus and Cressida,* see Council (see note 2), ch. 4. P.A. Jorgensen, *Shakespeare's Military World* (Berkeley, 1956), also offers helpful information on military conceptions of honor.

7. Dryden (see note 1), p. 125.

8. O.J. Campbell, who found Troilus "an expert in sensuality", a "sexual gourmet", was the earliest influential critic to notice that Troilus is not a faultless chivalric hero. See his *Comicall Satyre and Shakespeare's 'Troilus and Cressida'* (San Marino, Calif., 1938), pp. 211-212.

Stephen J. Lynch (essay date 1986)

SOURCE: "The Idealism of Shakespeare's Troilus," in *South Atlantic Review,* Vol. 51, No. 1, January, 1986, pp. 19-29.

[In the following essay, Lynch argues that the so-called idealism of Troilus is not as pure as some commentators have suggested, but is instead as self-absorbed and corrupt as the world Troilus himself inhabits.]

Troilus inhabits a world of near total corruption where honor serves ambition and love seems little more than lust. Yet within the confines of this bleak and hostile world, Troilus appears extraordinarily idealistic. He describes his will as "infinite," his desire as "boundless," and his truth as a "winnowed purity in love" (3.2.82-83, 167). Even after the betrayal scene he claims, "Never did young man fancy / With so eternal and so fix'd a soul" (5.2.165-66). Several commentators have interpreted this hero as a rare and noble exception to the characters that surround him (see, for example, Knight 60; Nowottny 291-93; Biswas 113). Yet when examined closely, the idealism of Troilus, however lofty and extreme, seems very much in keeping with the nature of his world. Though he makes repeated claims to purity and eternal constancy, he puts great emphasis on sensuality, and his actions are more moody and erratic than constant and true. Moreover, his energy and devotion seem concentrated not so much on Cressida as on an image of himself as a superlative and immortal paragon of love. His ideals, therefore, do not rise above the corruption of his world but are an integral part of it, ultimately as misdirected and self-serving as the pride of Achilles or the honor of Hector. Commentators have discussed the delusions of Troilus at some length (see Traversi 331; Dickey 126; Kaula 272-79; Marsh 37-45). Yet the central problem with Troilus seems not that he is deluded (we need no ghost from the grave to tell us this) but that his delusions emerge from an intense egotism in a love affair pursued primarily for self-glorification.

Troilus's egotism becomes evident in his first appearance on stage, as he strives, against all evidence to the contrary, to deify his love. He looks to the gods for a suitable parallel: "Tell me, Apollo, for thy Daphne's love, / What Cressid is, what Pandar, and what we" (1.1.98-99). Not only does Troilus attempt to romanticize the unmistakably perverse Pandarus, but he also tends to conceive of Cressida and himself in the most overlabored terms. His lovesickness verges on the artificial and affected—an impression that is reinforced by his frequent use of Petrarchan clichés:

> Why should I war without the walls of Troy,
> That find such cruel battle here within?
> 　　　　I tell thee I am mad
> In Cressid's love; thou answer'st she is fair,
> Pourest in the open ulcer of my heart
> Her eyes, her hair, her cheek, her gait, her voice,
> Handlest in thy discourse, O, that her hand,
> In whose comparison all whites are ink
> Writing their own reproach; to whose soft seizure
> The cygnet's down is harsh, and spirit of sense
> Hard as the palm of ploughman.
>
> 　　　　　　　　　　(1.1.2-3, 51-59)

In keeping with the Petrarchan convention that the beloved be not only divine but unassailable, Troilus envisions Cressida as "stubborn-chaste against all suit" (1.1.97). As we soon discover, he is not even remotely familiar with the earthy, crafty, and clever woman that we meet in the following scene. It appears that if Troilus is in love, he loves Petrarch and not Cressida; or, more precisely, he loves his own fabrication of a Petrarchan love affair.

When the two lovers finally meet, Troilus continues to ignore the real Cressida while imagining an ideal Cressida. In the grip of his fantasy, he barely listens to or comprehends the actual woman. She professes fears for her "folly," "craft," and "unkind self," concluding that "to be wise and love / Exceeds man's might" (3.2.102, 149-57). Troilus responds with a rather startling *non sequitur* in which he imposes upon Cressida a series of attributes and virtues that run counter to everything she has just said:

> O that I thought it could be in a woman—
> As, if it can, I will presume in you—
> To feed for aye her lamp and flames of love,
> To keep her constancy in plight and youth,
> Outliving beauties outward, with a mind
> That doth renew swifter than blood decays!
> Or that persuasion could but thus convince me
> That my integrity and truth to you
> Might be affronted with the match and weight
> Of such a winnowed purity in love!
>
> (3.2.158-67)

The speech is a curious blend of awareness and self-deception. Troilus seems to realize that Cressida is no match for his own constancy, but nevertheless he is willing to "presume" that she is. In a rapture of delusion, he overlooks the woman that stands before him and proceeds to fabricate and fall in love with essentially a female version of himself. His energy and devotion are directed not so much to Cressida as to an image of himself as a paragon of "integrity and truth." He loves Cressida only so far as she provides a necessary counterpart to his own self-image.

As Cressida serves Troilus's egotism as a lover, Helen serves his egotism as a warrior. Indeed the two women are closely associated in his mind: Cressida is a "pearl" in India, Helen a "pearl, / Whose price hath launch'd above a thousand ships" (1.1.100; 2.2.81-82). As with Cressida, Troilus perceives the inadequacy of Helen—"too starv'd a subject for my sword" (1.1.93)—but proceeds to disregard his perception in favor of a self-serving idolatry:

> She is a theme of honor and renown,
> A spur to valiant and magnanimous deeds,
> Whose present courage may beat down our foes,
> And fame in time to come canonize us.
>
> (2.2.199-202)

In both love and war, Troilus aspires to a profane version of sainthood, a type of deification through great fame. As Helen will "canonize" him as a model warrior, Cressida will "sanctify" (3.2.183) him as a model lover. His aspirations are given symbolic expression in the Trojan "towers, whose wanton tops do buss the clouds" (4.5.220)—symbols of overreaching pride.

Troilus's intense self-interest surfaces not only in his constant obsession with fame, but also in the very language he uses to pledge devotion to Cressida. Though he repeatedly vows simplicity and truth, he ironically speaks in convoluted grammar and hyperboles:

> Troilus shall be such to Cressid as what envy can
> say worst shall be a mock for his truth, and what
> truth can speak truest not truer than Troilus.
> I am as true as truth's simplicity,
> And simpler than the infancy of truth.
> True swains in love shall in the world to come
> Approve their truth by Troilus. When their rhymes,
> Full of protest, of oath and big compare,
> Wants similes, truth tir'd with iteration . . .
> "As true as Troilus" shall crown up the verse,
> And sanctify the numbers.
>
> (3.2.95-98; 169-70; 173-83)

It is difficult to accept such proclamations as genuine selfless love when we cannot detect in them even a hint of humility. In *All's Well That Ends Well,* Diana makes a comment that seems pertinent: "'Tis not the many oaths that make the truth, / But the plain vow that is vow'd true" (4.2.21-22). Troilus does just the opposite, making "many oaths" of which few are "plain." As in the opening scene, his language is overly labored, as if he were intent on being not simply a good lover but the most exceptional lover that has ever lived—an aspiration laden with egotism. Moreover, it is indicative of his self-obsession that he formulates his vow not in terms of fidelity to Cressida but in terms of loyalty to his own name as a synonym for truth. Assuming that Shakespeare used Chaucer's *Troilus and Criseyde* as a source (see Bradbrook and Thompson), Shakespeare certainly took pains to do away with the humility of Chaucer's hero who professes his vow strictly as a means of amending his unworthiness through dedicated service to his beloved:

> But herte myn, of youre benignite,
> So thynketh, though that I unworthi be,
> Yet mot I nede amenden in som wyse,
> Right thorugh the vertu of youre heigh servyse . . .
> This dar I seye, that trouth and diligence,
> That shal ye fynden in me al my lif.
>
> (3, 1285-98)

While Chaucer's Troilus hopes to attain virtue, Shakespeare's Troilus is confident that he is its very essence.

On the next morning, the deficiencies in his idealism become manifest in his behavior. As Cressida feared, he begins to lose interest:

>   Prithee tarry,
> You men will never tarry.
> O foolish Cressid! I might have still held off,
> And then you would have tarried.
>
> (4.2.15-18)

His refusal to tarry on the morning after seems particularly inconsistent when we remember the constancy and devotion he promised the evening before:

Tro. . . . This is the monstruosity in love, lady, that the will is infinite and the execution confin'd, that the desire is boundless and the act a slave to limit.

Cres. They say all lovers swear more performance than they are able, and yet reserve an ability that they never perform; vowing more than the perfection of ten, and discharging less than the tenth part of one. They that have the voice of lions and the act of hares, are they not monsters?

Tro. Are there such? Such are not we.

(3.2.81-90)

Though he boasted an infinite will and a boundless desire, he now acts just as Cressida had anticipated: "Things won are done" (1.2.287) (see Lynch 360-63). It seems peculiar that Troilus should consider himself a paragon of constancy when he is so obviously afflicted with a restless temperament: he refused to "tarry" (1.1.16-22) in winning Cressida, and now he refuses to "tarry" after having won her. The "monstruosity in love," it turns out, is not merely in the limitations of the world but in the limitations of the lover. This slacking off in his devotion to Cressida is even more evident when we compare his actions to those of his counterpart in Chaucer's narrative poem. After Criseyde urges him to make haste—"For tyme it is to ryse and hennes go, / Or ellis I am lost for evere mo!" (3, 1425-26)—Troilus almost refuses to leave, fearing that he may die from even a brief separation:

O goodly myn, Criseyde,
And shal I rise, allas, and shal I so?
Now fele I that myn herte moot a-two.
For how sholde I my lif an houre save,
Syn that with yow is al the lyf ich have?

(3, 1474-77)

Shakespeare reverses the situation: Troilus is up and ready to leave while Cressida pleads for him to tarry. Compared to his Chaucerian counterpart, Shakespeare's hero promises much more and delivers much less.

After he is informed of the plan to exchange Cressida for Antenor, Troilus again acts as Cressida feared. He "reserves an ability" that he "never performs" by not attempting to do for Cressida what he had so willingly done for Helen. Instead, he responds to the news of the transfer with instant and complete resignation: "Is it so concluded?" (4.2.66). Of course nothing really can be done. As Aeneas tells us, Priam is already "at hand and ready to effect it" (4.2.68). But nevertheless Troilus appears a bit too willing to concede. After Cressida inquires four times whether she must really be exchanged, Troilus responds with a distinct lack of energy: "No remedy" (4.4.55). Suddenly, he is willing to turn back the "silks upon the merchant" now that he has "soil'd them" (2.2.69-70). He becomes a "monster" when we evaluate him according to his own standards: "Praise us as we are tasted, allow us as we prove" (3.2.90-91). Confronted with an unfortunate turn of events, or what Agamemnon would call "the protractive

trials of great Jove / To find persistive constancy in men" (1.3.20-21), Troilus fails to "prove" any sustaining power in his vow of eternal constancy and devotion. He joins his brother Hector and his enemy Ulysses in betraying the very ideals he professes.

It is ironic that Troilus recognizes a "dumb-discoursive devil" in the Greeks (4.4.90), and he warns Cressida that "sometimes we are devils to ourselves" (4.4.95), but in his own nature he suspects no devil at all. His actions, however, suggest that he may indeed harbor desires that are less than saintly. The first indication of such a possibility occurs when Cressida proposes her challenge—"In that I'll war with you"—to which Troilus replies, "O virtuous fight, / When right with right wars who shall be most right!" (3.2.171-72). His eagerness to compete in love suggests something rather sinister in Troilus, a desire that he himself may be too young and naive to recognize. In his enthusiasm to prove himself "most right," he seems almost willing to have her prove false. Not only does he permit the exchange, but he also virtually tempts her to falsehood:

The Grecian youths are full of quality;
Their loving well compos'd with gifts of nature,
Flowing and swelling o'er with arts and exercise.

I cannot sing,
Nor heel the high lavolt, nor sweeten talk,
Nor play at subtile games—fair virtues all,
To which the Grecians are most prompt and pregnant.

(4.4.76-78, 85-88)

This unexpected shift from superlative self-esteem to unbounded modesty is matched with rather unusual advice: urging her to "be not tempted" (4.4.91), while assuring her that she will be tempted, and that she has good reason to be tempted. Caught up in a delusion of sanctity, simplicity, and truth, Troilus seems thoroughly blind to any possibility of corruption in his own nature. He seems completely unaware that a devil in himself may be planting in Cressida's mind the very seeds of temptation.

In the following scene, Ulysses speaks a tribute to Troilus that works to heighten our sympathy for the young Trojan moments before the traumatic betrayal he is about to suffer. We are reminded of his tender and susceptible age: "The youngest son of Priam, a true knight, / Not yet mature, yet matchless firm of word" (4.5.96-97). The speech is not altogether objective, as we discover when Ulysses names Aeneas as the source of his information. As Alice Shalvi says, Ulysses "ascribes to Troilus one specific trait which the action of the play shows him as singularly lacking: judgement" (294). Yet however much Trojan flattery may be in it, the speech works to highlight the more noble qualities in Troilus. At this critical point in the play, Shakespeare reinforces our sympathy for the young hero, portraying him not as an object of ridicule or satire (see Campbell 207-18) but as a sensitive hero blinded by the passions and excesses of youth and given over to an impossible idealism that only inexperience would allow.

Our sympathy for Troilus is heightened even more when we see his terrible anguish during the betrayal scene. His sudden disillusionment has no precedent in Chaucer's poem in which the hero is afforded weeks of letters, dreams, and growing suspicions before he finally accepts the awful truth. Moreover, the suffering of Troilus is of an intensity not found elsewhere in Shakespeare's plays. While Lear has time to travel from one daughter to the next before he recognizes their disloyalty, and Othello has time to dwell upon suspicions before he concludes that his wife has been unfaithful, Troilus has only moments to overhaul his elevated conception of Cressida. His suffering is made all the more poignant by his youth and inexperience. Unlike the older, more experienced, and more callous Ulysses, Troilus is not insulated against the slings and arrows of outrageous fortune. Naive and vulnerable, he suffers an almost unfathomable depth of human anguish as he looks with horror upon Diomed and Cressida enacting the irrevocable annihilation of his entire world view.

To make matters even worse, Troilus is accompanied by a very unsympathetic guide, Ulysses, who quickly assures him that Cressida "will sing any man at first sight" (5.2.9). And he watches himself being supplanted by a rather boorish no-nonsense Diomed, who even Cressida realizes will not love her as well as Troilus. He feels a sense of revulsion akin to that which Hamlet expresses when comparing his father to his step-father: "So excellent a king, that was to this / Hyperion to a satyr" (*Ham.*1.2.139-40). The revulsion of Troilus, however, may be even more sickening in that his feeling of betrayal is all the more personal. His suffering is so unbearable that he at first takes recourse in outright denial, desperately attempting to fabricate an illusion of two Cressidas:

> But if I tell how these two did co-act,
> Shall I not lie in publishing a truth?
> Sith yet there is a credence in my heart,
> An esperance so obstinately strong,
> That doth invert th' attest of eyes and ears,
> As if those organs had deceptive functions,
> Created only to calumniate.
> Was Cressid here?

> (5.2.118-25)

The irony in Troilus's reaction is that he suspects his senses are deceiving him now when in fact they have been deceiving him since Act 1. All along he has been subject to an "esperance so obstinately strong" that has created in his mind an ideal version of Cressida quite distinct from the "attest of eyes and ears." Now that he is confronted with an onslaught of irrefutable evidence to the contrary, the center of his philosophy—"What's aught but as 'tis valued?" (2.2.52)—can no longer hold. Cressida, like Helen, cannot attain great value solely by having value attributed to her. The illusions of Troilus disintegrate as he is forced to recognize that there is no Cressida other than the one who stood before him:

> Instance, O instance, strong as Pluto's gates,
> Cressid is mine, tied with the bonds of heaven;

> Instance, O instance, strong as heaven itself,
> The bonds of heaven are slipp'd, dissolv'd, and loos'd
> . . .

> (5.2.153-56)

Within the brevity of five minutes' traffic upon the stage, Troilus's whole world collapses in on him.

In his profound anguish, Troilus desperately sifts through the wreckage to find some means of salvaging his self-image. While his image of Cressida is hopelessly shattered and quickly discarded—"O false Cressid! false, false, false! / Let all untruths stand by thy stained name, / And they'll seem glorious"—his image of himself emerges virtually intact: "Never did young man fancy / With so eternal and so fix'd a soul" (5.2.178-80, 165-66). Though he abandons his illusions about her, he maintains steadfast fidelity to extraordinarily idealistic illusions about himself. (Chaucer's hero, in contrast, reacts with much greater modesty: "I have it nat deserved" [5, 1722].) To the very end, Troilus remains convinced that his vow of integrity and truth was a genuine vow of love for Cressida:

> If souls guide vows, if vows be sanctimonies,
> If sanctimony be the gods' delight,
> If there be rule in unity itself,
> This was not she.

> (5.2.139-42)

Yet this was she, a fact which implies that their souls did not guide their vows and their vows lacked divine sanctimony. Yet Troilus never realizes the inadequacy of his vow or his failure to live up to it. Unlike Lear or Othello, he suffers without gaining insight. Instead he remains stagnated in a delusion of his own sanctity.

In the final scenes of the play, Troilus struggles to sustain his pride through a double pledge of revenge, first against Diomed for seducing Cressida and later against Achilles for murdering Hector. Commentators such as Brian Morris (490) and Willard Farnham (264) have interpreted Troilus at the end of the play as a more mature and worthy champion of Troy. Yet Troilus's new-found devotion to "venom'd vengeance" (5.3.47) does not seem to differ entirely from his earlier devotion to love. Instead of rising in heroic stature, he exchanges in equal measure one form of excess for another: "as much as I do Cressid love, / So much by weight hate I her Diomed" (5.2.167-68). As he abandons his earlier lovesickness, he vents his frustration in a suicidal devotion to savagery and bloodlust. Recognizing the "sure destructions" of the Trojans, he will "dare all imminence" in pursuit of the one "Hope of revenge" (5.10.9, 13, 31). His persistently obsessive behavior, first with love and now revenge, recalls Hector's observation in the council scene: "pleasure and revenge / Have ears more deaf than adders to the voice / Of any true decision" (2.2.171-72). Metaphorically, Troilus's craving for sexual pleasure and now "venom'd vengeance" has transformed him into an "adder," deaf to the moderating effects of reason and deaf to the truth about his own nature. The change in Troilus at the end of the play can also be gauged by his treatment of Pandarus: in Act 1 he idealized Pandarus as a "bark" voyaging to India (1.1.104); in Act 5 he dismisses him as a "broker" and "lackey" (5.10.33). Troilus's shift from absolute idealism to absolute cynicism brings to mind the comment Apemantus makes to Timon after Timon's disillusionment: "The middle of humanity thou never knewest, but the extremity of both ends" (*Tim*.4.3.300-01).

The ending is perhaps the most bleak in all of Shakespeare's plays. There is no Malcolm or Edgar to give us any hope of a restored kingdom. Instead, the final scenes—violent, fragmented, chaotic—render the impression that Ulysses's apocalyptic vision has come about: the universal wolf of will and appetite has been loosed upon the world. The war for honor degenerates to a bloodthirsty quest for revenge. But unlike Shakespeare's other tragic heroes, Troilus does not attain any greater level of awareness or self-knowledge. The play contains almost no soliloquies, and Troilus, typical of his world, does not engage in a moment of penetrating self-analysis. He sees weakness and corruption everywhere but in himself. In distinct contrast, Chaucer's poem ends with the hero finally attaining greater understanding as he looks down from the eighth sphere of heaven:

> And down from thennes faste he gan avyse
> This litel spot of erthe, that with the se
> Embraced is, and fully gan despise
> This wrecched world, and held al vanite
> To respect of the pleyn felicite
> That is in hevene above . . .
> And dampned al oure werk that foloweth so
> The blynde lust, the which that may nat laste.
>
> (5, 1814-24)

Of course the transcendence and heavenly perspective at the end of Chaucer's poem would not be practicable at the end of Shakespeare's play. Nevertheless, Shakespeare's Troilus does not attain even a human level of enlightenment. It is ironic that Troilus should recognize his vanity in Chaucer's poem, where things are not so bad, but not in Shakespeare's play, where things could hardly be worse. He clings to his most prized accomplishment, that he remains as "true as Troilus," and in the narrow limits of sexual fidelity he may be right, but in the broader context of his persistent egotism and lack of self-knowledge he is as "false as Cressid."

Works Cited

Biswas, D. C. *Shakespeare in His Own Time*. Delhi: Macmillan of India, 1979. 90-114.

Bradbrook, M. C. "What Shakespeare Did to Chaucer's *Troilus and Criseyde*." *Shakespeare Quarterly* 9 (1958): 311-19.

Campbell, Oscar J. *Comicall Satyre and Shakespeare's "Troilus and Cressida."* San Marino: Huntington Library, 1938. 185-234.

Chaucer, Geoffrey. *The Works of Geoffrey Chaucer*. Ed. F. N. Robinson. 2nd ed. Boston: Houghton, 1957.

Dickey, Franklin M. *Not Wisely But Too Well: Shakespeare's Love Tragedies*. San Marino: Huntington Library, 1957. 118-43.

Farnham, Willard. "Troilus in Shapes of Infinite Desire." *Shakespeare Quarterly* 15 (1964): 257-64.

Kaula, David. "Will and Reason in *Troilus and Cressida*." *Shakespeare Quarterly* 12 (1961): 271-83.

Knight, G. Wilson. *The Wheel of Fire*. 5th rev. ed. New York: Meridian, 1957. 47-72.

Lynch, Stephen J. "Shakespeare's Cressida: 'A Woman of QuickSense.'" *Philological Quarterly* 63 (1984): 357-68.

Marsh, Derick R.C. *Passion Lends Them Power: A Study of Shakespeare's Love Tragedies*. Manchester: Manchester UP, 1976. 35-45.

Morris, Brian. "The Tragic Structure of *Troilus and Cressida*." *Shakespeare Quarterly* 10 (1959): 481-91.

Nowottny, Winifred M.T. "'Opinion' and 'Value' in *Troilus and Cressida*." *Essay in Criticism* 4 (1954): 282-96.

Shakespeare, William. *The Riverside Shakespeare*. Ed. G. Blakemore Evans *et al.* Boston: Houghton, 1974.

Shalvi, Alice. "'Honor' in *Troilus and Cressida*." *Studies in English Literature, 1500-1900* 5 (1965): 283-302.

Thompson, Ann. *Shakespeare's Chaucer*. Liverpool: Liverpool UP, 1978. 111-65.

Traversi, D. A. *An Approach to Shakespeare*. 3rd ed. Garden City: Doubleday, 1969. 323-40.

Peter Hyland (essay date 1993)

SOURCE: "Legitimacy in Interpretation: The Bastard Voice in *Troilus and Cressida*," in *Mosaic*, Vol. 26, No. 1, Winter, 1993, pp. 1-13.

[In the following essay, Hyland contends that the bastard, Thersites—though not always fair in his assessment of what is occurring around him—is nevertheless an important antidote to authoritarianism in the play by virtue of his apparent insignificance.]

One of the most significant aspects of radical academic activity over the past few years has been the liberation of previously suppressed voices into a new pluralism. In the field of literary interpretation these voices have brought issues of gender, race and class into the reading of texts, problematizing anew the question of authority or legitimacy in interpretation, and suggesting the possibility of a new openness in reading. At the same time there has been a growing recognition that there are no ideologically pure readings, and that the reader has to be aware of his/her own biases. This has, however, also resulted in acute attention to the biases of other readers. Literary studies have become more politicized than ever before, and there is the risk that they will turn into a site of contestation on which the urge to silence or exclude opposing voices is pursued with increasing vigor.

This struggle over the liberation or exclusion of voices in contemporary culture is inevitably reflected in current readings of earlier cultures. A very influential strain of new historicist criticism operating within the field of Renaissance studies argues that Renaissance drama always contains and silences the subversive, populist voices that it allows to speak. In an essay entitled "Invisible Bullets," the leading new historicist, Stephen Greenblatt, concludes that "the form [of drama] itself, as a primary expression of Renaissance power, helps to contain the radical doubts it continually provokes" (65). Leonard Tennenhouse, in his *Power on Display*, re-reads Shakespearean genres from a position similar to Greenblatt's. Shakespeare's theater, he argues, was allowed to exist only as long as it served court ideology; we cannot, he feels, conclude that Shakespeare and his company were capable of envisioning any different "political reality—one where the community of blood was not separated by an immutable principle from the people, or even one in which the power relations of the two social bodies were inverted" (38). This insistence on the absolute nature of official containment of the theater leaves us with a concept of Shakespeare's imagination as severely limited, and to a degree that seems to strain credibility. Annabel Patterson has recently described such totalitarian theories as "condescending to Shakespeare" (25), and has offered in their place a version of the dramatist as an author "unlikely to have unquestioningly adopted an anti-popular myth as his own" (1).

I want to consider in this essay the role of Thersites in Shakespeare's *Troilus and Cressida* in relation to the problem of containment. In a play that throws a harsh light on military and political idealism on the one hand and romantic idealism on the other, Thersites provides the most corrosive and anti-authoritarian condemnation of "wars and lechery." Within the play there are attempts to silence his voice, and in the critical history of the play the general tendency has also been to silence him. I shall argue that a strong case can be made for restoring authority to this "illegitimate" voice.

Much recent commentary on the play has indeed focused on silenced voices, but its concern has been with feminist issues, and it has made Cressida the center of its attention. Critics like Gayle Greene, Janet Adelman, Carol Cook and Linda Charnes, as well as males reading from a feminist perspective like Stephen J. Lynch and Paul Gaudet, have attempted to rescue Cressida from the condemnation of history and the play's masculine voices by revealing her as constructed by patriarchal discourses which suppress her own voice.

Some very recent critics such as Eric Mallin, James O'Rourke and Valerie Traub have extended analysis of what René Girard called "the politics of desire" beyond the heterosexual erotic into consideration of homosexual desire in the play; Traub, indeed, brilliantly brings the politics of AIDS into her reading. As one would expect, such critics have had more to say about Thersites than have the play's feminist readers; O'Rourke particularly, in his location of "Mistress Thersites" within a discussion of the homosexual and heterosexual implications of master-slave relationships, has some instructive comments on Thersites's place in relation to the Lacanian Symbolic Order, or Law of the Father. Thersites, according to this reading, takes the role of a woman, and is thus denied an identity within the Symbolic Order; as a result, however, he is also able to stand outside the mystifications of that Symbolic Order (155-56). Although this situation makes him a politically subversive voice, O'Rourke's concern is not to pursue this dimension, just as despite the increasing attention given to sexual politics and transgression in the play, little interest has been shown in the role played by Thersites's bastardy.

It is, of course, not until near the end of *Troilus and Cressida*, when he responds to the challenge by Margarelon, the bastard son of the Trojan King Priam, that Thersites first informs us, but then most insistently, about his illegitimacy:

> I am a bastard too; I love bastards. I am a bastard begot, bastard instructed, bastard in mind, bastard in valour, in everything illegitimate. One bear will not bite another, and wherefore should one bastard? Take heed, the quarrel's most ominous for us—if the son of a whore fight for a whore, he tempts judgement. Farewell, bastard.
>
> (5.7.16-22)[1]

In revealing his illegitimacy Thersites identifies himself as a version of the "other," and in doing so he also reveals his connection to issues of marginalization, subversion, sexual politics, and the social construction of identity. He becomes, in effect, a voice representing all those who are deprived of social identity, who are excluded and abused by the established hierarchy. To understand the significance of his bastardy, we need to consider the problem both in its theatrical context and in the historical context of the preoccupations of Tudor authority.

. . . . .

Commentators who have considered Thersites's bastardy have tended to take a moralist position, seeing it as just one more aspect of his detestable character. According to Robert Kimbrough's reading of his final speech, Thersites is dismissed "in a most ignominious way. He is made to confess to bastardy and cowardice" (148). In a more recent study Graham Bradshaw responds to the character with an outrage hardly less intemperate than Thersites's own: "His rancour is that of a 'ranke', despised bastard who is 'placed', within the play, as a physical and an emotional cripple." His judgments, therefore, are to be dismissed as the "filth" of a "puny performing freak" (141). This desire to silence Thersites's voice is handily epitomized by Kenneth Muir in the introduction to his edition of *Troilus and Cressida*. In discussing the play's two different endings in relation to the controversial question of its genre, he suggests that a modern director would be at liberty to follow either the relatively comic or the relatively tragic version, and to choose how sympathetic he wishes to make the Trojans, including Cressida. At the same time, however, Muir concludes: "It would not . . . be legitimate, in the interests of contemporary 'relevance', to offer Thersites as the fount of truth and wisdom" (38).

Well, fine word, "legitimate"! Muir's expression here is most interesting. He implies two things: that Thersites's reading of the events in which he is involved is not a legitimate reading, and that a reading of the play that would give power to Thersites's perspective is not a legitimate reading. That is, he is not only dismissing Thersites, but also denying space to a range of potential approaches to the play. On what authority, however, does Muir close down these ways of reading? I say authority, because this is an authoritarian position: to deny legitimacy to another is a means of asserting one's own legitimacy, for what is illegitimate cannot define itself or exist of itself, since it is defined by and in relation to what is legitimate. Further, the legitimate needs the illegitimate to authenticate or legitimate itself. Put more crudely (for Muir's chosen word provides a nexus of meaning nicely appropriate for my discussion), bastards do not make themselves.

Troilus and Cressida is a play whose critical history is grounded in a discussion of questions of absolute truth and legitimacy, the *locus classicus* of which is E.M.W. Tillyard's argument that the conception of order articulated in Ulysses's celebrated speech on degree was so much a part of the Elizabethan collective mind that it hardly needed to be expressed (18). Tillyard understood Ulysses as being "the fount of truth and wisdom." While there are few today who would wish to go along with the Tillyard view of the play (Muir does not; he sees Ulysses's speech as "a cunning piece of persuasion rather than a solid philosophical statement" [27]), it is rather disquieting to see that the play still encourages critics to make authoritarian statements about how it should (or in this case should not) be understood.

I would contend that the play does indeed present Thersites as a source of "truth," though truth must be understood as neither simple nor single. The ubiquity and insistence of his commentary on the action and other characters make it difficult to deny his voice a central place in the play, and his undiluted nastiness does not undercut its truth. After all, the fact that Ulysses is a cynical manipulator who uses noble-sounding ideas for narrowly pragmatic ends has not prevented critics from finding much "truth" in what he says, and some have found him to be the one true "reader" within the text of the play, presumably because what he says does not disturb them.

Thersites's voice constantly demands our attention, and the perspective that it embodies represents authentic experience and is potentially powerful. According to Robert Weimann: "his debunking and skeptical commentary serves to offer viable alternatives to the main or state view of things. In this sense characters like . . . Thersites help point out that the ideas and values held by the main characters are relative to their particular position in the play . . ." (228). Thersites, I would say, is indeed an illegitimate voice; he stands up for bastards, and he recognizes the precarious basis upon which the "legitimate" stands. As such he is a genuinely subversive figure, one whose voice is not finally silenced by the play, and one, I will argue, whose voice should not be silenced by theories of containment (it is perhaps noteworthy that Tennenhouse, who denies that Shakespeare could have imagined just such inversions as are imagined by Thersites, does not deal with *Troilus and Cressida*).

I shall begin by returning to Kimbrough's account of Thersites's final moment on the stage in which, according to Kimbrough, he is ignominiously "made to confess to bastardy and cowardice." The less interesting question is whether Thersites's refusal to fight Margarelon is the act of a coward, and we might wish simply to note that his early insistence on mocking Ajax with the "truth," in spite of the beatings he receives for it, hardly suggests that he is a coward. Further (though this is a matter of interpretation), the tone of his reply to Margarelon's challenge can surely be taken as ironically defiant rather than craven. The more interesting question is whether Thersites's "confession" of his bastardy is ignominious. Before the confrontation between Margarelon and Thersites, bastardy is mentioned only once in the play: when Agamemnon refers to the "bastard Margarelon," which he does with admiration for his colossal heroism (5.5.7-10). Margarelon himself, when challenged by Thersites, apparently sees no shame in proclaiming himself "A bastard son of Priam's" (5.7.15). So why should Thersites's response to Margarelon's confession of bastardy be ignominious if Margarelon's confession itself is not? Why, indeed, should Thersites's revelation of his illegitimacy even be seen as a confession, when for Margarelon it is no more than a way of identifying—and possibly a way of distinguishing—himself? One answer might well be that there is a difference between a royal bastard and other kinds, but that begs the question of what sort of judgment it is that would make such a distinction, a question that will take on ironic overtones in the course of the present discussion.

This whole brief scene between Margarelon and Thersites is distinctly odd. Why is it there? Agamemnon's reference to Margarelon is the only time we have previously heard of him, and he makes an appearance in no other scene. His sole function, therefore, seems to be to give Thersites a pretext for proclaiming his illegitimacy. As we have seen, the purpose of this cannot be to dismiss Thersites in a climactic humiliation. Furthermore, it equally cannot be simply a means of explaining his "villainy." In her study of illegitimacy, Jenny Teichman considers the conventions

A scene from Troilus and Cressida.

The function of this speech, I would suggest, is not to deepen the degradation of Thersites's character, but to proclaim him the "illegitimate voice," the spokesman for a whole constituency of those who have been marginalized and disaffected by the tyranny of "legitimate" power. After all, although this play is deeply concerned with the enforcement of hierarchical structure, we see very little hierarchy within the play itself (setting aside that of gender), because the Greeks are all kings and the Trojans are all members of the royal family. Of the mass of humble humanity there is almost nothing at all; it is Thersites, it appears, who lies at its social bottom. Further, this illegitimate voice is not silenced in the play when Thersites is "dismissed" by Margarelon, for, as many have noted, it re-emerges in the epilogue. The play's final speech belongs to Pandarus, and its first half is fully characteristic of him as he obtusely wonders at the meaning of a world that has so signally failed to reward his good offices, and, as he has done on other occasions, tries to give meaning to his experience through a fragment of a popular song. This closing voice, however, suddenly changes into that of Thersites, as he mocks the audience, accusing them of being pandars and whores, and laying his curse on them: "Till then I'll sweat and seek about for eases, / And at that time bequeath you my diseases" (5.10.54-55). The voice that rings in our ears as, picking at our dry serpigo, we leave the theater is the finally uncontrollable illegitimate voice.

. . . . .

In order to understand what this illegitimate voice can imply we need to know what bastardy meant in England in 1602 or 1603. The idea of legitimacy cannot be separated from the idea of authority. The first definition of "illegitimate" given by the OED is "not legitimate, not in accordance with or authorized by law," while "bastard" is defined as "illegitimate, unrecognized, unauthorized." Illegitimacy is, therefore, defined by authority and is, furthermore, a category which authority needs to legitimate itself; it is a form of the "other." When in his speech on order and degree Ulysses catalogs the horrifying effects of disorder he is, in fact, defining illegitimacy, for he expresses the result of a revolt against patriarchy through the metaphor of an act against husband and father that destroys the "unity and married calm of states" (1.3.99) and militates against the "primogeniture and due of birth" (1.3.105). In the light of this terror of the explosive force of illegitimacy we can understand the great glee that Thersites expresses over all the lechery he sees about him: it gives him a stake in the future by increasing the population of bastards in the world (much as Caliban's attempted violation of Miranda was prompted, or so he tells us, not by lust but by a desire to people his island with Calibans).

As is well known, the idea of patriarchal authority, and of the legitimate right of the ruling classes to rule and to engross wealth and property, was fundamental to the Tudor concept of social order, but it came under increasing pressure by the end of the sixteenth century. The center of power within the state, as within the family, depended

that have developed around the figure of the illegitimate in literature: "The bastard as usurper and murderer is an archetype. . . . Faulconbridge in Shakespeare's *King John* and Edmund of *King Lear* are striking examples—characteristic bastards" (127). If, however, we are to see Thersites as an archetypal bastard, his malice explained by his illegitimacy, we have to ask why Shakespeare left this crucial piece of information about his motivation to the end?

In both *King John* and *King Lear* the bastardy is made clear from the beginning, and in *Much Ado about Nothing* the bastardy of Don John, while not explicitly stated at the outset, is clearly enough implied as a cause of his sad and spiteful humor: "it better fits my blood to be disdained of all" (1.3.24). In *The Tempest*, too, the fact of Caliban's bastardy is early imparted to us (1.2.266-70). In each case the information sets up expectations, which are gratified by ensuing events, about the character's behavior. From this point of view Thersites's revelation of his bastardy seems to be gratuitous. Yet we cannot ignore it; it is peculiarly insistent (in a brief speech of some fifty words "bastard" is used eight times, "son of a whore" once, and "illegitimate" once) and, being his final speech, it draws particular attention to itself.

upon what Michel Foucault calls a "symbolics of blood" (148). It maintained itself through primogeniture and due right of birth, the acknowledged community of blood between father and legitimate first-born son. Yet the fragility of a claim on power that is justified by a metaphor involving sexual fidelity is poignantly indicated by Prospero in his account of the birth of Miranda: "Thy mother was a piece of virtue, and / She said thou wast my daughter" (1.2.56-57). Prospero has only his wife's word that Miranda is his legitimate daughter, a word that he knows may be nothing more than a word but that he must accept if he is to heal the rift between himself and the future. The tragedy for Leontes in *The Winter's Tale* is that he cannot accept the word of his "piece of virtue," and can find ironic comfort only in the idea that he is one of many thousands of men whose wives have been sluiced by their neighbors; the horrors of illegitimacy flood in on him.

The infidelity of the husband creates bastards who, like Edmund or Margarelon, can be tolerated but have no rights: from the thirteenth century onward bastards were legally excluded from the right to inherit property (Stone 30). The infidelity of the wife creates bastards who break the continuity of the bloodline, so threatening the stability of authority and the right to property (note that the central issue of the Trojan War is the restoration to Menelaus of his property rights by restoring to him control over his wife's body). Insofar as the bastard represented a threat to the clarity of blood connections and the safe transmission of power and property, he became in a sense a symbolic figure, diseased himself because he represented disease within the system.

The literary archetype of the characteristic bastard arises from this political dimension: the bastard is the pariah or malevolent outsider dedicated, like Edmund, to the destruction of the values represented by the "legitimate" authority of which he is the perverted product. This threat of disease is also the reason why established authority had to present bastardy as a moral problem, as reflected in the Church's homily "Against Whoredom, and Adultery." This homily, one of a number read out in churches at regular intervals throughout the reign of Elizabeth I, stated bluntly that sexual activity outside marriage was a sin which produced "so many bastardes and misbegotten children, to the hyghe displeasure of God" (Bond 180). The bastard, in effect, was the wages of sin.

We should not, however, allow the official insistence on bastardy as a moral problem to obscure the fact that it was much more extensively a social problem. What we have been observing up to now is the concern of the ruling classes with the impact of their own illegitimate offspring upon their own class interests. During the later years of Elizabeth's reign, however, bastardy in the lower classes offered a far greater threat to the system. Between about 1565 and 1604 the illegitimacy ratio almost trebled, from 1.31% to 3.36% (Laslett, "Introduction" 14); in some areas the proportion of bastard births reached as high as 10%

(Laslett, *Family Life* 104). A number of reasons have been suggested for this increase; Richard L. Greaves notes the possibility that it was a result of the unrestrained sexuality associated with festivity (214). David Levine and Keith Wrightson suggest that growing economic problems associated with a series of disastrous harvests, especially after 1594, decreased the opportunity for establishing marriage, particularly amongst the laboring poor, while failing to decrease the amount of sexual activity (171).

Whatever the cause, the effect was official fear of a drain on public financial resources and a consequent increase in the severity of penalties for producing bastard children (Stone 325; Youings 364). An Act of Parliament of 1576 gave Justices of the Peace the power to make fathers and mothers support their bastards, but it was, inevitably, the woman who usually became the victim of these penalties, with mother and child often adding to the numbers of vagrants and so-called "masterless men," as A.L. Beier has shown (54). Beier has analyzed in some detail the vagrancy problem of the sixteenth and seventeenth centuries and the threat to social discipline that masterless men were considered to constitute. As he demonstrates, the magnitude of the threat to order posed by vagrants was much exaggerated by a fearful ruling class in order to justify cruel penalties.

The official attitude toward the social problem is displayed to chilling effect in the words of magistrate William Lambarde, in a case at Maidstone in April 1582: "For, if you would find out the disorders of alehouses, which for the most part be but nurseries of naughtiness, then neither should idle rogues and vagabonds find such relief and harborow as they have, neither should wanton youths have so ready means to feed their pleasures and fulfill their lusts, whereby, besides infinite other mischiefs, they nowadays do burden all the country with their misbegotten bastards" (qtd. in Greaves 486). Given the congruency between illegitimacy and rootlessness as states of "other-ness" that evade or deny paternalist control, it is not surprising that the authorities came more and more "to regard bastardy as a symptom of disorder" (Youings 364).

The bastard had a grimly complex social reality because of the social need to keep people within rigid boundaries; the idea of the "archetypal bastard" arose from the *a priori* definition of the bastard as a bad character, as if the mere fact of illegitimacy made villainy inevitable. Consequently the bastard was made to fulfill the requirements of a social myth. Defined as a criminal, though he had committed no crime, he was the quintessential victim, punished for the actions of his parents by being marginalized, deprived of property rights and consequently of social identity. We can see, therefore, that the idea of the bastard had a less simple meaning than critics like Kimbrough and Bradshaw would appear to allow. In *King John* for example the injustice that underlies the stigma is acknowledged: "Your father's wife did after wedlock bear him, / And if she did play false, the fault was hers . . ." (1.1.117-18). In *King Lear* Edmund is allowed to articulate this same sense of injustice with greater eloquence:

> Why bastard? Wherefore base?
> When my dimensions are as well compact,
> My mind as generous, and my shape as true,
> As honest madam's issue? Why brand they us
> With base? with baseness? bastardy? base, base?
>
> (1.2.6-10)

The fact that Edmund is a villain and uses his illegitimacy as an excuse for his villainy in no way undercuts our sympathetic response to his words: what, apart from an act that was not his, makes the bastard automatically an object to be despised?

The bastard may also represent something larger than himself. Let us return for a moment to Thersites's revelation of his bastardy. He says to Margarelon that "the quarrel's most ominous for us," implying a community of interest between the two that is different from the interests of those running the war. Further, if it is true that they are fighting for a whore, then the whole basis of the war is brought into question, because a whore is no more "legitimate" than the son of a whore. Thersites's speech, far from being a base and cowardly confession, is an ideologically subversive gesture that creates a community of the "illegitimate" while at the same time bringing into question the validity of the claims of "legitimate" authority and the order for which the illegitimate are being asked to fight.

The play frequently expresses disruptions of order in terms of emulation and envy, and indeed Thersites himself locates the source of his own railing in "the devil Envy." Yet the disruptive envy of Achilles and Ajax is different from that of Thersites, for theirs is simply self-serving. They do not want to subvert the hierarchy, but to be at its head. Thersites's envy is something more; it is the rage of all those defined as "other" by established authority, all those whom the notion of hierarchy is intended to control; it is the rage of the dispossessed and disempowered, of bastards, but also of women, of the vagrant masterless, of the common soldiers who give their lives for the privileged likes of Pandarus and, who for their pains, are dismissed as "Asses, fools, dolts! Chaff and bran, chaff and bran!" (1.2.229-30)

Thersites is deliberately presented as the antithesis of Ulysses, who speaks on behalf of a ruling elite and articulates what is legitimate. Ulysses's speech on degree is such a fine piece of rhetoric that it became the foundation of the whole critical tradition represented by Tillyard, and summed up by Jonathan Dollimore and Alan Sinfield, "that Shakespeare believed in and expresses a political hierarchy whose rightness is guaranteed by its reflection of a divine hierarchy" (207). It is doubtful whether many critics today would insist on claiming that Ulysses's views are identical with Shakespeare's, but this speech nevertheless reflects official Elizabethan policy. It is no accident that the first mention of Thersites in the play comes in the lines that introduce Ulysses's speech:

> Speak, Prince of Ithaca; and be't of less expect
> That matter needless, of importless burden,
> Divide thy lips than we are confident,

> When rank Thersites opes his mastic jaws,
> We shall hear music, wit, and oracle.
>
> (1.3.69-73)

Muir, in his footnote to these lines, explains that they "forewarn the audience of Thersites' unsavory character" (71). Certainly, the evaluation of Ulysses and Thersites implied by Agamemnon sets them up as intellectual, esthetic, social and moral opposites, but this must be weighed in the light of Agamemnon's own intellectual deficiencies, amply demonstrated in his analysis of the Greek military position, and in the light of the fact that his own interests coincide with those of Ulysses.

The speech on degree is an ideological statement, intended to reassert the legitimacy of the class that Ulysses and those whom he is addressing represent. As Dollimore and Sinfield have it: "Ideology is composed of those beliefs, practices and institutions which work to legitimate the social order—especially by the process of representing sectional or class interests as universal ones. This process presupposes that there are other, subordinate classes, who far from sharing the interests of the dominant class are in fact being exploited by that class" (210-11). This exploitation may be achieved through an overt or a latent terrorism. The dominant class presents its interests through a set of norms, which are represented as being observed by all classes (cf. Tillyard's view that the concept of order was a part of the Elizabethan collective mind), though as Jurgen Habermas has argued, the subordinate classes do not necessarily believe in the legitimacy of those norms: "The factual recognition of such norms does not, of course, rest solely on belief in their legitimacy by those affected. It is also based on fear of, and submission to, indirectly threatened sanctions, as well as on simple compliance engendered by the individual's perception of his own powerlessness and the lack of alternatives open to him (that is, by his own fettered imagination)" (96). Thersites knows his own powerlessness against force: "He beats me, and I rail at him. O worthy satisfaction! Would it were otherwise—that I could beat him, whilst he railed at me" (2.3.2-4). He knows that the only power that he can wield resides in language, and through language he tries to keep his imagination unfettered.

Thersites's sense of the power of language, I think, accounts for the extreme violence and obscenity of his words—in order to have any authenticity, his own language must distance itself as far as possible from the mystifying rhetoric of authority. For Thersites sees clearly enough how the politicians use the concepts of hierarchy as a means of control, as he indicates to Achilles and Ajax: "There's Ulysses and old Nestor . . . yoke you like draught-oxen, and make you plough up the wars" (2.1.101-04). He sees things differently, and his only means of countering the oppressions of legitimate power is his own illegitimate vision. He is constantly uncrowning his superiors, re-categorizing them in terms of disease, of appetite, of bestial metaphor, or of the grotesque body: Ulysses as dog-fox, Agamemnon as botchy core, Ajax as itching scab or land-fish, Nestor as mouse-eaten cheese. We can hear in him clearly (if grimly) the voice of Bakhtinian carnival: "As opposed to the official feast, one might say that carnival celebrates temporary liberation from the prevailing truth of the established order; it marks the suspension of all hierarchical rank, privileges, norms and prohibitions. Carnival was the true feast of time, the feast of becoming, change and renewal. It was hostile to all that was immortalized and complete" (109).

Carnival is concerned with topsy-turveydom, with the world upside-down, with inverted hierarchies, and Thersites constructs hierarchies of his own, parodying the order that Ulysses is attempting to restore with his hierarchy of folly (in which he ironically locates himself): "Agamemnon is a fool to offer to command Achilles, Achilles is a fool to be commanded of Agamemnon, Thersites is a fool to be commanded of such a fool, and Patroclus is a fool positive" (2.3.58-61). More devastating is his treatment of Menelaus, on whose behalf the war is being fought; he is put at the bottom of a bestial hierarchy, lower than a louse on a lazar (5.1.55ff). Thersites surely performs the negative function proposed in R. Stamm's definition of the carnivalesque: "On the negative, critical side the carnivalesque suggests a demystificatory instrument for everything in the social formation which renders . . . collectivity difficult of access: class hierarchy, political manipulation, sexual repression, dogmatism and paranoia. Carnival in this sense implies an attitude of creative disrespect, a radical opposition to the illegitimately powerful, to the morose and monological" (55). In *Troilus and Cressida* the carnivalesque voice represented in the bastard Thersites is set up to oppose and expose the "illegitimately powerful."

I am not suggesting that we should like or approve of Thersites's character, but if we see him as a "demystificatory instrument" we can also see that moral condemnation of his scurrilous attitudes and behavior misses the point. What he says is all he can say; his words are the only weapons he has to represent the otherwise impotent rage of the oppressed and marginalized. His voice is not authoritative, but it does form part of a polyphony, and to deny interpretive legitimacy to it, to claim that it is simply "dismissed," is to perpetuate the kind of repression that created the voice in the first place. In our own troubled times, when the notion of "political correctness" has been used by authoritarian voices from both left and right to police language and thought, *Troilus and Cressida* takes on a special significance as a play in whose critical history the official, legitimate voice has for so long been heard to drown out the unofficial voice. Perhaps its illegitimate voice should be all the more carefully attended to, not "in the interests of contemporary 'relevance',," but because it represents, in however ugly a manner, a comprehensible account of the real and painful impotence of the great mass of the dispossessed whose voices we now never hear at all.

Note

1. All quotations from *Troilus and Cressida* are taken from Kenneth Muir's Oxford edition of the play. Quotations from other plays are taken from *The Complete Works* edited by Peter Alexander.

Works Cited

Adelman, Janet. "'This Is and Is Not Cressid': The Characterization of Cressida." *The (M)other Tongue: Essays in Feminist Psychoanalytic Interpretation.* Ed. Shirley Nelson Garner, Claire Kahane, and Madelon Sprengnether. Ithaca: Cornell UP, 1985, 119-41.

Bakhtin, Mikhail. *Rabelais and His World.* 1965. Trans. Helene Iswolsky. Bloomington, Indiana UP, 1984.

Beier, A.L. *Masterless Men: The Vagrancy Problem in England 1560-1640.* London: Methuen, 1985.

Bond, Ronald B., ed. *Certain Sermons or Homilies (1547) and A Homily against Disobedience and Wilful Rebellion (1570).* Toronto: U of Toronto P, 1987.

Bradshaw, Graham. *Shakespeare's Scepticism.* Brighton: Harvester, 1987.

Charnes, Linda. "'So Unsecret to Ourselves': Notorious Identity and the Material Subject in Shakespeare's *Troilus and Cressida.*" *Shakespeare Quarterly* 40 (1989): 413-42.

Cook, Carol. "Unbodied Figures of Desire." *Theatre Journal* 38 (1986): 34-52.

Dollimore, Jonathan, and Alan Sinfield. "History and Ideology: The Instance of *Henry V.*" *Alternative Shakespeares.* Ed. John Drakakis. London: Methuen, 1985. 206-27.

Foucault, Michel. *The History of Sexuality.* Vol. 1. 1965. Trans. Robert Hurley. New York: Vintage, 1980.

Gaudet, Paul. "'As True as Troilus,' 'As False as Cressid': Tradition, Text, and the Implicated Reader." *English Studies in Canada* 16 (1990): 125-48.

Girard, René. "The Politics of Desire in *Troilus and Cressida.*" *Shakespeare and the Question of Theory.* Ed. Patricia Parker and Geoffrey Hartman. London: Methuen, 1985. 188-209.

Greaves, Richard L. *Society and Religion in Elizabethan England.* Minneapolis: U of Minnesota P, 1981.

Greenblatt, Stephen. *Shakespearean Negotiations: The Circulation of Social Energy in Renaissance England.* Berkeley: U of California P, 1988.

Greene, Gayle. "Shakespeare's Cressida: 'A Kind of Self'." *The Woman's Part: Feminist Criticism of Shakespeare.* Ed. Carolyn Ruth Swift Lenz, Gayle Greene, and Carol Thomas Neely. Urbana: U of Illinois P, 1980. 133-49.

Habermas, Jurgen. *Legitimation Crisis.* 1973. Trans. Thomas McCarthy. Boston: Beacon, 1975.

Kimbrough, Robert. *Shakespeare's Troilus and Cressida and Its Setting.* Cambridge: Harvard UP, 1964.

Laslett, Peter. *Family Life and Illicit Love in Earlier Generations.* Cambridge: Cambridge UP, 1977.

———. "Introduction: Comparing Illegitimacy over Time and between Cultures." *Bastardy and Its Comparative History.* Ed. Peter Laslett, Karla Oosterveen and Richard M. Smith. London: Arnold, 1980. 1-68.

Levine, David, and Keith Wrightson. "The Social Context of Illegitimacy in Early Modern England." *Bastardy and Its Comparative History.* Ed. Peter Laslett, Karla Oosterveen and Richard M. Smith. London: Arnold, 1980. 158-75.

Lynch, Stephen J. "Shakespeare's Cressida: 'A Woman of Quick Sense'." *Philological Quarterly* 63 (1984): 257-68.

Mallin, Eric. "Emulous Factions and the Collapse of Chivalry: *Troilus and Cressida.*" *Representations* 29 (1990): 145-79.

O'Rourke, James "'Rule in Unity' and Otherwise: Love and Sex in *Troilus and Cressida.*" *Shakespeare Quarterly* 43 (1992): 139-58.

Patterson, Annabel. *Shakespeare and the Popular Voice.* Oxford: Blackwell, 1989.

Shakespeare, William. *The Complete Works.* Ed. Peter Alexander. London: Collins, 1951.

———. *Troilus and Cressida.* Ed. Kenneth Muir. Oxford: Clarendon, 1982.

Stamm, R. "On the Carnivalesque." *Wedge* 1 (1982): 47-55.

Stone, Lawrence. *The Family, Sex and Marriage in England 1500-1800.* 1977. Harmondsworth: Penguin, 1982.

Teichman, Jenny. *Illegitimacy: A Philosophical Examination.* Oxford: Blackwell, 1982.

Tennenhouse, Leonard. *Power on Display: The Politics of Shakespeare's Genres.* New York: Methuen, 1986.

Tillyard, E.M.W. *The Elizabethan World Picture.* 1943. Harmondsworth: Penguin, 1963.

Traub, Valerie. *Desire and Anxiety: Circulations of Sexuality in Shakespearean Drama.* London: Routledge, 1992.

Weimann, Robert. *Shakespeare and the Popular Tradition in the Theater: Studies in the Social Dimension of Dramatic Form and Function.* Ed. Robert Schwartz. 1978. Baltimore: Johns Hopkins UP, 1987.

Youings, Joyce. *Sixteenth-Century England.* Harmondsworth: Penguin, 1984.

Grace Tiffany (essay date 1993)

SOURCE: "Not Saying No: Female Self-Erasure in *Troilus and Cressida,*" in *Texas Studies in Literature and Language,* Vol. 35, No. 1, Spring, 1993, pp. 44-56.

[*In the following essay, Tiffany asserts that Cressida has been misread by most critics as either reprehensible or victimized, when in fact she is the product of a patriarchal culture still present today that misunderstands women who do not communicate forcefully.*]

> One half of me is yours, the other half yours,
> Mine own, I would say; but if mine, then yours,
> And so all yours.
>
> —Portia, *The Merchant of Venice* III.ii.16-18[1]

Like Shakespeare's Trojans and Greeks, scholarly evaluators of Shakespeare's Cressida divide themselves into two warring camps that only *seem* radically opposed. In fact, both camps share a common perspective and language that produce a disturbing vision of woman as passive creation of her patriarchal culture. Cressida as wanton and Cressida as victim present two sides of the same interpretive coin: both notions result from and re-create the idea of Cressida as a creature formed by male perceptions and values; thus both notions, by privileging male determination of female identity, reinforce female subjectivity. Missing from both categories of interpretation is an acknowledgment of female responsibility for self-creation within, but in defiance of, a patriarchal interpretive system. An alternative critical paradigm would inquire not only into the ways in which male valuations oppress women in Shakespeare's texts but into the ways in which characters such as Cressida support male valuations—in effect, give up the power of self-creation. This, I would argue, is a more powerful critical conversation: one which allows the female reader to "engage in the process of dislocation of the unconscious by which she begins to affirm her own reality."[2]

This paper's inquiry into Cressida's choices emerges from such a paradigm. My argument is not that Cressida is not false, nor that she is not oppressed; like others in the play, including some males, she is both.[3] I want to assert, alternatively, that a female character can be false without being wanton—can, that is, be acknowledged to fail morally without our subscription to homocentric evaluations of her failure—and that holding Cressida responsible for her moral choices, which include acquiescence in her own oppression, does her, and us, a service. It affirms her authoritative personhood and thus performs a healthy resistance to the masculine ethic that still controls the interpretation of female behavior in Shakespearean texts.

Therefore, after acknowledging some of the critical studies that demonstrate Cressida's erasure from Shakespeare's text—her disappearance into a male-authored symbol, first of beauty and value and ultimately of falseness—I propose to trace some of the steps by which Cressida participates in that erasure. To recuperate Cressida is, paradoxically, to assess her self-erasure and to demonstrate her horrifying negative control over her own ontology. The key action by which Cressida relinquishes authorship of her own identity is the surrender of her voice. Cressida voices herself— reveals, that is, her fundamental desires and interests—

only rarely in the first three acts, and in acts IV and V, as Janet Adelman, David Hale, and Stephen Lynch have noticed,[4] Cressida hardly speaks at all and shares no private thoughts in soliloquy. (E. Talbot Donaldson has determined that Cressida "speaks only 117 times" in the course of the play, "and a hundred of her speeches are of less than twenty words; eighty of less than ten," 74.)[5] Furthermore, with the exception of her early soliloquy in I.ii.282-95,[6] where she confesses her love for Troilus, and certain interchanges with Troilus and Pandarus in III.ii and IV.ii and iv, where she defies the male edict that she leave Troy and Troilus to join her father and the Greeks, when Cressida does speak, she adjusts her language to male discursive practices and her vision of reality to that dictated by male perception. Cressida initially hides her love for Troilus in order to conform to his Petrarchan image of her as indifferent love-goddess (I.i-ii); ultimately, she will affirm the equally limiting male-scripted role of frail, wanton woman. We see this where, after arriving in the Greek camp and arranging a tryst with Diomedes, she laments, "poor our sex! This fault in us I find, / The error of our eye directs our mind" (V.ii.109-10). In these lines, Cressida echoes Ulysses's previously stated judgment of her as fundamentally carnal, led by lust (IV.v.55-63), and thus not only accepts but actively promotes a negative male valuation of her behavior. Through this voluntary sacrifice of independent self-expression, Cressida authorizes her own displacement, affirming the erection of a male-authored "Cressida," an image first of disdainful beauty and finally of wantonness and frailty, where an authentic self might have stood.

Cressida is, of course, powerfully encouraged by her circumstances to validate male visions and participate in male schemes; the play does not allow her a clear alternative route for physical survival, any more than dramatic convention afforded Shakespeare the freedom radically to alter the Cressida myth.[7] Through exploiting and elaborating that myth, however, Shakespeare was able to dramatize how the human subject's ultimate valuation of physical survival might exact tragic cost. Unlike, for example, *Measure for Measure*'s Isabella, who frankly refuses Angelo's demand for her body and ultimately insists that her complaint against him be heard ("Hear me, O hear me, here," V.i.32),[8] the near-silent Cressida purchases survival at the price of being. She tacitly approves her character's displacement by a male idea by suppressing her own self-constituting voice.

Because Cressida remains silent or corroborates the male view of feminine weakness and "turpitude" (V.ii.112), critics have frequently reproduced Ulysses's condemnation of her. Negative descriptions of Cressida in this century range from Robert Ornstein's "a slut" to George Wilbur Meyer's "a whore" to Una Ellis-Fermor's milder "a light woman."[9] As unsettling as it is (or should be) for female readers to encounter the words "slut" and "whore" used unselfconsciously to describe a character who switches love interests only once (Romeo does no less) and who is not paid for sex, it is equally disturbing to read defenses of Cressida

that posit her fundamental powerlessness to do anything but inscribe herself into a masculine ethic which so (de)values her. Carol Cook, for example, ascribes creative ability to males but not to females where, demonstrating how Helen and Cressida are treated as "objects of exchange mediating the relations among men," she argues that "the play consistently reveals the operations by which women . . . are *produced* as objects" by an "economy of masculine desire" (254, 257). Gayle Greene also privileges male agency in the creation of female identity, calling Cressida the "victim of a strategy that costs her no less than her self" (145). (Since the strategy to which Greene refers is Cressida's own—her plan to replace Troilus with Diomedes—it is misleading to describe her as a "victim" of it.) Hesitant to assign responsibility to Cressida, Greene quotes Simone de Beauvoir's assertion that "'it is civilization as a whole that produces this creature'" (woman) and adds that women in *Troilus and Cressida* are "'formed in th' applause' (III.iii.1119) of others" (133-34). Cook's, Greene's, and de Beauvoir's passive constructions reproduce the reification of women to which they object; rather than produce herself in accordance with a masculine concept, woman, according to this view, gets produced. Carolyn Asp's similar passive voice structure likewise produces the image of a reified Cressida.[10] Noting that Troilus projects an "image of courtly, romantic love" onto his and Cressida's relationship, Asp adds, "This image had allowed Cressida to perceive herself as intrinsically lovable and valuable, but unfortunately this perception is unable to manifest itself in action; it remains vizarded in a hostile environment" (417). Asp might have said, "Cressida doesn't act on the basis of this perception," but she doesn't. Here the critic's insistence on Cressida's powerlessness creates logical and syntactical confusion, as she displaces Cressida's responsibility for action onto abstractions: an "image" that "allow[s]" and a "perception" that proves "unable to manifest itself." Thus, to varying degrees, all these critics reproduce in interpretation the dynamic they abhor in the text of the play: the objectification of the female character.

Acknowledging the dehumanizing potential of such defenses allows us to understand both Robert Ornstein's and E. Talbot Donaldson's seemingly conflicted arguments concerning Cressida. Ornstein pities Cressida for being "a daughter of the game which men would have her play and for which they despise her," but does not himself relinquish the term "slut" (315)[11] in his appraisal of her; and Donaldson, while pointing out Cressida's possible "innocence" (77), yet observes that we know she "will become a slut" (75) and that Thersites's reference to Cressida's mind having "turn'd whore" (V.ii.114) is "the appropriate last word on . . . Cressida . . . and on all the Cressid-kind" (68). These apparently divided judgments of Cressida's character are in fact reconcilable: if we straightforwardly echo Ulysses's claim that *Troilus and Cressida*'s women are "daughters of the game" (IV.v.63)—volitionless dummies created and controlled by what Cook has called the "economy of masculine desire"—the next logical step is to see them, as Ulysses also does, as "sluttish spoils of opportunity" (IV.v.62). Both formulations invoke an identity that is not self-generated but is imposed from without on the passive, choiceless female subject.

A critical strategy more likely to empower female readers might approach the text from an alternative standpoint. It might acknowledge the oppressiveness of a patriarchal environment that treats women as counters in a war game played to determine male identity and status—a game that achieves what Eve Sedgwick calls "homosocial" bonding (1).[12] But, and most important, it might also analyze the ways in which female characters suppress their independent voices in gestures of support for this game as they reconstitute themselves in imitation of male-authored images. Adelman employs this interpretive paradigm when she accuses Cressida of forfeiting her "sense of her own intrinsic worth" by "internaliz[ing] the principle of valuation that rules this society, the principle implied by Troilus's question, 'What's aught but as 'tis valued?' (2.2.52)" (120). I disagree with Adelman's reading of Cressida's betrayal of Troilus as the ultimate "assertion of her status as a separate person, not simply the creation of Troilus' fantasy" (134)—instead, I regard that betrayal as the final step in Cressida's passage into silent nonbeing as she conforms both to Ulysses's assessment of her character and to Troilus's fearful prediction for her (IV.iv.94-97). But I support Adelman's willingness to grant Cressida at least partial responsibility for her own "disappearance" as character—to draw attention to Cressida's collaboration with the interpretive system that produces reductive assessments of her behavior. Cressida's psychological investment in this male system in fact produces her struggles and self-division as, internalizing her oppression, she fights *against* (not for) self-expression.

Cressida's self-rejection is dramatized in her first scene, where she presents herself as something fundamentally other than she knows herself to be. Pandarus's entrance at I.ii.37 provokes her subterfuge. Determined to conceal her interest in his friend Troilus, Cressida launches a decoy dialogue in which she praises Hector at Troilus's expense ("Hector's a gallant man," I.ii.39). The wit she deploys here, seen by some as an expression of her best self,[13] is actually a protective strategy, produced in her encounters with men and designed for self-shielding. She loses this wit in her rare moments of honesty, as when she confesses her love to Troilus and then immediately asks, "Where is my wit? I know not what I speak" (III.ii.151), and she reactivates her wit when, recoiling from that act of courageous self-revelation, she repudiates her confession: "Perchance, my lord, I show more craft than love, / And fell so roundly to a large confession, / To angle for your thoughts" (III.ii.153-55). Cressida's reticence is indeed culturally approved; she complains of not having "men's privilege / Of speaking first" (III.ii.128-29). But it is worth noting that some Shakespearean heroines do assert "men's privilege" in defiance of social custom: *All's Well That Ends Well*'s Helena, for example, speaks first when she claims Bertram as mate. Unlike Helena, Cressida suppresses the voice of choice and assumes the defensive posture she earlier outlined to Pandarus, relying "upon [her] wit" to "defend [her] wiles" (I.ii.260-61); her tactics reveal a disturbing identification of self-revelation with self-loss.

Sadder yet, Cressida's conviction that her self-disclosure will inevitably result in her rejection, evident in her early soliloquy ("Things won are done," I.ii.287), betrays a fundamental assumption that she is intrinsically unlovable. Given the fact that Troilus does nothing to encourage this assumption, Cressida appears almost pathologically deficient in self-esteem, expressing offense at her "own company" once she has revealed herself to Troilus, as well as the desire to "shun [her]self" (III.ii.145-46). Her next words to Troilus reveal her longing to *be* what is actually her defense *against* being—her witty self—and her profound reluctance to identify herself as the lover she is:

> I have a kind of self resides with you;
> But an unkind self, that itself will leave
> To be another's fool. I would be gone.
> Where is my wit? I know not what I speak.
>
> (III.ii.148-51)

The simple meaning of these lines is that Cressida will leave Troilus for Diomedes; the more subtle and difficult meaning, and the one she intends, is that the self that craves relationship with Troilus—the "kind of self" that resides with him—is an unkind fool. Her "firm love" for Troilus, which earlier in soliloquy she has called her "heart's content" (I.ii.294-95), she here rejects as "unkind": not only cruel but unrelated to her. And immediately, disclaiming knowledge of that inner self, now manifest through its verbal disclosure, she calls for her subterfuge: her wit.

Having rejected herself, convinced in advance of her heart's valuelessness, any rejection by Troilus would be superfluous. Rejection is the emotional condition that Cressida brings to their tryst and out of which she chooses her next lover, Diomedes. Critics have readily attributed Cressida's wistful plea that Troilus "tarry" (IV.ii.15) after their lovemaking to Troilus's haste to leave her—have, in other words, validated Cressida's assumptions about the inevitability of her rejection, based on her notion of her own valuelessness to men. But Troilus is affectionate in this scene and displays only a reasonable interest in preserving their mutual secrecy by getting about the day's business:

> O Cressida! but that the busy day,
> Wak'd by the lark, hath rous'd the ribald crows,
> And dreaming night will hide our joys no longer,
> I would not from thee.
>
> (IV.ii.8-11)

For Cressida, however, their love is already over by virtue of her participation in it. "O foolish Cressid!" she accuses herself, telling Troilus, "I might have still held off, / And then you would have tarried" (IV.ii.17-18). She perceives herself as having lost Troilus by having been "won": won not only sexually but verbally. For Cressida, Troilus's affection is based on her absence—on the substitution of an image of a witty, disdainful beloved for the real Cressida who loves. He will love "her," she believes, as long as he cannot see—or hear—*her.*

Her view is as self-destructive as it is self-defeating. Convinced of the essential worthlessness of her own desires, Cressida reverts to suppressing them. She forestalls their expression, choosing instead to acquiesce in others' plans for her. Although she initially defies Priam's command that she depart Troy for the Greek camp, declaring, "I will not go from Troy" (IV.ii.110), her resolve evaporates in the face of Troilus's contrary assertion. She repeatedly looks to him for an interpretation of reality, asking, "is it true that I must go from Troy? . . . Is't possible? . . . I must then to the Grecians?" (IV.iv.30, 32, 55), and immediately stops protesting once he affirms that she must. She also looks to Troilus for a map of her future behavior, responding to his fearful warning that she may be tempted to betray him with, "Do you think I will?" (92), so that her subsequent treachery seems done almost in fulfillment of a role he has fashioned for her.

Cressida's privileging of Troilus's thoughts follows naturally from her sense of the unworthiness of her own. Up to this point, Cressida has intermittently manifested her authentic self through speaking—declaring her love for Troilus to the audience at the close of I.ii. and (however hesitantly) to Troilus in III.ii and proclaiming opposition to the men's plan to send her from Troy in IV.ii. From IV.iv on, however, Cressida reveals virtually nothing of what she wants, walling herself off from others with what Arnold Stein calls a "reserve that prevents her from ever saying or doing what might register the full feeling of her presence" (157).[15]

Her reserve is perhaps most self-damaging in the infamous "kissing scene," where, newly arrived in the Greek camp, Cressida participates in the sexual game initiated by the Greek commanders, tacitly enabling Ulysses's malicious assessment of her as "sluttish spoils" (IV.v.62). Cressida's participation here is not physical—Shakespeare's text, which keeps her silent throughout the men's kisses, gives us no reason to believe she is physically receptive, especially when her subsequent lines reiterate her *refusal* to kiss (IV.v.19-51). Yet Cressida, whatever her feelings, supports the male game through the obliqueness of her refusal. The kissing scene, in fact, dramatizes the two aspects of Cressida's reserve: her silence and the wit that, from the outset, she has used to divert attention from her real wishes. Earlier, Cressida wittily disclaimed interest in Troilus in order to mask real love; here, again using wit, she fends off Ulysses with a seeming promise of intimacy that is actually a refusal:

> *Ulyss.* May I, sweet lady, beg a kiss of you?
> *Cres.* You may.
> *Ulyss.*   I do desire it.
> *Cres.*   Why, beg then.
> *Ulyss.* Why then, for Venus' sake, give me a kiss
> When Helen is a maid again. . . .
> *Cres.* I am your debtor, claim it when 'tis due.
>
>   (IV.v.47-51)

Although Cressida, when she speaks here, says nothing but "no," that "no" is obscured by its embedment in witty banter, an idiom that for her, as we earlier saw, is not self-expressive. Choosing, instead of straightforward refusal, the habitual verbal strategy with which she hides herself from men—echoing, in fact, the flirtatious banter with which *they* address *her*—Cressida prevents her "no" from being heard.

Surprisingly few critics, even of those most sympathetic to Cressida, have recognized what Donaldson calls the "potential for ambiguity" in this scene (81), since Cressida does not authorize the kissing and seems to be trying, however jokingly, to fend off the men's advances. Lynch argues that the fact that Cressida "is kissed five times before she says a word . . . makes it difficult to interpret her behavior as blatantly provocative" ("Shakespeare's Cressida," 363), but the numerous examples of anti-Cressida criticism reveal that such an interpretation has *not* proved historically difficult (see Voth and Evans). In an extreme example, S. L. Bethell straightforwardly accepts Ulysses's view, expressed in this scene, that Cressida is "sluttish spoils of opportunity": Bethell cautions us against "search[ing] the morality of [Ulysses's] own conduct," since he is "the embodiment of wisdom in the play" (218).[16] But even some female critics generally sympathetic toward Cressida seem to blame her for going along with the men in IV.v; Anne Barton says Cressida "begins to play the coquette the minute she sets foot in the Greek camp" (446),[17] and Gayle Greene says she "allow[s] herself to be 'kiss'd in general' (IV.v.21)" (143)—a "sudden and complete violation of declared intentions" (135). Such readings of this scene come near to justifying the Greek commanders' view of Cressida as "the Troyan's trumpet" (with a pun on "strumpet") (IV.v.64). I believe that it is the oblique *manner* of Cressida's refusal in this scene that gives rise to these negative assessments of her behavior by critics and characters alike and that Shakespeare, through dramatizing Cressida's obliqueness and the men's response to it, is demonstrating the destructive effects of female nonassertiveness on interpretations of female character. One could not find better proof of those destructive effects than in our own habitual critical responses to Cressida.

This is not to make the absurd claim that straightforward resistance might have altered Cressida's fortunes either in this scene or in the earlier one in which she agrees to be led from Troy. Rather, I mean to point out the simple fact that Cressida does not offer such resistance—that, at every turn, she chooses either not to speak or to acquiesce in male discursive practices that do violence to what Greene calls her "best self" (145), eventually silencing that self altogether and thus accomplishing a virtual self-erasure from Shakespeare's text. Her language to Diomedes in act V borders on incoherence as, enacting the abandonment of integrity, she struggles between the impulse to flirt and the desire to declare a prior loyalty:

> Cres.: Sweet honey Greek, tempt me no more to folly.
>
> . . . . .
>
> Dio.: Nay then—
> Cres.: I'll tell you what—
> Dio.: Fo, fo, come, tell a pin. You are forsworn.
> Cres.: In faith, I cannot. What would you have me do?
>
> (V.ii.18-23)

The Cressida who loves Troilus ceases to matter, even to exist, through Cressida's refusal to speak her. She chooses to give up choice: she will do what Diomedes "would . . . have [her] do." When Diomedes and Troilus clash in V.vi, they thus fight over a nonentity; significantly, Troilus omits mention of Cressida when taunting Diomedes, instead challenging him to "pay thy life thou owest me for my horse" (which Diomedes has seized for Cressida) (V.vi.7). Like the "lechery" that, in Thersites's words, "eats itself" (V.iv.35), Cressida is self-swallowed: she is author of her own disappearance.

Ironically, those who argue that Cressida is victimized, intending sensitivity toward the female subject, unwittingly reinforce her erasure. Derek Traversi, for example, exempts Cressida from "moral evaluation" because, in his view, she is not responsible for her actions. His chivalric pardon seems inseparable from his "difficult[y]" in "conceiv[ing] of Cressida as a fully realized being" (202).[18] Such misfiring benevolence has also affected stage productions of *Troilus and Cressida*: Barbara Bowen writes of a 1965 version in which Joseph Papp, "influenced by the feminist movement," presented Cressida as "a victim 'of men, their wars, their desires, their double standards.'" Papp's investment in the creation of a totally controlled Cressida led to a defense of her so spirited that, in his own words, it "'created an unfortunate conflict between me and the actor playing the role of Troilus'" (Bowen, 272).[19] Significantly absent from Papp's report of this conflict is the actor playing Cressida; Papp here plays Diomedes fighting Troilus over a mere symbolic theme.

I am trying to show that sympathetic evaluations of Cressida that divest her of responsibility for choice, however well meant, are finally not helpful constructions but duplications of the objectifying principle that denies female subjectivity in the play (as where Troilus calls Helen a "theme of honor and renown," II.ii.199). Further, the fact that Cressida herself denies agency in her (mis)fortunes need not compel our own critical reinscription of the image of the powerless female. We may, for example, benefit from Linda Charnes's perceptive diagnosis of the particular stereotypes that afflict women in *Troilus and Cressida* without according these stereotypes full power to determine female identities in the play. Charnes argues that characters in *Troilus and Cressida* vainly resist their oppression by preinscribed historical identities

already known to Shakespeare's audience: that Cressida, like other characters, "act[s] out . . . a rebellion against a coercion and oppression of subjectivity that cannot and must not be directly confronted or openly challenged. Unable to construct alternatives, [she is] forced to be and not be '[herself]'" (414).[20] Cressida, in other words, is an unwilling victim of her own status as archetype of false womanhood—an archetype that she struggles to escape. I argue, alternatively, that Cressida's struggles are primarily produced not by historical *or* Greco-Trojan predefinitions of her character but by her own tacit acceptance of the principle that Charnes's words (ironically) reinscribe: the idea that her subjectivity "cannot and must not be directly confronted or openly challenged." In fact, Cressida's complaints throughout the play repeatedly express her sense of the fundamental, inescapable reality of the archetype that oppresses her; thus these complaints constitute not rebellion but aggrieved resignation. From her early observation that "Men prize the thing ungain'd more than it is" (I.ii.289), to her ironic affirmation of her future mythic status as archetype of feminine falsehood (III.ii.183-203), to her final reductive assessment of women as an error-driven "poor . . . sex" (V.ii.109-11), her lines validate the "Ulyssean" image of feminine frailty and relative worthlessness. The mythic "false . . . Cressid" archetype about which Cressida is dimly prescient, and the view of women as "sluttish spoils" suggested by the masculine ethic of her own society, in fact combine to create a powerfully seductive image of femininity for Cressida. This image, while cruelly oppressive, morally crippling, and fundamentally false, yet offers Cressida its own kind of escape—an escape from the responsibility of self-invention. Cressida's final lines in the play, which plot her future submission to Diomedes, enact her flight from decisive self-creation, as they dramatize her final surrender to a male-scripted role:

> Ah, poor our sex! this fault in us I find,
> The error of our eye directs our mind.
> What error leads must err; O then conclude,
> Minds sway'd by eyes are full of turpitude.
>
> (V.ii.109-12)

Revealing, schizophrenically, that she both perceives and is controlled by error, Cressida here enacts the destruction of her own integrity, disclosing her radical self-division and concomitant self-hatred. She thus disappears from the text. After this passage, Shakespeare allows her only the ultimate expression of acquiescent resignation to the story: silence.

Again, this is not to suggest that Shakespeare's Cressida *should* have displayed more strength than her mythic prototype. As I hope I have demonstrated, Shakespeare takes advantage of Cressida's prior negative symbolic value to *elaborate* the archetype of the dishonest person, from its origins in defensive hypocrisy to its final manifestation in nonbeing: the total disappearance of an integrated self. The Cressida myth affords Shakespeare the opportunity to dramatize the self-eradicating effects of resignation to a prescribed identity, and of choosing choicelessness. Shakespeare's play thus affords us a critical challenge, which may be met in this way. Rather than positing that female decisions are determined by a patriarchal universe, we may study the ways that universe is ratified by female consent: by silence or by acquiescence in discursive practices that discourage direct female self-expression. *Troilus and Cressida* demonstrates the danger of female voicelessness within an interpretive system dominated by masculine perceptions and justifies the warning of contemporary sociologist Jan Strout: "'Because men have been socialized to hear yes when women say no, we have to scream it.'"[21]

Notes

1. William Shakespeare, *The Merchant of Venice,* in *The Riverside Shakespeare,* ed. G. Blakemore Evans (Boston: Houghton-Mifflin, 1974), 254-83. All references to Shakespeare's plays are to this text.

2. Madelon Gohlke, "'I Wooed Thee with My Sword': Shakespeare's Tragic Paradigms," in *The Woman's Part: Feminist Criticism of Shakespeare,* ed. Gayle Green, Carolyn Lenz, and Carol Thomas Neely (Chicago: University of Illinois Press, 1980).

3. Gayle Greene, Janet Adelman, and Carol Cook note the way Helen and Cressida are treated as objects, the possession of which determines male status (see Greene's "Shakespeare's Cressida: 'A Kind of Self,'" in *The Woman's Part;* Adelman's "'This Is and Is Not Cressid': The Characterization of Cressida," in *The (M)other Tongue: Essays in Feminist Psychoanalytic Interpretation,* ed. Shirley Garner Nelson, Claire Kahane, and Madelon Gohlke Sprengnether [Ithaca: Cornell University Press, 1985]; and Cook's "Unbodied Figures of Desire," in *The History of Troilus and Cressida,* ed. Daniel Seltzer [New York: Signet, 1988]. Greene calls Cressida "the sum total of 'opinions' of men" (145) and sees the play as exploring "the effects of capitalism on woman" (137). Cook speaks of "the use of women as objects of exchange mediating the relations between men" (257), and Adelman refers to Cressida's "status as devalued object" after she passes to the Greeks, bearing out "the principle implied by Troilus' question, 'What's aught but as 'tis valued?' (2.2.52)" (122). Troilus's comment, however, applies to the male characters as well: Achilles loses value in Greek and Trojan eyes by resting on his laurels, and Troilus acquires value by virtue of his comparison to Paris (see Cressida's and Pandar's dialogue in I.ii.92-106), just as Cressida acquires hers through comparison with Helen (I.i.41-104). Both men and women are affected by this system of relative valuation, yet feminist criticism tends to avoid acknowledging its oppressive effect on male characters.

4. Adelman argues that Cressida's refusal to share her thoughts with the audience after IV.iv renders her "radically unknowable" and "irreducibly other" (128); I argue that Cressida's silence constitutes her total submission to the role in which men have cast her, but perhaps mine is just another way of describing the same phenomenon. David Hale argues that Cressida's voice is "overwhelmed" by other events and characters after the play's first two acts (p. 10 of "'Madness of Discourse': Language and Ideology in *Troilus and Cressida,*" paper delivered at "Seventeenth-Century Literature and Politics Conference," Orlando, Florida, March 1991). Stephen Lynch also notes Cressida's gradual lapse into relative silence ("Shakespeare's Cressida: 'A Woman of Quick Sense,'" *Philological Quarterly* 63 [1984], 357-67, 363). I differ with Hale and Lynch in my interpretation of what Cressida's authentic voice actually is: both these critics see it as her witty banter (a conclusion supported by Deborah Hooker in "Coming to Cressida through Irigary," *South Atlantic Quarterly* 88 [1989]: 899-932; and by Grant Voth and Oliver Evans in "Cressida and the World of the Play," *Shakespeare Studies* 8 [1975]: 231-40). Alternatively, I view Cressida's wit as a deceptive discursive practice, done in response to male teasing, which hides her genuine self.

5. E. Talbot Donaldson, "Cressid False, Criseyde Untrue: An Ambiguity Revisited," in *Poetic Traditions of the English Renaissance,* ed. Maynard Mack and George deForest Lord (New Haven: Yale University Press, 1982).

6. William Shakespeare, *Troilus and Cressida,* in *The Riverside Shakespeare,* ed. G. Blakemore Evans.

7. See chapter 2 of David Farley-Hills's *Shakespeare and the Rival Playwright, 1600-1606* (New York: Routledge, Chapman and Hall, 1990) for a comprehensive discussion of the treatment of the Troilus and Cressida myth on the English Renaissance stage.

8. William Shakespeare, *Measure for Measure,* in *The Riverside Shakespeare,* ed. G. Blakemore Evans.

9. See Voth and Evans for a catalog of negative critical assessments of Cressida's character.

10. Carolyn Asp, "In Defense of Cressida," *Studies in Pathology* 74 (1977): 406-17.

11. Robert Ornstein, excerpt from *The Moral Vision of Jacobean Tragedy,* in *Modern Shakespearean Criticism: Essays on Style, Dramaturgy, and the Major Plays,* ed. Alvin B. Kernan (New York: Harcourt Brace Jovanovich, 1970), 311-17.

12. Eve Sedgwick, *Between Men: English Literature and Male Homosocial Desire* (New York: Columbia University Press, 1985).

13. See n. 4.

14. See, for example, Stephen Lynch's "The Idealism of Shakespeare's Troilus," *South Atlantic Review* 51.1 (January 1986): 19-29, 22; and René Girard's "The Politics of Desire in *Troilus and Cressida*" in *Shakespeare and the Question of Theory,* ed. Geoffrey Hartman and Patricia Parker (New York: Methuen, 1985).

Both studies assert that Troilus is genuinely uninterested in Cressida in IV.ii. According to Girard, Troilus's attitude demonstrates that "a man loses interest in a woman who yields too easily to his desires"; Girard sees this as one of the "implacable laws" of "masculine desire" (189).

15. Arnold Stein, "*Troilus and Cressida:* The Disjunctive Imagination," *ELH* 36 (1969): 145-67.

16. S. L. Bethell, excerpt from *Shakespeare and the Popular Dramatic Tradition,* in *The History of Troilus and Cressida,* ed. Seltzer.

17. Anne Barton, introduction to *Troilus and Cressida,* in *The Riverside Shakespeare,* ed. Evans, 443-47.

18. Derek Traversi, excerpt from *An Approach to Shakespeare,* in *The History of Troilus and Cressida,* ed. Seltzer.

19. Barbara E. Bowen, "*Troilus and Cressida on the Stage,*" in *The History of Troilus and Cressida,* ed. Seltzer.

20. Linda Charnes, "'So Unsecret to Ourselves': Notorious Identity and the Material Subject in Shakespeare's *Troilus and Cressida,*" *Shakespeare Quarterly* 40 (Winter 1989): 413-40.

21. See p. 227 of Ellen Sweet's "Date Rape: The Story of an Epidemic and Those Who Deny It," in *Our Times: Readings from Recent Periodicals,* ed. Robert Atwan (New York: St. Martin's Press, 1989).

GENRE

Kristina Faber (essay date 1990)

SOURCE: "Shakespeare's *Troilus and Cressida:* Of War and Lechery," in *Colby Quarterly,* Vol. 26, No. 2, June, 1990, pp. 133-48.

[*In the following essay, Faber remarks that while* Troilus and Cressida *has been regarded by many critics as a "problem comedy," it is better described as a problem tragedy for which Shakespeare could not or chose not to provide a satisfactory conclusion.*]

Commentators have generally agreed that Shakespeare's *Troilus and Cressida* is one of his "problem plays." Others include *All's Well That Ends Well, Measure for Measure,* and sometimes *Julius Caesar;* less frequently, *Hamlet* and *Timon of Athens* are named. For critics, identifying the actual "problem" in a problem play, determining what causes the difficulty, and theorizing about how to solve it have traditionally represented three separate analytic tasks. I would like to treat all three as interrelated aspects of one critical misconception about *Troilus and Cressida*—that it

is a "problem comedy"—and offer an alternative explanation, though no solution, for the underlying "problem" of this play.[1]

The original problem seems to be the peculiar effect *Troilus and Cressida* and the other problem plays have on their audiences (Boas 345). At the end of these plays viewers may feel ambivalent, confused, dissatisfied, resentful, even repulsed. Playgoers and readers have suspected that Shakespeare himself did not know what he wanted or, worse, that in these dramas the playwright was cynically manipulating the spectators' reactions, but denying them his guiding vision and withholding his own emotional commitment to the dramatic material. Such plays have been called "dark," "satirical," "bitter and cynical pseudocomedies." I would concur that the ending of *Troilus and Cressida* will forever remain troubling, offering neither traditional comic release nor tragic catharsis.

A wide range of critics attempts to explain this difficulty. For instance, *Troilus and Cressida* may be a "problem" in the sense of a "botched" comedy; perhaps due to personal problems Shakespeare just wasn't up to his usual standard (Wilson 114-15). Or because the play's probable sources (Homer, Ovid, Chaucer, Henryson, Caxton, Lydgate, and Greene) were relatively well-known and thus resistant to major changes, *Troilus and Cressida* posed unusual dramatic challenges which Shakespeare was unable to overcome (Morris 483). Barbara Everett believes that the "absence of simple story-line . . . is the source of most of the other problems that disturb the play's readers" (119). But other commentators theorize that rather than the absence of story-line, too many story-lines cause the problem: Shakespeare could not successfully weld together two major plots in the story, the classical Troyan matter (the war plot) and the medieval invention of Troilus and Cressida's relationship (the love plot) (Palmer 49). More penetrating, I believe, are the observations of Marilyn French and F.H. Langman that "at every level" (Langman 66) these plots coterminate: in *Troilus and Cressida,* love is war (French 159; see also Yoder 19). French further argues that all of Shakespeare's problem plays cause difficulties because they "share an unusual donné [sexual disgust] and are all written in mixed gender modes" (136). This mixture, she explains, involves a conflict of ideals, which may or may not be embodied in individual male or female characters. "Masculine" principles encompass such values as unity, stability, order, control, reason, and power *over* (events, women, nature); "feminine" principles include plurality, mutability, flexibility, responsiveness, emotion, and power *to* (create, heal, transform). While I find feminist criticism particularly relevant to this troubling play and agree with French's assessment of it, this paper will discuss other approaches as well in an attempt to define more precisely its dramatic genre and its central problem.

One of the many difficulties affecting critical interpretation of Shakespeare's problem plays in general, and *Troilus and Cressida* in particular, has been the overriding tendency to speak of the group (however composed) as "problem comedies." The common assumption of the terms' synonymity has resulted in the decision by most modern editors to place *Troilus and Cressida* with the comedies, as do G. B. Evans in *The Riverside Shakespeare* (1974) and David Bevington in his most recent (1980) edition of the complete works. But in 1951 Hardin Craig grouped the play with other "Tragedies of the Third Period"; Kenneth Palmer proves another exception: in the 1982 Arden edition, we again find *Troilus and Cressida* with the tragedies. On the other hand, the *MLA Bibliography* continues to list it as a comedy. Ironically, early publishing history provides precedents for virtually any generic decision: the 1609 Quarto lists the play as a "history"; the second state of the Quarto, however, has an address to the "Eternal reader" which repeatedly refers to the play as a "Commedie"; the First Folio of 1623 calls it a "Tragedy." But as Brian Morris points out, "No real weight can be given to these ascriptions as critical terms, for the inchoate state of criticism in the first years of the seventeenth century did not admit of any precision in such labels, and terms like 'Comedy' and 'Tragedy' cannot bear their modern interpretations" (481). Yet immense critical weight has fallen precisely on the assumption that *Troilus and Cressida* is a comedy, albeit a problem one. This assumption creates its own problems. The average playgoer may well find it difficult to respond to the play as a comedy, given its cynical and bitter tone, its unrelievedly dismal appraisal of human virtues like love, loyalty, honor, courage, truth, and reason, its often savagely pessimistic language and ugly imagery, and its catastrophic conclusion—to say nothing of the virtual absence of lighthearted merriment.

Oscar Campbell tries to get around the difficulty of generic inconsistency by describing *Troilus and Cressida* as a "Comicall Satyre," thus redefining the play as a special subcategory of comedy. His argument is interesting, and unquestionably the play involves satire. But nagging doubts remain. Even if we concede that aspects of the play—the opening banter between Pandarus and Cressida, the tenderness between the lovers in their brief scenes together, the lighter pleasantries of Thersites—reflect something of the comic spirit, we must note that such moments are almost entirely confined to the first half of the play. Following the departure of the woeful Cressid to the merry Greeks in Act 4, things go rapidly to smash. Surely, the play is neither wholly comic nor tragic. Indeed, a far greater structural difficulty than the "tenuously" linked love and war plots is the clash between a certain comic tendency in the first part of the play and in the latter part a powerful tragic force which checks, turns, and obliterates the comedy.

In the problem plays Shakespeare seems to push generic experimentation further than usual. Some critics would say that, consequently, *Troilus and Cressida* fails dramatically by demanding too much of its puzzled and frustrated audiences. I would disagree, but would also caution that should an audience (or a director) expect primarily comedy from

it, this play will not work. In this drama I do not think Shakespeare was attempting comedy at all—a certain amount of humor, yes; comedy, no. Rather, in *Troilus and Cressida* Shakespeare was working primarily within the tragic mode, but for various reasons he failed, or chose not, to create true tragedy. This play is a problem tragedy, a tragedy without catharsis.[2]

Although famous for mingling comedy and tragedy, Shakespeare characteristically and immediately establishes a dominant comic or tragic mode in most of his dramas. But in the problem plays Shakespeare balances comic and tragic elements in more equal proportions than he does in other works. Freud has written that an audience is more strongly inclined toward finding a comedy funny if it *expects* comedy (408). The same psychological principle may operate in tragedy: if spectators anticipate tragic drama, they are more likely to make the appropriate responses to it; having already consented to suspend disbelief, they are predisposed to allow themselves to be manipulated toward catharsis. All the problem plays seem more generically ambivalent than Shakespeare's traditional comedies and tragedies, which from their opening scenes decisively announce and reinforce their dominant mode.

To create tragedy (or comedy) Shakespeare utilized many devices: plot structure, setting, language, and characterization. For instance, the audience is first influenced by setting, which helps establish a tragic or comic mode. The dark, dangerous alleys of Iago's Venice, the blasted heath in *Macbeth,* the ghost-haunted midnight of Hamlet's Elsinore, the increasingly claustrophobic confines of *Romeo and Juliet*—all help evoke the tragic world in which mistakes are inescapable and fatal, a world of narrowing and darkening vistas, limited possibilities, and doomed inevitability. Such spiritual landscapes ultimately mirror the tragic world view in which some central problem becomes the protagonist's whole universe; for the tragic hero sees but two solutions to his or her consuming dilemma: to attain heart's desire or to die. When Romeo learns of his banishment, his anguished cry expresses the characteristic myopia and extreme self-absorption of the tragic hero:

> There is no world without Verona walls,
> But purgatory, torture, hell itself.
> Hence-banished is banish'd from the world,
> And world's exile is death: then banished,
> Is death mis-term'd. . . .
>
>   (3.3.17-21)[3]

It is Juliet, of course, rather than Verona per se that he cannot fathom living apart from; their love now constitutes his world and his primary identity, without which he is a lost soul. So, too, Desdemona's "infidelity" damns Othello: "Perdition catch my soul, / But I do love thee! and when I love thee not, / Chaos is come again" (3.3.90-92). Troilus uses similar language to describe separation from Cressida: "I stalk about her door / Like a strange soul upon the Stygian banks . . ." (3.2.7-8).[4]

Troilus and Cressida has three settings: "Priam's six-gated city" (Pro. 15), Troy itself, as much prison as refuge for its inhabitants; the hideous, tedious, vermin- and plague-ridden Greek camp; and finally the Dardan plains. Significantly, the only open space in the play is this wasteland, alternately regarded as playing field and killing field. Here, as the bloody sun sets and "The dragon wing of night o'er-spreads the earth . . ." (5.9.17), Hector dies horribly. Curiously *Troilus and Cressida* both begins and ends *in medias res* (Arnold 39). While the play concludes in scenes of bloody battle and terrified flight from the field, it opens in an Ilium that seems orderly and civilized, if sterile. Rather than a brawl, like that which begins *Romeo and Juliet* and *Othello,* we are given "Brave / Troilus, the prince of chivalry!" (1.2.231-32), mooning about, a lovesick soldier shirking combat and complaining in stereotypical Petrarchan fashion about unrequited passion. This ambiguous opening scene could serve as well for comedy as for tragedy.

The Prologue operates similarly, mixing dramatic modes. Its language establishes major themes and images, prefiguring the entire play. The Prologue announces that it is "Beginning in the middle" (29). We learn that Greek "princes orgulous, their high blood chafed," have come to perpetrate "cruel war" (2, 5). These lines and that describing the war as "tickling skittish spirits" (20) begin the long process of deflating the heroes and trivializing the enterprise, whose unworthy cause is that "The ravish'd Helen, Menelaus' queen, / With wanton Paris sleeps . . ." (9-10). This point is emphasized: "—and that's the quarrel" (10). In short, it's a whore's war, as Thersites might put it. The Prologue further undercuts the traditionally heroic and tragic grandeur of the Trojan War by referring to it as "broils" (27), and Thersites calls it "clapper-clawing" (5.4.1). Characters often regard the war as mere sport—part gamble, part game—and the Prologue advises us to take it and the play lightly: "Like, or find fault: do as your pleasures are . . ." (30). Thus the Prologue sounds the theme of chaos come and fed and maintained by vain, self-indulgent, arrogant, brutal men obsessed with concerns simultaneously frivolous and bloodthirsty. The war is irrational and therefore indefensible from the first, and certainly in the final analysis. Shakespeare explores the ultimate human irrationality, the collective death wish that makes the compulsive, suicidal, tragic decisions of an individual Romeo, Hamlet, Othello, Antony, or Lear look like harmless child's play. In *Troilus and Cressida* Shakespeare grapples with the ultimate human tragedy—war.

This play is a tragedy because its underlying structure and themes are tragic, and it is a problem tragedy because it does not produce catharsis. Two forces in the play block catharsis; while they initially seem opposites, they actually represent a single, underlying problem. First, Shakespeare creates a more devastating catastrophe in this play than in any other of his tragedies; second, he chooses not to give us a tragic hero. The nature of the Trojan War determines both.

Whatever else it is, catharsis seems to be an emotional experience. This point is significant since most critics agree that the difficulty with Shakespeare's problem plays is the peculiar, often negative, emotional reactions audiences have to them. The "pity and fear" that Aristotle believed tragedy purged us of seem appropriate responses in an audience given that tragedies end in death or defeat for the hero. Comedies, of course, often end in marriage. This play concludes not with the marriage of Troilus and Cressida but with Hector's ignominious murder and mutilation. The fall of Hector has been explicitly linked throughout the play with the fall of Troy itself. Significantly for its problematic nature, then, this play's catastrophe has greater implications than that of any other Shakespearean tragedy, for while Egypt, Verona, Venice, Denmark, Scotland, and Lear's England survive, perhaps even benefit from, the death of their heroes, we know that Troy will vanish forever. The apocalyptic destruction of Troy may well push *Troilus and Cressida* beyond the tragic pale—in Juliet's words, ". . . past hope, past [cure], past help!" (4.1.45)—beyond redemption and restoration, even beyond fear and pity, into something very like existential despair.

Another aspect of this play's catastrophic ending is that Hector's death dooms, rather than saves, his society. Hector is murdered, not sacrificed. Traditionally, the tragic hero is something of a scapegoat: Romeo and Juliet "Do with their death bury their parents' strife" (Pro. 9), and their "Poor sacrifices" (5.3.307) allow Verona a space of peace; Hamlet's death restores stability and legitimacy to Denmark; Macbeth's fall signals a new era of prosperity in Scotland; Antony's and Cleopatra's suicides make possible the *Pax Romana*. Even in the more ambiguous final scenes of *King Lear* and *Othello,* when the protagonists die, their societies are also rid of their worst members, those "fiends," Edmund, Regan, and Goneril and the "honest Iago." Shakespearean tragedies emphasize the nobility and self-determination of the hero's ending.

The tragedies also stress the attendant restoration of the hero's society. Certainly, there is always the painful awareness of the terrible price paid for that restoration and the sense that it might instead have been effected "comically": Romeo and Juliet's marriage and children might have ended the feud as the play contains multiple clues that old Montague and Capulet are heartily sick of fighting; and how much better for Denmark a King Hamlet than a King Fortinbras. Still, even in the "glooming peace" (*R&J* 5.3.308) of Verona or in full view of the "dismal" sight (*Ham.* 5.2.378) of the catastrophe at Elsinore, one can imagine a collective sigh of relief arising from the long-suffering citizens. *Troilus and Cressida* concludes very differently: we know that an entire society is laid waste. For Priam's kingdom this is literally the war to end all wars. The scope of the coming holocaust is too great; we cannot emotionally grasp it. And the ugly ambiguity is reinforced by Shakespeare's choice to end the play not with a cathartic bang but with Pandarus' whimper.

Catharsis is also prevented in this play because Shakespeare does not give us a tragic hero with whom to identify, with whom to move through the intense process of suffering and clarification, to a cathartic climax. An emotional experience, catharsis enlarges us perhaps more than it uplifts. Eugene O'Neill believed that both the Greeks and the Elizabethans "felt the tremendous life to [tragedy]. It roused them to a deeper understanding of life. . . . They saw their lives ennobled by it" (qtd. in Clark 146). Tragic catharsis signals that shock of recognition we feel when, by a kind of emotional parasitism or identification, we experience with the protagonist a greater, fuller knowledge of himself, and therefore of humanity; in doing so we gain greater understanding of ourselves.

To understand better the "problem" of *Troilus and Cressida,* it is necessary, I believe, to place the play within the classical context that Shakespeare drew upon when he selected the Trojan War as a dramatic subject. Shakespeare's Troyan and Greek heroes may not have tragic stature, but they have the classical flaw (*hamartia* or sin) of the tragic hero: *hubris,* the overweening pride that causes man to forget his own humanity. *Hubris* is the compulsion to be as a god, to cross those boundaries that both define and restrain humans or, in Aeschylus' beautiful words, to trample "down the delicacy of things / inviolate" (ll. 371-72). Given the global influence of the American dream of unlimited upward mobility, it may well be difficult for twentieth-century audiences to relate to *hubris,* but it fascinated both the early Greeks and the Elizabethans, who feared "vaulting ambition." In the great Greek tragedies, *hubris* is usually made manifest when the protagonist breaks a taboo.

Often, the act which signals *hubris* specifically involves the destruction of a female, for *hubris* reflects a nihilistic willingness to destroy the future, symbolized by woman's procreative power. In the *Agamemnon* we learn that Agamemnon has killed a pregnant rabbit, sacred to Artemis (Aeschylus ll. 114-38). To "pay back" Artemis and to free the Greek fleet from her subsequent prohibition, Agamemnon chooses to sacrifice his young daughter, Iphigenia, on the altar of this goddess, to whom young wild animals (and, ironically, virgins) are sacred. While Artemis has posed this choice between killing his daughter or making impossible the Greek military expedition to Troy, the decision remains Agamemnon's. His final choice has implications that far exceed killing a rabbit, or even his daughter. Agamemnon chooses to align himself with "masculine" values and to dispossess himself of "feminine" claims. His is a death wish. The decision reveals his willingness to destroy the entire Troyan civilization, an evil whose consequences include not only Agamemnon's own death but the crippling of his own society: only a few of the thousand ships Helen supposedly launched survive to return to Greece a decade later.

Whether a man deliberately murders his daughter or turns his mistress over to his enemies, crimes against women and family reveal the hero's symbolic attempt to deny and destroy the "weak" emotional part of himself which he has been culturally conditioned to fear and loathe. But the hu-

man psyche violently resists being split, and psychologically appropriate retributive justice erupts—after all his efforts to evade his fate, to escape himself, Agamemnon is welcomed from Troy by his wife, Clytemnestra, who murders her daughter's murderer with a (phallic) knife as he luxuriates in a (uterine) bath. And Troilus' greatest fear is fully realized: Cressida does cuckold him, does make him a bastard through psychic analogy by calling into question the honor of his mother. That is, he describes Cressida's infidelity as a universal crime (like Eve's) that will "soil our mothers" (5.2. 1-3). Most important, Cressida moves beyond his control, just as he fears he will lose control over himself. Believing himself unmanned by the woman, he descends into pitiless violence to win back his virility, his honor, his identity.

For the tragic hero, *hubris* can only result in catastrophe, which precipitates *anagnoresis* (the recognition of who he is and what he's done—of his sin, thus of his human fallibility and of his bond with other humans). Ironically, then, *hubris* leads to *apotheosis;* the hero who once wished to be like a god comes through suffering to know and accept his limitations, his mortality, and in so doing experiences the revelation of a god. The hero becomes more like a god by having become more fully human. In modern parlance, the tragic hero integrates himself and achieves his full potential, even as he is destroyed. Paradoxically, by accepting human limitations, he transcends them. In tragedy the hero's death or defeat becomes a sacrifice which saves his society—rather than destroying the future, he makes it possible. Offstage, the audience undergoes sympathetic catharsis and, at some level, rational or emotional, conscious or unconscious, also comes to a fuller understanding of itself, its fellows, and the human condition.

In *Troilus and Cressida* all this is prevented because, while Shakespeare has given us many of the elements of tragedy, he withholds crucial ingredients: there is no tragic hero who can move us to catharsis, partly because Shakespeare has created a dramatic situation so terrible that it precludes heroism. If Shakespeare borrowed anything from Homer beyond general outlines of the Troyan story and occasional echoes of Chapman's language, he drew upon the Greek's preoccupation with the psychology of warfare. Homer recognized that war reflects a deep, ugly, ineradicable part of the human psyche and that, paradoxically, it can call forth in man the best and the bestial. Not only does the *Iliad* explore the dark, savage, ignoble waste of war, but it also celebrates martial glory. However, in *Troilus and Cressida,* Shakespeare's focus is narrower than Homer's. Both show the powerful attractions of war. But Shakespeare seems more intent on examining how war corrupts. Little that is redeeming remains in Shakespeare's Troy.

Aristotle argues that tragedy imitates a grand, serious, and complete action. The idea of grandeur ties in with the necessary appropriateness of a tragedy's elevated language to its main character—a hero who must, Aristotle argues, be "noble," though flawed. What constitutes the tragic hero's nobility? First, "nobility" (the potential for tragic stature) seems inherent, compounded of instinctive virtue, courageous strength, and insightful intelligence. Second, even the finest potential must still find expression in external circumstances. Perhaps certain forces are so powerful, or environments so degrading, that noble action becomes virtually impossible. Contrary to popular opinion, which tends to regard military conflict as ennobling and character-building, a world at war may be just such an environment.[5]

All of Shakespeare's tragedies open in desperate times; the difference is in the degree of desperation, its intensity and social influence, its reach in time and space. Troy and Greece have been locked in mortal combat for at least seven years (1.3.12). In contrast, Verona is plagued only with "discords" (*R&J* 5.3.294); there the "ancient grudge" (*R&J* Pro. 3), the conflict between Montagues and Capulets, is a local feud, not a war. In *Hamlet* Fortinbras and Norway threaten Denmark but have not actually invaded and seem, for the moment, to have been bought off. At the opening of *Antony and Cleopatra*, Egypt and Rome have had only skirmishes, apparently remedied by diplomacy. In *Othello* and *Julius Caesar* the wars commence after the plays begin. What discord Lear's England experiences is created by the King's own division of his kingdom. Only in *Macbeth* do we get full-scale warfare. Significantly, Marilyn French links *Macbeth* and *Troilus and Cressida*: "Both plays focus on war and on status; in both [masculine] power is not the greatest, but the only good" (155).

Troilus and Cressida have grown up in the shadow of the protracted conflict between Troy and Greece and learned its lessons well (Yoder 22). As Stephen J. Lynch explains, ". . . the war outside the gates of Troy has shaped the quality of love within, where relationships are characterized by combat and competition: women dominating the chase, men the kill" (359). While Lynch's first assertion is accurate—war has certainly formed these characters—his second seems absurd. Does the fleeing rabbit "dominate" the wolf? The remarkable similarity between the appetites of the wolf and the predatory lover—as both Lynch (359) and Gayle Greene (138) characterize Troilus—is revealed throughout the play by the young Prince himself as he characteristically uses food imagery to describe (and dehumanize) Cressida. Thus he distances himself from the real woman.[6]

It may be futile to ask whether Troilus or Cressida might have had "the right stuff," given less powerful forces arrayed against them. Unquestionably the play does not provide a character of tragic stature. Certainly the Greeks are never contenders. Thersites speaks fairly accurately of "That dissembling abominable varlet, Diomed . . . that stale old mouse-eaten dry cheese, Nestor, and that same dog-fox Ulysses . . . that mongrel cur, Ajax . . . that dog of as bad a kind, Achilles . . ." (5.4.10-15). All are fools: "Agamemnon is a fool to offer to command Achilles, Achilles is a fool to be commanded of Agamemnon, Thersites is a fool to serve such a fool, and this Patroclus is a

fool positive" (2.3.64-67). In the Troyan camp, Hector comes closest to being the play's tragic hero, but Shakespeare simply does not give him enough space in the play to dominate it. More important, Hector has limited insight. It is not merely that his younger, rasher brother Troilus outargues and overrides the more admirable Hector in two key scenes (the Troyan council and the final conflict) that suggests Hector's limitations; in fact, his wrongheaded decisions are the very kind that tragic heroes traditionally make, setting in motion the events that grind toward catastrophe. Rather, the problem is that in his death scene Hector gives no indication of having learned anything about himself or his situation. No revelation mitigates his brutal assassination by Achilles' mob of Myrmidons: Hector's wretched end is not a tragedy but a waste of shame.

Obviously, to dispense with Cressida as a noble heroine presents no difficulty. Critics have had field days slinging mud at this daughter of the game, and finding bad enough names to call her has often seemed the only real challenge. Thersites is probably the most creative: ". . . any man may sing her, if he can take her clef: she's noted" (5.2.10-11). Ulysses' words are cruelest: he calls her the "sluttish spoils of opportunity" (4.5.62). Actually, that Cressida is such easy game (if you'll pardon the pun) suggests a trap laid for us. Recently, however, a number of persuasive articles ably defending Cressida have appeared.[7] Cressida probably does not inherently possess, and she certainly never achieves, heroic stature, but her circumstances and her society help make her what she is—a survivor who sells her single commodity to the highest bidder. She knows only too well that she is not for all markets. Every man in her life, including Troilus, treats Cressida as though she were a whore. Why blame her for internalizing those expectations and acting upon them?

As the intensity of critical invective unleashed at the unhappy Cressida should surprise us, so too should the slavish adulation accorded Troilus. For instance, Brian Morris writes:

> Those very qualities which make [Troilus] a great warrior, his passion, ruthless single-mindedness, his refusal to compromise, cannot but destroy him if he should fall in love with a woman who is less than his ideal. The superlative nature of his qualities marks him as of the house and lineage of heroes.
>
> (488)

Still less objective is the judgment of William Lawrence: "[Cressida] is a seasoned coquette. . . . Troilus is an ardent, idealistic young fellow, thoroughly under the fascination of a sensual and calculating woman" (139). In assessing Troilus' vaunted nobility, we need look no further than his language. Troilus, rather than Cressida, is the sensualist, imaginative only in his ability to rationalize getting what he wants, which is to "wallow in the lily beds" (3.2.11). Throughout, Troilus is either explicitly critical of the female sex, viewing women as weak, cowardly, irrational creatures, or implicitly contemptuous of them (despite their allure), describing them as food, animals, diseases, or merchandise (including "soil'd" silks, 2.2.70-71). Both he and Cressida speak of love and war interchangeably, as when they agree to "war" with each other: "O virtuous fight, / When right with right wars who shall be most Right!" (3.2.169-70). Compare such martial language with that of Romeo's first meeting with Juliet: Romeo addresses her as "dear saint" (1.5.103), introducing the religious imagery that dominates their conversation and strikingly reveals his love and respect for her, as well as signaling his commitment to her.

To view Troilus as a sweet innocent in the clutches of the Spider Woman, or to castigate Cressida as a nymphomaniac opportunist, is to ignore the multitude of qualifying clues in the language and action of the play. The play cannot engage both our emotions and our intellect fully if we side wholly with, or against, Troilus and Cressida. Indeed, the preeminent functions of Pandarus and Thersites may be as distorting lenses through which we sometimes view the lovers and which help prevent our permanently adopting such extreme views. Thus the warping operation of Thersites and Pandarus acts to correct our own perspective on Troilus and Cressida, and on *Troilus and Cressida,* as eyeglasses correct defective vision by distorting it in the opposite direction.[8] Shakespeare presents this couple as flawed and ultimately ruined characters who almost achieve a moment of glory in their love for each other. What should come through is the sense of loss: "The expense of spirit in a waste of shame / Is lust in action . . ." (Sonnet 109). In this play it is predominantly war lust which disfigures the human spirit. Thersites once again clinches it: "Lechery, lechery; still wars and lechery; nothing else holds fashion" (5.2.195-96).

Carl Sagan has provided fascinating insights into man's capacity for evil—wars and lechery—in his book, *The Dragons of Eden.* He explains the tripartite structure of the human brain: the "reptilian" or "R-complex"; the limbic system which surrounds the R-complex; and the neocortex "surmounting the rest of the brain" (Sagan 58). As well as having different, though interrelated, structures and functions, these three neurological systems represent evolutionary stages in primate development: reptile, mammal, human. Sagan links the most primitive part of the brain, the R-complex, with "aggressive behavior, territoriality, ritual and the establishment of social hierarchies" (63) and also with "sexual function" (157-58). Although the neocortex, the neurological area that is most elaborately developed in humans, consists of "about 85 percent of the brain" (Sagan 64), the "old" or reptilian brain still exerts a powerful influence on us: ". . . it is striking how much of our actual behavior—as distinguished from what we say and think about it—can be described in reptilian terms" (Sagan 63).

Consider *Troilus and Cressida* in these terms. In both language and behavior, we see that love is war, that both involve aggression, territoriality, ritual, and social hierarchy. All these work to the detriment of women,

especially, in the play: Helen is "ravish'd" (Pro. 9); both she and Cressida are moved like pawns between Greek and Troyan "turf." Even the most attractive code in the play, that of chivalry, binds the women with absolute rituals—chaste constancy paradoxically within an adulterous relationship, for instance. Cressida knows the rules of that game; her pessimistic assessment of Troilus' self-proclaimed eternal vows, "tied with the bonds of heaven" (5.2.153), proves only too true:

> Women are angels, wooing;
> Things won are done; joy's soul lies in the doing.
> That she belov'd knows naught that knows not this:
> Men prize the thing ungain'd more than it is.
>
> (1.3.291-94)

Women occupy the very bottom of the Troyan and Grecian social hierarchies, kept firmly in their place by, again, violence and ritual.

Troilus explicitly links love and war in his first words: "Why should I war without the walls of Troy, / That find such cruel battle here within?" (1.1.2-3). Despite his later spirited defense of the enterprise in the Troyan council, here he admits freely that the Trojan war is irrational and its raison d'être, absurdly unworthy:

> Fools on both sides, Helen must needs be fair
> When with your blood you daily paint her thus.
> I cannot fight upon this argument;
> It is too starv'd a subject for my sword.
>
> (1.190-93)

His last line once more brings in food imagery to suggest that both love (lust) and battle (blood lust) are appetites—reptilian appetites. More than Troilus does, Cressida understands that love is as much danger as pleasure, for men hold the final advantage. In her witty exchange with her uncle, she mixes fencing, feeding, and erotic terms to describe her felt need to be forever vigilant: "Upon my back, to defend my belly [that is, trade sex for food]; upon my wit, to defend my wiles; upon my secrecy, to defend mine honesty; my mask, to defend my beauty; and you, to defend all these; and at all these wards I lie, at a thousand watches" (1.2.265-69).

When we reverse the original cliché, we have "war is love." This motto, too, the play illustrates. LaBranche explores an important motif in *Troilus and Cressida:* "the friendly meeting of enemies" (445). Such exchanges as that between Aeneas and Diomedes just before Cressida's departure for the Greek camp should strike us as curious, to say the least. Note Aeneas' first line, in which he defines the value that he then swears to violate:

> *Aeneas.* In human gentleness,
> Welcome to Troy! Now by Anchises' life,
> Welcome indeed! By Venus' hands I swear
> No man alive can love in such a sort
> The thing he means to kill, more excellently.
>
> *Diom.* We sympathize.
>
> (4.1.21-26)

Paris neatly sums up their dialogue: "This is the most despiteful gentle greeting, / The noblest hateful love that e'er I heard of" (4.1.33-34). After the contest between Ajax and Hector, Achilles says to the Trojan, "Tomorrow do I meet thee, fell as death; / Tonight, all friends" (4.5.69-70). LaBranche comments:

> However courteous and knightly, there is something inherently contradictory in a code which allows enemies to embrace, to chat like old friends, or to carouse the night away in good fellowship while hoping to kill one another on the field the next day. The code, as Shakespeare employs it in *Troilus,* perverts good sense. . . .
>
> (446)

Indeed, war certainly does pervert "good sense," that is, human rationality and humane kindness. But the oddity is not that warriors invented a chivalric code which to some small degree mitigates the horror of war. Nor is the real problem, as LaBranche believes, "conflicting demands of love and war" (445). In this play no conflict between love and war exists; rather, they are the same thing—appetite, impulse, manifestations of what Sagan calls the old brain. In *Troilus and Cressida* we witness reptilian behavior, whether the specific scene involves a battle or a bedroom.

War can be seen, then, as a *psychomachia:* a single human's struggle against himself. Arnold emphasizes that the Trojan War set ". . . 'kindred' speakers of the same language and worshippers of the same gods against each other . . ." (38). Even Troilus recognizes that the "Fools on both sides" are alter egos. More specifically, though, warfare symbolizes a *lost* battle against oneself—the warrior has surrendered to his reptilian self. That is why the language of war is always absurd: "We had to destroy the village to save it." Troilus calls such language "the madness of discourse, / That sets up with and against itself!" (5.2.141-42). Such rationalizations represent human ability (language and reason—the main functions of the neocortex) at the service of reptilian impulse, attempting to rationalize the irrational, justify the unjustifiable. The attempt only results in the kind of verbal hypocrisy and moral schizophrenia that occurs in *Troilus and Cressida,* a pathological duality that Cressida (and of all the characters, only Cressida) acknowledges in herself when she says that she has more than one "kind of self" (3.2.146). Troilus recognizes her duplicity when he witnesses her betrayal and cries in agony:

> This is, and is not, Cressid.
> Within my soul there doth conduce a fight
> Of this strange nature, that a thing inseparate
> Divides more wider than the sky and earth . . .
>
> (5.2.145-48)[9]

But he never sees his own duplicity, that he has led her to expect his protection, at the very least, and then abandoned her to his enemies.

Ironically the "false, false, false!" Cressida (5.2.177) is the only character in the play who expresses any regret for her

actions, who has at least some conscience and consciousness of her faults: "Cressida's movement in the play is from awareness to self-deception and back to awareness again, a counterpoint to Troilus's movement, whether it be from innocence to awareness or from ignorance to animal rage" (Voth and Evans 231). Lynch notes, "while Troilus engages in self-love and calls it a sanctified and winnowed purity, Cressida engages in 'folly' and 'craft' and calls it 'folly' and 'craft'" (360). In other words, Troilus falls to *hubris;* Cressida experiences *anagnoresis.* The fact that neither combines these characteristic attributes of a tragic hero reinforces the problematic nature of this play.

That the play offers numerous instances of broken vows has become a critical commonplace, and many commentators have studied the discrepancies between words and actions. For instance, Diomedes demands the impossible of Cressida, that ". . . your mind be coupled with your words" (5.2.15). Ulysses' great speech on order is followed immediately by his petty plot to manipulate Achilles into taking the field again. As LaBranche points out, this tactic ". . . demands a sudden reevaluation [of Ulysses], as he now reveals himself to the audience as a secret practitioner not only against his inferiors in the military hierarchy, but also against his superiors, from whom he has withheld the information about Achilles' love for Polyxena [Troilus' sister]" (444). But seen in the context of Sagan's neurological model, Ulysses' speech suggests two further interpretations. First, given that "aggressive behavior, territoriality, ritual and the establishment of social hierarchies" are linked to the old brain and reptilian behavior, the speech on order stands not in contrast to the irrational war effort but as part and parcel of it. Organized violence would be impossible without the military machine, itself dependent on aggression, territoriality, ritual, and hierarchy. Second, though the impulse to hierarchy and ritual is reptilian, language is neocortical, human (Sagan 77). As Thersites says, to be "languageless" is to be a "monster" (3.3.263). Our usual response to that which seems beyond our control, such as war, is to rationalize it, as for instance Ulysses does brilliantly in the Grecian council scene.

While others in the play may not be as eloquent as Ulysses (always excepting Thersites), being human, they have enough of the neocortical gift of gab to justify their broken vows and violent crimes. Thus Troilus tells Cressida that her exile "From Troy and Troilus" is "A hateful truth" (4.4.31, 29) rather than a diplomatic decision which might conceivably be revoked. Achilles announces that "It is decreed Hector the great must die" (5.7.8), moments before he commands his Myrmidons to batter the unarmed Troyan to death. Their wording—"it" is "a hateful truth," "decreed"—allows both men to shift the blame neatly off themselves onto . . . what? Fate? National security? After all, they're just following orders. What matters is that their language reveals their priorities: Troilus chooses the war (the familiar: reptilian violence) over love (change: nurture, equality, responsibility). His choice actually furthers the war effort: having Cressida in the Greek camp will provide yet another welcome rationale for more aggression, ritual combat, and territorial claims. So, too, Helen is the "cause" of the larger conflict (French 154-55), and Desdemona's "infidelity" is "the cause" of Othello's "having" to kill her (*Oth.* 5.2.1, 3). Perhaps Troilus gave Cressida up without a struggle so that the excitement of wooing and winning could be extended. Would he have relinquished her so easily had he not already "had" her? Cressida knows the answer: "Things won are done . . ." (1.3.292). Achilles' priorities are made equally plain by his behavior. The Greek jettisons without regret his vow to Polyxena and her mother, as well as all other rules of the chivalric code, which futilely seeks to make bloodbaths logical and heroic, to rationalize the reptilian.

Thus *Troilus and Cressida* operates within the tragic rather than the comic mode, but it ultimately withholds catharsis. From the Prologue, which evokes the audience's knowledge of the fall of Troy, creating specific expectations of catastrophe, Shakespeare has manipulated the audience toward a tragic conclusion. Despite the "lighter" first half of the play, its underlying plot structure, the overriding dramatic vision, as well as its language and spiritual landscapes, have been tragic. Typical of Shakespeare's tragedies and problem plays, the imagery in *Troilus and Cressida* emphasizes darkness, disorder, disease, dementia, deceit, dirt, decay, and death. Typically, too, sex and sexuality, especially as embodied in women, are treated as mere appetites and regarded as contemptible though pleasurable. The increasingly dreadful and claustrophobic settings also contribute to the tragic mode. The play properly concludes with Hector's death, not with the marriage of the lovers. But not even Hector achieves tragic stature: he never recognizes his own contribution to the catastrophe, and his death dooms, not saves, Troy. Moreover, the destruction of an entire civilization is too great a catastrophe to grasp emotionally. We see finally that the Greeks and Troyans all have surrendered, as Ulysses feared, to power, will, and the greatest, wolfish appetite of all: blood lust. And this terrible truth about ourselves—that our vaulting ambitions may lure us to the pit, that we are as reptilian as human—represents the final, unresolvable problem of *Troilus and Cressida*.

Notes

1. Portions of this essay were presented previously in a paper given at the Conference of College Teachers of English (of Texas), March 1987, and published in the *CCTE Proceedings,* 52 (Sept. 1987), 61-69.

2. For other discussions of *Troilus and Cressida* as a tragedy, see Brian Morris, "The Tragic Structure of *Troilus and Cressida,*" *Shakespeare Quarterly,* 10 (1959), 481-91; H. A. Hargreaves, "An Essentially Tragic *Troilus and Cressida,*" *Humanities Assn. Bulletin,* 18.2 (1967), 47-60; Emil Roy, "War and Manliness in Shakespeare's *Troilus and Cressida,*" *Comparative Drama,* 7 (1973), 107-20; G. K. Hunter,

"*Troilus and Cressida:* A Tragic Satire," *Shakespeare Studies,* 13 (1974-75), 1-23; Robert Wood, "*Troilus and Cressida:* The Tragedy of a City," *Philological Quarterly,* 56 (1977), 65-81; F.H. Langman, "*Troilus and Cressida,*" *Jonson and Shakespeare,* ed. Ian Donaldson (Atlantic Highlands, N.J.: Humanities, 1983), pp. 57-73; Margaret J. Arnold, "'Monsters in Love's Train': Euripides and Shakespeare's *Troilus and Cressida,*" *Comparative Drama,* 18. 1 (1984), 38-53; A.E. Voss, "Tragedy and History: The Case for *Troilus and Cressida,*" *Univ. of Capetown Studies in English,* 15 (1986), 1-11.

3. References to Shakespeare plays other than *Troilus and Cressida* are from the Hardin Craig edition of *The Complete Works of Shakespeare* (Chicago: Scott, Foresman, 1951).

4. References to *Troilus and Cressida* are from the Arden edition, edited by Kenneth Palmer (New York: Methuen, 1982).

5. For a brief but pertinent comparison of the Trojan and Viet Nam wars, see R.A. Yoder, "'Sons and Daughters of the Game': An Essay on Shakespeare's *Troilus and Cressida,*" *Shakespeare Survey,* 25 (1972), 11-25.

6. For an analysis of Troilus, the Greeks and Trojans locked in Oedipal conflict, see Emil Roy, "War and Manliness in Shakespeare's *Troilus and Cressida.*" In "Fratricide and Cuckoldry: Shakespeare's Doubles," Joel Fineman explores other psychological interpretations of the play, especially ". . . the problem that Shakespeare repeatedly represents in his plays— . . . [the male's] psychological need to build a distance between himself and his desire, lest he lapse into the psychotic discovery of No Difference between self and object, between his self-regard and his imagination of his mother, between his identity and the context of his identity" (103), *Representing Shakespeare: New Psychoanalytic Essays,* ed. Murray M. Schwartz and Coppélia Kahn (Baltimore: Johns Hopkins Univ. Press, 1980), pp. 70-109.

7. The tide may have turned; currently, Cressida's defenders seem to be catching up with her detractors in number and vehemence. For instance, see Robert Ornstein, *The Moral Vision of Jacobean Tragedy* (Madison: Univ. of Wisconsin Press, 1965), p. 245; R.A. Yoder, "'Sons and Daughters of the Game' . . ."; Camille Slights, "The Parallel Structure of *Troilus and Cressida,*" *Shakespeare Quarterly,* 25 (1974), 42-51; Grant Voth and Oliver H. Evans, "Cressida and the World of the Play," *Shakespeare Studies,* 8 (1975), 231-39; Carolyn Asp, "In Defense of Cressida," *Studies in Philology,* 74 (1977), 406-17; Arlene Okerlund, "In Defense of Cressida: Character as Metaphor," *Women's Studies,* 7.3 (1980), 1-17; Marilyn French, *Shakespeare's Division of Experience* (New York: Ballantine, 1981); Gayle Greene, "Shakespeare's Cressida: 'A Kind of Self,'" *The Woman's Part: Feminist Criticism of*

Shakespeare, ed. Carolyn Lenz et al. (Urbana: Univ. of Illinois Press, 1983), pp. 133-49; Mary L. Hurst, "Shakespeare, Chaucer and 'False Cressida': A Misinterpretation," *Selected Papers of the West Virginia Shakespeare and Renaissance Assn.,* 8 (1983), 1-8; Stephen J. Lynch, "Shakespeare's Cressida: 'A Woman of Quick Sense,'" *Philological Quarterly,* 63.3 (1984), 357-68; Linda LaBranche, "Visual Patterns and Linking Analogies in *Troilus and Cressida,*" *Shakespeare Quarterly,* 37.4 (1986), 440-50; Suzuki, "Shakespeare's *Troilus and Cressida,*" pp. 210-57.

8. I heard this wonderful description of Pandarus' and Thersites' function in R. Mark Benbow's Shakespeare class at Colby College, more years ago than I care to document publicly.

9. For a detailed examination of Troilus' speech in 5.2.145ff., see Elizabeth Freund, "'Ariachne's Broken Woof': The Rhetoric of Citation in *Troilus and Cressida,*" *Shakespeare and the Question of Theory,* ed. Patricia Parker and Geoffrey Hartman (New York: Methuen, 1985), pp. 19-36. And in "'This Is and Is Not Cressid': The Characterization of Cressida," Janet Adelman argues that in the first part of the play, "Our most intense engagement [and therefore much of our sympathy] is with her . . ." (124). However, after she reaches the Greek camp, Cressida "becomes radically unknowable, irreducibly other" (128) to us as well as to Troilus. Adelman explains this shift in terms of Troilus: ". . . Cressida's inconstancy is accompanied by a radical inconsistency of characterization; and both occur at once because both are reflections of the same fantasy" (120), *The (M)other Tongue: Essays in Feminist Psychoanalytic Interpretation,* ed. Shirley N. Garner et al. (Ithaca: Cornell Univ. Press, 1985), 119-41.

Works Cited

Adelman, Janet, "'This Is and Is Not Cressid': The Characterization of Cressida." *The (M)other Tongue: Essays in Feminist Psychoanalytic Interpretation.* Ed. Shirley N. Garner, Claire Kahane, and Madelon Sprengnether. Ithaca: Cornell Univ. Press, 1985, pp. 119-41.

Aeschylus. *Agamemnon. Aeschylus I: Oresteia.* Trans. Richmond Lattimore. Chicago: Univ. of Chicago Press, 1967.

Aristotle. "From *The Poetics.*" *Tragedy: Vision and Form.* Ed. Robert W. Corrigan. San Francisco: Chandler, 1965.

Arnold, Margaret J. "'Monsters in Love's Train': Euripides and Shakespeare's *Troilus and Cressida.*" *Comparative Drama,* 18.1 (Spring 1984), 38-53.

Asp, Carolyn. "In Defense of Cressida." *Studies in Philology,* 74 (1977), 406-17.

Boas, Frederick S. *Shakespeare and His Predecessors.* New York: Charles Scribner's Sons, 1886.

Campbell, Oscar J. *Comicall Satyre and Shakespeare's* Troilus and Cressida. San Marino: Huntington Library, 1938.

Clark, Barret H. *Eugene O'Neill: The Man and His Plays.* New York: McBride, 1929.

Donaldson, E. Talbot. "Cressid False, Criseyde Untrue: An Ambiguity Revisited." *Poetic Traditions of the English Renaissance.* Ed. Maynard Mack et al. New Haven: Yale Univ. Press, 1982, pp. 67-83.

Everett, Barbara. "The Inaction of *Troilus and Cressida.*" *Essays in Criticism,* 32.2 (April 1982), 119-39.

French, Marilyn. *Shakespeare's Division of Experience.* New York: Ballantine, 1981.

Freud, Sigmund. "Jokes and the Species of the Comic." *Theories of Comedy.* Ed. Paul Lauter. Garden City: Anchor, 1964.

Freund, Elizabeth. "'Ariachne's Broken Woof': The Rhetoric of Citation in *Troilus and Cressida.*" *Shakespeare and the Question of Theory.* Ed. Patricia Parker and Geoffrey Hartman. New York: Methuen, 1985, pp. 19-36.

Greene, Gayle. "Shakespeare's Cressida: 'A Kind of Self.'" *The Woman's Part: Feminist Criticism of Shakespeare.* Ed. Carolyn Lenz, Gayle Greene, and Carol Neely. Urbana: Univ. of Illinois Press, 1983, pp. 133-49.

Hargreaves, H. A. "An Essentially Tragic *Troilus and Cressida.*" *Humanities Assn. Bulletin,* 18.2 (1967), 47-60.

Hunter, G. K. "*Troilus and Cressida:* A Tragic Satire." *Shakespeare Studies,* 13 (1974-75), 1-23.

Hurst, Mary L. "Shakespeare, Chaucer, and 'False Cressida': A Misinterpretation." *Selected Papers of the West Virginia Shakespeare and Renaissance Assn.,* 8 (1983), 1-8.

LaBranche, Linda. "Visual Patterns and Linking Analogies in *Troilus and Cressida.*" *Shakespeare Quarterly,* 37.4 (1986), 440-50.

Langman, F.H. "*Troilus and Cressida.*" *Jonson and Shakespeare.* Ed. lan Donaldson. Atlantic Highlands, N.J.: Humanities, 1983, pp. 57-73.

Lawrence, William W. *Shakespeare's Problem Comedies.* 1933; rpt. New York: Chatto and Windus, 1969.

Lynch, Stephen J. "Shakespeare's Cressida: 'A Woman of Quick Sense.'" *Philological Quarterly,* 63.3 (Summer 1984), 357-68.

Morris, Brian. "The Tragic Structure of *Troilus and Cressida.*" *Shakespeare Quarterly,* 10 (1959), 481-91.

Okerlund, Arlene. "In Defense of Cressida: Character as Metaphor." *Women's Studies,* 7.3 (1980), 1-17.

Ornstein, Robert. *The Moral Vision of Jacobean Tragedy.* Madison: Univ. of Wisconsin Press, 1965.

Roy, Emil. "War and Manliness in Shakespeare's *Troilus and Cressida.*" *Comparative Drama,* 7 (1973), 107-20.

Shakespeare, William. *The Complete Works of Shakespeare*. Ed. David Bevington. 3rd ed. Glenville, Ill.: Scott, Foresman, 1980.

———. *The Complete Works of Shakespeare*. Ed. Hardin Craig. Chicago: Scott, Foresman, 1951.

———. *The Riverside Shakespeare*. Ed. G. Blakemore Evans et al. Boston: Houghton Mifflin, 1974.

———. *Troilus and Cressida*. The Arden Shakespeare. Ed. Kenneth Palmer. New York: Methuen, 1982.

Slights, Camille. "The Parallel Structure of *Troilus and Cressida*." *Shakespeare Quarterly*, 25 (1974), 42-51.

Suzuki, Mihoko. "Shakespeare's *Troilus and Cressida*." *Metamorphoses of Helen: Authority, Difference, and the Epic*. Ithaca: Cornell Univ. Press, 1989, pp. 210-57.

Voss, A.E. "Tragedy and History: The Case for *Troilus and Cressida*." *Univ. of Capetown Studies in English*, 15 (March 1986), 1-11.

Voth, Grant L. and Oliver H. Evans. "Cressida and the World of the Play." *Shakespeare Studies*, 8 (1975), 231-39.

Wilson, Dover. *The Essential Shakespeare: A Biographical Adventure*. Cambridge: Cambridge Univ. Press, 1932.

Wood, Robert. "*Troilus and Cressida:* The Tragedy of a City." *Philological Quarterly*, 56 (1977), 65-81.

Yoder, R.A. "'Sons and Daughters of the Game': An Essay on Shakespeare's *Troilus and Cressida*." *Shakespeare Survey*, 25 (1972), 11-25.

LANGUAGE AND IMAGERY

Juliet Dusinberre (essay date 1983)

SOURCE: "*Troilus and Cressida* and the Definition of Beauty," in *Shakespeare Survey*, Vol. 36, 1983, pp. 85-95.

[*In the following essay, Dusinberre maintains that Shakespeare's concept of beauty resides not in the bodies of such women as Helen or Cressida, but instead in the power of language to represent beauty truthfully—something which is impossible to accomplish in the corrupt world of* Troilus and Cressida.]

The problem of how to define beauty is central to *Troilus and Cressida*. Shakespeare depicts Helen as incapable of acquiring symbolic stature and this creates in the play questions about the nature of beauty.[1]

In the world of *Troilus and Cressida* beauty is defined by the beautiful woman, whether it be Helen or Cressida. But the idea of Helen as the archetype of beauty seems to have been challenged very early by shifts in perspective. The poet Stesichorus was legendary for a poem defaming Helen, for which the gods blinded him. He recanted and recovered, as Plato records in both *The Republic* and *Phaedrus*. Stesichorus' palinode asserted that the Helen story was a fabrication:

> False, false the tale
> Thou never didst sail in the well-decked ships
> Nor come to the towers of Troy.[2]

Dio Chrysostom, a first-century critic of Homer, declared that Homer was a beggar who told lies for a living and that the Judgement of Paris was an unlikely tale, in the first place because the 'consort of Zeus' would not have required Paris, a mere shepherd, to testify to her beauty, and secondly, because Helen was Aphrodite's sister, and the goddess would not have wished to disgrace her. Dio claims that Helen was lawfully married to Paris: 'If anyone does not accept this account under the influence of the old view, let him know that he is unable to get free of error and distinguish truth from falsehood.'[3] Euripides' version of the story in the play *Helen*, in which Paris abducts a phantom while the real Helen is taken to Egypt by Hermes, finds an echo in the Renaissance in the writings of the art historian, Giovanni Petro Bellori, who believed that the Trojan war was fought for art rather than nature:[4]

> Helen was not as beautiful as they pretended, for she was found to have defects and shortcomings, so that it is believed that she never did sail for Troy, but that her statue was taken there in her stead, for whose beauty the Greeks and the Trojans made war for ten years.[5]

In the late Dialogue 'Greater Hippias', Plato focuses on the intellectual dilemma which lies at the heart of the Helen myth.[6] Socrates presses the Sophist Hippias to define beauty, but ruthlessly demolishes each definition that is offered. Whether or not Shakespeare knew this Dialogue, its arguments throw light on the dramatist's preoccupations in *Troilus and Cressida*.

I

When Socrates asks Hippias what beauty is, he replies, as any of the characters in Shakespeare's play might do, that beauty is the beautiful maiden. Socrates refuses to accept the definition because it admits the possibility of comparison. The beautiful maiden is more beautiful than a mare, a lyre or a pot, but 'ugly in comparison with the race of gods'.[7] By the yardstick of heavenly beauty her human beauty is ugliness and therefore cannot embody the essence of the beautiful.

The opening scene of *Troilus and Cressida* sets up a competition between the beauty of Cressida and of Helen. Troilus sighs for 'fair Cressid', Pandarus declares that 'she look'd yesternight fairer than ever I saw her look, or any woman else', and is betrayed by his own tag into placing her in his mind's eye at Helen's side:

> An her hair were not somewhat darker than Helen's—
> well, go to—there were no more comparison between

the women. But, for my part, she is my kinswoman; I would not, as they term it, praise her, but I would somebody had heard her talk yesterday, as I did. I would not dispraise your sister Cassandra's wit: but—[8]

Troilus responds with poetic ardour:

> O, that her hand,
> In whose comparison all whites are ink
> Writing their own reproach; to whose soft seizure
> The cygnet's down is harsh . . .

> (1.1.54-7)

It seems as if Troilus, with true gallantry, disdains to compare his lady to another. But does he? The softness of the cygnet's down is tellingly evoked in Golding's translation of Ovid's *Metamorphoses*, XIII, where Polyphemus praises Galatea in words which recall the contest on Mount Ida:

> Of valew more than Apples bee although they were of gold. . . .
> More soft than butter newly made, or downe of Cygnet is.[9]

Troilus, despite the different contours of his imagination, like Pandarus measures Cressida's beauty by Helen's. Pandarus tries to heat the young man's passion with both praise and disparagement of his niece: 'An she were not kin to me, she would be as fair a Friday as Helen is on Sunday.' Troilus protests: 'Say I she is not fair?' and Pandarus retorts in a fit of pique, partly feigned and partly real: 'I do not care whether you do or no. She's a fool to stay behind her father. Let her to the Greeks; and so I'll tell her the next time I see her' (1.1.75-81). This is not all bluff; Pandarus calculates the effect which later in the play Cressida's beauty does have on the Greek camp. In Troy, cheek by jowl with Helen, she will always be black where beauty is counted fair.

Shakespeare might have known of an early Greek Cressida—very different both from Chaucer's Criseyde and from Henryson's—who was alert to the dangers of comparison. Dio Chrysostom's 'Sixty-First Discourse: Chryseïs',[10] gives substance to the shadowy Homeric figure of Agamemnon's concubine, whom medieval writers sometimes identified with Briseis, beloved of Achilles, when they looked for Criseyde's Homeric ancestry.[11]

When Dio's Chryseïs observed that the fall of Troy was imminent she contemplated the prospect of returning with Agamemnon to the household of Clytemnestra. But the king's propensity to compare her with his wife—'For he says that she is in no wise inferior in mind to his own wife'—alarmed the concubine:

> For Chryseïs knew that such talk breeds envy and jealousy. Then too, she observed Agamemnon's character and saw that he was not stable but arrogant and overbearing, and she calculated what he would do to her, a captive, when he ceased to desire her, seeing that he referred to his wife, queen though she was and

the mother of his children, in such disparaging terms. For though foolish women delight in their lovers when they are seen to disparage all other women, those who are sensible discern the true nature of the man who acts or talks that way.[12]

Another Cressida calculates how the successful lover will behave:

> That she belov'd knows nought that knows not this:
> Men prize the thing ungain'd more than it is.
> That she was never yet that ever knew
> Love got so sweet as when desire did sue;
> Therefore this maxim out of love I teach;
> Achievement is command; ungain'd, beseech.

> (1.2.280-5)

Dio suggests that the likelihood that Agamemnon's favourable comparisons would turn into unfavourable ones in the course of time, and that his devotion would be translated into tyranny, led Chryseïs to prompt her father to send for her to the Greek camp. Events proved her wisdom, for her successor in Agamemnon's love, Cassandra, another witty daughter of a priest, was murdered on her return with the king. Pandarus' boast that his niece is wittier than Cassandra may testify to the dramatist's residual memory of an earlier Chryseïs who chose to return to her father rather than suffer comparison with another woman. In the Greek camp it is Cressida who will do the comparing, as Troilus anticipates:

> I cannot sing,
> Nor heel the high lavolt, nor sweeten talk,
> Nor play at subtle games—fair virtues all,
> To which the Grecians are most prompt and pregnant.

> (4.4.84-7)

In her first scene in the play Cressida teases Pandarus by disparaging her lover: 'There is among the Greeks Achilles, a better man than Troilus.' Pandarus explodes: 'Well, well! Why, have you any discretion? Have you any eyes? Do you know what a man is? Is not birth, beauty, good shape, discourse, manhood, learning, gentleness, virtue, youth, liberality, and such like, the spice and salt that season a man?' 'Ay,' snaps the Beatrice of the ancient world, 'a minc'd man' (1.2.239-48). Dio's Chryseïs would have felt as sceptical as Socrates of Hector's challenge to the Greeks that:

> He hath a lady wiser, fairer, truer,
> Than ever Greek did couple in his arms.

> (1.3.275-6)

When Dio's second speaker admits Chryseïs' prudence but doubts Dio's version of the story, the critic retorts that the real is more worth writing about than the ideal: 'Would you rather hear how they [events] assuredly did take place, or how it would be well for them to have taken place?'[13] Cressida, Diomedes and Thersites are all governed by their regard for the unideal aspects of their world. Cressida has enough of Chryseïs' discernment to realize that in Troy her beauty is the casualty of the comparative mood.

Troilus is obtuse about the threat to beauty implicit in comparisons, but yet quick to deny Socrates' premise that the beautiful maiden is ugly compared with the gods:

> He brought a Grecian queen, whose youth and freshness
> Wrinkles Apollo's, and makes stale the morning.
>
> (2.2.78-9)

Such a claim would have been sacrilege in the ancient world. But one of the radical differences between the *Iliad* and *Troilus and Cressida* lies in Shakespeare's discarding of deities. In Homer the Trojan war is waged as much in heaven as in Troy. In Shakespeare the gods are names but not numina. Men and women have deposed them, so that Helen is more beautiful than Apollo and Agamemnon a 'god in office'. Compared with other plays set in the pagan world—*King Lear, Cymbeline,* even *The Winter's Tale*—*Troilus and Cressida* lacks religious dimension.[14] It is as though Shakespeare asked what the significance of beauty might be once the gods no longer cared about the fate of Troy. The impact of Troilus' comparison is poetic not religious. Socrates might have argued that Troilus, beautiful and appealing though his image is, sacrifices the intellect to the imagination, thus denying beauty immutability. For a man to find a beautiful maiden more beautiful than the gods demonstrates not her beauty, but how little his gods mean to him, a denial of order which looks forward to Ulysses' great speech, and which Hippias, wordly Sophist though he is, never contemplates. In *Troilus and Cressida* beauty translated into the form of the beautiful maiden must, like Helen and Cressida, come to dust.

II

Hippias abandons the beautiful maiden when logic forces him to. But turning triumphantly to his tormentor, he shifts ground, claiming that beauty is distinguished by gold. In *Troilus and Cressida* Greeks and Trojans alike identify Helen's beauty by what it costs.

Troilus, surprisingly enough considering his championing of Helen in the Trojan debate, is the first person in the play to claim that the cost of Helen's beauty is too high. Throwing down his arms he cries:

> Fools on both sides! Helen must needs be fair,
> When with your blood you daily paint her thus.
>
> (1.1.89-90)

Helen's beauty is grotesquely embellished not with vermilion but with blood, like a painted statue.[15] The image contains the two Renaissance themes of Nature improved by Art and yet corrupted by artifice. Troilus' outcry implies what Hector later argues: 'She is not worth what she doth cost / The keeping', but in the debate Troilus forgets his own scepticism, declaring: 'What's aught but as 'tis valued?' (2.2.51-2). According to this argument beauty is defined by what it costs, as Hippias tells Socrates. Yet Troilus had seemed in that first scene to value

Helen's beauty in Diomed's negative terms as 'a hell of pain and world of charge . . . a costly loss of wealth and friends' (4.1.59, 62):

> For every false drop in her bawdy veins
> A Grecian's life hath sunk; for every scruple
> Of her contaminated carrion weight
> A Troyan hath been slain.
>
> (4.1.71-4)

Paris's retort: 'Fair Diomed, you do as chapmen do, / Dispraise the thing that you desire to buy' (4.1.77-8), recalls the lightweight sparring of Shakespeare's comedies[16] and sounds incongruous amidst the carnage of war. Yet Bassanio's rejection of the golden casket at Belmont expresses a Renaissance distrust of beauty adorned by gold, which anticipates the buying and selling metaphor in *Troilus and Cressida:*

> Look on beauty
> And you shall see 'tis purchas'd by the weight,
> Which therein works a miracle in nature,
> Making them lightest that wear most of it;
> So are those crisped snaky golden locks
> Which make such wanton gambols with the wind
> Upon supposed fairness often known
> To be the dowry of a second head—
> The skull that bred them in the sepulchre.
> Thus ornament is but the guiled shore
> To a most dangerous sea; the beauteous scarf
> Veiling an Indian beauty.
>
> (3.2.88-99)

The language of gold, weight, light, fair, the Indian beauty and the dangerous sea suggests the eulogy of Cressida which follows Troilus's outburst against the folly of defending Helen's fairness:

> Tell me, Apollo, for thy Daphne's love,
> What Cressid is, what Pandar, and what we?
> Her bed is India; there she lies, a pearl;
> Between our Ilium and where she resides
> Let it be call'd the wild and wand'ring flood;
> Ourself the merchant, and this sailing Pandar
> Our doubtful hope, our convoy, and our bark.
>
> (1.1.97-103)

Here Cressida is the pearl sought by the merchant across perilous seas. In the Trojan debate Troilus defends Helen's beauty:

> Why, she is a pearl
> Whose price hath launch'd above a thousand ships,
> And turn'd crown'd kings to merchants.
>
> (2.2.81-3)

For Troilus beauty is defined by cost. To deny Helen's worth is to deny Cressida's, for in the world of Troy both are weighed in the same scale.

Troilus' image identifies a beauty measured by price. There are no gods in the play, but neither is there any royalty, despite a plethora of princes. Majesty has been devalued by merchantry. The pearl of great price, symbol of the spiritual life, is here both literal and secular. The word 'thousand' recurs in the play as part of its inflated currency, the thousand ships sent for Helen haunting Cressida's brag of love:

> But more in Troilus thousand-fold I see
> Than in the glass of Pandar's praise may be.
>
> (1.2.276-7)[17]

Hundredfold is the Biblical measure of perfection. The inflation of language describes an economy where beauty has proved not priceless but worthless. No one in the play is capable of understanding Juliet's: 'They are but beggars that can count their worth' (2.6.32). The pricing of beauty has forced it into the market-place to be valued, bought, sold, stolen or sullied: 'We turn not back the silks upon the merchant / When we have soil'd them' (2.2.69-70).

III

Having routed gold and the beautiful maiden as definitive of beauty, Socrates proposes to Hippias that beauty is perceived truly by the senses of sight and hearing. He rejects the witness of taste and touch as being rooted in the physical and incapable of ascent to the spiritual.

Troilus argues in the Trojan debate that Helen has been chosen through the consent of the eyes and ears, as all men choose beauty:

> I take to-day a wife, and my election
> Is led on in the conduct of my will;
> My will enkindled by mine eyes and ears,
> Two traded pilots 'twixt the dangerous shores
> Of will and judgment.
>
> (2.2.61-5)

Sight and hearing mediate between 'will', with its Elizabethan sense of sexual drive, and 'judgment', the operation of reason. But the thrust of the passage is to give greater dominance to will:

> How may I avoid,
> Although my will distaste what it elected,
> The wife I chose?
>
> (2.2.65-7)

Troilus' Platonic orthodoxy in recognizing eyes and ears as arbiters of the beautiful is here compromised by the word 'distaste'. In the *Commentary on Plato's Symposium* Ficino reinforces Socrates' distrust of the lower senses:

> What need is there of the senses of smell, taste, and touch? Odors, flavors, heat, cold, softness, hardness, and like qualities are the objects of these senses . . . Love regards as its end the enjoyment of beauty; beauty pertains only to the mind, sight, and hearing . . . Desire which arises from the other senses is called, not love, but lust and madness.[18]

Troilus' rhapsody on the softness of Cressida's hand is echoed later in Paris' plea to Helen to unarm Hector with her 'white enchanting fingers' (3.1.144). According to both Plato and Ficino the tactile imagination of wallowing in lily beds would demonstrate the local sensuality of lust or madness, as does Troilus' anticipation of the taste of loving:

> Th' imaginary relish is so sweet
> That it enchants my sense; what will it be
> When that the wat'ry palate tastes indeed
> Love's thrice-repured nectar?
>
> (3.2.18-21)

The sweetness of love for Cressida is tainted by its dramatic proximity with Pandarus' saccharine flattery of Helen in the preceding scene: 'My sweet queen, my very very sweet queen . . . honey-sweet queen' (3.1.75, 134). Sweetness has gone off in this play, as Thersites observes:

> *Hector.* Good night, sweet Lord Menelaus.
> *Thersites.* Sweet draught! 'Sweet' quoth 'a? Sweet sink, sweet sewer!
>
> (5.1.72-3)

Shakespeare knew as well as Socrates that beauty identified by taste turns swiftly to distaste. But where Socrates relies on the superior senses of sight and hearing, in *Troilus and Cressida* eyes and ears persuade the will of the form of physical beauty, but mislead the judgement about its relation to goodness. Cressida blames the eye for the vacillation of her affections:

> Ah, poor our sex! this fault in us I find,
> The error of our eye directs our mind.
> What error leads must err; O, then conclude,
> Minds sway'd by eyes are full of turpitude.
>
> (5.2.107-10)

The false logic almost parodies Socrates' methods of disputation. But Shakespeare refuses to endorse the gendered vision. Troilus, who had boasted of choosing with eyes and ears, is staggered by their false witness:

> Sith yet there is a credence in my heart,
> An esperance so obstinately strong,
> That doth invert th'attest of eyes and ears;
> As if those organs had deceptious functions
> Created only to calumniate.
>
> (5.2.118-22)

The eye and ear seemed to promise unity between the good and the beautiful where the judgement is forced to concede disunity.

In the 'Greater Hippias' Plato exposes the dilemma of the two and the one with brilliant if evasive wit. Socrates ties Hippias in knots over the problem of how the double sense of sight and hearing can perceive the single nature of beauty, forcing the Sophist to admit that he himself is two rather than one, and bidding an insouciant farewell to 'the two of you'.[19] Ficino, more concerned to elucidate than to obfuscate, explains Plato's premise in *Philebus* that the good and the beautiful are one, by pointing to the dissolution which attends their disjunction: 'All things are preserved by unity, but perish from disunity . . . Whoever departs from the good falls away from the one too.'[20] Observing a beauty fallen away from goodness, Troilus is confounded by the evidence of disunity where eyes and ears had claimed oneness:

> If there be rule in unity itself,
> This was not she.[21]

Identity cannot survive such division:

> This is, and is not, Cressid.
> Within my soul there doth conduce a fight
> Of this strange nature, that a thing inseparate
> Divides more wider than the sky and earth;
> And yet the spacious breadth of this division
> Admits no orifex for a point as subtle
> As Ariachne's broken woof to enter.[22]

Cressida's recognition of the two and the one parodies Troilus':

> Troilus, farewell! One eye yet looks on thee:
> But with my heart the other eye doth see.

                              (5.2.105-6)

Socrates chose eyes and ears as the registers of beauty because he believed that they created a harmony inherent in the beautiful. Cressida divides the organ of sight against itself, one eye looking one way and one another. The single nature of the beautiful and the good has disintegrated into a grotesque disunity of perception.

The philosopher Plotinus argued that beauty is inevitably fragmented by its embodiment in material form: 'In the degree in which the beauty is diffused by entering into matter, it is so much the weaker than that concentrated in unity.'[23] Plotinus shares Socrates' scepticism about the power of the beautiful maiden to embody beauty itself. Beautiful human beings are no more than the shadows of an eternal and immutable spirit of beauty: 'Whence shone forth the beauty of Helen, battle-sought; or of all those women like in loveliness to Aphrodite; or of Aphrodite herself; or of any human being that has been perfect in beauty?' Lovers of the beautiful, swayed by eyes and ears: 'Undisciplined in discernment of the inward, knowing nothing of it, run after the outer, never understanding that it is the inner which stirs us.' Beauty resides not in the 'concrete object' but 'in soul or mind'.[24]

In *Troilus and Cressida* Shakespeare seems deliberately to have rejected any consciousness of beauty in the mind. Troilus may cry despairingly: 'If beauty have a soul, this is not she', but can resolve despair into a complex pun: 'Farewell, revolted fair!' (5.2.136, 184). In the same spirit of resurgent parody on the part of the dramatist Paris' servant ushers Pandarus into his master's bedroom:

> *Servant.* With him the mortal Venus, the heart-blood
> of beauty, love's invisible soul—
> *Pandarus.* Who, my cousin, Cressida?
> *Servant.* No, sir, Helen. Could not you find out that by
> her attributes?

                              (3.1.30-5)

Shakespeare seems to burlesque the whole concept of inner beauty. Yet it is one which is recurrent in his drama as a whole. Viola in *Twelfth Night* bears 'a mind that envy could not but call fair' (2.1.26). She trusts the Sea Captain because she 'will believe thou hast a mind that suits / With this thy fair and outward character' (1.2.50). The play, despite transitory disruptions—'O, how vile an idol proves this god!' (3.4.349)—celebrates concord between the beautiful and the good, the inner and the outer man, the fair in body and the fair in mind. Even Iago perceives a relation between the two which is inaccessible to Paris and Troilus:

> If Cassio do remain,
> He hath a daily beauty in his life
> That makes me ugly.

                              (*Othello,* 5.1.18-20)

Shakespeare could have injected such awareness into the world of *Troilus and Cressida,* yet it remains conspicuously absent. Even Hector, the closest to owning a daily beauty in his life, cannot escape the debased values of his own society, its preference for will over judgement, its self-absorption, faded chivalry and domestic poverty:

> Andromache, I am offended with you.
> Upon the love you bear me, get you in.

                              (5.3.77-8)

The lack of religious dimension in the play has turned the worship of beauty as Plato conceived it into idolatry of its material forms.

Plotinus argued that the power to perceive inner beauty behind the outward is dependent on the purity of each man's soul. A man must shape his own nature to accord with the beautiful, just as the sculptor fashions stone according to his Idea of beauty: 'When you know you have become this perfect work, when you are self-gathered in the purity of your being, nothing now remaining . . . can shatter that inner unity.'[25] Beauty and identity are here one and the same, singleness of spirit defining the single nature of the beautiful. The fragmentation of identity everywhere apparent in *Troilus and Cressida,* which reaches its apotheosis in Troilus' recognition of a Cressida divided against herself,[26] is part of the dramatist's complex vision of the disintegration created by war. Ironically the defence of beauty in the Trojan retention of Helen, and its pursuit by the Greeks, creates a savagery and moral deformity which blinds men and women to the true nature of beauty itself. The eye which in other plays discerns the unity of the beautiful and the good can in this play only see the beautiful through the obscuring mists of its own imperfections.

The mirror into which a man looks in order to know himself, a favourite Renaissance image culled from both Socrates and Seneca, can easily become a means not to self-knowledge but to self-regard.[27] In Shakespeare's Sonnet 3 it serves both ends:

> Look in thy glass, and tell the face thou viewest
> Now is the time that face should form another.

The mirror reflects a self-devouring beauty vowed to sterility:

> Or who is he so fond will be the tomb
> Of his self-love, to stop posterity?

The poet advises the young man to defy Time by refusing to keep his beauty to himself. By embracing the destructions of age he will renew himself in youth. But in *Troilus and Cressida* the mirror offers no such advice. It betrays men and women into Narcissism. The self-loving man devours himself: 'He that is proud eats up himself. Pride is his own glass, his own trumpet, his own chronicle; and whatever praises itself but in the deed devours the deed in the praise' (2.3.149-53). Ulysses urges that men should cease to allow Achilles to see himself in the mirror of their deference:

> Pride hath no other glass
> To show itself but pride; for supple knees
> Feed arrogance and are the proud man's fees.
>
> (3.3.47-9)

Shakespeare no doubt recalled in this image of Pride gazing into its own glass Spenser's picture of Pride, 'a mayden Queene', in Book I of *The Faerie Queene*:

> And in her hand she held a mirrhour bright,
> Wherein her face she often vewed fayne
> And in her selfe-lou'd semblance took delight.[28]

The beauty, regality and vanity of Spenser's allegorical monarch audaciously laud and satirize the real Virgin Queen whose favour Spenser industriously and unsuccessfully courted. When Shakespeare came to show Richard II, a monarch whom Elizabeth I ruefully admitted to be her prototype, deposed by Bolingbroke, he has him call for a mirror in which to view his clouded majesty:

> Was this the face
> That every day under his household roof
> Did keep ten thousand men? Was this the face
> That like the sun did make beholders wink?
>
> (4.1.276-9)

The sun imagery looks back to Spenser's maiden 'that shone as *Titans* ray', forward to Helen, whose beauty 'Wrinkles Apollo's, and makes stale the morning' (2.2.79). But even more significant is the characteristic form in which Richard II's question is cast, with its obvious echo of Marlowe's Faustus:

> Was this the face that launched a thousand ships
> And burnt the topless towers of Ilium?[29]

When Shakespeare embarked on his own creation of Helen of Troy adulation of Elizabeth was over. The Queen who had seen herself mirrored in Richard II died the year that *Troilus and Cressida* was registered by the Stationers' Company. The Elizabethan myth she had cultivated was already dead. Shakespeare's Helen with her tarnished image, her vanity, her obsession, shared with Achilles and with Cressida,[30] with what other people see in her, bears witness to an emergent Jacobean consciousness of beauty corrupted by self-love and left succession-less. The maiden Queen fascinated by her own reflection had proved after all to be Time's subject, self-consumed in her own sterility.

When Achilles gazes into the mirror of the self, as Plotinus commands, he sees in his soul confusion rather than clarity:

> My mind is troubled, like a fountain stirr'd;
> And I myself see not the bottom of it.
>
> (3.3.303-4)

Shakespeare shows that eyes and ears fail to perceive a beauty at one with truth because the senses are deluded by self-regard. Unable to know themselves, the characters in *Troilus and Cressida* remain the slaves of beauty in its material forms, rather than the servants of its spirit.

IV

Troilus and Cressida dramatizes not the conjunction of the beautiful and the good but the inseparability of the fair and the foul in human experience. The consequence is the disintegration of language as the tool of rational discourse. This is evident early in the play when Paris argues for keeping Helen:

> I would have the soil of her fair rape
> Wip'd off in honourable keeping her.
>
> (2.2.148-9)

The antithetical responses evoked by the juxtaposition of 'fair' and 'rape' and of 'soil' and 'fair' rob language of stability. The word is no longer the signifier of the thing, but the evasion of its reality. The same coupling of beauty and falsehood in Cressida incites Troilus' outburst against discourse itself, which Ficino called 'the messenger of reason':[31]

> O madness of discourse,
> That cause sets up with and against itself.
>
> (5.2.140-1)

The same inner divisions in language appear in the dialogue between Hector and Troilus about the conduct of battle:

> *Troilus.*
> When many times the captive Grecian falls,
> Even in the fan and wind of your fair sword,
> You bid them rise and live.

Hector.
    O, 'tis fair play!
Troilus.
    Fool's play, by heaven, Hector.

(5.3.40-3)

The now commonplace expression 'fair play' was first coined by Shakespeare some ten years earlier in *King John,* where it is twice used with its modern meaning of fair dealing.[32] But the fact that the compound was so new to the language allows Shakespeare to exploit in *Troilus and Cressida* its willingness to regress into its separate elements of 'fair' and 'play'. Hector uses the words in the new sense to mean 'just behaviour', Troilus in their separate senses of 'beautiful sport' or even, in the context of the play, 'sport for beauty'. The word 'fool', so nearly related in sound to 'foul', contains a linguistic augury of where Hector's sport will lead him, to his own foul slaughter at the hands of Achilles, which follows hard on the fool's play of hunting the warrior in fair armour. Just as beauty in the play is the carcass of itself, lacking inner life, so the language of the beautiful, the rich Elizabethan word 'fair', has disintegrated into empty compliment:

> *Pandarus.* Fair be to you, my lord, and to all this fair company! Fair desires, in all fair measures, fairly guide them—especially to you, fair queen! Fair thoughts be your fair pillow.
> *Helen.* Dear lord, you are full of fair words.
> *Pandarus.* You speak your fair pleasure, sweet queen. Fair prince, here is good broken music.

(3.1.41-7)

The play records the breakdown of discourse as the badge of the rational being. At the end sweet notes fail. There is nowhere to go but silence.

V

The pursuit of beauty in *Troilus and Cressida* has thus brought its adherents to a vision of its worthlessness which trivializes even the burning of Troy. Shakespeare destroys the definition of beauty as the beautiful maiden more ruthlessly than Socrates himself without offering any alternative testimony to the reality of the spirit behind the physical form. Yet his other plays affirm that reality. He seems deliberately to have excluded from *Troilus and Cressida* some element vital to his drama as a whole.

In Plato's *Symposium* Diotima defines love as the desire to possess the beautiful and the good in perpetuity:

> All men, Socrates, are in a state of pregnancy, both spiritual and physical, and when they come to maturity they feel a natural desire to bring forth, but they can do so only in beauty and never in ugliness.[33]

Physical procreation is the lower form, spiritual the higher. But in *Troilus and Cressida* there is no time for the creation of the beautiful in spirit, any more than there is any place for the creation of children. Andromache is not allowed the luxury of her Homeric lament for Astyanax,

the child who will never carry his father's renown into the future. The legitimate are cut off, while gods stand up for bastards, as Thersites boasts in his absurd encounter with Margarelon, bastard son of Priam: 'One bear will not bite another, and wherefore should one bastard? Take heed, the quarrel's ominous to us: if the son of a whore fight for a whore, he tempts judgment. Farewell, bastard' (5.7.19-24). Defence, the aim of war, is also the aim of love, as Cressida, loving a thousand-fold, knows, lying 'at a thousand watches': 'If I cannot ward what I would not have hit, I can watch you for telling how I took the blow; unless it swell past hiding, and then it's past watching' (1.2.256, 259-62). The whore is the physical emblem of the barrenness of beauty in the play. Helen has no posterity:

> He like a puling cuckold would drink up
> The lees and dregs of a flat tamed piece;
> You, like a lecher, out of whorish loins
> Are pleas'd to breed out your inheritors.

(4.1.63-6)

From whores and wars men inherit only diseases. To such has the pursuit of beauty brought them.

The vital element missing from *Troilus and Cressida* is a commitment at the heart of the drama to the power of beauty to re-create itself. Dio Chrysostom recorded in his 'Twenty-First Discourse: On Beauty' his sense of decline in the Greek ideal of physical beauty: 'As if the beautiful have died out in the course of time just like some plant or animal—the fate which they do say has overtaken the lions in Europe.'[34] Perhaps Shakespeare meant Troilus' comparison of Hector's generosity to that of the lion to forebode extinction. The play shows beauty unable to survive in a world pledged, with deep irony, to its defence. Without the power to propagate, either in body or spirit, its men and women remain trapped in time, obsessed with the past and the future, powerless to own the present. Their stake in the future lies in the slanders of Time itself.

Troilus' question about whether he will lie in publishing the truth of Cressida's faithlessness recalls Greek scepticism about the story of Helen. Yet despite Shakespeare's destruction of the myth, outside the play Helen retains symbolic stature.[35] Shakespeare defines beauty by giving it the power to generate life not in the time-bound past of the Trojan war but in the recreating present of the work of art, the play itself.

Notes

1. John Vyvyan, *Shakespeare and Platonic Beauty* (1961), argues Shakespeare's familiarity with Neoplatonic thought. Since Vyvyan's study J.E. Hankins has discussed in *Shakespeare's Derived Imagery* (Lawrence, Kansas, 1967) and *Backgrounds of Shakespeare's Thought* (Hassocks, 1978) the extensive influence on Shakespeare of Pierre de la Primaudaye's *The French Academie,* of which the first three parts were translated into English in 1586, 1594

and 1601 respectively. I.A. Richards's essay, 'Troilus and Cressida and Plato', in *Speculative Instruments* (1955), pp. 198-213, contributes to an older debate about Plato's influence on the play, which is fully documented in the New Variorum *Troilus and Cressida,* ed. Harold N. Hillebrand and T.W. Baldwin, pp. 391-2 (Ulysses' speech on degree and *Republic* VIII), and pp. 411-15 (Ulysses' 'strange fellow' and Achilles' mirror speech, related to Plato's *First Alcibiades*).

2. *Phaedrus,* trans. R. Hackforth, in *The Collected Dialogues of Plato,* ed. Edith Hamilton and Huntington Cairns, Bollingen Series, 71 (Princeton, 1961), p. 475. I refer to this edition hereafter as Plato, *Dialogues.*

3. Dio Chrysostom, 'The Eleventh, or Trojan, Discourse', trans. J.W. Cohoon, I (Loeb Library, 1932), pp. 453-4. First translated—before any of the other Discourses—by Filelfo in 1428 and printed at Cremona in 1492, this one Discourse was followed by complete Latin translations of Dio in the mid sixteenth century (1555, 1585, 1604). Thomas Watson's Latin translation, *Helenae Raptus,* published in 1586, of the Greek Colothus' version of the Judgement of Paris (a manuscript discovered at the end of the fifteenth century) contains in the 1731 edition notes which refer to Dio's scepticism about the story.

4. Vyvyan, *Shakespeare and Platonic Beauty,* p. 164, records both Euripides' version of the Helen myth and the fate of Stesichorus.

5. 'The Idea of the Painter, Sculptor and Architect, Superior to Nature by Selection from Natural Beauties', reprinted in Erwin Panofsky, *Idea: A Concept in Art Theory,* trans. Joseph J.S. Peake (Columbia, 1968), p. 161.

6. Although Shakespeare might have read Ficino's translations of Plato and Plotinus in a number of editions, it is tempting to see the publication of the Basel *Opera Omnia* of Plato in 1602, with adjacent columns of Latin and Greek, as a spur to the composition of *Troilus and Cressida,* which appears in the Stationers' Register in 1603.

7. 'Greater Hippias', trans. Benjamin Jowett, in Plato, *Dialogues,* p. 1542.

8. 1.1.30, 32-4, 41-6. All quotations from Shakespeare are from *William Shakespeare: The Complete Works,* ed. Peter Alexander (1951).

9. Ovid's *Metamorphoses,* the Arthur Golding Translation, 1567, ed. John Frederick Nims (New York, 1965), p. 344. Shakespeare probably used some lines from *Metamorphoses,* XII, and the first 500 lines of XIII, as a source for the play (Geoffrey Bullough, *Narrative and Dramatic Sources of Shakespeare,* vol. 6 (1977), pp. 151-7). Having read Ovid's account of the Trojan war earlier in Book XIII Shakespeare might naturally have connected Polyphemus' worship of Galatea's beauty with Paris' giving of the apple to Aphrodite and with the goddess's promised reward of the most beautiful woman in the world, Helen of Troy.

10. Shakespeare might also have read Dio's 'Sixty-sixth Discourse: On Reputation', a mordant attack on seekers after fame in which the sequence of images of over-eating, uncurrent coin and beggary anticipate Ulysses' speech 'Time hath, my lord, a wallet at his back, / Wherein he puts alms for oblivion' (3.3.145-6). Dio remarks that Perseus carried in his wallet the Gorgon's head with which to turn men to stone but that 'most men have been turned to stone by just one word, if it is applied to them; besides, there is no need to carry this around, guarding it in a wallet' (v.109). He asserts that 'notoriety-seekers' become 'beggars and no longer would any one of all who formerly were fain to burst their lungs with shouting greet them if he saw them' (v.91). Achilles observes the neglect cast on him by the Greek generals: 'they pass'd by me / As misers do by beggars—neither gave to me / Good word nor look. What, are my deeds forgot?' (3.3.142-4). While Shakespeare might have found such images in other sources the cynical tone of the Discourse brings to mind not only *Troilus and Cressida* but also *Timon of Athens.* Dio recalls in the same Discourse Thersites' deflating jests.

11. Although the heroine of John Lydgate's *The Hystorye Sege and Dystruccyon of Troye* (1513), is called 'Cryseyde', in Caxton's translation of Raoul Lefevre, *The Recuyell of the Historyes of Troye* (c. 1474), her name is Breseyda. Dares Phrygius, writing in the sixth century, calls her Briseis in *De Excidio Troiae Historiae,* and in Benoît de Sainte-Maure's *Roman de Troie* she is again Briseida (Bullough, vol. 6, pp. 90, 94). Bullough notes that the translation of Benoît's romance into Latin prose by Guido delle Colonne in *Historia Troiana* (1287) 'became the chief medium by which the story of Troilus was disseminated' (vol. 6, p. 90).

12. Dio, *Discourses,* v.3, 15.

13. *Discourses,* v.21.

14. Philip Edwards, *Shakespeare and the Confines of Art* (1968), p. 106, remarks on 'the absolute lack of any sense of non-human guidance'.

15. Arnold Stein, '*Troilus and Cressida:* The Disjunctive Imagination', *ELH,* 36 (1969), 145-67; p. 148.

16. Compare *Love's Labour's Lost,* 2.1.15. 'Beauty is bought by judgment of the eye, / Not utt'red by base sale of chapmen's tongues.'

17. Chaucer uses 'thousand fold' in *Troilus and Criseyde* as a measure of intense feeling: the pain of love (I.546), curiosity (II.142), ardour (III.1540) and fulfilled passion (III.1684). But it is also used more ambiguously in flattery of Troilus by Pandarus (II.1103) and by Helen and the guests at the supper party when Troilus is sick and Pandarus contrives to bring Cressida to his room for him to declare his

love (II.1586). It acquires the dubiety it has in Shake-speare's play in Pandarus' prevarication with Criseyde about whether Troilus is in his house on the night on which he has planned for the love affair to be consummated:

> Soone after this, she gan to hym to rowne,
> And axed hym if Troilus were there.
> He swor hire nay, for he was out of towne,
> And seyde, 'Nece, I pose that he were;
> Yow thurste nevere han the more fere;
> For rather than men myghte hym ther aspie,
> Me were levere a thousand fold to dye.'
>
> (III.568)

All line references are to *The Works of Geoffrey Chaucer,* ed. F.N. Robinson (Boston, 1933; repr. Oxford, 1957).

18. *Marsilio Ficino's Commentary on Plato's Symposium,* trans. Sears Reynolds Jayne, The University of Missouri Studies, 19 (Columbia, 1944), 130, translating the Latin text, p. 41: 'Quid olfactu? Quid gustu? Quid tactu opus est? Odores, sapores, calorem, frigus, mollitiem et duritiem, horumque similia sensus isti percipiunt . . . Amor tamquam eius finem fruitionem respicit pulchritudinis; ista ad mentem, visum, auditum pertinet solum . . . Appetitio vero, quae reliquos sequitur sensus, non amor sed libido rabiesque vocatur.'

19. Plato, *Dialogues,* p. 1559.

20. *Marsilio Ficino: The Philebus Commentary,* trans. Michael J. B. Allen (Berkeley, 1975), pp. 102-3.

21. Hankins, *Backgrounds of Shakespeare's Thought,* pp. 68-70, discusses Troilus' use of 'unity' in relation to the mathematics of Plato and Macrobius (in *Timaeus,* in Ficino's *Compendium in Timaeum,* and in Macrobius' *Opera*). See also Vyvyan, *Shakespeare and Platonic Beauty,* pp. 169, 197, 199.

22. It is interesting that Ficino uses the image of the spider's web in his discussion of the difference between reason in human beings and instinct in beasts, in *Five Questions Concerning the Mind:* 'Thus all spiders weave their webs in a similar manner; they neither learn to weave nor become more proficient through practice, no matter how long' (trans. Josephine L. Burroughs, in *The Renaissance Philosophy of Man,* ed. Ernst Cassirer, Paul Oskar Kristeller and others (Chicago, 1948), p. 206). Shakespeare's reference to Ariachne's web in an outburst about the annihilation of reason might have been prompted by Ficino's Latin: 'Omnes arancae similiter texunt telam, neque texere discunt, neque tempore quamius longo in melius texendo proficiunt', where 'arancae' suggests 'Ariachne' (Marsilius Ficinus, *Opera* (Basileae, 1576), vol. I, p. 680).

23. *The Enneads,* trans. Stephen MacKenna (1956), p. 422. I am indebted to the very clear discussion of Plotinus' views on beauty in Panofsky, *Idea: A Concept in Art Theory,* pp. 25-32.

24. *The Enneads,* pp. 423-4.

25. *The Enneads,* p. 63.

26. Vyvyan, *Shakespeare and Platonic Beauty,* p. 197.

27. In Nannus Mirabellius' *Polyanthea,* a schoolroom compilation of extracts from Latin and some Greek authors arranged in dictionary form, which T.W. Baldwin argues was used in grammar schools, Socrates' advice about gazing into the mirror of the self is placed under two headings: *Pulchritudo* (Beauty) and *Amor Sui* (Self-Love).

28. Edmund Spenser, *The Faerie Queene,* ed. Thomas P. Roche, Jr. (Harmondsworth, 1978), I.iv.8, 10; p. 81.

29. *Doctor Faustus,* 5.1.99, in *The Complete Plays of Christopher Marlowe,* ed. Irving Ribner (New York, 1963).

30. Cressida's 'Tear my bright hair, and scratch my praised cheeks' (4.2.106) recalls Chapman's 'bright-cheekt Brysys' in *The Iliads of Homer,* I, reprinted in Bullough, *Narrative and Dramatic Sources of Shakespeare,* vol. 6, p. 118. The glass of other people's praise is equally vital to Achilles, as is apparent in the speech traditionally associated with Plato's *First Alcibiades:* 'The beauty that is borne here in the face / The bearer knows not, but commends itself / To others' eyes' (3.3.95).

31. *Five Questions Concerning the Mind,* in Cassirer (ed.), *The Renaissance Philosophy of Man,* p. 206.

32. 5.1.67: 'Fair-play orders'; 5.2.118: 'According to the fair play of the world'; *OED,* entry for 'Fair', 10(c).

33. Plato, *The Symposium,* trans. W. Hamilton (Harmondsworth, 1951), p. 86.

34. *Discourses,* II.273. Hardy notes this decline in the face of Clym Yeobright, the sign 'that a long line of disillusive centuries has permanently displaced the Hellenic idea of life', *The Return of the Native,* Book 3, chap. 1.

35. Douglas Cole, 'Myth and Anti-Myth: The Case of *Troilus and Cressida*', *Shakespeare Quarterly,* 31 (1980), 76-86, p. 84; R.A. Foakes, '*Troilus and Cressida* Reconsidered', *University of Toronto Quarterly,* 32 (1963), 142-54; p. 154.

Stephen X. Mead (essay date 1992)

SOURCE: "'Thou Art Chang'd': Public Value and Personal Identity in *Troilus and Cressida,*" in *Journal of Medieval and Renaissance Studies,* Vol. 22, No. 2, Spring, 1992, pp. 237-59.

[*In the following essay, Mead suggests that the instability of the Renaissance economy is reflected in the metaphors of coinage used in* Troilus and Cressida *to describe the shifting moral stances and unreliable characters within the play.*]

There are two sorts of wealth-getting . . . that which consists of exchange is justly censured; for it is unnatural, and a mode by which men gain from one another.

—Aristotle, *Politics*

As a dramatist and businessman, Shakespeare knew the vagaries of the theater business and the shifting faces of currency in the Elizabethan economy. Even in a period in which money was a frequent topic on the stage, Shakespeare distinguishes himself by using terms of coinage, currency, exchange rates, counterfeiting, and minting practices to dramatize the mutability of supposedly absolute ideals. With the concurrent phenomena of New World exploration (and the resultant import of precious metals), increased competition in the European trade markets, trade imbalances with Asia, shifting exchange rates at Antwerp, and the depletion of domestic treasure, even the common merchant, businessman, or theater owner would be forced to bring contemporary economic wisdom to his trade.

At this time in European literary and economic history, the traditional association of purse and person (with regard to monarchs as well as to other persons of wealth) becomes enmeshed in and complicated by contemporary anxieties concerning the very substance of wealth and value. Viewed from a perspective of economic history and theory, *Troilus and Cressida* reflects the impending chaos of a world in which people continue to rely upon a system of references even after their own betrayals of coded meaning have rendered such a system arbitrary and ruthless. The characters' belief that they live in a heroic world creates such a jarring discordance within the play that *Troilus and Cressida* has been a subject for every problematizing school of criticism.[1] For many critics, the play seems to compose a series of opposites that cancel each other out. For each promising Troilus there is a performing Diomedes, for the idealistic Hector a pragmatic Achilles, for the war-wisdom of Ulysses the whore-wisdom of Thersites. In this study I would like to suggest that the extraliterary debates over the meaning of money, wealth, and exchange show themselves in the very rupture that makes *Troilus and Cressida* the problematic play it is: the discrepancy between abstract ideals and manipulated commodities. The protean nature of money, as it was experienced and in part understood by the economic thinkers of Shakespeare's age, resonates with the characters' understanding of themselves and one another.[2] Reputation—that great commodity in both Ilium and the Greek camp—is inseparable from the historical discussions of coinage, national wealth, and the mercantilist policies pursued by early modern European principalities.

Although there had long been falsifications of coin such as clipping, sweating, restamping, and gilding, Shakespeare wrote in an age in which the substance of money was shifting in common understanding from coin specie of "intrinsic" worth to a representational signification. Bills of exchange, dependence upon long-term credit, and manipulation of exchange rates became commonplace among merchants and sovereigns in the second half of the sixteenth century as the exploitation of the New World and the gradual movements away from bullionist strategies made international trade boom. "Money of account," it has been argued, "lost its distinctness from real money with each variation."[3] But once money ceases to be worth its intrinsic value by being cheapened in fineness or weight, by being called up or called down, or by representation on paper, it begins to display many of the characteristics of language and loses its façade of absoluteness. *Troilus and Cressida* is about money as language and language as money: each is a signal system that claims its authority by relying upon the other. Shakespeare's play dramatizes this chaos by exploring the human impulse to validate meaning in a world where human beings constantly betray their very codes and constructions of meaning.[4]

Reputation, a product of language represented by Shakespeare in his metaphors of money, is a superimposed identity, just as the "intrinsic worth" of coin is a determination of declared value. Munro writes that "princes were naturally concerned to protect the integrity of their mints, their coinage, and their country's 'stock of treasure.' Their honor and sovereignty were at stake, as well as their purse."[5] Not only are money and reputation often similar; at times they can be one and the same. In Shakespeare's play, when someone's reputation is altered by the language of others, that person is "chang'd," both transformed and coined. To be coined, for currency and person, is to be a publicly declared value that may or may not correspond to substance. It is a move away from individual identity and toward a quantifiable function of circulation.

In spite of their growing awareness of the arbitrariness of money's valuation, the Elizabethans seemed reluctant to let go of the idea of intrinsic worth. Their insistence upon absolute value is demonstrated by royal attempts to control the exchange rate, by Elizabeth's great coinage reform, and by England's constant attempts to keep domestic specie in the realm and to import foreign bullion. Still, each royal machination to bring money back to some ancient, absolute value further served to prove the chimerical nature of intrinsic worth.[6]

Shakespeare's play, I shall argue, reflects these larger economic concerns. Moreover, Shakespeare uses contemporary economic ideas for dramatic ends. The playwright dramatizes Cressida's reputed falseness in economic terms to suggest that the declared value of money and reputation are constructs of a shifting human will. Even Cressida's identity—as it comes to Shakespeare—is a construct: by placing the story of Cressida's betrayal in terms of coinage, Shakespeare suggests that it is her reputation and not her character that is counterfeit. Furthermore, words such as "true" and "false" have no meaning in a discourse that remains bound to a defunct system of economic values. Cressida is not, therefore, a false coin that is exposed in a new market, but rather an ordinary piece of domestic currency that is set down when she is "chang'd" for Antenor.

The central idea of *Troilus and Cressida* is that what happens normally, if regrettably, to a coin occurs to a character, and it occurs because the language of currency has bled through to the language of human character and identity, where it assumes an absolutism that belies the natures of both currency and humanity. While an exposé of Cressida's reputation in literary tradition remains of great concern, *Troilus and Cressida* primarily insists that those who use language and live by wages understand both institutions as human constructs. To forget this is to become, paradoxically, a slave of one's own invention, as the Trojan characters sadly attest.

I

The idea of the English pound represents a correspondence of language and value: twelve ounces of sterling silver was a pound sterling.[7] From this mentality came the doctrine of bullionism, the belief in the absolute worth of precious metals.[8] *A Discourse of the Commonweal of the Realm of England* (1549) was a bullionist tract of which, it seems, the Tudors approved. Challis claims that "gold and silver were the sinews of power: with them munitions could be bought, mercenaries hired, and the country defended, but without them England stood at risk."[9] The mercantilist policy of bullionism was pursued vigorously by many European nations in the sixteenth and seventeenth centuries. Spain and Portugal were the most extreme, regulating trade so that the price of exports always exceeded the price of imports. By this method the governments piled up heaps of silver and gold, which either became worthless because they did not circulate or left the country because they did. Although English policies were not nearly so strict as those of the Iberian nations, the apparent necessity for coins to preserve the correspondence between character (face value) and integral worth (precious metal) did much to maintain a bullionist disposition, if not an outright governmental bullionism.[10] England's economic ideology at the turn of the seventeenth century was an uncomfortable mixture of the belief in gold- and silver-based wealth and the growing view that tradable goods more truly constituted wealth.

Still, its economy was essentially bullionist. Munro asserts that "medieval England's bullionist policies were the most severe of any in Western Europe," and that even in the Renaissance, "no other West European nation even approached such conservatism in its mint policies."[11] In 1607 the transportation of specie rose to such a height that a proclamation had to be issued against it.[12] English monarchs tried to limit the use of credit, fix exchange rates, demonetize base coin, and prohibit the export of specie—all policies that reflect a belief in bullion as wealth itself. Even paper money was directly backed by bullion.[13] In the middle of the sixteenth century, it was, consequently, common for merchants to keep balances to check the weight of coins, a practice that they would later abandon when bullionist practices and beliefs began to fade.[14]

As the late Middle Ages and the Renaissance proved times of devaluation, of coins called down, currency debased, reformed, and recoined, the whole process recurring over and over again, the practical value of a coin increasingly deviated from its appellation, from the language that gave it name. By the time Elizabeth came to the throne, the whole country was fully aware of the debased condition of the money. Coins of all finenesses were blanched (coated with silver) to improve their appearance. But coins of only one-third silver did not keep such appearances long. Feavearyear quotes an epigram of John Heywood: "These testons look red, how like you the same? / 'Tis a token of grace: they blush for shame."[15] Even a copious supply of bullion offered no security to a country's economy. Quite apart from exportation, coins simply wore out; good coins were hoarded; clipped coins were lightened—bullion disappeared. Munro explains that "a country's coinage can diminish drastically unless it is frequently and substantially replenished with fresh mintings. Coins do die."[16] The loss of metal from the coins themselves was astonishing. For example, conservative estimates of fourteenth-century metal loss noted that seven tons of silver simply vanished into thin air every decade, through wear alone.[17] As coins lighten, their decreed values are no longer accepted by merchants, who will eventually discount the entire coinage. The result of such discounting is that the monarchy must accept its own declared value (its public measure, for its own reputation) for the coins so that the domestic merchants will do the same. These domestic merchants will then pay their taxes with the light coins, thus impoverishing the crown, while foreign merchants will only trade for the better coins—and good coin leaves the country. Gresham's Law summarizes this process well: when good coins circulate with bad coins, the bad coins force the good ones out of the country.

The currency problems in sixteenth-century England began with Henry VIII's depletion of his father's hoard and his subsequent debasement of the coinage. Gresham writes that "the fall of the exchainge did growe by the Kinges Majesty, your latte Father, in abasing his quoyne From vj ounces fin too iij ounces fin. Wheruppon the exchainge fell From xxvi s. viii d. to xiii s. iv d. which was the occasion thatt all your Fine goold was convayd ought of this your realme."[18] Elizabeth's reform was, in short, to make only one kind of money current—surely a sound move, but one whose goal was to keep bullion in the realm. Hence, even the good advice she took reflected a purely bullionist understanding of wealth. It was not until the 1590s that Elizabeth instituted two finenesses of gold: 22-karat "crown gold" and 23½-karat fine gold. The crown gold was by far the more prevalent. From 1601 onward, fine gold was used almost exclusively for making angel coins by which monarchs ostensibly healed sufferers from scrofula.[19] By the second half of the sixteenth century and certainly by the turn of the seventeenth, money was manifestly becoming understood as a signifier, no longer specie of absolute value. Indeed, the value of money was becoming a matter of opinion.[20] Merchants, following the lead of the royal tax collectors, increasingly accepted the face value of coins and no longer passed coins by weight.[21] Money came to resemble language and to become more and more a *product* of language. One need only look at the royal proclamations that made England's a metal-fiat currency to see the self-consciousness with which Tudor and Stuart monarchs would "command" money to be worth what it used to be.

One particular change that Elizabeth made offers a striking illustration of how the coin changes the monarch as the monarch attempts to change the coin. Sir Albert Feavearyear tells the story of Elizabeth's attempts to pull base coins out of circulation by transforming the face of her half-brother. The base coins were supposed to be told from the better ones by the fact that on the latter, Edward had been given "a short neck and a round face," and on the former, "long neck and a lean face."[22] But the transformed Edward alone was not sufficient to distinguish the coins. Confusion arose, and indeed Edward the base often topped Edward the legitimate. The better coins were then stamped with a portcullis before the face of the king, a practice no doubt intended to frustrate the counterfeiting method of "washing out." This method of falsification removed a distinguishing feature from a coin to confuse it with another coin of higher worth. In the past, this method was used to change the three-farthing piece to a penny.[23] This anecdote seems especially apt, as it introduces the idea that there may be two particular individuals circulating, sharing the same name, but somehow distinct in value and identity.

The problem, of course, with developing a money system in which face value does not correspond to intrinsic value is not only the danger and relative ease of counterfeiting, but more profoundly, the world-view inherent in a multinational economy in which absolutes have been proven false. A merchant could refuse to accept paper money, for example, and insist on silver coins. To a bullionist, he would be refusing the signifier or promissory note in preference for the signified or the wealth itself. But as all bullionist mercantilist principalities were to learn, not even pure specie backed money, for specie itself was not backed by anything more than reputation: the signified was itself a signifier of language. Currency, then, came to represent an agreed-upon equivalence, and these agreements were constantly shifting.

The connection of currency and language is obvious from a twentieth-century perspective, but it was not necessarily so in an economy that predated established credit policies, corporations, bonds, and the stock market. Still, James I seems to have understood how important language can be in the perceived value of money. His ten-banner shield on the back of each coin tested the minter's art; his ubiquitous slogan *quae Devs conivnxit nemo separet* urged a congenial unification of Scotland and England.[24] But James proved himself sensitive to the economic power of language as well:

> 1606. On the 11th of November. in this year, a Proclamation was set forth to abolish the use of the word sterling, with respect to the coins of Ireland. It began with stating, that his Majesty had not only

reduced the base Money of the late Queen, first to one third of its current value, and afterward to one quarter, but also had established a new standard of nine ounces fine, being the old standard of the kingdom of Ireland, and had ordained that every piece thereof, which bore the name of a Shilling, should go current and be taken for Twelve Pence sterling, and the other pieces in proportion. Which word sterling had bred an error: being construed as if every of the said Harp Shillings should be taken for sixteen Pence of the Money of Ireland, and so should carry as high a valuation as the sterling Shilling of England; whereas in Truth his Highness meaning was, that every of the said Harp Shillings should have and bear the name and valuation only of Twelve Pence Irish, according to the old standard of that Realm; being in true value no more than nine Pence English.[25]

A *word* has "bred an error" and caused a coin to "go current" and be "taken" for something that it is not. And by another word, the King's proclamation, a "new standard" is established—which is the "old standard." What is also fascinating about this passage is the distinction between the "word" and the "meaning." A coin of intrinsic worth ought not to need anyone to do its explaining for it, especially if it has a "true value," but when currency can be "denominated," "called down," "called in," "descried," and "uttered," there is clearly more to a coin's value than its metal. Words prove as effective as fineness and weight. Elizabeth, for example, coined no crowns for twenty years, until the end of her reign, because of the possible confusion with the debased French crown.[26]

Coexistent with the concern of the unpredictable effect language could have upon money, there was a kind of economic nostalgia for a past that never was, in which one could set one's bearings and in which language, worth, and identity corresponded, a past in which absolute value was unconditionally guaranteed by unshakable collateral. Tudor and Stuart economic documents reveal a drawn-out period of royal attempts to reconcile face value and intrinsic worth, to reconcile the problematic present with the idealized past. Elizabeth's currency reform of 1560-61 sought to exchange the "old false" coins for "new coins" of the "old sterling,"[27] and here again we see an English monarch attempting to reclaim the old by establishing the new. Others have written that raising the face value of real money (devaluation) was the crux of every currency and price problem of the period.[28] The result of debasement is that "real" money becomes, in fact, money of account: imaginary money.[29] But much the same thing occurs when money is brought closer to the worth of the metal: "Her majesty is constrained to calling some of the base money to its true value."[30] By attempting to be faithful to an absolute measure, Elizabeth *established* that very measure; she did not submit to one. Further, if money can be demonetized, was it ever irrefutably money in the first place? Still, Elizabeth's proclamation of coin reform on 27 September 1560 intimates the nostalgic impulse that coexists with the economic imperative: "Her Maiestie well perceiveth . . . her Realme to be . . . impoveryshed [and] the auncient and singuler honour and estimacion . . . . is hereby decayed and vanyshed away.["31] Elizabeth's stated purpose in the reform was to "have the monyes of this Realme to be of one sorte of finenesse, richnes, and goodnes, as may be a treasure of estimacion."[32] Again, Elizabeth wished to bring the coin back "to the auncient standard . . . as it was in the time of her father."[33] The concern with reputation, it seems, is always connected to the spirit of nostalgia. Of course a coin reform also served to legitimize her own monarchy, both by strengthening the economy and by founding that strength on associations with Henry VIII.

Gerrard De Malynes's treatise on the exchange (1601) offers further information on the Elizabethan understanding of money: "Monie must alwaies remaine to be the rule, and therefore is called *publica mensura* . . . monie must be still the measure, and is valued by publike authoritie at a certaintie: whereby it doth not onely give or set a price vnto all other mettals: but receiveth (as it were) by repercussion a price in it selfe."[34] Money must be valued at a certainty, and yet the price it gives other metals in turn gives itself a price. It is the measure of all things, and yet it is measured by all things. De Malynes's repetition of the word *must* suggests that those in authority have a responsibility to keep money in this position of rule and certainty; the implication is that without supervision, money will naturally become merely another commodity. This concept reflects the understanding of Gresham, who wrote forty-three years earlier that "exchainge is the thing that eatts ought all princes, to the wholl destruction of ther comon well, if itt be nott substantially loked vnto."[35] The best that money can do is to serve as a vehicle to establish a standard which is arbitrary; the "price" that money "receives" is the public estimation of how successfully it establishes and maintains that standard. By the best reckoning of Elizabeth's advisors, the integrity of the coin kept money at a certainty. When the coins were not quite up to snuff, something else was called for. The exchange rate, Gresham wrote to the Queen in 1558, "is only keppt up by artte and Godes providence; for the quoyne of this your realme doeth not corresponde in finnes not x s. the pound."[36]

Part of "Godes providence" was the curious phenomenon that some economists believe occurs when bullion is scarce and coins are devalued.[37] Because base coins contain less specie than their face values express, bullion in cheap coins can be in more places at once. And because a swift circulation of bullion mitigates the effects of bullion scarcity, devaluation—the separation of intrinsic worth from declared value—can actually promote a healthy trade economy. Bullion is like reputation: it must circulate to have worth, and the lesser the worth, the swifter the circulation must be.

Not only were coins ("except those few gold coins that enjoyed international acceptance"[38]) reminted upon arrival in a foreign country, but even at home coins were of negotiable and transmutable value. Hence, it is not only the counterfeiter who exploits the arbitrariness of the mutable sign;[39] the currency system itself constitutes a veritable jungle of signals that often contradict one another. Art and Providence, as Gresham wrote, keep up the exchange—not absolute or easily negotiated worth.

II

In *Troilus and Cressida,* all debates reflect the common understanding of the elements that constitute wealth. The war itself may be understood as a bullionist contention between two principalities. The bullion, which these societies understand as wealth itself, is Helen, the signified. Those who win praise fighting to win or keep her become enriched with the currency of reputation—a currency backed by Helen's agreed-upon worth. As she is the origin of all esteem, Helen herself is deemed "inestimable" (2.2.88).[40] Troilus articulates the world view of many characters when he states that it is "a quarrel / Which hath our several honors all engag'd / To make it gracious" (2.2.123-25). His later speech at the Trojan council amplifies this theme:

> Were it not glory that we more affected
> Than the performance of our heaving spleens,
> I would not wish a drop of Troyan blood
> Spent more in her defense. But, worthy Hector,
> She is a theme of honor and renown,
> A spur to valiant and magnanimous deeds,
> Whose present courage may beat down our foes,
> And fame in time to come canonize us,
> For I presume brave Hector would not lose
> So rich advantage of a promis'd glory
> As smiles upon the forehead of this action
> For the wide world's revenue.
>
> (2.2.195-206)

Troilus's speech is replete with economic terms and sensibilities. The "promise" of glory signals the "performance" of spleens much as the promise of payment requires the performance of that debt. The Trojans and the Greeks, as the prologue reminds us, set all on hazard: they spend blood in anticipation of "rich" advantage that will be more profitable than all the world's "revenue."

But the very characters who construct Helen as an absolute value constantly try to enhance or denigrate that value. Paris "would have the soil of her fair rape / Wip'd off" (2.2.148-49); Menelaus "makes no scruple of her soil" (4.1.57); Diomedes measures her in scruples of her "contaminated carrion weight" (4.1.72); and Troilus, most importantly, likens Helen to a pearl (as he has also likened Cressida) "Whose *price* hath launch'd above a thousand ships, / And *turn'd* crown'd kings to merchants" (2.2.81-83, emphasis added). Troilus argues that Helen is the signified, a kind of economic *primum mobile,* the transmuter who turns royal crowns to numismatic crowns, kings to merchants. Shakespeare, however, suggests that it is the "chapmen" Greeks and Trojans who have turned Helen into a valuable pearl. Both Trojan and Greek play a losing game: they insist on the absolute value of Helen and yet ceaselessly attempt to negotiate, to transmute that value in their own interests. This strategy produces a preponderance of deceptive signals. Ulysses plots with Nestor:

> Let us like merchants first show foul wares,
> And think perchance they'll sell; if not,
> The lustre of the better shall exceed
> By showing the worse first.
>
> (1.3.358-61)

Paris accuses Diomedes of a similar practice when they meet in Troy:

> Fair Diomed, you do as chapmen do,
> Dispraise the thing that they desire to buy,
> But we in silence hold this virtue well,
> We'll not commend what we intend to sell.
>
> (4.1.76-79)

The Greeks have learned, as good merchants, to operate within a system of mutable signs: Calchas has sensed the blowing winds and becomes a Greek; the Greek commanders practice playacting in front of Achilles's tent; Patroclus playacts within that tent; Ulysses flatters Ajax; and two pairs of opposing warriors—Ajax and Hector, and Aeneas and Diomedes—declare in one breath their love and enmity.[41] Achilles himself, of course, is the terror of the Trojans while he woos Priam's daughter. The list could go on, and it would certainly include the Horse itself as an archetype of the art of counterfeiting.

The Trojans, though would-be manipulators of "absolute" value, nevertheless are deceived by their own constructions. Hector, for example, dies because he will not bend his word that he has given the day before. Achilles will kill Hector and effectively win the war because he breaks his word (not to mention the code of arms) several times. The Greeks seem to create deceptions consciously and casually. When his stratagem with Ajax fails, Ulysses blithely moves to another tack. One would be hard put to imagine him *disillusioned.*

To the Trojans, Helen is a priceless signified that determines the wealth of all else. To the Greeks, she is merely a finite supply of bullion in a time of scarcity, a quantity that Diomedes can weigh in scruples. Until Helen is returned to the Greeks, all things—including Menelaus's horns—are gilt. The conversation between Ulysses and Achilles reflects the necessity of swift circulation in a bullion-poor currency. Having just been scorned by the Greek commanders, Achilles understands that a warrior's worth is equal to his esteem by others:

> speculation turns not to itself,
> Till it hath travell'd and is mirror'd there
> Where it may see itself.
>
> (3.3.109-11)

Ulysses agrees and asserts that "no man is the lord of any thing . . . Till he communicate his parts to others" (115, 117). He then brings the analysis to specifically monetary terms:

> Time hath, my lord, a wallet at his back,
> Wherein he puts alms for oblivion . . .
>
> Let not virtue seek
> Remuneration for the thing it was . . .
> One touch of nature makes the whole world kin,
> That all with one consent praise new-born gawds,
>
> . . . . .
>
> And give to dust, that is a little gilt,
> More laud than gilt o'erdusted.
>
> (3.3.145-46, 169-70, 175-79)

Hoarded money, like dusty gold, is unpraised and hence virtually worthless. Reputation, like money, is movement, and that which does not move is bound for oblivion. As Troilus has argued in another context, what is anything but as it is valued? Like money, a man's fame does not even exist unless others say so. Each is inherently an unsignified value, a sign that points only to its very signifiers, in this case, the opinions of others. Therefore, Achilles's reputation says less about him than about his countrymen: if they say he is not a good soldier, then he is not. Achilles must pay for his fame continually with deeds; accordingly, a country's treasure must be frequently and substantially replenished, and that treasure must be one, in Elizabeth's words, of "singular honour and estimacion."[42] A country's treasure must inspire the esteem of domestic and foreign powers; if Achilles does not terrorize the Trojans, he is as worthless as a lost hoard of gold. He must "circulate" on the battlefield to achieve a reputation that will in turn give him an identity.

Had the Trojans understood the concessionary and circulatory nature of worth, they would have realized that Helen is without value as a treasure hoard inside Ilium. The Trojan cause, however, is predicated on the surety of absolute value, on the mentality that venerates the Palladium as a thing of immeasurable value *if* it remains within Troy. The Trojan council reveals the central condradicton of the sons' thinking. On the one hand, Hector argues, to declare the worth of a thing and then to be subservient to that thing because of its worth is both causeless and superstitious. On the other hand, by waging war, the Trojans effect an opportunity for gathering wealth in the form of honor and renown.[43] In what for many critics is the most frustrating speech of the play, Hector reverses himself and condemns his country to oblivion. Troilus, who has complained that the cause is too starved an argument for his sword, then argues that the cause is not Helen but honor (and so, presumably, a good enough argument for his sword); later, he will stop Hector on his way to the honorable war and chide him for showing mercy to wounded Greeks. Paris too thinks poorly: his pride (displayed in a later scene) in not commending what he intends to sell is indeed poor business and, in this play, poor warfare.[44]

III

As Cressida is central to Shakespeare's play, so she is thematically central to the Trojan War, which is as much a conflict about declared value as it is about anything else. Alone in Troy, save for a none-too-protective uncle, unmarried, and apparently virginal, Cressida is uncoined, an unknown, untested quality. It lies first for Troilus, with a prince's prerogative, to declare her worth something:

> Tell me, Apollo, for thy Daphne's love,
> What Cressid is, what Pandar, and what we:
> Her bed is India, there she lies, a pearl;
> Between our Ilium and where she resides,
> Let it be call'd the wild and wand'ring flood,
> Ourself the merchant, and this sailing Pandar
> Our doubtful hope, our convoy, and our bark.

> (1.1.98-104)

Like a pearl, like Helen herself, Cressida is a priceless abstract: a signified. Because it is unique, a pearl has no equivalent; it has no measurable or concrete value. A pearl is outside of currency; it cannot be minted or counterfeited. It is the perfect metaphor of abstraction: India is its platonic residence and Cressida its local image. But because Helen is the preeminent pearl, Cressida's value must in fact be finite and subordinate. In the Trojan council Troilus argues that Helen is

>   a pearl,
> Whose price hath launch'd above a thousand ships,
> And turn'd crown'd kings to merchants.

> (2.2.81-83)

In both cases, *pearl* denotes that which has worth, but whose price is incalculable. *Merchant* denotes those who nevertheless attempt to price that pearl. The war itself has augmented the inestimable value of Helen, as each day Greeks and Trojans die in partial payment of the cost of keeping or retrieving her. Cressida's pearl-like quality, however, is far less stable. She is, even by Troilus's infatuated reckoning, only a pearl so long as she is untaken, unbedded, unstamped, unimpressed—in short, she only has untouchable worth so long as she assumes a negative existence. She is money of account, with no physical reality.

But even though Troilus values the negative being of Cressida, he constantly asks what in fact she *is* (1.1.99). Cressida too thinks in these absolute terms; she knows well that "men prize the thing ungain'd more than it *is*" (1.2.289). She has a sense of her own calculable worth, for she implies that Troilus overrates her. After all, the conventional adage is that men prize the thing ungained more than the thing gained, but Cressida flatly states that men falsify the object of their desire and stamp upon it a face value that exceeds the object's intrinsic worth. The oppression that is the logical result of declared value occurs when Cressida is discovered by the prince. Once Cressida is "known," she is a calculable quality, assigned a concrete equivalent in quantity. She is bullion minted and ready for circulation, and it is no coincidence that her exchange is effected the morning after. No matter what worth Cressida is assigned, to be fixed at a certain amount is inherently to be debased.

If we understand the unbedded Cressida as an abstract signified, we may come to grips with Troilus's troublesome speech, in which he enthusiastically anticipates his tryst with Cressida:

> Th' imaginary relish is so sweet
> That it enchants my sense; what will it be
> When that the wat'ry palates taste indeed
> Love's thrice reputed nectar? Death, I fear me,
> Sounding destruction, or some joy too fine,
> Too subtle, potent, tun'd too sharp in sweetness
> For the capacity of my ruder powers.

> (3.2.19-25)[45]

The earthy desire of Troilus contrasts well with the platonic, mystical being he imagines Cressida to be. The virginal Cressida is too fine a thing to taste, too subtle a thing to know. She is an abstraction, a gross parody of the *caritas* that such humanists as Castiglione had written of. But once Troilus does know her, once she is impressed in the bed, she is a consumed, calculable commodity ready to be "chang'd."

As if on cue, Cressida is informed of her change the morning after, appropriately enough by Pandar, the broker. *Chang'd* incurs a complex of meanings that reveal themselves fully only en masse. Literally, of course, Cressida is exchanged for Antenor. Metaphorically, she is transformed from a Trojan girl sought by a prince to a traitor's daughter camping among the Greeks. Finally, Cressida is coined, made into change; specifically, she is brought to a lower denomination—literally "set down."[46]

The debate between Troilus and Diomedes during the exchange of Cressida closely resembles what happens to coins that leave the country in which they were minted. As we recall, coins were nearly always either set down (declared to have a lower value) or reminted when they arrived in another country, unles these coins were among the few that enjoyed international esteem. Helen represents the latter, Cressida the former. Troilus begins by asserting his sovereignty:

>   Here is the lady
> Which for Antenor we deliver you.
> At the port, lord, I'll give her to thy hand,
> And by the way possess thee what she is.

> (4.4.109-12)

Troilus attempts to transfer his authority regarding Cressida's worth to the Greek. Once again the verb *to be,* which speaks so eloquently of Troilus's world view, appears: it suggests that, to Troilus, Cressida *is* one thing, irrespective of time, place, supply, or demand, that a piece of consistent intrinsic worth ought to demand an equally consistent estimation. But as Joyce Appleby illustrates, while balance-in-trade theorists (the critics of bullionists) "recognized that silver constituted a universal standard and the principal source of value in coin, they also realized that because payments were made in the coin of a certain country that meant the demand for the products of a certain country would produce a demand for the coin of the same country."[47] The silver of a coin might remain constant, but an increased or decreased demand for the coin would alter its practical value. Appropriately, Troilus will take them to the "port," a word associated with international trade and exchange. Diomedes, a far less complex character, whose world view is consistently relativistic, asserts the empirical method: "The lustre in your eye, heaven in your cheek, / Pleads your fair usage," he tells Cressida (4.4.118-19). Diomedes's own assessment of her face value, and not Troilus's denomination, will determine Cressida's "intrinsic" worth. Shakespeare's audience, we should recall, would know that Diomedes's other great exploit during the Trojan War was to help Ulysses steal the Palladium from Troy. Such an association sets him squarely counter to the Trojan mentality of absolute worth. But Troilus insists on his princely prerogative: "I charge thee use her well, even for my charge" (126). Diomedes retorts, "When I am hence . . . To her own worth / She shall be priz'd" (131-34). That is, to Diomedes's determination of Cressida's own worth Cressida will be prized.[48] Economically, of course, Diomedes is perfectly right: outside of Troy, a coin or a prize will be worth what the market says it is worth. If her metal is deemed to be alloyed, Cressida will have to circulate swiftly to have any worth.

Although Troilus has set up Cressida as a priceless pearl, the exchange proves that nothing is priceless if someone agrees to let it go for a price. Cressida *is* not anything once and for all.[49] Cressida's introduction into the Greek economy is essentially a reminting.[50] All the Greek nobles are present, and Cressida is presented to them first as "Calchas' daughter." Before Cressida has spoken a word, the generals kiss her five times amid bawdy puns of losing heads and gilding horns. When Cressida denies Ulysses the impress of his kiss, he publicly stamps her:

> Fie, fie upon her!
> There's language in her eye, her cheek, her lip,
> Nay, her foot speaks; her wanton spirits look out
> At every joint and motive of her body.
> O, these encounterers, so glib of tongue,
> That give a coasting welcome ere it comes,
> And wide unclasp the tables of their thoughts
> To every ticklish reader! set them down
> For sluttish spoils of opportunity,
> And daughters of the game.
>
> (4.5.54-63)

Ulysses's speech articulates the general kissing, the declared stamp on Cressida's face. Assessing a foreign coin, Ulysses reads her face value interpretively, imposing upon her a language that he would have us assume comes from her. In short, he falsifies her appearance and declares that that appearance signifies Cressida's worth. *Set them down* crystallizes the influence of language upon a coin's value. To "set down" means to declare a coin at a lower worth than its face value.[51] For Cressida, it is a new, devalued estimation.[52] Ulysses's setting down of Cressida is then validated by the next stage direction and line: "*Flourish. / All.* The Troyans' [s] trumpet" (4.5.64).

Diomedes's tryst with Cressida completes her change. As Diomedes goes to Calchas's tent, followed by Ulysses and Troilus, Thersites prefaces the betrayal scene:

> Diomed's a false-hearted rogue, a most
> unjust knave. I will no more trust him
> when he leers than I will a serpent when
> he hisses. He will spend his mouth and
> promise, like Brabbler the hound, but when
> he performs, astronomers foretell it: it is
> prodigious, there will come some change.
>
> (5.1.88-93)

This speech connects the idea of falsification with that of "change" by means of promise and performance. The falsifying Diomedes will change Cressida; after promising to "use her" well, he will perform sexually. He will spend his mouth in anticipation of spending, and hence cheapening, Cressida.

The debasement of Cressida as coin is not a simple matter of counterfeiting, for such an assessment presumes an absolute value system that has been abused. Rather, Shakespeare suggests that simultaneously manipulating a value system and believing it to be absolute results in a loss of all reference and identity. It is then left for the characters either to accept reputation as identity or to disappear into oblivion. By promising to transmute her name to the "very crown of falsehood" (4.2.100) if she leaves Troilus, Cressida engages herself in the value system that will destroy her country as well as herself. She tells Troilus that she has only "a kind of self . . . an unkind self, that itself will leave / To be another's fool" (3.2.148-50). Her reputation is unnatural in that it will abandon the Cressida beneath the legend to be changed into the legendary Cressida.

Although Cressida intimates an understanding of the shifting currencies of identity and worth, Troilus maintains an absolutist philosophy that only recognizes a thing's being or nonbeing: "This is, and is not, Cressid!" (5.2.146). Perhaps his early assessment of the Trojan War is not sarcastic when he notes that "Helen must needs be fair, / When with your blood you daily paint her thus" (1.1.90-91). If so, then the war signifies Helen's worth. Why then has his attention, his "particular will," not signified the pearl-like Cressida? His absolutist philosophy leads him to an insoluble paradox: Troilus must choose one Cressida (his Cressida or Diomedes's Cressida) as true and consider the other Cressida an uncurrent illusion, much as Elizabeth's coin reform tried to rid the nation of the false Edward for the true. Like Ulysses, Troilus concludes that Cressida has sent erroneous signals: "O false Cressid! false, false, false!" (5.2.178). Because Cressida's declared value has changed in the Greek camp, Troilus assumes that her metal must always have been base. But calling Cressida a base coin is itself erroneous; Troilus does not realize that a system of human values is inherently a system of shifting values.[53]

Troilus's speech after having read Cressida's letter from the Greek camp is supremely ironic. Because he now sees

Act V, scene ii. Calchas's tent. Diomedes, Cressida, Troilus, Ulysses, and Thersites.

her as a base coin, he rejects her promissory note, then attempts to declare her old value as fraudulent:

> Words, words, mere words, no matter from the heart;
> Th' effect doth operate another way.
> *Tearing the letter.*
> Go, wind, to wind, there turn and change together.
> My love with words and errors still she feeds,
> But edifies another with her deeds.

(5.3.108-12)

Like a king whose coin has left the realm and been called down, Troilus no longer believes that words can declare anything meaningful. His declaration of Cressida's worth was unheeded by Diomedes; therefore, Cressida's own declarations of love are equally ineffective. Significantly, Troilus uses the words "turn" and "change" in their basest senses: Cressida has turned from him; she has changed lovers. He can no longer accept a declared value from her. To Troilus's mind, a word unbacked by a deed is a kind of nothing, like a promissory note whose collateral someone else is spending. But because he has seen his own declara-

tions invalidated, Troilus can only conclude that he has misread the face value.

Shakespeare suggests that Troilus, like coin-reforming monarchs, ought to scrutinize "ancient standard," his own role in manipulating that standard, and its applicability to one's perceptions of other human beings. Despite his dismissal of Hector's view that "value dwells not in particular will" (2.2.53), Troilus is unable to act upon his convictions. *Troilus and Cressida* asserts that when a value system becomes corrupt or ceases to be meaningful, it falls upon the individual—in the face of the general will—to determine worth as well as he or she can. In other words, as the ancient standard no longer holds, one must disengage the discourse of individual worth from the discourse of public currency. The desire of Elizabethan and Stuart monarchs to preserve the integrity of coinage was in part a facet of the deeper philosophical anxieties of the age—anxieties that juxtaposed metallic purity with estimable sovereignty, language that belies the coin it appears on with coins that belie the language stamped upon them, honor with treasure, and individual worth with economic equivalency. These anxieties Shakespeare explored through myths that transcend the economic exigencies of his time.

Notes

1. Linda Charnes's recent article, "'So Unsecret to Ourselves': Notorious Identity and the Material Subject in Shakespeare's *Troilus and Cressida*," *Shakespeare Quarterly* 40 (1989): 413-40, considers many of the issues brought forth in this study from a psychological and New Historical perspective. She argues that the play "represents neurosis in the form of subjectivity crippled by cultural inscription" (415). A history of responses to Shakespeare's most problematic "problem play" reveals an unusually broad spectrum of opinion. From Dryden's "heap of rubbish" and Evans's "a failure" to George Bernard Shaw's assessment of Cressida as "Shakespeare's first real woman," critics have sought ways to condemn, praise, or otherwise scrutinize *Troilus and Cressida*—but always to talk about it. Lawrence seems to have been the first to isolate the discordance in the play's world as a source of the "problem," a lead followed by Muir, Traversi, Tillyard, Campbell, Rossiter, Foakes, and Thompson. Feminist criticism has helped to sharpen this approach by focusing on Cressida's character as the cynosure of this discordance. See Oscar James Campbell, *Comicall Satyre and Shakespeare's "Troilus and Cressida"* (Los Angeles: Adcraft, 1938); E. Talbot Donaldson, *The Swan at the Well* (New Haven: Yale University Press, 1985); Bertrand Evans, *Shakespeare's Comedies* (Oxford: Oxford University Press, 1960); R.A. Foakes, *Shakespeare: The Dark Comedies to the Last Plays: From Satire to Celebration* (London: Routledge and Kegan Paul, 1971); Gayle Greene, "Shakespeare's Cressida: 'A Kind of Self'," in Carolyn Lenz et al., eds., *The Woman's Part: Feminist Criticism of Shakespeare* (Urbana: University of Illinois Press, 1980), 133-49; W.W. Lawrence, *Shakespeare's Problem Comedies* (New York: Macmillan, 1931); Priscilla Martin, *Troilus and Cressida: A Casebook* (London: Macmillan, 1976); Kenneth Muir, *Shakespeare's Comic Sequence* (New York: Barnes and Noble, 1979); A.P. Rossiter, *Angel With Horns* (London: Longmans, Green, and Co., 1961); Ann Thompson, *Shakespeare's Chaucer* (Liverpool: Liverpool University Press, 1978); E.M.W. Tillyard, *Shakespeare's Problem Plays* (London: Mouton and Co., 1966); D.A. Traversi, *The Moral Vision of Jacobean Tragedy* (Madison: University of Wisconsin Press, 1960); Edwin Wilson, *Shaw on Shakespeare* (New York: E.P. Dutton, 1961).

2. Concerning England's chronic shortage of coin and attempts to deal with it at the turn of the seventeenth century, Joyce Oldham Appleby writes, "The major difficulty lay with finding a definition of money that would be adequate to the many new roles it played during the decisive decades of growth and development." See *Economic Thought and Ideology in Seventeenth-Century England* (Princeton: Princeton University Press, 1978), 199.

3. E. E. Rich and C. H. Wilson, eds., *Cambridge Economic History of Europe*, Vol. 4 (Cambridge: Cambridge University Press, 1967), 383.

4. Marc Shell argues a point distinct from my thesis in *Money, Language, and Thought* (Berkeley: University of California Press, 1982). Shell proposes that money is not only talked about in particular works of literature, "but that money talks in and through discourse in general" (180). Such a claim, it seems, posits an authority to "money of the mind" that is not easily demonstrated. I recognize no such superiority of money over discourse; rather, I would suggest that both "money of the mind" and discursive constructions such as symbolization or metaphorization proceed from a commonly held, antecedent impulse.

5. John H. Munro, "Bullionism and the Bill of Exchange in England, 1272-1663: A Study in Monetary Management and Popular Prejudice," in UCLA Center for Medieval and Renaissance Studies, *The Dawn of Modern Banking* (New Haven: Yale University Press, 1979), 169-239, esp. 185.

6. Charnes argues that the characters of *Troilus and Cressida* exhibit symptoms of neurosis in that they not only mistake absence for loss, but they deny the loss itself ("'So Unsecret to Ourselves'," 415). Something similar was happening outside the play in English economic thinking: English economic manipulations manifested nostalgia by attempting to retrieve a value of money believed lost. It was not neurotic because no one would have denied its loss, even if one were to believe it was retrievable.

7. See A.B. Feavearyear, *The Pound Sterling: A History of English Money*, rev. E. Victor Morgan (Oxford: Clarendon, 1963), for the possible origins of sterling, penny, and shilling (7-9). Of course, as a physical object, the pound did not exist. The English pound was an idea—an abstract value about which all currency revolved and from which currency took its substance and significance.

8. See Munro, "Bullionism and the Bill of Exchange," 174.

9. C.E. Challis, *The Tudor Coinage* (Manchester: Manchester University Press, 1978), 185.

10. Munro, "Bullionism and the Bill of Exchange," muses with some surprise that "pre-Enlightenment Europe seems to have suffered the delusion that silver and gold was wealth *per se* and its sole form" (174). He reads Clements Armstrong's assertions as evidence of this. See R. H. Tawney and Eileen Power, eds., *Tudor Economic Documents*, 3 vols. (London: Longmans, 1924; reprint New York: Barnes and Noble, 1962), 3:105, 124.

11. Munro, "Bullionism and the Bill of Exchange," 187, 191.

12. William A. Shaw, *The History of Currency, 1252 to 1894* (London: Wilsons and Milne, 1895; reprint New York: Augustus M. Kelley, 1967), 134.

13. *Cambridge Economic History of Europe,* 4:386.

14. Challis, *The Tudor Coinage,* 281.

15. Feavearyear, *The Pound Sterling,* 63.

16. Munro, "Bullionism and the Bill of Exchange," 178.

17. Ibid., 179.

18. Quoted in *Tudor Economic Documents,* 2:146-47.

19. See Charles Oman, *The Coinage of England* (Oxford: Oxford University Press, 1931), 285; Challis, *The Tudor Coinage,* 228; Sir John Craig, *The Mint: A History of the London Mint from A.D. 287 to 1948* (Cambridge: Cambridge University Press, 1953), 131.

20. See Sandra K. Fischer, *Econolingua: A Glossary of Coins and Economic Language in Renaissance Drama* (Newark: University of Delaware Press, 1985), 14.

21. Harry A. Miskimin, "The Impact of Credit on Sixteenth-Century English Industry," in *The Dawn of Modern Banking,* 275-89, esp. 285.

22. Feavearyear, *The Pound Sterling,* 81.

23. Challis, *Tudor Coinage,* 284.

24. See Oman, *Coinage of England,* 292.

25. Rogers Ruding, *Annals of the Coinage of Britain and Its Dependencies, from the Earliest Period of Authentick History to the End of the Fiftieth Year of the Reign of His Present Majesty King George III* (London: Nichols, son, and Bentley, 1817), 2:199-200.

26. See Shaw, *History of Currency,* 130.

27. S.T. Bindoff, *Tudor England,* in *The Pelican History of England,* vol. 5 (New York: Penguin, 1978), 199.

28. *Cambridge Economic History of Europe,* 4:391.

29. It is about this time that paper money was becoming more familiar. The *Cambridge Economic History of Europe* states that paper money was used furtively in the fifteenth century, cautiously in the sixteenth, and insistently in the seventeenth (ibid., 389).

30. Oman, *Coinage of England,* 176.

31. *Tudor Economic Documents,* 2:196.

32. Ibid., 197.

33. Ibid., 193.

34. Ibid., 3:387-88.

35. Ibid., 2:148.

36. Ibid., 146-47.

37. See Miskimin, "The Impact of Credit," 285.

38. Munro, "Bullionism and the Bill of Exchange," 173.

39. See R.A. Shoaf, *Dante, Chaucer, and the Currency of the Word: Money Images and Reference in Late Medieval Poetry* (Norman, Oklahoma: Pilgrim Books, 1983), 35.

40. All references to Shakespeare's plays are taken from *The Riverside Shakespeare,* ed. G. Blakemore Evans et al. (New York: Houghton Mifflin, 1974). I have silently removed brackets.

41. See especially 4.1.15-31.

42. *Tudor Economic Documents* 2:196.

43. Cf. the immature sense of war as a marketplace for honor in *All's Well That Ends Well,* 2.1.32.

44. R.A. Shoaf's book carefully considers many of the issues in Chaucer's *Troilus and Criseyde* that I raise in this study of Shakespeare's play. Although we disagree on many principles, Shoaf also notes that in Chaucer's poem, Troy is "bad at business." See *Dante, Chaucer, and the Currency of the Word,* 258.

45. I have followed F1 in using "thrice reputed" instead of the *Riverside*'s use of the Q "thrice-reputed" for a number of reasons. First, "reputed" is an extremely rare term, cited in the *OED* as being used only twice besides the present use. The meaning in the only two other uses recorded is of something *returned* to a pure state, which is probably not Shakespeare's meaning. Second, "reputed" is a far more common word for the time. Third, all possible variants of "repure," such as "repurge" or "repurify," carry only the sense of a dirty thing having been cleaned. If "repured" were actually Shakespeare's choice, it would have to mean something like "so clean that it is three times purer than normal pure things." Although possible, this reading seems to me less likely than "reputed," especially in the context of Troilus's naive speech of anticipation. We should remember that while Shakespeare remains vague concerning Cressida's virginity, there is little question regarding that of Troilus.

46. Sandra Fischer's notes on *change* in *Econolingua* seem especially relevant to the legendary Cressida, who in other versions of the story (Henryson's *Testament of Cresseid,* for example) becomes a whore, a beggar, and a leper: "The implication is that women constantly have an eye out for new sexual partners and that their favors can be bought with money." Fischer notes associations with prostitution and the obliteration of the stamp or impress of the king that makes the coins tender (53). A scene probably written by William Rowley in *The Old Law* also demonstrates that other contemporary writers were noting the figurative and linguistic associations between Cressida and "lighter" economic units of measurement: in a discussion of Helen of Troy, Gnotho quips, "Cressid was Troy weight, and Nell [Helen] was avoirdupois." See *The Works of Thomas Middleton,* ed. A.H. Bullen, vol. 2 (Boston: Houghton Mifflin, 1885), 4.1.74-75. Although Feste remarks in *Twelfth*

Night that "Cressida was a beggar" (3.1.55) while trying to beg coins from Viola, Shakespeare does not suggest in *Troilus and Cressida* that Cressida becomes a whore; he rather asserts that she comes to be taken for one. Gayle Greene argues that "by showing Cressida in relation to the men and society who made her what she is, he [Shakespeare] provides a context that qualifies the apparently misogynist elements of her characterization." Greene further notes that "the stereotypical in her character occurs in a context that constitutes a critique of stereotyping." See "Shakespeare's Cressida: A Kind of Self," 145.

47. Appleby, *Economic Thought and Ideology,* 203.

48. The reappearance of the word *prize* puts Diomedes's speech in the context of Cressida's earlier self-assessment (1.2.289).

49. Writing of the betrayal scene, A.P. Rossiter makes a comment that is generally applicable: "For every participant in the scene there is a phenomenon called 'Cressida.'" See *Angel With Horns,* 135-36.

50. In *Dante, Chaucer, and the Currency of the Word.* Shoaf argues that what Criseyde was truly in Troy becomes manifest in the Greek camp: "Exchanged for Antenor and circulated to the Greek camp, her own alloy dominant again, her own character visible again, especially her 'slydinge corage' (5.825), Criseyde becomes Diomedes's coin, and he wastes no time in spending her" (258). Shakespeare's Troilus shares this opinion. Still, I believe that Shakespeare takes his cue from Chaucer in suggesting that Cressida's "worth" is entirely external to her.

51. See Munro, "Bullionism and the Bill of Exchange," 173-74.

52. "Calling down," synonymous with "setting down," is associated with prostitution. See Shaw, *History of Currency,* 123.

53. Cf. Troilus's metaphor on being true and being false when he and Cressida must part: "Whilst some with cunning gild their copper crowns, / With truth and plainness I do wear mine bare" (4.4.105-6).

David Hillman (essay date 1997)

SOURCE: "The Gastric Epic: *Troilus and Cressida,*" in *Shakespeare Quarterly,* Vol. 48, No. 3, Fall, 1997, pp. 295-313.

[*In the following essay, Hillman contends that Shakespeare wrote and produced* Troilus and Cressida *with a view to concentrating on the grossly physical aspects of the human body in order to bring life to a tale that had already been frequently told and whose language had thus been rendered abstract through overtelling.*]

Ignorance *in physiologicis*—that damned 'idealism.'

Friedrich Nietzsche, *Ecce Homo*[1]

1. THE MATTER OF TROY

Why did Shakespeare write *Troilus and Cressida?* Why, that is, did he turn his attention to a story that was so overdetermined as to have become, by the end of the sixteenth century, little more than a compilation of clichés? The Trojan story was enormously popular during the decades preceding composition of the play,[2] and the most obvious motive suggested by this popularity is the play's commercial potential (written by an already-famous playwright, reworking material that was all the rage in contemporary London). While this motive is called into question by the Epistle attached to the play's Quarto in the second state,[3] the pervasiveness and mass appeal of the matter of Troy was, I believe, nevertheless a decisive factor in Shakespeare's choice of this subject. For in placing these endlessly reiterated, rhetoricized, and textualized heroes onstage, he could not help but embody them;[4] and the limning of these "unbodied figure[s]" (1.3.16) in flesh and blood presented a perfect opportunity to wrestle with the issue that, I will argue, lies at the very heart of the play: the relation between language and the body out of which it emanates. Both within the play and in the cultural milieu that produced it, *Troilus and Cressida* enacts a restoration of words, and of the ideals created out of them, to their sources inside the body.

The play thrusts both its protagonists and the audience back into the body, recorporealizing the epic of the Trojan War. The story's unparalleled canonicity created heroes of a deeply textual nature, protagonists who by Shakespeare's time had become little more than, in Rosalie Colie's words, "rhetorical and proverbial figure[s]."[5] The play's "dependence on a prodigious literary and rhetorical legacy" entangles it (as most critics of the play agree) with issues of citationality and originality.[6] When Shakespeare turns to the legend, he places the relationship between origins and citations at the core of his play. He does this by reintroducing, as it were, the substance or "matter" of the body to the "Matter of Troy." Indeed, the very word *matter,* often associated in Shakespeare with the interior of the body, recurs no fewer than twenty-four times in the play.[7] The missing "matter" that Shakespeare reintroduces into the story is that of the truth of the body, which has been displaced over countless reiterations by something like pure citationality. "[T]ir'd with iteration" (3.2.174), the heroes' identities have become ever further removed from their material sources: the pun on *tir'd* (attired/tired) implies the increasing distance from the body, as if each retelling adds a layer of covering—a cover story—to the protagonists' flesh, with the overdetermined citationality that constitutes the "starv'd . . . subject" (1.1.93) of Troy rendering it disembodied, "pale and bloodless" (1.3.134). ("*Troy,*" apostrophizes Spenser's Paridell, "[thou] art now nought, but an idle name."[8]). By the time Shakespeare comes to write the play, these post-Homeric heroes have all become "Words, words, more words, no matter from the heart" (5.3.108).

Troilus and Cressida has often been described as being "consciously philosophical," as coming "closer than any other of the plays to being a philosophical debate."[9] There is little physical action in the play; mostly there are rhetorical arguments about degree, about honor, about time and value. Yet the play is compulsively body-bound; from start to finish, its language is replete with imagery of the body's interior, the ebb and flow of its humors looking out at every joint and motive of the text. There is, I think, a powerful connection between the play's intellectuality and its unyielding corporeality, a link that can perhaps be best elucidated by glancing briefly at what Friedrich Nietzsche says about the relations between philosophy and physiology. Entrails, for Nietzsche, are inherently anti-idealizing, undercutting metaphysics and transcendent aspirations of any kind: going *into* the body lies at the opposite pole from going *beyond* it. As Eric Blondel writes, "it is in order to contrast an abominable truth to the surface of the ideal that Nietzsche speaks of entrails."[10] Idealization usually involves a turning away from or repression of the messy truth of the body—toward what Agamemnon calls, in *Troilus and Cressida,* "that unbodied figure of the thought" (1.3.16)—or, alternatively, a conception of the body as a perfect, finished surface.[11] But while the exterior of the body is easy enough to idealize, its interior has a rather more offensive, unsavory reality, as Nietzsche repeatedly points out: "What offends aesthetic meaning in inner man—beneath the skin: bloody masses, full intestines, viscera, all those sucking, pumping monsters—formless or ugly or grotesque, and unpleasant to smell on top of that!"[12]

Reminding us of the existence of this monstrous "inner man" is, throughout Nietzsche's work, a way of revealing the reality *beneath* thoughts, systems, ideals. In "On Truth and Lie in the Extra-Moral Sense," for instance, Nietzsche points out the irony involved in the fact that "the urge for truth" is so often a product of our "proud, deceptive consciousness, far from the coils of the intestines, the quick current of the blood stream, and the involved tremors of the fibers. . . . "[13] Excavating the body is thus for Nietzsche—the "physiologist of morals"[14]—a foundational act of skepticism; in his view any hermeneutic undertaking must begin from the body—and, moreover, from its interior, which is why he speaks of the "hard, unwanted, inescapable task" of philosophy as a kind of vivisection; Socrates, for example, is "the old physician and plebeian who cut ruthlessly into his own flesh, as he did into the flesh and heart of the 'noble.'"[15] This, too, is what Nietzsche means when he speaks of "philosophizing with a hammer": "*sounding out idols. . . .* For once to pose questions here with a *hammer,* and, perhaps, to hear as a reply that famous hollow sound which speaks of bloated entrails—what a delight. . . ."[16] The hammer here is one that can both "sound out" the interior (like a tuning-fork) and, if necessary, smash through to this interior (like a sledgehammer).

I offer this brief reading of Nietzsche's conceptualization of entrails as a potentially instructive analogue to my reading of *Troilus and Cressida,* for both are uncompromising when it comes to revealing the distance between our proudly deployed language and the body's internal reality. Bloated entrails are a dominant image in the play; as Patricia Parker has recently argued, "the inflation or bloating that affects both bodies and words in *Troilus* also affects its presentation of its epic theme, matter, or argument, repeatedly said to represent an overheld or inflated value."[17] In foregrounding the physiological processes taking place within its protagonists' tumid bodies, the play "sounds out" the Homeric idols, the epic heroes at the very source of European culture; it finds at the center of their beings little more than disease and raw appetite, representing them all, more or less, as "idol[s] of idiot-worshippers" (5.1.7). "[M]ad idolatry" (2.2.57) is a subject repeatedly addressed by the play, which, we could say, depicts a kind of "Twilight of the Idols"—ending, as it does, as "the sun begins to set, / . . . [And] ugly night comes breathing at his heels" (5.8.5-6). The play uses a turn to the interior of the body to debunk time-honored ideals—to reveal the "Most putrefied core" (5.8.1) of the heroic ethos.[18] It depicts "the veins of actions highest rear'd" (1.3.6) in the most literal sense of "veins"; even Hector's honorable soldiership is—in his own words—no more than "th'vein of chivalry" (5.3.32) on a good day. In *Troilus and Cressida* the twin ideals of heroism-in-war and idolism-in-love are exploded in no small part through the attention directed to the "polluted" insides of the body, "more abhorr'd / Than spotted livers in the sacrifice" (5.3.17-18).

The idea that the play evinces a general disgust with corporeality was for many years practically undisputed; and indeed the vast majority of the play's references to the body insist on its internally diseased and utterly corruptible state. My argument here runs not so much "against the hair" (1.2.27) of these interpretations as *under* it; for to take this as a rejection of corporeality as such does little more than reproduce Thersites's bitter invective against the body—echoing his perspective rather than interpreting it. The main thrust in *Troilus and Cressida* is a turn not against but back toward the body, in the same way that Nietzsche's philosophy embraces corporeality with all its "formless or ugly or grotesque" aspects.

Shakespeare's response to the endless reiteration of the legend of Troy is simultaneously a response to the major genealogical project of Tudor mythographers—the tracing of the ancestry of the British nation to the Trojan War, a teleology culminating in the glories of the Elizabethan nation. But, as I am describing it, it was not so much this genealogy that Shakespeare was interested in as in a kind of Nietzschean genealogy, an enterprise of (re)linking words, and the values and ideals constructed out of them, to their bodily origins, to "the basic text of *homo natura.*"[19] Shakespeare's attempt to restore *materia* to the Matter of Troy constitutes a powerful countermovement to this founding narrative of English nationalism—as if to say that this narrative does not delve *far enough.*[20] That is: while Tudor mythographers sought a heroic site of origin in the Trojan epic, Shakespeare's skeptical satire seeks the origins *of* the legend of Troy *in* the bodies of its heroes.[21]

The implied repudiation of the idealizing narrative of Elizabethan nationalism simultaneously suggests a radical rereading of the progress-bound idea of time on which this history relies. *Troilus and Cressida* comes closer to a view of history as reiterative or circular in its perpetual return to human physiology as the source of action. The play, in fact, thematizes the question of what the perspective of time does to historical events. Time here is repeatedly personified—an all-consuming scavenger, a thief snatching at scraps of history with which to cram up his thievery, a vulture pouncing on the leftovers of every human deed. And as "raging appetite" is imagined as the origin of both the love plot and the war plot, this same appetite is figured as the terminus of all action, the universal wolf which last eats up itself.

Shakespeare's anti-mythologizing return to the body could be described as nostalgic, though it is anything but idealizing. It is in a sense a turning away from his medieval and early modern sources and back toward Homer, whose epic never for a moment flinches from describing the horror of the human body's utter destructibility. Both the *Iliad* and *Troilus and Cressida*—to quite different ends, to be sure—present the human being as "a bundle of muscles, nerves, and flesh" subjected relentlessly to "force, that is, in the last analysis, to matter."[22] It is this restoration of the body—a restoration of the heroically repressed, or the unveiling of what we might call the entrails of epic— which produces the play's ubiquity of corporeal images.

The return, as it happens, is simultaneously an etymological return, since the very name *Ilium* means, in Latin (in the plural form of *ile*), "intestines, guts." The play can thus be described as not only a genealogical excavation but also, in true Nietzschean fashion, a philological one. And (in case Shakespeare's "small Latine" did not extend this far) we might note that *Ilium* and *Ilion* (the two forms of the Homeric designation for Troy used alternately in the play) are—and were in the sixteenth century—alternative anatomical names for the largest part of the intestinal tract, the part affected in the apparently then-common disease called "iliac passion": bloating of the intestines.[23] If Tudor historiography traced the birth of the British nation to Ilium, Shakespeare traces "Ilium" back to the body. In this sense—and speaking hyperbolically—the entire play can be said to take place within one large, bloated intestine.

2. THE SATIRIST AND THE CANNIBAL

The ending of the Trojan legend, we might here recall, is inseparably linked to the idea of full intestines—to the Trojan horse, that is, with its bellyful of silent Greek warriors—a proverbial symbol of guile throughout the English Renaissance.[24] Writers of the period persistently figured the potential for deceit as a potential gap between words and the bodies out of which they emerge. A story particularly popular in early modern England was Lucian's version of the tale of Momus and Hephaestus. In *Hermotimus, or Concerning the Sects*—a satire of all manner of philosophical schools and pretensions—Lucian relates the

story of how Momus, mocker of the gods, judged a competition among Athena, Poseidon, and Hephaestus. To settle a quarrel among the three gods over which of them was the best artist, Momus is appointed to judge their creations; Athena designs a house, Poseidon a bull, Hephaestus a man. "What faults he found in the other two," writes Lucian, "we need not say, but his criticism of the man and his reproof of the craftsman, Hephaestus, was this: he had not made windows in his chest which could be opened to let everyone see his desires and thoughts, and if he were lying or telling the truth."[25]

Lucian—"the Merry Greek," as he was known to sixteenth-century Englishmen[26]—was a philosopher whose caustic, disillusioned perspectivism may well have influenced *Troilus and Cressida* directly (the epithet "merry Greek" is used twice in the play[27]); Shakespeare's comic satire shares with him a disenchantment with ideals, a deeply relativist attitude to questions of value, and a level of scoffing unparalleled elsewhere in the canon. But my interest here lies less in Lucian's influence on Shakespeare than in the way Momus's tale succinctly highlights a tendency that is central to satire in general and to *Troilus and Cressida* in particular. Momus's criticism of Hephaestus's man exemplifies a desire shared, in one form or another, by many skeptics and satirists: the desire to puncture pretense by revealing the body's innards. This skeptical impulse often takes the form of a desire to see into, or to open up, the body of the other. *Troilus and Cressida* partakes of this satirical tradition of figuring the puncturing of deceit and delusion as a puncturing of the body. The skepticism evinced by the play is itself described within the play in just such terms: "[D]oubt," says Hector, "is call'd / The beacon of the wise, the tent that searches / To th'bottom of the worst" (2.2.15-17).[28]

Such a penetrative impulse stems from an imagination of the interior of the body as capable of concealing an ulterior truth, a fantasy of the possibility of absolute knowledge of the other.[29] In "The Inside and the Outside," Jean Starobinski discusses the origins of such a corporeal schema in its archetypal form. Turning back to Homer's *Iliad*—"one of the first poetic documents in which the censure of duplicity is given full and emphatic voice"—Starobinski quotes Achilles's rebuke to Agamemnon ("For hateful in my eyes, even as the gates of Hades, is that man that hideth one thing in his heart and sayeth another") and comments: "the doubling, the splitting which causes *one thing* to be hidden and *another* said . . . takes on spatial dimensions: what goes unsaid is actively hidden in the heart, the space of the inside—the interior of the body is that place in which the cunning man dissimulates what he doesn't say."[30] The *Iliad* is, to be sure, a particularly effective place to look for such corporeal dimensions, as the exegeses of Bruno Snell and R.B. Onians have made abundantly clear: "emotional thoughts, 'cares', were living creatures troubling the organs in one's chest," writes Onians in elucidating the inseparability of body, mind, and soul in Homer.[31] But the bodily schema Starobinski points to has been too tenacious over the centuries to be dismissed either as a manifestation of primitive or archaic thought or as merely a convenient metaphor.[32]

The explicitly somaticized nature of the urge to puncture deceit and delusion was never more evident than during the English satire-vogue of the final decade of the sixteenth century, a vogue to which *Troilus and Cressida* was Shakespeare's main contribution.[33] "The Satyre should be like the *Porcupine,* / That shoots sharp quils out in each angry line, / And wounds the blushing cheeke," wrote Joseph Hall; and John Marston described the "firking satirist" as "draw[ing] the core forth of imposthum'd sin."[34] The strong corporealization of the satiric impulse owes much to the materialistic habits of early modern thought (and to the centrality of the practice of anatomy in particular); throughout this period, whether the trope is one of injury, anatomical dissection, or medical purgation, both the penetrative drive and the target of this drive—the bodily interior of the satirized object—are practically explicit.[35]

"The Gods had their *Momus, Homer* his *Zoilus, Achilles* his *Thirsites,*" writes the melancholy anatomist Robert Burton in his discussion of satirists and calumniators, adding that the "bitter jest . . . pierceth deeper then any losse, danger, bodily paine, or injury whatsoever."[36] *Troilus and Cressida*'s chief satirist, "rank Thersites," pierces each and every one of the play's protagonists with his "mastic jaws" (1.3.73). As this last phrase indicates, the penetrative drive of satire can appear at the same time as an impulse to devour the object under attack—it often manifests itself in a specifically oral form of aggression; as Mary Claire Randolph writes, "Renaissance satirists frequently picture themselves as . . . sinking their pointed teeth deep in some sinner's vitals."[37] This idea of oral sadism is a recurrent theme of satirists; it is often figured as a compulsion to bite. Marston, for example, writes that "Unless the Destin's adamantine band / Should tie my teeth, I cannot choose, but bite"; and Burton, quoting Castiglione, says of satirists that *they cannot speake, but they must bite.*[38] To say that the aggressive impulse of "byting" satire is predominantly oral is to approach redundancy (as Milton points out in dismissing Joseph Hall's "toothlesse Satyres": it is "as much as if he had said toothlesse teeth.")[39] But there is in satire, over and above this oral aggression, an urge to devour—an urge, moreover, specifically directed at the human body. The satirist typically fantasizes not only penetrating the other's body but devouring it, as if entering this body is a concomitant of being inhabited by it. The derivation of the word *satire*—from the Latin *satura,* meaning "full, satiated"—points to this cannibalistic drive; as Walter Benjamin writes, in his essay on Karl Kraus: "The satirist is the figure in whom the cannibal was received into civilization." And, he adds, "the proposal to eat people has become an essential constituent of his [the satirist's] inspiration."[40] The projective mechanism of satire, in this view, makes it both embody and thematize a cannibalistic urge, an urge epitomized by the delicious ending of one of the earliest Menippean satires, Petronius's *Satyricon,* where the rich Eumolpus

bequeaths his wealth to his friends "on one condition, that they cut my body in pieces and eat it up in sight of the crowd."[41]

The misanthropic cannibalism of satire is glimpsed in *Troilus and Cressida*'s relentless use of imagery related to food, eating, and digestion.[42] And while this alimentary obsession has often been noticed, a distinct pattern emerges when we examine its figurative trajectory through the course of the play.[43] The outline is one of more or less linear progression, from the early talk of culinary preliminaries ("[T]he grinding . . . the bolting . . . the leavening . . . the kneading, the making of the cake, the heating of the oven, and the baking" [1.1.18-24]; "the spice and salt that season a man . . . a minced man; and then to be baked with no date in the pie" [1.2.259-62]; the "bast[ing]" in one's "own seam" or grease [2.3.186]) and of "tarry[ing]," "starv'd" (1.1.15, 93), before the meal; followed by the promises of "tast[ing]" on the "fin'st palate" (1.3.337-38, 389), the readiness of the "stomach" (2.1.127), the "raging appetites" (2.2.182), and the preparation of "my cheese, my digestion" (2.3.44); then the "imaginary relish" (3.2.17) leading up to the meal itself, associated as it is with sexual consummation ("Love's thrice-repurèd nectar" [3.2.20]); and thence to the "full[ness]" (4.4.3; 4.5.271; 5.1.9) and "belching" (5.5.23) of engorgement, of having "o'er-eaten" (5.2.159)—and the ensuing nausea, associated with the "spoils" (4.5.62), the rancid leftovers, the "lees and dregs" (4.1.63), the "orts [i.e., refuse] . . . / The fragments, scraps, the bits, and greasy relics" (5.2.157-58). In view of this, it would not be going too far to call *Troilus and Cressida* a bulimic play, one that evokes in its audience (as has often been noted in a general way) a reaction akin to the figurative nausea of the imagistic trajectory delineated above. The play, in fact, begins with a "disgorg[ing]" (Pro.12) and proceeds through overeating to its anticathartic ending in Pandarus's stomach-turning Epilogue. The Prologue has referred to the ensuing action as "what may be digested in a play" (Pro.29), and—in spite of the Arden editor's rather severe gloss ("*Not* part of the food imagery of the play")—there is, I think, an implication of the nauseating effect of this "unwholesome dish" (2.3.122) on the digestive systems of its spectators.[44] What should also be noted here is that the lion's share of the imagery of food and eating in the play is cannibalistic—that is, it consistently imagines the object of alimentary consumption as a human being. The play thus places its spectators in the position not only of diseased "traders in the flesh" (5.10.46) but also of uneasy "eaters of the flesh"—of cannibals: little wonder that it was apparently "neuer stal'd with the Stage" in Shakespeare's time, and that audiences still find it somewhat unpalatable.

The notion of cannibalism is implicit, too, in the play's repeated evocation of images of self-consumption. The connection between the two is remarked on in Sir Thomas Browne's *Religio Medici:* "We are what we all abhorre, *Anthropophagi* and Cannibals, devourers not onely of men, but of our selves; and that not in an allegory, but a positive truth; for all this masse of flesh which wee behold, came in at our mouths: this frame wee looke upon, hath beene upon our trenchers; In briefe, we have devoured our selves."[45] The most prominent image of self-consumption in the play is of course Ulysses's speech on appetite, which "Must make perforce an universal prey, / And last eat up himself" (1.3.123-24)—a phrase that Kenneth Palmer calls an "image . . . of cannibalism as the last consequence of disorder";[46] but the disorder can take any of several forms (e.g., "He that is proud eats up himself" [2.3.156]; "lechery eats itself" [5.4.35]), so that, in this play at least, self-consumptive cannibalism appears pervasive. The entire project—comprising Shakespeare's relation to his sources, the audience's relation to the play, and the characters' relation to each other—is implicitly cannibalistic.

Forcing the idea of cannibalism on the audience entails, among other things, forcing it to come to terms with the corporeality—the very flesh—of the protagonists of the story. It is Thersites, above all, whose constant punning obsessively returns language to the body's internal "matter." Thersites even appears to know (and this is typical of the play's proleptic style) that he himself is destined to become, quite literally, a disembodied figure of speech, the rhetorical figure of "the standard rhyparographer" (or filth-painter).[47] When threatened by Ajax with "I shall cut out your tongue," he replies: "'Tis no matter" (2.1.112-13). Thersites's pun takes the material organ of speech to be immaterial, construing Ajax's "tongue" in its entirely figurative meaning (i.e., speech), and thus constituting himself, in one sense, as pure citation. (The irony, of course, is that the *actor* playing Thersites must use his material tongue to say these words, thereby revealing the odd status of the body in *Troilus and Cressida:* the play both depicts and—in its reiteration of the tale—enacts the body's displacement by speech even as it reverses this displacement by both foregrounding the role of the body and embodying the tale on stage.) Thersites's quibbling ways with the word *matter* begin earlier in the same scene: "Agamemnon—how if he had boils, full, all, over, generally? . . . And those boils did run—say so—did not the general run then? Were not that a botchy core? . . . Then would come some matter from him: I see none now" (2.1.2-9). With his first words in the play, Thersites, whose every third thought is of the body's putrefaction, points punningly to the gap between the substance of the body and the argument of words; as Patricia Parker explains, "The 'head and general,' supposed to be a source of ordered and reasoned argument, the generation of 'matter' for discourse as well as the hierarchical embodiment of order itself, is in this play only a 'botchy core,' the source of 'matter' in an infected body politic."[48] Here, though, Thersites's "Then would come some matter from him: I see none now" announces a *lack* of "matter" at the core of Agamemnon, thereby hinting, synecdochically, at a lack at the heart of the entire legend of Troy. The story's hero, Achilles, is figured in *Troilus and Cressida* as "a fusty nut with no kernel" (ll. 103-4); Ajax is a "thing of no bowels" (l. 52); and Agamemnon himself should be—and, in this play, is clearly not—a "great commander, nerves and bone of Greece, / Heart of our numbers" (1.3.55-56). Troy itself,

with the death of Hector, is deprived of interior matter: "Come, Troy, sink down! / Here lies thy heart, thy sinews, and thy bone" (5.8.11-12).

Critics of *Troilus and Cressida* tend to discuss its two salient imagistic strands—those of disease and of eating—separately. But the two are repeatedly intertwined in the play: they are twin manifestations of a pervasive "appetite"—"an appetite that I am sick withal" (3.3.237). We could say that as hunger is taken metaphorically for all beginnings of desire, disease is understood synecdochically as the terminus of all desire—hence the play's ending with Pandarus's bequeathal of his "diseases" to the audience's already "aching bones" (5.10.57, 51).[49] Nor is the disease imagery in the play solely a matter of syphilitic or venereal sickness, associated with a narrow (sexual) definition of desire:

> Now the rotten diseases of the south, the guts-griping, ruptures, catarrhs, loads o' gravel i'th'back, lethargies, cold palsies, raw eyes, dirt-rotten livers, whissing lungs, bladders full of impostume, sciaticas, lime-kilns i'th'palm, incurable bone-ache, and the rivelled fee-simple of the tetter, take and take again such preposterous discoveries!
>
> (5.1.16-23)

Thersites's cursing, while specifically attacking homosexual activity ("preposterous discoveries"), encompasses a dozen kinds of illness, most of which have nothing to do with sexuality but are rather the result of quite diverse forms of appetite. Disease and alimentary imagery are linked, first, by their relation to internal physiology and, second, by their relation to appetite in the broadest sense of the term. This is why the idea of self-consumption recurs so often in the play: appetite contains—or wills—its own end. For the play seems to me to conceive of appetite as something very like Nietzsche's "will to power"—an insatiable, appropriative urge that, for all its myriad manifestations, finds its sources in the physiology of each and every organism:

> Then everything includes itself in power,
> Power into will, will into appetite,
> And appetite, an universal wolf,
> So doubly seconded with will and power,
> Must make perforce an universal prey,
> And last eat up himself.
>
> (1.3.119-24)

The deflation of the ideals and of the high-flown rhetoric of these epic heroes centers on this idea of an insatiable, pervasive, polymorphous appetite. The Renaissance's hierarchy of desires, from the merely appetitive to the spiritual, is here portrayed as completely reducible to its lowest common denominator; it is only the arbitrary imposition of degree that stops this collapse. And it is this reduction of all forms of desire to the urge for food—the refusal to separate sexual, martial, and alimentary forms of desire—which makes the play so cannibalistic.

I am suggesting that we think of desire in *Troilus and Cressida* in a very broad scope. Catherine Belsey has recently argued that the play "shows a world where desire is everywhere. . . . Desire is the unuttered residue which exceeds any act that would display it, including the sexual act."[50] As Troilus himself puts it, "desire is boundless"—boundless, that is, not only in aspiration but in origin. Troilus's famous lament—"This is the monstruosity in love, lady: that the will is infinite, and the execution confined: that the desire is boundless, and the act a slave to limit" (3.2.79-82)—has too often been taken to imply little more than that all lovers fall short of their aims. But desire, the entire play seems to be saying, is not only unsatisfiable in relation to its objects—it is insatiable (or, to use Belsey's language, "excessive") at its very source; it is a "slave to limit" not only in that it can never fulfill its aims but also in that it must, perforce, *choose* these aims, these objects, though in and of itself it is "infinite." The various manifestations of desire here—alimentary, martial, amorous, hetero- and homosexual, mimetic—are all conceived of as just that: manifestations of some absolutely voracious and polymorphous physiological drive. All these expressions of desire are merely its protean forms, "Dexterity . . . obeying appetite" (5.5.27).

The theme of alimentary appetite appears everywhere in the very fabric of the play. As in Nietzsche, the alimentary process is here a central metaphor for *any* manifestation of a will to power; eating and digestion appear indiscriminately as tropes for the play's two main themes of love and war: the "generation of love" is figured as "eat[ing] nothing but doves" (3.1.127, 123), the origin of the "factious feasts" (1.3.191) of bellicosity as having a "stomach" to the war (3.3.219; 2.1.127; 4.5.263). This is not, I think, simply a matter of an interpretive reduction to the level of physiology; it is a way of understanding human activities and processes *metaphorically*. To describe the "spirit," Nietzsche—like Shakespeare in *Troilus and Cressida*—turns to the body: "The spirit," he writes, "is more like a stomach than anything else":

> This inferior being [the stomach] assimilates (*assimiliert*) whatever lies in its immediate vicinity, and appropriates it (property initially being food (*Nahrung*) and provision for food), it seeks to assimilate (*einverleiben*) as many things as it can and not only to compensate itself for loss: this being is greedy (*habsüchtig*).[51]

The "raging appetites" (2.2.182) of both Greeks and Trojans figure the insatiability of this process; their actions, again and again, constitute a display of "the will of the weak to represent *some* form of superiority."[52] *Troilus and Cressida*'s depiction of the endlessly shifting shapes that desire can take (the *folie circulaire* of heterosexual activity expressing itself as martial activity expressing itself as homosexual activity, and so on[53]) ultimately means that the protagonists "lose distinction" (3.2.25) between these shapes, as the spectators, by the end of the play, lose any sense of distinction between Greeks and Trojans, "hot" (3.1.125) lovers and "hot" (4.5.185) warriors: just about any of them could be described as wearing "his wit in his belly and his guts in his head" (2.1.75-76).[54] Nor, at this

level, is there a differentiation between male and female: entrails (in this play) are conspicuously ungendered; nowhere is "matter" linked (as it is, for instance, in *Hamlet*[55]) to *mater,* the maternal. All difference is, to use Nietzsche's term, "assimilate[d]"—"consum'd / In hot digestion of this cormorant war" (2.2.5-6)—even, it seems, the distinction between comedy and tragedy. The play displays an indifference to, or at least a profound skepticism about, the many forms of desire, including their generic concomitants; as Valerie Traub points out, "*Troilus and Cressida* declines to differentiate types of desire."[56] It is almost, as Joel Fineman puts it, "as though in *Troilus and Cressida* Shakespeare had turned against desire itself,"[57] exposing its ostensibly distinct manifestations as inextricable from each other at their source. The endlessly "dext[rous]" forms of desire seem to amount, in the end, to little more than "the performance of our heaving spleens" (2.2.197), the "pleasure of my spleen" (1.3.178), "a feverous pulse" (3.2.35), "the hot passion of distemper'd blood" (2.2.170), "The obligation of our blood" (4.5.121), "bawdy veins" (4.1.70), "too much blood and too little brain" (5.1.47), and so on; this approaches Nietzsche's "the coils of the intestines, the quick current of the blood stream, and the involved tremors of the fibers." Metaphors all, in a sense, but nonetheless figuring the distance between the deep sources of human motivation and their manifestations in rhetoric and action:

> However far a man may go in self-knowledge, nothing however can be more incomplete than his image of the totality of *drives* which constitute his being. He can scarcely name even the cruder ones: their number and strength, their ebb and flood, their play and counterplay among one another, and above all the laws of their *nutriment* remain wholly unknown to him. . . . Our moral judgements and evaluations too are only images and fantasies based on a physiological process unknown to us, a kind of acquired language for designating nervous stimuli.[58]

It is precisely the question of "the laws of their *nutriment*"—and of the "ebbs and flows" (as Agamemnon puts it) of the body's "humorous predominance" (2.3.132, 131)—that the play opens up.

Such a view goes some way toward explaining the strangeness of the play, the fact that *Troilus and Cressida* is so difficult to discuss profitably in terms of "character" or coherent "character development." The play seems almost perversely to flout any attempt to perceive full subjectivity in its dramatis personae; these are, without exception, flattened out, reduced to caricatures compared with their Homeric or Chaucerian predecessors.[59] As Shakespeare recorporealizes the story, he (quite uncharacteristically) "decharacterizes"[60] its heroes; they become little more than "ciphers" in the "great accompt" (*Henry V,* Pro.17) of the Trojan legend. As Matthew Greenfield points out, "the play works through two related theories of human behaviour, one physiological (humors) and the other psychological (emulation, or what René Girard calls 'mimetic desire'). Both are theories of damaged agency, of compulsive, involuntary action."[61] There is something entirely stripped-down, rather than fully rounded, about all the play's characters; Carol Cook speaks of "the play of drives" depicted here.[62] The unflinching nature of this vision can, again, be viewed as a return to Homer, to the "geometrical rigor" of what Simone Weil has called "the poem of force."[63] The entire spirit of the play drags any metaphysical or psychological pretensions back down to earth; indeed, the very word *spirit* is used repeatedly in *Troilus and Cressida* with strong overtones of its physiological sense (as the vital substance that inhabits the body's vessels).[64] In radically shifting our view of these heroes of the Western world, in its materialist reduction of motivation to something like the corporeal "will to power," *Troilus and Cressida* profoundly addresses the question of the relation between language and the body.

3. CANNIBALISM AND SILENCE

Let him who has something to say come forward and be silent!

      Karl Kraus, "In these Great times"[65]

For all its grand rhetoric—or perhaps, more accurately, as a necessary concomitant to this rhetoric—*Troilus and Cressida* reveals an extreme distrust of (not to say disgust with) language. If the play leaves one with a sensation of satiety with words, it is likely that this sensation was one that Shakespeare, in coming to write the play, was himself unable to avoid. Many writers of the period comment on this dilemma, several of them using a specifically oral metaphor: George Whetstone declares that "the inconstancie of Cressid is so readie *in every mans mouth,* as it is needlesse labour to blase at full her abuse"; Montaigne writes that "There is nothing, liveth so *in mens mouthes* as . . . *Troy,* as *Helen* and her *Warres*"; Burton describes the story's popularity vividly, in a phrase that evokes the play's nausea: "our Poets steale from *Homer, he spewes,* . . . *[and] they licke it up.*"[66] Perhaps it was this sense of verbal surfeit which impelled Shakespeare to turn the Trojan legend into material for satire, *satura;* such a sense may in fact be an inherent component of satire—oral satiety turned to oral sadism. Burton, in his discussion of satirists and calumniators, warns against "fall[ing] *into the mouths* of such men . . . for many are of so petulant a spleene, and have that figure *Sarcasmus* so often *in their mouthes,* so bitter, so foolish, as Baltasar Castilio notes of them, that *they cannot speake, but they must bite.*"[67] Confronted with a glut of retellings of the legend of Troy, Shakespeare may indeed have found, when he turned his attention to the writing of *Troilus and Cressida,* that he could not speak without biting; hence, perhaps, the play's turn toward cannibalism.[68]

This difficulty in speaking without biting perfectly figures the perplexed relation between language and the body in *Troilus and Cressida;* and for early modern Europeans the idea of cannibalism has a recurrent stake in interrogating this problematic matter. We are speaking here of a period of crisis in the understanding of this relation, a period dur-

ing which print technology and the exhaustion of the humanist project of "fattening up" language—to name just two factors—had resulted in a profound dissatisfaction with the hollowed-out discourses of European culture. It is at times of cultural crisis such as this, as Elaine Scarry has argued, that "the sheer material factualness of the human body will be borrowed to lend . . . cultural construct[s] the aura of 'realness' and 'certainty.'"[69]

The cultural construct of cannibalism was used in a similar way. Here I would like to turn briefly to Montaigne, whose "motivated confrontation of the philosophical and the anatomical"[70] recalls *Troilus and Cressida*'s linking of the two, and whose essay "Of the Cannibals" can provide us with some illuminating parallels to the play's staging of these issues. Both these texts portray attitudes toward love and war as exemplifying a society's ethical value. Montaigne displaces the idea of savagery back onto European civilization, describing his own countrymen's behavior as far crueler than that of the New World's cannibals; in the process of this displacement, as Michel de Certeau explains, "the word 'barbarian' . . . leaves behind its status as a noun (the Barbarians) to take on the value of an adjective (cruel, etc.)."[71] From one perspective, *Troilus and Cressida*'s trajectory is a diametric inversion of Montaigne's: instead of revealing and ratifying the deeply ethical imperative underlying the culture of cannibal society (and thereby assimilating the latter to "civilization"), it defamiliarizes (or disassimilates) the epic ethos, infusing it with a "cannibalism" that is seen as "savage strangeness" (2.3.128). The former society's "noble and generous"[72] heroism-in-war (the heroism of the victim) and polygamy-in-marriage (based on the love of the wives) are precisely inverted in Shakespeare's barbarism-in-war (the antiheroism of the perpetrator, exemplified by Achilles's butchering of Hector) and cuckoldry-in-marriage (based on the infidelity of the women—both Cressida and Helen). Yet the play ends up in more or less the same place as "Of the Cannibals," proclaiming the "barbarism" (5.4.17) of the heroes of the *Iliad*—the cradle of its own European culture.

Both texts evince a profound dissatisfaction with what Montaigne called, in the title of another essay, "the vanity of words."[73] But Montaigne's (idealized) savage culture is everything that Shakespeare's (debased) European culture is not. Where the former as de Certeau brilliantly shows, "is founded upon . . . a heroic faithfulness to speech [which] produces the unity and continuity of the social body," the latter's "Bifold authority" (5.2.143) emphasizes the antiheroic faithlessness of language, fragmenting any vestige of social—and, ultimately, individual—unity. Why is cannibal speech so reliable? Because it is "sustained by bodies that have been put to the test":[74] "These muscles," sings the cannibal prisoner before he is eaten, "this flesh, and these veines, are your owne."[75] Why is the speech of Shakespeare's Greeks and Trojans so unreliable? Because it contains "no matter from the heart."

The enigma of the relation between body and speech lies at the very center of both Montaigne's and Shakespeare's texts. Both are concerned with the question of the corporeal source of words, a question about the veracity or duplicity of voice. It is this turn from bodily source to disembodied discourse—the trope of voice—which is the target of much skeptical and satirical attack. Skepticism questions the accuracy of the connection between words and things; here, more specifically, it is the matter of the coherence of the link between the source of things (words, desires) within the body and their emanation in discourse that is at issue. Montaigne's cannibals have no need of skepticism, no use for it, since they are materially inhabited by the body of the other, and this inhabitation guarantees the quality of the link between language and corpus. Cannibalism, here, is a fantasy of speech as "a thing inseparate" (5.2.147) from the body. It is in this sense that what is taken into the body—the gastric—can be imagined as an antidote to the speech—the rhetoric—that leaves it: both Montaigne's cannibals and Shakespeare's protagonists are, in a sense, what they eat.

Montaigne's cannibal society is "a body in the service of saying. It is the visible, palpable, verifiable *exemplum* which realizes before our eyes an ethic of speech."[76] Shakespeare's *Troilus and Cressida* holds out no such hope of "faithful and verifiable speech."[77] But where Montaigne offers, as an alternative to the morally depleted discourses of early modern Europe, a new "ethic of speech," Shakespeare offers no hope of a language guaranteed by the body. Instead he offers the only other possible alternative: an ethic of silence. In the context of the play's outpouring of alternately high-flown, empty rhetoric and scurvy invective, one character stands out in his utter wordlessness: Antenor. A.P. Rossiter, the only critic (as far as I know) who comments on his existence, calls him "Shakespeare's one strong silent man."[78] Onstage on at least five separate occasions, mentioned by those around him a dozen times, he utters not a single syllable throughout. In his silence he is strikingly at odds with his traditional role: Homer, for example, calls him "strong in talking," and Caxton says of him simply that he "spacke moche."[79] His speechlessness in Shakespeare, then, is quite deliberate, a kind of rebuttal of the nauseatingly "cramm'd" (2.2.49) rhetoric circulating in and around the play. (And Shakespeare's knack for squeezing meaning out of the names he is given may be at work here, for *Antenor* can be related readily enough to the Greek private *an-* ["not" or "without"] prefixed to *tenor* ["the male voice"].)[80] If *Troilus and Cressida* as a whole shares with Montaigne a skeptical, Pyrrhonic sense of pervasive relativism, Antenor's tenacious muteness may be imagined as a Pyrrhonic commitment to aphasia, a "silence, / Cunning in dumbness" (3.2.130-31).[81]

Leaving behind (like Pyrrho) no textual trace of his voice, Antenor is the embodiment onstage of what de Certeau calls the "(t)exterior [*hors-texte*]"[82]—the space carved out by Montaigne for the figuration of the perfect corporeality of the savage. In his mimetic immediacy, Antenor literally fills this space of the "*hors-texte*." If *Troilus and Cressida* "thematizes the relationship between the mimetic and the citational,"[83] Cressida, upon being "changed for Antenor"

(4.2.94), becomes the purely citational to his purely mimetic. She is his precise opposite: "unbridled" (3.2.121) in her language, "glib of tongue" (4.5.58), she has betrayed herself from the outset by having "blabb'd" (3.2.123) to Troilus. She becomes, in the end, a figure of pure textuality—even her body, in Ulysses's mocking description of her, is a text: "Fie, fie upon her! / There's language in her eye, her cheek, her lip—/ Nay, her foot speaks; her wanton spirits look out / At every joint and motive of her body" (4.5.54-57). Her faithlessness is figured *as* the faithlessness of language itself: "I will not keep my word" (5.2.98). She is, we could say, the "whore-text" to Antenor's "*hors-texte*"—"right great exchange" (3.3.21) indeed.

Antenor, the man of silence, exists only as body, the word made flesh. His is an "art of *silence*"[84] which offers the only real space of alterity to the surfeit of degraded language with which he is surrounded, both inside and outside the play. "Compact, severe, with as much substance as possible, a cold sarcasm against 'beautiful words'"— this is how I imagine him.[85]

I imagine, too, that the actor who played Antenor originally was Shakespeare himself—his own silent, sly escape from the overwhelming citationality of his material. A playwright, though, cannot long remain silent. Shakespeare's great tragedies, written in the years following *Troilus and Cressida,* portray repeated—and often failed—attempts to recover the possibility of a meaningful language, a place for words that retain their integrity with the bodies from which they emerge, a way to heave the heart into the mouth—to love, without being silent.

Notes

I would like to thank Stanley Cavell, G. Blakemore Evans, Elizabeth Freund, Marjorie Garber, Jeff Masten, Ruth Nevo, and the members of the Harvard Renaissance Colloquium for their helpful and generous comments at various stages of the writing of this essay.

1. Friedrich Nietzsche, *Ecce Homo,* trans. Walter Kaufmann (New York: Vintage Books, 1967), 241.

2. According to J.S.P. Tatlock, "no traditional story was so popular in the Elizabethan Age as that of the siege of Troy and some of its episodes" ("The Siege of Troy in Elizabethan Literature, Especially in Shakespeare and Heywood," *PMLA* 30 [1915]: 676-78). For a good sense of how many competing versions of the legend were in circulation at the time, see Robert Kimbrough, *Shakespeare's "Troilus and Cressida" and its Setting* (Cambridge, MA: Harvard UP, 1964), 24-46; and Geoffrey Bullough, ed., *Narrative and Dramatic Sources of Shakespeare,* 8 vols. (New York: Columbia UP, 1957-75), 6:83-221.

3. According to the Epistle of *The Famous Historie of Troylus and Cresseid* (1609), the play was "neuer stal'd with the Stage, neuer clapper-clawd with the palmes of the vulgar" (¶2). All quotations from *Troilus and Cressida* follow the Arden text of the play,

edited by Kenneth Palmer (London and New York: Methuen, 1982). Quotations from other plays by Shakespeare follow the *Riverside Shakespeare,* ed. G. Blakemore Evans (Boston: Houghton Mifflin, 1974).

4. The very fact of putting these heroes onstage, in the inescapably embodied media of the theater, must have brought into sharp focus the disjunction between the rhetorical (and disembodied) and the mimetic (and corporeal). "I am half inclined," wrote Samuel Taylor Coleridge about the play, "to believe that Shakespeare's main object, or shall I rather say, that his ruling impulse, was . . . to substantiate the distinct and graceful profiles or outlines of the Homeric epic into the flesh and blood of the romantic drama" (*Coleridge's Writings on Shakespeare,* ed. Terence Hawkes [New York: Capricorn Books, 1959], 248-49). On this topic, see especially Harry Berger Jr.'s "Text vs. Performance in Shakespeare: The Example of *Macbeth,*" *Genre* 15 (1982): 49-79.

5. Rosalie Colie, *Shakespeare's Living Art* (Princeton, NJ: Princeton UP, 1974), 326.

6. Elizabeth Freund, "'Ariachne's Broken Woof': The Rhetoric of Citationality in *Troilus and Cressida*" in *Shakespeare and the Question of Theory,* Patricia Parker and Geoffrey Hartman, eds. (New York: Methuen, 1985), 19-36, esp. 21. Linda Charnes's "'So Unsecret to Ourselves': Notorious Identity and the Material Subject in Shakespeare's *Troilus and Cressida*" (*Shakespeare Quarterly* 40 [1989]: 413-40) similarly stresses issues of citationality in the play.

7. For occurrences of the word *matter* in *Troilus and Cressida,* see *The Harvard Concordance to Shakespeare,* comp. Marvin Spevack (Cambridge, MA: Belknap Press of Harvard UP, 1973), 798. On *matter* as bodily substance—and, more specifically, pus— see Alexander Schmidt, *Shakespeare-Lexicon: A complete dictionary of all the . . . words . . . in the works of the poet,* 2 vols. (Berlin: Georg Reimer, 1874-75), 2:700-701; and Elaine Scarry, ed., *Literature and the Body: Essays on Populations and Persons* (Baltimore: Johns Hopkins UP, 1988), xxii.

8. Edmund Spenser, *The Faerie Queene,* ed. Thomas P. Roche Jr. (Harmondsworth, UK, and New York: Penguin, 1978), 514.

9. S. L. Bethell, *Shakespeare and the Popular Dramatic Tradition* (London: Staples Press, 1944), 98; L.C. Knights, *Some Shakespearean Themes* (London: Chatto and Windus, 1959), 58. Cf. R.J. Kaufmann's comments in "Ceremonies for Chaos: The Status of *Troilus and Cressida,*" *ELH* 32 (1965), 139-59, esp. 145.

10. Eric Blondel, *Nietzsche: The Body and Culture* (Stanford, CA: Stanford UP, 1991), 220. My understanding of Nietzsche's use of the physiological metaphor is indebted to Blondel's excellent analysis,

as well as to Elizabeth Grosz's essay "Nietzsche and the Stomach for Knowledge" in *Nietzsche, Feminism, and Political Theory,* Paul Patton, ed. (London and New York: Routledge, 1993), 49-70.

11. This idealized, closed, opaque corporeal model has been described by Mikhail Bakhtin as the "classical" body, in contrast with the open, flowing, "grotesque" body that foregrounds its orifices and protuberances (Mikhail Bakhtin, *Rabelais and His World,* trans. Hélène Iswolsky [Cambridge and London: MIT Press, 1986], esp.18-30); Shakespeare's play adds to this binary a third model—the "abject" body whose interior organs and physiology are represented. For while *Troilus and Cressida*'s bodies are grotesque, it is not so much their orificial or protuberant status that makes them so as their internal ebb and flow, the diseased status of their visceral interiors.

12. Nietzsche, *The Will to Power,* quoted here from Blondel, 220.

13. Nietzsche, "On Truth and Lie in the Extra-Moral Sense" in *The Portable Nietzsche,* ed. and trans. Walter Kaufmann (New York: Viking Press, 1954), 42-50, esp. 44.

14. The phrase is taken from Georg Stauth and Bryan S. Turner, *Nietzsche's Dance* (Oxford: Basil Blackwell, 1988), 17.

15. Nietzsche, *Beyond Good and Evil: Prelude to a Philosophy of the Future,* trans. Walter Kaufmann (New York: Vintage Books, 1989), 137 and 138: "By applying the knife vivisectionally to the chest of the very *virtues of their time,* they [philosophers] betrayed what was their own secret: to know of a *new* greatness of man" (137).

16. Nietzsche, *Twilight of the Idols or, How One Philosophizes with a Hammer* in *The Portable Nietzsche,* 463-563, esp. 465.

17. Patricia Parker, *Shakespeare from the Margins: Language, Culture, Context* (Chicago: U of Chicago P, 1996), 224. Parker stresses the association of bodily swelling with rhetorical tumidity in the play.

18. The phrase has sometimes been taken as a symbol for the entire play; Eric Mallin's comment is particularly apt: "Hector discovers that the ideal has become entirely flesh, a corrupted thing" ("Emulous Factions and the Collapse of Chivalry: *Troilus and Cressida,*" *Representations* 29 [1990]: 145-79, esp. 168).

19. Nietzsche, *Beyond Good and Evil,* 161. Graham Bradshaw comments on this genealogical project in his excellent chapter on *Troilus and Cressida* in *Shakespeare's scepticism* (Ithaca, NY: Cornell UP, 1987), 126-63. Though Bradshaw addresses primarily questions of the construction of principles of value, his project shares with mine some basic assumptions about the play.

20. Cf. Matthew Greenfield's comment in "Undoing National Identity: Shakespeare's *Troilus and Cressida*" (unpublished paper presented at the 1995

annual meeting of the Shakespeare Association of America, Chicago): "The work of *Troilus and Cressida* is not to provide England or Elizabeth with a genealogy but rather to undo the genealogies created by other myth-makers" (5). In *Troilus and Cressida,* wrote Tucker Brooke, Shakespeare was, "however subconsciously, anatomizing the England of the dying Elizabeth" ("Shakepeare's Study in Culture and Anarchy," *Yale Review,* n.s. xvii [1928]: 571-77, esp. 576).

21. There is an analogous reversal in that the normative *end* of the Trojan story is in the belly of the Trojan horse; Shakespeare makes the belly the origin rather than the culmination of the tale. Troy and the belly are again linked—rather oddly—in Phineas Fletcher's *The Purple Island* (Cambridge, 1633), where the "vale" of the belly is described as "A work more curious, then which poets feigne / *Neptune* and *Phoebus* built, and pulled down again [i.e., Troy]" (20).

22. These quotations are from Simone Weil's description of Homer's epic in Weil, *The Iliad, or, The Poem of Force,* trans. Mary McCarthy (Iowa City: Stone Wall Press, 1973), 6 and 33. Cf. Sheila Murnaghan, "Body and Voice in Greek Tragedy," *Yale Journal of Criticism* 1 (1988): 23-43: "No reader of the *Iliad* fails to be impressed by the poem's vivid accounts of the body materializing as it is severed from the animating *psyche,* or spirit" (24).

23. For this etymology, see the *Oxford English Dictionary,* s.v. *Ileum, Ilion,* and *Ilium;* and A. Ernout and A. Meillet, *Dictionnaire Ètymologique de la Langue Latine* (Paris: Klincksieck, 1959), 308 ("ilia, -ium . . . *parties latérales du ventre*"). For the anatomical data, see, for example, Thomas Vicary, *The Anatomie of the Bodie of Man* (London, 1548; rpt. London: Early English Text Society, 1888), 65.

24. On the symbolic significance of the Trojan horse, see Robert Durling, "Deceit and Digestion in the Belly of Hell" in *Allegory and Representation: Selected Papers from the English Institute, 1979-80,* Stephen J. Greenblatt, ed. (Baltimore: Johns Hopkins UP, 1981), 61-93, esp. 74.

25. Lucian of Samosata, *Hermotimus, or Concerning the Sects,* trans. K. Kilburn (Cambridge, MA: Harvard UP, 1959), 297-99.

26. On the familiarity of Lucian to Elizabethan readers, see Douglas Duncan, *Ben Jonson and the Lucianic Tradition* (Cambridge: Cambridge UP, 1979), 82-96. Prominent allusions to Momus's tale appear in Francis Bacon's *The Advancement of Learning* (1605), where Bacon refers to "that window which Momus did require: who seeing in the frame of man's heart such angles and recesses, found fault there was not a window to look into them" (Bacon, *The Advancement of Learning,* ed. William Aldis Wright [Oxford: Clarendon Press, 1900], 228-29); and in Robert Burton's *Anatomy of Melancholy* (1621), where Burton observes, "How would *Democritus* have beene moved, had he seene the secrets of [men's] hearts? If every man had a window in his brest, which *Momus* would have had in *Vulcans* man. . . . Would hee, thinke you, or any man else say that these men were well in their wits?" (Burton, *The Anatomy of Melancholy,* ed. Thomas C. Faulkner et al., 3 vols. [Oxford: Clarendon Press, 1989-94], 1:55-56). On *Troilus and Cressida* as a Pyrrhonist play, see especially Robert B. Pierce, "Shakespeare and the Ten Modes of Scepticism," *Shakespeare Survey* 46 (1994): 145-58, esp. 151-52.

27. At 1.2.110: "she's a merry Greek indeed"; and at 4.4.55: "A woeful Cressid 'mongst the merry Greeks." Cf. Troilus's comment "Were it a casque compos'd by Vulcan's [i.e., Hephaestus's] skill, / My sword should bite it" (5.2.169-70).

28. A "tent" in this context is a surgeon's instrument for opening and probing a wound. Cf. Thersites's (typically somatizing) answer to Patroclus's "Who keeps the tent now?": "The surgeon's box or the patient's wound" (5.1.10-11).

29. For more on this fantasy in Shakespeare's plays, see my "Visceral Knowledge: Shakespeare, Skepticism, and the Interior of the Early Modern Body" in *The Body in Parts: Fantasies of Corporeality in Early Modern Europe,* David Hillman and Carla Mazzio, eds. (New York: Routledge, 1997), 81-105.

30. Jean Starobinski, "The Inside and the Outside," *The Hudson Review* 28 (1975): 333-51, esp. 336; Starobinski slightly modifies the translation of A. T. Murray in *The Iliad,* Loeb Classical Library, 2 vols. (London: Heinemann, 1930-34), 1:405.

31. Richard Broxton Onians, *The Origins of European Thought about the Body, the Mind, the Soul, the World, Time, and Fate* (Cambridge: The University Press, 1951), 86; Bruno Snell, *The Discovery of the Mind in Greek Philosophy and Literature,* trans. T.G. Rosenmeyer (New York: Dover, 1982), 1-22. See also Murnaghan, 23-24; and Jean-Pierre Vernant, "Dim Body, Dazzling Body" in *Fragments for a History of the Human Body, Part One,* Michel Feher, ed. (Cambridge, MA: MIT Press, 1989), 18-47, esp. 29-30.

32. The idea of an inherent connection between truth and entrails is at least as old as the practice of haruspices—or, in the case of human entrails, anthropomancy. In both Old and New Testaments, as Elaine Scarry has shown, "the interior of the body carries the force of confirmation [of belief]" (Scarry, *The Body in Pain: The Making and Unmaking of the World* [New York and Oxford: Oxford UP, 1985], 215).

33. Throughout this brief discussion of satire, I generalize about a wide field of material. The specific examples, which I take to be representative of the genre, can do no more than gesture toward this field. For more on early modern English satire, see

especially Mary Claire Randolph, "The Medical Concept in English Renaissance Satiric Theory," *Studies in Philology* 38 (1941): 125-57; O.J. Campbell, *Shakespeare's Satire* (London and New York: Oxford UP, 1943); and Alvin Kernan, *The Cankered Muse: Satire of the English Renaissance* (New Haven, CT: Yale UP, 1959).

34. *The Collected Poems of Joseph Hall,* ed. Arnold Davenport (Liverpool: The University Press, 1949), 83; John Marston, *Antonio and Mellida, Part One* in *The Works of John Marston,* ed. A.H. Bullen, 3 vols. (London: John C. Nimmo, 1887), 1:50. Cf. Marston's description of the satirist as a kind of barber-surgeon, lancing the sores of the world: "Infectious blood, ye gouty humours quake, / Whilst my sharp razor doth incision make" (*The Scourge of Villanie,* in Bullen, ed., 3:339).

35. Direct injury is usually figured either as biting or as scourging; but even in the latter case, the aim, as often as not, is to get beneath the skin: "Each blow doth leave / A lasting scar, that with a poison eats / Into the marrow" (Thomas Randolph, *The Muses' Looking Glass,* quoted here from Mary Claire Randolph, 150). Kernan writes that "gross, sodden, rotting matter is the substance of the satiric scene" (11).

36. Burton, 1:337-41, esp. 337 and 339.

37. Mary Claire Randolph, 153. The combination of impulses delineated here hints at what we might think of as a strongly preoedipal component to the satirist's aggression; Melanie Klein describes the first year of life as full of "sadistic impulses directed, not only against its mother's breast, but also against the inside of her body: scooping it out, devouring the contents, destroying it by every means which sadism can suggest"; so, too, the projective mechanisms crucial to this stage of life are central to the operation of satire. The satirist's oral sadism can be thought of, from this perspective, as an exacerbated version of this primary infantile position (Melanie Klein, "A Contribution to the Psychogenesis of Manic-Depressive States" in *Love, Guilt, and Reparation, and Other Works, 1921-1945,* Vol. 1 of *The Writings of Melanie Klein* [London: Hogarth Press, 1975], 1:262-89, esp. 282).

38. Marston, *The Scourge of Villanie,* in Bullen, ed., 3:355; and Burton, 1:337-38.

39. *The Works of John Milton,* Frank Allen Patterson, gen. ed., 18 vols. (New York: Columbia UP, 1931-38), 3:329. "Byting" comes from the title of Joseph Hall's first collection, "Of Byting Satyrs."

40. Walter Benjamin, *Reflections: Essays, Aphorisms, Autobiographical Writings,* ed. Peter Demetz, trans. Edmund Jephcott (New York: Harcourt Brace Jovanovich, 1978), 260-61. Despite the popular Elizabethan notion that the word *satire* came from the Greek *satyr,* the correct Latin etymology was not unknown at the time. See, e.g., Thomas Drant, *A Medecinable Morall* (London, 1566), A2^r (cited in Hallett Smith, *Elizabethan Poetry: A Study in Conventions, Meaning, and Expression* [Cambridge, MA: Harvard UP, 1952], 217), where the etymology of *satire* is traced to both the Greek and the Latin sources, as well as to the Arabic for a glaive (i.e., a lance or spear). See also *The Oxford Dictionary of English Etymology,* ed. C. T. Onions (Oxford: Clarendon Press, 1966), 790.

41. Petronius Arbiter, *Satyricon* in *Petronius,* trans. Michael Heseltine (London: William Heinemann; New York: MacMillan, 1913), 321. Swift's *A Modest Proposal* is English literature's most overt example of the satiric urge to eat people.

42. See Caroline Spurgeon, *Shakespeare's Imagery and What it Tells Us* (Cambridge: The University Press, 1936), 320-24.

43. There are, of course, images that don't fit into this trajectory, which is impressionistic rather than rigorous.

44. On the way *Troilus and Cressida* "work[s] to extend the logic of the play from the relations among characters to the relations between characters and audience," see Harry Berger Jr., "*Troilus and Cressida:* The Observer as Basilisk" in *Second World and Green World: Studies in Renaissance Fiction-Making,* John Patrick Lynch, ed. (Berkeley: U of California P, 1988), 130-46, esp. 141.

45. Sir Thomas Browne, *Religio Medici* in *The Works of Sir Thomas Browne,* ed. Geoffrey Keynes, 6 vols. (London: Faber and Gwyer, 1928), 1:48.

46. Palmer, ed., 130n.

47. Colie, 343-44. Kimbrough adds that "an Elizabethan audience would have recognized [Thersites] as a walking, talking figure of speech" (39). Shakespeare, however, seems to have associated Thersites less with language than with the body: "Thersites' body is as good as Ajax' / When neither are alive" (*Cymbeline,* 4.2.252-53). Cf. Burton's comment that all men "are in brief, as disordered in their mindes, as *Thersites* was in his body" (34).

48. Patricia Parker, *Literary Fat Ladies: Rhetoric, Gender, Property* (London and New York: Methuen, 1987), 89.

49. Is, for instance, "the open ulcer of [Troilus's] heart" (1.1.53) the source or the result of his love for Cressida?

50. Catherine Belsey, "Desire's excess and the English Renaissance theatre: *Edward II, Troilus and Cressida, Othello*" in Susan Zimmerman, ed., *Erotic Politics: Desire on the Renaissance Stage* (London and New York: Routledge, 1992), 84-102, esp. 93. Carol Cook's "Unbodied Figures of Desire" (*Theatre Jour-*

nal 38 [1986]: 34-52) relates desire not so much to the subject's body in the play as to its objects' corporeality.

51. Nietzsche, *The Will to Power,* quoted here from Blondel, 219 and 218.

52. Nietzsche, *The Genealogy of Morals,* trans. Walter Kaufmann and R.J. Hollingdale (New York: Vintage Books, 1967), 123.

53. Charnes's account of these complex circulations in the play is ingenious: "We might posit the circuit thus: possession of Helen generates desire for war, desire for war generates desire for Helen, desire for Helen generates mimetic desire, mimetic desire generates competitive identification between Greek and Trojan men, competitive identification generates homoerotic aggression, homoerotic aggression generates desire for more war, and finally, desire for more war reproduces desire for Helen" (437).

54. The phrase comes from Cornelius Agrippa and, interestingly, is used by Burton side by side with a reference to cannibalism: "To see a man weare his braines in his belly, his guts in his head, . . . or as those *Anthropophagi,* to eat one another" (1:53).

55. See my "*Hamlet,* Nietzsche, and Visceral Knowledge" in *The Incorporated Self: Interdisciplinary Perspectives on Embodiment,* Michael O'Donovan-Anderson, ed. (Lanham, MD: Rowman and Littlefield, 1996), 93-110.

56. Valerie Traub, *Desire and Anxiety: Circulations of sexuality in Shakespearean drama* (London and New York: Routledge, 1992), 84.

57. Joel Fineman, "Fratricide and Cuckoldry: Shakespeare's Doubles" in *Representing Shakespeare: New Psychoanalytic Essays,* Murray M. Schwartz and Coppélia Kahn, eds. (Baltimore: Johns Hopkins UP, 1980), 70-109, esp. 100.

58. Nietzsche, *Daybreak: Thoughts on the Prejudices of Morality,* trans. R.J. Hollingdale (Cambridge: Cambridge UP, 1982), 74-76.

59. See especially Colie's comment about the characters "refusing altogether to conform to the conventions of psychological illusionism" (326). Cf. Bethell, 102. This is where I part ways with Linda Charnes's powerful account of the play: it is not, I think, part of Shakespeare's enterprise here to take on "the task of giving mimetic spontaneity to, and representing viable subjectivity in" his Homeric characters (417)—quite the contrary.

60. The term is taken from Stephen Roderick's "Et Tu, Jello," *Boston Magazine* 87, no. 5 (1995): 66.

61. Greenfield, 10; Greenfield quotes René Girard's "The Politics of Desire in *Troilus and Cressida*" in Parker and Hartman, eds., 188-209.

62. Cook, 40.

63. Weil, 15.

64. See especially the Prologue's "expectation, tickling skittish spirits" (l. 20); Troilus's "spirit of sense" (1.1.58), echoed by Achilles's "most pure spirit of sense" (3.3.106); Ulysses's "her wanton spirits look out / At every joint and motive of her body" (4.5.56-57); and Achilles's "That I may give the local wound a name, / And make distinct the very breach whereout / Hector's great spirit flew" (4.5.243-45). Bradshaw calls *spirit* "a word to watch in this play"; beginning with the Prologue, the play "release[s] the perjorative senses the word spirit may have. These are many and include the clinical senses in humors psychology" (130). On the role of the "spirits" in humoral theory, see especially Gail Kern Paster, "Nervous Tension: Networks of Blood and Spirit in the Early Modern Body" in Hillman and Mazzio, eds. On premodern conceptions of "spirit" as a vapor or liquid inhabiting the body (and as "seed"), see Onians, 480-89, esp. 480-85.

65. Karl Kraus, *In These Great Times* (Montreal, Quebec: Engendra Press, 1976), 70-83, esp. 71.

66. George Whetstone, *The Rocke of Regard* (1576), quoted here from Bullough, ed., 6:97; Michel de Montaigne, "Of the worthiest and most excellent men" in *The Essayes of Michael, Lord of Montaigne,* trans. John Florio (1603), ed. Israel Gollancz, 6 vols. (London: J.M. Dent, 1897), 4:327-38, esp. 330; and Burton, 1:11. Emphasis added in all three quotations.

67. Burton, 1:337-38 (emphasis added except for the last phrase, which is italicized in the original). Perhaps we should think here of Shakespeare as attempting to displace his own anxieties about assimilating or digesting these "massively overdetermined" characters onto his audience; cf. Freund's observation: "Homer and Chaucer are sufficiently rich fare to daunt the digestion of even as voracious a literary imagination as Shakespeare's; and one cannot overlook the rancid flavor of o'ereaten fragments, scraps and greasy relics dominating a text which abounds in food imagery" (21).

68. One way of understanding this turn is as a return to a pre-verbal state—to infancy (speechlessness)—as a concomitant of the infantile oral sadism and projective mechanisms described above in relation to satire: cf. Klein's view of infantile sadism (see n. 37, above).

69. Scarry, *The Body in Pain,* 14.

70. Gary Shapiro, "Jean-Luc Nancy and the Corpus of Philosophy" in *Thinking Bodies,* Juliet Flower MacCannell and Laura Zakarin, eds. (Stanford, CA: Stanford UP, 1994), 52-62, esp. 60. On the bodiliness of Montaigne's skepticism, see Victoria Kahn, *Rhetoric, Prudence, and Skepticism in the Renaissance* (Ithaca, NY: Cornell UP, 1985), 115-51.

71. Michel de Certeau, *Heterologies: Discourse on the Other,* trans. Brian Massumi (Minneapolis: U of Min-

nesota P, 1986), 72. My understanding of Montaigne's essay is indebted to de Certeau's powerful reading of it.

72. Montaigne, "Of the Cannibals" in *Essayes,* 2:32-54, esp. 226.

73. Montaigne, 2:51. On the slipperiness of language in the play, see in particular C.C. Barfoot, "*Troilus and Cressida:* 'Praise us as we are tasted,'" *SQ* 39 (1988): 45-57: "*Troilus and Cressida* leads us to the conclusion that we can no more trust our heroes, or even our anti-heroes, than we can trust our words" (55).

74. De Certeau, 73.

75. Montaigne, 2:51.

76. De Certeau, 75.

77. De Certeau, 75.

78. A.P. Rossiter, *Angel with Horns: Fifteen Lectures on Shakespeare,* ed. Graham Storey (London and New York: Longman, 1961), 151.

79. *The Iliad,* 3:148; Bullough, ed., 6:194. It is perhaps not surprising to find that the only character to escape his predetermined citational identity is Antenor, the figure of pure mimesis.

80. I thank Jeff Masten for this observation. *Troilus and Cressida,* as we have seen, includes several such denominative jokes—"Ilium" and "Ilion," "the Matter of Troy," and the scatological play with the name "Ajax" (a jakes or privy) come to mind.

81. Silence is not, however, invariably an honorable way out of the degradation of language in *Troilus and Cressida.* Ajax's silent treatment of his compatriots in Act 3 is held up to merciless ridicule by Thersites: "Why, a stalks up and down like a peacock, a stride and a stand; ruminates like an hostess that hath no arithmetic but her brain to set down her reckoning; bites his lip with a politic regard. . . . He's grown a very land-fish, languageless, a monster. . . . Why, he'll answer nobody: he professes not answering; speaking is for beggars" (3.3.250-53, 262-63, 267-68): clearly, not all languagelessness stems from an *ethic* of silence.

82. De Certeau, 73.

83. Charnes, 429.

84. Nietzsche, *Ecce Homo,* 311. Sir Francis Bacon uses the same phrase—"the art of silence"—in *De Augmentis,* where he relates the story of Zeno, who, having remained silent throughout an audience with a foreign ambassador, told the latter to "'Tell your king that you have found a man in Greece, who knew how to hold his tongue'" (Bacon, *The Works of Francis Bacon,* ed. James Spedding et al., 14 vols. [London: Longman, 1868-90], 5:31).

85. Nietzche, *Twilight of the Idols* in *The Portable Nietzsche,* 556.

POLITICS

Christopher Flannery (essay date 1981)

SOURCE: "*Troilus and Cressida:* Poetry or Philosophy?" in *Shakespeare as Political Thinker,* edited by John Alvis and Thomas G. West, Carolina Academic Press, 1981, pp. 145-56.

[*In the following essay, Flannery remarks that in* Troilus and Cressida *Shakespeare demonstrated his understanding of the politically subversive nature of poetry when he portrayed Achilles' insubordinate use of language.*]

There was an article in the Chinese Communist Party newspaper, the *People's Daily,* not long ago, which is helpful in understanding the relationship between poetry and politics with particular reference to Shakespeare.[1] In the article, which, of course, expresses the authoritative views of the party leadership, the music of Beethoven and Schubert was blacklisted because of their "bourgeois and capitalist mentality," and because their music did not "reflect the class spirit." Beethoven's Sonata No. 17 was compared to one of Shakespeare's plays which, the article proclaimed, "only serves to disseminate the filthy nature of the bourgeoisie." Acceptable music or poetry, the piece continued, would glorify "the Red sun of Chairman Mao Tse-Tung and the Chinese Communist Party in the heart of the Chinese People." Every form of art "must be an instrument of the class struggle."

No serious person would characterize the mind and poetic genius of Shakespeare as "bourgeois" in the sense of the *People's Daily* or in any sense. The Chinese leadership is right, however, in deeming Shakespeare's poetry a deadly enemy of the Chinese regime. The political order maintained in China depends for its very existence upon the inculcation, "in the heart of the Chinese people," of a certain understanding of man, a comprehensive understanding of his internal make-up and his external relations, with other men and the world around him. This understanding must govern the lives of Chinese citizens, telling them what is good and what is bad, what is noble and what is despicable. And it must speak to their hearts, to govern their actions. But Shakespeare's poetry also reflects a comprehensive view of the soul of man and man's place in the universe. And in Shakespeare's universe there is no proper place for the class struggle. He is, indeed, the poet of "nature," not the poet of "history." Let the poetry of nature spring up "in the heart of the Chinese people," and the march of history must come to a dramatic halt.

Every political regime corresponds in some way with a certain view of man's place in the universe; and all great poetry reflects a view of the whole of man's life. Both universes, or views of the whole, are conjured up "in the heart" of their audience, an audience that is naturally made up of citizens. It is here, in their respective views of the whole, conjured up in the hearts of citizens, that poetry and politics meet.

That Shakespeare had considered this relationship between poetry and politics, and in much the same terms, I will try to show in my discussion of Act I, Scene 3 of *Troilus and Cressida*. I will then speculate briefly on the relationship that exists between the poetry of *Troilus and Cressida* and the human or political realm to which it is addressed.

Act I, Scene 3 is of course our introduction to the warring Greeks, who are holding council. When we first meet the "princes orgillous," encamped upon the Dardan plain, they no longer have a stomach for the war. They have lost the courage and resolution which carried them to Troy in their famous cause. The first utterance of the Great Agamemnon seeks the cause of this malaise: "Princes, / What grief hath set the jaundice on your cheeks?" (I.iii. 1-2).[2]

It is fittingly the wise Ulysses who addresses Agamemnon's concern, discovering and expounding the nature and causes of that fever whereof all the Grecian power is sick. The nature and substance of this sickness is, of course, the famed "neglection of degree," degree "which is the ladder to all high designs" (102, 127). Ulysses' great speech on degree has rightly been a favorite subject of critical interpretation over the centuries. Its political philosophy, imagery, and metaphysics have been traced by respected scholars, with varying degrees of success, not only to the obvious Chaucer and Homer, but, persuasively, to the *Ecclesiastical Polity* of Richard Hooker, Sir Thomas Elyot's *The Governour,* to Boethius, and, perhaps more hopefully than convincingly, to Plato himself.

To prove that Shakespeare drew on many or all of these sources in writing this passage does not tell us anything conclusive about the *substance* of Shakespeare's thought, any more than Thomas Jefferson should be considered a strict Lockean because he drew on the *Treatises of Government* in writing the Declaration of Independence. We should always be hesitant to take any single speech as fully representative of Shakespeare's final considered opinion on a matter. But that the substance of this passage should in depth and comprehension be comparable to such ostensibly serious works by such ostensibly serious men should be an added reason to take the passage seriously, certainly a reason *not* to consider the passage mere "rant," as at least one worthy critic has done, or as a mere "epitome of contemporary commonplaces" as another critic views it.

I leave aside the speech proper for the moment to consider the immediately succeeding passages. In these, having already expounded the nature of the profound malady afflicting the Grecian warriors, Ulysses turns to the *causes* of this sickness. These passages are less often honored with the close scrutiny of the critic, as they are obviously of less universal significance than the famous speech on Degree. But they tell us a great deal about the meaning of the preceding speech and, at the same time, about Shakespeare's understanding of the relation of poetry to politics.

We learn in these passages that the source of the political sickness that has undermined the great endeavor of the Greeks, the cause of that neglection of degree that "by a pace goes backward in a purpose / It hath to climb" (128-129), is nothing other than poetry itself, specifically, dramatic poetry. As Ulysses tells us, Patroclus, "with ridiculous and awkward action / (Which, slanderer, he imitation calls)" (149-150), pageants the Greek chieftains for the amusement of the Great Achilles. And further, "Like a strutting player whose conceit / Lies in his hamstring" (153-154), Patroclus acts out the greatness of Agamemnon and the old age of venerable Nestor, with such ridicule as to make Achilles burst in pleasure of his spleen. And Patroclus' imitations, or slanders, are not limited to the greatness of Agamemnon or the old age of Nestor. He presents a comprehensive imitation of the individual souls and collective purposes of the Greek camp. Again, to quote Ulysses,

> All our abilities, gifts, natures, shapes,
> Severals and generals of grace exact,
> Achievements, plots, orders, preventions,
> Excitements to the field, or speech for truce,
> Success or loss, what is or is not, serves
> As stuff for these two to make paradoxes.
>
> (179-184)

Shakespeare's Patroclus, momentarily assuming the classic role of the dramatic poet, imitates the whole Greek universe for the pleasure of Achilles. The paradoxes of Patroclus, paradoxically, find great favor in the "opinion" of the Greek camp. In the words of the venerable Nestor, ". . . in imitation of these twain, / Who, . . . opinion crowns / With an imperial voice, many are infect" (185-187). The sickness of the whole Greek camp can thus be said to derive directly from an imitation of Patroclus' scandalous imitation. There is an epidemic of scurrilous poetry in the Greek camp, poetry in the service of the imperial voice of opinion, that so reflects on the natures, virtues and stations of the Greek chieftains that the political order that depends on reverence for them is falling into factions.

What is the nature of that poetry that, in Ulysses' mind, makes it so destructive of the "high designs" of the Greeks? He tells us in lines 197-210, where his disquisition on degree properly comes to an end. The contagious flaw inherent in the poetry that infects the Greek camp is that it esteems the virtues of Achilles as the highest of all virtues. Falling prey to the communicable charm of this poetry, the whole camp places the virtues of the warrior above all others. Specifically, the Greeks

> Count wisdom as no member of the war,
> . . . and esteem no act
> But that of hand. . . .
> So that, the ram that batters down the wall,
> For the great swing and rudeness of his poise,
> They place before his hand that made the engine,
> Or those that with the fineness of their souls
> By reason guide his execution.

It is because *this* degree is neglected, the degree placing the "still and mental parts"—reason—above mere physical power—"the ram that batters down the wall"—that the Grecian "enterprise is sick" or literally suffering a political disorder.

Every political community, like the Greek camp, establishes some "degree" by which men are distinguished from one another for the purposes of rule; when this degree is shaken, chaos or disorder threatens. But in this scene Shakespeare clearly has in mind the question: "What is it that makes any such degree 'stand in authentic place'?" The answer given by Ulysses is, the recognition of the pre-eminence of "the still and mental parts" of man to all others, particularly to "the great swing and rudeness" of an Achilles. If this measure of distinction among men—this "degree"—is neglected, the argument runs, man is reduced to the level of beasts, for there is no sure ground to distinguish him from them. But this is precisely what the poetry infecting the Grecian camp *does* deny, leading unconsciously but inevitably to the conclusion, so aptly put by old Nestor, that "Achilles' horse / Makes many Thetis' sons" (211-212). It is when *this* degree is suffocate, that that universal chaos ensues, wherein,

> . . . everything includes itself in power,
> Power into will, will into appetite
> And appetite, an universal wolf,
> So doubly seconded with will and power,
> Must make perforce an universal prey
> And last eat up himself.

(119-124)

The particular sickness of the Greek camp is the failure of the Greek warriors to recognize the "degree" which is the ordering principle of the Greek polity. Recognition ultimately must mean viewing the ordering principle of that particular polity as reflecting the order of the cosmos itself, or the will of the gods. The scurrilous poetry of Patroclus and his imitators undermines that view by making "paradoxes" of all that "is or is not" for the Greeks. So much Ulysses tells us. But Ulysses' analysis of the causes of this sickness does not provide the political "remedy" sought by Agamemnon. According to Ulysses, as I have said, the decisive distinction among men, the distinction according to which one man rightly may rule another, is founded on the degree of wisdom possessed, a distinction in "the still and mental parts" of men, in the "fineness of their souls." This is hardly less revolutionary than the scurril jests of Patroclus, to a political order in which the basis of "degrees" among men is the authority of the gods. But this is the final formal argument made by Ulysses to defend such an order against the self-consuming poetry which threatens chaos in the Greek camp and would reduce Achilles, and all the other Greeks, to the level of Achilles' horse, or worse.

Having allowed Ulysses to make this argument, Shakespeare immediately shows us, not by argument but by action, that the conclusion arrived at is somehow not politi-

cally applicable. Consider: Ulysses' famous argument has just been concluded pithily by old Nestor when the stage is interrupted by a trumpet blast. Enter Aeneas from Troy. Aeneas has a message for the Great Agamemnon and, after some courtly formalities, which are not without a point, he asks—speaking of course to Agamemnon himself—"How may / A stranger to those most imperial looks / Know them from eyes of other mortals?"

> *Agamemnon.* How?
> *Aeneas.* Ay.
> I ask that I might waken reverence,
> And on the cheek be ready with a blush
> Modest as morning when she coldly eyes
> The Youthful Phoebus.
> Which is that god in office, guiding men?
> Which is the high and mighty Agamemnon?

(I.iii.223-232)

The mocking tone of this address is not lost on Agamemnon, who turns to his fellow chieftains saying, "This Troyan scorns us, or the men of Troy / Are ceremonious courtiers" (233-234). Nor should the irony of Aeneas' query be lost on the audience. Imagine Aeneas on stage staring the high and mighty Agamemnon square in the face, speaking directly to him and asking "Where is the divine Agamemnon, how am I to distinguish him from other mere mortals?" And all the divine Agamemnon, for all his glory, can reply is a lame—if imperious—"How?" It is a good question, one which he never answers. Of course, there is *no recognizable mark* of nature or divinity to distinguish Agamemnon from the other mere mortals over whom his sceptre holds sway. There is no *apparent* natural or divine ground to justify a blush of reverence on Aeneas' cheek. In fact, it would seem that the most obvious, if not the most satisfactory, mark of distinction among men, especially in a warring camp of Greeks, is precisely the one recognized by the factious elements in the camp—the "act of hand," the great swing and rudeness of an Achilles. The implication of Aeneas' puzzlement, in light of the discourse which precedes it, is that Agamemnon's position as ruler over the Greeks, the degree that sets him apart from those over whom he rules, and before which men should blush with reverence, though it claims the authority of the gods, is, in fact, purely a product of convention. This convention has been called into question by the infectious poetry which raises the natural, if insufficient, claim of Achilles or of physical power in general.

But more to the point: Suppose that Agamemnon possessed that "fineness of soul" proclaimed by Ulysses to be the only natural basis of rule. Would this be any more apparent to Aeneas, or to any Greek or Trojan, than the supposed touch of divinity in Agamemnon, which is not visible at all? No. The fineness of their souls may be Ulysses' and nature's final measure of degrees among men; this final degree, standing in authentic place, may be the ladder to all high designs; neglection of this degree may by a pace go backward in any purpose it has to climb; perhaps Ulysses would go so far as to say that this degree may somehow be the soul of the political community; but this degree is no more acceptable than the divinity of Agamemnon as the actual ordering principle of the Greek camp, or of any other body politic.

To return then to the relation of poetry to politics. An imitation of a slanderous imitation of the political universe of the Greeks has undermined both the actual ordering principle or degree of the Grecian camp, which is the divine authority of Agamemnon, and the true or natural ordering principle among men, consisting in the degrees of fineness of their souls. The nexus in the relation of poetry to politics, as it is reflected in this scene, is the view of the political universe, of the degrees within individual souls and the corresponding degrees in the external relations among the citizens, implicit in both politics and poetry. Poetry infects the body politic when it introduces into it an alien and hostile substance, a view of the political universe which is incompatible with that view which breathes life into the civil authority and reverence into the citizens. The disease is introduced into the body politic through the over-indulgence of the "spleen" of the citizens and the natural susceptibility of the imperial voice of opinion. Perhaps Ulysses would say that it becomes mortal when it cuts the body politic off altogether from its soul.

It is impossible to think that Shakespeare could have been unconscious of the parallel between the "imitation" of the political universe of the Greek camp by Patroclus and his imitators, and that which he himself was preparing for his own audience. In fact, quite the opposite must be the case. Shakespeare could not but have been acutely conscious that his imitation of the Greek and Trojan universes bore an inherent relation to the individual souls and collective lives of his audience and to whatever "high designs" his audience might affect. Just as the scurrilous poetry of Patroclus played upon the spleen and opinion of the Greek camp, Shakespeare plays upon the passions and sentiments of his audience.

The best efforts of earnest scholars leave us still unsure of the more immediate "political" purposes of Shakespeare's *Troilus and Cressida,* that is, of those idiosyncrasies peculiar to Shakespeare's contemporary audience, to which some specific passages of the play might, in whole or in part, be addressed. And we are not much the worse for that. We do, however, know with certainty that *Troilus and Cressida* contains some immortal verse, poetry with a significance not just for Shakespeare's time or some transient purpose of that time, but for all time and for the highest purposes. It seems best, then, to understand the play as it is addressed to men of all times, particularly as it bears upon any high design affected by them. This is the Grecian camp to which the best of Shakespeare's poetry is ultimately addressed.

How then does *Troilus and Cressida* affect the high designs of this universal camp of Greeks? For there can be no doubt that opinion has crowned its author with an "imperial voice," and that with imitation of him, of one sort or another, many are infect. Do all our abilities, gifts, natures, shapes, achievements, plots, orders, and preventions merely serve as stuff for the great poet to make paradoxes? And if so, what does this mean for our Helens and our wars?

The effect of a given work of drama on its audience is inseparably linked with its form. To oversimplify, tragedy incites admiration and tears; comedy incites ridicule and laughter. From the first, however, publishers and critics have been hard pressed to say what form of drama *Troilus and Cressida* is. The textual history of the play foreshadows the centuries of critical confusion that have followed its first publication.

In the quarto edition of 1609 the title page refers to "The Historie" of Troilus and Cressida. But there was a second issue of this quarto text to which was added an epistle describing the play as a comedy. In the Folio of 1623, the play is titled "The Tragedie" of Troilus and Cressida. Yet it is not placed properly with the tragedies, but in a nameless position between the tragedies and the histories. Later critics have tried, with limited success, to resolve this dilemma by placing the play in a new category altogether, naming it a "problem play" or a "comical satire." Clearly, the play does not fit comfortably into any traditional dramatic mold.

It has been possible for this confusion over the form of the play to persist through the centuries because of the confusing dramatic effect the play has consistently had on each generation of its viewers and readers. It is the common, if not universal, reaction to *Troilus and Cressida,* to feel that it is dramatically fragmented, that it lacks dramatic unity and completeness, and that as a result it is somehow dissatisfying or perplexing, even unpleasant. We must give due attention to this common effect of the play on the sentiments of its audience. It is an injustice not infrequently inflicted upon poetry, to reduce it prosaically to its supposed elements or philosophic implications, and to call this "understanding" it. When one ceases to be sensible of the laughter and tears and the whole range of subtler human passions brought to life in good poetry, one ceases to be capable of understanding it. It may be as impossible to understand poetry by "transcending" its pathos as to understand moderation and courage while being a glutton and a coward.

The confusion of the sentiments which is the common reaction to this play occurs in part, I think, because the play arouses in the audience passions and sentiments the *grounds* for which are contradictory. Everyone has tasted the bitter ridicule of Thersites which flavors virtually every character and every action of the play. Where Thersites is not at work, there is Pandarus, or Shakespeare himself, directly casting upon Homer's heroes and their heroic endeavor a shadow of ridicule and disgust. From the midst of all this ridicule, however, rise numerous instances of apparently unsullied nobility for which the audience is irresistibly moved to admiration. Yet neither admiration nor ridicule is dramatically resolved into the other. To be sure, the play is in part a debunking of the Homeric heroes; but it also debunks the debunkers. Dramatically, at least, a certain portion of heroism is left intact, if in doubt, at the end. The minute textual support demanded of such an argument is impossible to give here. But I will offer one example of what I think to be the contradictory sentiments aroused and left in contradiction by the play. In Act IV, Scene 5, Ulysses identifies Troilus for Agamemnon. Drawing on a private account given him by Aeneas, Ulysses describes Troilus as

> . . . a true knight,
> Not yet mature, yet matchless, firm of word,
> Speaking in deeds and deedless in his tongue;
> Not soon provok'd, nor being provok'd, soon calm'd,
> His heart and hand both open and both free;
> For what he has, he gives; what thinks, he shews;
> Yet gives he not till judgment guide his bounty,
> Nor dignifies an impair thought with breath;
> Manly as Hector, but more dangerous. . . .

(96-104)

The description is not without its ironies, but in the main the audience is here made to sense—to believe—the integrity, magnanimity, courage, judgment, and self-control attributed to Troilus by Ulysses. We feel that this is generally an authoritative account of the true Troilus, and we admire his virtues. But the play began by showing us the changeable nature of Troilus, who at one moment could not fight upon the argument of Helen, and at the next was off to the wars with Aeneas. And it ends showing him rapt in revenge, which we know to be at once characteristic of him and one of the primary destructive forces in the play, in as much as it is "deaf as an adder" to the voice of reason. Ulysses' attributions are partly untrue and partly overshadowed by the tragic flaws of Troilus. In addition they are diluted by the railings of Thersites for whom Troilus is a doting young Trojan ass who is willing to risk his arm for a sleeve. Still, this expression of Troilus' virtues does not completely lose its force over the sentiments of the audience. Our admiration is not dispelled, it is only unsettled. There are many passages in the play which convey a similar sense of self-sufficient nobility or virtue. This sense is not destroyed, even by all the railings of Thersites. It lingers, even to the end, but with a sense of doubt as to the grounds on which it stands. The audience is made to harbor simultaneously in its breast, the mockery of the empty heroism of the play, and the distaste for that mockery because it seems to destroy the grounds for the true heroism that the play allows us to believe is possible. Troilus himself senses a like dichotomy of soul and desperately wishes to resolve it in favor of all that is beautiful and noble:

> . . . there is a credence in my heart,
> An esperance so obstinately strong
> That doth invert that test of eyes and ears,
> As if those organs had deceptious functions,
> Created only to calumniate.

(V.ii. 128-132)

It is doubtful whether he succeeds. It is also doubtful that the play would endorse his success even if he were to achieve it. The play offers little comfort for the innocently noble. But it offers *no* comfort for the mockers of that nobility, and in this view cannot be better summed up than in the words of a great modern poet:

> Come let us mock at the great . . .
> Come let us mock at the wise . . .
> Come let us mock at the good . . .
>
> Mock mockers after that
> That would not lift a hand maybe
> To help good, wise or great
> To bar that foul storm out, for we
> Traffic in mockery.

One only wonders whether the author of *Troilus and Cressida,* when speaking about the mockers of the good, great and wise, would have spoken in the first person.

This explanation of the nature of the dramatic confusion or perplexity of *Troilus and Cressida* does not depart much from common opinion on the matter. However, many have been inspired by their dramatic confusion to seek the *causes* of the incoherence or fragmentation experienced in the play. And here common opinion is on less sure ground. Some argue that the "incompleteness" or lack of conclusion that one senses in the play results from Shakespeare's having "lost interest" in the play before he finished it; others argue that he did not finish it at all, but left it to some less skilled hand. Some blame the dramatic incoherence of the play on the supposed fact that Shakespeare was rewriting a play already in existence; still others claim that the "material" on which Shakespeare drew (meaning the diverse accounts of the Troy legend) was impossible to weave together into a dramatic unity. All of these explanations are alike in seeking the cause of the apparent incoherence of the play elsewhere than in the art of the author. It is as impossible to disprove as to prove them. But there is another more interesting and more fruitful explanation suggested also by common opinion.

It is almost as frequently said that *Troilus and Cressida* is "intellectual," "analytic," or "philosophic," as it is said that it lacks dramatic unity or coherence. And surely there is something to this, if we recall the Greek council scene and Ulysses' degree speech, its Trojan counterpart in Act II, Scene 2, and the great dialogue between Ulysses and Achilles in Act III, Scene 3. I am not concerned with whether, as some have maintained, Ulysses' speech on degree is drawn from Plato's *Republic,* or the Achilles-Ulysses dialogue is taken directly or indirectly from *First Alcibiades,* or with Hector's anomalous reference to Aristotle. The point is that all these passages, while they play a part in the drama, also evince a concern for the truth of their respective arguments, independent of the effect of that truth on the action of the play. Indeed, it is worth noting that in each case the effect of the argument on the action of the play is emphatically nothing.

We have seen in the case of Ulysses that the conclusion of his argument on degree does not solve the political problem facing the Greeks. In the Trojan council, Hector no sooner concludes his exposition on political morality than he dismisses his apparently true conclusions, with an abruptness that cannot but give pause, and follows the dictates of an empty honor. Achilles is temporarily moved by the arguments of Ulysses in their dialogue (though it is well to remember that it is not the profundity of those arguments that moves Achilles, but their success in eliciting his envy of Ajax). But in the end the arguments come to nothing when challenged by Achilles' previous engagement with Polyxena. If the arguments of these passages do not contribute to the action of the play, they nonetheless affect our understanding of it. And by their very detachment from the action they encourage us to consider their truth for its own sake. In this sense, they seem to be more philosophic than poetic, at least if we can say that philosophy aims more at discovering the truth, poetry at moving the passions.

It does seem to be the special province of the poet to have a deep sense of the human passions and sentiments and of the reigning opinions of his times. He plays upon them deftly, with utmost precision, instinctively sensing what image, word or phrase, what nuance of character or juxtaposition of scene, will stir elation, hope, anger, dread, or sorrow in the breasts of his fellows. When he takes his eye off this anticipated reaction of his audience, his poetry may be expected to suffer. Though he may hit upon a phrase truer in itself, it will not strike home as truly as it might. Though he follows a flawless train of logic, he may *seem* to discourse inconsequentially—not, to be sure, to that god among men, the philosopher, but poetry, in its nature, is not written for an audience of philosophers. Indeed, deception, which, in being opposed to truth, must be presumed to be anathema to a philosopher, is the very "bark" and "convoy" of the poet, carrying him unerringly to his intended effect. One might say, then, that by keeping his eye on the truth of his arguments, Shakespeare took his eye off the anticipated reaction of his audience; by seeking consistency of thought, he sacrificed the *appearance* of consistency in the drama. Or, perhaps, in seeking to inform our understandings, he failed to direct our passions and sentiments. It seems to be a prerequisite of good poetry that the poet himself should *feel* the passions he imitates, as Shakespeare surely does in some of the passages of *Troilus and Cressida.* But overall the play manifests the detachment of its author from the passions portrayed in it, a detachment similar to that of the philosophic passages cited above from the drama of the play.

From this point of view the dramatic confusion of the play comes to light as an *accident* of Shakespeare's preoccupation with the truth of his arguments as opposed to the appearance of truth. But one might say instead that the dramatic inconsistencies of the play are consistent with the truths sought in it, and that the discordant passions portrayed in the play and excited by it in the audience are harmonized, if not dramatically, then intellectually or philosophically. Such a reading of the play as a whole is suggested in both the council scenes, where reason and truth respectively put the unruly passions of Greeks and Trojans in their proper perspective. But just as in these scenes reason and truth prove incapable of actually governing the unruly, destructive passions guiding the political fortunes of both Greeks and Trojans, so in the play as a whole these passions prevail over the drama.

Philosophy puts the passions in perspective, but reason and truth are also put in perspective by the drama. They cannot be depended upon to govern the political life of men. That life will continue to be governed by such passions and sentiments as we see still ruling at the end of the play, passions swayed perhaps by poetry, through the spleen and the susceptible opinion of men, but not, as the play repeatedly shows us, by the truths of the intellect addressed to the understanding. The fineness of men's souls, to the extent that this consists in that reason which apprehends the truths of the intellect, does not govern the fates of political communities.

Also from the point of view of reason, both laughter and tears, ridicule and admiration, may seem insufficient, incomplete responses to the political or human universe, each reflecting perhaps a part of the truth about it, but in that very fact necessarily being blind to the rest of the truth. From this point of view, poetry itself, whatever form it might take, whatever passions it may elicit, might be incapable of representing the human or political world in its fullness. Each attempt of poetry to do so must end in the arousal of one passion or another, the implicit grounds of which reflect at best a partial truth, and therefore a partial falsehood, about the soul of man and his place in the universe.

Troilus and Cressida displays the contradictory or chaotic tendencies—the insufficiencies—of the passions governing the political life of man, and of the passions associated with poetry of any form. It suggests a resolution of this chaos, but it appears to be a resolution that is neither political nor poetic.

Notes

1. Quoted in the *Los Angeles Times,* January 15, 1974.

2. All quotations are from *The Tragedy of Troilus and Cressida* (New Haven: Yale University Press, 1965).

SEXUALITY

Barbara Hodgdon (essay date 1990)

SOURCE: "He Do Cressida in Different Voices," in *English Literary Renaissance,* Vol. 20, No. 2, Spring, 1990, pp. 254-86.

[*In the following essay, Hodgdon refers to several different stage adaptations of* Troilus and Cressida *to demonstrate how the play was constructed to keep Cressida in particular, and, through her representation, Renaissance women in general, under male control.*]

When Trojan Hector visits the Greek camp, *Troilus and Cressida* represents his meeting with Achilles as an exchange of male gazes, powerful speaking looks through which each constructs, or attempts to deconstruct, the identity of the other:

> *Achilles.* Now, Hector, I have fed mine eyes on thee;
> I have with exact view perused thee, Hector,
> And quoted joint by joint. . . .
> *Hector.* Stand fair, I prithee; let me look on thee.
> *Achilles.* Behold thy fill.
> *Hector.*   Nay, I have done already.
> *Achilles.* Thou art too brief. I will the second time,
> As I would buy thee, view thee limb by limb.
> *Hector.* O, like a book of sport thou'lt read me o'er;
> But there's more in me than thou understand'st.
> Why dost thou so oppress me with thine eye?
>
> (4.5.230-40)[1]

Among many other references to sight and bodily display,[2] this passage stands as an especially blatant instance of how Shakespeare's playtext consistently turns the act of spectatorship into a convention which interrogates, theatrically, propositions of identity and value concerning male—as well as female—bodies. Here, too, Hector voices a question that Cressida never asks. For like Hector, males feed their eyes on her "with exact view," quote her joint by joint, position her as a marketable commodity, read her "like a book of sport." But whereas Achilles' look searches Hector's body for a point of entry—"whether there, or there, or there" (4.5.242)—in Cressida's case the "local wound" already has a name; the passage through which men can "kill" her (and themselves) is known. In her case, too, the interpretive gap to which Hector alludes between reading o'er and understanding has (always) already been foreclosed.

To be sure, the playtext, like Cressida herself, "holds off" the final revelation of that foreclosure, a strategy which does indeed demonstrate that, like Hector, there's more in her than either the men who oppress her with their gaze or even she herself understands.[3] Ultimately, however, to read her is to recognize that "'As false as Cressid'" constitutes an almost inescapable constant amidst the generalized slippage of identity and value apparent elsewhere—particularly as that slippage concerns the heroic male image—in what Rosalie Colie terms a "monumental mock'ry" of language and form which "attacked literature at its very source."[4] Moving beyond Colie's argument, Elizabeth Freund observes, "In no other play does [Shakespeare] take on the redoubtable task of refashioning, decomposing, vulgarizing, declassicizing precursor texts quite so canonical and powerful, and nowhere does he strip *both* his sources *and* his own text of their 'original' substance with such spirited iconoclasm."[5] True, but not, I think, completely true of Cressida. *Refashioned* she undoubtedly is, but not stripped of her originary substance. Indeed the very process of slippage between prestigious and popular forms which hol-

lows out idealist myth to reveal the social seems to *require* that she retain her "true" identity, be proved false (by nature), be devalued as (common) property.

The facile answer to this seeming paradox—that further debasing the one character already demonized by literary tradition is somewhat unnecessary—conveniently occludes social process, and within that, the positioning of bodies and voices through which the culture defines gender relations in absolutist (moral) terms.[6] Yet *Troilus and Cressida,* as Jonathan Dollimore, among others, points out, consistently calls such absolutist constructions into question.[7] That is another paradox, and one I want to examine further by focusing especially on the issue of Cressida's authenticity. Like Cressida, who sees herself as divided, my project has a double vision. For I want not only to read Shakespeare's playtext in order to raise questions concerning Renaissance representation and reception, but, more importantly, especially since *Troilus and Cressida*'s performance history is concentrated in the recent past,[8] to look at a number of twentieth-century performance texts, specific instances of cultural reproduction which arrange, or rearrange, social meaning as theatrical meaning.[9] And I want to begin, as both the Trojan War and *Troilus and Cressida* do, with the question of Helen.

Troilus and Cressida is historically positioned to dramatize the change in gender relations occurring in the shift from feudal courtly love, which accorded women political as well as erotic power, linking the one with the other, to precapitalist social relations and the consequent double subordination of women to their husbands as well as to the prince.[10] Shakespeare's playtext constructs that shift as a binary opposition between idolatry and adultery, a move which foregrounds the cultural contradictions and strains of the social process. For in the case of Helen, *Troilus and Cressida* folds the one into the other, collapsing both into a single term: Helen's position as a Trojan icon derives from her adultery, which gives her value in the public realm of male discourse. But whereas Helen's trajectory (at least as she is theorized by the Trojans[11]) seems to insist that idolatry can contain adultery, Cressida's, which parallels Helen's experientially, suggests just the opposite. Far from containing adultery (or, let's be plain, in Cressida's case, faithlessness), idolatry precisely expresses and focuses it. In this sense, Cressida can be recognized as a transhistorically stable sign of an ideological process in conflict with itself. Indeed, *Troilus and Cressida,* which "turns" Cressida from idealized to fallen woman, may be viewed as a "set-up," for she begins by (perhaps) flirtatiously laughing at and with the jokes of a man who, through his mediatory role as a bawd, poses a sexual threat to her, and she ends by being positioned as the object of the gaze of several males who together reconstruct her as a whore. Literally as well as figuratively, she occupies the place that Freud assigned to women in the structure of the obscene joke: the place of the object between several male subjects.[12] In this scheme, which wrests power from the woman, in particular the power accruing to both body and voice, the men (and by association, male spectators) have the last laugh, thereby defusing not only the threat of woman's infidelity but also her potential to subvert patriarchal authority by transgressing its laws. In addition, of course, as an object of exchange within male subjectivity, the woman performs useful (patriarchal) cultural work by ratifying and reinforcing the very homosocial bonds that exclude her.[13]

Such a schematic outline of its gender economy offers an extremely attractive synoptic view of Shakespeare's playtext—attractive, that is, for male spectators. Certainly, as my earlier quotation suggests, *Troilus and Cressida* repeatedly calls attention to male looking relations. Troilus is led by "eyes and ears" (2.2.63); Ulysses speaks of how the "present eye praises the present object" (3.3.180); men search for their own reflections in each other's eyes (3.3.99). Obsessed as they are with their own looks and with recognizing (or pretending not to recognize) one another, their gazes become commodified as a source of knowledge, most especially so once they are turned on women, who are made accountable to them. As in classical Hollywood cinema, such relentless focus on male surveillance works to endorse similar mechanisms in a male spectator and so privileges the male gaze as well as the male project called the play, offering males particular, and particularly gendered specular competence, or what Laura Mulvey has called "visual pleasure."[14] But what of a female spectator? To view a spectacle which neatly accounts for her own position and attempts to frame her as false by nature surely constitutes an exercise in restrictive vision. For her, "visual pleasure" exists primarily in terms of intellectual mastery—in recognizing, to paraphrase Stephen Greenblatt, that there is pleasure, no end of pleasure, only not for a female spectator.[15]

This statement, however, assumes a point of view consistent with that of a late twentieth-century female spectator. And this in turn raises several important questions. Would a female spectator in the Renaissance share a similar outlook? And to what extent is it possible to historicize the gendered gaze? Given only negative or, at best, indeterminate evidence about *Troilus and Cressida*'s early seventeenth-century performance history, especially as to whether it was performed in public as well as private playhouses,[16] addressing the first question points toward the second, and any precise answers concerning audience positions and responses can only be broadly sketched in from existing documents, none of which were written by women.[17] Certainly women made up a definitely recognizable segment of the audience in the public theaters, but it is difficult to mark any decisive shifts in the composition of audiences in the private theaters around the turn of the century.[18] What can be said, however, is that female spectators, like males, spanned the social hierarchy to include representatives of all classes—apple-wives, fish-wives, citizens' wives, ladies and whores—and that, as Andrew Gurr cautiously notes, "their reasons for playgoing were most open to question and most subject to attack," primarily from anti-theatrical Puritan commentators. Home was the proper habitat for a respectable woman who, if she went to the theater at all, went with a male companion (preferably her husband); if alone, she could be considered, if not treated as, a whore. Indeed, even by appearing at the theater, a woman risked, with such public display, making a spectacle of herself.[19]

Although the assumption that women attended the theater for harlotry or adultery (rather than, say, to watch an all-male spectacle) begins to wane about 1600, shortly before *Troilus and Cressida* would have been staged, fresh accusations took its place. As Jonson and his fellow theater poets began to rail against unlearned spectators who came to the theater only to see sights, not to listen to and be edified by verse, such complaints were leveled specifically against women's "ignorant eyes."[20] Beaumont's *The Knight of the Burning Pestle* (1607) describes, in Nell, the Citizen-Grocer's wife, just such a spectator, one who, as a representative of a steadily growing middle-class audience fast becoming central to the theater's commercial enterprise, condenses many of the supposed attributes of playgoing women. Somewhat "virtuous" in that she has been pleading with George for a year to take her to the theater, her taste runs to romance, particularly to chivalric wandering knights, and particularly when played by Ralph, her husband's apprentice. From her seat on the stage among the gentlemen, a position which mocks her social pretensions, she reads all she sees with perfect comic literalness. Yet, however exaggerated by Beaumont's genial satire against the values of citizens' culture (as opposed to those of aristocratic playgoers) and their desire to see old scenes (primarily those acted in the public theater) replayed on the Blackfriars' stage, the case of Nell reveals one woman's power to alter the staged representation to suit her pleasures.

Apparently Nell was not alone. In the early decades of the century, the woman playgoer grew increasingly vocal about "see[ing] her shadow there"[21] in representative stereotypes—the shrew, the lusty widow, the country wench, the Amazon, the chaste wife or virgin, the adulteress, the ambitious female. Invited, on the one hand, to assent to such fictions being inscribed on their bodies, on the other, women were, as Jean Howard argues, "positioned as consumers, critics, spectators, and spectacles."[22] As early as 1600, the epilogue of Dekker's *Satiromastix,* by recanting the opinions of women expressed in the playtext, records some anxiety about pleasing female spectators, a trend which continues to accelerate throughout the early decades of the new century.[23] Although it was not until the late 1620s and early 1630s that stage plays show further signs of catering specifically to women's tastes, women spectators may have been partially responsible for the radical change, around 1610, in the drama's misogynistic portrayal of women.[24] If indeed, as Louis Montrose and others have observed,[25] the theater functioned as an agent of cultural transformation, the women who attended it seem to have played some part in creating new subject positions, perhaps even in remapping the representation of gender relations to redirect, and recirculate, the exchange of (visual) pleasure.

This brief history suggests that *Troilus and Cressida* is ideally suited to bring into sharp focus, for female spectators, the contradictions embodied in these heavily gendered looking relations. For Shakespeare's playtext rather precisely analogizes and reproduces in its theater of spectacle the prevalent male anxieties about their exclusive ownership of women, about woman's value and "place." In addition, it also analogizes the high visibility of women playgoers who were described, looked upon, "quoted joint by joint," classified, noted, and demonized by male observers. Even in the absence of women's own accounts of their material conditions, it would seem reasonable to assume that perhaps they saw themselves as owners of a potentially transgressive look and, simultaneously, as subject to the male gaze. It is precisely the relative historicity of these looking relations which I wish to investigate further.

In this regard, I see a useful connection between the models generated by recent feminist film theory, which assign gender to as well as psychoanalyze the relations between spectacle and gaze, and Katherine Maus's provocative conjectures about the relations between an eroticized Renaissance spectacle construed, by antitheatrical commentators, as a "whorish female" and the jealous male's scopic project as one figure for the Renaissance spectator "at his most agonizingly involved and his most scandalously marginalized."[26] Not only is a double standard of spectatorship that positions the male as perceiving subject and the female as perceived object common to both, but the deeply gendered split in subjectivity which both take as a given makes such modes of analysis entirely appropriate to examining looking relations in *Troilus and Cressida.* Indeed, such notions are peculiarly suited both to reading a playtext which positions women as unable to escape their transhistorical citations[27] and to examining its performance texts, which tend to re-produce, and thus re-inscribe, the ideological power of those citations on women's bodies. However, it is equally important to acknowledge at the outset the limitations of both Freudian and Lacanian theory, which, in presupposing the dominance of the male gaze, tend to endow it with a universal, even ahistorical, power. For that reason, I want to pursue a slightly different investigation of spectatorly desire by approaching issues of gender in performance not exclusively through an analysis of the male gaze but, rather, by re-examining the economy of exchange between performer and spectator in performance.[28] In this partial reading, my focus rests on Cressida's gaze, and the spectatorly gazes at her, both on the stage and from the audience, in two scenes: her first and last appearances. What I propose constitutes a somewhat subversive project which, by attempting to fix an eye on how Cressida is constructed, not only demystifies her ideological function but (potentially) diminishes the male pleasure of the text. What remains to be seen is whether destabilizing, if not dismantling, the hegemony of the male gaze can disclose some alteration in the looking relations—even, perhaps, some fissures along the gendered sightlines—that mark *Troilus and Cressida*'s recent cultural historicity.

II

Everything about Cressida's first appearance calls attention to sight, and beyond that, to the problematics of recognition and identity. Also at issue are the ownership of the gaze: whether it belongs to a knowing or unknowing spectator; whether these two positions are similar or different; and what exactly is being seen, and by whom. Cressida's opening words—"Who were those went by?"—together with Alexander's response—"Queen Hecuba and Helen" (1.2.1-2)—focus these concerns rather precisely. Her question invites reading her as unknowing—almost as though she is a stranger in Troy—and as a curious onlooker who may be searching for someone. Spectators in the audience, of course, are also strangers to this particular representation of Troy, lookers-on who (presumably) recognize that Troilus and Aeneas, not Hecuba and Helen, have just gone by. A number of puzzles, some of which impinge more specifically on Renaissance than on present-day representation, press into this exchange. For Alexander's reply not only invites offstage spectators to position Cressida in relation to Priam's queen (who never appears elsewhere) as well as to Helen (who does, but is never seen with Cressida) but calls attention to the possibility of misreading one gender for another. Why call into question either the possible (if highly improbable) theatrical doubling of warriors and women, or the convention of boy actors playing female roles, or both, just as Cressida is introduced? Although elsewhere, especially in *As You Like It* and *Antony and Cleopatra,* Shakespearean heroines undo, or risk undoing, their gender,[29] these instances occur well after the illusion has (presumably) taken hold. In Rosalind's case, it happens at the very point where the play, which rests on fictions of gender-bending, is about to dissolve. One answer, I think, points directly to Shakespeare's own source-bending. For rather than representing, as Chaucer does, Cressida's first sight of Troilus as a solitary spectacle—a twice-repeated pass-by on horseback (at a distance) arranged by Pandar (II. 1247-74)—Shakespeare's playtext rewrites and regenders a scene from *The Iliad.* There, in a similar spectacle of value, Priam asks Helen to tell him who the *Greek* warriors are; and in describing their attributes she identifies her own ambivalent, tenuous position in relation to Paris. By transforming these looking relations, *Troilus and Cressida* not only opens up a space for interrogating the gendered gaze but situates the scene, and Cressida's presence within it, as a potential site of gender anxiety.

Initially, this section of the scene positions Cressida as only slightly different from those who, as in Alexander's description of Ajax, are "all eyes and no sight" (1.2.30-31). If at the first the playtext denies her knowing gaze, however, later on as she and Pandarus watch the returning Trojan warriors, her gaze is, like Helen's in *The Iliad,* not only privileged but given potential power and agency. Although it is Pandarus who notices Aeneas, the first to enter, Cressida's language calls up the rest of the spectacle—a detail obvious in both Quarto and Folio but masked by edited texts which, in repositioning the stage directions so that it is Pandarus' words that "bring on" most of the Trojans, are complicit with subsuming her gaze in his.[30] But although Pandarus certainly attempts to direct her gaze, and although his running commentary seems more knowing than her questions, the play-text also suggests that she may not be "looking his way," for she is not only the first to see but clearly owns her own gaze. Indeed, it is this ability to know a man if "[she] ever saw him before and knew him" (1.2.66) which the playtext will eventually turn on her, deprivileging her gaze once she becomes looked upon, a spectacle not a spectator, no longer a subject but subjected to the male gaze. Throughout, Cressida's desire for secrecy—"Speak not so loud" (187)—as well as her punning "watch"-fulness (264-75) mask from Pandar how she reads what she sees; only when she is alone, in her sonnet-soliloquy, does she speak her looks, reveal that she is a woman who knows too much.

If the sudden shift in the gender of the spectacle—from a mass of male bodies to a single female body—works to subject Cressida to the gaze of offstage spectators, the position of her soliloquy as well as its rhetorical strategies contradict that subjection. Both accord her considerable power. For she not only allies herself with narrative process and determines her agency within it but appropriates a male discourse and undermines its idealizing strategies. Consider the last ten lines of this oddly deviant, even transgressive, sonnet:

> Women are angels, wooing:
> Things won are done; joy's soul lies in the doing.
> That she belov'd knows naught that knows not this:
> Men prize the thing ungain'd more than it is.
> That she was never yet that ever knew
> Love got so sweet as when desire did sue.
> Therefore this maxim out of love I teach:
> "Achievement is command; ungain'd, beseech."
> That though my heart's contents firm love doth bear,[31]
> Nothing of that shall from mine eyes appear.
>
> (291-300)

Throughout, Cressida's statements collapse toward emblematic summary, a feature which the rhyme scheme, with its repetitive coupleting, supports. Together with lines 296 and 298, lines 290-91 might stand as a gloss on Sonnet 129, "Th' expense of spirit in a waste of shame," one often evoked (especially by moralistic critics) to express *Troilus and Cressida*'s "essence."[32] Like that sonnet, Cressida's elides the speaking subject, which sets up a tension between a male agent (syntactically invisible but everywhere there); woman as object ("things," "thing," "it"); and the more specifically gendered subjects of following statements ("that she," "men," and "I"). In accounting for her own (constructed) position, Cressida hollows out sonnet discourse, destabilizes its terms, and exposes its contradictions, a stance that her "out of love" neatly condenses. In re-voicing the language praising women's erotic and political power, Cressida redoes it in terms of what it has become: a discourse of oppression.[33] Finally, as she expresses her own strategy in terms of vision, of an unreadable gaze, she acknowledges the tyranny

of the male gaze which, in decoding her looks and her look, can command her and so take away the power of her voice as well as her gaze.

Whereas Shakespeare's playtext endows Cressida, at this point, with a knowledge of gendered looking relations and with a carefully calculated glance, what it remains silent about—almost Cressida-like—is the worth of the public spectacle Cressida and Pandarus see. For aside from the "Prologue arm'd . . . , suited in like conditions as our argument" (*Pro.*, 23-25), the playtext remains open on this point, except perhaps to suggest, by representing six instead of nine worthies, that their diminished number (as well as the addition of "common soldiers") signals diminished worth. Such representation constitutes textual as well as generic politics: the spectacle of the returning heroes determines at least one sign of the value a particular performance text puts on the war action. Further, the stage directions (even when editorialized to include "and passes over" following each hero's entrance) allow for a possibly complex range of looking relations. Although Cressida's and Pandarus' dialogue suggests that the men may simply pass by, unaware of being seen by either onstage or offstage spectators, nothing in the playtext restricts their look. Moreover, although Cressida wishes to remain unnoticed (especially, it would seem, by Troilus [186; 233]), nothing *specifically* prevents the Trojans from looking her way or from acknowledging her presence as well as Pandar's. What is at issue here involves more than the obvious: the question of whether Cressida, already defined in relation to a male tableau, is further constructed by their gazes. For a particular looking dynamic can signal not only a *Troilus and Cressida*'s attitude toward male heroism but also its "turn" on Cressida and on its originary sources as well as toward locating itself within a particular genre. Indeed, the sexual politics of theatrical representation works to insert Cressida within a double frame, one erected by choices of mise-en-scène, the other by the discourse of a predominantly male interpretive community of reviewers.

Ben Iden Payne's 1936 performance text for the Shakespeare Memorial Theatre, for instance, suited itself in doublet and hose, with Cressida and Helen in panniered farthingales and feathered hats, as homage to continuing the tradition of William Poel's earlier (1913) Elizabethan revival, which sought to make topical allusions (particularly those to Essex) available.[34] Anxious to make all perfectly clear, Iden Payne includes Queen Hecuba and Helen and so explains Cressida's opening query to Alexander; furthermore, a communal spectacle becomes the scene's centerpiece. Each hero crosses the stage accompanied by supers; a group of citizens and "Three Girls" call out his name and cheer him; Helenus (the "priest") blesses the citizens as he passes. As though reading the scene through Chaucer, Iden Payne cuts all the language except for Pandarus' praise of Troilus, who, unlike the others, peeps out through a lancet window in the set's upper stage just before he enters, catching sight of Cressida and Pandarus. The three girls (apparently Troilus-groupies) flock to him; he turns toward Cressida and Pandarus and salutes smartly; Cressida curtseys to him. But Iden Payne's attempt to show an Elizabethan hero's progress reads more like the military homecoming parades of fairly recent memory; reviewers not only caught the anachronism but mourned the lack of classical costumes.[35] More significantly, the fawning women invite spectators both to read their hero worship and to see Cressida's curtsey within a context that already anticipates her subjection to an attractively breeched leg. Further, cutting Cressida's language takes away her voice, so that only her body language (which Ulysses later uses to demonize her [4.5.54-63]) and what one reviewer called her "cozening eyes"[36] code her presence. But when this Cressida did speak, she "dissimulated prettily, and . . . gave the giddy jilt a lisp, . . . a suggestion of levity and insincerity" that hinted at "her coming demoralization."[37] Moreover, the prompt copy, which rephrases her axiomatic "Achievement is command" as "Achieved men us command" and further underscores the line with music, provides yet another telltale sign of a transhistorical assumption, which locks a female spectator into an imaginary and illusory identification with Cressida, who is made to speak for, as well as to, all women.

If Iden Payne's scene absorbs Cressida's presence within the male spectacle and shows her gaze subservient to Troilus, Glen Byam Shaw's 1954 performance text, also for the Shakespeare Memorial Theatre,[38] focuses more exclusively on the difference between watchers and watched. Cressida and Pandarus stand high on Troy's massive mid-stage walls, a vantage point from which they look down on the entrances of the warriors, who pass beneath them, too self-absorbed to notice they are being observed. Their display seems directed to the offstage, not the onstage, audience; and their gestures—handing a helmet or gloves to an attendant servant, ordering a sentinel to the walls with a nod—reproduce those of aristocratic officers welcomed home by competent servants, actions which generate a communal sense of an exclusively upper-class wartime community and construct Cressida and Pandarus as outsiders commenting on a serious male ritual. In Shaw's *Troilus and Cressida,* all eyes focus on this display of male bodies: successful, assured, victorious, the idealized image of England's own recently returned soldiers.

Except perhaps for some eyes, who will surely notice Cressida's shimmering white "Grecian nightgown," and who, like W.A. Darlington, will "promptly recognize [her] for what she [is]," or who will see "her wanton spirits looking out 'at every joint and motive in her body.'"[39] For in this first appearance as elsewhere, Cressida's costume will permit spectators to read her body in relation to other bodies; and the alternate tradition of costuming *Troilus and Cressida* in period is just as likely to construct her as a product of male desire and male artistic practice by dressing her in flowing Attic robes which, like the drapery on any classical Venus, permits spectators not just to imagine but to see the contours of her body. Shaw's

performance text as well as the 1960 Peter Hall-John Barton and the 1976 Barton-Barry Kyle *Troilus and Cressida*s (both for the Royal Shakespeare Company) make precisely such choices.[40] In the 1960 "sand pit" production (part of a season of comedies), Cressida's gown, slit in front to the hip, undulates with her as she enters from upstage and crosses the large central circle of sand in a lazy, barefooted walk, sinking into it at every step: "a wisp of rippling carnality," according to Bernard Levin.[41] Whether she is positioned at a distance from the returning heroes, as in the 1976 Barton-Kyle performance text, where Cressida and Pandarus occupy a downstage-right balcony, or as in Terry Hands's 1981 bitterly black farce, quite close to the spectacle, such a Cressida constitutes a potentially fetishized icon, coded by conventional tropes of seduction addressed particularly to a male spectator. Moreover, when Pandarus is also costumed in a long flowingly "feminine" robe, as in each of these performance texts except for Iden Payne's, the scene is even more deeply gendered by opposing male and female codes of dress.

While in each of these versions, mise-en-scène and blocking make representational choices that give heroic value to the male spectacle, Terry Hands's 1981 Royal Shakespeare Company performance text reads the Trojans through Thersites' eyes.[42] Hands's Cressida, barefoot and wearing an ankle-length orange chiffon shift, sits with a nanny-like Pandarus (who carries a small parasol as well as a tiny basket filled with candies, which he shares with Cressida) on soft cushions placed on a siege machine that stands against Troy's blackened walls. Each entering hero crosses directly in front of the watchers, who see a parade of swaggering, self-important peacocks enacting cameo parodies of themselves. Aeneas drinks from an offered cup; Antenor does so as well but spits the drink out; a King Kong-like Hector poses and flexes his muscles, an about-to-go-to-seed footballer who draws audience laughter; Paris' servant hands him a mirror in which he rearranges his hair; Helenus limps in on a crutch ("Can Helenus fight, uncle?" [225]). When Troilus finally arrives, Pandarus grabs his hand and then pulls Cressida toward him, anticipating their later joining together (3.2). Troilus draws his (unbloodied) sword at Pandarus' urging, bending down so that Cressida can see the "hacks" on his helmet; imitating Ophelia's description of Hamlet leaving her closet, he exits backward, gazing at Cressida. In what Michael Billington aptly called "a cynic's *Iliad,*"[43] this mock-heroic spectacle deprives Cressida of at least some of the potential power of her gaze by co-opting that, at scene's end, for Troilus. Unlike the previous versions, Hands's does not represent a doubled spectacle which traces out gendered looking relations and thus marks the distinction between private and public spheres. Rather, only the male spectacle "counts," and because the heroes wittingly and witlessly showcase themselves as comic-opera buffoons, each displaying a quirky stereotype of male attributes, their masquerade offers a debased pageant which not only includes, and absorbs, its onstage spectators but increases the distance between performers and audience, displacing any potential emotional investment with ridicule. Later on, Hands stages Helen's only appearance as an orgy, which Michael Coveney described as "something like Zsa Zsa Gabor playing Dietrich in a camp floor show conceived by Giradoux,"[44] a not entirely different kind of spectator sport. As for the Cressida? According to another reviewer, she "establishe[s] herself from the start as that most dangerous commodity, a knowing and flirtatious virgin."[45]

In one or more features, each of these performance texts uses the openness of Shakespeare's playtext in order to exploit or disempower Cressida. While the playtext suggests that, as a relatively silent spectator, Cressida occupies a potentially dominant position, theatrical practice consistently limits and circumscribes her, perpetuating the structures of male desire and male looking which, as Peggy Phelan observes, "infect and inform all forms of representation."[46] Such practice constitutes a kind of early warning system, eagerly complicit with the demonizing literary tradition, with some form of contemporary cultural gender stereotyping, or with both. To be sure, at least one reviewer of each production carped at such anticipatory signals to note, for example, that "at times Shakespeare defeated [a "shallow" or "wanton" or "sensual" Cressida] by giving her words to say which she could not deliver other than sincerely."[47] Yet most reviewers also exhibited a certain relish at seeing Ulysses' opinion of Cressida come true. What seems to be operating here is a kind of inherited "cultural capital" which constitutes a particular mode of perception as essential, and therefore natural.[48] As Pierre Bourdieu observes, "The 'eye' is a product of history reproduced by education."[49] And in the case of these performance texts of *Troilus and Cressida,* such an "educated" vision depends on recognizing the "legitimacy" of the stories told of Cressida by Chaucer as well as Shakespeare. At least for one interpretive community, it is not simply a question of what is worth being seen but of the right way to see it.

Howard Davies' 1985 performance text for the Royal Shakespeare Company, however, goes against the grain of such inherited looking relations to redraw the map of Shakespeare's playtext. Davies' Brechtian project to recuperate *Troilus and Cressida* for nineteenth-century history began by inviting the company to do historical research on the period by assigning particular topics (which could be negotiated) to each cast member.[50] Although certainly not original to Davies, since both the 1968 and 1976 RSC productions were positioned within the context of Vietnam, his idea was to make connections between the attitudes available in the playtext and those of late nineteenth-century as well as late twentieth-century culture. One result was to re-envision Cressida, played by Juliet Stevenson, as a New Woman and so to read her as an historical subject.[51] Among several reviewers, Irving Wardle praised Stevenson's "feminist" Cressida by observing that she "reclaims a part for which some actresses apologize and anchors it in the facts of human behavior."[52] Yet a greater number leveled complaints against a Cressida who situates herself in history and thus counters the

familiar universalist-essentialist image. To quote several reviewers: "she has little of the mercurial inconstancy necessary for Cressida"; "the production showed only narrow-minded political anger where what was needed was mockery and a cosmic disgust for mankind"; and "it may be hard cheese on the RSC feminist puritans, but Shakespeare is writing about falsity and sexual wantonness, not rape."[53] Precisely because Davies' performance text questions the gendered economy of inherited looking capital and renders it transgressive, it offers a particular kind of "limit-text." Although some initial signs of this transgression appear earlier, they are most strikingly apparent in Cressida's first appearance, in which looking relations privilege not the male spectacle but the lookers-on.

Set in turn-of-the-century Crimea, Davies' *Troilus and Cressida* was housed within an abandoned, once-elegant mansion, shuttered, draped with dust sheets and no longer serving its proper function—a space reminiscent of a line from John Osborne's *The Entertainer:* "Don't clap too hard; it's an old building." In this "room with a view," Cressida and Pandarus stand far downstage and look out at the audience through binoculars, passing the pair of glasses back and forth. Cressida notices Troilus without the binoculars, so that when an embarrassed Pandarus finally does recognize the "sneaking fellow," she falls on her back laughing. By so turning her deliberate misrecognition of Troilus into a joke on Pandarus, she retains control of her own gaze, which not only singles out that part of the (unseen) spectacle that alone has meaning for her but privileges her look as more acute than Pandarus'. Moreover, her long-sleeved, sash-waisted, modest V-neck costume of rather stiff taffeta contributes to reading her as a buttoned-up Victorian who, within the privacy of her soliloquy, finally assesses her position ("Things won are done") somewhat regretfully ("Men prize the thing ungained more than it is") yet also, as a soft tune from the player piano covers her exit, remains sure of her ability to turn that to her own advantage. In denying an onstage representation of the returning heroes, Davies' performance text removes any opportunity at this point for an offstage audience to judge the "heroic" action. But by allowing neither the male spectacle nor the male gaze to dominate, his staging (potentially) undermines both and so overturns the conventions of representation to read presence as absence. As Cressida and Pandarus look out at the offstage spectators, this *Troilus and Cressida* sets up a mirroring or doubling process which calls attention to the act of spectatorship, locating its power and value as decidedly female. Certainly, given *Troilus and Cressida*'s misogynistic politics of gender, such a potentially disruptive gaze decidedly transforms the economy of looking relations to accord at least some visual pleasure to a female spectator. To the extent that it empowers Cressida's look, Davies' staging raises the question of whether her gaze can perhaps undermine patriarchal law or can possibly turn that law on the male spectator, secure with his own identity. But that question opens up further contradictions, for it has a short-term as well as a long-term answer, both of which clearly measure the cost of women's (historical) aversion.

III

Cressida's first appearance in Shakespeare's playtext and in Davies' performance text offers a female viewer particular specular competency. Both endow her look with difference (as well as *différance*) and permit her to stand apart from, if not completely outside, what Raymond Bellour calls the "place assigned to her by the logic of masculine desire."[54] Potentially, such "privilege" includes body as well as voice, a probability Davies' representational strategies bring into sharp focus, especially when compared to those of the earlier performance texts which (in varying degrees) stress Cressida's "to-be-looked-at-ness" and which limit (primarily through cuts) her voice. To the extent that these looking relations afford Cressida relative independence from the hegemony of the male gaze, they also free a female spectator's look, according to Mulvey by way of Brecht, "into dialectics."[55] The same is not true, however, of Cressida's final scene, the encounter with Diomedes observed by Troilus, Ulysses, and Thersites (5.2), where Cressida becomes doubly, even triply, specularized, a strategy which stigmatizes her worth as well as circumscribes and contains her voice and body. Yet the very heavy-handedness of the frames in which she is set also reveals the considerable anxiety that lies behind such misogyny.

As with Cressida's first view of Troilus, Chaucer positions him as a solitary observer of the meeting with Diomedes. But, by adding Ulysses and Thersites, Shakespeare's playtext not only calls attention to but overdetermines the male gaze. Further, on the two occasions when Cressida whispers to Diomedes (5.2.7; 34), neither onstage nor offstage spectators can hear what she says. At both points, however, Troilus, Ulysses, and Thersites speak her body and read it, in Thersites' words, as "secretly open" (24). For a female spectator, Cressida's voiceless text, deeply triangulated and elaborately mediated by a series of male gazes, may seem to flood this scene. But all that can literally be heard is the playtext's ability to "speak the father" in a weave of voices and looks which literalizes the gap Chaucer's text sets up between narrator and tale in his ambiguously ironic "men saye." To watch such a spectacle invites a female spectator to occupy one of two traditionally assigned viewing positions—those Tania Modleski recognizes as "the place of the female masochist, identifying with the woman as victim, or the place of the 'transvestite,' identifying with the active male hero."[56] But in this case, even the latter position is somewhat compromised, since the act of looking not only immobilizes Troilus in self-doubt ("I will not be myself" [63]) but threatens to destabilize his identity as well as Cressida's. Nowhere else in *Troilus and Cressida* do looking relations so clearly articulate the contradictory status of the female spectator as one who is and is not herself, a situation which not incidentally analogizes the fluid gender status of the original boy actor of Cressida's part. Moreover, any at-tempt to construct an alternative viewing position, and thus to escape from this highly structured economy of looking relations, also rather precisely analogizes the problem faced by feminist theory: that of constructing an Archimedean point from which to speak that is not already interpellated within Freudian or Lacanian discourse. Yet any such attempt creates an additional double bind. For to take up such a position involves refusing the (exclusively male) pleasure of the text[57] which, in staging the construction of "faithless woman," recuperates and rehearses the priorities of neo-chivalric culture.

These priorities are condensed, even emblematized, in the way the scene handles and dispenses with the threats woman poses to the ideologies sustaining that culture. With Cressida quite literally in the hands of the Greeks, she is ideally positioned to repeat (or revenge) Helen's story; she can become the agent linking Troilus with Menelaus. Also potentially dangerous because of her ability to make Troilus (as he himself claims) "weaker than a woman's tear" (1.1.9), thus feminizing his (naturally?) warlike nature,[58] Cressida becomes a pawn in *Troilus and Cressida*'s curiously contradictory logic of male valuation. For this scene shows Greek and Trojan, once drawn into war by their agreement that Helen is worth fighting for, *united*—not by their attitudes toward one another but by their gaze toward, and eventual demonization of, Cressida. Appropriately, one central element in this scene is a hand property, Troilus' sleeve, which Cressida herself calls to Diomed's attention: "You look upon that sleeve" (69). And it is through the handling—both woman-handling and man-handling—of this property that Shakespeare's playtext signifies Cressida's double transgression and inscribes it on her body.[59] Not only does it become a shorthand representation of the sexual encounter which is not (and cannot) be represented, but it also signifies Cressida's attempt, and ensuing failure, to manipulate correctly an emblem of the male chivalric system. In some sense the *un*-"virtuous fight" between Cressida and Diomedes for the sleeve constitutes a quarrel over Troilus' ownership: it seems to be the worth of that object rather than the ownership of Cressida (which Diomedes assumes that he has) which attracts him. As one of several shifting signifiers of value, among them Cressida's glove and the armor with the putrified core (5.8.1-2), the sleeve—passed from one pair of male hands to another through Cressida—functions as an emblem of her exclusion from a system which reduces her worth to that of an object within male exchange. In the earlier wooing scene with Troilus, Cressida saw herself, in Dollimore's phrase, "not only as subordinate to maleness but also obscurely derivative of it."[60] Now she becomes the means of authorizing maleness as well as of perpetuating male definitions of female faithlessness. Finally, the sleeve is redefined in the public realm as a mark that draws Troilus to Diomedes in the homosocial bonding of battle.

What this scene makes patently clear is that Cressida is read (or misread) as a split text. Her deeply specularized, even fetishized, body speaks against her voice, or for her lack of voice, much as though the several texts war with one another before being re-canonized, by the male gaze, to prove that woman's sexuality derives from and depends on its male use. At the last, Cressida herself acknowledges that division in terms of looking relations, and attributes it to a natural, universal flaw in gendered vision. In her soliloquy, Shakespeare's playtext once again takes a peculiarly contradictory turn toward her doubleness. On the one hand, by privileging Cressida's dramatic power, the soliloquy works to heal the split between body and voice; on the other, it erodes that power by confirming the proposition that oppression works best when it forces the oppressed to undermine themselves.

Especially striking here is the symmetry between this, Cressida's final appearance, and her first, both of which close on soliloquy. Indeed, the one seems designed to deconstruct the other:

> Troilus, farewell! One eye yet looks on thee,
> But with my heart the other eye doth see.
> Ah, poor our sex! this fault in us I find:
> The error of our eye directs our mind.
> What error leads must err; O, then conclude,
> Minds sway'd by eyes are full of turpitude.
> *Thersites.* A proof of strength she could not publish more,
> Unless she said "My mind is now turn'd whore."
>
> (106-13)

Compared to the earlier sonnet, this one is only half itself. Following a similar rhyme scheme, its language similarly emblematic, it pushes relentlessly toward resolution. Her vision split at first between a looking eye and an eye that sees "with the heart," Cressida's parallax is corrected through a pun equating "eye" with "I" to rewrite Helena's "Love looks not with the eye, but with the mind" (*MND,* 1.1.234) as "The error of our eye directs our mind." "Yet hold I off," Cressida's earlier phrase, here comes full circle: what the playtext has suspended within a complexly textured web of looks becomes refocused in terms of the disempowered female gaze, as Cressida internalizes the male looking relations which construct her, appropriating them as her own. In this regard she represents a perfect figure not only for the female spectator's mixed sexual body as well as her split gaze but for a spectator of either gender whose ability as a "meaning-maker" is led by visual "error."[61] This is also precisely the point of her final statements, which turn to address the offstage audience and so reinscribe not just a single "eye" but the communal, doubly gendered regard of those whose minds have been swayed by this particular economy of looking relations. Yet Cressida's are not the last words in this strangely broken-backed sonnet. That privilege belongs to Thersites. By revoicing her statement in an additional summary couplet, he wrests away her "I" and, in recuperating sonnet discourse for males, finally fixes and *publishes* Cressida as everyone's master-piece.

Although each is entirely complicit with the terms of the Freudian joke, performance texts differ markedly in setting up Cressida's encounter with Diomedes. Iden Payne's 1936 staging positions the two on a centrally located round bench with Troilus and Ulysses downstage right and Thersites at stage left, kneeling behind a column. Cressida and Diomedes, then, are quite literally framed by male gazes; moreover, the strategy of separating those looks by the entire width of the stage enforces, for offstage spectators, the double perspective which the scene appears to resolve in Cressida's own split vision. Here, Cressida seems the aggressor. Laughing at Diomedes' whispers, she kisses him first, just as Troilus remarks, "She strokes his cheek!", and then three times more: on Diomedes' "I do not like this fooling"; after her final "Good night"; and, finally, after "I prithee, come" (5.2.51; 101; 105). Because all the kisses mark physical advances by Cressida, she seems to be controlling her own seduction, even willing it on.[62] Indeed the prompt copy, which clearly marks actors' pauses, reveals no hesitations in either her speech or gestures; rather, any delays that might belong to Cressida are appropriated and ascribed to Troilus, written into his reactions, which the performance text privileges.

By titling this scene "Betrayal," even Glen Byam Shaw's 1954 prompt copy allies itself at the outset with Cressida's falseness. Although half as many kisses permit Cressida's lip to speak for her, their placement is carefully gauged. The first occurs almost as soon as Cressida enters, on "Hark, a word with you" (7), and seems to have little effect on Diomedes, for the choreography reveals that Cressida makes several further attempts to cling to a Diomedes who repeatedly thrusts her away, as though already tainted. The token she brings him, in fact, seems to be his objective, not Cressida, for once he actually has it in hand, his interest immediately shifts to thoughts of tomorrow's battle. Her second kiss, which precedes her "Well, well, 'tis done, 'tis past" (97), confirms her capitulation and accepts her "fate." Since her final soliloquy is cut, as is much of the exchange between Troilus and Ulysses (but not Thersites' pointed comments), the performance text seems to assume that the gaze of offstage spectators needs no further "attest of eyes and ears" (121) and that onstage and offstage looks are equivalent. Even more significantly, by depriving Cressida of both her voice and the self-directed gaze which her soliloquy incorporates, Shaw's performance text reads Cressida's infidelity as a completely "natural" attribute.

The performance texts directed by both Hall-Barton (1960) and Barton-Kyle (1976) construct a more complex frame of looking relations. Each stages the encounter between Cressida and Diomedes as a circling dance, watched in the earlier version by upstage rather than downstage spectators and, in 1976, by a Troilus and Ulysses positioned in a down-right stage balcony while Thersites perches on an up-left stage balcony, a strategy that reproduces and exaggerates the triangulated structure of vision. Yet another choice further complicates these sightlines, for the production's open-platform set includes a seating space for the audience which encircles the entire upstage area. Placed among these additional onstage spectators, Thersites can seem, to audience members seated off the stage, to speak for those he sits among; and with Troilus and Ulysses closer to the offstage audience, the visual economy simulates a carefully arranged debate, its spectators already divided. And because Troilus and Ulysses stand in the same place where Cressida and Pandarus earlier watched the heroes' return, the Barton-Kyle *Troilus and Cressida* draws the two scenes together, calling attention to their rhymed—and regendered—looking relations. As he enters, Diomedes carries a large "Helen doll," which he puts down midstage. At scene's end he retrieves it and slings it over his shoulder, a secondary, blatantly symbolic token, together with the sleeve, of his conquest, his use of women. When Diomedes exists, Troilus descends from the balcony to the main stage, as though he may be about to speak to Cressida, but her soliloquy stops him; he stands aside in the shadows to watch and listen. Her exit, in turn, is delayed until after Thersites' "Unless she say, 'My mind is now turned whore'" (113), which her cackling laugh indicates she may hear and concur with—a strategy that works to pull the sonnet's two voices toward one another, condensing them into a single, foreclosed expression.

As in the 1960 version (as well as the earlier performance texts I describe), the encounter between Cressida and Diomedes echoes and inverts the patterns of Cressida's "virtuous fight" with herself and with Troilus (3.2). While the earlier scene signals her "holding off" in her attempts to break away from Troilus, performances of this scene rewrite her delaying tactics as teasing provocation, in which it is Diomedes who wishes to leave. What is most striking about the Barton-Kyle version, however, is that both the Troilus-Cressida and Cressida-Diomedes wooings are replayed, once again, after Cressida's exit. Just before the "war" with the sleeve, Troilus puts Cressida's glove on his right hand; as she leaves the stage, his first gesture is to strip it off and throw it down—"think this not Cressid" (132). Now he, like Cressida, is the object of the male gaze; and his "recordation . . . of every syllable" (115-16) also replays, with her glove, the pattern of advance and retreat just witnessed—taking it up, throwing it down, taking it up again and then finally dropping it as he leaves, abruptly, at Aeneas' entrance. When Ulysses descends from the balcony, he picks up the glove and smells it, only to discard it at center stage, where it remains throughout Thersites' commentary, until he retrieves it and fits it on his own right hand—a token of Cressida as "whore" and "commodious drab," its power recommodified as "intelligence" destined for Patroclus' ears and hand (190-93).

If Barton-Kyle's *Troilus and Cressida* deprivileges as well as devalues Cressida by brutally reducing her to fetishized metonymy with the glove, it also makes explicit what the playtext remains somewhat indecisive about: that this is Troilus' tragedy. Certainly, in that Troilus' play with the glove suggests that Cressida, unlike her glove, cannot be so easily put on and taken off, the performance text re-privileges her meaning *for him*. Also, Ulysses' and Thersites' subsequent handling of the glove effectively protects Troilus to displace her final demonizing onto two voyeurs,

parceling her out in a final exchange between the most admired Greek and the most scurrilous Trojan. Such a strategy exempts Troilus to resituate the debate over Cressida's worth in terms of what is done to her in his absence; indeed, this particular instance of manhandling replays her arrival in the Greek camp (4.5). By exposing her construction through a fetishized property, this performance text offers its (doubled) audience a further opportunity to judge the extent to which value lies in the eyes, or hands, of the beholder.

However cruelly reductive to Cressida, the Barton-Kyle *Troilus and Cressida* also makes a spectacle of the two voyeurs, framing one, Ulysses, through the other's gaze, as though organizing male desire into a (descending) hierarchy. Committed to a different mode of disclosure, Terry Hands's performance text allows for no such careful anatomizing of the male gaze. By positioning Troilus and Ulysses upstage left and Cressida and Diomedes downstage center, Hands's staging exploits the playtext's split between sight and sound to differentiate at first between two sets of looking relations. As the tug-of-war over a scarf (rather than the sleeve) develops, an audience hears and sees an angry exchange that, since it ends with Cressida lying on the ground and Diomedes standing over her, reads to the distant upstage figures as seduction and submission. As Cressida stands, brushing herself off, she again lashes out at Diomedes as he starts to leave: "One cannot speak a word / But it straight starts you"; his biting "I do not like this fooling" tops her accusation (100-01). Then both laugh, as though recognizing each other's "game," which leads to a final reconciliation and to the promise of tomorrow's assignation. Rather than encompassing the exchange between Cressida and Diomedes within the structuring gazes of onstage spectators, Hands's staging privileges offstage spectators, inviting them to interrogate a double spectacle—those looked at as well as the lookers-on. But although this framing generates two *potentially* contradictory readings, Hands's representational choices ultimately flatten any possible ambiguities. Since offstage spectators see with unmediated clarity, Troilus' later refusal to believe that Cressida is neither "the real thing" nor herself invites, even enforces, his devaluation together with hers. At this and other moments of performance, Hands's own dis-illusionary eye seems to dominate the playtext's suggestions of multiple, overlapping layers of illusion, subsuming and absorbing all gazes into one.

Although Hands's performance text exaggerates its compass, such a powerfully panoptical male gaze certainly derives from, and is tied to, both textual authority and authoritative male interpretive strategies. Such strategies erect a standard against which to measure Davies' *Troilus and Cressida,* particularly its distinctly re-visionary moves. Not only does it reauthorize Cressida's history but it also dislocates the hegemony of the male gaze and thus renegotiates the exchange of spectatorly pleasure to accommodate another, less misogynous gaze at the heroine trapped within its visual economy. Certainly, up to the eavesdropping scene, Juliet Stevenson's performance had repeatedly undercut the possibility of defining Cressida as archetypally false by nature. Two scenes in particular contribute to reappropriating her "truth." Wary and distrustful of Troilus as well as of herself in the wooing scene, hers was indeed a Cressida whose "fears have eyes" (3.2.66) and who, when later forced to leave Troy, seemed to watch her own betrayal from an immense distance (4.4). At this point, costume functions as an especially telling sign. With her hair down, and wearing a loose white nightgown, she is suddenly put on view to the eyes of Pandarus, Troilus, Aeneas, Paris, and finally, Diomedes; as Cressida leaves for the Greek camp, Troilus puts a dark grey military greatcoat over her shoulders. On the one hand, his gesture acknowledges and seeks to protect her extreme vulnerability; on the other, the image of Cressida literally bearing a man's enveloping coat on her back precisely registers both her possession and the anxious strategies through which the men attempt to mask their own potentially guilty desires. Later, shaken at first by what amounts to a gang rape of speaking looks in the Greek camp (4.5),[63] she uses her exchange with Menelaus to buy time, so that when Ulysses desires a kiss, she snaps out, "Why, beg [then]" (48), and points her finger to the ground, as though commanding a dog to beg for a bone. By turning his desiring look back on himself, subjecting Ulysses to her gaze, she not only undermines his famous condemnation of her body language as the scornful revenge of a publicly humiliated man but also exposes the male hypocrisy which drives literary tradition, Shakespeare's playtext, and its interpretive communities. But, however much Stevenson's performance may offer Cressida (as well as a woman spectator) a satisfying opportunity to work through her anger (an emotion traditionally disallowed and unacceptable for women) and turn to look at those who would oppress her with their gaze, because Cressida's final appearance offers a more limited range of representational options, it constitutes the test case for re-envisioning the economy of looking relations.

Davies' staging positions Troilus and Ulysses downstage right and Thersites downstage left, both in deep shadows—a strategy which surrounds the bodies of Cressida and Diomedes with the onlookers' disembodied voices and so privileges the offstage over the onstage gaze. Diomedes enters up center, under a staircase-balcony, and lights a cigarette in the gloom. Cressida now has her blonde hair braided to one side and wears a gypsy-ish skirt and blouse, a costume more physically revealing than any she has worn before, and one which marks her as a "Greekish" possession, captive in a strange land. Their rather strained encounter, in which a briskly impatient Diomedes seems less anxious to own Cressida than to settle a bargain, echoes the earlier wooing of Troilus and Cressida only in that it replays their movements up and down the centrally positioned staircase. But the differences in Cressida's changes of mood and the awkward angle of her body as she bends over Diomedes to stroke his cheek invite spectators to read both language and gesture as "untrue," actions that a woman might play in order to ensure her own survival. As she takes back the sleeve-wrap she had given

to Diomedes, for example, her "It is no matter" (87) seems designed to downplay its importance to her and to close off the exchange. For Stevenson's Cressida, Diomedes indeed seems to represent simply a "guardian" who may protect her from the other Greeks; it is that fear which animates her self-absorption and, later, the interior quarrel which structures her soliloquy. When she speaks "I prithee, come" (105), she shrinks back into the deep shadows of the upstage staircase, calling out "Troilus" in anguish; after hearing no answer, her "farewell" marks her quiet resignation (106), splitting gaze and self even before she articulates that separation further. To privilege her desperation and sense of self-loss, the performance text gives her a long exit, from the main stage up the curve of the staircase, "walking in," this last time, alone.

Although positioning Cressida as the object of the male gaze remains "true" to Shakespeare's playtext, Davies' representational strategies also work to interrogate its predetermined looking relations and so exchange a visual for a verbal economy. For the (relative) darkness of the scene shifts focus from bodies to voices, with several telling effects, not the least of which emphasizes the narrative power of the three male onlookers' voices as well as their ability to control the meaning of the spectacle.[64] Further, just as neither onstage nor offstage spectators hear what Cressida whispers to Diomedes, her appeal to Troilus is met only by silence. Indeed, both Stevenson's performance and Davies' representational choices call attention to Troilus' lack of response and, beyond that, to his (chivalric?) loyalty, not to Cressida but to his fellow males. This strategy invites offstage spectators of either gender to turn their own gaze away from those of the (unseen) onstage spectators and to read in Cressida's final look—and its absent but (unknown to her) present subject, Troilus—a divided subject of their own fashioning. If the playtext's strategy depends on exploiting Cressida as subjected to the male gaze, Davies' decentering of that spectacle exposes how she is constructed by their looks and offers an alternative viewpoint. Moreover, it reveals Cressida as a special instance of what Dollimore calls "transgressive reinscription":[65] positioned as marginal to the male system which oppresses her with its gaze, at the last she not only internalizes, and so validates, its looking relations but simultaneously demystifies their power to construct and fracture her identity.

"Shakespeare dislocated"; "Shakespeare, modern master"; "Out of place"; "RSC's crime in the Crimea": these review titles attest to the wider implications of such demystification, its discomforting reception.[66] Citing "misinterpretation of Shakespeare's purpose," John Barber comments that "in attributing these vices [strife, lechery, crime, rage, and lust] to the Victorians, [Davies] destroys that universality which belongs to a great myth and makes it hurt us where we live."[67] Playing *Troilus and Cressida* as a piece of history threatens to destabilize myth, to exchange transcendental truths—"'as false as Cressid'" and "'as true as Troilus'" among them—for a more precisely politicized examination of specific social relations. Yet, while perceived as radically transgressive by some within the interpretive community, does not Davies' performance text simply take *Troilus and Cressida* further in the direction it was already going? In this regard, certainly the relation of present-day Britons to a legendary imperialist Victorian past rather precisely analogizes the relation of neo-chivalric Elizabethans to the heroic ideals of the ancient world—to its social text as well as to its texts. If as Elizabeth Freund writes, "*Troilus and Cressida* is all recognition scene, the recognition scene of Renaissance writing," then indeed Davies' performance text constitutes, for late twentieth-century spectators, another kind of recognition scene, one that most particularly reveals how fictions of gender, the product of looking relations, have been, and continue to be, transcribed onto the bodies of real women—and men. And largely because it accords power to a woman's look and thus incorporates a critique of the male-dominated visual economy which positions Cressida as the object of the male joke, Davies' *Troilus and Cressida* not only makes it possible for a woman spectator to see more deeply into the joke but also to take pleasure in understanding how it works, even though it works against women.[68] Indeed, perhaps the most significant and potentially threatening move resulting from such a performance is to topple the inherited cultural capital of the joke itself. But then this particular joke, like many of Freud's, has gone on too long.

IV

The two scenes I have examined mark the beginning and ending of Cressida's speaking role but not the end of her role as a spoken entity. In the final sign of her presence Troilus tears up her letter, brought to him by Pandarus— "no matter from the heart"—and consigns it to the wind, there to "turn and change together" (5.4.108; 110). Splitting her once more into words and deeds, he refuses to give her a public reading. At the last, his construction of the female subject, assimilating her within a male system of desire and representation, overrides any potential deconstructive turn, including Stevenson's and Davies' as well as my own. Suppressing her voice, Troilus writes his own (invisible) letter on Cressida's body, positioning her as she is written, not as she writes.

But Shakespeare's playtext also offers a further instance of Cressida—that is, an instance which once again seems designed to fetishize her absent body, censor her voice, and enclose her within legendary writing. At the close Pandarus reappears, only to be summarily dismissed by Troilus, presumably because he associates Pandarus with Cressida. Yet it is Troilus, not he, who exits: Pandarus remains to speak, first in prose and then in verse—as it happens, in fourteen lines of rhyming couplets interrupted by an apostrophe to spectators, calling them "Good traders in the flesh" (5.10.46). Pandarus' epilogue is unique, especially in its turn toward offending rather than entreating an audience, but also because it represents a textual trouble spot, one that seems both unusually Elizabethan and unusually local in its references. I want to trouble it a bit further, give both its locality and its gender another look.

Certainly Pandarus functions here as a kind of surrogate for Cressida,[69] and at the linguistic level, his overcomplete sonnet, which obeys the same deviant rhyme scheme as Cressida's two earlier sonnets (the last *in*complete), neatly supports such a relation between the two. Consider also the first four lines of his verse:

> Full merrily the humble-bee doth sing
> Till he hath lost his honey and his sting;
> And being once subdu'd in armed tail,
> Sweet honey and sweet notes together fail.
>
> (5.10.41-45)

In these lines, sentiment as well as syntax ventriloquize— and *regender*—Cressida's earlier "That she was never yet that ever knew / Love got so sweet as when desire did sue" (1.2.295-96). A similar gender-bending of voices and bodies occurred as Cressida entered. Now, just as her apparent surrogate is about to exit, and just as the representation stands on its edge, Shakespeare's playtext repeats it. To what purpose? And to what purpose, also, are Pandarus' subsequent references to "brethren and sisters of the hold-door trade," to their weeping eyes, to his legacy of disease (5.10.49-57)? All these features have to do with Cressida—that is, with her future written history, beyond the playtext. Yet they are represented as being *not*-Cressida. Displaced onto Pandarus, they are done in a different, and differently gendered voice, which issues from a diseased male body. Together, such signs engender the potentially transgressive suggestion that at the close Shakespeare's playtext exchanges Pandarus for Cressida, turning him, not her, into Hélène Cixous' figure for the female body confiscated by male systems of representation: "the uncanny stranger on display—the ailing or dead figure, which so often turns out to be the nasty companion, the cause and location of inhibitions."[70] Such a move may not precisely reclaim either Cressida's body or the bodies of those women spectators seated in a public playhouse "full of secrete adulterie"[71] (and, according to some, open to it) from being observed and written down by men. But it does at least locate the possibility of reclamation firmly within the fluid gender economy of a cultural institution that saw itself, in another famous, although perhaps equally false, written figure, as holding a mirror up to nature.

Notes

1. Quotations are from Kenneth Palmer's Arden edition of *Troilus and Cressida* (London, 1981).

2. Harry Berger, Jr. gives a neat summary in "*Troilus and Cressida:* The Observer as Basilisk," *Comparative Drama*, 2 (1968), 130-31.

3. For Cressida's difficulty in understanding herself, see esp. 3.2.116-49.

4. Rosalie L. Colie, *Shakespeare's Living Art* (Princeton, 1974), p. 317.

5. Elizabeth Freund, "'Ariachne's broken woof': the rhetoric of citation in *Troilus and Cressida,*" in *Shakespeare and the Question of Theory,* ed. Patricia

Parker and Geoffrey Hartman (New York, 1985), p. 35. See also Linda Charnes, "So Unsecret to Ourselves': Notorious Identity and the Material Subject in Shakespeare's *Troilus and Cressida," Shakespeare Quarterly,* 40, No. 4 (Winter 1989), 413-40.

6. Palmer, e.g., consistently reads the social as the moral (Arden edition, pp. 38-93). See also, among others, Douglas Cole, "Myth and Anti-Myth: The Case of *Troilus and Cressida," Shakespeare Quarterly,* 30 (1980), 76-84. Even apologist readings such as Gayle Greene's position Cressida as an inevitable product of a morally degenerate world ("Shakespeare's Cressida: 'A Kind of Self,'" in *The Woman's Part: Feminist Criticism of Shakespeare,* ed. Carolyn R. S. Lenz et al. [Urbana, Ill., 1980], pp. 133-49). In "The patriarchal bard: feminist criticism and Shakespeare: *King Lear* and *Measure for Measure,"* Kathleen McLuskie outlines an alternative project: "Feminist criticism need not restrict itself to privileging the woman's part or to special pleading on behalf of female characters. It can be equally well served by making a text reveal the conditions in which a particular ideology of femininity functions and by both revealing and subverting the hold which such an ideology has for readers both female and male" (in *Political Shakespeare: New essays in cultural materialism,* ed. Jonathan Dollimore and Alan Sinfield [Manchester, Eng., 1985], p. 106).

7. Jonathan Dollimore, *Radical Tragedy: Religion, Ideology and Power in the Drama of Shakespeare and His Contemporaries* (Brighton, Eng., 1984), esp. pp. 44-47.

8. Palmer conjectures that the first *possible* performances of Shakespeare's playtext might have occurred in late 1602 or early 1603, but this is conjecture only (Arden edition, pp. 17-18). Dryden's 1679 adaptation saw four productions in the first half of the eighteenth century; at the turn of the nineteenth century, John Philip Kemble prepared an edition that never reached the stage, and, by century's end, *Troilus and Cressida* had been performed in Munich. But the English-speaking stage history for Shakespeare's playtext begins, for all practical purposes, with a 1907 performance. Although William Poel revived it in 1913, it does not become regularly included in repertory seasons until after World War II. For a capsule stage history, see Kenneth Muir, *Troilus and Cressida* (Oxford, 1982), pp. 9-12. Joseph G. Price and Jeanne Newlin are in the process of preparing a full stage history.

9. For an argument legitimating theatrical performances as texts, see my *The End Crowns All: Closure and Contradiction in Shakespeare's History* (Princeton, 1990). For the relation between social and theatrical meaning, see McLuskie, "The patriarchal bard," p. 95; and Elin Diamond, "Brechtian Theory / Feminist Theory," *Drama Review,* 32 (1988), 82-94.

10. See Joan Kelly, "Did Women Have a Renaissance?" in *Women, History, and Theory* (Chicago, 1984), esp. pp. 30-47.

11. In 2.2, the Trojan council scene. See also, however, the exchange between Paris and Diomedes concerning who "deserves fair Helen best" (4.1.52-79).

12. I draw here on Tania Modleski, "Rape vs. Mans/laughter: *Blackmail,"* in *The Women Who Knew Too Much: Hitchcock and Feminist Theory* (London, 1988), esp. pp. 19-28.

13. For important distinctions between the homosocial and the homoerotic as well as a pertinent discussion of triangulated relationships, see Eve Kosofsky Sedgwick, *Between Men: English Literature and Male Homosocial Desire* (New York, 1985), esp. pp. 1-27.

14. Laura Mulvey, "Visual Pleasure and Narrative Cinema" (1975); rpt. in *Feminism and Feminist Film Theory,* ed. Constance Penley (New York, 1988), p. 62. For the notion of the play as a male project, with women as its stagehands, see Naomi Scheman, "Missing Mothers / Desiring Daughters: Framing the Sight of Women," *Critical Inquiry,* 15 (1988), 87.

15. Stephen Greenblatt's phrase, which concludes his "Invisible Bullets," is "There is subversion, no end of subversion, only not for us." See *Shakespearean Negotiations: The Circulation of Social Energy in Renaissance England* (Berkeley, 1988), p. 65.

16. For a summary of Peter Alexander's theory concerning Inns of Court performance, see Palmer, Arden edition, pp. 307-10. See also E.A.J. Honigman, "The Date and Revision of *Troilus and Cressida,"* in *Textual Criticism and Interpretation,* ed. Jerome McGann (Chicago, 1985), pp. 38-54; and Gary Taylor, *"Troilus and Cressida:* Bibliography, Performance, and Interpretation," *Shakespeare Studies,* 15 (1982), 99-136.

17. Andrew Gurr reports that very few women—and those few were among the aristocratic and upper classes—were literate; even in London, few women could write their names. See *Playgoing in Shakespeare's London* (Cambridge, Eng., 1987), p. 55.

18. Gurr, *Playgoing,* pp. 57-58, 79.

19. Gurr, *Playgoing,* pp. 57-58; I reproduce Gurr's index listing under "women" in the alphabetical order he uses, primarily because it nicely mixes class hierarchies. See also Jean Howard, "Crossdressing, the Theatre, and Gender Struggle in Early Modern England," *Shakespeare Quarterly,* 39 (1988), 440.

20. Gurr, *Playgoing,* pp. 92-94.

21. Thomas Randolph, *The Muses' Looking Glass* (1638), epilogue; reproduced in Gurr, *Playgoing,* p. 238.

22. Howard, "Crossdressing," p. 440.

23. Dekker's epilogue is reproduced in Gurr, *Playoing,* p. 214. See also Linda Woodbridge, *Women and the English Renaissance: Literature and the Nature of*

Womankind, 1540-1620 (Urbana, Ill., 1984), pp. 250-51; and Richard Levin, "Women in the Renaissance Theatre Audience," *Shakespeare Quarterly,* 40, No. 2 (Summer 1989), 165-74.

24. Woodbridge, *Women,* pp. 250-51; Gurr, *Playgoing,* pp. 102-04.

25. Louis Adrian Montrose, "The Purpose of Playing: Reflections on a Shakespearean Anthropology," *Helios,* N.S. 7 (1980), 51-74; and Howard, "Crossdressing," esp. pp. 437-40.

26. Katherine Eisaman Maus, "Horns of Dilemma: Jealousy, Gender, and Spectatorship in English Renaissance Drama," *ELH,* 54 (1987), 578. For the initial theoretical work on the gendered gaze, see Mulvey's "Visual Pleasure." Further studies respond to, extend and/or qualify her formulations. See Teresa de Lauretis, *Alice Doesn't: Feminism, Semiotics, Cinema* (Bloomington, Ind., 1984); Mary Ann Doane, *The Desire to Desire: The Woman's Film of the 1940s* (Bloomington, Ind., 1987); and Modleski, *Women Who Knew Too Much.* See also my "Kiss Me Deadly; or The Des/Demonized Spectacle," in *Othello: New Perspectives,* ed. Virginia M. Vaughan and Kent Cartwright (Cranbury, N.J., 1990).

27. For the notion of citation, see Freund, "'Ariachne's broken woof,'" p. 24.

28. I draw here on Peggy Phelan, "Feminist Theory, Poststructuralism, and Performance," *Drama Review,* 32 (1988), 111.

29. See Stephen Orgel, "Nobody's Perfect: Or Why Did the English Stage Take Boys for Women," *South Atlantic Quarterly,* 88 (1989), 27.

30. So, e.g., in the Pelican, Arden, and Oxford editions.

31. I use Folio's "that" and "contents" rather than Quarto's "then" and "content," primarily because both point to Cressida's dilemma, not to her "content." See Palmer, Arden edition, p. 119*n*. See also Gary Taylor's textual note in *William Shakespeare: A Textual Companion,* Stanley Wells and Gary Taylor (Oxford, 1987), p. 427.

32. Helena, in *All's Well That Ends Well,* uses similar syntactic constructions in 4.4.21-25; within women's discourse, her expressions resemble Cressida's.

33. For a view of the blazons of sonnet discourse as a language which oppresses women, see Nancy Vickers, "'The blazon of sweet beauty's best': Shakespeare's *Lucrece,*" in *Shakespeare and the Question of Theory,* pp. 95-115. For a fine reading of Cressida's first and last soliloquies as an especially intractable acting problem, see Lorraine Helms, "Playing the Woman's Part: Feminist Criticism and Shakespearean Performance," *Theatre Journal,* 41 (1989), 190-200.

34. Prompt copy at The Shakespeare Centre Library, Stratford-upon-Avon. My thanks to Sylvia Morris for supplying me with photocopies of all prompt copies I cite and of pertinent reviews.

35. "Shakespeare at His Bitterest," *Morning Post,* April 25, 1936. It was the "final proof," according to Sidney Charteris, "that this Elizabethan business can be carried too far" (*Birmingham Evening Dispatch,* April 25, 1936).

36. "Trojans Clad as Elizabethans," *Birmingham Gazette,* April 25, 1936.

37. *Times* [London], April 25, 1936; *Birmingham Post,* April 25, 1936. Most reviewers mention the lisp, a detail which links this Cressida to Hamlet's accusations against women: "You jig, you amble, and you lisp" (*Hamlet,* 3.1.144).

38. Prompt copy at The Shakespeare Centre Library.

39. W.A. Darlington, "Faithlessness in Women," *Daily Telegraph,* July 16, 1954; Claude L. Westell, "Mustard Cressida," *Birmingham Mail,* July 16, 1954.

40. Prompt copies at The Shakespeare Centre Library.

41. Bernard Levin, "If Shakespeare did suffer, then it was to good effect," *Daily Express,* July 27, 1960.

42. The material printed in the souvenir program—Sonnet 129, an extract from Juvenal's Satire 2, a quote from Heine about seeing "Melpomene dancing the Cancan at a ball of grisettes"—makes this point of view blatantly obvious. Prompt copy at The Shakespeare Centre Library.

43. Michael Billington, "Trojan workhorses," *Guardian,* July 9, 1981.

44. Michael Coveney, *Financial Times,* July 8, 1981.

45. Robert Cushman, "War Games," *Observer,* July 12, 1981.

46. Phelan, "Feminist Theory," pp. 124-25.

47. Darlington, "Faithlessness."

48. I borrow the phrase from Pierre Bourdieu, *Distinction: A Social Critique of the Judgement of Taste,* trans. Richard Nice (Cambridge, Mass., 1984), esp. pp. 22-26.

49. Bourdieu, *Distinction,* p. 3.

50. Some of the results of this research are reproduced, in place of the usual series of quotations from Shakespeare and critical opinions, in the souvenir program. Prompt copy at The Shakespeare Centre Library.

51. For Stevenson's own account of her attempts to reread other roles, see Carol Rutter, *Clamorous Voices: Shakespeare's Women Today,* ed. Faith Evans (London: Women's Press, Ltd., 1988), esp. pp. 26, 28-29; 37-52; 97-121.

52. Irving Wardle, "Full attention on the lovers allows a brief glimpse of hope," [London] *Times,* June 27, 1985.

53. In order, the comments are from Francis Barber, "Out of place," *Sunday Telegraph,* June 30, 1985; John Barber, "Shakespeare dislocated," *Daily Tele-*

graph, June 27, 1985; and Michael Coveney, *Financial Times,* June 27, 1985.

54. Janet Bergstrom, "Alternation, Segmentation, Hypnosis: Interview with Raymond Bellour," *Camera Obscura,* 3-4 (1979), 71-103; esp. 93.

55. "To-be-looked-at-ness" is Mulvey's phrase, "Visual Pleasure," p. 62; for her restatement of Brecht's dictum, see the same essay.

56. Modleski, *Women Who Knew Too Much,* p. 25.

57. Cf. McLuskie, "The patriarchal bard," p. 97, who in turn refers to Jonathan Culler's discussion of "Reading as a Woman" in *Theory and Criticism after Structuralism* (Ithaca, 1982), pp. 43-63, where he implies that positioning the reader as a woman is not only a matter of free choice but a coherent position that determines clear-cut readings.

58. Coppélia Kahn notes this feminizing tendency in *Man's Estate: Masculine Identity in Shakespeare* (Berkeley, 1981), pp. 131-32.

59. Only one other property, Desdemona's handkerchief, is so liberally handled, and so gendered and regendered with contradictory signs. See Lynda E. Boose, "Othello's Handkerchief: 'The Recognizance and Pledge of Love," *English Literary Renaissance,* 9 (1975), 360-74; and Karen Newman, "And wash the Ethiop white': femininity and the monstrous in *Othello,"* in *Shakespeare Reproduced: The Text in History and Ideology,* ed. Jean E. Howard and Marion F. O'Connor (New York, 1987), pp. 143-62.

60. Dollimore, *Radical Tragedy,* p. 48.

61. Annette Kuhn draws a useful distinction between spectator and audience by labeling the spectator a "meaning-maker," one who is not only constructed by a text but is part of a larger context, the "social audience." See "Women's Genres: Melodrama, Soap Opera and Theory" (1984), rpt. in *Home Is Where the Heart Is: Studies in Melodrama and the Women's Film,* ed. Christine Gledhill (London, 1987), pp. 18-28.

62. Editorial practice is willingly complicit with her seduction. A point of special interest occurs at 5.2.80-82 (Arden edition); Cressida is speaking of the sleeve she has just given to Diomedes: "And gives memorial dainty kisses to it, / As I kiss thee— Nay, do not snatch it from me: [*Diomedes snatches the sleeve*] / He that takes that doth take my heart withal." Re-examining the status of speech prefixes, Taylor assigns to Diomedes the phrase, "As I kiss thee," thus making Diomedes, not Cressida, the aggressor and changing considerably the performance options. For Taylor's note, see Wells and Taylor, *William Shakespeare,* p. 436.

63. David Burke, who played Hector, put it this way: "I'm not saying we could get Cressida down on the floor and rape her—that would be violating the text— but you can see brutal acts of lechery in the eye, in

the manner. A look between two men can tell you as much if not more than a hand stuck up a dress" (quoted in a program note).

64. For this function of the voice-over in film, see Kaja Silverman, *The Acoustic Mirror: The Female Voice in Psychoanalysis and Cinema* (Bloomington, Ind., 1988), pp. 48-49; 130-33; 136-40. Admittedly, cinema intensifies the effect of such vocal control over and above that of theatrical representation.

65. Jonathan Dollimore, "Subjectivity, Sexuality and Transgression: The Jacobean Connection," *Renaissance Drama,* N.S. 17 (1986), 57.

66. In order, the titles are from *Daily Telegraph* (June 27, 1985), *Sunday Times, Sunday Telegraph* and *Mail on Sunday* (all June 30, 1985).

67. John Barber, "Shakespeare dislocated," *Daily Telegraph,* June 27, 1985.

68. See Modleski, pp. 25-26. Cf. McLuskie, "The patriarchal bard," pp. 88-106.

69. Palmer, among others, notes their relationship, Arden edition, p. 303*n.*

70. Hélène Cixous, "The Laugh of the Medusa," in *New French Feminisms,* ed. Elaine Marks and Isabelle de Courtivron (New York, 1981), p. 250.

71. Stephen Gosson, *Playes Confuted in Five Actions* (1589), reproduced in Gurr, *Playgoing,* p. 207.

James O'Rourke (essay date 1992)

SOURCE: "'Rule in Unity' and Otherwise: Love and Sex in *Troilus and Cressida*," in *Shakespeare Quarterly,* Vol. 43, No. 2, Summer, 1992, pp. 139-58.

[*In the following essay, O'Rourke proposes that with Troilus and Cressida Shakespeare gave us universal characters that we can recognize as cynical sexual clichés even as we sympathize with them as romantic lovers.*]

Troilus and Cressida is not only a notoriously slippery play (comedy, tragedy, or history?) but one founded on a familiar contradiction. The play's relentless vulgarity constructs a scathing critique of the dominant forms of sexuality in Western culture, but at the same time the partners in its central romantic couple engage the sympathies of even the most sophisticated readers. When Cressida reflects sadly that "Men prize the thing ungained more than it is" (1.2.291),[1] and when Troilus wryly observes that Helen's reputation for beauty derives from the amount of blood shed over her (1.1.93-94), they appeal to our own knowingness about sexuality and expose the sexual clichés and conventions of their, and our, culture. But the complicity engendered by this shared knowledge has the paradoxical effect of making an audience identify with Troilus and/or Cressida as they reenact those conventions. Despite their worldly-wise cynicism, Troilus and

Cressida, as they enter into the romantic partnership, idealize each other without reserve and without self-consciousness about the utter conventionality of their behavior. Critical commentary about the destruction of their relationship reveals the intensity with which readers habitually identify with the position of one or the other of these characters; expressions of sympathy for one character are almost always overshadowed by condemnation of the other.

Contemporary feminist readings, for example, which have justifiably redeemed Cressida from the censure of a patriarchal (though not always male) tradition of interpretation that took Ulysses' and Thersites' descriptions of her at face value have filled out the spectrum of *amour-haine* in the romantic couple as they have fingered Troilus as the primary culprit in Cressida's betrayal.[2] But while Cressida-bashers have had to ignore the play's representations of the historical forces that have denied women the ability to make meaningful choices about their own lives, anti-Troilus readers face the burden of disagreeing with Cressida herself, who never blames Troilus for her plight. Even after her removal to the Greek camp, she laments to Diomedes that Troilus "loved me better than you will" (5.2.92), a line that conveys both the pathos of her loss and her ability to continue to make subtle and accurate judgments in the treacherous terrain of sexuality. While feminist and cultural-materialist readings of the play have given an accurate portrait of woman in history as a potential subject reduced to the status of a commodity, the affective force of *Troilus and Cressida* cannot be recovered through an ego psychology of individual will and choice that suggests Cressida would be better off without such a lover as Troilus. A Lacanian sexuality of relations rather than of drives, in which desire fails because of its alienation from a third term—the Symbolic Order or Law of the Father—can go beyond analysis of Troilus and Cressida as individual characters and can help to define the structures of power and sexuality in what sometimes seems Shakespeare's most disorderly play. At the final level of determination, though, the vulgarity of *Troilus and Cressida* exceeds even Lacan's account of the psychic powers of representation and follows the more elemental logic of what Kristeva calls the semiotic order.

The play's systematic critique of sexuality in a patriarchal culture culminates in the image of a venereal disease that is transmitted from a Greek brothel to an English audience. This disease, called by "Mistress Thersites" (2.1.35) the "Neapolitan bone-ache" as he wishes it on "those that war for a placket" (2.3.18-21), is, in the legends of the Trojan War, attached to Cressida. In Henryson's *Testament of Cresseid,* published as a supplement to Chaucer's *Troilus and Criseyde,* Cresseid is afflicted with leprosy.[3] Making Pandarus the communicator of Thersites' curse to the legendarily diseased Cresseid, Shakespeare treats Cresseid's leprosy as an obvious venereal image and the disease itself as a metaphor for Cressida's infamy. But by depicting Pandarus, and not Cressida, as both diseased and the source of disease, Shakespeare places the blame for the corruption of sexuality not on the woman but on the governing term of a patriarchal social order—the patriarch. The Law of the Father, as Lacan calls it, plays a range of roles as it regulates sexuality: it prohibits, as Calchas does when he is brought into the play to exceed the power of the conventional senex and to undo an already consummated union; it facilitates, as Pandarus does when he mediates between Troilus and Cressida; and it commodifies, as Pandarus does in his role as pimp. The legendary defamation of Cressida as a whore is a corrupted version of the metalepsis of Helen's idealization ("Helen must needs be fair, / When with your blood you daily paint her thus" [1.1.93-94]). Just as those who war for a woman will (as they do with Helen) blame the woman, those who drive women into prostitution will identify prostitutes as the source of disease ("gallèd g[ee]se of Winchester" [5.10.54]), when the real source is precisely the patriarchal sexual economy represented by Pandarus and the sexual practices it fosters. Shakespeare is presciently Blakean in his analysis of the sexual economy of London, characterizing prostitution both as a source of disease and as a dominant, not an aberrational, form of his culture's sexuality, and describing the violence in the oedipal triangle as coming from the side of the father and not from that of the son.[4]

The debased nature of this sexual economy shows itself in the interchangeability of the terms "whore" and "woman". The term "whore" is never used in the play to describe women paid for sexual services but refers to those who have been forcibly transferred from one man to another (Helen [4.1.68] and Cressida [5.2.117]), and to Patroclus, a man who, for lack of "stomach to the war" (3.3.221), has been made a sort of woman, a "masculine whore" (5.1.17). The sexuality of the Greek army is so fully relational, rather than biological, that, in the absence of biological women, Patroclus and "Mistress Thersites" play the role of woman to the heroes Achilles and Ajax.[5] The Hegelian master-slave dialectic that underlies Lacan's account of the negation of the woman in traditional heterosexuality perfectly describes the sexual behavior of the Greek heroes in *Troilus and Cressida*: their valor on the battlefield demonstrating that they prize honor above mere survival, Achilles and Ajax become masters and make others their slaves. In a sexual economy the names of master-slave roles are "men" and "women", and the greatest prestige accrues to the "men" who can keep possession of the most, or the most valued, "women." As Alexandre Kojève explains the activity of Hegelian masters in their pursuit of the specifically "human" value of prestige "It is human to desire what others desire because they desire it. Thus, an object perfectly useless from a biological point of view (such as a medal, or the enemy's flag) can be desired because it is the object of others' desires."[6] The complete irrelevance of the actual object being fought for is shown in Shakespeare's declension of the role of the *femme fatale* from Helen to Cressida to Thersites, as even Thersites' defection from Ajax' tent can serve as the occasion for the emulous rivalry of Achilles and Ajax. But even before Achilles "inveigle[s] his fool" (2.3.90) from Ajax,

Thersites shows why the heroic identity is so endangered by what it claims to dominate.

The imagery of Patroclus' confession of "little stomach to the war" is foreshadowed in the quarrel between Ajax and Thersites; when Ajax claims the privilege of the master to beat his slave, Thersites threatens to "tell what thou art by inches, thou thing of no bowels" (2.1.49-50). Since Ajax beats him anyway, Thersites tells Achilles what Ajax is "by inches," tells him that Ajax "wears his wit in his belly" and "Has not so much wit . . . As will stop the eye of Helen's needle" (ll. 74-81). Thersites thus demolishes the legend of Ajax, of whom Peele says in "The Tale of Troy" that "the stomacke of the man was great."[7] The slave, the subject reduced to an object, has the power of the fool (who can tell the demystifying truth about heroic ideology), and, as a sexual slave, Thersites can demystify Ajax in a particularly graphic and literal manner. Thersites' relation to Ajax is the classic Hegelian master-slave relation as it has been demystified by Lacan; the master claims prestige, but it is the repressed term, the Other, that carries the truth. Thersites' analogue in the Greek camp is Cassandra; while he curses those who "war for a placket," she tells her brothers that "Our firebrand brother, Paris, burns us all" (2.2.110). Cassandra is first spoken of in the play as the exemplar of "wit" as Helen is the pattern of beauty (1.1.43-49), but once Shakespeare equates the woman and the fool, Cassandra's prophecy is characterized as madness by Troilus (2.2.98) and as "divination" by Hector (l. 114); either way, it is outside the Symbolic Order and does not count. Cassandra, who tells the truth to which no one will listen, exemplifies the Lacanian Other, the site of a truth that could be liberating but that never will be heeded.

That this war is about male identity, and that male identity is cross-cultural and sexually based, is demonstrated by the ease with which Greek metaphors travel across to Troy. Achilles closes the scene in which Thersites derides Ajax' "bowels" and "belly" by describing Hector's challenge to "some knight . . . / That hath a stomach" (2.1.124-25); Hector begins the next scene by comparing himself to a "lady of more softer bowels" as he argues to "Let Helen go" (2.2.11, 17). Hector's sensible computation of the cost of keeping Helen is an ironic reversal of the terms of the challenge he has just sent to the Greek camp, and it is Troilus' invocation of the terms of that challenge, the equation of "Manhood and honor" (l. 47), that will eventually prevail. While the Trojan council scene shows the sons of Priam behaving in a more civilized manner than do the contentious Greek warriors, both societies are in the state of transition described by Freud in *Totem and Taboo;* the father-figure no longer dominates and controls, and as Priam's sons debate an offer sent to Priam, the younger males are now negotiating their own rights in the context of a war over the possession of the exemplary woman.[8] Troilus insists that his motivation is not in fact sexual, that it is "glory that we more affected / Than the performance of our heaving spleens" (ll. 195-96), but the imagery of this scene carries a graphic double-entendre as it purportedly serves the theme of glory. Hector introduces the suggestive imagery with his declaration that,

Act II, scene ii. Cassandra.

Though no man lesser fears the Greeks than I
As far as toucheth my particular, . . .
There is no lady of more softer bowels,
More spongy to suck in the sense of fear . . .
Than Hector is. . . .

(2.2.8-14)

Troilus continues it with his protest that "For my private part, / I am no more touched than all Priam's sons" (ll. 125-26). Priam's charge that Paris has the "honey" and the rest the "gall" (l. 144) brings a response from Paris that, within this field of imagery, cannot help but suggest, for just a moment, that he is about to propose sharing Helen with his brothers: "I propose not merely to myself / The pleasures such a beauty brings with it" (ll. 146-47). In the slightly less civilized Greek camp, such "sharing" nearly happens to Cressida. All that Paris actually proposes to share, though, is the fame of keeping Helen, and this is the argument that carries the day with Troilus, who proclaims her "a theme of honor and renown" (l. 199), and imagines that, in defending her, "fame in time to come [will] canonize us" (l. 202). The imagery of the scene suggests the complementariness of their fame in sexual terms; Trojan fame will be measured by this "pearl . . . inestimable," whom "The world's large spaces cannot parallel" (ll. 81,

88, 162). The thematic convergence of Helen and honor—in Troilus' "Will you . . . buckle in a waist most fathomless / With . . . fears and reasons?" (ll. 28-32)—allows the image of a "waist most fathomless" to float free of its tenor as Priam's honor and join its depth imagery to the "lady of more softer bowels" in the figure of the immeasurable Helen. In the sexual imagery of this war, Helen has not a tiny-eyed needle but a spongy, fathomless space, and Trojan honor will be recorded as the manhood commensurate with its depth.

The spurious autonomy of the penis as the phallus and the dependence of male identity on the woman it negates are the primary themes of Lacan's sexualizing of the Hegelian dialectic of the master and the slave. Although Hegel calls the relation between master and slave dialectical, and Lacan posits the "mirror stage" as the originary identification of the self through its consolidating reflection in the imago of the human form,[9] neither Lacan nor Hegel imagines a dyadic identity as more genuine than the identity imposed by a cultural order; Hegel's teleology of the state and Lacan's omnipresence of the Symbolic Order make the Aristophanic myth of perfect complementariness sheer fantasy. Lacan never even describes the mother performing the function of the mirror for the infant, and in fact seems to suggest that it is the father who will be the primary pattern of identification for "the ego," which is formed as a competitive, mimetic entity; the triad of ego/others/objects teaches the ego to imitate the desires of others and to compete with them for the objects of their desires.[10] Lacan thus grounds the Hegelian competition among masters in a phase of psychic development, as the subject learns to place a higher value on immaterial than on material satisfactions in the emergence of the gap between need and demand—the gap in which "desire" emerges. Lacan's assumption that the father's image will set the pattern of imitation for the ego raises obvious questions about the relation of women to "the ego." Kristeva has come closest, among Lacanian analysts, to entertaining the Aristophanic myth of the romantic couple as a form of identity, describing "the object of love [as] a metaphor for the subject—its constitutive metaphor, its 'unary feature.'"[11] Kristeva stresses, however, that this identification is liminal, an "idealization on the edge of primal repression,"[12] hovering between fragmentation and the Symbolic code; *Troilus and Cressida* will chart both the formation and the collapse of this idealization in the character of Troilus.

Shakespeare goes even further than Lacan or Kristeva in coupling the mirror imagery familiar in Lacanian analysis with imagery that, given the sexual charge of this play, suggests the imaginary grounding of male identity in the act of sexual intercourse. This conjunction of sexual and specular imagery is most fully developed in a conversation between Ulysses and Achilles that is pervaded by mirror imagery. Achilles is meant, in Ulysses' plot, to discover that "Pride hath no other glass / To show itself but pride" (3.3.47-48), and Achilles quickly discovers in the disdain of Agamemnon, Ajax, and Menelaus that "What the declined is / He shall . . . soon read in the eyes of others"

(ll. 76-77). Ulysses comes to explain the point to him and cites a "strange fellow" (who may be Plato)[13] who writes that "man, how dearly ever parted, . . . feels not what he owes, but by reflection" (ll. 96-100). Except for the potential phallicism of being "dearly . . . parted," Ulysses here remains within the dominant specular imagery of the scene, but then he adds, "As when his virtues, shining upon others, / Heat them, and they retort that heat again / To the first giver" (ll. 101-3). Achilles claims to know and understand the point and reiterates it with more mirror imagery: "The beauty that is borne here in the face . . . commends itself / To others' eyes" until, "eye to eye opposed," it is "mirrored there / Where it may see itself" (ll. 104-12).[14] Ulysses responds that Achilles has missed the most important part of the argument and repeats the imagery of parts and heat, explaining that

> . . . no man is the lord of anything . . .
> Till he communicate his parts to others;
> Nor doth he of himself know them for aught
> Till he behold them formed in the applause
> Where they're extended; who, like an arch, reverb'rate
> The voice again, or, like a gate of steel
> Fronting the sun, receives and renders back
> His figure and his heat.
>
>   (ll. 116-24)

The imagery of sexual intercourse is vivid, with extended parts entering a gate that responds to its own penetration, and the consummation of the sexual act is described as the final achievement of a male identity that is equated with mastery.

Lacan's interest in taking the psychoanalytic treatment of sexuality away from the "drive" follows the Hegelian course of distinguishing the specifically human desire for prestige from the merely biological satisfaction of the drive. These terms are difficult to disentangle in *Troilus and Cressida,* however; when Pandarus warns Troilus that he "must be witty" (3.2.30) when Cressida arrives, his surface meaning is that Troilus must retain his ability to speak in a properly courtly fashion. But the sexual imagery that Thersites attaches to "wit" in his quarrel with Ajax gives this line a subtext of performance anxiety, which is then developed in the possibility that lovers might "have the voice of lions and the act of hares," since "desire is boundless and the act a slave to limit" (ll. 87, 81-82). It would be a mistake, though, to return to a pre-Lacanian, "Freudian" mode of reading and characterize these lines as only a euphemism for sexual performance anxiety. Desire is "boundless" because there is far more at stake in sexuality than biological pleasure. While Troilus' doubt that "constancy . . . could be in a woman" (ll. 157-60) has been adduced as a sign of a misogyny that distrusts Cressida and all women, the symmetry should be noted between his fears and Cressida's ("They say all lovers swear more performance than they are able, and yet reserve an ability that they never perform" [ll. 83-85]) as they enter into the romantic couple. The primary signification of these fears is not a hostility toward the opposite sex but the stakes of the game when the desired object (Lacan's *objet petit a*) is raised to the level of the Other, the reflective surface of one's own sense of identity and worth. Kristeva's ability to imagine the couple as in itself a "utopic wager"[15] short-circuits the competitive triangles of ego/others/objects of Hegel and Lacan as the means of achieving such identity. Kristeva asks,

> If desire is fickle, thirsting for novelty, unstable by definition, what is it that leads love to dream of an eternal couple? Why faithfulness, the wish for a durable harmony, why in short a marriage of love—not as necessity in a given society but as desire, as libidinal necessity?[16]

It has often been noticed that there is no mention of marriage between Troilus and Cressida, but this omission should not be referred to a realistic economy of representation, where it can serve as a source of suspicion about the character of Troilus; the text does not support such a suspicion. The absence of a public contract suggests, rather, the romantic wager that the couple could sustain itself without the support of the Symbolic Order that is in fact hostile to it. Kristeva's answer to the question "why the couple?" is that, even after technological advances

> render the eternal couple socially and scientifically useless, and do the same for marriage as a social necessity that insured optimal conditions for the reproduction of the species . . . the faithful couple that the law used to wish for remains for many a therapeutic erotic necessity in the face of the loss of identity caused by the open multiplicity of pleasures and *jouissances*. . . . [T]he couple is a durable mirror . . . binding in self-esteem [*amour-haine*] partners who are tied to such and such a partial object furnished by the other. . . .[17]

For Hegel, the desire for prestige, or recognition by the Other, is the mainspring of the specifically human dialectic of desire, and the triangular relation of competition for the desired objects of others creates that recognition as the winners prove their ability to force others to recognize their claims. But if, as Kojève recognizes in unpacking Hegel, "to desire a Desire is to want to substitute oneself for the value desired by this Desire,"[18] why can't that recognition be given directly and self-esteem be achieved in a dyadic mirroring? The war over Helen is driven by a desire for recognition by an imaginary third term, called "fame" by Troilus; thus, Paris can ask Diomedes, "Who, in your thoughts, merits fair Helen most, / Myself or Menelaus?" (4.1.55-56). Achilles extends protection to Thersites because Thersites' primary value to Achilles is as a marker to others of Achilles' ability to defend such a possession; it is their opinion that proves Achilles' worth. The question remains of whether the relation between Troilus and Cressida is fundamentally different from the relations between Paris and Helen and between Achilles and Thersites.

The first place to look for an answer to this question is in the imagery of power in the courtship scene of Troilus and Cressida. Mihoko Suzuki believes that Troilus' initial fear of losing "distinction" as he distrusts his "watery palate"

(3.2.26, 20) means that "he does not see Cressida as a partner but as a vehicle for sexual experience that he simultaneously desires and fears."[19] While Suzuki is right to connect this fear of losing "distinction" with the terms in which male identity is defined in *Troilus and Cressida,* her not/but construction is a crucial oversimplification. "Distinction" and "palate" were the metaphors used by Agamemnon and Nestor earlier in the play to describe the trial of merit. Agamemnon proposed that "Distinction, with a broad and powerful fan, / Puffing at all, winnows the light away, / And what hath mass or matter by itself / Lies rich in virtue and unmingl̀ed" (1.3.27-30), while Nestor argued that the Greek response to Hector's challenge is important because "in this trial much opinion dwells, / For here the Trojans taste our dear'st repute / With their fin'st palate" (ll. 336-38). Thus Troilus' fear that "Death," or "some joy too fine, / Too subtle-potent" (3.2.21-23), will result from his first sexual encounter with Cressida derives from his anxiety over whether he can live up to the hyperbolic male identity that he championed in the argument over whether to continue the war for Helen. But the progress of the scene does not continue to cast him as a warrior. He eventually declares himself "simpler than the infancy of truth" (l. 169) in a metaphor of submission in which a chain of confessions of lack of power culminates. Despite Pandarus' exhortation that "You must be witty now," he feels himself, in anticipation of Cressida's entrance, "Like vassalage at unawares encount'ring / The eye of majesty" (ll. 37-38), and his immediate response to her appearance is a loss of his talent for Petrarchan wit: he tells her, "You have bereft me of all words, lady" (l. 54).

Anything can be made subject to suspicion of insincerity; Troilus' eloquence in other parts of the play has been used to argue that his interest is more in language than it is in Cressida,[20] and his silence here can be used to claim, as Cressida herself does, that he is employing "Cunning in dumbness" (l. 131) to draw her out. But Troilus' image of the vassal awed by the unexpected sight of a king marks him as more simple than Aeneas, whose self-conscious politesse reflects his awareness that the "high and mighty" Agamemnon will look just like other mortals and that he himself will have to put on a properly reverent face in order to observe the protocol for addressing a king (1.3.227-32). When Troilus assures Cressida that his will be "Few words to fair faith" (3.2.94) and that he will not be like "all lovers" who "swear more performance than they are able, and yet reserve an ability"—i.e., fidelity—"that they never perform," he uses a metaphor from the courtly love tradition that casts her as his sovereign: "Praise us as we are tasted, allow us as we prove; our head shall go bare till merit crown it" (ll. 89-91). The consequences of this metaphor will be mixed; at least at the level of intention, though, it describes the "therapeutic erotic necessity" of the couple from the male perspective. Hegel describes the inadequacy of the satisfactions belonging to the position of the master; having won the struggle for prestige by making the Other his slave, the master discovers that when "he [i.e., his value] is recognized by someone whom he does not recognize," this "is a recognition without value for him. For he can be satisfied only by recognition from one whom he recognizes as worthy of recognizing him."[21] A similar paradox can be described in gender terms. In Lacan's account of the primal triangle, the male baby initially sees the mother as having the phallus, since she is the source of the satisfaction of his needs. He learns, however, that he will have to give up the body of the mother in order to acquire the phallus from the father; this is his entry into the world of the fathers, the patriarchal Symbolic Order in which he has a place. Lacan's insistence that there is nothing but madness outside the Symbolic Order leads him to overlook the deduction that Kristeva (and Shakespeare's "strange fellow") makes about the couple: that in order to recover the pleasure that was deferred when the male infant forsook the body of the mother, he will have to return the phallus to the woman, so that she "tastes" him with the palate of her opinion. In order to obtain the pleasure of being the desired of the Other, he will have to grant her the power of recognizing or not recognizing his claim to a male identity, that is, his ability to provide a satisfying phallus.

Even this account of the libidinal value of the couple from the male perspective puts the woman in an ambiguous position in relation to an idealizing, courtly lover like Troilus. Can he really love her, or is the woman inevitably obliterated as she serves as the vehicle for his consummation of his own desire? Lacan derides the premises of courtly love, seeing its conventions as an "elegant" representation of the fact that the woman is merely the man's means of consummation with the Symbolic Order and declaring that chivalry "is always the discourse of the master," where the "lady was entirely, in the most servile sense of the term, his female subject."[22] But the literary record is not so unequivocal. Even one of the most misogynistic texts of the courtly love tradition, Capellanus's *Art of Courtly Love,* which shares with its predecessor, Ovid's *Art of Love,* a tolerance, under certain conditions, for rape, records a number of decisions of medieval courts of love which emphasize the importance of a woman's independent will and choice. Repeatedly, complicated cases in which knights assert claims based on a protocol or a promise made by a woman are settled by this precept: "The resolution of the immediate question depends more on the will or desire [*arbitrio vel voluntate*] of the woman than on an understanding of precept of law or special command of love." In such cases it is left to the woman to decide how she is moved by the "impulse to love [*spiritus movetur amandi*]."[23]

The reliability of Capellanus's text as historical document is problematic; it has been argued that the courts of love never existed, and that adultery could not possibly have been widely practiced in the tightly regulated sexual climate of medieval Europe. De Rougemont cites René Nelli's thesis that, in a society where marriages were contracted not out of love but from "material and social considerations . . . imposed on the parties regardless of

their feelings," the literature of courtly love, as it idealized adultery, offered to women "a *spiritual antipode* to marriage, a state into which they had been forced."[24] This would cast the Provençal lays as the medieval analogue to the romance novels sold on supermarket paperback racks today and would suggest the persistence of the Lacanian principle that, in a culture whose sexuality is structured around men's pleasure, women will uphold their *jouissance* "elsewhere," in a supplementary (not a complementary) *jouissance* that exists "beyond the phallus" and outside the law.[25] As Shakespeare exploits the medieval tradition of anachronistic revision of classical legends, he uses the resources of the literature of courtly love to create a highly sophisticated sexual psychology in his characters.

Cressida's first soliloquy shows that she fully understands the power of a woman's subjectivity in the realm of sexuality. She alludes to the possibility of being reduced to something subhuman, a "thing," and counsels that the only way to avoid such debasement is to "hold . . . off" (1.2.288-89). A woman who convinces men that her desire is difficult to attain thereby enhances its value; the recognition she finally confers gains in value directly in relation to the difficulty of its attainment. A woman who shows her desire too openly, on the other hand, does more than lower her own worth; she positively inspires male paranoia. In one of the most misogynistic passages in *The Art of Courtly Love,* Capellanus warns his young friend Walter against women who "grant favours readily," in a passage that shows why Cressida is initially so wary of sexuality and why she is ultimately defamed anyway:

> A woman of this type cannot unite herself to anyone with bonds of love because of her excessive sexual appetite; she seeks satiety through the lust of many. So in vain do you seek her love, unless you regard yourself as so virile in sexual matters that you can satiate her lust. But this would be more difficult than draining the seas completely of their waters. . . . Though you can obtain your will and win her embraces to the full, the consolations she offers will be the occasion of intolerable pain and the source of abundant griefs to you . . . [w]hen . . . you come to realise that she is lending herself to another's lust.[26]

If a woman's desire is independent of male inspiration, there's no telling where it might go, or what it might say; as Thersites' description of Ajax to Achilles shows, the woman's potential sexual mobility can threaten the very basis of male sexual identity. The reaction to this threat is the representation of the woman as promiscuous, a "whore."

While the courtship scene between Troilus and Cressida addresses the doubts of each about the other sex, Cressida displays a good deal more apprehension over the dangers of romantic idealization; she speaks in a vocabulary of fear and Troilus in a vocabulary of hope. Having confessed her desire, Cressida worries that he will "play the tyrant" (3.2.118) and she the "fool" (l. 149); Troilus hopes that "constancy . . . could be in a woman," so that (in elegantly sexual imagery) his own "integrity and truth" might be "affronted" by hers, and he could be "then uplifted" (ll. 157-67). The parrying and testing is inconclusive for most of the scene, as she threatens once to leave (l. 138), loses her composure at two other points (ll. 123, 149), and finally draws him out to her own satisfaction. Her assent to his suit is not final until the following exchange:

> TROILUS
>   . . . I am as true as truth's simplicity,
>   And simpler than the infancy of truth.
> CRESSIDA
>   In that I'll war with you.
> TROILUS   O virtuous fight,
>   When right with right wars who shall be most right!
>
>   (3.2.168-71)

The dramatic hinge of the scene is Cressida's line in that exchange; nothing is settled between them until she casts their relation as an inversion of the Hegelian struggle for mastery. As he adopts her metaphor, their vows to provide faithful service to the other cast each of them in the position of vying not for the position of master but that of servant.

This seeming mutuality is not symmetrical, however, as the terms of their succeeding vows show. Just as Troilus believed that fame would canonize his manhood if he stood by his honor and fought for Helen, so now he imagines that fame, through the agency of "True swains in love . . . in the world to come" (l. 172), will celebrate his fidelity to Cressida. Cressida imagines no such thing; her negative vows ("If I be false or swerve a hair from truth . . ." [ll. 183-95]) show that the most she can imagine asking from fame is anonymity. In Lacanian terms, what Troilus imagines is a positive evaluation by the Symbolic Order, an expectation that is the glue of social cohesion. The Troilus who is simple enough to believe his own metaphor about the vassal awed by the sight of a king truly believes in the premises of Ulysses' degree speech (which is probably more than Ulysses does)—i.e., that our earthly arrangements can and should reflect a cosmic order. To anchor this cosmology of an immanent natural order, both he and Ulysses imagine the earth as the center of the universe (1.3.85; 3.2.178). Cressida knows that her only place in such an order is not a happy one; when a simple mutuality of desire is alienated to the judgment of a totalizing authority, women lose their identities as they become the "things" men use to demonstrate mastery and achieve priority within the Symbolic Order. There is a fundamental incompatibility between the fame Troilus hopes to win by warring over Helen and the satisfaction Cressida can offer. Although Troilus describes Helen as a "pearl," he knows that her value is entirely a construct and that it is only the war itself that paints her as 'the most beautiful woman in the world'; in herself she's like any other "thing" in the Symbolic Order: "[n]aught but as 'tis valued" (2.2.52). In order to get satisfaction from Cressida, however, he needs to believe in her intrinsic value if her opinion of him is to satisfy his need for self-esteem.

The Symbolic Order that has brought about this war is, in linguistic terms, a metaphoric order of substitution in which Cressida stands for Helen and Helen for an abstraction. The romantic narrative that has joined Troilus and Cressida depends upon a metonymic (or Lacanian imaginary) order in which Cressida is simply herself. The shadow of the Symbolic is cast over the lovers by the omnipresence of Pandarus; Cressida's eventual willingness to set aside her fears of sexual exploitation derives from her belief that Pandarus is her ally and that what he represents as the guarantor of their vows could actually be friendly to her desire. Even this most benign form of the paternal metaphor will, however, betray her. The genius of the absolute distinction made in the courtly love tradition between love and marriage, and the insistence in that tradition on the complete secrecy of the true love bond,[27] is in the understanding that these practices manifest of the fundamental incompatibility of the binary (Lacanian imaginary) and triangular (Lacanian symbolic) structures of desire. There is nothing in the dyadic relation to satisfy a third term, be that a third person or the entire social order. Pandarus' voyeuristic pleasure in the courtship scene is often remarked upon, but in this he is like Juliet's Nurse in her vicarious enjoyment of Juliet's sexual prospects. When Juliet insists that she will have only Romeo, and the Nurse relishes the prospect of Paris, Juliet discovers that she must act alone. Those who insist on finding an identity within the couple will find no real support anywhere outside the couple. The Symbolic Order will seem to support, and even to legislate, monogamy as a means of its own reproduction, but it does so only by channelling desire into an idealization that, working metaphorically, turns the other (*objet petit a*) into one's marker of prestige within the Symbolic Order. When this function is at its peak, all men will fight to the death for 'the most beautiful woman in the world'. Pandarus' character is the mediating function of the paternal metaphor that has at one side the seeming affection of Juliet's Nurse and at the other old Capulet turning on his own daughter and telling her that she is nothing but his property. Pandarus' curse on Cressida, "Would thou hadst ne'er been born! I knew thou wouldst be his death" (4.2.86-87), illustrates that Capulet's actions were not the idiosyncrasies of a single, crotchety old man. They were an illustration of the fact, reinforced in the character of Pandarus, that a patriarchy does not really care about its daughters.[28]

Pandarus' betrayal of Cressida at the end of 4.2 is all the more painful because of her continuing trust in him. I do not consider the bantering just after Pandarus' entry in 4.2 to be nearly as hostile to Cressida as some other readers have found it. Pandarus' jokes about her sexual experience ("Has't not slept tonight? Would he not—a naughty man— let it sleep?" [ll. 33-34]) are the Nurse's jokes (". . . for the next night, I warrant, / The County Paris hath set up his rest / That you shall rest but little" [*Romeo and Juliet*, 4.5.5-7]), and Cressida's "Would he were knocked i' the head!" (l. 35) is not unlike her behavior towards him in 1.2. As for Troilus' behavior in this scene, René Girard has declared that his lines "O Cressida! But that the busy day, / Waked by the lark, hath roused the ribald crows, / And dreaming night will hide our joys no longer, / I would not from thee" (ll. 9-12) manifest such an obvious "highly artificial lyricism" that he "cannot be sincere."[29] To refer once more to *Romeo and Juliet,* this is Romeo's morning-after metaphor:

> It was the lark, the herald of the morn,
> No nightingale. Look, love, what envious streaks
> Do lace the severing clouds in yonder east.
> Night's candles are burnt out, and jocund day
> Stands tiptoe on the misty mountain tops.
>
> (3.5.6-10)

Lyricism is no proof of insincerity. Both Troilus and Cressida continue to try to maintain the secrecy of their love, as far as it can now be protected (4.2.41-42 and 73), and the difference in their responses to the news that they are to be forcibly separated can be traced to their differing beliefs in the existence of a governing natural order. The irony of Paris saying "I know what 'tis to love; / And would, as I shall pity, I could help" (4.3.10-11) is too obvious to be missed, but Troilus does miss it and identifies the agent of their separation as some omnipotent cosmic force, "the gods" (4.4.25) or "Time" (l. 42). From within his belief that the political system in which he lives is beyond question, Troilus can imagine no better response to the forced removal of Cressida than to continue to perform his knightly duty and risk his life in order still to see her. He "will throw [his] glove to Death himself" and "corrupt the Grecian sentinels, / To give thee nightly visitation" (4.4.63, 72-73), in contrast to Chaucer's Troilus, who thought of disguising himself as a pilgrim in order to sneak into the Greek camp but decided that it was too risky.[30]

The intensity of Cressida's response tells a different story. To Pandarus' admonition to "be moderate," she responds,

> Why tell you me of moderation?
> The grief is fine, full, perfect, that I taste,
> And violenteth in a sense as strong
> As that which causeth it. How can I moderate it?
> If I could temporize with my affection,
> Or brew it to a weak and colder palate,
> The like allayment could I give my grief.
> My love admits no qualifying dross;
> No more my grief, in such a precious loss.
>
> (4.4.2-10)

Unlike Troilus, who worried about the adequacy of his palate in relation to an ideal norm, Cressida takes the appetite metaphor that stands as an alternative cosmic order in this play (imaged as "appetite, an universal wolf" [1.3.121] just as Time is pictured as a devourer [3.3.146-51]) and turns it within—she now tastes herself—and joins that imagery to the narcissistic masochism of the male lover in the Petrarchan tradition[31] to create a subjectivity unsecured by any promises or patterns in any symbolic order. The primary modern theorist of such a subject is Kristeva, who writes of the "pangs and delights of masochism" as the lot of the "abject," the subject who has discovered that "all its objects are based merely on the inaugural *loss* that laid the foundations of its own being," and so experiences even its "own body and ego as the most precious non-objects; they are no longer seen in their own right but forfeited, abject."[32] Shakespeare's Cressida, motherless and abandoned by her father, believes for one moment that she can build "a life" (4.2.23) on one object of desire, one *objet petit a,* only to find that not only that object but her own body can be forfeited by an inexplicable law that demands everything and offers nothing in return.

Cressida's greatest terror in the scene of her parting from Troilus is that she could be betrayed from within the couple. Her response to his repeated exhortations to "be true" is "You love me not" (4.4.82), because his doubt suggests that the mirror effect was a mirage. She feels that her "love / Is as the very center of the earth" (4.2.104-5), and if he does not know this core of her being, then what is he in love with? Lacan argues that the mirror effect is always a mirage, that "When, in love, I solicit a look, what is profoundly unsatisfying and always missing is that—*You never look at me from the place from which I see you,*"[33] because there is no real center of one's being. The self that is projected into the romantic relation is an ideal I, an inevitable metaphor, whose function is to convince the other that I am worthy of love, while the *objet petit a,* who is, for the real, temporal self the cathexis of an already formed desire, is idealized into the cause of desire. The complementary subjects of a romantic mirroring are not the historical or "imaginary" selves (identical terms for Lacan) but idealizations that have been formed not from within but as patterns given by the Symbolic Order. As Pandarus sells Troilus to Cressida and Cressida to Troilus, he tells her that Troilus is like Hector (only better), and Troilus that she is like Helen (only better).

Shakespeare intensifies the pathos of the breakdown of the romantic construct by maintaining the sincere attachment of his characters to its terms. There is a perfect continuity from Troilus' entrance in the courtship scene "like vassalage at unawares encount'ring / The eye of majesty" through his culminating definition of himself in that scene as "simpler than the infancy of truth" to his final vow to Cressida that "The moral of my wit / Is 'plain and true'; there's all the reach of it" (4.4.107-8). In the realistic economy of the play, the simplicity of his character is brought out in the contrast between him and Diomedes. Troilus behaves courteously to Diomedes, and expects to be treated courteously; Diomedes, who has already engaged Aeneas in a round of ceremonious hostility, sees such ceremony as only a veil for a more brutal reality. The difference between them is emphasized by the later comments of Ulysses, who ratifies Troilus' depiction of himself as "firm of word, / Speaking in deeds and deedless in his tongue" (4.5.98-99), and of Thersites, who describes Diomedes as the exemplar of the "all lovers" Cressida fears, those who "promise . . . like Brabbler the hound, but when he performs, astronomers foretell it; it is prodigious" (5.1.92-94). It is Cressida's sensitivity to this difference that leads her to conclude that Troilus loved her better than Diomedes will. But in the mimetic geometry of the play, Troilus sets the pattern for imitation by Diomedes when he, in effect, tells Diomedes that he is Cressida's lover and casts her as a transcendent object of desire. The difficulty of assessing the nature of the romantic bond can be located in this moment of transition as Troilus praises Cressida to Diomedes: is this a sign of the intensity of his love, or is it a violation of the code of secrecy (which would be the only true marker of a self-sufficient mutuality) for the sake of prestige garnered from a third term? Is it any different than Paris' question to Diomedes about who deserved Helen more? Whatever the implicit reality, the appearance is the same.

Janet Adelman has found Shakespeare's account of Cressida's history in the Greek camp a disappointment and a failure of Shakespeare's artistry, seeing Cressida as a character who promised a great deal of depth but who becomes increasingly "opaque."[34] Cressida's motives in her first appearance among the Greeks are fairly obvious; she uses her wit as best she can to fend off a stylized gang rape. A scene is then omitted, as in her next scene with Diomedes they refer to a previous "oath" that the audience never witnesses, but the depth of her character does not disappear with that scene. The first words we hear her speak to Diomedes register her understanding of her vulnerability: "Now, my sweet guardian" (5.2.7). In a society that has made Patroclus and Thersites into a whore and a mistress, she knows that she needs a protector. What is intriguing about Shakespeare's Cressida is that, despite her previous vows to Troilus and her belief that Troilus' vows to her are worth more than those of Diomedes, she finds Diomedes more than a hateful necessity; she finds something in him that appeals to her "heart" when she says, "Troilus, farewell! One eye yet looks on thee, / But with my heart the other eye doth see" (5.2.110-11). Adelman believes that this shift does not come from within her character, and that she is the victim of Troilus', and Shakespeare's, inability to reconcile woman as a sexual being with woman as an idealized romantic object. But Cressida's simultaneous attraction to both Diomedes and Troilus makes psychological sense if it is viewed from within what Lacan calls a metonymic sexual economy, one that is not governed by the metaphoric Law of the Father.

The means of satisfying the human need for self-esteem in a metonymic economy of sheer contiguity is to be the desired of the Other, and it must be an Other whose opinion counts. This will be a good trick for Diomedes and Cressida; Diomedes needs to convince Cressida that she is the object of his free choice and not just the only woman in the Greek camp, and Cressida needs to satisfy Diomedes' desire for her "mind" and her "heart" (5.2.15, 85) along with her body. While Thersites characterizes her holding-off as a device for sharpening his desire, the stereotypically feminine strategem of enhancing one's value by seeming difficult to attain, it should be noted that Di-

omedes behaves in exactly the same way. He threatens twice to leave (ll. 33, 46) and insists that he will not play her "fool" (l. 33), suggesting that he, too, does not care to remain in this relationship unless he can be convinced of the sincerity of her desire for him. His pledge to wear her token into battle follows the courtly convention that equates a knight's valor and his mistress's honor; it is entirely plausible that the Cressida who was impressed by the hacks on Hector's helmet, asking "Be those with swords?" (1.2.210), would be susceptible to Capellanus's principle that "It is the daring of men above all which usually arouses women's love."[35] Whatever the intentions behind the ritual of casting one's desire as difficult to attain, both Cressida and Diomedes emerge from their dialogue satisfied with the libidinal value of this relation.

Cressida's character develops in a direction that follows the course of male paranoia as outlined by Capellanus, but Shakespeare makes her more than an effect of that paranoia. To see her as Adelman does, simply as an effect of Troilus' fear of women's sexuality, reads against the immediate dramatic situation, in which, after their sexual consummation, Troilus continues in romantic pursuit of Cressida and she discovers her own reasons for erotic ambivalence. If her idealization of him is less firm than his of her, this is not the revelation of individual character but the result of the different promises made to men and women in a patriarchal culture. The idealization of the Other, which is the support of monogamy, depends upon the psychoanalytic function of condensation, or, in linguistic terms, the metaphor, so that the *objet petit a* stands for a place in the grand Other, the Symbolic Order, where value is confirmed. In a subject with profound doubts about the promises of the Symbolic Order, desire is liable to take its naturally metonymic, promiscuous course. Shakespeare does not settle for the simple pathos of Chaucer, whose Criseyde tries to repair her "dishonor" as best she can, pledging that "to Diomede algate [at least] I wol be trewe."[36] Shakespeare's Cressida is a fundamentally divided figure who sends her last words to Troilus, where they become the play's most vivid metaphor of fragmentation as he shreds her letter and casts the pieces to the wind ("Go, wind, to wind! There turn and change together" [5.3.110]).

Troilus, of course, does not begin to understand her behavior. Having imagined himself as the cause of her desire, he cannot comprehend her being sexual in his absence. His disappointment is so thoroughly apocalyptic because he saw their union as proof of a cosmic order of values. His incredulity about the Cressida he now sees— "If beauty have a soul, this is not she" (5.2.142)—reflects his belief that the possession of her beauty was the means by which he had been gratified by that cosmic order for abiding by its principles. Troilus' expectation that he would be rewarded with eternal fame for maintaining his "honor" both in war and in love is a pre-Christian image of immortality, but his disappointment in Cressida embodies Lacan's principle that "in order for the soul to come into being, she, the woman, is differentiated from it. . . . Called woman [*dit-femme*] and defamed [*diffâme*]."[37] Troilus finds his world inexplicable because he tries to maintain his relation to two incompatible Others, one a stable, hierarchical system that could terminate in the permanence of immortality and another whose essence is mobility. Cressida's recognition confirmed his male identity, but the independence of her subjectivity—which was necessary for her recognition to matter within the couple—means that male identity cannot be self-grounded. Her defamation is identified precisely with the independence of her judgment as Thersites imagines her saying "'My mind is now turned whore'" (5.2.117). The woman is not defamed for her body's reduction to an object of male pleasure but for discovering in her "mind" any means of her own pleasure after having been so debased. It is ironic that Thersites, who gets his revenge on Ajax from the position of the sexual slave, should be the one to pronounce this judgment on Cressida, but, as Lacan puts it, what the Symbolic Order calls "perverts" have "a knowledge of the nature of things, which leads directly from sexual conduct to its truth, namely, its amorality."[38] Having been denied an identity within the Symbolic Order, Thersites is not subject to its mystifications about its practices.

Cressida does not want to see herself in these terms. She maintains an image of the ideal I, in relation to which the metonymic promiscuity of her desire seems to her like "turpitude" (5.2.115). But the woman—and this is not a biological entity, since "she" includes Thersites, who is a perfect example of Lacan's claim that real *jouissance* consists of talking—is the subject who is promised nothing by a transcendent Symbolic Order and so finds her *jouissance* elsewhere and is defamed for doing so. The only means of escaping this infamy is to take Juliet's course, suicide, which is what generations of Cressida-bashers have implicitly demanded of her. By choosing death over survival without Troilus, Cressida would make the Hegelian choice of preferring an idealized value to mere survival and would confirm that Troilus is indeed worth more than life itself. The mutual suicides of Romeo and Juliet are the confirmation that the couple has made love a value that transcends the biological instinct of survival. Troilus believes that he should make this choice, and so he risks his life for her. But for women—a category that includes Thersites and Patroclus—to meet this Hegelian standard and risk their lives for the sake of an identity better than that of slavery is, historically, not to take a risk but to commit suicide. Shakespeare's Cressida retells and explicates the position of the archetypal woman as it is told in the Troy legends: she does what she has to, she enjoys what she can, and she is condemned as a whore for it.

Adelman is right that for the remainder of the play, its point of view is focused through Troilus, and that the spectator who expected to enjoy an identification with Cressida is disappointed. But as *Troilus and Cressida* refuses to offer the vicarious pleasure of cathartic identification with the deaths of its heroine and hero, it tells a truer story as it represents woman in history as she whose story is forcibly suppressed. The audience is tantalized by one last possibility of hearing from Cressida when Troilus receives a letter from her, but that opportunity for dramatically ironic pathos is demolished when, instead of reading the letter aloud, he tears it and throws it away. With the play now funnelled through Troilus, it is no accident that the death of Hector follows immediately upon the loss of Cressida. As Kristeva explains the decline into abjection, "when the condensation function that constitutes the sign collapses"—and Cressida's beauty was to Troilus the signifier of a higher order—"in that case one always discovers a collapse of the Oedipal triangulation that supports it."[39] After the loss of Cressida from within the couple, Troilus no longer believes in a natural order or in following codes of conduct that would correspond with that order; his exhortation to Hector to kill "captive Grecian[s]" (5.3.40) is his means of serving notice to what's left of the paternal metaphor that he is no longer bound by any rules of fair play. Hector then becomes a victim of Achilles' practice of precisely the merciless and honorless policy that Troilus urged Hector himself to follow. The symmetry becomes even more precise when we remember that Achilles is enraged because the war that was to serve as an occasion for his glory has deprived him of his romantic Other.

As de Rougemont summarizes the literature of romantic passion, he finds that it is always a literature of suffering and death, and asks, "Why does Western Man wish to suffer this passion which lacerates him and which all his common sense rejects?" De Rougemont offers the Hegelian answer that "he reaches self-awareness and tests himself only by risking his life," and he sees this as "the most tenacious root of the war instinct."[40] But what Hegel sees as a field of human glory, Kristeva describes as an "infernal *jouissance*," much like Shakespeare's play, which declines into a disgusted parody of the heroic ethos. Kristeva's name for this is abjection, the "nocturnal reverse of the magnificent legend [of courtliness],"[41] whose logic Troilus revealed with his "common sense" when he described Helen's beauty as painted in blood and capable of turning crown princes into merchants, but whose lure he followed nonetheless. With his paternal metaphor completely dissolved by the death of Hector, Troilus can find no other pattern to emulate but can only "haunt" Achilles "like a wicked conscience" (5.10.28), imitating an Other with no object in view, risking his life with no possibility of satisfaction. The outcome, according to the legends of Troy (including Chaucer's version of the story), is that Troilus will be killed by Achilles. The nadir of the breakdown of the Symbolic Order is the play's final image, which turns this world's governing metaphor into an image of abjection, where even the "rule in unity" of the body itself is violated by Pandarus' body oozing its diseased fluids.

In suggesting that Shakespeare tells us, centuries before Lacan, that the patriarchy is not whole, this essay describes a familiar Shakespeare, the negatively capable, universal Shakespeare of the humanist tradition who can represent everyone's experience, including that of Cressida. A male critic who depicts *Troilus and Cressida* in these terms after Janet Adelman has described its denouement as a male fantasy about an objectified woman can only do so with a good deal of trepidation. But Adelman's analysis, like the assumption behind Hillis Miller's disbelief that Shakespeare could have known the extent of his subversions of the logocentric order,[42] depends upon a Hegelian view of the history of ideas as a story of progress, in which a modern systematic hermeneutic is inevitably more knowing than a Renaissance playwright. The structural relation to the past is then the Hegelian structure of the sublation (*Aufhebung*) that simultaneously cancels the force of Shakespeare's work while it preserves its insights in the critical commentary. Foucaul has gone furthest in our own time in following the Hegelian imperative to know and transcend history in the domain of sexuality, seeking to find the "strictly historical" grounds that have "imbued [sex] with the death instinct" and have sold us the idea that "Sex is worth dying for."[43] Reading Shakespeare at a Foucauldian remove is an adoption of the discourse of the master, while reading him as Virginia Woolf and Kristeva read him, both poetically and prosaically, draws one into the unstable material beneath the constructs of ego formation. The supplementary principle to Woolf's celebration of Shakespeare's androgyny[44] is Kristeva's abjection, which is the experience that *Troilus and Cressida* imposes on its audience as it refuses to provide us with the satisfying sublation of a definitive and glorious catharsis and instead simply deprives us of the characters whose libidinal resources had once seemed so promising. The erotics of art, if Kristeva is used as a guide, would not be a simple recovery of pleasure but a free fall into a primal and unstable calculus of pleasure and pain in which love neither lives happily ever after nor dies beautifully, and for which *Troilus and Cressida* is an exemplary text. To read Shakespeare as our contemporary is to believe, against Hegel, that art is never simply a thing of the past.

Notes

1. All quotations of Shakespeare are from *The Complete Works of Shakespeare*, ed. David Bevington, 4th ed. (New York: HarperCollins, 1992).

2. Troilus has been criticized for "inauthenticity," "predatory attitudes," and "jaded epicureanism" by Gayle Greene ("Shakespeare's Cressida: 'A Kind of Self'" in *The Woman's Part: Feminist Criticism of Shakespeare*, Carolyn Ruth Swift Lenz, Gayle Greene, and Carol Thomas Neely, eds. [Urbana: Univ. of Illinois Press, 1980], pp. 133-49); called "sanctimonious" and a "predator" by Stephen J. Lynch ("Shakespeare's Cressida: 'A Woman of Quick Sense,'" *Philological Quarterly*, 63 [1984], 357-68); found "insufferable" to the "sensitive spectator" by René Girard ("The Politics of Desire in *Troilus and Cressida*" in *Shakespeare and the Question of Theory*, Patricia Parker and Geoffrey Hartman, eds. [New York: Methuen, 1985], pp. 188-209); and condemned for "latent misogyny" and "infantile and narcissistic sensualism" by Mihoko Suzuki ("Shakespeare's *Troi-*

lus and Cressida" in *Metamorphoses of Helen: Authority, Difference and the Epic* [Ithaca, N.Y.: Cornell Univ. Press, 1989], pp. 210-57) and for "posturing aplomb" and "infantilism" by Deborah A. Hooker ("Coming to Cressida Through Irigaray," *South Atlantic Quarterly*, 8 [1989], 899-932). Other defenders of Cressida include Grant L. Voth and Oliver H. Evans, "Cressida and the World of the Play," *Shakespeare Studies*, 8 (1975), 231-39; Carol Cook, "Unbodied Figures of Desire," *Theatre Journal*, 38 (1986), 34-52; Janet Adelman, "'This is and is not Cressid': The Characterization of Cressida" in *The (M)other Tongue: Essays in Feminist Psychoanalytic Interpretation*, Shirley Nelson Garner, Claire Kahane, and Madelon Sprengnether, eds. (Ithaca, N.Y.: Cornell Univ. Press, 1985), pp. 119-41; Linda Charnes, "'So Unsecret to Ourselves': Notorious Identity and the Material Subject in *Troilus and Cressida*," *Shakespeare Quarterly*, 40 (1989), 413-40; and Claire M. Tylee, "The Text of Cressida and Every Ticklish Reader: *Troilus and Cressida* and the Greek Camp Scene," *Shakespeare Survey*, 41 (1989), 63-76. Cressida's detractors are too numerous to cite, but perhaps the most surprising member of their company is Joyce Carol Oates, who calls Cressida "evil," "villainous," and "impure before becoming Troilus' mistress" in "Essence and Existence in Shakespeare's *Troilus and Cressida*," *PQ*, 46 (1967), 167-85.

3. A modern edition that prints Chaucer and Henryson together is *The Story of Troilus*, ed. R.K. Gordon (New York: E.P. Dutton, 1963). Quotations of Chaucer will be taken from this text; for the passage referred to here, see page 362.

4. For Blake's description of prostitution, the well-known text is "London," *The Poetry and Prose of William Blake*, ed. David V. Erdman (Garden City, N.J.: Doubleday, 1965), p. 26; for his description of the oedipal relation, see "The Book of Urizen," *The Illuminated Blake*, ed. David V. Erdman (Garden City, N.J.: Doubleday, 1974), p. 293, esp. pl. 21.

5. My reading of the relation between Achilles and Patroclus differs greatly from those of Deborah A. Hooker (cited in n. 2, above), who believes that their relationship is a covert scandal within the Greek camp, exposure of which would violate the "hommosexual" order (a Lacanian neologism that appears in *Feminine Sexuality: Jacques Lacan and the école freudienne*, trans. Jacqueline Rose, ed. Juliet Mitchell and Jacqueline Rose [New York: Macmillan, 1982], p. 156), and Eric Mallin, who argues that Shakespeare depicts homosexuality as heroic and heterosexuality as unheroic ("Emulous Factions and the Collapse of Chivalry: *Troilus and Cressida*," *Representations*, 29 [1990], 145-79, esp. p. 163). My description of heterosexuality and homosexuality as fundamentally similar and operating on the same dynamics of power is consonant with the recent work of David M. Halperin, who argues that the distinction between homo- and heterosexuality did not

become rigidly encoded in Western culture until the nineteenth century (*One Hundred Years of Homosexuality* [New York: Routledge, 1990]). Shakespeare's descriptions of Thersites and Patroclus as mistresses and whores within the single-sex society of the army can profitably be compared to Jack Abbott's description of "women" in the population of contemporary American men's prisons (cited in Halperin, pp. 38-39).

6. *Introduction to the Reading of Hegel: Lectures on the Phenomenology of Spirit,* assembled by Raymond Queneau, trans. James H. Nichols, Jr., ed. Allan Bloom (New York: Basic Books, 1969), p. 6.

7. *The Life and Minor Works of George Peele,* ed. David H. Horne (New Haven: Yale Univ. Press, 1952), p. 197, l. 353.

8. Freud's account of this transition (in a more violent form) is in *Totem and Taboo,* trans. A. A. Brill (New York: Vintage Books, 1946), pp. 182-86.

9. Jacques Lacan, *Écrits: A Selection,* trans. Alan Sheridan (New York: W.W. Norton, 1977), p. 19.

10. *Écrits,* p. 19.

11. Julia Kristeva, *Tales of Love,* trans. Leon S. Roudiez (New York: Columbia Univ. Press, 1987), p. 30.

12. *Tales of Love,* p. 282.

13. For the controversy over the "strange fellow," see the New Variorum *Troilus and Cressida,* ed. Harold N. Hillebrand (Philadelphia: J. B. Lippincott, 1953), pp. 411-15.

14. The editorial question of Collier's emendation of Folio's and Quarto's "married" is treated in the New Variorum, where Hillebrand cites both the contemporary justification for the emendation and says, correctly, that "'mirror'd' has effectually established itself in modern texts" (p. 177).

15. *Tales of Love,* p. 222.

16. *Tales of Love,* p. 225.

17. *Tales of Love,* pp. 226-27. While "self-esteem" is an extremely loose translation of "*amour-haine,*" the two concepts are highly interdependent for Kristeva. Self-esteem is precisely what is at stake in the stabilization of *amour-haine.*

18. p. 7 (cited in n. 6, above).

19. p. 228 (cited in n. 2, above).

20. Greene, p. 142; Girard, pp. 188-89; Hooker, p. 917 (all cited in n. 2, above).

21. Kojève, p. 19.

22. *Feminine Sexuality,* p. 141 (cited in n. 5, above).

23. *Andreas Capellanus on Love,* ed. and trans. P. G. Walsh (London: Duckworth, 1982), pp. 206-7. This edition is a parallel translation. Other cases that are referred to the same principle of the woman's *arbitrio* occur on pages 254-55 and 258-59.

24. Denis de Rougemont, *Love in the Western World,* trans. Montgomery Belgion (New York: Pantheon, 1956), pp. 113-14.

25. *Feminine Sexuality,* pp. 144-45.

26. p. 221.

27. The importance of maintaining the secrecy of love is discussed by Capellanus and, in this century, by Peter Dronke, *Medieval Latin and the Rise of European Love-Lyric* (Oxford: Clarendon Press, 1968). Capellanus says that "He who is eager to preserve . . . his love undamaged ought to take the greatest precautions to ensure that his love is not divulged to anyone beyond its limits, but preserved secret from all" (p. 225), and Dronke that "The secrecy of *amour courtois* springs from the universal notion of love as a mystery not to be profaned by the outside world, not to be shared by any but lover and beloved" (p. 48).

28. See Claire McEachern's discussion of this idea in the context of two other Shakespeare plays in "Fathering Herself: A Source Study of Shakespeare's Feminism," *SQ,* 39 (1988), 269-90.

29. pp. 188-89 (cited in n. 2, above).

30. Chaucer (cited in n. 3, above), p. 340 (Bk. 5, st. 226, ll. 1576-82).

31. "I feed on these particular pains and sufferings with a kind of delight so poignant that if I am snatched away from them it is against my will" (Petrarch, *Secretum Meum,* quoted in de Rougemont, p. 183).

32. *Powers of Horror,* trans. Leon S. Roudiez (New York: Columbia Univ. Press, 1982), p. 5.

33. *The Four Fundamental Concepts of Psycho-Analysis,* trans. Alan Sheridan, ed. Jacques-Alain Miller (New York: W.W. Norton, 1978), p. 103.

34. p. 138 (cited in n. 2, above).

35. p. 265.

36. Chaucer, p. 326 (Bk. 5, st. 153, l. 1071).

37. *Feminine Sexuality,* p. 156.

38. *Feminine Sexuality,* pp. 157-58.

39. *Powers of Horror,* p. 53.

40. p. 51 (cited in n. 24, above).

41. *Powers of Horror,* p. 162.

42. J. Hillis Miller, "Ariachne's Broken Woof," *Georgia Review,* 31 (1977), 44-60, esp. pp. 58-59.

43. Michel Foucault, *The History of Sexuality: Volume One: An Introduction* (New York: Vintage, 1980), p. 156.

44. Woolf's comment on reading "poetically and prosaically at one and the same time" is on page 46 of *A Room of One's Own* (New York: Harcourt, Brace & World, 1929); her comment on Shakespeare's androgyny is on page 102.

Michael Yogev (essay date 1998)

SOURCE: "'War and Lechery Confound All': Identity and Agency in Shakespeare's *Troilus and Cressida*," in *Strands Afar Remote: Israeli Perspectives on Shakespeare,* edited by Avraham Oz, Associated University Presses, 1998, pp. 87-112.

[*In the following essay, Yogev observes that the courtly and chivalric codes found in earlier versions of the story of Troilus and Cressida are intentionally subverted in Shakespeare's play into opportunities for male sexual aggression and exploitation.*]

Shakespeare's *Troilus and Cressida* has occasioned a number of critical discussions of the psychodynamics of identity formation as well as poststructuralist accounts of how its powerfully ambiguous and enigmatic language subverts identity.[1] To my knowledge, however, these two approaches have not been combined to analyze the way in which language and "heroic" activity at once constitute and subvert the identities of the protagonists in Shakespeare's bitter drama. Like Chaucer and Boccaccio before him, Shakespeare juxtaposes the martial plot of the Trojan War with the amorous tale of Troilus and Cressida. But in sharp contrast to his sources, Shakespeare lends neither Troilus or Cressida any tragic depth of character nor even the very qualified comic closure we may find in such figures as Angelo and Isabella from *Measure for Measure*. Instead, Shakespeare reduces this medieval love story to a sordid mirror of the Trojan War itself. As Thersites succinctly puts it, "War and lechery confound all" (*Troilus and Cressida*, 2.3.77).[2] This caustic characterization of the world of the play recognizes the connection between the psychodynamics of love and war at the same time as it lays bare a fundamental instability in the codes of courtly love and chivalric honor that underlie this central legend of Western literature. Thersites' remark highlights the sexual desire and aggression that "con-found," coconstitute the individual and collective identities in the play—even as they erode and threaten to annihilate those identities. In its dramatic presentation of the erotic disintegration of Troilus, and its biting critique of the heroic ethos of the Trojan War, Shakespeare's text at once anticipates and offers a useful critique of contemporary psychoanalytic explanations of the development of male subjectivity. The stark discrepancy between the heroic ideals and the ultimate lack of chivalric integrity in heroes like Achilles and Hector suggests that this Shakespearean text also leaves room for a more extensive examination into the psychological roots of chivalry and courtly love.

Valerie Traub has argued persuasively that a central element in the sexual dynamics of Shakespeare's plays is the erotic vulnerability of men in a society preoccupied with female chastity as a linchpin of patriarchal, patrilineal culture.[3] Discussing the act of sexual intercourse as the familiar Elizabethan pun on death, she points out that

> in the act of orgasm, male experience of the female body is not so much that of an object to be penetrated and possessed, but of an enclosure into which the male subject merges, dissolves, and in the early modern pun, dies.

> (Traub 1992, 27)

This analysis, together with her reference to the famous Sonnet 129, "The Expense of Spirit," leads her to conclude that male orgasm in fact underlines the "myth of the unity and self-identity of the masculine subject," and thereby leads to an intense male anxiety about female erotic mobility, which "threatens the process by which male subjectivity is secured" (Ibid., 27).

While Traub's analysis helps us understand the tyrannical fathers and pervasive male suspicion of apparently chaste female characters in Shakespeare's plays, her description of the male experience of orgasm closely resembles the Freudian pre-Oedipal narcissistic union between male infant and mother. This "myth" of male unity and self-identity may therefore be based (as many myths are) on a related psychological phenomenon—the primary narcissistic phase of a self undifferentiated from the body of the mother, which in turn gives way to the crucial transition from the mother/infant dyad into a discrete male identity and (m)other. It is precisely this phase of male psychological development that appears to me to offer a useful paradigm for an analysis of the grim dynamics of love and war in *Troilus and Cressida*.

In his essay, *Beyond the Pleasure Principle,* Freud relates an anecdote that he claims has caused him to ponder a psychic economy that may exceed his view of the dominance of the pleasure principle in the process of identity formation. Observing a young boy at play in what Freud calls a *fort/da* game, the child throws away and retrieves a small wooden spool, repeating this action numerous times in connection with its verbal signs, *fort* (gone) and *da* (there); the child's articulations are in fact only the vowels *o* and *a,* but Freud provides the terms.[4] Freud speculates that this game is a means for the boy to achieve agency (and hence a first stage of identity formation) despite—indeed precisely *through*—the fact that his mother has begun to leave home:

> The interpretation of the game then became obvious. It was related to the child's great cultural achievement—the instinctual renunciation (that is, the renunciation of instinctual satisfaction) which he had made in allowing his mother to go away without protesting. He compensated himself for this, as it were, by himself staging the disappearance and return of the objects within his reach. It is of course a matter of indifference from the point of view of judging the effective nature of the game whether the child invented it himself or took it over on some outside suggestion.[5]

Freud's language, as always, is as suggestive as the observed phenomenon itself. While the "effective" outcome of a nascent male subjectivity may not be altered by the game's origins, the affective character of the game itself is very intriguing. By viewing this as a "great cultural achievement" Freud hints at a broader dimension to this phase of the male infant's abdication of the primary narcissistic connection to his mother. But Freud leaves ambiguous the question of whether this game is autogenetic or culturally defined and inherited, a lingering ambiguity that marks the affective nexus of individual psychology and culture. In this discussion of the *fort/da* game, then, it is my impression that Freud not only outlines a paradigm of male subjectivity acquisition, but also begins to reveal the entangled roots of the codes of chivalry and courtly love that continue to inform modern culture. Hence, we should examine a bit more carefully that discussion.

This *fort/da* game may also be, Freud admits, an enactment of revenge on the mother for violating the primary narcissistic unity her child has hitherto felt with her:

> Throwing away the object so that it was "gone" might satisfy an impulse of the child's, which was suppressed in his actual life, to revenge himself on his mother for going away from him. In that case it would have a defiant meaning: "All right, then, go away! I don't need you. I'm sending you away myself."
>
> (Freud 1961, 9)

This aggression is likewise remarked by Lacan in what he terms the "Imaginary register," when the child remains caught in a realm of visual experience before moving into the "Symbolic" register of language.[6] Lacan's Imaginary register is the phase in which the child enters the "mirror stage" and

> sees an image of himself as something "other." . . . an ideal image, not only in the sense of the root connotation "visibility," but because it is in fact the image of someone perfectly formed. . . . Hence his earliest "image" of himself is not only alienated, but ideal.
>
> (Kopper 1988, 155)

Such an ideal image can cause a sense of inadequacy due to the discrepancy between the male child's experienced self and its ideal image. Shakespeare's Troilus evidences something akin to this sense of inferiority in the opening scene of *Troilus and Cressida*:

> Call here my varlet; I'll unarm again:
> Why should I war without the walls of Troy,
> That find such cruel battle here within?
> Each Trojan that is master of his heart,
> Let him to field; Troilus, alas! hath none.
> . . . . .
> The Greeks are strong and skilful to their strength,
> Fierce to their skill and to their fierceness valiant;
> But I am weaker than a woman's tear,
> Tamer than sleep, fonder than ignorance,
> Less valiant than the virgin in the night
> And skilless as unpractis'd infancy.
>
> (*Troilus and Cressida*, 1.1.1-5, 7-12)

The "cruel battle within" and lack of mastery over his "heart" indicate that Troilus is caught in the Lacanian visual stage where he measures himself against an image

of the ideal warrior and comes up wanting. Troilus' alienation from this ideal image is also connected to the phase of primary narcissism by his self-comparisons with abstract qualities cast in feminine terms ("weaker than a woman's tear," "Less valiant than the virgin in the night") rather than with specific male warriors or ideal role models. Troilus' "unpracticed infancy" is not, however, so much linguistic as chivalric; rather than suffering from an inability to attain the Symbolic register of language (in a play whose language is so pervasively deconstructive),[7] Troilus instead dramatizes the cultural as well as individual affect of a pre-Oedipal drive to deal with a disrupted self-image.

Elizabeth Bronfen indicates indirectly how the *fort/da* game appears to articulate a different dynamic of identity formation than that Lacan would tie to the achievement of the Symbolic register.[8] Remarking that Freud's child has learned "to obey laws before it has learned the language of those laws," Bronfen continues:

> What Freud sets up in this preliminary description, then, is a different scene in the developmental stages of a child from the one governed by an Oedipal complex, another narrative for the way in which language acquisition and subjectivity are grounded on an acknowledged experience of loss. For the negation that serves both as catalyst for the game and as object or reference of its articulation marks a site independent of the father's castrative "no." The anxiety-engendering symbolization and self-consciousness in this narrative is of another kind. Initially, there is not father in this game at all, not even an absent one. Though the child plays in an intermediary zone connecting the imaginary register of the mother/infant dyad (governed exclusively by unrestrained drives) and the symbolic register (governed by forbiddances), the anxiety at stake does not involve the father as the disrupting third element.
>
> (Bronfen 1989, 969)

This distinction of the *fort/da* game from the mirror stage is denied by Lacan; he laughs off the notion that the *objet à* or spool of Freud's game is anything but a part of the alienated subject which helps lead him into the symbolic phase.[9] But Freud himself is genuinely puzzled by one aspect of the *fort/da* game:

> The child cannot possibly have felt his mother's departure as something agreeable or even indifferent. How then does his repetition of this distressing experience as a game fit in with the pleasure principle? It may perhaps be said in reply that her departure had to be enacted as a necessary preliminary to her joyful return, and that it was in the latter that lay the true purpose of the game. But against this must be counted the observed fact that *the first act, that of departure, was staged as a game in itself and far more frequently than the episode in its entirety, with its pleasurable ending.* . . .
>
> (Freud, 9; my emphasis)

Precisely at this point in his essay, Freud makes his own observations on what Lacan extensively develops as the "mirror stage":

A further observation subsequently confirmed this interpretation fully. One day the child's mother had been away for several hours and on her return was met with the words "Baby o-o-o-o!" which was at first incomprehensible. It soon turned out, however, that during this long period of solitude the child had found a method of making *himself* disappear. He had discovered his reflection in a full-length mirror which did not quite reach to the ground, so that by crouching down he could make his mirror-image "gone".

(Freud, n. 9)

What needs clarification here is precisely *which* "interpretation" of the *fort/da* game Freud's reading of this mirror stage fully confirms. There appears to be some deeper psychological compensation in the child's repetition of the first act itself, in the making "gone" of the spool/mother, and later of his causing his own image to vanish from the mirror. Lacan asserts that the repetition compulsion here simply confirms his sense of the *fort/da* game as equivalent to the mirror stage. As Barbara Freedman explains it,

Even if the child associates his mother's absence with his playing at his own absence, the association itself doesn't imply an effort to master maternal loss. Rather, it suggests a discovery of his own presence as predicated upon absence, and so a splitting that alone makes self-reference possible.[10]

Lacan himself is insistent that the distinction between the *fort/da* game and the mirror stage is a moot one, as far as the constitution of subjectivity is concerned:

If the young subject can practice this game of *fort/da,* it is precisely because he does not practice it at all, for no subject can grasp this radical articulation. He practices it with the help of a small bobbin, that is to say, with the *objet à.* The function of the exercise with this object [like the function of the mirror stage] refers to an alienation, and not to some supposed mastery, which is difficult to imagine being increased in an endless repetition, whereas the endless repetition that is in question reveals the radical vacillation of the subject.[11]

Shakespeare's text, however, *dramatizes* the "radical vacillation" of a number of male subjects, most prominently Troilus and Achilles. And *Troilus and Cressida* also presents the disturbing affective corollary of male subjectivity acquisition in an ethos of chivalry: erosion or erasure of female identity, particularly in the cases of Helen and Cressida. Precisely the same dynamic is involved in the transition of Freud's young boy from the *fort/da* game to the mirror stage, and in the remainder of this essay I will outline why poststructuralist and Lacanian analyses of Shakespeare's texts slight two very significant aspects of the play its representation of the affect of desire, and the dramatic and psychological outcomes of that desire for male and female identity.

Shakespeare's Ulysses articulates the limits of the "mirror stage" in affective terms which suggest those I find so interesting from Freud's essay. Ulysses turns to mirrors—

and language—to highlight the slippage of Achilles' stature and the subversion of his very identity among the Greeks:

> . . . A strange fellow here
> Writes me: "That man, how dearly ever parted,
> How much in having, or without or in,
> Cannot make boast to have that which he hath,
> Nor feels not what he owes, but by reflection;
> As when his virtues shining upon others
> Heat them and they retort that heat again
> To the first giver."

(*Troilus and Cressida,* 3.3.95-102)

We should note, however, that the "reflection" here is achieved only through the agency of the "others," not with a mirror that allows absenting and re-presenting of the self. The mirrors *are* others, and the "heat" is that generated by action, not by self-regard. Achilles, stung by the deliberate and exaggerated disregard of his fellow Greeks that has just been staged by Ulysses, acknowledges that the mirror is not sufficient to maintain the identity of the "man" he feels himself to be:

> The beauty that is borne here in the face
> The bearer knows not, but commends itself
> To others' eyes; nor doth the eye itself,
> That most pure spirit of sense, behold itself,
> Not going from itself; but eye to eye oppos'd
> Salutes each other with each other's form;
> For speculation turns not to itself,
> Till it hath travell'd and is mirror'd there
> Where it may see itself.

(3.3.103-11)

The aural pun of "eye-I" is relevant here, for if we are speaking about the self-construction of identity, Achilles acknowledges that it must involve another "eye-I." In fact, "eye to eye opposed" and its punning variations constitute a matrix of identity strategies that are dramatically portrayed in the play: self-reflection ("I to I"), reflection via another ("I to eye"), reflection on/by an ideal image ("eye to I"), and reflection or identity via active combat ("eye to eye opposed"); that each of the terms of this punning matrix are open to alternative and slipping interpretations strengthens my contention that the basis of identity in such characters as Troilus and Achilles is far from stable, and that it requires an *active,* ongoing reinforcement.

Ulysses' investment in this discussion is not merely theoretical, but instrumental. He brings up the subject of mirrors to suggest the vanity of the greatest Greek warrior resting on his mere image, and by contrast he presents the image of the foolish Ajax as the "I" to whom Achilles is now opposed. To Achilles" irritated query, "what, are my deeds forgot?" Ulysses responds:

> . . . to have done is to hang
> Quite out of fashion, like a rusty mail
> In monumental mockery.
>   . . . . .
> The present eye praises the present object.

Then marvel not, thou great and complete man,
That all the Greeks begin to worship Ajax,
Since things in motion sooner catch the eye
Than what stirs not.

(3.3.151-53, 180-84)

Shakespeare's text thus suggests, in Freudian terms, that the significance of the mirror stage lies in the male subject's active manipulation (and hence ongoing constitution) of his image. The affective dimension of this liminal phase of identity appears in the male characters" compulsion to continually measure themselves, in combat, "eye to eye opposed." While Kopper and other poststructuralists have focused on how language subverts the characters of the play, I propose to concentrate on how Troilus' jealous formulation of the Greeks as "Fierce to their skill and to their fierceness valiant" articulates an affective frustration. Shakespeare's play indeed seems to me to depict a both unconscious and explicit desire on the part of the male protagonists to continuously re-present themselves in the "mirror" of battle. Moreover, *Troilus and Cressida* painfully represents the reliance of chivalry and courtly love on a return to the reiterated first term of the *fort/da* game, a compulsion to make the (m)other *fort* or absent as a vain (in both its senses) attempt to constitute male identity. By deliberately maintaining as *fort* or "gone" the (female) object of their desire, the male protagonists inaugurate the potentially interminable "game" of martial combat, the only means through which their honor and distinction can be maintained.

Elizabeth Bronfen's summary of the work of Melanie Klein and D.W. Winnicott may provide insights into the complex dynamics of Shakespeare's knights' relationship to their "ladies." Recognizing the narcissistic wound that separation from the mother represents for the male infant, both Klein and Winnicott suggest that this wound engenders a latent violence and is countered by the construction of an idealized "internal mother" who neither threatens to engulf or to completely abandon the child. This "internal mother" then allows the male child to make the transition from an undifferentiated world centered in his union with the mother's body to the cultured external world of objects and signs. What Bronfen usefully highlights, however, is the paradox that the stability and effectiveness of Klein's "internal mother" is "contingent on the fact that the material maternal body is already fading before the child's ego":

> Thus a stable relation to the external cultured world not only doubles an internal stability, but in both instances stability is gained through a moment of destruction and loss. I wish to emphasize that Klein sees this emotional trajectory—from destructive impulse, through idealization and denial, to the ambivalent sense of guilty yet triumphant omnipotence in respect to a potentially wounding other—as "the central position in the child's development," a step in the process of organization and integration that is parallel to but different from and other than sexual development.

(Bronfen 1989, 974)

Winnicott, for his part, addresses the Freudian *fort/da* game directly, seeing in the spool of the game a "transitional object,"

> representing the child's transition from a state of being merged with the mother to a state of being in relation to the mother as something outside and separate, representing, that is, a wounding of the purely narcissistic type of object relating.

(Ibid., 974)

Bronfen's analysis of Winnicott then elaborates how this wounding is overcome by the stability of the returned object now invested as an loving, dependable, and amenable "internal mother." For Winnicott, then, the ultimate significance of the *fort/da* game is that "the child gains reassurance about the fate of his internal mother,"

> that is, that this internal representation will not fade, will not become meaningless. . . . Winnicott significantly shifts his interest from body to image—not the maternal body to be secured from fading, but rather the child's internal image. I would add that, if what is secured as "reliable" in the process of this game is the internal image created of the mother, then what is also secured is the child's ability to create. Thus the substitution from real, external maternal body to internal representation and external symbol (transitional object) is one that includes the move from disappearing/reappearing mother to revenging/representing child.

(Ibid., 975)

What emerges from Bronfen's able summary of the work of these two analysts is a paradigm of normal male subjectivity development. But the world of *Troilus and Cressida* is, as Pandarus continually points out, one of disease. Indeed, what we witness in *Troilus and Cressida* may be seen as a process of personal and cultural infantilization, in which the male protagonists cannot achieve a stable sense of identity due to the discrepancy between the women in their lives and the "internal image" of Woman they hold as a chivalric culture. Shakespeare's male characters, with the single exception of Pandarus (whose very name embodies the principle of constant transition and "trans-action") are fixated in the first phases of *fort/da* and mirror games, suggesting perhaps a summary judgment of the ethos of chivalry and courtly love that Shakespeare so often questions in his work.

What sets off Homer's account of the Trojan War from that of Shakespeare is precisely their different "internal image" of the most significant (m)other of the legend, Helen. While both sides to the conflict in *Troilus and Cressida* see Helen as the effective cause of the nine years' siege of Troy, they have nevertheless all but abandoned her as the basis of their justifications for this ongoing battle. This indeed makes her the sort of transitional object just described, but the problem is that Helen herself, in Shakespeare's version, is far from inspiring the sort of noble internal image of beauty that she represents in Homer. Shakespeare's Greek Diomedes describes Helen as he delivers a caustic formulation of the dynamic that has perpetuated the war. To Paris' question of who most deserves Helen, he or Menelaus, Diomedes replies in very unidealized terms:

> Both alike:
> He merits well to have her that doth seek her,
> Not making any scruple of her soilure,
> With such a hell of pain and world of charge;
> And you as well to keep her that defend her,
> Not palating the taste of her dishonour,
> With such a costly loss of wealth and friends.
> He, like a puling cuckold, would drink up
> The lees and dregs of a flat tamed piece;
> You, like a lecher, out of whorish loins
> Are pleased to breed out your inheritors.
> Both merits pois'd, each weighs nor less nor more;
> But he as thee, each heavier for a whore.
>
> (*Troilus and Cressida*, 4.1.55-67)

Shakespeare's text depicts a Helen vain to the point of being insipid, in contrast with Homer's portrayal of her as noble and inspiringly beautiful. In either case, however, the function of Helen is more significant than her identity, for Shakespeare and Homer alike the tale of Troy is one of the achievement and exercise of male agency, not of the redress of promiscuity. Shakespeare's Hector bluntly expresses the opinion that Helen herself is a "thing" not worth the cost of keeping:

> . . . Let Helen go.
> Since the first sword was drawn about this question
> Every tithe soul 'mongst many thousand dismes,
> Hath been as dear as Helen—I mean, of ours.
> If we have lost so many tenths of ours
> To guard a thing not ours nor worth to us. . . .
>
> (2.2.17-22)

For his part, however, Troilus immediately translates the loss of Helen into the loss of his father's and, by extension, of all Troy's honor (an ambiguity of identity instituted by a combination of Elizabethan political theory and the chivalric ethos):

> Fie, fie, my brother!
> Weigh you the worth and honour of a king
> So great as our dread father's in a scale
> Of common ounces? Will you with counters sum
> The past-proportion of his infinite,
> And buckle in a waist most fathomless
> With spans and inches so diminutive
> As fears and reasons? Fie, for godly shame!
>
> (2.2.25-32)

Hector's reply is one that indicates, similar to Freud, the psychological logic of completing the *fort/da* game. He recognizes the legitimacy of Menelaus' desire to regain Helen:

> . . . Nature craves
> All dues be render"d to their owners: now,
> What nearer debt in all humanity

Than wife is to the husband? If this law
Of nature be corrupted through affection,
And that great minds, of partial indulgence
To their benumbed wills, resist the same,
There is a law in each well-order'd nation
To curb those raging appetites that are
Most disobedient and refractory.
If Helen then be wife to Sparta's king,
As it is known she is, these moral laws
Of nature and of nations speak aloud
To have her back return'd: thus to persist
In doing wrong extenuates not wrong,
But makes it much more heavy.

> (2.2.174-89)

Yet while this is "Hector's opinion . . . in way of truth" (2.2.189-90), he nonetheless acquiesces in Troilus's appeal to their collective and personal honor as sufficient justification for keeping Helen as one of the "counters," in effect perpetuating her as *fort* in the chivalric game. She is *fort* for the Trojans as an "theme," and literally *fort* for the Greeks; on both sides her status as a cathected object of the game induces them to continue the war and thereby burnish their identities:

> My spritely brethren, I propend to you
> In resolution to keep Helen still,
> For 'tis a cause that hath no mean dependance
> Upon our joint and several dignities.
>
> (2.2.191-94)

Troilus seconds Hector's chivalric resolve to *not* end the conflict over Helen in terms that suggest an answer to Freud's question about the more numerous repetitions of the "departure" phase of the *fort/da* game:

> Why, there you touch'd the life of our design:
> Were it not glory that we more affected
> Than the performance of our heaving spleens,
> I would not wish a drop of Trojan blood
> Spent more in her defence. But, worthy Hector,
> She is a theme of honour and renown,
> A spur to valiant and magnanimous deeds,
> Whose present courage may beat down our foes,
> And fame in time to come canonize us
>
> (2.2.195-203)

The slight syntactic ambiguity of "Whose" here is symptomatic; it cannot refer to Helen, so it must refer to the "deeds" that become then the only way to constitute an enduring fame, to "canonize" their identity.

Hector not only endorses this cathexis of Helen as a "theme of honour and renown," but personally demonstrates its affective dynamic in his earlier challenge of the Greeks to single combat, delivered by Aeneas to the Greek camp:

> If there be one among the fair'st of Greece
> That holds his honour higher than his ease,
> That feeds his praise more than he fears his peril,
> That knows his valour and knows not his fear,

That loves his mistress more than in confession
With truant vows to her own lips he loves,
And dare avow her beauty and her worth
In other arms than hers—to him this challenge:
Hector, in view of Trojans and of Greeks,
Shall make it good, or do his best to do it,
He hath a lady, wiser, fairer, truer,
Than ever Greek did compass in his arms,
And will tomorrow with his trumpet call
Midway between your tents and walls of Troy,
To rouse a Grecian that is true in love.
If any come, Hector shall honour him:
If none, he'll say in Troy, when he retires,
The Grecian dames are sunburnt and not worth
The splinter of a lance. Even so much.

                                        (1.3.264-82)

The terms of address and challenge here collapse the courtly love ethos with the chivalry that idealizes Woman—but often demonizes actual women. Shakespeare's text continually presents the masculine heroes with the troubling discrepancy of their ideal Woman contrasted with those very real women in their lives. Hector's reaction to his own wife, Andromache (so chivalrically evoked in the above passage), who begs him not to fight due to her foreboding dreams, is dismissive to the point of being rude: "You train me to offend you; get you in" (5.3.4). Their ideal of Woman is what convinces the Trojans to continue to hold Helen, and the terms of Hector's challenge clearly reflect how such idealizations provide the psychosocial groundwork for chivalric action. Helen is the lover of Paris and the kidnapped wife of Menelaus, but she has become a "theme of honour and renown," due only to her status as "A spur to valiant and magnanimous *deeds*." Neither Hector nor his brothers will heed the dire warnings of Cassandra, their prophetic sister, for they are all, as Hector aptly puts it, "in the vein of chivalry" (5.3.32)—the pun on "vain" is psychologically telling.

Among the Greeks, the issue has almost stopped being Helen; the stalemated battle is the pressing problem. Achilles has been insulted by Agamemnon, and therefore refuses to take the field. In *The Iliad,* the insult to Achilles is Agamemnon's arbitrary decision to take the maiden, Briseis, from him after Agamemnon has been compelled to return one Chryseis, the daughter of a priest of Apollo, to her father. These two women are cousins, and they have in fact been tied to the emergence of Cressida in medieval legend, for there is no mention of her in the classic myths; she is in fact invented as eponymous of female treachery. Cressida's identity is hence even more ambiguous than Helen's, but her function will be much the same. Both Helen and Cressida become, in Shakespeare's text, a form of "anti-ideal image," so we should not be surprised that the male characters who base their identity to some degree on these women, even as objects, suffer from varying degrees of "dis-ease." In its representation of the medieval tale from Chaucer and Boccaccio, Shakespeare's text suggests a critique of the objectification of these women as part of the "gear" essential for the ongoing constitution of male identity in the chivalric world.

Our first glimpse of the Greeks (*Troilus and Cressida,* 1.3) opens with Agamemnon outlining the progress of the long and costly war and Ulysses continuing with the famous speech on the decay of degree as the chief explanation for the stalemate. Agamemnon, the king of the Greeks, discusses at length the need for "persistive constancy in men" (1.3.21) a solidity of character the martial dimensions of which he constructs in a metaphor:

. . . in the wind and tempest of her frown,
Distinction, with a broad and powerful fan
Puffing at all, winnows the light away,
And what hath mass or matter by itself
Lies rich in virtue and unmingled.

                                        (1.3.26-30)

The metaphor's physical lack of substance (mass and matter) and feminine gender are significant here, for Agamemnon's wind of distinction is to reveal male identity; "mass and matter" accrue only to male warriors who (as we have already seen in Ulysses' discussion with Achilles) persist in their combat.

For his part, Troilus is also anxious about "distinction." Imagining his first meeting with Cressida, Troilus' fear that "I shall lose distinction in my joys" (*Troilus and Cressida,* 3.2.25) voices a concern for self-presence that is threatened in the "death" of sexual intercourse. But the distinction between these two "distinctions" collapses in Cressida's most candid moment of the play, which Shakespeare masterfully places just prior to the political and philosophical discussions of Agamemnon and Achilles:

Things won are done; joy's soul lies in the doing.
That she beloved knows nought that knows not this:
Men prize the thing ungain'd more than it is. . . .

                                        (1.2.282-84)

Cressida here formulates the role women as objects of desire play in the constitution of male identity, and hence in the establishment of the "distinction" essential to any assessment of degree. Cressida recognizes the insubstantial or "thing" status of women in both the martial and marital plots, and the necessity for these things to be "ungain'd" in order to provoke and perpetuate male agency and desire. Joy (like its obverse, grief) is an intense experience of self-presence. Cressida outlines here the psychological roots of the idealization of Woman in the ethos of chivalry and courtly love, where she is at once desired and (at least initially) elevated above any actual possession or "en-joyment." Indeed, the desire of the beloved is "lust in action" until that beloved is in fact achieved, at which point the male lover may recoil from the experience that constitutes a death of that intenser self founded on desire:

Enjoy'd no sooner but despised straight;
Past reason hunted; and no sooner had,
Past reason hated, as a swallowed bait,
On purpose laid to make the taker mad:
Mad in pursuit, and in possession so;
Had, having, and in quest to have, extreme;
A bliss in proof, and proved, a very woe.

                                        (Sonnet 129, l.4-10)

As we have seen, Troilus sounds the most strident note of "joint and several honour," so we are not surprised to see from the opening scene of the play that his individual sense of honor—hence identity—is unstable. His deeds have not matched his heroic aspirations early in the play, a fact underscored by the debunking comments of Cressida in response to Pandarus' panegyrics in praise of Troilus (*Troilus and Cressida,* 1.1.256-276). Troilus is fixated in the Lacanian Imaginary register, where he must face both his ideal figure (and the figures of heroes like Hector and Achilles) and the real figure he has cut to this point. The discrepancy is painful, so he seeks a different mirror, or rather another object through which to attempt to constitute his identity. In effect, he has regressed in Freudian terms, moving back from the mirror stage to that of the *fort/da* game. Now the object against/through which he will establish his identity is Cressida, the amorous "counter" to his martial desire for honor. The terms in which he imagines their first "en-counter" are fraught with anxiety:

> I am giddy; expectation whirls me round.
> Th'imaginary relish is so sweet
> That it enchants my sense: what will it be
> When that the wat'ry palate tastes indeed
> Love's thrice repured nectar? Death, I fear me,
> Sounding destruction, or some joy too fine,
> Too subtle-potent, tuned too sharp in sweetness
> For the capacity of my ruder powers.
> I fear it much; and I do fear besides
> That I shall lose distinction in my joys,
> As doth a battle, when they charge on heaps
> The enemy flying.

>   (3.2.16-27)

In effect, Troilus here is the little boy contemplating the joy of the again present (*da*) (m)other, of a completely restored primary narcissism through total union with the maternal body (the metaphors of "wat'ry palate" and "sounding destruction" are only a few of the liquid, dissolving images associated with the female body in this play). Particularly in Chaucer but also in Shakespeare's text, Cressida emerges as a sexually experienced and worldly wise woman, a point Pandarus highlights in exasperation when he exclaims at her witty debunking of his fulgent descriptions of Troilus, "You are such another" (1.2.266). Cressida represents for Troilus not so much an other sexual conquest as "sounding destruction" and "some joy too fine," the paradoxical experience of psychic dissolution and intense joy in union with the (m)other. Troilus explicitly conflates Cressida with the figure of the mother in his shocked exchange with Ulysses after she has gone over to the Greek camp:

> *Ulysses.* . . . Cressid was here but now.
> *Troilus.* Let it not be believ'd for womanhood!
> Think, we had mothers; do not give advantage
> To stubborn critics, apt, without a theme
> For depravation, to square the general sex
> By Cressid's rule: rather, think this not Cressid.

>   (5.2.127-32)

The battlefield simile he has chosen to express this loss of distinction further indicates the interrelated character of courtly love and chivalric action. Both of these codes of male honor and distinction are, paradoxically, threatened by the prospect of Troilus actually *achieving* Cressida, or of Helen being returned to the Greeks by force of arms.[12]

When he finally does meet with Cressida, Troilus' imagined possession of her robs him of any symbolic distinction from her, leading him back to a preverbal phase of primary narcissism: "You have bereft me of all words, lady" (3.2.54). Again Shakespeare seems to have intuitively anticipated Freud and his interpreters, for now Troilus attempts to constitute a ideal image of himself prior to the physical union with Cressida, speaking of his "integrity and truth" as "true as truth's simplicity / And simpler than the infancy of truth" (3.2.163,167-68); his metaphor of childhood represents a return to the presexual phase of Freud's *fort/da* game, a desire for narcissistic union and not sexual conquest. Cressida, for her part, is allowed only negative formulations of her fidelity: ". . . let them say, to stick the heart of falsehood, / "As false as Cressid" (3.2.193-94).

Pandarus reinforces the dynamic tension of the courtly lover's simultaneous desire to have the woman of his idealized vision and the urge to "hold I off" (Cressida's turn of phrase is equally true of the male protagonists in the play), thereby maintaining the distinction that is threatened by their union. Pandarus, true to his name, recognizes and attempts to break the courtly stalemate Troilus and Cressida seem to have entered, even as he ironically voices the theme of deeds over words that I view as so central to the play, a critique of too close a focus on language at the expense of the dramatic plot:

> Words pay no debts, give her deeds: but she'll
> bereave you o' the deeds too, if she call your
> activity in question.

>   (3.2.55-57)

The activity she will call into question is in effect Troilus' own imagined version of the *fort/da* game, for he will soon become the victim of the inevitable narcissistic wound, the unavoidable loss of the (m)other.

After Cressida rather falteringly admits her love for Troilus, the courtly love tradition of the lady remaining aloof and untouchable begins to break down, and yet both Cressida and Troilus appear to "hold I off" yet a bit longer. One of Cressida's remarks that has become a favorite of those who would attack her touches upon this stasis and destabilization at the same time as it reinscribes the *fort/da* paradigm I have been discussing—but this time from the (m)other's perspective:

> I have a kind of self resides with you,
> But an unkind self, that itself will leave
> To be another's fool. I would be gone:

>   (3.2.146-49)

Kind as kinship or relation in human terms is a common Shakespearean pun, but here we find an ironic depth in Cressida's use of the term to describe her imminent connection with, and yet ultimate distinction from, Troilus. Deborah Hooker, discussing at length the nuances of the term *kind,* remarks usefully that in speaking of her "unkind self" Cressida is asserting "that part of herself, that region not specularized, not mirror-imaged, not resident in man, her "un-man-kind self"—the feminine."[13] It is as if the cathected object of the *fort/da* game, the (m)other made into a spool, now articulates the fundamental ambivalence of many Shakespearean heroines toward their comic or tragic situation as the means whereby male identity and agency are constituted.[14] The fragmented subjectivity she articulates here is one of Shakespeare's most keen anticipations of the bind of being an object of cathexis (an "unkind self"), a lover and/or mother ("a kind of self resides with you") and a counter in the games men play to assert their identity ("I would be gone"). Hooker states succinctly the psychology of the chivalric world and the role Cressida and other women play in it:

> Though the men of Greece and Troy, Troilus chief among them, fight in the name of women, what truly motivates them is a compulsion toward transcendence, to finally out-appetite appetite. This compulsion, ironically, invokes Irigaray's definition of hysteria. . . . Male hysteria manifests as an inescapable fixity, a paralysis-through-action, an inability to respond to any given situation outside the parameters prescribed by the male/warrior status quo.
>
> (Hooker 1989, 923)

Ulysses himself describes the self-perpetuating aspect of chivalric appetite in terms that are, ironically, intended to reestablish a proper sense of "degree" and identity as inherent in noble characters and paternal hierarchy, rather than being based merely in the brute achievements of "power:"

> Power into will, will into appetite,
> And appetite, an universal wolf,
> So doubly seconded with will and power,
> Must make perforce an universal prey,
> And last eat up himself.
>
> (1.3.120-24)

Ulysses has in fact been addressing what Hooker calls "paralysis-through-action," the stalemated war for Troy that neither side can appear to win. But winning is not the point, in fact; the alternative to the unbridled ambition/appetite he describes and the perpetual warfare it institutes is to find "a theme of honour and renown" through which to legitimate the ongoing warfare and somehow ennoble it. As we have seen, this involves a reinscription of the woman as an object that, paradoxically, must never in fact be won—"joy's soul lies in the doing."

On the morning after Troilus has finally "won" Cressida, the decision to send Cressida over to her father in the Greek camp has already been made. Thus, while the psychocultural machinations are at work to make Cressida a pawn in the male games of war, on the individual level we also see an affect of separation in Troilus himself. Standing outside the room in which their union occurred, when he is approached by Cressida, Troilus attempts to convince her to leave him and go back inside. Speaking in high, courtly terms, he nonetheless betrays a certain violence in his invocation to her to let "Sleep kill those pretty eyes" (again, a pun on "eye-I"?), and in a concise formulation of the narcissistic state of total union/oblivion: "As infants empty of all thought" (4.2.4-6). She, however, will not be put off so facilely:

> *Cressida:* Are you a-weary of me?
> *Troilus:* O Cressida! but that the busy day,
> Waked by the lark, hath roused the ribald crows,
> And dreaming night will hide our joys no longer,
> I would not from thee.
>
> (4.2.8-11)

Beneath his "I would not from thee" and his adjective "ribald"[15] we may read a desire to push her away from him, and Cressida reacts to what is clearly a sense of postcoital distance in his tone, remarking almost bitterly:

> Prithee, tarry:
> You men will never tarry.
> O foolish Cressid! I might have still held off,
> And then you would have tarried.
>
> (4.2.15-18)

More telling yet, however, is the flat tone of Troilus's response to the news that Cressida must go over to the Greek camp that very morning: "Is it so concluded?" is all he asks, and he then muses, "How my achievements mock me!" (4.2.68,71). The latter comment is indeed the heart of the matter, in psychological terms: Shakespearean men must look to "achievements" to constitute masculine identity, and while achievements may constitute them, in themselves they are as "rusty mail" for an idle Achilles, paradoxically inadequate and even subversive of identity. Hence, the love and war games must go on. Endless repetition is the only answer to a self-subversive mockery, and the spool/other must be sent *fort* again.

Troilus's rage is now directed toward the masculine figures who make Cressida their own object of desire. He does not evidence the extreme lover's grief that Cressida so movingly expresses (4.2.99-112). Instead, he questions her fidelity in a painfully repetitive insistence, "Be thou true" (4.4.61,64,65,73); we may see here precisely the process of Klein's ideal or internal (m)other being established. She must be true *for* him, not to him, and her anguished cry "O heavens, you love me not!" (4.2.81) is one of the deep truths of the play. Troilus sounds a chivalric warrior's challenge to Diomedes, and the latter's response to Cressida is only a function of the intensity and degree of Troilus' threat; the men have now established their identities as warriors, and Cressida will become no more significant than the glove Troilus gives to her—and that she ultimately gives to Diomedes.

Once she is in the Greek camp, Troilus' idealized and internalized image of her is radically undermined by her behavior. In this new dramatic context, we no longer have any view of her interior self, but can only uneasily calculate her exchange value as an object sent off and retrieved, lost and won. The scene in which she is welcomed by being kissed in common by all those present in the Greek camp would seem to totally undo any "kind" interpretation of her character. But Shakespeare's genius here is to recognize that her function in the psychocultural drama I have been describing has now changed. Cressida has become as little a "character" as his thinly depicted Helen. Both are merely "daughters of the game" (4.5.63) as Ulysses disgustedly puts it.

Indeed, immediately following the scene that begins the process of Cressida's denigration, we witness Hector arriving in a formal challenge, and hear Aeneas' inflated chivalric rhetoric underlining the two sides' view of themselves as noble "knights" (4.5.65-86). The same Ulysses who only moments before has described Cressida and other "daughters of the game" with undisguised loathing now waxes Homeric to set forth the chivalric warriors from Troy, including Troilus himself:

> The youngest son of Priam, a true knight;
> Not yet mature, yet matchless; firm of word,
> Speaking in deeds, and deedless in his tongue;
> Not soon provok'd, nor, being provok'd, soon calm'd;
> His heart and hand both open and both free;
> For what he has he gives, what thinks he shows;
> Yet gives he not till judgment guide his bounty,
> Nor dignifies an impare thought with breath;
> Manly as Hector, but more dangerous;
> For Hector in his blaze of wrath subscribes
> To tender objects, but he in heat of action
> Is more vindicative than jealous love.
>
> (4.5.96-107)

All the terms of the praise here are active, even those of an internal character ("Speaking in deeds," "what thinks he shows"), and in his loss of Cressida, then, Troilus has gained the chief distinction he holds in the eyes of his enemies, "dangerous." Because he has suffered his final disillusionment in the ideal, internal (m)other, his cry "This is and is not Cressid" (5.3.145) indeed indicates how dangerous he will become as a male stuck in the hysteria of chivalric honor and action. In his discussion with Hector in act 5, scene 3 about whether he will fight, Troilus confirms his sense of masculine identity and agency; both the brothers are "in the vein of chivalry" (5.3.32), and their vanity will not brook the misgivings or even the mention of the women with whom they have shared a constitutive bond. Shakespeare's Ulysses is the most callous example of this disregard of women, for he undercuts any sense of Cressida (or Helen) as particular, whole characters; they are simply "daughters of the game." Troilus' real pain over the loss of Cressida sets the stage for him to seek other "achievements" that will not "mock him," just as the male child in Freud's *fort/da* game overcomes his grief at his mother's departure by first play-

ing the game, then moving into a mirror stage that effectively substitutes self-presence for the absence of the (m)other.

More poignantly, however, Troilus here may also serve as a resonant figure for Freud himself. As Bronfen points out, Freud represses the fact that the mother and child of his essay, *Beyond the Pleasure Principle,* are in fact his own daughter, Sophie, and his grandson, Ernst. Sophie died at the age of twenty-six of influenzal pneumonia, "snatched away," in Freud's own words, "from glowing health, from her busy life as a capable mother and loving wife, in four or five days, as if she had never been" (Freud, 961). For Freud this event is a true crisis, for his grief threatens to paralyze him. He writes to Ernest Jones in a letter from 8 February 1920 that

> You know of the misfortune that has befallen me. It is depressing indeed, a loss to be forgotten. . . . Now I may be declining in power of thought and expression, why not? Everyone is liable to decay in the course of time."
>
> (Freud, 962)

Bronfen sees this as Freud's "rhetorical move from the Other to the self," a personalizing of the loss as a sign of his own vulnerability and mortality. But, she continues, this movement from the Other to the self also inaugurates a new phase and strategy of identity. Linking this moment to Lacan's analysis of the "destability" of the subject in the mirror stage, Bronfen points out that

> what is also contained in this second version of the [*fort/da*] game, not usually noted by critics, is the notion of imaging as a moment of erasure of the Other when this Other is substituted for an image of the self.
>
> (Bronfen, 976)

This accords well with Freud's own reaction to this terrible event, for rather than sink into a paralysis of grief, he plunges into his work—ironically enough, work on the essay that deals with his daughter and grandson, *Beyond the Pleasure Principle.* Like Troilus, Freud fears losing his distinction as the eminent psychologist and therapist in his terrible grief over Sophie's death, so again like Troilus (and Ernst), he engages in activity that simultaneously constitutes him as agent or actor while depersonalizing and finally erasing one of the women most close to his heart. Sophie is consigned to the status of an anonymous mother in a footnote, the same note in which Freud points out that what he earlier called the young boy's successful "cultural achievement" in accepting his mother's departure, has now become the fact that he evidences no grief over the real death of his mother (Freud, 10).[16]

The repressed always returns, however, for in his immersion into the writing of this little essay, Freud writes the story of his own struggle to gain and maintain his intellectual distinction and fame—over the dead body of his daughter, the "scar" in the footnote (Bronfen, 983). Indeed, the most significant parallel between Freud and Troilus is that the impending or actual removal of a beloved woman catalyzes their identity strategies at that same time as it erodes the subjectivity and individuality of the woman on whom those identities are at least initially and partially contingent. This is, and is not Cressid; even the elimination of the last vowel participates in her erasure as a fully human being in the male world of Shakespeare's play, and Freud more authoritatively yet expunges all reference to the identity of his daughter, focusing instead on little Ernst who has achieved a rather pathetic place in the symbolic order, the world of the Father and its chivalric laws of male self-constitution. Sophie Freud is one of the literal "daughters of the game," and Cressida is her invented and demonized literary sister.

The Trojan War, as a reiterated *fort/da* game played with the women whose presence/absence and erasure perpetuated it, emerges and reemerges throughout the culture of patrimony. The endurance of its chivalric renunciation/aggression complex in Western culture is remarkable,[17] enacted by Shakespeare's Troilus (heir to the medieval invention and demonization of Cressida, by Freud in his erasure of a daughter in service of his prestige and identity, and by any of the many variations of pre- and post-Rambos via the bodies of often anonymous, objectified, and/or dead women. This *fort/da* complex reflects a fundamental insecurity at the core of the male identity, which leads to compulsive attempts at reaffirmation through, on the one hand, the agency achieved in the patriarchal exchange of women, and on the other hand, through the competitive emulations of the mirror stage—in which the woman is simply erased. Neither strategy is wholly successful, however, in a world of "war and lechery," and Shakespeare's particular genius is to allow Pandarus the role of chorus at the close of his play. Eponymous of the uneasy traffic in desire that both determines and subverts male identity, Pandarus indeed can only promise one thing to a culture unwilling to acknowledge the voice of the "unkind" (m)other: an unbroken legacy of "dis-eases."

Notes

1. Most notable among the psychoanalytic approaches that also address the dramatic function of the characters' (particularly Cressida's) strategies of identity in the play are James O'Rourke, "'Rule in Unity' and Otherwise: Love and Sex in *Troilus and Cressida*," *Shakespeare Quarterly* 43, no. 2 (summer 1992); and Janet Adelman, "'This Is and Is Not Cressid': The Characterization of Cressida," in *The (M)other Tongue*, eds. Shirley Nelson Garner, Claire Kahane, and Madelaine Sprengnether (Ithaca: Cornell University Press, 1985), 119-41; a revised and expanded version of this essay appears in her *Suffocating Mothers: Fantasies of Maternal Origin in Shakespeare's Plays*, Hamlet *to* The Tempest (London: Routledge, 1992). See also Carol Cook, "Unbodied Figures of Desire," in *Performing Feminisms: Feminist Critical Theory and Theatre*, ed. Sue Ellen Case (Baltimore: Johns Hopkins University Press, 1990); Linda Charnes, "'So Unse-

cret to Ourselves': Notorious Identity and the Material Subject in Shakespeare's *Troilus and Cressida*," *Shakespeare Quarterly* 40 (1989); and Douglas B. Wilson, "The Commerce of Desire: Freudian Narcissism in Chaucer's *Troilus and Criseyde* and Shakespeare's *Troilus and Cressida*", *ELN,* Sept. 1983. More specifically deconstructive accounts of *Troilus and Cressida* are Gayle Greene's "Language and Value in Shakespeare's *Troilus and Cressida*," *SEL* 21 (1981); and Elizabeth Freund, "'Ariachne's Broken Woof': The Rhetoric of Citation in *Troilus and Cressida*," in *Shakespeare and the Question of Theory*, eds. Patricia Parker and Geoffrey Hartman (New York and London: Methuen, Inc. 1985) other deconstructive accounts of the play appear in the following notes. Coppélia Kahn's valuable study, *Man's Estate: Masculine Identity in Shakespeare* (Berkeley: University of California Press, 1981), while not discussing *Troilus and Cressida* at any length, provides an essential background to my more specific focus on the psychodynamics of chivalry.

2. All quotations from *Troilus and Cressida* are from the *Arden Shakespeare* edition, ed. Kenneth Palmer (1982; reprint, London: Routeledge, 1989).

3. Valerie Traub, *Desire and Anxiety: Circulations of Sexuality in Shakespearean Drama* (London: Routledge, 1992). The discussion of these fundamental sexual characteristics of late Elizabethan England occurs in chap. 1, esp. 27-28.

4. Derrida discusses this eruption of the paternal into the prelingual world of the child at length in his early essay on *Beyond the Pleasure Principle,* "Coming Into One's Own," trans. James Hulbert, in *Psychoanalysis and the Question of the Text,* ed. Geoffrey Hartman (Baltimore: Johns Hopkins University Press, 1978), 127-28.

5. All quotations from Freud are from *Beyond the Pleasure Principle,* trans. James Strachey (New York: Norton, 1961).

6. This discussion of Lacan is drawn in part from John M. Kopper, "Troilus at Pluto's Gates: Subjectivity and the Duplicity of Discourse in Shakespeare's *Troilus and Cressida*," in *Shakespeare and Deconstruction,* eds. G. Douglas Atkins and David M. Bergeron (New York: Peter Lang Publishing, 1988), 149-71. My basic contention, however, is that Kopper and others who read *Troilus and Cressida* as a play whose subversion of identity and values is to be found in language miss the psychologically cogent aspect of the actual drama, the action of the play, which is primarily that of the amorous encounter between Troilus and Cressida, her exchange for Antenor, and all the chivalric posturing and vengeful activity around the Trojan and Greek camps than accompany them. In a sense, I am using the words of the play to attempt to approach a preverbal analysis of the roots of the ethos of chivalry, an ethos of which *Troilus and Cressida* constitutes a devastating critique.

7. Kopper's essay finally takes essentially this position, arguing that the dissolution of order in the play is the result of a lack of the Lacanian "Law of the Father," an erosion of authority systems. But his remark that *Troilus and Cressida* enacts the moment of transition from comedy to tragedy, the fence on which confused editors have abandoned the play" (Kopper, 163) posits a sort of generic ambiguity to Shakespeare's dramatic examinations of chivalry and courtly love that coincides with the psychological oscillation and liminality I will suggest. Kopper usefully connects this play to the "problem plays" of 1602-4; I would add that it should be compared with the thoroughly sceptical, Jacobean treatment of chivalry that appears in *The Two Noble Kinsmen,* on which Shakespeare collaborated with John Fletcher.

8. Elizabeth Bronfen, "The Lady Vanishes: Sophie Freud and *Beyond the Pleasure Principle," The South Atlantic Quarterly,* 88, no. 4 (fall 1989): 961-91. Bronfen's essay has been extremely useful to me as a source of various interpretations of the *fort/da* game, as well as suggesting parameters for a feminist critique of chivalry that Shakespeare's play may offer.

9. For his discussion of the spool's significance in the *fort/da* game, see Lacan in "Tuche and Automaton," in *Ecrits: A Selection,* trans. Alan Sheridan (New York: Norton, 1977), 62.

10. Barbara Freedman, *Staging the Gaze: Postmodernism, Psychoanalysis, and Shakespearean Comedy* (Ithaca: Cornell University Press, 1991), 210. In this essay I have drawn extensively on Freedman's incisive analysis of Lacan's view of the *fort/da* game, though my ultimate focus is more cultural and affective than hers.

11. Lacan, "Of the Subject Who Is Supposed to Know," in *Ecrits,* 239.

12. As William O. Scott points out, Helen's own story has a variant in classical literature, one source of which is Plato's *Phaedrus.* This variant legend "keeps Helen faithful to Menelaus though separated from him, somewhat as Troilus had hoped for himself (in the case of Cressida)." Scott, "Self-Difference in *Troilus and Cressida,"* in *Shakespeare and Deconstruction,* 130-31.

13. Deborah Hooker, "Coming to Cressida Through Irigaray," *The South Atlantic Quarterly* 88, no. 4 (fall 1989): 922.

14. Many heroines come to mind here, but especially Portia, Hero, and Isabella. Portia, in particular, appears to enact a qualified vengeance on the male world that has imprisoned her through the casket test. By setting up the test of Bassanio through an inversion of the marriage ritual, giving him a ring which he is never to lose, she sets the stage for the weighing of Bassanio's love for her with his bond and love for Antonio. But she can only achieve her

small measure of vengeance on the Law of the Father by posing as a man, and the outcome of her test clearly indicates Shakespeare's awareness of the essentially male homosocial character of the chivalric world.

15. The *OED* lists one variant of "ribald" as *ribaude,* "a woman of loose character, a wanton." Although a rare and obsolete usage (*OED* cites two occurrences from the sixteenth century) it nonetheless adds metaphorical depth to the sort of postcoital distance we see in Troilus' affect here.

16. Derrida has discussed at length the significance of this footnote, and of *Beyond the Pleasure Principle* itself. See his "Coming Into One's Own," trans. James Hulbert, in *Psychoanalysis and the Question of the Text,* ed. Geoffrey Hartman (Baltimore: Johns Hopkins University Press, 1978), 139-42.

17. Julia Kristeva discusses this renunciation/aggression complex in her chapter on male sexuality through Plato's dual sublime and manic *eros* and in her examination of narcissism; see her *Tales of Love* (New York: Columbia University Press, 1987), 61-136.

FURTHER READING

Criticism

Adamson, Jane. "Drama in the Mind: Entertaining Ideas in *Troilus and Cressida." Critical Review* 27 (1985): 3-17.

    Examines the language of *Troilus and Cressida* in light of the play's confusing mixture of dramatic and tragic action.

Barfoot, C C. "*Troilus and Cressida:* 'Praise Us as We Are Tasted.'" *Shakespeare Quarterly* 39, No. 1 (Spring 1988): 45-57.

    Explores the shifting definition of human values in the play.

Clarke, Larry R. "'Mars His Heart Inflam'd with Venus': Ideology and Eros in Shakespeare's *Troilus and Cressida." Modern Language Quarterly* 50, No. 3 (September 1989): 209-26.

    Draws comparisons between the Trojans in *Troilus and Cressida,* whom he sees as representative of the aristocratic class of Renaissance England, and the Greeks, whom he sees as representative of the Renaissance bourgeoisie.

Engle, Lars. "Always Already in the Market: The Politics of Evaluation in *Troilus and Cressida."* In *Shakespearean Pragmatism: Market of His Time,* pp. 147-63. Chicago: The University of Chicago Press, 1993.

Argues that *Troilus and Cressida* is tonally unpleasant because it reflects the economic instability and moral flux of a newly emerging capitalism in Renaissance England.

Greene, Gayle. "Language and Value in Shakespeare's *Troilus and Cressida*." *Studies in English Literature 1500-1900* 21, No. 2 (Spring 1981): 271-85.
Contends that through the set speeches of Ulysses and the remarks of Troilus in *Troilus and Cressida*, Shakespeare criticized the disintegration of meaningful language in his own society.

Hillman, Richard. "*Troilus and Cressida*: Constructing Genre, Truth, and the Self." In *William Shakespeare: The Problem Plays*, pp. 17-53. New York: Twayne Publishers, 1993.
Argues that there are elements of three genres—tragedy, comedy, and satire—in *Troilus and Cressida*.

Hooker, Deborah A. "Coming to Cressida Through Irigaray." *South Atlantic Quarterly* 88, No. 4 (Fall 1989): 899-932.
Describes Cressida as a strong and admirable character who uses her wit as a weapon against male attempts to dominate her.

James, Heather. "'Tricks We Play on the Dead': Making History in *Troilus and Cressida*." In *Shakespeare's Troy: Drama, Politics, and the Translation of Empire*, pp. 85-118. Cambridge: Cambridge University Press, 1997.
Discusses the ways in which Shakespeare, like his literary and dramatic contemporaries, used the Trojan War and other classics to criticize his own, Renaissance, society.

LaBranche, Linda. "Visual Patterns and Linking Analogues in *Troilus and Cressida*." *Shakespeare Quarterly* 37, No. 4 (Winter 1986): 440-50.
Examines the ways in which Shakespeare deployed visual imagery in the play to depict Cressida and Achilles as more than mere clichés of classical mythology.

Lynch, Stephen J. "Shakespeare's Cressida: 'A Woman of Quick Sense.'" *Philological Quarterly* 63, No. 3 (1984): 357-68.

Illustrates the depth and intelligence of Cressida in contrast to other characters in the play.

McCandless, David. "*Troilus and Cressida*." In *Gender and Performance in Shakespeare's Problem Comedies*, pp. 123-66. Bloomington: Indiana University Press, 1997.
Identifies *Troilus and Cressida* as Shakespeare's "most problematic" problem comedy, pointing to the unresolved ending and to the manner in which Helen's perpetual inaccessibility emasculates the male characters.

Muir, Kenneth. Introduction to *Troilus and Cressida*, by William Shakespeare, edited by Kenneth Muir, pp. 1-40. Oxford: Clarendon Press, 1982.
Provides an overview of the play, including stage history, sources, and literary interpretations.

Owens, Roger. "The Seven Deadly Sins in the Prologue to *Troilus and Cressida*." *Shakespeare-Jahrbuch* 116 (1980): 85-92.
Asserts that the reference to the Seven Deadly Sins in the prologue lends moral weight to *Troilus and Cressida* without turning it into a conventional morality play.

Powell, Neil. "Hero and Human: The Problem of Achilles." *Critical Quarterly* 21, No. 2 (Summer 1979): 17-28.
Contends that Achilles is the only character in the play who is not trying to be someone or something other than what he is.

Spear, Gary. "Shakespeare's 'Manly' Parts: Masculinity and Effeminacy in *Troilus and Cressida*." *Shakespeare Quarterly* 44, No. 4 (Winter 1993): 409-22.
Discusses the ways in which the play reveals that the Renaissance period's focus on masculinity and femininity had more to do with social power than with sexuality.

Thomas, Vivian. "Shakespeare's Use of His Source Material: *Troilus and Cressida*." In *The Moral Universe of Shakespeare's Problem Plays*, pp. 23-61. London: Croom Helm, 1987.
Identifies Shakespeare's main sources for the play as Caxton, Lydgate, and Chapman, and describes the extent to which he relied on each of these sources.

Cumulative Character Index

The Cumulative Character Index identifies the principal characters of discussion in the criticism of each play and non-dramatic poem. The characters are arranged alphabetically. Page references indicate the beginning page number of each essay containing substantial commentary on that character.

Cumulative Topic Index

The Cumulative Topic Index indentifies the principal topics of discussion in the criticism of each play and non-dramatic poem. The topics are arranged alphabetically. Page references indicate the beginning page number of each essay containing substantial commentary on that topic. A parenthetical reference after a topic indicates that the topic is extensively discussed in that volume.

as dream-play
A Midsummer Night's Dream **3:** 365, 370, 372, 377, 389, 391; **29:** 190; **45:** 117; **58:** 181

Dreams in Shakespeare (Volume 45: 1, 10, 17, 28, 40, 48, 58, 67, 75)
Antony and Cleopatra **45:** 28
Cymbeline **4:** 162, 167; **44:** 28; **45:** 67, 75
Hamlet **45:** 28
Julius Caesar **45:** 10
A Midsummer Night's Dream **45:** 96, 107, 117
Romeo and Juliet **45:** 40
The Tempest **45:** 236, 247, 259

dualisms
Antony and Cleopatra **19:** 304; **27:** 82; **58:** 2, 71, 79, 105
Cymbeline **4:** 29, 64, 73

duration of time
As You Like It **5:** 44, 45
A Midsummer Night's Dream **3:** 362, 370, 380, 386, 494; **45:** 175

economic relations
Henry V **13:** 213

economics and exchange
Coriolanus **50:** 152
The Merchant of Venice **40:** 197, 208; **53:** 116

editorial and textual issues
Sonnets **28:** 363; **40:** 273; **42:** 296

education
All's Well That Ends Well **7:** 62, 86, 90, 93, 98, 104, 116, 126
The Two Gentlemen of Verona **6:** 490, 494, 504, 526, 532, 555, 568

education or nurturing
The Tempest **8:** 353, 370, 384, 396; **29:** 292, 368, 377

egotism or narcissism
Much Ado about Nothing **8:** 19, 24, 28, 29, 55, 69, 95, 115; **55:** 209

Elizabeth, audience of
Sonnets **48:** 325

Elizabeth's influence
The Merry Wives of Windsor **5:** 333, 334, 335, 336, 339, 346, 355, 366, 402; **18:** 5, 86; **38:** 278; **47:** 344

Elizabethan and Jacobean politics, relation to
Hamlet **28:** 232; **28:** 290, 311; **35:** 140; **58:** 79, 134

Elizabethan attitudes, influence of
Richard II **6:** 287, 292, 294, 305, 321, 327, 364, 402, 414; **13:** 494; **24:** 325; **28:** 188; **39:** 273; **42:** 118; **52:** 141, 144; **58:** 283, 293

Elizabethan betrothal and marriage customs
Measure for Measure **2:** 429, 437, 443, 503; **49:** 286

Elizabethan culture, relation to
General Commentary **50:** 34; **53:** 169; **56:** 2, 3, 15, 47
Antony and Cleopatra **47:** 103; **58:** 118
As You Like It **5:** 21, 59, 66, 68, 70, 158; **16:** 53; **28:** 46; **34:** 120; **37:** 1; **46:** 142; **57:** 23, 31, 64, 75
The Comedy of Errors **26:** 138, 142; **34:** 201, 215, 233, 238, 258; **42:** 80; **54:** 169, 200
Hamlet **1:** 76, 148, 151, 154, 160, 166, 169, 171, 176, 184, 202, 209, 254; **13:** 282, 494; **19:** 330; **21:** 407, 416; **22:** 258; **59:** 74
Henry IV, Parts 1 and 2 **19:** 195; **48:** 117, 143, 151, 175
Henry V **5:** 210, 213, 217, 223, 257, 299, 310; **16:** 202; **19:** 133, 233; **28:** 121, 159; **30:** 215, 262; **37:** 187; **49:** 260
Julius Caesar **16:** 231; **30:** 342, 379; **50:** 13, 211, 269, 280
King Lear **2:** 168, 174, 177, 183, 226, 241; **19:** 330; **22:** 227, 233, 365; **25:** 218; **46:** 276; **47:** 9; **49:** 67
Measure for Measure **2:** 394, 418, 429, 432, 437, 460, 470, 482, 503
The Merchant of Venice **32:** 66; **40:** 117, 127, 142, 166, 181, 197, 208; **48:** 54, 77; **49:** 37; **53:** 105, 111, 116, 127, 159
A Midsummer Night's Dream **50:** 86; **58:** 220
Much Ado about Nothing **8:** 23, 33, 44, 55, 58, 79, 88, 104, 111, 115; **51:** 15; **55:** 209, 241, 259
The Rape of Lucrece **33:** 195; **43:** 77
Richard II **58:** 267, 275
The Taming of the Shrew **31:** 288, 295, 300, 315, 326, 345, 351; **55:** 315, 322, 334
Timon of Athens **1:** 487, 489, 495, 500; **20:** 433; **27:** 203, 212, 230; **50:** 13; **52:** 320, 354
Titus Andronicus **27:** 282
Troilus and Cressida **3:** 560, 574, 606; **25:** 56; **59:** 225, 295, 306
Twelfth Night **1:** 549, 553, 555, 563, 581, 587, 620; **16:** 53; **19:** 42, 78; **26:** 357; **28:** 1; **34:** 323, 330; **46:** 291; **51:** 15

Elizabethan dramatic conventions
Cymbeline **4:** 53, 124
Henry VIII **24:** 155; **56:** 196, 248

Elizabethan literary influences
Henry VI, Parts 1, 2, and 3 **3:** 75, 97, 100, 119, 143; **22:** 156; **28:** 112; **37:** 97; **56:** 162, 180

Elizabethan love poetry
Love's Labour's Lost **38:** 232

Elizabethan poetics, influence of
Romeo and Juliet **5:** 416, 520, 522, 528, 550, 559, 575

Elizabethan politics, relation to
Henry IV, Parts 1 and 2 **22:** 395; **28:** 203; **47:** 60; **48:** 117, 143, 167, 175; **57:** 88, 94

Henry VIII **22:** 395; **24:** 115, 129, 140; **32:** 148; **56:** 201, 248
King John **48:** 132; **56:** 306, 314, 325
Richard III **22:** 395; **25:** 141; **37:** 144; **39:** 345, 349; **42:** 130; **52:** 201, 214, 257

Elizabethan setting
The Two Gentlemen of Verona **12:** 463, 485

Elizabethan society
The Merry Wives of Windsor **47:** 331

Epicureanism 50: 249

emulation or rivalry
Julius Caesar **16:** 231; **50:** 211

England and Rome, parallels between
Coriolanus **9:** 39, 43, 106, 148, 180, 193; **25:** 296; **30:** 67, 105

English language and colonialism
Henry V **22:** 103; **28:** 159

English Reformation, influence of
Henry VIII **2:** 25, 35, 39, 51, 67; **24:** 89; **56:** 201

epic elements
Henry V **5:** 192, 197, 246, 257, 314; **30:** 181, 220, 237, 252

erotic elements
A Midsummer Night's Dream **3:** 445, 491, 497, 511; **12:** 259, 262, 298; **16:** 34; **19:** 21; **29:** 183, 225, 269; **58:** 194
Venus and Adonis **10:** 410, 411, 418, 419, 427, 428, 429, 442, 448, 454, 459, 466, 473; **25:** 305, 328; **28:** 355; **33:** 321, 339, 347, 352, 363, 370; **51:** 345, 352, 359, 368

as experimental play
Romeo and Juliet **5:** 464, 509, 528

Essex Rebellion, relation to
Richard II **6:** 249, 250; **24:** 356; **58:** 293

ethical or moral issues
King John **9:** 212, 222, 224, 229, 235, 240, 263, 275, 280; **56:** 335
King Lear **52:** 1, 95;
Measure for Measure **52:** 69
Twelfth Night **52:** 57

ethnicity
The Winter's Tale **37:** 306

Euripides, influence of
Titus Andronicus **27:** 285

evil
See also **good versus evil**
Macbeth **3:** 194, 208, 231, 234, 239, 241, 267, 289; **20:** 203, 206, 210, 374; **52:** 23; **57:** 267
Othello **52:** 78
Richard III **52:** 78

Topic Index

Cumulative Topic Index, by Play

The Cumulative Topic Index, by Play identifies the principal topics of discussion in the criticism of each play and non-dramatic poem. The topics are arranged alphabetically by play. Page references indicate the beginning page number of each essay containing substantial commentary on that topic. A parenthetical reference after a play indicates which volumes discuss the play extensively.

All's Well That Ends Well (Volumes 7, 26, 38, 55)

appearance versus reality **7:** 37, 76, 93; **26:** 117

audience perspective **7:** 81, 104, 109, 116, 121

bed-trick **7:** 8, 26, 27, 29, 32, 41, 86, 93, 98, 113, 116, 126; **13:** 84; **26:** 117; **28:** 38; **38:** 65, 118; **49:** 46; **54:** 52; **55:** 109, 131, 176

Bertram

characterization **7:** 15, 27, 29, 32, 39, 41, 43, 98, 113; **26:** 48; **26:** 117; **55:** 90

conduct **7:** 9, 10, 12, 16, 19, 21, 51, 62, 104; **50:** 59; **55:** 143, 154

desire **22:** 78

transformation or redemption **7:** 10, 19, 21, 26, 29, 32, 54, 62, 81, 90, 93, 98, 109, 113, 116, 126; **13:** 84

comic elements **26:** 97, 114; **48:** 65; **55:** 148, 154, 164

conclusion **38:** 123, 132, 142; **54:** 52 **55:** 148, 154, 170

dark elements **7:** 27, 37, 39, 43, 54, 109, 113, 116; **26:** 85; **48:** 65; **50:** 59; **54:** 30; **55:** 164, 170

Decameron (Boccaccio), compared with **7:** 29, 43

desire **38:** 99, 109, 118; **55:** 122

displacement **22:** 78

education **7:** 62, 86, 90, 93, 98, 104, 116, 126

elder characters **7:** 9, 37, 39, 43, 45, 54, 62, 104

gender issues **7:** 9, 10, 67, 126; **13:** 77, 84; **19:** 113; **26:** 128; **38:** 89, 99, 118; **44:** 35; **55:** 101, 109, 122, 164

genre **48:** 65

Helena

as agent of reconciliation, renewal, or grace **7:** 67, 76, 81, 90, 93, 98, 109, 116; **55:** 176

as dualistic or enigmatic character **7:** 15, 27, 29, 39, 54, 58, 62, 67, 76, 81, 98, 113, 126; **13:** 66; **22:** 78; **26:** 117; **54:** 30; **55:** 90, 170, 176

as "female achiever" **19:** 113; **38:** 89; **55:** 90, 101, 109, 122, 164

desire **38:** 96; **44:** 35; **55:** 109, 170

pursuit of Bertram **7:** 9, 12, 15, 16, 19, 21, 26, 27, 29, 32, 43, 54, 76, 116; **13:** 77; **22:** 78; **49:** 46; **55:** 90

virginity **38:** 65; **55:** 131, 176

virtue and nobility **7:** 9, 10, 12, 16, 19, 21, 27, 32, 41, 51, 58, 67, 76, 86, 126; **13:** 77; **50:** 59; **55:** 122

implausibility of plot, characters, or events **7:** 8, 45

irony, paradox, and ambiguity **7:** 27, 32, 58, 62, 67, 81, 86, 109, 116

King **38:** 150; **55:** 148

language and imagery **7:** 12, 29, 45, 104, 109, 121; **38:** 132; **48:** 65

Lavatch **26:** 64; **46:** 33, 52, 68; **55:** 143

love **7:** 12, 15, 16, 51, 58, 67, 90, 93, 116; **38:** 80; **51:** 33, 44

merit versus rank **7:** 9, 10, 19, 37, 51, 76; **38:** 155; **50:** 59

"mingled yarn" **7:** 62, 93, 109, 126; **38:** 65

morality plays, influence of **7:** 29, 41, 51, 98, 113; **13:** 66

opening scene **54:** 30

Parolles

characterization **7:** 8, 9, 43, 76, 81, 98, 109, 113, 116, 126; **22:** 78; **26:** 48, 73, 97; **26:** 117; **46:** 68; **55:** 90, 154

exposure **7:** 9, 27, 81, 98, 109, 113, 116, 121, 126

Falstaff, compared with **7:** 8, 9, 16

reconciliation **7:** 90, 93, 98; **51:** 33

religious, mythic, or spiritual content **7:** 15, 45, 54, 67, 76, 98, 109, 116

romance or folktale elements **7:** 32, 41, 43, 45, 54, 76, 104, 116, 121; **26:** 117

sexuality **7:** 67, 86, 90, 93, 98, 126; **13:** 84; **19:** 113; **22:** 78; **28:** 38; **44:** 35; **49:** 46; **51:** 44; **55:** 109, 131, 143, 176

social and political context **13:** 66; **22:** 78; **38:** 99, 109, 150, 155; **49:** 46

staging issues **19:** 113; **26:** 15, 19, 48, 52, 64, 73, 85, 92, 93, 94, 95, 97, 114, 117, 128; **54:** 30

structure **7:** 21, 29, 32, 45, 51, 76, 81, 93, 98, 116; **22:** 78; **26:** 128; **38:** 72, 123, 142

youth versus age **7:** 9, 45, 58, 62, 76, 81, 86, 93, 98, 104, 116, 126; **26:** 117; **38:** 109

Antony and Cleopatra (Volumes 6, 17, 27, 47, 58)

allegorical elements **52:** 5

All for Love (John Dryden), compared with **6:** 20, 21; **17:** 12, 94, 101

ambiguity **6:** 53, 111, 161, 163, 180, 189, 208, 211, 228; **13:** 368

androgyny **13:** 530

Antony

characterization **6:** 22, 23, 24, 31, 38, 41, 172, 181, 211; **16:** 342; **19:** 270; **22:** 217; **27:** 117; **47:** 77, 124, 142; **58:** 2, 41, 118, 134

Cleopatra, relationship with **6:** 25, 27, 37, 39, 48, 52, 53, 62, 67, 71, 76, 85, 100, 125, 131, 133, 136, 142, 151, 161, 163, 165, 180, 192; **27:** 82; **47:** 107, 124, 165, 174

death scene **25:** 245; **47:** 142; **58:** 41

dotage **6:** 22, 23, 38, 41, 48, 52, 62, 107, 136, 146, 175; **17:** 28

Topic Index, by Play

Richard III (Volumes 8, 14, 39, 52)

ISBN 0-7876-4697-0